ASIA REBORN

ALSO BY PRASENJIT K. BASU

India as a New Global Leader
(with Brahma Chellaney, Parag Khanna and Sunil Khilnani)

ASIA
REBORN

A CONTINENT RISES
FROM THE
RAVAGES OF COLONIALISM
AND WAR
TO A NEW DYNAMISM

PRASENJIT K. BASU

ALEPH

ALEPH

ALEPH BOOK COMPANY
An independent publishing firm
promoted by Rupa Publications India

First Published in India in 2017
by Aleph Book Company
7/16 Ansari Road, Daryaganj
New Delhi 110 002

ISBN: 978-93-84067-19-9

1 3 5 7 9 10 8 6 4 2

This book is dedicated to

The pioneer
Ito Hirobumi

The pathfinders
Takahashi Korekiyo and Kishi Nobusuke

The liberators
Subhas Bose and M. K. Gandhi, Sukarno, Aguinaldo, Aung San, Zhou
Enlai and Liu Shaoqi, Sun Yat-sen and Lee Teng-hui, Phibunsongkhram,
Ahmed Boestamam, Atatürk, Mossadegh

The builders
Lee Kuan Yew, Park Chung-hee and Kim Dae-jung, Deng Xiaoping,
Mahathir, Narasimha Rao and Narendra Modi

CONTENTS

PROLOGUE

This book is an Asian telling of Asia's story in the twentieth century.

The twentieth century was both the most creative and the most destructive in human history. Humankind achieved extraordinary advances in scientific and technological achievement. Almost everything we consider necessities in today's consumer society (cars, televisions, computers, phones, tablets, etc.) was virtually unknown at the start of the century. And, yet, the century was unprecedented in its destructive force: two World Wars that brought untold destruction (including pogroms such as the Jewish Holocaust between 1938 and 1945, and the Great Bengal Famine of 1943–44), the great Communist killings (the pogroms of the Russian kulaks between 1929 and 1932, and the massive famine that followed China's Great Leap Forward between 1958 and 1961), huge wars in Korea (1950–53), Vietnam (1965–75) and the Gulf (Iran vs Iraq, 1980–88; Iraq vs the US, 1990–91), plus famine, civil war and deep-seated ideological conflicts in too many places to recount.

But perhaps the most extraordinary development of the twentieth century—one that few would have anticipated at its start—was the flowering of new nations around the globe, and especially in Asia. Many of the great currents that swept the world during the twentieth century had huge reverberations in Asia. But few could have imagined that this vast continent—seemingly inert and supine at the start of the century—would rise anew by the year 2000 and stand poised to re-emerge in the position of leadership that it held a millennium ago, but had largely surrendered by 1800.

This book seeks to tell the story of the renaissance of Asia during the twentieth century. One would expect this to be a well-chronicled tale, but it is a story that has hardly ever been told collectively. A single narrative about Asia is still considered inappropriate, because the Western media has led the world to believe that Asia is riven with deep-seated cultural differences that make it something less than a continent. A cursory traveller around the region would know that this assertion of divergence is absurd: the practice of popular religion has enormous similarities in China, Cambodia, Thailand, India, Indonesia and Japan; rice is a common thread that runs from eastern and southern India all the way to southern China (and all points in between), Korea and Japan; and the list can go on.

The historic experiences of the Asian continent have also been largely shared. Buddhism remains a source of cultural unity from Burma to Japan (with Thailand, Sri Lanka, Mongolia, Singapore and much of China thrown in), and before its advent much of Asia was bound together by the mythological legacies of the Ramayana (which continue to influence Cambodia, Indonesia, India, Thailand). The depredations of the Mongols affected virtually all of Asia—from China and Korea to present-day Russia, Iran and Iraq, and points in between. The kamikaze wind blew the Mongol navy away from the shores of Japan, but descendants of Genghis Khan ruled China (grandson Kublai was the emperor who united north and south China), Persia (where Genghis's descendants became Shiites and are still represented amongst Afghanistan's Hazaras) and, many generations later, India (where Babur was a descendant of Genghis on his mother's side and Timurlane on his father's). Common historical experiences, mythology, food preferences and religious practices—these factors apart from geography are surely enough to justify the classification of Asia as a continent.

But the triumph of European colonialism in the nineteenth century helped obscure much of Asia's cultural unity. At the start of the twentieth century, only Japan was not under the sway of a European colonial power: Iran, Afghanistan, Tibet, Nepal, Thailand, Korea and non-coastal China were nominally independent too, but at least partly in the thrall of one or more colonial power. The French ruled Indo-China (today's Vietnam, Laos and Cambodia) and some small enclaves in India; the Portuguese ruled Macao (on China's coast), Goa (on India's) and East Timor; the Dutch ruled the East Indies (all of today's Indonesia); the British ruled India (which then included what is now Pakistan, Bangladesh and Burma), Malaya (which included Singapore), Ceylon (today's Sri Lanka), Kuwait and neighbouring Gulf states, Hong Kong and some pieces of China (the control of whose ports was divided amongst the US, Britain, France, Germany, Russia, Holland and Japan). The Philippines had just passed from Spanish to American rule (which was being fiercely resisted by some). Central Asia (today's Kazakhstan, Uzbekistan, Turkmenistan, Tajikistan and Kyrgystan), Georgia and Azerbaijan were subsumed into Russia. And the Arab lands (modern Saudi Arabia, Iraq, Syria, Jordan, Israel and Lebanon) were part of the multi-ethnic Ottoman empire, although the British and French were beginning to make inroads from their North African colonial bases.

The umbrella of colonialism (and its post-colonial and Cold War effects) masked the underlying unity of the Asian continent. The post-colonial elites were variously influenced by each of their separate colonial experiences—and only slowly rediscovered their pre-colonial identities. Some of those identities still remain very different today from the Asian mainstream (especially for the post-Soviet Republics and in Arabia), so how do we define Asia for the purposes of a book focused on the twentieth century?

Asia in its broadest definition stretches from the Arabian peninsula in the west all the way to Japan. If the old land of Palestine is included, then all the world's religions originated in Asia—including the three great Semitic religions (Judaism, Christianity and Islam), which emerged at Asia's western fringes. All the great Semitic religions, however, initially expanded westwards, outside Asia (apart from a brief early foray by Islam into Iran). Christianity found its home primarily in Europe and parts of North Africa (notably Egypt and Ethiopia), while Islam spread to the Levant, North Africa (Egypt, Tunisia or old Carthage, Algeria, Morocco), Spain, Sicily and Turkey well before it had established itself in the rest of Asia (India, Pakistan, Bangladesh, Indonesia, Malaysia, China, Vietnam, the Philippines). And Judaism remained a minority religion in all the lands to which it spread—in all of which Christianity or Islam was the majority religion (with the exception of Kerala on India's west coast).

In that initial westward turn, the Semitic religions separated themselves quite clearly from all the religions of the rest of Asia—and one important doctrinal feature came to differentiate them from the other indigenous religions of Asia. The Semitic or millenarian religions asserted that non-believers were doomed to damnation and the only path to salvation lay in having faith in the doctrines of Islam/Christianity/Judaism. This belief differed profoundly from the belief systems of the rest of Asia where liberalism in the choice of belief (and ease of movement from one 'religion' to another during one's lifetime) was (and still is) the norm. The Sufi version of Islam largely fit into this pattern, mingling quite comfortably with Hindu and Buddhist beliefs in India and Indonesia (where the abangan continue to mix religious beliefs and mystical practices), and historically in what is now Iran, Bangladesh and Pakistan.

Asia's indigenous religions were not exclusionary. Individuals could mingle Shinto beliefs with Buddhist ones in Japan, Confucian beliefs with Daoist or Buddhist ones in China, Hindu beliefs with Buddhist or Jain ones in India. The experience of modernity and colonialism, however, altered this easy intermingling, as the exclusionary practices of the Semitic/millennial religions asserted themselves—and colonial anthropologists led bureaucrats into clearly defining each person's religious affiliation in the same exclusionary terms.

Although the two major Semitic religions—Islam and Christianity—are a dominant force in several Asian countries (Bangladesh, Malaysia, Indonesia, the Philippines), they differ from their counterparts in the rest of the world in one important aspect: religious pluralism. While Spain, Saudi Arabia, Germany and most other Christian- or Muslim-dominated countries outside Asia have virtually no 'native' (non-immigrant) adherents of minority religions, the Asian countries with Christian and Muslim majorities have substantial religious minorities (comprising at least a tenth of the population).

In drawing the boundaries of Asia in this book, I have included the countries in geographic Asia where religious pluralism is part of the current (or historic) reality. Iran and Turkey thus qualify (on historic grounds, although less so on the basis of current reality), but the story of how they moved away from the Asian tradition of religious pluralism is an important feature of their twentieth-century experiences. Pakistan and Afghanistan also fall narrowly into the same category, but Saudi Arabia and most members of the Gulf Cooperation Council (GCC) are outside it, as are Israel (narrowly) and Jordan. The UAE and other members of the GCC have substantial minorities of 'guest-workers' belonging to other religions, but they fail my Asia test since these guests are not native to the country (and cannot qualify for citizenship either). This book will therefore refer only in passing to the West Asian extremity of Arabia—although, of course, not neglecting to focus on its influence on Asia proper—while treating Iran as an integral part of Asia for most of the century.

Russia is certainly Asiatic by my definition—including, as it does, significant minorities of Buddhists (like the Buryats) and Muslims (in Chechnya, Dagestan and Tatarstan, for instance). So (with a few qualifications) are its former satellites in Central Asia. Russia and Turkey, however, are geographically part of both Europe and Asia—and both have sought quite clearly to emphasize their historic and future affiliation with Europe (as, indeed, have Armenia, Georgia and, to some extent, Azerbaijan). Their ambiguous status contributes to some ambivalence in my own approach to them. I have included them in the book, but they remain somewhat peripheral to the main narrative—players that walk on and off the stage as circumstances demand, rather than central characters. Mustafa Kemal Atatürk was clearly a hero to all of Asia, and Lenin, Stalin and their acolytes had considerable influence on Mao Zedong, Ho Chi Minh, Chin Peng, D. N. Aidit and a host of other communists around the region. Russia and Turkey therefore make important cameo appearances, slightly more intimate than the outside powers (the US, Britain, Netherlands, etc.) but not quite central to the narrative.

The central characters are, however, the nations of East Asia (China, Indonesia, Japan, Korea, Taiwan, Malaysia, Thailand, Vietnam, Tibet, Hong Kong, Singapore, Brunei, Burma, Cambodia and Laos), and those of South Asia (India, Bangladesh, Sri Lanka, Pakistan, Nepal, Bhutan, the Maldives), with significant roles for those of West Asia (Iran, Iraq, Afghanistan and the former Soviet Central Asian states). However, Cambodia, Laos, Tibet,

Brunei, Bhutan, Nepal and the Maldives—despite being geographically and culturally part of Asia—will not appear to be central characters, primarily because of their small size as economies; Burma (Myanmar to its military rulers) will feature significantly in parts of the book, but will naturally fade from view (along with its autarkic cousin North Korea) due to the deliberate myopia of their rulers.

The twentieth century in Asia was largely Japan's century. The apogee of its influence on not just the continent but the world was probably in the early 1990s. Bill Clinton ran for president with a platform aimed largely at emulating (and eventually outdoing) Japan. And the historian Felipe Fernández-Armesto began and ended *Millennium,* his magisterial thousand-year history of the world (published in 1994), with chapters about Japan, perhaps assuming that its influence was bound to be pervasive in the future too. From today's vantage point, that optimism about Japan's economic prospects appears profoundly ill-founded. But despite its struggles at the end of the century, there is little doubt that Japan's economy dominated Asia in the twentieth century.

One of the central arguments of this book is that Japan's role in twentieth-century Asia was akin to Napoleon's in nineteenth-century Europe. Although he eventually suffered a crushing military defeat, Napoleon Bonaparte's conquest of most of the European mainland enabled him to effect widespread institutional changes that helped 'modernize' Europe: codifying civil law, strengthening administrative structures, upgrading technology, etc. Similarly, although the atrocities allegedly committed by Japanese soldiers receive all the publicity in the Western press, the role of Japan in nurturing nationalism in the countries it conquered, and in building the institutions of modern economic development (especially in Taiwan and Korea, its two longest-lasting colonies) is often obscured. One of the questions I address in the book is why the countries that were longest in the Japanese embrace (Taiwan and Korea) have proved to be Asia's strongest economic performers (other than the city states of Hong Kong and Singapore, both of which, incidentally, were also Japanese colonies for at least three years during World War II).

The institutional legacy of Japan played a large part in determining the strategy of economic development in Taiwan and Korea. South Korea's President Park Chung-hee self-consciously sought to emulate Japan's economic institutions and strategy, having imbibed an admiration for the Japanese way of life while being trained in a Japanese military academy. In Indonesia, the Japanese helped nourish the early seeds of nationalism, and they subtly played a similar role in Malaysia and Vietnam too. And Lee Kuan Yew (the creator of modern Singapore) was candid in his admiration for the discipline and orderliness Japan introduced to wartime Singapore (while also deploring the atrocities committed by Japanese troops, or Korean ones acting in Japan's name).

While the institutional legacy of Japan is underappreciated, the alleged positive legacy of European colonial rule is much exaggerated. The British, French, Dutch and Portuguese came to Asia to trade. They eventually went on to rule, subjugating local populations and stripping bare the rich natural resources of Asia along the way. They imposed trading arrangements on their colonies that were egregiously discriminatory—forcing them to become markets for the industrial exports of the 'mother' (imperial) country, while banning imports of competing products from the colonies: most famously, the ban on imports of cloth from India—principally Bengal—destroyed the world's largest manufacturing base in the first half of the nineteenth century (through a complete ban on its exports to Britain) in order to construct the edifice of Lancashire's textiles that were the backbone of the First Industrial Revolution.

Eventually, the European imperial powers built some railroads, a few desultory highways and some rudimentary ports; they decidedly did not educate the populations of their Asian colonies (in contrast to their white-populated colonies, for instance, in Australia and Canada). Racism was the chief characteristic of their policies: it was considered normal for a British club in Calcutta to have a sign saying 'Dogs and Indians not allowed', and for the Australian embassy in London in the late 1950s to seek immigrants aggressively while explicitly stating that 'whites only' need apply. Unsurprisingly, there was hardly any economic growth in Asia during the first half of the twentieth century as the European powers sought to consolidate their hold on increasingly restive Asian populations. In the popular press, democracy and railroads are still routinely referred to as legacies of European rule in Asia. This book will show how ludicrous such claims are: democracy was not a conscious legacy of European rule anywhere, but an outcome that Asians had to fight hard to wrest from the imperialists (and only in India was a democratic outcome achieved, but even there at the expense of one of the great holocausts of the twentieth century—Partition). The hollowness of the claim of benign colonial rule was exposed quite starkly when many local populations initially welcomed the Japanese invaders in the Second World War (although eventually growing disenchanted when they proved to be only slightly less racist).

The two World Wars—especially the second—had a crucial impact on the nature of decolonization in Asia, while the role of the US (as the dominant global power) exerted enormous influence in virtually every aspect of Asia's fate in the second half of the twentieth century. Absolutely central to the

PRASENJIT K. BASU

post-war shape of Asia was the US decision to drop the nuclear bombs on Hiroshima and Nagasaki. When the bombs fell, Japan ruled about half of China (including all its main economic and industrial centres—Beijing, Shanghai, Nanjing, Guangdong, Hong Kong, and the great northern industrial belt in Manchuria), all of Indonesia, Malaysia, Singapore, Taiwan and Korea. The former colonial powers were far from ready to retake their old colonies (while Taiwan and Korea were suddenly orphaned into independence as their colonial master surrendered to the Allies). Thailand and Indo-China too were firmly under Japanese influence. The chaos in the aftermath of surrender created fertile ground for the advance of the Communists in China and elsewhere in Asia (especially Indo-China, with abortive attempts at gaining power in places such as Indonesia and India).

In regions unaffected by Japan's extraordinary military advance, its indirect influence (including the trial of three leading officers of the Japan-aligned Indian National Army) had a catalytic role in cementing nationalist aspirations. In those regions conquered by the great Japanese military juggernaut, the legitimacy and authority of European colonialism was forever dashed: in Indonesia, anti-colonial nationalist aspirations were immediately asserted, in Vietnam within only a short interval (although the fight to consolidate those aspirations eventually lasted twenty-five years). The nature of decolonization clearly had a big influence on the institutional features of the new nations that emerged from them. Malaya's more sedate path to independence preserved many of the characteristics of the colonial state while transferring political power to local hands. The local hands showed that circumscribed economic independence was not necessarily an impediment to economic advancement when the power to tax (and spend) was in local rather than imperial hands. Lee Kuan Yew's Singapore created this new paradigm of development—based on MNC-led export growth, a semi-colonial social structure without racism, and many of the institutional underpinnings of the colonial state—which eventually became a model for all of Southeast Asia and mainland China (although China, like Thailand but unlike the rest of ASEAN (Association of South East Asian Nations), did not have the baggage of a semi-colonial social structure).

While the US role as colonizer of the Philippines was hardly more benign than that of the European imperialists (except in one crucial aspect, education, in which the US was streets ahead of its Old World cousins), the US role as occupying power (in Japan and Korea) was largely beneficial to their futures, as was its subsequent role as chief benefactor to a fledgling South Korea and Taiwan through the fifteen years to 1965. Land reforms enacted during the US occupation (building on the incipient reforms in Japan during the

Meiji Restoration, and in Korea in the early years of Japanese colonial rule) played no small part in unleashing these countries' productive potential, while ensuring social cohesion through a notably egalitarian distribution of income and wealth. The enormously benign influence of the US in northeast Asia was partly a consequence of its innate idealism but also largely influenced by the crucial role of Japan, Korea and Taiwan in the emerging Cold War. A similarly benign influence was felt in the late 1960s and 1970s in much of Southeast Asia when the brutal US war against Vietnam raised the region's importance in the calculus of the Cold War.

But there was little that was benign about the US role in West Asia, where the depredations of that great charlatan Winston Churchill had created a minefield of resentments that the US inherited, and usurped wholesale in the 1950s at the behest of the Dulles brothers (one Secretary of State, the other CIA chief). The term charlatan to describe Churchill, of course, begs explanation, except to the Irish, Arabs, Iranians, Turks, Indians, Indonesians, and John Kenneth Galbraith, amongst others! Churchill was the man who, as head of the British Navy, suffered one of the greatest defeats of the First World War (at Gallipoli, where Australians and Gurkhas fell to the military genius of one Mustafa Kemal, later named Atatürk); then (as Chancellor of the Exchequer) took the sterling back into the gold standard at a catastrophically strong exchange rate; matched Hitler's rhetoric of a Thousand-Year Reich with an equally ringing promise to ensure a Thousand-Year British Empire (which he promptly squandered when his Impregnable Fortress in Singapore fell soon after the sinking of two capital ships that symbolized the demise of British naval superiority in Asia); presided over a famine in Bengal that killed at least 3 million (and possibly 6 million) people; eventually lost most of the empire he had fought for all his life; and yet, despite these repeated failures, wrote his own history with such facility that *Time* magazine seriously toyed with the idea of naming him as its Man of the Century in 2000. This book will hopefully demonstrate—as one small aside—just how wrong-headed it was to even consider Churchill for such an honour.

Churchill's convoluted tactics in gaining a deep and lasting foothold for Britain amongst the oil riches of West Asia only succeeded in creating deep resentments that persist to this day. Iran, of course, was most directly under British sway, with its oil resources controlled by the Anglo-Iranian Oil Company (the immediate progenitor of what became British Petroleum) from the turn of the century. Churchill's post-World War I redrawing of the map of the Ottoman empire's Arab dominions (by installing princes of the Hashemite family on the thrones of Arabia, Jordan and Iraq), granting Syria and Lebanon to the French and establishing a British Mandate over

Palestine sowed the seeds for much that ails today's West Asia. The even older Great Game between Britain and Russia for control of Central Asia in the nineteenth century—which was, to some extent, the continuation of an older Great Conflict of almost a thousand years between Russia and the Tartars (and their Turk Muslim cousins)—does bear part of the blame for what happened to Iran in the first half of the century and to Afghanistan in the second. But the seeds for the most deep-seated resentments were laid by Churchill, and will be fully explored in later chapters.

The second half of the twentieth century in Asia is better known to most readers today as the era of the emergence of prosperity in the east, but this book is devoted to the proposition that Asia's present conflicts, conundrums and challenges cannot be really understood without the context of what happened in the first half. West Asia too achieved a fleeting prosperity in the 1970s that far outstripped even what was to be achieved in non-Japan East Asia in the 1980s and 1990s. But built as it was on Allah's liquid gold (oil), it proved fleeting as the Organization of the Petroleum Exporting Countries (OPEC) countries succumbed to the curse of the Dutch Disease—the real appreciation of currencies resulting from excessively rapid growth in the exports of a single commodity, which in turn prices out the country's other potential exports. But the complex politics of oil—the Western oil companies' exploitative contracts (or concessions) from the kingdoms that contained the oil, the inability of the oil-producing countries to develop a skilled labour force of their own, and the emergence and eclipse of the great OPEC oil cartel— also make a compelling tale, and are part of the Asian story that cannot be neglected. Oil exists aplenty in East Asia's three Muslim-majority countries (Indonesia, Malaysia, Brunei) as well as in West Asia. An understanding of Islam, and the complex history of oil politics, is an essential part of the story of how Asia evolved in the last century.

To call oil Allah's liquid gold has been especially apposite in the past century because abundant oil resources have been found in virtually every Muslim-majority country or region, with the unfortunate exception of South Asia's threesome of Pakistan, Afghanistan and Bangladesh, although the last named has recently found an abundance of natural gas. Each of the Central Asian states of the former Soviet Union—with the exception of Tajikistan— have enormous reserves of oil or gas. Amongst the Caucasian states, Muslim-majority Azerbaijan has oil while its non-Muslim neighbours Georgia and Armenia do not. And just over the border from Georgia, the Muslim-majority regions of Chechnya and Dagestan (two Russian provinces) are floating on oil too. And the best story has to do with the Tatars: Stalin wanted to punish these hardy people for their perceived support to Germany during the War, so he banished them to a seemingly barren part of the desert. But he hadn't reckoned with Allah, because the Muslim Tatars soon found a bountiful supply of oil under the ground in their autonomous region, making it the single richest province in Russia!

The final quarter of the twentieth century proved to be the most fecund one for the region. The first batch of newly industrialized economies (NIEs) of Taiwan, South Korea, Singapore and Hong Kong moved into the developed economy category. Subsequently Malaysia, Thailand, Indonesia, China and India each achieved at least two decades of very rapid real GDP growth—of 6 per cent or more annually—that has been very rare indeed outside Asia. For a considerable period after the 'emergence' of Asia's dynamic economies (from Japan onwards) it was widely assumed that a free-market orientation was a principal contributor to their growth. While this was somewhat true, especially in comparison with the communist economies (Russia, China, Vietnam, North Korea, etc.) against which they were pitted in the popular press, the NIEs were in fact not very different from all 'late developers' in world economic history (starting with the US, Germany and France, and extending through Sweden and pre-War Japan) in assigning a very significant role to the government in protecting infant industries and/or directing credit to specific sectors. In fact, the role of government in driving the economy was substantially greater in Japan, Korea, Taiwan and Singapore than it was in the US in the period between 1880 and 1915.

East Asia is dynamic and independent today because Japan stood tall against Western imperialism between 1905 and 1945, helping to incubate nationalism across Asia. In contrast, West Asia was smothered longer in the colonial embrace, and suffers civil wars that are legacies of that embrace. This book tells the epic stories that flowed from the divergent pulls of colonialism and progressive nationalism in Asia's rebirth.

Chapter 1

IN EUROPE'S SHADOW:
ASIA'S POLITICAL LANDSCAPE IN 1900

As the twentieth century dawned, Asia lay largely supine. Most of the continent had been subjugated over the previous four centuries by European powers—the majority submitting fully to colonial rule, others seeing their sovereignty gradually erode away. Only Japan, in Asia's eastern extremity, had successfully used its insular geographic position to fend off European colonial rule, selectively adapt European mores, and thereby retain more than a semblance of independence. Persia (Iran) in the west, and China in the east, retained a semblance of independence—but the influence of European powers was already overwhelming and strangling them. Ironically, the ruling dynasties in both Persia and China were considered foreign to their native populations: Persia was ruled by the Qajar Turks, while the Manchu rulers of China did take a Chinese dynasty name (Qing) but were otherwise wont to frequently remind the Han Chinese that they were a subject people being ruled by the non-Chinese Manchu race.

Thailand, Afghanistan and Nepal were nominally independent monarchies, but retained little more than cultural autonomy from their European colonial neighbours, who exerted a strong political influence over them—and were not shy about demonstrating it on occasion. Nepal and Afghanistan, in fact, were formally British protectorates. Tibet was a mountain redoubt with its unique brand of lama rule. Like Korea, it theoretically acknowledged Manchu China's suzerainty, but was beginning to feel the press of European colonial competition. Tibet and Afghanistan were the final frontiers of the Great Game for control of Central Asia between Russia and Great Britain. And in the east, Korea's royal court was a den of international intrigue as Russia and Japan jostled to replace China as the power behind (and over) the throne of the ebbing Chosun dynasty.

THE BRITISH EMPIRE AND THE INDIAN RESISTANCE

At the dawn of the twentieth century, the British were the world's pre-eminent power, and their Asian colonies were the most important aspects of an empire that straddled every continent. The jewel in this imperial crown was India (which then included present-day Pakistan, Bangladesh and Burma), but also encompassed present-day Sri Lanka, Malaysia, Singapore, and various holdings along the coast of China including Hong Kong and the New Territories. A viceroy of the British queen Victoria ruled over her Indian realms from Calcutta (Kolkata) and, since 1877, Victoria also held the title of Empress of India (India having passed from Company to Whitehall rule in 1858); the official title was Kaiser-i-Hind, just as the Prussian ruler had been crowned Kaiser Wilhelm I of Germany and the Russian empire was ruled by the Tsar (Russian for Caesar). Succeeding a long line of aristocrats, the famously arrogant Lord Curzon was ensconced as viceroy in Calcutta, in the Governor General's mansion that was coincidentally an almost exact replica of his family's aristocratic seat of Kedleston Hall in Derbyshire.

The British East India Company had ostensibly come to trade in India, but (like its French and Dutch counterparts) it became engaged in military activity from the earliest years. The Mughals were still nominally the imperial overlords of India when 'John Company' acquired its trading posts in Surat, Fort St George (later Madras and Chennai), Fort William (later Calcutta and Kolkata) and the seven islands that were to form Bombay (Mumbai). The third and greatest of the Great Mughals (or more correctly Timurids, for it was their descent from the feared Timurlane that gave the dynasty its potent legitimacy as leaders of the flock), (Jalaluddin Mohammed) Akbar (r. 1556–1605), had established a distinctive form of syncretic rule, assimilating philosophical influences from the majority Hindus of his realms, as well as from Buddhists, Christians, Zoroastrians and others who peopled it. Emperor Akbar's syncretism was reflected in a new religion (Din-i Ilahi) which won fewer than fifty true converts—but left a lasting imprint in the form of a tolerant religious and cultural policy that enabled the Timurids to be seen as genuine emperors of India (unlike previous Muslim rulers of northern India in the previous four centuries, who had ruled over a surly populace from their garrison fortress towns with little real interaction with the countryside beyond, apart from revenue demands). Taking power at thirteen, the illiterate but highly intelligent Akbar had established a decidedly tolerant court, with his nine chief court nobles almost equally divided amongst Muslims and Hindus, and a relatively enlightened revenue policy.

Politically, Akbar established an alliance with the Rajput warriors (principally of Jaipur, Jodhpur, Ajmer and—more tenuously—Udaipur in Rajasthan), cemented through marriage. The alliance lasted through the terms of his two immediate successors, Jahangir and Shah Jahan (builder of the Taj Mahal), both of whose mothers were Hindu Rajput princesses. Shah Jahan was ousted by his austere son Aurangzeb, whose long quest to Islamize the empire, and desire to spread his realms to India's southern peninsula, combined to fatally weaken the Timurids' hold on their entire empire.

By the time of Aurangzeb's death in 1707 (just as Scotland was losing its own independence), the Marathas had emerged as a significant alternative source of power in western and southern India. Fratricidal conflict had been a feature of every Mughal succession, with Aurangzeb himself gaining the throne after a military victory over his elder brother Dara Shukoh. Had he succeeded to the throne, Dara Shukoh (who had translated the great Hindu philosophical treatise, the Upanishads, into Farsi/Persian) would have extended the great syncretic traditions of his great-grandfather Akbar and possibly prolonged and deepened Timurid imperial rule while assimilating even more thoroughly into the Indian milieu. In his preface, Dara Shukoh asserted that the Vedas and Upanishads were the 'secret book' that the Quran refers to as being the font of all sacred wisdom. Had Dara ascended the Timurid throne, India's and Asia's history would have taken a vastly different turn, but it was this syncretism that made him a dangerous and loathsome apostate in the eyes of his brother Aurangzeb (who had his naked, beheaded body paraded through the streets of Delhi as a final lesson to other apostates).

Instead, Aurangzeb's austere brand of Islam—and massive programme of temple-destruction—alienated the non-Muslims and heavily eroded the legitimacy of the Timurids, who had ruled north India and Afghanistan since 1526, with only a brief interruption in the 1530s, when Sher Shah Suri of Sasaram in Bihar had ousted the second Timurid emperor Humayun, and introduced many of the administrative reforms that were to be the bedrock institutions of India through the British period. Although still dependent on several Hindu generals, Aurangzeb reintroduced the jizya tax on non-Muslims, tore down prominent temples and built mosques in their stead (including in the most sacred of Hindu cities, Benares). Although this appeared to consolidate the Muslim conquest of India, it also bred growing resentment—culminating in Shivaji Bhonsle's epic Maratha resistance.

Fratricidal conflict, the rising challenge of the Marathas in the west and south, and the incipient rebellions of the Sikhs and Jats in the north, all had weakened the power of the Mughals by the time Emperor Farrukhsiyar (an almost forgotten figure in Indian history) signed a firman granting the British East India Company the right to trade freely in the industrial and fertile province of Bengal. In the key dominions of Bengal, Oudh (Awadh) and Hyderabad, the local satraps already had considerable autonomy, and the Company quickly came into conflict with the nominally-Mughal governors of those provinces, and in the south, with the rising power of the French (and eventually their key ally, Tipu Sultan). By then, the colourful cotton cloth from India was already ubiquitous in British homes—replacing the sweaty and scratch-inducing roughness of wool, especially in summer and as bed linen. Writing in January 1708, just a few months after Aurangzeb's death, Daniel Defoe (the creator of *Robinson Crusoe*) spoke of how 'it crept into our houses, our closets, our bedchambers. Curtains, cushions, chairs, and at last beds themselves were nothing but Callicoes or Indian stuffs.'

British historians ascribe great importance to the Battle of Plassey (1757)— in which Robert Clive, an intrepid clerk of the East India Company who had also proven to be an effective general—'defeated' Bengal's ruler Siraj-ud-Daulah by bribing his commander-in-chief, Mir Jafar (himself an Arab immigrant to India). This bribe actually had ample payoff, as Clive became jagirdar (feudal lord) of the Twenty-Four Parganas, or sub-districts, around Calcutta, and each British member of the Bengal Council received the equivalent—in today's money—of about £16.5 million sterling from the Bengal treasury. Siraj's earlier perfidy—of not only expelling the British from Fort William, but also stuffing several dozen Englishmen into a fairly small cell (that became infamous as the 'Black Hole of Calcutta' based on a wildly exaggerated account by a survivor)—was thus punished.

In fact, however, the pre-eminent power in India during the eighteenth century was that of the Marathas—spawned by Aurangzeb's imperial overstretch. Around 1655, Shivaji had established himself as an independent chieftain in territories that he split from the domains of the Sultan of Bijapur (in whose service his father was a prominent feudatory). Soon afterwards, however, he attacked the Mughal governor of the Deccan, Shaista Khan, captured his capital (Aurangabad) and entered his bedchamber in a daring manoeuvre. Eventually Aurangzeb sent his ablest general, the Rajput Jai Singh Kachwaha, with the full imperial army to subdue him. Although Shivaji agreed terms, and briefly entered the imperial system, he felt insulted by his treatment in Delhi and escaped from the imperial fortress. He then established an independent Hindu kingdom in 1674 in defiance of Aurangzeb, calling upon Brahmins from Benares (Varanasi) to invest him with a princely lineage from the Rajputs of Mewar (whose ancestors, Rana Pratap and Rana Sanga, had respectively resisted the Mughal emperors Akbar and Babur).

Although Shivaji only ruled as Chhatrapati (king) for six years, his sons continued to harry Aurangzeb's forces, leading the latter to move the imperial court to the Deccan, as he sought to separately subdue the Marathas, as well as the Muslim sultanates of Bijapur and Golconda. In this, Aurangzeb largely succeeded—although his empire was enfeebled in the long term by this prolonged engagement in the south, and by his intolerant policies towards non-Muslims, which broke the implicit compact between the rulers and ruled that had prevailed since the enlightened rule of Akbar. Although the Din-i Ilahi religion had died with Akbar, its spirit lived on in the tradition of Muslim–Hindu amity that prevailed both in the imperial realm as well as in smaller Muslim sultanates such as Golconda (which famously was ruled by the Hindu Gowda brothers at its apogee) and Hindu kingdoms such as those of the Marathas (which employed prominent Muslim generals and senior officials).

Shivaji established a highly efficient unitary state, with an uncluttered and effective civil administration that depended on cash payments rather than fiefs. Shivaji's land power was based on a series of massive hill fortresses, but he also established command of India's west coast and could thus charge the chauth (25 per cent tax) on all overland traffic from important western ports such as Surat. Plundering of territories outside those he ruled directly (especially in the Bijapur and Golconda sultanates) provided an important additional source of revenue; eventually, he took control of Bijapur and important districts further south in Vellore, Jinji and Tanjore (Thanjavur). An alliance with the Qutb Shahi dynasty of Golconda, which was facilitated by the Telugu Brahmin brothers who were its two leading ministers, further consolidated Shivaji's influence over south-central India.

Shivaji's unitary state did not much survive his death in 1680, as his youngest son Rajaram was quickly ousted by his wayward eldest son Sambhaji (who had once defected to the Mughal court for over a year upon being disciplined by his father). Over the next four years, however, the Mughal prince Akbar (not to be confused with his great-great-grandfather, the emperor Akbar) became the focal point of resistance to Aurangzeb's rule because he opposed his father's mistreatment of non-Muslims and enforcement of ulema rule. Sambhaji sheltered Prince Akbar in his court, especially after the latter proclaimed himself emperor in January 1681. But while Akbar wanted to mount a joint thrust northwards (combining his forces with those of the Marathas), Sambhaji was diverted to skirmishes with the English East India Company and with the Portuguese in Goa. Nonetheless, it was to subdue Sambhaji and Akbar that Aurangzeb was obliged to move his entire army and court (with bazaars and all its other accoutrements) southwards and to spend the final twenty-five years of his reign in this permanent encampment.

By 1688, Aurangzeb's armies had conquered the southern sultanates of Bijapur and Golconda. And, finding the Maratha ruler Sambhaji relaxing in his pleasure garden, a former Golconda general (then working for the Mughals) captured Sambhaji and his chief minister and brought them to Aurangzeb. They were tortured, their bodies cut to pieces and fed to the dogs. Although all his southern enemies were thus subdued, Aurangzeb was unable to move back to his northern capital. Shivaji's youngest son, Rajaram, was hastily crowned in February 1689 and escaped to the southeastern triple fortress of Jinji (just west of French Pondicherry—or Puducherry—and south of the emerging English fortress of Madras), but Aurangzeb brought Sambhaji's nine-year-old son Shahuji into the imperial encampment to be brought up as a Maratha Hindu prince in Mughal captivity (much like the fate of the child Panchen Lama in early twenty-first-century China).

Meanwhile, south of Jinji, the family of Shivaji's brother Vyankoji still ruled Tanjore. Several Maratha warrior chieftains continued to harry the Mughals with guerrilla warfare, and ran a parallel revenue system throughout the western Deccan, and eventually also in much of Bijapur and Khandesh. When his fortress of Jinji finally fell to the Mughals in 1698 after a siege that had lasted (with intervals) for over five years, Rajaram again managed to escape into the Maratha homelands and re-established his capital in Satara, his Bhonsle family's seat.

Aurangzeb then declared a jihad against the Marathas, and brought his entire imperial army to try and subdue Satara. Rajaram died of natural causes (and perhaps from battle exhaustion) in 1700, but his senior widow Tarabai continued to lead the Maratha resistance. The Mughal emperor offered to recognize Shahuji (the captive Maratha prince) as the rightful independent king of the Marathas if he would convert to Islam. Shahuji refused, and the emperor was forced to adopt varied stratagems to cajole other Maratha noblemen to desert to his side. But Tarabai's parallel administration continued to gain strength in the west and north, and mounted increasingly daring (and successful) raids into the Mughal cities of Hyderabad and Machilipatnam in the east.

The military stalemate with the Marathas (which lasted past Aurangzeb's death in 1707) weakened the Mughal empire economically, severely disrupting trade between the empire's northern and southern realms and leading to near-famine conditions in 1702–04. The emperor's obsession with the Marathas also created the space for the British, French and Dutch East India Companies to consolidate their coastal strongholds (aided by the immigration of impoverished peasants and traders fleeing the ravages of Mughal–Maratha conflict). And the Europeans also used their mild naval superiority to indulge increasingly in piracy at sea—the most celebrated episode being the 1695 rape and plunder of the *Ganj-i-Sawai*, a massive imperial ship returning from the Hajj that was attacked by two English pirate ships under the command of the English pirate Henry Bridgeman. After Aurangzeb's death in 1707, however, the Marathas gained almost absolute control of the western (Konkan) coast of India. Siddi Yakut Khan, the Mughal feudatory on the west coast, had failed in a punitive attack on the British fortifications at Bombay in 1702, and thereafter the Marathas increasingly emerged as western India's main naval power.

The Maratha admiral, Kanhoji Angre, was repeatedly challenged by the British, and repulsed numerous attempts by the British East India Company to capture his port strongholds of Colaba, Gheriah (Vijaydurg) and Suvarnadurg in 1718 and 1721. Angre gained fame as the chief protagonist in several histories of the period written by English contemporaries, in which he is, predictably, referred to as a notorious 'pirate'. As the Surkhail (grand admiral) of the Marathas—who were the sovereign rulers of India's west coast and much of central India at the time—Angre naturally saw the *British* as pirates, and any of their ships that did not carry a dastak (pass) issued by him were subject to seizure. The Company governor of Bombay, Charles Boone, requested his directors in London to seek the assistance of the Royal Navy, and a squadron under Commodore Matthews duly sailed out to subdue the Maratha admiral Kanhoji Angre. But in a joint Anglo-Portuguese assault (from the land) on Angre's fortress of Colaba in 1723—accompanied by an attempted naval blockade by Matthews's ships—Angre's Maratha forces clearly emerged victorious. Perhaps unfortunately for India's subsequent history (and fortuitously for the British) the Marathas did not pursue the retreating British forces, although much of the Portuguese force was destroyed. The latter then made their peace with Angre, while the British continued to skirmish with him until his death in 1729.

Meanwhile, in the north, the Mughal empire was crumbling. Bahadur Shah I (r. 1707–12) managed to hold on to most of his father's vast empire nominally, although he faced rebellions from the Rajputs (who had aligned with the Timurids since Akbar's time, but were alienated by Aurangzeb's policies) and was obliged to work out a modus vivendi with them that involved a dilution of the intolerant austerity of Aurangzeb's brand of Islamic rule, and granting substantially greater autonomy to Jodhpur and Jaipur. In the Deccan, Sambhaji's son Shahuji had been released from the imperial encampment soon after Aurangzeb's death, and became a competitor to his aunt Tarabai's claim to be the legitimate ruler of the Marathas. Although Bahadur Shah recognized Shahuji as the sovereign ruler of the Marathas (allowing him to collect 35 per cent of revenues in the region and take control of much of the Mughal Deccan), this did not enable Shahuji to defeat his aunt's forces— partly because Admiral Kanhoji Angre was still aligned with Tarabai. Finally, Shahuji's wily chief minister, (Peshwa) Balaji Vishwanath, pulled off a coup in 1715 by concluding an alliance with Angre, and the latter's defection to the Peshwa's side allowed Shahuji to assert himself as the legitimate king of all the Marathas. Although he now reigned, the Peshwas were effectively the rulers in an arrangement reminiscent of the Shoguns of Tokugawa Japan (and, later, the Ranas of Nepal). Under Balaji Vishwanath's son and able successor, Baji Rao I (Peshwa 1720–40), the hereditary Peshwas became the rulers of what emerged as the Maratha Confederacy, the pre-eminent imperial power in India between 1715 and 1803.

Balaji Vishwanath also intervened in the Mughal succession struggles following Bahadur Shah's death in 1712, aligning himself with the Sayyid brothers of Baraha, who became highly influential in the Mughal court between 1712 and 1720. By the end of Bahadur Shah's rule, the Timurids' only reliable source of revenue was from their richest—and most populous—province of Bengal. Aurangzeb's uncle Shaista Khan had substantially improved the fiscal situation of Bengal under the direction of his diwan (finance minister), Kartalab Khan (a Brahmin convert to Islam, who had previously made his reputation as diwan of the Mughal Deccan). Introducing the centralized administrative system that Emperor Akbar's finance minister Todar Mal had perfected, Kartalab Khan ensured that the most productive regions of Bengal and Bihar became khalisa lands (paying revenues directly to the emperor, with transferable officials appointed directly from Delhi), with most jagirdars transferred to Orissa. Aurangzeb was so pleased with the enormous surpluses he was generating that he gave Kartalab the title Murshid Quli Khan, made him governor of Orissa and allowed him to move his fiscal headquarters from Dhaka (the nawab's capital) to a new city called Murshidabad.

Meanwhile, in the north, the Rajputs, Jats and Sikhs were in rebellion, while Hyderabad was becoming increasingly independent. Bahadur Shah's period of rule was spent in subduing each of these rebellions. He broadly succeeded in each case, but was obliged to give substantially greater power to Ajit Singh Rathore of Jodhpur (who became governor of Gujarat) and Jai Singh Kachwaha of Jaipur (who became governor of Malwa). The assassination in 1708 of the tenth Sikh guru, Gobind Singh, who had transformed the Sikhs from a docile religious group into a highly efficient and loyal fighting force, made the Sikhs implacable foes of the Mughals. Their new leader, Banda Bahadur, began creating a rudimentary Sikh kingdom, even as he was obliged by the imperial forces to flee into the hills. Both Aurangzeb and Bahadur Shah used the Kachwahas to suppress the Jat revolt that emerged in the area around Agra, but that reliance only strengthened this Rajput dynasty, which (along with the Sisodias of Mewar and Rathores of Jodhpur) were to become largely independent of Mughal control after Bahadur Shah's death.

Farrukhsiyar—a nephew of Emperor Bahadur Shah who had been governor of Bengal—marched to Delhi amid the turmoil of a succession crisis in 1713. Although he was the emperor from 1713 to 1719, the real powers behind his throne were the two Sayyid brothers who had accompanied him from their strongholds in Patna and Allahabad. Farrukhsiyar's time on the throne was taken up largely with trying to outfox the Sayyid brothers who were wily and powerful but, as Indian Muslims, could never have the charisma of legitimacy that attached to those of Timurid stock.

The emperor sent one Sayyid brother, Husain Ali Khan, to the Deccan as governor while also sending secret messages to Shahuji, enlisting Maratha support in crushing his own governor. Having defeated another Mughal general who was sent to kill him, Husain Ali Khan discovered the emperor's secret communications—and the Sayyids now decided to open negotiations of their own with the Marathas. Eventually, terms were agreed, giving Shahuji virtually free rein over the Deccan in exchange for an annual tribute to Delhi, where (implicitly) the Sayyids would rule. Peshwa Balaji Vishwanath then marched to Delhi along with Sayyid Husain Ali Khan, and their joint forces ousted emperor Farrukhsiyar from the throne, blinded and jailed him, and installed a young puppet on the throne. The Marathas were now kingmakers in Delhi, although they continued to acknowledge the nominal overlordship of the Timurids: having been socialized in Timurid court etiquette, Shahuji always remained reluctant to challenge the Timurids either in Delhi or Hyderabad, although his Peshwas clearly had the military ability to do so.

During his brief period on the throne, however, Farrukhsiyar (who had been assiduously cultivated by English agents during his time in Bengal, including the period when his father was governor there) signed a firman giving the English East India Company the right to trade freely in Bengal. The previous ad valorem customs duties were removed and replaced with the payment of a meagre 3,000 rupees annually to Delhi! Although the British celebrated this—and it did give their exploitation of Bengal a veneer of legitimacy—Murshid Quli Khan was, by this time, ensconced as governor or nawab (not just diwan) of Bengal, Orissa and Bihar, and became almost completely independent from Delhi by 1720. The British would spend the next forty years trying to enforce this firman.

Lacking the legitimacy to hold the throne, the Sayyids ruled in Delhi for just over a year. Their initial puppet emperor died within six months, a second lasted another three, and a grandson of Bahadur Shah, who titled himself Muhammad Shah, ascended the Timurid throne in September 1719. By this time, the Peshwa had left Delhi after imperial coins were released to enshrine the Maratha–Sayyid understanding and recognize Shahuji's swaraj (independence). Within the imperial court, the Nizam-ul-Mulk began rallying the Persian (Irani and Turani) noblemen against the Sayyids. In August 1720, the Nizam won the battle of Shakar Kheda in the Deccan against a joint Sayyid–Maratha army. Soon after, one Sayyid brother was assassinated while marching with the emperor Muhammad Shah's forces; the latter then joined the Nizam in a battle against the other Sayyid brother, who was killed in November 1720. The Timurids were restored to the throne, but the Nizam (who was originally from Moradabad in north India) became the Nawab of Hyderabad by 1724, and became largely independent of Delhi in the vast territories of that south-central province. Along with Murshid Quli Khan in Bengal, Nawab Saadat Khan of Oudh too became largely independent of Mughal Delhi.

But Peshwa Baji Rao I, who took office upon his father's death in 1720 and ruled from Pune (Poona) until 1740, soon became the predominant Indian political figure of his time. The ablest Maratha general since Shivaji, Baji Rao fought thirty-eight battles and never lost one. The British general Bernard Montgomery considered Baji Rao one of history's greatest cavalry generals, using rapid troop movements that were later to be adopted by General William Tecumseh Sherman in 1864 during the US Civil War. He crushed the Nizam at Palkhed in 1728, conquered Rajasthan and Multan in 1735, recaptured Delhi in 1737, and reached Orissa and Bengal by 1740. The British built a 'Maratha Ditch' around their emerging capital of Calcutta to keep out the enemy, but the Marathas did not consider Calcutta a significant prize at the time, focusing instead on deltaic Bengal and bringing Orissa firmly under their sway. Baji Rao built an administrative system that is best described as a commonwealth, with vast lands being awarded to leading generals (most of whom were not the traditional deshmukhs or aristocratic landholders of the Marathas, but self-made men of humbler stock who had risen in the system by dint of their abilities).

Thus the Gaekwads of Baroda, the Scindias (actually Shindes) of Gwalior, the Holkars of Indore, and two sets of Bhonsle descendants of Shivaji (based in Nagpur and Kolhapur, the latter the successors of Tarabai) became the principal players in the Maratha Confederacy, owing allegiance to the Peshwa in Pune. Baji Rao was the Bismarck who held this system together, but its effectiveness naturally depended on the brilliance of the Peshwa. Just as Otto von Bismarck's system of alliances held Germany and Europe at peace in the late nineteenth century—while his successors were unable to hold the system together—so too the Maratha system in the eighteenth century inevitably frayed after Baji Rao's death. In the 1740s, the Bhonsles of Nagpur consolidated their control of Orissa, while the Holkars and Scindias gained control of much of Rajasthan.

By 1755, the Marathas ruled all the territory that comprises today's north, western and central India (apart from eastern Uttar Pradesh) and much of the south (with the exception of parts of Kerala, Karnataka and Andhra Pradesh). However, while the Scindias were effectively in control of Delhi, the Marathas did not explicitly challenge the legitimacy of the nominal Timurid emperor. The devastating Maratha raid of Delhi in 1737 had been followed by a far more destructive 'visit' from Nadir Shah of Persia two years later; ostensibly arriving as a guest of Muhammad Shah, he plundered the Red Fort (looting the Peacock Throne and Kohinoor diamond) and sacked Delhi. In 1756, an Afghan of the Durrani clan called Ahmad Shah Abdali launched an even more destructive raid on Delhi. In the south, however, the Peshwas defeated the Nizam in 1760, and were effectively the single biggest power in peninsular India, as well as in Lahore, Rajasthan and Delhi.

Four years after the skirmish at Plassey, where Bengal's Nawab Siraj-ud-Daulah was 'defeated', with Clive using the simplest expedient of all (a bribe to the opposing army's commander-in-chief, Mir Jafar, an Arab adventurer who had arrived in India penniless but risen to be bakhshi or military chief at Bengal's court), a much more climactic battle occurred at the famed battlefield of Panipat in 1761. This Third Battle of Panipat pitted the Afghan Ahmad Shah Abdali against a combined Maratha–Mughal army, commanded by Madhavrao (or Mahadji) Scindia. A panic (or perhaps treachery) amongst the Rohilla troops in the Maratha–Mughal ranks caused the tide of battle to turn decisively in favour of the Afghans (with whom the Rohillas shared ethnic kinship). A scion of the victor in that climactic battle (Zahir Shah) continued to rule Afghanistan until the 1970s, while the scions of the losing general (Madhavrao and Vasundhara Raje Scindia) became prominent politicians in both the Congress and BJP in modern India. In the immediate aftermath of 1761, however, the Peshwas lost their aura as the masters of India, as indeed the Timurids already had over the previous four decades of decadence.

Although 1761 took some of the sheen off their dominance, the Marathas were still largely unchallenged as the pre-eminent power in India through the eighteenth century. Mahadji Scindia quickly regrouped, recouping all his territories around Delhi and Agra, effectively making the Mughal emperor Shah Alam II his vassal, conquering the key Rajput kingdoms of Jaipur and Jodhpur and wreaking a heavy defeat on the Rohilla Afghans, thereby emerging as the dominant north Indian power. In the central Indian region of Malwa, Ahilyabai Holkar's benignly progressive rule (with low taxes and encouragement of enterprise) was justly earning her the title of 'Philosopher Queen'. Initially the British did not dare challenge the Marathas; more portentously for the future, however, the Marathas did not bother to challenge the British until it was too late.

In 1764, the British won a genuine military victory at the Battle of Buxar, in which they were pitted against an army representing Shah Alam II (the nominal Timurid emperor, albeit with little control over actual territory), the Nawab of Oudh (Shuja-ud-Daulah) and the deposed Nawab of Bengal (Mir Qasim). Company officer Major General Thomas Munro's forces were outnumbered 4:1, but he fortified the loyalty of his largely Indian soldiers by blowing twenty-four of them from cannons to demonstrate the price of disloyalty or lack of zeal. After the loss at Buxar, Shah Alam formally turned over the diwani (the revenue-collecting authority) of Bengal to the British East India Company in 1765; militarily, the British definitely owed much more to Munro than to Clive.

Now combining a monopoly of the external trade of India's wealthiest (and most industrialized) province, and its revenue-collecting authority, the East India Company officers went on a looting spree. The 'out and back' or 'carry trade' had, in any case, enriched innumerable generations of the Company's employees in India. Empty space on Company ships could carry the personal merchandise of its employees, and they invariably made massive fortunes. The prospect of those fortunes is what made Company employment especially attractive. Thus several generations of the great Pitt family which dominated British politics in the eighteenth century (including Prime Ministers William Pitt the Elder and the Younger) owed their fortune (and ability to finance political careers) to the massive wealth accumulated by an early governor of Madras, Thomas Pitt (1698–1709), while one of his predecessors Elihu Yale (1687–92) spent part of the fortune acquired in Madras to help establish Yale University in New Haven, Connecticut. But the new monopoly on trade and revenue took loot and rapine to new levels, and Bengal was hit by a devastating famine in 1770 that wiped out between a third and half of the population of the Bengal Presidency (which included today's Bangladesh, Bihar and parts of eastern Uttar Pradesh and Orissa).

Far from the mythology of an 'accidental empire' that British historians love to perpetuate, four Anglo–Mysore Wars, three Anglo–Maratha Wars, and two Anglo–Sikh Wars were required before most of what now comprises India was brought under British dominion over eight decades ending in 1849. Over this period, the mercenary army (comprising largely upper caste and elite Muslim troops who could rise no higher than an Indian rank equivalent to captain, and always commanded by British officers) was almost perpetually at war. Although the actual salaries of soldiers were meagre, loot and plunder of defeated palaces, treasuries and cities provided ample reward both to British officers and their Indian troops. However, the structure naturally required continual conquests in order to be viable.

The Mysore kingdom (much of modern Karnataka) was ruled by the Wodeyars, who claimed tenuous descent from the Vijayanagar rulers, the last great Hindu empire in southern India that had finally succumbed to a combined assault from the four neighbouring Muslim sultanates in 1565 at the Battle of Talikota. Vijayanagar had reached its zenith under King Krishnadevaraya, who ruled from 1509–29 and of whom Babur (his contemporary) spoke in some awe in his autobiography. The Portuguese traveller, Domingo Paes, reported in the 1520s that his capital was the 'best provided city in the world', larger than Paris and 'as large as Rome, and very beautiful'. Krishnadevaraya was described by Paes as an extraordinarily just king, but he sat atop a semi-feudal system consisting of about a hundred subordinates (called nayaks) who were appointed by the king and were responsible for maintaining the kingdom's military preparedness. It was from one of the more powerful nayak families that the Wodeyars sprung, although they retrospectively claimed descent from Krishnadevaraya himself. The First Anglo–Mysore War (1767–69), however, did not pit the Wodeyars directly against the British. Instead, it was an exceptionally effective general in the Wodeyar's employ, Haidar Ali, who rose to harry the British. After his initial successes, he ousted the Wodeyars—and he and his son Tipu Sultan proved major thorns in the British flesh in southern India in the late eighteenth century.

The Nizam of Hyderabad had been a French ally until 1759, when a small military detachment sent by Clive to the Nizam's Northern Circars (coastal Andhra) won an unexpected victory over French forces. The small detachment had only been meant to distract some French forces from Madras, which was being threatened by the brilliant French general Joseph-François Dupleix. But the unexpected British win led to the Nizam defecting to the British side and offering them considerable territory in the Northern Circars. The British then relieved the French siege of Madras, and won a decisive victory at Wandiwash; in 1761, the French capital of Pondicherry itself fell to the British. Although the 1763 Treaty of Paris (ending the Seven Years' War in Europe) restored Pondicherry to the French, the latter were never again a genuine threat to British imperial ambitions in southern India. But in 1769, the British suffered a defeat at the hands of Haidar Ali in the First Mysore War, after Haidar had secured the defection of the fickle Nizam. Although both his son Tipu and Haidar himself conducted looting raids on the grand streets of Madras, they did not seek territorial concessions from the British, instead choosing to sign an alliance treaty that committed the British to support Mysore if the latter was attacked by a third party.

Soon thereafter, when Haidar Ali was threatened by the Marathas, the British repeatedly failed to uphold their treaty obligations. This caused

Haidar and Tipu to turn decisively against the British, whom Haidar called 'the most faithless and usurping of all mankind'. During the decade of the 1770s, Haidar Ali held off the Marathas in the north while expanding his kingdom southward and became the master of the entire peninsula south of the Krishna and Tungabhadra rivers. As Anglo–French hostilities resumed with the American War of Independence, Haidar fortified his implicit alliance with the French, using the latter to improve the quality of his military's drills, training and equipment.

In the 1770s, the British began to interfere in the affairs of the Marathas, having found an ally in 'Raghoba' (Raghunath Rao), a disgruntled contender for the peshwaship, who had been ousted by the brilliant Nana Phadnavis (who headed the young Peshwa's Regency Council, and was holding the Maratha Confederacy together). The First Anglo–Maratha War (1775–82) was really a mix of treaties and intermittent clashes. Raghoba and the British signed a treaty in Surat in 1775, and jointly enjoyed some military successes against the Peshwa's forces in Gujarat. But Governor General Warren Hastings in Calcutta stopped his colleagues in Bombay in their tracks, and instead sent an emissary to negotiate with the Peshwa's Regency Council in Pune, which was led by the redoubtable Nana Phadnavis. The resulting treaty was honoured mainly in its breach, and hostilities resumed in 1778 when the British again rushed to Raghoba's aid. The British and Raghoba were thoroughly defeated, and the British governor of Bombay signed the Convention of Wadgaon (1779) under which the British had to give up all territories annexed since 1775. On the strength of this, Phadnavis was able to bring Scindia, Holkar and Gaekwad into a closer alliance and by 1780, had also formed an alliance with the Nizam of Hyderabad and Haidar Ali of Mysore. Hastings then dispatched a large army across India to the west coast, both to relieve Bombay and to try and weaken the emerging alliances (especially the intra-Maratha one). The Gaekwads of Baroda were the first to flinch, formally aligning with the British (and acquiring 'subsidiary' status by 1805).

Scindia was defeated by the British at Sipri, but the combined Maratha–Mysore–Hyderabad alliance inflicted another defeat on the British at Pune (1780). Scindia, however, now played peacemaker, and the Treaty of Salbai (1782) brought the First Anglo–Maratha War to an end. The British gave up advocating Raghoba, and the Marathas agreed implicitly to relinquish the alliance with Haidar Ali. The treaty did preserve Anglo–Maratha peace for over two decades. Meanwhile, Mahadji Scindia's professional army (trained by Benoît de Boigne, a Frenchman who had worked for the English East India Company) re-established his pre-eminence in north India, which continued until his death in 1794. He took Delhi, Agra, Jaipur and Jodhpur and became the guarantor of the Treaty of Salbai on behalf of all the Marathas.

The Second Mysore War (1780–84) began with a huge British defeat at Pollilur at the hands of Tipu, whose victory is commemorated with a massive painting that can be seen at his old palace in Srirangapatna to this day. The Company's Madras Army was clearly not up to the task of subduing Mysore, so Governor General Hastings had to send the Bengal Army from Calcutta (and considerable naval reinforcements) to take on first Haidar (who died of cancer in 1782) and subsequently Tipu Sultan. Eventually, the 1784 Treaty of Mangalore ended the war, but Tipu's relations with the French were frayed by the fact that they negotiated a separate peace with the British. Negligible support from Pondicherry had, in Tipu's view, kept him from winning a more decisive victory and he decided to henceforth negotiate directly with Versailles rather than merely the stragglers of Pondicherry.

In 1785 Tipu sent a diplomatic mission to Constantinople (Istanbul) to get the Ottoman caliph's imprimatur recognizing him as a legitimate padishah who was holding the British at bay in India. Two years later, this same mission was to proceed to France, but it got delayed in Iraq. Instead, a separate mission under the flag of Mysore arrived at Toulon in June 1788, and was received in grand style by Louis XVI at Versailles on 10 August. With the clouds of Revolution already forming (and the storming of the Bastille less than a year away), Louis and Marie Antoinette were in no position to conclude distant alliances, but a vast retinue of French technicians returned to Mysore with the mission. Tipu also began vigorously modernizing his realms in non-military ways, establishing a state trading company (on a joint-stock model, much like the East India Company), and setting up factories in the Arabian Sea and around the Persian Gulf, as well as in Pegu (Bago) in Burma. He was responsible for introducing sericulture to Mysore, and for the creation of factories for silk-weaving and processing, the production of sugar, paper, gunpowder, knives and scissors. More than eighty years before the Meiji Restoration in Japan, an Indian ruler was vigorously introducing Western methods to modernize and strengthen his realms and, to some, 'Citoyen Tipu's' methods and objectives were just as ambitious as French revolutionary contemporaries'.

At this time Governor General Cornwallis was seeking military redemption in India, following his defeat at the hands of George Washington (and his young lieutenants, Lafayette and Hamilton) in 1783 at Yorktown. Tipu's conquest of the Hindu kingdom of Travancore, a British ally on the Malabar coast, supplied the provocation. Cornwallis first secured a strong alliance with the Marathas and the Nizam. And a combined army of the three allies declared war on Tipu in 1790. Initially, Tipu got the better of Cornwallis, extending his hold over the British 'Carnatic', but the allied armies gradually gained the upper hand, conquering the Deccan, taking Bangalore and beginning to threaten Tipu's capital of Srirangapatna itself. Tipu held off the allied forces for almost a year before being obliged to accept humiliating terms in 1792, which included the surrender of almost half his territory, and an eight-figure indemnity (until the payment of which his beloved sons, aged eight and ten, were to be held by the British as surety).

Meanwhile, Cornwallis returned to Bengal, to introduce the Permanent Settlement—a system of land ownership that was aimed at granting secure property rights to zamindars (landlords), in the hope that they would become 'gentleman farmers' in the English manner. But the burden of taxation (although established at a fixed, permanent amount into the indefinite future) was set exceptionally high (at nearly 90 per cent of the value of the crop in the first year), and the system was doomed to failure from the outset. Zamindars typically farmed out their revenue-collection authority to other intermediaries, and the growing layers of the latter were to debilitate the productive capacity of agriculture in Bengal. One of the remarkable facts about the Indian subcontinent is that the parts that were ruled by the British the longest are today the poorest, while those parts that were conquered last are amongst the richest. Bengal, the richest province of the Timurid empire, was devastated in particular by the imposition in 1701 of a blanket ban on imports of Indian cloth into Britain—in order to protect and nurture the emergence of a new British textile industry in Lancashire. Until this time, Bengal was one of the world's leading manufacturing centres, producing much of the muslin and cotton that clothed the world (as Daniel Defoe had admiringly admitted in January 1708). British import protection—and the subsequent subsidized exports of British cloth into India—gradually destroyed the Bengal textile industry in the period between 1760 and 1850, contributing in particular to the devastating famine of 1770.

Tipu returned his reduced territories to prosperity, re-establishing trading ties with his far-flung network. The light tax burden he imposed generated substantial growth in agricultural and industrial production in his realms. But his continuing contacts with Napoleon Bonaparte, the new French ruler who had just conquered Egypt, provided the pretext for the Fourth Mysore War of 1799. Significantly weakened militarily, Tipu was no match for the 40,000 troops (and the 100,000-bullock baggage-and-armaments convoy) that invaded Mysore at the command of Governor General Richard Wellesley (whose brother Arthur, the future Duke of Wellington, was amongst the main generals in this army). After a three-month sacking that 'would not have disgraced Attila', Tipu was dead, his capital destroyed, and most of his territory annexed to the British empire. A small slice was restored to the scion of the Wodeyars, with all the panoply of British suzerainty, including a large British presence headed by a Resident. Similar arrangements were also made with the Nizam in 1800, who handed over all his Mysore territories to the Company in exchange for British protection.

The brilliant leader of the Marathas' Regency Council, Nana Phadnavis, died in 1800. The previous Peshwa had committed suicide four years earlier, opening the way for Raghoba's son Baji Rao II to become Peshwa (with the blessings of Daulat Rao Scindia). The other Maratha giant, Mahadji Scindia, had died in 1794, Ahilyabai Holkar the next year. Now Jaswant Rao Holkar and Daulat Rao Scindia went to war over control of the new young Peshwa, with the former emerging as winner. Baji Rao II fled and (in keeping with his father Raghunath Rao's predilections) sought shelter with the British. He was assured British support in his restoration as Peshwa, but his Treaty of Bassein (1803) effectively made him a 'subsidiary ally' of the British, with a large British troop presence. A renewed spurt of intra-Maratha conflict had provided just the opening for the British to end the independence of the Peshwa, and terminate the Maratha ascendancy in India.

Having thus secured control of the Peshwa through clever political manoeuvres, the Second Anglo–Maratha War (1803–05) was almost in the nature of a postscript—although the actual battles were still ferocious. Ostensibly fought by the British to restore the Peshwa to his throne (albeit a restoration that the British had ensured they would be fully in command of), the British were also aided by the Nizam's troops from Hyderabad in the main assault on Poona. Arthur Wellesley won decisive victories over Scindia at Assaye, and over the Bhonsles at Argaon. A large force under General Lake took Delhi (including a bedraggled Mughal 'emperor' Shah Alam) and Agra from the Scindias, and won a pitched battle against the main Gwalior army at Laswari. Two separate armies were required to subdue the awesome power of the Scindias in north India: Arthur Wellesley always considered the battle of Assaye a harder contest than Waterloo. The British annexed Gujarat from the Scindias, and Orissa from the Bhonsles, and the Doab (the area in north India between the Ganga and Yamuna, in today's Uttar Pradesh) came under direct British rule. The British frontier in 1805 was at the borders of Punjab, where a dynamic young Sikh ruler, Ranjit Singh, had been establishing himself as the pre-eminent ruler of much of the area from Peshawar to Lahore, having repeatedly raided and defeated Ahmad Shah Abdali's successors.

Meanwhile the financially and militarily weakened Maratha rulers struggled to maintain their moth-eaten authority, with many of their disgruntled troops defecting to join the central Indian marauders known as the Pindaris (whom the British suspected Holkar and Scindia of protecting). It was to subdue the Pindaris that the British began a new mobilization in 1818, ostensibly in alliance with the Marathas. But the latter's suspicions were aroused by the massive nature of the mobilization (which suggested that they, the Maratha rulers, were likely to be the real targets of the British moves). Peshwa Baji Rao II then turned against the British, and the Third Anglo–Maratha War began with the Peshwa's forces attacking the British Residency in Poona. But, by this time, the British forces were the only properly trained and drilled army in Poona, and they routed the Peshwa's straggling troops. An uprising of the Bhonsles in Nagpur was similarly put down by the British. The Peshwa was deposed and sent into internal exile (albeit with much of his wealth intact and a sizable 'pension') in the nondescript town of Bithur near Kanpur ('Cawnpore' in imperial parlance) in the Doab. The Bhonsles' realms were largely annexed, and they were reduced to two small 'subsidiary' principalities based in Satara and Kolhapur. The Marathas had been entirely tamed.

The British now began to turn their attention towards the Punjab, where Ranjit Singh Sukarchakia had established a powerful presence. In 1809, the Treaty of Amritsar defined the River Sutlej as the border between British India and Maharaja Ranjit Singh's empire. Ranjit had been only ten when he was first pressed into battle in 1790 and came out a hero. He was twelve when his father died, bequeathing him the Sukarchakia chieftainship. By the time he was sixteen, Ranjit had already been skirmishing with Shah Zaman, the ruler of Kabul, for three years. Inspired by the rousing speeches of his mother-in-law, Sada Kaur, a large Sikh army had rallied to Ranjit's side, and he inflicted a decisive defeat on Shah Zaman in 1798—and became the undisputed ruler of Lahore. In 1802, Ranjit took control of Amritsar (the location of the Sikhs' holiest site, the Harmandir Sahib, where Ranjit Singh added the marble and gold to make the magnificent Golden Temple). Although illiterate (like the Timurid emperor Akbar), he was curious about the world and (like Akbar) surrounded himself with men of learning, as well as a remarkably cosmopolitan set of military officers (from various parts of India, as well as Germans, Italians, Frenchmen and a smattering of Britishers).

His professional, highly capable army commanded sufficient respect from the British for them to adhere scrupulously to the Amritsar Treaty as long as Ranjit lived. The treaty also ensured that the 'Cis-Sutlej states' (including Patiala) between the Sutlej and the Yamuna rivers became British rather than Sikh vassals, giving the British an important toehold in the Punjab. By the time he died in June 1839, Ranjit Singh had united the rest of Punjab all the way south to Multan (plus much of what became the North West

Frontier Province all the way to Peshawar), conquered all of Jammu and Kashmir, annexed Ladakh from the realms of the Dalai Lama, and the Kumaon and Garhwal hills (much of today's Indian states of Himachal Pradesh and Uttaranchal) from the Ranas who ruled Nepal. Ranjit's formidable general Hari Singh Nalwa played the vital role in securing Peshawar and the Khyber–Pakhtunkhwa region for the Punjabi empire.

Although cosmopolitan and broadly secular in his approach to governance, Ranjit Singh's army, court and cabinet was predominantly Sikh: while Sikhs were only about 15 per cent of the population of his empire, they comprised more than half of all his troops and councillors, while Muslims made up half of the inhabitants but only about a fifth of his troops. This was a mirror image of what the typical Mughal alignment had been, with Muslims accounting for about a fifth of the realm's population but for between half and three-fourths of the court nobility, even under Akbar. A relatively light tax burden (especially in comparison with the 'Tax Britannica' that was decimating the rest of India) also ensured the rising prosperity in Ranjit Singh's realms. The year after he died, one of his Dogra generals, Zorawar Singh, actually invaded Tibet itself, but the invasion was poorly timed, in the bitter cold of winter, for which the Dogra army was thoroughly ill-prepared. The 6,000-man Dogra army was routed by a Tibetan force that was twice its size (including Chinese troop reinforcements), defeated primarily by frostbite rather than the strength of the opposing army.

Ranjit Singh's main army was a formidable Punjabi force with a Sikh core but incorporated Punjabi Hindus and Muslims, as well as Pathans. Both the rapidity of his rise and the brilliance of his generalship invited comparisons with his contemporary Napoleon from French and British visitors (the British acknowledged him to be a 'man of military genius', like Napoleon). And the proliferation of ex-Napoleonic officers at the top of his army (Generals Avitabile and Ventura, Colonels Court and Allard) helped create an 'army as effective as that of the Company.' In fact, the British were so in awe of Ranjit's army that they carefully skirted his realms on their march to Afghanistan in 1839 to fight the first Anglo–Afghan War with an army that was, naturally, overwhelmingly Indian.

The ostensible purpose of the Anglo–Afghan War was to secure this important buffer nation from the Russians, who had by then spread their rule all the way to Bukhara and Samarkand. Just as the Russians and the Americans were to discover in the twentieth and twenty-first centuries, the British learnt in the nineteenth century (1839–42) that it is easy to conquer the Afghans, but well-nigh impossible to rule them for long. The Army of the Indus comfortably conquered Kabul in 1839, and the British put in a puppet king of their choice, Shah Shuja, alongside a British Resident (or governor, who actually ruled), and set about establishing their cantonments and other accoutrements of control.

Imperceptibly, however, the Afghans organized a resistance, led by Mohammed Akbar, the son of the ousted king Dost Mohammed. One morning in November 1840, the British Resident Alexander Burnes and his family were hacked to pieces by their gardeners and retainers, and the British cantonment in the valley of Kabul found itself surrounded by guerrilla forces that had occupied all the high points on the hills surrounding the capital. The British were obliged to surrender Kabul in January 1842. Although offered safe passage, the British forces were massacred along the Kabul River and only a solitary Englishman, William Brydon (a surgeon), straggled into Jalalabad (along with a few Indian soldiers) on 13 January. The returning Jalalabad garrison, reinforced by troops led by Major General Sir Charles Napier, however, gratuitously attacked and conquered Sindh. Napier evidently did not send a telegram with the Latin pun, 'Peccavi' (meaning 'I have sinned') to Whitehall; that was attributed to him in a satirical piece in *Punch*, the late lamented epitome of British wit. Napier's sin was in running roughshod over numerous treaties with local Sindhi rulers and emirs that had supposedly guaranteed their neutral independence.

Unfortunately, like many of the greatest kings in Indian history, Ranjit Singh did not leave behind an institutionalized method of succession. And a mad scramble ensued amongst his legitimate and illegitimate children for control of his realm. When his son Sher Singh (the third holder of the throne since Ranjit's death, after eldest son Kharak Singh and his son Nau Nihal) was assassinated in 1843, the British (by then humiliated in Afghanistan) began to intervene in Sikh affairs. One of Ranjit Singh's wives, Rani Jindan, became regent to her infant son Dalip Singh, the new king, with two Dogra (non-Sikh) noblemen, Lal Singh and Tej Singh, holding substantive power. The British began massing their forces on the kingdom's borders, and the First Anglo–Sikh War began in December 1845. Possible treachery by Lal Singh and Tej Singh played a part in swinging the battle in favour of the huge British force (headed by Governor General Henry Hardinge and the commander-in-chief of the Bengal Army, General Lord Hugh Gough) at the Battles of Aliwal and Sobraon.

By the Treaty of Lahore that ended hostilities in March 1846, the British gained Kashmir—which they then sold to the Dogra raja of Jammu, Gulab Singh—and also the coveted Kohinoor diamond that Ranjit Singh had received as tribute from Shah Shuja of Afghanistan. The Sikh kingdom saw a shrinkage in its territory (with its boundary moving from the Sutlej to the Beas) and had to pay an indemnity, but continued to rule from Lahore. Gulab Singh, who had acknowledged the suzerainty of Ranjit Singh, now switched to British vassalage with the title of Maharaja of Jammu and Kashmir, a title his successors continued to hold until 1947.

Once it became clear that the British intended to rule the Punjab with the infant Dalip Singh as their hapless puppet, Punjabi sardars (noblemen) and soldiers began chafing at the British Resident's attempts at establishing authority. In April 1848, two separate rebellions began in Multan under Diwan Mulraj and Sher Singh Attariwala, and several English officers were killed. Governor General Dalhousie dispatched a strong Army of the Punjab under General Gough, but this only took the field in December. Despite overwhelming strength in numbers, Gough's army suffered a humiliating defeat in the Battle of Chillianwala in January 1849 at the hands of Sher Singh. Although British writers called it a draw or standstill, Chillianwala dealt a severe blow to British prestige in India, and indirectly contributed to the events of 1857.

Lord Gough was stripped of his command of the British Indian Army (replaced nationally by Sir Charles Napier). But he was saved in Punjab by Major General Whish, who (aided by a large column of troops from Bombay) subdued Diwan Mulraj in Multan, with a force of some 30,000 men confronting Mulraj's emaciated force of barely 10,000. The relief of Multan enabled Whish to bring large reinforcements to Gough's side in mid-February 1849, and he was able to win a decisive victory at the Battle of Gujrat on 11 March. On 29 March, Sher Singh and his father Chattar Singh formally surrendered to the British, and Dalip Singh signed the papers that enabled the British to annex the Punjab—bringing to a close ninety-two years of almost continual warfare that had enabled the British to conquer India.

By 1849, the East India Company had effectively conquered the whole of India, using a mix of subterfuge, bribery, clever manipulation of allies and the occasional straight military victory (usually after an adversary's forces had been infiltrated, bribed or otherwise compromised sufficiently for them to be easy prey for the Company's army). As the tide of conquest swelled, however, the East India Company's military rivals dwindled to fewer and fewer significant forces—first the Marathas throughout the eighteenth century, joined by Mysore late in that century, and the Sikhs (and remnants of the Marathas) in the first half of the nineteenth century. Throughout the period, some rulers had chosen to align themselves with the rising power of the Company rather than fight it, and these local rulers were officially called 'subsidiary allies', with a British 'Resident' in the court of a local ruler (nawab, maharaja, raja, nizam, etc.) being the only evidence of a formal British presence.

However, while the British had subsidiary alliances with a large number of rulers in India, the East India Company was still technically (and legally) a feudatory of the Mughal emperor. Although British chroniclers of the nineteenth century frequently speak of Emperor Bahadur Shah Zafar as a 'pensioner' of the Company, in fact Bahadur Shah received an annual tribute from the Company in return for the right to collect tax ('diwani') in Bengal. It was this right that the Company had parlayed into its vast territorial acquisitions across eastern, central and northern India, all made under the aegis of its Bengal Army; the East India Company's conquests in southern and western India (undertaken by the Madras and Bombay Army, respectively) were pure conquests without the veneer of legitimacy that the link to the Mughal emperor provided to its Bengal Army.

In the south, the nominal Mughal feudatory (the Nizam of Hyderabad) had become one of the earliest subsidiary allies of the British after Governor General Wellesley introduced the Subsidiary Alliance System in 1802; it was in alliance with the Nizam (and palace intrigues with Raghoba) that the Company had subdued the Marathas. The rest of southern India had been conquered in the 1750s primarily by buying over the Nawab of Arcot (one of whose descendants is the former English cricket captain, Nasser Hussain) and the Raja of Tanjore (a descendant of Shivaji's brother Vyankoji), and using their forces to subdue the rest of the peninsula. However, across north India the memory of two centuries of Timurid rule had left a more indelible impression—than compared to their more fleeting presence in the Deccan and points south—and the charisma of the Mughals contributed to the legitimacy of the East India Company's rule in the eyes of the common citizenry. It was natural for the sepoys (foot soldiers) of the East India Company's Bengal Army to rise in rebellion against their British officers in May 1857—and to do so in the name of the Mughal emperor, the legal overlord of the Company that employed them.

With the ascendancy of the Maratha Confederacy, the Mughal emperor Shah Alam came under the control of the Scindias of Gwalior, who still carefully maintained the official fiction of Shah Alam's position as emperor, while Shah Alam acknowledged Mahadji Scindia as the 'regent' who really ruled in his name. After the defeat of Gwalior at Assaye, the British styled the Mughal emperor as 'King of Delhi', with a 'pension' from the East India Company, although, of course, this nominal sum was formally a tribute in exchange for the diwani rights. Nonetheless, in the eyes of the common man in India, the legitimacy of the East India Company's rule continued to depend on that firman from Shah Alam's Timurid ancestor, Farrukhsiyar.

British East India Company coins were issued in the name of the Timurid emperor until as late as 1835 (seventy-one years after the Company had vanquished the Timurids at Buxar). Arguably, the shift to using the visage of King William IV of Britain in the coins after 1835 was one of the factors that bred deep-seated resentment of the foreign power, once it began to assert that it was indeed a power in its own right, rather than a licensed trading agent of the long-reigning Timurid dynasty. Governor General Dalhousie's 'Doctrine of Lapse' was an even more pernicious intrusion into the prevailing order.

By the 'Doctrine of Lapse', Dalhousie sought to take possession of any kingdom in which the king did not have a blood heir, repudiating the long-established practice of adoption that was a common form of inheritance in Indian law and tradition. This 'doctrine' tore the mask off Company rule, demonstrating with a sudden jolt that the traditional rulers of India had been shorn of their power and their realms could be annexed at the Company's whim.

The war of 1857 was, therefore, a collective roar of rebellion by the Company's Indian soldiers seeking to restore the natural order that had prevailed before this trading company usurped power (especially between 1835 and 1850). Although British historians persist in calling it *The Indian Mutiny* (the title of Saul David's book published as recently as 2003) there is no legal or historical basis to call the 1857 rebellion by the East India Company's Bengal Army a 'mutiny', since they were rising against their officers in the name of the Mughal emperor who was their formal ruler, and in whose name the East India Company ruled over India, and particularly the Bengal Presidency. British historians even today write about India in 1857 as if it was Britain's natural right to rule all India then. The Indians, particularly in north India (and specifically in the vast province of Bengal, which then extended from Assam in the east to Delhi, Agra and much of Punjab in the west) vehemently protested against this British claim, which was actually quite new, having been made only since 1835, when the Company ceased issuing coins in the name of the Timurid emperor. Ironically, the Bengalis of Calcutta (the Company capital) largely stood aside during the 1857 war—and did not formally join the rebellion, although they did not go out of their way to support the British either.

As the victors, the British were able to write the history of the 1857–58 war. The war of 1857 became synonymous with the memory of English women and children defiled, and generations of English schoolchildren were fed these apocryphal or exaggerated tales. British historians (and other chroniclers of empire) are past masters in the art of obliterating the memory of their 'arch-villains' by partly fabricating tales of their allegedly inhuman actions and erasing any memory of their actual successes against the British, including acts of great kindness. In their telling, Nana Saheb Peshwa (the adopted son of the last Peshwa, Baji Rao II) appears merely as the treacherous 'scoundrel' allegedly responsible for the Satichaura massacre. It turns out that Nana Saheb actually protected more than two hundred British women and children in Kanpur throughout the war, and only his defeat eventually led to their being killed. Although newspaper reports until the late 1880s suggest that the British lived in mortal fear of Nana Saheb's sudden re-emergence, his pivotal role in planning and executing the strategy for the war of 1857 is buried in the mists of British historiography.

It is an indubitable fact, however, that virtually all the key players in the planning and execution of India's First War of Independence—Nana Saheb himself, Azimullah Khan, Tatya Tope and Lakshmibai (the future Rani of Jhansi)—were schoolmates at the same school near Bithur. In 1855, Nana Saheb sent his trusted friend and adviser, Azimullah Khan, to Britain to argue his case before Queen Victoria and her court. As with all those 'defeated' in wars that they had fought against the British, the last Peshwa had been offered an annuity in perpetuity (conveniently referred to by British historians as a 'pension') in exchange for going into exile in Bithur (near Kanpur), far away from his family's dominions in the heart of the Maratha territory. Immediately upon the death of Peshwa Baji Rao II, however, this annual payment (which was part of a solemn treaty signed by the British) was summarily withdrawn from his successor, Nana Saheb, on the grounds that the latter was merely an adopted son (although adoption was perfectly legal under Indian law).

Azimullah Khan evidently generated great interest in contemporary British society, as the women of the British nobility quickly succumbed to his charms. The queen herself was sympathetic, but her politicians overruled her proclivities and Azimullah returned disappointed to India. On his way, however, he met the Ottoman emperor's representatives in Constantinople, and almost certainly also met senior representatives of the Russian tsar in an attempt to shore up global support for his master Nana Saheb's imminent rebellion. Upon his return, he and Nana Saheb undertook a tour of several cantonments of the British Indian Army, including Ambala, Meerut and Barrackpore (conspicuously the very places where rebellion was to break out a few months later); at Kalpi, he was said to have met representatives of the Rani of Jhansi. While the tour was described as 'leisurely', some white officers' servants informed them that Nana Saheb had used incendiary language in many of these appearances. The British had become extremely suspicious of Nana Saheb, but they were also complacent after their seemingly emphatic conquest of all India by 1850, and failed to pay sufficient attention to the actions of a supposedly neutered former ruler.

By the summer of 1857, chapattis with incendiary messages began spreading across north India, and sporadically across the south and west as well. The chapatti messages focused on the danger to Indians' religions (Hinduism and Islam primarily) from the evangelical zeal of the Company's Christian preachers—and, in particular, the danger to their religions represented by the Company's introduction of the new rifle cartridges coated with beef and pork lard. The chapattis created ferment across the country, well planned and executed by Nana Saheb and his followers, who were preparing to ignite a mighty nationwide rebellion to overthrow British rule around the centenary of the East India Company's 'victory' in the Battle of Plassey.

Unfortunately, some sepoys of the Bengal Army were aroused to a fever pitch by the message contained in the chapattis, and the taunts they regularly faced in the bazaars on account of the irreligious new rifles. One sepoy, Mangal Pandey, appeared to have ignited the rebellion three months too early by personally rising against his iniquitous British officers, shooting one dead and grievously wounding another on 23 March 1857. Mangal Pandey's summary execution only served to arouse even greater antipathy, and a full-scale rebellion amongst the troops began in Meerut (on 11 May) and quickly spread across all the main military stations across north India (i.e., in the vast Bengal Presidency). The British were already introducing the telegraph—a considerably superior mode of communication to the humble chapatti—but the innovative Indian response went a long way towards arousing all of India to the rising iniquities (and sheer illegality) of British suzerainty over India. But it didn't go all the way, and the early start upset Nana Saheb's carefully laid plans while giving the British an opportunity to regroup and plan their counteroffensive (which would have been much more difficult had there been a simultaneous uprising in several key locations across the country on a single day).

Nonetheless, the Indian forces scored a series of victories, as key British military bases across north India quickly fell to them, including Meerut, Ambala and most spectacularly Delhi, where Bahadur Shah Zafar was re-coronated as the Emperor of India. In a similarly grand ceremony in Bithur, Nana Saheb was formally proclaimed the new Maratha Peshwa on 1 July soon after the major British garrison at Kanpur was taken. Thus, the dominant powers in India between 1526 and 1707 (the Timurids) and in the period from 1710 to 1818 (the Marathas) effectively coalesced anew into a cohesive force to fight the foreign power (the British East India Company) that had sought to usurp them in the nineteenth century. Since both the Timurids and the Marathas had been largely defanged through incremental treaties over the previous century that decimated their military organizations, they depended crucially on the 'rebellion' of the Company's own sepoys to provide the foot soldiers (and much of the intermediate-level command-and-control structure) for the war against the foreign occupiers. The revolt of virtually the whole of the Bengal Army provided an ample army of foot soldiers. By August 1857, the whole of north India had been liberated from British occupation.

Unfortunately for the Indian forces, they suffered from a lack of able generalship and communications technology, while the British access to the new telegraph technology gave them a decisive advantage that became increasingly evident by early 1858. The British East India Company had ensured that the highest rank an Indian could rise to within its army was subedar major (i.e., a lower rank than second lieutenant). Thus, while the rebel army contained many highly decorated and brave soldiers, it contained no Indian officers who understood even the rudiments of war strategy. Prince Mirza Mughal (the eldest surviving son of Emperor Bahadur Shah Zafar) who took command of both the army and administration of Delhi soon after the old imperial capital was taken by the Indian forces, proved capable on both fronts but was unable to demonstrate decisive results quickly enough to hold off court intrigues that led to him being sidelined.

In Delhi, the British ensconced themselves atop the Ridge (where Delhi University now stands) for several months. Mirza Mughal decided to outflank this force by attacking from the rear—a manoeuvre that bore immediate results, demoralizing the British, but not resulting in any visible decline in their military position on the Ridge. Ironically, other courtiers were able to have Mirza Mughal replaced as commander-in-chief just as his strategy was beginning to work. In particular, the British had crucial allies within the imperial palace in Bahadur Shah Zafar's favourite (and youngest) wife, Zinat Mahal, and her ambitious father, who sent a steady stream of inside information from the Red Fort to the British. Zinat thought she had a secret agreement with the British to allow her son, Mirza Jawan Bakht, to be officially recognized as the heir to the throne. But even before 1857, the British had quietly decided that Bahadur Shah Zafar would have no successor as 'King of Delhi', and the events of 1857 made them even more determined to end the Mughal dynasty. While playing along with Zinat's fancies, and using every bit of information they received from her, the British never actually acceded to her request.

Mirza Mughal was eventually replaced as commander-in-chief (at the orders of Emperor Bahadur Shah Zafar) by Bakht Khan, the leader of a large phalanx from Bareilly that had augmented the Delhi Army at the beginning of July. Mirza Mughal then became adjutant general (head of the administration rather than military chief), while Bakht Khan (a much-decorated hero of the Afghan wars, but still only a subedar in the East India Company's hierarchy) took charge of the army. Bakht continued to harry the British forces on the Ridge—who often retaliated irrationally by punishing some of the Indians serving in the British army! But Bakht Khan failed to make a decisive breakthrough, and on 4 September 1857, the British forces were augmented by a large siege-train that arrived from the Punjab with more than a hundred bullock carts full of ammunition and thirty-two howitzers. Ten days later, the 11,000-strong British army stormed Delhi's Kashmere Gate, and a week-long battle for Delhi began, with fierce fighting for every street and alley of the old capital. The superior guns and artillery of the British forces enabled them to get steadily closer to the Red Fort. As his defeat became inevitable by 20 September, the Emperor (and some of his closest family) quietly slipped out of the fort, and initially took refuge in what was then the distant suburb of Nizamuddin. By the end of the day, British soldiers were uncorking wine and beer on the steps of Delhi's Jama Masjid, and General Wilson set up his headquarters in the Diwan-i-Khas (the Chamber of Special Audiences) in the inner sanctum of the Red Fort (much as American generals did in 2003 in Saddam Hussein's most ornate palaces).

Although Delhi had fallen, the imperial family and some 3,000 bedraggled soldiers and courtiers eventually sought sanctuary in the nearby tomb of Humayun. Captain Hodson and a small group of British soldiers negotiated safe passage for Bahadur Shah Zafar, Zinat Mahal and their youngest son Jawan Bakht (promising to spare their lives). They were imprisoned in Zinat's home in Chandni Chowk, tried for 'treason' and sent into exile in Rangoon (Burma), where they were imprisoned as nameless foreigners. The last Mughal emperor died there in 1862, seemingly unmourned until Subhas Bose's Indian National Army restored his mausoleum during World War II. But on 22 September, Hodson returned to Humayun's tomb to arrest the deposed emperor's other sons—Mirza Mughal, Mirza Khizr Sultan—and grandson (Mirza Abu Bakr). Once Hodson and his men had succeeded in separating the princes from their thousands of supporters, and disarming the latter, the princes were taken in a cart towards Delhi. After relieving them of their jewellery, swords and other valuables, Hodson summarily shot all three princes from behind.

Meanwhile, the ageing but highly effective Brigadier (later Major General) Sir Henry Havelock was engaging Nana Saheb in battle at and around Kanpur. Nana Saheb, with only limited military training (and virtually no experience), himself led his men into battle, exhorting them as they fought gamely for several days, but were pushed out of Kanpur by Havelock's well-equipped army on 16 July. Nana Saheb's troops regrouped at Bithur, and part of his army participated in the siege of Lucknow that went on through much of July and August. Sepoys rebelled in Indore, Mhow and Sagar in central India, and the seventy-nine-year-old Rajput Raja Kunwar Singh's forces defeated a British offensive in Arrah (in Bihar) and Danapur (Dinapore) near Patna. Through September and October 1857, Havelock and Lieutenant General Sir James Outram attempted—with occasional success and many setbacks—to relieve the siege of Lucknow. Eventually, the newly arrived commander-in-chief of British forces, Sir Colin Campbell, helped partially relieve the siege of the Lucknow Residency. But it was only in March 1858 that Lucknow was fully regained by the British after a six-week campaign by the full force of Campbell's army.

On 25 November 1857, Tatya Tope led a 5,000-strong contingent from Gwalior and defeated General Sir Charles Windham (a hero of the Crimean War) at Kanpur—thus briefly recapturing that vital city for the Indian forces. Campbell was thus obliged to move the bulk of his army back to the battle for Kanpur, where he was able to overwhelm Tatya Tope with the sheer numbers of his troops and weaponry on 6 December. He was subsequently forced to engage Bakht Khan and the Nawab of Farrukhabad at Khudaganj until early 1858.

Crucially, however, the Bombay and Madras armies did not join this First War of Indian Independence, apart from a few sporadic outbreaks that were quickly put down. Importantly, neither Nana Saheb nor any of the sepoy leaders devoted enough attention to fomenting rebellion south of the Vindhyas. In many of the recently conquered areas in the northwest, British officers took precautions against potential outbreaks by disarming the garrisons at Lahore and Peshawar in early May 1857. But they were unable to prevent sepoys from Jalandhar, Sialkot and (partially) Ferozepur in Punjab from joining the rebels, although the rest of the Punjab stayed loyal to the British side. And, while many of the main subsidiary allies of the British (including Jayajirao Scindia of Gwalior) appeared to hedge their bets through much of 1857 and early 1858, eventually none of the major Indian powers deserted their British allies.

Rani Lakshmibai of Jhansi and Tatya Tope rallied central India, leading a magnificent counteroffensive early in 1858 that almost turned the tide against the British. But while the army of Gwalior largely deserted their Scindia ruler and went over to Lakshmibai's side after she had captured Gwalior Fort, the ruler Jayajirao himself chose to flee (to the British-controlled area) rather than join the Independence War. Other British loyalists like the Rana rulers of Nepal and the maharajas of Patiala and Kashmir played crucial roles as British allies, supplying troops, logistical support and sanctuary to the beleaguered East India Company forces. Combined with the enhanced communication technology of the telegraph (available to the Company, but not to its opponents) and the automatic rifle (versus the muskets on which the Indian forces largely depended), these allies proved decisive in swinging the balance in favour of the British. The crucial role of Jang Bahadur Rana went a long way towards ensuring the permanent 'independence' of Nepal from British conquest, and helps explain why Nepal remains separate from India today, despite deeper cultural affinities to north India than many other parts of India have.

In 1878, Queen Victoria formally added the title 'Empress of India' to her numerous other honorifics, two decades after India was formally brought under her direct rule. Although the East India Company won the war of 1857–58, it lost its position as de facto ruler of India a hundred and one years after Plassey, and India came under the direct control of the British Crown and Parliament.

In retrospect, the war of 1857–58 was a collective attempt by a nation to reassert its independence from the creeping imperialism of the British. Just as Shivaji and the Marathas emerged as the unlikely opponents who fatally wounded the Mughal empire at its peak, Nana Saheb Peshwa (the adopted son of Baji Rao II) aligned himself with the last Mughal emperor and much of the Bengal Army to try and oust that perfidious Mughal feudatory (the East India Company) that had arrogated to itself all the trappings of imperial rule (including coinage after 1835). Mughals and Marathas, Muslim jihadis and Hindu religious and secular warriors, all combined to try and overthrow the newly assertive foreign power. Just as Aurangzeb overreached in repudiating the legacy of a syncretic civilization and policy of accommodative tolerance of Akbar, Jahangir and Shah Jahan—and consequently was obliged to confront a massive Maratha rebellion—so now the British faced a similar rebellion in the vast Bengal Presidency and its northwestern provinces. Neither rebellion succeeded entirely, but both fatally wounded the legitimacy and potency of empires.

Initially, in the first sixty years after Plassey, the British had sought to assimilate into the local scene (as the Mughals Akbar, Jahangir, Shah Jahan and Dara Shukoh did, and the Portuguese afterwards) with several prominent early luminaries of the Company marrying Indian women and becoming effectively Indianized. Warren Hastings (the first Governor General of British India) was fluent in Bengali and Farsi, was acquainted with Hindu and Muslim scriptures, and admired India's culture and history. And several early judges and administrators were even more deeply imbued with India's culture, most notably William Jones (who founded the Asiatic Society in Calcutta to deepen

England's awareness of the depths of this legacy). By 1805, with the advent of Lord Wellesley, a subtle change began to appear—with the British becoming increasingly aloof from the locals, and more stubborn in the enforcement of their supremacy over all things Indian. By the 1820s, James Mill (who had never visited India) began asserting that there was absolutely nothing of value in India's history, cultural heritage or literature, and this was taken to new extremes by Thomas Macaulay, the overtly racist imperial bureaucrat who asserted that 'a single shelf of a good European library was worth the whole literature of India and Arabia'.

Extraordinarily, the intellectually precocious Macaulay's supposedly insatiable appetite for knowledge did not extend to the literature or heritage of the country he was being sent to administer. On the ship to India in 1834 (to become the Law Member in the Governor General's Executive Council), this great bibliophile read books in Greek, Latin, English, French, Italian and Spanish, ranging from the *Iliad* through Horace, Virgil, Dante, Gibbon and Voltaire, but did not bother to read anything about India apart from James Mill's *The History of British India*, in which Mill virulently attacks the history, character, religion, laws and arts of India. The Hindustani and Farsi grammar texts he carried lay untouched. Mill and Macaulay's disdain for India's past became the prevailing ideology of the British empire after 1835 (and is still held unashamedly by the likes of historian Niall Ferguson). A small phalanx of urban Indians adopted these attitudes towards their past as well—epitomized by the talented Bengali poet Madhusudan Dutt, who converted to Christianity, took the name Michael and married an Englishwoman. Michael initially wrote poetry only in English, but eventually came to regret his disdain for India, and wrote a brilliant, inverted version of the Ramayana in Bengali, *Meghnadbadh Kabya* (*The Saga of Meghnad's Killing*), in which Ravana is a heroic figure (and his son, Indrajit or Meghnad, is the central figure).

Macaulay's 'Minute on Education' sought to create 'a class who may be interpreters between us and the millions whom we govern; a class of persons, Indian in blood and colour, but English in taste, in opinions, in morals, and in intellect'. There is little doubt that Macaulay succeeded, and lavishly so in urban India (as modern India, Singapore and Sri Lanka would attest, given their elites' facility with the English language). But a subversive element remained, biding its time and chafing at the insults that were being thrown at the ancient culture of India. The growing racism of the British rulers—in stark contrast to their respectful initial attitudes to India's cultures, languages and religions—created a critical mass of opposition that burst forth in 1857–58. The defeat of the Maratha–Mughal confederacy—and the attempted elimination of all traces of the Mughal dynasty, the brutal treatment of the 'mutineers' and sympathizers—did snuff out overt expressions of nationalism for the rest of the century. But memories of the heroism of 1857 remained, as with the ballad to Rani Lakshmibai of Jhansi ('Khub ladi mardani woh jo Jhansi-wali rani thi'... 'She fought valiantly like a man for she was the Rani of Jhansi') that is commonplace in India to this day. And they would provide the inspiration for the resurgence of Indian nationalism right through the first half of the twentieth century, starting in 1905.

The scornful contempt for Indian culture spawned some social reforms, especially under the Governor Generalship of the utilitarian William Bentinck, although this was also based on a vicious caricature of what constituted Hindu and Muslim culture. For instance, the notion of the caste system being absolutely central to Indian life emerged as an ideological view of the British at this time, and has since become seared into the minds of fresh generations of schoolchildren in the West ever since.

Caste (and the rules of Manu) had never been as rigidly enforced in India as the British interpreted it to be, primarily because their first interlocutors in India were the main literate groups, Brahmins and Kayasthas (the latter comprising a mixed-caste of scribes and accountants recruited over the centuries from amongst many different castes). The literal interpretation of the elaborate *Laws of Manu* (which included caste rules evidently cast in stone) resulted in the hierarchies of caste becoming much more entrenched in British India than they had ever been previously, especially in the first hundred years after Plassey, during which the Brahmins (and other upper castes) were seen as the primary allies of the British in Bengal and north India. Post 1857, this was inverted, with the upper-caste Hindus and elite Muslims being singled out for retribution because of their perceived role as instigators of the First War of Indian Independence.

Having defeated the great rebellion, the British first went on a rampage of pillage, plunder and rape to punish those towns and villages perceived to have participated in the 'mutiny'. Whole villages and towns were razed to the ground (including most of Delhi), captured rebels were blown from cannons, thousands of rebel soldiers were hung from trees and poles across the countryside in a campaign of vengeful reprisals aimed at stamping out the last hint of rebellion and instilling a deep-seated fear of the Englishman in the north Indian psyche. Most perniciously of all, history books were written with an inversion of facts, editing out any mention of Britain's inhuman brutalities or the massive famines that had bred the rebellious spirit, instead focusing entirely on the few Indian episodes of brutality (and dredging up the semi-mythological Black Hole of Calcutta from a century earlier) to demonstrate the supposed barbarism of the heathens that Britain was ruling, and that it now needed to 'civilize'. The ideology of the 'white man's burden' also emerged in this period, as Rudyard Kipling sought to rally America (the land of his in-laws) in particular to take up this 'burden' of 'civilizing' the heathens.

This curious inversion of facts also effectively erases from British history books (particularly those written for schoolchildren) all mention of how Britain enriched itself from the spoils of its Indian empire and, more importantly, how it caused the impoverishment of what had been (before the first British advent 450 years ago) the richest country on earth. With the largest population, and with per capita income only marginally lower than Britain at the time, India was easily the world's largest economy in 1700 and 1800, with China a close second. India and China each accounted for about a fifth of world manufacturing in 1800, although Britain's Industrial Revolution had already set in by 1750, driven primarily by industrial innovations.

England's population during the Elizabethan Age (i.e., the time of Shakespeare) was about 2.5 million (in 1560), while India's (during the reign of Akbar at the same time) was estimated at 75 million. By 1750, England and Wales had a population of 6.5 million, despite the massive migrations to the Americas, Australasia and India that had already occurred during the intervening period. The settled population of British America was just 1.5 million at the time, and Ireland's was 2.4 million. (As an aside, the population of all of Ireland today is 4.5 million, while about 45 million people claim to be Irish-Americans!) India's own population was estimated to have increased to 100 million by 1800, aided by the long peace of the seventeenth century in north India (during the zenith of the Timurids), and the relative peace of the eighteenth century enforced by the Marathas across western, central and southern India. Clive wrote in the 1750s that Murshidabad (a relatively new city, established and built up as Bengal's capital by Murshid Quli Khan only fifty years earlier) was larger and more prosperous than London (then already the largest city in Christendom, about twice the size of Paris).

British-run Calcutta, of course, was much smaller at the time, but had grown rapidly to a population of 120,000 with a promenade of magnificent palaces along the riverfront (in what later became Chowringhee). The 'victory' at Plassey resulted in Clive alone receiving a gift totalling about £400,000 from the Bengal treasury—and his associates receiving a total of £1.25 million—at a time when the ten richest noble families in England earned average annual incomes of £20,000 (in other words, Clive's personal prize from the Bengal treasury was twice the annual combined income of the ten richest noble families back home and approximately equal to the combined annual incomes of England's thirty richest noble families). Eric Hobsbawm quotes Joseph Massie's 1760 estimate of the annual earnings of the 150 noble families (who together controlled England then) as aggregating about £1.24 million. The spoils of just one war in India thus provided booty equal to the combined annual income of the entire English aristocracy at the time. Apart from this, there were of course the ongoing incomes earned by Company officials through the out-and-back trade, as well as the 'carry trade' permitted on Company ships that had empty space on either leg of the India–England or India–Malacca/India–China trade journeys. As we have seen, governors of Madras like Elihu Yale and Thomas Pitt (in the 1687–1710 period, at the crest of Mughal rule) were already able to amass enormous fortunes that helped found some of the Anglo-Saxon world's great institutions, with Thomas Pitt acquiring several rotten boroughs (including Stratford in east London) that became the political base for the dominant political dynasty of England in the eighteenth century.

As the East India Company began adding political and military might to back its trading privileges (including the control of virtually duty-free Bengal trade after 1719 that contributed to the prosperity of Calcutta by the 1750s), the annual profits remitted to England would have grown very substantially. Astonishingly, virtually no historians have attempted to quantify the size of the annual flow of remittances and other income that went back to England from India during this period (1670–1757), as the Company expanded its imprint across the land. The difference between Spain's enormous holdings in South America and England's in India was primarily that India was the world's major manufacturer at the time, particularly of the cotton (produced, then as now, in western and south central India) and Bengal's calicoes (yarn and muslin) that clothed the world. As English merchants gained control of this trade, they massively enriched themselves and helped lift incomes in England, expanding its economy and population, while also creating demand within England for cotton clothing. Because of its sheer size, there can be little doubt that the loot from India played a central role in financing the surpluses that helped fuel the Industrial Revolution.

Spain and Portugal, on the other hand, suffered an early form of what in the twentieth century was called the 'Dutch Disease' (or resource curse), as they exported mainly precious metals and minerals from their colonies rather than manufactures, as the English found in India. And, in the classic mercantilist strategy later emulated by other 'late developers' (starting with Bismarck's Germany and the US in the second half of the nineteenth century, as well as Japan, the Asian NIEs and China), England then imposed a ban on imports of cloth from India (by early in the eighteenth century, later changed to an 80 per cent import duty early in the nineteenth century) in order to provide 'infant industry' protection to the emerging textile industry of Lancashire.

Bengal, Bihar and the area around Benares were the workshop of the world in the sixteenth and seventeenth century, particularly for textiles and garments, which is what made them such valuable provinces for the Mughals. The ban on exports of cloth from India severely hurt the livelihoods of the artisans, weavers and spinners who (usually in small-scale and cottage industries, but also sometimes in rudimentary 'factories' of over a hundred workers) produced the textiles that clothed the world. Meanwhile, the peasantry working the land was also suffering from the depredations of the rapacious new English officials who were intent on sucking out as much as possible from the land, and hugely raised the revenue demands from them after 1757. Increased revenue demands from the land (to be paid to the English) combined with job losses amongst the artisans and weavers—which caused them to come back to seek work on the land—contributed to the impoverishment of the countryside, leading eventually to the horrific famine of 1770, which killed between a third and half the population of the vast Bengal Presidency.

In England, meanwhile, the vast riches from the loot of Madras, Bombay and the new Bengal Presidency (including Oudh, or eastern UP, and Bihar and Jharkhand) increased the wealth and lifestyles of the English aristocracy, while the middle class (and merchants) began to benefit from the imposition of a ban on imports of Indian cloth, which raised cloth (and wool) prices in England. The combination helped finance the innovations that made the Industrial Revolution possible. Clive, for instance, instantly joined the aristocracy (as the richest man in England) after his first tour of duty in India, and the 'nabobs' kept returning to England with massive riches in tow, which enabled many of them to purchase seats in the House of Commons (and occasionally in the House of Lords). By 1767, William Pitt the Elder, Earl of Chatham (and descendant of Thomas, the early governor of Madras), had risen to the prime ministership.

And with the ban on cloth imports from India, English innovation flourished in the 1760–1800 period with Hargreaves's spinning jenny (1764) enabling a sixteen-fold productivity gain in spinning, complemented by further gains from Arkwright's spinning frame (1768), Crompton's spinning mule (1779) and Cartwright's power loom (1784). The greatest of British historians of the Industrial Revolution, Eric Hobsbawm, is clear about why Britain rather than any other European power became the first industrialized nation and the venue for this proliferation of innovations: Britain had an enormous export market in India, and one that it was willing to break into and keep open with its navy (the procurement needs of which provided a vital domestic market for the early fruits of the Industrial Revolution, including demand for steel). Hobsbawm points to another distinguishing feature in England: the land was owned not by the monarch (as in continental European countries) but by the nobles and aristocracy. Thus the latter had an incentive to encourage mining on their land, and the development of manufacturing on it as well, because these enhanced their revenues and income. Unlike continental monarchies (and even the Netherlands, where the merchants were in control), the aristocracy (which controlled Parliament) developed a convergence of interests with the newly emerging manufacturing and middle classes in England. Additionally, the aristocracy was deeply involved in running the empire (as reflected in the Governors General of the East India Company and viceroys of the Raj, all invariably aristocrats from 1800 onwards), and Hobsbawm emphasizes the overall role of government (as reflected in the navy at home, the army and bureaucracy in India) in creating and maintaining the vital market that enabled the Industrial Revolution, which, of course, was primarily a cotton revolution (brought about by banning imports of Indian cotton textiles, and then flooding India with Lancashire's textiles imported duty-free into India). Steel was an offshoot of the Industrial Revolution, cotton textiles their heart.

Britain's raw cotton imports increased twentyfold between 1774 and 1820, but the majority of these imports came from the cotton plantations of America (driven by the slave economy) rather than western India and Egypt (which could not compete with the slave-driven plantations of America). The famine of 1770 in India caused a drastic reduction in revenue for the East India Company, and contributed to a crisis for the Company in 1772, which turned to the English Parliament for financial aid, which was easily obtained, given the large number of nabobs who had a decisive say in the House of Commons. However, one consequence was the passage of the Tea Act of 1773 (also aimed at aiding the Company to sell its crucial cargoes of tea to the American colonies), which led eventually to the Boston Tea Party in December 1773—the spark that led to the American War of Independence (1775–83). The independent USA did very well economically, reflected in the fact that its population tripled between 1760 and 1790 (to 4.5 million). Recurrent famines in the newly-conquered British territories in India were clearly a problem for the East India Company too, and Cornwallis (the English general defeated by Washington at Yorktown in 1783) set about creating the 'Permanent Settlement' in Bengal in 1793 to stabilize revenue demands.

Although the initial land revenue demand was extremely high (60–90 per cent of production in 1793), the amount was fixed in perpetuity in order to create a land-holding aristocracy loyal to the British, while entrenching capitalist property rights. Default in payment of land revenue (which was collected twice a year) would result in automatic auctions of those property rights, and well over half of all land in the Bengal Presidency passed into new ownership between 1795 and 1820. At the same time, duty-free imports into India of new mill-made cloth from Lancashire gradually destroyed what still remained of India's once-vaunted textile industry. Even domestic demand for silk products and textiles shrivelled in India during the 1750–1820 period, as the old aristocracy lost its livelihood, made worse by the transfer of ownership to new owners whose consumption habits aped the Western ways of Calcutta. Famines remained a recurrent feature—each time killing millions—right through the nineteenth century, with the 1890s facing both famine and bubonic plague.

The new depredations wrought on the countryside in 1858–59 did have a salutary benefit for the British colonial government. In most of what is today's India, the last vestige of resistance to British rule was stamped out, and the British administration no longer met regular resistance. Just before the turn of the century, the Pathans of the North West Frontier Province (a province that partly resulted from the Second Anglo-Afghan War) rose in revolt, and were put down with enormous brutality (although the young Winston Churchill, who fought as a lieutenant in that war, developed a grudging regard for the Pathan warrior as a result). But otherwise, orderliness was restored and the British ambition of replacing the Mughals as legitimate rulers of India was largely achieved through their decisive victory in the war of 1857–58.

The British were to ensure after 1858 that a fixed minimum proportion of the army would always comprise British soldiers and officers. In Bengal, the ratio of Indian to British soldiers was to be maintained at 2:1, while a 3:1 ratio was mandated for the Bombay and Madras armies. While all regiments were to be much more mixed in future, the British also introduced the concept of 'martial races and castes', the latter mainly comprising those races seen as loyal in 1857–58 (Sikhs, Gurkhas, Pathans). And though the Indians of Calcutta (and the urban elites of all Bengal) had remained largely loyal to the British during the Great Rebellion, the British subsequently discriminated against that entire region: there was a large expansion of irrigation in the 1860–1920 period, but this was almost entirely concentrated on the Punjab and Sindh.

Ironically, however, the lily-white British elite bureaucracy that had emerged in the 1830s with the creation of the Indian Civil Service (ICS) eventually began to admit a few Indians by the mid-1860s (with the first Indian ICS officer, Satyendranath Tagore, elder brother of the great poet, joining the service in 1864). And some Indians were also allowed to become officers in the British Indian Army. As a small, urbanized, English-speaking elite emerged amongst the Indians, an Indian National Association was formed in 1876 to represent their interests, based on an earlier association of zamindars that had been established four decades earlier by Dwarkanath Tagore. Surendranath Banerjea (who had briefly been in the ICS, but suffered racial discrimination and had been dismissed) led the Indian National Association, fashioning it into the first effective votary of Indian nationalism, aimed at 'advancing the political, intellectual, and material advancement' of the people of India. Banerjea's fiery speeches against racial discrimination led to his arrest in 1883.

The Indian Association's activities culminated in the establishment of the Indian National Congress in 1885. Technically, a Scotsman called Allan Octavian Hume is credited with creating the Congress, although he was at most a facilitator of a process that had been initiated by several Indian predecessor organizations. The first president of the Congress, Womesh Chandra Bonnerjee, was a classic Bengali bhadralok (gentleman) of the anglicized variety that the British caricatured as a 'baboo'. But by the turn of the century, the annual sessions of the Congress were beginning to demand some of the basic rights of citizenship that Britain extended to its white colonies but excluded the Indians from. Although Indians were now in the higher judiciary, for instance, even a senior Indian ICS officer or magistrate had no right to judge an Englishman. Congress was beginning to raise some of these uncomfortable issues, and the English establishment in India would soon come up with a classic stroke of 'divide and rule' enacted by one of the greatest of all imperial bureaucrats, Viceroy Lord George Curzon.

But there were other great currents of nationalism also emerging in India during this time. In Bengal, the semi-mythological novels of Bankim Chandra Chattopadhyay spread a subversive anti-imperial message, invoking patriotism as a semi-religious duty—very much continuing the spirit of 1857. Through the nineteenth century, several great Hindu reformers had emerged, the greatest of them being the Bengali mystic, Sri Ramakrishna Paramahamsa, and the Gujarati Sri Dayananda Saraswati (whose influence proved to be greatest in the Punjab). Sri Ramakrishna actually practised Christianity and Islam (as well as other religions) as part of his spiritual journey, and concluded (as had the emperor Akbar in the sixteenth century) that all religions were merely different paths to the same ultimate goal (which he interpreted to be the Vedantic one of uniting the soul with the Godhead).

Like Jesus Christ, Sri Ramakrishna did not have any elaborate formal education, but his universal message won acceptance from the elite and middle class of India, and eventually across the world for a short time through his great messenger, Swami Vivekananda, who created an elaborate network of schools, hospitals and cultural centres that remain vibrant to this day. At a time when India was considered an obscure, exotic colony smothered under the British yoke, the thirty-year-old Swami Vivekananda arrived in Chicago for the World's Parliament of Religions in 1893, and his inspiring universalist message became the dominant theme of the event, quietly subverting its goal of demonstrating 'that there is no teacher to be compared with Christ, and no Saviour excepting Christ'. When he first addressed the assemblage on 11 September 1893, Swami Vivekananda had electrified the audience with his stirring message of universal love and India's millennia-long history of welcoming adherents of every persecuted religion. On a subsequent lecture tour that took him from Minneapolis to Memphis, as well as New York and Boston, Swami Vivekananda demystified Hinduism for his urbane, well-heeled American audiences and many leading intellectuals were converted to the Vedantic way of thinking, including William James who persuaded Harvard to offer the thirty-year-old mystic a professorship in Eastern philosophy (which he declined). By the turn of the century, Swami Vivekananda's message of pragmatic spiritualism (stressing karma yoga, or the religion of work) was creating an idiom for the practice of Hinduism perfectly consonant with the demands of modernity and progress, and providing the underpinning for a new nationalism that would be proud of India's past rather than rejecting it.

In 1875 Swami Dayananda Saraswati established the Arya Samaj, which sought to go back to the purest Vedic form of Hinduism, asserting that the 3,000-year-old Vedas contained the eternal verities that should form the core of Hindu belief, with all other 'impurities' removed. The Arya Samaj also introduced a mechanism (called 'shuddhi') through which non-Hindus could be converted to Hinduism (which, until that point, had been considered a religion one had to be born into, but could not convert into). The Arya Samaj (which spawned a wide variety of schools and other public services that continue to exist today) was, to some extent, a response to the Brahmo Samaj, which had been started in the 1830s by Raja Rammohun Roy, as a syncretic religion merging Christian (and Muslim) beliefs onto a Hindu core. Roy is seen as the Father of the Indian (or at least Bengal) Renaissance, which later spawned the poetry of Tagore (as well as predecessors like Michael Madhusudan Dutt), the novels of Bankim and Sarat Chandra Chattopadhyay, and a tremendous flowering of scientific output from Jagadish Chandra Bose and Prafulla Chandra Ray (and later C. V. Raman and Satyendra Nath Bose of 'Boson' fame).

But Roy's religion, the Brahmo Samaj, remained confined to a small part of the elite of Bengal, Orissa and Assam. Maharshi Debendranath Tagore (the poet's father) was one of Roy's successors, but the movement split, with another of its leaders, Keshub Chandra Sen, becoming a devotee of Sri

Ramakrishna, who remains very influential amongst India's middle classes to this day.

With his freshly-minted first-class Classics Tripos from Cambridge, the young Aurobindo Ghose had just returned to India at the turn of the century and was beginning to translate Swami Vivekananda's robust spiritual message into a new nationalism that would not shy away from using any means (including violence) to overthrow British rule, clearly influenced also by the patriotic message of Bankim's novels. And far away in South Africa, another young Indian called Mohandas Karamchand Gandhi was undertaking his experiments with truth, trying out methods of civil disobedience to challenge the racism of South Africa's government while undertaking constructive service in his Phoenix Farm with the aim of building a self-reliant society. As the twentieth century dawned, the Britishers ensconced in Calcutta, Bombay, Madras or the plantations of Darjeeling, Munnar, the Dooars and Assam may have been forgiven for their belief that India was destined for permanent British occupation. But a new nationalism was bubbling just below the surface, some drawing inspiration from the spirit of 1857 but the majority creating a modern idiom of nationalism that drew on the wellsprings of Indian philosophy to reinterpret the ideologies of modern democracy.

THE LIGHT TOUCH OF THE SPANISH AND PORTUGUESE

As the century began, the people of the Philippines—the first Asian country to become a European (Spanish) colony—were engaged in a titanic struggle to resist becoming the colony of a rising new global power, the United States. The US had destroyed the Spanish fleet in Manila Bay in May 1898 in a brief seven-hour engagement. But a nationalist revolt had already been ignited in the Philippines a year before the US naval triumph, led by the diminutive mestizo (half-Filipino, half-Chinese) general Emilio Aguinaldo. The spark for this mighty nationalist uprising was Spain's myopic decision to publicly execute the cosmopolitan founder of Filipino nationalism, José Rizal, in 1896.

Aguinaldo's forces had gained control of much of the Luzon countryside, and were threatening Manila by May 1898. The Filipino general met US commodore George Dewey to discuss terms for cooperation. Aguinaldo came away from that meeting convinced that the US had offered guarantees of Filipino independence in exchange for revolutionary support against the Spanish, but he evidently misunderstood Dewey (who claimed to have made no such promise). Seeing signs of prevarication on the part of the Americans, Aguinaldo made the Declaration of Philippine Independence on 12 June 1898. It was not recognized by the Americans—making the Filipinos the unlikely pioneers of nationalism in colonial Asia, albeit a nationalism that was to be severely tested and circumscribed over the next half-century.

The Spanish–American War saw the final eclipse of Spain as a colonial power, culminating a process that had proceeded steadily through the nineteenth century. Amongst the great prizes of that war, the US had promised independence to the Cubans, and annexed Puerto Rico, but it also intended to take possession of the Philippines. A day *after* the peace terms were concluded in Paris, the US and Spain arranged a mock battle (without bloodshed) for the US to take Manila from the Spanish, while denying any glory to Aguinaldo's forces, which then numbered 30,000 men massed outside Manila and far outnumbered the 7,000 Spanish troops seeking to defend it. Aguinaldo kept hoping that the US Congress would not ratify the terms of the peace treaty, and President William McKinley (and his running mate, Teddy Roosevelt, the biggest political beneficiary of the war of 1898) would lose the 1900 election. But the latter was pre-empted by the beginning of full-scale hostilities in February 1899 between Aguinaldo's forces and the Americans (who had benefited from reinforcements that took their troop strength to 24,000 from 7,500 a half-year earlier). Although heavily outgunned, Aguinaldo's forces were strengthened by the tacit support of the rural populace. This obliged the US to raise its troop strength to 70,000 by early 1900 and the two sides were engaged in a full-scale war of independence at the start of the century.

Portugal had been the first of the colonial powers to descend on Asia. Beginning with Vasco da Gama's arrival in Calicut (Kozhikode) on the southwest coast of India in 1498 (where he encountered the Samoothiri raja, Europeanized as Zamorin), the Portuguese built a maritime empire encompassing the important port towns of Malacca (in Malaysia), Goa (in India) and Macao (in China), plus other possessions such as Ceylon (Sri Lanka) and East Timor (Timor–Leste). Ousted from Ceylon by the Dutch by 1658, the Portuguese at the dawn of the twentieth century retained possession of Goa, Macao and East Timor.

Intermarriage was the demographic key to Portugal's success as a colonizer—although this was much more manifest in Africa and Brazil than in Asia. When Vasco da Gama set sail in 1497, Portugal's population was just over a million. Today Portuguese is the lingua franca of Brazil (with a population of 182 million), Angola, Mozambique and (if its elites have their way) Timor–Leste. Liberally marrying into local communities, the Portuguese 'diaspora' is distinguishable not by the multi-hued colours of their skin, but the distinctiveness of their surnames. Names such as Gomez, Fernandez and de Silva remain common in Sri Lanka, Malacca and across India. On the tennis courts of the Atlanta Olympics, India's dark-skinned Leander Paes beat

Brazil's light-skinned Fernando Meligeni for the singles bronze medal: Vasco da Gama would have smiled in his grave regardless of the result!

Portugal's main maritime competitor in the fifteenth century—Spain—turned its attention westward, partly because Pope Alexander VI had divided the world in half, and given Spain the right (and responsibility) to proselytize West Africa and points west, while leaving the other half of the non-European world to Portugal. In 1492, Queen Isabella I of Castile and King Ferdinand II of Aragon planted the flag of Christendom on the great citadel of the Alhambra in Granada—the last bastion of the Muslim Moors who had ruled Andalusia for seven centuries and had been the predominant power in all of Spain for at least five. In the same year, they also financed the first voyage of Christopher Columbus—ostensibly setting off for 'India' (a realm then imagined to encompass most of Asia, despite the widely-known travelogue of Marco Polo, who visited Kublai Khan, the founder of the Mongol or Yuan dynasty of China, more than three centuries earlier). But it was Ferdinand Magellan (ethnically Portuguese but in the service of Spain) who captured a piece of Asia for Spain before meeting his own death in a local rebellion led by Datu Lapu-Lapu on the island of Mactan near Cebu (in today's Philippines), where the Chola Raja Humabon ruled (with Lapu-Lapu as one of his feudatory nobles). It was only after a Spanish fleet from Mexico had suppressed the Portuguese in 1541 that the archipelago was named the Philippines in honour of Philip II of Spain (although some assert that it was Magellan who coined the name in honour of the same man, who was then crown prince). The Spaniards predictably labelled the local Muslims Moros (Spanish for Moor), a label they happily flaunt to this day.

Because of its Spanish legacy, the Philippines (perhaps the only country still named for a forgotten king of another land) is often called an extension of Latin America into Asia. But the veneer of Spanish rule was thinner in the Philippines than in all of Latin America; local Asian traits were retained, and Spanish influence over the ethnic mix was much lighter than anywhere in Latin America. Alejandro Toledo was the first Amerindian to be elected president in Peru (where they comprise close to half the population) in 2001 and Bolivia (the one South American country with a clear Amerindian majority) was the only other country that had occasionally elected a vice president of mainly Amerindian descent until Evo Morales broke the glass ceiling to win the presidency in 2006. Proximity to China added an extra dose of Asianness to the Philippine ethnic mix as did its legacy of Indic and Malay civilizational influences, and every Philippine president has been decidedly Asian, despite the residual strength of the old Spanish business families that continue to dominate the Philippines' business elite.

And while Latin American countries came heavily under US influence, none of them formally became colonies of the United States as the Philippines did at the start of the twentieth century. Despite its early start (nationalism had barely stirred anywhere else in non-Japan Asia at this time), Philippine nationalism has remained stunted and diminished by a variety of disabilities— not least of which was its name itself. Nationalists attempting to name it Luzviminda (after the three main islands of Luzon, Visayas and Mindanao) have had little success. But the institutional and historic roots of the Philippines' aborted nationalism must be left to later chapters.

THE DUTCH AND THE RICH HISTORIC LEGACY OF JAVA

The Protestant Dutch were the next great mercantile power to explore non-European trading outposts. Briefly, in the first half of the seventeenth century, they were arguably Europe's greatest financial and mercantile power. Finding most of the Americas taken already (the South by the Spaniards and the Portuguese, the North mainly by the British), the Dutch only managed a small (and brief) toehold in New Amsterdam (today's New York). But it was to Asia—and the Spice Islands of the East Indies (Moluccas or Maluku)—that the Dutch turned their attention. In the early 1600s, the Dutch were the shipper, exchanger and commodity dealers of Europe—and had used this to consolidate their role as the centre of international finance. By 1610, they already had colonies in Amboina (Ambon) and Ternate, and had established a presence (through 'factories') at the mouth of the Amazon (in what is now Surinam), Nagasaki (in Japan) and in Malacca.

The Dutch had variable success in Europe's war-filled eighteenth and nineteenth centuries, and the ebbs and flows of Dutch fortunes on the mainland of Europe affected the degree and depth of Dutch control of the East Indies. Ceylon passed to British hands in 1796, when the British sent an expeditionary force to take control of the island after the fall of the Netherlands to France in 1795; by 1798, the whole of what is now Sri Lanka (with the exception of the kingdom of Kandy) had become a crown colony of Britain.

The Dutch, however, retained control over their most beloved colony— that of the East Indies (present-day Indonesia). At the turn of the century, the Dutch ruled all of Indonesia except Bali, Aceh and West Papua. They had established a cultivation system (cultuurstelsel) under which the heritable burden on landowners was not a rent or cash tax but a 'set aside' of land and labour devoted to commercial crops. So, in lieu of paying the government a cash rent/tax, landowners were required to set aside some of their land (and associated labour) for the cultivation of a commercial crop (coffee, sugar, tobacco, palm oil, etc.), a fixed amount of which was to be delivered to the government. The Dutch government thus acquired these commodities at a minimal cost and could control their supply and exports. The system naturally proved hugely profitable for the Dutch, but it caused increasing hardship amongst the locals who were obliged to set aside labour and land for the commercial crops. While the injection of cash did spark some entrepreneurial activity, the Javanese peasantry suffered grievously from the system.

There were famines in central Java in 1843 and again in the early 1850s. The rising death toll—and the rapid increase in the homeless immigrant population of Semarang, the main city in central Java—led to some soul-searching in the Netherlands. That, coupled with the rising political importance of the merchant class (represented in the Liberal Party), led to the gradual abolition (or at least dilution) of the cultuurstelsel by the turn of the century. In 1862, pepper was freed from the system, followed in 1864 by nutmeg and cloves, and in 1865 by tea and sugar. Only coffee—the main commercial crop of Java and Minangkabau—still remained subject to the old cultivation system at the turn of the century. Instead, new legislation passed by 1870 (the year marked as the beginning of the 'Liberal Era' of Dutch policy) ensured that only native Indonesians (those ethnic groups indigenous to the archipelago) could own land in Indonesia. However, land could be leased or rented to foreigners, and it was on this basis that the first plantations were established by private planters (European and Chinese) in the period between 1870 and 1885. But the plantation (especially sugar) economy of Java suffered a severe depression in 1883–85, and most private plantations were subsequently taken over by large Dutch conglomerates clustered around banks. This corporatization of agriculture did not significantly benefit the Javanese themselves—although it naturally enriched the new Dutch corporations. Average rice consumption amongst Javanese peasants declined from 119 kilograms annually in 1885 to 103 kilograms in 1900. And a government enquiry that year concluded that there had been a 'strong reduction of wages' paid to workers in the agribusinesses between 1885 and 1900. At the same time, Chinese entrepreneurs were displacing Javanese from traditional manufacturing such as batik, and also capitalizing on new areas such as gambling houses, opium dens and pawnshops.

The Indonesian islands had been famed for their trading acumen for at least two thousand years. They were trading with Bengal and Utkal (Orissa) as early as the first and second centuries CE. This trade resulted in the gradual dissemination of Indian culture and political norms to the Indonesian islands (either via the gradual immigration of Indian traders and scholars into Indonesian cities and towns, or through the knowledge gained by Indonesian traders spending time in Indian cities). The Chinese traveller Fa-Hsien and the princely Indian traveller Gunavarman of Kashmir both wrote of the existence of Sino–Indonesian trade in the fifth century CE, and an Indonesian-influenced language was also known to have spread to Madagascar by that time. By the seventh century CE, Chinese sources talk of trade between China and a Javanese kingdom called 'Ho-Ling' and one in Sumatra called Srivijaya. By the eighth century, Ho-Ling had merged with a kingdom called Mataram that had originated in the Dieng Plateau (where its first temples date from the fourth century) and was led by the Hindu Sanjaya dynasty. Both Hinduism and Buddhism were prominent influences in Mataram, one or the other being the dominant influence at various times. The Sailendra dynasty (which was Buddhist, claiming descent from the rulers of the Cambodian Hindu kingdom of Funan) originated in the Kedu Plain (in central Java), and became dominant in Mataram in the ninth century, during which it built the great Borobudur temple complex.

The Mahayana Buddhist empire of Srivijaya was perhaps Asia's (and so the world's) greatest trading empire of the eighth to tenth centuries, and controlled all trade through the Straits of Malacca for nearly 600 years (through the thirteenth century). Based in Sumatra (with its capital in Palembang), it extended through much of the Malay peninsula all the way to Kedah and Patani (which today is part of Thailand). Briefly (in the ninth century) the Sailendra dynasty united Java and Sumatra after its conquest of Srivijaya, but late in the ninth century it was ousted from its erstwhile Javanese stronghold by the Sanjaya dynasty, which subsequently controlled Mataram. As a great trading power, the Srivijayans spread their language (Malay) across the archipelago, and were also famed for their shipbuilding and navigational skills. They built the greatest seaworthy ships of their time, sailing them all the way to Arabia in the west and Canton (Guangzhou) in the east; and their capital (first Palembang, later Jambi) was notably cosmopolitan, housing Javanese, Gujarati, Bengali, Chinese and Persian traders. By the eleventh century, Srivijaya began to go into decline, partly as a result of the Chola invasion from southern India (1025) and a Javanese invasion by Mataram. Additionally, China too began building seaworthy ships at this time, contributing to a decline in demand for Srivijaya's shipbuilding skills.

Meanwhile, Mataram reached its zenith under its legendary hero Airlangga, the Balinese prince who married a daughter of the king of Mataram (where he ruled from 1016 to 1049). His wedding was celebrated in the great Javanese epic poem *Arjunawiwaha* by Mpu Kanwa, based on the Hindu epic, the Mahabharata. In 1016, Mataram suffered a military defeat at the hands of Srivijaya. Airlangga was one of the few members of the royal family to escape;

he rallied the forces of Mataram, and gradually reclaimed control of the whole of Java and Bali. Airlannga was responsible for unifying the various legal codes of Java. At his death, the kingdom was divided in two, and was reunited late in the thirteenth century by Kertanegara (r. 1268-1292). Under him, the kingdom (called Singhasari) expanded to include Bali, parts of Kalimantan and much of Sumatra and Malacca. But this westward expansion brought him into conflict with China, and the Mongol (Yuan dynasty) emperor, Kublai Khan, sent emissaries demanding tribute. Kertanegara ritually humiliated the emissaries, and Kublai Khan responded by sending a naval invasion party to Java. Kertanegara's son-in-law, Raden Vijaya, who had succeeded him by the time the Mongol army arrived, tricked the latter into laying down their arms, then attacked and defeated them and established the empire of Majapahit. Many members of the Chinese expedition stayed on in Java, injecting a dose of Chinese technology into Majapahit.

The archipelago that constitutes today's Indonesia (and parts of Malaya) was largely united by Kertanegara's great-grandson, Hayam Wuruk (1350–89), the greatest king of the Java-based Hindu kingdom of Majapahit. Ably aided by his heroic prime minister, Gajah Mada, he extended Majapahit's authority over Bali, Sumatra, Kalimantan and (according to the epic poem *Nagarakretagama*) over parts of the southern Philippines, New Guinea and Malaya. Majapahit benefited economically from the surging demand for Indonesian spices from Europe and China; trade between it and Ming China burgeoned, as was epitomized by the famous seven-state naval expedition across Asia of the Muslim eunuch and Ming nobleman Zheng He between 1403 and 1433, who stopped in Java to recharge on each journey. Apart from its military and political ascendancy over the archipelago, Majapahit's rich culture spread across the islands and Javanese myths and figures (attributed to Majapahit) became part of the founding myths of various small states across Sumatra, Malaya and the Maluku islands.

Islam began arriving in Indonesia in the thirteenth century, carried primarily by Muslim traders from Gujarat and southern India. The seaborne trade of the Indian Ocean and Arabian Sea was increasingly dominated by Muslims, and Indonesian traders found it commercially expedient to convert to the faith of their counterparties. Rulers too found that they could enhance their prestige by joining the brotherhood of the new faith that could link them to the rulers of the Ottoman empire, Arab principalities and much of India. The ruler of Aceh was the first to convert (in the mid-fourteenth century) followed about a half-century later by Parameswara, the ruler of Melaka across the Malacca Straits. Islam reached Gresik in the 1360s, the spice island of Ternate in Maluku in 1460, Demak (north-central Java) in

1480, Banten (west Java) in 1525 and Makassar (south Sulawesi) in 1605. While the rulers of many coastal principalities became Muslims, the interior of Java continued to be ruled by the Hindu kingdom of Majapahit, which owed its strength not only to trade but to the stable prosperity of its agricultural economy. Ultimately, Majapahit was undermined by the gradual loss of its quasi-monopoly of inter-island trade and Demak exploited that weakness to inflict a fatal military defeat in 1527 that marked the end of a thousand years of Hindu–Buddhist rule in Java.

Although militarily defeated, Majapahit continued to exert cultural influence over successor regimes throughout Indonesia. The founder of the Muslim state of Demak (Raden Patah) claimed descent from the last king of Majapahit. And a new Muslim kingdom called Mataram that emerged in the early seventeenth century in the vicinity of present-day Yogyakarta also claimed to be the legitimate successors of Majapahit. The new Mataram was heavily influenced by Sufism, the mystical sect of Islam that was largely compatible with most Hindu/Buddhist beliefs and practices. Mataram quickly defeated Demak and emerged as the dominant power in Java.

The era of European colonialism in the East Indies (Indonesia and Malaysia) was inaugurated with the Portuguese capture of the important port of Melaka in 1511 (just over a century after its elites' conversion to Islam after King Parameswara became Iskandar Shah in 1409), thus giving them control of the mouth of the commercially crucial Straits of Malacca. The following year, they established a base in the Maluku spice islands at Ambon. While the Portuguese sought to gain a monopoly of the spice trade and convert the population to Catholicism, Malay and Javanese traders increasingly gravitated towards Makassar, which became the greatest of the indigenous trading kingdoms, stretching at its zenith in the 1630s from Lombok to the outer islands of New Guinea. Militarily, however, Aceh (at the northwestern tip of Sumatra) was the greatest rival of the Portuguese. The great Acehnese sultan Iskandar Muda precipitated a war with the Portuguese in 1629, which the latter managed to win. But partly because of its festering struggle with Aceh, the Portuguese began to lose control of Maluku. The Dutch took Ambon and Ternate in 1605–06 and Tidore in 1666, while also gradually expanding in urban pockets of Java. The Dutch also snatched the port of Melaka from the Portuguese in 1641, by which time it was beginning to lose its lustre as the pre-eminent entrepôt of the region.

The Dutch Vereenigde Oost-Indische Compagnie (VOC, or United East India Company) was a joint-stock company established in 1602. Unlike the English East India Company (in which shareholders invested in individual journeys of company ships), shareholders bought shares in the VOC itself, giving it the ability to be more long-term in its orientation. The VOC initially tried to set up a base in Banten in west Java, then the centre of the China trade, but faced competition from the English and others. So it made an agreement with the ruler of Jayakarta, a principality just east of Banten, and set up a base called Batavia (today's Jakarta) in 1610. By the mid-1620s, Mataram's sultan Agung had gained control of most of the east Javanese ports (including Gresik and Surabaya) and soon came into conflict with the Dutch. However, Agung's two massive attempted invasions of Batavia (in 1628 and 1629) proved unsuccessful, partly because of his inability to properly control the sea supply lines to his 160,000-man army. The year 1629 clearly marked the gradual ascendancy of Europeans in the Indies, with both Aceh and Mataram suffering military setbacks that year at the hands of the Portuguese and Dutch respectively.

Makassar was a free-trading kingdom committed to the freedom of the seas, which naturally brought it into conflict with the VOC's desire to establish a monopoly over the trade in spices and other commodities. Makassar remained a cosmopolitan trading port, attracting Javanese, Gujarati, Portuguese and English traders. The VOC's early attempts to subdue the Makassarese failed, so they aligned with their regional rivals, the Buginese, and mounted a joint naval expedition against Makassar in 1667; two years later, the last of its forts fell to the joint expeditionary force, Makassar lost its independence and its foreign traders were expelled. Meanwhile, the Dutch had also secured the right to pass their pepper exports through the ports of a weakened Aceh Sultanate, and had similarly made Padang the centre for controlling the exports of the commodity-rich kingdom of Minangkabau in Sumatra. Although the English retained a toehold in Bengkulu (in south Sumatra) called Fort Marlborough, the Dutch had established a monopoly over the trade from the East Indies by the end of the seventeenth century. The old Javanese, Malay, Gujarati and Chinese traders' wealth was destroyed, while the monopolist VOC was able to sell spices in Europe at seventeen times the price at which they were procured in the east.

Late in the seventeenth century, the price of cotton began rising on account of political turmoil in India—arising from Aurangzeb's attempt to establish Mughal ascendancy over southern India. Traditionally, Minangkabau exported pepper to India in exchange for the valued cotton and cloth imported from India. While pepper's importance began to wane, the rising price and diminishing supplies of cotton led to increased cotton cultivation in Sumatra by the end of the seventeenth century. The Dutch and English also introduced tobacco to the island as an alternative cash crop.

In the eighteenth century, however, the spice trade gradually declined in importance, and the Dutch steadily lost their naval dominance to the British, and began concentrating instead on cash crops. From trading in cloves, nutmeg and pepper, the VOC became increasingly focused on cultivating cash crops like coffee, tobacco, sugar and indigo. This required a growing involvement in the interior of the islands, and the VOC tightened its grip over Java during the course of the century. Mataram was in decline, and the VOC intervened in each of the three Javanese Wars of Succession (1704–08, 1719–23 and 1746–57), gaining greater control over its realms with each intervention.

The pasisir (coastal principalities in the north of Java) were much more Islamized than the sultans of Mataram, to whom they owed nominal allegiance. In 1676–77, Raden Trunajaya of Madura led a rebellion centred on Surabaya and the north Java coast, using Islamic symbols to challenge the authority of Mataram's ruler Amangkurat. The Dutch intervened decisively on the side of Mataram, and in exchange obtained the rights to all the revenue from the pasisir ports, to build shipyards and forts wherever they wished in Java, and a monopoly over the trade in textiles, sugar and opium.

In 1740–41, the VOC itself faced a rebellion by the Chinese residents of Batavia; initially, Mataram's sultan, Pakubuwono II, intervened on the side of the Chinese and caused the ouster of the VOC from Kartasura (the capital of Mataram). The VOC then sought the support of Madura and began chipping away at the Chinese positions. With the tide of war turning, Pakubuwana began sending feelers to the Dutch—leading many of his courtiers and noblemen to defect. The rebellious Javanese–Chinese forces looted Kartasura in June 1742, and it took a combined VOC–Madura army half a year to help restore Pakubuwana to the throne. But the whole of the north coast was ceded to the VOC in return for its help, and Mataram's capital was shifted to Surakarta (Solo) in 1746.

But this settlement angered many of Mataram's princes, setting off the third (and final) War of Javanese Succession. In order to secure the company's support against his cousins, Pakubuwana II formally ceded sovereignty over Mataram to the VOC in December 1749. The VOC soon decided, however, that it would no longer seek to sustain the unity of Mataram, and instead worked towards an amicable partition. The Treaty of Giyanti (1755) divided Mataram in two, with Pakubuwono III (son of Pakubuwana II) ruling one part from Surakarta, and Pakubuwana II's half-brother (who took the title of Hamengkubuwono I) ruling the other part from his capital of Yogyakarta. Peace was not fully restored until 1757, when Pakubuwana's territory was further divided—with a portion going to his cousin, who took the title Mangkunegara I. This restored peace to Java, allowing the Dutch to resume their profit-making activities centred on cash crops. (But the struggle for supremacy between the three successor states of Mataram continued behind the scenes; Hamengkubuwono's territory too was split in 1813, with a part being hived off under Pakulam I—the founder of the fourth and smallest state formed from the splintering of Mataram. Those remain the four royal houses of Java to this day.)

Around 1700, the VOC brought coffee cultivation to Java from Arabia, centred around the Priangan region in the hilly interior of western Java that was already under direct VOC rule. The Sundanese 'regents' in the Priangan region were each required to deliver specific annual quotas of coffee. The regents in turn levied this on their subjects as a tax-in-kind, apart from continuing to levy their traditional taxes in rice and labour (for road-building, etc.). The Sundanese adopted many features of Javanese culture and grew very rich under this system, which was gradually extended to other parts of Java as the VOC's influence grew. In the north coast, the VOC farmed out river and road tolls to the Chinese, and also 'leased' many villages to them, who used these to grow sugar, indigo and other crops (with the labour rights that they gained). The essentially Javanese social structure persisted, albeit with the regents and other priyayi (noblemen) gaining substantially more power and wealth than they had in pre-Dutch times.

Although the Dutch ruled, daily governance remained in priyayi hands, and the latter often bribed the Dutch to gain greater office. Production was organized in familiar feudal forms, but became increasingly commercial. Dutch officials and priyayi became more wealthy (as the grant of office and the leasing of villages became largely privatized activities that benefited individuals rather than the VOC itself—in an early echo of the problems of today's Indonesia). The peasants, and the VOC as an institution, were increasingly squeezed. However, the eighteenth century also saw a flowering of Javanese (especially priyayi) culture, represented in court literature, the refinement of wayang kulit puppet theatre and the development of batik into an art form.

Its inherent institutional weaknesses—coupled with the ossification and waning efficacy of oligarchic rule in Holland, especially in the face of Britain's rising naval power—led to the gradual collapse of the VOC. On the last day of the eighteenth century, the Dutch government abolished the VOC (in the face of its mounting deficits and growing corruption) and assumed its assets, liabilities and possessions in the East Indies. Over the next three decades, Governors General appointed by the Dutch government struggled to reform the administration—attempting to alter the cosy accommodations the VOC had made with Javanese custom. The Netherlands was defeated by Napoleon Bonaparte in 1806, and his brother Louis became king of the Dutch. Louis appointed Herman Daendels as Governor General of the East Indies to implement the ideals of the French Revolution in the east. Daendels was determined to abolish both forced labour and forced deliveries of crop—the two illiberal features of the Dutch–Javanese economy.

But as the Napoleonic Wars spread east, the British began a naval blockade of the Dutch East Indies (today's Indonesia). Daendels was thus obliged to use forced labour to build a highway (or post road) along the north coast, and to lease land to European and Chinese entrepreneurs to boost agricultural output and revenues—at the cost of peasants' welfare (the opposite of his original reformist objectives). In September 1811 (a few months after Daendels's term had ended), Batavia fell to the British, who replaced the Dutch as suzerains of the East Indies until 1816. Thomas Stamford Raffles (an employee of the British East India Company) became Lieutenant Governor of British Java, and later Governor General of Bencoolen (Bengkulu). Raffles also attempted to abolish forced deliveries and forced labour and to replace them with a land rent tax, to be collected by the bupatis (regents) acting on behalf of the British government. However, with the end of the Napoleonic Wars, the Dutch regained their independence and so regained control of their old colonies.

However, the British held on to Padang in Sumatra until 1819; this, coupled with their continued control of Bengkulu, gave them a virtual stranglehold over the rich output of the Minangkabau highlands. The Minang had a unique culture, based on a matrilineal customary law that conferred a special status on women. In 1800–03, several Minangkabau scholars in Arabia began to come under the influence of the Wahhabis of the Arabian Peninsula and they tried to introduce these austere practices into their homelands on their return. The Wahhabi-inspired Paderis opposed alcohol, tobacco, cockfighting and the matrilineal system, and wanted to introduce Arab-style dress and other social mores of the desert (beards, tudungs, deferential women, etc.). These ideas brought them into conflict with the aristocratic elite—and indeed with most ordinary Minang—and set off a civil war amongst the Minangkabau. In 1815, the Paderi won a victory of sorts when they slaughtered the royal family. Raffles was then seeking to extend the influence of Padang into the highlands, and he sought to further this cause by aligning the British with the Minangkabau aristocracy. In exchange for British support, he sought trade concessions. But these moves were aborted when Britain returned Padang to the Dutch in 1819 despite Raffles's vehement protests. A chastened Raffles was obliged to turn his attention to the little island of Singapore, where he began to develop a British entrepôt that became the base of British expansion into Malaya over the next century.

In 1824, the Dutch and British concluded the Treaty of London, under which the Dutch handed over their remaining possessions in India and in

Melaka, in exchange for the British giving Bengkulu to the Dutch. In fact, a line through the Straits of Malacca was defined as the border between the British and the Dutch (and still forms the border between Malaysia and Indonesia today), while the Dutch recognized British sovereignty over Singapore. All of Sumatra became nominally Dutch, although the latter also inherited the Paderi Rebellion; in 1821, the Padang administration had made a deal with the Minangkabau nobility, under which the Dutch gained sovereignty in exchange for protecting the local leaders from the Paderi. War with the latter was the inevitable result. The Paderi War was inconclusive in the 1821–25 period. But after the end of the Java War (see below), the Dutch committed more troops to Minangkabau, and gained several decisive victories in the 1830s. The leader of the Paderi, Tuanku Imam Bonjol, surrendered in 1837 and the war was largely over the next year, although some resistance persisted for a few more years. With the capture of Minangkabau, the productive key to Sumatra, the Dutch gradually brought the whole of the island under their control by 1850.

Upon the Dutch return to Java in 1816, it was clear that the ruling elites were all much poorer than they had been a decade earlier. The Napoleonic Wars had drained Dutch resources; and local officials (especially in Yogyakarta) had been deprived of their source of living, having lost land to the annexations by Daendels and Raffles. The Dutch raised customs duties and tolls substantially, while also encouraging officials in Yogyakarta to lease out lands that remained in their control to Europeans and Chinese. As more and more land came under plantation agriculture (especially tobacco), the rice crop began to suffer, and there was a severe drought in 1821. These factors (coupled with a sense that Islam and Javanese practice were under threat) led to the Java War of 1825–30, the Javanese hero of which was Diponegoro, a son of Sultan Hamengkubuwono III of Yogyakarta (and so a legatee of Mataram and Majapahit). Diponegoro rallied all the Javanese enemies of Yogyakarta and the Dutch, and won a series of victories along the north coast; but, although he successfully besieged Yogyakarta, the city did not fall to his forces. By 1828, however, the war was at a stalemate. The Dutch were beginning to despair of their ability to hold on, as their resources were being steadily depleted. But in one final throw of the dice, the Dutch invited Diponegoro for truce talks. And, instead, in an act of treachery, they captured Diponegoro when he entered their camp for talks. With their leader's capture in 1830, the rebellion gradually petered out.

In Europe, meanwhile, the Dutch unsuccessfully fought a war in 1831–32 to prevent the creation of the kingdom of Belgium in their southern provinces. It was to recoup the losses from that war—as well as the costly Java and

Paderi wars—that the Dutch began introducing the cultuurstelsel cultivation system in the 1830s. The system proved hugely successful for the Dutch: between 1815 and 1830, the Dutch national debt had risen to 37.5 million florins; between 1830 and 1840, the cultivation system produced a net surplus of 9.3 million florins *per year*, the figure rising to 14.1 million annually in the next decade. The enormous profits from the forced delivery of plantation products from the East Indies fuelled the rising prosperity of the Netherlands, fully financing the building of its canals, railways and military defences. In Java, meanwhile, the former ruling elites engaged themselves in other pursuits, developing the arts and crafts of Java, leaving the political arena fully under the control of the Dutch after the last Java War.

Most of Sumatra (with the exception of the sultanate of Aceh) was brought into the plantation economy during the second half of the nineteenth century. Tobacco was the main crop planted by small holders along the east coast in the sultanate of Deli. Dutch planters soon began to take this over, winning leases from the sultan for massive plantations: since high-quality tobacco required that the soil be left fallow for eight years, the planters required eight to nine times the amount of land on which they grew a year's crop. Labour was initially procured from the Chinese populations of Singapore, Penang and mainland China, replaced largely by Javanese after about 1890. The notorious Coolie Ordinance of 1880 provided for a penal sanction against workers who ran away from their employers; if caught, such workers were subject to imprisonment and flogging before being returned to their employer. But the tobacco economy suffered a severe depression after the US imposed a protective tariff on tobacco amid a global glut, causing a halving in the world prices of tobacco in 1891. Production in Sumatra nearly halved between 1890 and 1892, and twenty-five tobacco companies collapsed. Thereafter, a concerted attempt began to diversify the economy, with coffee and rubber being aggressively introduced in the final decade of the nineteenth century. While the former failed to take permanent root, rubber became an increasingly important industry in Sumatra by the turn of the century. Also during the final decade of the nineteenth century, the first major oil strikes were made in Sumatra, and the Royal Dutch Company was established to exploit those opportunities, although its focus increasingly shifted to Kalimantan, where the Jewish businessman Marcus Samuel's Shell Transport and Trading Company became its chief rival.

In Aceh, however, the Dutch were still fighting a war that had begun in 1873 (and was not to end in victory for the Dutch before 1903). Aceh's prosperity was grounded in its role as a pepper exporter: in the first decade of the nineteenth century, Aceh's pepper exports were about 2,500 tonnes annually out of a Southeast Asian total of 9,000 tonnes. Most of its exports were routed through Penang, giving the British a vested interest in its independence from Dutch or other interference. With prosperity, however, the uleebalang (regional chiefs) who dominated the pepper trade were becoming increasingly independent of the Sultan of Aceh. Raffles interceded on the Sultan's behalf in the 1811–16 period, signing a concession agreement that gave the British exclusive trading rights in Acehnese ports in return for recognizing the Sultan as the sole legitimate ruler of Aceh. The 1824 Treaty of London, however, saw the British renounce all political connections with Aceh in return for the freedom to trade without impediment in all of Sumatra, while the Dutch agreed to respect Aceh's independence. By the 1860s, British interest in the independence of Aceh was waning, as its liberal access to all trade with Sumatra reduced the importance of an independent Aceh, and the British feared a US or French alliance with Aceh more than Dutch control of it. When the Dutch got news that the Sultan had approached the US consulate in Singapore for assistance, the Royal Netherlands East Indies Army (Koninklijk Nederlands Indisch Leger, or KNIL) attacked Aceh in 1873. Although the capital was initially captured with ease, the Acehnese fought back and regained control within ten days.

The KNIL was forced to send in a larger expeditionary force and, at its peak, a third of all its troops were committed to Aceh. Increasingly, the ulema rather than the sultan led the Acehnese resistance, and the war took on an increasingly religious aspect. Eventually, the Dutch decided to try and win the uleebalang over to the Dutch side by promising them high positions in the Dutch administration. This strategy broadly succeeded—although the war itself resulted in 15,000 deaths amongst the KNIL troops and some 25,000 amongst the Acehnese. The successful political strategy of the Dutch also drove a deep wedge between the secular and religious elites of Aceh by the turn of the century, which arguably continues to plague that region to this day.

More broadly, the first twenty-five years of the nineteenth century had clearly demonstrated that the Dutch ruled the East Indies upon the sufferance of the British, who had become the leading naval power in Europe and thus the world. Increasingly, Singapore became the locus of British interests in the archipelago, and it also became central to Dutch fortunes in the archipelago, both commercial (as represented by the plantation companies that dominated Sumatra's rubber, palm oil and tobacco industries) and military, as was to be repeatedly demonstrated in the first half of the new century. And the pattern of Dutch control over the East Indies had also (perhaps inadvertently) followed the British pattern in establishing control over their new colony.

Just as the British in India first established alliances with local rulers in India, militarily defeating some of their most intransigent opponents, and eventually assimilating (via a mixture of trickery and clever alliances) other long-recalcitrant rivals (especially the Marathas), the Dutch followed almost precisely the same pattern thirty to fifty years later (with Mataram replacing the Marathas in the story).

RUSSIANS AND TURKS (PLUS 'TARTARS' AND PERSIANS)

At the dawn of the twentieth century, Russia was actually the European power with the largest presence in Asia. Indeed, the Asian realms of Tsarist Russia were substantially larger than its European heartlands—albeit much more sparsely populated—and Russia's borders with China and Japan made it a full participant in Asian politics. In 1914, the explorer Fridtjof Nansen estimated that over the previous 400 years Russia had been expanding at the astounding pace of 55 square miles a *day*, or about 20,000 square miles a year. Genghis Khan's marauding Mongol forces had humiliated the princes of Muscovy and Kiev on their long journey of conquest that took the Golden Horde all the way to the gates of Vienna. One of the great speculative counterfactuals of world history involves the possibility of the Golden Horde conquering Vienna and leaving a firmer Mongol imprint on Europe: that continent escaped this fate primarily because Genghis Khan's successor Ogedei died just as his nephew Batu was at the gates of Vienna, obliging the latter to return to the Mongol heartlands to participate in the succession struggle.

Unlike the Viennese, the Russians and Ukrainians felt the full brunt of Mongol horsemanship and military might. Their brutality made the Tartars (and their successor Turks) the mortal enemies of Russians. So the Tartar successors of the Mongols in Central Asia became the villainous 'other' in Russian culture, as Russians and Tartars engaged in a titanic struggle for supremacy over the next eight centuries. (This enmity of course persists to this day in some parts of old Russia such as Chechnya.) From about 1500, Russia gradually gained the upper hand in this struggle, and steadily gained territory in Central Asia. With the Turkish conquest of the Byzantine capital of Constantinople in 1453, the struggle for control of Central Asia became largely a battle between Orthodox Christians (led largely by Russia) and Muslims (represented mainly by Turks, an ethnic category that came to largely subsume the less numerous Tartars and Mongols).

By 1900, the Muslim Turks were still demographically dominant in Central Asia, but their realms were mostly controlled by Tsarist Russia. The latter ruled all of modern Azerbaijan (Turkish-speaking Shias), Kazakhstan, Uzbekistan,

Kyrgyzstan and Turkmenistan (populated by Turkish Sunni peoples) as well as Tajikistan (dominated by Persian-speaking Sunnis). Throughout the nineteenth century, Russian mothers were mortally frightened of their children being kidnapped for the slave markets of Bukhara, where young Russian slaves were especially prized. Russia's conquest of Bukhara reduced, but did not eliminate, this flourishing (and frightening) slave trade. Although subjugated, the 'Tartars' and Turks did find ways of getting their own back at the Russians: Russian mothers even today warn their children of Tajik kidnappers.

The Mongol conquerors of Iran and Iraq (including the celebrated sacking of Baghdad in 1258 that destroyed the Fatimid Caliphate and fatally weakened the Seljuks) took just one generation to embrace the local faith, Islam, which became the predominant religion of all of West and Central Asia by the thirteenth century. The Mamluk (slave) dynasty in Egypt recruited its rulers and soldiers from the Central Asian steppe as well, and the slave-rulers' children automatically became Muslims too. At the start of the twentieth century, all of Arabia and the Levantine Fertile Crescent (Lebanon, Syria, Palestine), Egypt, Libya and Sudan were at least nominally part of the Ottoman (Turkish) empire, with its capital in Istanbul (old Constantinople).

The Ottomans used their beachhead in Constantinople to conquer much of Eastern Europe (Greece, Serbia, Bosnia, Albania and Bulgaria were part of the Ottoman empire at the start of the nineteenth century, and Croatia and Hungary had been for several centuries too); they turned their attention westward towards southern and Eastern Europe and never directly ruled Central Asia other than Dagestan and Chechnya. However, the Russian–Tartar struggle in Central Asia soon translated into a Russian–Ottoman struggle for control of southeastern Europe. Throughout the nineteenth century, the 'sick man of Europe' (the Ottoman empire) lost territory, as Russian aid and influence proved instrumental in securing the independence of its Slavic cousins in Serbia (in 1867, fifty years after the Ottomans had been forced to grant it limited self-government) and Bulgaria (which became an autonomous 'principality' of the Ottomans in 1878, with Prince Alexander of Battenberg— uncle of Lord Louis Mountbatten—as its ruling prince), and even earlier, its fellow Orthodox Greece (1821–30; at the end of this period, several European powers imposed the Bavarian prince Otto as king of Greece, and a grandson of Britain's Queen Victoria succeeded him in 1862, but Greece continued to seek to gain territory at Ottoman expense all the way until the start of the twentieth century). And in 1878 (apart from Bulgaria) the Ottomans were also obliged to give up Cyprus, which Prime Minister Benjamin Disraeli earned as a prize for British cooperation with Russia during the Congress of Berlin. At the start of the twentieth century, the Ottoman empire was much more clearly an Islamic empire, having been forced to shed most of the Christian possessions in Europe that had given it its cosmopolitan character.

Iran too was ruled by a Turkic dynasty, the Qajars, whose corrupt and arbitrary rule had largely frittered away the legacy of the great Persian civilization, and made it vulnerable to the competing imperial ambitions of Britain and Russia. One of the oldest nations on earth, it was first forged into a unitary nation in 559 BCE by Cyrus II, who was noted for the visionary benevolence of his rule and named his empire Persia after the Pars (later Fars) region from where his family sprang. He conquered Asia Minor (much of today's Turkey, particularly Anatolia) and Babylon, but his Achaemenid dynasty reached its zenith under Xerxes, who also conquered Athens, Macedon and Thermopylae. Persia became the great 'other' for the Greeks (and their Roman and Byzantine successors)—the perennial rivals for territory and civilizational pride. The Achaemenid were followers of the Zoroastrian faith, founded by Zarathustra sometime between the seventh and tenth centuries BCE (approximately the same time that the Buddha was preaching in India and Confucius lived in China). Amongst other things, Zoroastrianism bequeathed the notion of 'farr' to Iranians through the ages—which held that rulers earned a divine blessing through moral behaviour. The loss of farr inevitably led to defeat and upheaval. The spread of Achaemenid glory was halted when Darius lost the Battle of Marathon in 490 BCE, but a more decisive blow was defeat at the hands of Alexander in 334 BCE.

Zoroastrianism remained the basis for the three dynasties that ruled Iran over the subsequent ten centuries. The last of these, the Sassanians, were seen as breaking the implicit social contract between ruler and ruled that provided the foundation for farr; their intermittent wars against the Byzantine empire weakened them financially, and led to more tyrannical rule. Defeat by the Byzantines in 626 CE was a big blow, but the knockout punch was delivered when the Arabs (inspired by the zeal of their new faith of Islam) conquered the Sassanian capital of Ctesiphon (the historic capital of the Parthians, called Parthava in Old Persian, in present-day Iraq) in 638 CE. This defeat inspired much Persian poetry from such luminaries as Firdausi and Rumi in subsequent centuries, and Iran was the first of the newly-conquered Muslim domains to retain its pre-Islamic language (albeit adopting the Arabic script) and much of its culture. Politically, Persia was subsumed into Arab empires, until the latter were fatally wounded by the Mongol invasion of Iran in 1220.

In 1501, a Shiite dynasty, the Safavid, took control of Iran under the founder, Shah Ismail, who inaugurated a new Shia-inspired Persian renaissance. While Ismail reunited most of what is today's Iran (and much of Iraq, where the Shia holy sites of Karbala, Najaf and Kufa lie), the Safavids reached their pinnacle under Shah Abbas, who ruled from 1588 to 1629. Not only did Abbas encourage a cultural and scientific efflorescence, he built roads and created incipient industries by encouraging silk, ceramics and other factories to manufacture products that foreign traders sought. But he was also an absolutist whose paranoia about his sons led him to weaken them all, and the Safavids declined rapidly after him—until Iran was ravaged by Afghan invaders in 1722, who dealt the final blow. The Sunni Turk ruler Nadir Shah re-established order, conquered the then-effete Mughals in Delhi and sacked the city, but was himself assassinated in 1747.

The Qajars took control late in the eighteenth century (and were to rule until 1925), but these self-absorbed and corrupt rulers were ripe for exploitation by Russia and Britain; only the fact that there were two rival claimants for influence allowed Iran a modicum of independence. To maintain his harem of 1,600 wives and concubines, and his predilection for jewellery and foreign travel, Naser al-Din Shah sold a telegraph concession to the British in 1857 (amid the First War of Independence in India, whose leaders had forlornly hoped for Persian intervention on their side) and in 1872 awarded Baron Paul Julius von Reuter (a Briton of German descent) the concession to run Iran's industries, irrigate its farms, exploit its mineral resources, develop its railways, establish its national bank and print its currency! Russia's vigorous protests at this wholesale transfer of the national economy to a Briton obliged Naser al-Din to revoke the Reuter concession within a year, but much of it was then distributed amongst three British conglomerates, while Russia was placated with the selling of exclusive rights to the shah's caviar fisheries to Russian merchants. (Had Reuter retained his monopoly over Iran's economy, he might never have had enough time to develop the business that made him famous: an international news agency.)

When Naser al-Din gave the British Imperial Tobacco Company a monopoly in 1891 over both the purchase of raw tobacco from farmers and the retailing of cigarettes, there was a widespread revolt triggered by a fatwa from Iran's leading religious figure, Sheikh Shirazi, saying that smoking would be an offense against the Twelfth Imam of the Shia as long as tobacco was a foreign-owned industry. By the turn of the century, Iran was in ferment as the middle class began debating constitutional reform—inspired by the news from Europe, the Ottoman empire and across Asia. The assassination of Naser al-Din did not improve matters as his successor Muzaffar al-Din was perhaps even more prone to luxury and therefore to indebtedness. It was Muzaffar al-Din Shah who took the fateful decision in 1901 to sell to the London-based financier William Knox D'Arcy the exclusive right to 'obtain, exploit, develop...

carry away and sell natural gas [and] petroleum...for a term of sixty years'. Although it took D'Arcy more than a decade to finally strike oil, the grant of the concession set off a further flurry of protest that was to culminate in demands for major constitutional reform early in the new century.

CHINA UNDER THE WANING MANCHUS, BESIEGED BY 'TREATY PORT' POWERS

China, too, was ruled by a foreign dynasty at the start of the twentieth century. Despite it being an Asian dynasty, its self-image (shared by the subjugated Chinese) was that of a foreign imperial power lording it over the Han Chinese. The Manchus had conquered China in 1644 and, having been assimilated into the Chinese imperial system like most previous 'barbarian' conquerors of the sedentary Chinese peoples, had taken the dynastic title of Qing. As a reminder of their status as slaves of the Manchus, all Han Chinese men were required to shave the front of their heads and wear their hair in a ponytail/queue, while their women were obliged to bind their feet into severely constricting shoes. The Qing court was dominated by Manchu and Mongol nobles, as a further reminder of the inferior status of Han Chinese in this foreign-dominated regime.

The Sinologist W. J. F. Jenner points out that much of what we now know as China had spent most of the previous seventeen centuries under dynasties whose provenance was foreign (i.e., non-Han Chinese). This may appear an excessively broad claim, but over the last millennium the only dynasty that was clearly Han Chinese was the Ming, established in Nanjing by a former Buddhist monk (from the 'Red Turban' sect) named Zhu Yuanzhang in 1368. Zhu took the imperial title 'Hongwu' to refer to his reign, after having expelled the last ruler of the Yuan (Mongol, i.e., non-Han Chinese) dynasty from its imperial capital, Khanbaliq (Beijing) and razing all the Yuan imperial palaces to the ground. Hongwu established a brutal totalitarian regime based on fear and repression, and centred on a massive palace establishment run primarily by 70,000 eunuchs. At great cost, he did establish a ruthless peace in China, and the population doubled during the Ming dynasty's rule.

While the Ming dynasty lasted until its final ouster by another non-Han Chinese dynasty (the Manchu, who took the imperial title Qing) in 1644, it is clear that the Ming dynasty did not rule (or even have any claim of suzerainty over) Tibet, East Turkestan (Xinjiang) and Nei (Inner) Mongol (the territory of Inner Mongolia that is part of today's 'China'). The greatest of the Ming rulers, Yongle, moved his capital to Beijing to keep a closer eye on the persistent threat from the Mongols, but even he had no pretence to ruling over them.

At their height, the Ming were a great maritime power epitomized by the legendary voyages between 1405 and 1433 of the Muslim eunuch from the Ming court, Zheng He (sometimes thought to be the model for Sindbad the sailor) during the reign of Yongle. On his voyages, Zheng He established himself (as a resident, *not* as ruler) for long periods in the great maritime port of Malacca and in Java where there were thriving multinational communities from Bengal, Gujarat, Sumatra and parts of the Arab and African coast, apart from the Chinese communities established by Zheng He (mainly comprising Hui Muslims like himself). He himself was a sailor/soldier and not a merchant, but his vast fleets contained merchants too who conducted a vigorous trade across the region. In a typical Chinese conceit, however, his massive fleets also claimed to have collected 'tribute' from the various rulers he visited in Java, Sumatra, Brunei, Pahang, Malacca; Bengal, Cochin (Kochi) and other kingdoms on the east and west coast of India; as well as Madagascar and eastern Africa. In reality, those rulers probably saw themselves as merely exchanging gifts with another ruler whose envoy was visiting from China. In a similar vein, the Ming claimed that the Mongol ruler was a tributary of Ming China, while Altan Khan (the ruler of the Mongols) claimed that the Ming were paying tributes to the Mongols!

In reality, the Oirat Mongol leader Esen Taishi defeated the Ming emperor Zhengtong on 8 September 1449 and took him prisoner. Although this was the greatest single threat that Ming China faced from the Mongols, Altan Khan raided the Chinese empire in 1529, 1530 and 1542; in 1550 he attacked Beijing's suburbs and set them on fire, prompting the rebuilding of the Great Wall. But Altan Khan is remembered more for re-establishing ties between Mongolia and Tibet, and helping to spread Buddhism amongst his people.

In 1578, Sonam Gyatso (the third Dalai Lama) visited Altan Khan's capital at Kuku Khoto (Hohhot) and preached there to a huge crowd. Altan Khan had Mongolia's first monastery Thegchen Chonkhor built, and Buddhism was adopted as the state religion of Mongolia after the ruler of the Khalkha Mongols, Abtai Sain Khan, visited Sonam Gyatso in Altan Khan's realms. Abtai Sain Khan built a huge monastery complex (Erdene Zuu) at the site of the old Mongol capital, Karakorum, and a massive programme of translating Tibetan and Sanskrit texts to Mongolian was undertaken. In fact, it was Altai Khan who translated the Tibetan word 'Gyatso' into Mongolian as 'Dalai' (both words meaning 'ocean'). The term Dalai Lama is thus of Mongolian provenance and was adopted only during the term of the third Lama in that line! The Dalai Lama convinced the Mongols to give up animal sacrifices, and other past practices such as the burning of widows on their dead husbands' funeral pyres.

What most distinguishes the ties between Tibetans and Mongolians in this period is that the Ming Chinese had precisely *no* role whatsoever in mediating those ties. The only genuinely Han Chinese dynasty of the last millennium had absolutely no claim over Tibet or Mongolia; in fact, it had no significant contact with Tibet or Xinjiang, leave alone any claim of ruling over them, while its only link with the Mongols was on the battlefield, where the Ming were usually at the receiving end.

The Han Chinese dynasty of the Ming was preceded by the Mongol Yuan dynasty, which, in fact, united much of what constitutes China today after the divisions amongst the Southern and Northern Song dynasties (both of which ruled realms that were fractions of the territory claimed by today's People's Republic). Kublai Khan and his successors were decidedly non-Chinese. Although the People's Republic of China (PRC) now retrospectively claims even the great Mongol conqueror Genghis Khan, there is no doubt that Genghis spoke Mongolian, practised Shamanism, and did not consider himself remotely Chinese; even his grandson Kublai spoke very little Chinese, with Mongol being the court language. And the Ming were of course succeeded by the non-Han Manchu (or Qing) dynasty, who made their non-Sinitic ethnicity evident to those they ruled daily throughout their 268-year reign (1644–1912).

The first truly unifying Han Chinese dynasty had been the Tang who ruled from 618–906 CE, and created both the civil service examination system and the agrarian ownership structure that gave the bureaucratic state such enduring solidity. The Tang dynasty established Chinese influence over Korea, southern Manchuria and northern Vietnam, although this influence was well short of full sovereignty (probably closer to suzerainty, although the Koreans and Vietnamese may not have interpreted it as such). With the Central Asian tribes (such as the Uighurs of today's Xinjiang, the Kazakhs, Uzbeks, etc.), the Tang created a system of alliances that helped extend their influence. However, these alliances proved a mixed blessing: after the rebellion in 755 of the Tang general An Lushan, the Tang had to grant autonomy to many of the frontier chieftains who had helped put down that rebellion. By the ninth century, the Tang dynasty's political control was limited to Shaanxi—although the cultural flowering in China (set off by the splendour of the early Tang) continued even during this period of the Tang's declining political control.

Even the Tang ruled over most of what is today considered China (except northern Manchuria, Tibet, Xinjiang and Nei Mongol) for no more than 137 years, with the fuller period of dynastic rule only applying to Shaanxi province. Even as their realms shrank, however, the Tang extended the influence of

Confucianism—by aggressively purging Buddhism through the closure of 4,600 monasteries and the destruction of as many as 40,000 Buddhist temples and shrines. The Tang eventually succumbed to the depredations of the Khitan Mongols, who extended their Liao dynasty (907–1125) from their base in Mongolia and Manchuria to Hebei and Shanxi provinces, making Beijing their southern capital.

The period from 907–960 is considered the Five Dynasties period, with five short-lived dynasties in northern China and ten kingdoms in the south. In 960, Zhao Kuangyin established the Northern Song dynasty—although the Song were never able to regain Hebei and Shanxi (or Beijing) from the Khitan Mongols. In fact, after repeated defeats, the Song agreed in 1004 to pay an annual tribute to the Khitan Mongols in exchange for stopping their border wars. Similarly, the Song also agreed to pay an annual tribute to the Tibetan-speaking Xi Xia (Tangut) tribe after 1044. The Song entered into an alliance with the Jin (Chin) dynasty of northern Manchuria in 1120 in order to defeat the Liao, but eventually were forced out of their capital of Kaifeng by the Jin and obliged to flee south.

From 1135 until their final defeat at the hands of Kublai Khan in 1279, the Southern Song ruled from their new southern capital in Hangzhou (Zhejiang province). This was a period of great prosperity in the south, where the intellectual achievements and level of economic development greatly outstripped those of the conquered regions of northern China. Neo-Confucianism reached its apogee as the philosopher Zhu Xi synthesized the human-centred Confucian doctrines with some metaphysical elements borrowed from Buddhism. The bureaucracy grew too rapidly, reflecting some administrative decay, but there were no significant internal challenges to the Southern Song.

Once the Mongols were united under the dynamic leadership of Genghis Khan in 1206, northern China's Jin dynasty (with its capital in Beijing) was quickly defeated by Genghis in 1215 and brought under Mongol rule. The Southern Song were not immediately threatened, as the Mongols looked westward first and soon established a vast empire that included most of Russia, Persia and much of Central and Eastern Europe. The Golden Horde only stopped at the gates of Vienna and turned back towards the Mongol heartlands in order to return to the Mongol capital of Karakorum upon receiving the news of Genghis Khan's successor's death. In 1279, Genghis Khan's grandson, Kublai, used his vastly superior armies to defeat the Southern Song. Ironically it took a non-Chinese Mongol to unify much of what is now considered China for the first time. Although Kublai Khan took the dynasty title of Yuan, the Mongols were a decidedly non-Chinese dynasty.

Thus, in the period from 618 (when the Tang dynasty was established) until 1912 (when the non-Han Manchu dynasty was to give way to the semblance of a modern republic), there was no significant period during which a dynasty of Han Chinese extraction ruled over Tibet, Mongolia, Nei Mongol, Manchuria or East Turkestan (Xinjiang). Over the course of those thirteen centuries, Han Chinese dynasties—the Tang and the Ming—ruled China proper (i.e., excluding Tibet, Nei Mongol, Xinjiang and Manchuria) for just 137 and 81 years, respectively. In the preceding four centuries—since the fall of the later Han dynasty in 220 CE—there had been a protracted period of disunion in China, and much of northern China had been ruled by non-Chinese dynasties.

So W. J. F. Jenner's claim is indeed strongly grounded in historical fact. Over the seventeen centuries since the fall of the Han dynasty, China had not been ruled by Han Chinese for more than 218 years and, even during those years, no Han Chinese dynasty had ever ruled over or even dominated Tibet, Inner and Outer Mongolia, Xinjiang or northern Manchuria. China's historical founding dynasty, the Qin (also written Ch'in, founded by Shihuangdi in 221 BCE) extended over a subset of what constitutes China today: like its predecessors (the Shang and Zhou/Chou dynasties), the Qin dynasty was initially confined to Hubei, Shantung (Shandong), Henan and parts of Anhui province. Shihuangdi expanded his kingdom southwards to the Red River delta (in northern Vietnam), and also enlarged it towards the southwest to include much of what comprises Yunnan, Guizhou and Sichuan. In the north, his kingdom included the northern part of the Korean peninsula. Indeed, over the subsequent four centuries of Han dynasty rule, the Chinese empire exerted intermittent control over parts of Korea and Vietnam (especially their northern portions). But notably, no Chinese dynasty over those centuries laid any claim (leave alone exercising sovereignty) over Tibet, Turkestan, Mongolia or northern Manchuria (as opposed to southern Manchuria, which often merged with northern Korea and thus came under some Chinese influence).

It is therefore unsurprising that the Korean and Vietnamese languages have considerable Sinitic influences while Tibetan, Burmese, Nepali, Mongol and Uighur have none whatsoever. At the start of the twentieth century, Chinese ideograms would be recognized (and deciphered comfortably) by literate Japanese, Koreans and Vietnamese because of cultural intercourse stretching back between one and two whole millennia. Ironically, much of China's influence over Japan, Korea and Vietnam stemmed from the spread of Buddhism from China to those countries, which itself arrived in China from India via Tibet, Mongolia and Burma. Given the direction of influence, the Tibetan, Mongolian and Uighur languages are entirely unintelligible to the Chinese, and vice versa. The twists and turns of the first half of the

62   PRASENJIT K. BASU

twentieth century, however, have ensured that the Tibetans, Uighurs and (Inner) Mongols have come under the political control of China (despite being thoroughly non-Sinitic by culture and language), while the Koreans and Vietnamese (despite their greater cultural and linguistic affinity with China) have successfully resisted Chinese control.

Nurhaci (1559–1626 CE), the founding chief of the tribes that came to be known as the Manchu (who were so named only in 1636), united several adjoining tribes—all descended from the Jurchen (Ruzhen) tribes who had created the Jin dynasty in the twelfth century CE—and established his Later Jin dynasty with its capital in Mukden (Shenyang). His charismatic son Abahai (Hong Taiji in Chinese) conquered much of Korea, subdued several Mongol tribes in the west, gave his people the Manchu name and renamed the dynasty Qing ('pure'). By this time, the Manchus had a written language, into which many of the Chinese classics had been translated, and had institutionalized many of the trappings of Chinese kingship (including having Six Ministries), with a civil administration staffed by Manchus, Mongols and Chinese. For more than a decade before the actual conquest of China in 1644, the Qing were already preparing themselves to take power as a typically assimilated Chinese dynasty while clearly maintaining their separateness as Manchus.

Growing disaffection amongst the Ming nobility gave the Manchus the opening they needed. Wu Sangui, a Ming general in northern China, sought the Manchus as an ally to help suppress a rebellion against the Ming by a Chinese peasant rebel named Li Zicheng (who had raided northwestern China and taken much of Sichuan and the Yangzi Valley before capturing Beijing in April 1644). Wu believed the Manchus could be managed as the Ming forces in north China alone far outnumbered the Manchu military. The Manchus were, in fact, going through their own succession crisis, as Hong Taiji had died in 1643, and there was no clear succession mechanism. But once the Manchus were inside the Great Wall of China, they quickly established their military dominance over northern China, defeated Li Zicheng on 27 May 1644 and took control of Beijing on 6 June. Unusually for a conquering dynasty, the Qing (Manchus) immediately decided to make Beijing their new capital. Unlike Li Zicheng's forces, the Qing did not loot the city, instead pacifying it and keeping the Ming bureaucracy in their posts, thus quickly winning the support of the capital's inhabitants. The five-year-old Shunzhi emperor was installed on the throne with his uncle Dorgon (brother of Hong Taiji) as regent, and Dorgon proclaimed in October 1644 that the Mandate of Heaven had passed to the Manchu Qings. The Manchus had a sufficiently effective administrative infrastructure to seize control of China when the opportunity arose, with Dorgon's acumen as regent playing the vital role in smoothing the transition for his young nephew.

It took another generation before the Manchus were able to establish their sway over the whole of China; Wu Sangui himself led the rebellion of the 'three feudatories' in the south. Most Ming commanders and officials in the north as well as landed families in the lower Yangzi Valley, faced with a choice between loyalty and death, chose the former, choosing to shift allegiance from the Ming to the Qing. The infamous 'Queue Order' (requiring all Han Chinese men to shave the front of their heads in the Manchu manner, and to wear the rest of their hair in a queue or pigtail as a symbol of their submission to Manchu rule) was proclaimed in July 1645. Where the Manchus met resistance, they were ruthless in subduing it as, most infamously, in Yangzhou (on the Grand Canal) where almost 800,000 Ming holdouts were massacred. The rebellion of the three feudatories (who took control of almost all of southern China by 1653) was finally suppressed only by Shunzhi's successor, the Kangxi emperor, after eight years of fighting.

Since there were only a small number of Manchus, however, they had perforce to depend on Han Chinese to populate the bureaucracy and rule most of the country, having already developed the prototype for this pattern of rule by working with the Chinese in Southern Manchuria for several decades before their conquest of China proper. They paid particular attention to maintaining the efficiency of the central examination system for recruitment to the bureaucracy, and the early Qing emperors gained legitimacy by mastering the Chinese classics, demonstrating their personal scholarship and also showcasing their personal vigour by leading elaborate hunting expeditions that few predecessors could have matched. Most Ming Era officials were allowed to stay on (as long as they demonstrated their loyalty by wearing a queue and shaving the front of their heads), and the Six Ministries each had a Manchu and a Chinese minister. There was similarly a Han Chinese and a Manchu governor in each province (occasionally with one Manchu Governor General for two provinces, with Chinese governors in each). While Han Chinese provided most of the personnel for administration, Manchu placemen were entrusted with checking on the Han Chinese administrators, and reporting back directly to the palace in the Manchu language. The imperial palace household also maintained an elaborate treasury of its own—functioning as a secret echelon of government, with documentation in the Manchu language of revenues from land, customs (especially from Guangdong), trade monopolies (e.g., ginseng), taxes on salt and silk production, tributes, etc.—a remarkably similar list to the key sources of revenue for the British in India.

The Manchu innovation of 'bannermen'—military leaders personally attached to the king, who were responsible for maintaining cohesion within the military and protecting the borders—proved very effective as a military device. From the outset, there were Mongol and Han Chinese bannermen (as well as Manchu ones), and by the time the Manchus conquered Beijing, the majority of bannermen were already Han Chinese. Unlike the Ming (who had demonstrated their possession of the Mandate of Heaven through ruthless force), the Qing sought legitimacy through the meritorious actions of their emperors. The regime's stability was greatly aided by the fact that the first three emperors (who were paragons of Chinese kingship) ruled for a total of 133 years between them, with two (Kangxi, 1661–1722, and Qianlong, 1735–96) ruling for sixty years each, while Yongzheng used his relatively short reign of fourteen years (1722–35) to undertake widespread reforms that greatly aided the effectiveness of Manchu rule. All three studied the Chinese classics diligently, rose at the crack of dawn for meetings with their officials, and were active and conscientious rulers.

Thereafter, however, disenchantment with the later Manchu emperors began to set in, as China experienced 'growth without development' under the Manchu, while challenges from the west and east grew rapidly. This was exacerbated by the anti-entrepreneurial culture of old China, and the petrification of a legal system dependent on Confucian ethics, with patriarchal authority structures rather than individual rights, which militated against innovation and creativity.

By the turn of the eighteenth century, the Manchu dynasty was facing its first stirrings of rebellion with the Buddhist-inspired White Lotus Society mounting the first such rebellion in 1796 as rising corruption in the dying years of the by-then-senile Qianlong emperor provided a spark. The White Lotus Society mobilized the peasantry with the promised reincarnation of the Maitreya Buddha, but eventually also added an anti-Manchu racial message. Although the rebellion was comprehensively suppressed by 1804 (after the Jiaqing emperor ascended the throne in 1799 and reinvigorated the Qing armies), it punctured the myth of Manchu martial invincibility, as the bannermen struggled to suppress the impromptu peasant armies of the White Lotus.

A second, longer-term threat to the Manchu Qing dynasty began to emerge in the nineteenth century from the sea. Despite the Ming ban imposed in 1550 CE on official overseas trade ('Haijin', which ended the great official trade voyages that had culminated in Zheng He's storied journeys from 1405 to 1433 CE), Amoy (Xiamen) in Fujian had remained the hub of a vigorous private maritime trade with Chinese communities of long standing in Southeast Asia (where they were known as the Peranakan). Defying the ban, about a hundred Chinese junks continued to travel to Southeast Asia from Xiamen every year under both the Ming and Qing empires.

In the early years of the Qing, the depredations of Japanese traders (labelled 'dwarf pirates' by the Qing) as well as the ships of Koxinga (the Taiwan-based half-Japanese, half-Chinese admiral of the late Ming) had led to the reinstatement of the Haijin ban, with only limited success. Around the same time, the Spanish and Portuguese began to establish their own trading networks in East Asia, which competed with and complemented the native 'pirates' and traders. This growing trade helped enrich those who participated in it, but was largely outside the control of the imperial court. By the early seventeenth century, Manila already had a large community of 25,000 Chinese (mainly artisans and builders), and another more integrated group of Chinese–European mestizos (with names like Cojuangco, an amalgam of Koh-Huang-Koh) and Chinese converts to Christianity who were allowed to live in Manila proper and largely merge with the rest of the population.

Trade with the Muslim world also continued, and was officially sanctioned by the Ming and Qing, with Quanzhou (or Zayton, as it was known to Marco Polo and Ibn Batuta) in Fujian as the officially supervised port for this long-standing maritime trade. Thus, a string of Malay principalities such as Johor, Pahang, Trengganu and Patani were recorded as 'non-tributary trading countries' in Qing court records from 1818, while many of them had erroneously been referred to as tributaries in the Ming records of the 1580s. In 1759, the Qing dynasty made Canton (Guangzhou) the only official port for trade with the Europeans, and stationed a Manchu official from the inner court in Beijing as the customs supervisor (known to Europeans as the 'Hoppo') for the Guangdong region. Merchant-family trading houses (Hongs) acted as the intermediaries, and the British and Dutch East India Companies, in particular, rapidly developed the Canton trade. Two British emissaries (Lord George Macartney in 1793, and Lord William Amherst in 1816) and their large delegations bearing industrial manufactures were rebuffed by the imperial Manchu court, which remained oblivious to the enormous growth in Guangdong's trade and the growing indebtedness of the Chinese Hongs, which would give the British and other Europeans an opportunity to greatly expand their influence on China's coast.

Importantly, while the imperial strictures of China did not allow the emergence of a merchant subculture (unlike in contemporary Europe and Japan), the Overseas Chinese in Southeast Asia were able to accumulate capital and eventually use their trading networks to become great entrepreneurs (hugely benefiting from the legal frameworks that came to be established by the British, Dutch, Spaniards and Portuguese in their Southeast Asian colonies).

The Hokkien speakers, with their links to Xiamen, were the most prominent of the Peranakan business communities, but the Teochew (originating from seven villages in eastern Guangdong) became an even more closely knit and very successful business group (counting today's Bangkok business elite including the Sophonpanich and Chearavanont families, as well as Hong Kong's Li Ka-shing and Singapore's Lien Ying Chow amongst their number). But that was for the future.

A second, and more fabled, route for China's trade with the Muslim world was the ancient Silk Road. The Qing conquest of East Turkestan (renamed Xinjiang, or New Frontier) in 1759 facilitated this trade, conducted primarily through the western city of Kashgar. But merchants from the kingdom of Kokand (around the Fergana Valley in today's Uzbekistan) dominated Kashgar's trade, with Dzungar (Oirat Mongol) traders and soldiers also traditionally significant players in Kashgar and across Turkestan. The rulers of Kokand paid an annual tribute to the Qing court, but were also given a large yearly gift by the Qing for controlling potential rebels from charismatic Sufi Muslim families who might otherwise threaten Manchu control of East Turkestan. When Kokand's demands (for lower taxes on its trade, and the right to appoint its own representative to supervise Kokandian merchants in Kashgar) were refused by the Qing court, Kokand released its most prominent Sufi prisoner, Jahangir Khoja, who soon mobilized an army and invaded Chinese Turkestan in May 1826. It took a large Qing army more than a year to mobilize and defeat Jahangir in September 1827, and he was eventually captured a year later and paraded through the streets of Beijing in an iron cage before being presented to the Daoguang emperor, who had him executed, his body cut to pieces and literally thrown to the dogs. Despite that denouement with the individual scourge, the Manchu court came to an accommodation with Kokand, allowing some elements of extraterritoriality: Kokand was allowed to have a commercial representative at Kashgar, with subordinate agents in five other cities, and foreign/Kokand representatives were allowed to provide consular, judicial and police services to foreigners, with Kokand also allowed to levy customs duties on those foreigners' goods.

Such accommodations with distant bordering principalities were a hallowed tradition used by past dynasties with respect to the Jurchen, Jin, Manchus themselves and various Mongol tribes. But the threat from the Europeans—centred on Canton—was entirely of a different magnitude, as the Europeans (beginning with the British) wanted some forms of extraterritoriality to apply within China proper. Opium was the issue on which the Anglo–Manchu conflict came to a head. The obvious debilitating effects of the proliferation of opium within China spurred Qing attempts to regulate the trade.

The British East India Company had initially started a triangular trade involving opium cultivated in India (Bihar and Bengal) being imported into China (via Canton) by British and Indian traders licensed by the Company, in exchange for tea and silk (which were exported from China to Britain directly by the East India Company). Prominent amongst the exporters of opium from India was the managing agency Carr, Tagore & Company (owned and managed by Dwarkanath Tagore, grandfather of the poet), which also controlled the largest shipping line in the British empire, and ran British India's largest bank (Union Bank). Its main intermediary in Canton was Lancelot Dent & Company, the second largest of the managing agencies in the territory (whose chief executives came to be referred to as Taipan). The local Chinese brokers (Hongs) had handled the Company trade in Canton, collecting the duty payments on behalf of the Hoppo, whose venality was an open secret.

The cosy arrangements were destabilized once the British ended the East India Company's monopoly of the China trade in 1834. Prior to this, Canton trading houses like Jardine, Matheson & Company acted as intermediaries to the East India Company, loaning it their ships, importing opium from India, but not participating in the export of tea, silk, porcelain, etc. to Britain. The ending of the Company's monopoly opened up the trade to these trading houses, and also resulted in a sharp spike in the number of foreign traders from other European countries and the United States—massively expanding the volume of opium imports, which passed 30,000 chests in 1835 and 40,000 in 1838. The American vice consul in Canton was Warren Delano II (the grandfather of Franklin Delano Roosevelt, the thirty-second president of the US); his Russell & Company was the largest American shipper of opium to China. Most importantly, the British official sent to regulate this trade demanded to deal directly with the imperial Qing court on the basis of diplomatic equality (rather than as just another Taipan/Hong merchant) but this was impossible in the Chinese imperial scheme, in which all 'barbarians' were only considered to be bringing tribute to the imperial court, never dealing with it as equals.

The Daoguang emperor sought the advice of his senior officials on the issue of opium, receiving a split opinion (similar to current debates in the US and elsewhere) between those advocating the legalization of opium (as a means of regulating it better) and those demanding that it be ruthlessly stamped out. The emperor came out in support of the latter while the trading houses in Canton, who had also been following the debates closely, expected that legalization of opium would be the likely outcome. Amitav Ghosh's 2011 novel, *River of Smoke*, beautifully evokes the Canton of 1838–39, in the run-up to the Opium War. In March 1839, the cosy world of Canton and its waterfront dominated by the great foreign trading houses was shaken up by the arrival of the austere Confucian scholar Lin Zexu as imperial commissioner, with the clear remit to crush the opium trade.

Commissioner Lin began by interviewing each of the local (Cantonese) Cohong merchants, several of whom initially made futile attempts to obfuscate the role of Jardine, Dent, James Innes, etc. as opium traders. Lin wrote to Queen Victoria, appealing to her reason—erroneously asserting that opium was illegal in her realms, and surely ought to be in China too. (In Britain, opium was in fact legal, used most famously by the poet Coleridge but also put to much therapeutic use.) When this yielded no result, he ordered the arrest of the prominent British opium merchant Lancelot Dent, the very man who happened to be Carr, Tagore's intermediary—but the British refused to give him up, leading Lin to order an end to all foreign trade, and the blockading of all the foreign factories in Canton. The British superintendent of foreign trade, Charles Elliot (a retired naval captain, whose cousin was the 2nd Lord Minto, while another was then the Governor General of India, Lord Auckland) was also part of this blockade. This elevated the incident diplomatically unbeknownst to the Qing officials, who continued to treat Elliot like they had treated the East India Company officials in the past, as just another trader.

By the end of May 1839, Lin Zexu ordered the confiscation of all known chests of opium (without compensation), and had these chests destroyed on the beaches of Canton. Soon after Lin Zexu's arrival in Canton, the leading Taipan William Jardine (of Jardine, Matheson & Company) had already set off to London to personally intercede with the foreign secretary (and future prime minister), Lord Palmerston. When news of the blockade and unilateral destruction of British cargoes by Commissioner Lin reached London, a naval flotilla was dispatched for the China coast—which, led by Charles Elliot's cousin, Rear Admiral George Elliot (second son of the 1st Earl of Minto), arrived in Canton in June 1840 with 16 warships bearing 540 guns, 4,000 mainly Indian troops, 3,000 tons of coal and 16,000 gallons of rum! Lin Zexu had, by then, built up formidable defensive fortifications, but Admiral Elliot left just a small force of four ships to blockade Canton and instead sailed north to the Zhejiang coast.

He blockaded Ningbo with two ships, and captured much of the island of Chusan (Zhoushan, part of which was renamed after Charles Elliot) off the Zhejiang coast, where the Qing magistrate committed suicide. The capture of Chusan enabled the British to control traffic and trade in the Yangzi delta region. But Elliot's force swiftly moved further north, to the mouth of the

Bei He (North River) and the forts that guarded the outskirts of the strategic city of Tianjin (just over a hundred miles southeast of Beijing). Here, in August and September 1840, the trusted Manchu Governor General of the region, Qishan, engaged in serious imperial negotiations with the British force, persuading them to leave north China and complete the negotiations in Canton.

Qishan earned Daoguang emperor's approbation, and was appointed Governor General of Guangxi and Guangdong (in place of Lin Zexu, who had been promoted to that role earlier that year). He completed the negotiations, paying an indemnity of $6 million, agreeing to direct British contact with the imperial court, ceding the barren island of Hong Kong, and agreeing to reopen Britain's Canton trade within ten days. Both Daoguang and Palmerston were furious at the terms and both Qishan and Charles Elliot were dismissed forthwith (the former ordered executed, although his sentence was later commuted to exile). Palmerston disdained rights obtained over the barren rocks of Hong Kong, and was livid at Elliot having given up Zhoushan. Sir Henry Pottinger, appointed British plenipotentiary in Elliot's place, was expressly instructed to ensure that any new agreement must be with the emperor directly.

By the time Pottinger arrived in August 1841, hostilities had resumed and the British had come to occupy much of Canton, which they agreed to vacate only after the payment of a further $6 million. By the end of the month, Pottinger headed north again with the British fleet, capturing Ningbo, Xiamen and regaining control of Zhoushan. After reinforcements arrived from India by May 1842, the British began a campaign of squeezing Qing canal and river communication routes. In June, Shanghai fell to the British, and Zhenjiang the following month after some savage warfare and a string of suicides by Qing officials occurred as defeat became inevitable. With traffic on the Grand Canal and the Yangzi delta blocked, the Qing began seeking a truce, but Pottinger pushed further inland and reached the outskirts of the old Ming capital of Nanjing by 5 August.

On 29 August 1842, the First Opium War ended with the capitulation of the Qing and signing of the Treaty of Nanjing, which the historian Jonathan Spence calls the 'most important treaty settlement in China's modern history.' Article 2 of the treaty opened the first five 'treaty ports'—Canton, Xiamen, Fuzhou, Ningbo and Shanghai—to residence by British subjects and their families, and allowed the opening of British consulates in the five cities, while Article 3 gave Hong Kong 'in perpetuity' to Queen Victoria and her successors. There were also indemnities totalling $21 million ($6 million of which constituted direct compensation for the opium cargoes destroyed in

1839) that were to be paid by the end of 1845. Other powers immediately sought similar privileges, and US president John Tyler was the first to seek a similar treaty (in 1843). But the US treaty involved two further principles: Article 17, which allowed Protestant missionaries to operate in China, and the most portentous Article 21, which stated that Americans committing crimes in China could only be tried under American laws and by empowered American officials. This principle of 'extraterritoriality' significantly abridged Chinese sovereignty, and grievously harmed the prestige of the Manchu imperial court.

It was one thing for the Manchu court to offer extraterritoriality at the edges of China proper (as in Kokand), but quite another for such privileges to be offered to foreigners ('barbarians') in the very heartland of the Middle Kingdom. The British signed a supplementary treaty in 1843, which enshrined the 'most favoured nation' (MFN) principle so that any concessions offered to other treaty powers would also extend automatically to British subjects. The MFN clause was eventually extended to all the other European powers (France and Russia being the other treaty signatories). The 1842 Treaty of Nanjing inaugurated a 'century of unequal treaties' that was to last until 1943 when the Allied powers abjured their treaty rights amid the World War, although most of China was then under Japanese occupation, including almost all the treaty ports.

The Qing imperial court did not fully embrace all the privileges it had given up to the Europeans—with the senior Manchu official, Qiying, explaining to the emperor that these were temporary concessions aimed at feeding European commercial greed, in order to strengthen the imperial system. To the Europeans, of course, the treaties were seen as ironclad legal commitments that must be fully implemented. So the Second Opium War was necessary in 1856–60, fought by the British (and French) against the Qing, on the pretext of punishing the latter for the illegal seizure of a Hong Kong registered ship, the *Arrow*. Starting by conquering Canton in December 1857, the British repeated the 1840 campaign, taking the forts outside Tianjin and opening the path towards Beijing—forcing the imperial court to sign the 1858 Treaty of Tianjin, under which British and French ambassadors were to be stationed in Beijing with their family and staff, six additional treaty ports were opened, Christian preachers were to be protected, and the word 'yi' (for 'barbarian') was no longer permitted to be used to describe Europeans. Additionally, Russia (which had not participated in the actual war) also gained vast territories east of the Ussuri River totalling about 400,000 square miles.

When it was clear that the Qing had no intention of letting a British (or French) ambassador live in Beijing, the British attacked the forts outside Tianjin again but were repulsed by a bigger Qing force. Lord Elgin, the chief British negotiator, then determined to teach the Qing an unforgettable lesson. A joint British–French force under Elgin's command attacked Beijing itself and, in an act of supremely destructive philistinism, burnt to the ground Qianlong's magnificent Summer Palace and pleasure garden (Yuan Ming Yuan). The Xianfeng emperor had fled the capital for the royal hunting lodge in Jehol (Chengde, beyond the Great Wall, in an area that was originally reserved as imperial pastureland). His brother (Prince Gong), who negotiated on his behalf, affirmed the Treaty of Tianjin and added a 'Convention of Peking' that ceded Kowloon to the British, made Tianjin a treaty port, and added another massive indemnity.

The emperor's failure to vanquish the British barbarians in 1842, however, had inevitably shaken the Qings' claim on the Mandate of Heaven, irretrievably weakening imperial prestige. Domestic rebellions became a feature of the next two decades, with the regime facing its greatest challenge in the Taiping Rebellion (1850–64), which was far more destructive than the infamously brutal American Civil War (1861–65) or the First War of Indian Independence (1857–58) which all occurred during this same period of intense global bloodletting. The Second Opium War was a minor skirmish in the midst of the raging Taiping Rebellion, which ultimately caused between 20 and 40 million deaths, and untold destruction across central China; after 1860, however, the British (and other European powers) decided that stability in China required the restoration of imperial authority, and they provided crucial support in helping to bring that rebellion (and others) to an end.

Like many rebellions against imperial authority throughout Chinese history, a religious ideology animated the Taiping Rebellion, and it originated in southern China (Guangxi and Hunan provinces). The Taiping Rebellion's charismatic Hakka leader, Hong Xiuquan, had failed the civil service examinations four times, but began to see visions (after his third failed attempt) that he was Jesus Christ's younger brother. Like Jesus, he spent forty days and forty nights in a state of heightened religious consciousness (contemporary doctors called it a 'delirium'), after which he was convinced that God (and his son, Hong's elder brother) had sent him to spread his word, and transform China by stamping out idolatrous religions and restoring a 'heavenly kingdom of great peace'—Taiping Tianguo. Hong Xiuquan's religious ideology was not recognizably Christian, being driven much more by Old Testament tenets mixed with some Confucian beliefs. But it also had elements of social reform—seeking economic equality and fighting gender discrimination. Although anything but atheist, Taiping ideology had many elements that proved to be an inspiration to all of China's twentieth-century revolutionaries.

In Guangxi and Hunan, in particular, the end of the First Opium War (and the consequent disbanding of local militias mobilized for it) had created a large group of unemployed soldiers who found it difficult to find new employment as trade shifted northwards (from Guangzhou) after the opening of the northern ports to European trade. Additionally, Hong Xiuquan was able to tap a large and growing mass of disaffected people amongst his fellow Hakkas. This hardy community (then considered by some to be non-Han Chinese) had migrated southwards from north and central China over the centuries (the word Hakka translates as 'guest settlers'), spoke a separate dialect and were resentful of the Han residents of Guangxi, Hunan and Guangdong (who mainly spoke Cantonese and disdained the Hakka, many of whom had embraced Christianity—thus further distancing themselves from the Confucian norm of the settled Han Chinese communities they lived amongst).

It was in Guangxi province that Hong Xiuquan first began organizing his pseudo-Christian religious order, mobilizing disaffected peasants primarily amongst the Hakkas and other minorities, gradually building them into militias aimed at fending off the depredations of bandits. By 1850, Hong had built a strong enough army to sweep aside the Manchu defenders and take complete control of Guangxi and Hunan, and begin marching northwards up the Yangzi Valley, mobilizing Han peasants along the way, and moving well beyond its original Hakka character. In 1853, the swelling Taiping armies overwhelmed Nanjing, where Hong Xiuquan established his capital, and proclaimed the start of a new dynasty. In the Taiping realms, Mandarin was replaced with colloquial dialects as the lingua franca, and the civil service examinations were opened up to women as well as men and revamped with an emphasis on Hong's interpretation of the Bible. The family remained the unit of organization (with twenty-five families forming the basic social unit, under an overarching system of bureaucratic control that combined military and civilian duties), and peasants served dual roles as soldiers and farmers. But otherwise, the Taiping disdained all other Confucian principles of hierarchy, replacing them with egalitarian principles that prohibited excessive wealth and privilege, while also promoting the equality of men and women by banning polygamy and foot-binding.

In an unfortunate Orwellian touch, however, the egalitarian principles did not apply to Hong Xiuquan and his core leadership group who accumulated massive fortunes, and had large harems, while the movement's foot soldiers lived in harsh labour camps where contact between men and women was barred. Hong himself had more than eighty concubines, and the Eastern and Northern kings had broods of thirty to forty each. Hong, in fact, became increasingly dissolute and suffered a mental breakdown in 1855, brought on by his growing addiction to sensual pleasures. Ironically, this occurred just when the Taiping armies were at their greatest potency. Having repulsed a Qing counteroffensive, they had gained control of the lower Yangzi Valley and built a treasury reputed to be six times the size of that of the imperial government.

The Taipings' military discipline had been reinforced by a mix of religious fervour, social mobilization of land-starved peasants, and anti-Manchu nationalism. All these factors made them potent symbols for China's twentieth-century revolutionaries. But, eventually, vicious infighting amongst the Taiping generals undermined discipline, with Hong's mental breakdown being the major factor in weakening the chain of command; these negative aspects also served as a salutary lesson (sometimes learnt, sometimes not) for China's twentieth-century revolutionaries of all stripes. The Qing responded to the existential challenge presented by the Taiping by abandoning their erstwhile dependence on Manchu bannermen (and the system of divided authority that kept the Qing imperial edifice afloat), instead turning increasingly to the scholar-gentry class to build new regional armies. The gentry class—which had invested so heavily in the Confucian examination system and all its appurtenances—had the most to lose from the Taiping Rebellion, especially because of its intent to destroy Confucian values (which gave the educated gentry class a dual role as administrative as well as social/moral leaders). By using this class to mobilize new regional armies, however, the Manchu also fundamentally weakened their hold on China—as the regional gentry strongmen were all Han Chinese, and they eventually helped spawn a new nationalism.

One other, perhaps minor, consequence of the Taiping Rebellion was that the Hakkas—from being an 'out-group' in southern China—became very much a central part of the Han Chinese communities, having played such a crucial role in this first spurt of Chinese nationalism. Sun Yat-sen, the revolutionary nationalist leader and first president of Republican China, was a Hakka, as were his wife and sister-in-law (the wife of Chiang Kai-shek). One startling feature of the early 1990s was that all three of the great leaders of the world's Chinese-majority states were Hakka: Lee Kuan Yew in Singapore, Lee Teng-hui in Taiwan, and Deng Xiaoping in mainland China itself.

The most powerful of the gentry-warlords who emerged in the 1850s was Zeng Guofan, who mobilized the Hunan Army. Zeng began in 1853 by building a militia in his home district, recruiting scholar-gentry soldiers and encouraging them to draft peasants with whom they were personally familiar. These patrimonial ties were reinforced by a new levy on internal trade (called the 'lijin'), which gave the Hunan Army fiscal autonomy (with only about a fourth of the lijin collections being sent to the imperial government).

PRASENJIT K. BASU

Zeng countered the pseudo-Christian religious zeal of the Taiping with a strict adherence to Confucian principle, and his soldiers were taught that they were defending China's cherished cultural traditions. Each of these characteristics (personal ties between peasant-soldiers and their gentry-leaders, fiscal autonomy, Confucian nationalism) undermined key elements of the Qing system of authority. By 1860, the Qing were so weakened by the combination of the Taiping and Opium Wars that they readily agreed to give Zeng administrative authority in Hunan, and similar regional armies were allowed to sprout across the rest of China—becoming an alternative fount of authority to the Qing court. As with all previous waning dynasties, regionalism sowed the seeds of the Qing's demise.

But in the 1853–75 period, the regional gentry-led armies—bolstered after 1860 by European support for the Qing court (seen now as a bulwark against disintegration and chaos)—helped put down not only the Taiping Rebellion, but also other rebellions that bedevilled the Manchus. The most prominent of these was the Nian Rebellion of pillaging horsemen, who were only subdued in 1868 after multi-year battles, but there were also the twenty-year rebel government established by Muslims in Dali (Yunnan province), the revolt of the Red Turbans in Canton, and the Triads that overran Xiamen and Shanghai in 1853.

Zeng's protégé, Li Hongzhang, controlled the Huai Army of Anhui province. Once Li was appointed governor of Jiangsu province, the revenue from Shanghai's international trade came under his control, enabling him to build a muscular financial base. By cultivating ties with the treaty port powers, and learning from their commercial and technological knowledge, Li Hongzhang was able to build a formidable industrial edifice. He convinced the Qing court to allow him to use most of the revenue from the Shanghai trade by promising to work for the 'self-strengthening' of all of China. After 1860, the intellectual consensus amongst China's elite coalesced around the notion of using barbarian strengths (such as European technology) to help preserve the Confucian framework of Chinese culture. This period of reform came to be known as the Tongzhi Restoration (named after the six-year-old who became emperor in 1861).

But such use of technology had its limits, as Li Hongzhang discovered. The court (and most intellectuals) remained hostile to foreign trade, and Li was subjected to hostile criticism for amassing wealth through this trade, thus destabilizing social harmony by encouraging materialism. He was criticized even more fiercely for asserting that the examination system was too archaic to be conducive to any programme of industrialization and military reform. Only the intervention of the Dowager Empress Cixi (the former concubine of Xianfeng, and mother of the Tongzhi emperor) saved Li Hongzhang from calls for his execution from the entrenched reactionary wing of the imperial court. Despite such limits and setbacks, the Tongzhi Restoration expanded railways, factories and arsenals, boosted industrial productivity and established a period of relative peace by 1870 that encouraged the European powers to throw their support behind the Qing court (now effectively headed by the Dowager Empress Cixi). They were helped by the creation of the Zongli Yamen, the first Chinese equivalent of a foreign ministry (to deal mainly with the Europeans).

Despite these trappings of modernization, the Tongzhi Restoration was a pale shadow of its Japanese equivalent—the root-and-branch reform of the Meiji Restoration that began in 1868. Its economic vision was confined mainly to improving agriculture, with little focus on banking or industry. It was also fundamentally conservative and inward looking (while the Meiji Restoration's leaders eagerly sought out the best practices of every European power, and sought to introduce those into Japanese society). Li Hongzhang was a lonely visionary in industry (although Zeng Guofan was a key ally in military modernization). Li succeeded, in particular, in rapidly building a capable navy that impressed his European contemporaries. But the shortcomings of his headlong pursuit of naval modernization were brutally exposed by China's humiliation in the 1894–95 Sino–Japanese War.

China and Japan had long skirmished over who would have paramount say in influencing the court of Korea, which China considered to be a vassal state. Japan had signed a treaty with Korea in 1876, opening the country to foreign trade, and declaring its independence from China on foreign policy issues. In 1882, China and Japan had come close to war over Korea, but both sides agreed to stop short of full hostilities. The assassination of a pro-Japanese Korean activist in Shanghai in 1894 set off full-scale war (described in more detail in the Japan section later in this chapter). Li Hongzhang's much larger Northern Fleet suffered a series of defeats at the hands of Japan's smaller force of fast-moving ships. The Japanese army was also able to oust all Chinese troops from Korean soil, winning a decisive victory. Under the terms of the Treaty of Shimonoseki (1895), China ceded Taiwan and the Liaotung (Liaodong) Peninsula to Japan, and agreed to pay an indemnity that was more than double the annual revenue of the imperial government.

The defeat by Japan—a traditionally subservient culture, whose people were known to the Chinese as 'dwarf bandits'—was a particularly big blow to Qing prestige. But the European powers (especially Russia) were worried about Japan's territorial gains, and vigorously sought to undo them through the Triple Intervention (of Germany, France and Russia together; interestingly,

PRASENJIT K. BASU

Germany had, since 1882, been in an opposing alliance to the other two powers in Europe). Germany first gained the fishing village of Qingdao (or Tsingtao, now famous for the eponymous brewery that the Germans established there) and then gained a naval base and exclusive mining rights in the rest of Shandong province. France gained the lease of Guangzhou Bay and three southern provinces as its sphere of influence. But most importantly, Russia was able to get Japan to vacate the Liaotung Peninsula and (after payment of a large bribe to their Chinese interlocutors) was able to swiftly gain exclusive access to the warm-water port (Port Arthur) in Dalian that Russia had long coveted. Not to be outdone, the British gained a lease on Weihaiwei, and a sphere of influence in the Yangzi Valley. Another emerging European power, Italy, also sought a sphere of influence in China, but couldn't be accommodated (it was compensated with a similar sphere in North Africa, gaining Libya from the declining empire at Asia's other extremity, the Ottoman empire). The Japanese were left pondering the injustice of a European-centred world!

In China, the stimulus of the crushing defeat of 1895 spurred, first, the creation of a modern, professional New Army (under the command of Li Hongzhang's protégé, Yuan Shikai) and, second, the Hundred Days' Reform movement of 1898, led by the youthful philosopher Kang Youwei and his protégé, Liang Qichao. Like Rammohun Roy in India six decades earlier, Kang used classical sources to advance his radical agenda—always managing to find Confucian texts that were supportive of modern technological and political ideas. In a celebrated five-hour audience with the Guangxu emperor (who had succeeded his cousin Tongzhi upon the latter's death at nineteen), Kang persuaded the monarch to undertake a burst of reform akin to Japan's Meiji-era transformation—with radical institutional change grafted onto the traditional Confucian social edifice. In fact, Guangxu also formally consulted Japan's premier Ito Hirobumi to learn the lessons of the Meiji period. Guangxu's reform drive lasted 104 days (from 11 June to 21 September 1898), and included the introduction of capitalist principles into the economy in order to foster industrialization, the establishment of new universities (including technical institutes and a medical college) and railways, and an overhaul of the examination system (to include liberal arts and sciences, not just Confucian principles). The revamping of the examination system provoked intense opposition from the bureaucracy (and the broader scholar-gentry class, who had invested years in mastering the old examination system).

Guangxu also ignored his own cabinet, and instead relied on Kang, Liang and their young supporters to implement the reforms. He aroused additional suspicions by consulting Ito—and it was rumoured that the Japanese (along with Britain and the US) had proposed a federation with China (that would considerably abridge China's sovereignty). This rumoured scheme involving foreigners was the pretext that the Dowager Empress Cixi needed to mount a reactionary plot to end the reforms and depose Guangxu in a palace coup on 21 September 1898. Cixi had bypassed traditional procedures to install her nephew Guangxu on the throne upon her young son Tongzhi's death, but she was the effective ruler of China from 1861 until her death in 1908. Kang and his cohort underestimated Cixi's role as the real ruler behind the bamboo curtain; when they learnt of the evolving plot against the emperor, they turned to Yuan Shikai for support. Although General Yuan was known to sympathize with the reform movement, he quietly informed Cixi and her key Manchu courtier (and former lover) Ronglu—leading to Cixi's coup, the formal abdication of Guangxu (on grounds of grave illness) and the installation of Cixi as official regent.

The historian John K. Fairbank refers to the period from 1860 to 1908 as a period of 'Anglo-Qing co-dominion' over China, with the British (and other powers, including Japan) clearly in the ascendant. But, while British sympathies lay with Guangxu and his reformist cohort, the Dowager Empress was still able to get the better of them. Nonetheless, she continued to implement some reforms, particularly by strengthening the army and allowing quicker industrialization.

But first, the court had to deal with the Boxer Uprising, which began in Shandong province as a means to counter the Christian proselytizing of German missionaries who began to spread Catholicism especially amongst the impoverished peasants of Shandong. A severe drought in northern China contributed to the impoverishment of peasants and the consequent emergence of large groups of disaffected and hungry youth. Secret societies of 'boxers' (martial artists) emerged to counter the perceived arrogance of the Germans and (especially) their missionaries in an echo of what had happened in India in 1857. There were also shamanistic elements using techniques of 'spirit possession' that had been part of China's traditions especially under the Shang and Yuan dynasties, but were also a secret means of subversion. The Spirit Boxers (or 'Boxers United in Righteousness') combined the shamanist and martial arts elements into a potent call to action under the slogan 'Support the Qing, destroy the foreign' (in a faint echo of Japan in the late 1860s).

Cixi and the Manchu princes in the palace backed the Boxers, first implicitly and then quite explicitly, as a means of overthrowing the foreign yoke that had enveloped Qing China over the previous four decades. Skirmishes between the Boxers and foreign troops had occurred in Shandong right from the beginning of 1900, but the fighting spread to Tianjin and Beijing in June, after 400 foreign troops were sent into Beijing to guard the Legation

PRASENJIT K. BASU

(embassy) Quarter. Between 13 and 17 June 1900, the Boxers and the foreign troops clashed—amid the skirmishing, the Boxers swarmed into the Legation Quarter and burnt numerous Christian churches and cathedrals, while British troops and American marines killed many Boxers, alienating the populace of Beijing. Initially, Cixi ordered her confidant Ronglu to protect the Legation Quarter, but the foreign powers' attack on the Dagu forts in Tianjin tilted her view. The Dowager Empress and the princes were convinced they were responding to the voice of the commoner masses when they declared war on the foreign powers on 21 June.

Then began the fifty-five-day siege of the Legation Quarter of Beijing that affected 475 foreign civilians, 450 soldiers from the eight nations with embassies in the Legation Quarter (the UK, US, Russia, Germany, France, Japan, Austria–Hungary and Italy), and about three thousand Chinese Christians. The siege was relieved on 14 August by an allied force of 20,000 troops from those eight nations, which quickly captured and looted Beijing, while a field marshal sent by Kaiser Wilhelm II of Germany terrorized the nearby towns to exact revenge for the events of the previous two years (as the British troops had done in vast swathes of northern India in 1858–59). Ironically, the vast majority of the troops used by the Allies were Asian— more than half of them Japanese, with the next largest contingent comprising Indians in the British army and a small regiment of Chinese collaborators.

Governors like Li Hongzhang (Guangzhou) and Zhang Zhidong (Wuhan) had distanced themselves from what they labelled the 'Boxer Rebellion' and guaranteed stability and safe passage to the foreigners in central and southern China in exchange for keeping their troops and ammunition away. Yuan Shikai, the governor of Shandong province, also refused to back the imperial court's declaration of war on the foreigners, and used his troops to harry the Boxers instead. So, although the War of 1900 was the largest of the five wars that the Qing dynasty fought with foreigners in the nineteenth century, it was largely confined to northern China (and mainly to the area around Beijing and Tianjin).

The Boxer Protocol signed in September 1901 provided for an indemnity of US$333 million (greater than the annual revenue of the Qing imperial court) to be paid over forty years (at an interest rate that effectively doubled the sum) to the eight powers, the execution of ten high officials and punishments for a hundred others. The Imperial Maritime Customs Service (that had been effectively built up by Britain's Robert Hart in collaboration with the Manchu councillor Wenxiang in the treaty ports, providing a stable source of revenue for the Qing) was now instead focused mainly on levying charges on the Qing court for the repayment of indemnities, both to the eight protocol signers from 1901, as well as the additional indemnities to Japan from the 1895 treaty.

INDEPENDENT SIAM SURVIVES THE BRITISH CONQUEST OF BURMA AND THE FRENCH OF INDO-CHINA

The word 'Siam' (the old name for Thailand) was derived from the Sanskrit word 'shyama' (meaning dark or brown), and 'Shan' and 'Ahom' were amongst its other cognates. The Chakri dynasty had established Rattanakosin (later known as Bangkok) as the new capital of Siam in 1782, following the sacking of the Siamese capital city of Ayutthaya in 1767 by the forces of the Burmese king Alaungpaya of Ava, whose power had recently been augmented by his conquests of the Mon-speaking peoples in southern Burma, and Manipur in the eastern extremities of India.

Ayutthaya (thus named after the legendary lord Rama's capital) had served for more than four centuries as Siam's glittering capital, famed for its gold-tipped pagodas and palaces. It was far bigger than any Burmese city at the time, with a population said to rival contemporary London or Paris, and wealth to match. On their four-year journey towards Ayutthaya, Alaungpaya's generals Naymyo Thihapati and Maha Nawrata had conquered Chiang Mai in 1763, taken Lanna (northern Thailand) soon after, followed by the conquest of the Lao kingdom of Luang Prabang in March 1765, and the surrender of its rival, the king of Vientiane. When Ayutthaya finally fell in April 1767, following a siege lasting well over a year, most of the grand city was burnt to the ground, including its gold-tipped pagodas and palaces. Tens of thousands of Thai residents of old Ayutthaya—including a former king, ministers, noblemen and members of the royal family—were taken into captivity and resettled in Burma. The destructive brutality of the Burmese forces left a deep scar that continues to colour Thai–Burman relations to this day.

Fortuitously for Thailand, the all-conquering armies from Ava were not able to consolidate their conquest of Siam. The Manchu Qianlong emperor of China had sent his bannermen southwards—first to conquer Yunnan and its Dai people (who were ethnic cousins of the Thais and Shan), then to extend their conquests southward into north and east Burma, where some Shan aristocrats had been quite open to aligning with the Chinese from Yunnan against their Burmese overlords. But the armies of Qianlong—whose sixty-three-year imperial reign was the longest in China's history, and one of its most glorious—suffered a rare series of defeats at the hands of the Burmese.

The Chinese imperial army and Manchu bannermen were defeated as much by the weather as the force of Burmese arms, but defeated they certainly were, not once but in three great battles. In the first battle in the summer of 1766, the new Burmese king Myedu (son of Alaungpaya) laid a trap for the Chinese troops, luring them into the northeastern town of Bhamo without much of a fight, then surrounding them with two other Burmese armies. As thousands of Chinese troops began dying of cholera, dysentery and malaria, the Chinese commander Yang Yingjiu was ordered back to Beijing and forced to commit suicide.

After this initial defeat of a mainly Chinese army, Qianlong sent the veteran Manchu commander Mingrui as his viceroy for Yunnan and Guizhou, which made him the chief commander for the Burma war. Mingrui, the victor of numerous Manchu wars in Central Asia and Kazakhstan, won some early victories over the Burmese forces in the winter of 1767, leading his bannermen down the Irrawaddy Valley to conquer the town of Singu, just three days' march away from the Burmese capital of Ava. King Myedu personally entered the fray at that point, leading his men to the front, and sending another army to Hsenwi in the uplands, where it defeated a Manchu garrison. As it became warmer, the nomadic Manchu warriors (in their felt boots more appropriate to the steppes of the Manchu–Russia border) began to succumb to the heat of the central Burma plain. Mingrui abandoned any hope of capturing Ava, and instead directed his troops back towards Yunnan; but the Manchu commander himself was wounded before he could cross the border, and hanged himself from a tree rather than face the humiliation of reporting his losses to the emperor.

Qianlong then sent one of his most trusted military commanders, the chief grand councillor Fuheng—supported by the elite Manchu generals Agui, Aligun and Suhede—for a final confrontation with the intransigent Mien (the Chinese word for the Burmese). The Burmese offer of talks was spurned by the confident Fuheng, who made the fatal mistake of starting this last showdown in October 1769, at the height of Burma's monsoon. This debilitated the Manchu troops, who had by this point been reinforced by a Chinese naval squadron from Fujian, but so had the Burmese troops been reinforced by battle-hardened troops from the Siam front led by General Maha Thira Thura. Three Burmese army units successfully held off the might of Qing China's armies, and the latter failed to break through the Burmese lines after a month of heavy fighting, while commander Fuheng fell grievously ill (alongside many of his troops). Eventually, in December 1769, the two sides signed a peace deal under which the Yunnan–Burma border was established close to its current location. More crucially, with their noses severely bloodied by three years of fighting in tropical terrain, the Qing pledged never to attack Burma again.

During the three years that the Burmese armies were engaged in fending off the Manchu armies, King Taksin the Great (a former general and nobleman of Chinese origin from the Ayutthaya court) rallied Siamese forces, reunited the country, and regained most of the territory that had been lost to the Burmese. He also became an implicit vassal of China, and used his ethnic ties to bolster commercial links to the Teochew businessmen who dominated trade with China at the time. Taksin established his capital at Thonburi, but allegedly began to have religious delusions about his own exalted status, alienating the monks, and setting off a rebellion against his rule. When King Taksin was overthrown in a coup, his close friend and former confidant, General Chao Phraya Chakri, rushed back from the war front in Cambodia to take the throne and inaugurate the Chakri dynasty that rules Thailand to this day. In keeping with Siamese heritage, the founder of the Chakri dynasty (who was of Mon descent, with some Chinese and Thai blood) took the royal title of Rama I.

Succeeding kings of the Chakri dynasty have all had the royal title of Rama, but it was King Chulalongkorn (Rama V) who had to be especially deft in keeping the European powers at bay by playing one off against the other (primarily the British and French). The Thai monarchy was built on the Indic concept of the 'mandala' (of widening geographical 'circles' of authority, radiating from a powerful centre). The Shan, Lao, Cambodian and Malay states were variably part of the Mandala that the Siamese Chakri dynasty ruled over. King Mongkut (Rama IV), hero of the 1951 play and 1956 movie *The King and I* (adapted in 1999 into an animated movie), had first acquired Western knowledge during the two decades he spent as a wandering monk-prince, and came into close contact with British missionaries and other adventurers, from whom he learnt astronomy and other elements of modern science, and became a fluent speaker of English and Latin. In 1833, Prince Mongkut started a religious reform movement called Dhammayuttika Nikaya (which, as the Thammayut, remains one of Thailand's two main denominations of Buddhism), and later became a close friend of the Roman Catholic vicar of Bangkok, from whom he incorporated elements of Christian morals into his sect (while firmly rejecting most Christian doctrines and belief).

Mongkut's succession to the throne in 1851 was facilitated by Tish Bunnag, a powerful nobleman who was closely aligned with British agents operating in the kingdom. The Bunnags were a fascinating Siamese noble family of Persian descent: the founder, called Sheikh Ahmad (from the holy Shiite city of Qom) was originally appointed Siam's minister for the West (to deal with Indians,

Persians and Europeans) in the early seventeenth century, but suppressed a revolt amongst the Japanese (who had a colony of over a thousand refugees from the Shoguns in Ayutthaya) and was then named Samuha Nayok (First Prime Minister). One of his Buddhist descendants, Bunnag, married Nuan, the daughter of a wealthy Mon merchant-nobleman. Nuan's other sister, Nak, had married the man who became King Rama I and became Queen Amarindra. Given their close kinship to the founders of the dynasty, the Bunnag family remained key advisers to the royal court, with a status close to royalty, including as regents during the reign of Rama IV (Mongkut) and Rama V (Chulalongkorn). The Bunnags helped those two monarchs effectively negotiate their relations with the British in particular.

Mongkut's facility with English convinced many of his foreign visitors that he was pro-British, and the 'White Rajah of Sarawak', Sir James Brooke, praised him as 'one of our own'. Their confidence was borne out in the Bowring Treaty of April 1855, which opened Siam to 'free trade' on British terms (with a sharp reduction in import duties and other trade levies that did help to spur a substantial increase in Siam's exports, as the nobility gained control of large tracts of land to produce rice and sugar on a large enough scale to ensure exportable surpluses) but with the additional proviso of extraterritoriality (which exempted the British from being tried in Siam's courts). Rama IV also introduced considerable reforms to education, introducing Western-style geography (including the notion that the earth is round), obliged court nobles to begin wearing shirts (rather than appear bare-chested) and eliminated the practice of sending periodic envoys to the Qing court (which the latter viewed as tribute).

The implicit Anglo–Siamese alliance that Tish Bunnag (who was officially called Prayurawongse) negotiated on behalf of King Mongkut served to both reduce British pressure on Siam itself and increase British pressure on Siam's traditional enemy, Burma, which had steadily lost territory to Britain's expanding empire since 1826. That year (after the two-year First Anglo-Burmese War), Burma was obliged to cede its recently conquered territories of Assam, Manipur and Arakan to the British, who also took control of Tenasserim, the long, narrow strip of land inhabited mainly by Mons in Burma's south, with the intent of using it as bargaining chip with either Siam or Burma. Then, after the Second Anglo–Burmese War of 1852, the province of Pegu (Bago) fell to the British, who renamed the area Lower Burma and moved their headquarters to Rangoon (Yangon) ten years later. By this time, King Rama IV (Mongkut) was already on Siam's throne. Although his promised troop reinforcements were late, their potential support bolstered British morale in this war.

While Britain was otherwise engaged in the conquest of Burma, the French were not sitting idle. Starting in 1858 (after the conclusion of the Second Opium War against China), Napoleon III ordered the conquest of southern Vietnam. Like the British in Burma, the French first secured the south of Vietnam and then steadily expanded northwards. The use of Catholic missionaries to convert the locals was an added source of inspiration to the French, and a threat to the besieged Nguyen dynasty. Reinforced by Catholic soldiers arriving from Spain and its Philippines colony, the French navy captured Tourane (Da Nang) in 1858, Saigon and three southern provinces (Bien Hoa, Gia Dinh and Dinh Tuong) the following year. Eight years later, the French mounted another attack (claiming that the Vietnamese emperor was secretly trying to regain the lost provinces) and gained three more southern provinces, which were consolidated into Cochin-China in 1874. In the interim, King Norodom ('Narottam' or 'superior man' in Sanskrit) of Cambodia sought to reduce his dependence on Siam by petitioning to become a French protectorate in 1863. King Rama IV accepted this arrangement in 1867, in exchange for Cambodia's northwestern provinces of Siem Reap and Battambang being incorporated into Siam proper.

The French had pursued Catholic missionary activity in the northern part of Vietnam (Tonkin, and to a lesser extent Annam) since the late eighteenth century. French naval support enabled Emperor Gia Long to establish the Nguyen dynasty in the central region of Annam, with its capital at Hu in 1802. His successors in Hu faced relentless pressure from the French to accommodate Catholic missionaries and to themselves convert to that faith. This eventually brought France into conflict with Qing China over who should control Tonkin (the region around Hanoi in the north).

In 1883, the Sino–French War broke out, with control over Tonkin being the main prize, although much of the early fighting occurred in Taiwan and the Pescadores (P'eng-hu Islands), and across the straits in Fujian province. France was early in recognizing the potential for an alliance with Japan, which it explored in the middle of the war, especially when facing difficulties in Taiwan and Fuzhou. No alliance fructified (with many French officials reluctant to support Japan's desire to abrogate the unequal treaties, while Japan too was reluctant to openly antagonize China at that stage), but the Dowager Empress Cixi grew increasingly concerned about the pressure that Japan was exerting on Korea and ordered her officials in January 1885 to begin negotiating peace with the French. By April 1885, the contours of a peace settlement were agreed: Chinese troops were withdrawn from Tonkin, while France gave up its claims on Taiwan, Fuzhou and the Pescadores. Shortly thereafter, France consolidated its control over the whole of Vietnam, with the central region of Annam becoming a protectorate. The Nguyen dynasty and its vassals were only nominally in control, while a French Résident-Supérieur had supreme executive authority, and French Residents exercised their power in each province. A similar structure was to apply in Cambodia and Tonkin, and in Laos after Siam ceded it to France in 1893, while France directly ruled Cochin-China without intermediaries.

While one of Siam's traditional rivals (Vietnam) fell to the French in 1885, its crusty northern rival, the Burmese monarchy, finally succumbed to the British, both in the same year in which the Congress of Berlin had helped institutionalize the Scramble for Africa by apportioning that great continent amongst six European nations. Britain's new Conservative Secretary of State for India was the ambitious thirty-six-year-old Old Etonian Lord Randolph Churchill (Winston's father, and descendant of the Duke of Marlborough), who had decided that his path back to his parliamentary seat of Birmingham lay through the conquest of Upper Burma. Randolph Churchill dangled the promise of Burma opening an easier route to the great market of China, and rumours of French dealings with the Burmese court provided an additional urgency to his argument. The kingdom of Ava fell to the force of British guns in November 1885, when King Thibaw's fabled capital of Mandalay was captured by General Harry Prendergast's Burma Field Force, and the last Burmese king was sent away to exile in Ratnagiri on the western Indian coast, with his queen Supayalat, daughters and a small retinue of retainers.

The Burmese troops had submitted almost without a fight, partly because the Kinwun Mingyi (Chief Minister) had asked them not to resist the mighty British. His given name (U Kaung) became synonymous with treachery amongst the Burmese, especially after he became a high-ranking civil servant in the colonial administration. Amitav Ghosh's evocative description in *The Glass Palace* of the morose royal procession on ox carts out of the palace's auspicious east gate—where a pregnant Supayalat had entered the mirrored central hall a few weeks earlier to urge Thibaw's wavering advisers led by the Kinwun to fight rather than seek an accommodation with the British—is a classic of Asian literature. Thibaw's bristling subjects were prevented from intervening that November day by an escorting convoy of hundreds of well-armed British and Indian troops. But an insurgency had broken out across Upper Burma soon afterwards, and brutal British reprisals akin to India in 1858—with whole villages razed and burnt, public floggings and torture of captured guerrillas, and hundreds of summary executions across the countryside—had been needed to subdue the insurgency over the next half-year. And like in India, a famine hit Burma in late 1886, dealing the final deathblow to the insurgency.

With Indo-China in French hands and the whole of Burma now part of Britain's Indian empire, Siam's King Rama V (Chulalongkorn) felt increasing pressure from both European powers. After ceding Laos in 1893, he was obliged to relinquish Siem Reap and Battambang to the French in 1904, and that year's Anglo–French Entente Cordiale made life even more uncomfortable for Southeast Asia's last independent nation. Eventually, the Anglo–Siamese Treaty of 1909 would lead to the southern half of Siam's Malay tributary states being transferred to the British, while the latter allowed the northern ones to remain under Siamese suzerainty, judging that a strong Siam would serve as a useful buffer state against French encroachments into Britain's recently acquired colonies of Burma and Malaya. Siam was able to consolidate its independence thereafter as the European powers were increasingly caught up in the Great War (1914–18) and its aftermath. But European advisers would remain vitally important in many key positions through the next two decades, with the forest service manned mainly by Englishmen, a Frenchman serving as legislative adviser, an American as foreign policy adviser, a Dane training the provincial gendarmerie, and the Siamese State Bank being run first by a German and then an Englishman.

THE JAPANESE EXCEPTION: AN ASIAN SUN PIERCES
THE COLONIAL CLOUDS

Japan was easily the most advanced independent nation in Asia in 1900. The 'Britain of Asia' (an island-nation separated by a small strip of sea from the continental mainland, with similarly singular characteristics) was rapidly modernizing itself, having been roused to action by the appearance of the 'black ships' of US commodore Matthew C. Perry in 1853. Three hundred years earlier, the Dutch had established a trading presence in Nagasaki— but were confined to Deshima island (in Nagasaki harbour) when Japan's Tokugawa rulers found them proselytizing an alien faith (Christianity), which was promptly banned in the realm.

Japan was not only Asia's most prominent independent nation state at the turn of the century, it was a resurgent power—having announced its arrival as a regional power with its resounding victory in the Sino–Japanese War of 1894–95. The great reformist leader of the final quarter of the previous century, Ito Hirobumi, entered his fifth and final stint as prime minister in October 1900, having been preceded in that office by his great rival Yamagata Aritomo. Japan had been in ferment through the 1850s and 1860s, having responded with great alacrity to the rising challenge posed by the Western powers that had conquered most of Asia by this time and were scrambling to divide up the rights to exploit China amongst themselves. The arrival of Perry's ships in July 1853 heralded the start of the forced opening of Japan, which had been closed to commerce and significant intercourse with the outside world (and especially Europeans) since the 1620s, apart from the small Dutch trading post within Nagasaki at Deshima.

This autarkic closure occurred about two decades after the Tokugawa family established its dominance over Japan, ending a long period of civil wars in the fifteenth and sixteenth centuries, at the end of which Tokugawa Ieyasu established his hegemony over western Japan in 1600, and installed himself as shogun in 1603. Although the office of shogun was formally just the military deputy of the emperor, in reality shoguns had been the de facto rulers of Japan for several centuries—and they remained so until January 1868. Ieyasu's Tokugawa successors rarely proved capable after 1650 of exercising the autocratic power that he had won for them, so power was generally exercised by a centralized administration known as the Bakufu, made up primarily of Tokugawa vassals but a great repository of bureaucratic resources and administrative skill.

In the Tokugawa system, the shogun directly held 15 per cent of Japan's land as feudal lord, his direct retainers held a little over a further 10 per cent, and another tenth was held by Tokugawa branch families. The daimyos (feudal lords) operated like princes within each of their own domains (with a similar administrative structure), but were tied to the central Bakufu through the system of sankin-kotai (alternate attendance), under which the daimyo would spend half his time at Bakufu headquarters in Edo (today's Tokyo) and leave his family there as hostages upon his return to his province. (This system was remarkably similar to that adopted by the Mughals in India, who were near-contemporaries but did not develop the system as fully; it also had a distinct echo in twenty-first-century Afghanistan, where Ismail Khan, the warlord governor of Herat, was obliged to send his son, Mirwaiz Sadiq, to Kabul as a minister in Hamid Karzai's cabinet, although the Afghan experiment ended abruptly in tragedy with Mirwaiz's assassination in March 2004.)

In general, the system of daimyos, and the castle-towns that they ruled from, helped spawn urbanization and the seeds of capitalism on a far wider scale in Tokugawa Japan than anywhere else in Asia. By 1600, Japan already had a population of 18 million (over seven times the population of England at the time). The long period of relative peace under the Tokugawa caused the population to rise to 30 million by 1850, a sixth of whom lived in cities and towns, with Edo having a million inhabitants, Kyoto 400,000 and the commercial centre of Osaka 300,000. The samurai sat atop a social pyramid—ahead of farmer, artisan, merchant and burakumin (outcastes or untouchables)—although they were increasingly bureaucrats rather than soldiers in the times of relative peace that prevailed in the Tokugawa era. Despite retaining most of the rituals and ethos of their soldiering past, the samurai provided a readymade legion of more than 400,000 families of people with considerable experience of office routine and regulations. The samurai were to dominate Japan's politics at least through 1914, and people of samurai stock dominated most key ministries (especially the Ministry of International Trade and Industry, MITI, and the Ministry of Finance, MoF) in the post-1945 era too. Stability over 250 years was a boon to the merchant community, which helped build up the silk, sugar, cotton textile, indigo, chemical (dyes), paper, wax and even shipbuilding industries, and Osaka became a centre for commerce and financial innovation. The Dojima Rice Exchange was established there in 1697, and Osaka had a fully functioning futures exchange by 1730. As they grew wealthier (not least by lending to indigent samurai and cash-strapped daimyo alike), the merchant community sought to improve their social status through marital alliances with the samurai.

Tokugawa vassals (known as fudai) filled the ranks of the Bakufu and also held smaller domains in the centre of Japan around Edo, Kyoto (the imperial capital) and the routes connecting them, which together formed a 'central fortress' of Tokugawa power. The 'outside' daimyos, known as tozama, collectively controlled about 40 per cent of all land. The tozama were eventually to supply the ranks of the dissidents who led the revolt of 1867–68, but each of the larger tozama domains had fudai placed on their borders. The emperor's court in Kyoto was reduced to ceremonial functions, and the emperor himself was a Tokugawa pensioner and almost a prisoner of the Bakufu, who were the real rulers of Japan. However, the emperor had residual and traditional powers, which proved to be crucial during the years of ferment following the arrival of Perry on a second, more assertive trip to Japan—this time into Edo Bay itself in February 1854.

While the European powers had been scrambling across the Asian mainland, the Americans had remained silent bystanders. But with the addition of Oregon and California to its territory, the USA had become a Pacific power, and its interest in Asia began to grow through the second half of the nineteenth century. The China trade beckoned, and there was talk of a transcontinental railroad that would be linked to China by a trans-Pacific steamer route, which could make Japan a potential coaling station and its coastal waters a potential shipping lane for American ships. These concerns were reflected in the letter that Perry brought from US president Franklin Pierce (an ancestor of Barbara Bush) in 1853—referring to commerce, ports of refuge for coal and stores for American ships, and the treatment of shipwrecked sailors. When Perry returned with eight ships in February 1854 (twice the number he had brought the previous year) the Bakufu recognized the futility of resistance—and instead sought to avoid giving a direct answer to Perry's requests without provoking an altercation. Eventually a convention was signed opening Shimoda and Hakodate as ports of call, authorizing the appointment of consuls, but without any clear statement about opening trade.

That convention, however, prompted a scramble by the European powers—first Britain and Russia, and soon thereafter the French and the Dutch too—to seek similar or even larger concessions. Sir James Stirling signed a similar convention on behalf of the British in September 1854, and Yevfimy Putyatin signed one for Russia in December (with an additional codicil dividing the Kurile Islands between Russia and Japan). However, in 1856, with Britain and France at war in China, the US consul Townsend Harris was able to persuade senior Bakufu officials of the need to make additional concessions on trade.

The Dutch were the first to benefit, signing a treaty in October 1857 that abolished the annual limits on the total value of Dutch trade, but retained a high customs duty and a mass of regulations on the types of trade and the persons conducting it. The US's Harris was apoplectic at these seemingly desultory gains, demanding much wider concessions—including the key one of extraterritoriality (US citizens to be tried under US law). With the British capturing Canton, Harris persuasively reminded his Bakufu interlocutors that it was more advisable to make concessions to him rather than deal with the British, who would make their case with the backing of fifty naval ships. And in February 1858, the Bakufu appeared to accept a draft agreement allowing extraterritoriality, removing most restrictions on trade, drastically lowering the tariff, and opening additional ports (Nagasaki, Yokohama, Niigata, Kobe, plus the existing ones of Shimoda and Hakodate).

But when the Bakufu turned to the imperial court to obtain its customary assent to a decision arrived at by the Bakufu, its representative, Hotta Masayoshi, was merely able to return from Kyoto (the imperial capital) with a draft decree agreeing that foreign policy decisions were for the Bakufu to make. And even this decree—obtained after more than a month of hard bargaining by Hotta in Kyoto—broke down as Emperor Komei indicated to confidants that he had signed it unwillingly. The battle lines between Edo and Kyoto were being drawn, with the imperial court reinforced by a growing body of supporters—led by ten to twelve (out of a total of nearly three hundred) daimyos—who objected to this creeping abandonment of the principle of seclusion (and consequent limits on Christianity and trade) that had been staples of the realm for several centuries.

Nonetheless, with minds concentrated by the signing of the Treaty of Tianjin—which could free British and French forces to focus on Japan—Harris was able to sign (on behalf of the US) a draft treaty (on 29 July 1858) with the Bakufu represented by Ii Naosuke (a leading fudai lord and advocate of trade liberalization as a means of strengthening the country). The Dutch and Russian representatives made similar agreements the next month, the British obtained MFN treatment in October, and the French signed a treaty in November. By the end of 1858, Japan had been opened up to international trade with a low level of tariff and with foreigners subject to only their own consular courts. Japan had entered the age of Free Trade Imperialism.

The imperial court increasingly became the locus of opposition to the opening up of Japan as Ii Naosuke's move to sign the treaties without the emperor's assent provoked a growing storm of anger nationwide. The sentiment was reinforced in Kyoto by the dissident daimyos, thousands of disgruntled samurai, and a growing mass of students and other young commoners drawn to the imperial court by outrage at the Bakufu's swelling concessions to foreigners. Ii Naosuke (who by then carried the title of regent) did persuade the emperor to sign a compromise decree in February 1859, under which the Bakufu promised to try and prevent the opening of Osaka and Kobe—as permitted in the treaties—and to ensure that the treaties would all be revoked at an unspecified future date when Japan was stronger. But the growing body of dissenters in Kyoto—many of whom had been trained at the school of gunnery in Edo—turned increasingly to terrorism as a means to express their opposition to the Bakufu's signing of unequal treaties. Inspired by a young samurai from Choshu, Yoshida Shoin, these shishi ('men of spirit') planned to assassinate Manabe Akikatsu, the senior Edo councillor sent by Ii Naosuke to persuade/coerce the emperor to sign the decree of February 1859. Although Yoshida was discovered and executed while Manabe escaped narrowly, Yoshida's followers assassinated Ii Naosuke himself on 24 March 1860, inaugurating a decade of upheaval in which assassinations became common in Japan.

Satsuma (the area around Kagoshima at the southern tip of Kyushu), the second largest of the tozama domains, and Choshu (the region around Yamaguchi, on the straits between Honshu and Kyushu), about quarter the size of Satsuma, came to play the most important role in leading the opposition to the Bakufu. The leading shishi were mid- to lower-level samurai or goshi (rural samurai) from Satsuma and Choshu, and most of the leading shishi were killed in the violent period between 1862 and 1865—although their ideas had a more lasting impact. Others who played a key role in the Bakufu's overthrow were samurai who had chosen to join the bureaucracy in their respective domains, prominently Okubo Toshimichi and Saigo Takamori of Satsuma, and Kido Koin of Choshu. An important faction in Edo was also part of the opposition to the Bakufu—this included some Tokugawa branch families (prominently Matsudaira Shungaku of Echizen), Satsuma's Shimazu Hisamitsu and Choshu's daimyo, Mori Yoshichika. Although this noblemen's faction strongly opposed the Bakufu's concessions to foreigners, they did not wish to give up baronial privileges, which ultimately depended on maintaining the legitimacy of the Bakufu system. Once the battle lines between Bakufu and the rest were drawn after 1864, most noblemen (especially those belonging to Tokugawa branch families) usually sided with Edo rather than with the dissident samurai of Satsuma and Choshu.

A keen competition had developed in 1862–64 between the 'men of spirit' from Satsuma and Choshu to prove the intensity of their loyalty to the royal court. The Bakufu was able to persuade the British (in a mission to London in 1862) to postpone the opening of any more ports until 1868, as they were provoking increasingly severe disturbances. But soon thereafter, another 'anti-foreign' episode provoked British reprisals: when a British group from Yokohama failed to accord Satsuma's Shimazu the right of way on the road from Edo to Kyoto, his escorting samurai killed a prominent British visitor from Shanghai and wounded two of his companions. Although British residents demanded the immediate landing of troops, it took almost a year for the news to reach London and for naval reprisals to be mounted against Satsuma. In the ensuing naval engagement (in August 1863), much of Kagoshima was destroyed by British naval guns, but the British ships also suffered considerable damage and, upon the British withdrawal, both sides were able to claim victory (the Satsuma side with considerably less credibility).

But in the meanwhile, an attempt at Court–Bakufu unity had been launched in early 1863, resulting in a decree setting a date (25 June) for the foreigners to be 'excluded' from Japan. The Bakufu saw this merely as a pretext to open negotiations with the foreign powers, but the pro-monarchist 'loyalists' from Choshu took it as a signal to take action to actually expel the foreigners (and gain favour at the imperial court at the expense of Satsuma). Attacking American, Dutch and French ships, Choshu shore batteries succeeded in closing the Straits of Shimonoseki by July 1863. Thus emboldened, the loyalists in Kyoto were planning for the emperor to lead a loyalist army to expel the foreigners but, at the end of September 1863, they were thwarted by Shimazu, who captured the imperial palace gates by ousting the guards from Choshu and regained Satsuma's (and his own) leading role in the court. Having climbed back to the zenith of power, Shimazu (after his domain's recent experience of the power of foreign navies) opposed any further talk of expelling the foreigners or closing ports, and argued violently against Hitotsubashi Keiki (the Shogun's representative), who was still pressing for a negotiated closure of Yokohama.

Choshu had secretly sent Ito Hirobumi and Inoue Kaoru to study in London, where Ito read in 1864 about the danger to Choshu arising from the British decision to make an example of it for leading the loyalist faction that had instigated anti-foreigner demonstrations and forced the closure of the Straits of Shimonoseki. Ito and Inoue's attempts to intercede with the British having failed, the Straits of Shimonoseki were duly shelled by a combined Western fleet, forcing Choshu to pay an indemnity and agree to renewed uninterrupted passage through the Straits in future. Ironically, the shelling of the Straits of Shimonoseki by a combined Western fleet in September 1864, and the enforced reopening of the Straits proved pivotal in persuading the majority of samurai (including those from Choshu) that trade (rather than agriculture) and Western-style ships, guns and organization were the only way to achieve 'wealth and strength'.

By the second half of 1865, however, the Bakufu was being obliged to offer even more concessions to the British because it was finding it difficult to make the payments it had agreed to on behalf of Choshu. Hitotsubashi now managed to persuade the court to accept the terms of the 1858–59 treaties, and also accept further concessions (such as the opening of Hyogo or Kobe) on the pretext of 'building many more guns and ships' by 'using the barbarian to subdue the barbarian'. The Bakufu then began vigorously courting the French to help build a shipyard, iron foundry and dockyard, financed by profits from a Franco–Japanese trading company that dealt mainly in silk, and a French military mission to help modernize Japan's army. Hitotsubashi himself became shogun in January 1867 (as Yoshinobu) and promptly proceeded— with French assistance—to further modernize the Bakufu with the central bureaucracy streamlined into departments of army, navy, finance and foreign affairs, the military reformed, and steps taken to promote commerce and industry. Yoshinobu was getting the Bakufu to adopt most of the measures that would characterize the post-Meiji Restoration regime.

But the Bakufu's reform drive had come too late. In the intervening period, the Bakufu had moved to punish Choshu for an 1864 rebellion by 2,000 of its samurai. Troops from several of the major domains gathered in Osaka in January 1865, only to disperse when Choshu's council agreed to accept the Bakufu's terms. This provoked Kido Koin and Takasugi Shinsaku to overthrow Choshu's daimyo and his 'pro-Bakufu' followers, thereby precluding the implementation of the truce terms. In May 1865 the Shogun (Iemochi) announced he would lead a larger expedition to crush Choshu. Before it could assemble, Choshu and Satsuma came to a secret understanding in March 1866 aimed at overthrowing the Bakufu. By then, the modernizing reformers Okubo and Saigo were in control of Satsuma—sending students abroad, modernizing its military, improving ties with the major powers (especially Britain), and agreeing a trade-for-arms deal with the Belgians. Having been at the forefront of loyalist agitation, Choshu and Satsuma had initially competed for the imperial court's favour, then faced the full wrath of foreign military reprisals. Recognizing the West's strengths, they also became the first domains to accelerate modernizing reforms, and their young samurai leaders saw the clear benefits of aligning to overthrow the effete Bakufu leadership.

Reinforced by its secret alliance with Satsuma, and Takasugi's adeptness as a military organizer, Choshu was able to hold off the Bakufu's land and seaborne invasion that began in July 1866. Although severely outnumbered, Choshu's forces were better trained and organized, and managed to get the better of most engagements over the next two months. When Iemochi's death was announced in September, the Bakufu forces used that as an excuse to end hostilities, handing Choshu a major moral victory. Yoshinobu's French-inspired reforms were thus a response to the Bakufu's military defeat, and the new shogun showed he still had a controlling influence over the imperial court when he blocked Satsuma's attempt to get the court to pardon Choshu in exchange for allowing the opening of the port of Kobe. This manoeuvre, however, strengthened the resolve of Satsuma and Choshu to prepare a coup against the Bakufu, especially as Yoshinobu's reforms were beginning to strengthen the Bakufu. While the French continued to advise the shogun, the British moved to align themselves more closely with the emerging power centres of Choshu and Satsuma, displaying again their remarkably uncanny ability to side with eventual winners.

Tosa and several other domains were alarmed by the prospect of a coup, and suggested a set of moderate reforms that would entail the shogun resigning, and being replaced by a bicameral council: an upper chamber of daimyos and other lords, and a lower chamber consisting of samurai and commoners. These proposals were originally put forward as the basis of an alliance between Tosa and Satsuma, but Yamauchi Yodo (the daimyo of Tosa) instead sent them to Yoshinobu in September 1867, urging him to comply with them. The proposals surprisingly appealed to the shogun, who thought they provided the basis for him to give up the trappings of power while retaining their substance. And Yoshinobu resigned as shogun on 19 November.

The fear that the shogun would retain power as president of the new upper chamber was precisely what provoked the suspicions of Choshu and Satsuma. Okubo, Saigo and Kido began moving troops towards Kyoto, and in December informed four other domains (Tosa, Echizen, Hiroshima and Owari) that they intended to seize the palace. On 3 January 1868, Saigo Takamori led a contingent of troops from these six domains in taking over the palace gates, and an imperial proclamation stripped Yoshinobu of his powers. The text made it clear that the Meiji emperor (Mutsuhito, who had just succeeded his father Komei) would henceforth exercise the administrative authority that the heads of the Tokugawa house had arrogated for several centuries. The Meiji 'Restoration' was complete, but the coup led by Satsuma and Choshu still faced some challenges. Echizen and Owari were Tokugawa branch families, and they advocated that their relative Yoshinobu be permitted to keep his lands and be made a part of the new council.

But such issues were rendered moot when another Tokugawa relative, Matsudaira Katamori of Aizu, marched towards the imperial palace but was vigorously repulsed by forces from Satsuma and Choshu. The shogun fled to Edo, and the court named him a rebel. An imperial army then proceeded eastwards, collecting professions of loyalty from daimyos along the way. Yoshinobu forbade all resistance, and his capital of Edo was taken peacefully in April, he was sent into retirement and his successor was allowed to keep land near Shizuoka yielding about 10 per cent less than that of Satsuma. Aizu continued to resist for another six months, but by November the whole of Japan had been subdued. The victors in the political upheavals of the 1860s were popularly seen as advocates of 'sonno-joi' ('honour the emperor, expel the barbarian'), but they were acutely aware of their inability to actualize this slogan. Civil strife and anti-foreigner violence persisted in the early years of the new regime, but did not interfere with the vigour with which reform was pursued. An imperial proclamation on 6 April 1868 declared that 'knowledge will be sought throughout the world' and this became the central feature of the widespread reforms of the next few decades.

Dispersed authority had arguably contributed to some of Japan's strengths. Satsuma and Choshu on their own were able to withstand foreign powers to a degree, and rudimentary capitalism had developed around towns in domains across the country. But dispersed authority had ultimately proved the Bakufu's undoing. So the new regime sought to centralize authority in Tokyo ('eastern capital', as Edo was renamed in 1868, with the court's shift there aimed also at symbolizing the full transfer of the shogun's powers). By mid-1868, Kido Koin persuaded Choshu to surrender its territory to the emperor, provided Satsuma did so too. Eventually, he won over Tosa and Hizen too, and these four domains put their lands at the disposal of the emperor in March 1869.

By July 1869, virtually all daimyos had given up their land to the court. In a compromise, they were initially appointed governors of their old territories.

PRASENJIT K. BASU

But the court ordered that expenses of the former daimyos' household and those of administration were to be separated, samurai stipends reviewed, and reports prepared on demographics, military force and taxes, demonstrating the reach of central authority. The latter also relieved governors of their erstwhile responsibilities for revenue collection, and the domains were formally abolished on 29 August 1871, to be replaced by prefectures. The daimyos were offered one-tenth of their erstwhile revenues (but to be kept as private income) and samurais a reduced rate of stipend (without the old obligations of service); status rules forbidding members of the feudal class from supplementing incomes through farming, commerce, etc., were eliminated. The following year, the Tokugawa ban on land sales was also abolished, and land taxes (in cash rather than kind) were set at 3 per cent of land value or 30 per cent of annual yield. The institutional basis for capitalism had been laid.

The compensation package for daimyo and samurai proved too heavy a burden for the state. So an ingenious one-off payment was devised to replace it: in August 1876, a schedule was published of rates at which erstwhile feudatories of various ranks were to receive a final settlement of government bonds in place of annual allowances. Daimyo were given bonds worth five years of allowances at 5 per cent interest, the smallest pensions were compensated at fourteen years' income at 7 per cent interest—with various gradations in between. The ex-daimyo thus received a very substantial amount of capital that enabled them to live comfortably, and for some to form the first phalanx of capitalists who led the industrialization that was to soon ensue. For most samurai, the compensation was too small for them to live off, and they were obliged to gain an education or otherwise plunge into the newly competitive world.

The government managed to cut its annual budget for this head of expenditure by 30 per cent, while also managing to retain the loyalties of its erstwhile elite and turning their attention from land administration to other forms of enterprise. This was certainly a more collegial outcome than the bloodshed of revolutionary upheavals in France or even the US a century earlier, and infinitely more so than in Russia or China in the twentieth century. The one-off transfer of a massive amount of bonds did have inflationary consequences, and it required all the skills of a new finance minister, Matsukata Masayoshi (from Satsuma; appointed in 1881), to restrain inflation and create the conditions for the first stage of industrialization. But inflation was a small price to pay in the service of social stability.

The new regime then began a programme of vigorous institutional borrowing, choosing different European models for different aspects of the society, military, law and other institutions. In December 1871, a large delegation—led by the court official Iwakura Tomomi, with Kido and Okubo as his deputies (representing Choshu and Satsuma), fifty-nine officials of the new regime (including Ito Hirobumi) and fifty students—set sail by steamer for a 'learning' tour of the West. They spent seven months in the US, four in Britain, made shorter visits to France, Holland and Belgium, before arriving in Germany for an extended stay in March 1873. They were received everywhere by heads of state and senior ministers, including Bismarck in Germany. The delegation returned in two groups—via the Mediterranean and Russia—and published their findings in five volumes that were to serve as a compendium of Western modernization.

The Bakufu's relationship with a French mission continued in the training and organization of the army (at least in its lower reaches), but staff work and command followed German models—with Major Klemens Meckel being recruited from Germany to run the staff school and advise the general staff. The military was initially aimed largely at maintaining domestic order, but as Japan became more involved with disputes on the Asian mainland in the 1880s, the conscript army was expanded to prepare for external contingencies too. By the eve of the war with China in 1894, Japan's army was well-equipped with rifles and artillery (almost all manufactured domestically), and comprised 73,000 men in peacetime and 200,000 in wartime. Because of the always-acute foreign exchange constraint, the navy received less attention, with a Naval General Staff being established only in 1891 (three years after the naval officers' training school was set up), and the navy remained small by European standards (twenty-eight modern ships and twenty-four torpedo boats in 1894). The army and navy, however, remained closely linked to the emperor, who was their commander-in-chief and whose family members took up navy careers. The chiefs of the army and navy had direct access to the emperor on command matters (separate from their ministries)—and this enabled them to increasingly interfere in politics.

The domains were replaced by a smaller number of (seventy-two, then forty-three) prefectures (ken) with three cities (fu)—Tokyo, Osaka and Kyoto—given equivalent status, and all of them divided into districts. The prefectures and districts were staffed by a newly-created bureaucracy of appointed officials, and only the lower sub-divisions—villages and city wards—were under elected headmen. But the other key institutional innovation was that the entire structure of local government was centralized, with governors and district officials reporting to the (national) home ministry, which was headed in the crucial years of 1873–78 by Satsuma's Okubo Toshimichi, and (after his assassination in 1878) by Choshu's Ito Hirobumi. This administrative structure clearly owed much to the influence of Napoleonic France. In the early years, the bureaucracy was filled mainly by samurai who were close to members of the executive council (which represented the apex of the government until 1885, when a cabinet system was formally instituted) and it therefore acquired a reputation for being dominated by Satsuma and Choshu.

Although Choshu's Sanjo Sanetomi held the highest-ranking position in the executive council, Satsuma's Iwakura Tomomi had more influence with the emperor and was seen as more politically capable. Ito, the leading figure during the vigorous period of modernization from 1885 to 1900 was a protégé of Iwakura's. Princes, court nobles and daimyo survived in positions of power until 1871, but were replaced in the key ministries of Finance, Civil Affairs (Home after 1873), War, Justice, Imperial Household, and Foreign Affairs by samurai from Choshu, Satsuma, Tosa and Hizen. By 1878, the pioneers of the Restoration (Kido, Okubo and Saigo) were all dead, and a team of vigorous reformers had succeeded them, with Finance Minister Okuma Shigenobu (of Hizen) implementing the new land tax, Choshu's Ito Hirobumi (as minister of Public Works) responsible for the economic modernization programme, and Yamagata Aritomo (also from Choshu) spearheading the creation of the new army.

Ito Hirobumi, who became prime minister in the first cabinet in December 1885, further modernized the civil service and instituted examinations to determine both entry and promotion of officials after 1887. (Tokyo University graduates were exempted from examinations until 1893, a six-year head start that they parlayed into dominance of the bureaucracy over the next century!) By 1920, four-fifths of all bureau chiefs had entered the bureaucracy through the examination system (although only a third had by 1910), highlighting the gradualness of the process of change. The post office (established in 1871) was another redoubt for the ancien régime, with former noblemen being partly compensated with control of the postal system, which became pervasive as principal aggregator of the nation's savings and gradually emerged as the nation's largest financial institution (a structure that still persists, with the same families running local branches).

Earlier, just before a Western-style cabinet replaced the executive council in 1885, the emperor created a peerage (largely to accommodate the old feudal and court nobility) with princes/dukes at the head, followed by marquis, counts, viscounts and barons. Sanjo and Iwakura became princes, while Okubo and Kido were posthumously conferred the title of marquis, but most titles went to members of about thirty noble families. Accommodation and consensus were the perpetual hallmarks of change in Japan.

Japan's constitution, adopted in February 1889, was largely based on the German (Prussian) model, with some borrowing from Austria. As preparations for it began, the meticulous Ito paid a year-and-a-half long visit to Berlin and Vienna in 1882. While most of its principles were of Prussian provenance, the key area where Japan's constitution differed from the Prussian model was in the role of the emperor. The Japanese cabinet acted in the name of the emperor, but most decisions were to be made by the cabinet—and the emperor's senior *political* advisers (who were the senior councillors in the cabinet), *not* his *personal* ones—whereas the German kaiser not only presided over the cabinet but was actually responsible for its decisions (which merely had to be countersigned by ministers). In reality, of course, as long as a powerful figure (such as Bismarck) was Chancellor of the Cabinet, the German kaiser's role was also often to preside rather than to decide. But in Japan, the cabinet's constitutional position (as decision maker) was institutionalized, with the emperor only acting very occasionally as the arbiter when a decision could not be arrived at by the cabinet and the senior political advisers.

The Japanese emperor provided legitimacy to the cabinet, but the source of this legitimacy was further institutionalized by the propagation amongst the populace of Shinto doctrines of filial piety and loyalty to the emperor. Buddhism (the other major religion of the Japanese) was de-emphasized, with 18,000 temples being closed in the first decade after the Restoration, many subjected to violence, including idol-breaking. The Imperial Household ceased conducting Buddhist ceremonies in 1871. And Confucianism was installed as a secular creed (useful for its adherence to principles of filial piety) and no longer seen as a religion. In school textbooks at the beginning of the twentieth century, the orthodoxy encompassed an 'absolutist' Shinto-based interpretation of the emperor's position in the state, and a 'family' concept with respect to his subjects (who were to see him as a head of family to be unquestioningly obeyed) leavened by Confucian notions of duty and filial piety. It was a system of legitimacy more comprehensive than in most societies, although the implicit acceptance of Christian values, and the prime importance of 'manners' as a means of ensuring social compliance in Victorian England, certainly came close to doing the same thing.

Japan's pioneering role in Asia extended not merely to harnessing the forces of nationalism, constitutional government and industrial technology that had come to define European modernity. Like Britain, the social conservatism of its monarchic tradition contributed to an orderliness that was unique in Asia at the turn of the century. Asia's two great mother civilizations of China and India were severely in decay and humiliated by foreign rule—in one case by the Manchus, the other by the British—as indeed were the other smaller civilizations such as those of the Indonesian archipelago and Indo-China. Their humiliated peoples' standards of hygiene, in particular, were remarkably primitive in comparison with those of Europe. Japan's early focus on hygiene, cleanliness and literacy made it a unique pioneer in Asian (and perhaps even in world) history.

Only the US predated Japan's achievement of universal literacy (which Japan was close to achieving by the start of the twentieth century; by 1900, about 90 per cent of those of schoolgoing age were in school). With more than a million students enrolled in 10,000 temple schools and over 1,500 private schools by the 1860s, a high proportion of Japanese could read and write, rendering the dissemination of the edicts of the Meiji Restoration much easier than they could have been almost anywhere else in the world. Notices put up in villages and towns helped quickly bring about compliance with the often wrenching social and behavioural changes that the new regime was seeking. Thus Okubo Toshimichi, Ito Hirobumi and their fellow reformers from Satsuma and Choshu were able to introduce beef-eating to the Japanese Diet in 1888 (before which date, the cow was just as sacred—and forbidden as food—in Japan as it is in India and much of Buddhist Asia today). And their focus on inculcating civic consciousness amongst the Japanese helped foster an orderly cleanliness that is now one of the defining features of modern Japan and was admired and emulated by many of the peoples that Japan conquered in the first half of the twentieth century (most prominently by Lee Kuan Yew, who imposed an elaborate regime of fines to overcome Singapore Chinese and Indians' propensity towards messiness).

Even at the time of the Meiji Restoration, many farmers from the more advanced regions of Japan were familiar with the norms of a money economy, there was an effective distribution system, and many members of the ruling elite were acquainted with modern science and technology (especially as it related to military and medical matters). But although there was a considerable degree of knowledge of modern finance and commerce, there was little manufacturing expertise. The industrial section of Okubo's Home Ministry thus took the lead in providing government leadership in industrialization, supported by Ito's Public Works Ministry, and their main early focus was on improved transport and communication. Between 1871 and 1874, the new postal service had established 3,000 offices, including a telegraph network. The government played the lead role in creating a nationwide railway network (although two-thirds of this was privately owned by the start of the twentieth century) and in regulating shipping services to ensure they could beat foreign competitors. By 1873, Mitsubishi had emerged as a beneficiary of this: established by a samurai from Tosa, Iwasaki Yataro, who took over ships from the domain when it was dissolved in 1871, the new firm quickly established services between Tokyo and Osaka, as well as from Hong Kong to Osaka, having also obtained some ships from the government. In 1885, Iwasaki was obliged to merge his shipping interests with some rivals to form the Nippon Yusen Kaisha, although he retained the independence of Mitsubishi's non-shipping concerns.

Since the unequal treaties made it impossible to protect domestic industry with tariffs, Japan embarked on a vigorous export promotion drive. Exports in the 1860s were mainly confined to commodities like silk and tea, and coal was added in the next decade. The Meiji government invested in silk manufacturing (and skills training), and also regulated the industry to ensure quality standards. Silk production rose by 60 per cent between 1868 and 1883, while silk exports doubled over the period, with more than half of these exports going to the United States. Modest import-substituting investments were made by the government in relatively capital-intensive industries such as factories for cement (1871), glass (1876) and white bricks (1878). The Meiji government also invested in shipbuilding, expanding the shipyards inherited from the Bakufu in Nagasaki and Yokosuka and establishing a new one at Kobe. The government's total spending on industry and transport in the 1868–85 period amounted to about two years' tax revenues.

Finance Minister Matsukata's austerity drive meant that outlays for industry too had to be cut, and he announced in March 1882 that government factories would be sold to private buyers. The purpose of the privatization exercise was to withdraw from industry (which, he argued, should not be the government's business) and recoup some of the capital invested in loss-making enterprises. The latter goal was only partly achieved (as the privatizations succeeded only after reserve prices were reduced in 1884), but the future zaibatsu conglomerates acquired most of the key assets through this process: Mitsui purchased the silk-reeling mill, Mitsubishi the shipyard in Nagasaki, Furukawa the cement and white brick factories, and most mines were bought by Asano and Kuhara.

Since half the government's revenue still came from the land tax until the 1890s, and silk and tea were Japan's key exports, agriculture was still very important at the turn of the century. Japan did not have an agrarian revolution of the European variety (characterized by the establishment of property rights through land enclosures and consolidation), as Japanese agriculture involved the intensive cultivation of small plots by family labour. But technological innovations and investment helped lift yields per hectare by 30 per cent between 1880 and 1900, while land under cultivation increased 13 per cent. The index of agricultural production rose by 128 per cent between 1873 and 1900 as new seed varieties were introduced, fertilizer use increased sharply, irrigation benefited from both private and public investment, pest control improved and the government facilitated the spread of better planting techniques and other technical advice for farmers.

Significant advances had also occurred in finance and banking. In 1872, regulations were issued allowing private banks to function on the American model, albeit with the restriction that any notes they issued were to be exchangeable into gold. The 1876 withdrawal of this latter restriction helped the rapid growth of banks but also coincided with a sharp rise in government expenditure and inflation on account of the bond issues to fund samurai pensions (1876) and the suppression of the Satsuma rebellion of 1877 (led by Saigo Takamuri, who had led the final military assault on the imperial palace in 1868, but now led a rebellion of disgruntled samurai from Satsuma that took six months to suppress, at the end of which Saigo committed ritual suicide in the face of inevitable defeat). By 1881, the yen had been effectively devalued (relative to gold) by 45 per cent, and Finance Minister Matsukata set out to achieve a budget surplus over the next five years (through sin taxes on cigarettes and sake, and of course privatization) and used that to redeem the inconvertible notes in circulation. The resulting deflation caused bankruptcies and rural suffering, but established financial stability, which was institutionalized through the establishment of the Bank of Japan (as regulator of banks and the currency), and the Yokohama Specie Bank to regulate foreign exchange. And of course the post office savings scheme continued to provide a steady supply of investible funds for the Finance Ministry.

At the turn of the century, neither industry nor the banking system was as concentrated as they were to become by the 1920s, but the big five family-owned zaibatsu banking and industrial conglomerates (Mitsui, Mitsubishi, Yasuda, Sumitomo and Dai-Ichi) were already established. Mitsui had existed since the seventeenth century in domestic retail and finance, but was reorganized by 1876 along modern lines, including the establishment of an overseas trading company, a bank, and interests in sugar, paper, coal and shipping. Mitsubishi was the next biggest, including shipping, shipbuilding and mining (which was to lead to investments in heavy industry early in the twentieth century) and a bank (founded in 1880). Osaka-based Sumitomo developed from a pre-modern copper-mining firm and retained a focus on metals, but had added a bank too. Yasuda was created by an ex-samurai in early Meiji times who began with an initial stake in trade and banking.

The cotton textile industry had also grown significantly by the turn of the century, gaining from the growth in demand from China and Korea after those markets opened up to Japan following her victory in the Sino–Japanese War of 1895. Cotton textiles, however, had largely grown through private enterprise, the initial government attempts at import substitution having made little headway. In 1882, Shibusawa Eiichi founded the Osaka Cotton Spinning Company, using second-hand less-productive technology from the West, compensating by employing cheap labour on all-night shifts. Others copied his production methods, and Japan's yarn output expanded sevenfold between 1886 and 1890. This caused a glut of domestic supply, and set off a scramble for new markets; once these emerged after 1895, the textile industry resumed its rapid growth.

Meiji foreign policy began with the signing of a treaty with China in 1871, allowing for trade on equal terms between the two countries (although Japan had tried unsuccessfully to obtain terms on par with the European powers). A treaty was also signed with Russia in 1875, under which Japan forsook claims to Sakhalin Island, and instead received control over the northern Kurile Islands. However, Korea became the locus of disputes between China and Japan, with Russia lurking in the background as another power with interests in that peninsula. Korea had objected to the original proclamation of the Meiji Restoration—as its language allegedly assigned a lower status to the Korean king than the Japanese emperor. This Korean rejection was seen by some Japanese as a national insult, and a 'war party' emerged, whose leader (Saigo Takamori) persuaded the executive council that he should be allowed to take an expeditionary force to Korea either to seek a settlement or provoke a confrontation. However, this was thwarted by the 'reform party'—comprising Okubo, Iwakura and Kido—that had just returned from its European tour convinced that a war with Korea would be an unnecessary diversion at a time when Japan still needed substantial reforms to catch up with the West. Although the reform party was able to persuade the emperor to withhold his final approval for the war, it caused the first major split in the ruling coalition (and no doubt led eventually to Saigo's last desperate stand as leader of the Satsuma Rebellion of 1877).

Japan's growing influence over Korea in the 1870s and 1880s aroused an intense nationalist response by Korean patriots and students, partly because Japan's previous attempt at conquering Korea (in 1592–98) was seared into Koreans' collective memory, in ways that were never quite comprehended in Japan. During Japan's version of the Warring States (Sengoku) period, Japan's own 'great unifier', Toyotomi Hideyoshi had ordered an attempt to invade Ming China, which could only be accomplished with the cooperation of Korea's Chosun dynasty. When the latter refused to collaborate, Hideyoshi ordered a series of invasions—one of which was heroically repulsed by the 'turtle ships' of Korea's Admiral Yi Sun-shin (whose accomplishment is still commemorated with a monument on one of Seoul's most prominent boulevards).

Like Japan, Korea's socio-cultural homogeneity derives from more than a millennium of cohesive, unitary rule that forged a unique national identity. The Silla kingdom (668–918 CE) ruled about three-quarters of what constitutes Korea today (up to the Taedong River, on which Pyongyang stands). The Koryo dynasty (918–1392), ruling from Kaesong (just southwest of Pyongyang), ruled all of Korea and parts of southern Manchuria (where there still remains a considerable Korean minority, especially in Jilin province). Like China, Korea too was traumatized by a Mongol invasion in 1231. Although the Mongols did not establish a dynasty in Korea (as they did in China, uniting that country's north and south for the first time), they also left a distinct imprint on Korea. Japan, famously, was saved from a Mongol invasion by the kamikaze wind that blew away the Mongol fleet. The weakened Koryo dynasty was eventually overthrown in 1392 by General Yi Song-gye, the founder of the Yi (or Chosun/Joseon) dynasty that still ruled Korea at the dawn of the twentieth century.

By then, however, its capital of Seoul was a den of intrigue amongst competing diplomats from Russia, Japan and China. Within the first century of the Chosun dynasty's reign, scholars working for King Yi Sejong had invented Korea's unique twenty-six-character alphabet (known as Hangul), which was a huge simplification of the Chinese system of ideographs and added to Korea's sense of national cohesion. The key factor that had created the long period of stability (from 1392) under the Yi kings, also contributed to the ossification of society, and the intense weakness of the Korean state by the nineteenth century: a delicate balance of power existed between the Chosun monarchs and a hereditary aristocracy, which contributed to stability and order but prevented the mobilization of resources for development or defence. While Korea had produced the world's most exquisite celadon pottery during the Koryo era, the weakness of the Chosun state (and the monarchy's financial constraints) led to the demise of most domestic manufacturing as the Chosun royal household imported most of its luxury goods and other manufactured products from Ming China (the payment for which was considered a 'tribute' by the Ming court), a relationship that persisted under the Qing. The consequent demise of market-based exchanges meant that the money economy had not spread across Korea when Japanese traders began to appear in the 1870s and the yen soon replaced barley and rice as the most acceptable medium of exchange in Korea. And similarly, Korea's primitive distribution networks (based on animal or human transportation of goods) were quickly overwhelmed by Japan's modern transportation, distribution and retailing methods.

A Japanese naval expedition (ostensibly on an exploratory mission) clashed with Korean coastal batteries in September 1875, and this eventually led to the signing of a treaty between Japan and Korea in early 1876, which described Korea as an independent country 'with the same sovereign rights as Japan'. This was a shot across the bow to China, which had traditionally considered Korea a vassal state subject to China's suzerainty (and part of its tributary system). China's Li Hongzhang then quickly moved to ensure that Korea signed similar treaties with the Western powers in order to dilute Japan's influence. While China strengthened ties with Korea's royal family, Japan began encouraging Korean students to obtain a modern education in Japan, and sought allies amongst senior officials in the Chosun dynasty court. In December 1884, Korean reformers led by Kim Ok-kyun and Japanese activists (with at least the tacit approval of Japan's legation) attempted to stage a coup d'état. However, neither China nor Japan was yet prepared to take the conflict this far and a hands-off agreement was signed in Tianjin in the spring of 1885 between Li Hongzhang and Ito Hirobumi.

Over the next decade, China's influence over Korea greatly increased under the Chinese legation led by Yuan Shikai, with Sino–Korean trade increasing largely at Japan's expense. In June 1894, Korean traditionalists called Tonghaks (who opposed the growth of Western influence over the country) began a series of local rebellions. The pro-Japanese Kim Ok-kyun, meanwhile, was lured to Shanghai and assassinated, his body quartered and sent back to Seoul to be publicly displayed as a warning to other rebels. Acknowledging his vassal status, Korea's King Gojong asked China to intervene on his side, but Japan objected that China's dispatch of 2,000 troops violated the Tianjin agreement of 1885. Prime Minister Ito Hirobumi then sent Japanese troops into Korea too, and demanded that the Korean government implement a wide-ranging programme of reforms that would effectively substitute Japanese influence for Chinese. In July, Ito warned China not to send any more troops, and sank the British steamer *Kowshing* which was carrying Chinese reinforcements.

War was formally declared on 1 August 1894 and Japan swiftly made decisive gains. By the end of September, the Japanese army controlled all of Korea and its navy was in command of the Yellow Sea. In October, Yamagata Aritomo led two divisions into southern Manchuria, and three divisions under General Oyama Iwao captured Port Arthur (present-day Lushun in Dalian) in November. By March 1895, the Japanese had successfully invaded Shandong and Manchuria, and after the February capture of Weihaiwei, commanded the sea approaches to Peking. The Chinese sued for peace. In the Treaty of Shimonoseki, which ended the conflict, China recognized the independence of Korea and ceded Taiwan, the adjoining Pescadores, and the Liaotung Peninsula in Manchuria to Japan. It also agreed to pay a large indemnity, and to accord Japan the same trading privileges that the European powers enjoyed in China.

PRASENJIT K. BASU

The outcome of the Sino–Japanese War announced the arrival of a new Asian power that had hitherto been underestimated or overlooked. However, Japan could not fully savour the fruits of its great unexpected military victory as the Triple Intervention obliged Japan to give up her claim to the Liaotung Peninsula, in exchange for China paying an even larger indemnity. Japan was also allowed to hold Weihaiwei until China had paid the agreed reparations. However, another abortive pro-Japanese coup attempt in Korea (which led to the accidental death of Queen Min in October 1895) caused King Gojong to take refuge with the Russian legation, which, in turn, meant that Russia's influence over Korea grew manifold over the next few years, and strengthened Russo–Japanese rivalry.

Recognizing that she had still not earned the right to be treated on par with the European powers, and that Russia remained a more formidable rival with whom future conflict appeared inevitable, Japan embarked on a further rearmament and military modernization programme. Meanwhile, the three powers that had intervened at Shimonoseki on China's behalf now called in their debts from China: France carved up a sphere of influence in the south (near China's border with French Indo-China), Germany one in Shandong, and Russia one in Manchuria—where Russia formally took over Port Arthur and began building rail links that would link up with the Russian-owned China Eastern Railway. The Boxer Rebellion (1899–1900) broke out in north China, and Japan gained international repute for the lead role taken by Yamagata's army in suppressing it.

Japan's enhanced reputation also resulted in negotiations for a formal treaty with Britain, which the two powers began discussing early in the new century (in 1901) and signed on 30 January 1902. It provided for each power to stay neutral if the other became involved in a war, but to intervene on each other's side should one of them be attacked by two or more powers. Britain also recognized that Japan had political, commercial and industrial interests 'to a peculiar degree' in Korea. Japan had broken out of its splendid isolation as a major Asian power, and could deal with greater confidence with Russia.

Following the terms of the Treaty of Shimonoseki that proclaimed its victory in the Sino–Japanese War of 1894–95, Japan also ruled Taiwan, an island over which Japan and China had long contended. From the twelfth to the sixteenth century, Japan had controlled the eastern half of Taiwan, before the south of the island was visited by Portuguese ships (1590) and the southeast came under Dutch rule for a thirty-seven-year period (1624–61); it was the Dutch who named the island Formosa ('beautiful one'; actually Ilha Formosa, for the 'beautiful isle').

Taiwan's reputation as a redoubt for Chinese rebels was first established when a Ming pirate/general (Koxinga or Zheng Chenggong) escaped there after the defeat of the Ming by the Manchus. Koxinga (whose mother was Japanese, and whose Zheng family were known for their cosmopolitan trading network) drove out the Dutch and occupied much of the island in the name of the Ming dissidents. After coming under Manchu rule in 1683—and thus being incorporated into the Chinese empire for the first time—Taiwan saw waves of immigration from the Chinese mainland (chiefly from Fujian province across the Taiwan Straits), and Hokkien became the island's lingua franca. At the turn of the twentieth century, however, Taiwan was firmly under Japan's control after the suppression of some mild local resistance to the establishment of Japan's colonial rule. Eventually an active programme of 'Japanization' was to occur on Taiwan starting in the first decade of the twentieth century.

Over the course of the next fifty years, Japan would conquer most of East Asia and this formidable Asian power would only succumb to the nuclear bombs of the US in August 1945. Its rule would be seen as brutal in much of its future dominions, but only in Taiwan would the native peoples retain a residue of open admiration for the Japanese. Perhaps this is unsurprising as Japan, for several centuries, had considerable influence over Taiwan (which is geographically close to the Ryukyu Islands and Okinawa). Today, most native Taiwanese who grew up under Japanese rule retain a fund of goodwill towards Japan, epitomized by former president Lee Teng-hui, whose Japanese is said to be much better than his Mandarin (speaking which he often lapses into a Japanese accent).

While Japan's rule was to be remembered with considerably less fondness elsewhere in East Asia, it was to be the dominant institutional influence on the countries it ruled for longer periods (Taiwan, Korea, Manchuria) and a significant cultural one on those it ruled for shorter periods (Malaysia, Singapore, Indonesia, coastal China). A century earlier, Napoleon Bonaparte had re-established order in a chaotic post-Revolutionary France, but his subsequent conquests across Europe helped modernize much of Europe too. The French (and especially Napoleon) were not popular with those whom they conquered (starting with northern Italy, much of Eastern Europe—all of which was conquered from the Austrian empire—western Germany, Switzerland, the Netherlands and Spain). But the Code Napoleon not only became the basis of a new legal and administrative order in France, but was of equal significance in establishing administrative norms and a new legal code across much of the European mainland.

The imprint that Napoleon left on Europe was long-lasting, and it was his modernizing social reforms that Napoleon was proudest of. Similarly, he was arguably the catalyst for the first stirrings of Italian nationalism that was eventually developed most fully by Cavour, Garibaldi and Mazzini about seven decades later. And the legacy of unity under Napoleonic rule in western Germany played a large part in sowing the seeds of the German Customs Union of 1835 that eventually led to the unification of Germany in 1871 after Bismarck's victory in the Franco–Prussian War.

In much the same way, Japanese rule helped crystallize nationalism in much of Asia—indeed, as a later chapter will show, Sukarno (and his key Islamist collaborator Hatta) would incubate their Indonesian nationalist movement under Japanese rule, as indeed would Burma's Aung San and his college-student cohorts (whose Burma National Army would be created by the Japanese)—and modernize much of East Asia. While Taiwan's Lee Teng-hui and South Korea's late Kim Dae-jung were both fluent in the Japanese language, their national institutions would also be profoundly influenced by Japan. Trained in the Japanese imperial army and heavily inspired by it, General Park Chung-hee would remake South Korea more clearly in Japan's image—from the chaebols that replicated Japan's zaibatsu, to the planning machinery in the Trade Ministry, to the labour-market mechanisms, Park's Korea would be a conscious imitator of its former imperial power.

Manchuria (and the industries abandoned by the Japanese after their sudden surrender following the dropping of the nuclear bombs) would provide the basis of early industrialization in Mao's China, and it would be no accident that the most prosperous parts of today's China would be precisely those parts that were once conquered and ruled by Japan. In Malaysia, Prime Minister Mahathir Mohamad's 'Look East' policy of the early 1980s (while formally talking of emulating Korea) would consciously seek to remake its institutions in the Japanese image (including a Ministry of International Trade and Industry, MITI) and aggressively seek investments and credit from Japan to kick-start faster growth. The widespread influence of Japan over East Asian institutions in the twentieth century necessitated this extensive excursion into the details of how Japan came to be the most advanced Asian nation at the turn of the century. In an era of towering imperial ambitions, Japan was soon to leapfrog into the ranks of the colonizers in the first decade of the twentieth century.

Chapter 2

THE FIRST STIRRINGS OF NATIONALISM (1901–1913)

The first decade of the twentieth century in Asia was characterized by the flowering of nationalism. An abortive democratic revolution brought an end to millennia of monarchy in China, although democracy withered quickly in the newly republican country. Amid the chaos, the nations that had been yoked onto China by the Manchus, and subsumed into their Qing empire, broke decisively away—notably Tibet, Mongolia and East Turkestan. The sensational triumph of Japan (and especially its navy) in the Russo–Japanese War of 1904–05 had an electrifying impact on nascent nationalism across Asia—holding out the possibility that other nations too might aspire to overthrow their colonial overlords. Partly to nip those stirrings in the bud, the imperious Curzon gratuitously divided the British province of Bengal to punish the uppity Bengali elite in the first gambit in the long British game of 'divide et impera'.

Going against the tide of nationalism, the Dutch expanded their empire by completing their conquest of the Hindu island paradise of Bali. As the Dutch armies landed at Sanur in the south Bali kingdom of Bandung in September 1906 and besieged its capital of Denpasar for a fortnight, the king and his family and retainers tragically marched out of their palace in a collective act of suicide called 'puputan'. The Dutch cannons and guns went on firing until a thousand of Bali's finest went down to their sanguinary deaths. Such scenes were repeated across southern Bali until all of that idyllic island was subdued by the Dutch, while much of its intellectual heritage was decimated in an orgy that mixed cruelty with self-flagellation: in 1908, the last of the Balinese kingdoms, Klungkung, fell with the mass suicide of 300 people as the aristocratic priyayi of Bali were virtually exterminated. Bloodier and wider still was the war that the seemingly reluctant colonizers, the Americans, fought to subdue the Philippine bid for independence.

THE US AS COLONIZER, AND THE STUNTED NATIONALISM
OF THE PHILIPPINES

The Philippine War of Independence was the first genuine nationalist war in Asia, but its ultimate failure meant that it has left the lightest imprint on Asia's twentieth-century history. Historically, the Philippines is often thought of as a 'Latin American country that is only geographically in Asia'. The genesis of that phrase was the country's experience of Spanish colonialism, with the paramount role of the Catholic Church (and its resented friars) and large haciendas that are reminiscent of Latin America. However, its people have much deeper Asian (including Indian, Malay and Chinese) ethnic links than those of Latin America: the Spaniards referred to all natives of their colonies as 'Indios', but that appellation was ethnically more apt in the Philippines than anywhere in Latin America. Through much of the period of Spanish rule, though, the Philippines was in fact administered from Spanish Mexico. But while Spain lost most of its colonial possessions in Latin America during the revolutions of 1810–29 (themselves a consequence of Napoleon's conquest of Spain)—first in Argentina and Mexico, and then in the countries influenced by the charismatic leadership of Simón Bolívar—Spain retained control of Cuba, Puerto Rico, Guam and the Philippines.

The 1896–1902 War of Independence (first fought against the Spaniards, and then continued against the Americans) was heavily influenced by the Bolivarian revolutions, albeit with some peripheral influence from Hong Kong (where José Rizal spent several years in exile) and Japan (given his partly-Japanese heritage, and his frequent voyages there). After 330 years of Spanish rule, it was quite natural for Latin American and European influences to outweigh Asian ones on the Philippine elite, but the founding fathers of Philippine nationalism did attempt to rescue the pre-Spanish history of their archipelago from the depredations and distortions of the Spaniards' historiography.

It was as a novelist and remarkable polymath that José Rizal had the most profound impact on creating a Philippine identity and laying the seeds of the revolution, although he himself advocated institutional reform (including full Philippine representation in Spain's Cortes and other institutions of state, rather than outright independence for which he felt the Philippines was still far from ready). Rizal's most important vehicle was his satirical novel *Noli Me Tángere,* written while he was a medical student at the Universidad Central de Madrid, and published in 1887. (The Latin title refers to a phrase attributed to Jesus Christ, which means 'Touch me not', but the novel was written in Spanish.) The novel lampoons Catholic friars and the Spanish state, and critiques the backwardness of Philippine society. But, like Bankim's *Anandamath (The Abbey of Joy,* which was published contemporaneously in India), it was also a siren call to rouse the incipient nationalism of a supine people, and it duly had that impact (more immediately than Bankim's novel did in India).

The novel (and its sequel, *El Filibusterismo*, also known in English as *The Reign of Greed*) received a sensational response in the Philippines, and predictably attracted the wrath of both the colonial authorities and the Catholic clergy. Rizal created La Liga Filipina (The Philippine League) in 1892 to focus on institutional reforms, advance the cause of greater solidarity between Spain and the Philippines and to foster amongst the Spanish populace a greater understanding of the needs of their Asian colony. Although his second novel (*El Filibusterismo*) appeared to advocate a violent overthrow of Spanish rule, Rizal's public stance remained that the Filipino people needed greater education to be prepared for self-rule. By 1892, however, his writings had created enough of a national consciousness—and also attracted the ire of the Spanish colonial authorities and the church—and Rizal was exiled to Dapitan in the Zamboanga del Norte peninsula of Mindanao in order to nip the nascent nationalist movement in the bud. Instead, it had the opposite impact—with Andrés Bonifacio (along with associates such as Teodoro Plata and Ladislao Diwa) creating the Katipunan secret society (in July 1892, immediately after Rizal was sent into exile) to overthrow Spanish rule through a violent revolution. The revolutionaries reasoned (quite correctly) that a weakened Spain—already beset by rebellion in Cuba—would scarcely be able to fend off even a hastily organized military challenge.

In Dapitan, meanwhile, Rizal set about establishing a school (to inculcate 'self-sufficiency' and resourcefulness in young men), a hospital and a water supply system, and both taught and engaged in horticulture and farming. He was thus seeking to build the wherewithal of a nation state by creating a core of young men trained in leadership roles, and with a vision and commitment to doing the good works that would help build a nation. When the Katipunan sparked a national uprising by August 1896, José Rizal sought to dissociate himself from it by volunteering his medical services in Cuba. Instead, he was arrested in Barcelona (en route to Cuba), and accused of complicity with the uprising. Despite issuing a manifesto disavowing the violent revolution and again affirming that education and the building of a national identity were prerequisites to independence, Rizal was convicted of sedition, and executed on 30 December 1896. By February 1897, numerous other Filipino nationalists were also executed.

Andrés Bonifacio and the Katipunan had planned a coordinated attack on Manila for 29 August 1896. By the next day, their rebellion had spread to eight provinces. However, Bonifacio's forces had limited firearms, and instead depended on 'bolo knives' (similar to machetes) and spears as their main weapons. Besides, Spanish intelligence had captured Bonifacio's battle plans, and was able to thwart the coordinated attack on Manila, albeit only after some fierce battles. Meanwhile, in Cavite, Emilio Aguinaldo notched up some major victories, especially defeating the Spanish forces under General Ernesto de Aguirre at the Battle of Imus on 1 September. Aguinaldo gained further prestige through victories in various 'set piece' battles with Spanish troops, and soon set up a 'provisional government' headed by him, in direct competition to Bonifacio's Katipunan government. Eventually, at the Tejeros Convention in March 1897, the leadership question was sought to be settled through an election, in which Bonifacio was the presiding officer. However, with his numerous victories in war (in contrast to Bonifacio's defeats), Aguinaldo had gained prestige, and won the presidency over Bonifacio, who subsequently lost the ballot for several other positions, and was only elected Director of the Interior. With his qualification for even that position being questioned by some members of Aguinaldo's faction, Bonifacio (invoking his position as supremo of the Katipunan) declared the election null and void, and stormed out of the convention. He then began to force young Filipinos to join his army, and drew up plans for a coup against the elected government of Aguinaldo. Upon learning of these, Aguinaldo ordered the arrest of Bonifacio and his brothers (one of whom was killed in the operation).

Andrés Bonifacio and his surviving brother Procopio were executed in May 1897 by forces loyal to Aguinaldo—an episode quite typical of any revolution, but one that remains hotly disputed to this day. Bonifacio's lower middle class background lends the episode an additional edge when compared with the aristocratic (illustrado) lineage of almost all the leaders of Aguinaldo's faction. Aguinaldo had wanted to commute Bonifacio's sentence to deportation, but was swayed by his senior officers who insisted on execution as the only route to ensuring the unity of command that was essential to the success of the revolution.

Amid these signs of disunity amongst the revolutionary forces, the colonial authorities called for massive troop reinforcements from Spain. Thus augmented, the Spanish colonial forces began to peg Aguinaldo's army back, inflicting several defeats on them and obliging Aguinaldo to abandon his strongholds in Cavite and retreat northwards. The revolutionary army eventually made a stand in the mountainous caves of Biak-na-Bato (in Bulacan province, west of Manila), and the Spanish governor Fernando Primo de Rivera began negotiating a ceasefire. The eventual Pact of Biak-na-Bato (signed 15 December 1897) provided a pardon for Aguinaldo and his key military leaders in exchange for exile to Hong Kong and the payment of 400,000 Mexican pesos to Aguinaldo, with a similar sum offered conditionally to some of his other key followers. Most of the latter was never paid (and nor was the 900,000 pesos promised as compensation to the civilian casualties of the war), but Aguinaldo and his inner circle used the 400,000 pesos that they received to buy firearms and keep the embers of the nationalist uprising alive.

By the time the Spanish–American War began in April 1898, Aguinaldo's forces had regrouped and regained control of much of the countryside around Manila. Aguinaldo met the American consuls in Singapore in late April 1898, and he later claimed that they urged him to take command of the revolutionary forces. He also met with US commodore Dewey through these consuls, and came away from those meetings believing that the Americans had committed to an alliance, while Dewey always insisted that he had agreed to no such thing. The actual Battle of Manila Bay (between Dewey's fleet of seven warships, and the Spanish fleet of twelve ships) lasted only six hours on 1 May 1898, at the end of which all but one of the twelve Spanish ships had been sunk.

Dewey had written that Aguinaldo and the Filipino nationalist forces were 'intelligent' and 'capable of self-government', especially compared with the Cubans. But the McKinley administration sent clear instructions to Dewey to distance himself from Aguinaldo when he returned to the Philippines (on a ship provided by Dewey) in late May 1898. The Americans had promised Cuba independence at the start of the Spanish–American War, but there was little appetite for a similar pledge to the Filipinos, despite the best efforts of the steel tycoon and philanthropist Andrew Carnegie. Aguinaldo received a rapturous welcome from the Filipino people, and resumed the war against the Spaniards. His forces rapidly gained ground, and by early June had gained control of the entire island of Luzon except Manila, and much of the rest of the Philippines. Aguinaldo believed that his forces would control the land while the US provided naval support, but it soon became apparent that the US intended to take direct control of the whole operation, and sent for massive troop reinforcements, totalling nearly 11,000 soldiers partially led by Lieutenant General Arthur MacArthur (whose son, Douglas, was to be a pivotal figure in Asian history forty to fifty years later). With his relations with the Americans deteriorating rapidly, while his troops were effectively in control of much of the archipelago (despite many blandishments offered by the Spaniards), Aguinaldo decided on a unilateral Declaration of Philippine Independence on 12 June 1898, which put his forces in direct conflict with the putative American occupiers, although they were still confined to the blockading of Manila Bay, while their negotiations with the Spaniards continued in Paris. These concluded in the afternoon of 12 August 1898, and on that very day (perhaps a few hours before formal news of the accord reached Manila), the American forces captured Manila from the Spaniards, in what may have been a staged 'battle' to pre-empt Aguinaldo's forces, which were closing in on Manila.

Although the Americans disavowed any desire to become a colonial power—and Dewey is said to have told Aguinaldo that the US was in the Philippines to protect the country (and perhaps even facilitate its independence)—the reception that Dewey received on his return to the US in 1899 after the Battle of Manila Bay suggests that there was a groundswell of support for establishing an empire, especially in the wake of the patriotic fervour whipped up by the Spanish–American War. The Commodore was made 'Admiral of the Navy', a rank that no other US naval officer has ever been conferred, and received a rousing reception in Boston and New York. In the 1900 presidential campaign, the Republican ticket (McKinley–Teddy Roosevelt) campaigned on a platform supporting the gold standard and imperialism. And the enormous volunteer army of nearly 11,000 soldiers that assembled in San Francisco by mid-1898 was a culmination of the patriotic fervour of the times that was merely the final stage of the 'go west, young man' exhortation that had inspired the 'pioneers' who colonized the American West in the nineteenth century.

Those Americans had supposedly pursued their 'manifest destiny' in following Lewis and Clark's transcontinental journey of 1804–06, with wars against Mexico resulting in the incorporation into the United States of Texas (1841) and California (1848), while Alaska was purchased from the Russians in 1867. Chinese workers began to arrive in California in the second half of the century, mainly to help build the transcontinental railroads, and participate in the California gold rush.

The independent kingdom of Hawaii had its first known European visitors when Captain James Cook passed through in 1779, and more intrepid westward-bound Americans began arriving there to do business, spread Christianity and eventually settle throughout the nineteenth century. Like in much of Latin America, the white people also brought their diseases and the native Hawaiian population shrank drastically as a consequence, with about half the population succumbing to influenza, measles or smallpox by 1820, and a further fifth to measles in the 1850s. By 1885, Japanese immigrants began arriving, mainly to do the backbreaking work on the sugar and pineapple plantations being established by Americans and Europeans. In 1887, King Kalakaua of Hawaii was obliged to sign a new constitution that stripped the monarchy of all authority, and created a property-based voting system that disenfranchised most Hawaiians and Asians and gave electoral power only to white settlers. And in 1894, a Committee of Safety (comprising Euro–American businessmen primarily) overthrew the monarchy and established a 'republic' on those racist lines. President Grover Cleveland (a Democrat) was a friend of the Hawaiian monarch, and opposed its annexation. But only in June–July 1898, at Republican president McKinley's behest, was the formal annexation of Hawaii ratified by both houses of the United States Congress. American involvement in the Philippines followed logically from the long experience of colonizing and annexing Hawaii (which, incidentally, did not become a US state until 1959).

Given America's own anti-colonial history, the US was a reluctant imperialist but, while professing to work towards building nations (for the Filipinos, Cubans, Samoans, Hawaiians), there was little doubt that the 1898–1910 period was the heyday of US imperialism, and the US approach was best characterized as 'nation-building without nationality' (whether in the Philippines or Puerto Rico). Americans joined the scramble for empire especially in the Pacific with a gusto that matched the British, Germans and French—who had respectively gained Weihaiwei (and the New Territories), Kiaochow (Jiaozhou) Bay (including Qingdao city) and Kwangchow Peninsula (Guangzhouwan) from Qing China in 1898. In that spirit, American business sensed an opportunity to make Manila an entrepôt (much like Singapore was to the British) through which to exploit the emerging markets of Asia, and the rest of the Philippines was perceived as similar to the Malay sultanates that were then being incorporated more closely into the British empire.

By the time actual hostilities began between the Americans and Aguinaldo's nationalist forces in February 1899, the Americans were able to deploy an army of 24,000 troops, with more volunteers arriving every month, swelling the American army to 70,000 men by the end of 1899. Aguinaldo's forces were outgunned from the start, but they had unstinting support across the country. Much like India in 1857–58 (or Afghanistan after the Russian invasion of 1979), the Filipino nationalist army found refuge in the villages and hills and the Americans could never be sure that a 'pacified' village would not switch sides (back to the nationalist forces) as soon as the Americans had moved on. The American soldiers—many of whom had had their last military experience fighting Native Americans, or ('Red') Indians—were unabashedly racist in their attitudes to the brown 'Indios' they encountered, and their attitudes towards the use of torture and brutality were no different from those of the British in 1858. They were egged on by Rudyard Kipling's exhortation to 'Take up the White Man's burden' in suppressing 'Your new-caught, sullen peoples / Half devil and half child'.

Kipling, merely married to an American, met his literary match in the authentically American Mark Twain, who suggested that skull and bones replace the stars in the spangled banner for the US's 'Philippine Province'. He and Carnegie were amongst the luminaries in the Anti-Imperialist League, which had narrowly failed (by two votes) to dissuade Congress from ratifying the terms of the Treaty of Paris (December 1898) under which Spain ceded the entire Philippine Archipelago to the US. Politically, the leading anti-imperialist in the US was William Jennings Bryan, the Democratic Party's candidate for president in 1896 (at the age of thirty-six), 1900 and 1908. Bryan's advocacy of 'free silver' (as opposed to the gold standard) was ahead of its time, as was his populist emphasis on trust-busting and anti-imperialism. Had he won the presidency in 1900, Asia's history may well have taken a very different course, but the more conservative wing of the Democratic Party failed to rally behind Bryan; they (led then by incumbent president Cleveland) had supported a third-party candidate in 1896 who eroded Bryan's prospects of victory. This time, the advantages of incumbency and a pro-imperialist mood gave a larger victory to McKinley and Roosevelt.

The three-year war caused at least 20,000 Filipino nationalist warriors' deaths, and cost about 4,000 American soldiers their lives, plus at least another 200,000 Filipinos killed from starvation and diseases resulting from the war. The population of the archipelago declined from 9.5 million to just over 8 million during the period, so the toll from diseases and starvation might have been over a million. Amongst the senior American casualties was the hero of Wounded Knee (1890), Major General Henry Lawton, who was killed by Philippine sharpshooters at San Mateo. Given the generalized scramble for empire then underway in Asia (especially China) and Africa, the US was probably justified in arguing that any move towards Filipino independence would only invite other powers (Germany especially, but also possibly France or Japan) to intervene and circumscribe it. A strong current of opinion in the US (including the McKinley administration, albeit with the President's occasional ambivalence) argued that the US had to annex the Philippines in order to preclude other powers from doing so. But the notion of making the archipelago a protectorate—of the sort the French had established in nearby Indo-China and the British in Borneo—received short shrift, and was never seriously considered.

Soon after hostilities began in 1899, Aguinaldo had sent feelers to the Americans suggesting an honourable end to the fighting on the basis of McKinley's offer of 'the full measure of individual rights and liberties'. But General Elwell Otis ignored orders from Washington, and responded that 'fighting, once begun, must go on to the grim end'. Otis advocated unconditional surrender as the only possible outcome of the war, and used torture and press censorship to further his aims. But his tactics failed, and he was relieved of overall command a year into the war. The brutality that the US needed to deploy during the Philippines' War of Independence and the nationalist fervour of the Filipinos moved many of the Americans who faced them in combat. Amongst those who advocated a swift move towards Filipino independence was General Arthur MacArthur, who took over command from Otis in 1900, and ultimately overran Aguinaldo's capital of Malolos in April 1902.

Aguinaldo himself had been captured a year earlier, tricked by General Frederick Funston who came into Aguinaldo's encampment disguised as a prisoner of some Filipino troops who wore the revolutionary uniforms but were actually American recruits (called Macabebe Scouts); once inside, they quickly disarmed Aguinaldo's guards and captured him. A weary Aguinaldo soon pledged his allegiance to the Americans in exchange for a pardon, and called on his soldiers to lay down their arms. One amongst his generals, Artemio Ricarte (still considered the 'Father of the Philippines Army') refused to pledge allegiance to America, was imprisoned and eventually went into exile in Japan, where he established a restaurant called Karihan Luvimin, the latter a word that nationalists like to call their country (Luvimin or Luzviminda, after the three main islands of the archipelago that was named after Prince, later King, Philip II of Spain). But General Miguel Malvar continued the War of Independence for another year; amongst the prominent illustrado generals who continued to fight was one of Aguinaldo's earliest collaborators (who had been exiled to Hong Kong with him in 1897), Servillano Aquino, great-grandfather of the fifteenth president of the modern Philippines, Benigno Aquino III. Even after Malvar's formal surrender in April 1902 (and Aquino's in September 1902), some 'irreconcilables' continued to fight on until 1913, as did the Muslim Moros (originally aligned with the Americans, but disillusioned by 1903 once the Americans began to try and take control of their lands in Sulu).

Officially, the war ended in April 1902, and President Theodore Roosevelt (who had succeeded McKinley upon his assassination in September 1901) declared a general amnesty for all Filipinos who had participated in the conflict. The declaration was made on 4 July, which eventually became the Philippines' 'Independence Day' in a first sign of the tactics of assimilation that the US used towards the Filipinos. At the end of the war, General MacArthur's advocacy of a swift move to independence received scant support from Roosevelt (who only became convinced it was the right approach towards the end of his presidency in 1907–08). Imperialist sentiment was running high in America after the conquest of Hawaii, Puerto Rico and the Philippines (and the 'liberation' of Cuba from Spanish rule, and its opening instead to American corporate interests). The preferred approach to the Philippines was articulated by William Howard Taft, the rotund federal judge sent to the Philippines in 1900 at the head of a presidential commission who later became the US's first Governor General of the Philippines: Taft called his policy 'attraction', aimed at deluging the Filipinos with a wide-ranging development programme of benefits and privileges that would banish any thoughts of independence in favour of a durable bond with the US.

In the words of John Keay, 'the Philippines were therefore reinvaded, this time by an army of teachers, agriculturists, engineers, doctors, health workers, evangelists, statisticians and surveyors.' They energetically embarked on a programme of nation-building and Americanization, with ports, railroads, highways, and inter-island shipping improved and overhauled, and primary education extended to the remotest villages. The Catholic Church's influence was curtailed, with the friars' lands auctioned off to the highest bidders, who tended to be illustrados, even some (like Servillano Aquino) who had been implacable foes to the Americans during the revolutionary period. Political participation was also encouraged at every level, and the Philippines under American tutelage made substantial economic progress during the next decade, although this was a classic colonial relationship of mutual dependency, aided by American import preferences for the Philippines' exports, and a reciprocal system of preferences for American exports to the Philippines.

By ensuring that the new schools taught in English, however, Taft's 'policy of attraction' was also indirectly aimed at stamping out nationalism (and a sense of collective national identity) in favour of Americanization. (Tagalog was not taught in schools until 1940, and only fully established as the national language after Japan ousted the Americans during World War II and formally embarked on a programme to encourage Filipino nationalism.) Baseball, Hollywood, and the American Dream became the primary aspirations for most Filipinos, while the army of American 'experts' took most of the managerial and technical jobs—in an echo of colonial structures everywhere (especially India)—and the 'hill station' of Baguio provided the Americans a summer escape à la Darjeeling or Simla. Although the likes of Douglas MacArthur were appalled, American attitudes to their Indio natives became increasingly racist, exemplified by 'whites only' clubs that partially undid Taft's attempts at Americanization.

Even before Taft's arrival, several prominent illustrados, including members of Aguinaldo's first cabinet, had already begun advocating closer ties to the Americans, and openly collaborated with them. Pedro Paterno, prime minister in Aguinaldo's government, became the 'greatest turncoat (balimbing) in Philippine history' and one of the earliest advocates of collaboration with the Americans, as did Aguinaldo's secretaries for justice and foreign affairs, all going on to play prominent roles in the early years of the colonial administration. Paterno had predated Rizal as the author of the first novel written by a Filipino, *Ninay* (1885). Paterno, like Rizal, explored the ancient civilization of the archipelago, and wrote the novel's dedication in Baybayin, the pre-Spanish script for all the languages of the archipelago, which was based on the Brahmi script from India, reputed to have arrived in the Philippines from Bengal (having originated in Assam).

While some Spanish colonial officials had wanted him to also be tried alongside Rizal, Paterno was able to use his ties to Rivera and other colonial officials to avoid prosecution. He later played a leading role in negotiating the Pact of Biak-na-Bato, thus ingratiating himself with Aguinaldo sufficiently to join his cabinet as the second prime minister of the First Republic, succeeding Apolinario Mabini (the 'brains of the revolution' who drafted the first constitution, and was a late convert to Aguinaldo's cause, having been part of Rizal's La Liga Filipina until Rizal's execution radicalized him). Mabini, despite his polio-inflicted disability, remained steadfast in his opposition to the Americans, and was deported to Guam in 1901 because of his refusal to pledge allegiance to the US. Paterno, on the other hand, saw which way the winds were blowing and smoothly became the leader of the Federalistas, demanding that the Philippines be incorporated fully into the United States. He and his party had a prominent role in the first National Assembly, which comprised mainly officials appointed by the Americans, but gradually faded after elections to the assembly were held in 1907, giving way to parties demanding greater autonomy for the Philippines.

Manuel Quezon, the son of a Spanish former sergeant in the colonial army married to a Spanish primary school teacher in Manila, became the leader of the Nacionalista Party in the new Philippines Assembly (later called House of Representatives), becoming majority leader after the first election in 1907. Despite being Spanish on both sides, Quezon had earned his nationalist stripes by joining the revolutionary army in 1899, and soon becoming Aguinaldo's ayuda-de-campo (ADC), akin to Alexander Hamilton's role in Washington's army at Yorktown in 1783. Like Hamilton, he later distinguished himself in other military battles (especially in Bataan), and rose to the rank of major in the revolutionary army. The Nacionalistas were loud in their demands for independence while on the hustings, but were easily appeased by the trappings of office and autonomy afterwards. Promises from the Americans to create a vague timetable towards independence (epitomized in the Jones Act of 1916 promising independence once 'stable government' had been established) more than sufficed to appease the Nacionalistas. Quezon and his ally Sergio Osmeña were boisterous in their public demands for outright independence but 'invariably followed them with a private apology whispered in the ear of the nearest American official'!

The effective assimilation of Quezon, Osmeña and their ilk into the

American orbit aborted the nationalist aims of the Philippine War of Independence—a process that was greatly facilitated after Taft became US president in 1909. Taft had wanted to exile or execute Aguinaldo and his key generals; instead Teddy Roosevelt had pardoned them, but it was carefully ensured that those who had led the revolutionary army were effectively debarred from full political participation for the first three decades of the American occupation, and only assimilated and Americanized politicians like Osmeña and Quezon would carry the Nacionalista flag. William Jennings Bryan did rise to be Secretary of State in Woodrow Wilson's first administration (he resigned in 1915 as it became clear that Wilson was likely to take the US into war), but by then dealings with the Philippines were no longer a foreign policy matter, and the assimilation of the Philippines was no longer controversial in the US. Wilson's idealistic Fourteen Points—central to which was the right of all nations to self-determination—did not seem to apply to the Philippines (or Hawaii for that matter)!

THE ELECTRIFYING IMPACT OF JAPAN'S VICTORY OVER RUSSIA IN 1904–1905

Japan's victory over Russia in 1904–05—the first clear military defeat of a European power by an Asian one since the Mongols in the Middle Ages—had a truly electrifying impact on Asian nationalism. The young Jawaharlal Nehru (then studying at Harrow, the elite English boarding school) could hardly contain his excitement as the news emerged, and young nationalists across Asia felt a similar swelling of pride in this signal achievement by an Asian power, as it notched up victory after victory over the course of 1904 and early 1905. In 1910, the teenaged Mao Zedong listened enraptured to a paean to the victory composed by his Japan-returned schoolteacher (and could recall it precisely in later years, especially after his attitude towards Japan had become far more hostile); his teacher was amongst a wave of Chinese who had flocked to Japan after its victory in 1905. Those stirrings of nationalism also helped nudge Dowager Empress Cixi to finally agree to a comprehensive programme of reform—to be led by a delegation to the Western world (helmed by three Manchu princes and two Han officials) akin to the (much larger) delegation from Japan in the 1860s that preceded the Meiji Restoration—and to Curzon's ham-handed attempt to nip Indian nationalism in the bud with the partition of Bengal.

Although thwarted by the Triple Intervention (Russia, France and Germany) in gaining all the fruits of its victory over China in 1894, Japan had begun to be recognized by other European powers as an equal participant in Asian affairs by the turn of the century. The Dutch administrators of the East Indies began to recognize Japan as a 'European' power after 1899, and in that year (with British acquiescence in particular) the principal of extraterritoriality was abandoned in Japan. Immediately after the signing of the Boxer Protocol that ended the Boxer Rising in September 1901, Russian troops swept across Siberia and swarmed into Manchuria.

Russia's attempted annexation of Manchuria, however, was strongly resisted by the other powers, and Russia made pious promises to withdraw its troops as soon as order was restored on the Russian railroads in Manchuria. Although some troop withdrawals did occur, a substantial Russian troop presence remained in both Manchuria and Korea—where the Tsarist troops were a threatening presence for the waning Chosun dynasty. Russian nationalists had long sought a warm-water port (a quest that continues to this day), and the acquisition of Port Arthur was thus a turning point for Tsarist Russia, which energetically extended the Trans-Siberian Railway by connecting Port Arthur to both Beijing and Vladivostok by 1903 (having established a link between St Petersburg and Chita near Lake Baikal by 1899). In Korea, meanwhile, the official declaration of its independence (from Manchu and thus Chinese suzerainty) in 1895 had resulted in the emergence of pro-Russian and pro-Japanese factions in the Chosun court that tangled for dominance over the next decade.

Resentful of Tsarist Russia's expansionary motives, Japan first aligned itself formally with Britain—a power that had been in competition with Russia throughout the previous half-century, confronting it both in the Great Game of Afghanistan and Central Asia and in grabbing the spoils from the long disintegration of the European parts of the Ottoman empire. Partly to counter its global rivalry with Russia, Britain had been solicitous of Japan for some time, refusing to participate in the alliance that carved up Japan's spoils from eastern China in 1898, and pressing for its inclusion in the eight-power military force that countered the Boxers. Britain had supplied most of the warships in Japan's navy, and Japanese cadets had long been trained in British military academies. The Anglo–Japanese alliance, formed on 30 January 1902, safeguarded both powers' interests in China (while reaffirming their collective commitment to the 'Open-door' policy in China that had recently been advocated by the Americans) and the Yellow Sea region, while explicitly acknowledging that Japan had a special interest in Korea. Each power pledged to stay neutral if either one of them got involved in a war in defence of its interests, and to come to the other's aid if a third power were to enter into a war against it (thus preventing any coalition of powers against either of them, implicitly ensuring that Britain would enter on Japan's side should there be a repeat of the Russian alliance with France–Germany of 1898).

Thus fortified, Japan began demanding that the Russian troops be withdrawn from Manchuria and Korea. Tsarist Russia responded instead by sending reinforcements for its Far Eastern Fleet. In early February 1904, Japan informed the Korean emperor that war was inevitable to 'ensure the survival of the East Asian people'. On 8 February the Japanese navy (commanded by Admiral Togo Heihachiro) began torpedoing the Russian squadron in Port Arthur, and soon afterwards the Japanese army landed in Korea, crossed the Yalu River and besieged Port Arthur. Early in the engagements, Togo's fleet badly damaged Russia's two heaviest battleships and a large cruiser, and in April 1904, the Russian flagship *Petropavlovsk* sank and Russia's most effective naval strategist, Admiral Stepan Makarov, perished with his ship. Admiral Wilhelm Vitgeft, appointed as Makarov's successor, attempted to break out of the siege of Port Arthur on 10 August 1904, and Togo engaged his fleet in direct fire at the Battle of the Yellow Sea. After several hours of heavy bombardments on both sides, one of Togo's battleships hit the bridge of Vitgeft's flagship that evening, and he was killed instantly. Although the Russian fleet was in disarray, Togo chose not to expend further firepower as the Russians retreated back into Port Arthur.

With its Far Eastern Fleet rendered ineffective, Russia sent for its vaunted Baltic Fleet. Meanwhile a brutal land war continued in Manchuria, with Japan gaining numerous hard-fought victories especially in the Battle of Mukden in February–March 1905, at the end of which General Aleksey Kuropatkin's Manchurian Army was forced to retreat from Manchuria. Russia lost 90,000 men during this battle (fought around the city then known as Mukden, its Manchu name, but now called Shenyang in Mandarin) while Japan suffered 75,000 casualties. Although a clear victory for Japan, this battle of attrition was not decisive enough to end the war.

The Battle of Tsushima Strait involving the Baltic Fleet, however, was to be decisive. The Russian Second Pacific Squadron (the renamed Baltic Fleet) sailed 18,000 nautical miles around the Cape of Good Hope, and attempted to pass through the Tsushima Strait at night. Although his fleet was much smaller, Admiral Togo was well-prepared, and engaged the Russian fleet in battle on 27–28 May 1905, annihilating all eight of the Russian battleships, and most of their smaller vessels, only three of which managed to escape to Vladivostok. Russia lost 5,000 men in the Battle of Tsushima, while Japan suffered just 116 casualties and, after the battle, the Japanese army conquered the entire chain of the Sakhalin Islands.

Tsar Nicholas II could conceivably have prolonged the war by sending further troop reinforcements. But the war was unpopular in Russia—a classic case of imperial overstretch that exhausted an empire—resulting in the aborted 1905 Revolution, which began with Bloody Sunday (the killing on 22 January 1905 by Tsarist troops of over a thousand demonstrators as they approached the centre of St Petersburg and the Winter Palace). By February 1905, the Tsar had agreed to the creation of a Duma (parliament) with limited consultative powers, but this only ignited even more unrest when news of its small electorate and limited powers emerged. Beset by the ongoing revolution (including peasant uprisings in May–June 1905), and with his army and navy demoralized by debilitating defeats at the hands of the Japanese, Nicholas II sued for peace.

US President Theodore Roosevelt offered to negotiate peace terms, with the two sides meeting at Portsmouth (New Hampshire) in September 1905. Although Roosevelt won a Nobel Peace Prize for his efforts, his interventions (after initial courting of the Japanese side) were clearly aimed at leavening the pain for Russia, and the Russian negotiator, Sergei Witte, gained enough prestige to become the prime minister of Russia the following month. Roosevelt ensured that Russia would need to pay no reparations to Japan, and that only the southern half of Sakhalin Island would remain in Japanese hands. These terms were received with shock in Japan—resulting in riots across many cities, as the perception grew that Japan had again been deprived of its battlefield gains.

The Treaty of Portsmouth also recognized Korea as part of Japan's sphere of influence, while Russia agreed to evacuate Manchuria. These terms would have enormous consequences during the rest of the century. While three great powers (the US, Japan and Russia) negotiated their fates, neither Manchu China nor Korea was represented at Portsmouth. This was despite the fact that the Russo–Japanese War had been fought mainly in Manchu China's territory, and especially over the ancient homelands of the Qing dynasty, with Korea widely acknowledged to be the main prize of the war. Post-Portsmouth, Japan took over the Manchurian railways, and Japanese zaibatsu enthusiastically invested in the industrialization of Manchuria, with Mukden consequently toppling Shanghai as the most economically advanced city in China by the 1920s.

And, given a free hand by the other powers, Japan began to tighten its grip on Korea. In November 1905, the Japan–Korea Treaty made Korea a protectorate of Japan (i.e., Korea's foreign relations would be determined completely by Japan), and on 21 December, Ito Hirobumi, the leading genro (elder and privy counsellor) and four-time prime minister of Japan, became Resident General of Korea. While five Korean ministers (including those for foreign affairs and the army) signed the treaty, Emperor Gojong and his prime minister refused to sign. Gojong's letters to several of the great powers, however, went unanswered, indicating scant global support for the ebbing Chosun dynasty. Once Japan became aware of these letters (especially one to the Hague Conference on World Peace in 1907), Gojong was forced to abdicate in favour of his son Sunjong.

The Japan–Korea Treaty of July 1907 then turned over the internal administration to Japan, with secret protocols providing that all high-ranking officials in the Korean government must be Japanese, including the leadership of the army, and most of the top judicial and policing posts. Resident General Ito Hirobumi resisted the full annexation of Korea, but was overruled by the cabinet (then under the control of his rival, Yamagata Aritomo, the father of Japanese militarism) and forced to resign in June 1909. Ironically, Ito was assassinated in Harbin in October 1909 by a Korean nationalist who believed in the unity of the three great powers of East Asia (Japan, China, Korea) to effectively combat European colonialism: by assassinating Ito, however, he probably achieved the exact opposite of his aim, empowering Aritomo's militarist faction in Japan.

Within a year of taking full control of Korea, the Japanese abolished slavery, codified civil law, separated the royal household from affairs of state, outlawed all discrimination against commoners, abolished the Confucian system of national exams, separated the judiciary from the executive, instituted an independent court system, legalized the remarriage of widows, and instituted a new tax system based on payments in cash rather than kind. Vital reforms that had been neglected during centuries of dynastic rule were accomplished virtually overnight by the Japanese, who also undertook a cadastral survey of all landholdings, accounting for the ownership of every plot of land in Korea. (In England, the Norman invaders had done the same things after their conquest in 1066.) The survey took nine years to complete, but at the end of it, the Japanese introduced a significant programme of land reform that gave landlords ownership rights over the land (implying also the right to alienate and sell it); this had the benefit of creating a clear system of property rights, and the rudiments of a functioning market economy in rural Korea for the first time. But it also dispossessed the peasants of their traditional rights to live on the land they cultivated—turning them from serfs into tenants, with the potential menace of being driven from the land if they were unable to meet rental payments. Over time, Korean peasants' living standards clearly worsened, and they were increasingly driven towards seeking new jobs in the cities.

In Taiwan, the island that Japan had won as a prize for its victory in the 1895 Sino–Japanese War, an incipient agricultural revolution was underway.

Like the Normans in England, the Japanese began with a major cadastral survey of Taiwan's land, followed by a land reform initiative (similar to that undertaken in Meiji Japan) that transferred ownership from a class of absentee landlords to those landowners and cultivators who actually tilled the land. This newly empowered class immediately became the most loyal supporters of the Japanese regime. The Japanese invested heavily in irrigation, created farmer cooperatives, landlord-tenant associations to disseminate improved methods of cultivation, and vastly increased the use of fertilizers and better quality seeds (similar to the Green Revolution that was to occur in other parts of Asia only fifty-five to sixty years later). The outcome was a stable, fast-growing agricultural sector based on smallholder cultivation of the staple crops (rice and sugar), both of which were soon being produced in sufficient quantities to be exported. Within the first fifteen years of their rule, the Japanese also established an effective government, the first that Taiwan had ever had, with an effective police force that extended down to the village (much more than could be said for British India) and also helped perform important developmental tasks such as the spread of irrigation, drainage, fertilizers and seeds. And education and literacy received high priority in Taiwan under Japanese tutelage.

In the rest of Asia, however, the terms of the Treaty of Portsmouth were irrelevant. The fact of an Asian power inflicting a crushing defeat on a European power—and sinking most of its prestigious naval fleet in the process—was what grabbed the attention of Asian nationalists. In India, China, Vietnam, Turkey and the Dutch East Indies, Japan's victory had an electrifying impact, suggesting the possibility for the first time that Asia's colonized nations might well be able to throw off the European colonial yoke. Partly inspired by Japan, Haji Samanhudi established a batik traders' cooperative in Surakarta (Solo), Java, in 1905, which eventually spawned Sarekat Islam (1912), one of whose founders, H.O.S. Tjokroaminoto, was the mentor of both the secular-nationalist Sukarno and of his future Islamist rivals. Japan's victory spawned a more explicitly political movement in Java (and later the other Dutch Indies), Budi Utomo ('Prime Philosophy'), which was established on 20 May 1908, marked even now as Indonesia's 'Day of National Awakening'. Although a relatively conservative movement initiated by priyayi aristocrats, Budi Utomo gradually expanded its membership to incorporate the middle and working classes. Sitting in Damascus, the young Mustafa Kemal (later Atatürk, or 'Father of the Turks') was elated at this victory of this idyll of Asian modernity, Japan, while his future associate, the novelist Halide Edip went further, naming her newborn son Togo in honour of the victorious Japanese admiral. Sun Yat-sen, the exiled Chinese nationalist, was just as thrilled to hear the news while in London, although a bit embarrassed to be congratulated by port workers on the Suez Canal who mistook him to be Japanese! India was then aflame over Curzon's partition of Bengal, and the fervour of the nationalist uprising against this impending divisive move gained considerable momentum by mid-1905 as the sensational news arrived of an Asian nation's crushing victory over one of the great powers of Europe. Viceroy Curzon well understood that 'the reverberations of that victory have gone like a thunderclap through the whispering galleries of the East'.

'DIVIDE ET IMPERA': CURZON'S GAMBIT TO PARTITION BENGAL

George Nathaniel Curzon was not only reputed to be the finest British scholar-administrator of his generation, but was also descended from impeccable Norman stock. His ancestors had arrived in England with William the Conqueror in 1066, and occupied their aristocratic manor in Derbyshire—named Kedleston Hall—at least since the twelfth century. In keeping with the tradition amongst English aristocrats of the time, he married wealthy American heiresses: Mary Leiter, daughter of the co-founder of Chicago's great department store Marshall Field's (then known as Field & Leiter, and a Chicago institution until it was acquired by Macy's in 2005), and Alabama-born widow Grace Hinds. At both Eton and Oxford (where he was President of the Union), he inspired both admiration and revulsion amongst fellow students and teachers. Throughout his life, Curzon stirred extreme reactions and people were rarely neutral about this epitome of a self-assured imperial aristocrat. A doggerel composed at Balliol College, Oxford, defined him rather well: 'My name is George Nathaniel Curzon, / I am a most superior person...'

Curzon had prepared himself for the job he considered his destiny through extensive travels in Persia and Central Asia that entrenched in him a strong belief that Russia was the greatest threat to the jewel in Britain's imperial crown: 'For as long as we rule India,' he told Prime Minister Balfour, 'we are the greatest power in the world.' He churned out an array of books during those travels, elucidating on his conviction about this alleged Great Game, and he had ample opportunity to begin implementing his ideas as Undersecretary of State for India (1891–92) and for Foreign Affairs (1895–98). Upon his appointment as viceroy, he told Balfour that it would be 'best of all for the cause of progressive civilization if it be clearly understood that... we have not the smallest intention of abandoning our Indian possessions and that it is highly improbable that any such intention will be entertained by our posterity'. Inconveniently for this great votary of empire, there was a massive famine during his first year in office that is estimated to have caused at least 1 million deaths by starvation alone, and between 6 and 9 million deaths in all between 1899 and 1902, earning it a mention amongst 'late-Victorian holocausts'. Curzon cut back rations that he thought were 'dangerously high', arguing that 'any government which by indiscriminate almsgiving weakened the fibre and demoralized the self-reliance of the population, would be guilty of a public crime' (in whose eyes, he did not mention, as Curzon was apparently oblivious to his own culpability for those very crimes).

Famines had become so commonplace in British India during the 130 years since the first great famine of 1770 in Bengal that this humanitarian calamity barely affected Curzon's reputation amongst contemporaries. The previous famine (also killing well over a million) had occurred in 1896–97. Curzon pressed on with the Great Game, sending Francis Younghusband on an expedition to Tibet in December 1903 to try and ferret out Russian spies who were said to be all over Lhasa. Curzon had surmised, from his travels amongst the Buryat Mongols in southern Siberia, that their Buddhist faith would make them natural candidates to become Russia's spies on the rooftop of the world. In the event, Younghusband found no Russians in Gyantse (and no Chinese either), but Lhasa did contain a solitary Buryat scholar of Buddhism, Agvan Dorjiev, who was the intellectual sparring partner and confidant of the thirteenth Dalai Lama and had been sent to the Tsar's court as an ambassador of the Tibetans a few years earlier ('Dorjiev' itself being a Russification of the common Tibeto–Bhutanese surname 'Dorji'). Not the slightest evidence has ever emerged to support Curzon's contention that Dorjiev was a Russian spy; instead, given the historic ties between Mongols (including Buryats) and Tibetans, it was quite natural for a Buryat Buddhist scholar to spend a lifetime seeking knowledge in Tibet. He did, however, convince the Dalai Lama to escape from Lhasa (accompanying Dorjiev on a religious mission to Mongolia) before Younghusband's troops arrived, leaving a regent to confront the intruders in Lhasa.

But Younghusband's military force, commanded by Brigadier General James Macdonald, did meet stiff resistance from a woefully ill-equipped Tibetan army in March 1904 at Chumik Shenko—where 600–700 Tibetans perished, and Macdonald's force suffered no fatalities, as the Tibetans' muskets (and the occasional matchlock rifle) proved no match for the new Maxim machine guns and rapid-fire Gatling guns with which the British forces were equipped. The British force comprised mainly Gurkhas and Pathans accustomed to mountain warfare, plus some Sikhs from the hilly regions of Punjab (today's Himachal Pradesh in India and Murree in Pakistan). Descriptions and photographs of the massacre of the ill-equipped Tibetans at Chumik Shenko became something of a cause célèbre amongst radical elements of the British press. But Younghusband, egged on by Curzon, pressed forward to Gyantse, after first capturing and settling in to enjoy the farmhouse and manor of a Tibetan noble family called Changlo. Their idyll was disturbed by a Tibetan military detachment, and the renewed fighting resulted in further reinforcements of Gurkha troops from Lebong (in the lower reaches of Darjeeling town), with the augmented force mounting a massive assault on the fortress town of Gyantse between May and July.

At the Gyantse Dzong (fortress) the Tibetans mounted a stout defence, with a considerable artillery barrage, but were eventually overpowered in mid-July 1904 after a gallant battle, including acts of conspicuous bravery by the Gurkhas (and less celebrated gallantry on the part of the vanquished Tibetans). By this time, however, Younghusband and Macdonald were clashing over tactics—the latter much more focused on the need for clear supply lines, and consequent periods of rest to reinforce the base camp in the Chumbi Valley near Sikkim, while Younghusband was impatient to reach Lhasa as quickly as possible. Their differences reflected the growing hostility between their masters: Curzon and the military commander-in-chief in India, Lord Herbert Kitchener (hero of Omdurman and other battles in Sudan, and the earlier Anglo–Boer War).

Despite their lack of modern artillery, the Tibetans harried the rear flank of the British forces with guerrilla fire all the way from Gyantse to Lhasa, but these proved no more than irritants on the path to the Potala Palace, which the British forces reached on 3 August 1904. Camping outside Lhasa, Younghusband was told that the Dalai Lama had left his palace and 'fled' to Urga (today's Ulaanbaatar) in Mongolia, which, too, formally recognized the suzerainty of the Manchus. The Manchu 'amban' (high commissioner) in Tibet, Yu-t'ai, was of Mongol ethnicity himself, but the hostility of the local populace had led him to live on the outskirts of Lhasa. It was Yu-t'ai who agreed to accompany Younghusband's 10,000-strong force through Lhasa to the Potala Palace.

As we saw in Chapter 1, the Mongols and Tibetans had a complex historical relationship—with the Tibetans recognized as spiritual masters, while the Mongols took temporal control, in a mutually respectful relationship; it was when the Mongols were ruling China that Tibet first accepted the suzerainty of the Mongols (and consequently of China). When the Mongol Yuan dynasty was overthrown by the Ming (the last Han Chinese dynasty to rule from Beijing), most of the outlying subordinate states—Mongolia, Tibet, Xinjiang—immediately cut all ties to Beijing, and re-established full independence. But the Mongols and Tibetans retained their long-standing ties.

When the Manchus ousted the Ming, and established another non-Han Chinese dynasty in Beijing (the Qing) with Mongols restored to positions of eminence, second only to the Manchu bannermen, the Tibet–Mongol relationship was reinforced and the Manchus became part of this Mongoloid world.

In 1705, a Mongol called Lhabzang Khan deposed the sixth Dalai Lama (a maverick who rejected the monastic life) and proclaimed himself king of the Tibetans. He was ousted after twelve years by the Dzungar Mongols who began looting monasteries in and around Lhasa, resulting in Manchu intervention. Manchu emperor Kangxi's forces were initially annihilated by the Dzungar Mongols at Lhasa in 1718, resulting in Kangxi sending an even larger army to Tibet in 1720, accompanied this time by the legitimate seventh Dalai Lama, Kelsang Gyatso.

The Dzungars were crushed, and the line of the Dalai Lamas restored, but the Qing took advantage of the turmoil in Tibet to annex the Tibetan regions of Amdo and Kham (which today form the Chinese province of Qinghai) in 1724. The loss of the Kham region was particularly devastating for the Tibetans, as the Kham were known as the fiercest and most effective soldiers. (Indeed, most of the Tibetan soldiers at Chumik Shenko were in fact Kham, although their presence in the military had dwindled in Gyantse and Lhasa.) However, Qing China and Tibet signed a treaty in 1727 delineating the border between them—a treaty that remained in force until 1910. As part of this treaty, the Manchus were permitted to send an amban to Lhasa. The power of the amban ebbed and flowed: initially he was little more than an ambassador, but at other times a powerful Resident with an armed guard of 2,000 men (and occasionally more). Notably, 'amban' itself was a specifically Manchu word, and of the eighty ambans sent to Tibet between 1727 and 1910, just four were Han Chinese (including the last one sent in 1908), while fifteen were Mongols, but the majority (more than three-fourths) were Manchu bannermen.

In accordance with their interpretation of the 1727 treaty, the British had initially sought a treaty with Manchu China on the delineation of the Sikkim–Tibet border. But when this Sino–British treaty was signed in 1893, the Tibetans flatly refused to accept it, emphasizing again the ambiguous nature of the Manchu–Tibetan relationship. While Beijing interpreted its relationship with Tibet, Mongolia, Vietnam and Korea to be a suzerain–vassal arrangement, the 'vassals' operated independently, often treating the Beijing representative as no more than an ambassador, especially during these dying decades of the Manchu dynasty.

In August 1904, the amban advised the Qing court to depose the absent Dalai Lama but Tibetan representative institutions (the Council of Ministers led by the Regent Tri Rinpoche of Ganden, and the Tsongdu or National Assembly) directly negotiated with Younghusband. As the British exerted increasing military pressure—which neither the Tibetan defenders nor the Manchu amban could counter—the Tsongdu and Tri Rinpoche eventually were obliged to agree to British terms on 4 September 1904 (almost precisely a month after Younghusband's arrival in Lhasa). This British–Tibetan Convention of 1904 effectively made Tibet a British protectorate by prohibiting Tibet from maintaining relations with any other foreign power and also recognized the Tibet–Sikkim border, thus securing the two key outcomes that Curzon had enjoined Younghusband to obtain.

Additionally, the exquisitely beautiful Chumbi Valley—where Tibet, Bhutan and India's Sikkim meet at the Nathu-la and Jelep-la passes—was to be ceded to Britain until the payment of an exorbitant indemnity of 7.5 billion rupees, and Britain was granted the right to trade in Yatung (Yadong or Chomo), Gyantse and Gartok. The indemnity was reduced by two-thirds, and Britain held onto the Chumbi Valley for only nine months. However, Younghusband's intrepid Anglo-Sikkimese interpreter David Macdonald became the British trade agent at Yatung (and, after 1921, in Gyantse). The fading Manchu dynasty attempted to act on Amban Yu-t'ai's recommendation, deposing the Dalai Lama and refusing to accept the British–Tibetan Convention. The thirteenth Dalai Lama, Thupten Gyatso, travelled to Beijing from Mongolia in 1906 to negotiate with the Qing court, but refused to kowtow to the Qing emperor, believing that he should be negotiating as an equal. Unhappy with the insulting treatment meted out to him, he returned to Lhasa in 1908.

The Qing sent a 6,000-strong army to Lhasa two years later, forcing the Dalai Lama to escape again, this time to Darjeeling in India, aided by the fluent Tibetan and Nepali speaker David Macdonald, whose family became legends in the district. (One of his grandsons, Chris Macdonald, was the much-loved Junior School Headmaster at St Paul's School in Darjeeling, 1968–78, and another grandson, Tim, until recently ran David's Himalayan Hotel in Kalimpong that has been a key stopping-off point for most expeditions to Everest since the 1920s.) In 1911, the new revolutionary government of China apologized to the Dalai Lama for his mistreatment at the hands of the Manchus, and offered to formally 'reinstate' him; the revolutionaries were being rather presumptuous, because no Han Chinese dynasty had ever exercised suzerainty over Tibet. The Dalai Lama demurred, returned to Lhasa, declared the full independence of Tibet in 1913, and began instituting a series of judicial, penal and educational reforms.

With war looming in Europe, a border demarcation conference was attended in 1914 by representatives of China, Tibet and British India. The resulting Simla Convention of 1914 provided for Chinese secular (but not spiritual) control over 'Inner Tibet' (Qinghai province and the Tibetan parts of Sichuan), while China and Britain agreed to recognize the independence of 'Outer Tibet' under the rule of the Dalai Lama and also to respect the 'territorial integrity' and 'abstain from interference in the administration of Outer Tibet'. While Republican China agreed to these terms, its representatives failed to sign the Simla Convention because they objected to the inclusion of Tawang district (today the northern part of Arunachal Pradesh) in British India. (The Tibetan government in exile claims that 'Inner Tibet' too is part of Tibet, since China did not sign the other part of the Simla Convention, while Communist China insists that Outer Tibet is an integral part of China.) In 1911–12, a similar classification system was also adopted for Mongolia, with Nei Mongol becoming part of Republican China after the latter militarily suppressed the Mongols' attempt to unite the whole of Mongolia under the Bogd Khan (or Bogd Gegen, the eighth 'Jebtsundamba Khutuktu' or leader of the Mongol branch of Tibetan Buddhism who ruled 'Outer' Mongolia until 1924, when it became a Soviet 'peoples' republic').

In September 1904, however, Viceroy Curzon savoured a seemingly unmitigated triumph in Tibet, made all the sweeter as Russia's defeat by Japan over the next half-year effectively ended the Great Game across Central Asia as well. By 1907, ironically, Russia and Britain became formal allies with the signing of the 1907 Anglo–Russian Entente. This formally made Afghanistan a protectorate of Britain (and Russia agreed to forsake any contacts with its emir), endorsed Tibet's status as a British protectorate (although some disputes there remained unresolved), and divided Persia into three zones: a northern zone that was to be the Russian sphere, a southeastern zone that was to be the British sphere, and a neutral zone in the centre of Persia. This was precisely the sort of clarity that Curzon had long sought. But he was to have no role in these negotiations, having departed India with his career in some disarray after his grand bungle over Bengal.

Macaulay's Minute on Education from the mid-1830s had spawned a minuscule (but increasingly influential and articulate) 'class of persons, Indian in blood and colour, but English in taste, in opinions, in morals, and in intellect'. The more anglicized and articulate they became in the English language, however, the greater was the racist loathing that the British colonial elites expressed towards them: as Amitav Ghosh aptly shows in the first two novels of his Ibis Trilogy, the British in India much preferred the bumbling, easily-exploited elites of Bengal they initially encountered (who struggled to communicate in broken English and barely understood the new British laws). The word 'baboo' (usually extended to 'baboon') became the British colonials' preferred pejorative term for the articulate, English-proficient class that Macaulay's education reforms had spawned. Inconveniently, the 'baboo' was not only able to speak to his English counterparts as an equal, he (and increasingly, she) also understood the essence of European political ideology and philosophy, and had begun to ask polite questions about why 'liberty, equality and fraternity' were conspicuous by their absence in Britain's Indian empire.

About his proposal to partition Bengal (which he first mulled in 1901, and developed into a full-blown policy by December 1903), Curzon told the Secretary of State for India, 'The best guarantee of the political advantage of our proposal is its dislike by the Congress party.' Since its establishment in 1885, the Indian National Congress had seen itself as a forum for dialogue between Indians and the British colonial authorities, advancing modest demands for greater representation of Indians in the organs of state. The third president of the Congress was the prominent Muslim lawyer Badruddin Tyabji, who succeeded the Parsi (Zoroastrian) intellectual Dadabhai Naoroji. The next two presidents (for 1889 and 1890, respectively) were the Scotsmen George Yule (a prominent trader, whose brother founded the Calcutta managing agency, Andrew Yule & Company) and William Wedderburn (a judge, whose advocacy of equality of Indians before the law led to him not being appointed to the Bombay High Court). Naoroji and Womesh Bonnerjee (the first president) held the presidency twice each in the first dozen years of the Congress, but the tenth president was an Irishman (Alfred Webb), and there were two Muslim presidents, one other Bengali Hindu (Surendranath Banerjea), one Telugu-speaking Hindu (Panambakkam Anandacharlu) and a third Parsi (Pherozeshah Mehta). It was this very diversity of the Congress that the British Raj found especially subversive and dangerous, as the party was developing a pan-Indian sensibility and national temper that the Raj needed to break.

The strategic ideology of Britain's Indian empire was best captured by the veteran Company servant, Lord Elphinstone (then governor of Bombay presidency) in his 1859 'minute' to the commission investigating the causes of the 1857 War and determining how best to preserve British power in the future: '"Divide et Impera" was the old Roman motto, and it should be ours. I might perhaps hesitate to express my conviction so decidedly if I were not able to show that my views...are entirely in accordance with those of the Duke of Wellington.' In keeping with Elphinstone's dictum, the army was henceforth to also be divided along sectarian lines, with Muslims, Hindus, and Sikhs being segregated into different regiments. Secretary of State Charles Wood affirmed in letters to Viceroy Lord Elgin in March and May 1862: 'We have maintained our power by playing off one part against the other, and we must continue...to prevent all having a common feeling... If all India was to unite against us, how long could we maintain ourselves?' In that spirit, Curzon's home secretary formally floated the Risley Paper on 3 December 1903 proposing that the Bengal Presidency (encompassing 189,000 square miles and about a fourth the total territory of the Raj, with 78.5 million people or twice the population of Britain) be partitioned. In explanatory notes, Sir Herbert Risley was very clear about the reasoning behind his proposal: 'Bengal united is power. Bengal divided, will pull several different ways. That is what the Congress leaders feel: their apprehensions are perfectly correct and they form one of the great merits of the scheme.'

The fledgling Congress party was still controlled by its moderate, constitutionalist wing, which believed in engaging the British and seeking incremental political change. But it was their very use of the language of liberty and democracy that most thoroughly nettled the British colonials. Moderate constitutionalists like Gopal Krishna Gokhale (and indeed Muhammad Ali Jinnah) were to discover throughout the next fifteen years that the British would make them very few concessions, trusting perhaps to Britain's ability to militarily crush those of a more extreme persuasion, while keeping the moderate constitutionalists firmly in check, and certain of the permanent loyalty of their closest allies (the rulers of the myriad 'princely states'). Initially, the easy intermingling of Hindus and Muslims had led the British to believe that there were very few Muslims in Bengal. But the 1881 Census was an eye-opener, showing that Muslims comprised 48.5 per cent of the population of the predominantly Bengali-speaking districts of Bengal, while Hindus comprised 48 per cent, and that Muslims were preponderant in Dhaka, Rajshahi and Chittagong divisions. Bengali Hindus—the first community to adopt English education—had also spread far beyond the Bengali-speaking districts (going to work in Assam, Burma, Bihar and Orissa), thereby further depleting their demographic presence in their linguistic heartland. This presented the opportunity for the British to drive a wedge between Bengali Hindus and Muslims.

The American scholar of South Asia and Islam, Richard Eaton, has surmised that Islam spread across eastern Bengal primarily through 'pirs', charismatic preachers of Sufism, who doubled up as effective clearers of forests and thus helped more people settle the land. Even where land grants were made to Hindu landlords, a majority of their tenants turned out to be Sufi Muslims. Traditionally, religious identity in Bengal was very 'Asian' in its malleability, with Hindus revering pirs, liberal Muslims participating in the Durga and Saraswati puja festivities, King Hussain Shah in the sixteenth century providing protection to the saint Chaitanya (and being praised in turn as an incarnation of Krishna in Vaishnav ballads) while his son Nusrat Shah ordered the Mahabharata translated into Bengali. But the Muslims of succeeding generations were often subject to greater pressure to conform to more orthodox Islam in the nineteenth century, especially with the arrival of Wahhabi/Salafist influences in and from north India.

When the proposal for partition was first published in 1903, there was a united outcry against it across all of Bengal, with the Bengali Muslim elite (including the mouthpiece of educated Muslim opinion, *The Moslem Chronicle*, Dhaka's Nawab Salimullah, and the prominent aristocrat Kazemuddin Ahmed Siddiky who claimed descent from Abu Bakr Siddique, the first caliph of Islam) all expressing their abhorrence towards this planned attack on Bengali unity. Curzon toured eastern Bengal in 1904 to build support for his impending Partition, by extolling to the Muslim aristocracy of Dhaka (especially while staying with Nawab Salimullah) the chance for a restoration of a 'unity they have not enjoyed since the days of the old Musalman viceroys and kings'. Ironically, Salimullah's family themselves were unrelated to the old Muslim aristocracy, and had little to do with the Mughal nawabs: they were descended from a line of Kashmiri traders who had deployed their considerable wealth to acquire a large estate, and were designated as 'nawabs' by the British around 1875. Curzon's visit, however, did prove persuasive, as Nawab Salimullah shed his opposition to partition, created a Muhammadan Union on 16 October 1905 (the day partition came into effect) and eventually founded the Muslim League in December 1906.

When finally enacted in 1905, Curzon's imperial chess move proved to be catastrophic to his career and a major setback to the vision of an eternal British imperium over India. It mobilized India's collective nationalism like nothing had previously, and far more effectively than in 1857. Moderate politicians were outraged, with Surendranath Banerjea (hitherto and subsequently a loyal constitutionalist) leading the initial Swadeshi movement in Bengal—to shun the use of foreign cloth, chemicals, and other manufactures, and replace them with indigenously-produced ('swadeshi') substitutes. Curzon's confrontation with his military commander-in-chief Kitchener was already forcing him into a corner, and was the official reason offered for his resignation: he stood down as viceroy on 18 November 1905, less than five weeks after the implementation of Bengal's partition. But the national uproar his move had caused, and especially the enormous initial success of the Swadeshi and Boycott movements, fatally hurt his reputation: in May 1923, as he awaited with keen anticipation his long-desired call from the king to become prime minister (after the resignation of David Lloyd George upon the humiliating defeat of the British-supported Greeks in 'Asia Minor' or Turkey), Curzon was inexplicably passed over in favour of Stanley Baldwin (who he had described as a 'man of utmost insignificance'). His Bengal bungle finally caught up with this man of destiny.

As with any such attempt at import substitution, swadeshi indigenous products were often shoddy and invariably more expensive than the foreign product. So, implementing the Swadeshi programme became challenging—especially when it became clear that some of those affected by the boycott of foreign products were Muslim artisans (who used British cloth and implements to make their products) and traders. In the first flush of 1905, however, there was a united uproar against the Partition of Bengal, not only in Bengal but all across India. English clothes were burnt in great bonfires, 'national' schools and colleges were established across the land (one of which had Aurobindo Ghose as its principal, and still survives as Jadavpur University in Calcutta) and swadeshi production began across the country—most famously with the Tata Steel works inaugurated in Sakchi (later renamed Jamshedpur) in 1907. The chief commissioner of the (British) Indian Railways, Sir Frederick Upcott, said at the time: 'Do you mean...the Tatas propose to make steel rails to British specifications? Why, I will undertake to eat every pound of steel they succeed in making.' Not only did they succeed in making quality steel ingots by 1912, Tata Steel eventually bought the remnants of British Steel—by then amalgamated with their Dutch counterparts as Corus Steel—in 2006, and Ratan Tata reminded the audience of Dorabji Tata's jibe that Upcott would have suffered a 'severe case of indigestion' had he attempted to fulfil his promise!

Admittedly, Tata Steel was one of the rare examples of success. Most swadeshi products required real acts of patriotism to use. Amongst the exceptions was V. O. Chidambaram Pillai's heroic Swadeshi Steam Navigation Company, which successfully broke the monopoly of its British counterpart; despite the latter's attempts to undercut it with extremely low prices, and even free journeys, patriots still chose to use the swadeshi ships. Similarly, the great chemist Prafulla Chandra Ray's Bengal Chemical Works also gained enduring success, and the cotton mills of Bombay established in that era proved the genesis of India's textile industry. Perhaps the most enduring legacy of the national education movement was the Banaras Hindu University (BHU) established by Madan Mohan Malaviya in 1916 (based on plans developed in 1910–11), which particularly broke the British taboo against introducing engineering education to Indians. Until the creation of BHU, Indians were only allowed to be civil engineers and even such training was available only at a few institutions.

There was little doubt about the fervour of nationalism that spread across

India between 1905 and 1907, led initially by poets like Subramania Bharathi, Dwijendralal Ray, Rajanikanta Sen and especially Rabindranath Tagore (whose song from that era, 'Amar sonar Bangla ami tomay bhalobashi'—'My golden Bengal, I love you'—is still the national anthem of Bangladesh; indeed, when India played Bangladesh in the inaugural match of the 2011 Cricket World Cup, both anthems at the start of the tournament were compositions of this extraordinary polymath). Besides being a poet, though, Tagore was also a landlord, with most of his family's estates in eastern Bengal, where their tenants were predominantly Muslim. This eventually led him to appreciate some of the difficulties with the Swadeshi programme, and by 1907 he became a critic of both its occasional resort to violence and of its sometimes-coercive demands for destruction of foreign products, tools and implements. Tagore argued eloquently in his novel *Ghare Baire* (*The Home and The World*) against the extreme forms of nationalism. But his main critique (and that of subsequent Pakistani and Bangladeshi Muslim scholars) rings hollow: Tagore portrays Muslim traders and artisans as suffering disproportionately from the need to discard British cloth and other products and to use more expensive, lower-quality swadeshi products instead. In reality, the artisans/weavers (many of whom were Muslims) would have benefited enormously from the boycott of British products, as it would have bolstered demand for their products, partly reversing the impact of the deindustrialization of India in the previous century (and especially the collapse in demand for the work of artisans, metalworkers, silk- and cotton-weavers, the majority of whom were Muslims, and would now have benefited).

The nationwide programme of boycotts, tax resistance and destruction of foreign products was led primarily by the 'extremist' trio of 'Lokmanya' Bal Gangadhar Tilak, Lala Lajpat Rai, and Bipin Chandra Pal, although Pal was soon supplanted by the charismatic Aurobindo Ghose in Bengal. Educated at St Paul's School in London (where he was Head Boy), and King's College, Cambridge (where he got a double first in the Classics Tripos), Aurobindo's father had explicitly educated him purely in English with little knowledge of anything Indian. As desired by his father, Aurobindo easily passed the written examinations for the ICS, but intentionally arrived late for the horse-riding exam in order to ensure he wouldn't be selected. Instead, he went to work in the service of the Baroda state of Sayajirao Gaekwad, a relatively independent-minded and enlightened ruler who allowed him considerable intellectual freedom. There, Aurobindo immersed himself in learning Sanskrit and Bengali, and lectured at the local Baroda College (soon becoming its principal). He also established contact with the nationalist leader Lokmanya Tilak (considered the leader of the 'extremist' faction of the Congress party, which was impatient for independence—rather than the incremental, piecemeal gains that the 'moderate' faction led by Gokhale was willing to settle for).

At the 1905 Congress session, Gokhale was able to maintain the semblance of Congress unity by roundly condemning Curzon's regime as 'reactionary'. But Gokhale also succeeded in his main aim of confining Congress' support for the Swadeshi and Boycott movements to Bengal, with the rest of the country providing only moral support. Instead, Gokhale founded the Servants of India Society, aimed at educating his fellow Indians in their civic duties and responsibilities so that they would be capable of ruling themselves. In this, he was similar to José Rizal in the Philippines—in focusing primarily on education as a means to prepare the nation and its citizens for self-rule—while Tilak and Ghose were more akin to Aguinaldo and Bonifacio in their impatience for independence (and their willingness to use extra-constitutional means). In fact, notes from the 1906–07 Congress sessions show that the Tilak–Ghose faction were called Nationalists, and the term 'Extremist' was applied retrospectively by the mainstream (Moderate) faction.

Despite the lukewarm official support of the Congress leadership, both the Swadeshi and Boycott movements caught fire across India with 'boycott' also extending to social ostracism of those still using British products. At the 1906 Congress session (held in Calcutta), Gokhale again managed to fend off the Nationalists by nominating the veteran Dadabhai Naoroji as president, but the grand old man of the party rose to rhetorical heights by calling for 'swaraj' (self-rule, or independence) 'on the lines of the self-governing colonies' (i.e., dominion status like that of Australia, Canada and New Zealand), and passed resolutions in favour of Swadeshi, Boycott and National Education, accepting all the planks of the Nationalist faction. As part of a forty-five-member Muslim delegation to the Calcutta session, Muhammad Ali Jinnah had helped draft Naoroji's presidential address, and was hailed by the poet ('Nightingale of India') Sarojini Naidu as the 'ambassador of Hindu–Muslim unity'.

But that unity was being called into question at that very time by the British stratagem of divide et impera. Subtlety was always the preferred way to achieve British gains, and Curzon's methods had proven to be too ham-handed—creating strife without advancing British aims. The fourth Lord Minto (who succeeded Curzon) was the great-grandson of a previous Governor General of India, and was determined to proceed with greater tact. In August 1906, Minto's private secretary J. Dunlop Smith was contacted by William Archbold, the principal of the Mahomedan Anglo–Oriental (MAO) College, Aligarh, enquiring whether the Viceroy would be willing to receive 'a carefully drawn-up petition' from a delegation of Muslim feudal chiefs and landlords.

Aligarh's MAO College had been established by Sir Syed Ahmed Khan, scion of a family of minor Mughal noblemen who had become a munsif (junior judge) in Delhi, but who had seen the tide of history turn and switched vigorously to the British side in 1857. Sir Syed protected British families in Bijnor (including that of the local British collector, named Shakespeare) against the local nawab who sympathized with the rebels, and became an obsequiously eloquent advocate of Muslim–British cooperation afterwards. Sir Syed having died in 1898, the delegation to Minto was to be led by the Aga Khan (Sir Sultan Mohamed Shah), leader of the Ismaili Shia sect worldwide. He averred in a note to Dunlop Smith on 13 September: 'I have also asked [my colleagues] not to move in any matter before first finding out if the step to be taken has the full approval of the government privately.' The draft address was finalized three days later, approved on the 18th and formally presented to the Viceroy on 1 October 1906. After a loyal reference to 'the incalculable benefits conferred by British rule', the memorandum focused primarily on the nub of the delegation's demand: to create separate electorates for Muslims, a guaranteed percentage of jobs and promotion in the services without competitive examinations.

Minto responded effusively to the memorandum, expressing his 'appreciation of the just aims of the followers of Islam and their determination to share in the political history of our empire'. He assured them that British-style democracy was not about to descend on them, and that Muslim representation would be decided separately in accordance with their wishes. Dunlop Smith could not contain his exultant glee at the outcome in a note to his master's wife: '...a very, very big thing has happened today. A work of statesmanship that will affect India and Indian history for many a long year. It is nothing less than the pulling back of sixty-two millions of people from joining the ranks of the seditious opposition.' The only major dissenting Muslim voice was that of the thirty-year-old Jinnah, who continued to assert that the Congress was the only 'true political voice in the country', and wrote a scathing letter to a Bombay newspaper questioning the legitimacy of those who had presented the address to Minto on behalf of the Muslims of Bombay. The Aga Khan lamented that Jinnah remained their 'doughtiest opponent' with his assertion that 'our principle of separate electorates was dividing the nation against itself'. Nonetheless, reinforced by the explicit endorsement of Viceroy Minto, the Muslim League came into being as a political party on 30 December 1906 with the goal of achieving separate electorates for Muslims and extra representation (or reservation of seats in government and legislatures) to counter their economic weakness.

Like Muslim communities elsewhere in Asia, there was a clear dividing line between the Bengali-speaking mass and the aristocratic Muslim elite (who tended to trace their lineage either to Arab tribes—notably the Quraysh that the Prophet Muhammad belonged to, with his descendants known as Sayyids—or to Persia, Central Asia and Turkey, and so spoke Urdu or Farsi rather than Bengali). But by creating a province called Eastern Bengal and Assam with 31 million people (of whom 18 million were Muslims, 12 million Hindus), the British hoped to create a new, united and assertive Muslim leadership in that province. Sir Joseph Bampfylde Fuller, the new Lieutenant Governor of the province, began implementing the plan vigorously, encouraging Muslims to be aggressive in taking the lead in their province, and openly building an alliance between the Muslims and his administration in support of partition. In the colourful language of one interview, Fuller said 'of my two wives, the Mohammedan one is my favourite', as he cracked down hard on the agitation against partition. He sought to cancel the affiliation of two schools in Sirajganj where the teachers and pupils were said to be in the forefront of the boycott movement, but Viceroy Minto turned down this request: such blunt methods were unbecoming of the subtlety of British colonial manoeuvring, but Minto was quick to reassure loyalist Muslims that it connoted no change in policy, only a pullback of excess.

Swaraj had first been articulated as the goal for India's freedom fighters in 1897 by Tilak: he had built a large following in western India by reviving the Ganpathi festival (converting the private worship of Ganesh, the elephant-headed son of Shiva, into a public—'sarvajanik'—event), founded two popular newspapers (*Kesari* in Marathi and *Maratha* in English), and created the Deccan Education Society (DES) in 1880 (starting with the New English School) to teach nationalist ideas to India's young and imbue them with India's own cultural ethos. In 1885, Tilak's DES founded the Fergusson College in Pune where he himself taught Mathematics. It remains one of the pre-eminent colleges in India today, and *Kesari* remains a prominent Marathi newspaper. Tilak used religious festivals as a smokescreen to mobilize nationalist opinion, with his newspapers serving as an additional tool. Given the success of his educational programmes (that predated Gokhale's by two decades and have endured longer), Tilak had substantial organizational skills and a constructive vision of nationalism. In January 1897, Poona was afflicted by an epidemic of bubonic plague that had spread from Bombay, and the British responded by deploying troops in highly intrusive operations across both cities, forcibly entering private homes, arbitrarily destroying property, evacuating large numbers of people, and preventing patients from entering or leaving the afflicted cities. It had still taken five months to bring the epidemic under control, and Tilak had strongly criticized the government for both the initial failure to prevent the epidemic and its subsequently racist and intrusive method of dealing with it. In June 1897, two British officials (Rand and Ayerst) who had led the anti-plague campaign were assassinated by a trio of Chapekar brothers, and Tilak was arrested for incitement (based on an article in *Kesari* that argued that, according to the Bhagavad Gita, no censure applies to one who selflessly kills an oppressor), and sentenced to eighteen months in prison (while the Chapekars were executed). During his trial, Tilak made his famous remark: 'Swaraj is my birthright, and I shall have it.'

By contrast, Gokhale was made a CIE (Commander of the Order of the Indian Empire, one level below knighthood) by the British monarch in the New Year honours list of 1904, and was a member of the Governor General's Council of India, the highest (albeit symbolic) position an Indian could hold in 1905. At the 1907 session of the Congress in Surat (Gujarat), Gokhale attempted to water down the Congress' commitment to swaraj (as expressed the previous year) with a subtle change in language: 'The Indian National Congress has for its ultimate goal the attainment by India of self-government similar to that enjoyed by other members of the British Empire... and it seeks to advance towards this goal by strictly constitutional means....' In this formulation, Congress was not even seeking dominion status as its 'ultimate goal' and was quietly jettisoning the Nationalists' programme of Swaraj, Swadeshi, Boycott and National Education that had been adopted at the 1906 session in Calcutta presided over by Naoroji, with each of the four planks being diluted subtly to make it almost meaningless. Lala Lajpat Rai was the Nationalists' candidate for president of Congress in 1907, but Gokhale's faction refused to entertain the idea, and instead placed the anodyne Dr Rash Behari Ghosh in the chair. The venue, Surat, had been carefully selected to maximize the control of the Gokhale faction, and the delegates did not receive the revised programme until the day before the start of the session, with classic bureaucratic tactics of slight changes to the language that were actually of transformative significance. Most pernicious was a further clause that required strict adherence to this new formulation as a prerequisite for continued membership of the Congress.

It is difficult to escape the conclusion that Gokhale was acting to neuter Congress as a nationalist force, and take it back to being a loyalist debating society that would be acceptable to its British masters. In effect, the entire Nationalist faction led by Tilak, Aurobindo, Lajpat Rai, Bipin Pal, V. O. Chidambaram Pillai and the poet Subramania Bharathi was expelled from Congress at the end of 1907, although they had widespread and enthusiastic support across the nation, and probably had majority support within Congress too. The consequence of this breach was that Congress itself became a virtual irrelevance in India for the next decade, as the initiative passed to the Nationalists (now branded Extremists); with their moorings cut from Congress, they increasingly turned towards revolutionary violence as the only means to achieve their ends. Barindra Ghosh (Aurobindo's younger brother, who had received military training at Baroda) and Jatindra Mukherjee (later known as 'Bagha Jatin') had established the Anushilan Samiti in 1906 as a revolutionary organization to counter the partition of Bengal; this was a successor to the Bengal Revolutionary Society established in 1902 by Pramathanath Mitra, with Swami Vivekananda's brother, Bhupendranath Datta, as one of its earliest members. In 1906, they started a revolutionary newspaper called *Jugantar* (*Patrika*) and a secret society of the same name to advance their revolutionary programme, which gained support through cells established across cities, towns and villages across both parts of Bengal. Observing the spread of militant nationalism across Bengal and the rest of India, the British Director of Criminal Intelligence, Sir David Petrie, had a clear explanation: 'Japan's success (in defeating Russia) inspired India to the realization that it would be only a matter of time when her people would also be able to hold their own as free people in their own country.'

On 30 April 1908, two teenagers, Khudiram Bose and Prafulla Chaki, bombed the carriage of Douglas Kingsford outside the European Club in Muzaffarpur. Kingsford had previously been the chief magistrate in Calcutta, and was notorious for the harshness with which he dealt with nationalists brought to his court, including personal whippings and long sentences for minor infractions. While Bose and Chaki had meticulously watched Kingsford's movements over several days, their planning went awry on the occasion as Kingsford wasn't in his carriage that evening, and two English ladies were killed instead. Khudiram had also been involved in the attempted assassination of Andrew Fraser, the Lieutenant Governor of Bengal, four months earlier: they had derailed a train he was travelling in, but Fraser escaped with minor injuries. The outcomes of these early attempts at revolutionary violence showed their amateurishness, but the youngsters' actions and stirring words further galvanized the youth of India (...'for every Khudiram that dies, thousands of others will arise...' he said at his High Court trial, where he was ably defended free of charge by my grand-uncle, Narendra Basu, who poked several major holes in the prosecution; but Khudiram was executed despite the myriad legal weaknesses that had been exposed).

During the massive manhunt for Khudiram (Chaki having shot himself when cornered at Samastipur train station), the Jugantar 'bomb-factory' in the Ghose residence in Alipore was discovered, as was the Maniktala garden where the group had planned their activities. A total of thirty-nine 'conspirators' were brought to trial, including Tilak (as usual accused of incitement). Barin Ghose, having been born in England (but educated in India, unlike his three elder brothers), was offered the chance to be tried as a British subject, but refused. He and the bomb-maker Ullaskar Dutta were sentenced to death, but their sentences were commuted to life imprisonment—to be served at the Cellular Jail in the Andaman Islands, with extreme forms of torture sadistically administered as well. Bal Gangadhar Tilak was sentenced to exile in Mandalay Jail (Burma) for six years. But Aurobindo Ghose captivated the court with his charisma—and the effective defence of fellow Jugantar member Chittaranjan Das—and was acquitted. To the relief of the British empire, he also went through a spiritual transformation in prison, withdrew from politics, and spent the rest of his life as a sage in Pondicherry (a tiny French colony in the Tamil areas of India's southeastern coast). Although it is widely asserted that the nationalist movement (especially in its 'extremist' and violent incarnations) was exclusively Hindu at this time, there were several Muslims at its forefront too, including Maulana Abul Kalam Azad, who began publishing an Urdu nationalist journal, *Al-Hilal*, in 1908. Maulana Azad was intent on countering Syed Ahmed Khan's contention that Muslims' interests were best served by aligning with (and working on behalf of) the British; instead, Azad's *Hilal* argued that it was in Muslims' interests to join and fully participate in the nationalist movement. Azad had spent several years travelling in Turkey, Egypt and Arabia, and his interlocutors there had expressed surprise that India's Muslims were not at the forefront of the nationalist movement against colonialism. He returned to India determined to begin changing that. By 1914, *Hilal* had become the largest-selling Urdu publication in India, and Azad had attracted enough adverse attention from the British authorities for them to consign him to the first of his many prison terms.

Jugantar was to become much more effective a few years later, but in 1909 the most sensational assassination was committed in London by Madan Lal Dhingra of the Abhinav Bharat Society, led by Vinayak Savarkar. On the steps of the imposing Imperial Institute in London's posh Kensington neighbourhood, Dhingra assassinated Lieutenant Colonel Sir William Curzon Wyllie, ex-ADC to the Secretary of State for India, on the first day of July 1909. The assassination shocked Londoners, as the historian Arthur Herman points out, because 'Indians, especially educated Hindus, were supposed to be the placid and grateful beneficiaries of British rule'. Londoners were used to political murders, but these had until then been committed mainly by 'rowdy Irishmen'. They may have been less surprised had more Londoners chosen to read the *Indian Sociologist*, the journal started by Shyamji Krishna Verma and

Savarkar to 'remind the British people that they can never succeed in being a nation of freedom lovers...so long as they continue to send out members of the dominant classes to exercise despotisms in Britain's name upon the various conquered races that constitute Britain's military empire'.

Madan Lal Dhingra's trial lasted just two days at the Old Bailey, but his words impressed and rattled many an Englishman, not least of them Winston Churchill, then president of the Board of Trade (UK trade minister), who could recite Dhingra's words from memory two decades later, and told a friend that they were 'the finest ever made in the name of patriotism'. Dhingra had said upon being sentenced to death: 'I believe that a nation held down by foreign bayonets is in a perpetual state of war. Since open battle is rendered impossible to a disarmed race, I attacked by surprise. Since guns were denied to me, I drew forth my pistol and fired. Poor in wealth and intellect, a son like myself has nothing else to offer to the mother but his own blood... My only prayer to God is that I may be reborn of the same mother and I may re-die in the same sacred cause till the cause is successful. Vande Mataram!' Churchill's prediction that Dhingra 'would be remembered 2000 years hence, as we remember...Plutarch's heroes' appears not to have been borne out (so far), as his name is barely known by most Indians today (but some 1,895 years remain to test the robustness of that prediction!).

Savarkar himself was arrested near Marseilles in 1910, in a case that provoked an international storm over the right of arrest in a third country. He was accused of plotting a rebellion (over the Morley–Minto Reforms), and given a fifty-year sentence that was to involve hard labour at the Cellular Jail in the Andaman Islands.

Gokhale and his faction (including Pherozeshah Mehta and the redoubtable Surendranath Banerjea, initial leader of the Swadeshi movement who had broken with the Nationalists on the question of violence) had captured Congress at the end of 1907, and taken it back into constitutionalism (not seeking dominion status even as the 'ultimate goal') in the hope that Morley would deliver on his promise of substantive political reform—first made in August 1906. The Morley–Minto Reforms of 1909 proved a bitter disappointment. In the Central Legislative Council, there would still be an overwhelming majority of non-elected officials. While the provincial legislative councils would have a slight 'non-official' majority, the non-officials would include those nominated by the government. Elected non-official members were not only a minority, they would not be elected by a single electorate, but by separate ones for Muslims, Europeans, Sikhs, Graduates, etc. And the electorate itself was a narrow one—very far from universal suffrage—defined only as higher taxpayers (less than 1 per cent of the population). This was a severely moth-eaten version of diluted democracy akin to what the British offered Hong Kongers some eight decades later.

The most insidious aspect was the institutionalization of the system of separate electorates whereby only Muslims would be eligible to vote for Muslims, thereby solidifying the policy of divide and rule. The great chronicler of Islam and the Indian subcontinent, M. J. Akbar, puts it aptly: 'For nearly a quarter of a century the British had ignored or dismissed every Congress demand. But it took them just three years to institutionalize the guarantee to the Muslims through the principle of separate electorates in the famous Morley–Minto Reforms of 1909. The Muslims had been given critical advantages over Hindus... A Muslim could become a voter if he paid tax on an income of only Rs 3,000 per year while a Hindu had to have an income of Rs 3 lakhs (Rs 300,000). Similarly, in the graduate category, a Muslim needed to be a graduate of only three years' standing, while a Hindu required thirty.' Muslims thus elected would never have any incentive to cooperate with Hindus or other non-Muslims, as their electorate was purely Muslim, an invitation to focus exclusively on the sectional or communal interest of Muslims alone.

In December 1911, the British appeared to 'cave in' to Indian (and especially Bengali) sentiment by rescinding the Partition of Bengal. But this was packaged with the transfer of the capital from Calcutta to New Delhi, as an attempt to appease Muslim vanity. A hundred years later, Calcutta is yet to recover commercially from the consequences of that transfer, which also resulted in a gradual shift of India's financial capital to Bombay, which had been a close competitor until this point but had the disadvantage of not being the political nerve centre; once that handicap was withdrawn, it quickly surpassed Calcutta as a financial hub. In the flush of apparent vindication at the annulment of partition in April 1912, Bengalis failed to recognize that (when combined with separate electorates) the gerrymandered annulment was truly the death knell of a united Bengal.

A decade later, the world was to see Britain's mastery of gerrymandering, when Sinn Fein's Michael Collins was offered a take-it-or-leave-it map of Ireland that contained a carefully-gerrymandered boundary for parts of the old province of Ulster that was carved out to create a solid Protestant majority (which did not exist in Ulster) in the newly-invented territory labelled Northern Ireland. The short-lived province of (western) Bengal (with Bihar and Orissa) created in 1905 had a population of 54 million (9 million Muslims, 42 million Hindus) and an area of 141,580 square miles. It had a slight majority of non-Bengalis in theory, with Biharis and Oriya-speakers together slightly outnumbering the pure Bengali speakers. But this was a red herring. In reality, there is a linguistic continuum amongst all the languages of Eastern India:

Bengali, Oriya and Assamese are mutually intelligible, as is Maithili (the main language of northern Bihar, and southern Nepal), which used the same script (Mithilakshar) as Bengali and Assamese until 1947.

In the two parts of the Bengal created in 1905 (after removing five small 'Hindi-speaking' states, and adding a few Oriya-speaking ones), there were an aggregate of 54 million Hindus and 27 million Muslims. But in 1912, the British were able to create a new 'Bengal' that had a slight Muslim majority, which was bound to grow over time given the Hindu Bengalis' propensity to migrate wherever job opportunities arose across the whole of India and Burma. The British were able to gerrymander this Muslim majority in Bengal by removing Assam, Bihar and Orissa from the 'reunited' Bengal. There may have been a small argument for leaving out Orissa on the grounds that Oriya used a different script even if the language was mutually intelligible with Bengali. But no similar argument existed for Assam: while the historical Ahom kingdom (of Tai people who had arrived from Yunnan) had ruled Assam (and some northern parts of the rest of Bengal), the Ahom (never more than a tenth of Assam's population) adopted Assamese as their lingua franca too, a dialect that was akin to the neighbouring dialects of Jalpaiguri, Cooch Behar, Sylhet, Mymensingh and Chittagong. Had Assam or the Maithili-speaking parts of 'Bihar and Chhota Nagpur' (as the sub-province was called)—or even just the latter's urban centres—stayed within Bengal, there would still have been an overwhelming Hindu majority in the Bengal Presidency (as there always had been). British India was not administered along linguistic lines: the other two presidencies—Bombay and Madras—had much more linguistic diversity than did the pre-1905 Bengal Presidency. The other 'presidencies' (as large provinces in British India were called) were not sought to be partitioned, just Bengal was, because the obstreperous Bengalis were seen as the greatest threat to the endurance of the British empire. As others became more of a threat, more partitions and gerrymandering would ensue. But the gerrymandering of Bengal in 1912, which occurred with little more than a murmur of dissent from the Bengalis, was one of the masterstrokes of imperial divide and rule. It ensured that Bengali—then the fifth-most-widely spoken language in the world (now seventh)—would have its speakers divided by religion, and the largest linguistic community of India would forever be partitioned in two in 1947.

SUN YAT-SEN AND THE FRAGILE EMERGENCE OF A REPUBLICAN CHINA

Violent resistance was all the rage in China too in the first decade of the twentieth century, albeit with equal lack of success in the initial stages, and much ineptitude. The period of five years before the Boxer Rebellion, and the decade after it, were marked by innumerable attempts at the violent overthrow of the Manchu Qing dynasty as the clarion call of Han Chinese solidarity against this foreign dynasty steadily gained a greater voice. Of the 653 insurrections—all fairly small, and most in and around Beijing, with a few more serious ones elsewhere—that are estimated to have occurred between 1895 and 1911, ten were led or planned by the exiled leader of Chinese republicanism, Dr Sun Yat-sen.

Born to poor parents in Guangdong, the Cantonese-speaking southern province that was to remain a hotbed of rebellion and politico-economic experimentation throughout the twentieth century, Sun Yat-sen joined his brother in Hawaii as a teenager and became fluent in English—a vital resource in his drive to raise international funds for his republican cause from amongst the Overseas Chinese.

Sun went to Hong Kong to train as a doctor, becoming one of only two students to graduate from his twelve-person class at the Hong Kong College of Medicine. In Hong Kong, he also joined a revolutionary circle that was seeking to transform and modernize China, and only turned to the revolutionary overthrow of the Qing after his attempt to present a reformist petition to the Qing grandee Li Hongzhang in 1894 failed. During the first of the uprisings he had planned (in Guangzhou in 1895), Dr Sun gained wide acclaim after his arrest by the Qing legation in faraway London. Dr Sun's detention at the London legation became a cause célèbre there, and contributed greatly to his fame within China as a revolutionary.

In London, he also converted to Christianity before going into exile in Japan (with occasional forays to Europe, the US and Southeast Asia). But the main weakness of his Revolutionary Alliance or United League (Tongmenghui) was that it was based—like its leader—not in China itself but in Japan, where Japanese expansionists had played a vital role in helping to set it up. At the time of the Revolutionary Alliance's establishment (1905), this was much less of a handicap than it appears. Japan was widely accepted then, in the aftermath of its success in the Russo–Japanese War and the 1895 war with China, as the leader of Asia's resurgence. (Recall from Chapter 1 that the Guangxu emperor had sought Japanese prime minister Ito Hirobumi's counsel while implementing the Hundred Days Reform drive.) While Sun's slogans of democratic republicanism, the end of 'Tatar barbarian' rule, revitalization of the nation and equalizing land rights found considerable support overseas, they made only a modest dent back in China. All ten of his planned uprisings failed (four of them in 1907 alone), although one (at the Friendship Pass border between Vietnam and Guangxi) required a whole week of fighting before it was put down. In 1906, Sun spread the Tongmenghui's wings into

Nanyang (Malaya and Southeast Asia), establishing a subsidiary headquarters in Singapore. By 1908, the repeated failures of his uprisings led to a whispering campaign against Dr Sun in Tokyo, with specific allegations that he was profiteering from the Tongmenghui's activities in Nanyang. Although he was able to fend off this challenge, the pressure forced Sun to move the Singapore office to Penang in 1910, where he established the *Kwong Wah Yit Poh* newspaper, which remains Penang's leading Chinese newspaper to this day.

Other Japan-returned revolutionaries who were less impressed with Dr Sun had set up a rival Restoration Society based primarily in the entrepreneurial province of Zhejiang. Of these, perhaps the most famous was China's first modern feminist revolutionary, Qiu Jin, who swiftly became director of a modern girls' school, and then attempted to foment an uprising in July 1907. One of her cousins decided to take the gun into his own hands when he had a chance, fatally wounding the Manchu provincial governor two weeks ahead of Qiu Jin's schedule. Although some students managed to raid the local armoury, they were easily overpowered in a four-hour battle with imperial troop reinforcements, and Qiu Jin and her accomplices suffered a fate similar to Khudiram's: execution. But a posthumously published collection of her poems helped make Qiu Jin China's first revolutionary heroine.

Meanwhile, in the Forbidden City, a chastened Dowager Empress Cixi had responded to the debacle of the Boxer Rebellion with a tentative embrace of political reform, and an uncharacteristic openness: meeting commoners, gentry and even the children of the foreign legation within the palace premises. The veterans Zhang Zhidong and Yuan Shikai were allowed to expand their New Armies—although they were thus undermining the Manchu system of control—and Zhang was instrumental in creating the New Policies, especially education reform. Cixi's key Manchu confidant, Ronglu, died in 1903 and the Dowager Empress appointed Yuan Shikai as his successor to the vital position of viceroy of Zhili (the 'directly ruled' area immediately north of Beijing, and including Shandong and Henan provinces) that had hitherto been reserved for Manchu loyalists. Notably, like the other commanders of the 'new armies' like Zhang and Li Hongzhang, Yuan too had stood aloof from the palace during the Boxer Rebellion but was now being entrusted with a position that made him a potential military threat to the regime. In retrospect, this was probably the ageing but still shrewd Dowager Empress' attempt to appease the surge of anti-Manchu xenophobia that was sweeping China at the time. Influenced by Zhang Zhidong, large numbers of Chinese students were pouring into Japan to study, and demanding faster modernization upon their return.

Modern schools were established across the country, with more than

120,000 set up during the decade, with girls' schools accounting for nearly a tenth of the total. The traditional civil service examination system was modified substantially; but most students skipped the difficult modern content, and still focused on the traditional preparation for the old examination, so it was abandoned entirely in 1906. One important consequence of the educational reforms was that literacy rates had already risen to at least 30 per cent (and perhaps as high as 45 per cent) amongst males by the late Qing, and between 2 and 10 per cent amongst females. Even the low figure for males and females would put average literacy rates across the population in late Qing China well above the literacy rate in India at the end of British rule (an abysmal 14 per cent in 1947). Chambers of Commerce were also allowed to come into being, serving as an important lobby for a more business-friendly policy framework, and helping to incubate new industrial, mining and agro-processing enterprises.

After a delegation returned from a foreign tour to investigate constitutional practices in the West, the palace (Cixi) embraced their advice to create a constitution and dilute 'anti-Han' policies. The ban on intermarriage between Manchus and Han Chinese was lifted, and foot-binding was tentatively deprecated. Han Chinese were also allowed to migrate to the Manchu homelands in the northeast—a portentous step that was likely to demographically overwhelm the Manchu, and actually proved most beneficial to the Japanese corporations moving into that area. Provincial assemblies were created in every province by 1908, albeit with a very limited franchise estimated at about 0.42 per cent of the population, or essentially the educated gentry, but very similar to the electorate allowed by the British in India the following year (although the Qing assemblies were more democratic, since they had no non-elected official members)! As for the convening of a national parliament, the Manchus in China promised one by 1917; again, they were more forthcoming than the British in India (where the Morley–Minto Reforms made no mention of any timeline for the creation of a parliament), but the nine-year wait was already seen as too long by the restive gentry elite.

The neutered Guangxu emperor died on 14 October 1908. Although the Dowager Empress Cixi had numerous ailments by this point, she immediately took steps to arrange the succession of her preferred choice—Puyi, not yet three years old, who was the son of Ronglu's daughter. Puyi was given the imperial title Xuantong, with his father Zaifeng (or Prince Chun, a half-brother of Guangxu) serving as regent. Having swiftly put these key arrangements in place, Cixi died the following day, ending her extraordinary forty-seven-year reign as one of the most powerful women in China's long history, and the undisputed power behind the throne throughout that period. Although she had originally entered the royal household as a concubine, Cixi had mastered the art of palace power politics better than any of her contemporaries. And apart from the major error of judgement at the time of the Boxer Rebellion, she had steered the ship of state very ably from a Manchu standpoint despite being dealt an exceptionally weak hand at a time of growing foreign control over China.

In the period since 1905, one foreign power had somewhat unobtrusively expanded its presence in the old Manchu heartland. In accordance with the Treaty of Portsmouth, Japan had been given a free hand in southern Manchuria and had inherited the Russian lease on the Liaodong Peninsula, including the vital port of Dalian, which Japan developed into the primary outlet for China's exports of soya beans. Also within Dalian municipality stood the Russian-developed Port Arthur, which the Japanese modernized further in order to use it as the base for the export of southern Manchuria's rapidly expanding output of minerals (including coal and forest products) and manufactures. Japanese investors helped build the 700-mile-long South Manchurian Railway (SMR), with rolling stock imported mainly from the United States, and also energetically built tunnels and highways, parks, libraries, hospitals, schools and all the paraphernalia of modernity, quickly making the region a showpiece of development (in stark contrast to the northern part of Manchuria that remained a Russian sphere of influence). As Japanese capital and enterprise rapidly developed the region, Han Chinese migrated to the Manchu heartland in droves—taking advantage of the lifting of restrictions on settling there—and the population in the region tripled in six years to over 15 million. By 1913, Japan had a much bigger presence in China than Britain or any of the European powers in terms of the amount of trade and size of the resident population, besides a growing 'informal empire' of influence across China, starting with Sun Yat-sen, and the legions of Japan-trained former students who were at the vanguard of China's modernization. Those student returnees from Japan had helped fuel the growth of Sun's Revolutionary Alliance, the membership of which had grown from 400 at the outset to more than 10,000 by 1911.

Prince Chun had none of Cixi's political finesse and craftiness. Soon after taking charge as regent, he acted on his long-standing animosity towards Yuan Shikai, and had him removed as viceroy of Zhili. The court then displayed its utter disconnectedness from reality by creating a new cabinet that was dominated almost completely by Manchus and thus came to be known as the 'Clan Cabinet', further fuelling the antipathy of Han Chinese towards the fading Qing dynasty. The New Army movement had already created several regional power centres around the country, institutionalized further by the creation of elected provincial assemblies that consolidated the power of local gentries. Given these fissiparous tendencies, the attempted centralization of Manchu power appeared to go completely against the spirit of constitutionalism that had gained wider currency in China as a result of the success of Japan (a constitutional monarchy) over autocratic Russia, with the latter itself also moving towards constitutionalism after 1905. The most eloquent advocate of constitutional monarchy was the intellectually forceful Liang Qichao, a disciple of Kang Youwei, who popularized his ideas through plays and poems. While decrying Cromwell's beheading of the king, Liang believed that China needed a Cromwell-like leader who would bring 'iron discipline' to bear on the difficult tasks of modernization.

Leave alone a dictator like Cromwell, the Qing court had no equivalent of Ito Hirobumi to lead the modernization drive, and so it faced challenges even with alterations to its system of administrative communication. The biggest conundrum was fiscal: with the customs revenue almost completely earmarked for payments of the Boxer indemnity from 1901, expenditures far exceeded available revenues and Qing China ran persistently large fiscal deficits during its final decade. The lijin (or likin) levy, a transit tax on interprovincial trade (of between 0.4 per cent and 2 per cent of the value of goods in transit) was one alternative to the customs duty that was first introduced during the Taiping Rebellion, and remained in place until 1931. Although resented by foreign merchants, it was a vital source of revenue, but growing portions of it were held back by the provinces rather than sent up to the central government. In fact, this was a generalized problem with the attempted modernization of the entire revenue-generating structure: the provinces were expected to supply revenues and collect statistics for the central ministries, but were no longer seen as subordinate to them. Tax rates were set separately by the central and provincial authorities without coordination, so the inchoate system of budgeting crawled inexorably towards fiscal weakness and disaster.

In May 1911, the Qing court responded to these fiscal pressures by seeking to nationalize a number of privately financed railway projects—which had made much slower progress than the foreign-funded ones—in order to sell them on to foreign buyers, and so help defray the costs of paying the Boxer indemnity. When it became clear that some of the nationalized projects were actually going to be sold to a consortium of foreign banks (including the predecessors of HSBC, Deutsche Bank, Citibank, J. P. Morgan and a part of what became Lehman Brothers), a 'railway protection movement' arose, especially in Sichuan and Hubei, where investors in the rail projects were especially aggrieved at being compensated (for nationalization) in the form of bonds rather than silver. New Army troops especially from Wuhan were diverted to deal with the railway protesters, thus weakening the military position of the regime, particularly in Hubei province.

Ultimately, the spark that set off the Xinhai Revolution, which ended the Manchus' two-and-a-half-century-old reign over China, was an accidental explosion that occurred in Hankou, part of the Wuhan tri-city area, on 9 October 1911. Wuhan was a hotbed of revolutionary activity, as many returnees from Japan (some affiliated with the Revolutionary Alliance, others not) had established revolutionary cells in Hankou and the neighbouring city of Wuchang. Those two cities—and Hanyang, the third city in the Wuhan area—had large agglomerations of New Army troops, as well as Qing officials, boatmen and modern schools, which made them fertile recruiting ground for revolutionary activity. Like Tilak in India a decade earlier, these revolutionaries used an elaborate network of literary or fraternal societies as a cover for recruitment into secret societies. By the autumn of 1911, more than a third of the 15,000 New Army troops stationed in the Wuhan tri-city area had joined one or other of these secret societies.

The explosion on 9 October occurred while a group of young revolutionaries were making bombs at their hideout in the Russian Concession area of Hankou. Although being based in a foreign concession area usually provided implicit protection from the Qing police, the size of this explosion brought a police contingent into their hideout, and investigations revealed a great deal about the membership of the secret societies and their links with New Army troops. The three chief plotters were executed early the following morning, making that day ('Double Ten') a historic one in the unfolding story of Chinese nationalism. Those executions, and the discovery of the groups' membership registers and other secret information, forced the revolutionaries into a corner: they realized that they needed to mount an immediate uprising, otherwise they risked many more of their members being executed as more of their secrets were discovered by the authorities.

A Wuchang-based battalion of engineers mutinied that morning, and they soon captured the city's main arsenal. Transport and artillery units joined the rebellion later in the day, and the rebellious troops (joined by three other New Army units) captured Wuchang's main forts by day's end. Unable to muster any significant number of loyal troops, the Manchu Governor General and his Chinese divisional commander fled the city. The following day, the revolutionary cells were able to spark a successful uprising in Hanyang, and troops in Hankou mutinied on 12 October. With the whole of the Wuhan area under their control, the revolutionary forces needed a credible leader to take their uprising forward. They turned to Li Yuanhong, the popular commander of one of the New Army brigades in Hubei, who was both acceptable to the leaders of the provincial assembly and popular amongst his troops for having supported the activists during the railway protection movement. But he was a reluctant revolutionary, having been initially obliged to take the assignment at gunpoint.

The Qing court responded vigorously to the challenge, dispatching the war minister Yinchang to retaliate with force. He duly deployed two divisions of Beiyang Army troops, and swallowed Qing pride to invite Yuan Shikai to take command of the troops he had long commanded. Had he done so, Yuan Shikai could well have saved the Manchu dynasty yet again, but the shrewd Yuan held back from endorsing either side while he watched developments. By 22 October, the New Army mutinied in Shaanxi and Hunan, and massacred Qing loyalist troops and Christians especially in Changsha (capital of Hunan). Province after province now joined the rebels including Jiangxi (where the governor and his family were killed), Shanxi and Yunnan. At the end of October, a consortium of generals sent a 'circular telegram' of twelve demands to the Qing court, which swiftly complied with most of the demands. On 8 November, the members of the Beijing provisional national assembly named Yuan Shikai premier, and three days later the Qing court did the same and 'ordered' him to appoint a cabinet. Yuan Shikai appointed a cabinet filled with his partisans—all but one of them Han Chinese.

Although some (perhaps a majority) of the Xinhai revolutionaries belonged to his Tongmenghui, Sun Yat-sen himself was out of the country, raising funds in the US, when the Wuhan uprising began. He read about it in a Denver newspaper, and chose not to return forthwith to China, proceeding instead to Britain and France to reassure himself that the great powers would not again intervene to save the Qing. He was particularly pleased that Britain agreed not to make any additional loans to the Qing. But in Sun's absence, China appeared in November–December 1911 to be moving in the direction of the constitutional monarchy that the Qing loyalist reformer Kang Youwei had long advocated, rather than the republican constitution that Sun Yat-sen's partisans were passionately committed to achieving. The historian Jonathan Spence points out that Sun's Tongmenghui 'turned out to have a startling degree of mass support, which the alliance's leaders skilfully exploited' to expand their organization; they played a crucial role in nudging three key provinces—Jiangsu (3 November), Sichuan (22 November) and Shandong (12 December)—to declare their independence from Qing control. The fall of the symbolically important city of Nanjing, which had been the Ming capital for some time, and was also the venue of a major Taiping triumph in 1853, boosted Han Chinese morale, and severely undermined that of the Manchus.

As a consequence, Youlan (the mother of the now five-year-old emperor Puyi) overthrew the regent and came to the forefront of the negotiations. She effectively proposed moving to a full constitutional monarchy, with Puyi merely presiding at state functions and audiences while real power was to pass to Premier Yuan Shikai. But this was seen as too little, too late and also reminded too many people of the Dowager Empress Cixi.

When Sun Yat-sen arrived at Shanghai on Christmas Day in 1911, the final task of toppling the tottering Qing dynasty still remained. Within four days, delegates from the sixteen provincial assemblies gathered in Nanjing, and elected Dr Sun Yat-sen the first 'provisional President' of China, acknowledging the vital role of his Tongmenghui in the decade of revolutionary nationalist ferment, and particularly his own visionary leadership throughout that period. On 1 January 1912, China adopted the Western calendar, and Sun Yat-sen formally assumed office as the first president of China. However, Dr Sun recognized that his popularity amongst the assembled delegates was in stark contrast to his utter lack of military strength. Although he was the duly elected president in Nanjing, an emperor still nominally reigned in Beijing and his premier (Yuan Shikai) was militarily much the strongest figure in China. Dr Sun was quick to send Yuan a telegram, saying the presidency 'is actually waiting for you... I hope that you will soon decide to accept this offer.'

In Beijing, the month of January 1912 was marked by a series of assassination attempts, including on Yuan Shikai himself, as well as several Manchu princes and generals. Although most of these attempts narrowly failed, a bomb did kill one of the most intransigent Manchu loyalists—the deputy chief of staff, who had been organizing the Imperial Guard Corps as a final line of defence for the Qing. The assassination attempts were widely perceived to have been the work of the Tongmenghui, which continued its vigorous pursuit of the substance of a republican constitution. At the end of January 1912, forty-four senior commanders of the Beiyang Army sent a telegram to the Qing court calling for the establishment of a republic. The Queen Mother saw the writing on the wall and negotiated a settlement that would allow Puyi and her to remain in the Forbidden City, keep their imperial treasures and receive an annual stipend of $4 million. In exchange, she announced the abdication of China's last emperor, Puyi, on 12 February 1912. Although there would be a few additional twists in the tale with Kang Youwei leading an attempted restoration of Puyi in 1917, and the Japanese making him emperor of Manchukuo in the 1930s, this marked the formal, quiet end to over two millennia of imperial rule over China.

Despite having been duly elected by the provincial assemblies just six weeks earlier, Sun Yat-sen relinquished the presidency the day after the abdication of the last Manchu emperor. On 14 February, after Yuan Shikai had acknowledged that 'a republic is the best political system', Sun urged the National Council (a quasi-parliamentary body that had emerged over the previous three months, mainly at the behest of the Tongmenghui) to formally elect Yuan Shikai as president. Although he came to be much reviled by later generations of China's communists (and other nationalists), Yuan Shikai rose to office by dint of his pioneering role in creating and honing the New Army and his shrewd political moves during the final phase of tottering Qing rule. Sun Yat-sen, meanwhile, devoted himself to first developing and then attempting to implement a visionary blueprint for the development of China's railroad network. In 1913, Republican China's attempt to gain control of some of the outlying regions that had links to the Manchu were quickly rebuffed as the Dalai Lama declared Tibet's independence (abridged to exclude temporal authority over 'Inner Tibet', which later became Qinghai and western Sichuan), and the Bogd Khan did the same for ('Outer') Mongolia, with Republican China successfully using its military to keep 'Inner Mongolia' (Nei Mongol) within its fold.

Chapter 3

THE FIRST EUROPEAN CIVIL WAR AND ITS AFTERMATH
(1914–1925)

The Great War that engulfed Europe in August 1914, lasting more than four years, proved to be a major watershed in the three-century-old story of European dominion over Asia. European elites hark back nostalgically to the 'glorious peace' of 1871–1914—a period of harmony and concord, liberal economics, enhanced trade and free capital flows that led to prosperity across the western hemisphere, albeit interspersed with decadal financial crises. In the century between the end of the Napoleonic Wars and 1914, Europe had seen just one war involving more than two of the Great Powers (the Crimean War of 1853–56, pitting Russia against Britain and France). It was the heyday of European empire, and of the aristocratic way of life (with armies of servants living in basements) that was to disappear in the aftermath of that war—far sooner than the victor's empires.

For the rest of the world, the European Civil War of 1914–18 represented an opportunity to strike back at imperialism. Ultimately, the Europeans failed to resolve their civil war amongst themselves (with one of the major powers, Russia, succumbing to an internal revolution) and America's entry on the side of Britain and France proved the decisive factor in tilting the balance of battle. But America's studiously (and almost dreamily) idealistic president, Woodrow Wilson, entered the war conditionally, with the explicit goal of advancing the 'self-determination of peoples', as the principal one amongst the Fourteen Points that defined his (and so America's) war aims. Britain and France insisted that the phrase 'self-determination' would apply only to the empires of the Central Powers they were fighting—Germany, Austria-Hungary and the multi-ethnic Ottoman empire. But the genie was out of the bottle, and Wilson's idealism fuelled the dreams of colonized peoples all over the world—and especially in Asia. His Secretary of State, Lansing's, misgivings about 'self-determination' proved prescient: 'The phrase is simply loaded with dynamite. It will raise hopes which can never be realized. It will, I fear, cost thousands of lives. In the end it is bound to be discredited, to be called the dream of an idealist who failed to realize the danger until too late…'

The danger was especially real to Britain and France over the subsequent half-century, although those two powers were able to successfully *expand* their empires (especially in Asia and Africa) in the immediate aftermath of the war. Much of the damage caused by Britain's redrawing of West Asia's maps (especially at the behest of its impetuous colonial secretary, Winston Churchill, and the pair of Anglo–French diplomats Mark Sykes and François Georges-Picot) remains a pernicious thorn to peace in today's world. Ultimately, the war of 1914–18 was primarily fought in Europe, although it involved all the world's powers (including Japan, the one non-European power recognized by the others as a new Great Power in the previous decade). There were minor engagements in Africa and the Pacific Islands that had previously been colonized by Germany, and the only significant action in Asia was the seizure by Japan (with modest British–Indian support) of Tsingtao (Qingdao) and other German possessions in Shandong province, after a three-month battle that ended in an eight-day siege in November 1914. The climactic Battle of Gallipoli was a catastrophe for the vaunted British Navy (which had been integral to the notion that 'Britannia rules the waves' since Elizabethan England's defeat of the Spanish Armada in 1588). That British naval defeat prevented significant military action on the Asian side of the Ottoman empire, although minor skirmishes occurred (and one brutally destructive battle in Mesopotamia) as Britain and France sought to foment Arab nationalism as a means of weakening the Ottoman hold over the Arab lands.

With the exception of those few minor battles outside Europe, the war of 1914–18 was primarily a European Civil War. It only qualified for the appellation of a World War because troops from India, Australia, New Zealand and Canada fought on the British side, African troops on the French side, Chinese labour brigades were sent into battle on both sides and, most importantly, Wilson discarded George Washington's parting admonition to avoid 'foreign entanglements'. The US intervention in 1917 did make a decisive difference to both its own destiny and that of the world in the twentieth century. The United States had vigorously industrialized in the period since the end of its Civil War (1861–65), harnessing in particular the use of petroleum as a source of cheap illumination and heating, then as a broader source of electricity, and finally as the fuel for the development of the automobile industry that was beginning to revolutionize transportation. The US's eighteen-month intervention decisively turned the tide of the war, especially after Tsarist Russia ceased to be a factor on the side of the Allied powers with its Revolutions of 1917–23. Although much of the world was indeed involved in the war, the outside powers were intervening in what was primarily a *European* civil war, for dominance over Europe, and thence towards retaining or overturning possession over European empires around the world.

In Europe, the Triple Entente of Britain, France and Russia formed the initial core of the Allied powers, taking on the 'Central Powers' of Germany, the Austro–Hungarian and Ottoman empires. Italy, which was part of the Triple Alliance with Germany and Austria–Hungary before the war, did not join the Central Powers: Italy had been a natural ally of Germany (because of Italy's fear of France), but had a traditionally antagonistic relationship with its neighbour, Austria–Hungary. Italy chose to stay out of the war (claiming that Austria had taken the offensive against the Allies and Serbia, thus violating the terms of the Triple Alliance, which was a defensive treaty), but in 1915 was persuaded by Britain to switch sides and join the Allies via the Treaty of London under which Italy was promised Tyrol, Dalmatia (much of today's Croatia) and Trieste from the Austro–Hungarian empire. Eventually, with the exception of Spain, Switzerland and Sweden, all the other European powers joined one side or the other: Serbia, Belgium, Portugal, Romania and Greece joining the Allies, while Bulgaria joined the Central Powers. The war also marked a crisis of the European state system that had been established with the Treaty of Westphalia in 1648, with concerts of 'great powers' arbitrating the futures of the lesser powers in Europe. At Paris in 1919, the old European imperial powers made their last stand to preserve their empires, but Britain and France grasped too much, thereby planting the seeds for the ultimate demise of their empires, and perpetuating a crisis that was to last from 1914 to 1989. Arguably that crisis is not yet resolved, as the European Union faces an ongoing five-year economic crisis combined with a longer-standing demographic crisis arising from the combination of collapsing fertility rates in Europe and the press of immigration from the fecund but volatile nations of North Africa across the Mediterranean pond, which were once victims of European imperialism.

In Asia, Japan joined the Allies early in the war, while the Arab emirate of Jabal Shammar joined their Ottoman allies amongst the Central Powers. The emirate of Jabal Shammar was led by the al-Rashids, who were traditional enemies of the al-Sauds of the Nejd, and their religious backers, the al-Wahhabs. The al-Sauds had been forced to take refuge with their friendly neighbours, the al-Sabahs of Kuwait (a British protectorate) after the al-Rashids defeated the al-Sauds in 1891 to end the 'Second Saudi State'. During the first decade of the twentieth century, the al-Sauds had regained Riyadh and the neighbouring region from the al-Rashids. The British quickly exploited this opportunity during the Great War, sending in a spy with the unlikely name of William Shakespear to cultivate the al-Sauds. Upon Shakespear's death in 1915, his place was taken by an even more colourful character, Harry St John Philby, who converted to Islam in subsequent decades but became more famous as the father of Kim Philby, the double agent who led British counter-intelligence during the Cold War while spying for the Soviet Union.

But European empire was at its apogee when the (Bosnian) Serb nationalist Gavrilo Princip assassinated the crown prince of the Austro–Hungarian empire in Sarajevo on 28 June 1914 and the subsequent century was one of inexorable decline for Europe, creating the space for Asia in particular to gradually re-emerge as a significant player on the world's stage after a three-century eclipse. As sociologist Daniel Moynihan pointed out, there 'are just eight states on earth which both existed in 1914 and have not had their form of government changed by violence since then'. Moynihan was writing in 1993, and one of those eight (South Africa) had its form of government substantially altered the following year (at least partly through violence over the previous five decades), leaving just seven unaltered states from 1914: the United States, United Kingdom, Sweden, Switzerland, Australia, New Zealand and Canada.

Otto von Bismarck, the Iron Chancellor who united Germany in 1871 after his crushing defeat of France in the Franco–Prussian/German war, had created an elaborate system of alliances that underpinned a 'balance' in Europe that helped preserve peace. The alliance system became less stable with his dismissal by Kaiser Wilhelm II in 1890. But Bismarck also made Germany the most formidable economy in Europe, responding to the Depression of 1873 with a programme of protection for German industry and agriculture (through modest import tariffs) that strengthened Germany's economy. Although a conservative, Bismarck also inaugurated the welfare state with the modern world's first programme of social insurance—including old age pensions, accident insurance, medical care and unemployment insurance. He argued that providing such facilities for the new working class would guard against the appeal of socialism, and his social safety net played a large role in the ascendance of the German economic machine in the 1870–1914 period. His argument was similar to that made by Benjamin Disraeli who, in 1867, persuaded the Tories to support near-universal male suffrage, doubling the electorate, by arguing that a radical was in fact a true conservative, as radical change was sometimes needed to preserve the existing order.

Bismarck had initially kept Germany out of the colonial race, but by 1883–84 he too was caught up in the frenzy of colonialism, and Germany vigorously joined both the 'Scramble for Africa' and the race to scoop up choice ports in China. Germany was late. Much of the world had already been carved up, and this bred resentment in the less perspicacious men who succeeded Bismarck in the chancellery.

As Hobsbawm put it, the 'only war aim' for the two major protagonists, Germany and Britain, was 'total victory'. While British propagandists sought to make it a fight between German 'absolutism' and British 'democracy', the British were in fact absolutists in much of their empire, especially India (where even the fig leaf of limited democracy had been denied in the Morley–Minto Reforms) and the rest of Asia (Burma, Ceylon, Malaya, Hong Kong) and Africa (Kenya, Nigeria, Rhodesia). The vast majority of people in the British empire lived under absolutism, while Germany had more than a semblance of genuine democracy in its European domains. In fact, Germany made anti-imperialism its creed during the war, supporting insurgencies in Ireland and India, and the Bolshevik insurrection against Tsarist Russia and its republican successor state. The Irish–American Moynihan asked himself why the US—as the original anti-imperialist power—chose to side with the British rather than the Germans in 1916–17, especially given that the largest ethnic group in the USA at the time were Germans (about 19 per cent of the population), followed by Irish (13 per cent), and people of English and Scot descent well back in third place (11 per cent). Moynihan says Wilson saw the many 'American supporters of Irish independence...as little better than traitors.... In 1918, his administration prosecuted twenty-nine Indian émigrés for conspiracy to violate the neutrality laws—neutrality, that is, in favour of the Raj—and sent fourteen to prison in the circumstances of traitors.' Having examined the evidence, Moynihan 'reached no more satisfactory conclusion than that Woodrow Wilson, Scot...that he was, believed that Americans were of the "Anglo-Saxon race" and need come to the rescue of their brethren in Britain.' Of course, Wilson had other considerations in mind: the US was seeking to inherit Britain's role as the traditional 'balancing power' in Europe; with Britain and its allies arrayed against Germany and the Central Powers, Wilson would have calculated that the US could maximize its own payoff by aligning with the economically weaker Britain, rather than Germany, which was the more credible rival to the US as the pre-eminent industrial power of the age; 'democracy' was clearly not the real goal of the Allies, but ethnicity played a big role as well.

There were other ironies here: the First Sea Lord of the British Navy at the start of the war was Prince Louis of Battenberg, a cousin of Britain's King George V. The fact that he was born in Austria and had a distinctly German name became highly controversial amid the jingoism of the time, and Louis was obliged to resign his command of the navy and changed his name to Mountbatten. With that quintessentially English-sounding name, his son would rise to the same rank in the navy, after serving as Britain's last viceroy of India, and would also enable the family to regain royal status by arranging for his impoverished nephew, Philip (actually Philippos), to marry the princess who eventually became Britain's Queen Elizabeth II, thus ensuring that Louis Battenberg's great-grandson, Prince Charles, will someday be king. In World War II, both the key US commanders, General Dwight Eisenhower and Admiral Chester Nimitz, were of German descent, but the US had clearly assimilated them better than the older nations of Europe.

THE EMERGING STRATEGIC CENTRALITY OF BIG OIL

Air power had first been deployed during the Balkan Wars of 1912–13, but became a major strategic weapon during the Great War, especially in its final two years. By the second decade of the twentieth century, the automobile was not quite ubiquitous, but had begun to replace the horse-drawn carriage as the main means of transport for the elites of Europe—with resulting changes in road systems. Daimler and Benz began making car engines around the turn of the century, which they licensed to other European manufacturers. Amongst the most successful of the early users of the technology was Peugeot of France. And during the Great War, it was the French who first used automobile technology effectively in war. As the German army poured across the French countryside and reached the outskirts of Paris, the French army commandeered the entire taxi fleet of Paris to rapidly move troop reinforcements to the war front! This made a vital difference to the French resistance to Germany—thwarting the latter's push towards Paris, and enabling the Allied powers (primarily French troops with modest British reinforcements) to defeat Helmuth von Moltke's German army at the Battle of the Marne. Thus thwarted, Germany was forced to fight a two-front war, which the Schlieffen Plan had been explicitly aimed at avoiding. Four years of brutal trench warfare ensued on the western front.

But it was the United States, with a vastly larger potential market, that took the lead in the automobile industry by the end of the first decade of the twentieth century. Ransom E. Olds invented a basic assembly line and started Detroit's car industry with his Oldsmobile (the dominant American car from 1901 to 1904). But it was Henry Ford who truly revolutionized the industry with his Model T, which began to be produced in 1908, with foreign plants being established in 1911 in Britain, Germany and elsewhere, and the first true conveyor belt-based assembly line manufacturing process established in 1913. By the following year, Ford was able to produce a Model T in just ninety-three minutes. Just as the Great War was engulfing Europe, America was beginning to experience its automobile revolution: the Model T was priced at US$850 in 1909, but its demonstrable economies of scale enabled the price to drop to $550 in 1913, and its sales soared from 69,762 in 1911 to 308,162 in 1914 and 501,462 in 1915. The Model T was not only being mass-produced, the growing American middle class increasingly aspired to own a car and, to Henry Ford's great satisfaction, by 1914 an assembly line worker could buy a Model T with just four months' wages. The price fell further to $260 by war's end.

Oil had been the basis of the US industrial revolution following its Civil War. The pioneering uses of 'rock oil' as an alternative source of illumination and heating began in Titusville, Pennsylvania, when George Bissell invented the technique of drilling for oil, and production surged during the American Civil War. In western Pennsylvania alone, oil production soared from 450,000 barrels in 1860 to 3 million barrels in 1862. With the end of the Civil War, hordes of demobilized soldiers poured into the oil exploration business, which boomed over the next decade. But the industry was beset with extreme cycles of overproduction and price collapse helping to stimulate the market's evolution, while ensuring that all refiners and most explorer-producers were unprofitable. After 1870, however, a shrewd oilman called John D. Rockefeller began building his great Standard Oil trust, which was to gradually consolidate the industry.

Rockefeller used a mix of shrewd and sharp business practices to crush or acquire his rivals in the industry, becoming the unassailable monarch of the US oil market by the first decade of the twentieth century. Most of his myriad competitors after 1870 were offered a choice: either participate in a friendly acquisition, with key personnel from the acquired firm being absorbed into the Standard Oil management team, or be subject to a hostile takeover. By the end of the decade (1879), Standard Oil controlled 90 per cent of America's refining capacity and was a highly profitable machine. Gradually, thereafter, Standard Oil began a process of vertical integration, gaining control of the oil exploration and production process as well, especially in Ohio and Indiana, as the oil in Pennsylvania appeared to run out. Initially, the crude oil in the Lima–Indiana fields was 'sour', but Standard Oil soon invented a refining process to reduce its sulphur content. By the mid-1880s, it controlled more than a quarter of the world's kerosene refining capacity, even as new competitors emerged in Russia, Persia, Burma and Sumatra.

Rockefeller was the most successful of the entrepreneur-capitalists who characterized America's Gilded Age during the last quarter of the nineteenth century, but he certainly did not qualify for the appellation of 'robber baron', as his wealth primarily owed to the effective use of a new technology in a highly risky new industry, although some skulduggery was involved in the process of 'combination' he later utilized to create the vertically-integrated trust. The main entity (based at 26 Broadway in New York City) did not directly own all the companies in its stable, but controlled its 'associates' through having the same group of shareholders (with similar-proportioned holdings) in all those companies. By the 1890s, the Standard Oil trust controlled 85 per cent of America's refining capacity and about a quarter of its crude oil production, besides controlling the vast majority of the pipelines and transportation network for oil across the country, and accounting for four-fifth of US exports of kerosene. This level of control made it increasingly unpopular and a major target of the 'trust-busting' that began in the US after 1890. But it was able to avoid trouble until President Theodore Roosevelt adopted a populist platform in his second term, partly in response to the embarrassment caused at a crucial stage of the 1904 election campaign by the revelation that his Republican campaign had received a $100,000 contribution from key executives at Standard Oil.

The Teddy Roosevelt administration filed an anti-trust lawsuit against Standard Oil in 1906, but it wasn't until 1909 (when his chosen successor William Howard Taft, the former colonial administrator of the Philippines, had replaced Roosevelt in the White House) that the suit succeeded. Only in 1911 did the final appeal fail at the Supreme Court, requiring Standard Oil to be dissolved. By this time, the 'Esso' trademark was already ubiquitous around the world, and the company still refined more than 75 per cent of all the crude oil produced in the US, provided more than 90 per cent of the lubricants used by the railroads, marketed more than 80 per cent of all domestic kerosene and accounted for the same proportion of US oil exports. More importantly, the rapidly expanding automobile market was about to unleash a massive new surge in demand for oil, just as the market for kerosene and wax was waning with the spread of electricity as an alternative source of heat and light.

Breaking up this empire appeared a Herculean task, but was accomplished without too much disruption: the holding company, Standard Oil of New Jersey which had close to half the net value of the combine, was initially known as Esso and eventually Exxon, remained the dominant US and global oil company, while Standard Oil of New York (Socony, with 9 per cent of the net value) later became Mobil, merged with Exxon in 1999, and the successor combine remains the largest refiner in the world. Standard Oil of Ohio became Sohio, which became the US arm of BP (formerly British Petroleum) in 1978, and Standard Oil of Indiana became Amoco, which was also acquired by BP in 1998. Other smaller spin-offs included Socal (Standard Oil of California), which later became Chevron, Continental Oil that became Conoco, and Atlantic (which later became part of ARCO, also acquired by BP in 2000). Of the five 'super-majors' that dominate today's global oil market, three are direct descendants of Rockefeller's company, as is the sixth company sometimes included amongst the super-majors (ConocoPhillips).

By the time it was dissolved, Standard Oil already faced considerable competition both within the US from new independents based in Texas, and prominently from new oil producers based primarily in Asia. However, while oil helped fuel an industrial revolution in the US between 1861 and 1915, the new Asian oil producer-exporters saw no such benefit, since Asia was still almost universally under the heel of various European powers. It was those European powers—Russia, the Netherlands and Britain—that cornered all the benefits of the new oil finds.

Oil flares had been common enough in Azerbaijan from ancient times, with the Zoroastrian 'eternal flame' known to have been lighted by oil that gushed from the ground. Traditionally part of Persia (which gave it both a Zoroastrian past and then a Shiite legacy), the majority of Azerbaijan had been incorporated into the Russian empire by early in the nineteenth century. At the start of the 1870s, the Tsarist regime had opened Baku's oil fields to private exploitation, enabling the small-scale, disorganized exploration outfits to blossom into a spate of proper oil-drilling companies and twenty small refineries by 1873.

Ludvig Nobel was the first to recognize and effectively exploit the potential of the oil in and around Baku. The Nobels were a remarkable Swedish family of inventors and entrepreneurs, whose patriarch (Immanuel, the inventor of the underwater mine) had migrated to Russia in 1837, where his invention made him popular with the military establishment. Although his great industrial concern fell upon hard times when the Tsarist regime suddenly turned from domestic to foreign procurement, his son Ludvig had built on its ruins and created a great armaments company. Another son, Alfred, chose to move away from the arbitrariness of Tsarist Russia to Paris where he invented dynamite, and used it to build a huge global enterprise (and bequeathed the prestigious prizes that still bear his name). The eldest brother, Robert, had joined his younger brother Ludvig as an employee after the failure of several of his business ventures, and it was he who fortuitously discovered the potential of Baku's oil refineries. Having been sent to Baku by Ludvig to procure walnut and other wood for a large rifle order, Robert got caught up in Baku's oil frenzy and spent his brother's money on buying a refinery. Ludvig pumped additional funds into modernizing this, and by 1876 began shipping kerosene ('illuminating oil') to St Petersburg. Ludvig soon gained the blessings of the Tsar's brother (who was also the viceroy of the Caucasus), and used his considerable business acumen to build a huge integrated oil business that led to him being dubbed the 'Oil King of Baku'.

In 1878, Ludvig Nobel's company invented the oil tanker, naming the first bulk tanker *Zoroaster* in keeping with Baku's ancient history, and deploying it in the Caspian Sea. Later tankers proved themselves capable of crossing the Atlantic, thus revolutionizing oil transportation. Russian crude production soared from 0.6 million barrels in 1874 to 10.8 million barrels annually in 1884, almost a third of US production at the time. The Nobel company produced half of Russia's kerosene, and successfully forced out US kerosene completely from the Russian market. The main challenge that the Nobel company faced was the relative lack of dynamism in the Russian market— where the peasantry was unlikely to switch to illuminating oil—and the logistics of moving their product from Baku to the rest of the vast country. Part of the transportation problem was nearly solved by a railhead to Batumi (in Georgia on the Black Sea), but this independent Russian venture ran into trouble and had to be rescued by the Rothschilds, who subsequently became key rivals and collaborators of the Nobel company in Russian oil.

The Rothschilds, Nobels and Standard Oil all created subsidiaries in London in the early 1890s and Standard used these to pressure its global rivals into an 'alliance' or merger. Its rivals resisted, with the Rothschilds focusing primarily on finding a new market for their oil in the vast emerging markets of Asia, where Standard already had a presence. The Rothschilds' predicament over how to get their oil from Russia to Asia (through the Suez Canal that the Rothschilds themselves had helped finance) was solved for them by the intrepid Marcus Samuel. The son of a Jewish shell trader in London, Samuel had established himself as one of the first Western traders with Japan, riding the wave of its initial industrialization to sell British machinery, tools and textiles to Japan in exchange for rice, silk and copperware, and subsequently building links with the (mainly Scottish-owned) trading houses of Calcutta, Singapore, Hong Kong and Shanghai. In an audacious and secretive move in 1892, Samuel's tanker *Murex* sailed from Hartlepool in England to Batumi, where it picked up a large cargo of Russian oil, steamed through the Suez Canal and deposited its cargo in Singapore and Bangkok, breaking Standard Oil's monopoly over kerosene supply in Asia. By 1897, Samuel's company— named Shell Transport and Trading in honour of his father's profession—had deployed ten oil tankers to ship oil from Russia to Asia (with each tanker named after a type of seashell), which together moved about 90 per cent of all the oil shipped through the Suez Canal. Standard Oil was literally shell-shocked, and eventually offered Samuel an even better offer than those that many competitors had gladly embraced in the US: a huge payoff, and the opportunity to become a director of Standard Oil. But Samuel turned down the attractive offer, on grounds that he wanted his enterprise to remain British.

In Southeast Asia, Royal Dutch had already established a solid presence, with the first discovery of oil in northeast Sumatra (in the Dutch East Indies) in 1885. Here, too, local practices of using a mineral wax to light torches had first alerted a Dutch tobacco plantation manager called Aeilko Jans Zijlker to the possibility of discovering oil in the area and he threw himself into the business, eventually winning royal backing for his venture, which was publicly listed as Royal Dutch in 1890 (and was nearly five times oversubscribed). Zijlker died suddenly later that year, and was succeeded by an indefatigable trader and businessman called Jean-Baptiste August Kessler, who reorganized the firm and grew it dramatically against great odds—both financial constraints as well as the occasional raiding party by local 'pirates'. Between 1893 and 1897, Royal Dutch's production increased thirtyfold, the company became profitable in 1895, and began to pay large dividends the following year. In 1896, Kessler was joined by a gifted young marketing director called Henri Deterding, who was to play an increasingly important role in the firm over the next four decades. To begin with, Royal Dutch began deploying its own bulk-storage facilities and tankers, and the colonial government banned Samuel's tankers from the ports of the Dutch East Indies. Standard Oil's attentions also turned to Royal Dutch, but its overtures were firmly rebuffed by the Dutch, who also erected protectionist barriers to Standard's progress, especially in the Dutch East Indies.

Meanwhile, Shell had established itself in Malaya (with key oil depots in the Straits Settlements of Singapore and Penang) and made its first oil discoveries in Kutai in eastern Borneo (today's Kalimantan) in 1898 and also began exploring for oil in the British-controlled portion of Borneo, which was then run by the White Rajahs of Sarawak, the Brooke family, who had gained control of Sarawak from the Sultans of Brunei in 1842. The Borneo crude was heavier, so it yielded very little kerosene but it could be used as a fuel, and Samuel became a leading advocate for conversion of ships from coal to fuel oil.

Although Samuel was able to create much excitement about his Borneo oil wells, actual production was disappointing—it would be 1910 before Shell made major discoveries at Miri in Sarawak—and Shell's Borneo refinery faced numerous technical difficulties. Nonetheless, by bruiting his purported success in Borneo, Samuel obtained enhanced shipments of Russian oil on more favourable terms from the Rothschilds, and Shell's oil transportation business continued to boom. However, without faster expansion of its Borneo output, Shell remained vulnerable to Russian supplies and the 1905 revolution there proved a near-death blow to its key source of supply. The Bolsheviks (then a small revolutionary group) were able to capitalize on widening ethnic conflict in the Caucasus region in 1901–04, and Lenin's *Iskra* newspaper helped make Baku the 'revolutionary hotbed on the Caspian'. The leading organizer of the oil workers of Baku and Batumi was the former seminarian and son of a Georgian shoemaker, Joseph Djugashvili (then known as 'Koba', the Turkish word for indomitable, and later known to the world as Stalin).

When Japan defeated Russia in early 1905, the Russian revolution received an additional spur and Koba led his revolutionaries in helping to set the oilfields of Baku ablaze, although the Tsarist regime itself inflamed passions in the region by mobilizing the Tatars, who slaughtered numerous Armenian oilmen. The Nobels and Rothschilds gradually withdrew from the Russian oil business, and supplies from Russia began to diminish.

This coupled with the Panic of 1907 (and the run on US banks that eventually led to the establishment of the Federal Reserve system to regulate banks), obliged Shell to agree to a full merger with Royal Dutch Petroleum in 1907. The combined company would still have Marcus Samuel as chairman and its headquarters in London, although Royal Dutch would own 60 per cent of the combine and Shell 40 per cent. Deterding soothed English nerves by becoming a proper country squire, buying a grand estate in Norfolk. The two companies had already established a joint sales organization in 1903 (called Asiatic Petroleum Company) to combat the competitive pressures from Standard Oil and its near-ubiquitous Esso brand, and the combined company expanded rapidly under Deterding's able management after 1907, expanding from its Asian bases to establish large-scale exploration and production facilities in the US (especially Texas), Venezuela, Mexico (then still in the throes of its own revolution), Russia (where Royal Dutch/Shell bought the Rothschilds' assets in 1912 in exchange for shares in both companies) and Romania. And all the while, it also expanded in its traditional base in Sumatra and Borneo, particularly the British-controlled parts of it in Sarawak and Brunei, where its oil assets grew rapidly with substantial new discoveries.

In Persia, William Knox D'Arcy had struggled for seven years to exploit the oil concession he had received in 1901 from the Qajar Shah Muzaffar al-Din with little success. As D'Arcy began running out of money, and the Qajars were obliged to allow a revolutionary move to constitutional democracy in 1906, he sold a majority stake in his venture to Burmah Oil, a Glasgow-based company that had found oil in Assam in eastern India and in Burma (after it was annexed by the British in 1885), where it also built a refinery. Fortuitously, D'Arcy had also met Admiral John Fisher when he was Second Sea Lord in 1904 and this key naval officer had taken a keen interest in the progress of D'Arcy's ventures thereafter, especially after Fisher became First Sea Lord and the leading advocate for the use of oil in the British Navy's capital ships in order to perpetuate Britain's naval superiority over the rising challenge from Germany. The admiralty had even proffered a loan to D'Arcy, but was thwarted by other bureaucrats. In May 1908, the Scottish owners of Burmah Oil finally ran out of patience with their losses in Persia, and cabled their engineer George Reynolds to wind up operations. Fortunately, the cable took three weeks to reach Reynolds, and it was in that period (on 15 May 1908) that Reynolds struck a massive gusher of oil at Masjid-i-Suleiman (so named because it was near the site of a famous Zoroastrian fire temple). In 1910, Burmah decided to spin off and publicly list the Persian venture as the Anglo–Persian Oil Company (APOC), and the following year APOC built what was then the world's largest refinery at Abadan, an island in the Shatt-al-Arab waterway between Persia and today's Iraq.

When Winston Churchill became First Lord of the Admiralty (navy minister) in 1912, he appointed the recently-retired Admiral Fisher as his key adviser. It didn't take Fisher long to convince Churchill of the centrality of oil to any naval strategy, aided by an early discussion with Shell's Marcus Samuel (who failed to impress Churchill as a person, although his message proved very persuasive). On 17 June 1914—just weeks before the outbreak of hostilities in Europe—Churchill introduced a bill in the House of Commons for the British government to pay £2.2 million to take a 51 per cent stake in APOC. In justifying this extraordinary and near-unprecedented move towards government ownership of a private company, Churchill primarily used a 'Jew-baiting' argument, using the code word 'cosmopolitan' in conjunction with 'monopoly', arguing that Britain needed to counter the global duopoly exercised by Standard Oil and Royal Dutch/Shell. Given Marcus Samuel's act of British patriotism in fending off a highly attractive offer from Standard two decades earlier, this was the unkindest cut of all, as his brother (the MP for Wandsworth) tried to remind the House, to even more Jew-baiting taunts from Churchill. Later Churchill acknowledged that his 'attack on monopolies and trusts' was vital in securing overwhelming passage of the bill. A secret clause—not disclosed in Parliament—also provided for guaranteed supplies of fuel oil on favourable terms to the British Navy for twenty years. APOC (later renamed British Petroleum and BP) would remain wedded to Persia/ Iran for four more decades, with very few other assets elsewhere until the nationalization of the company by Prime Minister Mohammad Mossadegh in 1951. Forced out of Iran, BP would later take its cash hoard to buy Standard Oil of Ohio, then acquire Amoco to reconstitute Esso's subsidiaries from the US Midwest. That cash hoard was built up over a half-century in Persia, during which time APOC (BP) had only had to pay 16–17 per cent of its *reported* profits to the host government, and paid its Iranian local workers a pittance that left them in near-penury.

While Churchill had taken an instant dislike to Marcus Samuel, the

PRASENJIT K. BASU

British Jew who was in fact Lord Mayor of London, at Fisher's behest he also reached out to the Dutchman, Deterding, to whom Churchill took an instant liking. Deterding assured Churchill that Britain would not 'want for oil or tankers in case of war'. From a commercial standpoint, there was no particular reason for Britain to take a majority stake in APOC, except to fly the flag for British interests in Persia and claim that nation as being of strategic importance to the British empire (especially India). However, with control of Anglo–Persian, and a tight relationship with Royal Dutch/Shell, the British Navy plunged headlong into replacing coal with fuel oil in its ships, which helped maintain Britain's naval lead over Germany. In Curzon's words, the Allies 'floated to victory on a wave of oil'.

THE GREAT WAR IN ASIA: SHANDONG, GALLIPOLI, KUT AL-AMARA AND THE 'ARAB REVOLT'

The Anglo–Japanese treaty of 1902 did not require Japan to intervene on the British side once the Great War had begun. But when the Japanese government proposed to join the war on the side of the Allied powers in exchange for having the right to conquer German colonial territories in the Pacific, Britain readily agreed. In the event, some of Germany's Pacific territories were occupied by other powers who got there faster—German Samoa by New Zealand, and German New Guinea by Australia—within weeks of the outbreak of the war. But Japan gained control over the Mariana, Caroline and Marshall islands with very little German resistance. More importantly, Japan turned its attention to relieving Germany's hold over its treaty port of Qingdao and its sphere of influence in Shandong.

Japan's invasion of German interests in Shandong province involved one of the earliest uses of air power in war, with naval aircraft being used to land Japanese troops in Shandong and also conduct the first ever night-time bombing raids. The Kaiser made it clear to his commanders in the area that Qingdao must be stoutly defended as a matter of racial pride—losing it to Japan was simply unacceptable. The British sent a token contingent of 1,000 Welsh soldiers from Tianjin, later reinforced by 500 Sikh soldiers, to support the Japanese. The German commander chose to withdraw his forces from the outer defensive lines and concentrated them all in the innermost line of defence in the hills around Qingdao. Early in the skirmishes, German torpedoes sank two Japanese cruisers, but Japanese forces besieged the fort and city on 31 October 1915, digging parallel lines of trenches as they had done during the siege of Port Arthur during the Russo–Japanese War and steadily moved their trenches forward while continuing to bombard the German positions.

The bombardment continued for seven days, initially with return fire from the Germans but the latter soon ran out of ammunition. On 6 November, Japanese infantry attacked the final line of defences and overwhelmed them. The following morning, the German and Austro–Hungarian forces surrendered. Japan had suffered 236 casualties, the British 12, and the German defenders 199. But 4,700 Germans were taken prisoner by the Japanese, and sent to prisoner-of-war camps in Japan. They were treated well there, and 170 chose to remain in Japan even after the camps were closed after the signing of the Versailles peace treaties in 1919.

Meanwhile in Europe, the war had settled into a long stalemate of relentless, bloody trench warfare. Britain's First Lord of the Admiralty Winston Churchill decided that the vaunted Royal Navy would be deployed to break the stalemate with a grand victory in southern Europe by conquering the Ottoman capital of Constantinople. Churchill's plan envisaged an Anglo–French naval flotilla storming the Dardanelles (the strait separating Europe from Asia and also connecting the Aegean Sea to the small Sea of Marmara immediately to the south of Constantinople), then conquering the Ottoman capital, thereby opening up a direct route to the Black Sea via the Bosporus Straits that run through the city, so improving supply lines to Russia. The result was the eight-month Battle of Gallipoli, pitting the strategic 'vision' of Churchill against the daringly valiant Turkish lieutenant colonel Mustafa Kemal, whose forces doughtily defended their territory and inflicted a crushing defeat on the British Navy, forcing Churchill to resign in disgrace.

Born in the Macedonian town of Salonica (now Thessaloníki in Greece), Mustafa Kemal's upbringing combined the best of the Ottoman empire's cosmopolitan traditions. Although his family were largely of Turkish origin, his father had some Albanian blood (which explains his distinctly European features) while his mother was a Turk of Yoruk (nomadic) stock. Mustafa briefly attended a religious school at his mother's behest, excelled in mathematics at the private, secular school where he had most of his education, and defied his father's injunction to learn a specific trade—instead joining the Salonica Military School in 1893 (when he was twelve). By the time he graduated from the Ottoman Military Academy in 1902, Mustafa had been exposed to the subversive ideas of European thinkers, which had led him and a few comrades to start a clandestine newspaper. Subsequently, he was arrested and spent several weeks in a military prison for being part of a secret cell that studied the works of Voltaire and Tolstoy. The Ottoman realms were then gripped by a renewed conservatism after the Tanzimat reforms of 1839–76 (aiming at emulating the modern institutions of the West, which culminated in an attempted move towards a constitutional monarchy) were largely discarded by Sultan Abdulhamid II.

Although Mustafa's schooling had benefited from the legacy of the Tanzimat era, his brand of youthful inquisitiveness was already considered too radical for the times. He received a further rude awakening on a tour of duty in Damascus, which he found 'all bad' with its people weighed down by the deadening orthodoxy of medieval Islam and illiteracy, in stark contrast to all the cosmopolitan cities he had previously known (including, briefly, Beirut). The contrast helped deepen Mustafa's conviction about the need for quicker Ottoman reforms.

In 1905, the excitement generated by Japan's defeat of Russia led Mustafa to create a secret society called Vatan ('nation', or 'fatherland') committed to restoring the 1876 constitution and advancing sociopolitical reform. Vatan began in Damascus, but Mustafa was able to open branches in key towns like Jaffa, Jerusalem and Beirut while ostensibly travelling there on military duty. By 1906, when he was transferred back to his cosmopolitan home town of Salonica—where Turks, Albanians, Jews, Greeks and Armenians mingled freely—the town had become the locus of the reform-minded Committee of Union and Progress (CUP), and Mustafa happily merged his Vatan organization into it. He was to have some regrets about this in later years, as CUP leader Enver Pasha effectively sidelined him.

But those were heady days in Salonica, which became the centre of the ferment that was spreading across the Ottoman lands. The reformist spirit of rebellion spread rapidly, and protests erupted across more than a dozen cities, demanding a more receptive administration. Anger rose to a crescendo after the rapid loss of Bosnia–Herzegovina, Crete and Bulgaria (the latter going from de facto to actual independence) in the spring of 1908, boiling over into a full-scale rebellion in Salonica. Sultan Abdulhamid II sent troops from the capital to suppress the Salonica rebels, but these troops were themselves soon afflicted by the spirit of the uprising and jointly marched on Constantinople, demanding the abdication of the Sultan. Rather than continue to resist the inevitable, Abdulhamid announced an election and the restoration of the 1876 constitution, setting off a veritable flowering of liberty and democracy. In the election of 1908, the still-incipient CUP won less than a quarter of the seats but this did little to dampen the spirit of exuberance that resulted in a sprouting of free speech and rapidly-widening educational and business opportunities. An attempted counter-revolution by conservative forces in March 1909 was quickly suppressed by an 'Action Army' (of which Mustafa Kemal was one of the key leaders) and Sultan Abdulhamid was obliged to abdicate and go into exile immediately. His brother became caliph, but with virtually no temporal authority, as a constitutional monarchy was proclaimed with the

CUP—or Young Turks—firmly in control, especially after they swept 67 per cent of the seats in the 1912 election.

Despite the Young Turks' spectacular electoral victory, the 1912 cabinet was initially dominated by 'Old Turks', until the coup of January 1913 led by the Three Pashas—Enver Ismail (who became minister of war), Mehmed Talaat (the new interior minister) and Ahmed Djemal (the new navy minister)—who intervened to preclude the old cabinet's imminent concession to the Great Powers' demand to hand Adrianopolis (Edirne) to Bulgaria. While the CUP had been committed to secular nationalism—with the non-Turk minorities like Armenians, Jews, Albanians and Greeks strongly represented—the Three Pashas not only concentrated power in their own hands but also took the movement in a very different direction. They were far more committed to the creation of a pan-Turkish state—which meant they were especially hostile to Russia, which had subjugated most of the Turkic peoples of Central Asia over the past century—and began to pursue a policy of 'relocating' the 'dhimmi' (non-Muslims). Mustafa Kemal and other secularists were sidelined as the Three Pashas took the CUP in this narrowly Turkic direction and Enver's dictatorial triumvirate was closely connected to the Armenian genocide of 1915–16. The Three Pashas' anti-Russian stand also led them naturally to join the Central Powers when the Great War broke out, although many of the Young Turks were strongly inclined towards Britain and France.

Mustafa had returned to a posting in Constantinople in 1912, and so was closer to the centre of the action. But he loathed the narrow-minded Enver Pasha, and chafed at the direction his dictatorial triumvirate were taking the Ottoman empire. Mustafa found a soulmate in the urbane Corinne Lutfu, a multilingual pianist and the young widow of a Turkish officer whose salon in Pera (the European quarter of Constantinople, distinguished from the rest of the city which was known as 'Stamboul') became the centre of much drinking, partying and heady conversation for Mustafa. But, troubled by the direction Enver was taking, Mustafa Kemal was quick to accept an offer to become military attaché in the Ottoman embassy in Bulgaria and these fifteen months in Sofia proved to be another bracing period in his personal evolution. Mustafa marvelled at the fact that Bulgarian Turks ran successful businesses and their wives walked unveiled, no longer restricted by the 'fanaticism and intellectual slavery' he perceived everywhere in the Ottoman homelands.

Recalled to the capital once Enver Pasha had signed on with the Central Powers in August 1914, the young Kemal was assigned command of a key mobile division in the defence of the Gallipoli Peninsula in 1915. The initial attempt by the British Navy to storm the Dardanelles Strait had been thwarted by Turkish artillery fire, obliging a landing on Gallipoli by the Allied forces, mainly British–Indian Sikh and Gurkha forces, supported by a large phalanx of troops from New Zealand and Australia, who had outraged Cairo society with their wild carousing on the way to Constantinople. On 25 April 1915, one of the bloodiest marine landings of the war began, with nearly 1,500 allied troops dying on the first day alone (with just twenty-one survivors on the day) and Allied casualties mounting to more than 10,000 dead or wounded over the next three days in order to secure a narrow beachhead. Kemal was stationed away from the initial assault, but personally led his men towards the contested hills and exhorted retreating Turkish soldiers to fight on, by leading the way himself. Soon promoted to full colonel for his exploits in the early fighting, Kemal ensured that his forces held the high ground, thereby literally keeping an upper hand throughout the fighting. He is said to have 'fought like a man possessed', showing his military genius in the months that unfolded as he, almost alone, strategized and improvised to lead the Turkish defence of Gallipoli.

Drenched in mud as they got bogged down in trench warfare, the 'Anzac' and Gurkha troops attempted an August offensive, supported by forty British and French aircraft (twice as many as the Ottomans could deploy). The aim was to capture the high ground at Chunuk Bair. For two days, a detachment of New Zealand troops managed to gain the heights, but a massive counter-attack by Kemal on 10 August swept the two Kiwi battalions from the heights, with 711 casualties amongst the 760 New Zealand troops who had reached the summit. With the failure of the August offensive, the Allied forces fell into defensive mode in putrid, muddy trench warfare amid deteriorating morale. General Ian Hamilton, who had been leading the Allied offensive, was dismissed. But his successor could do little to regain the advantage that Mustafa Kemal had repeatedly gained for the Ottoman forces. In December, after eight months of futile battle, the Allied forces decided to begin a surreptitious withdrawal and by January 1916 they were gone. Churchill was forced to resign, and Mustafa Kemal emerged as an authentic Turkish military hero who had inflicted a crushing defeat on the Allies. By the end of the war, he was a general and had the right to be addressed as Mustafa Kemal Pasha.

One other offshoot of the Gallipoli campaign was the creation of the 'Anzac' legend, primarily through the writings of the Australian war correspondent and historian, Charles Bean. His tales of Australian and Kiwi heroism helped bind those two settler countries into nations, as well as strengthening their loyalty to the British empire. The area where the initial assault began on 25 April 1915 is still commemorated as 'Anzac Cove', and annual memorial services held—with the cooperation of the Turkish authorities.

Although humiliated at Gallipoli, the Allied powers continued to harry other parts of the Ottoman empire, especially fomenting an uprising amongst the Ottomans' Arab dominions in alliance with the Hashemite family who were traditionally called the Sharifs (descendants of the Prophet) who acted as custodians of the Muslim holy cities of Mecca and Medina. Since the tenth century, the emirs of Mecca had traditionally been Hashemites—members of the Banu Hashim clan within the prestigious Quraysh tribe of Arabs, who were descendants of the prophet's grandfather Hashim ibn Abd Manaf, and specifically through the prophet's daughter Fatimah and her second son Hassan. There were, of course, close to a thousand families who laid claim to being descended from the Prophet of Islam and several hundred Hashemites. Sharif Hussein bin Ali just happened to be the custodian of the holy sites when the Great War began. His son Abdullah had contacted the British in Egypt in early 1914 (well before the outbreak of hostilities), seeking support for a putative 'Arab Revolt' that he was planning against the Ottomans. Four of Sharif Hussein bin Ali's uncles had also been emirs of Mecca, but not his father, and soon after his appointment in 1908, Hussein found himself at odds with the Young Turks, especially as they questioned his claim to the establishment of a hereditary succession to the emirate of Mecca.

By June 1916, the Hashemite family's overtures culminated in the start of the 'Arab Revolt' led by Sharif Hussein's son Feisal, in alliance with T. E. Lawrence (whose florid and exaggerated account of his alleged exploits was immortalized by Peter O'Toole in the movie *Lawrence of Arabia*). Preceding this, however, the British Middle East expert, Sir Mark Sykes, had signed a secret agreement with France's François Georges-Picot, carving up the Ottoman domains between the three Allied powers: Russia (which already ruled much of old Armenia) would receive eastern Anatolia in order to build a Greater Armenia that would be more than thrice the size of Russia's existing province of Armenia; and a red line across the Arabian peninsula divided it between Britain (which was to gain control over Mesopotamia, and influence over the southern part of the Arab peninsula) and France (which was to control Lebanon and central Anatolia, and gain influence over Syria). When he learnt about Sykes–Picot after Lenin publicized this and other secret agreements amongst the Allied powers, Lawrence expressed outrage, and the Arabs still perceive it as a particularly perfidious example of imperial duplicity. But it is likely that the Hashemites were aware of the broad outlines of the agreement, and were quite willing to accept Allied support in exchange for perpetuating their dynastic claims over the Arab lands (even with an element of British suzerainty, although they had never bargained for any such French overlordship).

Importantly, there was no Arab nationalist rising against the Ottomans during the Great War, and no Arab units of the Ottoman army defected to Hussein's side. The vast majority of the Ottomans' Arab soldiers fought valiantly on the Ottoman side during the war except for a minority of Ottoman prisoners of war who were redeployed by the British to join Feisal's Arab Revolt, and proved its most effective soldiers. The majority of Feisal's army comprised a few thousand tribal irregulars who were subsidized by British money and proved much better at guerrilla attacks than at sustained battlefield warfare.

Just before the Arab Revolt actually began in June 1916, the Ottomans had inflicted a humiliating defeat on the British at Kut al-Amara in Mesopotamia (today's Iraq). Major General Charles Townshend, commanding a force that had relocated from Poona in India, had initially captured Basra in the south and marched triumphantly towards Baghdad with his Indian troops in November 1915. But after five days of inconclusive fighting against Ottoman colonel Nureddin's forces at Ctesiphon, sixteen miles south of Baghdad, Townshend soon found his supply lines running thin and he retreated to the seemingly more defensible town of Kut al-Amara. Nureddin had himself been planning a retreat, but he now pursued Townshend downriver to Kut, surrounded the town and sought to cut off its supply lines from Basra, thus beginning the Siege of Kut on 7 December 1915. Between January and March 1916, four major British–Indian attempts at breaking the siege failed and Townshend surrendered on 29 April. He and 13,164 mainly Indian soldiers were taken prisoner—Townshend in relative luxury (off the Sea of Marmara), his Indian soldiers in horrific conditions, which began with a forced march northward that resulted in hundreds of deaths. About half of the Indian soldiers, and 70 per cent of their British officers, died of starvation during Ottoman captivity, and those that survived were in a dire, emaciated state when Baghdad was finally captured by the Allied powers in March 1917—after the US entry into the war began turning the tide in Europe.

After the humiliation at Kut al-Amara, the British empire needed an alternative Muslim leader to act as a rallying point in order to stave off potential revolts amongst their Muslim subjects. Britain then ruled the largest Muslim empire on earth, ruling far more Muslims than the number who lived under the Ottoman or Persian empires. (Even today, there are more Muslims in the Indian subcontinent—over 450 million—than in the Arab world and Iran combined.)

Sharif Hussein, and his Hashemite family, was a very convenient rallying point for this cause, and Britain backed the Arab Revolt by mid-1916. General Edmund Allenby had also begun an offensive from the Sinai and Palestine using a British–Indian–Australian force, while a renewed assault on Mesopotamia was soon underway too; the Arab Revolt helped keep additional Ottoman troops engaged on a third front, and some acts of derring-do (such as the capture of Aqaba, and raids on trains carrying Ottoman supplies) did indeed occur in accordance with their later celluloid telling. Feisal and T. E. Lawrence were aided by a force of French artillery under Colonel Édouard Brémond, and by Ottoman prisoners of war recruited from Mesopotamia after the Kut campaign, prominent amongst whom was Nuri al-Said (who became prime minister of Iraq under the British Mandate in 1930, and then again from 1938 to 1958 after it became a Hashemite kingdom). But the only proper Arab Revolt occurred not against the Ottomans—despite Arab resentment of Enver Pasha and the Young Turks' 'Turkification' policy—but in Egypt in 1918–19, against the long-standing British rule over that Arab country.

General Allenby's forces conquered Jerusalem in late December 1917, with Allenby walking into the holy city (rather than riding a horse or car). Later, in September 1918, one of the great cavalry charges of the Great War occurred in the Battle of Haifa, where the 15th Imperial Service Cavalry Brigade (comprising the Jodhpur, Mysore and Hyderabad Lancers, from those three Indian-ruled states) fought heroically in capturing that city on 23 September (their heroism commemorated in New Delhi's Teen Murti statue). And in October 1918, Allenby's forces conquered Damascus, with regiments from Lahore and Meerut playing key roles alongside Australian forces, but Allenby ensured that Feisal was allowed to enter the fabled old city first as its conqueror (much as Charles de Gaulle was allowed to enter Paris as its 'liberator' in 1944 by the magnanimous Americans). Damascus and the rest of Syria, of course, were supposed to be within the French sphere of influence according to Sykes–Picot—and the British attempt to foist Feisal as king of Syria became controversial after the war—but the French did ensure that they took control of Lebanon by war's end. By the time of the armistice that ended the Great War, Mustafa Kemal was the only Ottoman commander who had remained undefeated, and he was holding fast onto Aleppo and the northern part of Syria, although fighting was still continuing in the Alawite-inhabited area of Latakia in the northwest.

THE END OF EMPIRES: BOLSHEVISM IN RUSSIA, AND THE EMERGENCE OF A NEW TURKEY

The major powers on both sides of the Great War attempted to foment revolutions and rebellions amongst the disgruntled peoples on the other side, and particularly amongst the colonized. While Britain and France cultivated rebellious and 'nationalist' elements amongst the Arabs of the Ottoman domains, the Allied powers had much larger empires, which provided fertile material for Germany to support revolutionary elements amongst the colonized people of those empires. Most prominently, Germany supported the maturing struggle of the Irish people for independence from seven centuries of British control over Ireland, and the attempt by India's Ghadar Party (mainly comprising exiles in the US, Japan and elsewhere) to foment a mutiny within the British Indian Army across garrisons from the northwest (Peshawar) to Calcutta and Chittagong in Bengal all the way southeast to Singapore. The Ghadar plan, known as the 'Hindu–German Plot', was blown open by British intelligence, which gained inside knowledge about it a few days before it was to occur (21 February 1915). The Irish succeeded eventually in gaining home rule, and eventual independence in 1922, albeit only over about two-thirds of their homeland, with a northern territory carefully carved out of the province of Ulster to create an artificial Protestant majority that would remain loyal to the British crown.

The Ghadar Conspiracy was organized within India by two revolutionaries who had prominently participated, but avoided incarceration, in the Alipore Bomb Case of 1908: 'Bagha' (because he had once fought off and killed a leopard with his bare hands) Jatin Mukherjee and Rash Behari Bose. The Ghadar organization outside India was led primarily by Lala Hardayal (a lecturer in Sanskrit and Indology at Stanford University), who became general secretary of the Ghadar Party (based in the US) and established close links with Savarkar's India House group in London, most of whose members (led by Shyamji Krishna Verma and Virendranath Chattopadhyaya, the elder brother of the poet Sarojini Naidu) had fled to Germany after Madan Lal Dhingra assassinated Curzon Wyllie, and London's India House was closed. The rest of the Ghadar party leadership included various Indian migrants to the US and Canada such as Baba Santokh Singh and Sohan Singh Bhakna, plus several Indian students from the University of California (Berkeley) such as Vishnu Govind Pingle and Taraknath Das, and a prominent revolutionary exile in Japan, Maulana Barkatullah. Pingle was sent to Benares to join Rash Behari Bose, who had previously planned the attempted assassination of Viceroy Charles Hardinge on 23 December 1912. Hardinge was travelling atop an elephant, celebrating the transfer of British India's capital from Calcutta to New Delhi when a bomb was hurled at him. The bomb killed the mahout (elephant driver) but the Viceroy was only badly injured and Bose again managed to evade detection. Thereafter, he became the key planner within India of the Ghadar rebellion, with Jatin Mukherjee playing the leading role in obtaining arms supplies from the Germans.

Their attempts at recruitment were greatly aided by the fracas surrounding the *Komagata Maru* incident. Over the previous two decades, several thousand Indians (particularly Sikhs) had migrated to Canada and the US, mainly to work as farm hands and labourers. They had faced increasing discrimination, especially in Canada (a fellow British colony), which was receiving about 400,000 immigrants a year but had passed legislation requiring any potential immigrant to travel directly from their home country to Canada, a provision aimed squarely at preventing arrivals from India, since journeys from there were impossible without stoppages in Hong Kong or Japan at the time. When the *Komagata Maru* arrived in Vancouver on 23 May 1914, it wasn't allowed to dock, and a Canadian tug was used to push it back out to sea. Eventually, just twenty passengers were allowed into Canada, and the rest were sent back to India. When the ship arrived in Calcutta on 27 September 1914, it was taken up the Hooghly River to Budge Budge, where the unarmed ship was met by a British gunboat and twenty of the passengers were arrested. There was a riot and nineteen passengers were killed in police firing, the rest sent to their villages in Punjab—where they were to be kept under close surveillance.

Bagha Jatin had already established links with the Germans, having obtained a promise of armed shipments when he met the German crown prince on his visit to India in 1912. Jatin's group (Jugantar, or 'dawn of a new age') helped seize a large shipment of arms from the Rodda gun-manufacturing company in 1914, and Jatin and Rash Behari began contacting senior Indian soldiers posted at Fort William to begin planning an 1857-style all-India mutiny in the army. The *Komagata Maru* episode inflamed passions in Punjab, so Vishnu Pingle was sent there and was able to recruit soldiers from several regiments (26th Punjab, 23rd Cavalry, 7th Rajput, 24th Jat Artillery and the 130th Baluchi, which was then posted in Rangoon). Rash Behari Bose set 21 February as the day for the coordinated mutiny, which was to start with the 26th Punjab and spread to the other regiments in a chain, with the Calcutta (Fort William) regiments to rise upon news of the cancellation of the Punjab Mail. However, the Punjab police was able to infiltrate the revolutionaries through a double agent called Kripal Singh, and got wind of the conspiracy about a week in advance. Thereafter, Rash Behari hastily advanced the plan by several days, but Kripal was able to inform the British about this too, and a series of arrests occurred across India (including Pingle, who was hanged shortly afterwards). The British were able to forestall putative mutinies in Rangoon, Lahore (where Rash Behari had himself gone), Firozpur and Agra. Some of the key leaders managed to escape, including Rash Behari (who fled to Japan, where he established links with the pan-Asian Black Dragon society, which protected him from persistent British demands for his extradition) and

Giani Pritam Singh and Swami Satyananda Puri, who fled to Thailand (where they were instrumental in keeping the flame of Indian freedom alive). In 1923, Rash Behari married the daughter of a pan-Asianist (Soma Aizo) and took a Japanese passport; they ran the Nakamuraya restaurant in Tokyo, which still serves the best Indian (as distinct from 'Japanese') curries in that city. In 1942, Rash Behari Bose and Giani Pritam Singh were to be instrumental in the formation of the Indian National Army.

Ironically, the only actual mutiny occurred in faraway Singapore, where news of the betrayal of the plot had not reached. On 15 February 1915, nearly nine hundred Indian soldiers of the 5th Light Infantry stationed in Singapore—joined by about a hundred soldiers from the Malay States Guides—mutinied there. The battle to suppress them lasted eight days (and required naval reinforcements from Japan and France), with forty-seven British soldiers killed—the worst mutiny the British colonial army in Asia had suffered since 1857. After a summary trial, forty-seven of the mutineers were lined up against a wall at Outram Road in Singapore and shot in public—with 3,000 people watching the spectacle in a scene not unlike Taliban-ruled Afghanistan—and about 200 others were imprisoned for terms of seven to twenty years, while another 500 were exiled to Africa.

Jatin Mukherjee continued to work with the Germans with the aim of fomenting another uprising on Christmas Day 1915. He dispatched his lieutenant Naren Bhattacharya (later better known under the pseudonym M. N. Roy as one of the leaders of the Communist International) to Batavia in the East Indies to liaise with two brothers of Karl Helfferich (the German finance minister) who operated out of Burma and Thailand. They arranged for the redirection of an arms shipment (originally meant to land at Karachi for the Ghadar plot) to the Christmas Day plot (to be received on the Orissa coast near Balasore). But this plan also became known to the British—through a Czech nationalist based in an Austro-Hungarian ministry who reported it to the Americans—and Bagha Jatin was trapped in Balasore with five comrades, while his cohorts in Calcutta were arrested. At Balasore in September 1915, Bagha Jatin made his last stand, fighting a seventy-five-minute gun battle (with just a Mauser pistol to defend himself) before being shot dead in an open gunfight against a large phalanx of armed policemen.

By far the most effective and far-reaching German intervention, however, was the financial and logistical support that Germany provided to the Bolshevik leader (Vladimir Ilyich Ulyanov) Lenin in his revolutionary quest to gain power over a crumbling Russian empire in 1917. The Bolsheviks were always embarrassed to acknowledge the centrality of Germany's support to Lenin's cause, but there is little doubt that Lenin was able to reach Russia from his exile in Switzerland primarily because of the special support provided to him by Germany. It is no longer a secret that the Germans provided Lenin, and his thirty-strong Bolshevik entourage, a sealed train carriage with two German armed guards to enable them to pass through German and Austro–Hungarian territory en route to Sweden, and thence to Russia. The sealed train stopped for twenty hours in Berlin, and Lenin almost certainly met his key German intermediaries during this vital stopover. German official papers—and secret communications intercepted by Lenin's political rivals (including interim Prime Minister Kerensky)—showed that Lenin and his Bolsheviks were receiving substantial financial support from the Germans, which enabled them to maintain an effective propaganda campaign in Russia even while almost the entire leadership of the party was in exile. Credible evidence suggests that the Germans had sanctioned about 50 million marks of financial assistance to the Bolsheviks in 1917, of which at least a quarter was paid directly to Lenin.

The investment in Lenin and his Bolsheviks paid off handsomely when they took power through a coup d'état on 7 November 1917 (still October according to the Russian or Julian calendar, which was thirteen days behind the Gregorian calendar used in the rest of the (Western) world). The upheavals in Russia had begun on 8 March that year, with a four-day mass rebellion, known as the 'February Revolution' as per the Julian calendar, during which the Tsar's troops refused to fire on the demonstrators and Tsar Nicholas II, already weakened by his overstretched army's massive losses in war, agreed to abdicate. The response of the people (especially in the cities) was the spontaneous creation of 'soviets' (workers' councils), which gained control of local affairs across the country. On 16 April 1917, Lenin's German-aided journey back to Russia culminated with his arrival at the Finlyandsky station in Petrograd: St Petersburg had been so renamed at the start of the Great War because it sounded too German. The leader of the Mensheviks (the other faction of the Russian socialist movement), who also headed the Petrograd soviet, was at hand to receive Lenin to the strains of the revolutionary Marseillaise anthem, but Lenin pointedly turned away from him to address the people directly with a stirring revolutionary call to arms.

Marxist theory posited that peasant societies (like those of Russia or China) needed to first go through a 'bourgeois-democratic' revolution and achieve conditions of relative 'abundance' through capitalism before they would be ready for a socialist revolution, and the subsequent 'withering away of the state' that would herald the arrival of true communism. Consequently, the Social Democratic Labour Party, led then by the Mensheviks but including most Bolsheviks like Stalin and Kamenev, supported Kerensky's provisional government. Lenin proposed a series of 'April Theses' that overturned this Marxist orthodoxy, and argued that imperialism (the 'highest stage of capitalism') needed to be fought internationally—and this could best be achieved by Bolsheviks forming a 'revolutionary vanguard' by taking power in Russia, and using it to foment revolutions in the most advanced capitalist societies (like Germany). Lenin developed this approach in close collaboration with the only other Bolshevik leader who advocated it, Leon Trotsky, and this 'international revolutionary' line continues to be associated with Trotsky to this day. For a start, Lenin and Trotsky argued that the Bolsheviks should support and strengthen the soviets (rather than the provisional government) as the basis of a true revolution in Russia.

The provisional government that took power in March under the liberal Alexander Kerensky had a tenuous hold on the country from the outset, and the Bolsheviks steadily gained ground across urban Russia (the only areas where they had a base) by infiltrating and influencing the soviets. When Kerensky rashly committed to a renewed war effort in June 1917, the Bolshevik ranks were greatly augmented by disgruntled soldiers (most of whom were peasants, as were four-fifths of Russia's populace at the time), which enabled Lenin's comrade Trotsky to begin creating the Red Army. And Lenin's decision to support the division of farmlands into family-owned units (going against the grain of communist orthodoxy) helped the Bolsheviks gain ground amongst the peasantry as well. But they were still a minority in most soviets until the attempted counter-revolutionary coup in August 1917 by a Tsarist general; when Kerensky turned to the Petrograd Soviet for help, the Red Guards (part of the Red Army) played the vital role in fending off the attempted Tsarist putsch. By the end of August, the Bolsheviks gained majority control of the Petrograd Soviet, and gained similar control over the Moscow Soviet in early September.

On 7–8 November, the Bolsheviks stormed the Winter Palace and completed the coup that ousted Kerensky. The Congress of Soviets then met in Petrograd, and it accepted Lenin's decrees on peace, and to transfer land ownership from the Tsar, monasteries, nobles and landlords to the soviets, and then elected the Bolsheviks to take control of government, which they did in a coalition with the left wing of the Mensheviks. Trotsky was initially asked to lead the new regime, but he demurred as he felt that his being a Jew would detract from the government's effectiveness and draw undue opposition. Lenin, whose mother belonged to a family of Jewish converts to Orthodox Christianity, took charge instead with Trotsky as his commissar for foreign affairs (and still commander of the Red Army). By February 1918, Soviet Russia withdrew from the Great War and signed a separate Treaty of Brest–Litovsk with Germany, under which it gave up Poland, the Baltic states and Ukraine, arguably an ample payback for Germany's investment in Lenin's Bolsheviks.

That was not the end of the war for the newly-created Union of Soviet Socialist Republics (USSR). A massive civil war ensued over the next two years, with most of the Allied powers sending troops in support of the White Russians who sought to overthrow Lenin's Reds—who, after all, were calling for revolutions across the world. During the course of that war, the Bolsheviks unleashed the 'Red Terror' under Dzerzhinsky (the new chief of the Cheka secret police) and 'war communism'—meaning the forced expropriation of farms and their produce, and nationalization of all industry—which caused economic havoc, decimating the economy and triggering a famine that killed 5 million people. But the Bolsheviks won the civil war, and the revolutionary message was spread around the world by international ideologues like M. N. Roy, the Indian communist sent as commissar to Mexico, where Roy ensured that Lenin joined the pantheon of Montezuma, Emiliano Zapata, and other native American heroes as icons of the Institutional Revolutionary Party (PRI). Roy then spread the message to China, where he helped found the Communist Party in 1921, and later helped align it with Sun Yat-sen's Guomindang (KMT, or nationalists).

With the victory of the Bolsheviks in November 1917, Lenin also gave up Russia's residual claims to a sphere of influence in Persia (hitherto enshrined in the 1907 Anglo–Russian Entente). Spurred on by Lord Curzon, who had been advocating British control over Persia since the 1890s, Britain moved quickly to cement its hold over Persia in mid-1918. First, Britain sent in 2,500 soldiers to disperse across the country and help underpin an extraordinary Anglo–Persian agreement (drafted by Curzon) that would make Iran a British protectorate, with Britain in control of its army, treasury, and transport and communication networks. This agreement provided for a much greater degree of British control over Iran than the sway Britain held over India's princely states and was exactly akin to the stranglehold that Japan had acquired (through the implicit acquiescence of the other great powers) over Korea in 1905–10. The three Persian diplomats who signed the agreement received generous bribes and the assurance of asylum in Britain 'should necessity arise'. When the Iranian people heard about the details of the agreement, the country was convulsed in outrage, with Parliament strongly opposing it, and mullahs issuing a fatwa against anybody supporting the agreement. Britain was unable to implement the one-sided agreement in full, but managed to install a pro-British journalist Sayyed Zia Tabatabai as Iran's prime minister in February 1921. Tabatabai (like the Maratha Raghoba in the final three decades of the eighteenth century) had already been on the British payroll for many years.

The charismatic Cossack soldier Reza Khan led a 600-man contingent from his Persian Cossack Brigade to Tehran, ousted the entire cabinet and replaced them with one headed by Tabatabai. The Cossack Brigade had come under British control in 1917, and the literally towering figure of Reza Khan had become legendary as 'Reza Maxim' for his effectiveness in fighting off various brigands and rebels—most notably a 'socialist' rebellion at Gilan in northern Persia—using his Maxim machine gun to lead his forces. Reza had joined the Cossack Brigade as a fifteen-year-old, starting as either a servant or stable boy, but quickly rose through the ranks as his fighting abilities came to be recognized and admired. On the night before the assault on Tehran, Tabatabai arranged for the British to distribute silver coins amongst the soldiers that Reza would lead and he highlighted to them the dramatic contrast between his own generosity (although he was loath to admit the British help then or in later years) and the soldiers' miserable conditions during their Gilan campaign. Within three months, Reza Khan led another coup against the British lackey Tabatabai and installed himself as prime minister of Iran.

Meanwhile, Lenin had also publicized the terms of the secret Sykes–Picot agreement between Britain and France to carve up the Ottoman territories between themselves and Russia after the war. The agreement had provided for eastern Anatolia to be ceded to Russia, thereby quadrupling the size of Russia's Armenian territories. By the end of the war, this was a fraught issue as Enver Pasha and the Young Turks had at least connived in the Armenian genocide of 1915–16, the spark for which was the perception of Armenian disloyalty to the Ottoman regime, and acquiescence in Russian designs on the Ottomans' 'Christian' territories. Eastern Anatolia had a significant Armenian minority at the time but was still a predominantly Muslim-majority region, with Armenian majorities only in towns such as Van and Kars (the locale for Turkish author Orhan Pamuk's novel *Snow*). In 1915, Armenian militants had launched an uprising with Russian support to carve a Greater Armenia out of five Ottoman provinces but (in what Mustafa Kemal later called 'a shameful act') Enver's triumvirate retaliated by forcing even Armenian civilians uninvolved in the revolt to leave their historic homes in Anatolia, leading to hundreds of thousands of deaths. The Allied powers had also made vague promises that parts of the Russian sphere of influence in eastern Anatolia, plus northern Mesopotamia, would form a 'Kurdistan'. Most of this became moot once Lenin both publicized Sykes–Picot and repudiated any Russian claims to territory deriving from that secret accord, although some parts of eastern Anatolia continued to be in Russian/Armenian control at the end of the Russian Civil War.

With the end of the Great War, the Allied powers moved quickly to actuate the key aspects of Sykes–Picot by occupying eastern Thrace (including Salonica and Adrianopolis/Edirne), the capital Istanbul, the whole of western Anatolia including the key port of Smyrna (Izmir) as well as the Arab territories and central Anatolia. The British provided naval support for Greece (under Prime Minister Eleutherios Venizelos, who was proclaimed the 'greatest Greek statesman since Pericles') to occupy Smyrna (which had a Greek and Jewish majority) and western Anatolia (which had a smattering of Greeks in a vast sea of Muslim Turks). The French occupied Lebanon and sent troops into central Anatolia, and Syria (part of France's sphere of influence according to Sykes–Picot, but promised by Lawrence and other Britishers to the Hashemite prince Feisal).

The Ottoman capital too was occupied by Allied troops borne through the Bosporus in a vast convoy of fifty-five ships, as Mustafa Kemal Pasha discovered when he disembarked at Istanbul's Haydarpasha station on 13 November 1918. Although the Ottoman armies had not been defeated in war— indeed they had won a great victory at Gallipoli under Kemal, and fought the British to a draw in Mesopotamia and other Arab lands—the dejected Sultan and his grand vizier had signed the humiliating Armistice of Mudros, under which most of the Ottoman armies were to be demobilized, the Allies were to gain sovereignty over all Arab territories, and would have the right to occupy Istanbul and any other Ottoman town or region where 'security problems' had emerged. The Sultan's regime thus aligned itself with the victorious Allies, although Britain's Prime Minister David Lloyd George considered the Turks 'a human cancer'—in keeping with the British Liberals' religio/racist antipathy towards Turks since the days of Prime Minister Gladstone (1892–94)—and was committed to carving up Anatolia into Greek, French and Italian spheres of influence, with Constantinople and Smyrna under British overlordship.

The occupying forces, however, made a series of errors that were to rebound on them. At Smyrna, the Greek troops humiliated Turk inhabitants of the town in their triumphal procession to take control of it on 15 May 1919; a Turkish colonel who questioned the advance of the occupying army was summarily shot in the streets, as were any other soldiers attempting to resist. And in the words of the British biographer Lord Kinross, 'The Greek troops then got out of hand, and some hundreds of Turks were killed. Their bodies were thrown over the sea wall into the harbour.' Elsewhere too, the likely emergence of Christian minority communities as overlords of the Anatolian Turks sparked resentment, and provided the basis for popular resistance should a leader emerge to mobilize it. Such a leader was soon at hand in the form of Mustafa Kemal Pasha, aided by his military comrade from Gallipoli, General Kazim Karabekir, and a senior civilian in the War Ministry, Ismet Pasha (later known as Inonu).

The Allied powers were running short of personnel, and asked the sultan to send Karabekir to Erzurum (in eastern Anatolia, in the region designated as part of the Armenian zone) to pacify a restive population. Similarly, the Allies also sought a commander to pacify the city of Samsun on the Black Sea coast, and the Grand Vizier decided to dispatch Mustafa Kemal to run the 'inspectorate' there. Sent to suppress unrest in Samsun, Kemal instead began to mobilize the troops there to rebel against foreign occupation from the day of his arrival—19 May 1919 (still commemorated as a national holiday in Turkey). He also used the efficient telegraph system to send tirades against foreign occupation and the subservience of the Sultan's regime to newspapers, embassies and military commanders. The British demanded that Kemal be recalled forthwith, but he ignored the order and instead gathered his comrades to issue the Amasya Circular, which proclaimed that the Turks must rule all of Anatolia with no partition, mandates, occupation or rule by Christians.

The victor of Gallipoli again proved a formidable foe, and power flowed swiftly away from the Grand Vizier to Kemal as the nationalists gained rapid ground, especially with the failure of an attempt to arrest Kemal with Kurdish troops in Sivas. Soon thereafter, nationalists ousted the governor of Trabzon, and the Grand Vizier resigned, being replaced by a new regime more sympathetic to the nationalist cause. With Kemal's assent, the new regime called a parliamentary election in December 1919. This was won overwhelmingly by nationalists owing allegiance to Kemal, who declared 'full independence' to be the new Parliament's goal, and rejected any partition or foreign occupation of Anatolia. The Turks were using Wilson's principle of 'self-determination' to overturn the authority of Britain and its allies (Greece, France, Italy) much as George Washington had done in the 1770s. Kemal used a parliamentary recess to ask the Grand National Assembly to reconvene in the remote, muddy central Anatolian town of Angora (Ankara), where on 23 April 1920 he was elected its president by an overwhelming vote of 110 of the 120 members, with Ismet Inonu elected chief of army staff.

The Allied powers responded to the Turkish acts of self-determination with the hubristic Treaty of Sèvres signed with the wilting regime of the Ottoman sultan Mehmed VI on 10 August 1920. Under the terms of Sèvres, the French, Italian and Greek spheres of influence were recognized, Syria and Lebanon were granted to France as League of Nations 'mandates', as were Iraq and Palestine to Britain, with Britain also enjoined to implement the

November 1917 Balfour Declaration for 'the establishment in Palestine of a national home for the Jewish people'. The British Mandate for the artificially created nation of Iraq included Mosul (which the Allies had promised as part of 'Kurdistan'), Kirkuk, and the Baghdad and Basra vilayets (provinces) of Mesopotamia, with all the oil concessions in the area given to the Armenian entrepreneur Calouste Gulbenkian's Turkish Petroleum Company, which had the Deutsche Bank as a significant pre-war shareholder but by this point was majority-controlled by British shareholders. Constantinople and the straits (Bosporus, Dardanelles and Sea of Marmara) were declared international free zones, as were the ports of Constantinople, Smyrna, Alexandretta (Iskanderun), Haifa, Basra, Trabzon and Batum (which had been ceded to Turkey by Lenin under the Treaty of Brest–Litovsk)—all to be policed by the British Navy. Armenia was initially supposed to become an American Mandate, but the US Congress rejected this. Instead, the four Ottoman vilayets of Erzurum, Van, Bitlis and Trabzon were to be added to the territory of the Republic of Armenia (carved out of Tsarist Russia) to create 'Wilsonian Armenia', although Trabzon had a minuscule number of Armenians. And, Sèvres also put the Ottoman government's finances directly under the control of British, French and Italian bondholders, completing its vassal status.

In response, Kemal and his nationalists opened discreet negotiations with Lenin's Bolsheviks, who saw the creation of a new Turkey as an effective buffer state between the USSR and southeast Europe, and the potential of war between the Allied powers and Kemal's Turkish revolutionaries as a useful diversion of Soviet enemies away from the Russian Civil War. In exchange for a promise of future arms shipments, Kemal agreed a new border between the future Turkey and the USSR, ceding Batumi (the key oil port in Georgia) and Nakhichevan (an Azeri Turkish enclave, which remains a region of conflict within today's Armenia).

The British pulled out their old colonial rule book of divide and rule—which had also been employed during the 'Arab Revolt'—and tried to arm various minority communities, including the Armenians, Kurds, Circassians and Anatolian Greeks, some of whom were Muslim descendants of Janissaries, the old elite guard unit of the Ottomans. But these irregulars proved no match for Kemal's inchoate army, and for Karabekir's XV Corps (the only Ottoman corps that was still intact) in Erzurum. Kemal and his revolutionary army decided to attack each element of the Sèvres Treaty, and dismantle it clause by clause, beginning with the new Armenian Democratic Republic. Kemal ordered Karabekir to attack Armenia immediately (September 1920). His army quickly defeated any Armenian resistance in Erzurum, and then took the key city of Kars. By November 1920, the Armenians had surrendered and the new

Turkish revolutionary army had gained control of the old Ottoman territories claimed for Armenia, including those lost to Russia in 1878. Soon after, the Bolsheviks fomented an uprising in the Armenian republic, overthrowing the government there and restoring Russian/Soviet control. The successor (Soviet) Armenian regime signed the Treaties of Kars and Moscow renouncing all claims to the former Ottoman vilayets included in Armenia at Sèvres.

Meanwhile, the British gave up their attempts at arming irregular units of ethnic minorities in western Anatolia and instead redeemed their old promises to Venizelos to allow substantial Greek gains in Anatolia. At the Versailles peace negotiations, Lloyd George gave Venizelos enormous importance and he expounded his grandiose 'Megali Idea' for an expanded Hellenic Republic that would encompass all the territories of the Byzantine empire, with its capital in Constantinople. These were truly audacious claims as there were non-Turk majorities only in Pera (the European part of Constantinople) and the city of Smyrna, while the rest of western Anatolia was overwhelmingly Turkish and Muslim. The Allies insisted that Constantinople must remain under joint international (i.e., direct British) control, but allowed Greece to occupy eastern Thrace and the vilayet of Smyrna (although the latter would be subject to a plebiscite on Greek or Turkish control after five years of Greek occupation). The British then gave the Greek Army carte blanche to occupy western and north-central Anatolia. Given the long-standing enmity between Greeks and their former Ottoman Turkish overlords, this inflamed Turkish Muslim opinion, and allowed Kemal to invoke the cause of 'Islam in danger' to mobilize even greater support for the nationalist revolutionary army. Meanwhile, the French had occupied Cilicia and several other Ottoman vilayets (Maras, Urfa, Antep and Adana) in south-central Anatolia—with a promise to resettle Armenians there, further inflaming local Turkish anger.

According to Sykes–Picot, southern Anatolia was to be directly occupied by France, while Syria (starting at Aleppo and southwest to Damascus) was merely part of the French sphere of influence. On the Mediterranean coast, Italian forces attempted to occupy Antalya and its neighbouring regions. In Cilicia, the French were interested in coal and copper mines, but Kemal recognized that France's greatest interest was Syria. He sent his revolutionary armies to support local uprisings against the French occupation, and the French Armenian Legion suffered a series of military defeats, each of which resulted in reprisals against the local Armenian and other Christian inhabitants of liberated areas. By February 1921, the last French bastion in Antep crumbled after Mustafa Kemal had led his forces to a crushing victory over the French at the Battle of Marash. The Turkish forces were well positioned to conquer Aleppo next, a city Kemal knew well, as he had successfully defended it at the end of the Great War. But Mustafa Kemal consciously decided to stop at what he considered the border of ethnic-Turk habitation and agreed a Peace of Cilicia with France in March 1921. Skirmishes continued until the Treaty of Ankara (as Angora was now called) in October 1921, which ended all French claims to any territory in Anatolia. Italian forces had crumbled even earlier, as Kemal's incredible advance continued—having started with a small force of just over 4,000 loyalists in the little town of Angora, and grown steadily as the Allied powers' hubris and atrocities spurred tens of thousands of recruits to join Kemal.

With the defeat of the French, Armenians and Italians, only the Greeks remained. While Kemal's revolutionary army was engaged on the western and southern fronts, the Greek Army had advanced all the way to the banks of the Sakarya River less than eighty miles west of Ankara. This is where Kemal decided that his army would make its stand, taking up positions on the other side of the Sakarya River (of which the Ankara River is a tributary). The Greek king Constantine I had taken command of his army in early 1921, after Venizelos was defeated in an election in late 1920 soon after the death of his son, King Alexander, after a freak accident (following a monkey bite). Constantine had been fighting wars against Turkey (and skirmishing politically with Venizelos) all his adult life: in 1897, he suffered a crushing defeat in the Greco–Turkish War (after which Venizelos ensured that his and the other princes' roles in the military were diluted), but in 1913 Constantine (by then king) led the army to victory over Bulgaria in the Balkan Wars and also captured Salonica (thus ensuring that it became Thessaloníki) just ahead of the Bulgarians. Yet, when the Great War began, Constantine's German descent (as well as the fact that he was married to a princess of Prussia) became highly controversial, and Venizelos forced him to abdicate in favour of his son Alexander. Upon the latter's death, Constantine was restored to the throne through a plebiscite, and he took command of the Greek Army. In June–July 1921, King Constantine led his army to victories over Ismet Inonu that resulted in the fall of Eskisehir to the Greeks and Inonu's demotion to a staff position. Mustafa Kemal's counsel prevailed, and the Turkish revolutionary army took up a more defensible position on the banks of the Sakarya at a bend in the river, where Greek supply lines would be very overstretched.

An overconfident Constantine committed to go for the jugular and made for Ankara, including a nine-day march through the Salt Desert (Lake Tuz) that further tested his supply lines. His forces got to within thirty-one miles of the Turkish nationalist capital, after capturing some of the key heights on one bank of the Sakarya. But by then, Mustafa Kemal himself took command of the Turkish nationalist forces and began a flanking manoeuvre behind the Greek Army to emasculate their supply lines. The flow of armaments from the USSR also reinforced Kemal. The Battle of Sakarya River lasted from 23 August to 13 September. On 8 September, Mustafa Kemal personally led a ferocious counter-attack against the Greek positions on the key high point of Mt Chal. Six days later, Constantine and his general Anastasios Papoulas were forced to retreat towards Eskisehir. This was the decisive moment, described in Turkish history as the turning point that ended 238 years of steady retreat by the Turks that 'began with the retreat from Vienna on September 13th 1683'. Mustafa Kemal returned to Ankara, and was hailed by the Grand National Assembly (GNA) as a Gazi (Muslim military hero), and given the military title of Field Marshal.

The intransigent British were still oblivious to the battlefield victories of the Turkish nationalists, and attempted to continue enforcing the Sèvres terms. But Kemal's GNA signed treaties with the French and the USSR that ended all hostilities on the southern and eastern front by October 1921, and the Italians too began selling arms to Kemal's forces. There was a seeming stalemate in the war against the Greeks over the next year, but with incremental retreats by the demoralized Greek forces, which committed awful atrocities of rape and pillage, killing at least a million Turk civilians in their wake. In August 1922, Mustafa Kemal launched an all-out assault on the Greek lines at Afyonkarahisar in central Anatolia, and inflicted a crushing defeat on the Greeks at the Battle of Dumlupinar on 30 August 1922. The Greek commander-in-chief, General Nikolaos Trikoupis was himself taken prisoner. The GNA forces recaptured Eskisehir three days later, and swept to victory after victory thereafter, pushing into the Greek stronghold of Smyrna (which was additionally protected by the British Navy) on 9 September 1922. The Greek Army headquarters was evacuated before the Turkish forces entered Smyrna (thereafter known as Izmir). Despite Mustafa Kemal's proclamation in Turkish and Greek against looting, and the threat that any soldier who harmed non-combatants would be sentenced to death, the victorious army pillaged the properties of Greeks and Armenians (partly to avenge terrible atrocities wrought by the Greek Army over the previous two years across Anatolia). The Great Fire of Smyrna blazed through the Greek and Armenian quarters of the city, virtually destroying them.

Thence the GNA forces pressed on to Constantinople, which was still under Allied occupation. Lloyd George's government was determined to defend the great city straddling two continents, and support the Greek defence of eastern Thrace. But the Italian and French troops quickly abandoned their positions, and none of the British dominions apart from New Zealand was willing to provide any support. This itself caused a crisis: the dominions were asserting an independent position on a foreign policy issue for the first time. Shorn of significant support, Lloyd George's position became untenable: even the British commander on the ground, General Charles Harington, asked his troops to refrain from firing on Kemal's forces as they marched in to retake Constantinople (thereafter to be known as Istanbul) in October 1922, and the Greek forces withdrew from eastern Thrace by 15 October. With his policy in tatters, Lloyd George resigned as Britain's prime minister four days later. The Treaty of Lausanne endorsed the modern borders of Turkey, fully in keeping with the National Pact that Kemal's GNA had always insisted on— that the whole of Anatolia must be part of it, plus eastern Thrace including Edirne (henceforth called Adrianopolis). The Lausanne Treaty also provided for an exchange of populations between Greece and Turkey, resulting in about 500,000 Greek Muslims being resettled in Anatolia in exchange for 1.3 million Greek and Turkish adherents of Orthodox Christianity being resettled in Macedonia (including Thessaloníki) and Thrace.

Hailed as Atatürk ('Father of the Turks'), Mustafa Kemal quickly set about creating a republic—a concept completely unknown in the annals of Muslim history. He also introduced a new alphabet (the English one, with a few modifications) to replace the Arabic one, liberated Turkish women by abolishing the use of the hijab in public places, and abolished the sultanate, although he allowed a cousin of the Sultan, Abdul Mejid, to become caliph in 1923 with exclusively spiritual powers. However, when this too became a competing source of parallel authority, the caliphate was abolished in March 1924, and Atatürk's Turkey became a secular republic. Each of these planks— the liberation of women, a new written script, the creation of a republic—were completely radical nation-building ideas, requiring heroic educative efforts to explain their rationale and ensure they would spread to the common folk, who were thinking of their Gazi as their sultan. Over the subsequent fifteen years, Atatürk broadly succeeded in entrenching these secular, republican ideas, which went largely unchallenged for six decades after his death in 1938. With the departure of the Greeks, Armenians and (after 1948) Jews, most of Turkey's commercial class departed as well. Although this was initially debilitating, Atatürk's economy almost naturally became a state-capitalist one.

Thus it was that the dissolution of the Ottoman empire resulted in the creation of a new secularist state in Turkey (all of Anatolia or ancient Asia Minor, plus Istanbul and eastern Thrace in the southeastern corner of Europe including Edirne or Adrianopolis). Every inch of this territory had been won for Turkey by Kemal Atatürk's new army and, thus sanctified, would continue to be defended implacably by that army into the future. Having nearly ended the career of one British titan (Churchill) on the battlefield of Gallipoli in 1915, Atatürk now decisively ended the career of another—David Lloyd George. With the failure of his gambit to use Greek troops to enforce the British blockade and Allied occupation of Anatolia, Lloyd George was forced to resign—and his Liberal Party ceased to be a major player in British politics for the next eighty-five years.

THE FAILED HOPES OF INDEPENDENCE: PARIS 1919
AND THE MIRAGE OF 'SELF-DETERMINATION'

At the Versailles Peace Conference of 1919, which was actually held at several venues across Paris apart from the opulent Versailles Palace (which French Prime Minister Georges Clemenceau picked precisely because it was where France had signed the humiliating terms of its capitulation to Prussia/Germany in 1871), Japan expected to have a seat at the high table, as it saw itself as one of the victors of the war, having entered it early and won quick victories over the German territories in Asia. But the negotiations were dominated by the triumvirate of Britain's Lloyd George, France's Clemenceau and America's Wilson. It had been a Council of Four, until Italy left once some of its territorial demands were rejected.

The exclusion from the highest councils bred resentment in the Japanese delegation. Their leader, Prince Saionji Kinmochi, was a liberal internationalist, whose refinement and background should have made him a sentinel of peace during the conference. Belonging to a kuge family (of noblemen close to the imperial family in the old capital of Kyoto), he was amongst the few noblemen who personally participated in the Boshin War of 1867–68 which led to the Meiji Restoration, conquering several castles in a decisive intervention; he spoke French fluently, having studied it for several years at Marseilles and Paris before taking a law degree from the Sorbonne (where Clemenceau remembered him as a classmate). He later became a leading light in Ito Hirobumi's Seiyukai political party, which believed in peaceful cooperation with other nations (and strongly opposed the militarists led by Yamagata Aritomo, especially on Japan's conquests of southern Manchuria and Korea), twice serving as prime minister. In 1913, Saionji was appointed a genro (Crown's senior statesman, with the responsibility of choosing prime ministers), and was the last holder of that title when he died in 1940—adhering throughout to his belief that the one with the greatest support in the Diet (national assembly) should lead it.

Japan's primary focus was on the principle of 'racial equality'. Given the *Komagata Maru* episode, this had great resonance in India too, while the spread of the noxiously racist rhetoric of the 'yellow peril' in the US,

South Africa and Australasia united Japanese, Chinese and Koreans on this issue. This 'yellow peril' rhetoric had emerged in the late nineteenth century, primarily as a means of limiting the inflow of Chinese, Japanese and Korean workers, who had been arriving on the west coast of the US to work on the railways and in the gold and other mines of California. In 1868, the US and China signed the Burlingame Treaty, which encouraged the flow of Chinese labour to the US, with reciprocal protections against religious persecution in both countries. But by 1882, xenophobia against Chinese workers was running high—they were perceived to be depressing wages—and US president Chester Arthur signed the Chinese Exclusion Act (which remained in force, in some shape or form, until 1943). In the first decade of the twentieth century, US fears of the 'yellow peril' began to focus more on Japan, as the two nations' interests in the Pacific began to clash: US strategic planners saw further expansion into the Pacific (beyond the recent acquisitions of Hawaii and the Philippines) as part of America's 'manifest destiny', and Japan's naval expansion after her 1902 treaty with Britain was increasingly seen as a threat to US aspirations. In the years before the war, Japanese nationals were debarred from buying or even leasing land in California, and eventually prevented from bringing their wives along on business trips. The San Francisco school board segregated Chinese and Japanese students (although they numbered fewer than a hundred) and all Asian migrants were facing extreme difficulties in the US and Canada, and were completely excluded by whites-only Australia.

Wilson, a southerner himself, found racial equality troublesome, and knew it would be inconvenient and unpopular at home. He had prevented black American troops from fighting under American commanders during the Great War, albeit allowing them to fight under French command. A half-century after the US Civil War, racial segregation was still very much a reality in the US (especially in the south). The Australian prime minister Billy Hughes was strongly opposed to any racial equality clause—believing that it would result in Japanese and Chinese swamping Australia's shores—and his New Zealand counterpart endorsed his view. Britain, given its 1902 alliance with Japan, could not openly disagree with Japan. Additionally, Britain (along with France and Italy) had signed secret agreements with Japan in early 1917 in exchange for additional help from the Japanese Navy, which had sent destroyers to counter Germany's submarines. One important aspect of these agreements was an assurance that Japan would gain control of the Pacific Islands—Marianas, Carolines and Marshalls—that Germany had previously controlled. The first of Wilson's Fourteen Points forbade 'secret agreements' amongst nations, so the US treated this as a private agreement that had no standing in their eyes. But Britain supported Japan and, despite American objections, the Pacific Islands did become Japanese Mandate territories under the auspices of the League of Nations (just as Palestine, Egypt, Transjordan and Iraq became British mandates, and Lebanon and Syria French ones). The islands were to play an important role during the Second World War.

The US and Australia were also concerned about Japan's increasing economic might. By 1914, Japan already accounted for more than a third of the world's output of cotton yarn, and was the biggest exporter of silk and silk textiles. While Japan had large trade deficits in the 1900–14 period—as it imported machinery for its rapid industrialization—those trade balances turned into large surpluses during the war, as Japan's exports boomed, with shipments to the US and UK doubling over the four years, those to China quadrupling and exports to Russia rising sixfold. During the Russian Civil War, Japan moved into Siberia; while almost every European power participated on the White side against the Russian Reds, Japan's participation came to be seen as much more of a threat by the other powers—a fact that was regarded with some bemusement in the Japanese press, reflecting yet another manifestation of the double standards that continued to bedevil Western approaches to Japan.

Despite backchannel attempts by the British to dissuade them from introducing it, the Japanese delegation tabled the racial equality clause and put it to a vote. The clause was passed comfortably, despite the opposition of the US and British empire delegations. But Wilson performed a manoeuvre to scuttle the clause, and the Japanese decided not to immediately raise further objections. Racism was thus allowed to remain enshrined in immigration policy by the white/Western nations as part of the Versailles/Paris peace treaties!

Instead, it was over their claims in Shandong that the Japanese decided to make their stand. They would only allow the 'racial equality' clause to be excluded from the covenant of the League of Nations if Japan's claims over the former German territories and concessions in Shandong—and the subsequent treaties agreed between Japan and China in 1918—were accepted in full. After much handwringing, the other powers agreed to Japan's demands over Shandong on 30 April 1919 despite eloquent and learned speeches by young Wellington Koo (China's ambassador to the US, who had just received a PhD in international law from Columbia University). Koo correctly referred to Shandong as the cradle of Chinese civilization (being the birthplace of Confucius and Mencius), and Japan's demands as 'a dagger pointed at the heart of China'.

China itself was in a state of disarray at this time, with a new disintegration into warlord fiefdoms and a particularly clear North–South divide. After Yuan Shikai became president of Republican China in March 1912, he had gradually aggrandized power—first by insisting that the seat of government (and the National Assembly) move from Nanjing closer to his power base in Beijing, then by gradually reducing the power and effectiveness of the National Assembly (which had originally picked Sun Yat-sen as president, then turned the post over to Yuan Shikai at Sun's urging). In January 1913, a new election was held to the National Assembly, which resulted in a clear plurality (392 out of 800 seats) for Sun Yat-sen's Guomindang, who were led into that election by Sun's young political organizer, Song Jiaoren (who was just thirty years old at the time). Although the electorate only comprised about 40 million or a tenth of China's population, the 1913 election was the freest ever held in China. Three parties that had finished second, third and fourth merged under the leadership of the intellectual Liang Qichao to form the Progressive Party, which was critical of Sun Yat-sen, and broadly supportive of Yuan Shikai within Parliament.

President Yuan was irritated by having to deal with the obstreperous KMT in the National Assembly, especially as Song Jiaoren's campaign had focused specifically on creating effective checks on the powers of the presidency. By the time the newly elected National Assembly met, defections had given the KMT a clear majority (438 of the 800 seats) and Song Jiaoren was widely expected to become prime minister. But Song was shot twice on 20 March 1913 while driving with friends to the legislature (and died two days later) and circumstantial evidence suggested that President Yuan Shikai himself had arranged the assassination through the incumbent premier (who resigned in May 1913, and was murdered a year later), although no watertight evidence was ever found to directly implicate Yuan.

The assassination dominated initial meetings of the new assembly, and in July 1913 Sun Yat-sen began an open rebellion against Yuan within the Assembly (including on issues relating to the national budget) but failed to carry his party, as many succumbed to Yuan's threats, bribes and intimidation, while Liang's party continued to oppose Sun, thus defeating him by September. In November, Sun Yat-sen fled to Japan and called for a Second Revolution to overthrow the incumbent, but this was defeated militarily over the next few weeks. Yuan Shikai then banned the Guomindang, expelled it from the Assembly and disbanded the Assembly itself in January 1914 on the pretext that it lacked the quorum to convene. He proclaimed a new constitution that gave him almost unlimited powers, and appointed his trusted Beiyang Army lieutenant Duan Qirui as prime minister. However, in December 1915, Yuan Shikai went one step too far and proclaimed himself emperor. This attempt at making himself emperor stirred enormous opposition to Yuan Shikai, from even amongst some of those in his inner circle. By March 1916, he moved to rescind his decision but died of uraemia in June 1916 (at just fifty-six, after an eventful career that had begun nearly three decades earlier with him being sent to Korea as Resident, then playing a key role in the New Army movement, and subsequently in the final overthrow of the Qing). Yuan was succeeded by his vice president, Li Yuanhong (the reluctant leader of the October 1911 Wuhan mutiny) who quickly came into conflict with Premier Duan over the question of participation in the Great War (which Duan, and Liang Qichao, favoured as a means to improve China's bargaining position in any post-war settlement).

During the half-year following Yuan's monarchist turn, however, China had started disintegrating: in December 1915, a huge uprising had begun in Yunnan, as warlords based in Kunming (led by Cai E and Tang Jiyao) declared their independence from Beijing, and sent a National Protection Army northwards to defy the new emperor. Yuan Shikai's army of 80,000 sent to counter it suffered a crushing defeat in Sichuan, and the warlords in Guizhou and Guangxi also declared independence by March 1916. By the time of Yuan's death, several other provinces had followed suit, including Guangdong, Shandong, Hunan and Jiangsu. Only the former Qing general governing Muslim-majority Xinjiang province had expressed open support for the new emperor. Yuan's death led to most of the provinces rescinding their independence declarations. President Li Yuanhong attempted to restore the old National Assembly on 1 August 1916, but most KMT members stayed away, still suspicious of Premier Duan, who refused to accept the 1912 constitution. Sun Yat-sen consequently convened an alternative parliamentary session in Guangzhou, where he established a rival military government (called the Constitution Protection Movement), receiving support from Tang Jiyao and the leadership of the National Protection Army, as well as most of China's naval leadership.

As the conflict between president and premier came to a head in Beijing, President Li Yuanhong dismissed Premier Duan Qirui in May 1917 when it was discovered that Duan had secretly taken several large loans from Japan. Li also sought to strengthen his military position by seeking the support of the monarchist general, Zhang Xun. After initially bolstering President Li, Zhang displayed his royalist predilections by supporting an attempt at restoring the Qing dynasty, this time initiated by the former reformist intellectual of the late Qing era, Kang Youwei, who had spent several years in quiet contemplation in Darjeeling (India) before this attempt at restoring Puyi to the throne on 1 July 1917. His former protégé, Liang Qichao, was horrified at this turn of events, and denounced it. But Kang's attempted Qing restoration—led by the warlord Zhang Xun—lasted less than two weeks, with Duan moving his troops into Beijing within a week, and retaking the capital on 12 July. Fed up with the constant intrigues in Beijing, President Li Yuanhong resigned, and Duan Qirui became the undisputed strongman of Beijing (and northern China), with Liang Qichao as a key minister. They took China formally into the Great War soon afterwards on the side of the Allied powers. It was a token presence, as China's main contribution was to send 96,000 labourers to Europe to help build and reinforce trenches. Two thousand labourers died during the war.

More importantly, Duan used the pretext of war to secretly negotiate the Nishihara Loans from Japan—ostensibly to fight the Great War, but actually to strengthen the army to crush resistance in the south and in Hunan, which was ruled by a pro-KMT governor. In exchange for those loans, Premier Duan (negotiating on behalf of the legitimate government of China) agreed on 29 September 1917 to allow Japan to place its troops in Shandong, and to build and take full control of two railroads there. It was this partly secret agreement with the government of China that Japan decided to publicize at Versailles in January 1919, which helped to thoroughly undermine the young diplomat Wellington Koo's brilliant rhetoric.

Until that point (and in most subsequent re-narrations), the primary focus of the Sino–Japanese negotiators at Versailles had been on Japan's Twenty-One Demands from 1915. The original Twenty-One Demands had been presented in January 1915 and were grouped into five categories: (i) confirming Japan's annexation of German concessions and territory in Shandong province, and expanding Japan's sphere of influence over its ports, railways and other key cities; (ii) demanding a ninety-nine-year lease for Japan's South Manchurian Railway, and allowing Japan to extend its sphere of influence into eastern Nei Mongol, where Japan sought mineral rights; (iii) providing an effective debt-for-equity swap that would give Japan control over the vital Hanyeping mining and metallurgical complex that was deep in debt to Japan; (iv) barring China from giving coastal or island concessions to any other power apart from Japan; and, most controversially, (v) requiring Japanese 'advisers' to be appointed to oversee China's finances and police, allow Japan to build three new railways, several Buddhist temples and schools, and gain effective control over Fujian province (across the straits from the Japanese colony of Taiwan).

This fifth group of demands was what Fairbank and other historians refer to when alleging that the Twenty-One Demands were aimed at making China a protectorate of Japan. They were initially kept secret (unlike the other four groups of demands, which were merely affirming what Japan already had gained in China). But the canny President Yuan Shikai immediately had them publicized, in order to garner the sympathy of the other great powers, which would lose some of their influence in China at Japan's expense. The US, in particular, raised strenuous objections and insisted on its long-standing demand for China to maintain an open-door policy towards all the powers. The raging negative publicity led the genro elder statesmen (including Saionji) to intervene, and modify the demands—eliminating the fifth group altogether. A modified set of Thirteen Demands was presented to China, with a two-day ultimatum for China to accept (apparently added at Yuan's request, in order for him to appease public opinion) or risk war. The Thirteen Demands were actually quite lenient, demanding less than what the Chinese negotiators had already conceded in previous weeks, and not going much beyond what Japan had already gained in China over the previous two decades. It was this relatively lenient version of the Thirteen Demands that China signed with Japan on 25 May 1915. While Japan gained very little of substance, it lost a great deal in terms of international public opinion, which to this day focuses on the Twenty-One Demands as Japan's first attempt at making China a protectorate, although the demands were in fact withdrawn within a couple of months, and modified by Japan's genro elders.

In the end, it was only the 'Group 1' demands relating to Shandong that were introduced and endorsed by the Allied powers at Versailles on 30 April 1919. Considering that Britain and France had divided up the Arab world into mandates, and US president Wilson's gambit to take on mandates (in 'Greater Armenia', for instance) had been thwarted by his own Congress, Japan 'gained' very little in Shandong (having actually conquered the entire area from the Germans early in the Great War, thus gaining control of areas that had already been 'conceded' by China to Germany, and were now merely endorsed on to Japan). But by this time, the raised expectations of 'self-determination' (via Wilson) and 'dignity and quid pro quo' (via Liang Qichao) had aroused China's intelligentsia, especially the young and restless in the vibrant new colleges and universities. When word got out about the Shandong settlement (the fact that it would become a Japanese sphere of influence rather than reverting to full Chinese sovereignty, as implicitly promised by Wilson), there was outrage in China itself and also amongst Chinese expatriates in Paris. A group of Chinese students from French universities surrounded the Chinese delegation's hotel in Paris, and physically prevented them from signing the 'humiliating' terms of the Versailles Treaty. Thus while the US, European powers and Japan signed, China itself did not.

More significantly, there was an uproar in China itself, and on 4 May 1919 a portentous gathering of 3,000 students from thirteen colleges occurred at the Tiananmen Square (the Gate of Heavenly Peace which leads into the Forbidden City) in Beijing. The occurrences of that day were to take on great symbolic significance, and the Tiananmen Square itself was to attract protesters (and fear in incumbent regimes) at many key subsequent turning points in China's history. On that May afternoon, the angry crowd attacked the home of Cao Rulin, communications minister for the Republic of China, who was seen as particularly close to the Japanese. Cao himself nimbly jumped over a wall of his home and escaped, but his furniture was destroyed, some of his visitors assaulted and his house set alight. The spontaneous eruption (in both Paris and Beijing) marked a key democratic milestone for China—albeit one that remains aborted and incomplete to this day.

Most significantly, Sun Yat-sen—himself a frequent exile in Japan, and occasionally a believer in pan-Asian unity (implying close ties between China and Japan)—now became very disillusioned with the West. In that disenchantment, he turned instead to the only rising new power that was unrepresented at Versailles: the Soviet Union. Working with Comintern agent Mikhail Borodin, Sun Yat-sen in 1923 knitted together an alliance between his KMT and the Chinese Communist Party (CCP), which had been created two years earlier in Shanghai with help from the Comintern's representative, M. N. Roy. A group of Chinese workers in France, including a young man called Zhou Enlai and a teenager called Deng Xiaoping, had already initiated a CCP but were to eventually merge it with the Shanghai party. Under Soviet auspices, the KMT and CCP were to create a National Revolutionary Army aimed at driving out the warlords and uniting China. Two men stood out at the military academy established at Canton: a young military tactician called Chiang Kai-shek, and the communist propagandist Zhou Enlai. Chiang would come to the fore after Sun's death, using his key role in the National Revolutionary Army to begin gaining control of the KMT in 1925. By the following year, he was leading the joint forces of the KMT and CCP towards the north, conquering most of the densely-populated provinces on the coast all the way to Nanjing and Shanghai, then massacring his key communist rivals at Shanghai in 1927, and forming a National Government of China in 1928.

Japan had itself faced a nationwide uprising in Korea, which began on 1 March 1919. Nearly a decade into the formal annexation of Korea by Japan, a minuscule middle class was emerging in Korea's cities, and the first department stores, cinemas, and universities had come into being. It was from amongst university students that this first rebellion began. Although inspired by Wilson's Fourteen Points (and their implicit call for the 'self-determination' of all subjugated nations), Korea's 1 March 1919 movement had its roots in the intense nationalism that had been evident amongst Korean students and other patriots since the 1870s. It drank from the chalice of ethno-linguistic homogeneity, and an abiding distrust of the outsider. The land reform of

1919—which granted property rights to landlords, and allowed Japanese settlers to buy substantial chunks of agrarian land—almost certainly catalysed the patriotic sentiments of young Koreans, some 2 million of whom joined the nationalist revolt. However, the yangban class of bureaucrats largely cooperated with the Japanese, working out an accommodation with the foreign rulers (as most elites inevitably do).

While one of the leading rebels, Syngman Rhee, and some of his colleagues, fled Korea after the suppression of the uprising—and settled in the US, primarily in Denver—other leading intellectuals of the time (including Yi Kwang-su) later became key supporters and ideologues of Japan's empire in Korea, and many Korean aristocrats continued to collaborate with the Japanese regime throughout the period. The extensive degree of collaboration ensured that about half of the national police comprised Koreans by 1920, and Koreans were being increasingly recruited into the army and bureaucracy too.

For Korean elites—landlords, bureaucrats, former Confucian scholars—cooperation with the Japanese proved to be bountiful, giving them an opportunity to participate in a very successful agrarian economy: in Japanese-ruled Korea, agricultural output grew 2.3 per cent annually between 1910 and 1941 (far more rapidly than was ever achieved in British India). After 1930, Korea (particularly the north) was rapidly industrialized alongside Manchuria, acquiring heavy industry, including steel and cement plants and munitions factories. It was true that about half of all agrarian land in Korea, and much of industry, was Japanese-owned, but Koreans perforce occupied middle management and technical (engineering) jobs, acquiring skills that were to prove useful to post-war independent Korea. Japan's relationship with Korea was much more akin to England's links to Scotland and Ireland, with large settler populations helping to develop the colony far more than the English ever developed distant India, where they stayed far more aloof from the 'natives' than the Japanese did from their ethnic cousins across the Sea of Japan in Korea.

The highly centralized bureaucracy created for Korea by the Japanese penetrated all the way down to each village, where the police maintained a presence, as did an agricultural extension service that disseminated better production methods. By contrast, the British presence in rural India barely extended to an aloof civil servant (magistrate) in a sub-district, but never reached most villages, which were administered by their traditional rulers (who, nonetheless, were responsible for paying the high taxes that the British demanded of them, failing which they would be dispossessed of their land).

At Versailles, 'India' was represented by a delegation led by the Secretary of State for India, Edwin Montagu; the only Indian ever made a hereditary peer, Lord Satyendra Prasanna Sinha (of Raipur in Bengal's Birbhum district); and a loyalist prince, Maharaja Ganga Singh of Bikaner, a rotund figure whose tales of tiger-hunting regaled the Paris party set more than any contribution to the peace negotiations. Maharaja Ganga Singh had also led some of his troops (notably in a 'Camel Corps') during the Great War in France and elsewhere (having previously served Britain during the Boxer Rising in China) and was rewarded (like Lord Sinha) with a token place in the Imperial War Cabinet. He later formed the Chamber of Princes in 1920, along with Prince Ranjitsinhji of Nawanagar, one of the greatest cricket batsmen of the nineteenth and early twentieth century. Lord Sinha, as a distinguished judge, proved useful in committees, but by this stage was not seen as representative of India, despite being Congress president in 1915, before the return of stalwarts like Tilak and the gradual transformation of Congress into a more mass-based party during the war years. Montagu steered well clear of any notion of self-determination, and the mainstream Congress made few attempts to force him to do so, awaiting instead his promised constitutional reforms. But he did keep emphasizing that Indian Muslims' interests not be forgotten, and that the caliph not be humiliated—leading to Lloyd George's retort that Montagu was behaving not as a British member of the War Cabinet but like a 'successor on the throne of Aurangzeb'!

The Chamber of Princes was committed to thwarting the advance of democracy, and in particular the growing independence movement led by the Indian National Congress. It was formed via a royal proclamation by King-Emperor George V expressly to represent the 'needs and aspirations' of the princely states, and unite them against India's nationalists. Ranjitsinhji succeeded Ganga Singh as head of the Chamber of Princes, and also took his place as India's delegate to the League of Nations (1920–23). Over the next three decades, Britain's imperial strategy in India was aimed at: (a) dividing Muslims from Hindus, and attempting to create further fissures in Hindu society (through, for instance, dividing Brahmins and non-Brahmins in south India, and fomenting other forms of caste conflict elsewhere); (b) deepening the commitment to the princely states (through the Chamber of Princes) to ensure that these British allies would remain committed to thwarting any moves towards national consolidation and unity; and (c) providing token concessions (but never any substantive ones) towards Congress demands for greater self-governance of India by Indians.

More than a million Indian troops had fought on the Allied side during the Great War (more than ten times the number of Chinese labourers sent into the war theatre), an estimated 74,187 Indian soldiers had died and 67,000 were wounded. Before the war, Indians were still banned from becoming officers in the armed forces, but by the end of the war the sheer demographic challenge obliged the British to allow Indian-born soldiers to finally be commissioned as officers in the army (although it was carefully arranged that Indians would not command white soldiers). Some Indian ace pilots had already been commissioned into the Royal Air Force before the war's end.

Loyalist Indians like Gopal Krishna Gokhale, Muhammad Ali Jinnah and Motilal Nehru had expected that their support of the British war effort (and the valiant fighting by Indian soldiers on the Allied side in West Asia and Europe) would result in significant political concessions after the war. Soon after Austen Chamberlain was replaced (after the humiliation at Kut) as Secretary of State for India by Edwin Montagu, the latter made a momentous statement in the House of Commons on 20 August 1917 acknowledging the need for 'the gradual development of self-governing institutions with a view to the progressive realization of responsible government in India as an integral part of the British Empire'. This promise of Dominion status was, at a minimum, a clear attempt at buying India's support in the midst of war. In November 1917, Montagu also became the first British Secretary of State for India to actually visit the country, ostensibly to solicit Indian opinion on constitutional reform.

The high hopes thus aroused were dashed when the actual Montagu–Chelmsford reform proposals were published in May 1918 (and enacted in December 1919). They provided for 'diarchy' at the provincial level, but with the main subjects (finance, revenue, law and order, army, police, etc.) still firmly 'reserved' to the unelected governor (and his nominated councillors), while the less vital subjects—public health, education, agriculture, local self-government—were transferred to ministers who were responsible to the elected legislature. But even here, the provincial legislatures were to be elected by a small proportion of the population (about a tenth of all adult males), the central legislature by just 1 per cent of the population, and the principle of 'separate electorates' was extended to Sikhs, Europeans, and Anglo–Indians, further enshrining and deepening the 'divide and rule' policy. The viceroy still reported only to London, and could dismiss the national or provincial legislatures at any time; he also appointed 40 of the 144 members of the Central Legislative Assembly, and 26 of the 60 members of the Council of States. Far from moving towards dominion status, India was still not even close to the limited democracy that was offered to Hong Kong in 1997.

As usual, India's political leadership was well ahead of their British rulers when it came to visualizing the future democratic shape of India. During the war years, the mainstream ('moderate') Congress party had moved to pre-empt the imperial policy of divide and rule by working out a pact with the Muslim League at Lucknow in 1916. Maulana Muhammad Ali, a foppish and fun-loving Muslim who had become the unlikely leader of the Khilafat Movement (to protect the institution of the caliphate in Ottoman Istanbul) also invited Jinnah to join the Muslim League in 1913, which the latter did on condition that it would 'at no time imply any disloyalty to the larger national cause'. As a member in high standing of both the Muslim League and Congress, Jinnah agreed the Lucknow Pact with Motilal Nehru, which provided for 'special electorates' for Muslims (who would only vote in those electorates and not for seats open to others) in the provincial legislative councils. The special electorates for Muslims would cover half of the Punjab council, one-third in Bombay Presidency, 30 per cent in the United Provinces, and 15 per cent each in the Central Provinces and Madras Presidency. By acknowledging 'special electorates', Congress was accommodating the imperial gambit of divide and rule for the first time, with a view to finding a permanent democratic solution to the Hindu–Muslim wedge that Britain was trying to create in Indian politics. But the Montagu–Chelmsford Reforms pointedly ignored this solution that had been meticulously prepared and accepted by the two mainstream nationalist parties. The British demonstrated again that any solution arrived at by even the moderate (loyalist) wing of the Congress would not be acceptable to the imperialists, and instead went ahead to try and create additional sources of division in Indian society through separate electorates for Sikhs, Christians, Anglo–Indians and Europeans.

This failure to appease even the Congress 'moderates' created an opening for the nationalists ('Extremists') committed to an early achievement of 'swaraj' or home rule. Bal Gangadhar Tilak, who had returned from his six-year jail term in faraway Mandalay in June 1914, now embraced the constitutional methods that his rivals (principally Gokhale) had advocated a decade earlier. Mellower after the years of forced labour in Mandalay that had severely worsened his health, Tilak rejoined the Congress and signed the Lucknow Pact, building close ties with Jinnah (especially after the death of the latter's mentor, Gokhale). But Tilak then devoted his attention to creating the Home Rule Leagues in alliance with the radical Anglo–Irish theosophist, Annie Besant, who had devoted the previous decade to Indian causes, including philosophy and religion, but increasingly politics, where her approach was modelled on the practices of the nationalists in her native Ireland. Both were able to expand the base of the nationalist movement significantly, with Tilak focusing increasingly on making the future India a federation (with separate linguistic states for the Telugu, Kannada and Marathi-speaking regions where he operated). Montagu's August 1917 promise of future dominion status was at least partly a response to the success Tilak and Besant achieved in their campaigns for home rule in India, and they were thus in the vanguard of the national opposition to the final form of the Montagu–Chelmsford Reforms announced in 1918–19. Surprisingly, however, neither the nationalist nor the moderate wings of Congress ever attempted to take their legitimate demand for self-determination to the peace-makers at Versailles, although a Vietnamese waiter (later known as Ho Chi Minh) and Chinese students (as we have seen) made their presence felt. India's claim to be heard at Versailles was much stronger, given the contribution of more than a million troops, and the promise of dominion status made in 1917 by Montagu in the House of Commons.

Soon after the 'Montford' reforms were announced, but before their final enactment, the British government instead took an extraordinary step to kill off the last vestige of moving towards 'self-determination' or democracy in India. Through its Imperial Legislative Council, it passed the Rowlatt Act on 18 March 1919—extending the Defence of India Rules introduced during the war to deal with violent revolutionaries. This Act permitted the colonial authorities to arrest and detain without trial anyone perceived to be seditious, giving accused persons no access to their accusers, stricter restrictions on the press, arrests without warrant, and in camera (secret) trials for proscribed political acts. The timing of this Act (smack in the middle of the Versailles Treaty negotiations) surely suggests that the British empire had been shaken to its core by the Ghadar, Jugantar and other violent uprisings before and during the war and remained extremely wary of their potency. Coming so soon after the promises of dominion status during the war, the Rowlatt Act united Indians of all shades of opinion against it. Almost all Indians in the central legislature resigned in protest, including Jinnah. And a new, far more effective adversary of the British empire now stepped to the fore: having built an extraordinary nationwide following over the previous two years, Mohandas Karamchand Gandhi called a 'hartal' (general strike) for 6 April 1919 to protest this murder of democracy.

Gandhi had returned to India in early 1915, having completed two decades of 'experiments with truth' in South Africa, where he had gone in 1893, a year after qualifying as a barrister from the Inner Temple, London. His considerable reputation preceded him in India, based on constructive work programmes at his Phoenix and Tolstoy farms (respectively near Durban and Johannesburg), political actions against the racism already rampant in Boer- and English-ruled South Africa, and latterly his organizational and social work on behalf of indentured labourers brought to Africa from India. From his earliest times in South Africa, Gandhi had become convinced of the primacy of two things in his work and the future of India: the need for

Hindu–Muslim unity, and the need to root out the scourge of untouchability. On the latter, he had made it an early conviction to clean the chamber pot of his law clerk (who happened to be from the untouchable caste) and his insistence that members of his family do so too almost broke his marriage. Through his own example, Gandhi fought untouchability throughout his life; in his experimental farms and ashrams, cleaning one's own toilet (and keeping it spick and span) was a founding principle, and cleaning the refuse of anyone from the untouchable caste was a second principle followed scrupulously to demonstrate to all members that untouchability was abhorrent and must be stamped out. Soon after setting up his first ashram in India, Gandhi was again faced by a similar furore over taking in a Dhedh (tanner) as a resident, and he again took his marriage to Kasturba to the brink in order to get his way, and did.

In South Africa, Gandhi's first few clients were Gujarati Muslim merchants, and his first political speech there was made in a mosque. In Durban and Pietermaritzburg (where he was famously thrown off a first-class train compartment because of the colour of his skin), he gained a deep empathy for the Muslim sensibility, which helped him hone an abiding commitment to Hindu–Muslim unity. In keeping with the advice of his ailing mentor Gokhale, Gandhi spent his first year back in India observing and travelling around the country (rather than plunging into politics). But the one person with whom he kept in close touch was Maulana Muhammad Ali who was leading the Khilafat campaign to preserve the rights of the Muslim caliph (khalifa), even as Britain went to war against the Ottomans. When Muhammad Ali and his brother Shaukat were arrested and jailed, Gandhi was amongst the first to protest.

Within his first week back in Bombay, a reception was organized in Gandhi's honour by the Gujarati Sabha, addressed by the leading young Congress leader of the time, M. A. Jinnah, who (like Gandhi) was seen as a protégé of the ageing Congress 'moderate' leader Gopal Krishna Gokhale. The two, already seen by some as rivals for the future leadership of India, started off on a sour note. Gandhi had observed, after his first interactions with the Indian National Congress fourteen years earlier, that Indians needed to operate in their own languages, rather than the language of their ruler, as English was spoken and understood by merely a million of India's 300 million people. Jinnah, clad in his immaculate Savile Row suit and tie, cut a very different figure from the dhoti-clad Gandhi at this reception, and he spoke in clipped English. Responding, Gandhi thanked Jinnah saying he was delighted that a Gujarati Muslim should be introducing him, but then saying it was unnecessary for them to speak in a foreign language when they shared a common one. There were two snubs in those opening lines (one calling attention to Jinnah's religion), and their relationship never got any better.

In early 1917, Gandhi travelled to west Champaran district in northern Bihar to act on behalf of the indigent indigo workers who were treated much like the indentured labourers of South Africa by British indigo planters, with very similar terms of service. Arriving at Champaran, the dhoti-clad Gandhi was initially refused entry (by a guard) into the home of the leading Indian lawyer of the town, Rajendra Prasad (later to be the president of India's Constituent Assembly and the first president of the Republic of India). Instead, Gandhi spent the first night at the home of a friend from his London days, Mazharul Haque, the president of the Muslim League in 1915. Rajendra Prasad hurried across the following day with an embarrassed apology, which proved to be the start of a close relationship, starting with Prasad refusing a judgeship in order to become a satyagrahi. Gandhi also spent another night at the hostel of the government college in Muzaffarpur, where J. B. Kripalani was a professor. He too was to become a lifelong devotee of Gandhi, and was president of Congress in the final months before independence in 1947. Both Prasad and Kripalani were mesmerized by Gandhi's personality, as was Vallabhbhai Patel, who was similarly cosmopolitan in his sartorial and personal habits until he encountered Gandhi during his second great satyagraha ('truth-force') campaign in Gujarat's Kheda district.

Gandhi had been travelling the country campaigning against the practice of indentured labour, and massive crowds greeted him at every station he stopped at in Bihar. In Champaran, his polite missive to the local British planters' representative, J. M. Wilson, brought forth an apoplectic response from the latter. Gandhi met L. F. Morshead, the district commissioner, and told him that his 'mission is that of making peace with honour', to enquire about the truth regarding the peasants' situation in Champaran and let the world know the facts. Morshead responded with a prohibitory order forbidding Gandhi's presence in the district; Gandhi defied the order and travelled on elephantback to several remote villages to fulfil his mission. For four days, the nation's attention was riveted on this frail man in his modest dhoti and kurta defying the might of an empire, as he had done successfully so often in South Africa. When arrested on 17 April, Gandhi made a simple statement that flummoxed the magistrate: he was responding to the 'higher law of our being, the voice of conscience', and so pleaded guilty to breaking the law of the British Raj. The magistrate now sought time to think, reserving his judgement until four days later, and asking Gandhi to post bail of a mere Rs 100. Gandhi said he did not have the money and the confused magistrate let him off anyway. At every step, Gandhi was winning the battle for public opinion, exposing the unjustness of an empire that spoke of the rule of law and fair play, but allowed nothing of the sort in an area of extreme injustice—near-slave conditions of employment in an imperial industry that produced dyes for the global clothing and chemical industries. A thoroughly mortified Lieutenant Governor ordered that the case be withdrawn on 20 April and Gandhi had his first big victory over the British government of India.

Gandhi had quickly become a national hero, and he only added to his growing reputation with his next two satyagraha campaigns—both in his native Gujarat. The first was in Kheda, where he and Patel organized peasants in a no-tax campaign following a terrible drought that had severely reduced the crop, and made it impossible to pay the land and other taxes. The imperial government's approach in all such cases was to confiscate land soon after taxes had gone unpaid. Having instilled fearlessness into the indentured labourers and landless peasants of Champaran, Gandhi (with Patel) did so now for their counterparts and their landlords in Kheda. Hundreds voluntarily gave up their land, while Gandhi demanded that the government cease the unjust and inhuman practice of confiscation. Before long, the government caved in and most of the confiscated land was returned (some voluntarily sold back to previous owners by the shamefaced new ones). Gandhi also turned his attention to the millworkers of Ahmedabad, where he used a new technique— fasting—to first get the workers to persist with their struggle, and then to get the mill owners to agree to pay them higher wages.

These were all consciously apolitical actions, as Gandhi tested the waters and moved slowly forward. In March 1919, however, his own, and the nation's, outrage over the Rowlatt Act led Gandhi to plunge headlong into the political fray, calling for boycotts and non-cooperation. Protests were even more vehement because 6 to 12 million Indians had died in the influenza epidemic during the past year. News of Gandhi's call for a hartal spread quickly around the country, but not always without distortions: Delhi shut down a week early (on 30 March), but there was a complete shutdown on the appointed day (6 April) in Punjab and Bombay. Such 'lawless' methods did cause consternation amongst most of the senior leadership of the Congress, including Tilak, Besant, and Motilal Nehru (who was appalled that his thirty-year-old son, Jawaharlal, had joined Gandhi's bandwagon). On 8 April, Gandhi was pulled off a train from Bombay to the Punjab and arrested. Two days later, two key leaders of the movement in Punjab, Dr Saifuddin Kitchlew and Dr Satya Pal, were arrested—inflaming a storm of outrage the following day, as massive processions were taken out in protest. The British police fired indiscriminately into this crowd, killing twenty to thirty people. This set off a riot, and five Europeans were killed in the aftermath. Gandhi decried this breakdown of discipline, and immediately called off the satyagraha campaign while sitting in jail.

Governor Michael O'Dwyer imposed martial law on Punjab, and brought in Brigadier General Reginald Dyer to maintain order. They rounded up a large number of Punjabis, and made them crawl through the streets where the riots had occurred, forcing some vegetarians to lick the ground where European blood had spilt and dried. On 13 April, a crowd of some 10,000 unarmed people (including many villagers unaware about martial law) had gathered at Jallianwala Bagh (an enclosed garden) to celebrate Baisakhi, a day of festivity for Punjabis to ring in the New Year. The overzealous Dyer brought in Gurkha and Baluchi troops, blocked the only exit from the garden, and asked his troops to fire indiscriminately into the crowd until the troops' ammunition ran out. The subsequent report into the episode found that 1,650 rounds had been fired into the unarmed and peaceful crowd, killing 379 men, women and children and injuring another thousand, of whom some 200 later succumbed to their wounds. Press censorship ensured that almost no news of the arbitrary and brutal massacre emerged until several weeks later; when it did, the whole nation was outraged. Tagore resigned his knighthood at the end of May 1919, and Gandhi returned the Kaiser-i-Hind medal he had been given for recruiting soldiers for the British cause in the Great War, and other medals for his work in the ambulance brigades during the Boer and Zulu wars.

And a most surprising intervention occurred at this point: Amanullah Khan, the new king of Afghanistan, sent his troops across his border into British India in May 1919 in solidarity with his Indian brethren (over Jallianwala). That border was disputed, in any case, although the Anglo–Russian treaties of 1907 had made Afghanistan a British protectorate (with Britain in control of its foreign policy). Lenin had repudiated this Tsarist treaty too, emboldening Amanullah to make his bid for full independence. Britain sent the Royal Air Force into action in June 1919, bombing Kabul and Herat. Chastened, Amanullah arrived at a peace treaty with Britain on 8 August 1919—but, weary of war, Britain relinquished control over Afghan foreign policy, leading promptly to the opening of Soviet consulates in the country.

General Dyer was hailed as a hero back in Britain, with the conservative *Daily Mail* raising a large collection of £26,000 in his honour, and the House of Lords officially condoning his actions for having saved the empire. That reaction infuriated politicians of all stripes in India, and Gandhi announced a new programme of satyagraha and protest, which gained ground especially after the publication in early 1920 of the Hunter Committee Report (into the

Jallianwala massacre) which whitewashed Dyer's role. Over this period, the emerging contours of the Versailles settlement provided an additional spark, and Gandhi reached out to his close Muslim allies—Maulana Abul Kalam Azad, Maulana Muhammad Ali, and the latter's cricketer brother Shaukat (all three of whom were in British jails)—to build an impregnable wall of Hindu–Muslim unity over the Khilafat issue. Gandhi told Hindus that, to show solidarity with their Muslim brethren, all Indians should support Muslims in their time of greatest need (when Muslim holy places were under threat), and he urged Muslims to adopt his non-violent methods in return for this pledge of unconditional support from non-Muslim Indians. Between May 1919 and August 1920, Gandhi developed a programme of Non-Cooperation with the British government, especially to pressurize Britain and its allies not to partition Turkey or interfere with the institution of the caliphate.

However, events at the other edge of Britain's Asian empire initially took centre stage after March 1919. On the very day that the Rowlatt Act passed in London—giving the British new authoritarian powers of arbitrary arrest and detention without trial in India—the leader of Egypt's nationalist Wafd Party, Saad Zaghlul, and three of his colleagues were arrested and deported to Malta. Although Britain had effectively ruled Egypt since 1882 through the khedive, an Ottoman satrap, Egypt had been formally turned into a British protectorate at the start of the Great War in 1914. Khedive Abbas II first sought to align with the Ottomans but was promptly deposed by the British, and the more compliant Sultan Hussein Kamel agreed to make Egypt a British protectorate. This caused outrage amongst Egyptians like Zaghlul, and the broader population was even more disgusted by the licentiousness of the British and Australian troops that swept through Cairo and Alexandria on their way to Gallipoli and the Ottoman front.

At the end of the war, Egyptians were just as enthused about Wilson's promise of 'self-determination' as were many other nationalities of the Central Powers' empires in Europe. Zaghlul, a distinguished lawyer, litterateur and former education minister, demanded complete autonomy (if not full independence) when he met Reginald Wingate, the British administrator of Egypt in November–December 1918. He requested that a wafd (delegation) be allowed to go to Paris to present the nationalists' demands to the Great Powers—a request that Wingate summarily rejected. In response, hundreds of thousands of Egyptians signed petitions in support of Zaghlul's demands and his movement was appositely named the Wafd. Now Zaghlul urged the Khedive to demand complete independence, which is what provoked his deportation to Malta, in turn stirring a massive storm of protests and demonstrations on the very day that Britain outraged India with the passage of the 'black'

Rowlatt Act. The protests in Egypt turned violent, with telegraph lines and railway tracks being vandalized. A mob killed eight British soldiers and the British were suddenly confronted with a genuine Arab revolt, not in one of the Ottoman vilayets, but in the one country that Britain had wrenched from Ottoman rule and made a British protectorate.

In Egypt, the British responded to the violence of the crowds in a notably more benign manner than they were to do in Punjab a few days later. General Allenby, the hero of the British 'liberation' of Jerusalem and Damascus during the war, was sent to Cairo to deal with the ferment there. Unlike O'Dwyer and Dyer in Punjab, Allenby concluded that Egypt could not be pacified without releasing Zaghlul and his nationalist comrades; he duly let them out of their Maltese prison, and allowed them travel to Europe, thus belatedly fulfilling the original demand for a wafd (delegation) to Paris! Zaghlul received little support from the other powers in Paris (just as a delegation from the Korean monarchy in 1907 had been brushed off by the Great Powers when it sought aid against Japan's imperial ambitions); this was after all the high noon of imperialism, and pious declarations of 'self-determination' were never meant to apply to the Great Powers!

Nonetheless, after many months of negotiations (during which Zaghlul was again exiled—this time to Seychelles—for thwarting the formation of a pro-British government), Britain gave Egypt her 'independence' in 1922. After winning 90 per cent of the seats in the first election, Zaghlul himself became prime minister in January 1924. However, it was a severely circumscribed independence since Britain retained control over the Suez Canal (which it did not relinquish until 1956) and also continued to run Egypt's foreign policy. More significantly, while the khedive (now called sultan) was also the king of Sudan, the British insisted on retaining full military control over Sudan. It was over his disagreements with the British about Sudan that Zaghlul resigned after just ten months in office. Independence proved to be a mirage for the Egyptians, as Britain continued to exert control and subsequent governments came to be seen as little more than puppets of the British, provoking the formation of Egypt's Communist Party in 1925 and the Muslim Brotherhood in 1928.

Britain had, of course, taken control of Egypt since 1882 primarily in order to bolster its control over the trade routes to India and, in particular, the Suez Canal (built with French assistance), which drastically cut the cost of the passage between Europe and India, and thence to the rest of Asia. In India in 1919, the events in Egypt registered only very slightly as the Congress first decided to investigate exactly what had happened at Jallianwala. On 8 June 1919, a five-member Congress committee (comprising Gandhi,

Abbas Tyabji, Motilal Nehru, Fazlul Haq and Chittaranjan Das—who had defended Aurobindo at the Alipore Bomb trial in 1908) began investigating the atrocities committed by the British in Punjab.

Just as the 10 April arrests had involved a Muslim and a Hindu leader, now the investigative committee had three Hindus and two Muslims, and this unity was also evident in the slogan of 'Hindu–Musalman ki jai' (victory to Hindu–Muslim unity) that resonated across Punjab and India through 1919. That December, to remind the nation of the awful atrocities of Jallianwala, the annual session of the Congress Party was held in Amritsar and Motilal Nehru, in his report as Congress president that year, mentioned that 108 people had been sentenced to death, and a total of 7,371 years' worth of imprisonment had been handed down for agitations against the Rowlatt Act. During the Congress session, the Montagu–Chelmsford Reforms were finally enacted, and most political prisoners (other than those transported to Mandalay or the Andamans) were released at the end of the year, including Maulana Abul Kalam Azad and Maulana Muhammad Ali.

By this point, the partition of Ottoman territories appeared to be a settled fact, but Muhammad Ali led a four-man delegation to London to press for the Ottoman caliph to continue to control the Muslim sacred places—Mecca and Medina—which had just passed out of Muslim control for the first time in twelve centuries. London stories about the exploits of Lawrence of Arabia and the Hashemite Sharifs of Mecca cut little ice with India's Muslims, as Feisal was seen as little more than a British puppet; his father Hussein's antecedents notwithstanding, he too was seen as a British surrogate. When Muhammad Ali's delegation met Prime Minister Lloyd George, the latter said clearly that he did not want 'any Muslim in India to imagine that we are going to abandon, when we come to Turkey, the principles which we have ruthlessly applied to Christian countries like Germany and Austria'. By May 1920, the partition of Turkey was complete, and the Ottomans' Arab domains had been divided up between Britain and France: Mt Lebanon (where France had established links since 1861 with the Maronite Christians, who owed allegiance to the same Pope as the French rather than to the Orthodox church based in Constantinople) plus the Bekaa Valley and some coastal Muslim- and Druze-dominated regions would constitute the French Mandate of Lebanon, with a slight Christian majority; the new nation state of Syria (where Feisal had been ensconced as king) was to become a French mandate too, in a compromise that Lawrence and his friends like Gertrude Bell found tawdry and outrageous. Palestine was to become a British Mandate, as would the new country of Iraq (the former Mesopotamian vilayets of Basra, including Shia holy sites such as Karbala, and the Sunni-majority vilayet of Baghdad, plus Kurdish-dominated Mosul, where the Turkish Petroleum Company was to be renamed the Iraqi Petroleum Company, with France given a quarter of the shares in exchange for giving up its claim on Mosul, which had been assigned to France under the Sykes–Picot accord). The Hijaz (including Mecca and Medina) would remain under the nominal control of the Hashemite Sharif Hussein, although it was understood that the Hashemites had the cover of military support from Britain.

These forms of 'indirect rule' were familiar to Indian nationalists, who were aware how 'subsidiary alliances' had just been the first step towards exerting full British control in the eighteenth and nineteenth century in India and Malaya. Although the mandates (for Britain over Palestine and Iraq, and the French over Syria and Lebanon) were only ratified by the League of Nations in 1922, their contours were already clear by the middle of 1920. The veneer of Hashemite control of the Hijaz was seen as little more than a smokescreen for British rule and in India, the Khilafat Movement gained additional wind in its sails with the national outpouring of rage over the attempted whitewashing of Dyer's atrocities by the Hunter Committee Report in May 1920. Gandhi and Muhammad Ali formed an eight-member Khilafat Committee (with Gandhi, a Hindu, as its chairman!), and began to organize nationally for a Non-Cooperation Movement that would involve Indians withdrawing from all forms of representative government, the bureaucracy, schools and colleges, boycotting British goods, shunning the courts, returning all honours, refusing all nominated positions, and repudiating the recruitment of Indians for further military services in Mesopotamia. This last would especially hurt Britain, as a tribal revolt had just broken out in the new Iraq, and Indian troops had always been crucial to maintaining Britain's hold over that territory, although the British protectorates along the coast of the Arabian peninsula (the Trucial States of Oman, Dubai, Qatar, Kuwait, Abu Dhabi, etc.) remained an important strategic asset for Britain to control Basra and the southern part of Mesopotamia/Iraq.

When the leadership of the Mahomedan Anglo–Oriental College at Aligarh (which had been established by Sir Syed Ahmed Khan as a pro-British institution for Muslims) refused to join the boycott, the vast majority of its Khilafatist students walked out, and an alternative institution was established on Delhi's outskirts called the Jamia Millia Islamia. Gandhi requested the poet Muhammad Iqbal to become its rector, but had to settle for his friend Muhammad Ali (as Iqbal turned down the offer). Nationally, however, the summer and monsoon of 1920 was the high noon of Hindu–Muslim unity, as a tidal wave of support emerged for Gandhi and any programme for which he sought support: on 1 August 1920, he announced the details of his

Non-Cooperation programme, and called for a united nationwide agitation in favour of the Khilafat demands, and the restoration of the khalifa of Islam—the Ottoman sultan—to full authority over the Islamic holy places. That day, coincidentally, the other titan of India's nationalist movement, Bal Gangadhar Tilak died, further clearing the way for Gandhi to dominate the national scene; already, he had been elected president of Annie Besant's India Home Rule League.

At the Calcutta session of the Congress in September 1920, however, the old guard of Congress decided to oppose the Non-Cooperation Movement because it would contribute to anarchy and the breakdown of order, and (as articulated by Jinnah) unleash potent religious forces that would be impossible to control. In the days before the Congress session in Calcutta, Gandhi (alongside Shaukat Ali) prepared the programme of Non-Cooperation, while the rest of the Congress leadership—Motilal Nehru, Chittaranjan Das, Lala Lajpat Rai, Bipin Pal, Annie Besant—confabulated to prepare a befitting response. At the session itself, it was clear that the tide of the young and Muslims was strongly in favour of Gandhi, but the veteran leadership was strongly opposed, and the balance of opinion seemed evenly poised. When it came to the voting, however, one of the key veteran leaders of Congress (Motilal Nehru) defected to Gandhi's side, ensuring a narrow victory (144 to 132). His coup thus complete, Gandhi was quickly able to merge the masses (loyal to him) with the classes (as represented by the Congress leadership) in mounting a unified non-violent assault on British rule.

With the programme of Non-Cooperation generating spectacular support across the land, in December 1920 Gandhi promised his compatriots that he would deliver 'swaraj within a year'. Only a few important voices (including Rabindranath Tagore, the poet-sage of India who was not formally in Congress, but an important voice of conscience outside it) counselled caution. At the Nagpur session of Congress in December 1920, the acclamation and support for Gandhi was near-universal, with all Muslims but one strongly on his side: the one exception was Muhammad Ali Jinnah, who attempted to speak out against this dangerous mixing of religion and politics; he was shouted down, and walked out of Congress, never to return.

Ironically, the future maker of a nation state for the subcontinent's Muslims was opposed to Indians taking up the cause of Islam in its Arab homelands, while the father of the future secular nation state of India was urging his people to take up this sectarian Muslim cause. In the euphoria of 1921, the departure of Jinnah (who had been a Congress titan on par with Motilal five years earlier) was barely noticed. One of the founding members of the Muslim League, Hakim Ajmal Khan, was elected Congress president for 1921.

Another prominent Muslim doctor, M. A. Ansari, who was president of the Muslim League in 1920, left the League for the Congress (and remained a steadfast Congressman for the rest of his life).

All other organizations were irrelevant now, as Gandhi was increasingly seen as the saviour of peasants and workers, of India's rich and poor alike. Swami Shraddhanand of the Arya Samaj was invited to preach from the pulpit of the Jama Masjid in Delhi. Maulana Abdul Bari urged Muslims to stop eating beef as a gesture to their Hindu brethren (although Gandhi had insisted that Hindus' support for Khilafat must be unconditional). The Non-Cooperation Movement spread like wildfire across the country, literally, with great bonfires of foreign cloth being held, and charkhas (spinning wheels) being distributed and taken up across the country as Indians sought to spin their own khadi (coarse homespun) clothes instead. The battle cries of Swaraj and Khilafat rang through the land, although some confessed not to know what the latter meant (often mistaking it for 'khilaf', the Urdu word for opposition!).

Gandhi kept insisting on non-violence (ahimsa). For most of his followers (including the Muslims), the commitment to non-violence was tactical at best—in keeping with their leader's exhortation. Three or four major outbreaks of violence did occur, including one that caused the deaths of fifty-eight people in Bombay during the Prince of Wales' visit. Gandhi undertook a fast to bring the Bombay violence (against Parsis, Anglo–Indians and Christians perceived as pro-British) to an end, which was duly achieved within three days. But the most dangerous outbreak occurred in Kerala, where the Moplahs (or Mappila, a Muslim community that was believed to be descended from Arab trader-settlers from a millennium earlier, but were now mainly peasants) had been agitating for tenant rights since 1916 against their landlords (who were mainly Hindu) and the British government. This had occasionally turned violent, but on 29 August 1921, the police attacked a mosque in Tirurangadi looking for stored arms. A raid on a mosque by security forces almost always has incendiary consequences and it did on this occasion too, as the Moplah leaders began exhorting their followers to rise up in a jihad to establish 'Khilafat republics' or kingdoms. There was an orgy of violence, with Hindus being targeted in particular, as hundreds were forcibly converted to Islam, and numerous temples and shrines were desecrated. Gandhi took Maulana Muhammad Ali and set off for Kerala but the British, sensing an opportunity to drive a wedge into the Hindu–Muslim relationship, arrested Muhammad Ali from the train and jailed him and his brother Shaukat. After letting the violence flare on for some time (with Hindu killings being increasingly highlighted in the press), the British government sent in the army to suppress what, by then, was a major rebellion. More than 45,000 people were arrested and as many as 2,337 rebels were killed in the army response, including 60 who were found asphyxiated in an overstuffed train compartment.

Despite those significant setbacks and exceptions, the Non-Cooperation Movement remained largely non-violent. By December 1921, however, the goal of 'swaraj' (defined then as dominion status) was still elusive, as Gandhi's one-year deadline approached, and some former opponents of non-cooperation (prominently Annie Besant) were taunting Gandhi about this. But the British had been shaken too, and were struggling to devise a solution to the impasse, made worse by discontent sparked by a sharp increase in inflation since the end of the war, which had also been accompanied by a decline in India's exports (and overall economic climate) with the evaporation of wartime demand, and the failure of the monsoon in 1921. At the Ahmedabad session of Congress in December 1921, organized efficiently by Vallabhbhai Patel, the British viceroy Lord Reading sent word through M. M. Malaviya and M. A. Jinnah, offering to open negotiations for dominion status for India by January 1922, and setting 14 January as the specific date for the talks. Malaviya also visited Chittaranjan Das in his Calcutta prison cell, and Das and Maulana Azad sent a telegram to Gandhi urging him to take up Reading's offer of talks on dominion status. This was a dramatic advance on the mealy-mouthed Montford Reforms of just two years earlier.

In retrospect, historians question whether Reading was acting on his own or really had London's backing for his move. But Gandhi made the release of the Ali brothers (Muhammad and Shaukat) a precondition for any talks with Reading. This was unacceptable to the British, who were keen to create a breach between Gandhi and his Khilafatist supporters, and were unwilling to release Muhammad Ali, whom they accused of treason, especially for his alleged invitation to Afghanistan's king to attack India (in April 1921), which was supposed to have enthused the Moplah leaders too. Maulana Abul Kalam Azad later wrote in his book *India Wins Freedom* (in one of the sections that he held back for publication until thirty years after his death) that Gandhi made a strategic error by not taking up the British offer of dominion status (or talks towards them) and standing by Muhammad Ali (who was later to desert him). While this judgement is easy to make (and appears completely correct) in hindsight, Gandhi had to consider the British record of divide and rule tactics and he could just as easily have been drawn into possibly futile talks at the expense of a breach in the solidity of the Hindu–Muslim alliance.

Given what was to happen over the first two months of 1922, Gandhi surely missed his best opportunity to win India its freedom, with a united India taking its place as a British dominion alongside Canada, Australia and

New Zealand, but with a demographic clout that would have quickly made it one of the great powers of the 1920s and 30s. The British, exhausted by war and facing defeat in Turkish Anatolia while struggling to hold on to their gains in Arabia, had been brought to their knees in India by the Khilafat and Non-Cooperation movements. Amid inflation and economic stagnation, plus the nationwide support for boycotts and non-cooperation that had caught the imagination of rich and poor Indians alike, Britain (as represented by Lord Reading) had run out of ideas to counter the united uprising that Gandhi was leading. Independence was his for the taking.

Instead, Gandhi ignored Reading's overture and pressed on with plans for his next political programme: Civil Disobedience in Bardoli, Gujarat, to protest land confiscations after a drought. He sent a charter of demands to the Viceroy on 1 February 1922, and they were all rejected within the week. Nationwide support for a mass civil disobedience campaign had been mobilized. But then, an episode occurred in the village of Chauri Chaura in Gorakhpur district of the United Provinces, to which Gandhi had a most unexpected reaction.

Like in many other villages across the country, a procession had been organized at Chauri Chaura in solidarity with the impending civil disobedience campaign. The police had intervened, and the crowd had responded with taunts about the police constables' treachery in defending the foreign power's oppressive tactics. A scuffle initially occurred between stragglers in the procession and the police constables, and the rest of the crowd had returned to help their comrades. With the crowd swelling, the panicked policemen began to fire into the crowd but their ammunition was insufficient to deal with the situation, and it soon ran out. Having angered the crowd with their unnecessarily armed response, killing three and wounding several more in the crowd, the policemen ran back into their police station, which the incensed crowd surrounded, and set alight. Twenty-two police constables died in the resulting fire on the night of 5 February 1922. It took three days for the news to get out to the rest of the country, and Gandhi's response to it was immediate and emphatic: he called off the entire Non-Cooperation (and impending Civil Disobedience) Movement on 8 February. Instead, Gandhi announced that he would undertake a five-day fast of purification and penance and regretted, in particular, his equable responses to the previous episodes of violence that had occurred. As with everything else that Gandhi had decided since 1920, Congress immediately fell in line, suspending the Non-Cooperation Movement, and instead announcing a 'constructive programme' of education, charkha spinning, reform and temperance.

The rest of the nation was quite another matter. India was shell-shocked, and angered by the leader's strange and inexplicable decision. He had not suspended non-cooperation even after thousands of deaths over the Moplah riots. Here it was the *police* that had responded with armed violence, and the crowd had only reacted to the armed actions of the police. Young India was simply astounded that inches from securing the triumphal outcome of independence for a united India, the leader had suddenly called off the movement. Amongst the many young leaders who expressed their anger and astonishment was the twenty-five-year-old Subhas Chandra Bose, who had qualified for the prestigious ICS (where Jawaharlal Nehru had failed, and Aurobindo Ghose had passed the written exam but chosen to fail the riding test) but amazed his family—and electrified the nation—by becoming the first qualified member of the ICS to resign rather than take up the 'covenanted' position. Bose had gone to meet Gandhi immediately after his decision to resign, and came away not entirely convinced that non-violence was the only acceptable path; his conviction was only reinforced now, and he remained an adversary the British regarded with altogether more guardedness than Gandhi or Nehru. Another young man, Bhagat Singh (whose uncle Ajit Singh had been one of the leaders of the Ghadar uprising in the Punjab a decade earlier) also expressed a sense of anger and betrayal at Gandhi's capitulation to the imperial power at the very cusp of victory, and he was to lead a popular movement during the rest of the 1920s that did not eschew targeted violence in the pursuit of freedom.

The Khilafat leadership was particularly flabbergasted: they had made a tactical compromise with the idea of non-violence, and now it was shown to have failed. Maulana Muhammad Ali, in defence of whose interests Gandhi had rejected the Reading–Malaviya–Jinnah initiative of 14 January, drifted away from him. Many prominent Muslims did not—including Maulana Abul Kalam Azad and M. A. Ansari—but from here on, the initiative in Muslim leadership passed from Gandhi's associates, and the spirit of Hindu–Muslim solidarity ebbed as the British worked to deepen animosity amid a growing number of episodes of Muslim–Hindu violence. When Mustafa Kemal Atatürk abolished the caliphate after successfully creating a new Turkey, the last embers of the Khilafat Movement died a natural death.

For the British, Gandhi's decision to suspend non-cooperation when Britain was on the verge of capitulation was an absolute godsend. On 10 March 1922, Gandhi himself was arrested and jailed for a six-year term, although he was released in 1924 on medical grounds, when faced with an acute case of appendicitis. Many prominent leaders of Congress—including Motilal Nehru and Chittaranjan Das—decided that a dose of cooperation with the moth-eaten legislative bodies created by the Montford Reforms was worthwhile, and they participated in the 1923 elections to those legislative bodies under the banner of their newly-created Swaraj Party, and the Swarajists became the largest single party in most provincial assemblies as well as the central legislature. C. R. Das himself became the first mayor of Calcutta, appointing twenty-six-year-old Bose as his chief executive officer, and they plunged into the tasks of education reform, as well as the mundane work of cleaning up the administration of the city with aplomb. Jinnah, having resigned from Congress, was elected to the central legislature as an independent but voted almost exclusively with the Swarajists on most issues. Although the central legislature had forty unelected members (more than the thirty-eight Swarajist members, who were usually joined by seven independents), a prominent Swarajist, Vithalbhai Patel (the elder brother of Vallabhbhai) was elected the president (or speaker) of the central legislature, and played an important role in institutionalizing its parliamentary practices, some of which survive today.

Never slow to capitalize on a political opportunity, the British began to create other wedges in Indian society, apart from deepening the emerging Muslim–Hindu divide. In the large Madras presidency, local British bureaucrats had helped launch an anti-Brahmin movement during the war years and had attempted to spread the canard that the Congress was a 'Brahmin' party (conveniently missing the fact that its national leader himself was non-Brahmin). The result was the creation of the Justice Party, which remained a pro-British and anti-Brahmin party with a detailed mythology of 'Dravidians' being separate from the rest of India, mixing a loathing of North Indians ('Aryans') with its initially caste-based appeal. Despite active British patronage, the Justice Party was slow to gain actual ground amid the nationwide appeal of Gandhi, and the Congress continued to grow in Madras too. Additionally, at the start of Gandhi's non-cooperation campaign, the British encouraged the creation of a Moderate Party, but this was hamstrung by the absence of a stalwart like Gokhale (who had performed the role so effectively in 1907). Although led by Surendranath Banerjea, one of the titans of the 1905–08 agitation against the partition of Bengal, the Moderate Party (even after it was rechristened as the National Liberal Federation of India) gained no more than a moderate following, although participating as a bit player in the constitutional dance that Britain attempted to play with those willing to collaborate with it over the next two decades—much like the now-forgotten roles of Bishop Abel Muzorewa in 1970s Zimbabwe (Rhodesia) and Mangosuthu Buthelezi in 1990s South Africa. In the restricted electorate for the 1923 election, the Moderates were nonetheless the second-largest party bloc, with 27 of the 105 elected seats in the central legislature.

Back in the Arab world, Britain's Hashemite allies and proxies were facing divergent fates. Feisal, although appointed king of Syria by the British, was left high and dry in September 1919 when Lloyd George and Clemenceau agreed that Syria should become a French Mandate, but that Britain should have Palestine and Mesopotamia (including Mosul) as British Mandates. Feisal put on a brave face, and mobilized Arab opinion in favour of his definition of a Greater Syria that would encompass Lebanon and Palestine, and had a Syrian national assembly endorse this idea on 7 March 1920. A few days later (20 March), the Christian-controlled state of Lebanon repudiated this idea, and adopted a new national flag for itself with a Lebanese cedar in the middle of the French tricolour. In July, the French sent an ultimatum to Feisal, and a French army crushed Feisal's Arab force on 24 July to re-establish the French Mandate over Syria—separating it clearly from its other mandate, the greater Lebanon (with a slight Christian majority) described earlier.

Feisal fled Syria, but eventually, on 23 August 1921, was crowned the king of Iraq, albeit within a British Mandate territory with an array of British advisers led by Gertrude Bell. He had always been the favourite of the Mesopotamian assembly, but they had initially picked his brother Abdullah in his stead (when Feisal had been designated as king of Syria). Now, a smaller but completely artificial and new state called Transjordan, carved out from the territories on the east bank of the Jordan River within the British Mandate of Palestine and including some of the historic sites made famous by the Lawrence movie, was found for Abdullah. His great-grandson (with the same name) still rules as king of Jordan. The Hashemite handed the least promising kingdom eventually settled down to become a surprisingly effective ruler and his is the only branch of the family that still rules a small chunk of the Arab homelands that his father Hussein's British allies hoped to hand over to the loyal Hashemites.

The Hashemite patriarch, Hussein, was able to rule only briefly as king of the Hijaz, before he was defeated militarily and driven from his ancestral homeland in 1924 by Abdul Aziz ibn Saud and his Wahhabi allies with their extreme Salafi interpretation of Islam. Ibn Saud had first regained control of his family's traditional seat of Riyadh in 1902 from their rivals the al-Rashids, who had ousted the al-Sauds from the Nejd central highlands in 1890 (obliging the al-Sauds to seek refuge with the al-Sabah rulers of Kuwait). But by the time the Great War began, the al-Rashids were still in control of most of Arabia apart from the Nejd (which ibn Saud had incrementally regained control of by 1912) but the al-Rashids made the fateful decision of aligning themselves with the Ottomans (and the Central Powers) during the war. Interestingly Abdul Aziz ibn Saud's tutor in Islamic jurisprudence, Abdullah bin Abdullatif al ash-Sheikh (of the al-Wahhab family), defected to the al-Rashids when they conquered the Nejd in 1890, but eventually switched loyalties back to the al-Sauds in 1902. He was accepted back unconditionally, with ibn Saud even marrying his daughter Tarfa bint Abdullah; the son she bore, Faisal, was to be king of Saudi Arabia from 1964 to 1975, and the leading figure in the OPEC boycott and oil crisis of 1973.

By 1914, British intelligence had made contact with Abdul Aziz ibn Saud, through a spy named Captain William Shakespear who gained his confidence and helped to build him up as an alternative and more credible leader of any 'Arab Revolt' than the Hashemite Sharif. The aura and strength of ibn Saud's forces came from the fanaticism of the Ikhwan brotherhood of Bedouin tribes he had created, convincing them that the only way to truly practise pure Islam was to abandon their nomadic lifestyles and settle around oases. Being new converts to the Wahhabi ideology, the Ikhwan were easily convinced that a state of jahiliyya (anarchy and idolatry) prevailed in much of the Muslim world (akin to its alleged condition in the seventh century during the lifetime of Islam's prophet).

In December 1915, the Treaty of Darin made the inchoate Saudi state a 'protectorate' of Britain, with the latter promising to support the al-Saud in their battles against the al-Rashids. After Shakespear's death in 1915, Harry St John Philby became the British intelligence link to ibn Saud. He became a close personal friend and eventually converted to Islam, married a Muslim, and resigned from the British political service to become an adviser to ibn Saud. With the end of the war in 1918, an abundance of British munitions were made available to ibn Saud and this enabled him to begin a final campaign against the al-Rashids in 1920. By 1922, the al-Sauds had defeated the al-Rashids and added the eastern and southern parts of the peninsula to their existing stronghold of the Nejd. With the doubling of Saudi territory after the defeat of the al-Rashids in 1922, a new British–Saudi treaty was signed at Uqair, under which the Saudis recognized British suzerainty over Iraq and Britain's long-standing protectorates along the Persian Gulf coast (Kuwait, Oman, Dubai, Abu Dhabi, Qatar, etc.), which were vital trading links and coaling stations on the trade routes between the Suez Canal and British India. Now the Saudis inevitably came into conflict with the Hashemite rulers of the Hijaz, having already won a skirmish with Abdullah in 1919.

Sharif Hussein proclaimed himself the new caliph once Atatürk abolished the Istanbul-based caliphate in 1924. The Ikhwan were immediately roused to turn on this claimant to Islam's leadership, and they captured Ta'if in September 1924. Sharif Hussein turned to his supposed British allies for assistance, but Britain turned him down, as did his son, King Abdullah of Transjordan.

When ibn Saud and the Ikhwan arrived at the holy city of Mecca in December 1924, they were able to take it without a fight, as Sharif Hussein had already fled to Jeddah. Thus ended 700 years of Hashemite ascendancy over Mecca, and over the following few months the Saudis conquered Medina and Jeddah as well. In January 1926, Abdul Aziz ibn Saud was proclaimed the new king of the Hijaz, and he installed his son Faisal (an al-Wahhab from his mother's side) as the first Saudi governor of the Hijaz. By 1927, ibn Saud had unified most of the Arabian peninsula into a new Kingdom of Saudi Arabia, whose independence (over the Nejd and Hijaz) was recognized by the British in a new Treaty of Jeddah in May that year. Ironically, the newly Muslim Harry St John Philby proved rather too zealous in his loyalty to his Saudi masters, advising them in the ways of the world with diligence—and an objectivity that included shedding any residual loyalty to Britain. While his son was to betray Britain to the Soviets, Harry advised ibn Saud to hitch his wagon to the rising Americans, which he was to duly do in 1938—forging a rock-solid oil-for-security alliance deal that endures to this day.

Chapter 4

THE NASCENT CLASH OF IMPERIAL TITANS
AND NEW IDEOLOGIES (1925–1939)

Globally, the years from 1925 to 1939 were characterized by the clash of contending ideologies—Communism, Socialism, Imperialism, Fascism and Democracy—and the advent of a severe financial crisis, which began in Britain (after Churchill took sterling back onto the gold standard at an unsustainably high parity rate) and eventually spread to the US with the October 1929 Wall Street crash. The Smoot–Hawley import tariffs imposed by the US (which had an especially negative impact on Japan's textile exports) set off an orgy of 'beggar-thy-neighbour' currency devaluations and other protectionist steps that made the Great Depression a global phenomenon. Russia and Japan were the first to bounce back from the economic shock, although many of Asia's politically conscious leaders and writers missed the Japanese recovery in their ideological enthusiasm for Soviet Russia. Britain and France greatly expanded their empires by exploiting the mechanism of 'mandates', and Britain's disdain for its wartime promises to the Arabs and Indians became one of the themes of the period. In retrospect, Japan's actions in Manchuria (where it reinstalled the Manchu king, with Manchu or Chinese heads of all government departments) were less autocratic than anything Britain did in India or Iraq at the time, or that France was doing in Syria and Lebanon, although the fog of European historiography has helped obscure this.

THE UNRAVELLING OF CHURCHILL'S ARABIA

By the mid-1920s, Britain controlled almost all of peninsular Arabia, having gained substantially more than was supposed to be its lot under the Sykes–Picot Agreement with France. During the Great War, the tiny principality of Qatar had been added to the list of British protectorates along the Arabian coast (which had included Kuwait since 1899, Bahrain since 1860, and the Trucial States—Dubai, Abu Dhabi, Sharjah, Ras al-Khaimah and the rest of what is now the UAE—since 1821). The crucial port of Aden had been administered as part of the Bombay Presidency since 1839, and by 1863 the British had also established an Aden Protectorate over 285,000 square kilometres (of what later became South Yemen). Oman, once a great empire that had controlled not only the Arabian coastline but extended all the way to Zanzibar in east Africa and included Gwadar on the coast of Baluchistan, lost the Trucial States (previously dubbed its 'pirate' protectorates by the British) in the 1820s, and became part of the British sphere of influence by the 1860s when the British brokered a succession plan under which Zanzibar and Oman proper were separated, with one prince becoming emir of each. Although never formally part of the British empire, Oman (like Kuwait, Qatar, Aden, the Aden Protectorate and the Trucial States) used the (British) Indian rupee as the official currency. In 1924, the League of Nations had endorsed the British Mandate over Palestine (including Transjordan) and Iraq (the Mesopotamian vilayets of Baghdad and Basra, plus the mainly Kurdish vilayet of Mosul). By 1926, the British-allied King Abdul Aziz ibn Saud had conquered the Hijaz (including the holy cities of Mecca and Medina), adding them to his kingdom of Nejd, which had doubled in size after he defeated the Saudis' traditional enemies, the al-Rashids, in 1922 (as we've seen in earlier chapters).

The Treaty of Jeddah, signed on 20 May 1927 between ibn Saud and the British, recognized Saudi sovereignty and independence, distinguishing the relationship quite clearly from the unmistakably subordinate ones that the Hashemite family had with the British. Abdul Aziz ibn Saud had grown powerful enough for his independence to be recognized by the British, in exchange for his assurance not to attack the British protectorates of Kuwait, Qatar, Bahrain and the Trucial States. His Ikhwan forces, however, were unwilling to abide by any such agreements as they viewed these states as being insufficiently Muslim, and branded them infidels for not adhering to Wahhabism. When they attacked Transjordan, southern Iraq and Kuwait, ibn Saud went to war to suppress his former allies, the Ikhwan, and eventually defeated them in the Battle of Sibilla in March 1929, aided by British aerial bombardment. However, the austere Wahhabi doctrines—which outlawed almost all the popular forms of Muslim worship (including all forms of Sufism, as well as the use of music during the Hajj pilgrimage to Mecca)—brought the inchoate Saudi state into conflict with Egypt and other Muslim nations, who were used to a more relaxed approach during the Hajj.

In September 1932, ibn Saud formally proclaimed the establishment of the Kingdom of Saudi Arabia. The Salafi branch of Sunni Islam that the Saudi state promoted was based on a literalist and puritanical interpretation of the Quran and Hadith and rejected all later accretions (including especially the veneration of the graves of saints, and the use of amulets or beads for protection). Instead they sought to emulate the 'salafi' ('predecessors' or earliest

Muslims) as being the epitome of true Islamic practice. These austere and puritanical beliefs (which some Muslims found obscurantist, especially in their apparent rejection of modernity and science) inevitably brought the Salafi into conflict with other Muslims, especially the Shia (whom they branded as heretical). Islam in the Indian subcontinent, Egypt and Indonesia had been strongly influenced by Sufism (and the synthesis of Islam with other forms of mysticism), but this was vigorously opposed by Saudi Arabia, which sought to enforce its interpretation of Islam through its control over the Hajj and Umrah pilgrimages.

At the behest of Colonial Secretary Winston Churchill, British spies had sought out an authentic leader for post-Ottoman Arabia, and had hoped to find a pliable one. In 1921, Churchill had specifically ensured that the annual subsidy for ibn Saud was equalized with the subsidy Britain provided to Sharif Hussein (at £100,000 each). By backing two different leaders (the Hashemite Hussein, and the Salafi ibn Saud), the British had attempted to hedge their bets. In the end, Saudi Arabia proved a menace to peace in the Muslim world with its puritanical Salafism often spilling over into fanaticism. The founding king of Saudi Arabia had twenty-two wives from whom he had forty-five sons, of whom thirty-six remained in contention to succeed him on the throne in turn (right up to the present day). The enormous royal family's luxurious lifestyles appeared at odds with the austerity that they advocated for all other Muslims. This contradiction, coupled with hatred of the Saudi regime's alliance with the US, eventually spawned Al-Qaeda in the 1980s as an alternative Salafi force (led by Osama bin Laden, himself an authentic product of Saudi Arabia's school system). The Saudi state itself backed and funded the Jamaat-e-Islami in the Indian subcontinent and further east to propagate (and eventually enforce) Salafi/Wahhabi doctrines, playing a key role in radicalizing the practice of Islam across Asia. In the first few years after the Saudi takeover of the Hijaz, there were frequent clashes between Saudi police/Ikhwan and Muslim pilgrims from Egypt, India and the East Indies with the Saudi police beating up pilgrims who sang/danced or played music on their journey (as they had done for centuries).

Worse for the British, Abdul Aziz ibn Saud proved to be far more independent-minded than the British had bargained for. Harry St John Philby 'went native' upon resigning from the British secret service and became a personal adviser to the Saudi king: he advised his boss to diversify away from his early dependence on the British and instead cultivate the rising new power, the United States. When a massive gusher of oil was finally discovered in Saudi Arabia in 1932, it was Standard Oil of California (Socal) that found it and received the early concessions. Britain's long investment in the creation of Saudi Arabia came to nought, as it was to be an American consortium in alliance with the Saudi state that created the oil company (Arab-American Oil Company, or ARAMCO) that was to fully exploit Saudi Arabia's colossal oil reserves after 1938. With the enormous wealth from its oil, Saudi Arabia's influence grew greatly across the Muslim world, and the obscure lifestyle and cultural practices of this once-isolated nomadic tribe from the Nejd increasingly came to be seen as the epitome of Muslim orthodoxy.

In 1921 Churchill had briefly toyed with the idea of making ibn Saud king of Mesopotamia as he contemplated the challenges of dealing with the new British Mandate there. Upon becoming Colonial Secretary, Churchill quickly discovered that Britain was the 'greatest Mohammedan power in the world' after the demise of the Ottoman empire. He sought to 'appease' the Muslim world (a word used repeatedly by the British historian Christopher Catherwood, based on Churchill's extensive correspondence with Lloyd George), first by joining France and Italy in withdrawing from Anatolia (in favour of Mustafa Kemal's Turkish army, which, after all, had almost destroyed his career on the mud fields of Gallipoli). Lloyd George had invested too much in backing the Greek invasion of Smyrna and Anatolia, so he (and Foreign Secretary Lord Curzon) refused to countenance the idea of withdrawal. But Churchill's appeasement of ibn Saud—and especially the increase in the 'subsidy' Britain paid him monthly at a time when he had few other sources of revenue apart from the loot of warfare—was to prove hugely destructive to the world. His failed advocacy of appeasement for Mustafa Kemal's Turkey also had a strategic element, which in Churchill's case always meant some link to oil. Churchill feared that a powerful new Turkey would threaten Britain's vital new province of Mosul, with its existing and large potential oil reserves. Churchill wanted an accommodation with Kemal so that Turkey would not stake any claim to the Kurdish vilayet of Mosul that had been part of the Ottoman empire, but which Britain had controlled since the war, having received French endorsement for making it a British Mandate territory (in exchange for France gaining full control of Syria).

Churchill convened the Cairo Conference in March 1921 to decide the fate of the many British territories and mandates in Arabia including the Hijaz, Nejd, Iraq, Transjordan and Palestine. This 'conference' was attended by forty British 'experts' on the region, chaired by Churchill who insisted that Arabs must specifically be kept well away from the opulent hotel where the conference was occurring. So much for Wilsonian self-determination! After some initial doubts about the legitimacy of the 'Sharifian' family's claims to leadership of the Arab world (having discovered there were other claimants within the same family other than Hussein, who had himself been appointed

Sharif by the Ottomans only a few years before the onset of the Great War), Churchill eventually went along with T. E. Lawrence's strong advocacy of Feisal being anointed king of Iraq, and his elder brother Abdullah being given Transjordan. This was a portentous decision, since Jordan (as Transjordan was eventually called) could well have become the homeland for the Arabs of the old vilayet of 'Palestine'; specifically, Jewish settlement was prohibited in Transjordan, while it was permitted to continue on the territory west of the river Jordan. Jews from elsewhere in the Ottoman empire (mainly the Sephardim who had left Spain to move there since the 1490s) had been settling in that region for about two to three decades, but still comprised less than a fifth of the population there. But Britain's Balfour Declaration of 1917 had led to a new surge of Jewish immigrants, spurring a Syrian-led revolt in Jerusalem in 1920 soon after Herbert Samuel (Britain's most prominent Jewish politician, and a self-confessed Zionist) was appointed high commissioner for Palestine (two years before the League of Nations formally made Palestine a British Mandate territory). Now Churchill decided to give Abdullah (and his Arab armies from the Hijaz) control of Palestine east of the Jordan river—a partition of Mandate Palestine aimed at creating a British-aligned state, and also rewarding Abdullah for his loyalty to the British (but notably without seeking the opinions of the residents of the area). Abdullah proved an able ruler (his descendant Abdullah II is still king there), but he was an outsider imposed on a population he knew little about. T. E. Lawrence argued that Abdullah would also help to stem anti-Zionist discontent, and that 'in four or five years...the opposition to Zionism would have decreased, if it had not entirely disappeared'. This prediction has, of course, proven wildly over-optimistic!

Much more controversial was the decision to impose Feisal as king of Iraq (the combination of the Ottoman vilayets of Basra, Baghdad and Mosul). As one of the major Asian theatres of the Great War (including the horrific Siege of Kut), Iraq expected to receive self-determination and independence. But in the words of Catherwood, 'Churchill's scheme was, in effect, to establish a series of pro-British client monarchies, all of whose rulers would owe Britain a debt of considerable gratitude simply for the fact that they were in power at all'. Like in India, Africa and Malaya, the British intended to grant the appearance of independence while retaining real control in their own hands. When it first became apparent that Britain did not intend to give them independence, an Iraqi revolt had begun in May 1920, starting mainly in the Shia south of the country (especially in the Shia holy cities of Najaf and Karbala, as well as Basra), but then spreading to Baghdad and Mosul too. Churchill had asked for troop reinforcements—bringing in sixteen Indian battalions, and four British battalions—but had mainly used the Royal Air Force to strafe the population, including authorizing the use of mustard gas and other chemical weapons against the civilian population. Close to 10,000 Iraqis died in the revolt, which ended in November 1920.

The one lesson Churchill took away from the Iraqi revolt was the need to minimize expenditure, that he felt could best be done by deploying a small (and hence inexpensive) military force on the ground, aided by local British-trained troops, but backed especially by the Royal Air Force (with the right to use 'gas bombs') to pacify the restive population. Churchill was particularly keen to demonstrate to Lloyd George that he was good at reducing expenditure as he was eyeing the job of Chancellor of the Exchequer. In August 1921, Churchill staged a 'plebiscite' amongst various tribal chieftains and their supporters (and without a secret ballot), declared that 96 per cent had voted in favour of Feisal, and had him proclaimed king of Iraq on 23 August 1921. Churchill had imposed Feisal as ruler of Iraq by neatly ignoring the fact that he was a Sunni from the Hijaz, with no relationship or base amongst the Shia-majority people of Iraq. The Kurds (mainly a Sunni Indo–European people who spoke a non-Arabic language more akin to Farsi) had been promised an independent Kurdistan, but were left high and dry— partly for fear that the 'southern' Kurds of Mosul would align with Mustafa Kemal, just as their northern brethren in Anatolia had done. Acutely aware of his lack of legitimacy, Feisal immediately set about making nationalist (and hence anti-British) statements, as he had done in Syria two years earlier. In particular, he sought to establish an Anglo–Iraqi treaty that would serve as a badge of sovereignty while also seeking Iraqi representation in the League of Nations. After much back and forth, an Anglo–Iraqi treaty was, in fact, signed on 10 October 1922. This was virtually the last thing that Churchill did as Colonial Secretary, just nine days before the Liberal–Conservative coalition government was toppled by the Tories, and Churchill himself lost his seat at the next parliamentary election. The 1922 treaty still gave Britain control over Iraq's military and foreign affairs, while conferring a modicum of self-rule over economic and social matters. Although the act of signing a treaty gave Iraq a veneer of sovereignty, its autonomy was little better than that of a typical Malay, African or Indian chief/maharaja, and the treaty was treated with smouldering contempt by Iraqi nationalists.

The disastrous consequences of creating an artificial state like Iraq which had a Shiite majority, but with a Sunni Arab outsider imposed by the British as king, supported by an unrepresentative Sunni cabal as the ruling elite, would become evident after 1960, and all the way to the toppling of Saddam Hussein in 2003. (Only the 1958 coup leader, Abd al-Karim Qasim, had some Shia blood, through his mother; otherwise, Iraq was ruled by Sunni Arabs, who constituted 24–28 per cent of the population, throughout the period from 1921 to 2003.) Churchill's cynical use of a rigged plebiscite was a further blow to any residual claims of fair play and self-determination. Feisal brought in more 'outsiders' from his short-lived regime in Syria, causing further resentment. In 1927, however, Calouste Gulbenkian's renamed Iraqi Petroleum Company (IPC)—in which the founder's share was down to 5 per cent, but in which Deutsche Bank's quarter share had gone to France, with a similar shareholding controlled by the APOC—discovered a huge oil well in Kirkuk in northern Iraq. This fundamentally altered Iraq's strategic importance, and put paid to any hopes Feisal still harboured of real independence. Instead, a second Anglo–Iraqi Treaty was signed in 1930 (in preparation for Iraq obtaining nominal independence in 1932, and finally joining the League of Nations). Under this treaty, Britain obtained the right to use Basra and Habbaniya as air bases 'in times of peace', and the use of all transport facilities—by railways, air, river barge, roads and ports—in times of war. The latter was the basis on which Churchill was to order the invasion of Iraq in 1941 (to oust a nationalist government that was seeking to remain neutral in World War II). Additionally, Britain obtained a slew of commercial and military rights (including the exemption of British soldiers from any obligation to pay taxes in Iraq or be subject to the jurisdiction of Iraqi courts), which would severely circumscribe the moth-eaten 'independence' that Feisal's Kingdom of Iraq would receive in 1932.

Back in the UK, Winston Churchill's second political demise proved short-lived. Fighting the 1924 general election as a Constitutionalist (rather than a Liberal) expressing virulent opposition to the Labour Party's alleged lack of fidelity to Britain's (unwritten) constitution, Churchill's group won 7 seats but dissolved soon thereafter. Nonetheless, his long-standing ambition to be Chancellor of the Exchequer was soon fulfilled when Stanley Baldwin invited him into his cabinet, and Churchill thus returned to the Conservative Party. As if the damage he had wrought in Arabia weren't enough (and perhaps because the damage was not yet fully visible), the 'Great Bumbler' now proceeded to nearly destroy the British economy!

Churchill's major action as Chancellor was to take the pound sterling back onto the gold standard in 1925 at an artificially high exchange rate. This decimated what remained of Britain's export industries, forced interest rates to stay too high, and led to deflation and unemployment, leading to the twelve-day General Strike of 1926. John Maynard Keynes wrote *The Economic Consequences of Mr Churchill* (1925), excoriating Churchill's decision to take Britain back onto the gold standard (at the pre-War parity of US$4.87 to the pound, compared to an exchange rate of US$3.85 per pound in 1921) as likely to lead to a worldwide depression. John Kenneth Galbraith called it 'perhaps the most damaging error of modern economic and financial policy', which inevitably led to 'a period of economic stagnation and unemployment that extended over the decade'. Churchill's decision was a purely ideological one (quite akin to calls by Ron and Rand Paul, and assorted Austrian economists, for the Obama-era US to return to the gold standard), and one shot through with nostalgia for the glorious pre-War past. In reality, Churchill had dealt the final blow to sterling as the world's reserve currency and started the inexorable process that led to the worldwide Great Depression of 1929–39. Facing the intransigence of the unions, Churchill suggested machine-gunning the strikers and extolled his fascist contemporary Benito Mussolini as a 'Roman genius...the greatest law-giver amongst modern men' who had shown a 'way to combat subversive forces', particularly the threat of communism.

Compared to Churchill's follies in creating a theocratic Saudi Arabia, a minority-ruled Iraq, and the fragile monarchy of Transjordan, the French Mandate of Syria might even be considered a relative success. Here too, though, imperial ambition led to some bizarre outcomes. In their keenness to widen the remit of their Christian allies in Lebanon, the French created a Greater Lebanon that extended past Mt Lebanon into the Anti-Lebanon Mountains east of the Bekaa Valley. This attempt at augmenting the power of Lebanon's Christians (by doubling the extent of their territory) has proved disastrous to this enterprising community in the long run, as it increased the Sunni Muslim population eightfold, and the Shiite population fourfold, while giving Lebanon a substantial Druze minority too. The 1932 census still gave the Christians a slight majority in this Greater Lebanon and formed the basis of constitutional negotiations. But the Christian proportion of the population declined steadily through emigration (with successful Lebanese Christian businessmen prospering in West Africa, and points further west including Mexico, Argentina and the US), while the Muslim population increased through rapid procreation. The French drew up a constitution for Lebanon in 1926, which created a Parliament with a 6:5 ratio of Christians to Muslims, and provided for the president to always be a Christian (usually Maronite, although they constituted slightly less than half of all Lebanese Christians) and the prime minister to be a Sunni Muslim. By the time Lebanon became independent in 1943, it was already believed that Muslims were a majority (and the proportion of Shias was rising especially rapidly), making Lebanon a ripe candidate for civil war. Syria itself (despite its territorial losses to Lebanon) was administered as a federation of four regions with a small

Druze region in the south, an Alawite region on the west coast with Latakia as its capital, and the two large Sunni-dominated states of Damascus (in the centre) and Aleppo across the north.

In 1933, France attempted to grant Syria independence on terms similar to those that had been offered by Britain to Iraq in 1932, with power transferred to a puppet president. But this was strongly opposed by the National Bloc (the largest group in the representative legislature) led by Hashim al-Atassi, who himself went on a sixty-day hunger strike in protest. Eventually, in 1936 (when the left-wing Popular Front coalition led by Léon Blum gained power precariously in France, amid the outbreak of socialist idealism in Republican Spain next door), France offered Syria formal independence, including a reduction (but not elimination) of French troops, in exchange for France having two air bases and full access to all air and other military facilities in the event of war. This was acceptable to al-Atassi, who returned to Damascus in triumph but was blindsided by the failure of the French National Assembly to ever ratify the treaty, ensuring that Syria remained in political limbo.

LENIN, TROTSKY, STALIN AND THE SOVIET CHALLENGE TO ASIA'S STATUS QUO

Marxist theory held that if the first Communist revolution occurred in a relatively backward ('feudal') country like Russia (or China), it would only succeed if it could be internationalized, and particularly by involving a properly industrialized economy, where the phase of bourgeois democracy would have helped achieve economic abundance. The Bolshevik seizure of power in Russia did have an electrifying impact on socialist and revolutionary parties around the world, with attempted revolutions in as distant places as Spain, Argentina's Córdoba, amongst the Finnish–Americans of Minnesota, and amongst the working classes of Bulgaria (who did actually establish a short-lived revolutionary regime). The communists felt their best opportunity existed in the dissolving Austro–Hungarian empire, and Hungary did turn briefly to communism. But the force of nationalism—encouraged in particular by Wilson's Fourteen Points and their emphasis on self-determination—proved a much more potent force in Europe, and a series of small nation states (Czechoslovakia, Romania, Hungary) were carved out of the Hapsburg (Austro–Hungarian) empire.

Peasants and the middle class proved an insurmountable bulwark against the advance of communism. Meanwhile the Treaty of Brest–Litovsk had helped carve Poland, the Baltic states (Estonia, Latvia, Lithuania), Ukraine and

Transcaucasia from Russia. (The latter two were won back by the Bolsheviks in the Russian Civil War.) In Germany, too, a revolutionary environment was afoot at the end of the Great War, but despite the romantic idealism of Karl Liebknecht and Rosa Luxemburg, the communists stayed a minority tendency, although the socialists and social-democrats gained a combined 45 per cent of the vote in the first election after the war. By mid-1919, it was clear that no industrialized economy would fall durably to the communists. Hence Lenin was obliged to pursue War Communism: nationalization of the 'means of production', including workers' control over factories, and the forcible takeover (by government) of large estates and farms.

Lenin made further pragmatic compromises with the ideological orthodoxy of War Communism while the Civil War raged—allowing soldiers and military officers to keep larger land holdings in order to win their crucial loyalty in that precarious struggle. Once the Civil War was won (by the end of 1920 in the European theatre), Lenin made much larger compromises with Marxist orthodoxy, inaugurating the New Economic Policy (NEP) in March 1921 at the Communist Party of the Soviet Union's (CPSU) 10th Congress. NEP allowed for a much smaller tax-in-kind to be charged to peasants, who were then free to sell any of their surplus produce on the open market. Like Deng Xiaoping's agricultural reforms in China more than half a century later (1978–79), it was hoped that NEP would induce peasants to produce substantially more, since they could keep anything they produced beyond the tax-in-kind paid to the government. Unfortunately for Lenin, 1921 was the second year of a severe drought and crop failure that led to starvation deaths from famine, which killed 5 million people and displaced millions more. So the agricultural reforms were initially a failure, and Soviet Russia had to turn to the West for food aid: the US, amongst others, responded to a formal appeal for food aid from novelist and political activist Maxim Gorky, with the future president Herbert Hoover administering the aid supplies. In 1921, there was also a widespread 'Antonov Rebellion' by Russia's peasants (especially in the Volga region, but also in western Siberia), and Lenin responded by reducing the tax-in-kind, especially in regions faced with crop failures.

But the NEP's dose of market-based reforms was otherwise a big success: the denationalization of small-scale industry and services, and the opening up to foreign trade with the West (which Lloyd George's Britain responded to with alacrity) helped revive industry. Lenin viewed the NEP as a 'retreat' by the state to the 'commanding heights of the economy' (large-scale industry, foreign trade, and banking)—language that was to be employed subsequently by other 'late-developing' (or emerging) economies, including Jawaharlal Nehru for India. The NEP also encouraged foreign investment, and the US businessman Armand Hammer was prominent amongst those who invested in Russia at this time; despite using 'arm and hammer' as one of his brands, and being the son of a Russian Jew (Julius Hammer) who helped found the US Communist Party, Armand was a dyed-in-the-wool capitalist. And though the NEP did generate substantial angst amongst Soviet communists about a revival of capitalism and its excesses (including 'kulak' landowners and capitalist NEPmen), it was a huge economic success, helping to reverse the economy's collapse: by 1926, most output indices had surpassed the pre-War levels that were the apogee of Russian economic vitality. By then, though, Lenin was dead, succumbing in January 1924 to a series of illnesses, including a stroke that partially immobilized him during his final months.

Lenin's death (and the embalming of his body to serve as a permanent icon of the revolution in the Kremlin) resulted in a no-holds-barred contest for power between Trotsky, the commissar who had created the Red Army and co-led the revolution with Lenin, and Stalin (who had been appointed general secretary of the party a couple of months before Lenin's first stroke). Stalin advocated 'socialism in one country', while Trotsky believed in 'permanent revolution'—and the initial argument was over which of them was more faithful to Lenin's own thinking. Stalin triumphed primarily because he was far more effective in intra-party combat—having quickly built an organizational base in the provinces, while Trotsky's base was in Moscow. The latter was accused of having insufficient faith in Soviet socialism (with his advocacy of world revolution), and was isolated within the party by the end of 1924. Although allowed to remain in the politburo for another three years, Trotsky was thereafter seen as the Leader of the Opposition to the main party led by Stalin. It was over China that Stalin and Trotsky had their final disagreement, which led to Trotsky's expulsion from the CPSU, and his exile (first to Kazakhstan, then Istanbul, and finally to Mexico).

On China, Trotsky and his supporters argued that the CPSU should support a proper proletarian revolution with the Communist Party at its vanguard, while Stalin backed the United Front of the communists with the KMT led by Chiang Kai-shek. Although recognizing Chiang as a rightist, Stalin argued that he was far more capable of creating a successful revolution because of the finances he could raise from the wealthy in China. Collaboration between the CPSU and the KMT had been initiated by Sun Yat-sen in early 1923, with Mikhail Borodin (a Jewish stalwart of the CPSU) serving as the key intermediary. Borodin himself had been given refuge in 1919 in Mexico by the founder of that country's communist party, M. N. Roy, a Bengali revolutionary (and former associate of Bagha Jatin Mukherjee) who had originally been tasked with arranging German arms shipments to India from Java during the

Great War. Subsequently (in 1915), Roy had sought to enlist Sun Yat-sen's assistance in the Indian revolution that the Ghadar party was planning, but Sun had rebuffed him, suggesting that he place more faith in Japan's liberating mission. Hounded out of Japan, Roy fled to Palo Alto (California), and thence to New York where, ironically, just before the Russian Revolution, he first discovered the works of Marx in the public library, proceeding thence to Mexico, where he founded the communist party to help direct the Mexican revolution in a more leftist direction.

Roy had mixed success in Mexico: Marx and Lenin joined Montezuma and Zapata amongst the Mexican pantheon of revolutionary icons, but his communist party was eventually marginalized at the end of the Mexican revolution (won by the centre-left PRI) in 1920. M. N. Roy was inducted into the presidium of the Communist International (Comintern) that year, and remained in it for eight years (until expelled by Stalin, because of Roy's perceived closeness to Trotsky and Nikolai Bukharin). One of his first tasks was to create communist parties in the East—and he began with the creation of the Communist Party of India (CPI) in 1920, and then solidified what was to become the PKI (Indonesian Communist Party) the following year through a split in the Sarekat Islam, the main nationalist movement in the Dutch East Indies. The CPI remained little more than a fringe party until World War II, when it further isolated itself from the mass nationalist movement by following the Soviet lead to support Britain wholeheartedly during the war.

A Dutch socialist called Henk Sneevliet had already established a Social Democratic Party of the Indies in 1914, and he and his followers steadily became more Marxist in their orientation—especially after the Russian Revolution. Sneevliet was the key local organizer of the new communist party in the East Indies once it broke off from Sarekat Islam, which now took a course towards Islamic modernism under Agus Salim (who was later to be Indonesia's first foreign minister). The PKI acquired its final name only in 1924—having initially been named the Perserikatan Komunis di Hindia (Communist Union of the Indies), with three of its founding committee members being Dutch, although the chairman and vice-chairman were local Indonesians. Tan Malaka was soon to take the baton from Sneevliet, and he attempted a general strike amongst the industrial workers in the East Indies as early as 1922. Thereafter, in keeping with the Comintern's strategy, the PKI sought to capture trade unions across the archipelago. But restive young members were dissatisfied with the United Front strategy that the Comintern wanted, and instead attempted to foment a revolution in November 1926—defying Tan Malaka's express commands, based on his correct assessment that the PKI was still too weak to attempt a nationwide revolution. The PKI faction's attempted revolution was suppressed within a few days, and the party was banned in 1927, forcing it to go underground—where it remained until the Indonesian independence war in the 1940s.

With the PKI banned, a new nationalist party, the PNI (Indonesian National Party) came to the fore, founded in 1927 by the charismatic twenty-six-year-old Sukarno as a blending of the varied ideological strands of the inchoate nationalist movement. Born of a Javanese father and a Balinese Brahmin mother, Sukarno (whose name was Javanese for 'good Karna', the heroic but tragic warrior of the Mahabharata who is the half-brother of the Pandavas) epitomized the syncretism that was both central to Javanese mysticism and religion, and was to characterize Sukarno's definition of Indonesian nationhood. From the start, Sukarno had been amongst the fortunate few native Javanese to be admitted to a Dutch primary school and then a Dutch college-preparatory school (Hogere Burger) in Surabaya (Indonesia's second city). There, from the age of fifteen, Sukarno lived in a boarding house owned by Tjokroaminoto, the founder of the Sarekat Islam, and fell in love with Tjokroaminoto's daughter (who he later married). But living as a teenager in the home of the leader of Indonesia's budding nationalist movement—which included both socialist and Muslim wings, besides being influenced by Javanese mysticism—was the finest education possible for a future leader of his country.

Sukarno subsequently went to the Bandung Institute of Technology to study civil engineering and architecture, and established an architecture firm in that hill resort city. He also used his schooling to learn a slew of languages—not just Javanese, Balinese, Sundanese and Melayu Riau (today's Bahasa Indonesia), but also English, Dutch, German, French, Arabic and Japanese. But his focus soon turned to strengthening the anti-colonial struggle amid the disintegration of the Sarekat Islam. The failure of the PKI's aborted revolution provided him just the opening, and he founded the PNI as the embodiment of secular nationalism and anti-colonialism, creating a revolutionary creed that blended Marxism with Javanese mysticism and Islamic solidarity in the sort of syncretism that was to epitomize his future nation state's founding Pancasila ideology. Many other young men—like Mohammad Hatta and Sutan Sjahrir—used the opening provided by the Dutch 'Ethical Policy' to obtain university degrees in the Netherlands during the 1920s. As that cohort returned from the Netherlands, they joined and strengthened the PNI.

By 1929, Sukarno and Hatta were discussing their hope that Japan would invade the East Indies some day to liberate it; failing that, they and the PNI began demanding complete independence at about the same time that Subhas Bose was attempting to persuade the Indian National Congress and Gandhi to adopt the same goal ('purna swaraj'). Sukarno and the PNI began programmes of non-cooperation with the Dutch, and fomented workers' strikes. In 1930, Sukarno was arrested by the Dutch colonial authorities, and sentenced to four years in jail, but not before a two-day peroration in court that became a florid exposition of his nationalist creed, and a severe critique of capitalist injustice and colonial oppression. Arguing that the PNI was merely the instrument and reflection of a nationalist stirring, not its initiator, he said 'The sun does not rise because the cock crows; the cock crows because the sun rises.' And he adumbrated his vision for 'the future united Republic of Indonesia at one in friendship and respect with other countries, of an Indonesian national flag adorning the Eastern sky, of a nation strong and healthy'. In ringing tones that were heard and read around the archipelago, Sukarno said, 'We hear the promise of a life for our people that will be happy and safe, of social benefits which will meet and fulfil our needs, of an open and democratic system of political life, of unbounded progress in the arts, sciences and culture.' The Dutch authorities sentenced him to a four-year jail term, but at twenty-nine, Bung (Brother) Karno was thus already anointed the leader of the nationalist movement. While he was in prison, though, the Dutch banned the PNI and sought to break it up.

After Sukarno's early release in 1932, he attempted to reconcile the two wings of the nationalist movement—one called Partindo, which was committed to immediate mass agitation to press for independence, and the other (called PNI Baru or New), led by Hatta and Sutan Sjahrir, which was committed to a long-term programme focused on education to build up a cadre of intellectuals capable of leading an effective nationalist movement. Failing in his attempts to unite the two wings, Sukarno assumed leadership of Partindo, and published a series of pamphlets outlining the path to the attainment of an independent Indonesia. He was arrested again in 1933 and sent into internal exile without trial to the relatively remote island of Flores, being transferred to Bengkulu in Sumatra in 1938, but remaining imprisoned until freed by the Japanese in 1942. In Indonesia, the communists had overplayed their hand, and been supplanted by a secular-nationalist force (the PNI) which incorporated elements of Marxism. But this too was suppressed by the Dutch—although it was always widely known (since the events of the first two decades of the nineteenth century) that the Dutch hold over the East Indies was tenuous at best, and dependent on British naval support from Singapore.

In China, the United Front was much more of a success initially, having been initiated by the non-communist Sun Yat-sen, who took Borodin's advice in reconstituting his KMT party along Leninist lines. Soviet-style local cells of the KMT were established, which were to help elect a national congress and executive for the party, and undertake propaganda to build a mass base. In 1922, the CCP had only about 300 members (rising to 1,500 by 1925), so Sun Yat-sen believed that the United Front would enable him to co-opt the 'young men' from the CCP whom he accepted into the KMT (which had 50,000 members by this time). Leninist discipline did reinvigorate the KMT and Sun's nationalist movement. Until this point, Sun Yat-sen was merely the well-accepted figurehead of China's nationalist movement, but had signally failed to unite China or become its leader for more than a short period after the establishment of the republic. His Guangdong-based warlord-supported nationalist regime also proved short-lived, and he had been forced to flee to Shanghai in 1922 where, at a low ebb in his personal quest to unite China, Sun forged the alliance with the Comintern through Borodin in January 1923. After the launch of Lenin's New Economic Policy, Sun viewed even the communist programme as being quite consistent with one of his three Principles for the People of China: People's Livelihood (the other two being Nationalism, and People's Rights or Democracy). The CCP, of course, viewed the United Front as an opportunity to infiltrate the KMT and capture it from within. Chiang Kai-shek, who went on a three-month apprenticeship to the USSR soon after the United Front was established, returned from that sojourn as a dedicated anti-communist, deeply suspicious and realistically aware of the CCP and the methods it was likely to employ.

By the time Sun Yat-sen died suddenly in March 1925, the KMT had been greatly strengthened through its alliance with the Comintern. In May–June 1925, the KMT helped to spearhead an anti-foreign (primarily anti-British) agitation by workers and students across urban China—which also engulfed British-controlled Hong Kong, and shook it to its core on 30 May. Capitalizing on this momentum, and Russia's armed support, Chiang Kai-shek gathered the KMT's six armies and mounted a Northern Expedition—preceded by well-trained propagandists, who applied Borodin's Leninist lessons in building mass support for the KMT cause. Moving up north from Guangzhou, the KMT's forces decimated the armies of about thirty-four warlords in southern China. Sun Yat-sen's leading acolyte, Wang Jingwei, worked closely with Borodin in February–March 1927 to establish a revolutionary government in the industrial city of Wuhan, which was seen as fertile recruiting ground for the CCP, with two CCP members joining the revolutionary cabinet as ministers.

But soon thereafter, a clear split in the KMT began to appear between a left wing—led by Wang Jingwei and Sun Yat-sen's widow, Soong Ching-ling (herself the daughter of the itinerant American Bible salesman, Charlie Soong, who had later become a missionary in Shanghai and then a successful businessman who bankrolled his friend, Sun Yat-sen)—and the right wing led by Chiang Kai-shek. Wang Jingwei and the left were keen to strengthen relations with the CCP and Comintern, while Chiang was suspicious of the communists. The dispute mirrored one that had emerged in the Soviet Union itself between Trotsky and Bukharin on the one hand—who advocated the fomenting of an indigenous revolution in China by building up and strengthening the communist party—and Stalin, who asserted that China was too underdeveloped for the communists to organize the small industrial working class (proletariat) within a largely peasant society. Stalin comfortably won that debate by 1925, enabling the USSR to throw its weight behind the KMT's Northern Expedition in 1926–27. Stalin had rightly judged that Chiang was militarily much stronger than his rivals, and Chiang began to develop an alternative base of power in the Lower Yangzi region, centred around Nanjing, having already arrested many leftists at the start of his campaign in Guangzhou, allegedly to thwart a plot by them to kill him.

Despite the fact that both Sun Yat-sen and Chiang Kai-shek were each to marry daughters of the Christian proselytizer Charlie Soong, a central tenet of their nationalist movement was anti-foreigner, and particularly inimical to the persistence of foreign concessions and treaty ports. Anti-imperialism was a fundamental creed of the nationalist armies, with their ire particularly directed at the British, who were still quite appropriately considered the primary imperialist power. As they entered Nanjing in March 1927, the revolutionary army attacked foreigners and six foreign residents were killed. British and American gunboats went into action to provide covering fire for other foreigners to depart. Christian missionaries working in Nanjing and the interior of China had fled well in advance of the arrival of the revolutionary army, fearing its virulent anti-foreignism.

In the meanwhile, however, Britain had amassed an international force of 40,000 troops to guard Shanghai and its international concession area while also returning the small British concessions in Hankou and Jiujiang. The threat to the foreign residents of Nanjing and Shanghai provided an opportunity for Chiang Kai-shek to consolidate his hold over those cities. He did so with a surprising manoeuvre: while communist labour unions confronted foreign troops in Shanghai in April 1927 and—on Comintern orders—awaited additional support from their supposed KMT allies, Chiang Kai-shek instead turned his guns on the communists, annihilating them in a bloody massacre in alliance with the city's underworld Green Gang. Chiang then ousted the left-leaning government in Wuhan, sending one of his generals to defeat its leader (and Chiang's KMT rival) Wang Jingwei. He then expelled all the communists and launched a nationwide campaign to root out and destroy communist cells across the country in a campaign labelled the 'White

Terror'. Apart from an aborted coup by communist troops in Guangzhou in December 1927, Chiang Kai-shek's crackdown on the communists was a complete (if temporary) success driving the remaining communists into the rural mountains of Jiangxi province in central China, well away from the prominent industrial cities. The expulsion of the communists also endeared Chiang Kai-shek to the Western powers, and his marriage to Soong Mei-ling (youngest daughter of Charlie Soong) and formal conversion to Christianity strengthened their support for him. Sun Yat-sen's leading disciple (and preferred successor) Wang Jingwei, fearing for his life, fled to Europe, returning in 1929 to lead or participate in several abortive attempts to oust Chiang in 1929 and 1930. Sun Yat-sen's young widow, Soong Ching-ling, fled to Moscow and bided her time there awaiting communist advances, and never reconciled herself to her new brother-in-law Chiang Kai-shek's politics.

Sun Yat-sen still remains the nationalist icon of China—both in the KMT redoubt of Taiwan, and on mainland China (where the PRC's acknowledgement of his vital republican role was reinforced by the fact that his widow, Ching-ling, remained a devout communist to the end of her days, including a fortnight as the nominal president of the PRC shortly before she died in 1981). Ironically, however, it was only in the two years after Sun had aligned with the Soviet Union in January 1923 that his party acquired the organizational capacity to attempt the republican reunification of China that was accomplished by his successor, Chiang Kai-shek, who had received most of his military training from the Soviets too. An important reason for the failure of the Soviet strategy (nominally espoused by Stalin) of getting the young CCP to infiltrate and gradually take over the KMT from within, was precisely because the KMT too was organized along Leninist lines by this time and it was just as well-schooled in the arts of subterfuge and sabotage as its much smaller, communist rival. Stalin clearly preferred Chiang Kai-shek to the intellectuals at the top of the CCP (led by Chen Duxiu); both Stalin and Chiang were ruthless political bruisers well-versed in the dark arts of assassination and violence.

In 1928, Chiang Kai-shek led another northern expedition up the Yangzi delta and captured Beijing (which he renamed 'Beiping', or 'northern peace'). Zhang Zuolin was the warlord general who Chiang Kai-shek's forces defeated to take Beijing in late May 1928. Zhang was a monarchist warlord based near Mukden, who had played a role in the attempted restoration of Puyi in 1917, and had been the undisputed master of all three provinces of Manchuria since 1920, when China's government acknowledged him as Governor General of all three provinces. Zhang had been loosely aligned with the Japanese— who operated from their base in the rapidly growing and prosperous port of

Dairen (Dalian)—although he often used anti-Japanese rhetoric in building political and military support for his Fengtian Army ('Fengtian' being the Manchu word for Liaoning province). From 1920 to 1927, Zhang Zuolin had provided stable and effective governance in Manchuria and, aided by Japanese investment, this region became an oasis of stability and prosperity amid the chaos of warlord-wracked China, attracting legions of settlers from the rest of China, who were offered homesteads and cheap land by Zhang's regime. In 1924, Zhang had gained control of three other provinces—Shandong, Anhui and Jiangsu—but the frontiers of his territory ebbed and grew frequently until he finally gained control of Beijing in 1926, and briefly became the internationally-recognized ruler of China.

The renewed conflict of 1925–27, however, weakened the hitherto-stable economy of Manchuria, and made Zhang vulnerable to Chiang Kai-shek's expanding nationalist armies. Japan's prime minister General Tanaka Giichi sought to persuade Chiang Kai-shek (when he visited Tokyo in November 1927) to stay behind the Manchurian border, and Tanaka sent troops into Shandong as a warning sign. As the KMT armies approached Beijing, however, Japan's Tanaka cabinet persuaded Zhang to withdraw from the capital and a series of surprises occurred.

As Zhang Zuolin's train passed through territory controlled by the Japanese South Manchurian Railway, he was assassinated by a bomb planted by a Japanese colonel, who was subsequently court-martialled for this bizarre action. The militarist faction of Japanese were evidently angry with Zhang Zuolin for his failure to hold off the KMT (which, after all, was aligned with Japan's long-term enemy, Russia), and hoped that his son and successor, Zhang Xueliang, would be a stronger ally of Japan. But while this is the historically-accepted story, the writer Jung Chang cites Soviet intelligence as claiming credit for assassinating Zhang Zuolin, and then placing the blame on the Japanese.

But Xueliang provided an even bigger surprise by throwing his support behind the new Nanjing regime headed by Chiang Kai-shek, with whom he was to have a tempestuous relationship (including the Xian Incident of 1936 described later), but to whom he generally stayed loyal through the rest of his life. With the vital support of the young warlord of Manchuria, Zhang Xueliang, Chiang could finally claim by late 1928 to have reunited China proper for the first time since 1912. Notably, of course, the reunited China did not include Tibet, Qinghai, Nei Mongol, Taiwan and Xinjiang (just as Ming China had excluded these regions).

Having benefited greatly from Soviet training and support in his climb to the top of China's greasy pole, Chiang Kai-shek was quick to neutralize

Soviet influence over his government by seeking enhanced ties with the other European powers; their recognition was key to his new regime's legitimacy as the true international representative of all China. He was helped along by the fact that Stalin, having comfortably defeated Trotsky in their internal fight for control of the CPSU, had turned his attention to agrarian reform, and devising the best methods for 'extracting the surplus' from agriculture to invest in the rapid industrialization of the Soviet Union. There had been an esoteric debate in the Soviet Union between 1925 and 1928 pitting the Left (represented by Preobrazhensky) and the Right (led by Bukharin) over the best way to accumulate the 'surpluses' that would be needed for backward Russia to catch up with the industrialized West. The two intellectual leaders of the Left and Right in this debate were, ironically, the co-authors of the 1919 Bolshevik manual, *The ABC of Communism*. Initially, Stalin supported Bukharin's view that the incentive structures of the NEP would be the best way to develop the economy, and gradually build up the surpluses needed for industrialization. Preobrazhensky argued that the state sector needed to appropriate peasants' surpluses (either through raising non-agricultural prices sharply, or procuring peasants' output at low prices); he lost the argument initially—partly because the Left was associated with Trotsky—and Stalin purged him from the party leadership in 1927.

But, in one of the ideological about-turns that were to mark his career, Stalin then adopted Preobrazhensky's strategy in 1928 and now purged Bukharin and his former allies of the Right! Stalin began the collectivization of agriculture in 1928, a deeply unpopular policy aimed at both increased food production (in large mechanized farms) and using the surpluses (or 'primitive capital accumulation') garnered from agriculture to invest in industry. Lenin had freed the peasants from serfdom in 1919 (completing the process of emancipating serfs that began in 1861), and many had responded to their new freedom (and landownership) with big increases in output, especially under NEP. Peasants who had become rich through this process were known as 'kulaks' and they stringently resisted Stalin's Collectivization programme. Stalin responded by aligning with poorer, smallholder peasants and mobilizing them to oppose the supposed greed and selfishness of the kulaks.

In 1928, about 82 per cent of the Russian population lived off agriculture and rural services, so it was truly audacious (and profoundly anti-democratic) for the Left of the CPSU (first represented by Trotsky and Preobrazhensky, later by Stalin) to attempt any form of expropriation of their land and output. Although the CPSU purportedly was serving the interests of landless peasants, there were very few of them, as almost all peasants owned at least some land after 1919. Stalin dressed up his programme as being aimed at improving the condition of the whole country, as only a rapid charge towards industrialization would enable the Soviet Union to resist the 'inevitable' invasion from the West. Peasants and kulaks were both horrified by Stalin's attempt to appropriate their farm output at throwaway prices and responded as farmers everywhere would, by withholding output, burying it in underground silos or consuming it themselves. Similarly, when Stalin's activists arrived to try and take over livestock and farmland for the Collectivization programme, they often found that cattle, sheep and pigs had been slaughtered ahead of their arrival. Meat, grain and milk production plummeted in the next few years as the agricultural aspect of the programme failed miserably, but Stalin then got approval from the Central Committee in November 1929 to begin forced collectivization and the official end of Lenin's New Economic Policy.

The resulting forced evictions (of kulaks and those deemed to be their 'agents') to regions remote from their homes caused the deaths of at least a fifth of all those deported, and led directly to the horrific famine of 1932. The primary agricultural outcome was a drastic reduction in the livestock population, which halved across the Soviet Union within the next five years, and did not return to the 1928 levels until the late 1950s. Kazakhstan and its neighbouring Central Asian republics were affected most drastically, because ownership of livestock there (as in India and Africa) was a cultural aspect of community living and an emblem of individual and family self-worth, especially for nomadic herders. The peasants of Soviet Central Asia resisted collectivization with particular fervour: more than a million of them emigrated to neighbouring countries (particularly to Xinjiang), but a similar number died of starvation, and the livestock population was literally decimated. Kazakhstan's cattle population declined from 7 million to 1.6 million, and its sheep population plummeted from 22 million to 1.7 million between 1929 and 1932. In Soviet-controlled Mongolia, forced collectivization was abandoned after 8 million cattle and sheep perished. A catastrophe of similar proportions occurred in Siberia, a land that had been populated by Russians and Ukrainians over the previous century and was thus dominated by hardy farmers now deemed to be kulaks, after their successful advances in farm output during the first decade of the twentieth century. Almost all their farms were collectivized, and the kulaks uprooted.

In contrast to the deleterious consequences for agriculture, Stalin's industrialization programme under the auspices of the 'Gosplan' (a centralized planning agency established in April 1928) met with quite astonishing quantitative success, albeit at the expense of great suffering on the part of workers (many of whom were, in fact, convicts forced into conscripted labour to achieve near-impossible industrial goals). Most of the goals of the

First Five Year Plan (1928–32) were met in four years, with coal output rising from 35.4 million to 64 million tonnes, and iron ore from 5 million to 19 million tonnes. To aid the process of mechanizing agriculture, three massive tractor plants were established (in Stalingrad/Volgograd, Kharkiv and Chelyabinsk), automobile plants came up in Moscow and Gorky (Nizhny Novgorod), and heavy machinery complexes in Magnitogorsk and Kuznetsk. Notably, only Kuznetsk was in the Asian part of Russia, the rest all inside Russia's European heartlands (including eastern Ukraine). Marxists everywhere extolled the glories of this success story, often overlooking what enabled the economic successes—the fact that, in the workers' paradise, workers' rights were heavily suppressed. Workers' living standards plummeted, and by 1932 a worker could be fired for being absent for a day (and by 1938 could receive six months' probation for being just twenty minutes late); losing a job meant the loss of an apartment, and the right to commodity and ration cards. Writing his magisterial *Glimpses of World History* in 1933, Jawaharlal Nehru was one of the unabashed admirers of what Stalin had achieved in his first Piatiletka (or Five Year Plan): 'One thing is clear: that the Five Year Plan has completely changed the face of Russia. From a feudal country it has suddenly become an advanced industrial country. There has been an amazing cultural advance; and the social services, the system of social health and accident insurance, are the most inclusive and advanced in the world. In spite of privation and want, the terrible fear of unemployment and starvation which hangs over workers in other countries has gone.' The last sentence (particularly the reference to workers losing the fear of 'starvation') showed just how prone Nehru was to seeing the Soviet experience through rose-tinted glasses.

And, while we now have access to the unpleasant truths hidden away in Soviet archives, Nehru (writing in 1933) was able to see mainly the positive bits of evidence put out by Soviet propaganda. He pointed out, in particular, that the backward regions of Central Asia—including 'Tadjikistan' and Uzbekistan—had seen dramatic advances in social services. He noted Tajikistan (with a population under a million) went from just six schools in 1925 to 2,000 in 1931 (with 120,000 students), and witnessed huge improvements in 'roads, irrigation and agriculture, industries, education, and health services'—basing this on the observations of a 'competent American observer' who visited Tajikistan in 1932. Nehru's admiration for Soviet achievements in education was not misplaced: communism did fire the ideological imaginations of young people in greater Russia and indeed around the world. Committed young socialists and communists contributed, in particular, to rapid improvements in basic and secondary education, as the Soviet Union quickly achieved universal literacy (including especially in the Central Asian republics, where the enrolment of women in schools—and their gradual discarding of the veil—was a remarkable social transformation). Similarly, basic health services were extended to millions of people who did not previously have access to it and the Soviet Union quickly achieved universal access to basic health services. Life expectancy consequently improved, and Nehru pointed out that the population of the Soviet Union rose from 130 million in 1917 to 165 million in 1933 with a massive increase in urbanization, as the number of cities (with populations of over 100,000) rose from twenty-four in 1917 to over fifty by 1933. This was indeed one of the consequences of forced collectivization: as the rural economy collapsed, more and more people flocked to the cities, where industrial job opportunities beckoned, albeit in harsh factory conditions (including sixteen- to eighteen-hour work days in the mines, and seven-day work weeks).

By the end of the Second Five Year Plan (1933–37), working conditions did begin to improve aided also by the spread of education, which relieved some of the disjuncture between the demand for skilled labour (especially engineers) and the rapidity of industrial growth. By 1937, coal output jumped to 127 million tonnes, and pig iron output leapt from 6.2 million tonnes to 14.5 million, enabling rapid advances in broader industrialization, including heavy machinery, truck and tractor production and especially in the armaments industry. In 1937, Stalin launched his Great Purge—aimed not only at 'class enemies', but also at eliminating all those who had been his rivals or near-equals in the CPSU, including Bukharin, Kamenev and Kirov (with Trotsky himself assassinated in Mexico in 1940). As war beckoned in Europe, Stalin tried to reach out to rekindle the pre-WWI alliance with Britain and France, but found them reluctant. So, on 23 August 1939, he signed the Nazi–Soviet pact, which allowed for huge territorial gains for the Soviet Union (including Eastern Poland, Latvia, Estonia, Eastern Moldavia, and Finland) in exchange for the opening of economic relations and the cession of Western Poland and Lithuania to Germany.

JAPAN'S MILITARY ADVANCE INTO CHINA AMID THE RISING SPECTRE OF COMMUNISM IN ASIA

Japan's delegation to Versailles in 1919 (led by Prince Saionji) had returned with egg on its face, after its main goal—of achieving 'racial equality' (i.e., an end to overt racism) in immigration policies—was rejected outright at the behest of the two main immigrant/settler nations, the USA and Australia. Its subsidiary goal—of receiving an official imprimatur to consolidate the gains it had won in Shandong (from Germany) in the Great War (and which Britain,

France, Italy and the US had endorsed in secret agreements in 1916–17)—was strenuously challenged by the May Fourth Movement in China, which quickly spread from Beijing to Shanghai, Guangzhou, Nanjing, Xiamen and other cities across China.

In the Meiji Era, the genro elders had played the key coordinating role in holding together the various institutions of the state: the cabinet (and its separate ministries), military, Diet, and privy council. By the 1920s, just one genro remained (Saionji), and he was weakened by the perceived failure of the delegation he had led at Versailles. The consequent breakdown of authority meant that the cabinet was often a mute spectator as the other institutions of state pursued their own (often conflicting) agendas. In the previous three decades, the weakness of the cabinet had been offset by the authority enforced (in the name of the palace) by the genro (who preferred to keep the cabinet weak in order to exercise their own authority). With the waning of the genro, managing elite competition and decision-making became impossible, although societal order was still easily maintained through the social norms and common manners/courtesies to which the Japanese populace were naturally wedded. The start of the Showa Era (the rule of Emperor Hirohito) in 1926 inaugurated an internal contest for power between conservatives seeking a 'Showa Restoration' that would hark back to the essence of 'Japanese-ness', and liberals seeking to continue Japan's progress towards 'modernity', notably through fostering trade and enhanced relations with China. Both factions believed that Japan and China needed to join forces to fend off Western domination of Asia, but the liberals believed post-Manchu China was worthy of cultivating as an ally, while believers in the 'Showa Restoration' felt that China was too weak and thus needed to be shown the way by Japan (through military control if necessary).

In the immediate aftermath of the Great War, Japan also got entangled in the Russian Civil War, after a Czech army captured the east Russian port of Vladivostok (just north of Manchuria) in late 1918 and also gained control of the eastern sections of the Trans-Siberian Railway. With communists and socialists gaining ground around the world, the Japanese elite felt it necessary to try and forestall the creeping spread of communist ideas in China and also to fend off the threat Bolsheviks represented to the whole treaty port system in China (and particularly the Russo–Japanese parcelling out of spheres of influence in Manchuria). The US and Japan agreed to send a division each to relieve the overstretched Czech forces, and Japan soon took control of the Amur river basin all the way to Lake Baikal. This area, particularly Buryatia, also contained a large Buddhist population (mostly of Mongol ethnicity) that would have felt some affinity to the Japanese. However, the loose anti-Soviet coalition squabbled constantly, and there was no effective anti-Bolshevik Russian force to back them locally. The Czechs were the first to withdraw, while the American forces were also withdrawn in early 1920, quickly followed by the British, French and Canadian forces in the area. Japan alone remained in the field, and extended operations into the island of Sakhalin after a massacre of Japanese citizens there. With the Reds gaining increasing support from the locals, however, Japanese forces also withdrew from the Amur basin in 1922 and from Sakhalin Island in 1924. Lenin and Trotsky's Red Army had proven itself substantially more effective than its Tsarist predecessors had been on both the western and eastern fronts two decades earlier.

Even before that final denouement, the US had become alarmed about the potential consequences of its growing rivalry with Japan on numerous issues (immigration into California, the US advocacy of an 'open door' in China versus other powers'—including Japan's—preference for the treaty port system). In particular, the 1902 Anglo–Japanese Treaty was a thorn in America's side, which led the US to call for a naval conference in Washington (starting in December 1921) to deal with all the relevant naval issues in the Pacific. The US advocacy of an 'open door' in China, of course, was a veiled attempt at gaining greater scope for American corporations to exploit opportunities in China with as much alacrity as the treaty port powers were exercising in their respective ports within China. The first step involved breaking the Anglo–Japanese alliance, which was deftly achieved through the Washington Naval Conference. This agreed in January 1922 to establish a Four-Power Treaty (involving Britain, France, the US and Japan) aimed at respecting each other's rights in the region, and 'consultations' amongst them all if any crisis arose in East Asia. The Washington Conference also agreed to limit the tonnage of capital ships in a ratio of 5:5:3 for the US, Britain and Japan, with the other two powers persuading Japan to accept this unequal arrangement in exchange for a promise not to increase any naval fortifications in Guam, Hong Kong or Singapore (which, then, would purportedly ensure Japan's naval superiority in the western Pacific). For the US, the key benefit of the 1922 Washington Naval Conference was the ending of the two-decade-old Anglo–Japanese alliance.

Additionally, a Nine-Power Treaty was signed in February 1922 (by the above four powers, plus China, Belgium, Italy, Holland and Portugal), which institutionalized what historian William Beasley calls 'the platitudes associated with the Open Door', and promised to reconsider the aspects of the treaty port system relating to tariffs and extraterritoriality. However no enforcement mechanism was put in place to implement the treaty powers' undertakings to respect China's independence and territorial integrity, especially the treaty's first clause under which the powers agreed not to interfere with China's attempts 'to develop and maintain... a stable and effective government'. This was unenforceable at the time, partly because China's own warlords were undermining any moves towards a single stable government in China.

But, on the sidelines of the Nine-Power Treaty, Japan and China also came to an agreement on Shandong—with Japan effectively giving up all the rights it had won during the Great War. Japan agreed to withdraw her troops from the Qingdao–Jinan Railway, while China bought back the railway itself and transferred the formerly German mining rights in Shandong to a Sino–Japanese company.

The contrast between this outcome and that in the Arab parts of the old Ottoman empire was strikingly noteworthy: Syria and Lebanon became French colonies (under the guise of League of Nations 'mandates'), Iraq, Palestine and Transjordan became British colonies using the same fig leaf, while Egypt (including Sudan) and the states of the Arabian peninsula (the new 'Saudi' Arabia, plus the small coastal states) all became British 'protectorates' to varying degrees. Not only had Britain and France vastly expanded their sphere of influence in what they called the Middle East, they had acquired vast new territories rich in mineral (and especially oil) wealth—all on the basis of a few tenuous military victories. Japan, on the other hand, had won legitimate victories in the Great War, been promised by the other Allied powers that it would be able to keep those spoils of war, but had eventually been obliged by the other powers to give up its territorial gains. This followed a pattern akin to what had happened to Japan since 1895: while the Europeans rarely ever gave up any territory they had acquired in Asia (Britain in India, Malaya and the China coast, France in Indo-China, the Dutch in the East Indies), the Japanese were always obliged to give up those gains and often (as in the late 1890s) suffered the additional indignity of seeing those territories taken over by other (European) powers. One classic example of this was Weihaiwei in Shandong province: the final naval battle of the 1894–95 Sino–Japanese War was the Battle of Weihaiwei, in which Japan won a crushing victory and sank much of the Chinese (Qing) navy. Japan administered Weihaiwei until 1898, but was persuaded to give it up that year and Britain then took control of it, and Weihaiwei remained a British naval base until 1930. And furthermore, at Versailles, the Japanese delegation's request for racial equality in immigration policies had been rejected too.

Shidehara Kijuro was the career diplomat (and foreign minister in 1924–27 and 1929–31) most closely associated with the foreign policy that Japan adopted towards China—based on 'economic diplomacy' and accommodation with China's nationalist aspirations, while maintaining the treaty port system. Shidehara's policy predilections were partly animated by the fact that he was related by marriage to the Iwakura family, who were the founders of the large Mitsubishi zaibatsu. He belonged to the same political party as Kato Takaaki, who was married to the eldest daughter of Iwakura (and was thus an heir of Mitsubishi). Kato, who led a party that was less beholden to the establishment than the Seiyukai (that had been headed previously by Ito Hirobumi, Saionji and then Hara Takashi, who was assassinated in 1921), began crucial reforms, including the introduction of universal male suffrage in 1925. Kato also made important cuts to government spending, to bring them into line with the shrinkage in the post-War economy (and a consequent decline in government revenue). Importantly, he cut the size of the bureaucracy by 20,000 and reduced military spending to 30 per cent of the national budget (from 40 per cent), thereby eliminating four army divisions. But, in keeping with the prevalent practice in the West at the time, Kato also took important steps to stamp out socialist and communist influences in Japan through the Peace Preservation Laws.

Kato and Shidehara, and the 'liberals' in Japan, argued that Japan should avoid making 'enemies of our neighbours' (in Siberia just as much as in China), eschew territorial adventures as they interfered with trade, and instead focus on 'economic diplomacy' while maintaining the essence of the treaty port system. But while Shidehara thus sought an accommodation with the rising tide of Chinese nationalism, the latter frequently manifested itself in anti-Japanese actions and rhetoric—especially in the aftermath of the May Fourth Movement of 1919, and the deep feeling of antipathy towards Japan that had grown amongst Chinese youth in the 1920s. This was fed by Chinese nationalists' animosity towards Zhang Zuolin, the Manchu-Era general and advocate of a Qing restoration (who had also supported Yuan Shikai's bid to become emperor of China). With Japan's unstinting support, Zhang had become the 'warlord' in control of the three main Manchurian provinces. (In China's historiography of the 1920s, the KMT and CCP are the two parties who are exempt from the 'warlord' moniker, although Chiang Kai-shek—with his alliance with the underworld Triads—and Mao Zedong—with his predilection towards banditry—certainly were no less prone to behaving as warlords during this period.) Hatred towards Zhang, which was mixed in with the nationalists' residual anti-Manchu racism, manifested itself in boycotts of Japanese goods and anti-Japanese strikes in China. Shidehara's concessions during the Washington Conference (1922) came to be seen within Japan as a profligate giveaway of rights that Japan had painstakingly acquired over the previous three decades, with virtually nothing gained, since China's hostility towards Japan had only seemed to increase with time.

During discussions on extraterritoriality and tariff concessions towards the end of the decade—after Chiang Kai-shek and his nationalist armies had gained control of most of China (having purged their communist rivals in 1927)—Japan was often seen as less generous than the Western powers. Britain, for instance, gave up its naval base of Weihaiwei in 1930 but, of course, did not give up any of its rights to extraterritoriality in (and tight control over) Hong Kong and its New Territories. Japan, which should have been holding Weihaiwei since 1898 (but had surrendered those rights to Britain) was expected to make more concessions despite having made far larger concessions on Shandong in 1922. China's nationalists never gave Shidehara or Japan any credit for its sacrifices in 1922; and, unlike the other European powers, Japan had also made large loans to the legitimately constituted government of China during the Great War years (the Nishihara Loans), but received little support from the other powers in enforcing its rights over these credits.

The manifest failures of Shidehara's attempts to engage the world (in his pursuit of 'economic diplomacy') played right into the hands of the many 'patriotic societies' who were emerging at this time—advocating a return to the essence of 'Japanese-ness'. The more extremist groups (including one led by Kita Ikki) advocated a military coup to restore a direct relationship between the emperor and his people, followed by confiscation of all large estates—including the emperor's—and all wealth above 100,000 yen per family, with the seized assets helping to fund the nationalization of industry and the rebuilding of Japan's military might in order for Japan to advance into mainland Asia and become a bulwark for Asia against European expansionism. Others—advocating agrarian nationalism as being the true essence of Japanese culture—shunned the 'modernity' of the Meiji Restoration and its industrialization altogether, instead calling for a Showa Restoration that would extol the clans and family lineages of Japan's pristine farming communities. The latter's ideologue Gondo Seikyo thus sought to make the village the centre of this more pastoral life, eschewing capitalism, centralized bureaucracy and all the trappings of 'Western' modernity. But other agrarian nationalists were more militant: Tachibana Kozaburo established a bucolic village school to teach agriculture blended with patriotism, but he also established a blood brotherhood committed to assassinating bankers and industrialists in order to achieve his pastoral idyll.

Increasingly, advocates of a Showa Restoration blended an anti-capitalist (and hence agrarian) appeal with hatred for socialism and a greater focus on militarism, and the need for Japan to lead Asia in fending off Western imperialism. They looked at the zaibatsu conglomerates as the embodiments of corruption, and excoriated the links between bureaucrats, ministers and businessmen who—they believed—were weakening Japan's will. The children of shopkeepers, small businessmen and farmers were typically attracted to these right-wing causes: as new opportunities were seemingly opened by Kato's reforms, many of them felt thwarted by the economic contraction of the 1920s, especially during the second half of the decade. Then, America's Smoot–Hawley tariff (a 32 per cent impost on textile imports) hit Japan especially hard, leading to a halving in Japan's silk and other textile exports.

The strategic implications of such thinking were best encapsulated in the teachings and writing of Ishiwara Kanji, one of the most accomplished of the Military Staff College instructors in Tokyo. Ishiwara taught that Japan needed to eventually conquer Marxism and other such Western ideological perversions through a just war, in which Japan had to take the lead in fighting Asia's corner against the Western imperial challenge. To vanquish the new epitome of Western capitalist corruption, the USA, Japan needed to first take on the Europeans who already dominated Asia—Britain, France and Russia. And in order to do this effectively, Ishiwara argued, Japan needed to control and develop Manchuria, with its rich deposits of coal and iron, and potential (along with Taiwan) as a food supplier.

Ishiwara was influential amongst groups of lower level officers (lieutenant colonel and below), and the advocates of the Showa Restoration were nowhere near achieving political power in Japan. But what they could not achieve through the political process, they sought to achieve through assassinations and coups, of which there were a spate in the late 1920s. The most prominent early victim was Prime Minister Hara Takashi (of Ito's conservative but anti-imperial Seiyukai party), who was assassinated on 4 November 1921 by a Japanese ultranationalist. Ironically, the founder of his party, Ito Hirobumi, had himself been assassinated in 1909 by a Korean ultranationalist (who failed to distinguish between the ameliorative approach towards Korea that Ito pursued and the militarism of his rival Yamagata Aritomo). As prime minister, Hara had suppressed the anti-colonial Samil (1 March 1919) Movement in Korea, but had then adopted a conciliatory approach, introducing Korean history and culture into school curriculums (including the use of Korean as the means of instruction), replaced military with civilian administrators and instituted a degree of self-rule for Koreans.

Hara was the first prime minister since the Meiji Restoration from a domain other than Choshu and Satsuma, and he was a commoner who helped advance democracy—but not to the extent of supporting universal male suffrage—and also reformed the bureaucracy to improve its performance.

Hara's assassination was a major setback to the cause of liberal democracy in Japan, but much worse was the assassination of the Seiyukai party's Prime Minister Inukai Tsuyoshi in May 1932 after he attempted to withhold imperial recognition for the Kwantung Army's conquest of Manchuria (and its renaming as Manchukuo). In the intervening years, there were numerous other assassinations of liberal politicians and zaibatsu business leaders—the two main targets of the ultranationalist Black Dragon Society (Kokuryukai, or Amur River Society, with the overt goal of keeping Russia behind the Amur River boundary in northeastern China). Kokuryukai remained influential through covert links with myriad mainstream politicians, and virulent opposition to leftists and the perceived tendency of liberals to pursue left-wing policies. The ultranationalists gained increasing ground at the expense of the liberals throughout the 1920s as the engagement policies of Shidehara and the more centrist Seiyukai (with its conciliatory approach towards the rest of Asia) appeared to be gaining little for Japan from the Western powers or indeed in China and Korea.

As we have seen, one militarist faction of Japan's Kwantung Army assassinated Japan's key Manchurian ally, Zhang Zuolin, on 4 June 1928, soon after Zhang had been persuaded by the Tokyo cabinet to withdraw from Beijing (and his three north China provinces) and return to Manchuria. The Tokyo cabinet, however, was strongly opposed to the militarist faction's advocacy of direct Japanese military intervention at this time, and thwarted those moves. After Tanaka's Seiyukai ministry fell, the next (Minseito party) cabinet continued the conciliatory policy towards Chiang Kai-shek's new regime in China. By this time, however, Ishiwara Kanji was the operations head of the Kwantung Army, and he spearheaded preparations for a possible future occupation of Manchuria pending a suitable opportunity. Foreign Minister Shidehara was still participating in negotiations over tariff concessions and extraterritoriality at a time when the global economic depression (brought on by the October 1929 stock market crash in the US) was causing a dramatic shrinkage in Japan's exports. Exacerbated by the Smoot–Hawley tariffs, Japan's exports plummeted from 2.5 billion yen in 1929 to 1.4 billion yen in 1931, spelling disaster for small firms in the textile trade. Farmers were even more severely affected by plunging prices as the raw silk price declined by 56 per cent between 1929 and 1931, while rice prices halved in 1930 alone. In this atmosphere—and amid fears of communist encirclement as Chiang Kai-shek was still perceived as being aligned with Stalin despite improving ties with other European powers—militarist proponents of 'Japanese-ness' gained ground against both the effete 'establishment' parties.

The London Naval Treaty of 1930 proved the last straw. It was strongly opposed by Japan's naval leadership, which felt that the asymmetrical restrictions on smaller ships (coupled with those already agreed in 1922 for aircraft carriers and battleships) would make it impossible for Japan to defend the western Pacific against the might of the United States. But the Minseito cabinet, eager to sustain good relations with world powers while also paying heed to the necessity for economic austerity, overruled the navy's objections and ratified the treaty. This set off a constitutional crisis, as the naval leadership questioned the right of the civilian leaders to make decisions about national security without reference to the views of the navy and army. Ironically, both political parties that dominated the Diet in the 1920s—the liberal Minseito, and the centrist Seiyukai (the legatee of Ito Hirobumi and Saionji Kinmochi)—had sought to foster cordial relations with the other global powers, but Britain and the US had continually dealt treacherously with Japan, forcing deals that were one-sided and detrimental to Japan's interests. The two main political parties continued to win well over 90 per cent of the seats in the Diet, but only rarely did one of them have an outright majority in Parliament, thereby weakening the resulting governments. By the 1929–32 period, Seiyukai was seen as being close to Mitsui and Minseito to Mitsubishi. The patriotic societies and advocates of a Showa Restoration came to see both parties as being hopelessly corrupted by their zaibatsu ties and, in particular, pursuing policies that placed the commercial interests of the large business conglomerates above the national interests of Japan.

Prime Minister Hamaguchi Osachi (like his US contemporary Herbert Hoover) was pursuing fiscal austerity in the face of the global depression, hoping that deflation, industrial retrenchment and keeping the yen on the gold standard would eventually restore the health of the economy. Instead, these policies proved disastrous, exacerbating the severity of the downturn and severely affecting Minseito's reputation. Their Seiyukai opponents aligned with the naval leadership to argue that the London Naval Treaty was unconstitutional, as Article 11 of Japan's constitution made planning and operational matters for the army and navy the responsibility of the military chiefs rather than of ministers. Amid rising anger over the London treaty and the economic collapse, Hamaguchi was shot at Tokyo train station in November 1930 by an ultranationalist. Hamaguchi was badly wounded, but remained in office for another three months (and eventually succumbed to his wounds in August 1931). His Minseito successor, Wakatsuki Reijiro, pursued very similar policies after taking office in March 1931, which enraged the patriots even more. They planned a coup d'état within Wakatsuki's first month but were thwarted by the military leadership, and tried again six months later (with elaborate plans for the aerial bombardment of the cabinet), but were thwarted this time by an internal betrayal. Meanwhile, Ishiwara Kanji and his fellow Kwantung Army lieutenant colonel, Itagaki Seishiro, were becoming concerned about the South Manchurian Railway's financial viability amid the collapse in global trade and were also growing fearful of the rising military threat to Japanese interests in both Korea and Manchuria from Chiang Kai-shek. They began putting in place contingency plans to occupy certain key strategic points in Manchuria in order to secure it from a possible KMT attack.

With rumours about these plans swirling, the imperial court and cabinet decided to take pre-emptive action to stave off any military adventures by Kwantung Army units. The cabinet sent an emissary to Manchuria to forestall the conspiracy but the emissary chosen was himself a party to the conspiracy, and he warned Itagaki and Ishiwara about his mission well in advance of his arrival in Mukden. They were thus able to fabricate the 'Mukden incident', in which a bomb went off under a railway carriage on the Japanese section of the South Manchurian Railway outside Mukden on 18 September 1931, providing the pretext for the Kwantung Army to invade and formally occupy all three provinces of Manchuria. Japan's Kwantung Army was able to do this with relative ease as their long-standing knowledge of the capabilities and weaknesses of Zhang Zuolin's forces gave the Japanese an overwhelming advantage over Zhang Xueliang's Northeastern Army. Despite the latter being twenty times as large—and equipped with tanks and aircraft—the Japanese were able to quickly secure the key cities of Dalian and Mukden. Xueliang happened to be recuperating at a Beijing hospital when an initial force of a thousand Japanese troops overwhelmed the 7,000 Chinese defenders of Mukden. Apparently passing on orders from the KMT, Zhang Xueliang had ordered his men not to resist a Japanese invasion and instead preserve their weapons for future skirmishes (instructions that the Japanese had become aware of). Other Chinese generals did put up some resistance in Heilongjiang, but within the next five months, Japan controlled all three Manchurian provinces—Heilongjian, Jilin and Liaoning. Initially, the whole operation had been a surprise to even the commander of the Kwantung Army and had been strongly opposed by the War Ministry and General Staff in Tokyo. But once Japanese troops were already in the field, the chain of command closed ranks around their forces, and provided full support—including diplomatic cover.

Tokyo also thwarted Ishiwara and Itagaki's plans to impose military rule over the three Manchurian provinces. Instead, the former Manchu (Qing) emperor, Puyi, was brought out of retirement and installed as the constitutional monarch of the region—which was renamed Manchukuo— with the commander of the Kwantung Army becoming Japan's ambassador to Puyi's court. The arrangement was rather similar to the way in which British colonialists had established their 'indirect' rule (through 'Residents') over the Indian subcontinent in the nineteenth century and much of the Arab world in the twentieth. There also was more than a grain of truth in Foreign Minister Uchida's assertion that 'China is not an organized state; its internal conditions and external relations are characterized by...many abnormal and exceptional features; and that, accordingly, the general principles...which govern the ordinary relations between nations are found to be considerably modified in their application as far as China is concerned.'

Manchukuo also comprised the three provinces that were the ancestral homelands of the Manchu people, and Emperor Puyi's ancestors had ensured that they remained a Manchu stronghold by limiting Han Chinese migration into the three provinces. Ironically, however, the very success of Japan in rapidly developing the region had attracted a legion of new Han Chinese settlers, thus altering the Manchu character of Manchuria (fatally for the Manchus). And while Zhang Zuolin had been an unreconstructed monarchist, and punctilious in his loyalty to the Qing (Manchu) throne, he himself was originally of Hakka rather than Manchu stock (despite his family having moved to Manchuria when he was a boy); his son Xueliang proved to be a Chinese nationalist, and thus less welcoming of the Japanese occupation of Manchuria despite his family's close links to Japan.

The League of Nations sent Lord Lytton (the British governor of Bengal from 1922 to 1927 and the son of a former viceroy of India) to investigate the rival claims of Japan and China in Manchuria. There was a rich irony here, as Britain was still ruling Iraq as a colony, and was about to impose a nominal 'independence' there that would keep Iraq's military and foreign policy completely in British hands. Had Manchuria still been predominantly Manchu, even the arch-imperialist Lytton may have been convinced that there had been a popular clamour for a Manchu restoration. But he instead confronted a largely Han population, and found in favour of China (ignoring the fact that China's armed forces had appeared to almost invite the conquest of Manchuria by failing to put up a fight despite a 20:1 advantage in regional military numbers). Japan left the League of Nations in 1933 rather than face the European powers' condemnation. But by this point, political power in Japan had also decisively passed from civilians to military leaders.

With the economy collapsing, Prime Minister Wakatsuki resigned on 13 December 1931, and was replaced by the Seiyukai's Inukai Tsuyoshi. Initially hobbled by a divided cabinet, Inukai's finance minister Takahashi Korekiyo floated (and sharply devalued) the yen, spurring a robust recovery in exports, and shored up the domestic economy with retaliatory tariff increases (to counter the Smoot–Hawley hikes by the US). Takahashi inflated the economy with new public spending, and helped spark a strong recovery in 1932. But Inukai's first fortnight in office was marred by additional military activity in China, which Emperor Hirohito expressly forbade—orders that Inukai passed on to his army commanders, to little avail. Instead, his hawkish army minister obliged Inukai to dispatch additional troops to Manchuria as well as Tianjin in contravention of the Emperor's wishes, and skirmishes between those troops and Chinese forces began on 28 January 1932 (in the 'First Shanghai Incident') after five Japanese Buddhist monks were attacked by a Chinese mob near a factory outside Shanghai. Two of the monks (who also belonged to a patriotic society) were seriously injured, and one died, provoking the retaliatory attack on Shanghai by the Japanese imperial army. This time, China's 19th Route Army and Fifth Army (reinforced by doughty Cantonese troops) put up a stiff resistance, and it took almost a month of fighting (including the naval bombardment of Shanghai harbour from a Japanese aircraft carrier) before Shanghai fell.

Riding on its popular opposition to the ratification of the London Naval Treaty, the electorate's disillusionment with Minseito's mishandling of the economy, and the patriotic fervour generated by military victories in China, Seiyukai won Japan's February 1932 general election in a landslide (301 of the 466 Diet seats). But this electoral triumph proved a poisoned chalice for Inukai, as the militarists too wanted their pound of flesh for helping to bring it about. The League of Nations negotiated a truce that made Shanghai a demilitarized zone, prohibited China from garrisoning any troops in areas surrounding Shanghai, Suzhou and Kunshan but allowed some Japanese military units to remain. This negotiated agreement—despite being more favourable to Japan than most previous negotiations with the Great Powers—was seen by the militarists as being a capitulation by Inukai, and also appeared to hurt his popularity with the general public. Inukai's continuing attempts to rein in the military resulted in the League of Blood Incident of March 1932, in which an ultranationalist pseudo-Buddhist sect planned the assassination of several leading figures of Japan's establishment, but only succeeded in assassinating two (Inoue Jonnosuke, a former finance minister, and Takuma Dan, director general of the Mitsui holding company). Ultimately, that sect acted in concert with several junior naval officers (all aged just over twenty) and army cadets to assassinate Prime Minister Inukai himself on 15 May 1932 as part of an elaborate coup plot that was to have resulted in a military takeover of Japan's government. The coup failed, despite the bombing of genro Saionji's house, as well as a grenade attack on the headquarters of the Mitsubishi Bank. The plotters had also planned to internationalize the issue by assassinating the inimitable movie star, Charlie Chaplin, who had arrived in Japan as Inukai's guest the previous day. But they failed to accomplish this either, as Chaplin was away watching a sumo wrestling match with Inukai's son at the time!

Although failing in their immediate objective of a military takeover of government, the coup plotters had the satisfaction of winning in the court of public opinion and also of effectively ending the period of democratic political party governance. Although the Seiyukai still had a strong majority in the Diet, the next two prime ministers Saito and Okada (who served two years each until 1936) were former naval officers, albeit carefully selected by Saionji from the small faction of naval officers who had supported the 1930 London Naval Treaty (with Okada, in fact, helping to negotiate it). By 1940, the political parties were dissolved into a single Imperial Rule Assistance Association as Prime Minister Konoe Fumimaro made Japan a single-party state. The tussle between Tokyo politicians and the militarists in Manchukuo continued, with the latter gradually gaining ground. They were continually surprised, however, by the resistance of the Chinese to Japan's bid to create a 'co-prosperity sphere' comprising Japan, Manchukuo and northern China, although the non-Han communities (including the Manchus and Mongols) were often keen to collaborate with the Japanese.

In 1933–35, the Mongol regions of Jehol and Chahar were added to Manchukuo (with the Mongol prince and pan-Mongol nationalist, Demchugdongrub, as leader of Chahar), while Hebei province was made a kind of buffer region. Prince Demchugdongrub (the Tibetan form of 'Chakrasamvara Siddhartha') had been working with other Mongol princes from Chahar and Suiyuan (the region that includes the Inner Mongolian towns of Hohhot and Ordos) with the intent of creating an independent pan-Mongolian federation. (Outer) Mongolia itself had been independent for a decade after 1911, but got caught up in the Russian Civil War, and became a satellite state of the Soviet Union in 1921, with the theocratic nationalism of Bogd Khan being replaced by the atheist communism of Lenin and Stalin. Mongol nationalism still had a constituency, and it found an outlet in the vast Mongol provinces that had been a central part of the Manchu domains but were now being called 'Inner Mongolia'—formerly within Qing China, but now up for grabs. Prince Demchugdongrub stepped neatly into this void and, at a conference at the temple of Bat Khaalga (or Bailingmiao) just north of Guihua (or Guisui, present-day Hohhot) in September 1933, the princes agreed to bury their differences and create a confederation of (Inner) Mongolia. They sent a missive to the Nanjing government threatening to seek Japanese assistance for their cause and were promptly granted the right to create a Mongol Local Autonomy Political Affairs Committee (sometimes called the 'Bailingmiao

Council'). This was an intermediate step to independence, as the council had three times as many independent Mongol nobles and bannermen as the number of KMT-linked Mongols and Tibetans. Demchugdongrub was made the council's Secretary General, and the former Qing dynasty nobleman and feudatory Yondonwangchug (or Yunden Wangchuk in Tibetan) its chairman.

In May 1935, Demchugdongrub and Emperor Puyi of Manchukuo cemented another Manchu–Mongol alliance, and Puyi conferred on the former a first-rank Manchu princely title. The Mongol region was renamed Mengjiang, with an autonomous Mongol government that was independent of Nanjing. Demchugdongrub initially rejected the terms offered by the Japanese for their support. After some Japanese soldiers were detained by Nationalist (KMT) Chinese guards in a region of north Chahar still controlled by the KMT, the Japanese intervened and the KMT emissary signed an agreement with the Japanese diplomat Doihara Kenji, which provided for the expulsion of KMT troops from all of Chahar, and banned the settlement of any Han Chinese in north Chahar. This helped win over the Mengjiang administration, and Demchugdongrub agreed to cooperate closely with Japan in return for substantial financial assistance. Mengjiang remained independent of China for the whole of the next decade (until the Soviet invasion of Manchukuo in August 1945).

Fighting was continuing, meanwhile, between the KMT and communists along the coast of China. The communists occasionally gained ground in Guangdong, but in 1931 were cornered in their fastness of Jiangxi and Fujian, where Mao Zedong created a soviet, with Zhu De as his key military confidant. That year, Zhou Enlai became the party's leader but by November 1935, he had subordinated himself to Mao, and remained the latter's key deputy throughout the rest of his career, serving as a suave commissar to the rest of the world while surviving the many bitter purges within the party. Mao aligned himself with a local bandit in 1931, and himself operated like one initially in order to survive those early years of tough fighting against the KMT. The Comintern sent a Bavarian communist called Otto Braun (known as Li De) to China to establish the Red Army with Bo Gu in 1933, and the two were able to overcome four encirclement campaigns. Defeated in the fifth of these encirclement campaigns, the Red Army began the Long March to escape the KMT's grip in October 1934—a story mythologized in the West by the journalist Edgar Snow, who wrote in 1938 about the heroic rearguard action led by Mao that allegedly covered 8,000 miles (12,800 kilometres), probably double the actual distance covered. In fact, Mao and the rest of the party leadership did not 'march' much during the Long March, being carried in palanquins (litters) through most of it! From early on, Mao had a retinue of servants that belied his image as an egalitarian who lived the rough life.

In early 1935, Zhou led a purge of the party, in which Otto Braun and Bo Gu were denounced; during that year, Zhou and Mao effectively escaped the grip of Chiang's KMT forces, feinting their way south into Yunnan before heading northwards. In June–July 1935, Zhou and Mao's forces briefly merged with the larger forces of Mao's rival and CCP founder Zhang Guotao. But their paths soon diverged again, with Mao and Zhou heading north towards Shaanxi while Zhang Guotao went south, where Chiang Kai-shek (with Muslim Ma allies) decimated most of his forces. Soon after the Red Army reached Shaanxi in November 1935, Mao officially became its chairman, with Zhou and Deng Xiaoping as deputy chairmen, establishing a new base in Yan'an in Shaanxi province. Although only a tenth of the army that had begun the Long March survived it, the trek through eleven provinces proved an invaluable recruiting device for the CCP, enabling it to build a powerful reputation amongst the peasantry. But above all, Edgar Snow and other journalists' mythologizing gave an immeasurable boost to Mao's reputation in China and amongst romantic radicals around the world, helping to convert a series of strategic disasters into the epic triumph called the 'Long March'.

In 1936, Zhang Xueliang staged the extraordinary Xian Incident to force Generalissimo Chiang Kai-shek to begin cooperating with the communists to fend off further Japanese advances. Zhang, the son of Japan's key military ally in Manchuria during the 1920s, had thrown in his lot with Chiang and the KMT—as opposed to Japan—right from the start of Japan's intrusion into Manchuria, and remained the key KMT military commander in north China. In October 1936, Chiang had flown to Xian from his capital, Nanjing, to announce a new mobilization to defeat the communists. But when he failed to persuade Chiang of the need for a united front with the communists to defeat Japan, Zhang Xueliang kidnapped Chiang Kai-shek on his next visit to Xian on 13 December 1936. In what came to be known as the Xian Incident, the purported President of China was a captive of Zhang for the next eleven days, while the latter negotiated with the communists to send a delegation to begin unity talks with Chiang. Mao was inclined to use the opportunity to kill Chiang, but was dissuaded by Stalin, who believed it was more important to re-establish a united front. Eventually, Zhou Enlai led a delegation to Xian, and Zhang Xueliang was able to broker an agreement between the two rival parties to establish a new United Front of the KMT and CCP to fight Japan. Zhang accompanied Chiang Kai-shek back to Nanjing, but was arrested soon afterwards and spent much of the rest of his life as a prisoner of the KMT, suspected of being a communist agent. But Zhang Xueliang's two interventions (to support the KMT over Japan in 1928, and then to kidnap Chiang to force a United Front) had been absolutely vital in fending off the Japanese military's advances into Manchuria and China proper.

On 7 July 1937, the Marco Polo Bridge Incident occurred at this crucial bridge connecting the walled city of Wanping outside Beijing to the KMT's southern strongholds. After the initial skirmishes, both sides refused to accede to the others' demands, and the incident soon escalated into full-scale war, as the Tokyo government proved unable to restrain its army commanders. By early August, Japan's newly established North China Army had captured Beijing and Tianjin. At this stage, neither the Japanese nor Chiang Kai-shek's KMT wanted the hostilities to widen, and the Japanese in particular felt that their forces were already overstretched and needed to consolidate their control over northern China. Only Stalin had a strong interest in diverting Japan's military attention away from northern China and its long border with Soviet Russia, all of which was vulnerable to any potential attacks by Japan. And in Zhang Zhizhong, the general commanding the Shanghai–Nanjing garrison, Stalin had a useful mole embedded in the heart of Chiang's army.

Zhang Zhizhong had been an instructor at the Whampoa military academy funded by Soviet Russia in 1925 and had developed close ties to the Soviets; he claimed to have wanted to join the Communist Party then, but was advised against it by Zhou Enlai, who suggested he remain within the KMT while retaining secret ties to the CCP and Moscow (through its embassy). After the fall of Beijing and Tianjin, Zhang repeatedly cabled Chiang requesting him to launch a pre-emptive strike against the Japanese forces in Shanghai a thousand kilometres to the south of where the fighting was then occurring. Chiang ignored these requests: Shanghai was too close to his capital of Nanjing, and he had no interest in provoking Japan to shift its attention to the industrial heartland of China. But Zhang Zhizhong forced the issue, by first getting one of his army units to kill two Japanese officers outside Shanghai airport on 9 August, and then having a Chinese prisoner dressed up in Chinese army fatigues and shot at the airport gate to make it appear as if the Japanese had fired first.

Chiang Kai-shek continued to caution Zhang against attacking the Japanese, but the latter pre-empted his leader by getting Chinese planes to attack the Japanese flagship *Izumo* on 14 August, and following it up with false claims that Japan was shelling Shanghai. With anti-Japanese sentiment flaring up, Chiang Kai-shek was obliged to acquiesce, and he ordered an assault on the small Japanese naval force near Shanghai on 17 August. Within a day, Chiang asked his forces to halt the offensive, but Zhang ignored those orders and expanded operations—obliging Japan to send in substantial reinforcements on 22 August. Eventually Chang Kai-shek removed Zhang Zhizhong from his position of command, but Zhang was to stay on in Communist China after the 1949 revolution.

As the hostilities spread south, heavy fighting occurred in and around Shanghai, causing nearly 400,000 Chinese and 40,000 Japanese troop casualties, and virtually all of Chiang's fledgling air force and several vital warships were destroyed before the great metropolis fell to the Japanese, who then attacked Chiang's capital of Nanjing in December 1937. The fierce fighting included gruesome atrocities committed by the Japanese forces there. The civilian population of Chiang's capital of Nanjing were the victims of a six-week period of horrific atrocities, including rape, killing between 40,000 and 300,000 people (the latter being close to the entire population of the city at the time, and thus perhaps an extreme figure). Defeated in his capital, Chiang Kai-shek was forced to move to Wuhan, but heavy naval bombardments by the Japanese forces all along the coast pushed the KMT-CCP united front steadily inward. Eventually Chiang established his new capital inland in Chongqing (then the largest city in the heavily populated and largely agricultural province of Sichuan), while the communists remained in their redoubt of Yan'an. Japan's North China Army gained control over the entire Yangzi Valley, and captured all the key economic and political centres of northern China. In 1938, the Japanese won the Battle of Wuhan, and took control of Hankou, before the North China Army linked up with another Japanese force in the south to capture Canton. The diversion of Japan's military southwards was a boon to Stalin, who immediately arranged for major weapons supplies to be sent to Chiang in pursuance of a genuine 'united front' strategy. Stalin sent Wang Ming, his Comintern representative to the CCP, with a clear message for the CCP to 'fight the Japanese'. Mao's strategy throughout the war was to ensure that Japan and the KMT did most of the fighting, so that Japan would destroy Chiang's army and the CCP would be able to consolidate behind the Japanese lines, steadily gaining ground there. Mao's secret line for the CCP was a 'don't fight Japan' policy that directly contravened Stalin's orders conveyed via Wang Ming. Through the first half of 1938, Mao was in a minority within the politburo and Wang Ming was in the ascendant, but Mao's military colleagues (Zhu De and Peng Dehuai) were the first to see the benefits of Mao's approach, especially as Japan kept gaining victories over Chiang's forces, steadily decimating them along the way. Ironically, Liu Shaoqi (who was to fall out with Mao in 1961–62 and die from torture at the hands of Mao's Red Guards) played a vital role in swinging the politburo away from Wang Ming's line (which had been supported by Zhou Enlai), and falling behind Mao in the autumn of 1938. Zhou eventually switched to Mao's side too, staying his loyal henchman for the rest of his life.

All the focus on the military manoeuvres over Manchukuo and coastal China have partially obscured the fact that the early 1930s also marked the start of Japan's heavy and chemical industrialization drive—one that was even more successful than Stalin's contemporary industrialization drive (and without requiring the kulak killings). Nehru, for instance, spent just a couple of paragraphs on Japan's industrialization, describing how Japanese goods flooded European markets because they were cheap (on account of the weak yen and 'low-wage female labour') in contrast to the two chapters he devoted to extolling the achievements of Stalin's Piatiletka. Political economist Alice Amsden points out that Japan's success—even in cotton textiles and piece-goods (in which Japan's share of world exports soared from 22 per cent in 1929 to 44 per cent in 1935)—was not based on low wages alone, as explained in a study (published in 1938) by G. E. Hubbard, a British economist. Amsden quoted Hubbard as arguing that wages for females were lower on average in Japan primarily because most of them were girls under twenty, and the discrepancy between their wage rates and those of 'young learners in the British cotton trade... is not very marked'; instead, group control to 'check overproduction and uneconomic competition', large manufacturing units with the latest technology (ring spindles), low shipping costs, bulk buying of the raw material (cotton) at the lowest costs to the spinner, and efficiency in marketing (based on close cooperation between manufacturers and traders) helped explain their success. Amsden adds that Japanese management was far superior to that of their Lancashire counterparts, aided by the fact that there were many more graduates amongst Japanese managers—reflecting the lead Japan already had over Britain in education. The blinkered glasses worn by Marxists of every hue globally (including Nehru) blinded them to the remarkable achievements of Japan's industrial leap of 1931–34, which the great economic historian Charles Kindleberger dubbed Japan's 'Keynesian policies as early as 1932 without a Keynes.' Between 1931 and 1934, Finance Minister Takahashi Korekiyo's industrial policies (backed at their outset by Prime Minister Inukai) enabled Japan's industrial output to increase by 81.5 per cent in three years.

While Takahashi's reflationary deficit financing was undoubtedly Keynesian, political scientist Chalmers Johnson was quick to point out that there was far more to Takahashi's policy success than just Keynesian fiscal policy! After a brief six-month term as prime minister in 1922, Takahashi became minister of agriculture and commerce in 1924–26, and played the key role in bifurcating the ministry into a separate Ministry of Commerce and Industry (MCI) and another of Agriculture and Forestry. In his earlier bureaucratic career, Takahashi had been the first chief of Japan's patent bureau and effectively organized the patent system after spending his early career in the Bank of Japan, where he rose rapidly through the ranks.

Within the MCI (the precursor to the post-WWII Ministry of International Trade and Industry, or MITI), two of Takahashi's protégés—Yoshino Shinji and Kishi Nobusuke (maternal grandfather of Abe Shinzo, Japan's current prime minister)—were to become the key formulators of Japan's approach to industrial policy. Takahashi himself was finance minister right through the period from 1931 to 1936, providing a remarkable degree of policy continuity during the period—marked by expansionary monetary and fiscal policies that brought Japan out of the Great Depression far more effectively than any other capitalist economy. Over five years from 1930 to 1935, wholesale prices declined in Britain, Germany and France and were broadly unchanged (falling sharply for three years, then rising) in the US, but rose about 12 per cent in Japan (and nearly 30 per cent between 1931 and 1935). Similarly, Japan's index of mining and manufacturing output rose 50 per cent over the period, while the USA's declined 6.3 per cent, France's fell 27 per cent, Germany's rose 9.4 per cent and Britain's rose 14.4 per cent (aided by the strength of its captive colonial markets).

Keynes wrote his great treatise in 1936, but by that time Takahashi (tragically assassinated in February that year) had already demonstrated the effectiveness of 'Keynesian' macroeconomic policy. More important, Yoshino and Kishi created the framework of complementary industrial policy—based on rationalization of industry through a system of self-regulation that created cartels in 'important industries' and an oligopolistic structure—that facilitated rapid industrial growth, ensuring that Japan could take full advantage of the macroeconomic stability fostered by Takahashi. The industrial cartels were aimed at rationalizing industries through superior organization, cost cutting and labour peace—the formula that helped not just cotton textiles and garments (as we have just seen) but a slew of other industries ranging from steel to shipbuilding and chemicals.

The Important Industries Control Law enabled the creation of cartels in any industry in which two-thirds of the members requested it, which would then be administered by the MCI. By 1933, the MCI had the right to approve new investments by cartel members and approve members' decisions to restrict output. The surge in Japan's heavy and chemical industries output during this period was made possible by the effective rationalization and planning of capacity and investments by the Temporary Industrial Rationalization Bureau, under which cartels were authorized in twenty-six 'important industries' including iron and steel, coal, silk thread, rayon, paper, cement and even wheat flour, with the MCI playing a key role in restricting competition in key

PRASENJIT K. BASU

industries that suffered from excess capacity such as shipbuilding, electrical machinery and cotton spinning. Then, beginning with the petroleum industry in 1934, the MCI facilitated a series of sector development laws that would restrict competition in the sector, and license participants in the industry who would receive substantial incentives if they achieved key targets.

The Petroleum Industry Law of 1934 specifically gave the government the right to license the importing and refining of petroleum, as well as to set quotas and prices, and compulsorily requisition petroleum products when necessary; it also required license holders to stockpile at least six months' supply of petroleum in Japan at all times. The next key sectoral law was the Automobile Manufacturing Industry Law (May 1936), which licensed just two car manufacturers (Toyota and Nissan), but supplied them half their capital, and eliminated all taxes and import duties for five years while also providing some protection to their end product. With the sharply depreciated yen, competitors (Ford and General Motors) who needed to import components quickly went out of business. Over the next three years, similar sector laws were passed for the steel industry, machine tools, aircraft manufacturing, shipbuilding, important machines manufacturing and artificial petroleum. Despite the widespread direction by bureaucrats that these sector laws entailed, private ownership remained central to the Japanese approach, with the developmental state always working primarily through privately-managed businesses, the best of which were chosen to lead.

The zaibatsu had become unpopular partly because they were seen as profiteering from the dollar crisis of 1929–30, during which many of them hoarded dollars in anticipation of the inevitable yen devaluation that was to come. Following the assassination of Takuma Dan, his successor as head of Mitsui, the Harvard-educated Ikeda Seihin made a public 'conversion to patriotism' to forestall potential attempts by the military and bureaucracy to nationalize the zaibatsu. Ikeda was to become the MCI minister in 1938 (succeeding Yoshino, who rose through the ranks to become minister for about one year). Throughout the 1930s, there was a tussle between the MCI bureaucrats' (especially Yoshino's) preferred approach of self-regulation by the zaibatsu, and the military's predilection for state control and, at its extreme, nationalization. The latter was tried out in Manchukuo between 1932 and 1936, with the military (led by Ishiwara Kanji) and the South Manchurian Railway (SMR) attempting to develop a state-led and anti-zaibatsu industrial model there. But this largely failed, mainly because of the lack of capital and expertise—especially in the complex management of the new heavy and chemical industries. Eventually, in 1936 the SMR leadership and army commanders specifically asked for Kishi to be deputed to Manchukuo to help implement the 'five-year plan for Japanese and Manchurian industry'. (The term 'five-year plan' reveals one motivation for Japan's turn towards aggressive industrialization after 1930: the fear of Soviet progress, as announced with its first five year plan in 1928.) Amongst Kishi's earliest moves was to invite the head of the Nissan conglomerate, Ayukawa Gisuke, to Manchukuo to help manage and implement the plan. Nissan was acceptable to the military as a 'new zaibatsu' focused primarily on the new technology-heavy industries (including cars and trucks, in which it was one of the two licensed producers). Ayukawa shifted the headquarters of his Nissan zaibatsu entirely to Hsinking (Changchun), the new capital of Manchukuo (in Jilin province), where it was renamed the Manchurian Heavy Industry Corporation (or Mangyo for short) with Ayukawa as its president. After his one-year stint as minister for the MCI, Yoshino too went to work for Mangyo in Manchukuo. Changchun became one of the primary centres of China's automobile industry (with Nissan's first major plant established there), and retained that role through the 1950s. And Manchukuo industrialized rapidly through the next decade, becoming the centre of China's heavy industry until at least 1960.

Although historians almost instinctively refer to Manchukuo's constitutional monarchy as being a 'puppet' regime, it is worth noting that the bureaucratic structure established in Manchukuo had Manchurians as heads (directors) of all key government bureaus, albeit each with a Japanese deputy director. The police force was the one exception where the Japanese were fully in charge. (In September 1935, Tojo Hideki became chief of the Kempeitai or the military police in Manchukuo, a stepping stone to becoming Chief of Staff of the Kwantung Army in 1937, and leading the conquest of Chahar in Inner Mongolia.) Compared to British India, Manchukuo had a much more localized—Manchurian (including Han Chinese)—bureaucratic structure than British India had in the 1930s, where the British were completely in charge of the police and military. There were some slight nods to political change at the provincial level in India (with the 1937 provincial elections being won almost completely by the Congress party), but these provincial governments had little influence on national policymaking. When Britain declared war on India's behalf in 1939, the provincial governments were not consulted, which led them to resign. More importantly, of course, most bureaus of the national administration remained firmly in British hands throughout, and Manchukuo had much more administrative autonomy than Indians had in India in the 1930s.

Between 1930 and 1940, the MCI was able to bring about a more than doubling of Japan's mining and manufacturing production, and its composition shifted dramatically from light to heavy industry. The latter (comprising metals,

260   PRASENJIT K. BASU

machines and chemicals) rose from 35 per cent of all industry in 1930 to 63 per cent of the total by 1940. And while there were three textile firms amongst Japan's top ten largest companies in 1929, by 1940 there was just one. In 1940, the top five largest companies in Japan were Japan Steel, Mitsubishi Heavy, Oji Paper, Hitachi and Japan Mining; the first two were to retain those positions until the 1970s, while Oji Paper (which, with Fuji Paper, was amongst the top three in 1929 too) and Japan Mining would fall off the map in the post-War years. Toshiba (number eight in 1940) and Sumitomo Metals (number ten in 1940) were the other two that would remain amongst the top ten in the 1972 list.

However, the assassination of Takahashi Korekiyo (the last great Seiyukai stalwart, and surely one of the world's greatest economic policymakers in the twentieth century) in February 1936 proved a huge setback to the cause of macroeconomic stability in Japan. One vital reason the militarists hated him was because he had begun to reduce military spending in order to both contain the fiscal deficit and keep the balance of payments from falling into deficit. Takahashi's assassination removed all constraints on military spending but also resulted in a rapid deterioration of the twin deficits, and a sharp rise in inflation in the late 1930s. Japanese planners visited the Dutch East Indies during these years, seeking greater access to its petroleum and other mineral resources. Southeast Asia became increasingly important to Japan during this period both as a market for its exports and a source of vital raw materials for its industry. In fact, the military and MCI saw eye-to-eye on one area: the importance of export promotion, which became a key focus for both in the 1930s, with a special Trade Bureau being carved out from the MCI to focus on it.

And not all Chinese patriots scorned the Japanese. Wang Jingwei, the leftist KMT leader who Sun Yat-sen had designated his successor (but who had been outwitted by Chiang Kai-shek in 1926–27), came to believe that China and Japan needed to cooperate with each other in order to fend off Western imperialism. In the years between 1928 and 1931, Wang had participated in various rebel governments opposed to Chiang, but those had been defeated by Chiang in the Central Plains War (1930) and in Guangzhou (1931). Thereafter, Wang had reconciled with his old rival, who made him premier of the KMT regime based in Nanjing in 1932. From the outset, however, Wang disagreed strongly with Chiang, and their relationship remained turbulent even as the regime was constantly on the retreat in the face of Japanese advances. Wang resigned as premier in December 1935 after a failed assassination attempt against him; he advocated strong punitive action against Zhang Xueliang during and after the Xian Incident, but was opposed by Chiang's wife, Soong

Mei-ling, and brother-in-law, T. V. Soong, who feared that Chiang might die in the ensuing internal warfare, paving the way for Wang Jingwei to take power—suggesting he still remained a potent rival to Chiang.

After the KMT's withdrawal to Chongqing in 1937, Wang gradually began to advocate the need for a negotiated settlement with Japan, followed by a Sino–Japanese alliance as a bulwark against Western imperialism, which remained the much bigger threat to China. Wang began to send feelers to the Japanese in 1938–39, after he moved to Hanoi in French Indo-China, and the negotiations bore fruit in early 1940. On 30 March that year, Wang Jingwei became president of the Reorganized National Government of China—the rival to Chiang Kai-shek's regime based in Chongqing. Derided as heading a 'puppet' government, albeit one that was no less independent than the British-supported regimes established in Egypt in 1922 or Iraq in 1932, Wang Jingwei in fact presided over all of China's economically-significant cities and provinces. Ruling from Nanjing, his territory covered Beijing, Shanghai, the entrepreneurial province of Zhejiang, Hebei, Anhui, Jiangsu, Shandong (with its German industrial heritage), the coastal regions of Fujian (including the key cities of Fuzhou and Xiamen), Guangzhou and Hong Kong. Puyi's Manchukuo operated as a separate nation state.

THE GANDHI-BOSE RIFT OVER NON-VIOLENCE AND INDIA'S LOST OPPORTUNITIES OF THE 1930s

India's more well-established nationalist movement proved much less prone to communist influences, although socialism gradually took root—especially amongst younger nationalists who were disillusioned with Gandhi after he called off Non-Cooperation following Chauri Chaura (1922). Upon his arrival in Bombay from Britain on 16 June 1921—after becoming the first Indian to resign immediately from the elite Indian Civil Service (ICS) to which less than a dozen Indians qualified each year—Subhas Chandra Bose had hastened that very afternoon to meet Gandhi. During the journey home by ship, Subhas had also been fortunate to have the poet Rabindranath Tagore as a fellow passenger, and the two had had many meaningful conversations, during which Tagore expressed some misgivings about the effect of the Non-Cooperation Movement on another generation of India's youth, who would be missing school and college classes in order to agitate. Bose had closely questioned Gandhi during that first conversation, and come away not entirely convinced about the strategy to achieve independence by the end of the year. Gandhi had suggested he begin work with Chittaranjan Das in Bengal, and Bose had taken that advice to heart, soon accepting the job of principal of the national college established as an alternative to the British-run universities (where Aurobindo Ghose had been the founding principal, and which is now Jadavpur University). During the Prince of Wales' visit to India in October 1921, Bose and Das had effectively organized a complete boycott of his visit to Calcutta, unlike in Bombay, where opponents and supporters had clashed violently.

The British reacted by imprisoning both Bengali leaders. They grew closer in jail, where other inmates joked about Das acquiring an 'ICS cook' as the younger man soaked up wisdom from his new leader. Disillusioned by Gandhi calling off the Non-Cooperation Movement after Chauri Chaura, Das proposed (as Congress president) in December 1922 that the Congress should try and work the Montford Reforms through 'council entry'. Although Gandhi (from prison) and Congress rejected that plan, Das and Motilal Nehru floated the Swaraj Party and emerged as the single largest party in the country at the 1923 election. Das then had legislation passed to strengthen the municipality of Calcutta (by far India's largest city at the time, and the 'second city of the British empire') and became its first elected mayor in 1924, with one of his lieutenants, Hussain Shaheed Suhrawardy (a future prime minister of Pakistan) as deputy mayor and twenty-seven-year-old Bose as chief executive officer. The trio focused on improving social services, aiming at widening their delivery to the poorest denizens of the city: Bose set up free primary schools across the city and health associations in every ward. Inspired by Das, CEO Bose took steps to strengthen Hindu–Muslim unity by appointing Muslims to three-quarters of senior jobs in the municipality—to help redress the historic wrong of inadequate Muslim representation. Bose won commendation from Gandhi for this bold step, although he also upset orthodox Hindus.

But Bose was only able to function for half a year, before he was peremptorily arrested in October 1924 under the obscure Regulation III of 1818, which gave the British colonial authorities the right to detain any Indians without trial, or even making the charges public. The ostensible reason for Bose's arrest was that he was allegedly 'the leading organizer of the revolutionary movement in Bengal' including consorting with 'Bolshevik propagandists'. There was absolutely no basis to the charge of a communist link: Das had been approached by the Comintern but had firmly rejected the overture, and Bose was always suspicious of the communists and their tendency to follow Moscow blindly. He was not wedded to non-violence, but did not believe in random acts of individual terrorism; instead, he believed that India needed to acquire some coherent military capabilities over time, in case non-violent means failed. Bose sued three newspapers for libel (for alleging he had terrorist links) and won damages in court from two of them.

Nonetheless, Bose was imprisoned and soon taken away to Mandalay. Bose was also inspired by the fact that he was in the same prison in Mandalay that had once held Bal Gangadhar Tilak, the nationalist (labelled 'extremist' by the British) who had led the Swadeshi Movement of 1906–08 before spending six years imprisoned in Mandalay. The British had a hierarchy of their Indian adversaries: virtually no Muslim League politician (including Jinnah) was ever imprisoned by the British (unless the person also had dual membership in Congress at the time); prominent Congress leaders like Gandhi and Nehru (both father and son) were sent to prisons within India, sometimes to fairly luxurious ones (like the Aga Khan's palace) and at other times to such well-appointed places as Yerwada prison in Pune; but the British reserved their severest sentences—imprisonment in Mandalay (outside India proper) or the Andaman Islands—for those seen as the empire's most dangerous enemies (Tilak, Subhas Bose, V. D. Savarkar), who were frequently exiled from India when they weren't imprisoned. That Bose was sent to Mandalay within three years of his return to India suggests the British had marked him out from the outset as a potentially most dangerous subversive.

Bose spent his two-and-a-half years in Burmese prisons feverishly gaining knowledge about empires and revolutions (with Irish history a particular favourite), and read memoirs, philosophy (Nietzsche and Bertrand Russell), and works on comparative religion, criminology and social anthropology. A year into his imprisonment, Bose received the tragic news that his mentor, C. R. Das, had died—a loss that he felt deeply, as Das had become a father figure to him. Bose was physically assaulted by jailers on several occasions, once being seriously injured, and in February 1926, he undertook a fast to protest inhuman conditions in prison. This three-week fast weakened him severely, and his brother Sarat began petitioning the authorities to move him back to India. Instead, they offered him exile to Europe, which Subhas refused. He plunged into a study of Burma's culture and history, India's history and Bengali literature, and concluded that traditional Burma had created 'the most classless country', with empowered women and an inexpensive system of primary education that had resulted in much higher levels of male and female literacy there than in India. Subhas was already getting to the nub of some of the social challenges that an independent India needed to address: literacy and women's empowerment.

With his health deteriorating rapidly, Bose was released in May 1927, and quickly rejoined the Congress movement, becoming general secretary of the All India Congress Committee (alongside Jawaharlal Nehru) that December and president of the Bengal Provincial Committee of the party. Jawaharlal had just returned from touring Europe, and was freshly imbued with the ideological certainties of Marxism. After some years of dormancy, Congress had been galvanized into action with the premature arrival (February 1928) of the Simon Commission to assess the first decade of the Montford Reforms of 1919. Baldwin's Tories had brought forward this commission, in order to control any proposed reforms, fearing that a future Labour government may be 'too inexperienced' to deal effectively with India, and therefore needed to be pre-empted. Headed by Sir John Simon (a Liberal MP who was soon to join the Conservatives), the all-white commission comprising four Conservative British MPs and two Labour MPs (including the future prime minister Clement Attlee) raised the hackles of all Indians—Congress, Swarajists, the 'Jinnah group' of the Muslim League and the relatively pro-British Liberals. That it had absolutely no Indian representatives raised one major red flag in India. Its attitude—of looking at India as a disparate congeries of regional, religious and sectional interests, rather than as a single nation state—was even more offensive to Indians. As had been evident since 1909, the British colonial authorities were determined to keep India divided into as many smaller units as possible, starting with creating a Hindu–Muslim divide, but also encouraging the princes to stay separate, and stoking sectional interests in the major provinces (non-Brahmins in Madras, Muslims in Bengal and Assam, the Scheduled Castes in Bombay) to keep the nationalists off-balance, prevent the emergence of a single nationalist voice, and provide a justification for Britain's rule to persist as the only arbiter amongst these supposedly disparate voices.

Lord Birkenhead, Secretary of State for India, was blunt in a letter to Viceroy Irwin: 'We have always relied on the non-boycotting Moslems; on the depressed community; on the business interests; and on many others, to break down the attitude of boycott.' He ordered that, in order to 'terrify the immense Hindu population', any meetings between Simon and 'representative Moslems' should be widely publicized. In April 1928, Birkenhead privately expressed the Conservative government's attitude to India in clear terms: 'the phrase "Dominion Status" should not be used to describe the ultimate goal ... since ... Dominion Status means "the right to decide their own destinies", and this right we were not prepared to accord India at present, or in any way prejudge the question of whether it should ever be accorded.'

Gandhi had demonstrated the futility of such British attempts at sowing division over the previous decade, but the attempts continued. The Simon Commission proved a particular spur towards national unity, and after an all-party meeting in May 1928, Gandhi's Congress responded by appointing the Motilal Nehru Committee to formulate the outline of a constitution for India (in defiance of the British taunts that India was incapable of creating her own statute). Both Subhas Bose and Jawaharlal Nehru were in the

Motilal Committee (as were a couple of Muslims—Ali Imam and Shuaib Qureshi). Annie Besant had, in consultation with some Congress leaders, put together another draft constitution for India in 1925 and had it introduced in the British House of Commons, where it was quickly killed. Jinnah took a delegation (comprising his young acolytes, M. C. Chagla and Liaquat Ali Khan; the former would become India's education and foreign minister while the latter would become the first prime minister of Pakistan) to confer with the Nehru Committee. In 1916, Motilal and Jinnah had negotiated the Lucknow Pact that had cemented Hindu–Muslim unity, blessed in particular by Tilak strongly endorsing the pact—which allowed for separate electorates and other electoral safeguards for Muslims. But the climate had changed substantially by 1928, and the (Motilal) Nehru Report of September 1928 set aside separate electorates, instead allowing for 'reserved constituencies' for minorities within each state, but with joint electorates. This was actually an interesting innovation in that it ensured that Muslims (and other minorities) would be guaranteed a minimum number of elected legislators, but they would have to contest through joint electorates. This neatly countered the long-standing British tactic of divide and rule, central to which were separate electorates which ensured that each community had no reason to moderate its message, as only members of its own community would be electing its representatives. Unfortunately, the Muslim League and Khilafat Committee rejected these recommendations, as did Jinnah, who touted his 'Fourteen Points' that were rejected by even the mainstream Muslim League.

As the Simon Commission's seven members toured India starting in February 1928, they were met by black flag demonstrations everywhere, countered by police repression. One of the worst police atrocities occurred in Lahore in October 1928, when the police baton-charged a peaceful demonstration and severely injured the veteran Congress leader of Punjab, Lala Lajpat Rai, who succumbed to his wounds and died on 17 November. This inflamed many young men, particularly Bhagat Singh, whose uncle Ajit had been a revolutionary in the Ghadar campaign of 1914–16. Already unhappy about the abandonment of the Non-Cooperation Movement after Chauri Chaura, twenty-one-year-old Bhagat Singh had joined the Hindustan Socialist Republican Association (HSRA), alongside his comrades Sukhdev Thapar and Shivaram Rajguru, led by Chandrasekhar Azad (one of the founders of the HSRA and its predecessor the HRA, which had raised funds through raids on trains and armouries, including the Kakori revolutionary raid, after which Ram Prasad Bismil and Ashfaqullah Khan had been hanged by the British). The four revolutionaries decided that Lala Lajpat Rai's murder by the Punjab police had to be avenged, and Bhagat Singh and Rajguru assassinated J. P.

Saunders, an assistant superintendent of police involved in the assault on the Lala, on 17 December 1928 (exactly a month after Lajpat Rai's martyrdom), with Azad providing covering fire. More remarkably, all four were able to escape without detection —as Chandrasekhar Azad had also done after Kakori.

When Subhas introduced a resolution at the Congress session of December 1928 advocating 'purna swaraj' (complete independence), Jawaharlal supported him, but the resolution was defeated, with Gandhi and Motilal Nehru insisting on dominion status as the Congress goal. Gandhi, however, promised that if dominion status did not arrive within a year he too would become an 'independence-wallah' (akin to his 1921 promise). The previous month, Subhas and Jawaharlal had formed an 'Independence for India League', which kept the pressure up even after the defeat at the Congress session. The 1928 session was held in Calcutta, and was thus organized by Subhas (like the Ahmedabad session of 1921 had been by Vallabhbhai Patel). Subhas demonstrated his superb organizational skills and also used the occasion to instil a dose of military discipline into the Congress cadres, training his Congress Volunteer Corps in military drill (albeit without arms) to show that an alternative approach to Gandhi's ahimsa was available in reserve. Although Gandhi was particularly contemptuous of this display of military discipline, it resonated with India's youth, and Subhas had a very successful tour of all corners of India advocating his line of complete independence.

Soon thereafter, Bhagat Singh and his HSRA upped the ante further, when Singh himself along with Batukeshwar Dutt (a Bengali chosen to demonstrate the all-India nature of the revolutionary campaign) dropped two small bombs and a shower of leaflets into the Central Legislature on 8 April 1929. The bombs were deliberately chosen 'to make the deaf hear', but specifically not to kill anybody. Bhagat and Dutt made no attempt to escape, as they wanted to use this protest as a pulpit to get their voice heard across the land, and publicize their opposition to newly repressive legislation being introduced at that assembly in the name of 'public safety' and industrial disputes. Subhas too had peacefully protested those two bills, and had organized the workers of the Tata Steel plant in Jamshedpur to demand better working conditions (which they did obtain).

Bhagat Singh and Dutt made their justification clear: 'The bomb was necessary to awaken England from her dreams.... We have only marked the end of an era of utopian non-violence of whose futility the rising generation has been convinced beyond the shadow of doubt. The new movement which has arisen in the country... is inspired by the ideals which Guru Govind Singh and Shivaji, Kemal Pasha and Reza Khan, Washington and Garibaldi, Lafayette and Lenin preached.' The British responded with sweeping arrests of young men from across the country allegedly involved in the 'Lahore Conspiracy Case', which soon encompassed the killing of Saunders as well. When the Assembly Bomb trial began in May 1929, one of New Delhi's most prominent building contractors, Sir Sobha Singh (father of Khushwant Singh, the pioneering novelist and leading Indian journalist of the 1970s) identified Bhagat Singh and Batukeshwar Dutt in court. Both of them (as well as Sukhdev) were initially sentenced to transportation for life, which Dutt was to spend at the Cellular Jail in the Andaman Islands.

The young revolutionaries revelled in getting their propaganda and messages broadcast to the nation during the trial of the Lahore Conspiracy Case, singing patriotic songs in court and disrupting proceedings with speeches and slogans. The nation, especially its youth, was aroused to a fever pitch in their support, and many Congress leaders (including Bose, Jawaharlal and Motilal) visited them in prison. On 15 June 1929, they began a hunger strike to protest being treated as common criminals, and demanding that they be treated as political prisoners. Jinnah spoke eloquently on their behalf in the Central Legislature: 'The man who goes on hunger strike has a soul. He is moved by that soul and he believes in the justice of his cause; he is not an ordinary criminal who is guilty of cold-blooded, sordid, wicked crime.' The colonial authorities were unmoved. While many of his comrades called off their hunger strikes after several weeks, twenty-five-year-old Jatindranath Das (who had joined the HSRA to help manufacture bombs) died in prison on 13 September, having fasted for sixty-five days. Jatin Das had been part of Subhas Bose's Congress Volunteer Corps during the Calcutta Congress the previous year, and Subhas took charge of his funeral rites. Tagore composed a moving song that remains popular to this day ('Shorbo khorbo tare dahe'—'All meanness is devoured by the fire of your anger') with the beautiful line: 'Death will render trivial the zeal of your life' ('mrityu-re koribe tuchchho pranero utshaho'). A throng of several hundred thousand accompanied Jatin's body through the streets of Lahore to a huge public meeting addressed by Gopi Bhargava and Mohammed Alam (who had resigned from the Legislative Council in protest), and large crowds greeted the cortège as Subhas accompanied it back to Calcutta, where a crowd of over 600,000 accompanied them all the way to the cremation grounds.

Back in Britain, there had been a change of government with Labour's Ramsay MacDonald becoming prime minister in June 1929, and inaugurating a new India policy enunciated by his progressive Secretary of State for India, William Wedgwood Benn (father of Tony Benn, the maverick leader of Labour's left wing in the 1980s). Viceroy Irwin was summoned back to London by Benn, and empowered to make the announcement in New Delhi that the 'logical culmination' of Montagu's promise of August 1917 was 'dominion status'—an announcement that Irwin made only on 31 October 1929, twelve years and two months after Montagu's wartime promise to India (which had instead been followed by the Rowlatt Act). By this time, Subhas and the left wing of Congress were well past accepting mere dominion status, but Irwin's announcement gave Mahatma Gandhi an opening, with two months left in his deadline to achieve dominion status by the end of 1929. Irwin proposed a round-table conference once the Simon Commission had submitted its final report. (The Nehru Report had been public for more than a year.) In response, Gandhi got a majority of Congress leaders to sign a manifesto that looked forward to the framing of a dominion constitution for India.

One of the founders of the Independence for India League, Jawaharlal Nehru, chose to align with Gandhi rather than stick with the programme Nehru and Bose had initiated a year earlier. His reward was to be made the next president of the Congress party at its Lahore session, succeeding his father. Subhas Bose, along with Saifuddin Kitchlew of Lahore and Abdul Bari of Patna, issued a clarion call to reject the round-table conference and seek complete independence. Consequently, Bose was excluded from the Congress Working Committee. However, the Gandhi–Irwin talks failed to deliver any agreed basis for dominion status by the end of 1929. The Simon Commission had not yet submitted its report, and when it eventually did (in May 1930), it was to still recommend full self-government only at the provincial level, with the national government still largely British-controlled (i.e., well short of even proper dominion status). Prime Minister Ramsay MacDonald had also hinted at full self-determination (i.e., the elimination of diarchy) at the provincial level, with the viceroy retaining control of defence, military and foreign affairs. The dream of even dominion status was still a rather distant prospect as the year 1929 drew to a close, and Gandhi was obliged to redeem his pledge to become an 'independence-wallah'.

When the Congress met at Lahore on the banks of the river Ravi, the tricolour was unfurled on the final day of 1929 as the national movement finally made the momentous decision to seek 'purna swaraj' (complete independence), and declared that 26 January 1930 would be observed as 'Independence Day'. The Congress constitution was amended to reflect Mahatma Gandhi's new proposal to make 'purna swaraj' the movement's goal. Bose introduced a resolution aimed at actuating this objective by establishing a parallel government with the aid of organizations of workers, peasants and youths—but this was predictably defeated. Nonetheless, Congress was now, for the first time, in open defiance of Britain's colonial objectives, having acknowledged that India was under an alien army of occupation. Civil disobedience would soon become the only logical approach for Congress to adopt. Jinnah was particularly perturbed by what this turn of events meant for India's security, and he importuned MacDonald's government to immediately announce a plan to introduce dominion status. This was not forthcoming: despite Baldwin's support for MacDonald's proposals, Birkenhead had expressed outrage especially at the fact that they pre-empted the Simon Commission's findings and obliged it to take a particular course (the Labour one, precisely what the Tories had wanted to avert through the commission's premature appointment). More pertinently, Winston Churchill had started a shrill campaign against even the mild concessions to Indian self-determination that MacDonald and Benn were seeking. On 26 January 1930, Congress celebrated the first 'Independence Day' with joyous songs and slogans, but Subhas Bose was unable to join in as he had been arrested again three days earlier on charges of sedition and unlawful assembly.

In secret meetings at his Sabarmati Ashram in February 1930 with some of his closest lieutenants, Mahatma Gandhi began chalking out a programme of civil disobedience. He had settled upon a simple but highly effective form of protest: he would gather a core group of satyagrahis from all over India (mainly from amongst those already living in his ashram, and thus committed to non-violence), and march to the sea at Dandi. There, the group would defy the British prohibition on the private production of salt. This programme had the virtue of not being disruptive to business interests, barely material to the actual workings of the empire, and hopefully inclusive of all religious communities in India. Yet it was highly symbolic—focusing on an emblem of foreign rule that needlessly hurt the lives of Indians of every hue and social strata, reflecting the arbitrary discrimination Indians faced every day.

Irwin cabled London that 'the prospect of a salt campaign does not keep me up at night.' Most Anglo–Indian newspapers found the idea risible. Even many of Gandhi's close associates were dubious. But, in fact, this was a brilliant ploy to unite the nation in a simple cause that all Indians could readily understand and identify with. And the pilgrimage-style Dandi March had an electrifying impact not just on Indians, but also on world public opinion. Gandhi reasoned that 'after air and water, salt is perhaps the greatest necessity of life' and there was no more meaningful way of symbolizing the need for purna swaraj than by highlighting the injustice of not being able to make salt for yourself in your own country.

Setting off on 12 March 1930 from his Sabarmati Ashram, Gandhi attracted massive crowds along the way, and he addressed them with a powerful yet simple message about the injustices of foreign rule: 'The British government in India has not only deprived the Indian people of their freedom but has based itself on the exploitation of the masses, and has ruined India economically, politically, culturally and spiritually. We believe therefore, that India must sever the British connection and attain Purna Swaraj or complete independence.' On the first day, he addressed more than 100,000 people outside the ashram before setting off with a core group of seventy-nine carefully selected marchers from every state and region of India, including two from Nepal! Every day, the 'river of white' flowed steadily towards the sea, inspiring millions and calling the world's attention to this 'most remarkable call to war that has ever been made' (in the words of the US journal, *Nation*). India's favourite poetess, Sarojini Naidu, joined the march for several days, and further lifted spirits. The river of people swelled every day as more and more joined it, singing spiritual songs to keep their spirits up, and the throng of marchers was soon more than two miles long. In the distant North West Frontier Province, home of the rugged Pathans, Khan Abdul Ghaffar Khan began organizing his Khudai Khidmatgars (Servants of God), and training 50,000 of them in Gandhian methods of non-violent resistance. Finally, the marchers arrived at Dandi on 6 April—the day Gandhi had chosen, to commemorate his call on that day in 1919 for the first national hartal to protest the Rowlatt Act. A crowd of 50,000 greeted the marchers at the railhead of Dandi, and Gandhi gave speeches and wrote articles (as he had all along the way). The world press—especially in the US—was mesmerized by the drama of the Dandi March, and Gandhi was anointed *Time* magazine's 'Man of the Year' for 1930. *The New York Times* carried long front-page stories on the final two days of the march, having covered the whole journey extensively. Finally, on the morning of 6 April, Mahatma Gandhi said a prayer, and then proceeded to the beach, where he picked up a clump of salty sand, and said, 'With this, I am shaking the foundations of the British Empire.' He then boiled the salty mud in seawater to make salt, and urged all his hundreds of thousands of followers to emulate him and defy the authorities to make salt.

The Civil Disobedience Campaign spread like wildfire across the land, as millions of people defied the colonial government's salt monopoly, and other forms of boycott (especially of alcohol and foreign cloth) spread as well. The British soon began a crackdown, arresting 60,000 people by the end of the month. But the movement now had an unstoppable momentum. On 23 April, Khan Abdul Ghaffar Khan was arrested, and his Khudai Khidmatgars came out in large numbers to offer peaceful protest. But the army was called upon to fire on this peaceful crowd, and between 200 and 250 peaceful Pathan satyagrahis were killed in a brutal massacre, as they stayed true to their oath of non-violence and refused to retaliate against the cold-blooded murders by British troops. One regiment, the Royal Garhwal Rifles, refused to shoot at their compatriots, and most of these soldiers were arrested and sentenced to long terms in jail, including life imprisonment. The brutality of the massacres of peaceful protesters in the North West Frontier Province (NWFP) was especially noteworthy, because this was a region that the British considered strategically vital to Britain's hold over the buffer state of Afghanistan and oil-rich Persia beyond. The success of Gandhi's ally, Ghaffar Khan, in converting the rugged Pathans (considered by the British to be amongst the most warlike and ferocious peoples of the subcontinent) to non-violence was seen as a particular threat, which the British colonialists countered with fierce determination over the next seventeen years (with consequences that reverberate to this day in the form of the Taliban movement that is the diametric opposite of what Khan Abdul Ghaffar Khan stood for).

Chakravarti Rajagopalachari (Rajaji) led a parallel salt march on the east coast from Trichinopoly (Tiruchirapalli) to Vedaranyam, where his marchers broke the salt laws on 30 April and were promptly arrested—starting with their leader, Rajaji. Gandhi, meanwhile, began planning another satyagraha, this time aimed at disrupting the Dharasana Salt Works twenty-five miles south of Dandi. He was arrested on 5 May 1930 using an 1827 law that allowed detention without trial for people engaged in 'unlawful activities'. But the Dharasana Satyagraha went ahead as planned, led now by Abbas Tyabji (a Bohra Muslim who had formerly been the Chief Justice of the Baroda High Court). Justice Tyabji (whose nephew Salim Ali was to become independent India's most eminent ornithologist) had Gandhi's wife Kasturba at his side as he led the Dharasana Satyagraha, but both were arrested before they could reach Dharasana. The poet Sarojini Naidu then stepped into the leadership breach, and she urged her followers to stay scrupulously non-violent, even in the face of the gravest provocation. The United Press International's correspondent, Webb Miller, broadcast the result to the world: 'Not one of the marchers even raised an arm to fend off the blows. They went down like ten-pins. From where I stood I heard the sickening whacks of the clubs on unprotected skulls… Those struck down fell sprawling, unconscious or writhing in pain with fractured skulls or broken shoulders. In two or three minutes the ground was quilted with bodies. Great patches of blood widened on their white clothes. The survivors, without breaking ranks, silently and doggedly marched on until struck down… Finally the non-resistance enraged the police… They commenced savagely kicking the seated men in the abdomen and testicles…' Women had joined the movement in their thousands, and this was a source of consternation for Irwin and his aides. Gandhi's ideal of non-violence was now being adhered to scrupulously, and the world's conscience was aroused.

While the Gandhian core of the movement was spotless in its disciplined adherence to its leader's non-violent principles (unlike in 1922), the national mood did not remain non-violent everywhere. With the leading Bengali politician, Subhas Bose, again imprisoned since January 1930, Bengal's youth was especially restive. On Good Friday, 18 April 1930, 'Masterda' Surya Sen led a group of sixty-five young male and female revolutionaries in a daring raid of the Chittagong armoury. The date was chosen in commemoration of the Easter Rising in Ireland (1916), but when they captured the European Club (where they had planned to assassinate some officials) they found it largely empty, while the two armouries (those of the police and auxiliary forces) were stacked with weapons but no ammunition. Surya Sen hoisted the national tricolour outside the police armoury headquarters, the auxiliary forces' armoury was emptied of its weapons, and a Provisional Revolutionary Government was proclaimed. But the revolutionaries decided to disperse into the nearby hills early next morning as British troop reinforcements began to arrive. Several thousand troops surrounded the revolutionaries in the Jalalabad Hills near Chittagong's cantonment, and engaged them in a fierce firefight, which resulted in the deaths of twelve revolutionaries and as many as eighty British troops. Surya Sen himself, and several of his associates, were able to escape the military dragnet and dispersed in small groups into nearby villages. Of those captured during the fighting, twelve were deported for life and two were given three-year jail terms.

Although reduced in size, the revolutionary group was able to assassinate twenty-two officials and kill about 220 other Britishers over the next two years. And in September 1932, the European Club was captured by a group of eight rebels led by Pritilata Waddedar (a female comrade of Sen's). Surya Sen's safe house was revealed to the British by a disgruntled comrade in February 1933, and he was eventually captured and hanged, but the legacy of his revolutionary group's daring activities were etched into Bengal and India's collective soul.

Bhagat Singh, Sukhdev and Rajguru were also sentenced to be hanged when the Special Tribunal finally delivered its verdict on 7 October 1930. Their other comrades all received long sentences, including several to be served at the Cellular Jail in the Andaman Islands. There was an immediate nationwide outcry for the three heroes' sentences to be commuted to life, with Motilal Nehru making an appeal from his deathbed. But the British did not relent. The revolutionary spirit was kept alive by three young men—Benoy Bose, and brothers Badal and Dinesh Gupta—who attacked Calcutta's venerable Writers' Building, the seat of Britain's Bengal government, and assassinated the Inspector General of Prisons in December 1930. They then engaged the police in a running gun battle along the corridors of the building until their bullets were exhausted. While Benoy and Badal died of the injuries they had sustained, Dinesh was tried and executed. The Esplanade in Calcutta's business district has been renamed BBD (Benoy–Badal–Dinesh) Bagh (Garden) in honour of the three martyrs.

Amid this ferment, and while still in prison, Subhas Bose was elected mayor of Calcutta in August 1930, defeating Jatindra Mohan Sengupta (also a member of the Congress party, but one who adhered more closely to the Gandhi line, obeying the dictates of the Congress 'high command' far more than the rebellious Bose). Bose set about strengthening municipal administration, especially in the areas of education and health, but he was brutally attacked by mounted police while leading a peaceful 'Independence Day' procession on 26 January 1931. The British colonial authorities would rarely abide leaving Bose out of prison for more than a few months at a time! Produced in court in his blood-soaked shirt, Calcutta's elected mayor was hauled off to prison once more on a charge of 'rioting'.

The Simon Commission's long-delayed report satisfied nobody when it was finally released in June 1930. It provided for the end of diarchy in the provinces, where full authority over almost all subjects would pass to newly elected governments (with the unelected governor retaining some residual powers, including the right to dismiss governments over issues of 'peace and tranquillity' and the protection of minorities' rights). But extraordinarily, at the national level, no substantive changes were recommended and the viceroy would still be in complete control, with a toothless Central Legislature being granted no additional powers, although the size of the electorate and number of seats in the Legislature were increased. Despite the Labour prime minister, the Conservative approach to India had won out. The Nehru Report of two years earlier was ignored. Instead, the Simon Commission recommended a 'federal' structure that sounded like an excuse for Balkanizing India into many smaller units (with the 550 princely states being only loosely federated into the structure). However, in keeping with the commission's pious intent of seeking 'constitutional advance' for India, Irwin announced there would be a Round Table Conference in London in November 1930, which Congress naturally decided to boycott, given that Irwin's 'logical culmination... being dominion status' promise of less than a year earlier appeared now to have been indefinitely postponed!

In keeping with the spirit of Simon's Balkanizing ideas, this first Round Table Conference was organized to demonstrate the divisions of Indian society, with a sixteen-member delegation of Indian (princely) states (including the loyal English cricketer Ranjitsinhji), four other landlords, a ten-member Muslim delegation (including Jinnah, Fazlul Huq of Bengal, and Zafarullah Khan who was to become Pakistan's first foreign minister until hounded from office because he was Ahmadiyya), three (including B. S. Moonje and M. R. Jayakar) to represent the majority Hindus, plus five for the Liberals (all five nominally Hindu, but generally loyal to the British), four Europeans, three Parsis, two Sikhs, one Anglo-Indian and another one for Indian Christians, two representing the 'Depressed Classes' (including the British loyalist B. R. Ambedkar) and three representing the Justice Party that also was an advocate of the same classes/castes, two representatives each for women, Labour and Universities, three for Burma (which was still administratively part of India), two for Sindh (including Shahnawaz Bhutto, father of Zulfikar and grandfather of Benazir), one each for Assam, NWFP and Central Provinces, and four representatives of the 'Government of India'. In the absence of Congress (Gandhi himself called it *Hamlet* without the prince of Denmark), it was little more than an unwieldy academic exercise, apart from Ambedkar raising the issue of a 'separate electorate' for the 'Untouchables'—the sort of divisive manoeuvre that endeared him to Britain's imperialists—and the princes agreeing to participate in a loose federation. Winston Churchill, meanwhile, continued his tirade from the backbenches and barnstormed across the country railing against the conference. On 11 December, Churchill told the India Empire Society, 'the British nation has we believe no intention whatever of relinquishing effectual control of Indian life and progress.' Not for him Wilsonian notions of self-determination: 'The truth is Gandhi-ism and all it stands for will, sooner or later, have to be grappled with and crushed.'

Although there were signs that Churchill's intransigent wing was gaining ground within the Tory party, his voice could for the moment be ignored by the Labour-led government. Prime Minister MacDonald and his Secretary of State for India, Benn, were disillusioned by the manifest failures of the conference and made it clear at its final session (in January 1931) that the next such conference could only make progress if Congress was represented. Viceroy Irwin finally took the hint, released Gandhi from Yerwada jail, as well as all the members of the Congress Working Committee on 26 January (itself a symbolic acknowledgement of Indian aspirations), and offered to begin serious talks with Gandhi, who reciprocated on 7 February. Over eight sessions, each lasting an average of three hours in February and March 1931, the 'two Mahatmas' (to use Sarojini Naidu's phrase) confabulated. Irwin had thus risen in Indian eyes partly because of his graciousness at his first meeting with Gandhi on 17 February, accompanying him to the door with the words, 'Good night, Mr Gandhi, and my prayers go with you.' Irwin was compensating with personal charm (and a religious connect) what he could not offer in substance.

Churchill went apoplectic at the very idea of the talks, with his infamous words: 'It is alarming and also nauseating to see Mr Gandhi, a seditious Middle Temple lawyer now posing as a fakir of a type well known in the East, striding half-naked up the steps of the Viceregal palace... to parley on equal terms with the representative of the King-Emperor. Such a spectacle can only increase the unrest in India and the danger to which white people there are exposed.' As always, Churchill was raising the bogey of 'danger to white people', although they would be far safer as long as Gandhi's movement dominated, and would face much more danger were he to lose control of the Independence movement. But as the old racist revealed in secret letters to his son Randolph, he was making a bid to oust Baldwin as Tory leader and ascend to the prime ministership, which had eluded his father at the final step. On 5 March 1931, the rug was pulled from under Churchill's feet when the Gandhi–Irwin Pact was announced and Gandhi agreed to participate in the next Round Table Conference. In a characteristically symbolic touch, Gandhi fished out a paper bag containing salt, poured it into the cup of tea that Irwin offered him to toast their pact, and good-naturedly joked that the salt was intended to remind them of the Boston Tea Party.

Ironically, the reaction to the pact amongst Gandhi's own followers was one of utter shock and dismay: most importantly, the pact did not provide for independence (purna swaraj), the goal that Congress had proclaimed at the end of 1929 and was the objective of the Civil Disobedience Movement— or even any real promise of dominion status. Irwin had promised only to release all political prisoners arrested because of participation in the Civil Disobedience Movement, allow people living close to the sea to make salt (i.e., even the ban on salt-making was not fully withdrawn!), and allow 'peaceful propaganda' against foreign cloth and alcohol consumption. In exchange, Gandhi had agreed to call off the Civil Disobedience campaign and participate in the Round Table Conference—in effect, participating in talks that could, at best, result in the implementation of the Simon Commission's recommendations, which fell far short of even dominion status (leave alone independence)—providing only for provincial autonomy and self-government. This was a considerable step backward for Gandhi than the deal that had been offered by Lord Reading in January 1922.

Crucially, the 'Delhi Pact' between Gandhi and Irwin ignored the fate of violent opponents of the British empire like Bhagat Singh and his comrades who were languishing on death row. To the extent that Bhagat Singh's fate was part of the talks, Irwin appears to have been able to persuade Gandhi that it didn't behove an apostle of non-violence to plead on behalf of those who used violent methods. Despite all the goodwill garnered by the talks (and the especially warm feelings towards Irwin that had been expressed by many Indian nationalists during the talks), Irwin and the British were quick to take advantage of the opportunity provided by the Delhi Pact: on the morning of 23 March 1931 (barely eighteen days after the pact between Gandhi and Irwin had been agreed), Bhagat Singh, Rajguru and Sukhdev were hanged. The news set off an outcry across India, and severely undermined Gandhi's credibility. Jawaharlal Nehru pointed out that the twenty-three-year-old Bhagat Singh's valiant bearing and single-minded patriotism had made him and his young comrades almost as popular as Gandhi himself. Bhagat Singh was seen as an icon of young India, capable of rising above the sectarian conflicts of his native Punjab, and uniting the whole of India. After their sudden execution, the three became instant martyrs, and the whole of urban India mourned.

Since Bose was not a member of the Congress Working Committee, he had only been released in March, but he immediately visited Gandhi in Bombay. They travelled together to Delhi, and Bose saw for himself just how popular Gandhi was across the country. He received assurances that the goal of independence was not being compromised, but Bose (and Jawaharlal) continued to harbour doubts about the wisdom of participating in a jamboree like the Round Table Conference, where Congress would be seen as just one party amongst more than a hundred others representing various sectional interests. By the time the Karachi session of Congress began a few days after Bhagat Singh's martyrdom, Gandhi's popularity had taken a beating, especially amongst the young, and radicals/Marxists, who showed their disapproval of Gandhi with a black flag demonstration soon after he arrived. The Karachi Congress session deplored the execution of Bhagat Singh (while decrying all acts of violence), but this formula did not satisfy Young India. Subhas was invited to become president of both the Naujawan Bharat Sabha (of which Bhagat Singh had been a key leader) and the All India Trade Union Congress. He used the opportunity to outline his vision of what socialism would mean in India—stressing in particular that socialism needed to be adapted to India's circumstances, and he did not believe in aping the Soviet Union or other Marxist ideas blindly, but instead seeking to synthesize them with Indian conditions. Pragmatically adapting socialist ideas to build an effective economy would also entail India fully gaining from her innate entrepreneurial skills. Bose would eventually use the Buddhist notion of equality, 'samyavada', to encapsulate his political philosophy.

The Karachi Congress session decided that Gandhi would be the sole representative of Congress at the Round Table Conference, and that Congress must be seen as representing all Indians. But the Congress session was also marred by the outbreak of serious communal riots in Kanpur. Churchill's apologists (like his biographer Martin Gilbert or the historian Arthur Herman) point to the Kanpur riots as proof that his dire warnings about sectarian conflict were borne out almost immediately after he had made them (Herman claims 'thousands' died in the Kanpur riots, when even the official figures showed about 400 had died).

In fact, the riots had little to do with the Gandhi–Irwin Pact, and were sparked by the response to the execution of Bhagat Singh. The British colonial authorities had used the years since 1922 (during which the Congress leadership had been largely incarcerated) to foment—or at least connive in—an orgy of communal strife. Some of this strife (in Kerala and Punjab, for instance) was really peasant risings against either landlords or moneylenders. If the latter were of a different religious community from the peasants, the incidents were played up in the English language, pro-British press as being inter-communal. The colonial police, so quick to crack down on Congress agitation, usually stood aside for days and weeks while the violence between classes of people (played up in the press as between two religious communities) raged on. Kanpur in the last week of March 1931 had witnessed precisely this phenomenon: Bhagat Singh's leftist supporters had called for a strike and closure of shops to mourn and protest the martyrs' execution. Some shopkeepers had failed to heed the call, and been attacked by the sponsors of the shutdown. Many of the shops that were thus attacked happened to be owned by Muslims—a fact that was mercilessly played up in the press, instigating retaliatory attacks on Hindus. Some 60 mosques and over 200 temples had been attacked, and the incident was a propaganda coup for those arguing against India's independence. Congress responded by appointing a six-member commission (three Hindus and three Muslims) to investigate the riots, and they came up with a comprehensive report going back several hundred years to examine the nature of amicable relations between Hindus and Muslims prior to the British arrival. The commission's report was immediately banned by the colonial authorities when it was published (despite the fact that the report criticized some Congress leaders for having a 'communal' attitude themselves). Any report that spoke of amity between Hindus and Muslims, and the role of the police in allowing (or occasionally fuelling) riots was simply not going to get past colonial censors!

By the time the Second Round Table Conference finally began in September 1931, Ramsay MacDonald was heading a National Government in which the Conservatives were heavily represented and Samuel Hoare (rather than William Wedgwood Benn) was Secretary of State for India. The situation had altered quite significantly, and the October 1931 election would further erode

MacDonald's standing: although the National Government won a landslide victory (thereby nominally re-electing MacDonald), the Conservatives led by Baldwin were by far the dominant party in the coalition and MacDonald's 'National Labour' party had just fourteen seats. Irwin had been replaced as viceroy by Lord Willingdon, an old India hand who had nothing but contempt for Irwin and his pact with Gandhi. With such hostile interlocutors, Gandhi was already at a disadvantage. Worse, the other hundred or so participants were at the conference to highlight a wide variety of sectional interests. Much as Abel Muzorewa in Zimbabwe, and Mangosuthu Buthelezi in South Africa (in the 1970s and 1990s respectively) were used by the white regimes to downplay the importance of the liberation leaders (Mugabe/Nkomo and Mandela), so Ambedkar was Britain's key man in 1931—attacking Gandhi as being unrepresentative of India, or even of Hindus. Ambedkar's demand for separate electorates for the Depressed Classes (who Gandhi called 'Harijans', or God's People, and had worked tirelessly to uplift throughout his life) became a major focus of the conference. Although Gandhi's delegation included such luminaries as the poets Allama Muhammad Iqbal (the future poet-advocate of Pakistan) and Sarojini Naidu, they did not appear at the conference, where Gandhi alone represented Congress.

Although he scored many propaganda coups with the ordinary people of Britain, mingling happily with farmers and workers, Gandhi was frustrated and isolated at the conference itself and returned to India empty-handed. The high hopes of the Delhi Pact had been completely dashed, and Gandhi soon announced the resumption of the Civil Disobedience Campaign. The long delay before the start of the conference, and its leisurely progress towards a fruitless outcome, had enabled Willingdon to prepare his responses. The novelty of the Salt Satyagraha was never going to be repeated, and this time Willingdon responded with a repressive crackdown. The Congress was proscribed and almost its entire leadership (from Gandhi down) was imprisoned.

Meanwhile, MacDonald announced the 'Communal Award' in August 1932 codifying the divide and rule tactic of separate electorates for the 'minorities', albeit with some minorities (especially Muslims, and 'Europeans' and Anglo–Indians) clearly treated as more equal than others: the Sikhs, for instance, only received 19 per cent of the seats in Punjab (lower than recommended by the Simon Commission), while Muslims received 51 per cent, thereby ensuring Sikhs' permanent electoral subservience to the Muslims in that large province. (Sikhs were about 15 per cent of the population, but 24.1 per cent of the electorate at the time). Ambedkar's efforts in favour of the British during the three Round Table Conferences were rewarded by creating separate electorates for the Depressed Classes (or Untouchables) who alone would be able to vote in constituencies carved out for them. Gandhi, imprisoned in Yerwada jail in Poona, strongly opposed this latest scheme to divide not only Indians from each other, but also to create new categories of separation within the Hindu community itself. When the British failed to budge, Gandhi announced that he would go on a fast unto death unless this aspect of the Communal Award was withdrawn. Ambedkar reluctantly went to Poona to meet the Mahatma, and they worked out an agreement under which the Depressed Classes (thereafter known as Scheduled Castes and Scheduled Tribes) would have seats 'reserved' for them in the legislatures (where candidates could only be from those classes) but the election to those seats would not be by a separate electorate (comprising Depressed Class voters alone) but by a generalized electorate.

The Government of India Act of 1935 was prepared and passed by the British Parliament, essentially on the lines of the Simon Commission's report, giving provincial autonomy (but with the non-elected governor having the right to dismiss the provincial government) and with the central government of India still an autocracy firmly controlled by the viceroy. The most extraordinary aspect was the bicameral Central Legislature: here, in the Upper Chamber, 110 of the 260 seats were reserved for the Indian princes, while 125 of the 375 seats in the Lower Chamber were reserved for the princes—who would nominate their representatives as they wished (and without consulting any electorate). Thus a third of the Lower Chamber and more than 42 per cent of the Upper Chamber of the federal legislature were reserved for the pro-British princes, with not an iota of democracy involved! Churchill sent representatives to persuade the princes to reject even this (because he feared that any federal structure would inevitably lead to dominion status), so the federal portion of the Act never actually came into force. But separate electorates ensured that even the rest of the seats would never yield a single-party majority nationally, while the proposed over-representation of princes (without any recourse to democratic choice) would further hobble the democratic parties. And 80 per cent of the expenditure of the central legislature (for 'British-retained' subjects such as defence, foreign policy, debt servicing, railways, etc.) was not subject to voting by this legislature, and could only be introduced with the viceroy's consent, so the legislature could direct no more than a fifth of all the spending of the proposed federal government on social issues like education, health and infrastructure. India was too important to Britain to even be considered for Iraqi or Egyptian-style 'independence', leave alone dominion status.

After much internal debate, Congress eventually agreed to participate in the first election held in February 1937 under the 1935 Act. Many Congress leaders (including Jawaharlal Nehru and the still-imprisoned Subhas Bose) argued before the election that Congress should enter the provincial legislatures merely to undermine the system from within, but cooler heads—such as Maulana Azad—argued that the non-participation of Congress would open the doors to other parties and entities, and thus could prove more detrimental to India's future, and this view eventually prevailed. In the intervening years, most of the Congress leadership including Gandhi, Azad, Vallabhbhai Patel and Nehru were in jail, while Bose (after falling grievously ill in 1933) was sent into exile in Europe, and not allowed to return to politics until after the 1937 election.

Although the electorate was still only confined to about 14 per cent of India's total population, the 1937 election was the first opportunity to actually gauge the relative strength of the various parties claiming to represent India's people. The turnout was reasonably good (51.5 per cent of eligible voters) and the elections proved a triumph for the Congress party. The system of separate electorates (which meant that Muslim constituencies would comprise exclusively Muslim voters and candidates, with some other minorities also separated in this way) was a significant disadvantage for a broad-based non-sectarian national party like the Congress. But Congress still won 707 of the 1,585 seats, including an overwhelming 617 of the 864 'general constituencies' (i.e., those open to all voters). Congress also won 26 of the 59 Muslim reserved constituencies it contested. The All-India Muslim League (led by Jinnah) finished as the second-largest party, with 106 seats—just marginally ahead of the Unionist Party (a non-sectarian party in Punjab uniting Muslim, Hindu and Sikh and dominated by landlords), which won 101 seats.

The 1935 Act was specifically aimed at keeping the Congress away from national power, and severely circumscribing it within the provinces. Bengal (where Hindus still comprised over 48 per cent of the population) was a case in point: of the 250 seats in Bengal, only 80 (32 per cent) were 'general' seats (open to all voters) of which 30 were reserved for Scheduled Castes and 2 for women, which actually meant that only 48 seats (19.2 per cent of the seats) were truly 'general'; of the rest of the seats, 16 were reserved for European, Indian Christian and Anglo–Indian voters (who together comprised about 1 per cent of the population, but had 6.4 per cent of the seats), and a further 19 seats for Commerce, Industry and Plantations (almost exclusively British interests, thus reserving 14 per cent of the seats for the 'Europeans', who were 0.004 per cent of the population, and Indian Christians who were less than 1 per cent); 119 seats (111 rural, 6 urban, 2 women) were for Muslims alone. The Bengal Congress leader Subhas Bose, who had long advocated that Congress adopt a strongly pro-tenant policy, had been exiled from India for over three years and not allowed to return to public life until after the election (being under house arrest in Kurseong and Calcutta in the final half-year until the election). His brother Sarat too had been imprisoned, and was released only weeks before the 1937 election; the right wing of Congress (led by Bidhan Roy since the death of Jatindra Mohan Sengupta in 1933) remained wedded to landlords' interests. Congress won 54 seats in Bengal (including 43 of the 48 truly 'general' seats), to 37 for the Muslim League and 36 for Fazlul Huq's Krishak Praja (Farmers and Tenants) Party, which advocated the right of the tiller to have security of tenure (i.e., not be evicted by landlords)—the programme that was eventually adopted by the CPI(M) in West Bengal in the 1970s and 1980s.

Fazlul Huq was able to form a coalition government in Bengal (with the Muslim League and some independents such as Nalini Sarkar), as Congress refused to cooperate with the colonial authorities; initially, Fazlul Huq had proposed a coalition with Congress, and only formed one with the Muslim League when Congress turned down the idea (partly because Nehru was opposed to Congress joining any coalitions and Sarat Bose was initially opposed to joining a ministry, feeling that this would amount to cooperation with the colonial authorities).

Congress comfortably won the 1937 elections in provinces where the 'general' constituencies were more than half the total. For instance, in Bombay presidency, 97 of the 175 constituencies were 'general', and Congress won a total of 88 of the 110 seats that it contested (including some Muslim reserved constituencies); in Madras presidency, where 116 of the total of 215 constituencies were in the 'general' category, Congress (led by Rajagopalachari) won 159 seats, the Justice Party (which was loyal enough to the British to have participated in all three Round Table Conferences, and was a predecessor of the Dravida parties) won just 18 seats, and the Muslim League won 11 (of the 28 seats reserved for Muslims). Of the 11 provinces for which elections were held in 1937, Congress won a clear majority in 6 provinces (including 92 out of 152 in Bihar, 70 out of 112 in Central Provinces, 36 out of 60 in Orissa, and 133 out of 228 in United Provinces, plus Madras and Bombay). In those six provinces, Congress was thus able to form its own governments without any outside support. Additionally, Congress won 19 of the 50 seats in the almost completely-Muslim NWFP, and was able to form a government with the aid of seven independent members, with Ghaffar Khan's elder brother Dr Khan Sahib elected as Congress' chief minister. Only in two provinces—Punjab and Sind—did the Congress fail to win a plurality of seats, paying the price in Punjab particularly for having acquiesced in the British hanging of Bhagat Singh within days of the Gandhi–Irwin Pact.

In Punjab, the Unionist Party (led by Sir Sikandar Hayat Khan) won 95 of the 175 seats and should have been able to form a stable government; here, however, the Muslim League won just 2 of the 84 seats reserved for Muslims, and one of these members soon defected to the Unionists too. But Jinnah was determined to weaken the unity of the non-sectarian Unionist party, and gained steady ground amongst the newly elected Muslim legislators towards the end of 1937, once his relations with Congress had broken down. In the recently-created province of Sind, where 34 of the 60 seats were reserved for Muslims, the Congress won just 7 seats, while the Hindu Mahasabha won 11 seats. The Sind United Party (which aspired to recreate a party akin to the Unionists in Punjab) won 21 seats, but no Hindu contested on its platform and its leader Shahnawaz Bhutto lost his own seat.

In both Bombay and Sind, the British governors initially tried to form pro-British governments comprising smaller parties, but this soon collapsed in both places. In Sind, however, the governor instigated defections from the Sind United Party—the one party that was closest to the mainstream of Indian nationalism—and asked Sir Ghulam Hussain Hidayatullah (leader of the Sind Muslim Party, which had won just 4 seats) to form the government, as he was the most pro-British of the politicians elected; the governor then aided Hidayatullah to concoct a majority in the Sindh assembly. One of the biggest losers in the 1937 election was Ambedkar, whose Independent Labour Party failed to make any impression outside Bombay (where it won 12 seats) and Sind (where it won 1 seat reserved for Scheduled Castes, SCs). In Bihar, Congress (led by Jagjivan Ram) won 23 of the 24 seats reserved for SCs, in the United Provinces Congress won 18 out of 20, and in Madras it won 26 of the 30 SC-reserved seats.

The breakdown of Congress-Muslim League relations was a result of the intense personality clash between Jinnah and Jawaharlal Nehru, who had led the Congress campaign, particularly in the United Provinces (UP), where the Muslim League won only 27 of the 64 seats reserved for the Muslims. Had Nehru shown a degree of magnanimity towards the Muslim League—as his father and Tilak had done in 1916—Hindu–Muslim unity could have been solidified, and a joint effort been mounted to move India towards dominion status. Congress had put up candidates in only 9 of the 64 Muslim-only seats in UP (itself a quiet acknowledgement of a seeming pact with the League), but failed to win a single one of them (although it subsequently secured the single Muslim-only seat of Bijnor in a by-election). Similarly, while India's Congress-inclined historians frequently mention how badly the Muslim League fared in the Muslim-only constituencies across India, little mention is made of how Congress performed in those constituencies: putting up just 59 candidates in the 482 Muslim-only constituencies, Congress won just 26 of those seats. The Muslim League could not be the exclusive spokesman for Muslim interests after this election, but could speak much more for them than the Congress could. But Nehru failed to show statesmanship, admittedly because Jinnah took an unreasonable position too. The latter argued that all the Muslim ministers in a coalition ministry in the UP should be from the Muslim League; this was unacceptable to Nehru, as he had many able Congress Muslims who deserved to be ministers too. Given that Congress had a majority on its own, it did not need Muslim League support in that province, but securing such support nationally (at a time when the Muslim League was at an electoral nadir) would have enabled India's nationalists to negotiate with a much stronger hand with the colonial authorities at a time when the war clouds were gathering over Europe. Instead, Nehru insisted that the Muslim League should dissolve into the Congress in the UP (and wherever else it wished to join a coalition) in order to strengthen nationalist voices. This rather extreme demand was impossible for Jinnah and the League to comply with, and it caused a severe breach between him and Jawaharlal that became impossible to repair in subsequent years. The arrogance of the Congress under Jawaharlal—particularly the Congress decision not to accommodate the League in a coalition ministry in either the UP or Bombay—dealt a grievous blow to Hindu–Muslim unity at a time when Jinnah and Congress had much in common (including opposition to the British plan of a weak federation with excessive power to the princes).

The leading Muslim stalwart of Congress, Maulana Abul Kalam Azad, later blamed Nehru (and Patel) for failing to show statesmanship in two other states. In the Bombay Presidency, the provincial Congress was led by Khurshed Nariman (a Parsi), who had successfully served as mayor of Bombay in 1935–36. He was widely expected to be picked as chief minister, but was passed over by Nehru and Patel, who instead appointed B. G. Kher (a Marathi Brahmin) as chief minister, with the Gujarati Brahmin (and able administrator) Morarji Desai as minister for revenue, agriculture and forests. Nariman made his displeasure known very publicly, asked for an inquiry (which found against him), left the Congress and later joined Bose's Forward Bloc in 1939. Mumbai's Nariman Point is named for him, but that was scant compensation for being passed over for the chief ministership, and the optics of Nehru picking a less accomplished Hindu over the Parsi leader of Congress in the province also left a bad odour nationally. Similarly, in Bihar, Dr Syed Mahmud was the acknowledged leader of Congress in the province and was expected to become chief minister after the Congress won an overwhelming majority. But Rajendra Prasad instead intervened to call Sri Krishna Sinha (a member of the central rather than provincial assembly) back to Patna to be chief minister, and Nehru failed to show statesmanship again, although Dr Mahmud was at least accommodated as a minister. On these actions, Maulana Azad contrasted Nehru's approach particularly to that of C. R. Das in the 1920s—when he had gone out of his way to accommodate Muslim interests in Bengal and, he implied, across the country when he took the lead in creating the Swaraj Party that became a real beacon of Hindu–Muslim unity against the colonial authorities in the 1920s, when Das was successful in winning substantial support for the Swaraj Party even in Muslim reserved constituencies.

Subhas Bose had been imprisoned in Seoni in the Central Provinces in 1932 when he again fell grievously ill with severe abdominal pain that caused him to lose thirteen kilograms in body weight over a short period. He was transferred to Jabalpur Jail, and when doctors were unable to treat him adequately, sent into exile in Europe in February 1933. He lived in Austria, Switzerland, and France for the next three years, strengthening the Congress organization and propagating the case for India's independence in Europe: the German empire was a major diasporic space for Indian nationalists since the Great War, and Indic studies had flourished in Germany since the nineteenth century with the great Indologist Max Mueller, but Bose's passport was not valid for Germany (although he still found ways to overcome this restriction and visit it on occasion). Bose linked up with Vithalbhai Patel, the former speaker of the Central Legislative Assembly, and they issued the 'Patel–Bose Manifesto' in May 1933 (when Gandhi called off the Civil Disobedience Movement) calling for a more radical new leadership of the independence movement. A. C. N. Nambiar, a leader amongst Indian students in Europe (and brother-in-law of Sarojini Naidu) became their key lieutenant at this time. They established especially strong relationships with the Czechoslovak, Polish and Irish nationalist movements. Vithalbhai had established the Indian–Irish Independence League, and this proved an effective organization for Bose to advance India's cause across Europe. Both Subhas and Vithalbhai were hospitalized at a place called Gland in October 1933, where the latter died on the 22nd. He left a large part of his fortune for Subhas to spend 'for the political uplift of India and preferably for publicity work on behalf of India's cause in other countries.' But his younger brother Vallabhbhai filed a case against this, and ensured that Subhas was unable to inherit a single penny for the cause.

Subhas built particularly close ties to Edvard Beneš, the foreign minister of Czechoslovakia, with whom he developed a bond right from their first meeting in 1933. When he visited Prague again just before returning to India,

Edvard Beneš was president of Czechoslovakia and they had another warm meeting. In 1936, Subhas paid a fortnight-long visit to Ireland, during which President Eamon de Valera treated him like a visiting head of state, giving him an official reception as well as a private dinner, and Bose held long discussions with him and several of his key ministers, including a session on land reform with the agriculture minister. Upon disembarking at Cork, Subhas had immediately paid a floral tribute to the city's late mayor Terence MacSwiney, who had (like Jatin Das) fasted unto death in a British prison.

Bose also found time to frequently visit and take care of Jawaharlal's ailing wife, Kamala, in Austria and Switzerland. When she and her daughter Indira arrived at Vienna in June 1935, Subhas Bose received them at the train station, and visited Kamala every day at her hospital. Later, when Jawaharlal was released from prison on compassionate grounds in September, Subhas received him at Basel, and they drove together to be by Kamala's side at Badenweiler, just across the German border. When Kamala Nehru breathed her last at Lausanne on 28 February 1936, Subhas Bose was present beside her, Jawaharlal and Indira, and helped his close political comrade with the funeral arrangements. As he became better known in Europe, Bose published *The Indian Struggle* to critical acclaim in Europe (including Britain), but the book was immediately banned in India. In the book, Bose laid out a vision for India's future that was rooted in India's soil, and proposed that India would find a middle way between the two prevailing ideologies of the age: 'the next phase in world-history will produce a synthesis between Communism and Fascism. And will it be a surprise if that synthesis is produced in India?' While Nehru saw a stark choice 'between some form of Communism and some form of Fascism', and declared that he was 'all for' communism, Bose believed there was no reason why the options should be 'restricted to two alternatives'. In particular, Bose held that communism's hostility to nationalism, and ideological antipathy to religion, made it unsuitable for India, where a unique approach would need to be adopted—albeit with 'all the modern sociopolitical movements and experiments in Europe and in America' having a 'considerable influence on India's development'. He called his synthesis 'Samyavada—an Indian word, which means literally the doctrine of synthesis or equality'. Bose condemned Italy's invasion of Ethiopia in late 1935, and Britain's hypocritical non-response, drawing the conclusion that any nation could 'hope to be free only if it is strong'. He urged the Federation of Indian Students to strongly refute Hitler's speech claiming that it was the destiny of white races to rule the world, and sent a statement to India's press calling for a trade boycott of Germany. But during the first year of his friend Jawaharlal's two-year term as Congress president (1936 and 1937), the British ensured that Subhas would remain imprisoned or exiled, with the Secretary of State sending him a direct communication in March 1936 that Bose 'cannot expect to remain at liberty' if he returned to India. Sure enough he was arrested immediately upon arrival in Bombay on 10 April 1936, and soon moved to the same yard in Yerwada Jail where Gandhi had recently been held. With Bose's health deteriorating, Nehru called an 'All-India Subhas Day' to press for his release, but the British merely shifted his detention to Kurseong in the hills of north Bengal.

Only after ministerial formation in the provinces had been completed—and British governors had kept the Congress out of governments in both Bengal and Assam despite being the largest party in both legislatures—did Bengal's Governor Anderson feel confident enough to release Subhas Bose on 5 April 1937. After spending some time convalescing in the home of his friends the Dharmavirs at Dalhousie, Subhas plunged back into political life with a tour of the country and an essay on 'Japan's Role in the Far East'. While he had long considered Japan 'the British of the East', and now wrote admiringly of Japan's role as a bulwark against European imperialism and a beacon of inspiration for Asia at the dawn of the century, he pointedly asked why Japan's aims could not be achieved 'without humiliating another proud, cultured and ancient race? No, with all our admiration for Japan… our whole heart goes out to China in her time of trial.' And he committed India to seeking 'self-fulfilment… in every direction, but not through the bloody path of self-aggrandizement and imperialism'.

By October 1937, a jilted Jinnah was raising the bogey of 'Islam in danger', claiming that the new Congress governments were anti-Muslim. He had unexpected success in the large province of Punjab, where the Muslim League was down to just a single member (Malik Barkat Ali) of the Legislative Assembly. The Unionists' Sir Sikandar Hayat (who had the Jat leader Sir Chhotu Ram as his revenue minister) came under considerable pressure in the Assembly from the Congress (which had 18 of the 175 seats), and an alliance of Sikh and Hindu parties (that had 35 seats). The Unionists' leader Fazli Husain had died in 1936, and Chhotu Ram had succeeded him as party leader. Although the Unionists were seen as a 'landlords' party' and relatively pro-British (having participated in the legislatures created by the Montford Reforms, attended meetings with the Simon Commission, and been at all the Round Table conferences), Chhotu Ram had propagated the idea of 'peasant brotherhood' and soon brought in reforms of money-lending to restrict or ban usurious practices.

There were clearly many elements of the Unionist platform (including the party's secular character) that meshed well with that of the Congress. Yet

Jawaharlal Nehru urged a dogmatic approach, fighting the Unionists (because they were 'pro-British', although not significantly more so than Motilal and C. R. Das's Swaraj Party had been, and 'feudal'). This drove the inexperienced Sikandar Hayat into a surprise alliance with the Muslim League (called the Sikandar–Jinnah Pact) in October 1937, after which he urged Muslim members of the Unionist party to also acquire membership in the League. Sir Sikandar thought he was thus emasculating the Punjab Muslim League (while acquiring no more than a nominal membership in it for himself, not enough to alienate Sir Chhotu Ram), but Jinnah's biographer Stanley Wolpert was convinced that this was the moment of triumph for Jinnah's campaign for Pakistan, as the 'P' had been secured in a startling turning point, especially because Fazlul Huq too became a Muslim League member at this October 1937 session in Lucknow and made inflammatory statements against Hindus and Congress, reflecting the zeal of the new convert. Both Sir Sikandar and Fazlul Huq, however, retained control over their own political bases within their provinces—and neither ever became a staunch adherent or a stable ally of the Muslim League. The poet Allama Iqbal, who had by this time become the key ideologue for the creation of 'Pakistan', frequently complained to Jinnah about Sikandar Hayat, and demanded his dismissal, but Jinnah never felt strong enough to remove him, given his political support base. Between 1940 and 1942, while Viceroy Linlithgow worked hard to advance Jinnah's cause amongst the Muslims of Punjab, Sikandar Hayat strongly objected to any attempts at dismembering the unitary, multi-religious province of Punjab.

Meanwhile, Subhas Bose was touring the country and getting a strong response from the peasantry in particular for his radical programmes for reforming land tenure. N. G. Ranga and Swami Sahajanand, the respective peasant leaders of Andhra and Bihar, began urging Gandhi to make Subhas the next president of Congress. Gandhi had been observing Subhas's progress too, and noted the enthusiasm of the country for this fiery patriot, and Subhas himself acknowledged that non-violent resistance was now the more appropriate strategy for India (while not giving up other options should the need arise). By October 1937, on a visit to Calcutta where he stayed at the Bose family home in Woodburn Park (rather than at the home of G. D. Birla, as he usually did), Gandhi told Subhas to prepare to become Congress' rashtrapati (president), at the next session to be held at the Gujarati village of Haripura in early 1938. But before that, he sought Rabindranath Tagore's counsel on how to deal with Jinnah's claim that 'Vande Mataram', the song by Bankim that was the nationalist battle cry, was fundamentally repugnant to Muslims. Tagore and Subhas devised a solution, by ensuring that only the first stanza of the song would be sung from nationalist platforms; there was nothing objectionable in that stanza, with anything that could be construed as anti-Muslim or expressing religious veneration of Mother India (embodied as a goddess) being part of the succeeding stanzas that were to no longer be sung in public. This was an innovative solution, although one that caused much heartburn amongst orthodox Bengali Hindus.

In a long, rousing speech, Bose laid out his practical vision for India, with population control being one focus (the first time any Indian leader had broached it), radical reform of agriculture (including abolition of landlordism, liquidation of rural indebtedness, freer credit availability), the organization of cooperatives, and socialist planning and control to advance the cause of rapid industrialization. There would be a role for Gandhian cottage industries, but India needed to embrace the best of technology to industrialize rapidly too—with a judicious mix of private entrepreneurship facilitated by public investment in heavy industry. Subhas Bose also proposed a solution to the vexed question of what script to adopt for the national language Hindi (which had been adopted by a previous Congress session in a very close vote ahead of Bengali). Bose proposed a via media between those who advocated the Arabic script used for Urdu (and occasionally for Hindustani, which was the hybrid of Hindi and Urdu used in north India) and those who wanted Devanagari for a more Sanskritized Hindi. Bose proposed that Hindi be written in the Roman/English script (with appropriate adaptations), like the new Roman script adopted by Atatürk's Turkey. Although the Congress did not accept this proposal, the Indian National Army would adopt it at Subhas's behest later.

As the president of Congress, one of the first tasks that Subhas Bose decided to undertake was the creation of a National Planning Committee that would devise a plan for India's industrialization and provide practical ideas for the provincial ministries to implement. In May 1938, he held a conference of Congress chief ministers at which he obtained their support and also some seed money for the planning committee. Subhas persuaded civil servant Hari Vishnu Kamath to resign from the ICS (like Subhas himself had done), join the Congress and take charge as member-secretary of the National Planning Committee. And, in yet another fraternal gesture towards Jawaharlal (who was in Republican Spain as an eyewitness to the civil war there), Subhas requested Nehru to come back and become chairman of the committee. Bose envisaged private businessmen taking the lead in light industry, the government helping to kick-start heavy industries, and land reform and better credit availability as the basis for a rejuvenation of agriculture. But while Bose and Kamath were focused on the practical aspects of planning—and especially on providing practical advice and specific ideas for the provincial industry ministers (who were invited to a conference on 2 October, Gandhi's birthday, to chalk out concrete plans)—Nehru (who took over as chairman only in December 1938) balked at implementing the ideas, fearing that they would scare away businessmen and the middle class. Although Nehru had often expressed his romantic commitment to socialism, he soft-pedalled planning now, creating a plethora of committees that buried the objectives of planned industrialization in a bureaucratic thicket. Recriminations with Nehru led a disgusted H. V. Kamath to resign from the committee.

Halfway through his first term as president of Congress, Subhas Bose came to the conclusion that the Congress Party should aim to be part of all the provincial governments, in order to be able to speak to the colonial authorities in a single, strengthened voice. Drawing on his deep knowledge of contemporary Europe, Bose argued that German aggression—especially on Czechoslovakia, where his friend Beneš was president—would inevitably draw Great Britain into the conflict, and the Congress needed to be in the strongest possible bargaining position when that happened. While Congress governments were in power in seven provinces, Bose argued that taking power in the remaining four provinces was crucial to forcing Britain to the negotiating table. To that end, he worked with the Congress leader in Assam, Gopinath Bordoloi, to topple Muhammed Saadulla's government. Saadulla was leader of the Assam Valley Muslim Party (which had won 24 seats in the assembly) and was in a coalition with the Muslim League (which had won 10 seats). Congress had 33 seats in the assembly (of a total of 108), but could easily form a coalition with the help of some of the 27 independents. This is what Subhas enabled Gopinath Bordoloi to do in September 1938—the same month in which the Munich Agreement (Neville Chamberlain's 'peace with honour') allowed Nazi Germany to acquire the German-populated areas of Czechoslovakia that were renamed 'Sudetenland'. Saadulla had also begun proposing the resettlement of Bengali Muslim farmers in the tribal areas of Assam (today's Meghalaya, Nagaland and Mizoram), which was also causing much consternation, until Bordoloi's ministry stalled the scheme.

In Sindh, where the Congress was especially weak (with just 7 seats, while the Hindu Mahasabha had 11), Subhas had supported Allah Bux Soomro (a founder of the Sind United Party, which had won 21 seats in Sindh's 60-seat assembly), who was able to overcome the governor's shenanigans and become chief minister in March 1938. After Subhas Bose's own breach with the Congress, that party voted against Allah Bux Soomro in a confidence motion at the Assembly in 1940, but Soomro formed another government in Sindh in alliance with the Congress in 1941 and gave up his British titles to support the Quit India Movement in 1942. Allah Bux Soomro became one of the most prominent 'nationalist Muslims' (aligned with Maulana Azad of Congress), and attended a convention of nationalist (i.e., anti-partition) Muslims in 1942 during Cripps's first ministerial mission to India that year. But Soomro was assassinated by 'unknown assailants' (i.e., likely either a British or Muslim League agent) in 1943 during the Quit India Movement, thus silencing one of the strongest emerging Muslim voices for a united India. Ironically, one of his leading opponents in the Sindh assembly was G. M. Syed of the Muslim League, who, after 1954, was to found the Jiye Sindh Movement (advocating the secession of Sindh from Pakistan), and spent the last three decades of his long life in Pakistani prisons!

In May 1938, Bose engaged Jinnah in talks to try and work out a nationwide settlement between Congress and the Muslim League. The Bose–Jinnah talks proceeded on cordial terms, and Chaudhry Khaliquzzaman (who might have been the first UP minister nominated by the Muslim League in the aborted Congress–League coalition there) told Maulana Azad later that the 'Bose formula' had been acceptable to the League and Jinnah. But the memory of Jinnah's acerbic exchange in 1937 with Jawaharlal, which had continued in an exchange of letters in February–April 1938, vitiated the atmosphere. Jawaharlal had said after the 1937 elections that there were only two parties in India—the Congress and the British. And, in his 1938 letters to Jinnah, Nehru took his rhetoric further by claiming that he had 'looked through a telescope' for a Hindu–Muslim problem, but 'if there is nothing what can you see?' Nehru repeatedly irritated Jinnah by refusing to acknowledge even the existence of any communal problem. Nehru was being disingenuous, because there had been several communal riots in the UP in particular, where the absence of Muslim League ministers enabled that party to heap blame on the Congress. Nehru launched a 'mass contact' programme to reach the UP's Muslim peasants directly, but this effort had failed. To Subhas Bose's plaintive question in late July 1938, 'is it not enough that the Congress is not only willing but eager to establish the friendliest relations with the League and come to an honourable understanding on the much vexed Hindu–Muslim question?', Jinnah replied that Nehru's having questioned the 'very existence' of the League, the only 'basis' for negotiations would be the acceptance by the Congress of the League as the 'sole spokesman' for India's Muslims. Bose was willing to share power with the League in the provinces and at the all-India level, but the two parties failed to agree to the 'basis' on which to begin negotiations, and Subhas called off his all-India attempt in December 1938. This was yet another tragedy of the period engineered by Nehru.

Subhas Bose had long-standing ties to some of Bengal's leading Muslim politicians: Suhrawardy was a colleague from their time together in the Calcutta municipality, and Subhas had written a warm letter of congratulations (from Europe) to Fazlul Huq when the latter was elected mayor of Calcutta in 1935 with Congress support. In the final quarter of 1938, Subhas and Sarat Bose began discussions with Huq's Krishak Praja Party to form a coalition in Bengal (with the Congress still the largest party in the assembly). Sarat Bose had also introduced a number of bills in the assembly to reform land tenure in Bengal, which endeared him to Huq's party legislators. By December 1938, the Bose brothers were ready to form a ministry in Bengal.

Then Gandhi suddenly intervened—responding to a plea from the businessman G. D. Birla and Huq's finance minister Nalini Ranjan Sarkar (who did not belong to the Congress party). They brought Maulana Azad along with them, and petitioned Gandhi not to 'disturb' the existing Huq ministry—presumably because Birla's business interests were in safer hands under a Huq–Muslim League ministry than under a more left-wing ministry led by Congress. Azad often had his way within Congress on matters concerning Muslims anywhere in India. But here, a non-Congress politician (Nalini Sarkar) was appealing to Gandhi over the head of the Congress president—and Gandhi chose to side with Birla and Sarkar over the national president of the Congress and his brother Sarat (who was likely to become chief minister). This was an extraordinary act of betrayal (some would say treason), for which knowledgeable Bengalis have never forgiven Gandhi and the Congress. By sabotaging his own party and its president, Gandhi effectively ensured that Bengal would have Muslim League ministries for most of the period from 1940 to 1946, which had a major role in vitiating the amicable relations between Muslims and Hindus in Bengal, leading eventually to the partition of the province. In an ironic postscript, Fazlul Huq (who had helped move the Lahore Resolution in 1940 for the creation of Pakistan) became quickly disillusioned by the idea of Pakistan by 1941. In early 1943, Fazlul Huq joined his fellow chief ministers, Allah Bux Soomro (of Sindh) and Dr Khan Sahib (of NWFP) in sending a telegram to Churchill demanding that Britain immediately grant India self-rule—refuting Churchill's persistent contention that all the Muslims of India were opposed to the creation of a unitary India. Fazlul Huq rejected the 'two-nation' theory that was the basis of Pakistan, and he was able to cobble together several coalitions in alliance with Sarat Bose (who was by then in the Forward Bloc) and even the Hindu Mahasabha led by Shyama Prasad Mukherjee. But the British governors strongly favoured the Muslim League and helped the latter topple Huq's coalitions with non-Muslim parties repeatedly. What is clear, though, is that a Bose–Huq alliance could have been cemented in 1938–39—and this would have precluded Fazlul Huq going against his natural instincts to support the Pakistan Resolution in 1940. Had Gandhi not intervened to thwart Subhas Bose's initiative (in order to benefit Gandhi's friend and financier G. D. Birla), Huq would not have become the implacable foe of Gandhi he became thereafter and Bengal may have never needed to be partitioned again.

In September 1938, as the clouds of war darkened over Czechoslovakia, the All India Congress Committee (AICC) adopted a weak resolution 'appealing to the good sense of the British to do the right thing by India if a crisis came' (as Mihir Bose put it in his biography of Subhas). This 'sloppy' and ambiguous resolution, introduced by Rajaji (who was considered a leader of the Right of Congress that was more accommodating towards British tactics), was strongly opposed by the Left nationalists. Subhas expressed his personal support for the Left's proposed amendments, but eventually played the conciliatory role as president and supported Gandhi and Rajaji's resolution, even though he disagreed with it. Several communist members (including P. C. Joshi and Somnath Lahiri) walked out of Congress at this time, but Subhas and his key leftist supporters (particularly Jayaprakash Narayan and Acharya Narendra Deva) decided that the next Congress president must be from their side.

There was a very clear fracture within Congress over the issue of 'federation' as envisaged by the 1935 Government of India Act. Congress found it repugnant, as did almost every other party in India (including the Muslim League, despite the fact that it incorporated most of Jinnah's 'Fourteen Points'). But Birla had reported to Viceroy Linlithgow that Gandhi did not object to the federal provisions that reserved Defence and Foreign Affairs for the centre (where the viceroy had overriding power). Although this private communication was not widely known at the time, Subhas Bose's followers sensed that the Right was willing to work out a compromise with the British (as Gandhi had done in 1931). Bose had, since 1928, been at the forefront of the campaign for purna swaraj. The 1935 Act was clearly aimed at postponing even dominion status for India for another whole generation, with the interim arrangements being aimed at keeping Congress on the defensive, while separate electorates ensured that minorities (especially Europeans) were over-represented in the provinces, and the princes were massively over-represented in the federation. While the princely states accounted for only a quarter of the population, the princes would get to nominate 33 per cent of the members of the Lower House and 40 per cent of the members of the Upper House. The princely states would thus not only be immune to democratic governance, but there would be massive over-representation of their despotic rule at the federal level! About 80 per cent of all federal expenditure—on the army, foreign affairs, debt servicing and railways—would be directly controlled by the viceroy (in turn reporting to the Secretary of State for India, sitting in London), and the already-emasculated federal legislature would only be able to spend about a fifth of the federal budget. Even Hong Kong in the last years of British rule had more real authority transferred to locals than was envisaged for India in the federal aspects of the 1935 Act, with the viceroy having the power to dismiss governments at will—something that the provincial governors had already shown their willingness to do, despite being more constitutionally circumscribed than the viceroy.

Bose and his supporters within Congress were determined not to compromise with this British Tory vision of perpetual empire, as they suspected Gandhi was willing to do. The Bose camp wanted, in particular, to capitalize on the opportunity offered by the war clouds in Europe to force the British to negotiate on equal terms with Congress as the main representative of India, given that the party was now in power in nine of India's eleven provinces. Subhas Bose thus decided to run for re-election as Congress president—although he offered Narendra Deva as an alternative president from his camp, and decided to put himself up only when the latter decided not to run. Bose also made a public statement about 'a prospect of a compromise on the Federal scheme between the Right-wing of the Congress and the British government... Consequently, the Right wing do not want a Leftist president who... may put obstacles in the path of negotiations.' Gandhi had initially sounded out Jawaharlal Nehru as the candidate to take on Subhas, but turned to Maulana Azad when Nehru declined. As the day drew closer, Azad too got cold feet and Gandhi nominated Dr Pattabhi Sitaramayya from Andhra as his candidate to take on Subhas Bose. On 29 January 1939, Sitaramayya telegraphed his 'hearty congratulations' to Subhas, who had won by a narrow but decisive margin of 1,580 votes to 1,377. Gandhi took it as a personal defeat: '...since I was instrumental in inducing Dr Pattabhi not to withdraw his name as a candidate when Maulana Sahib withdrew, the defeat is more mine than his.' But in the spirit of Mark Antony's speech upon the assassination of Caesar, Gandhi added: 'After all, Subhas Babu is not an enemy of his country. He has suffered for it. In his opinion his is the most forward and boldest policy and programme. The minority can only wish it all success.' He urged Subhas to form his own Working Committee and run the party in his own style.

In effect, though, Gandhi had declared war on Subhas—and he was a far more bruising intriguer than Bose would ever be. Bose attempted to be conciliatory, saying 'it will be a tragic thing for me if I succeed in winning the confidence of other people but fail to win the confidence of India's greatest man.' But Bose's main enemy was his frail body: having spent long years in exile and prison, Subhas was wont to fall ill frequently and he was now afflicted with bronchial pneumonia, plus liver and intestinal complications. Citing his illness, he sent a telegram requesting the postponement of the Congress Working Committee meeting on 22 February at Wardha. Twelve of Gandhi's acolytes (led by Patel) sent in their resignations citing this telegram as being symptomatic of Bose's autocratic streak, although Nehru's letter was sent separately and was ambiguous about whether he was resigning. By the time the main Congress session began at Tripuri (near Jabalpur) in central India on 6 March, Subhas was still grievously ill with pneumonia in both lungs and his relatively brief presidential speech had to be read out by his brother Sarat. It emphasized the need to present the nation's demands before the British government in the form of an ultimatum and to begin civil disobedience if an acceptable response was not received. He accurately predicted that war would arrive in Europe within six months, and this presented a unique window of opportunity to press India's cause. Bose's opponents had spread the rumour that he was malingering, and the UP chief minister Govind Ballabh Pant passed a resolution saying that the Congress executive needed to command Gandhi's 'implicit confidence, and requests the President to nominate the Working Committee in accordance with the wishes of Gandhiji.' In five weeks, the party's high command had asserted itself quite emphatically.

Ironically, Gandhi himself did not attend the Tripuri session at all, instead focusing on his agitation against the ruler of Rajkot (close to his own birthplace), demanding more democratic rights for his people; and sure enough, Gandhi's fast diverted attention from the centrality of the annual Congress session. Subhas Bose's presidential address alluded to this too, calling for the Congress to guide democratic movements in all the 560 or so princely states on a 'comprehensive and systematic basis' rather than a 'piecemeal' attack on a single small fiefdom like Rajkot. Later, Bose personally requested Gandhi to turn his considerable powers to such a comprehensive democratic solution across all the princely states, but Gandhi demurred. Subhas also sent Jawaharlal a long twenty-seven-page letter containing withering criticisms of a man he considered 'as politically an elder brother and leader' who had let him down terribly and, more importantly, let down the causes they both held dear. This did have a salutary effect on Nehru, who intervened with Gandhi, saying any attempt to 'push' Subhas out 'seems to me to be an exceedingly wrong step'. (In a mellower time twenty-three years later, Nehru was to confess to an interviewer that he had 'agreed with' what Bose wanted to do, but had 'let him down'.) Bose and Nehru then held a long, cordial consultation before the former went back to Gandhi—at a meeting of the

AICC in Calcutta in late April—and requested the patriarch to nominate a Working Committee. When Gandhi still refused, Bose said on 29 April he had no option but to resign in the higher interests of the Congress party. The whole episode spoke poorly of internal democracy within the Congress party, which operated a High Command structure despite its commitment to non-violence, with Gandhi as a permanent super-president. Bose's impertinent observations about his colleagues (including in *The Indian Struggle*, which was released in India in early 1939) also created awkwardness with them. But overall, Gandhi had responded in a peevish manner against a young challenger to his ideological line and, given the imminent opportunities that could have accrued to India and a united Congress over the next few months, the timing of the Gandhi-Bose breach was a tragedy for India.

Bose then decided to create a 'Forward Bloc' *within* Congress to provide a platform for those committed to more radical methods. The Congress Socialist Party (with two factions headed by Jayaprakash Narayan and Minoo Masani), other leftists such as M. N. Roy, and the communists operating in a National Front, decided to retain their distinct identities but created a Left Consolidation Committee with Subhas as chairman. However the president of the All India Kisan Sabha, Swami Sahajanand Saraswati of Bihar and his key Andhra and Gujarat allies N. G. Ranga and Indulal Yagnik, joined the Forward Bloc, as did Khurshed Nariman and H. V. Kamath from Bombay province, Sardul Singh Caveeshar from Punjab, Mian Akbar Shah from NWFP and the Congress party's Karnataka president, S. K. Hosmani. As Bose's group gained more adherents, the Congress leadership passed two resolutions in late June 1939 banning Congress members from offering satyagraha or civil disobedience without permission from the Provincial Congress Committee. The Left Consolidation Committee held a day of protests against this decision on 9 July, and Gandhi himself drafted the resolution disciplining Bose, removing him as president of the Bengal Provincial Congress Committee and banning him from holding elective office within Congress for three years. Henceforth, the Congress in Bengal split into two blocs—further weakening its position in the Bengal Assembly. The vindictiveness was persisting even at a time when the Congress needed to present a united face—not only within its own house but across India—in order to force the issue with the colonial authorities as they confronted the prospect of war in Europe.

On 3 September 1939, Bose was addressing a mammoth rally in Madras of more than 200,000 people when someone slipped a newspaper into his hands, which showed that Britain was at war with Germany. Bose immediately expressed his solidarity with the Poles, but also expressed outrage at the other piece of news—that Linlithgow had unilaterally declared war on India's behalf, without so much as informing (leave alone consulting) the Congress party, which was in power in nine of the eleven provinces of British India. Bose urged Congress to launch a final fight for freedom, given that Britain was far more amenable to pressure than it would ever otherwise be. Gandhi met Viceroy Linlithgow the following day, expressed his personal solidarity with the British, and spoke with some emotion about his horror at the prospect of Westminster Abbey and 'any monuments of (British) civilization' being defaced by an enemy. As he had done in the First World War, the viceroy's notes from this meeting showed that Mahatma Gandhi pledged to help with recruiting Indians into the war effort. But Gandhi was in a minority in Congress, as (with the slight exception of Rajagopalachari) the Congress leadership wanted an unequivocal statement from the British that India would be freed at the end of the war.

On 8 September, the Congress Working Committee surprisingly invited Subhas Bose to join a special meeting to discuss the Congress attitude to Britain during the war. Nehru had been in China visiting Chiang Kai-shek in Chongqing when the war was declared, and he hurried back to join the meeting. When Nehru passed through Calcutta, Bose organized demonstrations that declared 'Britain's adversity is India's opportunity'. But Nehru had asserted, 'This is not the time to bargain. We are against the rising imperialism of Germany, Italy and Japan and for the decaying imperialism of Europe.' That last clause was truly bizarre! Nehru still drafted a resolution critical of Britain, but it was toned down and the Working Committee passed a resolution condemning fascism, while asking Britain to define its war aims (i.e., to clarify whether it meant to grant India self-rule). Bose thought this was a pussyfooting resolution that represented yet another lost opportunity. But Linlithgow then called the Congress leaders—and Bose separately—to talks at the viceregal mansion.

Linlithgow responded to the Congress demand to clarify Britain's war aims by saying it was too early to do so and would not serve any purpose. Jinnah had met Linlithgow immediately after Gandhi on 4 September, and pledged 'the loyalty of the Muslim community everywhere' (although he clearly could not be speaking for the whole Muslim community, since his Muslim League had won less than a quarter of the Muslim reserved seats in the 1937 election—106 out of 482). Jinnah also told the Viceroy that 'Muslim areas should be separated from "Hindu India" and run by Muslims in collaboration with Great Britain'—an idea that Linlithgow was determined to capitalize on during the war. When Gandhi met Linlithgow a second time on 26 September, Gandhi offered his personal assurance that control of the military would not be a major concern for a future Indian government, but here he was going out on a personal limb, and Linlithgow was much more cold to him, knowing (from his own Intelligence) that Gandhi's views were in a minority in Congress. The Viceroy asserted that the 1919 Act, seen together with the 1929 declaration of the aim of dominion status, provided enough substance regarding the meaning of the 1935 Act. In a private interview, Linlithgow was much clearer: Britain had no intention of granting dominion status (or setting India free) for at least another fifty years, given the 'many differences amongst Indian political parties'. Here was the heart of Britain's position: the 1935 Act had proposed a federal structure in which no Indian political party could have a majority, since more than 40 per cent of the seats were reserved for unelected representatives nominated by the princes, and Britain expected to run a 'federal' government in which the British viceroy still remained in unfettered control.

In the face of this British intransigence, Congress asked all its governments in the eight provinces it controlled to resign in late October 1939. In retrospect, this was a major strategic error by Congress. If, instead, the Congress had followed Bose's lead in 1938, strengthened its provincial alliances, and stayed in government while putting united pressure on the British, it would have been in a much stronger bargaining position. By resigning, Congress gave the British governors free rein to remake their provinces, foment communal tensions and deploy the full panoply of divide and rule tactics. Most crucially for the future of the Indian subcontinent—and indeed Central and West Asia—Britain intervened to obliterate Congress control over the NWFP, which was 92 per cent Muslim but had been ruled by Congress since its success at the 1937 election. Now Linlithgow asked Jinnah to form an alternative government there, although the Muslim League had won no seats (even amongst the 36 reserved for Muslim voters alone) in the NWFP.

Britain's hypocrisy cannot go unremarked upon: while claiming to be fighting for freedom and democracy, Britain's policy in India murdered democracy; having promised 'self-determination' in August 1917 in the heyday of Woodrow Wilson's idealism, Britain rolled back steadily. First in March–April 1919 had come the draconian Rowlatt Act and the massacre at Jallianwala Bagh; then, faced with Gandhi's unprecedented mass mobilization, Britain had come close to conceding dominion status in January 1922. Once Gandhi called off his campaign—on the high-minded grounds that his followers had strayed from his non-violent path—the British took full advantage, steadily whittling away at the initial moves towards democracy, adding an array of anti-democratic measures, culminating in more than a third of the seats in the federal legislature being assigned to the princes, and about a quarter of the rest being reserved for various contrived minorities (Muslims, Europeans,

Anglo–Indians, Sikhs, Christians, landholders, Depressed Classes, etc.) until less than 40 per cent were open to the broad citizenry of India. Britain was to use similar tactics in every one of its colonies, including the last one, Hong Kong, where the successor power (Communist China) today only has to point to the utter lack of democracy in British Hong Kong to justify its own reluctance to allow full democratic choice there.

Chapter 5

THE GREAT ASIAN WAR
AND THE EBB OF EUROPEAN EMPIRE (1940–1946)

The British historians Bayly and Harper wrote apropos the late 1930s that 'the Japanese regarded China in rather the same way that the previous generation of Britons had regarded France, as a cultural reference point, but a contemptible nation state.' This has the ring of truth, as we saw in the previous chapter, with the Japanese military and bureaucratic elite adopting a mission to use their knowledge and technology to remake and revive an effete Chinese nation. Japan was very much the Britain of Asia—an island-nation off the mainland, which used that redoubt to become far more advanced economically than the rest of its continent. Just as modern Britain is the product of a French remaking of the country (the British aristocracy traces its lineage back to the Norman invasion of Britain in 1066, although the francophone element of that heritage is now obscured), Japanese culture was periodically infused with influences from China (including some influences that China itself received from India). Thus, Zen (the Japanese version of Mahayana Buddhism) was imported from Song China, where it was referred to as Chan—the Chinese pronunciation of the Sanskrit word 'dhyana' (meditation)—and had arrived in China during the Tang dynasty in the sixth century CE from India, spreading gradually to Vietnam, Korea and (in the thirteenth century) to Japan. Although Buddhism did not get a foothold in Japan until the thirteenth century, the first written form of Japanese can be traced to Buddhist documents that circulated in Japan (using Chinese ideographs) dating to the eighth century.

The Japanese adapted and evolved these beliefs in uniquely Japanese ways: the Kiyomizu-dera temple in Kyoto, for instance, with its punctilious cleanliness in a beautifully tranquil wooded hilltop setting, has few parallels in India, China or Vietnam. Similarly, neo-Confucianism arrived in Japan in the fourteenth century, but was only adopted more widely in the sixteenth century after the Edo period philosopher Fujiwara Seika and his disciples gained access to the Tokugawa shoguns and were able to establish academies with state patronage. The Tokugawa shoguns' Kansei Edict of 1790 established neo-Confucianism as the official state ideology, cementing Chinese influence. However, the British–French parallels cannot be taken too far, as Japan also had a powerful indigenous cultural heritage, which gained ground during the late Tokugawa period as the Kokugaku (or National Revival) movement. This elevated Shinto (including its central belief that the emperor was a direct descendant of the Sun goddess Amaterasu) to a central role, even as Japan adopted outwardly Western institutions and practices.

Japan's sense of mission in China inexorably clashed with those of the old imperial power, Britain, and the emerging one, the United States of America. Those two powers were determined to keep the embers of Chinese nationalism alive by backing Chiang Kai-shek's regime in Chongqing and points west. Ironically, with the exception of Chiang's base province of Sichuan, most of China proper (i.e. the territory that was ruled by the Ming dynasty before its conquest by the Manchus) was in fact under Japanese control by 1939. Chiang Kai-shek controlled Yunnan (once dominated by the Dai, but conquered and Sinicized by the Manchu Qing), Qinghai ('Inner Tibet', also gained by the Qing) and Xinjiang (still dominated by the Muslim Uighurs), while Mao's communists based themselves at Yan'an in northern Shaanxi province. The northern provinces of Shaanxi, Gansu, and Shanxi were contested between Chiang and Mao's forces, and various residual warlords, but Mao's strategy of not directly fighting the Japanese had paid off in allowing the communists to steadily gain modest amounts of territory in the north, while Chiang Kai-shek's much larger forces shrivelled from their fierce confrontations with the Japanese.

The American interest in China had grown steadily since the 1850s with trade (and the opportunity to exploit China's potentially enormous domestic market) being one major motivation, and the possibility of converting China's people to Christianity being a close second. Madame Chiang Kai-shek (Soong Mei-ling), the daughter of an itinerant Bible salesman made good (Charlie Soon) helped cultivate the China mystique in the US: having spent her teenage years in Georgia (including a year at Wesleyan College), she spoke American English with an authentic and endearing southern drawl. And having graduated with honours from Wellesley College (the same college that Hillary Clinton attended several decades later), Mei-ling had a Rolodex of influential American friends that she cultivated with elan throughout her life. Christian missionaries from the US had always looked upon China's enormous population as a particularly fertile source of convertible souls. And President Franklin Roosevelt's maternal grandfather, Warren Delano II, was one of the biggest American traders with China (in opium and other products) in the previous century, giving the president a particular interest in the country. As Bayly and Harper put it, Americans hoped that 'China would one day be the United States of Asia: prosperous, Christian and free'! Specifically, Roosevelt sought to keep Chiang's Chongqing-based government adequately supplied through the famous Burma Road that snaked out of northeastern India through Burma and onto the boomtown of Lashio in Burma's northeast; another part of the Burma Road linked Lashio to the ports of Rangoon.

Although the US was still (in 1939–41) ostensibly neutral in the war, its role in supplying the Burma Road was yet another provocation to the Japanese—who were already angered by the collapse in US demand after the imposition of the protectionist Smoot–Hawley tariffs, and positively incensed by the US imposition of an oil and defence-equipment embargo on Japan in 1940 and 1941. That the US general Joseph Stilwell had become a key military adviser to Chiang Kai-shek was an act barely short of war, and there was also an American Volunteer Group led by Claire Chennault that acted as an auxiliary air force for China, clandestinely managed from the FDR White House by the young economist Lauchlin Currie and his assistant John King Fairbank (who was to later become a famed historian and Sinologist). Stilwell had been the military attaché at the US legation in China from 1935 to 1939, and became a fluent Mandarin speaker. He then took up key command positions back in the US in 1940–41, but was sent back to China (against his wishes) to help set up and lead the 'China–Burma–India theatre' for the US in the summer of 1941 (well before the Japanese bombing of Pearl Harbor), after FDR announced that the defence of China was vital to the national interests of the US. Chennault had ostensibly retired from the US Army in early 1937, and instead devoted himself to helping to train an air force for Chiang Kai-shek (working under the direct 'supervision' of Madame Chiang). In 1940, Chennault and T.V. Soong (brother to Madame Chiang, and a key financier to the KMT regime) were able to persuade the FDR administration to send additional equipment to reinforce the shambolic Chinese air force, including 100 P–40B Tomahawk aircraft. By the summer of 1941, Chennault had a team of 300 American fighter pilots and ground crew based in Burma (where they posed as tourists) and ready to help China fight the Japanese with their sixty crack fighter aircraft.

Ironically, the effective closure of the American market had obliged Japan to cultivate Southeast Asia as an alternative market in the 1930s. British-ruled Malaya and French-ruled Indo-China had, by then, already become two of the largest sources of rubber for the booming global automotive industry, and both also had expanding metal mining industries. Relatively sparsely populated Malaya became a booming market for Japan's manufactured exports: by the end of the decade, more than half of Malaya's imported goods came from Japan. Japanese-owned barber shops, chemists, photo shops and taxidermists were ubiquitous in towns throughout Malaya. Across Asia, Japan was still seen as a beacon of Asia's economic renaissance, although this was diminished in some eyes by Japan's invasion of China: Subhas Bose, for instance, remained positively inclined towards Japan, but asked pointedly whether Japan's revival could not have been achieved 'without dismembering the Chinese republic, without humiliating another proud, cultured and ancient race.'

Admiration for Japan was more unalloyed amongst the Malays, the indigenous people of Malaya, who already felt besieged by the influx of European, Chinese and Indian immigrants who were gaining all the fruits of Malaya's economic progress. The Egyptian nationalist Mustafa Kamil's travels through Japan in 1906 (the year after Nippon's great naval triumph over Russia) had stirred admiration across Muslim Asia, including amongst the Malays, helping them develop their first notions of 'nation' from the Japanese example. Prominently, Sultan Abu Bakar of Johor had visited Japan soon afterwards in the same year; his son, Sultan Ibrahim, followed him there in 1934 and was feted by Japanese aristocrats on that trip, acknowledging Johor's growing economic importance to Japan. The sprawling state of Johor had been the last of the Malay sultanates to become a British protectorate (in 1914), although it had lost arguably the most valuable part of its territory— the island emporium of Singapore—to Britain a century earlier. By the late 1920s, one large iron ore mine in Johor supplied nearly 40 per cent of Japan's needs for that vital industrial raw material, and other Japanese mines there and in the northeastern backwaters of Kelantan and Trengganu produced bauxite, tin and manganese. Japanese-made bicycles were ubiquitous in Southeast Asia as the common person's mode of transport, and were to play a vital role in the conquest of Saigon in September 1940 and Singapore in February 1942. And even the great gun emplacements at Pengerang Point at the southern tip of Malaya—meant to protect the new British naval base in northeastern Singapore—could only be approached via a large Japanese-owned rubber estate. The British Special Branch began waking up rather late to the stranglehold that Japan's economic network had quietly built up over Malaya. The British empire in the east was to pay grievously for its hubris.

The Japanese foreign office (aided by large corporations) had also been assiduously cultivating students from all over Asia, and had started language and 'area studies' schools for Japanese to learn the languages of Burma, Malaya, Thailand and India—where they also received sumo and other martial arts training, while being imbued with nationalism and a sense of Japan's leadership role in Asia. Colonel Suzuki Keiji established the Minami Kikan—a clandestine subversive organization devoted to furthering the cause of independence movements in Asian nations then under European colonial rule. And the final piece of the puzzle of Japan's strategy for Southeast Asia was cemented with the implicit alliance that Japan built with Thailand—the other East Asian monarchy that was an eager student of Japan's methods—and was soon to capitalize on that alliance to deal a severe blow to the other European power, France, in the Franco–Thai War of 1940–41. Colonel Suzuki began operating in Bangkok from the late 1930s, establishing contact with Indian nationalists such as Giani Pritam Singh (of the Ghadar movement), who helped establish the Indian Independence League (IIL). More portentously, Suzuki was able to establish links with young Burmese nationalists, one amongst whom, Aung San, arrived in Tokyo (from China) in November 1940, just in time to witness the elaborate celebration of the '2,600th anniversary' of the supposed establishment of Japan's imperial dynasty.

THAILAND'S CHESS GAMES TO STAY INDEPENDENT BEFORE AND DURING ASIA'S GREAT WAR

Thailand was the only Southeast Asian nation to have successfully resisted European colonization in the nineteenth century—having fended off the French by ceding its Laotian provinces to them in 1893, and then ceding Kedah, Kelantan, Perlis and Trengganu to the British in 1909 (who later instituted them into the Unfederated Malay States; the four are today the northern states of Malaysia). Siam had previously controlled several Malay principalities to its south, of which it retained Pattani, Yala, Narathiwat, Satun, and southern Songkhla as part of the 1909 Anglo–Siamese Treaty.

In late 1917, King Rama VI (Vajiravudh) expelled his Austrian railway adviser and German administrator of Siam Commercial Bank, and joined the Allied side in the war. Siam's token participation at the end of the war was aimed at bargaining for the elimination of extraterritoriality, but the European powers did not oblige, although the US agreed to renounce its unequal treaty rights. In 1912, there had been a palace coup attempt (inspired by the Republican revolution in China), and immediately after the war discontent grew as rice prices soared following a drought. An accomplished poet and playwright, Vajiravudh's attempts at political reform (through decentralization of power to provincial uparajas, or viceroys) and modernization made only modest headway, and he never escaped the long shadow of his accomplished father. The lavish spending of the ever-growing royal household (including the thirty-three sons and forty-four daughters of his father, Chulalongkorn, and their progeny) was one aspect with which Vajiravudh grappled unsuccessfully, but his mastery of Sanskrit and Pali enabled him to write and stage many plays and stories based on the Ramayana. He also established Vajiravudh College (an English-style boarding school for boys) and strengthened Chulalongkorn

University, extended the nation's railway line all the way north to Chiang Mai, and constructed Don Muang airport.

During his reign (which ended with his death at age forty-four in November 1925), calls for constitutional reform grew, reaching a crescendo during the reign of his brother Prajadhipok (Rama VII), the youngest of Chulalongkorn's thirty-three sons. By this point, Siam's finances were in parlous shape, with a soaring fiscal deficit amid a slumping global economy, and a new king ill-equipped to deal with the challenges (despite his education at Eton and Woolwich Military Academy, as well as its French equivalent). Admitting he knew little about fiscal issues, Rama VII appointed a Council of State, but fatally constituted it primarily from members of the royal family and nobility. The most influential member was the interior minister, Paribatra Sukhumbhand (the king's half-brother, whose grandson Sukhumbhand Paribatra was Bangkok's mayor from 2009 to 2016).

In June 1932, a group of soldiers and civilians who had formed the Khana Ratsadon (People's Party) executed a near-bloodless coup d'état that was later dubbed the Siamese Revolution. The revolution ended a century and a half of absolutist rule by the Chakri dynasty, and replaced it with a constitutional monarchy. Prajadhipok was away from the capital when the coup occurred on 24 June, but he quickly returned to meet the coup leaders—and disarmed them when he stood up as they entered his throne room (breaking the royal custom of remaining seated when addressing commoners). He quickly accepted a new constitution and agreed to rule in accordance with it. The co-leaders (or 'promoters') of the Khana Ratsadon were seven individuals who had first met at a Paris hotel five years earlier, but Pridi Phanomyong and Plaek Phibunsongkhram respectively became its most prominent civilian and military leaders (and eventually came to lead its left and right wings).

In order to foster national reconciliation, Pridi nominated Phraya Manopakorn Nititada (a privy councillor since the reign of Rama VI) to become the first prime minister. But Pridi's proposal to nationalize all land, labour and enterprise in 1933 was violently opposed by the military, and he was briefly forced into exile. The reverberations from the proposal eventually led to a military coup in June 1933, following which General Phahon Phonphayuhasena (the commander of the Royal Siamese Army, and himself the son of a Teochew Chinese father) became prime minister. It was the first in a long line of military coups that have periodically 'stabilized' Thailand in the subsequent eight decades. Within four months of Phahon becoming prime minister, there was a royalist revolt, but its successful suppression eventually led to the abdication of King Rama VII (Prajadhipok) in 1935. He was succeeded by Ananda Mahidol (Rama VIII), who was just nine years old at the time, and continued his schooling in Switzerland for another decade.

Plaek Phibunsongkhram had played the key role in crushing the royalist revolt in November 1933, and he became defence minister soon thereafter. After elections in 1937 and 1938, Phibun gained further ground at Phahon's expense, and in 1938, Phibun replaced Phahon as both prime minister and commander of the Royal Siamese Army. One of his earliest acts was to rename the country Thailand (in 1939). With the young king absent from the country, Phibun became the undisputed leader of the country in a near-republican government and was to play the key role in the modernization of Thailand over the next two decades.

The 1930s in Thailand were also marked by legislation aimed at forcing the cultural assimilation of the Chinese who had become the dominant ethnic community in Bangkok (and, indeed, in every major Southeast Asian city from Singapore to Penang, Kuala Lumpur, Jakarta, Medan and Manila). This obliged the ethnic Chinese to take on Thai names—for instance, the successful Chia family of the Charoen Pokphand business conglomerate became 'Chiaravanont'—and all Chinese schools were compelled to ensure that at least three-quarters of all instruction (for all subjects) occurred in the Thai language. King Vajiravudh had published a pamphlet referring to the Chinese as the 'Jews of the East', claiming that Chinese men remained Chinese even when they married Thai women (as they often did), while Thai men who married Chinese became more Chinese! Commercial restrictions, discriminatory taxation and the obligation for Chinese teachers and students to learn Thai helped homogenize society, and only the length of a surname (or the telltale presence of 'Chia', 'Wong' or 'Leong' within it) hinted at Chinese descent. Ironically, the discriminatory legislation was introduced by leaders who were themselves of Chinese descent (but perhaps saw themselves as better assimilated than the majority of their ethnic brethren). Both parents of the first prime minister, Manopakorn, were of Chinese descent, and Plaek Phibunsongkhram's grandfather was a Cantonese-speaking immigrant. Phibun's ideological rival, Pridi Phanomyong, came from a more assimilated family but both he and his wife traced their ancestry back to a Cantonese immigrant called Heng from Chenghai district of Guangdong province, who arrived in Siam in the 1760s. With the exception of the impeccably Thai Prem Tinsulanonda (who was prime minister for eight years in the 1980s, and remains president of the Privy Council to this day) and some other coup leaders (including 2006 coup leader Sonthi Boonyaratglin, a Muslim), virtually all of Thailand's prime ministers over the past eighty-four years have been the sons of ethnically Chinese fathers.

Having consolidated his power in 1938, General Phibun began negotiations with Léon Blum's left-wing Popular Front government in France to regain some of the territories in Laos and Cambodia that France had seized in 1907. Although Blum's regime was willing to make small territorial concessions, events were soon overtaken by the outbreak of war in Europe. In May 1940, Germany invaded France and advanced quickly into Paris. The French hero of World War I, Marshal Philippe Pétain, negotiated an armistice with Germany on 22 June 1940 that signified the ignominious Fall of France. Paris and the whole of northern France came under formal German military occupation, while a small sliver of the southeast was occupied by Italy. Pétain was allowed to rule over the central and southern part of France (covering close to half of France's territory) from his capital of Vichy, and theoretically oversaw all civil servants across France (including in the two occupied zones).

With metropolitan France in disarray, Japan demanded safe passage of its troops through French Indo-China, especially in prosecuting its military operations in southern China. Japan also demanded that Vichy France close the railway line from Hanoi to Kunming (in China's Yunnan province) that was being used as one of the supply routes for Chiang Kai-shek's regime. Although the Vichy regime was willing to partially comply, it sought formal recognition from Japan of French sovereignty over Indo-China. Japan did agree to make this allowance, and France retained its colonial authority right until 1945—in distinct contrast to the fate of the British and Dutch colonies. But in order to secure their key strategic objectives, Japanese forces invaded French Indo-China on 22 September, and overran French resistance after four days of heavy fighting on land, sea and air. Pioneering a technique that was to be used later in Malaya, Japan's 'bicycle infantry' was at the vanguard of its invasion of Saigon. With the defeat of the French, the Vichy regime agreed to allow Japan to station 40,000 troops in southern Vietnam (a right Japan did not exercise until the German invasion of the Soviet Union in June 1941 relieved pressure on Japan's troops in Manchukuo). Japan immediately moved about 1,500 troops into an airbase outside Hanoi and a key railhead from Vietnam into Kunming, while the French retained authority over the local populace. On 27 September 1940, Japan signed a tripartite pact with Germany and Italy, which demarcated their respective spheres of influence (with 'Greater East Asia' left to Japan).

Major General Phibun, Thailand's prime minister, had established cordial relations with Japan, and now sensed an opportunity to regain the territories that Thailand had lost to France over the previous forty-five years. Border skirmishes began in October 1940, and the well-trained Thai air force began to make effective and virtually unimpeded bombing runs over Vientiane in Laos, and Battambang, Phnom Penh and Sisophon in Cambodia. Admiral

Decoux, the governor of French Indo-China, sought American support—to impose an economic blockade—but was rebuffed. On 5 January 1941, the Thai army (using mainly Isan forces from the northeast of Thailand who are ethnically and linguistically akin to Laotians) launched a ground offensive into Laos and Cambodia. The French forces in Laos were quickly overrun, and Thailand regained the whole of Laos with relative ease, but met more resistance from the French forces in Cambodia. On 16 January, France launched a counteroffensive on two border villages, but by the end of the day had been beaten back.

The following day, the French navy attacked the island of Ko Chang in the Gulf of Thailand and won France's only victory of the Franco–Thai War, sinking two Thai torpedo boats and a coastal defence ship. But Thai mastery of the air and land was reinforced in subsequent days with bombing raids by Thai aircraft on the main French airfield in Angkor (in Siem Reap province), and destructive raids on Phnom Penh and Sisophon. On 31 January, Japan intervened to negotiate a ceasefire and in May 1941 the final peace terms were agreed. France agreed to hand the western half of Cambodia (Battambang, Pailin, Siem Reap, Preah Vihear, Banteay Meanchey and Oddar Meanchey) to Thailand, along with the western provinces of Xaignabouli and Champassak (including part of Luang Prabang) in Laos. Prime Minister Phibun became a national hero for this decisive military victory over a European power, and especially for having regained all the territories lost to that European power during the halcyon days of the reign of Chulalongkorn. Thailand lost just 90 soldiers and sailors during the war (and just 21 were taken prisoner), while 321 French (and colonial) soldiers were killed, and 222 taken prisoner. Thailand was able to shoot down twenty-two French aircraft (about a third of all fighter planes in French Indo-China), while it lost only ten. It was a decisive military victory on land and in the air, and Phibun built a grand Victory Monument that still stands in Bangkok.

Phibun is said to have made a secret compact with Japan, pledging Thailand's support for any future Japanese invasion of British-ruled Burma and Malaya. On 8 December 1941 (which was still 7 December across the International Date Line in Hawaii's port of Pearl Harbor), Japanese troops landed on the east coast of Thailand at dawn. After some token fighting, a ceasefire was declared by noon the same day and Thailand became a Japanese ally, signing a mutual assistance treaty on 14 December 1941. This provided Japanese troops safe passage through Thailand on their way to Burma and Malaya, and proved invaluable to Japan's war effort; in February 1942, Thailand also signed on to the Tripartite Pact (between Japan, Germany and Italy). Although Phibun had become a hero with Thailand's general public, his decision to align with Japan divided the Thai elite—with a large faction led by Pridi Phanomyong strongly opposing the alliance. Phibun sacked all ministers who were opposed to the alliance, and offered sinecures to some others including Pridi, who was made regent to the absent young king. When Phibun's Thailand acquiesced in Japan's request to declare war on the Allies in January 1942, the Thai declaration of war was duly delivered by the ambassador in London to the British government. But in Washington DC, the Thai ambassador (the aristocrat Seni Pramoj, whose mother was a Bunnag) refused to deliver the letter and instead sought political asylum in the US. Seni Pramoj persuaded US Secretary of State Cordell Hull to unfreeze Thai assets in the US, and used those funds to organize the Seri (Free) Thai movement of resistance—which linked up with prominent members of the Thai government such as Pridi and foreign minister Direk Jayanama. Although they had very little impact during the war itself as a resistance army, the Seri Thai were able to seize power soon after the war ended, and help restore Thailand's good standing with the West despite its wartime alliance with Japan.

THE BRITISH CRESCENT IN THE LEAD-UP TO ITS CONQUEST BY JAPAN

British interest in the Malay Peninsula had begun with the East India Company's acquisition of Penang in 1786. This became an important stopping-off point in the British East India Company's China trade, especially in opium and tea, but two other entrepôts were acquired for the same purpose— Singapore (1819) and Malacca (1824, as part of the Anglo–Dutch Treaty). Those three free ports and Dinding (now Manjung) constituted the Straits Settlements that were administered from Calcutta until 1867, when they became a Crown Colony administered directly from London. But a tenuous historical link to Calcutta remained, and the region from there to Singapore could still be thought of as a 'British Crescent' on the eve of war. Given their key role in the China trade, all three British ports were soon inhabited mainly by Chinese merchants, labourers and refugees who assimilated into local Malay society to create a unique Peranakan culture based on a hybrid form of Malay that was spoken in those ports as well as those of the Dutch East Indies. A smaller Chitty (or 'Indian Peranakan') community also emerged in Malacca, while all three cities had growing enclaves of other Indians who settled temporarily in these cities while conducting the India–China trade, mingling with indigenous Malays. By the time control of the former Straits Settlements was transferred to the Colonial Office in London in 1867, tin mining was already flourishing across the Malay Peninsula and the Chinese (with their long presence in all three free ports) were now the partners or compradors of British capitalists seeking to exploit the mining potential of Malaya, and to bring some 'order' to the sultanates of the interior. 'Piracy' at sea (citing an episode when a British merchant ship was attacked by Chinese and Malay attackers off Selangor in 1871) provided one excuse for intervention, and 'anarchy' in Perak led the governor of the Straits Settlements, Andrew Clarke, to conclude the Pangkor Engagement under which Perak acquired a British resident with plenipotentiary powers (except in matters of Malay religion and customs), in the time-tested manner honed in India.

Selangor and Sungei Ujong (later called Seremban) were soon brought under the sway of the same Pangkor Treaty. Pahang followed in 1888, and the following year so did Negeri Sembilan (a confederation of nine Minangkabau states, ruled from Seremban). In 1895, Britain formalized the arrangement by centralizing authority in a Resident General, but naming the newly contrived union the Federated Malay States (comprising Perak, Pahang, Negeri Sembilan and Selangor). Frank Swettenham, as the first resident general, got down to showing how to wed centralization with federalism in this loose agglomeration of states. By 1940, almost all the district officers in the four Federated Malay States were Britishers, so they were subject to quite direct British rule, albeit not to the intricate municipal governance of the three great port cities that had constituted the Straits Settlements. The Unfederated Malay States (the four northern states acquired from Siam in 1909, and Johor—which had accepted British 'protection' only in 1914) were subject to more indirect rule: Johor, for instance, had virtually no British district officers, and the prince (tunku) Abdul Rahman was a district officer in his native state of Kedah. Although British Malaya (including the Straits Settlements) had a population of only 5 million (not much more than, say, Mymensingh or Murshidabad district in Bengal), it was one of the more prosperous parts of the British empire—idyllically described in Somerset Maugham's novels and short stories. That prosperity was built primarily on 'narco-colonialism', with more than half of the revenue of the Straits Settlements even in the 1930s coming from the export duty on opium, which was produced primarily from a factory on Pepys Road in Singapore.

An elaborate racism was an integral feature of British Malaya. This can be discerned obliquely in Somerset Maugham's short stories about Malaya—in which locals are barely people, as British planters and officials lament that the closest person lives several miles away! But the wealthy Straits Chinese, who had been partners of the British from the start of their adventures in Penang and Singapore, were accorded a more exalted status: uniquely amongst British colonial subjects, they were eligible for British citizenship. Many had grown wealthy through 'concessions' that gave them monopolies in specific aspects of commodity trade—rice, sugar, coffee—or the tin mining boom of the early twentieth century, or in providing services within the hill stations of Cameron or Fraser's Hill. The Straits Chinese elite truly believed in the imperial project, acquired British habits, and wrote yarns about the global cosmopolitanism of which the Straits Settlements were supposedly a harbinger.

The Eurasians (including 'burghers' from Ceylon with hints of Dutch and Portuguese blood) had a more ambivalent position in the social milieu—disdained by the British, but holding themselves aloof from the locals as they clung to their partially European heritage. The Malays were either aristocrats at the courts of the sultans, or peasants, and by this time the British were past masters at sidelining the majority community in each of their colonies. Consequently only a tiny proportion of Malays (often those with some non-Malay blood, i.e., either Arab, Turk, Bugis, or Indian) were able to join the urban middle class—which was dominated by Chinese (including 'hwaqiao', or the China born) and specific groups of Indians (Jaffna Tamils, a smattering of Bengalis, Sindhis, Gujaratis and Sikhs). Most of the newly arrived hwaqiao of course worked the tin and other mines in the interior. And at the very bottom of the social pile were immigrant indentured labourers—largely Tamils (and a smattering of Telugu and Malayalam speakers)—who worked the new rubber plantations that had prospered on their labour during the inter-war years, while keeping the workers themselves in abject poverty. The Depression of the 1930s had been cruel on both the tin and rubber industries of Malaya, and the workers' plight had been especially acute.

In this atmosphere, nationalism took two forms in the 1930s—with the Chinese (led by the former tycoon and educational philanthropist Tan Kah Kee) turning towards Mao and his communism steeped in Chinese nationalism, while an inchoate Malay nationalism was incubated in Ibrahim Yaacob's KMM (Kesatuan Melayu Muda, Union of Malay Youth) movement. Ibrahim Yaacob had emerged from the Sultan Idris Training College that was set up by the British just north of Kuala Lumpur to train Malay schoolteachers. The British hope of creating a docile group of preceptors to impart basic knowledge to farmers and fishermen was quickly belied, as Sultan Idris College became a new laboratory of nationalist thinking amongst the Malays, and a fertile source of alumni recruits into Ibrahim Yaacob's KMM.

Aligning early with Japan, Ibrahim Yaacob was able to obtain Japanese funding in 1939 to acquire a successful newspaper, *Warta Malaya* (*Malaya News*), having previously edited the Kuala Lumpur paper *Majlis*. Yusof bin Ishak (who was later to become President of Singapore) founded a rival Singapore newspaper that still exists in Malaysia today, *Utusan Melayu* (*Malay Courier*). Through his newspapers, Ibrahim Yaacob extolled the glories of the

Melaka empire and centuries of Malay literature, and began to incubate ideas of a 'bangsa Melayu' (Malay nation) that had been reduced to a minority in its own homeland by 1931. While he initially sought to distinguish Malays from other 'outsiders' to the peninsula like Arab and Indian Muslims, the definition of Malay gradually widened to embrace the many Indonesian immigrants to the peninsula—from whom the word 'merdeka' (independence) entered the language. Eventually, Ibrahim Yaacob became an advocate of a Greater Indonesia, with Malaya being absorbed into the East Indies, an idea that made him persona non grata in post-War Malaya.

Earlier, the British had created an even more elite school, the Malay College in Kuala Kangsar, to train a new cadre of officers for a Malay Administrative Service. In this English-style public school known (like St Paul's School in Darjeeling) as the 'Eton of the East', young Malays learnt English history and literature, played rugby, cricket and Eton Fives (squash with gloved hands rather than racquets), ate with knives and forks and became authentic 'brown Englishmen'. As with all such colonial projects, however, the outcomes were sometimes contrary to imperial plans: one Malay College alumnus, Onn bin Jaafar (whose father and brother were prime ministers to the Johor sultans) turned in a republican direction, writing pamphlets against the exploitative ways of Johor's sultans, and edging towards a broader Malay nationalism. He was to eventually become the founder of the United Malays National Organization (UMNO) that has ruled Malaysia since its independence in 1957. Later alumni of Malay College were to include Anwar Ibrahim (the deputy prime minister to Mahathir Mohamad, who led the Opposition after 1998), Tun Abdul Razak Hussein (Malaysia's second prime minister) and Azman Mokhtar, who led the remaking of corporate Malaysia through his legendary leadership of Khazanah Nasional after 2004.

Tan Kah Kee (known as the 'Henry Ford of Malaya' for both his philanthropy and the extensiveness of his business interests in rubber plantations, manufacturing, trading and canneries) had been one of Sun Yat-sen's most avid supporters in Malaya. By the 1930s, he was a KMT member of the Legislative Yuan based in Chongqing but found himself appalled by the corruption he saw in Chiang Kai-shek's regime on a visit to Chongqing in late 1939. Although born in Fujian province, Tan had come to Singapore as a teenager and lived in Malaya all his life, so this was his first trip to China in two decades. He arrived at a time when Edgar Snow's eulogy about Mao, *Red Star Over China,* had introduced the Chinese communists to the English-speaking world in a rather romantic and glamorous light. Mao had given Snow many long interviews during which he greatly exaggerated the struggles and triumphs of the Long March, but most of all Snow had emphasized that Mao was a Chinese nationalist and patriot, apart from being radically egalitarian. (I first read Snow's book as an impressionable seventeen-year-old in 1981, having chosen it as a school prize for History; despite knowing about the depredations of the Gang of Four, and admiringly following the remarkable political comebacks and emerging economic reforms of 'Teng Hsiao-ping', I remember being thoroughly absorbed by its narrative—to the consternation of my father, who had confronted Maoist mobs as a tea estate manager near Naxalbari in the late 1960s.) Tan Kah Kee had been the key organizer of Malaya's China Relief Fund in 1937, to help raise money to support the new United Front in China (between the KMT and CCP) against the Japanese. That had introduced him to the romance of the communists, and he decided to travel over land to Mao's redoubt in Shaanxi province.

This was an interesting decision, as it came at a time when the communist movement had been thrown into disarray by the Hitler-Stalin (or Molotov-Ribbentrop) Pact of August 1939. His visit to Mao in Yenan had a profound effect on Tan Kah Kee, who was moved by Mao's austerity, social commitment and seeming simplicity, and became convinced that Mao was far more capable of uniting China than his better-supplied rival, Chiang Kai-shek. On his return to Malaya, Tan Kah Kee went on a speaking tour extolling the virtues of Mao's party. Soon thereafter, he was joined in Singapore by Hu Yuzhi, a secret member of the CCP who had been sent to Nanyang to energize the anti-Japanese movement there. Hu became editor of *Nanyang Siang Pau,* a Singapore newspaper, and his translation of Snow's *Red Star Over China* became very popular in the region—keeping Mao's flame alight amongst Overseas Chinese even as the National Salvation alliance back in China was fraying. Tan Kah Kee himself supported Britain during the war, raising money to support Londoners during the Blitz—and eventually took refuge in Java after the Japanese invasion. Given his communist sympathies, Tan migrated to China after the 1949 revolution, but his daughter married another Singapore tycoon, Lee Kong Chian (of Lee Rubber), who was one of the founders of OCBC Bank.

Tan Kah Kee's philanthropy resulted in several educational institutions—including Amoy (now Xiamen) University in his native Fujian, and Singapore's Chinese High School (now Hwa Chong Institution). A schoolteacher at the latter, Ng Yeh Lu, became one of the most effective anti-Japanese propagandists after 1938, and many of his students became early recruits to the Malayan Communist Party (MCP). The fifteen-year-old Ong Boon Hua of Setiawan in Perak became one of the earliest MCP members to go underground in July 1940, after immersing himself in the Maoist canon for several months. Fierce in his commitment to China, he was to lead a guerrilla war in Malaya first against the Japanese, and eventually against the British, under his better-known pseudonym of Chin Peng.

•

Ceylon was quite similar in its social structure to Malaya, and indeed many of Malaya's best schoolteachers and railway clerks/managers came from Ceylon, maintaining the link. Here too, the local Sinhala Buddhist majority was disdained and isolated. After three centuries of rule by the Portuguese and Dutch, the Sinhala elite had learnt to assimilate effectively with their colonial masters, embracing their religion, language and other social mores much more willingly than their Indian neighbours were willing to. Like in India and Malaya, however, the British were punctilious about maintaining the separateness of different ethnic communities in Ceylon and developing elaborate mythologies about their distinct alleged characteristics and traits. The burghers—with names like Ondaatje, Pieris, Fernandez, La Brooy, et al.—were very much at the top of the social heap, naturally filling the top levels of the bureaucracy despite being less than 1 per cent of the population.

The main interlocutor between the Sinhala and the British was the Maha Mudaliar (chief headman)—a position that was held by Sir Solomon Dias Bandaranaike, who (as his name suggests) was a High Church Anglican whose ancestors (many of them also mudaliars to the Portuguese) had converted to Catholicism (while still retaining their claim to being Govigama or the 'highest' caste of paddy farmers, who convinced the British of their primacy in Ceylon's caste hierarchy). His son S. W. R. D. Bandaranaike created the Sinhala Maha Sabha in 1936 to further the interests of the Sinhalese people—although he did not adopt the full chauvinistic programme (of making Sinhala the sole national language and Buddhism the national religion) until well after Independence (and his own ostentatious conversion to Buddhism). With the elites seemingly so well assimilated (including Govigamas with names like *Dudley* Senanayake and *Junius* Jayawardene), the British granted Ceylon universal franchise in 1931—in distinct contrast to neighbouring India (which was always seen by the colonialists as far more difficult to control).

Ceylon also had a large Tamil community of which one group (from Jaffna and the northern part of the island) were the original inhabitants of Ceylon (having long predated the arrival of the Sinhalese), while another group comprised Indian Tamils brought over as indentured labourers to work on the coffee, rubber and (especially) tea plantations. Through the first half of the twentieth century, the Tamil Hindus were a little over 25 per cent of Ceylon's population, with the 'Indian Tamils' slightly outnumbering the Ceylon Tamils after 1911. Ironically, the kingdom of Kandy (the flag of which has been adapted as Sri Lanka's national flag, because it was the lone part of Ceylon which had remained independent of the Portuguese and Dutch, and only succumbed to the British after a war in 1815) was ruled for several generations until 1815 by a Telugu-speaking royal family called Nayak. They traced their ancestry to the Nayaks of the Vijayanagar court and had been invited over to Kandy from Madurai in southern India. In ousting the Nayak kings, the British made a pact with the Sinhalese noblemen of Kandy, promising that (unlike the Dutch and Portuguese) the British would not seek to convert the local people to Christianity. When this promise was openly flouted by the British, the Sinhalese nobility of Kandy rebelled, and this Uva Rebellion was suppressed after two years of guerrilla warfare were countered by an orgy of brutality to demonstrate to the inhabitants of Ceylon that opposing the British could be very costly indeed. One of the Sinhalese signatories of the Kandyan treaty in 1815 was the ancestor of S. W. R. D. Bandaranaike's wife, Sirimavo (who herself, like her husband and daughter, was to eventually become prime minister of Sri Lanka). With a socially stable, assimilated elite in a plantation economy (worked by Indian Tamil near-slaves), Ceylon was the most prosperous of Britain's colonies on the eve of the World War, and the one with the greatest degree of political autonomy. Resentment of the oppressive colonial social structure was brewing far below the surface, but the appearance of social order was to make Ceylon an ideal location for the British (and the Allies) to base their Southeast Asia Command headquarters.

◆

Between 1886 and 1936, Burma was ruled as part of Britain's Indian empire, although curiously, the Indian National Congress never attempted to expand into that country, treating it as quite separate in an implicit acknowledgement of Burma's separate nationality, despite the fact that Burma elected members to India's Central Legislative Assembly between 1921 and 1935. The Great Depression had hit Burma especially hard, with a 50 per cent decline in Burma's exports—especially of rice—in turn causing a massive rise in rural indebtedness and poverty. Two destructive earthquakes in 1930–31 caused more damage to rural livelihoods, and an itinerant mendicant called Saya San had stepped in to crown himself king of Burma in 1930, and led a growing rebellion against British rule. This was eventually put down after 8,000 troops were flown in from India (contributing to a further deterioration in relations between the Indians who were ubiquitous in urban Burma, and the small elite of English-speaking Burmese). After a summary trial (in which he was ably but unsuccessfully defended by the rising politician and nationalist barrister Ba Maw), Saya San was executed for sedition.

In 1936, while implementing the Government of India Act of the previous year, Burma was formally separated from India and vicious anti-Indian riots began across Burma that year, to protest the fact that the best jobs in Burma were cornered by the British, Indians and Anglo–Burmans. The riots had been sparked by a clash between striking dockworkers (who were almost all Indians) and Burmese sent to break their strike. Several hundred Indians died in the generalized rioting that then ensued. In 1938, there had been Muslim–Buddhist riots that were further inflamed by the fiery writing of the politician U Saw.

Many prominent politicians, including Ba Maw (whose father had been one of Thibaw's courtiers) and the Buddhist clergy, initially opposed the separation of Burma from India (as they thought this was a ploy to exclude Burma from the political reforms that were inevitable in India). Eventually, Ba Maw accepted the 1937 constitution for Burma that made it rather like a Crown Colony—with an elected legislative assembly with powers similar to those of an Indian province (albeit with key powers reserved for the British governor). Ba Maw himself was elected the first premier of British Burma. When he opposed Britain's declaration of war (on behalf of Burma), Ba Maw was ousted from the premiership, and resigned from the legislature. In August 1940, he was arrested for sedition and spent more than a year in jail until freed by the invading Japanese and eventually restored to office as the executive head of the new administration in August 1942. In the interim, U Saw had succeeded to the premiership with some unctuous words of praise aimed at ingratiating himself with the British.

The British, pursuing their divide and rule strategy, had always ensured that recruitment into the army in Burma was restricted mainly to the minorities—Kachins, Karen, Shans, even Rohingyas—with a predominance of Christians (and a smattering of Muslims), but with Buddhist Burmans explicitly kept out. Similarly, Anglo-Burmans, Indians and Chinese were favoured for clerical and government positions, and as business partners and suppliers. It was to counter these forms of isolation that a group of radical students and other Burmese youth began to plan the creation of a more authentically Burmese army to fight colonialism. The young radicals were called Thakins (the Burmese equivalent of 'sahib', the word for a colonial 'master' in India), and most of them belonged to middle-class families, generally from outside Rangoon and just below the top echelons of colonial Burmese society, educated in the Anglo-vernacular and nationalist schools, rather than elite ones like St John's and St Paul's. Inspired by Sinn Fein and the militant faction of the Irish nationalist movement led by Michael Collins, the Thakins included communists, socialists and nationalists (including some with distinctly fascist tendencies).

Aung San, whose kinsman had been a minister to King Mindon (Thibaw's father), was emerging as the natural leader of the Thakins. An admirer of Lincoln and the Mexican nationalist Benito Juárez, Aung San sought (with only modest success) to improve his English by memorizing the speeches of the English rhetorician Edmund Burke. In August 1940, Thakin Aung San and another comrade set sail for China with the aim of reaching out to Mao's communists. When they arrived at Amoy (Xiamen), however, they were contacted by Colonel Suzuki Keiji, 'Japan's Lawrence of Arabia' who was a passionate supporter of Burmese independence (and Asian self-realization). Arriving in Tokyo on the day the Tripartite Pact (with Germany and Italy) was signed, the two Thakins spent the rest of 1940 getting military and ideological training in Tokyo. In early 1941, Aung San landed back in Burmese territory (in Bassein), and soon contacted his core group of Thakin friends. The famous Thirty Comrades then gathered together, and were flown to Hainan Island (then under Japanese control) for six months of intense, rigorous military training. Aung San took the nom de guerre of Teza ('Fire'), while his two other senior colleagues (each, like him, about twenty-five years old) became Setkya ('Magic Weapon') and Ne Win ('Bright Sun')—each prefixed by the title 'Bo' to designate an officer or person of standing. In the autumn of 1941, the Thirty Comrades were moved to Field Marshal Phibunsongkhram's capital of Bangkok, where they created a new Burma Independence Army (BIA) under the stewardship of Colonel Suzuki, who himself took the title of Bo Mogyo ('Thunderbolt') in fulfilment of the fabled prediction that the 'umbrella' of British rule would ultimately be ousted by a thunderbolt!

With Britain at war, U Saw travelled to London to try and persuade Churchill to grant Burma independence, but was summarily rebuffed. On his journey back to Burma from London, U Saw travelled through the US, stopping in San Francisco and Hawaii—where British intelligence agents found evidence of his secret meetings with the Japanese (immediately before and after the bombing of Pearl Harbor), and some British special agents briefly considered the possibility of assassinating U Saw. Better sense prevailed, but U Saw was taken off a plane in Europe and packed off to exile in Uganda for the duration of the war, remaining under close British surveillance. Meanwhile, Ba Maw had aligned himself with the Thakins in a Freedom Bloc, demanding that Britain recognize Burma's right to independence, begin preparing for a constituent assembly, and bring the governor's authority within the ambit of the cabinet. The British jailed Ba Maw for his trouble, and kept him confined until the Japanese freed him following the liberation of Burma by Japanese forces.

In the first half of 1940, Subhas Bose's Forward Bloc and radical elements of the Muslim League worked out a coalition in the Calcutta Corporation and the Bengal assembly. Subhas Bose had grown increasingly popular with the Muslim peasantry of eastern Bengal and he got elected to the Central Legislative Assembly from a Dhaka constituency. Although Subhas had given sufficient cause to be arrested—with his continuing public calls for India to aggressively push for a constitutional settlement with the British while they were at war—Muslim ministers in Bengal were very reluctant to arrest him for fear of alienating their electorate. Subhas Bose used this opening to plan a major agitation in Calcutta on 3 July 1940, which was commemorated as Siraj-ud-Daulah Day. On that day, Subhas decided he would lead a rally to agitate for the demolition of the Holwell Monument that commemorated the partly-apocryphal story of the 'Black Hole of Calcutta' by which the city was perhaps best known globally.

This was an emotive issue sure to unite Muslim and Hindu Bengalis, both of whom felt acute anger at the heavily exaggerated (and perhaps concocted) story of the Black Hole of Calcutta, which was calculated to show the barbarism of the 'natives'. Bose pointedly asked why there were no monuments to the thousands of Indians killed by the British in 1857 and other wars, or to those who had been martyred fighting the British in more recent decades. Subhas Bose lauded Siraj as an authentic Bengali Muslim patriot, and Fazlul Huq's cabinet agreed to tear down the offending monument, causing outrage amongst the local European elites of Calcutta. Prodded by the latter, the British governor invoked the autocratic Defence of India Act to arrest Subhas on 1 July 1940—in order to forestall the massive demonstrations he had organized for the next two days.

Following the progress of the war from prison, Subhas Bose—the quintessential man of action—decided that he could not waste the war years whiling his time away in jail. In November 1940, he began a hunger strike to protest conditions in prison; despite attempts by the colonial authorities to force-feed Subhas, his health deteriorated alarmingly. Rather than risk allowing the popular leader to die in jail, the British transferred him to house arrest at his father's home on Elgin Road in Calcutta. Immediately, Subhas got in touch with Akbar Shah, his Forward Bloc's NWFP representative. On 16 January 1941, having told his family he was not to be disturbed for several days as he had taken a vow of silent reclusiveness, Subhas left home in disguise and drove to Gomoh in Bihar. Thence, he travelled incognito to Peshawar, where he was met by Akbar Shah, who helped him get over the international border to Afghanistan—where a nationalist shopkeeper called Uttam Chand Malhotra became his host for several days while he sought to contact the German, Soviet and Italian embassies. The Italian embassy eventually obliged him with a new passport and it was as Count Orlando Mazzotta that the former president of the Indian National Congress crossed the Amu Darya (Oxus River) in northern Afghanistan, drove to Samarkand, traversed the vast length of the USSR by train and eventually reached Berlin via Italy.

It had taken the British more than a fortnight to discover that Subhas had left Calcutta and they were initially misled into believing that he had joined Sri Aurobindo's ashram in Pondicherry as a reclusive monk. When the colonial authorities eventually learnt that Subhas was in Kabul, secret agents of Britain's Special Operations Executive were instructed to assassinate him in Basra, Baghdad or Turkey—the likeliest route the British expected Bose to take on his way to Moscow or Berlin. Instead, Count Mazzotta was able to re-establish a base for Indian nationalists in Berlin and soon attracted a diverse group of followers who met at his mansion in the Charlottenburg neighbourhood of Berlin, which had previously been occupied by the American military attaché. He established a Free India Centre, which was run by young enthusiasts N. G. Swami (an employee of Siemens, the German engineering firm) and his electrical engineering-student friend Abid Hasan. Later, Bose's old friend A. C. N. Nambiar (Sarojini Naidu's brother-in-law) and Girija Mookherjee joined the group, and began making broadcasts to India (albeit without using Bose's own voice, since he was still living as Mazzotta). Although unaware of where he was, the British press had begun a vicious propaganda offensive against Bose—labelling him 'India's Quisling No. 1', an absurd charge, as transcripts of his meeting with German foreign minister Ribbentrop in December 1941 show: Bose demanded at the meeting that Hitler's derogatory references to India in *Mein Kampf* be repudiated, and that a clear plan for India's liberation be announced.

Soon thereafter, Subhas Bose began speaking to Indian prisoners of war in Germany and persuaded over four thousand to enrol in India's freedom movement by joining a newly established Indian Legion (which he preferred to call the Azad Hind Fauj, or Free India Army). Initially, the Indian POWs were hostile, but Bose's rhetoric, historical references and appeals to nationalism strongly motivated thousands to join the Azad Hind Fauj, for whom Subhas and Abid coined a unique form of nationalist greeting, 'Jai Hind!' that remains popular in today's India. Meanwhile, in October 1941, Bose established contact with the Japanese legation in Berlin and began efforts to persuade both Japan and Germany to allow him to move back to Asia so that he could more effectively coordinate the effort to foment a revolution in India. Back in India, some of the communications between Subhas and his brother Sarat (wired from Berlin to Tokyo, then delivered by the Japanese consul in Calcutta) were intercepted by the British. By December 1941, Sarat had succeeded in replacing the Krishak Praja Party–Muslim League coalition with one between his Forward Bloc and Huq's Krishak Praja Party in which Sarat himself was to become home minister, in charge of the police. But the British authorities would have none of this, and the colonial police swooped in to arrest Sarat Bose on 11 December 1941 (three days after Japan's invasion of Southeast Asia and the bombing of Pearl Harbor) with instructions from Secretary of State Leo Amery himself to ensure that Sarat would not become a minister. He languished in prison through the rest of the war, while British provincial governors sought to ensure that the Muslim League remained at the core of government in Bengal and across India, fomenting more inter-communal clashes between Muslims and Hindus.

JAPAN'S CONQUEST AND LIBERATION OF THE WEST'S ASIAN COLONIES (DECEMBER 1941–MAY 1942)

On Sunday, 7 December 1941, the world awoke to the astonishing news of Japan's attack on the US naval base of Pearl Harbor in Hawaii. By the time of the attack, it was already 8 December in Asia (across the International Date Line), although Hawaii was geographically almost equidistant from Japan as from the mainland of the US, had a plurality (well over 40 per cent) of Japanese in its population (far more than the white American proportion) and was still only a colony of the US (and was not to become a state until 1959). The Japanese navy used six aircraft carriers to launch the attack on Pearl Harbor; they damaged all eight American battleships berthed there—sinking four of them—and destroyed 188 US aircraft. Fortuitously for the US, however, all three US aircraft carriers normally stationed at Pearl Harbor were away at sea on that day and escaped the attack. They were to prove vital during the war, much more so than battleships (the importance of which the Japanese overestimated, ironically basing their thinking on the theories of the greatest nineteenth century American geostrategist, Alfred Thayer Mahan; the Americans, in turn, learnt quickly from the effectiveness of Japan's attack, and made aircraft carriers the centrepiece of their naval strategy through the rest of the war).

Although the attack on Pearl Harbor—and the near-simultaneous assaults on Malaya, the Philippines, Hong Kong, Wake, Guam and Midway, followed by the invasion of the Dutch East Indies—was brilliantly executed by Admiral

Yamamoto Isoroku, it was not an unalloyed success. Admiral Yamamoto was aware that all three US aircraft carriers were away, and the shallowness of the waters around Pearl Harbor would enable many of the sunken battleships to be salvaged (as indeed six of them were). But he went ahead nonetheless, partly because Japan was running out of supplies and time, and did not want to lose the element of surprise (lest its large naval flotilla be discovered). The lack of a knockout blow to the US navy was to prove fatal to Japan's military prospects by 1944.

President Franklin D. Roosevelt, who was to rise to great heights in prosecuting the Second World War and leading the Allies to victory, gave a brief (seven-minute) but highly effective speech to Congress the next day, starting with the famous words, 'Yesterday, December 7th 1941, a date which will live in infamy, the United States was suddenly and deliberately attacked by naval and air forces of the Empire of Japan.' A Gallup poll of Americans conducted a few weeks before the attack had found that 52 per cent believed war with Japan was imminent, but it was the 'suddenness' of the attack that Roosevelt and his administration repeatedly invoked to justify the US declaration of war on Japan within an hour after this speech. Although the precise moment and place of the attack was a surprise, the Americans were not completely unprepared for war. They were well aware that the US embargoes on oil, metals and other key supplies were throttling Japan. The US already had a significant military presence confronting Japan in China (where General Stilwell was working closely with Chiang Kai-shek), and Chennault had created an air force for China (with more than 100 aircraft supplied that year) and had three squadrons (totalling 60 aircraft) with 300 American fighter pilots and crew based in Burma (with their distinctive 'shark-faced' fighter jets that prompted the name 'Flying Tigers'). Together, they were helping to keep Chiang's regime afloat through a steady stream of supplies via the Burma Road.

Japan had been feeling the pressure from its 'ABCD encirclement' (American, British, Chinese, Dutch) right through 1941. The conquest of Manchukuo and Inner Mongolia had provided substantial supplies of coal and iron, and Japanese investment in those regions resulted in big increases in production, with 23 million tonnes of coal and 5 million tonnes of iron ore produced in 1941. About a fifth of Japan's output of pig iron and 8 per cent of its steel was coming from Manchukuo—and the southern part of this region continued to industrialize during the war years, despite the fact that war needs diverted it from the original industrial plans (and kept it from achieving envisaged targets). But oil was a key resource that Japan was short of, and it also lacked sufficient supplies of rubber, tin, tungsten and nickel—all of which were available in Southeast Asia. The US had remained Japan's main supplier of petroleum and scrap metal, but the US began to tighten the noose during the summer of 1941.

The Japanese leadership had, since 1939, been debating whether to 'defend the north, and advance south' or vice versa as it faced increasing pressure particularly from the USSR to the north. In July 1938, Japan's Kwantung Army had suffered a reverse at the hands of the Soviet army in the Battle of Lake Khasan (Changkufeng) in the Russian Far East, and had been similarly bested in the summer of 1939 at Nomonhan (Khalkhin Gol) near the Soviet border with Mongolia, as the Soviets successfully defended their territorial integrity. This induced Japan to sign the Tripartite Pact with Germany and Italy in September 1940 and a neutrality pact with the USSR in April 1941, but Japan was completely taken aback by Hitler's invasion of the Soviet Union in June 1941. At a Tokyo leadership conference in early July 1941, some leaders urged that Japan should take advantage of Soviet difficulties by attacking its vulnerable provinces in the far east, but others argued that advancing in the south (for its resources) was the greater imperative. No decision was arrived at, but on 29 July Japan decided to exercise its right (won in September 1940) to reinforce its military position in Indo-China and moved to occupy Cochin-China (the region around Saigon that was to become the core of the post-War regime of South Vietnam).

The US used this excuse to impose a freeze on Japanese assets in the US and a complete oil embargo on 1 August 1941. The Dutch followed with an embargo on oil and bauxite exports. Although officially not at war, the US had first imposed licensing for any US exports of oil and scrap metal to Japan a year earlier, imposing an embargo on scrap metal exports in September 1940, and extending it to iron and steel in November 1940 (after the US election). The new Dutch and American embargoes made war inevitable, as Japan's stockpiles (especially of oil) would otherwise run out in 1942 and an invasion of the Dutch East Indies was the only way to secure the vital raw materials that Japan needed. Prime Minister Konoe Fumimaro (descendant of the Fujiwara clan of kuge courtiers and regents to the imperial dynasty, and grandfather of Hosokawa Morihiro, who became prime minister in 1993) had spent most of 1941 trying to negotiate an agreement with the US. But Konoe's numerous attempts to call a summit meeting with Roosevelt proved futile over the summer and he steadily lost support within Japan, especially from the navy (which had previously been his ally). The latter began arguing that if Japan was to be forced into war with the US, it would be sensible to declare war as soon as possible. On 16 October 1941, Konoe resigned as prime minister, and was succeeded by his war minister Tojo Hideki. Prime Minister

Tojo continued to attempt negotiations with the US until 5 November, when it became apparent that they were futile and the die was cast for war, as both sides were aware. The Japanese sent a formal statement to the US government breaking off relations, which was supposed to be delivered just before the attack on Pearl Harbor, but did not reach the Roosevelt administration until a little after the attack (due to secretarial inefficiency).

About an hour before the attack on Pearl Harbor, a Japanese landing force had begun bombarding the beach at Kota Bharu, the capital of Kelantan in Malaya, at half past midnight on 8 December. Japanese landing craft, facing heavy artillery fire from the British Indian Army defenders of the beach (mainly the Dogra regiment), were able to land a large invasion force of Lieutenant General Yamashita Tomoyuki's 25th Army on the beaches. A separate invasion force had landed in Yala and Pattani in Thailand, agreed a truce with Phibun's Thai regime by noon, and proceeded south towards Kedah in Malaya by the end of the day. Japan's land forces, reinforced by the presence of tanks from their base in Indo-China, were able to overwhelm the stout defence of the British Indian Army units—commanded universally by British officers but with no tanks of their own—and the British and Australian air forces, which had their Malayan bases in Kota Bharu. The white officers quickly abandoned this vital airbase, leaving it to be defended by its Malay and Indian soldiers—a bizarre racist pattern of behaviour that was repeated across Malaya, undermining British prestige in East Asia.

Two days into the battle, the British Navy, which had dominated Asia's seas for two centuries, suffered its worst humiliation in Asia since the sinking of Commodore Matthews's flotilla by the Maratha admiral Kanhoji Angre in 1720. The Japanese sank Britain's vital capital ships, the Royal Navy battleship HMS *Prince of Wales* and battlecruiser HMS *Repulse*, on 10 December. The former was the British Royal Navy's most modern battleship, on which Churchill had sailed for the Atlantic conference with Roosevelt. Admiral Tom Phillips was commanding Force Z—comprising that vital battleship, a battlecruiser and four destroyers—tasked with intercepting the Japanese naval convoy bound for Malaya. Phillips had chosen not to have any air support, in order to maintain radio silence. Japanese aircraft attacked and sank the two capital ships, partly because the *Prince of Wales*'s state-of-the-art anti-aircraft high angle control system failed to function. It sank with Admiral Phillips and 840 men on board, and the *Repulse* went down soon after. Awoken by the First Sea Lord with this catastrophic news, Churchill was quick to recognize what had happened, as he wrote later: 'In all the war, I never received a more direct shock.... As I turned over and twisted in bed, the full horror of the news sank in upon me. There were no British or American ships in the Indian Ocean or the Pacific except the American survivors of Pearl Harbor.... Over all this vast expanse of waters Japan was supreme, and we everywhere were weak and naked.' British naval ascendancy over Asian waters had ended, never to be fully restored.

The defence of British Southeast Asia—Malaya and Burma—depended crucially on the 'impregnable fortress' of Singapore. The pride of this supposed fortress was the new naval base of Sembawang, ironically constructed mainly with iron and steel from the Japanese-owned iron ore mine in Johor. The decimation of Force Z suddenly made Singapore's naval position extremely vulnerable. Nearly a quarter of all British trade in Asia passed through the port of Singapore, as did 60 per cent of Australia's trade. If Singapore were to fall, Australia's position would become very fragile and Burma, India and Ceylon too would be susceptible to a Japanese attack. Britain's General Archibald Wavell and his commanders had been considering a pre-emptive strike on southern Thailand, code-named Operation Matador, but had vacillated over thus violating Thailand's neutrality, which was likely to provoke American ire too. They were well aware that the 'fortress' of Singapore could only be defended if its perimeter (Malaya) was in British hands, so the elite III Corps of the Indian army and Australian troops were assigned to the defence of northern Malaya. Singapore's 'big guns' were alleged to be facing the wrong way but their real inadequacy was that, although capable of being rotated, they only had armour-piercing shells for use against naval ships, not the high-explosive shells that could be used against infantry and artillery. And the actual number and size of these gun emplacements (many of which had been rumoured to be camouflaged in the thick forests along the edges of the island-city) was much less impressive than they were reputed to be. With its main naval squadron decimated, the vaunted guns of Singapore were redundant, and the Japanese strategy unfolded accordingly.

By 10 December, Matador was moot, as Japanese armoured forces poured into Kedah in northwestern Malaya (across the Thai border). At Jitra, where the Japanese had expected to meet a three-month-long resistance, their tanks smashed through the British defensive lines, causing confusion in their ranks and a chaotic flight southwards. Bizarrely, the British Indian Army was not equipped with any tanks in Malaya, believing that the thick jungles were 'impenetrable' by tanks—a disastrous miscalculation, because Malaya had some of the best roads in the British empire outside Britain itself. The two Indian divisions were also woefully unprepared for jungle warfare, having been hastily shipped to Malaya from north Africa: comprising mainly Rajput and Pathan soldiers, they were trained for desert warfare! Jitra fell in fifteen hours, and the Japanese commander Yamashita was soon celebrating in the captured state capital, Alor Setar. Giani Pritam Singh arrived there from Bangkok to establish a branch of the IIL, and Major Fujiwara Iwaichi recruited Captain Mohan Singh (of the 1/14 Punjab Regiment) to help form an Indian National Army (INA), which soon acquired 229 initial recruits. Mohan Singh told Fujiwara that the INA needed a charismatic leader like Subhas Bose who 'people worship... like a god' and word quickly reached Subhas about this promising new branch of the Azad Hind Fauj.

The oldest British 'fortress' in Malaya, Penang, was now within Japan's sights. On 11 December, Japanese aircraft began bombing both Singapore and Penang, but at the latter, they met almost no resistance to their reconnaissance and bombing runs. With the decimation of Force Z, Penang's naval base had been evacuated southwards—partly to Singapore, but mainly much further west to Colombo in Ceylon—and Wavell had decided to move his defensive lines south to the central area of Malaya, leaving Perak to the Japanese. The European residents of Penang were evacuated in a hasty, chaotic manoeuvre that demonstrated the racism that underpinned the British imperium: one local Chinese judge had been told he could board one of the ships, but was disallowed at the last moment; instead, the governor of the fortress ensured his own car was evacuated ahead of the Chinese judge!

Penang fell on 16 December, but there were no Europeans left in town to formally surrender, apart from a very busy doctor at the general hospital. Three days earlier, all civic functions (including traffic control) had been taken over by temporary Eurasian and Asian volunteers. It fell to M. Saravanamuttu, the editor of the local English newspaper, the *Straits Echo*, to lower the Union Jack, bringing to an unceremonious end 156 years of British rule over Penang, while a Eurasian racehorse trainer cycled across to the Japanese command centre in Sungei Patani to inform them that Penang had been abandoned and the bombing should stop. The abandoned residents of Penang were even more infuriated to hear Duff Cooper, Churchill's resident minister in Singapore (who had resigned as First Lord of the Admiralty in protest against the Munich Pact in 1938) claim on the radio that 'the majority of the population had been evacuated from Penang'—speaking with the implicit racism of Somerset Maugham's characters who overlooked the very existence of Chinese, Indians and Malays who had lived and worked alongside the British in Penang for a century and a half. Similarly, a reader of Margaret Shennan's *Out in the Midday Sun* (about British life in Malaya from 1880 to 1960) would be blissfully unaware that the vast majority of soldiers in the regiments bearing English and Scottish names that defended Malaya were, in fact, Indians!

On the same day that Penang fell to the Japanese, so did the two vital oilfields of Miri (in Sarawak) and Seria (in Brunei) in British-controlled Borneo.

A Japanese naval convoy that had set off on 13 December from Cam Ranh Bay in French Indo-China secured the two oilfields by dawn on 16 December 1941. Sarawak had a uniquely colourful history, having been ruled for a century by the 'White Rajahs'—the Brooke family, who had been ceded control of Sarawak in 1842 by the Sultan of Brunei as a reward for help in crushing a rebellion by the indigenous Iban and Bidayuh tribes. James Brooke, a British adventurer born outside Benares in India, had resigned from the East India Company's army and arrived in Kuching in 1838 with a ship, some inherited money and plenty of gumption. James Brooke befriended the Rajah Muda (crown prince) of Brunei, and aided him in fighting both the tribal rebellion and the widespread threat of 'piracy' and was rewarded in September 1841 by being made Rajah of Sarawak. The position was initially akin to governor, but by August 1842 also included a large grant of land (substantially more than what remained with Brunei itself), after James Brooke helped restore the sultan to the throne of Brunei (with the help of part of Britain's China squadron). The Brookes had become absolute rulers of Sarawak, with a loose affiliation to the British empire, which was cemented by the gift of Labuan Island to the British (who made it a Crown Colony) in 1846, and a treaty of 'protection' (akin to that signed by other Malay sultans/rajahs) in 1888. In the same year, Brunei itself also became a protectorate—explicitly requesting that status because the White Rajahs had been acquiring or leasing more and more of Brunei's territory; the British did little, however, when the Brookes acquired another small piece of Brunei in 1890, although that proved to be the last.

North Borneo (Sabah) had also become a British protectorate in 1888, but was otherwise thoroughly under the corporate control of the British North Borneo Company. Sabah's fortunes rose and ebbed with rubber, while Brunei was primarily an oil economy (then as now) driven mainly by Shell, and Sarawak had both oil and rubber. The North Borneo Company's fortunes had taken a severe hit during the global Depression as rubber prices collapsed, and it fell to the Japanese with virtually no resistance. Brunei too fell without a fight, but the Sultan and his administrative machinery (including the secretary to the British Resident) refused to be evacuated, and largely cooperated with the Japanese in administering Brunei during the course of the war.

The third White Rajah of Sarawak, Charles Vyner Brooke, had rejected Straits Settlements governor Cecil Clementi's plans in the early 1930s for a confederation of British Borneo (including Sabah, Brunei, Sarawak and Labuan), and expressed abhorrence towards even tentative suggestions of a broader customs union covering all of British Malaya and Borneo. (The North Borneo Company, on the other hand, had been willing to be bought out for £1 million.) In early 1941, however, Rajah Vyner had sprung a surprise by introducing an element of representative government into the 'most absolute monarchy in the world'—although his motivation for doing so was primarily to circumscribe his purported successor, the Rajah Muda Anthony (his nephew), whose vigorous administrative reforms in the late 1930s had won him plaudits from the bureaucracy. The Rajah had taken $2 million (£200,000) from the kingdom's treasury in exchange for this constitutional change, although the new Supreme Council still had a clear British majority, and the indigenous representatives were non-elected. In November 1941, the Rajah had left for Australia, with Anthony still in limbo and Sarawak's international position somewhat ambiguous. While it was recognized as a sovereign power, Britain sent a representative to fill the constitutional void and take over Sarawak's foreign affairs. Earlier in 1941, about a thousand soldiers from the Punjab Regiment had been posted to help bolster a similar number from the Sarawak Rangers that the Rajah had created as the only military force within his territory. When the Japanese invaders arrived, this notional defence force proved entirely inadequate, and Sarawak was overrun by the Japanese within a week, although some of the doughty Punjabis continued a guerrilla resistance from the jungles for another couple of months. And crucially, the British (aided by the Punjabis) had succeeded in filling most of the oil wells of Miri and Brunei with cement—thus disabling much of Borneo's oil supply, which only returned to about half its pre-War production levels over the course of the next year.

The British decided to adopt a scorched earth policy as they evacuated any part of Malaya, often to the detriment of Chinese entrepreneurs, who had spent decades creating some of the businesses and assets that were now to be abandoned or destroyed. And Britain's Indian and Australian troops were constantly on the retreat, as the Japanese steadily gained ground. As they rattled down the Malay Peninsula on their bicycles, people often mistook the sound for that of tanks; Japan's actual tanks did, in any case, give their troops a decisive advantage on the battlefield. On 11 January 1942, the capital of the Federated Malay States, Kuala Lumpur, fell to the Japanese, as did the industrial heartland of Selangor. Wavell had withdrawn his troops to Johor, where they hoped to make a last, stronger stand against the Japanese advance, while he himself moved his own headquarters to Java in preparation for the coming assault on the Dutch East Indies.

In contrast to Singapore and Penang, Hong Kong had no pretensions to being a British fortress—impregnable or otherwise! It was well known that the defence of Hong Kong needed robust British control of the New Territories, over which Britain's lease only ran until 1997. Once Guangzhou

(Canton) fell to the Japanese in 1938, Hong Kong's vulnerability increased. At a minimum, Britain needed to considerably reinforce its military presence in the New Territories if a Japanese attack was to be deterred or repulsed. But Britain was unwilling to militarily reinforce territory over which its hold was so tenuous. In 1935, there had been some suggestion that Britain should attempt to turn its ninety-nine-year lease over the New Territories into a permanent freehold arrangement, but its putative interlocutors, the KMT, were soon distracted by the Xian Incident and the war with Japan.

Hong Kong society on the eve of war was even more racist than that of Malaya, with divide and rule taken to extremes. The local Chinese were at the very bottom of the social heap, deeply distrusted by the British, who preferred to use Indians (mainly Sikhs, and some Gurkhas) to police Hong Kong. All managerial staff at British-owned banks, industrial companies, and the colonial bureaucracy were Europeans, with Eurasians permitted to be clerks, and the local Chinese not employed in any roles other than as manual labour. The small military garrison in Hong Kong consisted of mainly British, Australian, Portuguese and Indian troops and the Chinese, even if they were recruited as police constables, were rarely allowed to bear arms. Only Europeans were allowed to enter the Peak (the literal height of society in Hong Kong). Non-Europeans were not permitted to lease property on the Peak, with Chinese permitted to enter only to deliver goods (and this they could only do by walking up the perilously steep slope, not taking the tram which was limited to Europeans).

The Mid-Levels were for Eurasians, Portuguese and middle-class Britishers (including Scottish traders), while the Chinese were confined to the lowest reaches (and usually lived in Kowloon and beyond). Similarly, the first-class upper tier on the ferry between Central and Kowloon was reserved only for Europeans, with Chinese only allowed in second and third class below. Like in India, only a thin sliver of the elite was given access to a modern education (at the Queen's College, and later the University of Hong Kong) and this tiny group of loyal anglicized Chinese stood just below the British and Eurasians in the social hierarchy. The British strongly disapproved of miscegenation, and admission into clubs (such as the jockey and yacht clubs) was strictly regulated by race (with no non-Europeans being allowed as members until the late 1920s, when a small number of Eurasians and Chinese were admitted into the Jockey Club).

Some Eurasians were able to break the glass ceiling, simply by virtue of the wealth they had accumulated, after taking advantage of the educational opportunities that were made slightly more available to them than to the local Chinese (and especially recent immigrants from China). Robert Ho Tung and Robert Kotewall were two Eurasians who had, by virtue of their wealth, been allowed into the upper echelons of Hong Kong society, including taking the two seats on the Legislative Council that were opened to locals. Robert Ho Tung was sufficiently successful in business to have circumvented the law against non-Europeans renting property on the Peak by *buying* a bungalow there instead! Kotewall was, strictly speaking, not a Eurasian as his father was Parsi and his mother Chinese. But his looks gave him Eurasian status, and he rose to be chief clerk in the colonial secretariat before resigning to embark on a successful business career. They served as key intermediaries between the British rulers and their Chinese subjects—some of whom, despite all the restrictions, had successfully established textile businesses, world class shoe export houses and banks (such as the Bank of East Asia) that served the Chinese community effectively.

The Anglo–Japanese Treaty of 1902 had been the basis for considerable economic engagement between Japan and Hong Kong, with many British officials spending holidays in the cool mountains of Japan and a small but growing community of Japanese businesses establishing themselves in Hong Kong, resulting in a community of about 1,500 Japanese in Hong Kong by the late 1930s (compared with half a million Chinese there). The problem of where to accommodate these Asiatic peoples from an emerging great power was solved by allowing the Japanese to live in the lower reaches of Mid-Levels (on McDonnell Road or below). Additionally there was a growing community of Taiwanese (nominally citizens of Japan too) who operated successfully in Hong Kong, fitting into local society despite speaking a dialect (Hokkien) that was considerably different from the Cantonese spoken by Hong Kongers. But Japan was able to use its community of Japanese and Taiwanese residents to establish a successful espionage network in Hong Kong—reinforced by strengthening ties with the Triads (both in Hong Kong and in Canton) who were willing to cooperate with a power hostile to their own enemy, Britain. Of particular value here was a Triad with 5,000 members who had been expelled by the British to Macao, and were particularly keen to join hands with the Japanese and gradually find their way back to Hong Kong.

The Japanese air force began the assault on Hong Kong at 8.20 a.m. on 8 December 1941, starting with an attack on Kai Tak Airport and, within the first five minutes, had destroyed Hong Kong's few operable fighter aircraft— three ageing torpedo bombers and a couple of flying boats. The British had 12,000 troops in Hong Kong—mainly Sikhs, Gurkhas, Rajputs and some Scots, recently reinforced by a French-speaking Canadian battalion, who could barely communicate with the rest of the troops. Hong Kong's defences had been built on the assumption that any attack was likeliest to come from the sea, so twenty-nine of its heaviest guns pointed south and could provide no support to the infantry. Most of the British troops were concentrated on Hong Kong Island itself, but the first line of defence was the 'Gin Drinkers' Line' in the southern part of the New Territories (just north of Kowloon), a fortified warren of tunnels and trenches that was expected to hold back any assault for six months. Although the size of Japan's invading force of 15,000 was not much larger than the British troop presence, Japanese scouts soon discovered that the Shing Mun Redoubt (which could hold as many as 120 troops, and was supposed to be the line's headquarters) was a weak area with just 30 soldiers and the Japanese poured into this area on 9 December. Major General Christopher Maltby decided at noon on the 10th that it would be impossible to hold the Gin Drinkers' Line, and decided to withdraw all troops to the main island of Hong Kong itself, leaving only the Rajput Battalion to fight a rearguard action for a further three days.

With the decision to retreat into Hong Kong Island, all European (including Portuguese) residents of Kowloon were evacuated to the main island, and ferry crossings between Kowloon and Central were then closed down. This caused enormous outrage amongst the Chinese residents of Kowloon, who were both denied access to their jobs and bank accounts on Hong Kong Island, and also stranded defenceless in their homes in Kowloon. A full-scale insurrection broke out amongst the Chinese residents of Kowloon, partly instigated by the pro-Japanese partisans of Wang Jingwei and their Triad allies. Medical workers, police constables, hotel staff and street cleaners all joined the rebellion, and by the time the final British–Indian troops (from the Punjab Regiment) were evacuated from Kowloon on the morning of 12 December, they did so amid a hail of bullets from arms that had been abandoned by previous groups of police and army units leaving in haste. The KMT admiral on Hong Kong offered to help the British defend the island, but the latter were reluctant to provide additional ammunition to the KMT garrison for fear of losing moral authority over their colony. The British had always been squeamish about arming the local population, and they remained reluctant to hand ammunition to any group of Chinese partisans even in the teeth of the rapid Japanese advance. Hopes were briefly lifted by news of possible KMT troop reinforcements, but the inordinate delay in their arrival was mired in continuing disputes over how much ammunition the British would be willing to provide them. Eventually, in the early afternoon of Christmas Eve, the British finally agreed to provide adequate ammunition and Robert Kotewall sent a cable to Chiang Kai-shek requesting troops.

But by then, the British resistance was crumbling. The Japanese were already in control of Wan Chai, the area immediately west of the main business district, and were launching a relentless barrage of artillery and aerial bombardment of Victoria. Governor Mark Aitchison Young was determined to follow Churchill's instruction to 'fight to the last man', but General Maltby had had enough by the evening of Christmas Day 1941, and the military's view prevailed. He and Young gave themselves up to the Japanese at Wan Chai, and were taken by motor boat to the Japanese headquarters at the Peninsula Hotel in Kowloon—where the Japanese conquest of Hong Kong was completed in a candlelit surrender ceremony, ending approximately a century of British rule.

The KMT's one-legged admiral on Hong Kong, Chan Chak, managed to escape with the help of a British launch and torpedo boat and eventually was able to join up at Huizhou in Guangdong province with the general who was leading the KMT relief force meant to come to Hong Kong's aid. The dispute about how much ammunition the British would part with was one factor that had stalled the advance of this KMT force, but a second was a Japanese attack from the rear, aimed primarily at capturing Changsha, which had diverted the KMT army's attention after 13 December. After news of the British surrender, the KMT army abandoned its effort to provide relief to Hong Kong on 30 December, partly also because Chan Chak insisted that Churchill had urged Young to surrender to the Japanese as this would be more likely to enable Britain to regain Hong Kong after the war than if Hong Kong were to be rescued by a Chinese Nationalist army.

In the immediate aftermath of the conquest of Hong Kong, the city was subjected to a week-long orgy of looting and violence, beginning with the Triads, who were essentially given free rein over the city for the first twenty-four hours (before military authority was established fully by the Japanese on 26 December evening). During the conquest of Hong Kong Island, the Japanese soldiers had been angered by the doggedness of the resistance, and had responded with violence towards civilians—including awful atrocities in the hospitals. A few days into the occupation, nine Japanese soldiers were executed on account of those atrocities but looting persisted until the first few days of January 1942, with the Chinese in Kowloon suffering most from random violence and looting by a combination of Triad members and Japanese soldiers. Although the Japanese soldiers had been given strict orders not to repeat the atrocities and misbehaviour that had besmirched the conquest of Nanjing and other cities in China, it proved difficult to enforce this in the early days after the conquest. Besides, valuables like metal from statues, iron gates, etc., were shipped to Japan, and other valuable supplies (like six months' supply of rice for the expected siege) were expropriated for use in Hong Kong, Japan and elsewhere. By mid-January 1942, however, Major General

Yazaki Kanju, the intelligence chief of the Japanese forces in Hong Kong (and himself a disciple of Ishiwara Kanji, the military ideologue of Japan's 1931 invasion of Manchuria, who had later become the leading advocate of an attempted accommodation with Chiang Kai-shek) began a charm offensive to undo the damage done by the initial atrocities, and return to the ideas and practice of the Asian values that supposedly underpinned the Greater East Asian Co-prosperity Sphere. The English language and Cantonese newspapers began to highlight ways in which the British had discriminated against locals, and the Japanese began to invite groups of local citizens to banquets where they were promised substantially better treatment.

This charm offensive gained more momentum with the arrival of Isogai Rensuke, the new Japanese governor of Hong Kong, at the beginning of February. Isogai had a rather inglorious military career (commanding his troops to defeat in Nomonhan and elsewhere in north China), but spoke some Cantonese, was an expert calligrapher in Chinese, and was rumoured to have known Sun Yat-sen well in his Canton and Tokyo days. Even before Isogai's arrival, the Japanese commander General Sakai Takashi had organized a series of luncheons for groups of potentially sympathetic locals, starting on 8 January 1942 with Hong Kongers who had been educated in Japan (and could thus serve as interpreters between the Japanese and the locals). Two days later, Sakai organized a grand lunch banquet in the Rose Room of the Peninsula Hotel for 137 of the local 'gentry' (Chinese notables)—of whom 133 actually attended.

Sir Robert Kotewall and Sir Shouson Chow, the two leading gentry figures, gave speeches of fulsome praise for their new Japanese overlords, and were soon assimilated into the new leadership group for Hong Kong, with their names suitably Asianized or Sinified: Robert Kotewall became Lo Kuk-wo and Sir Shouson saw a milder change to Chow Shou-son. And the Japanese were especially solicitous to the minority communities: the Punjabi and Rajput troops, and the large numbers of Indian police officers (who had been disdained by almost all inhabitants of Hong Kong previously) were given access to special rations as well as large pay hikes, and were reminded of how the British had fled their posts with such alacrity and left the Indian soldiers to make a last stand across the island (with disrespectful neglect of their war dead). Eurasians too received similarly special treatment, as the Japanese sought to win over the local middle class, while humiliating the English former ruling classes—who were frequently marched through the streets of Hong Kong to banks and other posts, and made to hand over their roles to local successors. On 25 February 1942, a large reception was organized for Hong Kong's Asian elites to welcome Isogai as the new governor, which gave many Chinese, Indians and Eurasians the first opportunity ever to enter some of the hallowed portals of Hong Kong's society that had previously been exclusively open to Europeans. Joyrides up and down the elevator in the HSBC building became a favourite activity for non-European locals.

Governor Young and the British notables made initial entreaties to persuade the Japanese to let them serve their internment in the luxurious environs of the Peak. They received a rude shock when it became clear that the Japanese wished to bring them very much down to earth, and show the local populace that there was nothing exalted about Europeans, and Asians could do just as well if given a chance. Consequently, local notables replaced the British across the length and breadth of government, giving many Hong Kongers their first opportunity to partake fully in the administration of their own affairs. Apart from the regular humiliations (including occasionally having Britishers pull Chinese customers on rickshaws, with the local populace frequently being presented with the spectacle of a long line of former British notables being marched to various menial tasks), the British faced a geostrategic challenge too by the end of 1942. Madame Chiang Kai-shek wrote in the *New York Times* that the British and Dutch capitulation in Asia contrasted markedly with the doggedness of the Chinese resistance to Japan over several years (which was still continuing); consequently, she argued, China should be treated as a great power at least on par with the effete British.

This was an argument that found resonance in the US, reinforcing Stilwell's disdain for the British (who, he claimed, were still drinking their gin and tonics, and spending lazy days playing golf while Burma and Malaya fell rapidly to the Japanese). Specifically, China used the opportunity to get the Western powers to repudiate extraterritoriality and their special rights in the treaty ports of China (almost all of which were then under Japanese occupation). Most piquantly for the British, China demanded during the negotiations that Hong Kong's New Territories be included amongst those ports over which Western powers were relinquishing rights. Although Hong Kong had been given to Britain in perpetuity, the Japanese invasion had shown again that it was militarily impossible to hold Hong Kong without the New Territories. Although many in the US were urging that Hong Kong too should be included, Chiang Kai-shek agreed not to specifically name the New Territories in the treaty, partly because he was confident that, at the end of the war, the KMT rather than the British was much more likely to be capable of liberating Hong Kong from the Japanese.

Meanwhile, the Japanese advance through Malaya proceeded apace—moving southwards from Kuala Lumpur and Selangor in the second half of January 1942, steadily gaining ground in the vast southern state of Johor.

Educated Malays were quick to note that 'Malaya' seemed to refer just to the British residents of the area, and Malays were simply being abandoned. Amongst the outraged was Abdul Razak Hussein, who would become the second prime minister of Malaysia in the 1970s but was then a student at Singapore's prestigious Raffles College. Remarking on the fact that Malays were simply being ignored in all the discussions about the war (despite having two battalions and many other volunteers serving in the British Army in the region), Abdul Razak left for his home in Pahang, along with thousands of other Asians who moved north to their homes now under Japanese rather than British occupation, increasingly recognizing the latter for what it was. British rule over the Malay states was based on treaties of 'protection' signed between the Malay sultans and the British, but the latter were plainly incapable of fulfilling their obligation to 'protect'. The British attempted to hustle some of their favoured sultans away to India, but they all refused to leave. The ailing Sultan of Kedah was one who was vulnerable, as his son (the regent) appeared ready to acquiesce on his father's behalf, but the regent's brother Tunku Abdul Rahman (himself a district officer in the British service) intervened to take his father away to a 'kampong' (village) where he was placed in the care and protection of the villagers.

Sultan Ibrahim of Johor refused to leave his palace, ordered that there should be no destruction of assets within a twelve-mile radius of his capital of Johor Bahru, and prohibited British artillery from firing at his administration building. The British were suspicious of his sympathies, but all their intelligence reports suggested that he remained intent on maintaining the integrity of his state without taking sides (despite past business dealings with Japan). Indian and Australian troops put up a stout defence at Muar and further south at Batu Pahat and Mersing, but by 27 January General Arthur Percival received permission from Wavell (the overall commander of the ABDACOM, American–British–Dutch–Australian Command) to withdraw from Johor, causing a massive traffic jam on the causeway to Singapore, as some 85,000 troops and civilians attempted to cross into the island-fortress. Once they had crossed over into Singapore by 31 January, an attempt was made to blow up the causeway, but only making a relatively small seventy-foot hole, in an area where it was possible to wade across. The battle for Malaya was over, with 50,000 Commonwealth troops killed or captured. When the explosion from the causeway was heard in Singapore, the principal of Raffles College asked students nearby what that might be and the brightest of the lot replied, 'That is the end of the British Empire.' That young man's name was Harry Lee Kuan Yew.

General Yamashita had been accompanied by Tokugawa Yoshichika, a scion of the last shogun family who was a good friend of Sultan Ibrahim. They were welcomed into the Istana Bukit Serene (royal palace) in Johor, which stood atop a hill from which a magnificent view was available of Singapore. From there, Yamashita plotted the invasion of Singapore while carrying out an aerial and artillery bombardment of the island. Percival concentrated his forces in the northeast of the island, expecting that to be the likeliest focus of any Japanese invasion. But Yamashita, with just 30,000 troops available, marshalled his limited forces much better—outflanking Percival by coming ashore with some 5,000 troops in the lightly-patrolled northwest on 7 and 8 February 1942, using the causeway too (to bring cycles ashore) and a surprise smaller landing in the southwest, where they fought pitched battles with the 44th Indian Infantry Brigade. The Australian troops manning the northwest of Singapore were easily overrun by late on 8 February, as their communications lines with the rest of the island had already been severely disrupted by the earlier bombing, and their supplies were running thin too. The airfields of Seletar, Sembawang and Tengah were within range of Japanese artillery fire from Johor Bahru, so all ten of the British Hurricane fighter aircraft were forced to use Kallang airfield near the heart of the city. They gamely engaged in dogfights with a squadron of eighty-four Japanese bombers during the first twenty-four hours, but by 9 February Percival decided to withdraw his remaining eight aircraft to Palembang in Sumatra, where the Allies were assembling the strongest possible naval and air defences. Kallang airfield itself was pitted with bombs and was no longer usable by this point.

The loss of communication led to some of the Australian troops being removed from Kranji in the north of the island, just west of the causeway. Here, the Japanese were able to bring tanks—with buoyancy aids—ashore unopposed, and they rapidly advanced into the heart of Singapore on Woodlands Road on 10 February, outflanking the 22nd Brigade that was holding the Jurong Line and the 11th Indian Division which was defending the naval base. Citing the examples of the doughty Russians, and the Americans who were so 'stubborn at Luzon', Churchill cabled Wavell that day: 'There must at this stage be no thought of saving the troops or sparing the population. The battle must be fought to the bitter end at all costs.... Commanders and senior officers should die with their troops. The honour of the British Empire and of the British Army is at stake. I rely on you to show no mercy to weakness in any form.'

The following day, however, the Japanese forces captured Bukit Timah and the area around it—which gave them control over most of Singapore's water supply, and much of the Allies' fuel and ammunition. A Malay platoon led by Second Lieutenant Adnan Saidi held off the Japanese for two days at the Battle of Pasir Panjang, but the Allied forces were by this point confined in a narrow area on the southeast of the island, within the precincts of the city of Singapore itself. Any further fighting would involve brutal urban combat with substantial civilian casualties. Yamashita, ironically, was wary of street-to-street combat too—as his supply lines were severely depleted, and he knew he was outnumbered three to one.

But the Allies were far more vulnerable, with a million people (more than nine-tenths of them helpless civilians) tightly packed into a narrow urban space with diminished supplies of food, water and fuel that were controlled largely by the Japanese, who also had complete air superiority over Singapore. Churchill's admonition to fight to the last man was, in fact, a reckless and imprudent order for the mass suicide of several hundred thousand Chinese, Malay and Indian residents of Singapore (and some 85,000 Europeans, including those who had fled to Singapore from all over Malaya). On the morning of 15 February, Percival called his senior staff and commanders to a conference at Fort Canning to decide on the best course of action—and the consensus was that surrender was the only option.

Ordering the destruction of all important documents, secret papers, codes, and heavy guns, Percival prepared to surrender, which he was eventually obliged to do that evening at the Ford Motor Factory building in upper Bukit Timah Road. At a little after 5.15 p.m. that day, Japan's rising sun flag was raised over the tallest building in Singapore, and some 80,000 British, Indian, Australian and Malayan troops were taken prisoner—to add to the 50,000 taken during the Battle of Malaya—in what Churchill dubbed the 'worst disaster' and 'largest capitulation' in British military history. In an infamous scuttle, Major General Gordon Bennett (the commander of the Australian forces in Singapore) handed charge to a brigadier, took some of his senior staff officers and escaped on a boat; most of them did eventually make it to Australia via the East Indies, but his soldiers were left to their fates.

At Farrer Park on 17 February, Colonel J. C. Hunt brusquely told 45,000 Indian soldiers (including officers) that they were now in Japan's captivity and must follow Japanese orders; having said that, Hunt left to join his British colleagues incarcerated in Changi. Fujiwara then spoke soothingly, saying 'the Japanese Army will treat you not as POWs but as friends', and Japan was committed to helping India's freedom struggle if the soldiers pledged their allegiance to Mother India and joined the INA. He received a rapturous response, and British intelligence estimated that 40,000 of the 45,000 Indian POWs joined the INA shortly thereafter. On 19 February, the people of India heard a familiar voice speaking to them over the 'Azad Hind Radio' from Berlin, shedding his identity as Mazzotta and identifying himself as Subhas

Chandra Bose, with the prophetic words: 'The fall of Singapore means the collapse of the British Empire, the end of the iniquitous regime which it has symbolized and the dawn of a new era in Indian history. Through India's liberation will Asia and the world move forward towards the larger goal of human emancipation.'

Singapore's Chinese majority was not so lucky. It was well known to the Japanese that a significant proportion of Singapore's Chinese community had been closely tied to both Chiang Kai-shek's regime, and latterly to the communists, and that many of them had provided monetary and other forms of assistance to both Japan's mortal enemies in China. As they had no intelligence about who exactly amongst the Chinese was a KMT or CCP sympathizer, the needle of suspicion initially fell on the whole community and the Japanese (including the Korean soldiers in their ranks) behaved with great brutality towards the Chinese in Singapore (and, to a more limited extent, the rest of Malaya). Many thousands of Chinese were gratuitously murdered in the notorious Sook Ching massacre in Singapore. My former work colleague, Chia Tse Chern, told me how his grandfather was taken away and never heard from again, and such tragic stories remain etched in family histories across Singapore to this day. Many Chinese in Malaya naturally gravitated towards the only significant resistance movement to the Japanese, the communist-dominated Malayan Peoples' Anti-Japanese Army (MPAJA) led by Chin Peng. Towards the end of the war, this led to inter-ethnic violence between Malays and Chinese amid food shortages and a scramble for land ownership.

The Japanese were to foster nationalism in Java, but they were less supportive of Ibrahim Yaacob's KMM in the initial years. Despite this, Dato Onn bin Jaafar, the founder of the United Malays National Organization (UMNO) later remarked: 'Under the Japanese I learnt that an Asian is just as good as a European.... [The Japanese] were brutal, true, but they inspired us with a new idea of what Asia might become.' And, by redrawing the map of the region—including Sumatra and Malaya in a single entity ruled from Syonan (as Singapore was renamed by the Japanese)—they indirectly fostered the KMM's notion of 'Indonesia Raya' (Greater Indonesia). Malay pride was hurt later, in 1943, when the four northern Unfederated Malay States were returned to Thai sovereignty (as a reward for the latter's loyalty). In 1945, some prominent Malays (including Abdul Razak Hussein) joined the Allies' secretive Force 136 guerrilla organization to aid in a future reinvasion of Malaya by the British. But in July 1945, the Japanese finally endorsed the idea of Malay autonomy within Greater Indonesia, and Ibrahim Yaacob was allowed to meet Sukarno and Hatta to make plans for a revolutionary organization called KRIS (Kekuatan Rakyat Indonesia Istimewa, or Indonesian

Peoples' Special Force) that would work closely with Pembela Tanah Air (PETA, Indonesian Volunteer Army) and the MPAJA guerrillas to defy any attempts at an Allied invasion. After the nuclear bombs fell on Hiroshima and Nagasaki, however, recriminations rather than unity occurred between the MPAJA and KRIS, and the former began attacking all Japanese 'collaborators', including the mainly Malay police force. This worsened race relations in Malaya, and Ibrahim Yaacob himself fled to Indonesia, where he spent the rest of his days.

◆

Six hours after the attack on Pearl Harbor, Japanese aircraft also began a bombardment of Manila and other urban centres in the Philippines, which had, since 1935, been called a 'Commonwealth' rather than a colony of the US (the status that Puerto Rico continues to retain even today). Within an hour and a half, the Japanese bombardment had destroyed more than half the American bomber fleet and most of its aircraft on the crucial island of Luzon. Field Marshal Douglas MacArthur (the second generation of his family to have spent much of his career there, and the first US general ever given five stars) had relocated to the Philippines as military adviser to President Manuel Quezon of the new commonwealth (from his previous job as chief of the US Army, during which he had frequently clashed with FDR over the latter's allegedly pusillanimous attitude towards communist infiltration and other threats). In July 1941, MacArthur was appointed chief of the new US Army Far East Command—encompassing both US troops and the fledgling Philippines Army (comprising about 200,000 troops trained mainly under his own tutelage) to counter the threat from Japan's growing presence in Indo-China. During the summer of 1941, Quezon (believing that the Pentagon was about to abandon the Philippines) had started making peace overtures to the Japanese—offering to stay neutral in any war—but his spine was considerably strengthened when his close friend MacArthur received this vast new military command.

During the crucial hours after he heard about the attack on Pearl Harbor, however, General MacArthur's response was woefully inadequate. In the preceding weeks, he had started an ambitious (but still incomplete) troop redeployment to defend the whole archipelago, rather than stick to his previous 'Plan Orange' aimed mainly at holding Manila Bay. In the hours before the Japanese attack, MacArthur made no contingency arrangements to revert to Plan Orange—and the effectiveness of the bombardment gave Japan complete air superiority over the Philippines by the end of the first day of bombing. Over the next few days, most US ships (apart from submarines) were forced to retreat southwards from the main Philippine naval base at Cavite, and the Japanese began to land troops on beaches that were inadequately defended. These sporadic beach landings preceded the main invasion on 22 December 1941 by Japan's 14th Imperial Army led by Lieutenant General Homma Masaharu. With Japan's air and sea superiority well established by this stage, supply lines to the Philippines were largely cut off. On 24 December, MacArthur activated 'Plan Orange–3', to evacuate most of his forces to Bataan and Corregidor (at the mouth of Manila Bay), and to declare Manila an 'open city' on 26 December, which resulted in an orgy of looting in the abandoned capital—until some order was restored a week later, once Japanese troops had occupied the city.

In 1935, while the British were passing an act providing some provincial autonomy in India (but retaining autocratic control at the national level), the US finally acted upon the 1916 Jones Act that had promised Filipino sovereignty 'as soon as a stable government can be established therein'. While the Republicans held the White House (from 1921 to January 1933), there was very little progress on Filipino sovereignty—and this obduracy helped the Nacionalista Party leaders Manuel Quezon and Sergio Osmeña to bolster their support with rhetoric (while quietly continuing secret negotiations). Quezon had secretly agreed a twenty-year transition period, but when Osmeña negotiated an agreement that was passed by the US Congress in 1933 promising independence in ten years—with the status of a self-governing commonwealth in the intervening years—Quezon led the campaign opposing it, ensuring that it failed to be ratified by the Philippines Congress. Instead, Quezon (as Senate president) led a delegation to Washington and secured the Tydings–McDuffie Act of 1934: this specified a two-year period within which a constitution was to be drafted for the Philippines (to be ratified by the US president and the people of the Philippines), and a ten-year transition period as a commonwealth before becoming a separate and self-governing nation in 1946. In the intervening years, the US would retain its military presence and would have the right to call on all Philippine armed personnel—and there would be a two-year period after independence during which naval and other basing rights would be negotiated. Filipinos were immediately to be classified as non-Americans, with a quota of fifty immigrants per year! Having secured this credible timetable for independence, Quezon united with Osmeña to run on a joint ticket for the newly-created presidency of the Commonwealth of the Philippines—defeating the ageing lion of the original war of independence (1898–1901), Emilio Aguinaldo.

President Franklin Roosevelt was proud of these constitutional reforms, and cited them as the reason why the Filipinos had mobilized in support of their colonizers far more effectively than the citizens of Britain's and Holland's colonies. The Dutch East Indies had a Volksraad (People's Council) since 1918, although only thirty of its sixty members comprised indigenous people—while twenty-five were selected from amongst the Europeans who comprised 0.5 per cent of the population, and five from amongst Chinese (2 per cent of the population) and other minorities. The Volksraad initially had only an advisory role, but after 1925 it became a semi-legislative body (members being elected to four-year terms by a very small electorate), with the Dutch Governor General enjoined to consult it on all major issues. But despite the 'ethical policy', which had opened up educational and social opportunities for a small slice of the indigenous elite, the administration of the East Indies was still heavily dominated by the Dutch and 'Indos' (or Eurasians), with very little indigenous representation. Some prominent locals did get elected to the Volksraad (including the Javanese Tjokroaminoto, the founder of Sarekat Islam, the fountainhead of all three streams of Indonesian nationalism, and M. H. Thamrin, as well as the Sumatran Agus Salim, foreign minister of Indonesia after 1947). But, as beautifully evoked in Pramoedya Ananta Toer's novel *Bumi Manusia* (*This Earth of Mankind*) and the rest of his Buru Quartet, an elaborate racist hierarchy characterized Dutch colonial society, with marriage to the Dutch depriving a woman of status in local society while giving her little legitimacy amongst the Dutch. The Indos were beginning to clamour for greater political rights in the 1930s despite comprising only about 0.4 per cent of the population, and already having substantial representation in the Volksraad.

When, in 1936, the Soetardjo Petition (formulated by Soetardjo Kartohadikusumo) was introduced in the Volksraad, it passed (by twenty-six votes to twenty, albeit with several abstentions which prevented a majority in favour) but was summarily rejected in November 1938 by the Dutch, who argued that the Indonesians were not 'ready' for self-government, even within the Dutch commonwealth. This had led in 1939 to the formation of an Indonesian Political Federation (GAPI), comprising all political parties other than the PNI (whose leader, Sukarno, was still jailed). After the German invasion of Poland, GAPI again called for an independent Indonesia (while retaining a link to the Netherlands), but this too was rejected. In January 1941, some of GAPI's leaders were arrested for passing information to the incoming Japanese. Prominent amongst these was T. H. Thamrin, who had close ties with many Japanese businessmen operating in the East Indies; he was placed under house arrest on 6 January 1941, and died in Dutch custody five days later, just as the invasion began.

By contrast, the Philippines had a duly elected president (Quezon) and vice president (Osmeña), and an elected Congress. Despite MacArthur's support, FDR had denied President Quezon the twenty-one gun salute he wanted at his inauguration (being limited to nineteen guns because of his nation's status as a Commonwealth of the US, rather than a fully sovereign state). And the new 200,000-strong Philippines Army was still very much under the tutelage and control of the Americans (even if MacArthur thought of himself as almost a Filipino, on his fourth tour of duty there). But commonwealth status within the US certainly gave the people of the Philippines much greater say in the running of their country than the people of Iraq or Egypt enjoyed under the British definition of 'independence' at that time, and vastly more than India had been granted after the 1937 election (which only gave a limited degree of provincial autonomy, itself abridged further once the war began and the provincial governments resigned). In the British colonies of Malaya (including Singapore) and Hong Kong, there was no pretence of self-government at all.

The two factions of the Nacionalista Party of Quezon and Osmeña had won a clear victory in the 1934 congressional elections, but they still faced a revolt from a more radical party, the Sakdalistas led by Benigno Ramos, who demanded immediate and complete independence from the US, and a radical reform of land tenure, including an 'investigation of religious lands'. Ramos had established a Tagalog newspaper called *Sakdal* ('to accuse' in Tagalog) in 1930, which had gained great popularity in rural areas. The Sakdalistas ran candidates in the 1934 election, and won all three of the congressional seats that they ran for, as well as a few surprising victories for municipal offices in Cavite, Rizal and other areas near Manila. Although they were still a small minority party, the surprise victories gave the Sakdalista movement great prestige and the critique of the Tydings–McDuffie Act (especially its eleven-year time table to independence) in *Sakdal* gained substantially greater credence with the public. It was partly to counter the growing clout of the Sakdalistas that Quezon and Osmeña united for the presidential campaign of 1935, and the Americans threw their support behind their illustrado allies by stifling the circulation of *Sakdal*, and requiring that public meetings could only be held with a government permit. Ramos had visited the US in 1934 to try and forestall the Tydings–McDuffie Act and, when that failed, he visited Japan to seek support for his campaign for complete independence. In April 1935, he was able to partly circumvent the attempted stifling of *Sakdal*'s circulation by printing broadsheets in Japan and having them widely distributed in Manila and rural Luzon.

On 2 May 1935, the Sakdalistas planned a massive uprising and 68,000 protesters thronged key areas with a plan to march on several municipal centres. They were hoping that the police would be sympathetic to them and some had been led to believe that Japan would intervene if the colonial authorities cracked down. Instead, sixty-nine protesters were killed and about a thousand others injured in the harsh police crackdown that crushed the Sakdalista uprising. Ramos himself went into self-imposed exile in Japan, returning to the Philippines in 1938—where he established a strongly pro-Japanese party called Ganap (meaning 'complete' in Tagalog) to continue the fight for complete independence. Ganap was one of three parties allowed to participate in the November 1941 election, but Benigno Ramos himself was imprisoned before the election, and the party consequently failed to stop the Quezon landslide.

The Philippines Army—along with their American officers and trainers—fought valiantly on Bataan and Corregidor until May 1941. But they were poorly supplied, especially in Bataan, where thin rations resulted in emaciated soldiers by March, breeding resentment towards MacArthur's better-supplied troops on Corregidor. There in late February, Quezon again revived the idea of neutrality—proposing that, in return for an American declaration of full independence for the Philippines, he would disband the Philippine Army and call for both Japanese and American troops to withdraw. MacArthur, somewhat surprisingly, supported Quezon's suggestion, but Roosevelt would have none of it—insisting that resisting Japanese aggression trumped all other priorities, including any obligations to the Filipinos. Japan was promising the Philippines independence under its Greater East Asia Co-Prosperity Sphere and many prominent Filipinos were already collaborating with them, including Jorge B. Vargas, who had been designated by Quezon as mayor of Greater Manila to administer the open city and deal with the arrival of the Japanese. The Filipino people were growing increasingly resentful about the lack of military reinforcements or supplies from the Allies, who appeared to be concentrating their forces primarily in Europe. MacArthur argued that, if Bataan was likely to fall anyway to the Japanese, it would be more sensible to agree to a mutual withdrawal and Philippines' neutrality. FDR ordered instead that Quezon and MacArthur both be evacuated from Corregidor to Australia, so that MacArthur could take on more crucial military responsibilities than the defence of the Philippines.

FDR appointed MacArthur head of a new Southwest Pacific Command, and he was evacuated on 12 March 1942 to Australia, from where he would lead the defence of Papua New Guinea and Australia and help turn the tide of war in the Pacific. It was from Australia that MacArthur broadcast his famous promise to the Filipino people, 'I shall return' (a promise he was determined to keep, no matter what the circumstance). Quezon moved to Visayas and Mindanao before arriving in Washington DC, in mid-May 1942 after a brief sojourn in Australia—just after the fall of Corregidor to the Japanese forces on 6 May, Bataan having fallen on 9 April. This was the largest surrender of US military forces anywhere since the Civil War and was soon followed by the horrific 'Bataan Death March', in which 80,000 already-starving soldiers were forced to trek towards their imprisonment, during which nearly an eighth of the soldiers perished (many of starvation and exhaustion). Quezon established a government in exile in the US and was feted in that country, but eventually succumbed to ill health before the end of the war and was succeeded as president-in-exile by Osmeña in August 1944.

Homma's invading force had included the pro-Japanese General Artemio Ricarte, one of the heroes of Aguinaldo's army (the Katipunan) from the 1898–1901 revolutionary war. Ricarte had famously refused to take an oath of allegiance to the US after that war, and had spent his life in exile (first in Hong Kong and then in Japan, where—like Rash Behari Bose—he opened a restaurant along with his wife, called Karihan Luvimin in Yokohama) and was convinced that Japan would finally give his nation real independence. Soon after the fall of Manila, the Japanese forces freed Benigno Ramos and his Ganap party helped mobilize the populace in favour of the new regime. The Japanese presided over the establishment of the Second Philippine Republic and duly granted the country independence on 14 October 1943, with José P. Laurel as president and Benigno Aquino as speaker of the national assembly. The new regime introduced Tagalog as the official national language, endorsed it as the main language of instruction in schools, and created a thousand-word version of the language to facilitate its wide acceptance and quick learning.

In the midst of war, the Japanese did not wish to overturn Filipino society completely, so they accepted the collaboration of the illustrado elite as well, rather than establish Ganap as the ruling party, which could have been socially disruptive. Most remnants of the Nacionalista Party who had stayed on in the country, led by Vargas and Laurel, participated in the creation on 30 December 1942 (the anniversary of José Rizal's martyrdom) of a new all-encompassing nationalist party called KALIBAPI (Association for Service to the New Philippines), with Benigno Aquino as its first director general and Benigno Ramos (of Ganap) as an executive committee member. Aquino, who had been secretary of agriculture and commerce in Quezon's cabinet, toured the country alongside Ramos to spread awareness about the 'New Philippines' that would adhere to authentic Asian values.

The preparatory commission for the new constitution of the independent Philippines comprised largely of members of the existing national assembly. While Laurel himself was a Supreme Court judge (after serving as a senator for six years prior to that), he was known to be pro-Japanese, having sent a son to the Imperial Military Academy in Tokyo, and been a well known critic of US rule. Of the fifty-four members of the new National Assembly established under the new Constitution, thirty-three had been members of the outgoing Assembly. Although there had been a few dissenting voices (including Chief Justice Abad Santos) who were violently silenced, the majority of Filipinos appeared to welcome the independence declaration and more than half a million of them joined the KALIBAPI party/movement. Manuel Roxas, who had been Quezon's finance secretary and had stayed on (as a newly enlisted lieutenant colonel) with the Filipino and American forces in Bataan and Corregidor after Quezon fled, was captured in mid-1942—and also brought into Laurel's cabinet as president of the Economic Development Board. He always claimed afterwards that he joined the cabinet under duress, but like most of his compatriots, Roxas too was probably swept up in the spirit of patriotism engendered by the Japanese fulfilment of the promise to grant the Philippines independence under a new, nationalist constitution. Laurel, despite being favourably disposed towards the Japanese, refused to formally declare war on the US and UK, concentrating instead on the many problems (especially food supply) that he faced. But there could be little doubt that the Philippines received independence and a constitution—and the widespread use of a binding national language—during the war from the Japanese, well before the US actually came anywhere close to granting it independence. Although the war economy was a complete shambles, literacy advanced rapidly with the widespread use of simplified Tagalog.

With the capture of Singapore on 15 February, the Japanese turned their attention to their most vital economic target: the Dutch East Indies. In the second half of January, following their conquest of British Borneo (Sabah, Sarawak and Brunei), the Japanese had decided on a three-pronged attack on weak points of the East Indies: an Eastern force was to attack the Celebes (Sulawesi), Amboina (in the Maluku islands) and Timor; a Central force was to capture the rest of Borneo (particularly the oilfields and refineries of Tarakan Island off the east coast of Borneo, and the airfields and oil of Balikpapan); and a Western force was tasked with capturing Palembang, the capital of South Sumatra which housed a major Royal Dutch Shell refinery (and, historically, had been the first capital of the Srivijaya Buddhist empire). By 17 January, the Japanese had captured Tarakan and were able to use it as a forward airbase, and a week later they captured Balikpapan as well— although the Dutch had succeeded in destroying the oil facilities in both places. Restoring them proved a challenge, especially as a Japanese transport ship with several hundred petroleum engineers on board was sunk on its way to the East Indies. By the end of January, Japanese forces had taken control of most of Sulawesi and the rest of Kalimantan. In early February, they began coming ashore in northern Sumatra, where the Japanese helped foment an Acehnese uprising against the Dutch.

Just as the Battle of Singapore was reaching its climax, the Japanese navy turned its attention to Palembang—where the Allies had assembled a force of seventy-five fighter-bombers, albeit most of them ageing ones that had been transported from Egypt and Iraq. Several squadrons of British aircraft from the Malaya and Singapore campaigns, and one squadron of American heavy bombers from the Manila area had also assembled in Palembang, although the latter were withdrawn to help defend Java by early February. The Royal Netherlands East Indies Army (KNIL) also had about 2,000 troops guarding the Palembang refinery. On 13 February, Japanese aircraft began dropping paratroopers into the Palembang area, and the 270 paratroopers were soon able to gain complete control of the undamaged Pladjoe refinery complex. A KNIL counter-attack, aided by anti-aircraft gunners, managed to retake the refinery the next day, while suffering heavy casualties; they were able to set the stored oil ablaze, but did little damage to the refinery. By then, the Japanese were mounting a massive amphibious landing, using the aircraft carrier *Ryujo* and a fleet of cruisers, destroyers and transport ships. Just one of the transport ships was sunk, as wave upon wave of Allied naval attacks were repulsed and several Allied cruisers and destroyers sunk, while others began to withdraw south of Sumatra. Another sixty Japanese paratroopers were dropped near Palembang, and they helped regain both the refinery complex and the nearby airfield by 15 February. The Japanese now had control over a vital strategic and oil asset, and with it gained control of Sumatra by 16 February as the key Allied aircraft and remaining ships either withdrew to Java—to help mount a stout defence of the island that held the majority of the East Indies' people—or further west to India and Ceylon.

The Allies had concentrated most of their naval and air assets from across Southeast Asia for the defence of Java and its nearby islands (including Bali). But the Allied strategy depended crucially on the KNIL providing stout resistance on the ground, so that the ABDACOM navy and air forces could counter the strength of the expected Japanese assault—reinforced as they were with control of Sumatra, Singapore, Malaya and Borneo, with all their resources (including vital, albeit diminished, oil supplies). The rapid and virtually unimpeded conquest of Bali on 18 February was a bad portent as, in the words of one eyewitness, the Dutch 'threw away their uniforms or whatever else they wore, and donned native clothing and stained their faces brown. The panic grew as the Dutch set fire to all the military installations.' The barbed wire, anti-aircraft guns and searchlights installed on Kuta beach proved to be of little more than academic value during the first days of Japanese aerial bombardment, and soon afterward the Japanese navy came ashore to take control of Bali and install a relatively benign administration over the tranquil Hindu island.

The airfield at Bali gave the Japanese a vital airbase from which they could threaten the ABDACOM air headquarters in Surabaya, so Rear Admiral Karel Doorman brought a large fleet into the Bandung Strait off Bali to engage the Japanese flotilla there. Although the Japanese were heavily outnumbered and outgunned, the four Japanese destroyers were able to defeat the ABDA force—comprising seven destroyers, three cruisers, two submarines, and twenty aircraft—in the Battle of Bandung Strait, sinking one Dutch destroyer and inflicting heavy damage to the rest of the Allied force. Having secured this victory on 20 February, the Japanese navy went on to conquer Timor by the 23rd and also inflicted severe damage to the naval base in Darwin (in Australia's Northern Territory), disabling it as a supply base for the East Indies.

The Allied defence of Java was led by ABDACOM's overall commander in the area, Field Marshal Wavell, with Lieutenant General George Brett (of the US Air Force) as his deputy. Reporting to them, Lieutenant General Hein ter Poorten of the KNIL was ground forces commander, US Admiral Thomas C. Hart was the naval commander, and Air Chief Marshal Sir Richard Peirse was the air commander. Despite the seeming unity of command, this was a disparate force with divergent goals, which had been hastily put together and never quite gelled. Wavell himself had distinguished himself early in the war as commander-in-chief, Middle East, when he had defeated the Italians in western Egypt and Libya, but had then suffered a defeat at the hands of Rommel in the western desert of Libya in April 1941. Thereafter, Wavell had been appointed commander-in-chief for India—a post in which he served from July 1941 to June 1943, with his detour to ABDACOM in Southeast Asia almost a last-minute afterthought. Just before an Allied naval squadron from Surabaya (in east Java) set off to try and counter the Japanese forces converging on the northern shores of Java, Wavell resigned as supreme commander of ABDA on 25 February, handed power to his local commanders, and recommended the creation of two separate commands—a Southwest Pacific one (which was soon to be placed under MacArthur) and another based in India (where he returned), to take charge of the defence of Burma, which was by then rapidly succumbing to Japan's advances.

In the Battle of the Java Sea on 27 February, Admiral Doorman's task force from Surabaya fought the biggest surface ship engagement since the Battle of Jutland in 1916. The ABDA fleet was based on two seaplane tenders—including the USS *Langley*, the oldest US aircraft carrier that had been converted to a seaplane tender only in 1936. The fleet included two heavy cruisers (USS *Houston* and HMS *Exeter*) and seven light cruisers. Of these eleven large ships, just one (an old US cruiser) survived the Battles of the Java Sea (27 February), Sunda Strait (28 February) and 2nd Java Sea (1 March); the other ten were destroyed or sunk by the Japanese air and naval forces, including *Langley* (sunk off Cilacap harbour on the first day), *Houston* (sunk in the Sunda Strait) and *Exeter* (sunk at the Second Java Sea battle). In the crucial engagement of the first Battle of the Java Sea, a Japanese torpedo attack sank two Dutch cruisers *De Ruyter* and *Java,* killing Admiral Doorman himself. Just before his cruisers sank, Doorman had ordered the two other large cruisers (*Houston* and *Perth*) to withdraw, but both were sunk early the next day. By the morning of 1 March, the ABDA command structure was completely dismantled and Japan had established thorough naval and air supremacy over the East Indies, especially after sinking *Exeter* and its two supporting destroyers by noon that day.

The previous day, Japanese ground troops had invaded Java proper and had been greeted by jubilant crowds in most towns and cities, as the Javanese welcomed them as liberators from three centuries of hated Dutch rule. Facing the prospect of much bloodshed—and with little air or naval support from the rest of the ABDA command—the Dutch surrendered on 9 March 1942, giving Japan unfettered control over the nation that was then the world's fourth-largest oil producer.

As the prospect of Japan's ground invasion loomed, the Dutch colonial leadership had moved nationalist leader Sukarno from his prison in Flores to Bengkulu in February 1942 and then hastily to Padang in west Sumatra, with the aim of shipping him out to Australia. But amid the chaos of battlefield losses, the Dutch were unable to execute the final aspect of their plan, and the Japanese leadership were quick to find and release Sukarno soon after they conquered Sumatra. Sukarno was treated with great respect, as were his former comrades (and occasional nationalist rivals) Mohammad Hatta and Sutan Sjahrir—who had both also been moved around frantically by the Dutch from Banda (where they had been sent from initial internment at the penal colony of Boven-Digoel in Papua) to Sukabumi in west Java.

Although there was an element of tension between the Japanese desire to use the nationalist stalwarts to bolster their control over the East Indies and Sukarno and his mates' intent to gain Indonesian independence as soon as possible, both sides worked largely in tandem initially. Hatta and Sjahrir were sent to Jakarta on 22 March, and Sukarno was able to join them there by July 1942. The three stalwarts decided that Sukarno and Hatta would work closely with the Japanese to further the aim of obtaining their consent for Indonesian independence, while Sjahrir would help the triumvirate hedge their bets by leading an underground resistance movement (alongside fellow socialist Amir Sjarifuddin).

The novelist Pramoedya Ananta Toer has written that, 'with the arrival of the Japanese, just about everyone was full of hope, except those who had worked in the service of the Dutch.' New vistas of opportunity were opened up for the Indonesian middle class under Japanese rule. Dutch bureaucrats across the broad swathe of government offices and administrative positions were replaced by Indonesians. Perforce, many of those who replaced the colonial officers were very inexperienced, and struggled initially with their new positions. But the three years of governance experience was far more than any Indonesian could possibly have obtained under Dutch colonial auspices. Bahasa Indonesia was standardized using Melayu Riau, which was already the trading link language of the archipelago. Although Javanese was spoken by about six-tenths of the population, the leaders of Java had consciously decided against making their language the national one in order to be more inclusive, and the Japanese went along with this nationalist sentiment. The Japanese helped Sukarno and Hatta create the Pusat Tenaga Rakyat (Centre for People's Power, or PUTERA) as a galvanizing force for Indonesian nationalism, although the organization was also misused for recruiting 'romusha' (forced labour) for various projects in the outer islands and elsewhere in the Japanese empire, something that Sukarno was always shameful and apologetic about subsequently. More crucially for Indonesia's future, Sukarno and Hatta worked with the Japanese after October 1943 to create the PETA to resist a possible Allied invasion of Indonesia. Over the next two years, PETA recruited and trained 37,000 soldiers in Java and 20,000 in Sumatra.

PETA was to form the core of Sudirman's nationalist army, which fought a four-year war to resist Dutch and Allied efforts to recolonize Indonesia after August 1945. The Japanese also helped create Masyumi as an encompassing organization for Indonesia's Muslims—incorporating both Nahdlatul Ulama (the traditional group that ran the Islamic pesantren schools) and the modernist Muslim organization Muhammadiyah. It was only under Japanese rule that the many threads of Indonesian Islam were welded into a single entity: while the purpose may have been for the Japanese to have visibility into the Muslim leadership, it also played a vital role in uniting disparate elements through PUTERA and Masyumi. Ironically, the youth (pemuda) resistance movement led by Sjahrir and Sjarifuddin also created a spirit of unity amongst youth opposed to Japanese rule that was to prove useful in providing a supplementary source of volunteers to PETA during the independence war. When Sjarifuddin was arrested by the Japanese in 1943 and faced the prospect of execution for treason, Sukarno intervened to convince the Japanese authorities to spare him. Despite the deference accorded to Sukarno and Hatta, the Japanese had not promised independence to Indonesia (or Malaysia)—unlike their promises to Burma and the Philippines, where there already were representative governments and leaders to whom institutional control could be turned over. In Indonesia, the Japanese saw their role as fostering nationalism and nurturing the anti-Dutch leadership, and it was only in September 1944 that the Japanese began contemplating Indonesia's independence. Finally, on 29 April 1945, an Indonesian Independence Exploratory Committee was formed under Japanese auspices. (Such a body was also formed in Burma and the Philippines several months before their independence declarations.) Importantly, the Japanese army encouraged nationalist mobilization on Java, while the navy administered the outer islands more stringently—so their political development during the period was more limited than Java's.

◆

The main Japanese assault on British Burma began almost simultaneously with its onslaught on the East Indies, and the danger that posed for British India was a crucial factor inducing Wavell to abruptly abandon Java to return to India. The Japanese military had learnt from the experience of 7–8 December 1941 that simultaneous assaults were an excellent device to outwit an underprepared enemy. By February 1942, Burma was already in disarray after the massive aerial bombardment of Rangoon on 23 December 1941—which killed 3,000 (out of a population of 400,000) in Burma's capital, and scared a complacent population into the shocked realization that Burma was likely to slip out of British control soon. Rangoon's Indians (who outnumbered all other nationalities in that city) felt they would be especially susceptible in a city under new rulers (especially if they were Burmese), given the experience of 1937–38. Many tens of thousands of Indians began streaming out of Rangoon—headed towards India by car, ship, bullock cart or on foot by January in a chaotic and massive migration of nearly a million people over the course of the next two months; more than a tenth of them perished in the attempt, while the majority of others staggered into India emaciated and impoverished, forced to walk because all other means of transport had been monopolized by the British, Anglo–Indians and educated or richer Indians, with the lack of fuel often forcing the abandonment of cars too (as beautifully evoked in Amitav Ghosh's *The Glass Palace*). Meanwhile, coastal towns around the southern border like Mergui and Tavoy fell to the Japanese in January, and Moulmein (the third largest city in Burma, just east of Rangoon across the Salween river) fell on 1 February. By the second half of February (even before Wavell flew back to India from Java), the British began evacuating Rangoon, although the dogged Irish governor Reginald Dorman-Smith was determined to stay in Burma to the bitter end.

On 22 February, the British blew up the bridge over the Sittang River less than a hundred miles east of Rangoon, although the 17th Indian Division was still caught on the other side. Churchill then ordered Australia's Sixth and Seventh Divisions, which were sailing back home from the Middle East, to be rerouted to Burma. But Australia's Prime Minister John Curtin demurred, eventually persuading Churchill that Australia needed these crack troops back home to defend their homeland from a possible Japanese attack. Nonetheless, General Harold Alexander arrived to take overall command of the Allied forces, and General Stilwell arrived in Burma at the head of the Chinese armies deployed there by Chiang Kai-shek, although these were generals without new divisions, chiefs with no 'Injuns'!

On 7 March, the British Burma army began evacuating Rangoon, but only after implementing a scorched earth policy—blowing up the oil terminal and destroying the port. The oil wells of the great Glasgow-based Burmah Oil Company near Pagan were blown up, sending billowing clouds of black smouldering soot into the sky over that town's medieval ruins. (In 1965, Burmah Oil won a judgement in its favour from the House of Lords granting compensation from the British Crown for the damage to its property, but the government of the day passed the War Damages Act of 1965 to retrospectively exempt the Crown from having to pay damages for acts lawfully committed by the British during a war.) The military authorities had imposed a limit of 5,000 civilian evacuees per day in order to keep the roads clear for military withdrawals, and the civilians (mainly Indians) suffered most grievously. With the southern half of Burma in Japanese hands, Dorman-Smith fled to the hill station 'summer capital' of Maymyo, but this too had to be evacuated soon, and General Alexander decided to take his army west towards India—leaving Stilwell's Chinese forces to fend off the final Japanese thrust.

By this point, Roosevelt was putting enormous pressure on Churchill to resume negotiations with Gandhi, and come to a settlement that might enable India's wholehearted participation in the war effort. In his memoirs, Churchill gave vent to the elation he felt on learning of the Japanese bombing of Pearl Harbor, and the US entry into the war: 'So we had won after all… Britain would live. The Commonwealth and Empire would live.' He immediately made plans to go to Washington DC, to review all the war plans, including those regarding production and distribution. Churchill was apoplectic when Roosevelt used the opportunity in January 1942 to raise 'the Indian problem… on the usual American lines', but Churchill 'reacted so strongly at such length that he never raised it verbally again'. Sensing the threat, the British prime minister acted quickly to devise a strategy and a unified formulation that would appear to address America's concerns while containing clauses that would make it impossible for Congress (the largest party in India by a long way) to accept it. A new source of pressure on the British emerged, when Chiang Kai-shek and Madame Chiang arrived in India on 9 February (just before the fall of Singapore), determined to parley with the Congress leadership and urge the British to offer genuine self-determination to the Indian people in order to gain their full support in the war effort. After a fortnight in India, Generalissimo Chiang cabled Roosevelt on 25 February, saying that the British had mismanaged the Malay states but now 'should voluntarily give the Indians real power and... not allow different parties in India to cause confusion'.

When Averill Harriman, FDR's personal representative, broached the India issue with Churchill in London the next day, he was told (as recounted in a telegram he sent his president) that, 'Approximately 75 per cent of the Indian troops are Muslims... The Muslim population exceeds 100 million. The fighting people of India are from the northern provinces largely antagonistic to the Congress movement.' This was a bald-faced lie. Field Marshal Wavell, the commander-in-chief in India, had cabled London that very week that only 35 per cent of the Indian troops were Muslims. And a large proportion of those Muslims were Pathans from the NWFP, a province that had elected the Congress to power in 1937. (In deflecting American pressure, it also helped Churchill that Harriman was, at the time, having an affair with Churchill's daughter-in-law Pamela, and was to later marry her!)

On 27 February 1942, the British cabinet (with Deputy Prime Minister Attlee of the Labour Party in the chair) adopted the principle of the 'provincial option', giving every Indian province (or group of provinces) the right to decide whether or not they wished to stay within or secede from a future union of India. Sir Stafford Cripps (until recently the popular British ambassador to the Soviet Union), brought into the War Cabinet on 19 February as Leader of the House of Commons, was to be sent to India in March 1942 to confer with India's leaders. As a friend of Nehru (whose guest he had been at Allahabad in 1939) and Gandhi (a fellow-vegetarian with whom he had conferred at Wardha on that trip), the choice of the socialist Cripps was specifically aimed at softening Congress. Cripps's cabinet colleagues were, however, emphatically clear in the nature of the 'offer' that Cripps was permitted to make to India's leaders: (a) after the war, India would have independence on the basis of a constitution framed by Indians, and in the interim Indian political leaders would enter the Viceroy's Executive Council where they would frame policies in all areas other than the conduct of the war (which would stay in British hands); (b) the caveat was that every Indian province, or princely state, would have the right to stay out of the Indian Union at Independence; and (c) this proposal must be 'accepted as a whole or rejected as a whole'. The first clause was received positively by the Americans (as Churchill had calculated it would be) while the final clause meant that any Indian parties who agreed to enter the proposed Executive Council would thereby commit themselves to accept the principle of the potential partition of India when the British withdrew from India after the war.

These were the War Cabinet's secret instructions to Cripps. In public in early March 1942 (as the East Indies and southern Burma were falling to the Japanese), Secretary of State Amery told the House of Commons, 'Our ideal remains a united India.' But in his top-secret recommendation to Churchill's War Cabinet on 28 January 1942, Amery had referred to the '1940 declaration' giving minorities a veto over India's constitutional development as 'the only long-term policy which can achieve a settlement.' On 8 August 1940, Linlithgow had made a British declaration (that was repeated, at Jinnah's request, by Amery in the House of Commons on 14 August 1940) offering dominion status after the war, Indian representation in the Viceroy's Executive Council, and the following specific guarantee to the minorities: 'It goes without saying that they [His Majesty's Government] could not contemplate transfer of their present responsibilities for the peace and welfare of India to any system of Government whose authority is directly denied by large and powerful elements in India's national life. Nor could they be parties to the coercion of such elements into submission to such a Government.' From that point on, the British interpreted 'large and powerful elements' to mean the Muslims—as represented by their 'sole spokesman', M. A. Jinnah.

As we saw in the previous chapter, Jinnah (and his Muslim League) had singularly failed to earn the electoral right to be the sole spokesman for the Muslims of India in the 1937 election. Jinnah had specifically asked for this 'August 1940 Resolution' as a permanent block against the 'likes of Cripps and Wedgwood Benn' who might 'at some future date sell the Muslims to the Hindus'. Meanwhile, as he noted in a report to London, Linlithgow did everything possible to 'shepherd all the Muslims into the [Muslim League] fold'. The timing of the August 1940 resolution was a bolt from the blue for Congress too, as Nehru and Azad had persuaded their colleagues in the Congress Working Committee in July 1940 (after the fall of France) to set aside 'the creed of non-violence in the sphere of national defence', thus dropping a key reason Gandhi had been citing for staying aloof from the war. (Gandhi's non-violence had reached somewhat bizarre extremes earlier that year, when he suggested to Linlithgow that Britain should allow Hitler to occupy their 'beautiful island' and offer non-violent resistance instead. He stepped aside from Congress when this resolution was passed.) The Congress failed to understand that, once it had demonstrated its electoral sway over India in the 1937 election, the British became even more resolute in thwarting them at every turn, and developing strong alternatives to that party. Nehru's altered resolution of July 1940 was aimed at creating an opening for discussions with the British, who rebuffed it quickly.

The Congress party's reaction to the arrival of Cripps in Delhi on 24 March 1942 bordered on the euphoric, as Congress president Maulana Azad and his predecessor Nehru prepared to meet him. But Cripps's secret report to the cabinet after his meeting with Jinnah the following day was more telling: 'I think he [Jinnah] was rather surprised in the distance that it [the British offer] went to meet the Pakistan case.' Jinnah had also arranged a big demonstration of his supporters in Delhi on the day that Cripps arrived in Delhi (which also happened to be the second anniversary of the League's acceptance of the 'Pakistan Resolution' in Lahore). But, if Cripps was really there to observe and draw independent conclusions, he would have taken greater note of his discussions with his first host in India—the Sindh chief minister, Allah Bux Soomro, who had hosted him in Karachi two days earlier. Allah Bux was a 'nationalist Muslim' committed to a united India, and he had organized a convention of nationalist Muslims attended by 1,400 politicians just before Cripps's visit.

Unfortunately for hopes of a united and independent India, Cripps's mission was clear from the start: he was in India to fulfil previous British 'promises of self-government to the Indian peoples', Cripps said at his first press conference. Most of his listeners were quick to note that he was no longer talking about Indians as one 'people', but many 'peoples', and Balkanization was what Britain was determined to offer if Indians wished to be independent. Gandhi saw through the scheme right away, and rejected what he saw immediately as 'an invitation to the Muslims to create a Pakistan'. A delegation of Sikhs met Cripps the same day, and expressed strong opposition to their community being marooned permanently in a Muslim-majority nation such as the proposed Pakistan. The Sikhs—being disproportionately represented in the army (and having suffered more casualties than any other Indian community in both World Wars)—could not be easily ignored, and Cripps's suggestion that Sikhs could eventually carve an 'autonomous' area within the new nation failed to reassure Master Tara Singh and the three other members of his delegation.

Gandhi also requested that Cripps postpone the official announcement of his proposals until wider consultations had been held, but Cripps went ahead with his official announcement three days later. Narendra Sarila (later aide-de-camp to Mountbatten) remembered hearing it on the radio at his school, and being struck immediately by the reference to the 'peoples' of India. George Merrell, then head of the American Commissariat in Delhi telegraphed US Secretary of State Cordell Hull on 2 April that 'Congress will oppose the scheme on the ground that it presupposes vivisection of the country whereas the declaration should only promise Dominion Status and a Constituent Assembly after the war leaving details to be worked out by the Indian leaders themselves.' Within a couple of days, FDR sent Colonel Louis Johnson as his personal envoy to India to intercede with Cripps.

Maulana Azad and Jawaharlal Nehru were rather naive in ignoring the clear language of Cripps's official announcement and his similar public statements to British civil servants and army leaders, which reiterated the right of the Muslim-majority provinces and princely states to secede from a future Indian union individually or jointly. Continuing their parleys with Cripps based on his personal assurance that the viceroy's role would be like that of a constitutional monarch (except in the area of defence, which would remain the domain of 'the British Commander-in-Chief for the duration of the war'), Azad and Nehru thought they had worked out a settlement that they would be able to sell to their colleagues and the country which would, in effect, make one of them the new empowered head of the Executive Council (and so the de facto prime minister of India). Here, however, Cripps had exceeded not only his brief (as Churchill angrily pointed out), but also existing British law: the viceroy's veto powers were a result of the Government of India Act of 1935 (passed by the British Parliament) and any abridgement of those powers required a further reference to Britain's Parliament. Had Cripps been able to persuade Linlithgow to voluntarily forego his veto powers, a settlement might still have been possible, but there was never the slightest possibility of Linlithgow going along with such a scheme!

On 9 April (five days after a Japanese naval attack on Colombo and Trincomalee in Ceylon sank the aircraft carrier *Hermes* and killed more than 500 people), Colonel Johnson brokered an arrangement under which the 'Defence' department (to handle all matters of production, distribution, canteens, etc.) would be controlled by Indians, and a new 'War' department would handle the armed forces. This subterfuge only convinced Johnson, Cripps, Nehru, Azad and their only supporter in the Congress leadership (Rajagopalachari, the former chief minister of Madras province, whose daughter was married to Gandhi's son). Wavell and Linlithgow protested about it to Churchill, who quickly shot it down. So on 11 April 1942, a frustrated Cripps ended his mission and departed for home, to Churchill and Amery's unconcealed glee.

Gandhi memorably called Cripps's offer a 'post-dated cheque on a crashing bank', and the majority of the Congress leadership agreed with him—including Working Committee members Vallabhbhai Patel, Rajendra Prasad, J. B. Kripalani, G. B. Pant and young socialists like Jayaprakash Narayan, Asoka Mehta and Narendra Deva—although Gandhi himself was no longer formally a Congress member. Nonetheless, President Azad and Nehru had agreed that the Congress would not publicly air their objections to the long-term proposals in Cripps's offer and especially to the 'provincial option' while Cripps was in India negotiating with them. Just before Cripps left, Azad lamented to him the 'progressive deterioration' in their negotiations which had strayed so far from Cripps' initial discussion with Azad in which he had been led to believe that the position of the viceroy would be 'analogous to that of the King in England' relative to the new cabinet that was to be formed in India.

That was never the British intent because, as Colonel Johnson cabled Cordell Hull, Churchill had made clear he would 'give no approval unless Wavell and Viceroy endorsed the change', and it was obvious to Johnson that 'London wanted a Congress refusal.' When Churchill reported Cripps's failure to FDR by asserting, 'I feel absolutely satisfied we have done our utmost,' FDR immediately wrote back saying, 'I am sorry to say I can't agree... that public opinion [in the US] believes that the negotiations have failed on broad general terms... The feeling almost universally held is that the deadlock has been caused by the unwillingness of the British government to concede to the Indians the right of self-government, notwithstanding the willingness of the Indians to entrust technical, military and naval defence control to the competent British authorities'. Unaware that Cripps had already left India, FDR requested Churchill to urge Cripps to 'make a final effort to find a common ground of understanding.' That was not to be, particularly because General George C. Marshall had just arrived in Britain to begin chalking out the joint Anglo-American plans for the invasion of Europe. India gradually took a back seat: FDR kept an eye on progress towards India's independence but never took as active an initiative as he had in 1942.

Meanwhile, soon after Cripps's departure, the Congress passed a resolution (and publicized it) opposing the Cripps offer because it had advanced 'beforehand' the 'novel principles of non-accession for a Province' that it judged to be a 'severe blow to the conception of Indian unity'. But the Congress Working Committee muddied the waters by stating that it 'cannot think in terms of compelling the people in any territorial unit to remain in an Indian union against their declared and established will.' The collapse of the Cripps Mission and subsequent recriminations led straight to Gandhi's calls for the British to leave India to her own devices and the formal 'Quit India' resolution of 8 August 1942. In July, Gandhi had sent a letter of friendship to FDR, to which Roosevelt sent a supportive reply on 1 August, but that reply did not reach Gandhi before he was arrested by the British colonial government (under the draconian Defence of India Rules) before dawn on 9 August along with the entire Congress leadership and about 100,000 other members. Although British censors attempted to destroy the letter, FDR ensured that Gandhi did receive it upon his release in 1944. It said: '[The] US has always supported policies of fair dealing and of fair play... I shall hope that our interest in democracy and righteousness will enable your countrymen and mine to make common cause against a common enemy.'

Azad held on to the lonely belief that he, Nehru and Cripps might have worked out an agreement and later blamed the Congress' attitude partly on the fact that 'Subhas Bose's escape to Germany had made a great impression on Gandhiji. He had not formerly approved many of his actions, but now I found a change in his outlook. Many of his remarks convinced me that he admired the courage and resourcefulness Subhas had displayed in making his escape from India. His admiration for Subhas Bose unconsciously coloured his view about the whole war situation.' That situation was indeed looking increasingly unfavourable to the Allies in Asia, with Japan capturing their first (albeit small) part of British India—the Andaman and Nicobar Islands which had been partly used as a penal colony—and shelling Visakhapatnam (Vizag) and Kakinada on India's east coast on 6 April (while Cripps was still in India), two days after the devastating bombardment of the ports of Colombo and Trincomalee in Ceylon. In retrospect, had Congress accepted the Cripps offer (swallowing the unlimited right of princely states and other provinces to secede from a future independent India), it might conceivably have checkmated Churchill. But the latter would then have surely introduced other features to make Council entry unpalatable to Congress leaders. British cabinet discussions (and the nature of the original offer) made it clear (as the Americans too saw very clearly) that Britain had no interest in bringing Congress into actual positions of power in 1942. But Azad betrayed a profound naivety about the nature of Britain's geopolitical strategy, wilfully ignoring what Gandhi and most of the Congress leadership could see: the British determination to hold on to parts of northwestern India that were essential to Britain's control over the oil of Iraq and Iran (while also keeping the princely states as a further bargaining chip to keep Congress on the back foot).

Wavell's military career in the year before his return to India in February 1942 could have provided Azad and Nehru one important lens into Britain's grand strategy for India and the Middle East, if they had paused to consider the immediate past. As commander-in-chief, Middle East, Wavell had commanded the Allied forces in two wars—the Anglo–Iraqi War of April–May 1941 and the joint Anglo–Soviet invasion of Persia in August–September 1941. Both were aimed at nipping nascent nationalism in the bud, particularly any hints of neutrality in the war. Remarkably, in histories of the period, these two blatantly illegal invasions of independent nations are hardly mentioned, while reams of newsprint are expended on Japan's invasion of Manchuria. In the first half of the twentieth century, imperial Britain had the implicit right to act with impunity against any nation—and international law be damned! In Iraq, Rashid Ali al-Gaylani led the largest nationalist bloc in Parliament and had stringently opposed the Anglo–Iraqi Treaty of 1930 (giving Britain the right to station the RAF in Iraq, and maintain numerous other bases across the country). After Iraq became 'independent' in 1932 (and a member in good standing with the League of Nations), Gaylani's parliamentary bloc attempted to assert Iraq's genuine independence from Britain, but was thwarted by the pro-British Hashemite king Ghazi bin Faisal. When the latter died in 1940, Gaylani became prime minister and began to prohibit the free passage of Allied troops through Iraq, while refusing to break diplomatic ties with Italy and Germany. Britain responded with tough economic sanctions, and eventually persuaded the regent to oust Gaylani on 31 January 1941 after ten months in office. Following a power struggle, Gaylani was able to oust the regent and take power as prime minister again on 3 April 1941. A fortnight later, he sent artillery units to take control over the RAF base in Habbaniya.

Churchill ordered military reinforcements to be sent in from India—which duly arrived in Basra on 18 April 1941—and the mobilization of another force from the British Mandate of Palestine. The two military units commanded by Wavell and Field Marshal Claude Auchinleck then attacked Iraq on 2 May, and were able to regain control over the RAF Habbaniya base by 29 May, leading Gaylani to flee to Persia, after which a British puppet regime was installed in his place. This new Iraq Force (dominated by the Indian army units that had arrived in Basra) was then sent into action in Persia too in August 1941 to oust Reza Shah Pahlavi, the reformist king of Iran who (despite having initially been installed in power with British help) had steadily asserted his autonomy over the years, including a slightly more favourable renegotiation of the APOC concession agreement (after he cancelled the old D'Arcy concession in 1931). Emulating and learning from his northern neighbour Atatürk of Turkey, Reza Shah had reformed education and society (especially improving the status of women and emasculating the role of the mullahs), and begun a vigorous attempt at industrializing Iran. In 1935, he had established Tehran University (following the establishment of Istanbul University in 1933, when Atatürk invited German Jewish professors expelled by Hitler to help him start a world-class university) and, in 1936, Reza Shah went even further than Atatürk by banning the use of the veil by women.

Reza Shah Pahlavi had also chipped away at other aspects of Britain's stranglehold over his country, taking over the Post and Telegraph service from British control, and removing the currency-issuing power of the British-owned Imperial Bank of Persia (predecessor of HSBC in Iran and the Gulf states) and replacing it with Bank Melli Iran (his country's first modern bank) in 1931. Exercising Iran's sovereign rights, Reza Shah had also greatly expanded his country's commerce with Germany: by 1940, nearly half of Iran's trade was with Germany. He declared Iran's neutrality in the war, and refused British demands that all German advisers be expelled from his country—pointing out there were only 690 German nationals in Iran, compared with 2,590 British nationals. Once Germany invaded the Soviet Union, Iran's strategic importance to the Allies increased substantially, as the Trans-Iranian Railway was the easiest way for Lend-Lease supplies to reach the Soviet Union by sea from the US, especially as the northern routes were often too icy. On 25 August—a week after a diplomatic note demanding the expulsion of German nationals—about 200,000 Allied troops invaded Iran, supported by air and naval forces. Ironically, less than two weeks earlier Churchill and Roosevelt had signed the Atlantic Charter, reaffirming that they both 'respect the right of all peoples to choose the form of government under which they will live'.

Three Soviet divisions from the Caucasus invaded northern Iran with the aim of annexing Iranian Azerbaijan, while Wavell invaded southwestern Iran (where the British owned the world's largest oil refinery in Abadan) with the 8th and 10th Indian Infantry Divisions, the 21st Indian Infantry Brigade, the 2nd Indian Armoured Brigade and the 4th British Cavalry Brigade. The Indian troops enabled Britain to gain complete control within three days over the southwestern oil complex around Abadan, Bandar Shahpur (later to be renamed Bandar Khomeini) and Masjid-i-Suleiman. By the next day, key towns near Tehran like Qazvin were given up to the British, as generals were receiving mixed signals from the pro-British prime minister Ali Mansur. (He was sacked by the Shah on 27 August.) Reza Shah's reforms had improved the army and air force, but not enough for them to withstand a joint invasion by two great powers. By the end of August, Reza Shah Pahlavi had opened negotiations with the British (after receiving little more than pious words and no support from President Roosevelt), but the Allies demanded that all

German nationals be handed over. Reza Shah resisted this demand, and enabled most Germans to escape through Turkey. But with Soviet troops already inside Tehran, Reza Shah Pahlavi himself abdicated on 16 September 1941, and was succeeded by his pusillanimous son, Mohammad Reza. The former Shah was flown to Bombay, and then to South Africa where he died in 1944.

Britain's use of the Indian Army in 1941 demonstrated yet again—as it had also in 1914–18—that India was the most important cog in the wheel of Britain's ability to exert its prerogatives as a great power, especially in the Middle East. The oil in southwestern Iran and in Iraq was vital to fuelling the British war effort, and to sustaining Britain's future as a great power—especially were it to ever lose control of the Jewel in its Imperial Crown, India. This is why Cripps—despite professing to be a friend of India and especially Congress leaders like Gandhi, Nehru and Azad—avoided substantial meetings with Sir Sikandar Hayat Khan, the chief minister of Punjab (the province that provided the largest proportion of Indian army recruits), where he ran a delicate coalition government encompassing Muslims, Hindus and Sikhs. In the only credible election held in British India (in 1937), Sikandar Hayat's party had won almost as many constituencies as the Muslim League had across the whole of India, and won the overwhelming majority of seats in Punjab (where the Muslim League won just one of the seventy-five seats reserved for Muslims). A fair-minded interlocutor would have listened to Sikandar Hayat's views (which were, still, strongly opposed to partition—as the Punjab was bound to face the greatest upheaval from it—but also likely opposed to any quick timetable to independence, as Sikandar Hayat's Unionist Party was dominated by landlords who were broadly loyal to the British). Similarly, Cripps kept the Sindh chief minister, Allah Bux Soomro (a nationalist Muslim who opposed partition and wanted an early timetable towards independence for a united India) waiting several days in Delhi and only met him for an hour on his penultimate day there, after Azad had interceded on Soomro's behalf. Cripps avoided substantive discussions with Allah Bux Soomro both during his stopover in Karachi and during their hour-long meeting in Delhi, as he could not deviate from the British cabinet's script, in which the Muslims of India had only one spokesman, Muhammad Ali Jinnah of the Muslim League.

Allah Bux, Sikandar Hayat and Dr Khan Sahib (the Congressman who had been elected chief minister of NWFP, another great recruitment province for the army) would complicate the simple picture that the British were determined to see—of Muslim 'disenchantment' with Congress and Hindus, and the desire for Partition. When Cripps came to India in 1942, *none* of the elected chief ministers of the three provinces that were to eventually form

West Pakistan were in favour of partition, but even Cripps was not permitted to scratch the surface of this overwhelming reality. Britain either would rule India for at least another fifty years (as Linlithgow wanted; forever if Churchill had his way), or a Pakistan needed to be created in the northwest of India to ensure British control of the oilfields of its protectorates (Kuwait, the Trucial States, Qatar) and sphere of influence (Iran, Iraq and Oman). Over the next twelve months, Sikandar Hayat Khan died of heart failure aged just fifty (apparently succumbing to the pressure of dealing with the widening complexity of the political conundrums he faced) and Allah Bux Soomro (who supported Gandhi's call for the British to Quit India) was assassinated in 1943 (either by the League or the British), thus removing these two potential obstacles to the favoured British narrative of the inevitability of partition. Conveniently, the mystery of who killed Allah Bux has never been solved.

In Burma, March and April 1942 saw the Japanese advance steadily northward, facing resistance primarily from Chiang Kai-shek's armies, trained and led by Stilwell, and supported by Chennault's fighter-bombers. General Alexander had taken the bulk of the British Indian Army across the border to India to guard against a possible invasion of Bengal or Assam, and the rest of the troops and supporting staff were left to manage the longest retreat in British history. Only Governor Dorman-Smith (another veteran of the Middle East wars of 1941) was doggedly determined to share the local population's fate and not be seen to be abandoning them, as the peoples of Malaya had been abandoned. When Maymyo fell, he moved to Myitkyina on 28 April—a town that was overflowing with Anglo–Indians and Anglo–Burmese, the most loyal denizens of the Raj who were now desperate to escape the reprisals that seemed inevitable against them once Burma fell. Churchill had to order the ailing Dorman-Smith to fly out to Calcutta (rather than fulfil his professed desire to die in the jungles or walk with the thousands braving the hazards of the monsoon rain and thick jungles of the India–Burma border to escape the onrushing Japanese).

On 1 May, Aung San's BIA entered the smouldering ruins of King Thibaw's old capital of Mandalay, accompanying the Japanese troops, who they and much of the Burmese population looked upon as liberators. The BIA had gathered increasing numbers of volunteers as it advanced—swelling its ranks, but also contributing to a disorganized unprofessionalism as untrained recruits swarmed in. In the villages of Burma, the BIA stirred enormous pride, particularly because uniformed Burman soldiers had become such a rarity in the previous six decades, during which a wide chasm had been cleaved between the cosmopolitan cities (with their swarms of immigrants and minorities) and traditional Burmese villages. The latter helped Aung San and his comrades and foot soldiers grow roots (including through marriage) that made rural Burma a bastion of the BIA (which its successor national army has maintained to this day). But in the western Irrawaddy delta, the seeds of Britain's divide and rule policy began to bear poisonous fruit. The ethnic Burmese (or Bamar) BIA troops sought to disarm ethnic Karen soldiers who were returning home (from service in the defeated British Burma army). As in Malaya, the locals had rejected the opportunity to join the exodus to India, and instead sought to return quickly to their home villages to protect families and homesteads.

After more than a half-century of colonial occupation, the novel spectacle of ethnic Burmese in military uniform sent a frisson of excitement amongst the majority ethnic group, but also stirred rumours and fears amongst the Karen Christians, who had been more favoured by the colonialists, including serving as soldiers of the hated occupying army. The Karen elder statesman, Sir San C. Po, intervened to avoid a conflagration in Bassein, but when the Burmese soldiers discovered a plot by Karen in Myaungmya to go on a pre-emptive killing spree against Burmese, the BIA soldiers shot the Karen leader Saw Pe Tha and his family. Despite San C. Po's attempts to negotiate peace, vicious reprisal killings began—with the Karen burning Burmese villages, after several dozens of Karen had been killed and a church burnt down. The communal violence went on for several weeks before Japanese troops intervened to re-establish peace. The civil war that began in May 1942 between the BIA and ethnic minorities like the Karen has, arguably, continued until the present day.

The immediate consequence of the inter-ethnic carnage in Burma, however, was that the Japanese had to concentrate on subduing the violence within, rather than consider chasing British–Indian troops across the Arakan border or into Assam. And the Chinese armies too caused enormous destruction as they straggled back to Yunnan. Angry at the humiliation they had suffered at Japanese hands, the Chinese troops burnt villages and massacred civilians as they departed. Arguably the antipathy then engendered between the people of northeastern Burma and the Chinese has also persisted in a subdued form to this day. But resistance from those soldiers and the disarming of the ethnic minorities who dominated the colonial army took most of May. And by the time they had been dealt with, the monsoons had arrived, thereby putting paid to any thoughts of even a modest invasion of British India. British intelligence (which, admittedly, had failed spectacularly in Southeast Asia) had concluded that Japan did not feel confident enough—especially of its supply lines—to attempt to invade India. In fact, after the initial scare of naval bombardments of the ports on India's east coast and in Ceylon, the Japanese began to divert their best naval assets back to the Pacific to deal with the challenge from the US armed forces there, now being commanded by MacArthur.

Nonetheless, in that extraordinary half-year period from 8 December 1941 to mid-May 1942, Japan had liberated all of East Asia from non-Asian imperial domination. Many of its most dramatic advances had occurred within the first three to seven days, but it had then consolidated its gains—and eliminated British rule over Malaya, the Straits Settlements (Singapore, Penang, Malacca), Hong Kong and Burma; Dutch rule over the East Indies; and American control of the Philippines. Japan was also in control of Cochin-China (what eventually became South Vietnam), and the rest of French Indo-China was within its sphere of influence, while Japan's ally Thailand had greatly expanded its territory (including parts of Laos and Cambodia that it had won back from France, and parts of northern Malaya that it was soon to receive from Japan in appreciation for its vital aid in the early stages of the war). Korea and Taiwan were incorporated into Japan's empire (sending elected representatives to Japan's Diet), while Manchukuo was back under the rule of the last Manchu emperor, Aisin-Gioro Puyi. And Japan's ally Wang Jingwei (the former leftist rival of Chiang Kai-shek within the KMT) presided over Nanjing, Beijing, Shanghai, Jiangsu, Zhejiang, Fujian and Guangdong.

The Japanese military leadership redeemed its pledge to Burma by granting it independence on 1 August 1943. In the preceding twelve-month period, Ba Maw had been officially in control of Burma's civil governance, although he and the BIA faced initial resistance from the Japanese army, which had quickly isolated Colonel Suzuki and his Minami Kikan, and their strong commitment to Burmese nationalism. (This was very much in keeping with Suzuki's reputation as Burma's 'Lawrence of Arabia'; like Suzuki, T. E. Lawrence too had found his Arab nationalism quickly set aside in favour of Britain's imperial interests in the region.) The BIA had raced Japanese forces into many of the cities and towns of Burma, and a keen rivalry had emerged—leading the Japanese army leadership to become particularly sceptical about the young Thakins, many of whom they perceived to be communists or crypto-communist. Two of the Thirty Comrades—Aung San and Hla Pe (Bo Let Ya)—were indeed amongst the six founders of the Communist Party of Burma (CPB), with Aung San as its first secretary general; once they became key players in the BIA, both distanced themselves from the CPB (two of whose six founders were Bengalis: H. N. Goshal or Thakin Ba Tin, and Dr Amar Nath or Yebaw Tun Maung) but did not sever all links. The Thakins' growing support base with rural Burmans, however, made them difficult to ignore, and the military was eventually forced to accommodate them, despite their persistent complaint that the diminutive Aung San was simply not imposing enough to be the nation's leader. The Japanese had, from the start, emphasized Buddhism as a common binding force, and their radio broadcasts about 'Asia for the Asians' made a big impact on the Burmese population. The ceremony for the installation of Ba Maw (who had, after all, been elected prime minister in 1937 when Burma became a quasi-Crown Colony under the 1935 Government of India Act) had most of the trappings of a royal coronation, including liberal use of the music from Thibaw's court, and quasi-royal costumes and ceremonies. Ba Maw took the ancient Sanskrit title of Adipati ('he who stands first', or head of state), combining the roles of president and prime minister, with twenty-eight-year-old Thakin Aung San as his deputy and war minister. Thakin Nu (himself only thirty-six years old) became foreign minister. Ba Maw and Aung San had been co-founders of the Freedom Bloc in 1939, but had had a chequered relationship since.

Another communist ideologue, Thakin Than Tun, became minister of land and agriculture in Ba Maw's government. Than Tun's co-author of the 'Insein Manifesto' (of July 1941) advocating a temporary anti-fascist alliance with Britain, Thakin Soe, led the CPB during the war years and maintained close ties with four of the CPB's leaders who had fled to British India (including the two founders of Bengali origin). Thus like Indonesia's Sukarno and Sjahrir, the Burmese nationalist leadership also ensured that some key factions were aligned with the Allies while the major faction worked with Japan to attain nationalist goals. Aung San had married Khin Kyi (mother of Aung San Suu Kyi) in September 1942 and soon afterwards Than Tun married Khin Kyi's sister, Khin Gyi. Their father-in-law was a leading timber merchant and the communist Than Tun is said to have enriched himself considerably through his control of the land ministry. But in the period leading up to the formation of the newly independent government, both Ba Maw and Aung San consulted closely with Subhas Chandra Bose in Singapore and Rangoon—as the arrival in Southeast Asia of this titan of India's freedom struggle had transformed the nationalist movements there—and Bose was an honoured guest at the independence celebrations.

SUBHAS BOSE, THE INA, QUIT INDIA, CHURCHILL'S FAMINE AND THE PATH TO INDIA'S INDEPENDENCE

Subhas Bose had met Hitler at the Reich Chancellery in Berlin on 29 May 1942, nearly a year (eleven months and seven days) after Hitler had launched his surprise attack on the Soviet Union, to Subhas Bose's extreme consternation and surprise. The actual meeting did not go very well, as Bose was unable to persuade Hitler to formally declare his support for the tripartite powers' endorsement of India's full independence. Such a joint declaration of support for India and the Arabs had been proposed on 11 April (the day the Cripps mission failed) by Prime Minister Tojo Hideki of Japan, who had earlier promised 'India for the Indians'. After toning down Tojo's original draft, Ribbentrop's foreign office forwarded it for Hitler's approval on 16 April. Hitler had balked, not wanting to support Japan with such alacrity, apparently because he was envious of Japan's spectacular success against the European colonial powers in Asia. Mussolini was keen to support Japan's declaration, but was dissuaded by Hitler when they met at Salzburg on 29 April. Subhas had immediately travelled to Rome to meet Mussolini and his son-in-law and foreign minister Galeazzo Ciano on 5 May (after an adulatory article about Bose appeared in a popular Italian journal), and persuaded him to write to Hitler to alter his opposition to the declaration. Hitler would not be moved and he only 'extended his best wishes to Bose for the success of his journey and plans'.

As a practical matter, the sudden collapse of the Molotov–Ribbentrop Pact on 22 June 1941 had made it impossible for Subhas to travel quickly back to Asia, and also sundered parts of his Forward Bloc in India. For instance, Bhagat Ram Talwar—the party operative who had helped arrange his passage through Peshawar to Kabul—secretly joined the communist party and became a double agent, providing information to the British about Subhas's movements. During that first year in Germany, Subhas had established a Free India Centre, from where he broadcast inspiring messages to India and built up the Azad Hind Fauj to over 4,000 soldiers, and (with German military help) trained several hundred new recruits, including Abid Hasan and N. G. Swami. Their passage back to India too became impossible once Germany declared war on the Soviet Union. Subhas Bose's broadcasts made it abundantly clear that he did not agree with the Axis on their domestic policies, but it was his patriotic duty to find help wherever he could to rid India of the unyielding British yoke: 'While standing for full collaboration with the Tripartite Powers in the external sphere, I stand for absolute self-determination for India where her national affairs are concerned, and I shall never tolerate any interference in the internal policy of the Free Indian State.' His main interlocutor in the German government was Foreign Minister Ribbentrop and more specifically the head of the India department of the Foreign Office, the aristocratic Adam von Trott, and his deputy Alexander Werth. The latter had been jailed for anti-Nazi activities in 1934, and the former was eventually to be executed in 1944 for his role in Claus von Stauffenberg's plot to assassinate Hitler in July that year. Both were sympathetic to Bose's political outlook and views, and provided him considerable cover and protection when his publicly expressed opinions may have provoked Hitler's ire. During the meeting, Bose asked Hitler to repudiate his racist remarks about India in *Mein Kampf*, a demand that Hitler parried by saying he had not wanted 'passive resistance for the Reich of the Indian pattern'. But he did agree to make a German submarine available for Bose to travel to Asia.

Eight crucial months were to elapse before Bose was finally able to begin that perilous journey to Asia on 8 February 1943, while the Germans and Japanese squabbled over when and how he could travel. In the interim, however, Subhas Bose provided robust support to Gandhi's call for the British to Quit India. In fact, Bose had told Ribbentrop more than a month in advance that a major revolt in India was likely on 8 August, and it was urgently important for Bose himself to be able to reach Asia by then. Instead, he was only able to use radio broadcasts to support Gandhi's efforts at a time when the two estranged leaders were ideologically closer than they had ever been. Gandhi gave a call to the Indian people to 'Do or Die', and the people of India were galvanized into action, but so were the British colonial authorities, who unleashed a brutal crackdown. Subhas Bose's broadcasts over Azad Hind Radio became a favourite clandestine activity for the youth of India, who partly followed his instructions in planning their fight. The full repressive machinery of the British empire—including the military mobilized supposedly for the defence of India from a Japanese invasion—was unleashed on India's civilian protesters. Police bullets killed more than a thousand people in Calcutta and Bombay alone, and over 100,000 people were imprisoned—all within the first month. Even with this massively brutal crackdown, the mid-level leadership of Congress—mainly left-wingers like Jayaprakash Narayan, Aruna Asaf Ali and Narendra Deva—went underground to continue the struggle, which intensified especially in Bengal, Bihar, Orissa and the United Provinces. Unlike previous Gandhian movements—which Gandhi himself had tried to keep scrupulously non-violent—the Quit India Movement quickly turned violent in the forced absence of its leader, with the torching of police and railway stations, post and other governmental offices, and the destruction of rail tracks and other infrastructure. For some time in September 1942, supply lines to eastern India were cut off completely—just as the danger of a Japanese invasion was most feared as the monsoons ended.

Fortunately for the Allies, disagreements between Germany and Japan had thwarted Subhas Bose's desire to reach Asia. He had twice flown to Italy when it appeared that the Italians were ready to arrange for him to fly to Asia from there. But on the first occasion an intelligence leak by the Italians jeopardized his flight out in October 1942, and the following month the Japanese opposed a route over the Soviet Union (a country with whom they were not yet at war) while the Italians thought the southern route proposed by Japan too risky. By then, the massive repressive machinery of British India had largely crushed the Quit India Movement in most urban centres, although several pockets of resistance remained, where the colonial machinery was overthrown and parallel governments established by the rebels. Such parallel governments functioned effectively in Midnapore district (Contai and Tamluk) in Bengal, Satara and Saurashtra in Bombay province, Talcher in Orissa and Ballia in eastern UP. The vast majority of the country was quiet by December 1942, and it appeared that Gandhi's last political campaign had ended in failure in the face of a gruesome counter-attack by the colonial army and police. Bose said in a broadcast to India, 'The whole world now sees that the velvet glove, which ordinarily hides the mailed fist of Britain, has now been cast away and brute force—naked and unashamed—rules over India... the soul of India asks: "Where are the four freedoms?" ...After a pause, the soul of India asks "Where is the Atlantic Charter, which guaranteed to every nation its own Government?" This time Downing Street and White House reply simultaneously: "That Charter was not meant for India."'

Once it became clear that Bose would be able to take a German U-boat in February 1943 and transfer to a Japanese submarine, he was finally able to say his farewells, which he did at a reception to celebrate India's 'Independence Day' on 26 January, which was attended by the recently-ousted Rashid Ali al-Gaylani of Iraq and the Grand Mufti of Jerusalem. Accompanying Subhas on this arduous undersea voyage was Abid Hasan (whose nephew, Abid Hussain, became a prominent Indian bureaucrat in the 1980s and India's ambassador to the US from 1990 to 1992). They set off from Kiel on a U-180 submarine of the IXD type; the German U-boat evaded British depth charges in the North Sea, refuelled off the coast of Spain (from where Subhas posted a new edition of his *Indian Struggle* to his publisher), rounded the Cape of Good Hope and entered the Indian Ocean in April 1943. From their intelligence intercepts, the British knew that Subhas was on the move, but remained completely unaware of precisely how. The day after Bose began his journey, Gandhi had begun a fast and Churchill had ordered that he be allowed to die, rather than address the issue of Muslim–Hindu inter-communal riots that the British were fomenting; pressure from FDR's personal envoy, William Phillips, forced an eventual compromise that ended the fast on 4 March, although Gandhi remained imprisoned for another fourteen months.

During the subsequent months, Churchill unleashed his most vicious weapon against the Indian people: famine. In the words of the British historians Bayly and Harper: 'Quite apart from the demands of war, it is difficult to escape the impression that the War Cabinet was simply hostile

All areas that were ever under British control

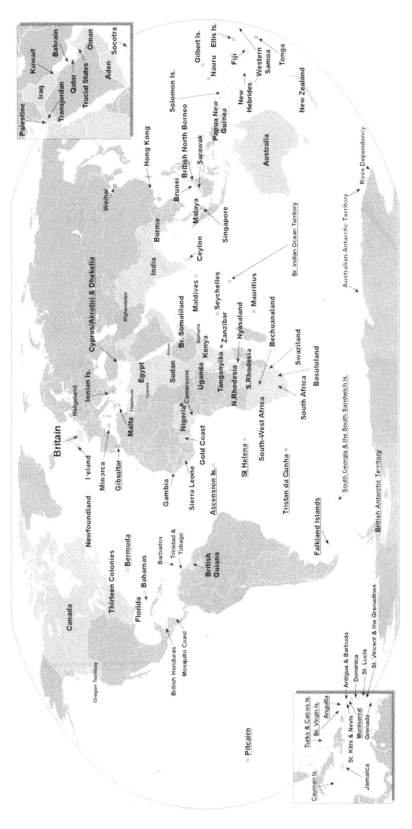

The Second World War: The Pacific Theatre (1941–45)

THE SECOND WORLD WAR
THE PACIFIC THEATER
1941 - 1945

Ito Hirobumi, Japan's first prime minister, played a vital role in creating the institutions that cemented the gains of the Meiji Restoration during nearly eight years as prime minister (in four different stints).

Takahashi Korekiyo, 'Japan's Keynes', who demonstrated in 1931–36 how capitalism could counter a Great Depression through expansionary fiscal and monetary policies.

The sunken ships of Russia's vaunted Baltic Sea fleet at Port Arthur (in Manchuria), 1905. Had Russia won this climactic battle, Asia might never have turned back the European tide.

Prime Minister Subhas Bose with his cabinet colleagues after the formation of the Provisional Government of Free India, 21 October 1943. Front row (R-L): A. C. Chatterjee, J. K. Bhonsle, Dr Lakshmi Swaminadhan, Bose, A. M. Sahay, S. A. Ayer. Back row (R-L): Gulzara Singh, Shah Nawaz Khan, Aziz Ahmed, M. Z. Kiani, N. S. Bhagat, Ehsan Qadir, Loganathan.

Mustafa Kemal Atatürk launches what he considered the biggest war of his career, the battle against ignorance, through a new script that would be easier to learn and link Turkey to the world.

Aurobindo Ghose (seated at table) presides over a meeting of the Nationalists being addressed by Bal Gangadhar Tilak (standing) in 1907 after Gokhale's faction had jettisoned their programme of Swaraj, Swadeshi and Boycott in favour of more cooperation with the British.

Gandhi at the 2nd Roundtable Conference (1931). The Government of India Act, 1935, was its outcome—giving Indians less democratic representation at the national (federal) level than Hong Kong had in 1996.

Mao Zedong and Chiang Kai-shek at their last meeting in August 1945, after Zhang Xueliang's Xian intervention had forced them back into a precarious united front in 1936. Stalin's invasion of Manchuria soon afterwards gave Mao and Lin Biao a decisive edge in the civil war that followed.

PM Attlee meets Aung San and his team in a frigid London in January 1947 to negotiate the path to Burma's independence. Tin Tut, the first Burmese to qualify for the Indian Civil Service, is on Aung San's other flank.

Iran's Mossadegh meets US president Truman in 1951, after Mossadegh had transfixed the UN General Assembly with his speech about the APOC's depredations.

Egypt's Nasser with an ecstatic crowd in Cairo after announcing the nationalization of the Suez Canal.

Lee Kuan Yew welcomes Deng Xiaoping to Singapore in November 1978, in the early stages of Deng's ascent to the pinnacle of power in China. The ethnically Hakka leaders hit it off immediately, and Deng was to implicitly implement a variation of the Singapore model of economic development in China's SEZs.

Two of the makers of modern Asia together: Singapore's Lee Kuan Yew visits South Korea's Park Chung-hee in October 1979, just a week before Park was tragically assassinated. (His daughter and acting first lady, Geun-hye, is also in the photograph; she was elected president in her own right in 2013, but was hounded from office in 2017.)

towards India. The prime minister believed that Indians were the next worst people after the Germans. Their treachery had been plain in the Quit India Movement. The Germans he was prepared to bomb into the ground. The Indians would starve to death as a result of their own folly and viciousness.' On 16 October 1942, there had been a devastating cyclone in the Midnapore district of Bengal, and Japanese radio broadcasts claimed it had killed 100,000 people, while British officials initially told Indian newspapers to hush it up altogether (later estimates put the death toll at 30,000, versus an official government underestimate of 11,000). Since this was an area where the Quit India rebellion was still raging, the colonial police continued severe repression and thwarted the local district official, Binay Sen (who was later to head the UN's Food and Agriculture Organization), in his attempts at providing effective relief to the victims. Instead the police raided any villages suspected of 'harbouring' rebels, wantonly raped women and burnt whole villages to the ground (including poor families' food stockpiles).

Bengal's finance minister, Shyama Prasad Mookerjee, resigned on 16 November and called Chief Minister Fazlul Huq's attention to the devastating effects of the cyclone and the rising risk of famine—decrying official callousness as having 'no parallel in the annals of civilized administration'. But Huq's hands were tied by Governor John Herbert, who was determined to continue diverting rice supplies to Calcutta (to pacify the urban population) and keep the military well supplied. Herbert's minions had been buying up rice from rural markets for use by the military, including for export outside India, and Herbert travelled to Midnapore to decorate policemen for their 'loyal service' in combating Congress, raping women and confiscating their rice. The price of rice tripled in Midnapore as supplies diminished rapidly, and reports began coming in of severe deprivation in Bhola Island and Noakhali district of eastern Bengal, where Fazlul Huq ordered an inquiry into reports of rapes and murder by soldiers posted there.

In March 1943, demonstrating again the severely circumscribed democracy India's provinces were allowed, Governor Herbert forced the resignation of Fazlul Huq (who still had a majority in the provincial assembly) and replaced him with the pro-British Khwaja Nazimuddin of the Muslim League. James Blair, chief secretary of Bengal, who had expressed concerns about the repression in Midnapore, was eased out too, with Secretary of State Amery commending Herbert for giving 'good support to the Military authorities'. The rural cultivators of Bengal were no more than cannon fodder to be allowed to die while the produce of their hard work was unavailable to feed their own families. On 10 March Churchill wrote in a memo, 'I am glad to learn...that a strict line is being taken in dealing with requests for cereals from the Indian

Ocean area. A concession to one country at once encourages demands from all others.' (The policy of grain denial to the colonies also caused famines in Kenya and other British colonies in Africa.) Over the previous couple of months, even the phlegmatic Linlithgow had been warning of a food crisis in India, responding to concerns of a famine in Calcutta and Bombay raised by his council member, Sir Ramaswami Mudaliar. All ships that might have plied from Australia to India (possibly carrying Australian wheat) had already been diverted, as Churchill insisted that all attention must be focused on stockpiling massive amounts of grain for the British home population. Grain stockpiles in the United Kingdom were 14.6 million tons at their lowest point (in March 1943), still well above the 9.8 million tons that the Cabinet's food supply committee considered an adequate grain buffer (and also well above the 12.5 million ton estimate of the Ministry of War Transport).

British India typically was a net importer of 1 million tons of foodgrain annually before the war. Yet in the fiscal year from April 1942 to March 1943—a year in which cyclone and pests had cut grain output, and the loss of Burma to the Japanese also reduced potential supplies—British India was a net exporter of 360,000 tons of foodgrain (with gross exports of nearly half a million tons), the exports going to Ceylon and Arabia (which had previously imported from Burma) as well as to Britain itself. Had this grain been distributed properly in Bengal and Bihar instead, it could have fed over 3 million people. The total shortfall of rice and wheat in India in 1943 was estimated at between 2 million and 3.5 million tons. Churchill and his intensely racist scientific adviser Frederick Lindemann (Lord Cherwell) were intent on importing 27 million tons of grain into Britain, mainly as a stockpile for the post-War period, when (they anticipated) Britain would have few other liquid assets. Churchill and Cherwell (who felt physical revulsion at the presence of any black person in a room and, according to Bayly and Harper, believed that 'overbreeding and eugenic unfitness were the basic reasons for the scarcity') were also livid that the war had caused India to become a creditor to Britain because Britain was 'buying' grain and other resources from India on credit (with a promise of future repayment rather than any actual cash outflow); Churchill wanted to 'charge' India for the expense of its defence, neatly forgetting that taxes from India paid for its own army, which was fighting all over the world (including in Britain's only significant victory in the war, at El-Alamein in North Africa).

An additional factor inducing the build-up of food stocks was Churchill's quixotic quest to attack the Balkans (and hopefully get Turkey to enter the war on the Allied side, rather than staying neutral, in a personal reprise of his failed Gallipoli campaign two decades earlier). In Bengal, as in Burma earlier, the British instituted a 'scorched earth' policy in 1942–43, removing most river barges (a vital lifeline of transportation in eastern Bengal) in order to deny easy passage to a potential Japanese advance—apart from instituting the rice denial strategy that was so evident in Midnapore and elsewhere.

The consequence was a devastating famine that killed 3 million people in Bengal alone (as estimated by the economist Amartya Sen). The actual death rate in Bengal in 1943 was 5.3 per cent, compared to a mortality rate of 2.1 per cent in normal times for India as a whole. Using that figure (to subtract normal deaths that would have occurred each year), the death toll from famine in Bengal was 5.4 million. (In the worst affected sub-division of Bhola on the east Bengal coast—where the ban on barges, boats and bicycles hit hardest—the mortality rate in 1943 was nearly 15 per cent of the total population). The historian Paul Greenough estimated that deaths from the famine in Bengal alone totalled 3.8 million in 1943–45 but even his estimate did not account for the deaths in 1942, when the combination of the cyclone and scorched earth policies resulted in close to half a million unnatural deaths.

Additionally, the famine had also devastated parts of Madras province (particularly the Andhra coast), Bihar and Orissa. The latter two saw a sharp spike in famine deaths in mid-1943, when Bengal's Muslim League food minister H. S. Suhrawardy began to buy grain aggressively from those two provinces, causing prices to spike sharply there and spread the impact of the famine. The consequence was that famine killed between 3 million and 6 million Indians in 1942–45 as a direct consequence of Churchill's policy of exporting grain from India to other parts of the British empire (and his obsession with stockpiling grain within the United Kingdom)—especially his refusal to allow any imports into India even after it was evident that famine was killing millions there. In August 1943, after Amery recognized the enormity of the famine and pleaded with his Cabinet colleagues for some grain to be diverted to India, Churchill again emphatically refused to allow it. In July, Subhas Bose had arranged for 100,000 tons of rice to be sent from Burma to any port in eastern India, but the British specifically refused this offer, and placed a complete blockade on any information about Bose's offer (which could have fed 1.6 million people for the next half-year) from reaching India. Similar sized offers from Australia and Canada were blocked too. The famine of 1942–45 was a truly gruesome war crime committed by Winston Churchill to punish the people of India for the Quit India campaign; that it was committed against a civilian population of non-combatants who were under colonial occupation made it all the more appalling. Churchill wrote his own history (with a retinue of 'researchers' and assistants), but his six volumes neglected even a whiff of a mention of the Indian famine. Other historians ought not to let him get away so easily.

Meanwhile, in extremely choppy seas off the coast of Madagascar on 28 April 1943, Subhas Bose and Abid Hasan were transferred from the German U-boat to a Japanese submarine—the only submarine-to-submarine transfer successfully completed in World War II. It was accomplished in seas over which the Allies had clear air and naval supremacy, using a flimsy rubber dinghy and a rope; just how daring the journey was is evident from the fact that the mortality rate on German submarines in the war was 80 per cent. The Japanese submarine, an I–29, was more spacious and the Japanese commander vacated his cabin for Subhas and Abid to use; they immediately felt more at home in the Asian ambience of the Japanese submarine, on which special arrangements had been made for curries to be cooked. On 6 May 1943, the I–29 made landfall in the little island of Sabang off the coast of Sumatra, having been diverted from Penang because Bose's potential arrival there had become too widely known. A few days later, Subhas Bose boarded a Japanese combat aircraft and flew to Tokyo via Penang, Saigon, Manila, Taipei and Hamamatsu before arriving on 16 May at the Imperial Hotel in Tokyo (designed by Frank Lloyd Wright) just opposite the Imperial Palace grounds.

Tojo was apparently unenthusiastic about the INA at this stage. After the initial euphoria at Farrer Park, there had been recriminations within the ranks of the INA, especially because Mohan Singh did not prove to be a natural leader: to his credit, he proved a great early recruiter, and had always said that the INA would only be effective with a charismatic leader like Subhas. Mohan Singh having promoted himself to General (from Captain) also rankled with some of the other officers, especially the large number who had been senior to him in the British Indian Army. Two senior Bangkok-based leaders of the IIL, Giani Pritam Singh and Swami Satyananda Puri (both veterans of the Ghadar Movement of 1911–16, the latter also a member of the Anushilan revolutionary group) were killed when a plane taking them to a conference in Tokyo crashed in March 1942—leaving the movement somewhat bereft, as Mohan Singh and the INA leadership felt that Rash Behari Bose was too close to the Japanese. And amongst the latter, the replacement of the empathetic Fujiwara with Colonel Iwakura (an intelligence operative) and his cohort of arrogant surrogates further vitiated relations. In December 1942, Mohan Singh sought to dissolve the INA and was himself arrested by the Japanese, who eventually sent him to detention in Sumatra. Although Rash Behari had been able to salvage the situation somewhat, Subhas Bose had an uphill struggle to regain credibility with Tojo and the Japanese leadership, which he proceeded to do with elan over the next three weeks.

By the time Prime Minister Tojo met Subhas Bose on 10 June, the latter had built up a strong constituency of supporters in the foreign ministry, and the senior leadership of the army and navy. Tojo himself was thoroughly impressed by the force of Subhas's personality, became an enthusiastic advocate of Indian independence and quickly shed the doubts he had harboured about the Indians' ability to fight. The two men met again on 14 June, when Tojo pledged 'unconditional support' to India's struggle, but requested time to consult his army commanders about Bose's request for a Japanese attack on India from Burma in which the INA would fight shoulder to shoulder with them. Two days later, Subhas Bose was invited to be a special guest at the Imperial Diet, where Tojo declared unequivocally that Japan would do 'everything possible' for India's independence.

Subhas Bose flew to Singapore with Abid and Rash Behari at the end of June, and was received by the INA's top commanders, J. K. Bhonsle (a direct descendant of the Maratha warrior king Shivaji) and Mohammad Zaman Kiani. In the interim, he made several rousing radio broadcasts to Southeast Asia which stirred enormous enthusiasm amongst Indians there: 'The freedom we shall win, through our sacrifices and exertions, we shall be able to preserve with our own strength', promising to 'throw open the prison gates' so that Indians could 'step out of the darkness of prison cells into the light of freedom, joy and self-fulfilment'. On 4 July 1943, at the Cathay theatre in Singapore (a building whose facade still stands) Rash Behari turned over the baton of the IIL and INA to Subhas in a moving ceremony amid unbridled joy for the newly enthused soldiers of the Azad Hind Fauj who sat in the audience. He promised to create a Provisional Government of Free India (which was formally established as the Arzi Hukumat-e-Azad Hind on 21 October 1943), and promised that 'when the revolution succeeds... the task of the provisional government will be over. It will then make room for a permanent government to be set up inside India, in accordance with the will of the Indian people.' British propagandists had tried to insinuate that Subhas was a fascist, but this quote from his founding speech laid that canard to rest. He did believe that a strong, development-oriented party should have decisive powers in the initial years, but Bose neither envisaged himself in the role of leader of such a party nor ever advocated any abridgement of democracy in India, referring always to Gandhi as 'Father of our Nation'.

On 5 and 6 July 1943, Subhas Bose took the salute at two INA military parades on the Padang in front of the City Hall of Singapore, which is flanked on one side by the Singapore Cricket Club (used before the war exclusively by the British) and the other by the Singapore Recreation Club (which used to be reserved for the Eurasians). By then, Bose's presence had electrified Singapore. As the British historians Bayly and Harper described it, 'Subhas Bose drew crowds to public rallies on an unprecedented scale; Chinese and Malays as well as Indians.... This was the true dawn of mass politics in Malaya. As one young Indian recalled, "It was really the first speech, you see, I had heard in my life. Like magnetic power."' Thenceforth, Bose always appeared in military uniform (but conspicuously without medals or other accoutrements and, unlike Mohan Singh, without any grandiose military rank), and on the second day Japan's Prime Minister Tojo himself accompanied Bose on the podium.

By then, excitement had reached a crescendo amongst Indians in the region. S. Rama Nathan (a future president of Singapore) told me that he was a policeman in Johor Bahru at the time, and his curiosity had been aroused by all that he was hearing about Bose, so he came to attend the second rally. Bose's electrifying speech changed his perspective on life, introducing notions of patriotic duty and nationalism that had been totally alien to an audience that was taught from primary school that 'King George VI is our king. Long Live the King!' Nathan joined the IIL, and at least one member of almost every Indian family in Singapore and Malaya joined either the IIL or the INA over subsequent months.

On 9 July, Subhas Bose made a pledge to a crowd of 60,000 civilians which his army was to fulfil in its entirety: 'Indians outside India...are going to organize a fighting force which will be powerful enough to attack the British army of occupation in India. When we do so, a revolution will break out, not only amongst the civilian population at home, but also amongst the Indian Army, which is now standing under the British flag. When the British government is thus attacked...from inside India and from outside—it will collapse, and the Indian people will then regain their freedom.' Bose's rallying call, 'Chalo Delhi' (On to Delhi) was inspired by the slogan of the rebels of 1857, and the symbol of his movement, the Springing Tiger, was a tribute to Tipu Sultan (who had fended off the British in the second Anglo–Mysore War in the 1790s before succumbing in the fourth). And in his most evocative tribute to the spirit of 1857, Bose recruited a prominent female Indian, Dr Lakshmi Swaminathan (scion of a prominent Madras family of freedom fighters who had started a free medical clinic for migrant workers in Singapore) to lead the Rani of Jhansi Regiment, the first all-women's combat unit of any army in Asia (and one of the rarest such units on any side during the World War). Led by 'Captain Lakshmi', the regiment was named after the valiant warrior queen Lakshmibai of Jhansi, the heroine of 1857. In 2006, I spent time with two prominent early recruits: Janaki Nahappan (née Davar) and Rasammah Bhupalan (née Navarednam). The ailing Janaki's eyes lit up when talking about the INA and the Rani Jhansi regiment; she proudly told me of the time she 'finally kissed the soil of India for the first time, with a rifle in my hand' near Imphal in 1944. Rasammah, who had become one of Malaysia's leading educationists (and two of whose former students had become prime ministers of Malaysia) spoke movingly of the most inspirational person she had ever known: 'my leader, Netaji'.

Immediately after taking charge, Subhas Bose realized that what India needed most at this time was food. The famine, of course, provided the perfect justification for declaring war on Britain as the INA was doing. But Subhas did not care about the propaganda potential of the famine, he was instead seized by a fervent desire to provide relief to his starving compatriots. He went to Burma before the end of July to arrange those rice supplies, and met Ba Maw just before and immediately after he became Burma's Adipati on 1 August. Ba Maw wrote that 'when Bose really got down into his subject, he gave you a feeling that you were listening not to a man but to...a long-pent, primordial force suddenly breaking through.' Aung San and his Thakins' Freedom Bloc also had built close ties to Bose's Forward Bloc.

Bose was quickly able to arrange for 100,000 tons of rice to be sent to India, escorted by two Japanese patrol ships, with further similar supplies to follow. Such wartime collaboration between enemies for a humanitarian cause was not unprecedented: in late 1941, Germany had permitted the International Red Cross and other relief agencies to ferry crucial humanitarian supplies into Greece when it was threatened by famine. But the British were 'of course particularly anxious to discredit Subhas Bose in every possible way' (as numerous intelligence operatives at the time noted), so the most stringent press censorship was imposed to ensure that Bose's offer was never reported in the Indian press. But almost every young Indian who possessed a radio listened clandestinely to Subhas Bose's broadcasts whenever it was safe to do so and many millions heard his offer. The British knew the offer was real, because they would surely have called his bluff if they felt Bose could not deliver. But they responded instead with censorship, compounding Churchill's crimes of diverting foodgrain away from India, continuing exports (of 71,000 tons of rice between January and July 1943) from India while famine raged, and of denying rice even to farmers who had cultivated it in areas where the rebellion still persisted, while eliminating all means of transport from within eighty kilometres of the coast.

Thwarted by the inhumanity of the British imperial authorities, Subhas redoubled his effort to recruit volunteers into the IIL and INA. He went to Bangkok as an honoured guest of Prime Minister Phibunsongkhram (who said later, 'if you want to know what personality is, look at Subhas Bose'), and addressed a massive public meeting at Chulalongkorn University on the first anniversary of Gandhi's Quit India resolution. Bose then visited Kuala Lumpur, Ipoh, Penang, Manila, and in subsequent weeks went to Shanghai, Nanjing, Saigon and Jakarta—drumming up funds and recruits wherever he went. At Kuala Lumpur, he was greeted by a rapturous multi-ethnic crowd of 60,000 on the Padang (between the Moorish railway station and the Royal Selangor Club), and amongst the hundreds who enrolled in the Azad Hind Fauj that very day were the two sixteen-year-old girls, Janaki and Rasammah, the former having to overcome parental objections but happily persuading her wealthy father to enrol in the IIL as well. Malaya, which had nearly a million Indians at the time (over a fifth of the total population) became the key recruiting base for the INA, followed closely by Burma (where 400,000 Indians still lived, even after the big emigration of nearly a million before and during the Japanese invasion), while Thailand's well-established community of 60,000 Indians served as a major funding base (as it had already done for the IIL since its founding in Bangkok).

The INA comprised just 12,000 men when Subhas took over, having recovered slightly from the low of 8,000 reached in December 1942. He wanted to build up a force of 50,000 soldiers, but met resistance from the Japanese: Field Marshal Count Terauchi Hisaichi (the Japanese military commander in Southeast Asia) initially agreed to provide training and equipment only for 30,000 men (or three divisions). Bose encouraged his own officers to provide basic training to the thousands of local Tamil, Malayali, Bengali, Punjabi and Telugu speakers who flocked to join the army of liberation, which grew to nearly 60,000 in time, with half of them recruited from amongst the local population. For many of the local plantation and construction workers, the opportunity to associate with Azad Hind was the first chance at dignity they had had in the region where they had worked as indentured labourers in conditions of near-slavery.

What most distinguished the Azad Hind Fauj (literally 'Free India Army', albeit better known in English as the INA) was its conscious attempts at breaking down the barriers of religion, caste and language that the British had erected. While encouraging all soldiers to maintain their religious and linguistic affiliations, Bose ensured that meals were had together, and no regiments were ethnically identified, instead ensuring the full mingling of India's many communities in the three main brigades that he named after the leading Congress figures (Gandhi, Nehru and Azad). Bose himself was a devout Hindu—who spent an hour or more in meditation at the Ramakrishna Mission every evening he was in Singapore—but his religious affiliation was strictly personal, and he worked hard to break down barriers such as the reluctance of Hindu priests to allow non-Hindus into temples: Bose urged that all Indians should have access, as the agnostic Abid Hasan recalled with pride after attending a benediction ceremony for soldiers at a Chettiar temple on Dussehra.

On 21 October 1943, Bose created a Provisional Government of Free India to which over 240,000 Indians in Southeast Asia formally signed oaths of allegiance and another 1.5 million Indians resident across the region were joyfully governed by, voluntarily paying taxes and giving donations. (Subhas often claimed that there were 3 million Indians across East Asia, but this number would only be possible by including those living in Fiji and South Africa!) The new cabinet and INA leadership were truly representative of India as a whole with the Rajput Muslim Mohammad Zaman Kiani as commander of the 1st Regiment (which was soon moved to Rangoon), the Maratha J. K. Bhonsle as overall INA commander, the Sikhs Gulzara Singh and Gurbaksh Dhillon, and the Pathan Muslim Shahnawaz Khan and Punjabi Hindu Prem Sahgal as senior commanders, the Bangalore-born A. D. Loganathan, Bengali A. C. Chatterjee, Kerala Christian John Thivy and Tamil S. Appadurai Ayer (father of the famed social anthropologist Arjun Appadurai), the Tamil Muslim Karim Ghani (previously a parliamentary secretary in Ba Maw's pre-War government), the Bihari A. N. Sahay, the Assamese Debnath Das and the Sikh Sardar Isher Singh amongst its ministers.

Apart from the innovative greeting of 'Jai Hind', Bose's references to Gandhi as 'Father of the Nation' also spread, although his use of a Hindustani translation of Tagore's 'Jana Gana Mana' as the national anthem did not endure (the original Bengali words being adopted by independent India instead). Bose had worked hard on mastering Hindustani (the language understood most widely by Hindu and Muslim troops) and it became the language of the INA, but Bose also taught himself rudimentary Tamil to be able to communicate with the new local recruits. Bose used Hindustani in the Roman script (akin to Atatürk's Turkey) as the official language of Azad Hind—as he had previously suggested to Congress when he was its president—but this sensible idea was dropped by India later.

The Provisional Government of Free India was recognized by Japan, Germany, Italy, Thailand, Croatia, Manchukuo, China (as represented by the Nanjing-based government headed by Wang Jingwei), Burma and the Philippines, while Ireland's Taoiseach (prime minister) Eamon de Valera sent a note of congratulations to Subhas Bose on the day of his inauguration. Two days later, the Azad Hind government declared war on Britain and the US (primarily because of the presence of US troops on Indian soil at the time) although the inclusion of the US was opposed by several cabinet ministers (including Loganathan) and proved problematic for Bose when he publicly sought US support in November 1944.

The week after the proclamation of the Arzi Hukumat, Subhas Bose set off to attend the conference of the Greater East Asia Co-Prosperity Sphere in Tokyo (on 5 and 6 November), insisting that his provisional government would have observer status as it did not intend to join the Japanese-sponsored sphere. Sukarno too was an observer, because (unlike Bose, Ba Maw, Wang Jingwei and Philippines president José Laurel) he did not yet have a provisional government. The Japanese evidence suggests that 'Chandra Bose' was a dominant presence at the conference, his speech 'held the entire assembly in awe' and his powerful personality produced an 'admirable effect'. As soon as Bose finished speaking, Tojo announced that the Andaman and Nicobar Islands would soon be transferred to the Azad Hind government, and that Japan remained fully committed in its support for India's independence. Japan's army chief, General Sugiyama, agreed to treat the INA as an allied army of Japan—and not in any way subordinate to it, with Indian soldiers subject to Indian and not Japanese jurisdiction—and also accepted Bose's plan to send three INA divisions into India. Subhas was to find, however, that Japanese military commanders on the ground were much less willing to implement his operational plans than the ever-solicitous leadership in Tokyo.

Bose then went to Nanjing as a guest of Wang Jingwei's government, from where he broadcast an appeal to Chiang Kai-shek in Chongqing, although this predictably fell on deaf ears, with Chiang increasingly accorded great power status by the Allies. Earlier that year, the Western powers had finally given up extraterritoriality and their rights over treaty ports (quite conveniently, of course, since Japan controlled all those ports at that time!). Wang Jingwei had responded swiftly, ensuring that his government (and not the Japanese military) took charge of all those ports relinquished formally by the Western powers.

Subhas recruited several hundred Sikh soldiers in Shanghai, and continued his recruitment drive in Manila (where he was President Laurel's guest) and across the East Indies—Jakarta, Surabaya as well as Kalimantan and Sumatra. By late November, preparations began for the deployment of the INA's first division to India, with the first guerrilla regiment arriving on the India–Burma border. A small party of spies (headed by S. N. Chopra, a former schoolteacher from Batu Pahat in Johor) landed by submarine on the Kathiawar coast in western India in December 1943, and fanned out across India to their respective destinations.

Subhas flew to the Andaman and Nicobar Islands from a state visit to Bangkok on 29 December 1943, and unfurled the flag of Azad Hind over the Cellular Jail in Port Blair where so many hundreds of nationalist revolutionaries had been incarcerated and tortured by the British authorities. He appointed Major General Loganathan (who had been a military doctor in the British Indian Army and was—like his fellow doctor Major General A. C. Chatterjee—amongst Azad Hind's ablest administrators) as the chief commissioner of the newly renamed Shaheed (Martyrs) and Swaraj (Independence) islands. Loganathan was very unhappy, however, with the way the Japanese treated him—handing him control over only a few civilian affairs (particularly education) as the Japanese navy considered the islands too strategically important to give up their own tight control over policing, including extremely harsh treatment of anyone accused of spying for the British. (Some critics have bizarrely attempted to blame the INA for the atrocities committed by the Japanese troops during the March–April 1942 Japanese invasion of the islands; this is an absurd charge, as the INA did not formally take control of the liberated islands until twenty-one months later.)

On 7 January 1944, Bose moved his forward headquarters to Rangoon, where he had earlier paid obeisance at the mausoleum of Bahadur Shah Zafar, the last Mughal emperor of India. Now he gave special attention to preparing his 'bahadur' (fearless) units for their coming assault on British-held Manipur and Nagaland, while also reorganizing his cabinet to provide logistical support, and assemble the civilian administrators who would take control over any areas that fell to the combined forces of the INA and Japan. These civilians had already received several months' training at a Reconstruction College in Singapore run by a former district magistrate from India. General Mutaguchi Renya had planned a two-pronged attack, one on Arakan inside Burmese territory that the British still held (with the aim of pushing them back, and then reaching Chittagong) and another thrust further north aimed at taking Imphal and Kohima. The INA's objective was to get to either Chittagong in eastern Bengal or the plains of Assam (just north of Kohima) as soon as possible in order to spark an uprising amongst the people of Assam and Bengal.

The Japanese were primarily interested in pre-empting a British reinvasion of Burma. Subhas had a raging argument over a couple of days with General Kawabe Masakazu, the commander-in-chief of Japanese forces, over how best to deploy the INA troops. Bose insisted that, 'The first drop of blood to be shed on Indian soil should be that of a member of the INA.' Kawabe argued that it was impossible for the INA to be used as a spearhead (as Bose wanted), since the INA force was barely 2 per cent the size of the Japanese force on the Burma border. Kawabe thus wanted to attach small detachments of INA troops (200–300 each) to each Japanese formation but Subhas insisted that the

INA must retain its separate identity throughout, and this could not happen if the INA operated in units smaller than a battalion. The guerrilla regiment of the INA's first division had undergone advanced training in the jungles of northern Malaya, and its soldiers (led by Shahnawaz Khan) had dubbed themselves the Subhas Brigade (despite Bose's strong objections). Finally, on 24 January, Bose agreed that the first battalion of the Subhas Brigade would help oppose the British West African Division in Arakan's Kaladan Valley, while the other two battalions would help guard routes over the Chin Hills (that formed the border between Burma and India's Manipur and Nagaland regions). He was clear that this would be a test of the INA's fighting qualities.

On 3 February, Bose gave his men an emotional send-off: 'Arise! We have no time to lose. Take up your arms.... We shall carve our way through the enemy's ranks, or, if God wills, we shall die a martyr's death. And in our last sleep we shall kiss the road which will bring our army to Delhi. The road to Delhi is the road to Freedom. Chalo Delhi!' The very next day, the Azad Hind Fauj covered itself in glory in its first engagements on the Arakan front: a Bahadur group led by Major L. S. Misra conducted highly effective reconnaissance and subversion which enabled Japan's 55th Division to trap the 7th British Indian Division east of the Meyu range and cut off its communication links with headquarters of the British 15th Army. Japanese survivors were to wistfully recall the joyous ringing tones of the marching songs of the INA: 'Kadam kadam badhaye ja, khushi ke geet gaaye ja' (March forward step by glorious step, singing freedom's happy song), and their sheer unadulterated joy on re-entering the 'pavitra bhoomi' (sacred soil) of India.

Unlike in Malaya and Burma in 1942, however, the British Indian Army did not easily capitulate, and instead chose to fight on even in the face of such early setbacks. A major factor helping the British was the security of overwhelming American air power—unlike in 1942, when the Japanese had air superiority in Malaya and the East Indies (and eventually also in Burma). This time, the American aircraft outnumbered the Japanese ten to one, and this became of increasing importance as the battle ensued. The Japanese failed to fully capitalize on Misra's breakthrough, and the hoped-for thrust into Chittagong did not materialize. But the Arakan-based battalion led by Major P. S. Raturi captured Kaladan, Paletwa and Daletme as they steadily moved northward on the Kaladan Valley and gained a foothold on the Indian side of the border at Mowdok.

In the early skirmishes, about a hundred British Indian troops came over to the INA side—although a few were shot by British officers in the attempt. Meanwhile, Shahnawaz Khan's 2nd and 3rd Battalions began an offensive in the Haka–Falam sector on 10 February and, with the swift advance of the

Japanese–Indian forces into Nagaland and Manipur, Major General Zaman Kiani (commander of the 1st Division) set up his divisional headquarters in Chamal on 17 April. Some 9,000 INA troops were soon fighting in eight different sectors on the plains near Imphal and the neighbourhood of Kohima (then little more than a large village, albeit the seat of a colonial district commissioner). An INA detachment led by Colonel Shaukat Ali Malik captured Moirang in Manipur and planted the Indian tricolour there on 14 April 1944, aided by the young Manipuri Mairembam Koireng Singh (who, in 1963, was to become Manipur's first chief minister when it acquired a legislative assembly). Malik's forces advanced swiftly with the Japanese 33rd Division in the Tiddim–Bishenpur sector of Manipur, successfully establishing a spy network of local Manipuris. Subhas Bose transferred Colonel A. C. Chatterjee (previously finance minister of the provisional government) to the India–Burma front as Chief Administrator of Occupied Territories, which now included a considerable part of Manipur and Nagaland. (The businessman N. S. Raghavan replaced Chatterjee as finance minister.) Amongst the local notables who joined the INA in the vicinity of Kohima was Angami Zapu Phizo—the future leader of the Naga nationalist uprising against India, whose 1948 manifesto of rebellion specifically referred to the shabby treatment INA veterans like him had received from Nehru's government; in his 16 May 1951 speech demanding a plebiscite too, Phizo mentioned his role in helping the INA to free 'most of Nagaland as far as Kohima' from 'the dominating control and influence of the British'.

For about a month, the hills around Kohima were under INA control, but the Japanese failed to take Bose's advice to circumvent Kohima and instead focus on taking the key railhead at Dimapur (then a larger town, northwest of Kohima); while Tojo and Sugiyama in Tokyo were persuaded of Bose's strategy of aiming to rapidly reach the plains of Assam or Bengal, Kawabe was never convinced, preferring to fight a holding action. The fighting at Kohima and later around Imphal was fierce, with territory changing hands frequently, and some of the most climactic battles occurring on either side of an Imphal tennis court. The Japanese had set 29 April as the date on which Imphal would fall to them, and the INA troops had taken just three weeks' worth of supplies with that date in mind—and in the hope that 'Churchill rations' would fall into their hands as they captured new territories. But the stiff British resistance proved unexpected. Air support from the Americans enabled exhausted British Indian and African troops to be flown out and replaced with fresh contingents of troops, apart from receiving supply reinforcements, and bombing runs by the United States Air Force on Japanese positions. Three hundred soldiers from the INA's Gandhi Brigade made a valiant attempt to capture the main British airfield at Palel on 2 May; they came close to capturing it, but were eventually beaten by covering fire from US planes.

Subhas Bose's intelligence chief, N. G. Swami, had successfully infiltrated some twenty-five operatives behind the British lines by sea, and they now considered sending some over land as well, but the key was a breakthrough towards Bengal or the Assam plains. On their side, the Japanese air force was exhausted and overstretched in the island-to-island combat that was occurring in the Pacific. It proved incapable of even acting as a source of new supplies and rations to their forces. The early onset of the monsoon that year on 21 May infinitely worsened the supply situation for the INA and their Japanese allies, as rivers of mud began to flow, and the torrential rain made the exhausted and ill-fed troops even more vulnerable to pests and disease. Morale deteriorated as supplies ran out and soldiers were forced to subsist on grass and small fish caught in streams. Colonel Inayat Kiani (Zaman's cousin) was leading the Gandhi Brigade in fierce fighting against the Scots of the Seaforth Highlanders, but they received a severe setback when Inayat's deputy, Major B. J. S. Garewal deserted to the British side, taking key operational plans with him. Abid Hasan was appointed to replace him, and managed to rally his forces and disentangle them from a dire situation. (Garewal was assassinated by a fellow Sikh on a Lahore street soon after the war ended.)

Even the official British history of the war acknowledged that the fall of Imphal would have led to 'a revolt in Bengal and Bihar against British rule in India... on a far greater scale than the riots of 1942'. As it happened, the Allied forces' successful defence of Imphal proved to be the most decisive turning point of the Asian war. On 10 July, the exhausted Japanese forces gave the signal to suspend the Imphal campaign and M. Z. Kiani reluctantly followed suit, ordering all regiments of the INA's 1st Division to withdraw on 18 July. The retreat was an exhausting and chaotic affair, made worse by a severe dearth of rations and transport amid the rain, mud, pests and snakes. Upon meeting his supreme commander, Abid Hasan reported that 'the situation is slightly not so very good'—still holding on to his impish sense of humour, as he repeated words he had heard from a Japanese officer. One motor transport company led by Colonel Raja Mohammed Arshad and the civilian Zora Singh did yeoman service in moving wounded soldiers from Kalewa to Yeu in Burma. The 2nd Division of the INA had moved up to Mandalay by this time, and Bose rallied his forces and inspired them to regroup and fight on, for their goal was still to show that Indians could create a freedom army of their own that was ready to spill their own blood and sacrifice their lives if necessary, in order to gain India her independence.

On 26 July 1944, Tojo resigned as prime minister, and his successor Koiso invited Subhas Bose to Tokyo in late October 1944. In the intervening period, Bose went to the front, tending to his wounded soldiers and organizing their treatment by his medical corps and Ranis (many of whom had received nurses' training). His presence and spirited words helped rally the demoralized forces, and large amounts of donated funds poured in to reinforce the INA. Bose was able to create a well capitalized, viable Azad Hind Bank against the objections of Japanese area commanders.

During his two-week trip to Tokyo, Bose's government formally received diplomatic recognition from Japan, and Ambassador Hachiya was dispatched to Bose's headquarters in Rangoon soon afterwards. (This formal diplomatic representation was aimed at overcoming the glaring difficulties that had emerged between the INA and its liaison, Hikari Kikan, which was not influential enough to have its voice heard by local Japanese commanders; a diplomat would be able to convey Bose's requirements more clearly to Tokyo, and ensure early redress of any problems: had this arrangement been put in place a half-year earlier, the outcome and strategy in Imphal might have been different!) Bose also used his time in Tokyo to reach out to the Soviet Union (through a diplomatic missive sent to Moscow via the Soviet ambassador in Tokyo, Jacob Malik, to which Moscow's response is unknown) and the people of the US (via two radio broadcasts). He explained to his 'American friends' that Asia was 'surging with revolutionary fervour', but Americans hadn't helped Asia when it had a chance to do so. The Asians had 'plunged into the struggle alongside her' not to help Japan but 'we are helping ourselves—we are helping Asia'. On 10 January 1945, Bose went back to Burma to rally the INA to wage a final heroic rearguard action to show that 'Imphal has given us the knowledge and the certainty that in the fight for independence, which Indians at home will join as soon as they receive the call, we shall ultimately prevail.' Now, Bose argued, the army needed to pay the ultimate price of freedom—spilling their own blood in Burma (and if necessary in Malaya) to both earn the right to independence, and defend their million compatriots there: 'Tum mujhe khoon do, main tumhe azadi dunga. Give me blood, and I will give you freedom. Die for your country, that through your death your country may live.'

The INA put up a valiant last stand in February–April 1945 at Mt Popa in Burma, led by three men whose names were to become synonymous in India with patriotic valour before the end of the year: Sahgal, Dhillon, Shahnawaz. Prem Sahgal had been Bose's military secretary (and was later to marry Lakshmi Swaminathan), but he specifically requested to be sent to the front and took up a defensive position on the western slope of Mt Popa on

13 February. A few days earlier, American B–29 bombers had flattened an INA hospital at Myang, just ten kilometres outside Rangoon, despite the fact that it was marked with a large Red Cross sign. Dhillon's Nehru Regiment (comprising less than 1,500 men with just four machine guns, three light mortars with twenty rounds of ammunition each, and rifles) held off Major General Frank Messervy's 7th Indian Division on 14–15 February where the mighty Irrawaddy narrows markedly at Nyaung-U (just northwest of Meiktila and Mt Popa). Churchill had wanted to recapture some part of erstwhile British territory, so that all the glory of defeating (or at least pushing back) Japan did not accrue to the Americans alone. Although Malaya was strategically much more important, an amphibious landing would be required there, and would take many months, with the probability of success uncertain. Although Burma would be strategically incidental to the course of the war elsewhere in Southeast Asia (since it was isolated from it by Japanese-aligned Thailand), it was its symbolic importance that propelled Sir William Slim (knighted in Imphal) and his 14th Army.

Slim was especially dismissive of the INA in his memoirs, but one of the few places he acknowledges them is Nyaung-U, claiming that his army faced 'variously reported as between five and ten thousand' men of 'the 2nd Indian National Army Division' in the Nyaung-U-Pagan area. This is a backhanded compliment to Dhillon and especially his battalion commanders Hari Ram (7th Battalion) and Chandar Bhan (9th Battalion)—who fought so valiantly that Slim estimated they had four to eight times as many men as they actually did! Hari Ram's 400 men (mainly with those four machine guns) sank many of Messervy's boats as they attempted to cross the Irrawaddy at Nyaung-U, with many other boats being overturned in the melee. Further southwest in Pagan, Chandar Bhan's 500 troops stalled the attempted diversionary advance of a Sikh battalion with rifle fire. Just when it seemed Dhillon's two battalions had won the day (without the use of his reserve battalion of 500 men at his command post of Tetthe), another British Punjabi battalion made for Nyaung-U in the wee hours of 15 February aided by a bombing run by aircraft overhead and heavy firing by a tank brigade and 25-pounder howitzers. When the British forces made it onto his bank of the river, Hari Ram (with about 100 troops) surrendered. But several hundred INA soldiers gave their lives fighting, there and near Pagan. By the evening of the 15th, the overwhelming superiority in numbers of the British forces was obvious to Dhillon, and over the next two days, he prudently withdrew his remaining troops to Mt Popa—a mountain-oasis rising to 4,000 feet above an arid plain west of Meiktila.

Against heavy odds and with limited ammunition and even lower morale amid news of Allied victories in Europe and the Pacific, Dhillon and Sahgal (later joined by the commander of the INA's 2nd Division, Shahnawaz) held Mt Popa for two months. Some of the British troops circumvented the scenic mountain to get to Meiktila and made for points south. On 25 February, Bose himself decided he would go to Mt Popa to urge his troops on, but Shahnawaz objected strongly: 'You are proposing to risk your life, but… your life is not your own, it is a precious trust for India, held in our keeping: we are responsible.' Two days later, Bose was almost trapped in Meiktila as the British approached; he took a loaded tommy gun, boarded a car with Shahnawaz and two others, and reached Pyinmana the next day after being strafed by machine guns fired from aircraft over the village of Yindaw. At Pyinmana, Bose created a new X Brigade from the remainder of his 1st Division, and decided he would himself go down fighting there with them. Again Shahnawaz persuaded him that this would not serve any real purpose at that point.

The INA's defence of Mt Popa—coupled with occasional victories for General Kimura's Japanese forces around Meiktila—almost succeeded in preventing Slim from reaching Rangoon before the monsoons arrived. But during this period, one major setback for Japan and the INA was the decision of Aung San (still official war minister and number two in Ba Maw's cabinet) to take his Burma National Army (BNA) over to the British side on 27 March. Ten days earlier, he had ceremonially set off with his seven battalions, supposedly destined for the front in Meiktila, a couple of hundred miles away. Having made arrangements for his family (and those of other BNA generals) to find safe haven away from the Japanese, Aung San's BNA turned their guns on the Japanese on 27 March near Pegu (just seventy kilometres north of Rangoon). The British began to refer to the BNA as the Anti-Fascist Organization, although only the communists had insisted previously on calling the Japanese 'fascists' (the term Mussolini used to describe his political philosophy). The Japanese notion of Asian values ('Asia for the Asians') had very little in common with Mussolini's views, especially as they applied to Indians, Burmese, Filipinos, Indonesians or even the majority of Chinese. Later, the British more appropriately referred to the BNA as Patriotic Burmese Forces.

The BNA's decision to switch sides made a considerable (and perhaps decisive) difference in Slim's 14th Army reaching Rangoon about a week after the monsoons arrived that year towards the end of April. Although the BNA had been envious of the INA's larger premises in Rangoon (partly a consequence of its stronger financial footing), the two nationalist armies had put aside the pre-War racial bitterness between Burmese and Indians, and developed close fraternal ties. They reached an understanding not to fight each other after March 1945 even though they were suddenly on different sides in the war. (M. Z. Kiani suggested to Subhas Bose that the INA should consider emulating what the BNA had done, but Subhas rejected the idea outright—partly because he felt responsible to the nearly 2 million Indians in Southeast Asia who still remained under Japanese control, and could all face reprisals if the INA were to switch sides. Besides, Bose's life's work made it unlikely he would ever align with the British until they had quit India.) At Mt Popa, Sahgal's men fought two heroic actions in April 1945: between the 1st and 6th of that month, Sahgal and Kanwal Singh led their men valiantly in the Battle of Legyi a few kilometres from the summit of Mt Popa, and Captain Bagri went down fighting with 600 of his men at Taungdwingyi on 20 April. In both actions, the British used tanks, armoured cars and heavy guns, while the INA had little more than their rifles and a few mortars. Ten days earlier, the British had bombed an INA field hospital at Kyaukpadaung—killing eighty patients and injuring thirty others.

Eventually, Prem Sahgal was captured near Slim's headquarters at Allanmyo on 29 April, fighting on with almost no rations and rapidly diminishing ammunition. The monsoons had broken over Burma by then, but the lack of Japanese air support—and the crucial intelligence provided by the BNA—had turned the tide decisively in favour of the British. Dhillon and Shahnawaz were captured on 18 May near Pegu, ten days after the German surrender in Europe. The historian Peter Fay asserts that it was this 'battling with no hope along the Irrawaddy' over more than three months 'that justified the freedom army and gave it in the end such moral leverage'. The dignity with which the senior INA officers (Shahnawaz, Dhillon, Sahgal, as well the Rani Jhansi regiment's Lakshmi Swaminathan) behaved upon their capture began to build their reputations, and also change the minds of their interrogators, especially when they were Indians. When General Douglas Gracey asked Prem Sahgal, 'What did you mean, you people, by going on fighting? We had armour, artillery. You chaps had nothing. But instead of surrendering, you fought. It was madness. Why did you do it?' Prem responded that it was 'madness of a deliberate, revolutionary sort' and a 'revolutionary army lives on the spirit of madness'. It was the kind of answer that got him branded a 'bad sort'.

Bose learnt on 20 April that the Japanese were preparing to abandon Rangoon, and that Ba Maw would be leaving with them. Bose destroyed most of his papers and files as the Japanese too were doing. But while the Japanese were abandoning their station completely, Bose decided that an INA contingent would stay on to maintain order in the city and offer the formal surrender when the British troops arrived. He left Loganathan and 5,000 INA troops behind to accomplish this task and they successfully prevented any looting in the already ravaged Burmese capital (that the British had nearly destroyed with their scorched earth approach on their way out in 1942), and handed the city over peacefully to the British troops on 4 May 1945. Meanwhile, Bose sent the X Regiment and several of his senior commanders ahead to Moulmein, and thence on to Bangkok. But he insisted that he himself would not leave until transportation had been found for every last INA soldier who was to leave, and especially for the 100 or so remaining women of the Rani Jhansi regiment.

They set off on 24 April in a convoy with twenty-one trucks, but within a few days were down to just two trucks—some hit by enemy fire, others stuck in the mud or out of fuel—and eventually Subhas Bose walked with his Ranis and men, even as British aircraft strafed them from the air, unaware that their Enemy Number One was amongst the group of marchers heading towards Moulmein. They walked mainly at night to avoid easy detection, taking cover in villages during the day. Rasammah Bhupalan and Janaki Davar never forgot their leader's personal sacrifice of walking heroically with men and women soldiers, his feet full of blisters and sores, through southern Burma until they all reached safety in Moulmein on 3 May. Then they were able to board trains that took them safely to Bangkok, where Bose began reassembling his cabinet on 15 May, and sent one senior minister each to Saigon, Hanoi, Kuala Lumpur and Singapore to guard against their simultaneous capture.

Wavell (now Viceroy of India) called the Simla Conference in mid-June 1945 to make preparations for post-War political changes. His main purpose was to put arrangements in place that would ensure that Britain's strategic interests in the subcontinent were protected ahead of the July election that might give Labour a bigger role in the government (perhaps even a Commons majority). Bose was worried about this development, and urged in his radio broadcasts to India that Gandhi and Congress leaders should not negotiate with Wavell and, instead, await the Labour government that he felt was inevitable after the elections. (This was remarkable prescience, and quite contrary to most analysts' expectations at the time.) Bose believed (like much of the Congress leadership) that Attlee, Cripps and Bevin would be much more sympathetic to India's interests but this belief was naive. In reality, the Simla Conference proved to be a farce, because Wavell's constitutional suggestions were even more pro-Jinnah than Cripps had proposed in 1942. Wavell was offering that all members of his Executive Council (apart from Viceroy Wavell himself and Commander-in-Chief Auchinleck) would be Indians, but offered an equal number of seats to Hindus and Muslims, with the Muslim League having the exclusive right to appoint all Muslim members. The Congress president, Maulana Azad, himself was a Muslim as was the former Congress premier of NWFP (Dr Khan Sahib), who was also at Simla. As we saw in Chapter 4, the Muslim League had won less than a third of the Muslim seats in the provincial elections of 1937, so there was no objective basis on which the Muslim League had earned the exclusive right to have every Muslim seat on the Executive Council (and demographically, no basis for Muslims and Hindus to have an equal number of seats). The Congress rejected these proposals outright.

Meanwhile, as Subhas Bose said, the fall of Burma had one positive side effect: 'The British Indian Army have now seen us [the INA] with their own eyes. What is the result? There is no longer any talk of a puppet Army—of a Japanese Indian Force, or "J. I. F.". Even enemy propagandists now talk, at last, of an I. N. A.' Hugh Toye, the British intelligence officer who wrote a biography of Bose in 1957, understood that the long period of 'fraternization' that began in May 1945 (and gathered pace after September) between INA soldiers and the arriving soldiers of the British Indian Army, navy and air force resulted in a 'political consciousness which the Indian Serviceman had never before possessed. He received a picture of the INA uncorrected... by any official statement. He saw it as a band of oppressed heroes and listened eagerly to the hospitable and now fully politically conscious Indian civilians of South East Asia, who had their own tale to tell about an independent Indian Government and the departed glories of Bose's Cabinet.'

The INA trials (of captured members) began on 5 November 1945 at the Red Fort in Delhi, as three stalwarts of the Azad Hind Fauj—one a Muslim (Shahnawaz Khan), one a Hindu (Prem Sahgal) and one a Sikh (Gurbaksh Dhillon)—arrived at Subhas Bose's 'Chalo Delhi' destination in ironic ironclad circumstances. The commander-in-chief of the British Indian Army, Claude Auchinleck, had reported to his bosses on 31 October that the Indian Army would accept the INA trials as 'the majority view is that they are all traitors'. And he believed that stories about the INA's returnee troops (who numbered no more than 23,000 survivors) would be overwhelmed by those of loyalist British Indian Army troops (numbering nearly a million) who would be returning to those same villages and towns. Hugh Toye, who delved into Subhas Bose's life and became a grudging admirer, knew that there already were underlying problems with this view because the nature of demobilization in Malaya had allowed the intermingling of INA prisoners and British Indian Army loyalists for too long. It had taken several months to evacuate the Indian troops, who were still the last ones to be repatriated after the British and Australian ones, so even the loyalist troops' views and opinions about the war and nationalism were coloured.

During the war, there had been a complete blackout in India of any news about the INA. If any news reports mentioned them at all, they were scornfully dismissed as no more than small clusters of JIFs. While young Indians had been listening in to Bose's broadcasts, their newspapers contained almost no reports about the INA's actual role as a freedom army that fought a war for India's independence. So, when the newspapers began to carry detailed reports about the INA trials, the vast majority of Indians (and, especially, British residents of India) began hearing for the first time about the heroic fighting by an ill-equipped and poorly-supplied but valiant freedom army of soldiers and civilian recruits, men and women, who had been prepared to lay down their lives so that India could be free. It had an electrifying impact on the nation, spurred further by the upright and attractive personalities of the three officers facing trial. S. A. Ayer recalled the thrill of realizing (upon his arrival in Delhi from Tokyo to testify at the trials) that the 'INA had literally burst upon the country… From the Himalayas to Cape Comorin was aflame with an enthusiastic fervour unprecedented in its history'.

On 20 November, a secret note from the head of the Intelligence Bureau (IB), Norman Smith, agreed that 'there has seldom been a matter which has attracted so much Indian public interest and, it is safe to say, sympathy.' The evidence was everywhere: massive demonstrations and a strike (hartal) had been called across Punjab on the first two days of the trial, with thousands of students demonstrating in Lahore, Lyallpur and Rawalpindi, and 'INA Days' had been held in Karachi, Madras, Vellore, Salem and right across the length and breadth of India. In Madurai, two people were killed in police firing, and three days of strikes and police firing in Calcutta followed by rioting resulted in thirty-five deaths and several hundred injured there between 21 and 24 November. Demonstrations in sympathy with the Calcutta victims occurred in Dhaka, Patna, Benares, Allahabad, Karachi and Bombay (with several killed in police firing) and the IB was especially concerned about a growing undercurrent of anti-European feeling evident in these demonstrations. Posters had appeared in Delhi and Calcutta threatening to kill twenty Englishmen for the hanging of every INA hero.

British bosses were startled to hear their employees refer to Subhas Chandra Bose (who had been so demonized in the English-language press) as 'the George Washington of India', with photos of him and the three INA officers taking on iconic status throughout the country. Shops refused to serve British clients, and increasing evidence of racial hostility towards the British was manifested in mounting stories of insubordination across the country. The governor of the Central Provinces was amongst the first to voice doubts about the willingness of Indian troops to fire on mobs—comparing the atmosphere to that which prevailed in 1857, the epitome of British fears about their presence in India.

The Congress party—moribund in the wake of the crushing of Gandhi's Quit India Movement—had been revived partly by this rush of patriotic fervour. And the Muslim League too came out strongly in favour of the INA, somewhat ironically so, given Bose's hostility to Jinnah in his broadcasts. The very fact that Muslims had such a prominent role in the Azad Hind army and government made it impossible for the Muslim League to ignore the INA, and joint Congress–League demonstrations were held in support of the INA in Delhi, Calcutta and Lahore in a rare moment of unity. Jawaharlal Nehru, having effectively retired from the bar some twenty-five years earlier, decided to join the INA officers' defence team alongside the veteran Congressman Bhulabhai Desai and the seventy-three-year-old ailing barrister Tej Bahadur Sapru. This was an ironic twist for Nehru: when the INA was fighting in the trenches and forests of Manipur and Nagaland, Jawaharlal had provocatively travelled to Bengal and Assam and said that he would personally oppose Subhas Bose even at the head of his army. INA veterans like John Jacob and Janaki Davar told me how bitter they were about this act of treachery by a man whose name adorned one of the INA brigades. It was, no doubt, an important reason why the British were far more willing to have Nehru as an interlocutor in 1945–46 than Gandhi (who Wavell described as 'shrewd but devious and malevolent' and refused to meet), apart from the fact that, like Churchill and Amery, he was an old Harrovian, albeit one with Fabian Socialist leanings (which, in turn, were later to prove appealing to Attlee and Cripps, who shared many of those leanings).

In the end Nehru's membership of the defence team was little more than symbolic, as Bhulabhai Desai's eloquent advocacy needed no substitutes. In a brilliant ten-hour summation, Desai argued that it was 'not a case of three individuals waging war against the King, but the right of the Indian National Army—the organized army of a duly-constituted Provisional Government of India—to wage war for India's liberation.' A war for the liberation of a people, if properly declared and conducted, gave those waging such a war the rights and immunities of belligerents, as Britain had in the past conferred through support of Bolivarian rebels in South America, of the Confederate Army in the US Civil War, of Garibaldi in Italy and Byron in Greece, or indeed of Dutch, Polish and Yugoslav governments-in-exile during World War II (even while they had no territory to call their own). While acknowledging that some of the INA men had a previous allegiance, Bhulabhai argued that their 'king' and 'country' did not coincide, as they had not in 1776 for George Washington and his men, who had consequently repudiated their allegiance to the British crown in order to fight for the rights and independence of their country. Shahnawaz, Sahgal and Dhillon had done precisely the same thing as the Americans whose descendants were now the friends and allies of England and 'their warmest and greatest supporters in the task of saving civilization'.

Desai argued that at Farrer Park on 16 February 1942, when Colonel Hunt had handed the Indian soldiers over to the Japanese, their bond of allegiance to Britain was broken, and 'to insist upon an everlasting allegiance on the part of a subject people would be tantamount to...perpetuation of their slavery'. Since the Provisional Government controlled territory (Andaman and Nicobar Islands for eighteen months, Manipur and Bishnupur areas for four months, and the area of Ziawadi), it had more legitimacy in declaring war than the Czech and Polish partisans that Britain had supported in World War I. The 'municipal law' of British India on treason therefore did not apply, argued Desai, but the provisions of international law did. And while the latter had not acknowledged the rights of non-European peoples until the nineteenth century (including their right to sovereignty and self-determination), they surely did in the twentieth century.

Brilliant and colourful as this argument was, the three were inevitably found guilty of waging war against the King, but not murder. On 3 January 1946, they heard that their sentence was not execution—the first surprise. Instead, they were to be cashiered (dismissed from service), forfeit all pay and allowances, and receive transportation for life. Then, as the American historian Peter Ward Fay described it, 'the officer added, in a low matter-of-fact voice, that with respect to transportation for life...the sentence had been remitted by the Commander-in-Chief'. The three INA men were confused and asked what they should do now. They were told that they were free to go! Where? 'If you have people in Delhi, go there. Otherwise we'll make a booking for you on a train to Lahore.'

In Delhi the next day, Asaf Ali of the Congress organized a massive rally attended by well over 100,000 people, rapturously chanting 'Azad Hind Fauj Zindabad!' (Long Live the INA) and other slogans. When they took the short train ride to Lahore the next day, the Senior Police Superintendent there reported that 'a seething mass of humanity stretching back into the heart of the City' had gathered to welcome 'the three heroes of the Delhi Trial... and celebrate their victory'. The tumultuous welcome from an ecstatic crowd of nearly a hundred thousand of their fellow Punjabis was the ultimate vindication for the three heroes and the army they had fought valiantly for. 'It was the triumph of the INA', as historian Fay put it.

Auchinleck had made the extraordinary decision to remit the sentences because the turmoil induced by the INA trials of November–December 1945 had fundamentally changed his mind about the loyalty of the Indian Army. The first bombshell came from the Governor of Punjab, Sir Bertrand Glancy, on 17 November. Glancy said in his memorandum that Shahnawaz, Sahgal and Dhillon are considered heroes in the eyes of most Punjabis, and treating them as 'traitors' only adds to their popularity. A death sentence for these heroes would result in far worse violence than in 1942 or 1919 (preceding the Jallianwala Bagh massacre) and make a constitutional settlement extremely difficult. In particular, Glancy asserted that the trials were serving no useful purpose; although the current trial could not be abandoned (as that would embolden Congress too much), he advised that future trials should be dropped, and must not carry the charge of treason, which was inflaming the greatest resentment. He was also certain that the presence of even the small number of INA returnees to the villages was bound to 'infect' all demobilized soldiers, and nationalist feeling was now spreading fast across the Punjab. If this vital recruiting ground for the Indian Army were no longer securely loyal, Britain's hold on India would erode rapidly.

Three days after receiving Glancy's memorandum (and the minutes of a conference called to discuss it), Auchinleck recommended that treason trials should cease. And he began his own investigations of what Indian officers really felt. On 27 November, Sir George Cunningham, Governor of NWFP, went further than Glancy, advising Auchinleck that 'as Indian opinion is opposed to the trial of these persons, he wipes the whole thing out and takes no further proceedings against anyone.' He urged Auchinleck to halt the first trial and cancel all subsequent ones. Despite the strong opinions of the governors of the two provinces from which the majority of soldiers were still recruited, the Commander-in-Chief was not convinced at first, and pressed on with trials of those accused of 'brutal acts' while forestalling new treason trials. But by December he was reporting to London that, in the event of an insurrection, British battalions alone would need to be deployed to suppress them, but there were too few of these in India to accomplish the task. 'To regain control of the situation, nothing short of an organized campaign for the reconquest of India is likely to suffice.' He requested three additional British battalions, but the British Cabinet flatly denied those to him: troops were being rapidly demobilized, and there simply was no appetite amongst soldiers to return to new battle duties in India. And when pressed, Indian officers had quietly admitted to Auchinleck that they could not be sure of their men's loyalties if an insurrection occurred, and most were not able to assure their own personal loyalty in such a situation either.

Auchinleck had concluded that every Indian soldier was a 'nationalist' now, with only the degree differing. In a 'personal and secret' letter to all senior British officers explaining his decision to remit the sentences on Sahgal, Dhillon and Shahnawaz, Auchinleck wrote that while most Indian officers acknowledged the 'gravity' of the charges, 'practically all are sure that any attempt to enforce the sentence would have led to chaos in the country at large, and probably to mutiny and dissension in the Army, *culminating in its dissolution*'.

The historian Peter Fay concluded: 'In the autumn of 1945 India was swept by a storm of excitement and indignation, a storm that Bose and his renegades ignited. It was a storm the Indian officer, and the jawan too, could not ignore. They did not ignore it. In 1942, at the time of Quit India, there had been no question of their reliability. Now their own commander doubted it. Three years of campaigning, three years climaxed by battlefield victories in Europe and the Irrawaddy, do not explain the change. Only that autumn storm can. It was the Indian National Army that forced Britain's hand.' At the height of the Quit India agitation of 1942, a hundred thousand new recruits were enrolling in the British Indian Army every month. In the aftermath of the patriotic fervour induced by the INA trials, soldiers and officers had all become nationalistic for the first time and could no longer be relied upon to fire on their compatriots in the event of an insurrection. The basis of the British empire—the unquestioning loyalty of the Indian armed forces—had been thoroughly undermined by the INA trials. Thwarted in its advance on Chittagong and the plains of Assam in 1944, the Azad Hind Fauj had succeeded in its ultimate goal in late 1945: of inciting the patriotic fervour of the Indian people, and spreading that ardour from civilians to airmen, sappers and soldiers of the armed forces on which Britain's imperial rule depended.

General Francis Tuker too noted that anger over the INA trials was threatening the edifice of the Indian Army, the implicit loyalty of which underpinned the British imperium. The Congress president, Maulana Azad, who had always been sceptical about Bose—and especially of his decision to form an army of liberation—felt the anger tangibly on streets across India: 'Wherever I went during this period, young men of the Defence Forces came out to welcome me and expressed their sympathy and admiration without any regard for the reaction of their European officers.' Gurkha soldiers lined up to meet him in Lahore, and police constables in Calcutta shouted pro-Congress slogans when they saw him. In Karachi, naval officers told him they would support Congress in the event of any confrontation with the government.

In January, there was a near-paralysing strike by 5,200 officers and pilots of the Royal Indian Air Force (RIAF). On 11 February, riots broke out in Calcutta and elsewhere after the sentencing of an INA soldier called Rashid Ali to seven years' rigorous imprisonment for murder. Simultaneously, trouble was brewing since 8 February on the HMIS *Talwar*, a signals training ship based in Bombay. On 18 February, this became a full-scale revolt, with demands for the release of all INA prisoners, the equalization of pay between British and Indian sailors, and the withdrawal of Indian troops then fighting in Indonesia on the British and Dutch side against Sukarno's nationalist army. Being a signals ship, the *Talwar* mutineers were quickly able to communicate with other ships and soon seventy-eight of the eighty-eight ships of the Royal Indian Navy (RIN) had joined the mutiny, which spread to all the key ports along the west and east coast of India. A massive sympathy strike amongst the civilian population of Bombay paralysed life in that city for several days.

The day after the full-scale RIN mutiny began, Britain's Prime Minister Attlee announced he would be sending the Cabinet Mission to India to begin negotiations for India's independence. As late as 14 January 1946, the Attlee cabinet had agreed that if India and/or Pakistan could not 'stand on their own feet economically' or for purposes of defence, Britain had 'a moral responsibility' not to hand over the country until India's people had appropriate plans to solve those problems. 'We should not, therefore, in fact be able to divest ourselves of our responsibilities, however much we might appear to do so.... If no solution is reached...we should continue governing India even if it involved rebellion which would have to be suppressed by British troops.' The RIAF and RIN mutinies, rumblings of growing dissent in the British Indian Army itself, and Auchinleck's clearly expressed opinion that the British could no longer rely on Indian officers or soldiers to put down an insurgency, all had combined to change the mind of Attlee's cabinet within five weeks.

India's national politicians were more concerned about the ongoing provincial elections, but appeared to have been convinced by the sincerity of Attlee's declaration of 19 February. Sardar Vallabhbhai Patel hurried to Bombay on 22 February, went aboard several of the mutinous ships and urged their leaders to surrender: Patel had done a deal with Auchinleck to spare them any punishment. Jinnah had similarly discouraged Muslim sailors, Gandhi scolded the navy men for the 'unbecoming example' they were setting, and Nehru expressed the need to curb the 'wild outburst'. The British now needed Indian politicians to help them restore order within the armed forces, which had provided the vital if implicitly coercive underpinning of their rule since 1858. Although the sailors largely did respond to Patel, it took military intervention to subdue the civilian population—and only after the deaths of 228 civilians and injuries to 1,046. It had still been the biggest mutiny faced by the British since 1857 and militarily a much more dangerous one. The army was not unaffected, as the Jabbalpore regiment mutinied, and several engineering units of the Madras Regiment also joined the rebellion. Subhas Bose's prediction on 9 July 1943 at Singapore's Padang ('When the British government is thus attacked...from inside India and from outside—it will collapse, and the Indian people will then regain their freedom') came fully to fruition in February 1946. Nehru's biographer, M. J. Akbar, wrote: 'It was the first time since 1857 that the military had revolted, and the British caved in. The Empire was over.'

Yet there are no commemorations of February 1946, the month in which Britain's Indian empire was finally brought to its knees by the force of arms, when the INA trials convinced Britain's Indian sailors, airmen and soldiers that they were indeed what Subhas Bose had called them: 'an army of occupation'. Once thus edified, they rose in revolt and Britain decided within weeks that the empire could no longer hold. It suited both the Congress and the British to foster the myth of a peaceful 'transfer of power', which flattered the alleged British commitment to 'fair play and the rule of law' and the Congress' conceit that Gandhi's non-violent movement alone had enabled India to achieve independence in the 'noblest' manner possible. The reality was more complicated—although the Congress party has worked assiduously to obliterate the role of the INA, in particular, in bringing India her independence. When I broached with Vayalar Ravi (then India's minister for overseas Indian affairs) the subject of merely commemorating the 25,000 volunteer soldiers from Southeast Asia who had fought for India's independence, he said, 'Mr Basu, your view of why India got its independence is quite different from our Congress view.' He did not let me convince him that my view was not that different from his. India could never have won its independence without Gandhi's nationwide mass mobilization; but that alone was not enough (as 1930 and 1942 showed quite emphatically), and it needed the INA to undermine the implicit loyalty of the British Indian armed forces for the British to finally concede India its independence.

Gandhi, in particular, knew he could not depend on the British sense of fair play. Like most nationalists, he had learnt that bitterly from the experience of 1919, when the British reneged on their pledge of 20 August 1917 (by Montague in the House of Commons) to move 'progressively towards self-government' for Indians after the war, and instead implemented the draconian Rowlatt Act of 18 March 1919 and the desultory 'diarchy' of the Montague-Chelmsford Reforms. After all the platitudes of the 'saintly' Irwin, Gandhi got precisely nothing but classic colonial tactics highlighting dissonant Indian voices at the Second Round Table Conference (1931). This eventually led to the Government of India Act of 1935, under which India's provinces got some autonomy (but still subject to the whims of the British-appointed governor of each province). The 1935 Act conceded less self-rule at the federal (national) level than Hong Kongers were to have in 1996, with more than half of India's federal parliamentary seats appointed by Britain and her allies (the princely states). In the end, Gandhi and Bose were allies after 1942 with Gandhi's slogan of 'Do or Die' after Quit India far more compatible with Bose's views than those of Nehru or Rajagopalachari.

THE TURNING OF THE TIDE, AND THE SURPRISING CONSEQUENCES OF JAPAN'S NUKE-INDUCED SURRENDER

Roosevelt's firmness in ordering MacArthur to abandon the Philippines and move to Australia in order to take charge of the Southwest Pacific Command began to pay off as early as June 1942, when the Allied forces under his command won their first major victory at Midway—where the US Navy sank three Japanese aircraft carriers, dealing the Japanese their severest blow after their six-month run of victories in Asia. The previous month, the US and Japanese navies fought a pitched Battle of the Coral Sea, the result of which was indecisive, but with a slight edge (in terms of carriers sunk) in favour of the US, which also succeeded in frustrating the Japanese attempt to capture Port Moresby in Papua New Guinea. That successful Allied defence also effectively ended the threat of a Japanese invasion of Australia. After Midway, MacArthur slowly began to turn the tide of the war in the Pacific—fighting the Japanese island by island, gradually chipping away at its archipelagic possessions built up over the previous two decades. The biggest contribution this made to the eventual Allied victory was that it tied up a large proportion of Japan's naval and air assets in the Pacific, so reducing any commitment it could make to other theatres (for instance, Burma, as we have seen).

By September 1944, MacArthur had secured the Mariana Islands (particularly Guam, Saipan and Tinian which were captured between June and August that year), and annexed two small bits of the former Dutch East Indies—Irian Jaya (or West Irian) and Morotai in the Moluccas. The US navy wanted thence to attack Taiwan, the Japanese colony that had by then become an economic jewel in Japan's crown—a well-developed industrial and agricultural base. Alternatively, the economically crucial East Indies were a potentially vital target worth pursuing, and Okinawa at the southern tip of Japan itself was strategically important. But MacArthur would not forget his pledge ('I shall return') to the Filipinos, and it is there he decided to turn in October 1944, having convinced FDR at a meeting in Hawaii two months earlier that the Philippines was the vital strategic staging post for any invasions of Japan's homeland or Taiwan. Having secured his president's assent with that argument, however, MacArthur embarked on a crusade to take back the Philippines island by island—oblivious to the strategic relevance of such a costly and tedious endeavour. With a massive force of 200,000 troops armed with 200,000 tonnes of ammunition, 235,000 tonnes of combat vehicles and 700 ships, MacArthur came triumphantly ashore on the island of Leyte, but his men were obliged to fight ferociously as the Japanese declined to roll over as the Spanish had done five decades earlier. Manila, the capital that MacArthur improbably named the 'Citadel of Democracy in the East', fell in February 1945 but only after the street by street (and sometimes house to house) fighting had claimed 200,000 lives.

Once the war turned against them, President Laurel and most of his cabinet colleagues were evacuated—first to the hill resort of Baguio, and then at the end of April 1945 to Tokyo. After Japan's surrender, Laurel announced the dissolution of his government, and both he and Benigno Aquino were arrested at Osaka airport and taken into custody by the US occupation authorities. Osmeña had returned to Manila via the Leyte landings with MacArthur to reclaim his position as president. He arranged the summary trial and execution of Lieutenant Generals Homma and Yamashita, and advocated taking action against all those who had 'collaborated' with the Japanese, including especially 'quislings' like Laurel and Aquino. This was an interesting position, since his late boss Quezon had been quite willing to negotiate a treaty of neutrality with the Japanese both before and two months after their invasion. MacArthur favoured a less antagonistic approach, preferring to pardon those who had not committed any atrocities or violence against civilians; thus his friend Manuel Roxas avoided facing trial as a collaborator (having allegedly escaped from his cabinet colleagues in April 1945), as did Laurel and Aquino—thus limiting social disruption, but earning the ire of leftist guerrillas who had resisted the Japanese regime and gained substantial ground in rural areas. With MacArthur's implicit support, Roxas successfully challenged Osmeña for the presidency in April 1946 and became the last president of the Commonwealth, and subsequently the first president of an independent Philippines. But this was a strange kind of independence: critics (especially from the Left) always asserted that Roxas had purchased his personal freedom from prosecution by bartering away the Philippines' own independence. In reality, the US committed itself to a heavy programme of foreign aid to help with the Philippines' reconstruction (albeit nothing on the scale of Europe's Marshall Plan), and in return received the right to maintain twenty-two military bases in the country, where extraterritoriality would rule, with American soldiers not subject to Philippine law but having the right to be judged only by American law (which also applied to Filipinos—and the many Filipinas—working on those bases).

And in trade, US exports to the Philippines had preferential tariff arrangements that protected them from competing countries' exports; while the Philippines' exports could enter the US duty-free, this privilege did not apply to products that might compete with the US (for instance, manufacturing), thus confining the Philippines to eternal dependence on US brands and technology, and a classic post-colonial relationship based on exports of commodities by the Philippines and import of manufactures and technology. MacArthur had gained the eternal gratitude of most Filipinos by his fidelity to his promise of personally returning to liberate the Philippines. But the American form of independence for the Philippines turned out to be even more abridged than what had been given in wartime by the Japanese in 1943 (although very few remarked on it at the time) and considerably more circumscribed than what India, Indonesia and North Vietnam would obtain over the next few years.

The consequence of the protracted (and still incomplete) reconquest of the Philippines was that it was the only nation other than Burma that the Allies had largely regained by August 1945, when the nuclear bombs on Hiroshima (6 August) and Nagasaki (9 August) suddenly brought the war to an abrupt end. On 1 August, General Stilwell had responded to a memo from President Truman, telling him that he anticipated that it would take up to three years to regain China from the Japanese. The US invasion of Okinawa was already turning gorily costly, with the ratio of US to Japanese casualties rising to 1:2 (from 1:5 in the Philippines). Japan, recognizing that the Allies would next make a landing on the southern island of Kyushu and then begin a multi-pronged attack on the main island of Honshu, reinforced the defences on those two islands. The Americans had firebombed Tokyo in March 1945, a ghastly attack that incinerated thousands of wooden homes and killed 83,000–100,000 civilians across the ancient city and rendered at least a million people homeless. Using Guam and Saipan as bases, similarly destructive firebombing raids were conducted by the United States Army Air Forces against Nagoya (and its industrial base), the commercial city of Osaka, and the industrial cities of Kobe and Yokohama, with multiple attacks that continued until June 1945, after which the firebombing campaign was redirected to smaller cities.

But still the Japanese fought on, with their deadliest response being the suicidal dive-bombing flights into American navy ships by pilots known as 'kamikaze' (named after the wind that had blown the Mongols away from the Sea of Japan). Stilwell's memo estimating that it would take another three years to retake China—and the prospect of having to fight on grimly for another twelve to fifteen months to subdue and conquer Japan itself—led

Truman to his fateful decision to use mankind's most destructive weapons.

On 26 July 1945, the Allies (US, UK and China) made the Potsdam Declaration laying out the stark terms for Japan's surrender (which needed to be unconditional), failing which, Japan was to face 'prompt and utter destruction'. The full horrific meaning of that threat was made plain when the *Enola Gay* dropped the atom bomb on Hiroshima on 6 August. Flying six hours from Tinian in the Mariana Island chain, the B–29 bomber (named for the mother of Colonel Paul Tibbets, its pilot) dropped the 'Little Boy' nuclear bomb filled with sixty-four kilograms of Uranium–235 over Shima Surgical Clinic in Hiroshima (about 800 feet wide of the actual target, the T-shaped Aioi Bridge). Almost everything within a 1 mile radius of the hypocentre of this blast in the heavily built-up area was destroyed, and at least 70,000 people were killed (of a total population in Hiroshima of 340,000), with another 10,000–20,000 dying of burns and other wounds over the next few months resulting from the fires that raged across eleven square kilometres from the blast site; injured survivors numbered over 100,000—many of them suffering the ghastly after-effects of radiation. Amongst those killed were twelve American POWs held in the city, and the Korean Prince Yi Wu of the Chosun dynasty, who was a lieutenant colonel in the Japanese army: the prince was estimated to be one amongst more than 10,000 people of Korean origin killed in Hiroshima. Although Japan's own nuclear scientists confirmed the horrific destructive power of the new weapon, the Japanese cabinet initially decided to fight on, believing that the US was unlikely to be able to quickly produce significant numbers of these bombs. When US intelligence picked up chatter about Japan's dogged determination to fight on, the decision was made to drop an even bigger bomb on 9 August; initially the target was Kokura, with Nagasaki as the secondary target. Both were major industrial cities.

Three attempted bombing runs over Kokura (which housed the well-defended Yawata Steel Works) failed because of cloud cover and the black smoke from burning coal tar. So, just after 11 a.m. on 9 August 1945, the 'Fat Man' bomb—containing four and a half kilograms of plutonium—was dropped over a tennis court in the Urakami Valley, halfway between the Mitsubishi Steel and Arms Works and the Mitsubishi–Urakami Torpedo Works. This was about three kilometres away from the original target and, because the area was surrounded by hills, most of the urban population of Nagasaki was protected from the impact. Despite 'Fat Man' being a bigger and more destructive weapon (generating an explosion equivalent to twenty-one kilotons of TNT) than 'Little Boy' (equivalent to sixteen kilotons of TNT), the casualties in Nagasaki were somewhat lower. Of the 7,500 working at the Mitsubishi arms factories, some 6,200 were killed immediately, as were 17,000–22,000 others working in other munitions plants nearby. Only about 150 of those killed were Japanese soldiers. Estimates of the total number killed immediately by the Fat Man bomb vary between 22,000 and 75,000, with total deaths in subsequent months estimated at between 39,000 and 80,000. Of the total number killed in both nuclear bombings, about a seventh were said to be of Korean origin. The effects of radiation on survivors were severe, with about 2,000 subsequent cancer-related deaths directly attributable to the bombs, and unknowable numbers of deformed children born from parents who had suffered the after-effects of being exposed to radiation from the bombs.

The Soviet Union was represented at the Potsdam Conference (held at a Hohenzollern palace in eastern Germany), but did not sign the declaration as it was not yet at war with Japan. Despite their long-standing rivalry over Manchuria and Korea going back at least five decades, both Japan and Soviet Russia had scrupulously avoided declaring war on each other over the previous six years—each upholding the terms of the Soviet–Japanese Neutrality Pact of April 1941 (the five-year validity of which was supposed to last until April 1946); the Soviet Union had informed Japan in April 1945 that it did not intend to renew the pact, while reassuring Japan that the USSR had no intention of violating the pact before the end of its term (April 1946) either. However, the Allies had agreed at Yalta that the Soviet Union would invade Japan within three months of the German surrender (9 May 1945, Moscow time). In June–July 1945, Japan sent several peace feelers to the Soviet Union, which included very attractive territorial concessions to the Soviet Union. (Japan was in control of southern Sakhalin Island, the Kurile Islands, the whole of Manchuria, Inner Mongolia or Mengjiang, and the whole of Korea—all territories that had been coveted by Russia or the Soviet Union in times past.) Stalin appeared to express interest in a negotiated peace until as late as 2 August 1945, stringing Japan along while feverishly making preparations for a possible invasion of Manchuria.

About ten minutes after midnight on 9 August 1945 (i.e., still 8 August in Moscow, and thus barely hours before the deadline for it to fulfil its Yalta promise to invade Japan), the Soviet Union declared war on Japan and began its invasion of Manchuria. Knowing that the nuclear bombs were fatally impairing Japan's ability to wage war, Stalin took the opportunity to gain ground in Manchukuo which, after fourteen years of full Japanese control and forty years of de facto Japanese hegemony, was by far the most industrialized part of the mainland territories of the former Manchu (Qing) empire. The proximity of Manchukuo to Mao Zedong's base in Yan'an made it even more attractive to Stalin, who ordered his Red Army to aim at capturing munitions depots, weapons and armour from the Japanese forces and to make these clandestinely available to his communist allies. Stalin's forces also crossed the Soviet–Korean border near Vladivostok and advanced into northern Korea, another heavily industrialized area: about a fifth of Imperial Japan's industrial output came from Korea, most of it from the north.

The Soviet invasion occurred over a vast area the size of Western Europe, with the biggest invasion force arriving from Mongolia (which, since 1921, had been a Soviet communist vassal state). Although the Mongol nationalists in Mengjian had created an autonomous, largely Mongol area for themselves, they were poorly armed and proved no match for the Soviet forces, whose surprise invasion they were completely unprepared to combat. The Japanese had also moved a lot of their heaviest weaponry and several divisions to defend the homeland and fight in the Pacific island campaigns, but the remainder of the Japanese Kwantung Army still put up a stout defence of Manchukuo. The Soviet forces faced major resistance at Hailar in northeastern Inner Mongolia (close to the Soviet border), but also used their air force to attempt to take airfields and land troops in city centres, and later began to use their navy to land troops and marine units into northern Korea, eastern Manchukuo and the Kurile Islands. The Soviet units were able to move fast, while the Kwantung Army was sluggish even when it retreated. Within a week, the Soviet forces penetrated deep into Manchukuo (about halfway into Jilin and part of Heilongjiang) and had gained a toehold in northern Korea, but a week was too short to achieve anything more in that vast land mass.

At noon on 15 August 1945, the Japanese people heard Emperor Hirohito say, in archaic and formal words of classical Japanese that few fully understood, that he had ordered his government to 'communicate to the Governments of the United States, Great Britain, China and the Soviet Union that Our Empire accepts the provisions of their Joint Declaration' (referring to Potsdam). Japanese militarists had virulently opposed what they considered a dishonourable course of action. The previous night, about 1,000 soldiers raided the Imperial Palace in an attempt to destroy the recording of Hirohito's speech but failed to find it, partly because the layout of the palace confused them. The recording was smuggled out of the palace in a laundry basket filled with women's underwear, and successfully broadcast after a last-minute attempt to stop it at the radio station. Stunned by what they had heard, most Japanese civilians retreated into their homes, fearing reprisals. For the first time ever, Japan was brought under foreign military occupation as US airborne forces took over Tokyo and other cities, and the US navy came ashore in Yokosuka and elsewhere.

The peremptory nature of the surrender, following the shock of the two nuclear bombs (which Hirohito described as 'a new and most cruel bomb' with the power to do 'incalculable' damage), had a dramatic impact across the vast swathes of Asia that Japan still controlled (Indonesia, Vietnam, Malaya, Borneo, Singapore, Korea, Taiwan, Manchukuo, coastal China including Beijing, Nanjing, Shanghai, Jiangsu, Zhejiang, Fujian, Guangdong and Hong Kong). Indonesia and North Vietnam quickly declared their independence under their respective charismatic leaders, Sukarno and Ho Chi Minh, while the Soviets continued fighting in Manchukuo (using the argument that many of the Japanese forces—although far from all—were still fighting on, and not heeding their emperor's call to surrender). Most of the territory that the Soviets gained, including almost all of northern Korea, was gained in the period between 15 August (the day Japan officially surrendered) and 22 August, during which the Red Army continued to advance in the face of limited (and, in many places, no) resistance from the Kwantung Army—most of whose generals and soldiers were hesitantly adhering to their emperor's command to lay down their arms. The Soviet effort was akin to a team that enters a soccer field in the eighty-fifth minute of a ninety-minute soccer match, and then keeps playing for a further five minutes after the referee has blown the final whistle—scoring one goal after another, subsequent to most of the rival side's defenders having left the field (heeding the referee's final whistle)!

In Indonesia, Japan's Supreme Commander for Southeast Asia (Marshal Terauchi) had finally sanctioned a Preparatory Committee for Indonesian Independence on 7 August (the day after the Hiroshima bomb), having created an exploratory committee just over three months earlier. Sukarno and Hatta rushed to meet him at his headquarters in Saigon, and were told upon their arrival (on the 11th, two days after the Nagasaki bomb) that independence would be granted on 24 August. On their way back to Jakarta, they met Ibrahim Yaacob on the 12th and made plans for KRIS to work towards creating an autonomous Malaya within Greater Indonesia. (For Ibrahim Yaacob, these plans came too late, and before long he would have to flee to Indonesia.) By the time Sukarno and Hatta returned to Jakarta on 14 August, Japan was preparing to surrender, and restive pemuda and other youth groups aligned to the socialists Sjahrir and Sjarifuddin (who had opposed the Japanese presence throughout) were clamouring for an immediate declaration of independence, with some of them actually circulating draft declarations.

The Japanese surrender terms included an assurance to the Allied powers that Japan would maintain order and not alter the status quo in any of the countries that Japan still controlled. Terauchi was inclined to abide by these Allied injunctions. Sukarno and Hatta appeared to have missed their chance; they recognized that the only way to declare independence would be to do so as a revolutionary body, but this risked provoking a bloodbath, with the new revolutionaries battling for legitimacy against the demoralized Japanese armed forces and police, who were still charged with maintaining order. Eventually, a group of hot-headed pemuda led by Adam Malik (who was to become Sukarno's ambassador to the USSR in the late 1950s) forced the issue by kidnapping Sukarno and Hatta. They were taken to the house of a sympathetic Japanese rear admiral, Tadashi Maeda, where they faced an ultimatum to sign the proclamation of independence or be cast aside. They agreed to sign a proclamation that was drafted on the night of 16 August, but on Hatta's condition that it be signed by all twenty-seven members of the Preparatory Committee (who represented Indonesia's vastness and unity in diversity).

At a hastily organized ceremony outside his own house at 10 a.m. on 17 August, Sukarno (with Hatta standing behind him) read out this proclamation: 'We the people of Indonesia hereby declare the Independence of Indonesia. Matters concerning the Transfer of Power, etc., will be executed by careful means and in the shortest possible time.' For Sukarno—he of the florid speeches and extravagant rhetoric—this sounded like no more than a stage whisper. A national flag sewn by Sukarno's wife, Dewi, was raised, and the new national anthem, *Indonesia Raya*, was lustily sung. It was the signal for the start of a four-year revolutionary war to secure the independence that had been proclaimed that day. The Allied powers took nearly two months to figure out through whom and how they would attempt to regain Indonesia. But during that period Sukarno's revolutionary government had taken charge and run Indonesia with considerable competence, and despite being challenged by the Japanese armed forces who were trying hard to serve their new masters (the victorious Allied powers).

French Indo-China, led militarily by Admiral Jean Decoux (with Georges Gautier as the civilian governor of Tonkin in the north), had remained officially neutral in the Pacific War until March 1945, albeit submitting to a series of Japanese demands for use of military facilities, bases, resources and even financial contributions. By having allowed the French to retain sovereignty over Indo-China, the Japanese also forfeited any right to spread their doctrine of 'Asia for the Asians', especially amongst the Vietnamese. The communist-linked Vietminh headed by Nguyen 'the Patriot' Ai Quoc (better known as Ho Chi Minh) had, from its base on the China–Vietnam border, led the resistance to the French (and Japanese) presence.

Once de Gaulle created a provisional government in France following its liberation by the Americans (on 25 August 1944), he began to try and establish a parallel administration in Indo-China, the nucleus of which was headed by Major Jean Sainteny from Kunming, just across the Tonkin border, from where (with British assistance) he sought to infiltrate intelligence operatives into Indo-China. Eventually, with portraits of de Gaulle popping up in more and more government offices, and leaks about Japanese troop movements apparently enabling the Americans to direct bombing runs over the railway lines through Annam (thus cutting off their ability to move rice supplies quickly across the famine-hit country), the Japanese gave Decoux a two-hour ultimatum on 9 March 1945 to give up all administrative, military and police control of the country. When he failed to respond within two hours, the Japanese troops moved out of their barracks and formally took over Indo-China, arresting Decoux in Saigon and Gautier in Hanoi. The following day, Japan announced that Indo-China was now independent and no longer under colonial rule. The Francophile playboy prince, Bao Dai, who had (nominally) been emperor of Annam since 1932, was now encouraged by the Japanese to repudiate all ties to France and proclaim himself the ruler of all 'Vietnam'. King Norodom Sihanouk similarly proclaimed the independence of Cambodia, as did Sisavang Vong for Laos. Bao Dai's remit, however, was very light in the country's central spine of Annam and virtually non-existent in Tonkin—where the Vietminh effectively held sway. On 15 August 1945, Ho Chi Minh's guerrilla army marched unchallenged into Hanoi, preaching a new egalitarian doctrine, while Sainteny watched from the Governor General's palace, where he was effectively a prisoner. Ho Chi Minh and his colleague Vo Nguyen Giap (a brilliant doctor of law) had worked closely with American intelligence during the war, and now made a point of including a large extract from the US Declaration of Independence in their own proclamation, and a couple of American planes flew overhead to salute this potential new ally (while the hapless French fumed).

Subhas Bose was in Seremban in central Malaya when he heard (on 11 August) about the bombing of Nagasaki, and the Soviet advances into Manchuria. He had come to Seremban to investigate reports about a mutiny in the INA training centre, which turned out to be a storm in a teacup. Two days later, he learnt that Japan was preparing to surrender, and soon drove back to his wartime home in Mayer Road in Singapore (the site now houses a condominium called the Altria). On 15 August 1945, the INA was the only Japanese ally that had not, in fact, surrendered. That night, after a meeting with his cabinet that went on until dawn, Subhas Bose decided that he would try and head to Dairen (the Japanese name for Dalian) in Manchuria to meet the advancing Soviet forces, certain that they were the likeliest allies for India in its final battle for independence. Leaving M. Z. Kiani in charge of the INA troops in Singapore and Malaya, Subhas flew on 16 August to

Bangkok with Habibur Rahman (chief of staff of the INA) and S. A. Ayer (information minister), conferred with General Isoda (of the Hikari Kikan liaison organization), picked up Abid Hasan and flew onto Saigon. Either there, or at its unscheduled stop in Tourane in Vietnam, the plane picked up Lieutenant General Shidei Tsunamasa, vice-chief of the Japanese Kwantung Army and then flew on to Taihoku (now Taipei) in Taiwan (which, for fifty years, had been part of Japan, and consequently the most economically developed part of Asia after Japan itself). What happened next remains a matter of conjecture—and even some official secrecy in India.

Habibur Rahman, who was supposedly on the plane when it took off from Taihoku airport, claimed that it lost a propeller, dived steeply and crashed within a few minutes of taking off. He and Bose managed to extricate themselves from the burning wreckage (in which Shidei and the pilot are said to have perished), but Bose had severe burns all over his body and a terrible head injury. Habib managed to get a truck to take Bose to a hospital where he is said to have died between 9 and 10 p.m. on 18 August 1945, aged just forty-eight, a martyr to the cause for which he had given his life—India's independence. His ashes were taken to the Renkoji Temple in Tokyo, where they still supposedly reside. The news reached India on 23 August, and even Gandhi did not initially believe it—and the legend of Subhas alive (like that of Nana Sahib after 1858) has reappeared in many guises during the decades since. In 1964, some CIA reports also speculated about the reappearance of Bose after Nehru's death! And most intriguingly, an official inquiry commission (headed by Justice Manoj K. Mukherjee) was told by Ma Ying-jeou (then the mayor of Taipei, and subsequently the president of Taiwan from May 2008 to May 2016) that records showed no evidence of any plane crash at Taihoku airport between 15 August and 30 September 1945. Anuj Dhar, an Indian journalist, has investigated the matter closely but has faced stonewalling from the Indian government, which still has hundreds of files concerning Bose that are marked 'Top Secret', including several new files created in the 1970s, apparently because they might 'compromise relations with friendly powers'.

Dhar believes that Bose reached Manchuria (probably with Shidei, who acted as his interpreter), and spent years in Siberia. The historian Purabi Roy told me she has seen GRU (Soviet military intelligence) records that suggest Bose was killed by Khrushchev in 1956, but she was unable to photograph the evidence. Dhar believes that Bose may have lived as a recluse in Ayodhya (Uttar Pradesh) until 1985. While some of his evidence is persuasive, Bose seemed too vigorous and action-oriented to have lived as a recluse for forty years, especially at a time when India needed strong leadership. So the mystery persists!

On the Allied side, the Supreme Commander of Southeast Asia Command (SEAC) was Lord Louis Mountbatten, cousin of King George VI (although he had been friendlier with his elder brother, Edward VIII) and son of the Louis Battenberg we met in Chapter 3. Louis the son ('Dickie' to friends) had little apart from his royal lineage to thank for his exalted military title. His mother was sister to Russia's last tsarina, which meant he was a cousin to almost every king in Europe, although he himself was only forty-ninth in line for the British throne at his birth in 1900. He had accompanied his cousin David (the future Edward VIII) on his trip to India in 1921 (at the height of the Non-Cooperation Movement, when black flag demonstrations greeted them in most cities), but his time as a navy captain (the equivalent of an army colonel) commanding the destroyer HMS *Kelly* proved to be a comedy of errors for Dickie.

Early in World War II, while surging through a turbulent North Sea at two times the destroyer's recommended speed, Dickie suddenly ordered the ship to turn, which caused it to list dangerously, losing most of its provisions and some of its men. A few weeks later, he sailed smack into a mine in the Tyne estuary, and soon afterwards hit a fellow British ship (HMS *Gurkha*).

His destroyer was hit by German torpedoes, and immediately after it had spent six months in the repair yard, Captain Mountbatten again rammed it into another British ship! This would have surely earned any other officer of less noble birth an immediate court martial. Then, on 23 May 1941, HMS *Kelly* and its sister ship HMS *Kashmir* were both sunk by German dive-bombing aircraft off Crete, albeit after they had helped British aircraft retake an airfield that had previously fallen to the Germans. Mountbatten managed to survive by swimming ashore, and the heroic retelling of this story by his friend Noel Coward in the Hollywood movie, *In Which We Serve,* won Coward an Oscar nomination and Mountbatten great fame. So much so that this blundering naval officer with a catalogue of bumbling failures to his name was suddenly promoted by Prime Minister Churchill to Chief of Combined Operations (which meant a triple promotion to Vice Admiral of the navy, and the acting ranks of Lieutenant General of the Army and an Air Marshal of the RAF) on 4 March 1942. In his first major operation, on 19 August 1942, Mountbatten attempted a joint Allied landing on the French coast at Dieppe—which was a comprehensive catastrophe, largely because he had appointed incompetent cronies to all his staff, planning and intelligence positions, and they mounted a shoddy and poorly planned operation that caused thousands of needless Allied deaths.

The reward for this act of folly was a further promotion (with an additional stripe that made him a full Admiral) to Supreme Commander of

SEAC in August 1943. Churchill, given his own propensity towards quixotic military quests (like Gallipoli), was partial towards military risk-takers, even if those risks invariably failed to pay off. With no really successful combat experience, Mountbatten was treated with scarcely concealed contempt by his key generals—who all operated completely independent of him. After spending a year in Delhi (where there was a concentration camp for Japanese civilian prisoners at Purana Qila, the old fort), Mountbatten moved his headquarters to the pleasant environs of the Botanical Gardens in Kandy (Ceylon), about 3,000 kilometres from the war's front line. General William Slim led his 14th Army into Burma with US air cover but little more than a glance backward to the SEAC at Kandy. From his headquarters, Mountbatten was planning a grand reconquest of Southeast Asia by sea, in what he termed 'Operation Zipper'. When the nuclear bombs on Hiroshima and Nagasaki pre-empted him, Mountbatten decided to mount the grand spectacle of conquest anyway, in order to at least have the ceremonial pleasure of restoring British rule over Malaya in the regal style that came naturally to him and his wife Edwina.

They duly 'conquered' Malaya, arriving unimpeded on the shores of Port Dickson and Port Swettenham with the 'Zipper' armada manned by 100,000 beribboned sailors and soldiers, and ceremonially accepted the Japanese surrender at Singapore two days later. The only firing they did was to blow up the INA memorial on Singapore's beachfront, commissioned by Bose just two months earlier. At the museum displays of the two surrender ceremonies in Singapore, the striking difference between the one for 15 February 1942 and this one on 11 September 1945 was the all-white composition of the Allied contingent in 1942 contrasted with the considerable smattering of Chinese and Indian faces amongst the Allied generals in 1945. One of them was Brigadier K. S. Thimayya, whose brother had fought bravely on the other side of the conflict—as an officer of the INA.

Meanwhile, the British moved as quickly as possible to send a naval flotilla to retake Hong Kong, ahead of any KMT move to do so on behalf of China. Britain had assembled a large naval task force to aid the Americans in the Pacific Islands, but this was very much under American command and could only be detached with American permission (which was unlikely to be forthcoming, especially for the purpose of re-establishing British colonial control over Hong Kong, since Nationalist China too was a US ally). So, within two hours of Hirohito's radio broadcast, a flotilla under the command of Rear Admiral Cecil Harcourt set off from Sydney (Australia) for Subic Bay in the Philippines en route to Hong Kong—where it arrived, somewhat surreptitiously, on 30 August to accept Japan's surrender.

During the intervening period, about a thousand communist partisans loyal to Mao had entered the New Territories, capturing Japanese arms as they swept through several villages and also briefly showed up in Kowloon. A KMT military force was also massing near Hong Kong, but on 17 August US president Truman (who, unlike FDR, was not particularly committed to decolonization) had sent a cable to Attlee allowing the British to accept Japan's surrender in Hong Kong. Until that point, the official understanding (based on Truman's Order No. 1 after the surrender) was that the chief Allied commander of each area would accept Japan's surrender within that area. Hong Kong fell under the 'China Area', where Chiang Kai-shek was supreme commander. Mountbatten's SEAC remit ran only up to Saigon, and the Pacific Area command belonged to MacArthur. The British were also helped by the fact that the latter was sympathetic to them, but most of all the British were helped in regaining control of their old colony by the cooperation of the Japanese military and civilian authorities. This enabled Franklin Gimson, the colonial secretary, to regain authority by 20 August, but Harcourt's naval flotilla (led by three aircraft carriers) still entered Hong Kong harbour fearing resistance that, fortunately for them, proved quite desultory. During the intervening period, the local Chinese newspapers had moved from gingerly praising Japan, to talking about Chiang as the 'Old Father from East Zhejiang' who was about to restore China's dignity, to being solicitous towards the returning British—nicely encapsulating the chameleon-like qualities that Hong Kong's gentry had acquired over the previous four years.

On the very day of the surrender ceremony in Singapore, Mountbatten's representative, General Gracey, also arrived in Saigon to assert the Allies' control over Cochin-China. One of Gracey's key responsibilities, he asserted, was to protect the French denizens of Saigon, which was the casus belli for Ho Chi Minh's Hanoi-based Vietminh government to declare war on the British empire (and their new French allies), specifically demanding that they vacate Saigon. And Mountbatten also soon became aware of 'local resistance forces' in Java and the East Indies, who would also need to be dealt with; it would take him another six weeks to turn his full attention there, and by then Sukarno's revolutionary government would be commanding almost universal support, especially in Java. So, as of mid-September 1945, the British Indian Army was again at war—and by the end of October 1945, it would be fighting in both Indo-China and Indonesia to help re-establish 'Allied' imperial control over two erstwhile colonies that had tasted the pleasant fruits of independence largely as a consequence of Japan's liberation of both countries from European domination.

Chapter 6

FREEDOM, REVOLUTION AND JAPAN'S MIRACLE
AMID THE COLD WAR (1947–1971)

The true victor of the Second World War was the United States of America. Not only did the US have the decisive role in the Allied victory in western Europe (as epitomized by the liberation of France by Eisenhower's forces) and Asia (through the nuclear bombs that forced Japan's surrender after the island-by-island advance of the US navy through the Pacific, the Philippines and the eastern extremity of the East Indies), but the US economy gained new vitality during the war. Keynesian fiscal spending—financed through the issuance of war bonds to the public—enabled the US economy to grow rapidly during the war years, decisively ending the period of feeble economic expansion during the first decade after the Great Depression (including the 'double-dip' into recession after 1937). Aided also by the fact that US exports and manufacturing had ready markets in a Europe where industry had been devastated by war (while its own homeland did not suffer invasion), the US economy expanded rapidly. By 1950, the US accounted for 27.3 per cent of global GDP, up sharply from 19.1 per cent in 1913. Protected geographically by two great oceans, the US had gained enormous economic benefits from the two World Wars, and its per capita GDP was the highest in the world in 1950 (higher even than neutral Switzerland). Without doubt, the US military intervention two years into each World War had also made the decisive difference in the outcomes of both. The post-War Pax Americana was underpinned by its economic and strategic predominance—challenged only by the USSR (the genuine liberator of Eastern Europe, and a last-week interloper in North Asia). The Pax Americana was immediately evident in Japan, its two erstwhile colonies (Korea and Taiwan) and the Philippines.

In the rest of Asia, Britain made an audacious attempt to use the Indian military to extend its own colonial reach, and also to restore the colonial authority of the Dutch and French empires. In both France and the Netherlands, 'collaborators' with the German occupiers during the war years were being exposed and disgraced, and their colonial officials tried to tar any Asian nationalists seen as having 'collaborated' with the Japanese with the same brush being applied back home. Sukarno, Hatta and Ho Chi Minh were treated by many of these colonialists as beyond the pale, despite the fact that they had substantially greater legitimacy with their local populations than the returning colonialists did (and Ho should have had legitimacy with the Allies too, having collaborated with US intelligence). East of India's borders, the British Indian Army operated in the guise of Mountbatten's SEAC to help re-establish French and Dutch control over the Asian colonies. But as we saw in the last chapter, the war and the INA trials had fundamentally altered the loyalties of the British Indian navy, air force and army, and by early 1946 almost every Indian soldier, sailor and airman was a nationalist.

Britain's Prime Minister Attlee was forced to call an end to the British Indian empire on 19 February 1946, but over the next eighteen months he was able to successfully ensure that India was partitioned in two, with the accompanying gory brutalities permanently embittering relations between the two successor states. But the refusal of India's political leadership to allow the use of the Indian Army to fight colonial wars spelt the end of Dutch rule over the East Indies (except West Papua) by 1949, France's rule over Indo-China by 1954, and Britain's unfettered control over Iran's oil after 1951. Anglo–French colonial hubris received its ultimate comeuppance during the Suez crisis of 1956, when Egypt's Gamal Abdel Nasser (an anti-colonial ally of Nehru and Sukarno) succeeded in establishing Egyptian sovereignty over the Suez Canal despite an Anglo–French–Israeli military invasion attempting to restore Anglo–French ownership of it.

But one factor was absolutely decisive in determining the post-war trajectories for East Asia's fledgling new nation states. At the time of Japan's surrender on 15 August 1945, almost all of East Asia was still in Japanese hands, and in little realistic danger of being conquered by the Allies. In every national territory controlled by Japan there was thus a scramble to gain first access to Japanese arms, ammunition and materiel, because control over this was bound to make a decisive difference to the future of each territory. The Soviet Union, in particular, marched its Red Army as rapidly as possible into Manchuria—the territory that Russia and Japan had been battling over since 1905—and northern Korea. This led eventually to the division of the Korean peninsula between the USSR and the US, and almost inevitably towards the Korean War that began on 25 June 1950. But Soviet control over Manchuria (which was then by far the most industrialized part of Asia after Japan and Taiwan) enabled Stalin to give his ally Mao a huge head start in the Chinese Civil War that raged over the next four years.

Two features of the post-war Pax Americana—cheap oil and access to the US market—created a propitious environment for other economies to expand. Learning the lessons of the protectionist orgy of the 1930s, the US (with significant intellectual input from Britain's John Maynard Keynes) attempted to create an International Trade Organization (ITO) during the Bretton Woods deliberations, but the US Congress demurred, as other countries were demanding too many exceptions. The alternative Generalized Agreement on Tariffs and Trade (GATT) nonetheless proved an effective way to liberalize global trade, and particularly to steadily liberalize the US market (for manufactured goods trade, but not initially agriculture or services) without much resistance from Congress. Brazil and Mexico were key beneficiaries of GATT and the opening of the US market. But in Asia, only Japan succeeded in fully capitalizing on that conducive climate for economic growth in the two decades starting in 1950, although Taiwan jumped on the bandwagon by 1960 and Korea by 1965.

PERVERTED WAR CRIMES TRIALS, AMID THE CONTINUANCE OF BRITISH–INDIAN IMPERIALIST WARS

Japanese soldiers committed many atrocities against civilians during the war years, including the Sook Ching massacre in Singapore and the Nanjing Massacre in China's old capital. Insulting behaviour by insensitive Japanese soldiers—such as slapping people randomly on the streets—was common. With the collapse of the wartime economy, and the throttling of supply from the Allies, some of the Japanese-controlled parts of Asia suffered famine in 1944–45. But this famine was not a deliberate act of war by Japan on the civilian populations, while the famine in India (under British occupation) was caused by deliberate acts of policy by Winston Churchill. And the Allies committed massive atrocities against Japanese civilians too, including the carpet firebombing of Tokyo in March 1945 which killed about 100,000 non-combatant civilians, followed by similar incineration campaigns against civilians in other cities, which killed in excess of a million civilians. And the final choice of Hiroshima as the target of the first nuclear bomb was precisely a consequence of the fact that (since it had escaped any significant bombing until that point) Hiroshima would serve as a very effective 'laboratory' for the destructive capacity of that ultimate weapon, the atom bomb.

The International Military Tribunal for the Far East was established to administer victors' justice on the vanquished, and so did not consider the question of Allied culpability for crimes against civilians. Of the eleven members of the tribunal, only one (Radhabinod Pal of India) had any background in international law—as historian Richard Minear pointed out—and five of the others were either not judges at all, did not understand the languages used (Japanese and English), or had prior involvement in the issues and so should have recused themselves (or been disqualified in a normal law court). During the years that the trial lasted (1946–48), pressure was brought to bear on Justice Pal by Rama Rao, India's ambassador to Japan, to agree with the majority opinion in order 'not to damage the international relations' of newly independent India. Justice Pal ignored this pressure and, in his dissenting judgement, pronounced that 'each and every one of the accused must be found not guilty of each and every one of the charges in the indictment and should be acquitted of all charges.' At least three other members of the tribunal had strong doubts about the majority judgement by the 1960s, and Pal believed that they had succumbed to the type of pressure being brought on him (as well as the fear of opprobrium in their home countries amid the frenzied atmosphere of the immediate post-war period).

Justice Pal grouped the fifty-five crimes of which the Japanese were accused into three distilled categories: conspiracy to commit aggression, aggression and conventional war crimes. He pointed out that 'conspiracy to commit aggression' was not considered a crime under international law, until the law was changed just before these trials began. Aggression (the main charge) too was not designated a crime in international law by the US, Britain and France until 1944, primarily because they wanted to retain an absolute right to retaliate in self-defence. Pal asserted that any executions of prisoners 'otherwise than under a due process of international law' would itself amount to a war crime. Additionally, the failure to try war criminals on the victors' side—for instance, for the firebombing of Tokyo and the atomic bombs dropped on Hiroshima and Nagasaki—meant that even bigger violations of the Geneva Convention were being set aside. Even critics of Pal admitted that Japanese atrocities were 'perhaps not the result of an organized governmental plan'.

And since eight of the eleven judges came from nations that were victims of Japanese militarism—and all were from the victor nations (rather than from neutral ones)—there was never any pretence at impartiality. Yet there were clear hints of dissent, with the first American judge appointed to the tribunal resigning quickly, and being replaced. There was a clear racist element involved in the treatment of the Japanese relative to the Germans: one astonishing fact is that 927 Japanese were executed after all the trials, compared with fewer than 100 Germans (not counting the Dachau military trials, at which another 300 Germans were put to death). US Supreme Court Justice William O. Douglas was quite forthright in saying later that the Tribunal 'did not act as a free and independent tribunal to adjudge the rights of petitioners under international law'. Despite these deep-seated flaws, the global media treats the notion of a 'Japanese Class A war criminal' as a settled factual category, decrying the annual visits of some Japanese politicians to Yasukuni Shrine (where millions of souls are commemorated, including fourteen who answer to that descriptive category). With the supposed end of war, Britain led the way in committing more war crimes against the people of Indonesia and Vietnam, just as Churchill had committed clear war crimes against the Iraqis in 1920, when he strafed them from the air with chemical weapons (using planes from the RIAF), and then against Indians whom he deliberately starved to death in 1943–45.

After Sukarno and Hatta's declaration of independence on 17 August 1945, they moved quickly to consolidate their hold on power, particularly on the island of Java (home to more than six of every ten citizens of Indonesia, the former Dutch East Indies). But there were spontaneous declarations of support for the new Republican government from all the other islands and provinces, as the period of Japanese rule had cemented a romantic attachment to Indonesian nationalism across the archipelago, not least through the Japanese regime's universal use of a unifying language (Bahasa Indonesia). The new regime's egalitarian rhetoric soon led many of the aristocrats in the outer islands to grow more ambivalent about their early endorsement of it, but by that point events were already beginning to slip out of the old elites' control, as roving bands of ideologically-motivated pemuda (revolutionary youth) groups increasingly took control of public opinion, and the streets reverberated to their popular cry of 'Merdeka' (freedom). The charismatic poet Chairil Anwar was emblematic of the pemuda spirit, challenging the settled bureaucratic ways of the old elite. The pemuda used an egalitarian (and seemingly crass) language that cut through the niceties of old Javanese, replacing priyayi hierarchies with the everyday term 'bung' (brother). The long-haired and gun-swinging Sutomo (popularly 'Bung Tomo'), with his revolutionary rhetoric redolent of Paris 1789, became the rallying point for the pemuda, counterpoised to the relatively staid approach of the Republican government led by Sukarno and Hatta.

The Japanese, in keeping with the surrender terms, needed to find a senior Allied prisoner of war to hand over formal control to, and they settled on Colonel Laurens van der Post, a South African who later became a famous author, explorer, conservationist, and friend of Britain's Prince Charles. Having arrived in the East Indies only weeks before the Dutch surrender in March 1942, van der Post had been on an undercover espionage mission and only surrendered to the Japanese in May 1942. However, his knowledge of Dutch, English and more than a smattering of Japanese greatly increased his importance during the years of internment, as did his energetic pursuit of educational and other schemes of social uplift in the internment camps. The largest group of Allied prisoners were held (as was van der Post) in Bandung, the city in the uplands that was the third largest on Java (after

Jakarta and Surabaya). After assuming control, van der Post travelled to Jakarta and elsewhere around Java, and quickly became apprised of the near-universal support that Sukarno's Republican government commanded across Java and Sumatra.

Mountbatten, despite being an atrocious naval officer, proved to be relatively astute when dealing with the emergence of nationalism across Asia, and especially within his SEAC bailiwick. He sent for van der Post in mid-September 1945, and after hearing his sobering appraisal, sent him on to London to meet Attlee and then to The Hague to alert Dutch Prime Minister Wim Schermerhorn, but his warnings about an impending explosion in the East Indies fell largely on deaf ears, with the Dutch prime minister being particularly dismissive of Sukarno and Hatta as Japanese 'quislings'. When Mountbatten's SEAC troops—comprising the 23rd Indian Division under the command of Major General Douglas Hawthorne—arrived in Java on 29 September, they still expected to be handed temporary charge by the Japanese, until the Dutch retook permanent control. Another British officer with a Dutch-sounding name (derived from his father, who was of Flemish descent) and a past in espionage and reconnaissance, the future actor Dirk Bogarde, was Hawthorne's ADC and newsreader on local radio. But the pemuda had their own riposte to Bogarde in 'Surabaya Sue', a former hotelier from Bali of Scottish descent who went by her Balinese name K'tut Tantri, and became famous for her English-language broadcasts advocating the Republican cause.

During the six-week interregnum between Japan's surrender and the arrival of SEAC troops in Java, the Japanese had attempted to maintain order but without ever seriously challenging the authority of Sukarno's fledgling republic based in Jakarta. The latter, however, also acted with great caution—not wishing to provoke the Allied powers—and this had incurred the wrath of the pemuda radicals. President Sukarno, for instance, asked the PETA to accede to Japanese demands to give up their weapons. Most did, although some (including the PETA battalion under the command of Sudirman) regained a lot of these weapons, and there were other raids on Japanese armouries in and around all three of Java's biggest cities, resulting in the Republic's informal army being very well stocked with arms and ammunition by the time the SEAC troops arrived. Some of the confused and disoriented Japanese soldiers were lured into joining the Republic's forces, a small number joined those forces out of conviction about Asians' right to rule themselves, and numerous others who were sympathetic to the Republic let Indonesian nationalists gain access to Japanese weaponry. Apart from about 3,000 soldiers, the majority of Japanese troops obeyed their commanders, seeking to maintain order in the

East Indies while they awaited the Allies' arrangements for their repatriation to Japan.

Led by the iconic house of Yogyakarta (where Sultan Hamengkubuwono IX quickly threw in his lot with Sukarno's Republic, and was rewarded with a promise to become Yogya's governor for life), most royal houses had thrown their support behind Sukarno, as had most of the leadership of the outer islands. Recognizing this reality, the Japanese troops stayed largely within their military bases, allowing the Republic to take charge of most of the institutions of government across Indonesia, many of which had, in any case, been staffed by Indonesians (replacing previous Dutch incumbents) during the war years. In mid-September, a series of triumphal 'ocean' rallies were held across Indonesia's major cities to celebrate the spirit of Merdeka and the reality of a month of unfettered Indonesian independence. The communist PKI's elusive founder, Tan Malaka, had quietly slipped back into Indonesia in 1942, working unobtrusively as a clerk in a Japanese-owned mine while clandestinely organizing workers and peasants around the country. He and the PKI likely played a key role in organizing these 'ocean' rallies, but Tan Malaka was outraged when Sukarno spoke emolliently at the biggest of these rallies in Jakarta's Ikeda Square (later renamed Medan Merdeka), instructing the 200,000-strong crowd to disperse so as not to provoke the ring of Japanese sharpshooters who were guarding the square.

Hawthorne's 23rd Indian Division did not have enough troops to take control of the whole of Java, so it initially concentrated on taking charge of 'Batavia' (as Jakarta was renamed), Surabaya and Semarang. At van der Post's urging, Bandung was added, taking account of the fact that it contained the Japanese military headquarters with 15,000 troops and about 50,000 Allied prisoners. The Allies were greatly aided in Bandung by the Japanese troops, who acted to clear the city of pro-Republican forces, which were forced beyond the railway tracks at the edge of the city after some deadly skirmishes. In these first few weeks, Sukarno's Republic was observing the SEAC troops warily—cooperating with them on the implicit condition that the Allies would not facilitate the return of Dutch (KNIL) troops, and would work out a modus vivendi with the new Republic. But their suspicions were immediately aroused by the arrival, along with the British Indian troops, of Charles van der Plas, the former Dutch governor of East Java, and a couple of senior Dutch military commanders who had spent the war years at a camp outside Brisbane (in Queensland, Australia) plotting their return amid much racist rhetoric. Completely oblivious to the vast metamorphosis that had occurred in their formerly placid East Indies, the Dutch made matters much worse with their colonial haughtiness: van der Plas made several broadcasts to the people of the archipelago, promising swift retribution to 'traitors and collaborators' (meaning Sukarno and Hatta), ignoring the fact that he did not possess the military means to enforce his threats. Already, the Dutch internees who had sought to return to their homes and offices (after being released from Japanese internment) had seen the initially empathetic response of Indonesians turn to anger, resentment and violence once the Dutch allowed their pre-War racial haughtiness to return.

Indonesian resentment was especially sharp over Dutch attempts to reassert racist prerogatives at their exclusive clubs and other watering holes. On 19 September 1945, a large group of Dutchmen and Eurasians had gathered to celebrate at the Yamato (the pre-War name for which was the Oranje Hotel), a favourite watering hole in the volatile city of Surabaya in East Java. In a triumphal gesture, they raised the Dutch tricolour flag atop the hotel in an atmosphere of drunken rowdiness, provoking the ire of Indonesians in the street outside, who began stoning the building. Some young Indonesians climbed to the top of the building and tore out the blue part of the Dutch flag, and cheered lustily as it was thus converted into the 'merah putih' (red-white) flag of the Republic. In the ensuing melee, a Eurasian called Ploegman was fatally injured. Adding fuel to this fire, when the SEAC troops arrived at Surabaya (the largest naval base in Southeast Asia after Singapore, and the most industrialized city in Indonesia), they were preceded by a senior Dutch naval officer, Captain P. J. G. Huijer, ostensibly tasked with defending Dutch ex-internees. Although Huijer had just five armed men with him, he was hardly lacking in swagger.

Possibly going beyond his brief, Huijer decided that in Surabaya, a Dutchman (rather than a British SEAC representative) would accept the Japanese surrender. With large numbers of ex-internees accompanying Huijer, the local Indonesians assumed that they had all arrived by ship with Huijer in an attempt to reassert Dutch control over their city. They saw red, especially as it became clear that a Dutch reoccupation of the city was precisely Huijer's objective.

Japanese Vice Admiral Shibata Yaichiro was relieved to give up responsibility for Surabaya to Huijer, but the agreement between them provided for the Republican forces to take custody of the Japanese arms and ammunition in the city, recognizing that there was no real alternative. Soon afterwards, Huijer's car was stolen, and the Republicans took Huijer himself into custody when he sought to take a train out to Jakarta. Meanwhile, an impromptu trial of Dutch soldiers and ex-internees was conducted in the billiard room of the hitherto-exclusive Simpang Club, and several of them were severely beaten up on the dance floor of this club that Indonesians had previously been barred from. Bung Tomo urged his pemuda to seize their chance in ringing tones: 'We extremists, we who revolt with a full revolutionary spirit... would rather see Indonesia drowned in blood and sunk to the bottom of the sea than colonized once more! God will protect us! Merdeka!' The conventional Republican forces in Surabaya were under the command of Sudirman, the strength of whose battalions was greatly reinforced by the Japanese tanks, artillery, small arms and transport that had fallen into their hands.

By the time Brigadier Aubertin Mallaby arrived with the 49th Infantry Brigade of the 23rd Indian Division (comprising about 4,000 Rajput and Maratha troops) on 25 October, Surabaya was already in full revolutionary mode, ready for a veritable storming of the Bastille. Mallaby, who had spent much of his career in staff rather than combat situations, added fuel to the fire by seeking immediately to rescue a Dutch reconnaissance party that had been detained for several weeks by the Republicans. On 27 October, the situation was inflamed further when SEAC planes from Jakarta (supposedly without informing Mallaby) began showering Surabaya with leaflets demanding that all weapons in Indonesian hands be surrendered. The following day, Mallaby's Indian troops duly began seizing arms and impounding trucks. That afternoon, Sudirman's Republican forces mounted a fierce counteroffensive. There were 20,000 well-armed and equipped Republican troops in Surabaya, plus close to 120,000 armed pemuda. The fighting blazed on all night, and isolated Maratha and Rajput units suffered more than 200 casualties. Many Dutch civilians they were seeking to protect also died. There were Indonesian casualties too in the fierce fighting, but Mallaby's brigade was in greater danger of being wiped out, and appealed to Jakarta for urgent reinforcements.

Again, the Republic's President Sukarno and his deputy Hatta proved to be the sobering voices, and were flown into Surabaya on 29 October 1945 to help calm the building tensions. Sukarno broadcast an appeal for a ceasefire, and Sudirman and Mallaby toured the city jointly as a symbolic gesture. The following day a wider conference (including Bung Tomo and Hawthorne) agreed peace terms: safe passage for ex-internees in exchange for an end to arms seizures by SEAC troops and their withdrawal from 'forward positions' in the city. The bigwigs left on the morning of 30 October, but that evening Mallaby and Sudirman went to the downtown area to help end a siege of a Maratha unit by a pemuda throng. Having sorted out this dispute, they dispersed in different directions, but Mallaby's car was soon besieged by another Republican militia near the Jembatan Merah (Red Bridge). What happened next remains in dispute: according to a Captain Smith who was in Mallaby's car, a Republican soldier shot Mallaby dead after a short conversation, and Smith claims to then have thrown a hand grenade in the general direction of where the shooter had run to hide. The resulting explosion blew out the back seat of the car, and others credibly claimed that Mallaby was actually killed by that explosion. The upshot, however, was that Mallaby had been killed and *The Times* of London screamed on 1 November: 'MALLABY KILLED; ALMOST WAR IN EAST JAVA'.

Lieutenant General Sir Philip Christison, the overall commander of SEAC troops in Indonesia, immediately began preparing for all-out (undeclared) war. He sent an ultimatum to the Republican forces in Surabaya to yield up the killers of Mallaby and surrender all arms and ammunition, or face the full brunt of British reprisals. (If Captain Smith's account was true, Mallaby's killer(s) may have died in the grenade explosion, but this was never given a second thought at the time.) Over the next week, a further 24,000 troops of the 5th Indian Division led by Major General E. C. R. Mansergh with twenty-four Sherman tanks, twenty-four armed aircraft, three destroyers and two cruisers were sent as reinforcements to Surabaya. Sukarno broadcast a fervent appeal to the pemuda to desist from a foolhardy war: 'Don't let us be forced to face alone the whole military power of England and all the Allies.' He ordered all fighting with the Allies to stop.

By this time, however, Sukarno's regime formally had an army too. After initially resisting calls to form one (for fear of provoking the Japanese and the Allies), Sukarno had authorized the creation of the Tentara Keamanan Rakyat (TKR, People's Security Army) on 5 October, with Major Urip Sumoharjo (the highest-ranking former member of the colonial KNIL) as its first chief. Urip had the near-impossible task of uniting relatively well-trained ex-KNIL units with the less well-trained but passionately nationalist and more numerous ex-PETA battalions (comprising 37,000 troops in Java, 20,000 in Sumatra and about 3,000 in Bali). Additionally, the new TKR also sought to incorporate the inchoate but even more numerous forces of the ill-disciplined pemuda. Reflecting the democratic spirit of the times, the senior leaders of the TKR met on 12 November at Yogyakarta to formally elect their leader; in a close ballot, Sudirman edged out Urip but sought to keep the latter onside as the TKR's chief of staff. In keeping with President Sukarno's orders, most TKR units had been withdrawn from Surabaya by this time, in order not to provoke the SEAC.

But the British were determined to act on their threat of reprisals in the absence of an abject surrender by Surabaya's pemuda. Mansergh issued a final ultimatum on 9 November for all arms to be relinquished by dawn the next day, knowing very well that it was impossible for Surabaya's leadership to comply, and effectively obliging them to prepare for battle. As students from the religious schools in neighbouring regions poured into Surabaya to bolster the resistance amid growing calls to jihad, Bung Tomo responded through his Radio Pemberontakan (Revolutionary Radio): 'Our slogan remains the same: Freedom or Death! Allahu Akbar!'

On 10 November, the SEAC (actually the 5th and 23rd Indian Divisions under British command) began a massive air and naval bombardment of Surabaya, which began early that morning and went on virtually non-stop for four days, during which over 500 bombs were dropped on the city. The hugely disproportionate bombing campaign (in reprisal for the killing of a single officer) was ostensibly aimed at easing the path of SEAC troops as they fought from street to street to gain control of Surabaya. RAF Thunderbolt and Mosquito aircraft strafed buildings that were identified as being under Republican control, but (according to eyewitness accounts) also bombed fleeing civilians on the road south from the city. Far from a peacekeeping operation, the SEAC commanders fought and bombed just as fiercely as during the Burma campaign, and the Battle of Surabaya (lasting through the rest of November) became a fight to the bitter end.

It was fought on behalf of the British empire by the Rajputs, Marathas, Jats and Gurkhas of the Indian Army just as, unbeknownst to these soldiers, the INA trials were reaching their climax at the Red Fort in Delhi, still too distant to influence them directly. K'tut Tantri wrote that some of the Indian troops became susceptible to the nationalism of their fellow Asians, and occasionally supplied arms to them surreptitiously. The British tried to insinuate that the Japanese were secretly fighting the battle on behalf of the Indonesians, but this charge could never stand up to scrutiny, as very few Japanese bodies were discovered later in the smouldering ruins of the city. The three-week resistance was authentically Indonesian—a heroic emblem of the Indonesian people's passionate commitment to their fledgling independence. Forever afterwards, 10 November has been commemorated as Hari Pahlawan (Heroes' Day) in Indonesia. The official SEAC estimate was that perhaps 10,000 Indonesians had died in the fighting (compared with 600 Indian soldiers killed fighting on the SEAC side), although a more realistic estimate of Indonesian deaths put them closer to 15,000, plus over 200,000 rendered homeless by the fighting.

At the end of November 1945, the Battle of Surabaya ended in a pyrrhic British (SEAC) victory—a final triumph of imperial hubris that demonstrated the impunity with which the British could flout the Geneva Conventions, and use troops from their Indian empire while doing so. From a military standpoint, it was a disaster for the Indonesians who lost not only 15,000 young soldiers and civilians but also a great deal of their military equipment and ammunition, and suffered the destruction of their most industrialized city.

But the Battle of Surabaya also served to invigorate the Republican forces in Indonesia, strengthening their resolve and demonstrating to the world the depth and seriousness of Indonesia's determination to free itself of any vestige of colonial rule. And while war crimes trials would soon begin against the Japanese, and the INA trials were winding down in India, the British faced no criminal charges for this wildly disproportionate attack against the civilians of Indonesia's second-largest city as 'punishment' for the killing of a single brigadier. The aftermath of the INA trials, and particularly the RIN and RIAF mutinies that followed, were to ensure that Indian troops could never again be used to pursue Britain's imperial ambitions.

In the immediate sanguinary wake of Surabaya, however, Britain and the Allies came to be seen as enemies of Indonesia's revolution, fighting a proxy war to help restore Dutch rule. At Bekasi in West Java, the downing of a Dakota plane on 22 November led to the horrific hacking to death of 23 British and Indian survivors from that plane—and the British reprisals (reminiscent of India in 1857–58) involved the indiscriminate incineration of 600 homes (and their inhabitants) in the village deemed responsible, including 60 homes belonging to Chinese families who were neutral in the conflict. The TKR, despite its horrific losses in Surabaya, prepared under Sudirman to take the fight to the Dutch; they briefly took control of Semarang from the SEAC, and the latter had to deploy both air power and Japanese troops to regain control there. The town of Magelang in Central Java fell to the Republicans, and fighting was extended to Medan and other places in Sumatra. But even while the Battle of Surabaya was raging, Sukarno's Republicans took steps to prepare the way for negotiations with the Allies.

On 14 November, Sutan Sjahrir was appointed prime minister by Sukarno, who remained president but with less of a role in day-to-day governance. This was a transparent step to facilitate negotiations with SEAC and the Dutch, by removing the taint of 'collaboration' with Japan from the Republican government: the socialist Sjahrir had led the underground resistance to Japan (along with Sjarifuddin), and had particular cache with the pemuda that he had helped create. That the tensions within the Republican side ran deep was evident in papers that Sjahrir and the crypto-communist Sjarifuddin published, excoriating Sukarno and Hatta for aligning with Japan.

The Dutch Lieutenant Governor, Dr Hubertus van Mook, had returned to Jakarta at the beginning of October to derisive slogans from the Indonesian public. Although born in Indonesia, both van Mook and van der Plas were utterly disdainful towards Indonesian nationalism—indeed, to the very idea of Indonesian nationhood in the absence of the Dutch (much like Churchill's attitude towards India). They were wedded to the notion of a partnership between the Dutch and the Indonesians, believing that the paternalistic role of the Dutch and the 'natural' affinity between them and the Indonesians would be restored as soon as an iota of peace prevailed. Having ruled out negotiations with the 'quislings', van Mook could hardly reject talks with the cosmopolitan and untainted Sjahrir. The way for talks was cleared further when Sukarno and Hatta decided, in late December 1945, to move much of the apparatus of government to Yogyakarta—the heartland of Javanese culture and the erstwhile capital of the legendary kingdom of Mataram—leaving Sjahrir in sole charge at Jakarta. That city was turning increasingly lawless by this time, with large numbers of returning Dutch settlers turning especially rowdy—on one occasion physically assaulting Sjahrir in the streets (an incident that sparked the Sukarno–Hatta flight to Yogyakarta).

While sporadic fighting continued, van Mook and Sjahrir's talks meandered on, with the Dutch attempting to turn the clock back to 1942, and to Dutch queen Wilhelmina's pre-War plans for a 'Commonwealth'. Sjahrir refused to consider any proposals until the Republic had been recognized, while van Mook felt he had time on his side, as more and more Dutch troops were returning to the East Indies, slowly taking the place of their SEAC counterparts. The newest challenge to Sjahrir's legitimacy came from Tan Malaka, who finally came overground in January 1946 and announced a 'minimum programme' involving '100 per cent merdeka' with 'people's ownership of the economy'. Despite his iconic status, Tan Malaka had no organizational base in Indonesia, and in mid-March Sjahrir resigned, but was persuaded by Sukarno to return once it became clear that the alternative coalition led by Tan Malaka was too disunited. Thus strengthened, Sjahrir ordered Tan Malaka's arrest and he remained in detention until September 1948.

Once Jawaharlal Nehru became India's 'interim prime minister' in September 1946, he immediately demanded that all Indian troops be expeditiously repatriated, saying it was outrageous that they should still be fighting Britain's colonial wars (as the naval mutineers had said with even greater eloquence in February that year). The new deadline for an agreement was 15 November 1946 since British Indian troops were to begin being withdrawn on that day. With Sukarno joining Sjahrir in the negotiations that went to the wire, an agreement between the Dutch and the Indonesian Republic was finally reached at Linggadjati in West Java on 15 November.

Both sides had grave misgivings about aspects of the Linggadjati Agreement, each side believing that it had conceded too much. The Republic's leaders were desperate to get formal international recognition of Indonesia's independence, which they believed they had secured with the Republic (comprising Java, Sumatra and Madura) recognized as one of three states (the others being Borneo, and the 'Great East' comprising Sulawesi, Nusa Tenggara, Maluku and West New Guinea) that were together styled the United States of Indonesia (USI). Defence, foreign policy, and currency would be determined by the central USI government in Jakarta, with all other powers devolved to the federating units. At the apex would be a Netherlands–Indonesian Union (including Suriname and the Dutch Antilles) under the Dutch crown, where formal sovereignty would reside, albeit with a very woolly definition of what powers would be reserved to it (apart from symbolism).

Republican leaders saw the federalist scheme as a transparent attempt to divide and rule, by seeking to create puppet regimes that would be beholden to the Netherlands and only nominally independent. In 1947, these disputes steadily widened the gulf between the two sides, with the Dutch focusing on bolstering their military preparedness, while the Republic sought primarily to gain greater international legitimacy. The Dutch harboured particularly fond hopes for the Great East, where there appeared to be strong support for the federalist scheme and a more friendly attitude towards the Dutch. Australian troops had taken over most of this region after the Japanese surrender, and although most islands had declared their loyalty to the Republic, the Dutch were hopeful that they would welcome the Dutch as protectors against the sheer demographic weight of the Javanese and Sumatrans.

The new constitutional arrangements were scheduled to come into effect only in January 1949, but the Republic demanded that in the interim Dutch troops must be removed from within its territory. The Dutch disingenuously argued that they needed to remain because the Republic was incapable of policing its own territory. Sutan Sjahrir was obliged to take the blame for the continuing disputes over the terms he had negotiated, and resigned as prime minister in June 1947, but was succeeded by his good friend and fellow socialist, Amir Sjarifuddin (who later admitted that he had been an undercover communist since 1935). Armed clashes between the two sides steadily increased, culminating in a full-scale invasion of the Republic's territory in July 1947 by Dutch ground forces supported by aerial bombardment—which the Dutch termed a 'police action'. Dutch forces swiftly overran West Java, much of East Java, and most of the productive areas in Sumatra (including Medan and Palembang), reducing the Republic to a rump of less than a third of its erstwhile territory (which had been equal to Germany and France combined, with a larger population). But the plight of the Indonesian Republic soon garnered global sympathy and attention, not least because the British were increasingly contrite about the gruesome brutalities they had unleashed in November–December 1945.

Crucially, a flamboyant ace pilot from India called Bijayananda ('Biju')

Patnaik (who would later serve two terms as chief minister of Orissa) flew into Jakarta on 21 July 1947—tasked by Nehru with flying Sjahrir and Hatta out of Java, so that they could broadcast the Republic's plight to the rest of the world. The former prime minister was trapped in a remote area, so Biju Patnaik had to land his Dakota in an improvised airfield surrounded by rice paddies on 22 July. He then snatched Sutan Sjahrir from hostile Dutch-held territory and flew him out to Jakarta. From there, Biju flew Sjahrir and Hatta to Singapore, and onto New Delhi where they held a press conference, and Nehru took time out of fraught negotiations over the partition of India to condemn Dutch brutalities and formally throw India's support behind the Indonesian cause. He arranged for Sutan Sjahrir to be flown to New York, where India and Australia jointly sponsored a United Nations resolution condemning the Dutch invasion, and Sjahrir made an impassioned speech that resulted in the creation of a Good Offices Committee (GOC, comprising Belgium, Australia and the US) to help the two sides reach a settlement. Sjahrir was aided at the UN by an able team of Republican representatives led by Sumitro Djojohadikusumo, who had a doctorate in economics and whose father (Margono) headed the Republic's central bank. (Sumitro's eldest son, Prabowo, was the losing candidate for president of Indonesia in 2014). Sumitro had reached New York by charming a secretary in the US embassy in Singapore to finagle a visa for him, and smuggled rubber in order to raise the funds to travel there!

Patnaik remained a lifelong friend of the Sukarno family, and was showered with national honours by Indonesia. He was particularly happy to accept these, given the long-standing pre-colonial ties between his home state of Orissa (in eastern India), known then by its ancient name Kalinga, and the islands of Suvarnadwipa (Sumatra), Javadwipa and Bali (to which there used to be annual trading and pilgrimage ships from Orissa called the 'Bali-jatra', leading to 'Keling' becoming the colloquial term for ethnic Indians in Southeast Asia).

The combination of the GOC and Sjahrir's eloquence at the UN, however, could not dislodge the Dutch from their entrenched military positions. The Renville Agreement signed between the Dutch and the rump Republic aboard the USS *Renville* in January 1948 legitimized Dutch military gains in exchange for another promise of future independence and a plebiscite to be held across all of Java and Sumatra. Despite that promise of a plebiscite that might restore Republican rule over the two main islands, this blatantly one-sided deal caused a massive uproar in Republican ranks, and the left-wing government headed by Amir Sjarifuddin was immediately forced from office. Sukarno now appointed his respected vice president, Hatta, as prime minister. Hatta (like Sjahrir and Sjarifuddin) was from Minangkabau in West Sumatra, but (compared to his two socialist predecessors) had a much stronger political base in the umbrella Muslim organization Masyumi that had been created under Japanese rule.

Since the Dutch now controlled most of the food producing and export earning regions, Hatta confronted an economic crisis in the rump Republic, and ordered a programme of fiscal austerity, which only fuelled further discontent. At this moment of crisis, the communist PKI began to mobilize behind its recently returned leader, Musso, who had led the failed uprising of 1926–27 and had spent the intervening years in the Soviet Union. At Madiun in East Java, Musso's PKI mounted a coup, killed the governor of East Java and declared an Indonesian Soviet Republic in September 1948! Musso announced a full-scale communist uprising, aided by a People's Democratic Front led by former prime minister Amir Sjarifuddin. In the brief ensuing civil war, Musso was killed, several other communist leaders including Sjarifuddin were summarily executed, and thousands of others put behind bars. The Republic had triumphed against a determined ideological foe and, more importantly, the US took notice of a Southeast Asian power that had subdued and crushed a communist uprising at a fraught moment in the early months of an incipient global Cold War. Domestically, Madiun became a symbol of the treachery of the PKI that the Indonesian Army continues to cite to this day.

In December 1948, the Dutch mounted a second 'police action', this time aimed at obliterating the Republic altogether. They captured its capital Yogyakarta, and arrested Sukarno, Hatta, Sjahrir and most of the cabinet. But the Republic's army, the TKR, under Sudirman's command (although himself ailing with tuberculosis), continued to hold out as the final independent and non-communist bulwark against Dutch control, gradually regaining ground from their original fastness of Bukit Tinggi in Sumatra. And despite their fond hopes of collaboration, the Dutch met resistance even in the Great East, and unleashed brutal repression in order to sustain their newly installed regimes. Captain Paul 'Turk' Westerling (so named because of a youth spent in Istanbul) unleashed a reign of terror in Sulawesi, indiscriminately shooting inhabitants of any village thought to harbour Republicans—killing close to 10,000 people in the process. In the island of Bali, Ngurah Rai led a stout resistance to Dutch rule for several weeks and eventually committed ritual suicide (puputan) in time-honoured Balinese fashion (as his ancestors had done during the first Dutch invasion four decades earlier), thereby sanctifying the Republican cause. US policy was particularly swayed by the failure of the Dutch to secure a quick victory, and the danger that a persistent guerrilla war might embolden communists and their allies to mount another putsch.

As one of the three members of the UN's GOC, and a co-sponsor of the Renville Agreement, the US could not stand by in good conscience while the Dutch ran roughshod over the terms of the accord. The US attitude to the Republic changed noticeably after it crushed the communist Madiun uprising, as well as the Islamist Darul Islam uprising that followed. Using the threat of withdrawing Marshall Plan support for the Netherlands' economic recovery, the US pressured the Dutch into releasing Sukarno and Hatta, and resuming negotiations at a Round Table Conference in January 1949. The tide of global opinion had turned decisively in favour of the Republicans by this point, and the Dutch also miscalculated the degree of support they might command from the outer islands. As Dr Ide Anak Agung Gde Agung, the Balinese raja who was chief minister of the Great East archipelago put it, 'I am a federalist, yes, still a federalist; but not a separatist.' During the course of 1948, the Republicans had worked out a modus vivendi with the states' representatives—accepting the principle of federalism (and generous representation for the regions in national institutions) in exchange for their staunch support for the Republican cause.

At the Round Table Conference, there were three parties represented—the Netherlands, the Republic and the States. (The Netherlands had wanted the Republic to be one of sixteen entities at the conference, parroting the British approach to Gandhi in 1931, but the moment for such shenanigans was past.) To van Mook's chagrin, the States supported the creation of a unitary nation fully independent of the Netherlands, to be called (in a nod to the federalist idyll) the Republic of the United States of Indonesia (RUSI). On 27 December 1949, Queen Juliana signed away 350 years of Dutch rule as jubilant crowds celebrated the arrival of their militarily hard-won independence.

RUSI still had a federal structure, but the long years of war with the Dutch had discredited the federal idea, which had come to connote Dutch attempts to undermine the national unity of Indonesia by dividing it into the many states. Economically, independence was somewhat hollow, with seven foreign-owned banks controlling the financial system, the private Dutch-owned Java Bank having all the functions of a central bank (owning the foreign reserves and issuing currency), the Dutch KPM shipping line having a near-monopoly of inter-island shipping, and four Dutch firms controlling more than half of all consumer goods imports into Indonesia. Political unity, at least, was quickly achieved. Over the first seven months of 1950, the fifteen other states of RUSI were each, one after another, persuaded to merge with the Republic of Indonesia based in Yogyakarta. The only resistance was from southern Maluku (a largely Christian region), but it too eventually agreed to amalgamate into the Republic. The western half of New Guinea still remained in Dutch control, but the rest of the formerly Dutch East Indies had been merged into the unitary Republic of Indonesia by 17 August 1950, when the fifth anniversary of Indonesia's independence was celebrated with a grand ceremony encompassing the whole of the country (sans West Papua).

◆

Indo-China (Vietnam, Cambodia and Laos) had lived through a strange twilight zone during the Great Asian War. Formally ruled by France (which itself was overrun by Germany in June 1940), it was brought under the control of the Vichy French regime. Japan began to exert significant influence over French Indo-China, demanding and obtaining safe passage for their troops through its territory in exchange for a promise to respect (Vichy) French sovereignty over the region. The French remained in control of Indo-China until March 1945, although the degree of control was steadily eroded. First, after a four-day war in September 1940, the Japanese inflicted a severe defeat on the French, and obtained the right to station 40,000 troops in Cochin-China (the southern half of Vietnam, with its capital in Saigon, where the Japanese established their key southern command headquarters; the full troop deployment only occurred in mid-1941). Second, General Phibun's Thailand defeated France in the Franco–Thai War in early 1941, and after May that year the western half of Cambodia and more than a third of Laos reverted to Thai sovereignty. Third, on 10 March 1945 Japan abruptly declared the independence of Indo-China, following which four regimes emerged—independent kingdoms in the rump of Cambodia (headed by Norodom Sihanouk) and Laos (led by Sisavang Vong of Luang Prabang), Annam (nominally led by emperor Bao Dai) and Tonkin (where the Vietminh under Ho Chi Minh held sway, gradually extending their influence over Annam in the central neck of Vietnam).

Cochin-China was where Japan exerted its most direct control, and Saigon remained the headquarters of the ailing Field Marshal Count Terauchi (who had suffered a stroke earlier in the year). So Cochin-China (south of the 16th parallel, which soon came to be called 'South Vietnam') was really the only part of Indo-China where there was a Japanese military leader who could surrender to the Allies, since the rest of Indo-China was formally independent. Here, a nationalist coalition regime had been established in March 1945, including several heterodox religious sects that the Japanese had encouraged and helped arm. The Vietminh too was represented in this coalition in Saigon, and the communists Tran Van Giau and Dr Pham Ngoc Thach eventually came to lead it, albeit in an uneasy balance with other groups.

The remit of Mountbatten's SEAC also extended up to the 16th parallel, while points north of it were part of MacArthur's US Pacific Command, with Chiang Kai-shek's KMT regime directly responsible for its military security.

In theory, Cambodia fell within the SEAC zone, and most of Laos in the Chinese one. Mountbatten and the British insisted that Thailand too needed to be within the SEAC perimeter, since it had formally declared war on Britain in 1942, and been closely aligned with Japan. The French were even more insistent on an Allied occupation of Thailand, and blocked Thailand's accession to the United Nations until Cambodian and Lao territories lost by France in the Franco–Thai War of 1941 were returned, and Britain similarly demanded the return of the Malay states (Kelantan, Terengganu, Perlis and Kedah) that Japan had transferred to Thai control during the war.

In Thailand, General Phibun's government had been ousted in a parliamentary manoeuvre in August 1944, and been replaced by one dominated by his long-standing civilian rival, Pridi Phanomyong. Pridi's initial period in power after 1932 had lasted less than a year when his radical programme (calling for nationalization of land and labour) met stiff resistance; yet he had returned to become a minister in the late 1930s and served as regent to the young King Ananda Mahidol from 1941 to December 1945. His protégé served as prime minister, but Pridi and the aristocrat Seni Pramoj ran the civilian governments of 1945–47. Although Mountbatten later acknowledged that he had been receiving military and intelligence secrets from Pridi in 1945 despite him being the head of a state technically at war with the Allies, Britain still insisted on sending the 7th Indian Infantry Division (commanded by Major General Charles Evans) to occupy Thailand and enforce the surrender. Britain wanted reparations, and to reduce the size of Thailand's armed forces. But the United States opposed the imposition of punitive terms, since Thailand and the United States had not been at war (recall that ambassador to the US, Seni Pramoj, had instead used frozen Thai funds in the US to create and run the Pridi-aligned Free Thai movement).

Backed by the 7th Indian Infantry Division, Britain was quickly able to sign the Anglo–Thai Peace Treaty on 1 January 1946 at Singapore, and Britain and the United States restored diplomatic ties with Thailand four days later. The Anglo–Thai Treaty provided for the return of the Shan States and the four Unfederated Malay States to British sovereignty, forbade the building of a canal across the Kra peninsula (presumably to preserve the primacy of Singapore and Penang as entrepôts) and provided for the free shipment of 1.5 million tonnes of Thai rice that year to Malaya (the last being a form of reparation, albeit a modest one-off one). No restrictions were placed on the size of Thailand's armed forces. Pridi then agreed to the return (to France) of the provinces that Thailand had gained from French Indo-China in 1941 in exchange for French acceptance of Thailand's accession to the United Nations, as French diplomats again showed their ability to maximize returns even with a weak hand!

Ironically, for about half the time between August 1944 and April 1948 a 'Cambodian' from Battambang province (which had been Thai before 1907, and again from 1941 to 1946, but part of French Cambodia between 1907 and 1941) served as the prime minister of Thailand, and became one of the founders of the conservative Democrat Party which remains influential in Thailand today. Khuang Aphaiwong was a descendant of Khmer (i.e., Cambodian) royalty, and his father had been the Thai governor of Battambang before 1907; another member of their clan, Princess Suvadhana married Thailand's King Vajiravudh (Rama VI). Khuang Aphaiwong himself became a major in the Thai army and led the military reconquest of that province from the French in 1941. Subsequently, his brother-in-law Poc Khun (or Phra Phiset Phanit) led the Khmer Issarak movement to resist French colonial rule in Cambodia, and later became chairman of the Khmer National Liberation Committee (after briefly serving in the Thai Parliament in 1946). However, the resistance to French rule in both Cambodia and Laos was relatively mild, especially as the Free French (de Gaulle's) forces moved into both countries early after the Japanese surrender, and secured Japanese arms and ammunition quickly. Although the incipient version of the Ho Chi Minh Trail helped infiltrate communists into Laos, the French succeeded in incorporating both Laos and Cambodia into a 'French Union'—a loose federation with France, alongside all French colonies around the world, in a legislative arrangement that ensured that metropolitan France would always be in a majority.

The notion of an Indo-Chinese Federation (with five entities, i.e., Vietnam still divided into three parts) within a French Union had been floated in March 1945 by de Gaulle's Free French government as an alternative to Japan's offer of independence to Indo-China. It made little impact on nationalists, as the federation would still be headed by a French Governor General, while the Japanese could offer them genuine independence over territories directly within their control. In Tonkin (the northern region of Vietnam with its capital at Hanoi), a moderate nationalist regime led by Tran Trong Kim (with strong sympathies and ties to the communists) was initially installed. Ho Chi Minh's Vietminh forces quickly established their sway, with the Japanese essentially looking the other way while this region (which, along with Annam in central Vietnam, was supposed to be under the nominal control of emperor Bao Dai) steadily came under the left-nationalist Vietminh's control (and formally so just before Japan's surrender to the Allies).

From April 1945 onwards, Ho Chi Minh also established clandestine relations with the US spy Archimedes Patti of the Office of Strategic Services (OSS), the predecessor to the CIA. Although the Vietminh were primarily

Vietnamese nationalists and Ho's close colleague Vo Nguyen Giap, for instance, was a French-trained professor of history who appeared perfectly assimilated into the francophone world, there can be little doubt that Ho Chi Minh was deeply imbued with communist ideals, having spent much of the previous quarter-century in the Soviet Union and amongst Mao's forces in China. He was heavily involved with the Comintern after 1923, led the creation of the Vietnamese Communist Party in 1930 and later the Indo–Chinese Communist Party, and was briefly imprisoned by Chiang Kai-shek in 1942, before being rescued by Mao's forces. Most of Asia's nationalists (particularly those demanding full independence rather than any compromise with the colonialists) were either socialists or communists, so Ho Chi Minh was not unusual in that respect. He did, however, reach out to US intelligence (the OSS), and collaborated closely with Patti and his OSS team (also benefiting from OSS healthcare when he contracted malaria in mid-1945); like Subhas Bose, Aung San or Sukarno, he would align with whoever would help him end colonial rule.

Between 15 and 19 August 1945, Ho's Vietminh took control of Hanoi and other major cities across Tonkin and Annam (the future North Vietnam), and extended its iron grip over the villages throughout the area north of the 16th parallel. In his public speeches at this time, Ho Chi Minh quoted extensively from the US Declaration of Independence and frequently invoked the Atlantic Charter in seeking US recognition. But the Atlantic Charter, and especially its anti-colonial principles, had been advanced and advocated primarily by the late president Franklin Roosevelt (a New York patrician of Dutch descent, who was wedded to anti-colonialism). His successor, Harry S. Truman of Missouri, had less well-formed views of international affairs and so was much more prone to Winston Churchill's influence in his first months. Although Churchill had been ousted by late July 1945, some of that influence lingered as the new Attlee government found its feet and Truman determinedly ignored Ho Chi Minh's many overtures in August–September 1945. By doing so, in a region that was formally within the American security ambit at the time, Truman effectively allowed Britain and France to dictate the course of Vietnam's future, sparking the thirty-year war against Vietnam's nationalists that the West (including the US) was to fight.

In their wartime exile in the north Indian hill town of Simla, Burma ex-governor Reginald Dorman-Smith and his acolytes had been discussing with Churchill and Anthony Eden plans for extending Britain's sphere of influence further in Southeast Asia. A British protectorate over Thailand was part of these dreams but the US thwarted this. On Vietnam, President Roosevelt had wanted to create a United Nations protectorate after the war, as he loathed French colonial rule. Churchill, though, felt a particular obligation to his Free French and Dutch allies who were determined to regain their old colonies (just as he was to retain the British ones) and he got his opportunity once FDR died. Although the Labour Party was ostensibly committed to decolonization, Attlee's Labour government faithfully followed Churchill's script in Indonesia (as we have seen), but also in Indo-China, Burma and India—particularly while finding its feet in the early months (which proved decisive for the long term too).

On 2 September 1945, the Vietminh organized a 'Fête de l'Indépendance' across Vietnam, including in the south (Cochin-China), where the disparate Saigon-based coalition (including such religious groups as the Cao Dai and local Buddhists, all of whom had been armed and encouraged by the Japanese) had acknowledged the leadership of Ho Chi Minh a few days earlier. Unlike the orderly and impressive ceremony in Hanoi, however, chaos had ensued in Saigon on 2 September: after the mysterious shooting death of a priest outside a Catholic cathedral, shots rang out on all sides—killing scores of Vietnamese demonstrators and French settlers (and their families, including Vietnamese wives and mistresses of Frenchmen). The Vietminh police arrested a number of 'Trotskyites' and other 'troublemakers' to calm the situation. A key difference between Vietnam north of the 16th parallel and to its south was that the former had had a Vietnamese administration for five months prior to mid-August 1945, while the southern region had been turned over to Vietnamese hands (by the Japanese) only days earlier. So, apart from the northern government being more cohesively led by the Vietminh, it also had much more control over the levers of government (including the middle-rung officials, and crucially the police force).

When Chiang Kai-shek's 160,000-strong army marched into Hanoi and Tonkin, they acknowledged the local authority of Ho Chi Minh's government, and concentrated on releasing French prisoners of war and disarming the Japanese soldiers. But when Major General Gracey arrived in Saigon leading the 20th Indian Division (representing SEAC) on 13 September 1945, he and his delegation pointedly ignored the representatives of the Vietnamese government who had come to the airport to receive and greet them. Much more emphatically than Christison in Jakarta, Gracey made it abundantly clear in Saigon that he would act on behalf of the French colonialists, while disarming and containing the Japanese, but would have nothing to do with the Vietnamese.

In frustration, the Vietminh called a strike that closed down Saigon and its twin port city of Cholon on 17 September. Given the government's relatively thin writ over the population, rogue elements were able to mount further attacks on French property that day in Cholon. Gracey made his partisan preferences completely clear, stating that 'the Annamite government was a direct threat to law and order through its armed Police Gendarmerie': his very use of the term 'Annamite' to refer to the Vietnamese government (which had southerners in office in Saigon, not people from Annam) betrayed his and the British–French armies' antipathy towards this Vietminh-dominated coalition.

On 21 September 1945, Gracey declared martial law, warning anybody challenging the order that they would be 'summarily shot', imposed a curfew, gagged the press and radio, banned meetings and demonstrations, and demanded the surrender of all arms. Far from adhering to the tenets of the Atlantic Charter, Gracey was using the Indian Army to suspend civil liberties in all of Cochin-China, impose draconian military rule, and oust the Vietnamese nationalist government.

His forces methodically took control of key buildings including banks and police stations, and handed them to French control. Two days later, at 3 a.m. on Sunday 23 September, the coup d' état was completed when a heavily armed posse of 300 Frenchmen moved into all the important government offices, killed Vietnamese guards, and imprisoned or hanged members of the Vietminh People's Committee. South Vietnam (Cochin-China) had become French again, heavily buttressed by the force of British–Indian arms. Gracey had, in fact, helped the Free French representative to arm more than a thousand French ex-POWs to make this coup possible. The following day, the newly empowered French army (just recently released from Japanese internment) went on a rampage in Saigon; along with local French 'colons', they assaulted the Vietnamese, ransacked their homes, and went about settling real and perceived scores. Two days later, Vietnamese nationalists retaliated, with a general strike that paralysed and blacked out the city, leading to blazing fires that were uncontrollable without fire engines, and an attack on a tony French residential quarter in which about 150 French men and women were murdered.

The Japanese were technically considered 'surrendered personnel', not prisoners of war, so they were still ranged as a disciplined army with a chain of command from top to bottom. The British and French began using Japanese soldiers as 'coolies' to undertake reconstruction and infrastructure-building activity, and soon enlisted them as an army as well in attacking the Vietnamese nationalists. General Jacques-Philippe Leclerc (legendary amongst Frenchmen as a 'liberator of Paris' alongside de Gaulle) arrived in Saigon, accompanied by a large army that was fresh from France, as opposed to the jaded forces of colons and ex-Vichy troops that had been bested in initial engagements with the Vietminh. The combined forces of Gracey and Leclerc quickly reclaimed Cambodia for the French, and pushed northward into central Vietnam, steadily gaining ground. As the British historian John Keay pointed out, the most 'telling legacy of the Allied occupation was SEAC's disposal to the French of all arms collected from the Japanese and much of its own military hardware including transport, aircraft and artillery.' Those arms and hardware proved decisive.

On 10 October, Gracey attempted to explain himself to Dr Pham Ngoc Thach, who was by then leading the resistance forces of the Vietminh against the French dominion being enforced behind the veneer of the British Indian Army. Although Gracey began by attempting to assert that the British were not interested in taking sides in the political conflict 'as between you and the French', he was soon threatening the use of 'armed cars, guns, mortars and aircraft'.

The Vietminh began to drop leaflets in October and November seeking to persuade the Indian troops not to fight fellow Asians. The language barrier proved insurmountable: one of the Gurkha veterans of this campaign and of the later battles in Malaya, Dilman Mothe, later joined the support staff at the public school I attended in Darjeeling. Like his fellow Gurkha soldiers, Dilman's English was halting at best—certainly insufficient to be persuaded by the florid call to 'the sons of Gandhi' to rise up against European imperialism; and Dilman spoke Malay with some facility but had picked up no Vietnamese at all. Apart from the Gurkhas, most of Gracey's other troops were Muslims from Punjab or Hyderabad. Gracey's own Urdu was reasonable (he was to later become Pakistan's first army chief) and he was able to retain most of his troops' loyalty. When the Vietminh mounted a counteroffensive from Bien Hoa towards Saigon in December and January the 20th Indian Division repulsed the poorly-armed Vietnamese with machine gun fire as the Gurkha and Indian Muslim troops stayed disciplined. By then, however, the British Indian Army's engagements in Indonesia and Indo-China were becoming a live political issue in India—with the naval mutineers of February 1946 demanding the repatriation of Indian troops from those two East Asian theatres. The 20th Indian Division did indeed begin withdrawing from Vietnam before the end of February 1946, having delivered the whole of Cochin-China into French hands.

In Ho Chi Minh's Democratic Republic of Vietnam in the north, tensions had begun to emerge with the 200,000-strong Chinese army and support staff of the KMT's General Lu Han to whom the US had delegated the responsibility for taking over the region from the Japanese. The surrender of the latter and protection of the 20,000 French POWs were accomplished quite well by the KMT, and the Vietminh government also accommodated some other nationalists to appease the KMT, while implementing an extensive land reform programme and alleviating the famine.

Initially, the KMT was ambivalent between the Vietminh and the French—certainly unsympathetic to the latter's colonial claims, but also suspicious about Ho Chi Minh's communist past (despite the fact that he had apparently been expelled from the Comintern sometime in the previous decade, something that might have endeared him to Chiang Kai-shek). But soon Lu Han's forces began to take full control of the northern borderlands of Vietnam near Yunnan, and the long-standing Vietnamese suspicion of the Chinese quickly came to the fore.

Major Sainteny, appointed France's commissioner in Tonkin, developed a deep mutual respect for Ho Chi Minh, whom he came to describe as the 'Gandhi of Indo-China', praising his 'wide knowledge, his intelligence, his unbelievable energy, his abstemiousness and his total dedication' which 'had earned him incomparable prestige and popularity in the eyes of the people'. Other French interlocutors, including the parliamentarian Max André, were also favourably impressed by Ho Chi Minh's moderate approach. But, like Nehru and Azad in India, Ho Chi Minh trusted too much in the good faith of not only Sainteny but also of the French Left which, he expected, would soon attain power in France and be sympathetic to Vietnam's nationalist aspirations. (He was wrong; not only did Léon Blum prove to be surprisingly committed to France's imperial project, so did the French communists.) Thus, on 6 March 1946, Ho signed an agreement with Sainteny that allowed for the peaceful return of Leclerc and a French army to Hanoi in exchange for French recognition of the Republic of Vietnam as a 'free state having its own government, parliament, army and finances', and a referendum to allow for the reunification of Tonkin, Annam and Cochin-China. They were all still to be part of an Indo–Chinese Federation within the 'French Union'—remarkably similar to the fond hopes and widely differing assumptions amongst the two parties to the Linggadjati Agreement in Indonesia.

The inevitable recriminations followed almost immediately afterwards, at the peace negotiations aimed at ironing out the details of the agreement in Dalat (in Cochin-China) and Fontainebleau (France). Vo Nguyen Giap held the fort at Dalat, while Ho Chi Minh proceeded to the Paris suburbs, where he expected that the French Left's parliamentary strength would bolster his negotiating hand. French perfidy began in Cochin-China, where Admiral Georges-Thierry d'Argenlieu, the newly arrived French high commissioner for Indo-China and former Catholic priest, constituted an 'advisory council' which endorsed Cochin-China's separate status, and so, he claimed, precluded the need for a referendum. This was a replica of the dubious methods Churchill had used in Iraq in 1921. Cochin-China, with its abundance of rice and rubber, was too important to the French imperial project (just as Mosul and Iraq's oil were to Britain in 1921), and propriety was abandoned in the blink of an eye. While the discussions at Fontainebleau were stalled by the inability of the French to agree on their own government, d'Argenlieu announced the creation of a separate 'free republic' in Cochin-China without the slightest hint of legitimacy.

With the rug pulled from under his feet, Ho Chi Minh importuned Sainteny and other interlocutors at Fontainebleau to give him at least a few crumbs of credibility to fend off his colleagues' calls for war. But the muddle of French metropolitan politics made decision-making impossible, so the person on the ground (d'Argenlieu) had a relatively free hand. Ho knew that war was a last resort, one that would cause ten times as many Vietnamese deaths as French ones, but as he told Sainteny, 'it is you who will end up wearing yourselves out.' While low-level skirmishing persisted in the French puppet state of South Vietnam (with the French incorporating the southern part of Annam into it as well), the war arrived in Tonkin in November 1946, after a French attempt to impose customs duties at Haiphong resulted in firing, the deaths of several French officials, and a massively disproportionate response by d'Argenlieu—involving artillery, naval and air bombardment that killed about 6,000 people in Haiphong, causing most of the city's Vietnamese inhabitants to escape to the countryside in an almost exact replica of what had happened in Indonesia's Surabaya a year earlier.

The French soon captured the key town of Lang Son on the Chinese border, and the strategic port of Da Nang (near the historic city of Hué, capital of Annam) and the war raged most fiercely just as Léon Blum, the socialist who had taken charge of France's provisional government, began speaking publicly of an offer of independence for Vietnam. It had come too late, effectively pre-empted by the colons led by Thierry d'Argenlieu. On 19 December 1946, the Vietminh began to retaliate in Hanoi, first shutting electricity to the city and then attacking French installations across the capital. By then, French naval, air and ground forces had moved into Hanoi and other urban centres in Tonkin with troop reinforcements having arrived from France throughout the course of 1946. A fierce battle ensued for the next fortnight, but at the end of it, Ho Chi Minh and his cohorts abandoned the capital and melted back into the countryside and forests, from where they were to fight a dogged guerrilla war for the next seven years.

Importantly, unlike Sukarno and his Indonesian forces (who were initially seen as Japanese 'quislings' and thus started with even less support from the Allies, but were eventually able to seek and win international support—

especially after the suppression of the 1948 communist uprising in Madiun), international support for Ho Chi Minh steadily diminished over time. One important difference was that France—despite having played almost no part whatsoever in the Allied victory in World War II—was made a permanent member of the UN Security Council. With its large armaments industry and much larger population, France was seen as more vital to the future of the Cold War than the Netherlands. That the Vietminh had strong communist leanings did not help, regardless of their close ties to the precursor of the CIA, through Archimedes Patti of the OSS. And, unlike the East Indies, Indo-China was a genuinely French economic enclave with other European powers having few commercial or financial interests there (unlike in Indonesia, where Britain had 40 per cent ownership of Royal Dutch Shell, its key oil producer, and stakes in other large Anglo–Dutch enterprises such as Unilever). The US became less supportive of the Vietminh once it became clear that French centrists and centre-right parties were strongly committed to colonialism; given the precarious state of French politics, the US did not wish to weaken its natural allies on the centre and right of French politics in pursuit of the American tradition of anti-colonialism. There had been elections in 1945 across Indo–China, with independence-minded majorities emerging in the assemblies for Tonkin and Annam (most of whose members now went underground), as well as in Cambodia and Laos. In the former, King Norodom Sihanouk and his cohort of elite bureaucrats neatly sidestepped the national assembly (by suspending it!) and negotiated an autonomy agreement with the French, leading to the status of an 'associate state' within the French Union.

In Laos, such a neat solution was impossible, as the 'Three Princes'—two of them nephews of King Sisavang Vong—aligned themselves with various sides in the emerging Cold War, leaving the royal palace isolated in its fastness of Luang Prabang. In 1946, the French created a provisional government based in Vientiane (in an obvious attempt to distance themselves from the palace), and eventually received the support of one of the Three Princes, Prince Boun Oum of Champassak (a kingdom in the southern extremity of Laos that he merged in 1946 into the Kingdom of Laos, based in Luang Prabang). Boun Oum then served as prime minister in the French-backed regime from 1948 to 1950. But the French faced fierce opposition from the Lao Issara (Free Laos) movement led by two sons (from different wives) of the vice-king of Luang Prabang.

In a devoutly Buddhist country, where monkhood was traditionally seen as the path to an education and social mobility, the two half-brother princes (Souvanna Phouma and Souphanouvong) eventually represented various shades of socialism, respectively leading the 'neutralist' (mildly pro-US but politically socialist) and communist (pro-Vietnam) factions in the 1950s. But in 1945–46, they were aligned in the Lao Issara movement led by Souvanna Phouma's eldest brother, Prince Phetsarath Ratanavongsa, who had been the pro-Japanese prime minister of the Kingdom of Laos in 1941–45, and whose supporters remained in power until April 1946, when the French reclaimed Laos after the March 1946 agreement with Ho Chi Minh and withdrawal of Chinese KMT troops. Prince Phetsarath was perceived to possess supernatural powers, and some of the amulets he wore remain popular in Laos today. But after France reclaimed Laos, Prince Phetsarath fled to Thailand, where he and his two brothers were instrumental in keeping the nationalist Lao Issara afloat.

A monarchist solution was eventually tried in Vietnam as well, with Bao Dai being persuaded to formally return to the throne in March 1949. But Bao Dai only agreed to return after France promised the reunification of the whole of Vietnam, and conceded formal 'independence' to Vietnam within the 'French Union' (which did of course constrain the degree of actual independence). Laos also became formally independent in 1950, albeit with its foreign policy, defence and finances still largely controlled by France (which caused the USSR to veto the Laotian application to join the UN). Soon afterwards, US arms supplies began to flow to the French in Indo-China. By 1954, four-fifths of France's war effort was being financed by the US. What turned such a reflexively anti-colonial power as the US into a full-blown supporter of French colonialism, of course, was Mao's victory in the Chinese Civil War and the advent of the Cold War.

Mao's triumph also helped the Vietminh break out of their international isolation and, militarily, provided a vital rearguard that Ho Chi Minh could fall back on inside China (albeit one he was reluctant to use, given a millennium of Sino–Vietnamese history). The USSR and China were quick to recognize the 'Democratic Republic of Vietnam', and that recognition immediately became a literal and metaphorical red flag to the Americans. The former ally of the US OSS during the 1940s was now a full-blown enemy, as the Korean War caused a complete polarization across Asia. As the intensity of the Korea conflict eased by 1953, Vietnam increasingly came to be seen as the front line of Asia's Cold War, especially as Britain was by then fully engaged in fighting the Communist Party of Malaya. By 1953, the former history professor Vo Nguyen Giap was developing a reputation as a brilliant military genius; that year, he shifted the Vietminh's military emphasis from the Red River delta to the highlands of Tonkin, and began to develop the rudiments of what eventually became the Ho Chi Minh Trail through Laos into Cambodia and a possible backdoor to South Vietnam. After Phibun returned to power in

Thailand, he cooperated more with the French, which was ironic given his heroic role in the Franco–Thai War of 1941. The Lao Issara gradually became less welcome in Thailand, and were forced either to make their peace with the French (as Souvanna Phouma did, returning to Laos, winning a landslide electoral victory and becoming prime minister in 1951) or fall fully into Vietnam's embrace (as his half-brother Souphanouvong did, becoming the leader of the communist Pathet Lao or Free Laos movement).

Seemingly somnolent Laos was suddenly on the front line of Asia's last great colonial war. With the Pathet Lao in control of the highlands on the Laos side, and Giap in control of the Vietnamese side, the French began to build up a massive concentration of forces in the strategic valley of Dien Bien Phu—primarily to cut off supply lines to the clandestine routes that were feeding into Laos and Cambodia, and threatening to reach Cochin-China. In 1953, Souvanna Phouma's government had obtained full independence for Laos, although its recommendation to attempt a coalition with the Pathet Lao (which was already in control of the northeastern and southern regions) was vigorously opposed by the royalist Boun Oum. Nonetheless, the Pathet Lao were militarily well positioned to provide cover to their Vietminh allies, as Giap began a final assault on the French military complex at Dien Bien Phu on 13 March 1954. The relatively new Eisenhower administration—with the Dulles brothers taking particularly hawkish positions on Cold War conflicts—briefly considered deploying US ground troops and nuclear weapons in this conflict, but demurred because the British (burnt once too often in colonial wars) were not willing to get involved.

After two months of fierce warfare, in which the elite of France's multinational Expeditionary Force (including Russians and Germans from the famed Foreign Legion) suffered more than 15,000 casualties and lost 60 aircraft, Vo Nguyen Giap's Vietminh claimed a decisive victory. France's colonial pretensions in Asia suffered a final crushing blow with the abject surrender of French troops at Dien Bien Phu on 7 May 1954.

Politically, too, the defeat came at an inopportune moment for France—just as the Geneva Conferences to discuss Indo-China's future were reaching a climax, and the Radical Socialist Pierre Mendès-France was taking office as prime minister of France, promising to complete the negotiations within a month. Mendès-France had been a brilliant lawyer and fiscal expert who had challenged the Vichy regime and escaped into exile during the war to join de Gaulle's Free French. But after representing France at the Bretton Woods monetary conference in 1944, he became a leading advocate of decolonization. Already in the previous year, France had offered nearly full independence to Laos, Cambodia and Bao Dai's (South) Vietnam. Now, Mendès-France went the whole way, offering independence, the withdrawal of all French troops from Vietnam north of the 16th parallel, and elections across North and South Vietnam to determine the whole country's future status. By this time, however, the US was already underwriting Bao Dai's regime in South Vietnam, so France's role was naturally withering away. Neither side ever fully ratified the Geneva Accords, but they nonetheless effectively ended France's colonial involvement in Indo-China. Cambodia, Laos and North Vietnam (above the 16th parallel) were now fully independent, while South Vietnam remained part of the unfinished business of the Cold War, tenuously holding on as a separate nation state propped up by the United States, which would expend considerable money and manpower over the next twenty-one years to prevent the Vietminh from fulfilling their long-thwarted nationalist destiny.

BRITAIN'S DECOLONIZATION AND THE WAGES OF DIVIDE AND RULE

Two elections were held in quick succession in British India in 1945–46: first, to the Central Legislative Assembly in December 1945, and then to the provincial assemblies in February–March of 1946. Since the federal aspects of the Government of India Act of 1935 had been rejected pre-emptively by the princes and the main political parties, the election to the Central Legislature had to be held under the 1919 Government of India Act. This bizarre aspect of this election is neglected by almost all observers, particularly Pakistani ones who cite this election as the biggest justification for Pakistan's creation. While the 1935 Act widened the electorate to about 14 per cent of the Indian adult population, the 1919 Act restricted the electorate to 1 per cent of the adult population. Replying to a House of Commons question in 1942, Secretary of State for India Leo Amery said that the total electorate for British India's Central Legislative Assembly '...for the last General Election (1934) was 1,415,892'. (That year, India's total population was 350.7 million, so barely 0.4 per cent of the population was eligible to vote!) The 1945 election was also conducted using a similarly narrow electorate. One of the unanswered questions of the time is why Congress did not insist on universal suffrage, which would have resulted in a better outcome for it. Perhaps fighting for a wider franchise would have only delayed matters, and Congress did not want to lose time.

Wanting to capitalize on the nationalist fervour generated by the INA trials, the Congress announced that Sarat Bose would lead its electoral campaign for the Central Legislature. This was quite extraordinary, as Subhas Bose's elder brother Sarat was no more than a part-time politician; he had remained a practising barrister in order to earn a living, and so provide financial support to his younger brother's full-time commitment to India's fight for independence. Led by Sarat Bose, and the indefatigable campaigning of his colleagues Nehru and Patel, the Congress won a clear majority: of the 102 contested seats, Congress won 59. But the biggest gainer was the Muslim League, which won all 30 of the seats reserved exclusively for Muslim voters and candidates. The Akali Dal won the 2 seats reserved for Sikhs. Although the Congress (with 91 per cent of the vote in the 'general' constituencies open to all voters) won a decisive majority, the Muslim League celebrated the fact that it had won all 30 seats reserved for Muslims (with nearly 87 per cent of all votes cast in the Muslim-only constituencies), and it declared that this vindicated Jinnah's claim to be the 'sole spokesman' of the Muslims.

Despite the narrowness of the electorate, there was little doubt that the Muslim League had taken massive strides forward amongst Muslims during the war years—while Congress leaders were imprisoned. Two episodes, however, contributed significantly to elite Muslim opinion swinging increasingly towards Jinnah, whose claim to being the 'sole spokesman for the Muslims' appeared to have been endorsed by both the other parties in India's political triangle: (a) after Gandhi's release from prison in mid-1944, he had held talks with Jinnah during which he offered (after the departure of the British) a district-wise referendum to determine which areas wanted to be part of Pakistan (although Jinnah rejected this offer, it was the first time the Congress leader had acknowledged that Pakistan was a legitimate possibility or goal; that Gandhi was formally no longer a Congress member was an obscure fact ignored by almost everyone in India); and (b) at the Simla Conference in late June 1945, Wavell offered to expand his Executive Council by offering an equal number of seats in it to Hindu and Muslim members (itself an extraordinary offer highly favourable to Muslims, who comprised less than a third of British India's population), and resolutely supported Jinnah's demand that he (Jinnah) alone would nominate all the Muslim members of the Council. This strong British endorsement of Jinnah as the 'sole spokesman' for India's Muslims signalled to the Muslim elite that their future lay in aligning with Jinnah if they wished to have any prospects in British India (as well as in the Pakistan that was inevitable), especially since Congress was barred from nominating any Muslims to high office. After July 1945, there had been an exodus of ambitious Muslims from the Unionist and Congress parties to the Muslim League that they had disdained until that point (especially in Punjab).

The results of the provincial elections—based on a substantially wider franchise (still only 14 per cent of the population, and with separate communal electorates)—were broadly similar, although less decisively in favour of the Muslim League within the Muslim-only constituencies. It was extraordinary that Congress did not insist on universal suffrage even at this election, as a wider electorate would clearly have been to its advantage; but challenging the British on yet another vital issue did risk delaying the process (and the experience of 1919–20 was probably high on Congress leaders' minds). With so much apparently at stake, the polarization of votes continued and the Muslim League made massive gains in 1946 compared with its dismal tally at the 1937 election, but the Congress too won many more seats than in 1937.

Nationwide, Congress won 923 of the 1,568 seats (up from 707 in 1937), but the Muslim League dominated the Muslim-only constituencies, taking its tally to 425 (from just 106 in 1937) of the total of 492 seats reserved for Muslims. In particular, the Muslim League gained at the expense of the non-sectarian Unionist party in Punjab (where the Unionists' leader Sikandar Hayat Khan had died in 1943, and been replaced by the less-experienced Khizar Hayat Tiwana): from just 2 seats in 1937, the Muslim League's Punjab tally jumped to 73, while the Unionists' tally slumped to 20 (from 95 in 1937). But Congress (51 seats in 1946, from 18 in 1937) and the Akali Dal (22 seats in 1946, from 10 in 1937) also gained at the expense of the Unionists, and Congress and the Akali Dal together had the same number of seats as the Muslim League; a stable Unionist–Congress–Akali coalition government was formed in Punjab, with Khizar Hayat continuing as chief minister.

Congress won large majorities, and was able to form ministries of its own, in eight provinces (Assam, Bihar, Bombay Presidency, Central Provinces, Madras Presidency, NWFP, Orissa, and United Provinces). Notably, the Communist Party (which had opposed Gandhi's Quit India Movement on orders from Stalin's USSR) put up 108 candidates, but won only 8 seats (including 3 seats in Bengal, one won by Jyoti Basu). The Muslim League won 113 seats in the 250-member Bengal assembly, gaining hugely at the expense of Fazlul Huq's Krishak Praja Party (which won just 4 seats, compared with 34 in 1937); the Congress won 86 seats in Bengal, including several Muslim-only seats and a near clean sweep of the 48 general seats and the 30 reserved for Scheduled Castes. In both Bengal and Punjab, the Muslim League promised tenant-farmers that it would confiscate the land of Hindu landlords without compensation (a more sectarian version of the tenurial reform programme that had made Fazlul Huq the leader of East Bengal's peasants in the 1930s).

With the active help of each governor (and the European bloc within the assembly), Bengal and Sindh were the only provinces in which the Muslim League was able to cobble together a ministry in 1946. In NWFP (where Muslims constituted 92 per cent of the population), Congress won a decisive victory (with 30 seats in the Assembly, to 17 for the Muslim League, out of a total of 50) and was able to form a majority government. In Sindh, Congress won 18 seats (up from 7 in 1937), and the Muslim League won 27 in an Assembly comprising 60 members. G. M. Syed's bloc (which had been expelled from the Muslim League before the election) won 4 seats; it soon aligned with a 3-member bloc led by Haji Maula Bux and 4 independents to throw their support behind Congress. Consequently, the two main coalitions in the Sindh Assembly comprised 29 members each (two short of a majority). Congress' national leaders Maulana Azad and Sardar Patel went to Sindh and proposed a broad-based coalition of all the parties. A significant faction of the Muslim League led by Hashim Gazdar agreed to this proposal. But it was vetoed by Jinnah and the British governor, Sir Francis Mudie, who invited Sir Ghulam Hussain Hidayatullah of the Muslim League to form a minority government. When G. M. Syed (the Congress-led coalition's candidate to be chief minister) met Mudie to stake his claim to form a government, Mudie shocked him by advising that he align with the Muslim League in the interests of Pakistan!

The evidence overwhelmingly suggests that by 1945 Britain was committed to creating Pakistan before departing the Indian subcontinent. The Conservative Party (and particularly its dominant faction led by Churchill) expected that Britain 'would have to continue responsibility for India for at least thirty years' (as Viceroy Linlithgow told his successor Wavell), and during that interval British India would have to be divided amongst 'Pakistan, Hindustan and Princestan' (as Churchill expressed it to Wavell on 29 March 1945; this was of course implicit in the design of the federal features of the 1935 Government of India Act); the assumption was that Princestan and Pakistan would remain military allies of Britain. The Labour Party, despite the apparent 'friendship' between some of its leaders and the Congress leadership, was just as committed to this goal by September 1945, partly convinced by Viceroy Wavell. Attlee himself was an alumnus of Haileybury, the public school that was established to prepare pupils for careers in the ICS, so he was steeped in imperial lore (particularly about India), and had been a member of the 1929 Simon Commission that failed to advance reform. While most observers (including the US historian Stanley Wolpert) blame Mountbatten for the 'haste' with which he implemented the partition plan within weeks of his arrival as viceroy in March 1947, he was merely completing the plan that Wavell had meticulously prepared.

Wavell's antipathy towards Congress stemmed from his experience in 1942, when (as he wrote in a letter to King George VI soon after becoming his viceroy in India): 'Congress made a deliberate effort to paralyse my communications to the eastern front by widespread sabotage and rioting' at a time when, as Commander-in-Chief ABDACOM Southeast Asia, he was seeking 'to secure India with very inadequate resources against Japanese invasion'. But his strategic understanding of India was in accord with the top-secret assessment prepared by the Post-Hostilities Planning Staff of the British War Cabinet in late May 1945: 'The USSR is the only major power which would be capable of seriously threatening our interests in India and the Indian Ocean area by 1955–60... It is of paramount importance that India should not secede from the Empire or remain neutral in war.' As the Second World War was ending, the British military clearly did not expect to relinquish control of India until 1960!

Britain's military planners saw India as a valuable base for deployment of the military in 'the Indian Ocean area and in the Middle East and the Far East' (as indeed it had been in both World Wars), vital to air and sea communications from the UK to the Far East and Australia, and a source of enormous 'reserve manpower' that could contribute to the 'war effort of the British Empire'. The May 1945 report asserted that Britain 'must ensure that whatever constitutional changes occur, we retain the right to station military strategic reserves in India... after she has been granted Dominion Status.... Central Headquarters India have suggested Baluchistan as an alternative to India proper, on the ground that it may be relatively easy to exclude this territory from the Dominion of India'. So the British military envisaged a form of dominion status for India akin to what was offered to Egypt in 1922 or Iraq in 1931, with a substantive residual British military presence in India (the form of 'independence' that Egyptian and Iraqi nationalists had emphatically opposed).

As long as Churchill was Britain's prime minister, Wavell conducted 'negotiations' with Indian politicians primarily to deflect American pressure, while offering proposals (such as Jinnah having the sole right to nominate half the members of the Executive Council) that were bound to be rejected by Congress. With Churchill's defeat in the July 1945 general election, Wavell needed to change tack as he was initially unsure whether the new Labour government would adhere to the War Cabinet's strategic vision for India. His initial response was to aggressively assert Britain's need to accept the principle of Pakistan. Within weeks of Attlee becoming prime minster, Wavell warned on 20 August 1945: '[His Majesty's Government] must be most cautious in any immediate announcement they wish to make [on India]. It is easy to say that the Muslims cannot be allowed to hold up the settlement; but they are too large a proportion of the population to be bypassed or coerced without grave danger.'

Arriving in London a few days later, Wavell asserted that accepting the principle of Pakistan was a precondition to any discussions: 'It was most unlikely that Mr Jinnah would now enter into discussions without a previous guarantee of acceptance in principle of Pakistan.' More ludicrous was his 'own judgement…that Jinnah spoke for 99 per cent of the Muslim population of India in their apprehensions of Hindu domination'—and this before any elections had been held, with the only previous one having shown that Jinnah spoke for less than a third of India's Muslims. Wavell's claim regarding Jinnah was an even more egregious falsehood than Churchill's 1942 remark to FDR about the Indian Army being more than 75 per cent Muslim (in the same week in which Wavell had told him the correct figure was 35 per cent). In a note to the Cabinet on 31 August 1945, Wavell asserted that the 1942 Cripps offer, which 'proceeded on the assumption that partition in the last resort provided solution of the Hindu–Muslim question', was no longer acceptable to Jinnah in 1945 since he could not be sure that Bengal and Punjab (with their slim Muslim majorities) would vote definitively for Pakistan in a plebiscite of the whole population. Thus, Wavell implied, Jinnah would reject the idea of a Constituent Assembly unless Pakistan was accepted in principle.

So Wavell was again recommending that Britain accept the principle of Pakistan at the outset of any negotiations. However, he did add an important rider: that it would be unfair to the Hindus and Sikhs to hand all of Punjab to Pakistan, just as it would be unfair to Bengali Hindus to hand Calcutta and West Bengal (with their large Hindu majorities) to Pakistan. So he was recommending—as early as the last day of August 1945—that Punjab and Bengal be partitioned as well. At the time, the British military was adamant about retaining bases in India for future operations against the USSR and to defend Britain's oil interests in the Middle East—and Wavell's emphatic recommendation was that this goal could only be achieved through partition, since Congress would not cooperate on military matters. While Attlee's cabinet was not immediately convinced, a degree of continuity in strategic thinking was ensured when Attlee appointed General Hastings Ismay (Churchill's chief staff officer and military adviser throughout World War II) as a senior member of the Cabinet Secretariat, and his chief liaison with the British chiefs of staff. Ismay was a second generation officer of the British Indian Army (born in Nainital, although educated at Charterhouse and Sandhurst). He remained personally loyal to Churchill throughout, and was to accompany Mountbatten to India as his chief of staff in 1947, later being appointed the first secretary-general of NATO (1952–57) by Churchill. Attlee's decision to persist with Churchill's alter ego, Ismay, as such a key defence adviser was the ultimate guarantee of policy continuity—especially when it came to strategic issues relating to India.

Clement Attlee's approach to India did differ significantly from Churchill's. The latter would have pursued his Balkanization plan (Pakistan, Hindustan, Princestan), which would have provoked extreme reactions from India's leaders with unpredictable consequences (even in mid-1947, the British chiefs of staff expected to have access to military bases and airfields in friendly princely states like Hyderabad and Kashmir). Attlee, on the other hand, was determined to maintain a positive relationship with an independent India, although he had been fully immersed in the strategic necessity of partitioning India after his years as deputy prime minister in the War Cabinet. The US Secretary of State, Dean Acheson, said Attlee was apt to 'operate behind smokescreens'; while Attlee was cognizant of the strong sentiment in favour of a united India within a wing of his Labour party, he pursued the ultimate goal of partition (or at least the maintenance of key military bases in northwestern India) while appearing to appease (and use) that wing of his party. Stafford Cripps's strong relations with Nehru proved particularly useful. Cripps's close friend and Labour Party collaborator, V. K. Krishna Menon (who had been secretary of the India League in London since 1929), proved a valuable interlocutor between Labour leaders in the UK and Menon's friend and political mentor in India, Jawaharlal Nehru.

Krishna Menon had been a theosophist and disciple of Annie Besant's in the early 1920s (a time when Besant's star was on the wane with the rise of M. K. Gandhi). But Besant arranged for Menon's passage to London in 1924 (when he was already twenty-eight), and Menon became a serial collector of master's degrees from the London School of Economics and Political Science. Between 1930 and 1934, he obtained separate first-class MA degrees in Philosophy and Political Science, and was called to the Bar at the Middle Temple, finishing his studies at the ripe age of thirty-seven, while also building a formidable reputation as an agitator for left-wing causes. Harold Laski, the left-wing professor and Fabian ideologue at LSE who gathered around him a galaxy of admirers from India (especially) and elsewhere in Asia and Africa, is said to have considered Krishna Menon the 'most brilliant' student he ever had (but, of course, most of his other students would have been much younger in age and intellectual maturity when Laski first encountered them). Although Laski was one of the leading members of the Fabian Society (which believed in 'evolutionary' rather than revolutionary socialism), his speeches and teaching often shaded into revolutionary rhetoric that appeared to advocate violence. This is what made him an iconic figure with Indian communist students like Jyoti Basu and Mohit Sen, while the likes of Feroze Gandhi (Indira's husband) were in the periphery of Laski's circle.

In 1945–46, Laski was also chairman of Britain's Labour Party—a title that sounded grander than it was in reality, because the chairman was more a symbolic (and intellectual) figure (a constitutional monarch of the party, if you will) and not the party's leader or policy formulator. While Attlee was disdainful of Laski, the latter retained his large circle of admirers within the Labour Party (including Cripps and Frederick Pethick-Lawrence, the two key men who would be influencing India policy). Attlee kept Laski firmly away from actual policy formulation, but he was wont to use his network to his advantage—including via his favourite radical former student, Krishna Menon.

Menon had a gift for self-promotion, which led to his claim of having 'co-founded' the Penguin publishing company with his friend (and colleague at Bodley Head), Sir Allen Lane. Penguin's own official history makes clear that Allen Lane was emphatically (and solely, alongside his brothers) the founder of Penguin. Krishna Menon, however, played a key role (as the first editor) at Penguin's new affiliate, Pelican (focusing mainly on non-fiction writing), and can rightly be thought of as the founding co-editor of Pelican Books. This, along with his radical nationalist rhetoric at India League, helped Krishna Menon build a devoted following of his own amongst Indian students in London. But both then and throughout his career, Menon was to maintain a lofty, theoretical and romantic view of global politics, seeking out ideological causes rather than pragmatic solutions. So he and Jawaharlal Nehru plunged into the politics of the Spanish Civil War (and created a Spain–India Committee) in 1936–38, when the Spaniards had no commensurate interest in India; and this at a time when new provincial governments had been formed by Congress in India, and the challenges of governance should have occupied their minds more than romantic support for the supposedly 'just' and 'universal' cause of the Republicans in Spain.

It was at Krishna Menon's urging that Cripps reached out to Jawaharlal Nehru in November 1945. Nehru was then just one amongst several important Congress leaders, whereas Maulana Abul Kalam Azad was Congress president, and had been the chief negotiator with the British on behalf of Congress since 1942 (including at the June 1945 Simla Conference, which Nehru had not even attended). Even during the war years, while Nehru and the entire top- and mid-level membership of Congress was languishing in British jails, the British Labour Party had kept a channel open to Nehru via Krishna Menon, using Fabianism as the binding ideological factor. That he was an Old Harrovian (like Churchill and Amery) made Nehru the most acceptable face of the Congress to Britain's leaders of all stripes.

On 6 November 1945 (the day after the INA trials began, accompanied by massive demonstrations that resulted in deaths from police firing outside the Red Fort in Delhi), Wavell sent a top-secret memo to Secretary of State for India, Pethick-Lawrence: 'We are now faced in India with a situation of great difficulty and danger.... The Congress leaders intend to provoke or pave the way for mass disorder...counting on the INA as a spearhead of the revolt. They would suborn the Indian Army if they could.' Yet, Cripps wrote to his friend Nehru, and Nehru wrote back warmly: 'Many things that have been done during the past few years have hurt me...but at no time did I doubt that you had the cause of India at heart.... We shall do our utmost to avoid conflict and to restrain the hotheads.' This last sentence was astonishing, since Wavell (who had accused Nehru of being inflammatory in his election speeches) considered Nehru to be the embodiment of a hothead! As the nation responded with patriotic fervour to the INA trials, and anti-European demonstrations occurred across India amid the election campaign for the Central Legislature, Cripps wrote to Jawaharlal: 'I am so glad you are as convinced as I am, that we must do our utmost to restrain the use of force on either side,' and added a question bound to stir Nehru's ego: 'If you were in the Viceroy's place what line of action would you lay down to be followed after the elections?' and requested an 'off-the-record answer to that!'

In a rambling 3,500-word response dated 27 January 1946 that began 'My dear Stafford', Nehru said the British government needed to state clearly that it accepts the independence of India, and that the constitution of free India would be determined by India's elected representatives without any British interference. Nehru asserted that the ideal would be a loose federation with safeguards to protect the minorities; all power would be left to the federating units apart from defence, foreign affairs, communications and currency. While asserting that Jinnah's threat of bloodshed was not credible, since the 'Muslim League leadership is far too reactionary...to dare to indulge in any form of direct action', Nehru said Britain 'cannot force Pakistan on India, in the form demanded by Jinnah, for that certainly will lead to civil war'. But Nehru left a door open, saying that if inhabitants of any territorial unit wanted to opt out they could do so via a plebiscite, but would not take with them inhabitants within the same unit who did not wish to opt out. He effectively conceded that a future Pakistan could only comprise a part of Punjab and part of Bengal, but not all of those provinces. Nehru was going out on a limb here, as this letter expressed his own opinions, almost certainly without any consultation with his colleagues. After Gandhi's June 1944 talks with Jinnah, this was the first time a Congress leader was discussing the possibility of an 'acceptable' concept of Pakistan, diluting the party's seeming intransigence on partition.

There is no evidence that Nehru's letter to Cripps was shown to Wavell, but there is no reason why it should not have been, since it was not confidential. But the olive branch Nehru had offered (in the form of a partition of India, as long as Punjab and Bengal were further partitioned) was incorporated into a very detailed proposal for the partition of British India that Wavell sent to the British Cabinet on 7 February 1946. Wavell's letter contained a blueprint that was followed in almost every detail in the August 1947 partition plan, recommending that Sindh, NWFP, British Baluchistan, and Rawalpindi, Multan and Lahore divisions of Punjab (less Amritsar and Gurdaspur districts) be included in Pakistan, as should (from Bengal) the Chittagong and Dacca divisions, the Rajshahi Division (less Jalpaiguri and Darjeeling districts), the Nadia, Murshidabad and Jessore districts of Presidency Division, and Sylhet district from Assam. Wavell made clear that there was no basis for Calcutta (with its large Hindu majority) to go to Pakistan. The only change that occurred to this plan eighteen months later was that Murshidabad stayed in India, in exchange for Hindu-majority Khulna going to Pakistan on account of contiguity, while Nadia was partitioned into Kushtia (which went to Pakistan) while the smaller western part with a slight Hindu majority stayed in India. The western part of Pakistan was to be formed precisely in accord with Wavell's informal demarcation of February 1946: the district of Gurdaspur (51 per cent Muslim) would stay in India because of contiguity with Amritsar, which had to stay with India because of its religious importance to Sikhs.

The fortnight following Wavell's memo to the British Cabinet proved to be especially turbulent in India, with the outbreak of the naval mutiny forcing Attlee to precipitately announce (on 19 February 1946) the dispatch of a Cabinet Mission to negotiate the terms for India's freedom. Given the animosity between Wavell and the Congress leaders (especially Gandhi), Attlee saw the Cabinet Mission as a way to secure Congress agreement for the British plan, and saddle the Indians with the responsibility of partitioning India. In order to mollify Congress, the Cabinet Mission was led by Cripps, and included Secretary of State for India Pethick-Lawrence, and the working-class First Lord of the Admiralty A. V. Alexander who had never visited India (and found dhoti-clad politicians 'baffling and tricky'). Francis Turnbull, assistant secretary in the India Office, sent a memo to Cripps and Pethick-Lawrence on 13 March 1946 suggesting how best to advance the partition scheme: 'If the Mission can avoid a discussion with Mr Gandhi in the opening stages there may be advantage.... If there is any hope of compromise, it is likely to be best worked out with Azad and Nehru.... If Mr Gandhi has not committed himself [at the start] he may be affected by the views of supporters if they are sufficiently unanimous.'

Attlee's explicit instructions to the Cabinet Mission were that they were to adhere to the following cardinal principles: (a) Constitutional protection for the minorities; (b) provision for the defence of India and the Indian

Ocean; and (c) allowing princely states to freely make whatever arrangements they thought fit upon Britain's withdrawal. The princes and Jinnah's Muslim League were still Britain's trump cards to ensure that the defence/strategic role of the British–Indian military could be perpetuated. Within three weeks of their arrival in India, Cripps wrote to Attlee on 11 April 1946 that two 'possible bases of agreement' had emerged: (a) 'a unitary India with a loose federation at the Centre charged with control of Defence and Foreign Affairs (Scheme A)'; and (b) a 'divided India and the smaller Pakistan (Scheme B)' (as in Wavell's proposal of 7 February 1946). Two days later, Attlee responded: 'you may work for an agreement on the basis of Scheme B (Pakistan) if it seems to be the only chance of an agreed settlement.' On 12 April, Attlee had convened a meeting of his top generals, at the end of which Field Marshal Francis Alanbrooke asserted that Pakistan 'was in fact militarily unsound' but he feared that 'chaos would probably take place in India if this scheme, which was a political one, was not put into effect'. Attlee had even worked on convincing the Chiefs of Staff that partition was the only political solution.

With serious negotiations underway with the British, Congress needed to elect a successor to Maulana Azad, who had been president of the party for an unprecedented six-year term, primarily because war and imprisonment prevented the Congress from functioning effectively through that period. Azad himself claimed that five provincial committees of Congress sent entreaties for him to continue as president, and that he himself chose to stand down, and nominated Jawaharlal to succeed him on 26 April, following an hour-long meeting with Gandhi. Azad later wrote that 'the way things have shaped since then has made me realize that this [withdrawing from the Presidency of Congress] was perhaps the greatest blunder of my political life.' And he came to believe that his 'second mistake was that... I did not support Sardar Patel. We differed on many issues but I am convinced that if he had succeeded me as Congress President he would have seen that the Cabinet Mission Plan was successfully implemented. He would never have committed the mistake of Jawaharlal which gave Mr Jinnah the opportunity of sabotaging the plan.'

In reality, as Patrick French pointed out (quoting Alan Campbell-Johnson's memoirs), twelve of the fifteen Congress provincial committees chose Sardar Vallabhbhai Patel to become Congress president in 1946, and Nehru was not even nominated (Acharya J. B. Kripalani being the only other nominee). While Gandhi had in 1942 reiterated '... for many years that Jawaharlal would be my successor', the widespread feeling within Congress was that Jawaharlal was too impractical to be India's first prime minister, and he was not nominated by any of the provincial committees. There was to be an election in mid-May, but it was clear that Sardar Patel would win Congress's nod handily, despite

PRASENJIT K. BASU

Azad and Gandhi's support for Jawaharlal. At this point, Gandhi intervened directly with Patel to request that he (and Kripalani) stand aside in favour of Jawaharlal Nehru. Gandhi pointed to Nehru's 'international outlook', and to the fact that, having been 'educated at Harrow and Cambridge', he would be best positioned to 'carry on the negotiations with the Englishmen'. Somehow, then or since, nobody ever asked why there needed to be a successor to Gandhi at all; he was seventy-six years old, but still in vigorous health and clearly the ultimate decision maker in Congress.

The Congress party's paradox was that, while almost all policy decisions were made through a democratic process (explaining why democracy has survived so long in India, quite unlike almost all of Britain's other former colonies), questions of leadership were almost always settled by Gandhi as long as he lived (in 1939 with Bose, here between Patel and Nehru). Gandhi was ruled out as leader in 1946 primarily because he was no longer acceptable to the British, while Nehru (after his loyal-to-the-British foray into Assam and Bengal in 1944 when the INA and Japanese troops were threatening Britain's control over India) had proved his loyalty to the British, and was more acceptable as a result.

So Nehru, the avowed democrat, was nominated (by Gandhi) rather than elected to the leadership of Congress (and hence to the prospective prime ministership) and that too, primarily because he was the most acceptable Congress interlocutor for the British. The anglicized atheist, Jawaharlal was by now being called 'Pandit Nehru' or simply 'Panditji', to call attention to the fact that he was, by birth, a Brahmin. This was an especially hypocritical moniker for a politician who made modernity and 'secularism' his political touchstones, but 'Panditji' became central to the creation of the Nehru political brand.

In late March 1946, Jawaharlal had visited Singapore and Malaya, where Dickie Mountbatten treated him like a visiting head of state, both flattering him and signalling to India that Nehru was the favourite British choice for the leadership of India. Dickie and Edwina Mountbatten had an open marriage, with each talking to the other about their various affairs (with both men and women in the case of the bisexual Dickie). Edwina was charmed by Jawaharlal on this trip, and they began a relationship that was soon to develop into an affair.

Eventually, on 16 May 1946 the Cabinet Mission settled on a new plan (Scheme C) that would provide for a federal government to deal with foreign affairs, defence and communications, with all other powers vested in the autonomous provinces. An election to a new Constituent Assembly would be held in July 1946, with each federal legislator representing one of the three groups of provinces: Group A would comprise the non-Muslim-majority provinces except Assam (Madras, Bombay, Orissa, Central Provinces, Bihar and United Provinces); Group B would comprise Punjab, NWFP, Sindh and Baluchistan; while Group C would comprise Bengal and Assam. An interim government would be established as soon as the parties accepted this Scheme C, with Indian party politicians replacing the nominated members of the Viceroy's Executive Council in preparation for the British withdrawal once the newly elected Constituent Assembly had settled on a new Constitution, with separate sub-constitutions for each of the three Groups. After ten years, Groups B and C would have the opportunity to choose whether or not to secede from the Indian confederation; secession would be on the basis of a majority vote of the Group legislators sitting together.

Effectively, Groups B and C comprised the 'larger Pakistan' that Jinnah had always hoped for (with Muslims in a slight majority, 51 per cent, in Group C too). The princes would each have the right to decide their own territories' fate—so a third of the land of British India could theoretically break free into little principalities. The larger ones amongst these—Hyderabad, Kashmir, Travancore—were seen by the British military chiefs of staff (in memoranda dated as late as July 1947) as excellent potential bases and aircraft-refuelling stations, so they would be encouraging them to declare independence or autonomy. The weak and divided federal government would hardly be in a position to intervene.

The Cabinet Mission proposals were only marginally different from what had been proposed at the Simla Conference in July 1945 and by the Cripps mission in 1942, both of which Gandhi had rejected outright, even if some Congress leaders (notably Azad, Nehru and Rajagopalachari) had been tempted into negotiating variations of them at various times. Yet again, Congress leaders (Patel and Nehru this time) had cooperated with the British (by intervening with the mutinous sailors at the height of the naval mutiny in February 1946), but received no more than crumbs in return. Now, many of the younger radicals in the Congress (particularly the socialists) began calling for a renewed Quit India mass movement, including calls for subversion of the armed forces. The British too were cognizant of these risks: they prepared a top-secret plan (code-named 'Bedlam') to deal with the potential for chaos unleashed by such a mass movement, during which the 100,000 European civilians in India were to be evacuated to fortresses and other safe havens; additionally, despite the strong opposition of Auchinleck (who opposed any division of the British Indian armed forces), Wavell sent another evacuation or scuttle plan to the British cabinet. Calling this 'Operation Breakdown', Wavell suggested that, in the event of a new mass mobilization by Congress, all British military personnel would be withdrawn from the Congress-ruled provinces and relocated to the 'northwest and northeast' of India (i.e., to the territories of a putative Pakistan).

But in the face of calls for a new mass mobilization à la 1942, the Congress leadership balked. Internally, Congress leaders argued that since the British had always insisted on the 'provincial option' of seceding from the federal union, such a provincial option also applied to each of the provinces within each Group. Thus Congress-ruled Assam and NWFP could choose not to join their respective groups, thereby rendering their Group rudderless. The British were insistent that such an option did not exist; only the Groups had the right to secede from the federal union, not provinces from Groups. But both sides were clutching at straws! Jinnah too had initially rejected the Cabinet Mission Plan, but was soon persuaded that it laid the seeds for Pakistan, and began proclaiming that it was a victory for the Pakistan idea. Once Jinnah began insisting that the Plan 'conceded Pakistan', the Sikh leader Baldev Singh immediately objected to the Sikhs being potentially trapped within it, and began demanding redress.

On 7 July 1946, the AICC voted overwhelmingly in favour of the Cabinet Mission Plan, after an impassioned speech in its favour by outgoing Congress president Maulana Azad, who argued that 'independence without a violent and bloody uprising' while guaranteeing 'the unity of India' represented a great victory for Congress. For three tantalizing days, it appeared that a solution had been achieved that the British, Congress and Muslim League all agreed to live with, and India would indeed gain independence without Partition. But on 10 July, the incoming Congress president Jawaharlal Nehru made some bizarre statements at a press conference that put a spoke in this delicately-poised wheel. In response to a question asking whether Congress had now accepted the Cabinet Mission Plan in its totality, Nehru said Congress would enter the Constituent Assembly 'completely unfettered by agreements and free to meet all situations as they arise'. To a further question asking if this meant the plan could be modified, Nehru replied that Congress felt free to change or modify the Cabinet Mission Plan.

Jinnah, already facing criticism from within the Muslim League for seemingly agreeing to a plan short of partition, now had his excuse to repudiate it in full. First he demanded that, now that the Congress president had effectively rejected the Cabinet Mission Plan (by claiming that Congress could use its brute majority to modify it), the Viceroy ought to invite the Muslim League (which had accepted the Cabinet Mission Plan) to form the interim government. When the British did not respond, Jinnah called a meeting of the Muslim League council for 27 July, at which the League repudiated the

Cabinet Mission Plan, and announced that it would instead take 'Direct Action' to achieve its goal of Pakistan.

While the country waited with bated breath to see what 'direct action' meant, Jinnah prepared the way in Bengal—the one large province where the Muslim League ran the government—and designated 16 August 1946 'Direct Action Day'. On 8 August, the Congress Working Committee released a tortured statement explaining that it remained committed to the Cabinet Mission Plan in full (while also saying that the Constituent Assembly was the place to discuss such issues); Azad had requested the Working Committee meeting to reiterate that Nehru had spoken for himself and not on behalf of Congress, but Jawaharlal had additional phrases added to the resolution to avoid the impression that Congress was admonishing its president. Patel wrote to D. P. Mishra (a senior Congressman in the Central Provinces, and father of Brajesh Mishra, the National Security Adviser to PM Vajpayee in 1998–2004) about Nehru: 'He acts with childlike innocence.... He has done many things recently which caused us great embarrassment.... His acts of emotional insanity... put tremendous strain on us to set matters right.' Clearly this was one of those.

In July–August 1946, elections for 296 seats in the Constituent Assembly assigned to the provinces of British India had also been completed, with the Congress winning 208 seats (including 3 of the 4 from NWFP) and the Muslim League winning 73. (The 93 seats reserved for the princely states were yet to be filled, but Congress was still certain to have a majority in the 389-seat Constituent Assembly). The unequivocal acceptance of the Cabinet Mission Plan by the Congress triggered Wavell's invitation to Nehru (as Congress president and leader of the majority party in the assembly) to form an Interim Government, an invitation that he immediately accepted.

On 15 August, Nehru visited Jinnah at his home in Bombay to undo some of the damage he had done, and explore whether the League could join the interim government, but to no avail. The genie of communal hatred was out of the bottle; on 13 August, the Muslim League had proclaimed to its members: 'It was in Ramzan that the permission for Jehad was granted by Allah. It was in Ramzan that the Battle of Badr, the first open conflict between Islam and Heathenism, was fought and won by 313 Muslims... and again it was in Ramzan that 10,000 Muslims under the Holy Prophet conquered Mecca.... The Muslim League is fortunate that it is starting its action in this holy month.'

At 4 p.m. on 16 August 1946, the Muslim League's massive rally at Calcutta's Maidan ended, and as the League's supporters dispersed, they began attacking shops and homes owned by Hindus from trucks flying the

Muslim League flag and filled with bayonets, sticks and stones, which an American Consul reported seeing from a building overlooking the Maidan.

At that rally, Chief Minister Hussain Shaheed Suhrawardy announced that he 'had seen to police arrangements' in order to ensure 'they would not interfere'. Since Suhrawardy was also the home minister (with overall control over the police) of Bengal, this was interpreted as an open invitation to the aroused multitude to riot without fear of police intervention. The British governor, Frederick Burrows, also pointed out that Suhrawardy spent many hours of the next twenty-four at the control room of the police headquarters, explicitly directing the rioting by his supporters. Burrows had the constitutional right to intervene but did not. His report failed to mention that Brigadier J. P. C. Makinlay, the military officer in charge of law and order in Calcutta, had specifically ordered his troops confined to barracks for the day, leaving the city totally vulnerable to the riots that the British authorities had known would occur (as they had seen the Muslim League proclamation of 13 August, although the public had not).

An English resident of Calcutta reported that 'it is the unanimous decision of all that the Mohammedans struck the first blow and took many lives before the Hindus were ready.' It took Hindus (and Sikhs, who then as now drove most of the city's taxis) close to a day to organize a response. Although Hindus comprised close to two-thirds of the city's population, the police was controlled by Suhrawardy and the Muslim League, and the Great Calcutta Killings took many hundreds of Hindu lives before the inevitable retaliation occurred; in one gruesome episode, about 800 Hindu cotton mill workers (about 500 of them from Orissa) were massacred by an armed mob of Muslims. A total of 5,000 people were reported to have died over the next four days, and the rioting spread to Noakhali and Tippera in eastern Bengal, where tens of thousands of Hindus were killed in the first half of October 1946. The killings were designed by the Muslim League to be as gruesome as possible to provoke a response from Hindus, and this inevitably occurred, with retaliatory killings of Muslims in the neighbouring state of Bihar in late October.

Although it was clear that Chief Minister Suhrawardy and the Muslim League had cynically organized this horrific outbreak of criminal brutality, Wavell and Burrows took no action against the Muslim League. The head of the IB, N. P. A. Smith, wrote a memo to the Viceroy explaining that 'communal disorder' was 'a natural, if ghastly, process tending in its own way to the solution of the Indian problem,' especially as it was a rather desirable alternative to 'anti-British agitation', which was what the British needed to avoid. In November 1945, forty-six Europeans and Christians had been killed in the riots to protest the INA trials, and thirty-five Europeans were killed in the February 1946 riots in the city, but no Europeans were killed between 16 August and 17 September 1946. Wavell forwarded Smith's memo to London (evidently agreeing with it), and began pushing even harder for the Muslim League to be accommodated in the interim government, and for London to clearly express its opposition to the notion of NWFP and Assam opting out of Groups B and C.

Wavell was determined to 'saddle Indians with responsibility', particularly for the eventual partition of the subcontinent. So it was a great personal triumph for him when Nehru agreed to lead the interim government, and Patel to join it as the powerful Home Member at its inception on 2 September 1946. (Nehru was, formally, the Vice President of the Viceroy's Executive Council, but was then and ever since called 'Interim Prime Minister'.) Nehru had been yearning for power, which is what had led him to naive negotiations with the British since 1942 (even after Gandhi had emphatically rejected Britain's proposals). But the surprise was Patel's decision to join. He had calculated that it would be impossible for Congress to fight both the British and Jinnah, and so it made sense for Congress to cultivate the British as an ally, since Patel was convinced that Jinnah's Muslim League was determined to be intransigent. From India's longer-term standpoint, the biggest calamity of this interim government was Nehru's decision to take control of foreign affairs directly. This provided a great opportunity for Nehru to showcase his alleged abilities as a global statesman and leader of anti-colonial causes. Nehru's global grandstanding—at a time when India was struggling with its own existential crisis of unified nationhood—was to prove highly counterproductive in the months ahead. On one issue, however, he had an immediate impact: Indian troops were still fighting colonial wars on behalf of the British in Malaya, Indonesia and Burma, and keeping the peace in Japan and Iraq. They had been withdrawn only from Indo-China earlier in the year. Nehru immediately ordered that they all be withdrawn, to the evident consternation of the British chiefs of staff.

The US went out of its way to immediately recognize the interim government, and Henry F. Grady was sent as the first US ambassador to India. Throughout 1946–47, the US was indefatigably committed to maintaining a united India, interceding repeatedly with the British to ensure that the integrity of India was upheld. Unfortunately, Nehru had a blinkered view of the US, failing to recognize its rising strategic importance; he thus failed to effectively utilize US goodwill towards the idea of a united India. As his first ambassador to the US, Nehru sent the eminent Muslim lawyer Asaf Ali, who had never before visited the US and whose wife Aruna, née Ganguly, belonged to the left of the Congress's socialist wing. (Although her brother was married to Rabindranath Tagore's daughter, and her father was a prominent businessman, Aruna Asaf Ali would formally become a communist in the 1950s, resigning from the communists' women's wing only in protest of Khrushchev's criticisms of Stalin! By 1946, she was famed for having hoisted the national tricolour at Gowalia Tank on 8 August 1942 after Gandhi was arrested following his Quit India call, and for breaking with the Congress leadership to strongly support the naval mutiny in February 1946; none of those credentials would necessarily endear her to the Americans.) In distinct contrast, a few months later, Jinnah sent his good friend, M. A. H. Ispahani, a savvy businessman, as the Muslim League's representative to the US—the sort of articulate and pragmatic envoy likely to establish an instant rapport with Americans.

At the UN, Jawaharlal's sister who headed India's delegation, Vijaya Lakshmi Pandit sparkled, especially in taking the lead on opposing apartheid and other vestiges of colonialism in the teeth of strong resistance from the Europeans (who argued that apartheid was an 'internal' matter for UN member South Africa). The anti-apartheid resolution won plaudits for not-quite-independent India from fellow-colonized nations in Asia and Africa, but also thoroughly embarrassed (and hence irritated) Britain. It reminded Tory opponents of Indian independence of yet another reason why 'unreliable' India needed to be countered with a determined push for partition that would preserve Britain's military presence in the Indian subcontinent. Already John Foster Dulles (then a mere member of the US delegation to the UN, and still seven years away from becoming Secretary of State) was reporting (after an encounter with Krishna Menon during the UN session) that Nehru's India was tending strongly towards communism! Secretary of State George C. Marshall went out of his way to have his Delhi chargé d'affaires speak to Nehru to reassure him that Dulles's speech to the US press corps about the interim government did not represent US official views about India.

But the fact that Nehru had, within weeks of becoming interim prime minister, sent Krishna Menon to Moscow to meet Foreign Minister Vyacheslav Molotov, did nothing to reassure twitchy British officials. Nehru had sent a letter assuring India's hand of friendship to the USSR, but Menon went well beyond his brief, and sought a visit by Soviet military experts to India, something that Patel and most of the Congress leadership strongly disapproved of. Gandhi, Patel, Azad and most of their senior colleagues had always been highly suspicious about the communist fellow-traveller Krishna Menon; in Maulana Azad's scathing words he 'was, to take a charitable view, unreliable'. Of Krishna Menon's undue influence over Jawaharlal, Azad was even more cutting: 'We all like our admirers but perhaps Jawaharlal likes them a little more than others.'

While Nehru's foreign policy team pursued its own erratic path, he was also under constant pressure from Wavell to invite Jinnah's Muslim League to join the interim government 'in the interests of communal peace'. The well-developed Congress policy on this was clear: the Muslim League was welcome to join the interim government as soon as it entered the Constituent Assembly (the official body constituted legally to create the constitution of unified India in accordance with the Cabinet Mission Plan) and after the Muslim League had called off its 'Direct Action' policy to foment violent anti-Hindu terrorism across India. Wavell urged Nehru to accept League participation in his government at their meetings on 11, 16, 26 and 27 September. And the capricious and impulsive Nehru proved to be anything but a disciplined negotiator: directly contradicting the Congress policy, Nehru (on his own initiative) agreed on 2 October 1946 (Gandhi's seventy-seventh birthday) to let Wavell invite the Muslim League into the interim government despite the fact that it was then engaged in 'Direct Action' against the government to incite more communal bloodshed. Sure enough, League provocations resulted in horrific pogroms against Hindus in the heavily Muslim-majority Noakhali and Tippera districts of eastern Bengal later that month. Whenever communal trouble worsened, Bengal chief minister Suhrawardy would cynically invite Gandhi to Bengal in order to help contain the violence. Gandhi's acts of selfless saintliness over the next twelve months—in helping to douse the fires of communal hatred that had been unleashed by the Muslim League—inadvertently provided political cover, legitimacy and succour to the League, and especially Suhrawardy.

But although he was willing to lend his support (and personal authority) to the cause of inter-communal peacemaking, Gandhi (through his acolyte Sudhir Ghosh) expressed his dismay to Nehru at his unilateral decision to accede to Wavell's requests to invite the Muslim League into his government. Ghosh pointedly asked Nehru why he had not resigned rather than submit to a policy to which the Congress had always expressed strong opposition; Nehru never gave a satisfactory response. During April–June 1946 (while the Cabinet Mission was still negotiating with all sides), Congress had stringently opposed the notion of parity in numbers between Congress and Muslim League within the Viceroy's Executive Council, and the League's demand that Congress not nominate any Muslim minister. On the few occasions that the Cabinet Mission had met Gandhi, he had made it abundantly clear that a coalition (between Congress and League) was the worst of all outcomes; he had suggested that if it was impossible to have a government headed by the majority Congress party, then Jinnah should be invited to head it (and

Gandhi assured the Mission that his own full authority would be deployed to ensure Congress' legislative cooperation with Jinnah in such a government; the Mission never acted on this, although a year later Mountbatten was rather more enthused by a similar suggestion from Gandhi).

The decision to invite the League into a coalition of equals with Congress proved calamitous. The League not only continued to unabashedly pursue its Direct Action programme of communal violence, but it also used its presence in the interim government (including control of the finance portfolio which had gone to the League stalwart Liaquat Ali Khan) to wreck it, while still refusing to enter the Constituent Assembly. Wavell was, of course, complicit in this reckless scheme to reward the reprehensible violence unleashed by Jinnah and the Muslim League.

But it was only made possible by the collusion of Nehru who, owing his own position as interim prime minister to the support of Cripps (that had been secured previously by Krishna Menon) gave in to every irrational British demand that Congress had always officially opposed. The reality was that the British demands conveyed by Wavell to Nehru were profoundly anti-democratic. There was a Central Legislative Assembly elected in December 1945 (under rules aimed at over-representing the Muslim League and under-representing the Hindu majority), and a Constituent Assembly (also elected under 'separate electorates' that gave extra weight to Muslims). Those ought to have been the bodies through which the Constitution and new laws of India should have been written; but Wavell and the Cabinet Mission were, in fact, proposing ways of further diluting these democratically-constituted legislative bodies. The technique of circumventing a legitimately constituted legislature by creating intermediate tiers to weaken the federal centre was exactly the same technique being used at the time by the Dutch in Indonesia—aimed at demonstrating to the world that the colony was ungovernable without the colonial power.

Sukarno, despite starting with a much weaker hand (having been a 'collaborator' with the Japanese), was able to secure a unitary Indonesia by August 1950. Nehru, on the other hand, despite his cooperation with the British from November 1945 onwards, steadily gave ground to British designs but failed to preclude the sundering of India.

The blame for Partition, and especially the rapid path towards it between March and August 1947, is usually placed on Mountbatten (prominently by the pro-Jinnah US historian Stanley Wolpert in his 2006 book *Shameful Flight*). But while Jinnah was totally disciplined in his negotiating strategy (refusing to budge from his claim to be the 'sole spokesman' for India's Muslims, and hence to speak for every Muslim-majority province, even those, like Punjab and the NWFP, where his party had repeatedly lost electoral tests), Nehru proved to be fickle and malleable. He and Azad were especially gullible in their attitude to the British, unlike Gandhi, whose long experience of futile negotiations with the British made him naturally suspicious about their goals. The Congress negotiators (Azad first, then Nehru) in 1942–47 showed a deplorable incomprehension of strategic and military considerations, and never understood that India was a vital military asset to Britain's empire, and they needed to assuage British concerns about that asset's future (e.g., via a continuing military link). By contrast, Attlee's government focused like a laser beam on securing Pakistan as a dominion where Britain would be able to maintain military bases to help secure Britain's vital interest in the oil of Iran, Iraq and the British protectorates of the Persian Gulf.

On 8 September 1946 (in the week after Nehru's interim government took charge), Britain's military chiefs of staff had prepared a report titled 'The Strategic Value of India to the British Commonwealth', and Lord Ismay wrote a fortnight later to Attlee that they 'would like to suggest... the necessity to do everything possible to retain India within the Commonwealth'. The report said India was 'an essential link in our Imperial strategic plan,' so it was vitally important to ensure that no 'hostile power' would be able to establish bases in the Indian Ocean area, because it was crucial to ensuring safe passage for oil from the Persian Gulf (which Britain controlled). It reiterated the importance of India's ability to supply 'almost inexhaustible' military manpower to the Commonwealth, and recommended that Britain should not give up the Andaman and Nicobar Islands, which could serve as vital outposts from which to control Burma and Malaya. When Sir Terence Shone arrived as high commissioner to New Delhi on 19 November 1946, his first reports back to London confirmed Whitehall's worst fears about the Nehru government's foreign policy path that asserted that 'Asia was for the Asians' (in an inadvertent echo of Japan's wartime slogan).

The Constituent Assembly was to finally begin its first session on 9 December 1946, but Jinnah refused to allow Muslim League representatives to enter it until Attlee had confirmed that all the 'Group B' and 'Group C' provinces' legislators would vote as a collective (and not as individual provinces) when deciding issues relating to their Group. Attlee called representatives of the Congress, League and Sikhs (Baldev Singh) to London for a conference just before the convening of the Constituent Assembly, and at the end of it (on 6 December) confirmed that decisions of the Groups (or 'sections') would be taken 'by simple majority vote of representatives of the sections (and not by majority votes of representatives of individual provinces)'. This set the cat amongst the pigeons, sparking outrage in India, especially in Assam and amongst the Sikhs, who were in danger of being 'trapped' within a future Pakistan. Congress leaders like Nehru, Patel and Azad always insisted that Cripps had given them private assurances that the right of provinces to opt out of Groups was just as much part of the plan as was the right of Groups to opt out of the federal union. Once Attlee showed his hand, the Congress felt betrayed, and took countervailing steps.

Patel, sensing what the London conference was likely to be about, had refused to attend. Nehru, embarrassed by what had transpired at the London conference, began the session of the Constituent Assembly on 9 December by tabling an 'Objectives Resolution' that 'solemnly' resolved 'to proclaim India as an Independent Sovereign Republic'. With the Muslim League's seventy-three and princes' ninety-three seats in the assembly still unoccupied, the reach and credibility of this resolution left something to be desired. But it immediately alienated the British establishment in India—who still manned most of the civil service, and the upper echelons of the military. And back in Britain itself, Whitehall and the Cabinet grew even more determined to back Jinnah's Muslim League as the only hope for Britain to retain a vital strategic toehold within the Indian subcontinent. Before the end of the year, Patel had been convinced by his key bureaucrat, V. P. Menon, of the importance of India becoming a dominion 'to begin with' in order to allay British fears, and more crucially the need for a 'strong, united and effective' central government that would be capable of framing a 'truly democratic constitution unhampered by any communal considerations'. V. P. Menon (no relation to Krishna Menon, and from a very different social background) was a 'promotee' from the ranks of the clerical service rather than a member of the prestigious ICS. But he was a highly effective civil servant, and played the vital behind-the-scenes role in much that happened in India between 1946 and 1949. Patel promised V. P. Menon that he would work to convince Congress of the need for both a strong Centre and for temporary acceptance of dominion status.

The US Undersecretary of State Dean Acheson (he became Secretary of State in 1949) had cabled his envoy in the UK just before the London conference, cautioning that 'any halt in the constitutional process' in India risked 'chaos similar' to what was happening in China, but instead that the US 'looks forward to mutual advantageous economic relations with stable powerful united India.' The professional diplomat Girija Shankar Bajpai had told Acheson (just before he was replaced as India's representative in Washington DC by the politician Asaf Ali) that India looked forward to a relationship with Britain that would be more akin to the Republic of Ireland's rather than to those of Canada, Australia and New Zealand. Asaf Ali, despite being a leading lawyer and graduate of India's best liberal arts college (St

Stephen's, Delhi) was a novice at diplomacy, and he surprised the incoming Secretary of State George C. Marshall by speaking of India's 'indebtedness to the British for their stand on Indian independence' rather than India's true feelings about Britain's nefarious designs!

Nonetheless, the US kept up the pressure on Britain to commit to a united India. On 7 February 1947, Congress (and the minority members of the interim cabinet) demanded that the Muslim League ministers be dismissed, since Congress had accepted the British 'grouping formula' the previous day, while the League had yet to enter the Constituent Assembly. Four days later, the new US Secretary of State Marshall cabled his envoy to enquire 'whether or not Brit are disposed to instruct Viceroy dismiss Muslim League ministers... and whether they are planning to bring pressure on princes to reach definitely agreement with Congress'. But before this clear démarche could be delivered, Attlee made a statement to the House of Commons on 20 February 1947 that the British would leave India by 30 June 1948, and that if 'a constitution will not have been worked out by a fully representative Assembly... [His Majesty's Government] will have to consider to whom the powers of the Central Government in British India should be handed over... whether as a whole to some form of Central Government of British India or in some areas to the existing Provincial governments or in such other way as may seem most reasonable and in the best interests of the Indian people....' More crucially, Attlee played his second trump card by stating that '[His Majesty's Government's] powers and obligations under Paramountcy would not be handed over to any government of British India' (referring to Britain's relations with the princes, who were thus left open to make their own arrangements, including the distinct possibility of declaring independence).

Attlee also replaced Wavell with Mountbatten as viceroy. That one military man was being replaced by another as Viceroy of India was telling enough: Britain looked at India as a vital strategic asset within its empire, and only military hands could adequately deal with its disposal while protecting Britain's strategic objectives. By asserting that a constitution had to be formulated by a 'fully representative assembly', Attlee had again given Jinnah an opening to keep his members out of the Constituent Assembly, thus making it less than 'fully representative'. Nehru actually welcomed Attlee's statement, believing it allowed Congress to establish a 'strong unitary government' while the League interpreted it as meaning that their refusal to participate in the Constituent Assembly would enable them (through the Group scheme) to receive their larger Pakistan. In fact, Attlee's statement of 20 February 1947 was an invitation to a free-for-all: every province was free to declare independence, and every princely state was similarly given the right to secede; it still held out the possibility of Balkanizing India if the minimum British demand of Pakistan was not achieved.

Mountbatten was really coming out to India to implement Wavell's detailed blueprint of 7 February 1946. This meant that Mountbatten's two main tasks were to ensure that the NWFP was prised from Congress hands and made part of Pakistan, while ensuring that the latter would be the 'truncated' Pakistan, with Punjab and Bengal partitioned (so that India, and especially the Sikhs, would not become hostile to Britain). Tragically, one community was being left out of these discussions—the Hindus of Sindh (and Baluchistan). Although the Muslim League was precariously positioned in Sindh, that province had a clear Muslim majority, and had been separated from the larger Bombay presidency in 1936, after the issue of Sindh's separation had first been raised at the Congress session of 1917 (in Sindh's capital, Karachi). In the heyday of Hindu–Muslim amity (as represented by the Lucknow Pact between Jinnah and Motilal Nehru recognizing separate electorates), the separation of Sindh had been considered an act of magnanimity by India's Hindus to empower Muslims in another province. Three decades later, the large Hindu community of Sindh (comprising over a quarter of the province's population, about half the population of Karachi and 60 per cent of Sindh's total urban population) was left unrepresented and forgotten, and many soon fled to other parts of the world, including East Africa, Singapore, Hong Kong and Japan, mainly becoming entrepreneurs. Today Hindus are 5 per cent of Sindh's population. A similar fate befell the Hindus of Baluchistan, a region that primarily comprised princely states (particularly the giant state of Kalat) with a flourishing Hindu minority (albeit only 15 per cent of the population) that was indigenous to the region; today Hindus and Sikhs constitute barely 1 per cent of the population of Baluchistan.

The US continued to press for a united India, deeming it the best solution for the post-War world. In particular, Acheson and Marshall were concerned about reports of Hyderabad seeking to become independent, and the potential this held for other princely states (like Travancore, which believed its thorium deposits made it attractive as a supplier for nuclear power) to also seek independence. The British were subtly encouraging these ideas, fully utilizing both their trump cards—the separatist Muslim League, and its longer-standing princely allies—to keep the Congress off-balance, as they had done since 1909, and especially in the federal structure of the Government of India Act of 1935. But the Congress failed to utilize its potentially strongest ally—the US, which had maintained relentless pressure on Britain to retain India's unity, especially since 1945 (and also in the first half of 1942). Instead, the next momentous shock to the US came not from the British but from

Congress, which passed a resolution (despite Gandhi's strong opposition) on 8 March 1947, calling for 'a division of Punjab into two provinces so that the predominantly Muslim part may be separated from the predominantly non-Muslim part'. For the first time, the Congress organization itself (and not just its leading representatives like Nehru, Azad or Patel) had accepted the principle of partition, and implicitly accepted Jinnah's 'two-nation theory' positing that Muslims and Hindus could not live together. The ostensible reason for this resolution was to placate the Sikhs, who otherwise risked being trapped unhappily in Pakistan. But additionally, the Congress reasoned that, since the NWFP was in Congress hands, the smaller Punjab (plus Sindh) surrounded by Indian territory could not be the basis of a viable state, and Jinnah would never accept it.

Events had moved quickly in the Punjab after Attlee's statement of 20 February. With partition now a near certainty, Khizar Hayat Tiwana's coalition government of the Unionists, the Akali Dal and Congress fell apart, resigning on 2 March, as Muslim members of the Unionist party began to desert it. The Unionist–Akali alliance had been Britain's gambit to keep this vital province loyal to the British. The Akali Dal had emerged as a reform movement aiming to cleanse the Sikh gurudwaras of corruption—sweeping away the British-appointed priests at the Golden Temple of Amritsar and other gurudwaras. Despite its anti-British antecedents, the colonial authorities eventually cultivated the Akalis in the hope of creating a Unionist–Sikh alliance that would be loyal to the British, especially given that a large proportion of Sikh families depended on military pensions. The election results of 1946—which left the Muslim League short of a majority—led to a Unionist–Congress–Akali coalition, an ominous development for the British, as it held the seeds of a non-sectarian future for Punjab. This was nipped in the bud by the fall of the Tiwana coalition, and the outbreak of anti-Sikh and anti-Hindu riots in Rawalpindi and other Muslim-dominated towns and villages. The Akali leader Master Tara Singh responded with his slogan of 'Pakistan Murdabad' (Death to Pakistan), and March–April 1947 was a sanguinary period of violence for Punjab, providing the backdrop for the Congress decision to call (on 8 March) for a partition of the province. Responding to the virulent terrorism unleashed by the Muslim League in the Rawalpindi area, the Akali Dal called on Sikhs to abandon their fertile ancestral lands in western Punjab and instead prepare for retaliation in eastern Punjab where they organized themselves into 'jathas' (formations) aimed at 'cleansing' the region of Muslims and taking their land.

When Mountbatten arrived on 22 March 1947 in Delhi (a city he knew well, as he had proposed to the heiress Edwina Ashley there soon after accompanying the Crown Prince, the future King Edward VIII, to India in 1921, and had initially had Delhi as his SEAC headquarters), the 'interim Prime Minister' Nehru had his head firmly in the clouds, basking in his dream project of an Asian Relations Conference. This brought representatives of all shades of Asian opinion (the KMT and Mao's communists, Palestinians and the Hebrew University, republicans and monarchists from Malaya, Sukarno and his opponents from Indonesia) to Delhi to discuss Nehru's vision of 'Asia for the Asians'. Both Chinese delegations (especially the KMT one) protested at the presence of a large delegation from Tibet, but Nehru and Patel firmly insisted that Tibet was an independent nation that was a traditional buffer state between India and China, and had every right to be there.

Nothing, however, came of Nehru's proposal to create an Asian Relations Organization. Holding such a conference was a singularly impolitic move by Nehru. Alongside the strongly independent foreign policy (on issues of apartheid and decolonization) that Nehru had pursued, this served only to highlight to the British that an independent India would not be a reliable ally, and perhaps not a military ally at all. The British Foreign Office had prepared a memo in 1946 stating that 'India will continue to be dependent upon the United Kingdom for defence, and will follow the United Kingdom's lead on all major issues of foreign policy,' although a 'self-governing India within the Commonwealth may well wish to take the lead in Asia and to assume a more important role than China'. The memo acknowledged that 'it seems somewhat rash to assert that strategic considerations will necessarily be the decisive factor in determining Indian policy.' But the actual contours of that policy still came as a rude shock to the British establishment, especially Krishna Menon's flirtation with the USSR and inflammatory anti-Western rhetoric. Mountbatten was thus committed to making sure that India would stay within the Commonwealth, but also to ensuring that the NWFP would switch out of Congress hands so that Pakistan became viable.

Despite his myriad well known shortcomings as a naval officer, Mountbatten's meteoric rise had been aided by his charm, his aristocratic birth, and his marriage to a prominent socialite and heiress. From the moment of his arrival in India, Mountbatten deployed all three to his and Britain's great advantage. Unlike Wavell, Mountbatten did not ignore Gandhi; instead he began his deliberations in India with four days of 'getting-to-know-you' meetings with Gandhi, at which Lady Edwina was photographed allowing Gandhi to lean on her for support. At the second of their meetings, Gandhi suggested that the 'Indian problem could be solved if Mr Jinnah were to form a new interim government' with the freedom to name his own Cabinet. Gandhi gave an assurance that he would secure fair and sincere cooperation with the new administration by Congress. Mountbatten was tempted, but asked that the full Congress Working Committee would need to give it its backing. On 11 April 1947, Gandhi wrote back to the Viceroy that he had been unable to 'obtain the agreement of the leading members of the Congress'. In reality, Azad had supported Gandhi's proposal, but Nehru and Patel vehemently opposed it. This last possible path to maintaining India's integrity too fell apart.

Mountbatten never discussed Gandhi's proposal with Jinnah himself, having first sworn Gandhi to 'complete secrecy' about it. Azad, whose hand Jinnah had refused to shake for years, denigrating him as a 'showcase Muslim' and worse (although Maulana Azad was a genuine scholar of Islam, unlike the anglicized Jinnah), set aside personal animosity and strongly supported Gandhi's plan, believing it would involve a short-term sacrifice by Congress for the greater long-term good of a united India. But Nehru told Mountbatten that Gandhi was now 'far out of it' and they together shelved Gandhi's idea, which was predicated on the necessity of a single-party government (rather than the unwieldy coalition that had rendered the interim government utterly ineffectual).

Jinnah was forthright in making his case for Pakistan: 'the new Pakistan is almost certain to ask for Dominion Status within the British Empire', the League had been loyal to the British throughout ('none of our leaders has ever had to go to prison for disloyalty'), and none had been in the Constituent Assembly when it passed the resolution calling for an Independent Sovereign Republic. Although Lord and Lady Mountbatten found Jinnah stiff and stilted, they were able to persuade him to accept the smaller Pakistan. On 10 April 1947, Jinnah told them, 'I do not care how little you give me as long as you give it to me completely.' Mountbatten had heard what he needed to: although Jinnah would persist in demands for an independent Bengal, joint control of Calcutta, and a corridor linking East and West Pakistan, his private statement of 10 April was what Mountbatten held him to. The demand for Calcutta represented exceptional overreach: less than a third of that city's population was Muslim at the time, and the Congress did not (for instance) ever demand Lahore or Karachi, two cities where there was a slim non-Muslim majority at the time.

Nehru was initially the most obdurate, especially asserting that 'for psychological and emotional reasons India cannot remain in the Commonwealth'. Mountbatten then used the same tactic as Cripps, asking Nehru what he would do if he were in the Viceroy's shoes. Merely a fortnight after his initial obduracy, Nehru told Mountbatten 'it would not be right to impose any form of constitutional conditions on any community which was in a majority in a specific area.' Mountbatten used this opening to soon begin demanding that a fresh referendum be held in the NWFP. This was extraordinary, as the NWFP delegation had already entered the Constituent Assembly and was participating in it fully. But Wavell had sent Sir Olaf Caroe (who had been the member for foreign policy in the Viceroy's Executive Council during the war years, and so had a good understanding of strategic issues) as the British governor of NWFP, and he had energetically set about winning over the Maliks (lords) of the various tribes (especially in Waziristan and the other tribal agencies) to the British (and hence the Pakistani) side, and inciting violence against Sikh and Hindu landowners in the province. Nehru, against the strong advice of Patel and Azad, visited NWFP in October 1946—soon after Caroe had arrived there to begin his campaign against Chief Minister Dr Khan Sahib, Khan Abdul Ghaffar Khan (the leader of the Khudai Khitmatgars or non-violent Servants of God) and their Congress government. On past visits, Nehru had received a rapturous reception, but this time Caroe organized Muslim League black flag demonstrations wherever Nehru was supposed to visit (although there were no demonstrations at unscheduled stops on his tour, giving the game away).

Now, in late April 1947, Nehru acquiesced in a unique scheme to determine NWFP's fate: a referendum. No other province of British India was being subjected to a referendum; in other provinces (such as Bengal) where there was a dispute over its future, the legislators would be the determining factor (since Muslim League legislators were in a majority there). The reason was obvious: Britain wanted NWFP in Pakistan, because it would serve as a vital strategic base for Britain (and eventually the US, as became evident when the CIA pilot Gary Powers was shot down over the USSR in 1960, and it turned out that his U–2 spy plane's flight had begun from the secret CIA airbase at Peshawar, the capital of NWFP). The world is still paying the price of British perfidy over NWFP in 1947. The non-violent and modernizing Khan brothers were the natural leaders of the Pathans of NWFP (who, then as now, outnumber the Pathans of Afghanistan itself), and had demonstrated their electoral hold in both the 1937 and 1946 provincial elections. The British jettisoned the Khan brothers' peaceable interpretation of Islamic tradition in favour of the rabid violence of Muslim League 'Direct Action', which amounted to little more than atrocities against non-Muslim minorities, incited by Caroe, the father of jihadism amongst the Pathans.

By early May, Mountbatten had secured broad acceptance of partition (for India as a whole and Punjab and Bengal in particular) from Nehru and Jinnah. Lord Ismay, who had been Churchill's chief military staff officer during the war, had accompanied Mountbatten to India as his chief of staff (again underlining that the end of Britain's Indian empire was primarily seen from a military perspective by the British). On 2 May, Ismay set off for London with the contours of Mountbatten's plan for the future of India. This has come to be known as Plan Balkan, as it sought to implement Attlee's statement of 20 February 1947 almost to the letter, by handing power to each of the provinces, who would then be free to decide whether to become part of India or Pakistan, or indeed stay independent. The princely states would similarly be free to determine their own future in whichever way they saw fit. Neither Nehru nor Jinnah had been shown the details of this proposal, although they had approved its broad contours. On 7 May, Dickie and Edwina Mountbatten took Nehru on a short holiday into the salubrious mountain air of Simla and Mashobra, where Jawaharlal and Edwina's affair flowered, while Mountbatten sought to convince Jawaharlal to allow India to become a dominion and stay part of the Commonwealth. Mountbatten's key intermediary on securing dominion status was Krishna Menon, who advocated India joining the Commonwealth to limit US influence over India; he agreed to persuade Nehru about dominion status in exchange for Mountbatten lobbying Nehru to appoint Krishna Menon as India's first high commissioner to the UK (while V. P. Menon worked on persuading Patel).

On 10 May, while still holidaying in Simla, Mountbatten received word that the British Cabinet had approved his plan, which astonishingly was still known only to Ismay, Mountbatten and the British Cabinet itself. On a 'hunch', Mountbatten decided to show the details of the plan to Nehru that night. For once, Jawaharlal set aside all other considerations and worked furiously on a long letter to Mountbatten that he finished at 4 a.m., vigorously opposing everything that was in the plan, as it would Balkanize India, allowing tens of little nation states to emerge, including numerous possibly princely states, and thoroughly demoralize the army and police by destroying their integrity. Mountbatten and Ismay were seeking to undermine the Constituent Assembly even more thoroughly with this plan, and Nehru made it clear that it would be completely unacceptable to Congress, which remained committed to a united India, from which some parts could be allowed to secede if the people of those regions so chose. Most of the princely states within India had actually joined the Constituent Assembly by early 1947, after the independence-minded Nawab of Bhopal was ousted as head of the Chamber of Princes by the Maharaja of Patiala. Only Bhopal, Hyderabad and Travancore were still seeking independence, but more would be likely to follow suit once 'Plan Balkan' became more widely known.

Faced with a new crisis that could end his career prematurely, Mountbatten turned to V. P. Menon for a solution. The latter had observed closely that

Nehru and Patel wanted an early transfer of power, and were amenable to dominion status if that would secure early independence. He therefore proposed a partition of India in accordance with the Wavell plan of 7 February 1946 (i.e., the 'smaller Pakistan'), via an amendment to the Government of India Act of 1935 to allow power to be transferred to two independent British dominions. This would still not be acceptable to Jinnah without the chance to keep NWFP and Baluchistan within Pakistan, so the Congress leaders needed to be persuaded to allow a referendum in NWFP and Baluchistan (to prise them from participation in India's Constituent Assembly). Menon suggested that Mountbatten give a solemn assurance to Patel that Britain would oppose the princely states becoming independent, and instead persuade each of them to join either of the two new states (which would ensure that 90 per cent of them would be likely to join India) in exchange for Congress support of a fresh 'reference to the electorate' in NWFP and Baluchistan. In less than half a day, this new plan (formulated by V. P. Menon) was adopted by Mountbatten and presented to Nehru, who was much more receptive. The rapidity with which these events proceeded in the rarefied air of Simla suggests that Plan Balkan was simply Mountbatten playing his ultimate trump card to bring Nehru (with his lofty dreams of Asian unity) down to earth, and force him to accept the two outcomes dearest to Britain (dominion status, and the separation of NWFP from India).

Mountbatten now went to London himself with his final plan for partition and the 'transfer' of power. He was able to persuade the Cabinet to go along with his quick change of plan by playing the trump card he had just secured—that both India and Pakistan had agreed to dominion status and remaining members of the Commonwealth—and his other ace (the promise of a referendum in NWFP). Attlee's Cabinet endorsed the plan, and Churchill (hitherto glowering at every twist and turn of what he saw as Britain's capitulation to Congress) was also delighted that India had agreed to dominion status. Mountbatten showed him written evidence of Congress support. And when told that Jinnah had not yet endorsed the plan, Churchill retorted, 'It is a matter of life and death for Pakistan to accept this offer with both hands. By god! He is one man who cannot do without British help'. Mountbatten may have been mildly disingenuous with Churchill, not mentioning that he was precluding independence for any of the princely states, because Churchill wrote a letter to Attlee endorsing the plan on the basis of 'an effective acceptance of Dominion status for the several parts of a divided India'. When he next met Mountbatten (in November 1947), Churchill publicly snubbed him, making clear that he felt betrayed that India had only been divided in two!

In Calcutta, chief minister Suhrawardy had begun to reach out to Congress leaders with a proposal to create an independent Bengal in late April 1947, with the enthusiastic backing of Governor Burrows. Eventually Sarat Chandra Bose and Kiran Shankar Roy joined Suhrawardy on 11 May in putting forward a vision of a sovereign United Bengal, including some areas of Bihar and Assam that were Bengali-majority districts and towns. May 1947 was a month in which the future of India was truly fluid and malleable, and the united Bengal was one idea that some members of Attlee's cabinet were keen to press on Mountbatten, as British businesses were enthusiastic about it. But Shyama Prasad Mookerjee led the way in strongly opposing the United Bengal move, alongside key Hindu Mahasabha leaders of Bengal such as Narendra Basu. Most of the Bengal Congress deserted Sarat Bose and went along with Shyama Prasad on this occasion, and the Bengal legislature endorsed the idea of partition, reducing one potential headache for Mountbatten.

On 3 June 1947, Mountbatten was able to bring Jinnah, Liaquat, Abdur Rab Nishtar, Nehru, Patel, Kripalani (as Congress president) and Baldev Singh together around a small conference table, where they collectively endorsed Mountbatten's partition plan, under the watchful gaze of Lord Ismay. Photographs of the occasion show an assemblage of universally morose individuals (with the exception of the gleaming Ismay): none of the Indians present could possibly be happy with the full outcome, but each had received just enough to give his endorsement. The minutes of that meeting show that the first issue Liaquat brought up was the need to control the language not only of their subordinates but also of 'super-leaders', specifically Gandhi. Liaquat said Gandhi 'preached "non-violence", but that many of his speeches could be taken as an incitement to violence'. But Mountbatten had spent the previous day charming Gandhi, saying that the 'Mountbatten Plan' should really be christened 'Gandhi Plan', as it met all his conditions (the choice left to the Indian people, avoiding coercion, and a rapid transfer of power). He had secured a promise from Gandhi not to speak against the plan, and Gandhi told his prayer meeting that evening that the Viceroy 'had no hand' in partition; 'if Hindus and Muslims cannot agree on anything else then the Viceroy is left with no choice.' That evening, the Indian Independence Bill was introduced into the House of Commons, and a simultaneous declaration was made from New Delhi and London that power would be transferred to two new dominions—India and Pakistan—on 15 August 1947.

A Boundary Commission (eventually headed by Cyril Radcliffe, a London barrister who had never previously visited India, aided by two Hindus and two Muslims) would delineate the precise boundaries between India and Pakistan in the provinces of Bengal and Punjab. British suzerainty over all princely states would lapse on 15 August 1947, and with it all treaties and agreements between the British and those princely states. A referendum would be held in NWFP (as Nehru had agreed six weeks earlier), and another would be held in the Muslim-majority Sylhet district of Assam (the rest of which would remain in India). Remarkably, no referendum was called for the Chittagong Hill Tracts, where non-Muslims (Buddhists, Hindus and Christians) were in a strong majority, or indeed for the cities of Karachi or Hyderabad (Sindh), which (with clear non-Muslim majorities) would almost certainly have voted to remain within India. Mountbatten acknowledged afterwards that Nehru had been 'indispensable' to Britain achieving all its chief goals during that vital summer of 1947.

In his unseemly haste, Nehru had sacrificed all that Congress had stood for steadfastly over the previous twenty-five years. In January 1922, Lord Reading had offered India dominion status with no question of partition. A quarter-century later, Nehru had acquiesced in a plan to vivisect India in two, tying himself in verbal and logical knots that inevitably led to Britain and Jinnah achieving all their goals at his expense. At the beginning of 1947, NWFP was firmly in the Congress camp with a popular Congress government, Punjab had a non-sectarian coalition government of Muslim, Sikh and Hindu ministers (supposedly the Congress idyll) and the Khan of Kalat (whose domains covered most of the territory of Baluchistan) was amenable to either declaring independence or joining the (Indian) Constituent Assembly. Despite the terrorism (aka 'Direct Action') unleashed by the Muslim League since 16 August 1946, Nehru agreed to allow the Muslim League to take half the portfolios in his interim government in October 1946, only to see even more terrorism unleashed upon Noakhali and Tippera two weeks later, while Liaquat (as finance minister) imposed a 25 per cent tax on capital gains, aimed specifically at squeezing traders and industrialists aligned with Congress, while cutting funding to Congress ministries. The Muslim League was focused solely on separatism, and Nehru never explained why he had acquiesced in Wavell's scheme of bringing them into his interim government (apart from holding on to his own job).

While Jawaharlal Nehru pursued his lofty ambition of becoming a world statesman, Jinnah steadily pulled the rug from under his feet, with a great deal of British support. Nehru (and to a lesser extent Patel) acquiesced in the British sidelining of Gandhi during the crucial final year leading up to independence. While the Congress party and Nehru's family descendants are scrupulous in giving credit for the arrival of independence to Gandhi, they quietly skirt the fact that Nehru (not Gandhi) negotiated all the terms under which the 'transfer' of power to him occurred. And, in each case, Nehru inexplicably capitulated to the British, ignoring the support proffered by the

Americans (for fear of what Mountbatten and Krishna Menon called 'dollar imperialism') in order to give the British everything they wanted. The most inexplicable capitulation was over NWFP, and the ones who felt most betrayed by this were the Khan brothers. The Congress had agreed (on 8 March 1947) to the partition of Punjab on the assumption that NWFP would still stay with India (since the Constituent Assembly members from NWFP were already participating in its deliberations), and there was a likelihood that Baluchistan too would do the same. Since Kashmir's most popular leader, Sheikh Abdullah, was a Congress ally, the putative Pakistan (comprising west Punjab and Sindh) would be encompassed on either side by Indian territory, greatly reducing its viability. Yet, just over a month later, Nehru inexplicably and unilaterally agreed to a referendum to determine NWFP's future, for no other reason than to burnish his credentials as a democrat in the eyes of Mountbatten (and, perhaps more pertinently, Edwina).

Rumours of Nehru's ambivalence over NWFP's future encouraged Caroe to prise more Maliks away from Khan Abdul Ghaffar Khan. Indeed, Caroe now went further still, urging NWFP's chief minister, Dr Khan Sahib, to push for an independent Pakhtunistan since Congress appeared likely to abandon NWFP. The Congress party's acceptance of Partition by end-April 1947 was a tragic blow to long-standing Congress Muslims like Maulana Azad, M. A. Ansari and Ghaffar Khan, who were all suddenly left in the lurch, their lifelong commitment in tatters. But the most poignant plight was that of the Khan brothers, who would also find themselves abandoned in hostile Pakistani territory. When the Congress met to consider Mountbatten's partition plan, Ghaffar Khan made a final impassioned plea not to throw 'the Khudai Khidmatgars to the wolves' (as Azad remembered his words). Having stood by the Congress (especially Gandhi) through thick and thin, their enemies would now laugh at Ghaffar Khan, and all Pathans would consider it an act of treachery if Congress abandoned the red-shirted Khudai Khidmatgars. Gandhi appealed to Mountbatten to intercede with Jinnah to provide some assurance that the Khudai Khidmatgars would not suffer in Pakistan, but brief Jinnah–Ghaffar Khan talks made little headway.

Jinnah had sent Iskander Mirza (a Bengali Muslim civil servant known for his effective past service in NWFP) to foment 'jihad' there in March-April 1947, given the League's weak presence in the province; he only called off Mirza's mission after the referendum was called. Iskander Mirza would eventually be rewarded by being made the first president of Pakistan. This was especially ironic given his family antecedents: Iskander Mirza was the great-grandson of Mir Jafar, the infamous traitor of 1757 who had taken a bribe from Clive to concede the Battle of Plassey. In the run-up to the referendum, Dr Khan Sahib strongly advocated the creation of an independent Pakhtunistan and demanded the introduction of this as a third choice (other than joining India or Pakistan) on the ballot paper.

Mountbatten refused to allow that third choice (independence) on the ballot (for fear, he said, of encouraging others to demand the same), but did agree to replace Caroe with a more neutral governor, Lieutenant General Rob Lockhart, who would conduct the referendum. With no independence option, the Frontier Congress decided to boycott the referendum (which was hastily held on 6 July 1947). Dr Khan Sahib wanted to fight the Muslim League's violence with his own party's toughs, but his brother Ghaffar Khan was committed to non-violence and refused to countenance the bloodshed that would result from a full-blown fight with the Muslim League. Of the narrow electorate (15 per cent of the population of NWFP), 50.5 per cent voted in the referendum, about 15 per cent lower than the turnout in the 1946 provincial election. But, with no concerted opposition from the Khan brothers, whose supporters were boycotting the plebiscite, almost all ballots cast (99 per cent) were in favour of Pakistan. Abandoned by Nehru (and hence by India), Khan Abdul Ghaffar Khan spent much of the rest of his life in Pakistani prisons, especially after his calls for Pakhtunistan became too much for Pakistan's military establishment to bear. Grateful refugees (Muslim, Sikh and Hindu) from the NWFP named the iconic Khan Market in the heart of New Delhi after him. (Some of Ghaffar Khan's idealistic Muslim followers—including his nephew Mohammed Yunus, and the actor Shah Rukh Khan's father—chose to migrate to India rather than stay on in a Pakistan they simply could not abide).

Patel too had acquiesced in the quick timetable towards partition and independence; but while Nehru made concession after concession to the British (gaining nothing in return), Patel acquiesced only after striking a tough quid pro quo. Looking back on this time two years later, Sardar Patel made explicit in the Constituent Assembly (in July 1949) the deal that he had struck: 'In exchange for Indian acceptance of partition, Britain had agreed to withdraw not only within two months but not to interfere in the question of Indian states.' As home minister, Patel's finest hours were to be the period between 25 July (when he drew up the 'Instrument of Accession' that princes were to sign) and 15 August 1947, by which time almost all the princes had acceded to India, with the notable exceptions of Hyderabad and Junagadh (overwhelmingly Hindu-majority states with Muslim rulers), and Jammu and Kashmir (a multi-religious state with a Muslim majority but a Hindu ruler).

One-third of the territory of British India was occupied by 320 nominally independent states of varying sizes (and there were another 240 very small states in Gujarat comprising only a village or two each). The princes were initially required to accede by surrendering their control of foreign affairs, defence and communications to India (while also giving up any rights to issue currency). Almost all the states were surrounded by Indian territory, and were heavily dependent on the rest of India for water, communications, railways, and most other resources; integration into India therefore seemed natural, and only modest amounts of persuasion (and occasional threats of coercion by the States' Peoples' Organization mass movement that Congress had floated) enabled Patel to secure their accession (with V. P. Menon's support). Jinnah expended a lot of time trying to lure several border states (Jodhpur, Junagadh, Bikaner) and some states that had Muslim rulers (Junagadh again, Bhopal, Rampur) to accede to Pakistan rather than India; some large states (Hyderabad, Travancore, Indore, Baroda) initially thought they could go it alone, perhaps by offering to serve as military or air bases for the British, but Mountbatten could not go back on his solemn promise to Patel. Jodhpur was amongst those tempted by Jinnah's lavish promises (to deal with food shortages, free access to Karachi port, and free import of guns by Rajputs), all of which Patel matched (replacing Karachi with a port in Kutch, to which he promised a railway line from Jodhpur). Jodhpur's ruler Hanwant Singh eventually acceded to India but was reported by Mountbatten to have threatened V. P. Menon by drawing his revolver and promising to shoot him if Patel's promises to him went unfulfilled!

On 11 August 1947, Pakistan signed an agreement with the Khan of Kalat recognizing the latter as an independent, sovereign state. Kalat had been treated on par with independent Oman (to which it had leased the Baluchi port of Gwadar) when the British held an imperial assemblage at Delhi in 1877 to mark the accession of Victoria as Empress of India; this was only right, the Khan of Kalat asserted, since the British had recognized Kalat as an independent state in their 1876 treaty. Although it was mentioned as an Indian state in the 1935 Government of India Act, Kalat's status (being at one extremity of British India) was at least ambiguous (almost exactly akin to Sikkim). Importantly, however, Kalat's treaty with the British granted the latter a perpetual lease over the large strip of strategic territory between Kalat and Afghanistan (including the crucial city of Quetta, and the towns of Nushki, Nasirabad and Bolan); once all treaties with the princely states lapsed, those territories would ironically have to be ceded by Britain to Kalat! Jinnah is said to have agreed to acknowledge Kalat's sovereignty in order to ensure that Pakistan rather than Kalat would inherit the vital strategic area of British Baluchistan abutting Afghanistan (including the border town of Bolan and the provincial capital of Quetta); as we have seen, the British military chiefs had always stressed that Baluchistan and NWFP needed to be kept separate from India in order to ensure that they could continue to serve as British military bases.

The Khan of Kalat continued to resist Jinnah's attempts to abridge Kalat's sovereignty, and Jinnah instead adopted the stratagem of getting Kalat's southern feudatories (Kharan and Las Bela) to defect to Pakistan, cutting off Kalat's access to the sea. In the elected assembly of Kalat state (which covered more than the territory of British Baluchistan), a strongly nationalist party held sway, and Mir Ghaus Bux Bizenjo spoke powerfully of the Baluchi people's historical right to sovereignty. The Khan insisted, quite rightly, that his feudatories did not have the right to make treaties independent of their Khan. Eventually, the Khan began to make secret overtures to Afghanistan especially through his brother (who had married into the Afghan royal family), and also to India. In fact, in mid-March 1948, All India Radio reported that the Khan of Kalat had signed and sent the Instrument of Accession *to India*, but that Nehru had rejected it. This little-known episode showed yet again just how willing Nehru was to do Britain's bidding rather than act in India's national interest.

That All India Radio report caused such a furore in Pakistan that the Khan of Kalat (already isolated by Nehru's rejection of his overture) finally agreed to accede to Pakistan on 28 March 1948, after Pakistani armed forces moved in to assert their plans: given Pakistan's own recognition (on 11 August 1947) of Kalat as a sovereign state, this was clearly an invasion, but one that attracted no global opprobrium! The Khan's brother (who had fled to Afghanistan) came back to Kalat a few months later, rejected his brother's treaty with Pakistan, and resumed a nationalist struggle, which was joined by the chief of Bugti and several other feudatories. The nationalist struggle of the Baluchi people to secede from Pakistan continues unabated to this day, having reached a crescendo in the 1970s (under Ghaus Bux Bizenjo's leadership), but having been brutally repressed during periods of military rule, especially under Muhammad Zia-ul-Haq (1977–88) and Pervez Musharraf (2000–07).

Speaking at the British Labour Party's annual conference during the week after the momentous agreement on 3 June 1947 to partition India before its independence, Ernest Bevin (Britain's foreign secretary at the time, and an ideological stalwart of the Labour Party) stated that India's partition 'would help to consolidate Britain in the Middle East'. From May 1945 onwards, every important British military or strategic document (most of them marked 'top secret' at the time) had emphasized the vital importance of holding on to Baluchistan and NWFP, from which 'British air power could threaten Soviet military installations'. On 12 May 1947, General Leslie Hollis wrote to Attlee on behalf of the chiefs of staff: 'From the strategic point of view there are overwhelming arguments in favour of a western Pakistan remaining in the Commonwealth [i.e., maintaining defence ties with Britain].' On 7 July 1947, the chiefs of staff noted that '[t]he area of Pakistan is strategically the most important in the continent of India and the majority of our strategic requirements could be met... by an agreement with Pakistan alone'. In May 1948, they emphasized, 'The Indus Valley, western Punjab and Baluchistan are vital to any strategic plans for the defence of the all-important Muslim belt... the oil supplies of the Middle East. If one looks upon this area as a strategic wall (against Soviet expansionism) the five most important bricks in the wall are: Turkey, Iran, Iraq, Afghanistan and Pakistan.' By May 1948, Britain had secured the key pieces of the puzzle by creating the Pakistan that was essential to NATO's strategic interests in the region, and within a decade all those nations (except Afghanistan) would be part of the Baghdad Pact which evolved into the CENTO (Central Treaty Organization).

But in the intervening period, Pakistan had been created on 14 August 1947, as a British dominion with Jinnah as its first Governor General (overruling Mountbatten's ambition of staying on as Governor General of both dominions until 30 June 1948, the original end of the term to which he had been appointed by Attlee). In one of the more embarrassing episodes of that day, Jinnah had prepared plans for a grand luncheon banquet in his adopted home town of Karachi on Pakistan's first National Day—forgetting (as only a non-practising Muslim could) that it was still the holy month of Ramzan, and most devout Muslims would be fasting (and so, unable to eat at such a banquet)! When this was pointed out to Pakistan's Quaid-e-Azam (Supreme Leader), he hastily changed this to a dinner banquet (after sunset, when Muslims would be able to break their fast). Mountbatten attended the ceremony and banquet as a guest before flying back to New Delhi, where he would become the 'independent' Indian dominion's first Governor General. The army and bureaucracy were quickly divided amongst the two nations, with the vast majority of Muslim military men and bureaucrats choosing to join Pakistan, whose army would be commanded by Lieutenant General Gracey (who had commanded the British Indian Army most recently in Vietnam).

'At the stroke of the midnight hour, when the world sleeps, India will awake to life and freedom,' intoned Nehru as the midnight of 15 August 1947 arrived, in the second sentence of one of the finest speeches of his career, which began with the famous words: 'Long years ago, we made a tryst with destiny, and now the time comes when we shall redeem our pledge, not wholly or in full measure, but very substantially.' That lofty rhetoric masked the massacres that were then occurring in Punjab especially, and to a much lesser degree in Bengal, where Suhrawardy had again requested the 'one man boundary force', Gandhi, to intervene. The Mahatma spent the night of 15 August 1947 (and several more besides) fasting in a Calcutta slum, with Suhrawardy for company, in an attempt to maintain communal harmony in that city. The import of Gandhi's intervention is sometimes glossed over, but it was extraordinary that a Muslim League chief minister (who had been directly responsible for launching the terrorism of 'Direct Action' a year earlier, thus setting in motion the events that led towards partition) was now seeking the help of the one man who had been most steadfastly opposed to the very idea of partition; it was an act of enormous magnanimity (and innate humanity) for Gandhi to respond to Suhrawardy's call.

One consequence of this intervention was that only a small proportion of Calcutta's Muslims (who then comprised about a third of its population) left for Pakistan, and large proportions of East Bengal's Hindus initially chose to remain in what was to become East Pakistan. Of the 21 million Bengali Hindus who suddenly found themselves Pakistani citizens in the second half of August 1947, only 344,000 initially left East Bengal; but Punjabi Muslim thugs soon arrived in East Pakistan to terrorize the population, and 786,000 Hindus were forced out in 1948, and a further 213,000 in 1949, all arriving at Calcutta's Sealdah station with little other than the clothes on their bodies, swelling that city's population of vagrants, and severely straining the creaking infrastructure of what had once been the Second City of the Empire. Nonetheless, as late as 1970, nearly 20 per cent of East Pakistan's people were non-Muslim (although that proportion has now declined to 9 per cent, with the diminution beginning with the Pakistani military massacres of 1970–71, which led to an exodus of Bengali Hindus and Muslims to India, most of the former never returning), while Muslims comprise over 25 per cent of West Bengal's population, 31 per cent of Assam's, 16 per cent of Bihar's and 15 per cent of Jharkhand's (based on the 2011 census).

By contrast, the bloodletting was concentrated in its severity in the Punjab. Muslim League terrorism had started in Rawalpindi and its surrounding villages in February–March 1947, and most towns and villages in western Punjab had already been emptied of their Sikh and Hindu inhabitants by mid-August 1947, while a similar retaliatory process had also begun in parts of eastern Punjab expected to stay in India. The precise details of Radcliffe's partition line were deliberately kept secret by Mountbatten until after 15 August 1947. Whether Punjab's capital city of Lahore (or its twin city of Amritsar) would be in India or Pakistan was not certain until after 15 August. Lahore's commerce and services were dominated by Hindu landlords, lawyers, doctors and architects (who, along with Sikhs, formed nearly half the population). Most wealthy and middle-class Hindus and Sikhs in Lahore and many other towns and villages across central and western Punjab only became aware that they were in Pakistan (rather than India) after the Radcliffe award was announced on 17 August 1947. By then, the cities of Pakistani Punjab were literally burning, as Hindu and Sikh homes were attacked relentlessly and most families fled with virtually no preparation, locking their homes where possible, in the forlorn hope of returning some day. My wife's grandfather, who had a flourishing grain business in Lahore and whose brother had been mayor of the city, fled in a truck with literally no more than the clothes on his body. Stories about a train full of murdered Hindus and Sikhs arriving into Amritsar led to a fearsome retaliatory response, as Muslims were massacred in response on the eastern (Indian) side of Punjab.

Punjab thus saw a chaotic exchange of population, with Hindus and Sikhs leaving Pakistani Punjab for India while Muslims from Indian Punjab (including today's Haryana and Himachal Pradesh) and Delhi similarly fled to Pakistan. Unlike the formal exchanges of population that occurred between Greece and Turkey in 1923, there was nothing formal about the population exchange in the Indian subcontinent; nobody expected that the division between India and Pakistan would become set in stone, and that movement between the two parts of Punjab would soon be near-impossible. My father-in-law (having left his home in Lahore as a twelve-year-old in early August 1947 ostensibly to take a short holiday in Simla) returned to Lahore for the first time in 2014, and was visited by ISI operatives after attempting to visit his old school and see his home near the Badshahi Mosque. Similarly, General Pervez Musharraf first revisited his family home in Old Delhi (which he had left as a little boy in 1947) only when he came to India as Pakistan's military ruler in 2002.

The violence in western Punjab had built up to a crescendo, starting with the rumble of gunfire and arson in Rawalpindi and its surrounding villages in March 1947, and reaching Lahore by June. During that month, Hindu and Sikh homes were regularly being incinerated across western Punjab, including in the new flashpoint of Lahore, where the police appeared complicit in perpetrating violence on non-Muslims. Nehru (still interim prime minister of undivided India) requested Mountbatten on 24 June to persuade Punjab's governor, Evan Jenkins, to use the military to restore order. Jinnah too agreed that the imposition of martial law was necessary to restore peace, as the military was a relatively neutral force, and had the necessary means to intercede effectively in the growing crisis (Jinnah specifically asked that Muslims too must be shot at sight if found rioting). But Jenkins refused to countenance the use of the military for fear that the involvement of British troops would ostensibly result in violence against British residents of the Punjab. This utterly spurious argument let the real cat out of the bag: crusty colonial administrators were determined to foment (or at least connive at) the bloodletting between Muslims and non-Muslims as a kind of insurance policy against anti-British violence. Of course, no Indians were then advocating anti-British violence, and there had been virtually none of it after February 1946, once India's leaders became convinced that Britain did indeed intend to leave India within a year or two.

The truth was that the British colonial rulers were ever ready to use violence against Indians, and to foment and encourage bloodletting amongst India's communities, while Indians only resorted to violence as a last option (if ever) against the British; even Bhagat Singh and Subhas Bose only reluctantly took up the gun when other means had failed, and they (or their followers) never advocated (or perpetrated) random violence against British civilians. In the summer of 1947, Jenkins's actions and (ultimately) Mountbatten's inaction were emblematic of the deep-seated cynicism of British colonial rule: using the concocted red herring of possible Indian violence against British civilians (in retaliation for British military involvement in basic *peacekeeping*), the British abdicated their responsibility for maintaining even a modicum of law and order in their colonial realm. Instead, Mountbatten and Jenkins sat idly by while mayhem and violence were unleashed across the Punjab, killing thousands of Indian civilians, and all before the actual dividing lines were known. Punjab had been a peaceful province ruled by a multi-religious coalition for a decade; but the Unionist–Congress–Akali coalition's ouster at the behest of the Muslim League (and its armed 'National Guards') before the Ides of March in 1947 proved disastrous. With no ministry in place, Governor Jenkins had full control over the law and order machinery of the Punjab after 8 March 1947: then, as now, the police were directly under the control of the provincial government, which was fully British at the time. Culpability for the horrendous violence that engulfed the Punjab between June and September 1947 rests wholly with Governor Jenkins and his boss Mountbatten, made infinitely worse by their refusal to call in the army to restore order (then, as now, standard procedure when communal trouble got out of hand).

The consequence was that western Punjab (Pakistan's main province) was, within half a year, emptied of almost all its Hindus and Sikhs (who together had comprised a third of that region's population). A less traumatic movement the other way also occurred, with Muslims leaving eastern Punjab in droves too. However, there can be no moral equivalence about the process that occurred on either side of Punjab's dividing line. The very name Pakistan connotes 'land of the pure', so those who weren't Muslims ('pure') had no place there. Hindu and Sikh women were forcibly converted to Islam, or raped in order to ensure that they converted (as rape victims' families might be too ashamed to accept them). In India, where the Congress was avowedly secular, no such pressure to convert was exerted on Muslims. Many nonetheless chose to migrate to Pakistan, but substantial others stayed in India. Today, Muslims comprise about 2 per cent of the population of Himachal Pradesh, 6 per cent of the population of Haryana, and 1.5 per cent of India's Punjab (which, at independence, also included those two states), whereas Hindus, Sikhs, Parsis and Ahmadiyyas (no longer 'pure' enough to be classified as Muslim) together comprise less than 0.5 per cent of the population of Pakistani Punjab. (The few Hindus who remained were mainly 'Bhangis' who cleaned the toilets and refuse of Punjab's Muslims as well as Hindus: Jinnah specifically requested them to stay, and stopped some from leaving both Punjab and Sindh for fear of having a massive sanitation problem were they to leave).

At least 500,000 people were killed in the violence of June–September 1947 in Punjab (especially) and Bengal, although some estimates put the death toll as high as 3 million. It was a last, gruesome act of revenge by the British on the Indian realms they were being forced to vacate, and their greatest triumph was that they escaped all blame for the tragedy they had wrought. Mountbatten had admitted that announcing the Radcliffe 'award' as soon as he received it could have averted many tens of thousands of deaths, by giving people about a week to make plans to leave if they happened to find themselves in the 'wrong' country. But (despite having urged Radcliffe in July to expedite his work) Mountbatten deliberately chose to lock the document away until after the celebrations (indeed, precisely in order not to interfere with the celebrations) of Independence.

That Nehru and Jinnah went on with those celebrations, seemingly oblivious to the gory violence that had overtaken their capitals and most of Punjab, was appalling, too. But the military and police were still very much under British control. At the beginning of 1947, all positions above colonel in the army were held by Britishers (K. M. Cariappa becoming the first Indian brigadier later that year), and 60 per cent of all police officers were British across India, as were just over half of all senior civil servants. While steps were being taken to relieve British officers (and replace them with Indians and Pakistanis), the British officers were still very much in control of the military and police as of 15 August 1947, and would remain so for at least another nine months. Most British military and police officers offered a choice picked Pakistan, looking at it as the more closely allied of the two new dominions. To them, Mountbatten 'lost India of course', and he became an object of hatred amongst the British colonials, also because, unlike his predecessors, he made it a point of principle to ensure that Indians made up at least half of all invitees at his garden parties (something that most old colonial hands found utterly confounding).

Hindu and Sikh landowners in western Punjab lost far more, both in property and financial resources, than their Muslim counterparts in eastern Punjab. Hindus and Sikhs were far more urbanized, and owned a disproportionate amount of property in Lahore, Rawalpindi and other cities of Punjab (and indeed even more so in urban Sindh). Having taken to capitalism sooner, Hindu landlords owned vast tracts of agrarian land across western Punjab. The agrarian dominance of Hindu landlords was even more pervasive in eastern Bengal, and in the Sylhet district of Assam that became part of Pakistan. Fazlul Huq's political platform of extensive land (especially tenurial) reform was particularly popular in eastern Bengal because it was implicitly an attack on Hindu landlords' property—a point that the Muslim League picked up on, and exploited much more fully in 1946 (because the League was more explicit in mixing its agrarian message with religious bigotry and a Muslim call to arms, while Fazlul Huq's appeal was to all peasants and workers, not necessarily just to Muslims). Partition was an absolute bonanza for the Muslim elites of the Punjab, Bengal and Bihar who quickly acquired the 'enemy property' of Hindu and Sikh evacuees from western Punjab and eastern Bengal, particularly their vast holdings of agrarian land. Since Fazlul Huq's party (with a genuine commitment to agrarian reform, and giving 'land to the tiller of the soil') had been isolated in the 1946 election, the opportunity for genuine land reform in eastern Bengal was also lost: Hindu and Sikh landlords were disenfranchised through the 'Enemy Properties Act' and similar acts (which allowed the Pakistani state to take possession of any property belonging to the family of a landholder who was deemed as an 'enemy of the state'; all members of a Hindu family could be deemed enemies of the state if some members of the family 'abandoned' Pakistan because of religious persecution, and their property could be expropriated by the state). Unfortunately, property acquired by the state in this way from Hindus in East Pakistan (and later Bangladesh) was quickly acquired by leading Muslim League politicians rather than transferred to tenants' ownership.

By contrast, there was very little Muslim-owned property in western Bengal that could be given to the Hindu refugees from the east, and relatively little urban property owned by Muslims in eastern Punjab (except in Old Delhi, and pockets of Amritsar, Ludhiana and Jalandhar); many Muslim landowners chose not to leave India, further reducing the potential supply of land for Hindu refugees from Pakistan, whereas virtually all Hindu/Sikh landowners were forced out of Pakistani Punjab, creating a very substantial land pool that could have been distributed more widely amongst Muslim refugees from India (had it not been grabbed mainly by Muslim League politicians). And since relatively few Hindus initially left East Bengal during 1947—the exodus only gathering pace in the subsequent two to three years—rehabilitating them properly in West Bengal proved much more onerous for the Indian government than the refugee rehabilitation that occurred in northwestern India, which entailed a swift programme of resettlement aided partly by being able to swap a considerable proportion of them into evacuated properties. The chaotic arrivals of hundreds of thousands of Bengali Hindus over the next three years made the newly impoverished and property-less refugees perfect candidates for recruitment into the CPI, which developed a strong core of followers amongst the refugees from East Pakistan, especially amongst the scion of formerly wealthy rural landlords of the area, and amongst middle class and poor East Bengalis, for whom the CPI provided basic services and support.

Before their departure, the British also executed a neat final coup in Kashmir. The strategically most vital part of the princely state of Kashmir was the Northern Area, comprising the Gilgit Agency that shared a border with China's restive province of Xinjiang, otherwise known for several of the previous decades as the East Turkestan republic. Kashmir's Gilgit region abutted NWFP, and was separated from the USSR only by a long, narrow strip of Afghanistan. The British were worried that Xinjiang would become a vital battle arena in China's Civil War, especially as Mao's armies were threatening to enter the region with Stalin's, and that Nehru would oppose using Gilgit for any moves against the communists.

The Gilgit Agency, which included the strategically important and beautiful mountainous regions of Swat and Chitral—which have more recently become dens of Islamist terrorism—had been leased by Kashmir state to Britain in 1935 (for a term that was to last until 1995). Gilgit consequently became an 'Agency' (like the Malakand and Khyber Agencies in NWFP) administered directly from Delhi, by British members of the elite Indian Political Service. However, on 1 August 1947, with the abrogation of all previous treaties between the princely states and Britain, the Gilgit Agency was returned to full Kashmiri sovereignty. Srinagar sent Brigadier Ghansara Singh to take over as governor of Gilgit that day, but the British forces did not withdraw fully. Major William Brown and Captain A. S. Mathieson remained in command of the Gilgit Scouts, which ostensibly now owed full allegiance to Maharaja Hari Singh of Kashmir, but actually still reported to their former British commander, Lieutenant Colonel Roger Bacon, who was transferred at the start of August 1947 from Gilgit to Khyber (which, after 14 August, became part of Pakistan).

Hari Singh initially entertained the idea of declaring independence, but he also faced pressure from a popular democratic movement led by Sheikh Abdullah, a close ally of the Congress party (and specifically of Nehru) and the dominant politician in the Kashmir Valley (the small but breathtakingly beautiful area that housed more than half of Kashmir's people, and that was 80 per cent Muslim; the Jammu region, from where Hari Singh's Dogras originated, had a Hindu/Sikh majority, while the sparsely populated but vast Ladakh region—occupying well over half Kashmir's land—was a Buddhist-majority region). In 1946, Hari Singh had arrested Nehru when he visited Kashmir in support of Sheikh Abdullah.

Jinnah had also sought to use the Muslim Conference led by Agha Shaukat Ali to initiate 'direct action' to foment Hindu–Muslim riots in 1946, but failed mainly because Abdullah's National Conference opposed such moves. Some riots occurred in the Poonch region of Jammu, but these were swiftly controlled by the Maharaja's forces. In June 1947, Mountbatten visited Maharaja Hari Singh, telling him that independence was not an option, and that he needed to accede to either India or Pakistan, but that Mountbatten had 'assurances from the Indian leaders that if he acceded to Pakistan they would not take it amiss'. Hari Singh decided to play a waiting game, with his prime minister, Ram Chandar Kak, continuing to hold the pro-Indian Sheikh Abdullah in prison, while he conducted discreet negotiations with Jinnah. Eventually, however, in mid-September 1947, Hari Singh replaced Kak with Mehr Chand Mahajan, one of whose first acts was to declare a general amnesty, which resulted in the release from prison of Sheikh Abdullah. Jinnah, recognizing that the replacement of Kak signalled Hari Singh's decision to end the negotiations with Pakistan, began to immediately pressurize Kashmir with an economic blockade that would become even more effective in the impending winter months. On 10 October 1947, Pakistan invaded Kashmir using tribal forces from the NWFP (Afridis, Masoods from Waziristan, and Hazaras).

During this interregnum, there was a raging dispute in India's cabinet between Nehru and Patel over Kashmir; the former insisted that Sheikh Abdullah must be made the head of Kashmir's government, while Patel asserted that this demand was unnecessary at the time, and was the only reason why Maharaja Hari Singh was hesitating on accession to India. The Pakistani invasion, though, helped make matters much clearer to Hari Singh.

Narendra Singh Sarila, military ADC to Mountbatten, published a brilliant book in 2005 exposing the detailed British planning of partition from 1941 onwards, including the close coordination between British and Pakistani policy over Kashmir. Sarila quotes the memoirs of Colonel (later Major General)

Akbar Khan, military member of Pakistan's Liberation Committee, who described in detail how Pakistan's prime minister Liaquat Ali Khan personally supervised the 'tribal operation' of Afridis, Masoods and Hazaras, with Colonel Khan himself (one of the seniormost non-British officers in the Pakistan Army) as its military leader. The use of irregular 'tribal' forces (mixed in with a few regular Pakistani troops in disguise) became standard operating procedure for Pakistan in future invasions of Kashmir (for instance in 1965 and 1999, on both occasions through use of the road to Kargil into Ladakh). Pakistan's proxy war to take Kashmir (that began in the first half of October 1947) has never ended, although there are periodic lulls in its offensive.

The Pakistani troops and irregulars proved to be difficult to discipline—stopping for a couple of days in Baramulla (at the entrance of the vale of Kashmir) to indulge in rape, looting and murder of the local civilians (most of whom were Muslim, although the incident that grabbed global attention was their raid on the Convent of Jesus and Mary, and Pakistani troops' raping of nuns there, which led Auchinleck to contemplate the use of British troops to protect British residents of Kashmir). The Kashmiri forces, led by Dogra commander Rajinder Singh Jamwal, put up a stiff resistance for three days before he was killed in battle. On 14 October 1947, Colonel Akbar Khan found himself trapped in Uri, west of Baramulla, as his forces began to retreat from Srinagar, where they were pushed back by the Maharaja's forces. Nehru's India had refused to send military reinforcements to support Kashmir's government, but did send planeloads of civil (and some military) supplies, with the first plane flown into Srinagar by the ace pilot (and aviation hero in Indonesia a few months earlier) Biju Patnaik. Almost all commercial aircraft available in India were commandeered for this operation to drop supplies into Kashmir (particularly Srinagar), in an aerial version of the French response (using the taxi fleet of Paris) to the German invasion in the First World War.

In the face of the Pakistani invasion, Maharaja Hari Singh of Kashmir signed the Instrument of Accession to India, which was accepted and signed by Governor General Mountbatten on 27 October 1947, thus completing the legal accession of Jammu and Kashmir to India. The United States was amongst the first to recognize this accession. Mountbatten, however, also wrote a personal letter to Hari Singh, stating: 'As soon as law and order have been restored in Kashmir and her soil cleared of the invaders, the question of the State's accession should be settled by reference to the people.' Pakistan has always cited this letter as being evidence of Kashmir's 'conditional' accession to India, although Mountbatten clarified (after he had left India) in an aide-memoire to Ismay that 'the decision to hold a plebiscite in no way invalidated the legality of the accession of Kashmir to India. The position then was that Kashmir was legally part of the Dominion of India and the voluntary, unilateral decision to hold [a] plebiscite to confirm this was only intended to be held after the tribesmen had been withdrawn and peaceful conditions had been restored throughout Kashmir.' India's position ever since has been that a plebiscite was impossible as long as Pakistani troops remained in any part of the original state of Jammu and Kashmir.

On 31 October 1947, a coup was completed in Gilgit by the British officers commanding the Gilgit Scouts, Major William Alexander Brown and Captain A. S. Mathieson (who still reported to Lieutenant Colonel Bacon although they were now sworn to obey the orders of Kashmir's Maharaja Hari Singh). Upon the accession of Jammu and Kashmir to India, Brown and Mathieson opted for service in Pakistan. They should thus have left Gilgit (which had become part of India on 27 October). Instead, acting on orders from Bacon in Khyber, Brown got his Gilgit Scout troops to surround the Residency during the night of 31 October, capture it after a short gun battle in which he lost one 'scout', and imprison Governor Ghansara Singh. The following day, Brown informed Peshawar about the 'accession' of Gilgit to Pakistan, not mentioning on whose authority he was proclaiming this 'accession'. On 2 November, the Pakistan flag was raised over the headquarters of the Gilgit Scouts, and Britain's quiet military coup to secure a vital region of Kashmir was complete! An attempted rebellion against this accession, led by several chiefs in the region who declared a republic of 'Gilgit–Astore' was quickly crushed by Pakistani troops led by Major Aslam Khan. Major Brown received an OBE in the next year's New Year Honours List as his reward for his military coup in Kashmir's Gilgit.

Nehru effectively acquiesced in this British coup to secure Gilgit for Pakistan (and for the West in the emerging Cold War), never raising the issue globally (for instance at the UN) although this was clearly an act of war by the departing colonial power (acting, eventually, to acquire territory that was part of India in international law and hand it to a neighbouring country). Gilgit was a sparsely populated but vast region (accounting for more than a third of the territory of Jammu and Kashmir), albeit with just three widely dispersed towns (Gilgit, Skardu and Chitral) in the craggy, hilly terrain. But, of course, it was of vital strategic importance. Nehru's benign neglect of Britain's coup there was of a piece with the other bizarre decisions he made at the time—prominently his decision to let Mountbatten chair the Indian Cabinet's Defence Committee. This tied India's hands at a time when the newly independent country's territory was under attack by neighbouring Pakistani troops (thinly disguised as a 'tribal invasion', although Jinnah admitted to

Mountbatten that all that was required for these 'tribals' to withdraw from Kashmir was a direct order from him).

Major General Kulwant Singh, India's general officer commanding (GOC), Kashmir Operations, prepared a plan at the beginning of November to clear out Pakistani troops (and 'tribals') from the western belt of Jammu—Poonch, Mirpur, Naoshera—and Muzaffarabad. But his plan was shot down by General Roy Bucher, the (British) acting commander-in-chief of the Indian Army, and by Mountbatten. Patel then encouraged Mountbatten to attend his nephew Philip's wedding to Princess Elizabeth on 10 November in London—a marital alliance he had himself done so much to encourage and facilitate. Soon after Mountbatten left for London on the 9th, Kulwant Singh swung his troops into action, and within the next fortnight they had cleared Naoshera, Jhangar and Kotli of Pakistani troops and irregulars, and also relieved their siege of Poonch town. But he could not reach Muzaffarabad, Domel and Mirpur before his superiors ordered him to stop. Upon his return from London on 14 November, Mountbatten remonstrated with Nehru via a long admonitory letter protesting the 'change' in the Government of India's 'purpose' (during the time he was away) towards imposing 'their military will on the Poonch and Mirpur areas.' This was a surreal war, because the commanders-in-chief of both the Indian and Pakistani armies were still British generals, and the British officers leading the Pakistani Army were much more eager to fight than those in the Indian Army, since the British officers saw India increasingly as the enemy.

General K. M. Cariappa, who became GOC in the area by December, found himself facing the British general, Messervy, who had fought in Burma and commanded the British forces in Indonesia (including during the Battle of Surabaya) and now led the Pakistani Army in the parts of Kashmir occupied by Pakistan. Cariappa, during his operations to secure Naoshera, Rajouri and Jhangar, also had to dodge the commands of his boss, Bucher, who remained in close contact with his Pakistan counterpart, General Gracey (who we met previously in command of British Indian forces in Vietnam). Bucher (although ostensibly the commander-in-chief of the Indian Army) suggested to his Pakistani counterpart Gracey that 'three battalions of the Pakistan army should be employed in Kashmir opposite the Indian forces at Jhangar in or around Poonch and at Uri', and he (Bucher) would then work to evacuate Indian forces from Poonch, which the British wanted to deliver into Pakistani hands.

Another dispute had emerged by this time between India and Pakistan— having to do with Rs 550 million (worth about US$500 million in today's money) that India 'owed' to Pakistan as part of the Partition settlement and division of assets. Of this, India had paid Rs 200 million, but Patel strongly opposed paying the rest as long as India was in a state of war with Pakistan which, he argued, would use the money to buy more weapons to use against India. For once, Nehru agreed with Patel, but Mountbatten went over their heads to appeal to Gandhi on grounds of morality and ethics. Gandhi then began campaigning publicly for India to make the payment to Pakistan, and went on a fast unto death in January 1948 to persuade Patel and Nehru. He was able to eventually convince his former acolytes (and the Government of India reluctantly acceded to Gandhi's demand to make the full payment to Pakistan), but his public campaign enraged many of the refugees who had been forced to leave their ancestral properties and homes, and flee for their lives from Pakistan.

One amongst them, Madanlal Pahwa, made an abortive attempt to assassinate Gandhi in mid-January and his associate, Nathuram Godse, killed Mahatma Gandhi on 30 January 1948 in the bucolic garden of Birla House in New Delhi just after one of his prayer meetings. It was a tragic end to the life of the icon of India's independence campaign. Subhas Bose had acknowledged him as Father of the Nation, a title he achieved and lived up to emphatically in 1919–22, after which the subsequent twenty-six years were like those of any ageing father, often challenged by the impetuosity of his children while attempting to lay an ethical path for them to follow, as the energetic amongst them went ahead to find other pathways that ultimately helped deliver the same end through more realistic means.

Although Nehru led the eulogies with an emotional speech, this masked the fact that Nehru had sidelined Gandhi from the moment he was picked by Gandhi (ahead of Patel, the near-unanimous choice of his colleagues) as Congress' next leader in May 1946. Thereafter, Nehru and Congress did not abide by Gandhi's wishes and, in fact, acted explicitly against them, especially in their actions on Punjab (in agreeing in March 1947 to its partition) and NWFP (in agreeing to a referendum there). Sidelined, Gandhi spent the final two years of his life primarily as a saintly social worker—succouring the weak and dying, ameliorating conflict, and working indefatigably to alleviate the human pain of partition. The apogee of his career had been January 1922, when he had the British on their knees but suddenly chose to call off his campaign after Chauri Chaura in the first week of February 1922. From that point on, Gandhi's principled non-violent approach was repeatedly defeated by the amorality of the British, and it was the INA's undermining of the military's loyalty to the British that ultimately undid Britain's dominion.

Nehru, although opposed to making the payment to Pakistan, had remained solicitous of Mountbatten's military views—and fearful, in particular, that taking military and diplomatic actions that Mountbatten opposed might provoke him to leave India before the end of his term, and thereby embarrass India internationally. This became Britain's trump card in the final half-year of Mountbatten's time in India. Ironically, having Mountbatten as the first Governor General of 'independent' India proved an albatross around India's neck, while Pakistan (with Jinnah as Governor General) had greater freedom of action, coupled with the strong military support of the 500 British officers who enthusiastically led Pakistan's army, believing it to be a bulwark against the proto-communist tendencies of Nehru's India.

By 20 December 1947, Nehru had decided that the Indian Army needed to enter Pakistani territory to clear the invaders' training camps and cut off their communication links. When Nehru proposed this to his cabinet's Defence Committee, Mountbatten (who chaired it) suggested that a reference be made to the UN Security Council, since he asserted that 'India had a cast-iron case'. This was a pernicious suggestion, because Mountbatten was also apprising Attlee of the likely military action by India, and Attlee in turn was alerting the US of the likelihood of a formal escalation of the situation in Kashmir to an 'inter-dominion' war. The Indian Cabinet had agreed to Mountbatten's suggestion of a reference to the UN Security Council, but only on the assumption that any such reference would be preceded by an Indian military attack on the training camps and communication facilities inside Pakistan.

But Mountbatten and Attlee then worked on Nehru, convincing him that the British military officers would have to leave forthwith if full-scale war broke out (which Nehru unilaterally took to mean that Mountbatten himself would leave, the one thing that Nehru appeared to 'fear' above all, as he mentioned in a letter to Patel on 29 December). Bizarrely, therefore, the Indian Army made absolutely no preparations for mounting an attack inside Pakistan (even on the part of Kashmir that Pakistan still occupied) in the final week of 1947, but India did deliver a stiff letter to Pakistan's Prime Minister Liaquat Ali Khan on 22 December demanding that Pakistan 'deny all help to the raiders.' This letter was instead used by Attlee to raise alarm in Britain and, more importantly, with the Americans, who (until this point) had been strongly supportive of India, acting on the basis that all of Kashmir had legally acceded to India. Now the US envoy in the UK asked if it was possible not to refer the matter to the UN—and Attlee's government said it was absolutely necessary. Using that argument, Britain was able to persuade the American envoy to write identical letters to India and Pakistan asking to restrain irresponsible elements (presumably Pakistan's 'irregulars') while also asserting that precipitate action would seriously jeopardize international goodwill (words presumably aimed at Nehru). Ironically, the Indian Army made no preparations at all to attack 'training camps and communication lines' in Pakistan, but the reference to the UN Security Council was duly made by India on 1 January 1948, ignoring the fact that the Indian Cabinet had agreed to the UNSC reference only on the condition that prior military action would be taken against the camps and communication lines. (This has had eerie echoes in Indian actions on the Kashmir border ever since: while Pakistani proxies attack Indian territory in Kashmir with impunity, Indian troops never go beyond planning/threatening to attack the training camps and communication centres of terrorists and other infiltrators from the Pakistani side of the 'border' which, supposedly, India does not recognize; Narendra Modi's 'surgical strike' into Pakistan Occupied Kashmir in September 2016 was a marked exception).

Philip John Noel-Baker was Britain's ambassador to the UN at the time. Fortunately for Pakistan, Noel-Baker's main assistant on Indian subcontinent issues—especially on Kashmir—was the ubiquitous Lord Ismay, who had been posted there at the start of 1948 (to coincide with India's reference to the UNSC). Ismay's view on Kashmir had been clear: he believed that the international community should recognize Pakistan's legitimacy in Kashmir by acknowledging the presence of its 'raiders' and troops there, the government led by Sheikh Abdullah should resign, and a UN-supervised plebiscite should be organized instead. This now became the British position at the UN, thoroughly belying Mountbatten's contention to India's Cabinet that 'India had a cast-iron case' and should take its case to the UN. Instead, Britain now openly took Pakistan's side.

Noel-Baker's UN speeches and policy were also heavily influenced by his principal staff officer, General Sir Geoffrey Scoones, who had written an 'appreciation' for the British cabinet a week before Pakistan's invasion of Kashmir asserting that an Indian invasion would unite India (and hence was attractive to India's leadership 'and even Gandhi'), but that the 'effect of the disappearance of Pakistan on the Middle East would be considerable.' Scoones, with the vast majority of British military officers, believed that multilingual India had very little chance of surviving (and would soon succumb to internecine warfare amongst north and south, and various other fault lines) while Pakistan's religious cohesiveness would give it a purpose and ensure its enduring success. Nehru's 22 December letter to Liaquat became a convenient handle for the British trio at the UN to raise the bogey of an imminent Indian invasion (and divert attention from the reality of an ongoing Pakistani invasion and military operations on India's territory). In reality, of course, no Indian military moves were occurring or even being planned!

Britain's foreign secretary, Ernest Bevin, also kept warning Attlee that Britain 'should be very careful to guard against the danger of aligning the whole of Islam against us'. Noel-Baker, Ismay and Scoones mounted a concerted behind-the-scenes campaign in the Security Council in favour of Pakistan, arguing that Kashmir should 'naturally' be part of Pakistan since it was '77 per cent Muslim'; in particular, they sought to convince the US representative, Warren Austin, that Pakistani troops needed to be deployed in Kashmir to 'protect the Muslim population' and monitor a plebiscite, that Indian troops should withdraw to the southern Hindu-majority part of the state, and that an interim UN administration should replace the government of Sheikh Abdullah in Srinagar and the Valley. While Austin was often willing to go along with these ideas (and be used as a front by the British to suggest them publicly at the UN), his boss, the US Secretary of State George C. Marshall sent him periodic instructions that Kashmir was officially part of India, so any changes to Kashmir's governance and policing needed India's acquiescence first of all.

But India's diplomats—and eventually Nehru—did not help matters with their equivocation. Pakistan's UN delegate, Chaudhry Sir Muhammad Zafrullah Khan, mounted a verbal assault accusing India of securing Kashmir's accession through 'violence and fraud'. Although all the violence in Kashmir had in fact been perpetrated by Pakistan and its proxies, India's delegate Gopalaswami Ayyangar was punctilious in distinguishing between the tribal raiders and the formal armed forces of Pakistan, and insisted that the accession was conditional on a plebiscite. This Nehruvian attachment to the niceties of international law and propriety only ended up making India seem apologetic about its legal position, and greatly strengthened Pakistan's standing on the issue in the eyes of the world. When the Czech-American diplomat Josef Korbel (father of Madeleine Albright) led a UN delegation to India in July 1948, Nehru further muddied India's diplomatic waters by telling him that India would not be averse to Kashmir being divided between India and Pakistan. Sheikh Abdullah had mentioned this too in January that year (at a time when he was a member of India's UN delegation) and in February told US envoy Grady that another option worth considering was Kashmir's independence (except for foreign policy, which could be controlled jointly by India and Pakistan). Grady strongly discouraged the idea of Kashmir's independence.

But Nehru repeatedly betrayed his complete lack of basic negotiating skills. As with Partition, Nehru was cutting the ground from under his own feet (and that of the US, which had been a supporter of India's unity, and now was strongly supportive of India's legal possession of Kashmir). Having never practised law, Nehru was remarkably impractical and idealistic, repeatedly altering his positions while Jinnah and his successors were disciplined negotiators who never deviated from the singularity of their goals and line of argument. Mountbatten and Attlee succeeded not only in advancing Pakistan's position at the UN, but also managed to convince Nehru that it was the US that was behind the pro-Pakistan stand, although memos from Marshall, the acting US delegate John Foster Dulles (who wrote that the British position on Kashmir was invariably 'pro-Government of Pakistan') and ambassador Grady all show that the US was staunchly committed to recognizing the accession of Kashmir to India, and so according India all commensurate legal rights there. Nationalist (KMT) China also rendered support to India's positions. Occasionally Mountbatten succeeded in tempering the British position in order to ensure that India would remain part of the Commonwealth. In the end, that was the one bargaining chip that prevented Britain from wholeheartedly supporting Pakistan's positions and, in particular, it helped purge the proposal to replace Sheikh Abdullah's government with a UN one. But India never demanded that Pakistani troops withdraw from the vast territory of Gilgit, and quietly came around to accepting the partition of Kashmir with Muzaffarabad and Mirpur incorporated into Pakistan by the time the Kashmir ceasefire came into effect on 1 January 1949. In a sad postscript to his pioneering role in Pakistan's diplomacy, Zafrullah Khan was hounded out of the Pakistan Cabinet in 1954 because he was Ahmadiyya, and thus deemed not Muslim enough to represent the Land of the Pure!

India did become a republic on 26 January 1950 with a Constitution drafted principally by B. R. Ambedkar, the man who had been an unrelenting opponent of India's independence and a staunch ally of the British against Gandhi. Arguably, Nehru and India's Constituent Assembly rose above partisanship in according this honour to a conservative opponent of India's independence, but one who was an eloquent advocate for India's former untouchables and also one of India's best lawyers. Ironically, the far more successful statesman from the former untouchable caste, Jagjivan Ram (who became India's first labour minister, and went on to serve with distinction as a minister in all India's governments between 1946 and 1979, including as agriculture minister at the start of India's Green Revolution and defence minister during the 1971 India–Pakistan War) has now been forgotten, while Ambedkar (the unrepentant British collaborationist) is eulogized. A special arrangement was worked out to enable India (and later Pakistan) to remain in the Commonwealth without acknowledging the Queen as head of state.

THE RAPID COLLAPSE OF BRITAIN'S PARAMOUNTCY IN WEST ASIA
IN THE ABSENCE OF INDIA'S MILITARY

At the end of British rule, India was the least-developed society on earth as measured by a mix of socio-economic indicators, including literacy and life expectancy. Angus Maddison's authoritative data showed that, in 1950, life expectancy at birth in India was just 32 years, well below the African average of 38 years, the Asian average of 40 years and the Latin American average of 51 years. At that time, life expectancy at birth for the world as a whole was 49 years, for Western Europe 67, for the US 68, Russia 65 and Japan 61 years. Life expectancy at birth epitomizes socio-economic attainment, providing a summary measure of well-being, living standards and access to healthcare. Despite all the chaos and social upheavals of the first half of the century, China's life expectancy at birth in 1950 was 41 years (nine years more than for India); this was probably helped by the fact that about half of China's population had been ruled by the Japanese since 1937, and life expectancy continued to improve there even in conditions of war (while supposedly peaceful British India lagged far behind in social attainment and life expectancy). Life expectancy in the former Japanese colony of Korea was affected by the outbreak of war there in 1950, but by the second half of the 1950s, life expectancy at birth in Korea was 54 years—vastly better than British India.

Maddison estimates that India accounted for nearly a third (32.9 per cent) of world GDP in the year of Christ's birth, with China accounting for 26.2 per cent, Japan 1.2 per cent and the whole of Asia 76.3 per cent. India was still the world's largest economy and the world's dominant trading power a millennium ago, accounting for 28.9 per cent of world GDP in 1000 CE. Unsurprisingly, Indic cultural influences spread right across Asia during that millennium, to the archipelagos of the Philippines and Indonesia, Cambodia, Laos, Malaysia, Thailand, Vietnam (especially in the Champa kingdom) and China (whose scholars travelled regularly to India in search of knowledge, both scientific and spiritual).

And in the west, Old Persian was a linguistic cousin of Sanskrit (albeit with 'S' pronounced as 'H', as it still is in Assam). In the mythology of Old Persia, the evil ones are called 'daiva' (a cognate of the Sanskrit 'deva', for the Vedic gods) while the benign gods are called 'ahura' (which would be pronounced 'asura' in Sanskrit, signifying the evil ones), led by the Zoroastrian supreme god, Ahura Mazda. Some ancient battle must have separated the devas from the asuras, and the latter's followers appear to have settled in Persia (although some small tribes called Asura do still exist in parts of eastern India) while the (winning) deva followers stayed on in India!

Further afield, the original inhabitants of Iraq, the Yazidi (now a persecuted minority in the Sunni and Kurdish-dominated parts of that country) have a tradition that they moved there from India six thousand years ago, and the conical spires above their temples do suggest a Hindu influence, as does their dominant religio-cultural motif of the peacock (which is non-existent in Iraq, but native to India). In 1380 BCE, the Hittites of the Arab peninsula signed a treaty in the name of three Vedic gods with the Mitanni people of northern Iraq and Syria, suggesting Indic civilizational influences were extant there too. From being the world's largest economy and trading power two millennia ago—and retaining those positions with only a marginal decline in share over the next millennium—India has suffered a thousand-year decline in its economic influence and weight in the world. Despite invasions and subjugation by foreign tribes (Arabs, Turks, Uzbeks, Persians) in the period from 1200 to 1750 CE, however, India's share of global economic output declined only slightly (to 24.5 per cent, second to China's 25 per cent in 1700)—and Bengal, in particular, remained one of the wealthiest and most productive regions of the world at the time of the British 'victory' at Plassey (aided by the perfidy of Siraj-ud-Daulah's foreign mercenary commander, Mir Jafar). At the end of 190 years of British rule, that realm of Bengal (including Bihar, Orissa and Bangladesh) was amongst the poorest regions on earth, and the whole of India had a lower life expectancy at birth than any other major region of the world. British rule had been an unmitigated catastrophe for India.

As mentioned earlier, the main purpose of partitioning India, as explained by Britain's foreign secretary Bevin to the Labour Party conference at Margate on 10 June 1947 (just a week after the Partition decision had been announced) was that it 'would help to consolidate Britain in the Middle East.' A first test of this dictum came in Iran, where the Anglo–Iranian Oil Company (AIOC) held almost complete sway over the government of Iran's shah Mohammad Reza Pahlavi (who had been installed as Britain's puppet on the throne after the joint Anglo–Soviet invasion of Iran in 1941 toppled his father, the nationalist modernizer Reza Shah Pahlavi).

In April 1951, a seventy-year-old patrician and Persian patriot called Mohammad Mossadegh was elected prime minister of Iran. A long-standing member of the Majlis (national assembly) from an aristocratic family, Mossadegh was incorruptible and determined to reduce the AIOC's stranglehold over Iran's governance. Briefly finance and foreign minister soon after Reza Khan took control of Iran in 1921, Mossadegh had fallen out with Reza once he found the latter insufficiently committed to either democracy or anti-imperialism. Instead, he was elected to the Majlis in 1924, where he became a trenchant critic of Reza Shah's authoritarian rule (although supportive of his social reforms) and later an implacable foe of the pro-British Mohammad Reza Shah.

Mossadegh's formidable intellect (he was the first Iranian to obtain a PhD in law from a European university, Neuchatel in Switzerland) and unswerving probity made him a singular figure amongst Iran's elite—who loathed him as a traitor to his class. After 1943, Mossadegh focused increasingly on the iniquities that the AIOC had rained upon Iran—paying a paltry share of its under-declared profits, and failing to comply with a 1933 agreement to improve workers' pay and training, and build schools, hospitals, roads and telephone systems.

The consequences of AIOC's perfidy were summarized in a report in 1949 by Manucher Farmanfarmaian, head of Iran's petroleum institute: 'Wages were fifty cents a day. There was no vacation pay, no sick leave, no disability compensation. The workers lived in a shantytown called Kaghazabad, or Paper City, without running water or electricity…. In winter the earth flooded and became a flat, perspiring lake…. Summer was worse…. The dwellings of Kaghazabad, cobbled from rusted oil drums hammered flat, turned into sweltering ovens…. To the management of AIOC in their pressed ecru shirts and air-conditioned offices, the workers were faceless drones…. In the British section of Abadan there were lawns, rose beds, tennis courts, swimming pools and clubs; in Kaghazabad there was nothing—not a tea shop, not a bath, not a single tree.' Inevitably, riots broke out amongst Abadan's thousands of impoverished oil workers in 1946, but AIOC's management rejected the very idea of compromise. The British government (as 51 per cent owner) already took more than half of AIOC's profits, and the company provided fuel to the British Navy at below-market prices. The Shah attempted to pack the Majlis with loyalists by rigging the 1949 election, but Mossadegh staged a sit-in on the royal palace lawns alongside thousands of his supporters—forcing a fair election, which resulted in him and six other members of the newly-constituted National Front being re-elected to the Majlis, where they formed a centrist bloc with a redoubtable anti-imperialist and democratic voice—opposed to both the Shah and the communist Tudeh (Masses) party.

After he was elected to chair the Oil Committee of the Majlis, Mossadegh sought merely to negotiate better terms between the AIOC and Iran's government: instead of paying a meagre 17 per cent of the profit (as determined by the AIOC's own accounting methods) to the government of Iran, Mossadegh sought half of the profit with the precise quantum to be jointly determined, via joint preparation of the AIOC's accounts by AIOC and the Iranian government. In December 1950, ARAMCO had agreed to share 50 per cent of its profits with the Saudi government, so Iran's request was not outrageously unique. The AIOC—and indeed the British government of Attlee, Bevin and Morrison—refused to countenance this, because they believed that the oil of Iran, and the products of the AIOC's Abadan refinery (the world's largest), were not Iranian at all, but were legitimately 'British'. The British obliged the Shah to sack a series of hapless prime ministers who failed to do the AIOC's bidding. Britain's obduracy inflamed the Majlis, where a broadening anti-imperialist coalition began to form around Mossadegh and his secular liberals.

The British government's intransigence stemmed from the fact that the Shah was beholden to the British (who had placed him in power after ousting his father in September 1941), and a large faction of Majlis members was secretly on Britain's payroll. Britain's foreign secretary Herbert Morrison and his intelligence service had arranged for Sayyed Zia Tabatabai (a key British stooge since 1921) to be nominated for the prime ministership on 28 April 1951 during a highly-charged Majlis session at which Mossadegh was expected to lead the opposition's rhetorical assault against the AIOC. But the British-paid deputy who was tasked with nominating Sayyed Zia instead made a speech taunting Mossadegh for his constant carping, and challenged him to 'try being prime minister himself and see how difficult the job was'. Mossadegh paused for effect, and then stunned the hushed chamber by accepting the challenge—saying he was honoured and gratified at the suggestion that he become prime minister and would accept in all humility. The resulting motion to make Mossadegh prime minister was passed by an overwhelming 79–12 margin in the Majlis. As a precondition for taking office, Mossadegh asked the Majlis to pass a bill he had drafted for the nationalization of AIOC: it sought to create a new National Iranian Oil Company (NIOC), set up a parliamentary committee to audit AIOC's books, and send Iranians abroad to learn oil industry skills. The Majlis passed the bill unanimously that very afternoon, as the rising tide of nationalism overwhelmed any deputy's private misgivings.

From the outset, the British government and media denounced Mossadegh, demonizing him as a demagogue and 'communist'. This latter epithet came to be associated indelibly with Mossadegh throughout the Cold War, despite the fact that it was patently untrue. Mossadegh was an arch anti-imperialist, who was just as implacably opposed to the Soviet Union as he was to Britain—the two powers that had jointly invaded Iran a decade earlier. The communist Tudeh party was not even informally aligned with Mossadegh, who was highly suspicious of its strong ties with the Soviet Union. Instead, Mossadegh had an informal alliance with Ayatollah Abolqasem Kashani, the spiritual leader of Iran's majority Shia Muslim community (although the thirty-year-old Ruhollah Khomeini refused to join the secularist Mossadegh's coalition). The BBC and other British media outlets painted a bizarre portrait of Mossadegh as a whimsical man given to feigning illness, breaking down in tears often, and working from his bed; that Churchill too often worked from his bed naturally escaped their notice. Mossadegh had a chance to refute this image when he addressed the United Nations on 16 October 1951, pointing out 'that in 1948, according to accounts of the former Anglo–Iranian Oil Company, its net revenue amounted to 61 million pounds; but from those profits Iran received only 9 million pounds, although 28 million pounds went into the United Kingdom treasury in income tax alone.... If foreign exploiters continue to appropriate practically all of the income, then our people will remain forever in a state of poverty and misery.' Mossadegh's sincerity and transparent probity electrified the chamber, and had a profound influence on American public opinion.

President Truman opposed all British attempts at a military retaliation—although three British Navy frigates had moved into the Persian Gulf. Truman sent a trusted diplomat, Henry Grady (the same man previously sent to India in the 1940s to facilitate the path towards independence without partition) as ambassador to Iran. He was sympathetic to Mossadegh's nationalistic project, although exasperated by his inflexibility on questions regarding Iran's sovereign control over its oil.

Upon nationalization, the British withdrew all their staff and employees, and organized a global boycott of Iranian oil—threatening sanctions against any country that bought Iranian oil. The blockade worked extremely well, especially as Britain and the AIOC increased output from their other oil sources around the Persian Gulf (including the protectorates of Kuwait, Abu Dhabi, Qatar and the puppet monarchy of Iraq). Most portentously for Iran, Winston Churchill regained Britain's prime ministership ten days after Mossadegh's climactic speech at the UN—and belligerence towards Iran was one of the planks on which Churchill rode to his narrow electoral triumph.

Mossadegh appointed one of Iran's leading engineers, Mehdi Bazargan, as the head of the newly renamed NIOC. The Azeri Bazargan was a brilliant engineer, but of thermodynamics, not anything more closely related to oil.

Iranians were only employed as low-paid labourers in AIOC, so very few Iranians had the capability of effectively running the Abadan refinery in the face of global sanctions. Iran's output of crude oil and refined petroleum quickly plummeted, and the absence of royalties from oil began hurting Iran's fragile economy, reducing the strength of Mossadegh's coalition. Ratcheting up the pressure, Mossadegh expelled all British diplomatic personnel from Iran in October 1952, and the British began consultations with the US for an invasion of Iran. The Truman administration had its hands full fighting the Korean War, but did not wish to antagonize their British allies either. The US persuaded the British not to invade, and instead proposed a 50/50 profit sharing agreement (without any Iranian audit of AIOC), but this was rejected by both sides. Once the Republican Eisenhower administration took office in January 1953, the British warnings about Iran's strategic oil reserves and Abadan refinery falling into Soviet or communist hands found a more sympathetic audience in Washington DC. Allen Dulles, the new CIA chief, led the way in persuading a reluctant President Eisenhower to back Britain—especially after Churchill intervened directly with Eisenhower by falsely claiming that Iran was about to fall into Soviet hands.

Kermit Roosevelt, the Harvard-educated grandson of President Theodore Roosevelt, led the CIA's 'Operation Ajax' into Iran in 1953, working closely with Britain's MI6 intelligence service. Using techniques of black propaganda and bribery, Kermit Roosevelt was able to peel away some of Mossadegh's key allies, starting with Ayatollah Kashani. Then the CIA/MI6 operation settled upon General Fazlollah Zahedi to lead a coup against Mossadegh. Zahedi had impeccable nationalist credentials, having been kidnapped by the British during the war years for allegedly plotting a nationalist uprising with German support. Kermit Roosevelt began his plot by getting the Shah to sign a 'firman' dismissing Mossadegh (although this was unconstitutional, since Mossadegh commanded majority support in the Majlis), and distributing this in strategic places around the capital. The first coup of 15 August 1953 nonetheless failed, as Mossadegh got wind of it, and troops loyal to him managed to reach his home just before the Imperial Guard troops that Roosevelt had recruited to lead the coup. The tremulous Shah, following events on the radio at a Caspian Sea resort, quickly fled to Baghdad, and the CIA ordered Kermit Roosevelt to leave Iran immediately. But, as narrated in Stephen Kinzer's scintillating book *All the Shah's Men,* the entrepreneurial grandson of Teddy Roosevelt refused to throw in the towel and coordinated a second coup four days later with Kashani and Zahedi's support. This time, Roosevelt arranged a mob of wrestlers and other 'sportsmen' or toughs to parade through Tehran, and artfully infiltrated them to ensure that they turned against Mossadegh. In the end, the CIA coup culminated in a gun battle outside Mossadegh's home that killed at least 300 soldiers on either side before the troops loyal to Mossadegh finally ran out of ammunition. Zahedi became prime minister, and a grateful Mohammad Reza Shah returned to his royal palace to lead a pro-Western regime. Mossadegh was arrested, subjected to a show trial, sent to a high-security prison for three years, and then spent the rest of his life in house arrest, closely guarded by the Shah's SAVAK secret police. To Iranian patriots in exile, however, Mossadegh will forever remain Persia's Gandhi.

Mehdi Bazargan, the engineer appointed to be the first chief executive of the NIOC, eventually succeeded Mossadegh as the head of his nationalist political party. In 1979, in a distant echo of the original alliance of nationalism and Shiism of 1952, Bazargan was appointed the first prime minister of the Islamic Republic of Iran. He lasted only about half a year in office before resigning in frustration as the Revolution began shedding its secular allies (which had included the Tudeh Party, which the mullahs later purged and crushed with particular brutality).

Ironically, British Petroleum (the new name that the AIOC took on in 1954) never regained full control of Iran's oil. After the CIA's coup, the NIOC remained the formal owner of Iran's oil, but a new holding company called Iranian Oil Participants Limited (IOP) would operate and manage the oil facilities on behalf of the NIOC, with the profits to be shared 50/50 but without Iranians being allowed on to its board or to audit its accounts. British Petroleum owned 40 per cent of IOP, Shell 14 per cent, Gulf Oil, Exxon, Mobil, Chevron and Texaco 8 per cent each, and Total (of France) the remaining 6 per cent. Having leaned on US support during the coup, the British had been quietly obliged to swallow a great deal of pride and ownership.

Mossadegh had had no time to mobilize world opinion against Britain's colonial shenanigans, hampered partly by his dearth of experience in foreign affairs, and partly by the fact that nationalization became an unplanned fait accompli when he assumed office as prime minister. By the time of the Suez crisis of 1956, however, Gamal Abdel Nasser of Egypt had built up a network of supporters in the developing world—primarily Sukarno, Nehru and Tito (of Indonesia, India and Yugoslavia), the prime movers of the new Non-Aligned Movement that was building a new majority in the UN General Assembly around its anti-colonial agenda. Nasser could thus nationalize the Suez Canal while still retaining a considerable hold over global public opinion, and despite the inevitable propaganda barrage of opprobrium unleashed against him by the Anglo–French media. The French asserted that they had built the Suez Canal, while the British had become co-owners soon thereafter, and therefore jointly owned it in perpetuity—implying that, like Mossadegh, Nasser too was engaging in 'expropriation' of British (and French) property. The anti-colonial alliance in the UN General Assembly, however, countered that the entire project of colonialism with all its effects, including the building of the Suez Canal over Egyptian land, was illegitimate.

Unlike in 1952–53, when Britain (and the US' CIA) used covert action against Mossadegh, the Anglo–French–Israeli alliance went a step further against Nasser in November 1956, resorting instead to the overt methods reminiscent of nineteenth-century gunboat diplomacy. Britain's prime minister Anthony Eden badly miscalculated the likely response of global public opinion and its effect especially on Britain's key twentieth-century ally, the USA. When Eden launched the joint Anglo–French–Israeli invasion of Egypt, both the USA and USSR separately brought Security Council resolutions condemning the invasion, and the British and French were obliged to twice use their veto powers to kill each resolution. But the force of global public opinion was represented by the moral power of the UN General Assembly's 65–5 vote condemning the Anglo–French–Israeli invasion (with those three countries voting against the resolution, joined only by Australia and New Zealand).

The British badly misjudged the likely US reaction to Egypt and the Suez crisis. Nasser's Free Officers Movement had overthrown the British-installed King Farouk of Egypt in July 1952 and some asserted that the CIA had aided Nasser in his coup. In reality, Nasser had had contacts with the CIA, but the latter was probably not involved in executing the coup, despite maintaining cordial relations with his group. The coup itself had been triggered partly by anti-British agitation by Egypt's populace following the killing of forty-one Egyptian civilians in January 1952 during protests against the continuing presence of 80,000 British troops in their Suez military base. The US wanted to prise the Arab world away from the iron grip of Anglo–French post-colonial influence, and Egypt was one country where the US and Britain were in friendly competition. John Foster Dulles invited Nasser to join an anti-Soviet alliance in 1953, but Nasser demurred, as Britain (with its presence 'sixty miles away in Suez') was seen as a much bigger threat by Egyptians than the distant Soviet Union, which (unlike Britain) had never invaded Egypt. Thus, when Britain established the Baghdad Pact in 1955—centred on the Hashemite (hence pro-British) kingdom of Iraq, plus Iran (with the pro-British shah restored to power), Pakistan (created specifically in 1947 to be a British military ally) and Turkey—it raised a major red flag for Nasser.

Facing pressure from the US to agree not to use any US-supplied arms against Israel (a condition that was near-impossible for him to fulfil), Nasser agreed an arms deal with Czechoslovakia (a key member of the Soviet bloc) in September 1955, a few months after attending the Bandung Conference where the Non-Aligned Movement was launched. Disputes with the US over the funding of the Aswan High Dam further alienated Nasser, who eventually nationalized the Suez Canal in July 1956. In the British and French press, Nasser was depicted as a new Hitler or Mussolini, so 'appeasement' was quickly discarded as a policy option in dealing with him. In late October that year, Israel invaded Egypt, secretly coordinating its action with Britain and France, which dropped the fig leaf a week later and joined the invasion too. At the UN, US President Eisenhower refused to support Anglo–French actions, instead coordinating his response with Nehru of India. The latter was circumspect at first (since India's trade went through the Suez Canal too), but eventually threw his support fully behind Nasser, criticizing Eden bitterly.

Despite the existence of the Baghdad Pact, Pakistan failed to come out in open support of its British ally. The US coordinated its actions with Saudi Arabia, which was informally aligned with Nasser's Egypt (particularly because of its long-standing antipathy towards the Hashemites of Iraq and Jordan, who Nasser too loathed). At the start of the crisis, the Democratic-controlled US Congress voted down Eisenhower's decision to withdraw US$100 million of aid from Israel, but President Eisenhower soon regained the president's prerogative to make foreign policy, and he chose to side with Arab nationalism over his NATO allies—a decision that had far-reaching implications, eventually leading Nasser's successor Anwar Sadat to switch alliances from a non-aligned (or Soviet-leaning) position to alignment with the US twenty-two years later.

The Saudis imposed an embargo on oil supplies to Britain (France still had ample supplies of oil from Algeria), and the UK was obliged to turn to the IMF for assistance to tide over the crisis, as a run on the pound sterling began, and the UK rapidly lost foreign exchange reserves. Eisenhower refused to support Britain's application for assistance from the IMF, and this meant IMF assistance would not flow to Britain, demonstrating starkly the decline of British financial clout. Eden's Chancellor of the Exchequer, Harold Macmillan (a potential successor to Eden), made it clear that Britain's foreign reserves would be rapidly depleted and he offered few credible pathways out of the economic dilemma. On the night of 6 November 1956, the UK's Prime Minister Anthony Eden ordered a unilateral ceasefire without consulting his French and Israeli allies. While Port Said had just been taken, and his military commanders later asserted that they were just twenty-four hours from reaching (and perhaps taking) the Suez Canal, Eden felt he could not risk Britain's financial stability any further in pursuit of an uncertain military campaign. Britain's role as a major global power was over.

The Suez Crisis of 1956 marked the end of Anglo–French ascendancy in the Arab world: in the absence of British India's army, it was no longer possible for Britain to do to Egypt in 1956 what it had successfully done to Iraq and Iran in 1941—crush nationalism with Indian troops under British command. France's pretensions to being a world power had received a fatal blow when Germany overran and occupied France at the start of the Second World War (repeating more emphatically what Bismarck had done seventy years earlier); French independence was only restored by American military intervention. French imperial pretensions—already dented by Thailand's military defeat of it in 1941—received a final body blow at Dien Bien Phu in 1954, with the last rites administered in Algeria and Tunisia over the next decade. For Britain, Suez was the most decisive turning point. In January 1957, Eden resigned and was succeeded by Macmillan, and the Suez Canal was reopened by April 1957, with UN troops patrolling the violent areas, and British ones withdrawn.

The loss of India, Ceylon and Burma was a severe setback to Britain's financial power and, by making it more difficult to reach Australia and New Zealand, also reduced Britain's global military might. This became evident during the Suez Crisis, following which the baton of Western leadership in West Asia passed quietly from Britain to the US. Two years later, the pro-British Hashemite regime in Iraq was overthrown by General Abd al-Karim Qasim, born of a Sunni Muslim (half-Arab, half-Kurd) father and a Shia (also partly Kurd) mother. He thus literally embodied Iraq's ethno-religious diversity, and was the only Iraqi leader in the twentieth century with any known Shia blood (in a nation where Shias were the majority community).

During the Suez Crisis, the Harrow-educated and impeccably anglicized Faisal II was still on Iraq's throne, with the diminutive Nuri as-Said as prime minister and the truest bulwark of Britain's effective control over Iraq. Faisal and his cousin, King Hussein of Jordan had been schoolmates at Harrow—where the likes of Churchill, Nehru and Amery had previously been schooled. Faisal II (grandson of Faisal I, the founding king of Iraq who had briefly been king of Syria) had been much the more accomplished student at that elite school, but the two had become close friends and made adolescent plans to merge their realms to create a united phalanx against pan-Arab nationalism. As the start of the Lebanese Civil War seemingly threatened Jordan, Hussein requested military support from his cousin in Iraq. Faisal II persuaded a reluctant Nuri as-Said to release sufficient ammunition for a couple of brigades to go to Jordan, to be led by Brigadier Abd al-Karim Qasim and Colonel Abd al-Salam Arif. They set off, ostensibly for Jordan, on 13 July 1958, but instead made for Baghdad, where they arrived early the next morning.

Faisal II had become King of Iraq at the age of four after the death of his nationalist father, King Ghazi, in April 1939. Although Ghazi too had been educated at Harrow, he was an introvert who had not been particularly happy there and had grown up to be an Arab nationalist, and the only anti-British member of his family. The official British story about his death—that Ghazi was driving an open-topped sports car with two young women in the rear when he lost control and hit a lamp post—was widely disbelieved in Iraq.

Ghazi had supported a military coup by nationalist officers, and his death resulted in a revolt during which the British consul in the Mesopotamian city of Mosul was brutally murdered. The bout of anti-British ascendancy ended in 1941, when the nationalist politician Rashid Ali al-Gaylani was ousted following Wavell's British–Indian invasion of Iraq, and Faisal II's uncle Abd al-Ilah (son of Faisal I's elder brother Ali) and Nuri as-Said were restored atop a properly pro-British regime, with the latter as prime minister and Prince Abd al-Ilah as regent to his six-year-old nephew, King Faisal II, who was already attending the English preparatory school that Anthony Eden had previously attended. While Abd al-Ilah lived the life of an English aristocrat transplanted into Arabia—and indulged his penchant for fox hunting and attractive women—resentment towards the regime became ever more vehement. While the Iraqi Petroleum Company (IPC, Gulbenkian's creation, but with his share down to 5 per cent, with the company majority-controlled by the British, and significant minority stakes for the US and France) basked in bountiful revenues from oil, the vast majority of Iraq's people remained dirt poor and illiterate.

Iraq's oil exports had soared to 6.5 million tonnes by 1950, from just 600,000 in 1934. During that period, oil production from West Asia increased ninefold—far ahead of the merely 50 per cent increase in global oil production—highlighting clearly for the British the strategic importance of the region, where Britain controlled most of the oil production (in Iran and Iraq, but also potential future producers in Kuwait, Abu Dhabi, Bahrain and Qatar). The importance of retaining control over this region was precisely the reason cited by the British chiefs of staff in their White Paper of May 1945 advocating the partition of India in order to retain a British foothold in Baluchistan and NWFP, and thereby maintain Britain's stranglehold over the oil in Iran and Arabia.

The British indifference to the socio-economic development of its colony proved its undoing. After thirty-eight years of formal British control (first via the League mandate, then the British-controlled Hashemite regime), just 14 per cent of Iraqis were literate in 1958—the same proportion as in British India at independence eleven years earlier. The contrast between the abject poverty of the mass of Iraq's people, and the opulence of the ruling elite—with some crumbs from their extravagance flowing to a minuscule middle class—was too dramatic to ignore. Iraqis did not ignore it. When Qasim and Arif's tanks approached Baghdad's royal palace, the Qasr al-Rihab, at dawn on 14 July 1958 they were accompanied by a swarm of angry young men. King Faisal II, the crown prince and some of their servants quickly succumbed to a hail of sub-machine gun fire.

The crown prince's dead body was dragged through the streets, shredded to pieces and hanged from a pole in front of the Defence Ministry. Nuri as-Said went into hiding for thirty-six hours, but in attempting an escape wearing a woman's chador, his trousers were spotted by a teenager and he was immediately shot dead. His body too was dragged behind a truck for miles, mutilated beyond recognition. The palace and Nuri's home were plundered by angry crowds and burnt to the ground, bringing a gruesome and ignominious end to British domination of Iraq.

Qasim led a regime that was nationalist—with socialist, communist, Nasserist and Baathist elements all represented. (The Baathists briefly gained power in 1963, lost it after a year, and regained it more durably in 1968, ruling for thirty-five years thereafter—with Saddam Hussein as vice president until 1979, and president for the next twenty-four years.) Qasim withdrew Iraq from the Baghdad Pact, which was then renamed the Central Treaty Organization (or CENTO), with the US effectively taking over its leadership from Britain.

In 1960, when the US U–2 spy plane piloted by Gary Powers was shot down over the Soviet Union, it emerged that he had set off from a secret American base in Peshawar, and the world learnt that British bases in Pakistan had largely been turned over to the US, the new paramount Western power. Britain's strenuous efforts to prise NWFP away from India and attach it instead to Pakistan had finally paid some dividends, albeit not to Britain itself, but to its ally, the US. It was to pay many more dividends to the US after 1979, but at the cost of turning the peaceable land of Khan Abdul Ghaffar Khan's Khudai Khidmatgars into the killing fields of the Taliban and other terrorist groups claiming to be the only credible voice of the Pathans.

Pakistan itself shed dominion status to become an Islamic republic only in 1956, and was to hold its first general election in 1959. But a year ahead of this first test of popular will, it became clear that the election was going to be won comfortably by the left-wing National Awami Party (NAP), headed by the Frontier Gandhi's son and Pashtun-nationalist successor Khan Abdul Wali Khan, Baluch nationalist Ghaus Bux Bizenjo and in East Pakistan by the Bangla nationalists Maulana Bhashani and Sheikh Mujibur Rahman, who headed the allied Awami League. Pakistan's army chief Ayub Khan decided that the democratic experiment had gone too far, declared martial law and put most of the NAP's leading lights in prison—accusing them of being communist sympathizers (although their main crime was that they wanted to normalize ties with India).

In the name of the Cold War, the US made a Faustian bargain with the Pakistan military (that has broadly held to this day): the military retains real power in Pakistan by abrogating democracy, and in exchange the US has a substantial security and intelligence presence in Pakistan. The arrangement persists with a thin veneer of secrecy, but the veil occasionally falls: once in 1960 over the Gary Powers episode, and most dramatically when the operation to kill al-Qaeda leader Osama bin Laden on 2 May 2011 was accomplished by US Navy SEALs deep inside the heart of Pakistan's national security headquarters in Abbottabad.

The inevitable outcome of Britain's loss of strategic paramountcy in the Middle East was its decision in the mid-1960s to begin closing its military bases 'east of Suez', and instead focus on entering the European Economic Community (the European Union's precursor). Amid the last throes of a pro-British Iraq in 1957, it was still not obvious that the remainder of Britain's empire would be dissolved within a decade. In March 1957, Kwame Nkrumah (the elected leader of the British Gold Coast since 1951) declared the independence of Ghana, the first African colony to free itself from European rule, albeit as a dominion, with Queen Elizabeth II still the head of state. On 31 August 1957, amid the dying embers of the Malayan Emergency (the decade-long war pitting the Gurkha and Malayan soldiers of the British Malayan Army against the guerrillas of the Communist Party of Malaya), Malaya was granted its independence, with British companies remaining in firm control of its economy, and the British Navy securely in control of its bases there and in Singapore.

Having relinquished control of Suez (and with it Egypt), and lost its leading role in Iraq and Iran, it soon became infeasible for Britain to maintain its string of military bases across the rim of the Indian Ocean, from Aden to Singapore. In 1968, Britain announced it would be closing all its naval and other military bases east of Suez by 1971, including in Singapore/Malaya and its protectorates of what became the UAE, Kuwait, Bahrain and Qatar.

When Mustafa Kemal Atatürk defeated the British-inspired attempt to divide Anatolia amongst Greece, Italy, France, Armenia and Britain in 1923, it was the first shot across the bow for ending Britain's Asian empire. In January 1922, as Britain faced expulsion from Ireland and Anatolia, Gandhi had his best chance to obtain independence for a united India as a British dominion. He did not grasp the opportunity. The British would have had their empire in some form even today had the Japanese military not exposed Britain's soft underbelly with its six-month blitzkrieg in 1941–42 during which it conquered all European territories east of India. But India itself would not have fallen without Subhas Bose's INA undermining the loyalty of the Indian soldiers, sailors and policemen who enabled Britain to control its empire. And as long as Britain controlled the Indian military, its grasp over its empire was unshakeable. Nelson Mandela, on his first visit to India in 1990, was repeatedly asked how Gandhi had inspired his struggle. He quietly responded, 'Your heroes of those days became our heroes. Netaji

Subhas Chandra Bose was amongst the great persons of the world whom we black students regarded as being as much our leader as yours. Indeed, Netaji united all militant youth of all the colonially oppressed world. We followed with pride his great contributions, as we did that of the Mahatma and Pandit Nehru.' The British have worked hard to obliterate Bose's memory (aided by the Congress party's machine in India), as indeed they have largely succeeded in obliterating the memory of Nana Sahib and blackening his name and that of Sinn Fein (which won the majority of Ireland's parliamentary seats in 1918, but has never held power in Ireland in the subsequent ninety-eight years). History, and future generations, will hopefully shed this collective amnesia, as Mandela reminded us.

THE CONVOLUTED AND GORY PATHS TO A POST-COLONIAL SOUTHEAST ASIA

Burma's capital, Rangoon, had fallen to British, Indian and West African troops on 3 May 1945—a couple of days after Hitler committed suicide in his Berlin bunker. Major General Aung San's defection to the Allied side in late March 1945 with his BIA played a crucial part in hastening the Allied advance down the Sittang Valley to Rangoon, and Aung San was quick to emphasize that his newly established Anti-Fascist People's Freedom League (AFPFL) was going to do all the running in Burma's politics. On 16 May 1945, Aung San marched into British General Slim's headquarters clad in his full Imperial Japanese Army regalia, introduced himself as the War Minister of the Provisional Government of Free Burma, declared that the BIA was now a British ally, expected to be treated as such, and would be taking charge when (not if) Burma became free at the end of the war. Slim was startled, but agreed to integrate the BIA troops into the Allied force, while deferring the political questions to his superiors.

Churchill, with a particular fondness for British rule over Burma (which he considered his father's key political legacy), was especially keen to ensure that the 'notorious Quisling', Aung San, would face justice as a 'war criminal'. Well before the formal Japanese surrender in September, Churchill had Whitehall's mandarins spell out Britain's plans for Burma in a White Paper in June 1945. This did envisage 'eventual' self-governance for Burma (but in some distantly indefinite future, perhaps ten years), with a prominent role (autonomy or secession) for the Karens, Kachins and other British war allies, and all within the British Commonwealth. The first order of business was to be reconstruction (naturally, led by British firms), the restoration of law and order, and only subsequently elections under the 1935 Act (which, of course, limited the electorate to about a sixth of the population, while giving the British governor the right to dismiss the government at his will). Even dominion status was envisaged to be at least five years in the future. Whitehall appeared to be completely oblivious to the situation on the ground, with a mobilized population and several radicalized political groups (including the communists) having developed strong networks of support during the war, with Aung San and his AFPFL clearly in the nationalist vanguard.

Even before the war, Prime Ministers Ba Maw and U Saw had competed in seeking independence from the British, with the former being imprisoned by the British for his exertions. On his way back from a rebuff from Churchill in 1941, U Saw had secretly contacted the Japanese (and been exiled to Uganda when the British got wind of this). Eventually, Ba Maw (having served a year in British jails for sedition) was liberated by the conquering Japanese, and restored to the premiership of a formally independent Burma, heading a cabinet that contained the brightest youth leaders of the country, including Deputy Premier Aung San, Land Minister Than Tun and Foreign Minister U Nu. And despite defecting from the Japanese to the British side on 27 March 1945, Aung San had never resigned from Ba Maw's cabinet, so his self-introduction to General Slim was factually unimpeachable! The people of Burma had tasted the sweet fruit of freedom during the war, with peasants freed of debts to moneylenders who had fled to India, and they were unwilling to countenance Britain's proposed return to the pre-1937 political situation.

After the fierce fighting in the major cities, Burma lay in complete ruins. Rangoon, where the INA (led by Loganathan's residual force of 5,000 troops) had maintained order and delivered the city peacefully to the Allied force, was the relative exception. Mandalay had been completely incinerated for the second time in the war and virtually none of its buildings was left standing, while Meiktila, Prome and Bassein had been similarly obliterated. The country's infrastructure—already largely destroyed by Britain's scorched earth policy in 1942—was smashed to smithereens a second time as the Allies regained the country. The former governor Reginald Dorman-Smith and his key bureaucrats (alongside the anglicized politicians of the pre-War era) had spent the war years in the Indian hill resort of Simla, contemplating Burma's future. They were marginally more realistic than their Whitehall colleagues; Dorman-Smith made it clear that elections would be a top priority and 'Burma would be free', but even he envisaged that in the run-up to the election he would run Burma for at least five years with a 'representative council' primarily reflecting the pre-war alignment of political forces with some space created for Aung San's group.

Aung San counter-offered a council where more than half the members would be from the AFPFL, which most importantly would control the Home Department (i.e., the police). With Whitehall urging that Aung San be shown his place (as one amongst many legitimate political players), Dorman-Smith rejected the AFPFL's scheme and insisted on implementing the White Paper. These tactics had worked in India in 1931 (following the Gandhi–Irwin talks, which were followed by a Round Table Conference in London where Gandhi's Congress was surrounded by hordes of pro-British voices). But in the Burma of 1945–46, the AFPFL was better organized as a nationalist umbrella organization that encompassed Aung San's BIA (led by a phalanx of former ministers in the Japanese-supported war-era cabinet, including the communist leader Than Tun as secretary-general of the AFPFL), the rest of the communist party (including those who had gone into exile in India during the war) and the socialists (led by Nu). Aung San (himself the founding general secretary of the CPB, despite aligning later with Japan and briefly Britain) was the unchallenged nationalist leader. The AFPFL continued to mobilize support across the cities and villages of Burma, organizing them into a People's Volunteer Organization, which became a private army comprising tens of thousands of ex-BIA soldiers with a leftist orientation and strong personal loyalty to Aung San.

In September 1945, Mountbatten had invited Aung San and his key loyalists to his headquarters in the tea-growing highlands of Kandy in Ceylon. They had worked out an agreement to create a small, united national army for Burma comprising 5,000 soldiers from the BIA (led by Aung San's comrades Bo Let Ya and Bo Ne Win) and an equal number from the old British Burma Army, which (apart from just three ethnic Burmese officers) mainly comprised soldiers from the Karen, Kachin and Chin (Mizo) ethnic groups. While half this new Burma Army was also fiercely loyal to Aung San, the latter's People's Volunteer Organization was much more of a menace to British designs, especially since the Indian Army was no longer available for deployment to Burma, and British battalions were being rapidly demobilized. And right from the outset, Aung San was crystal clear and unwavering in his only demand: complete independence.

Beset by problems in India, Palestine and elsewhere in their empire (including the East Indies and Indo-China where British Indian Army troops were still fighting to restore European imperial control), the British bureaucrats in Burma were caught in two or three minds. Some urged early elections, certain in their conviction that Aung San would fail to gain a majority, while others (including Whitehall) urged that arresting Aung San would soon make him irrelevant, while a third group insisted this would be utterly foolhardy and would set off an uncontrollable mutiny. Dorman-Smith, in a provocative move, took Thakin Tun Oke (a former member of the Thirty Comrades who had fallen out with Aung San) into his Executive Council. When the legislative council began meeting in March 1946 (before there had been any election), advocates of the immediate arrest of Aung San got an 'unexpected' opportunity: Thakin Tun Oke accused Aung San, in an open session, of having personally murdered a village chief (an Indian called Abdul Rashid) near Moulmein during the early stages of the Japanese invasion (when Rashid was found to still be in contact with the British and organizing resistance to the Japanese). The astonishing accusation was splashed all over the newspapers in Rangoon and London. (Those reports usually failed to note, however, that Tun Oke himself was facing American accusations of atrocities in the early stages of the war when he had murdered three British soldiers, and had their heads impaled on stakes outside a village with an offensive notice attached.)

Dorman-Smith quickly called a meeting of his chief lieutenants on 27 March 1946, and was given conflicting advice, with the civilian chief secretary saying Aung San had to be arrested if the accusation was true, but the police chief insisting that an arrest would lead to rebellion and rioting. The commander of all British armed forces in Burma supported the police chief, saying that arresting Aung San would lead not just to rebellion but to a mutiny in the Burma Army that he was simply in no position to counter. Word of all this soon reached Aung San and, in typical fashion, he walked into the governor's office the next day, acknowledged that the story was true and took full responsibility for his actions.

The governor told Aung San that he might have to be arrested; but Dorman-Smith waited for instructions from Whitehall before acting. A fortnight later, with British credibility in Burma continuing to erode amid the uncertainty, orders finally arrived for the arrest of Aung San. The police began to prepare to act the following day, while also hastily bracing for the potential start of civil war. Burma hands gloomily contemplated the prospect of a gory and hopeless war far worse than what Indonesia and Vietnam were already enmeshed in. But by the following day, Whitehall changed its mind and rescinded the arrest order, primarily because Attlee's Cabinet colleagues (Cripps and Pethick-Lawrence) counselled from India (where they were already in fraught negotiations with the Congress and Muslim League) that the consequences of arresting Aung San would be impossible to contain. British rule over Burma was effectively over, and Aung San had won the battle of nerves hands down!

Recognizing reality, Governor Dorman-Smith finally recommended that Aung San be brought into the Executive Council. But Attlee's Labour government had finally lost confidence in this Tory grandee and decided to replace him. His successor, Major General Hubert Rance (who had been the director of civil affairs in Burma since the Japanese withdrawal and had worked out a close relationship with Mountbatten), inherited a country in shambles, with food prices soaring (as some of the rice crop had been exported to India to ameliorate the famine), crime rampant in a country awash with guns, and no sign of any reconstruction amid the recriminations of the past year. After the horrendous destruction wrought by the war, Burma's standard of living had regressed to below the level of twenty-five years earlier. The *New York Times* had asserted in early June 1946 that Burma was on the brink of revolution.

After the British House of Commons finally held its first debate on Burma, with Tory MPs demanding that Aung San and his cohorts be arrested in order to regain the confidence of the Burmese people, Attlee made clear that there was no alternative to working with Aung San towards a roadmap for independence. In reality, though, the only official roadmap for Burma was still the June 1945 White Paper which postponed self-rule into the indefinite future, while holding out the prospect of secession by the Karens, Kachins and other hill peoples. By the time Rance took formal charge as governor in September 1946, Burma had been paralysed by a wave of strikes starting with the police, spreading to the rest of the government machinery, and then the railways and oil industry. Nehru took charge as vice-chairman of the Viceroy's Executive Council in India on 2 September. At his first meeting with the AFPFL on 21 September, Rance offered the same role in Burma to Aung San, and within a fortnight a deal was done: the AFPFL would have a prominent role in the Governor's Executive Council ('provisional government'), with Aung San as its vice-chairman (hence de facto prime minister) and minister of defence and foreign affairs, but the minorities and other political persuasions would also be accommodated, including followers of Ba Maw and U Saw.

From that point on, the still only thirty-year-old Aung San combined the roles of agitator (for a swift path to full independence) with that of statesman (particularly in reaching out to the minorities, including key British allies like the Karen). He quickly made Tin Tut—educated at Dulwich and Cambridge, the most accomplished Burmese official of his generation (and the very first Burmese to become a member of the highly exclusive ICS)—his key adviser, and finance minister. During October 1946, the new government offered substantial pay increases to government workers, and then cracked down on further agitation, a decision that was hailed with a big pro-AFPFL rally in Rangoon. Before the latter, however, there was a parting of ways between Aung San and his old communist friend, Than Tun, undoubtedly a personally painful decision given that the two men's wives were sisters. The communists had already split once in January 1946, when Thakin Soe formed the Red Flag Communist Party accusing his former comrades of 'Browderism' (compromising with imperialists, as the US communist leader Browder is said to have done). Now in October 1946, Than Tun's White Flag Communist Party of Burma was expelled from the AFPFL as it continued to oppose participation in the Governor's Executive Council (interim government).

Nehru began communicating directly with Aung San from early October—a signal both were sending of their independence from British control. In particular, Nehru told his Burmese counterpart that the 12,000 Indian troops still in Burma would soon be withdrawn, but only at a time that would not inconvenience Aung San. They also agreed to convene a conference of Asian leaders in March 1947. Having stabilized the social situation (and averted a general strike) in October, Aung San laid out his goals in November: universal suffrage for the election in March 1947 (and without the separate electorates for Europeans, Indians, and other ethnic minorities under the Government of India Act of 1935 that were aimed at keeping the Burmans from a stable majority); an end to the governor's discretionary power over 'imperial' subjects, bringing all such subjects within the Cabinet's purview; and bringing the frontier areas into the remit of the national government and its cabinet. Tin Tut was particularly insistent that constitutional progress should occur at the same pace as for India. Over the next few weeks, preparations were completed for a Burmese delegation (including Aung San and Tin Tut) to travel to London in early 1947 for talks with Attlee. Aung San stopped in New Delhi on the way, where Nehru treated him with great affection and regard, including having a new, more appropriate suit, overcoat and other clothing tailored for him to replace the longyis he had brought along, which would be utterly inadequate in an especially frigid London.

Tin Tut's role was crucial when Aung San arrived in London for the first time, to negotiate the terms of independence with Attlee. After a fortnight, on 27 January 1947, Attlee agreed to recognize the interim government as a dominion, and both sides agreed to an early election to a new constituent assembly, the product of which would be presented to the British Parliament for approval—and all this would be achieved within Aung San's self-imposed deadline for independence of 31 January 1948. Attlee agreed to let the newly elected Burmese Parliament decide whether or not Burma would stay in the Commonwealth, but to sponsor Burma's UN membership regardless of its choice. U Saw, who was part of the Burmese delegation to London, ostentatiously rejected the Attlee-Aung San pact, and became one of its loudest critics (with the implicit backing of British conservatives, including Dorman-Smith). Upon his return from London (where he had thrown a well-attended farewell reception at the posh Dorchester Hotel), Aung San first invited all the 'hill peoples' to talks in February 1947 and an agreement on autonomy within the Union of Burma was reached by all present on the 13th, with the Shan, Kachin and Chin areas negotiating hard to gain autonomy and development assistance. They were all given the right to decide whether they wished to secede after ten years.

Conspicuously missing from these discussions about regional autonomy were the Karen, who were being egged on to hold out by several intransigent British officers led by a long-standing advocate of the minorities called Noel Stevenson. He privately decried Britain's 'betrayal' of the hill peoples, and succeeded in getting the Karen National Union to boycott the talks, despite the fact that Aung San had made special efforts to reach out to the Karens and had good relations with several Karen leaders. U Saw and the Karen National Union remained the key recalcitrants who preferred a closer relationship with Britain—dominion status with guarantees for British companies and a strong defence relationship. Aung San, too, had agreed to a small residual British troop presence, and was attacked sharply by the communists for this. That was more than satisfactory for the Attlee government. Although British grand strategy for Burma had been predicated on supporting the Karen, Kachin, Shan, Anglo–Burmans and Indians as counterweights to the majority Burmans, the Attlee government expressly opposed the creation of a separate Karen state, partly because the Karen were not concentrated in a contiguous area (being in the majority in just one district), and the growing threat from China's contending armies created an additional strategic imperative for a united Burma.

On 7 April 1947, Burma held its general election based on universal suffrage (something that never happened in India prior to Independence). U Saw and the majority of Karens boycotted the election, and despite a low turnout of 49.8 per cent, the AFPFL won a landslide victory with 173 of the 210 seats, the communists winning 7 seats, two Karen groups taking 24, Anglo–Burmans 4 seats and 2 going to independents. After the new Constituent Assembly was inaugurated on 11 June, Aung San convinced Mahn Ba Khaing, leader of the Karen Youth Union, to become minister of industry, while Sao Hsam Htun (a Shan chief) became the minister of hill regions, Abdul Razak (a prominent Muslim leader of the AFPFL) became minister of education and national planning, and Tin Tut continued as finance minister. The cabinet reflected Aung San's earnest effort to conciliate groups that had been outside the nationalist movement and to build a representative cabinet that reflected Burma's unity in ethnic diversity.

Before this unity cabinet could settle down, Governor Rance reported some very disturbing news to London on 16 July 1947: three weeks earlier, 200 Bren guns had been issued to 'unknown' persons on the basis of a forged 'demand note' from the Base Ordnance Depot of the still British-controlled Burma Command. Around the same time, about 25,000 rounds of Sten gun ammunition and 100,000 rounds of small arms ammunition had mysteriously 'gone missing'. This threatened to drastically alter the balance of power in Rangoon, by providing enormous firepower to those who had got hold of this cache of ammunition. Rumours were afoot that British rogue elements were seeking to arm the opposition in order to overthrow the government and replace it with one that would agree to dominion status rather than the complete independence (and departure from the Commonwealth) that Aung San wanted.

On 19 July 1947, Aung San was chairing a meeting of his Executive Council at the main Secretariat building in Rangoon, when three gunmen with Sten guns burst in at a little after 10:30 a.m. and opened indiscriminate fire. Aung San had stood up when he heard the commotion outside, and was the first one to be felled by the hail of gunfire; the founding national hero of Burma died instantly. He was only thirty-one years old.

The gunmen then fired at all the other men in the room, killing four other council members and mortally wounding two others. Tin Tut was seriously injured too, but survived, only to be assassinated the following year. Burma's founding national government had been eliminated within just six weeks of its birth. It was as if George Washington, Jefferson, Adams, Hamilton and Madison had been assassinated in the Spring of 1789 before the new US republic could begin to settle down. Burma had been mortally wounded at birth.

U Nu was the only council member absent from the meeting at the Secretariat, and Rance quickly turned to him to take Aung San's place. Another set of assassins had also gone to Nu's residence but found him away. By that afternoon, the Special Branch had concluded that neither Than Tun's White Flag nor Thakin Soe's Red Flag communists were involved in the assassination. Instead, they raided U Saw's home, and found a Sten gun and eighteen rifles concealed there, and a suspicious Jeep without a number plate parked in his compound. When they drained a lake on U Saw's property, the police discovered thirty-seven Bren guns, fifty-nine spare barrels and eight revolvers. At the home of another key member of U Saw's party, the police found forty-four hand grenades and forty-nine detonators. Evidence emerged that U Saw had paid two British Army officers, and another British officer had reported to his senior that U Saw himself admitted to stealing the arms, but this superior officer simply filed this information away instead of reporting it to the police. U Nu, recognizing that evidence of such widespread British involvement would set off a conflagration (including possibly severe reprisals against Britishers) that could delay the progress towards independence, chose not to reveal most of these facts. U Saw and the actual assassins were convicted and hanged.

British divide and rule had claimed another victim, ensuring that Burma would become the archetype of a failed state. Having honed their techniques over 130 years in India before they conquered Burma in 1886, the British had perfected their methods. In Burma, the government bureaucracy was dominated by Anglo–Burmans and Indians (apart from the top layer of Britishers), the colonial army by Christian Karens, Kachins and Chins, and business was dominated by British, Indian and Chinese companies. The Buddhist Burmans were only able to gain an army (and a modicum of administrative experience) through collaboration with Japan; given their exclusion from business, the ethnic Burman antipathy to private business (and predilection for nationalization) was understandable.

With the war's end, Dorman-Smith (using the Churchill government's White Paper as the template) had set about implementing the divisive strategy. He was thwarted by the dearth of efficacious partners, although he and his cohorts succeeded in keeping the Karens away from the nationalist mainstream represented by Aung San and his AFPFL. When the Labour government removed him from office, Dorman-Smith retained close ties to a network of operatives from the clandestine Force 136 espionage organization of the war years, and a slew of key mid-level officers who had been in exile with him. U Saw's correspondence from prison showed that he had fully expected to be rescued by his many British friends (including three ex-governors and several ex-ministers). During the weeks before the assassination, U Saw had had extensive discussions with John Stewart Bingley of the British Council regarding ways he would protect British business interests in a future Dominion of Burma if he could be allowed to lead a non-socialist government. It turned out that U Saw's business associate, Captain Vivian (who ran a trucking business with him), was involved in the arms theft. He was arrested, but escaped from prison, and fought on the Karen side in Burma's ensuing civil war, until his death in 1951. Captain Moore, the commandant of the Base Ordnance Depot, turned out to be a regular drinking companion of U Saw's, and revealed during interrogation that Saw told him he had enough arms for a private army hidden in his lake. Another British friend of U Saw's, Major Daine, testified that Saw was expecting another five lorry-loads of weapons from a British officer. The evidence of British involvement in modern Burma's founding act of national infanticide was widespread, but hushed up in the interest of relative political stability. U Nu duly took office at the head of a new cabinet in August 1947, the Independence of Burma Bill was endorsed by the House of Commons in November that year, and Burma became fully independent on 4 January 1948. Unlike India, Pakistan and Ceylon, the Union of Burma left the British Commonwealth that day.

During the Commons debate, Winston Churchill (the leader of the opposition) said that the 'White Paper of May 1945' laid out the goal of attaining 'a status equal to that of the Dominions', after 'three years' breathing space for rehabilitation' during which the objective was a 'return to the constitution of 1935'. He excoriated Attlee's government for dealing with Burma from a position of weakness rather than strength (because British troops were 'squandered in Palestine on a policy now abandoned') and viciously attacked the late Aung San for having 'raised what we might call a Quisling army to come in at the tail of the Japanese'. While Churchill acknowledged that he had accepted Aung San's overture to Mountbatten to switch sides during the war, he 'certainly did not expect to see U Aung San, whose hands were dyed with British blood and loyal Burmese blood, marching up the steps of Buckingham Palace as the plenipotentiary of the Burmese Government'. Churchill demonstrated his complete divorce from reality: Dorman-Smith had in fact sought to implement the White Paper for a whole year (May 1945– June 1946) but failed because the 1935-era politicians had no credibility; had Attlee still tried to bamboozle Burma with the 1935 constitution (with its inbuilt mechanisms to keep the ethnic Burmans in a minority in the legislature) in 1946, there would have been a massive nationalist uprising (with Aung San likely aligning fully with the communists). Churchill's speech nonetheless laid out the even worse nightmare Burma would have suffered had he won the 1945 election.

For, even as U Nu was ascending to power, he already faced rebellions by the Stalinist Red Flag communist forces led by Thakin Soe, and a mujahideen insurgency led by Rohingya Muslims in the north of Arakan province bordering East Pakistan. In February 1948, CPB (White Flag) leader Than Tun held a massive rally in the middle of Rangoon, assailed the AFPFL as a stooge of British imperialism and called for a people's revolution. His speech was based on the 'thesis' formulated by the ideologue (and co-founder with Aung San) of the CPB, H. N. Goshal, that this tool of British imperialism needed to be overthrown in order to set up a true 'people's government'. The thesis was adopted by the CPB within a month of the British departure from Burma. Strikes and violence ensued, and U Nu's government made a futile bid to achieve a peaceful compromise, including an offer by Nu to resign. Than Tun and his cohorts based themselves at their stronghold in Pyinmana, and their 20,000-strong army began capturing one town after another in the Irrawaddy Valley. Soon, various battalions of the Burma Army (itself only 15,000 strong) began to mutiny; in June and July, three of its ten battalions mutinied, with most of their officers and men joining the communists. Aung San's orphaned People's Volunteer Organization also joined the rebels in July 1946.

Lieutenant General Smith Dun, the ethnic Karen commander-in-chief of the Burma Army (who had graduated from the Indian Military Academy with the Sword of Honour for best cadet in 1934) then led the mainly Karen and Kachin battalions in a counter-attack, regaining Prome, Pyinmana and Thayetmyo. Helped by his deputy chief, Major General Ne Win, the Burma Army was able to entirely drive out the communists from their headquarters in Pyinmana by December 1948, and 3,000 communists surrendered in Toungoo. Then, the rebellions took another bizarre turn when disaffected Karens from the military police took control of Moulmein. Instigated by two British former members of Force 136 (the wartime Special Forces guerrilla unit)—who were caught smuggling arms to them—the Karen National Union began building up its military wing, the Karen National Defence Organization (KNDO), and preparing to follow the path of little Laos to independence. U Nu's government tried to work out an autonomy deal with the Karen, setting up a credible commission to work out the details and quietly retaking Moulmein. But in December 1948, bloody inter-ethnic killings between ethnic Burmese and Karens poisoned the atmosphere, especially after nearly 200 Karens died in attacks on a church and Baptist school, following KNDO attacks on an armoury in Insein and the port city of Bassein.

On 1 February 1949, General Ne Win replaced the loyal Karen General Smith Dun as head of the armed forces. Soon afterwards, three Karen battalions of the army rebelled and began marching on the capital—hesitating just outside the city because they lacked a leader. But General Ne Win's Fourth Burma Rifles, reinforced by hastily-raised Gurkha and Anglo-Burman militias, pushed the Karen forces back, and steadily gained ground against the other rebel forces over the course of 1949. The Karen rebels (and a Kachin battalion that rebelled in April 1949) often aligned themselves closely with the communists. In the Cold War era, this factor increasingly drew the sympathy of the West, bringing arms supplies and financial aid from Britain (with whom Burma had signed a defence treaty, as Labour MPs had pointed out to Churchill during the Commons debate of November 1947) and its allies, including the US, Australia, India and Ceylon. Although the rebel armies had over 30,000 men under arms (while Ne Win started with a paltry 3,000 loyalists from the Fourth Burma Rifles) General Ne Win emerged as the hero of the hour, marshalling his scant resources superbly to gradually regain control of much of the country by early 1950.

The affable Buddhist socialist U Nu proved the perfect civilian foil to Ne Win's military genius as the two old comrades of Aung San struggled against near-impossible odds to consolidate their fragile new republic. Charming and loveable in his eccentricity, U Nu was slightly out of his depth as prime minister, a job for which his friend and natural leader, Aung San, had always been destined. Nu's personality made him an ideal negotiator and diplomat, but he was uncomfortable with the exercise of power, had a theoretical and literary bent, and was frequently impractical in his ideas. Had better sense (from others) not prevailed, he would have resigned (in favour of Than Tun or other communists) in February and April 1948: in happier, youthful days he had once told Than Tun, 'You'll be the Lenin of Burma and I'll be your Maxim Gorky'! As a devout Buddhist, however, U Nu could not reconcile Marxism with his religious beliefs, and so preferred to be a socialist, as he would not have wanted to shed blood merely for his political beliefs. Yet his charm and natural garrulousness made him an extremely popular politician.

In September 1948, U Nu's government lost its most experienced minister when Tin Tut (the former ICS officer who had served in the Central Secretariat in New Delhi after a stint in the military in Mesopotamia during the Great War) was killed in a grenade attack on his car. After serving as a very effective finance minister to Aung San's government, Tin Tut had become U Nu's foreign minister, and his assassination was yet another blow to his government's effectiveness. Nu turned to his old friend (and fellow school headmaster) from the town of Pantanaw, U Thant, to become his chief of staff and eventually foreign minister. In the former role, U Thant helped organize and systematize his eccentric friend's life and policy implementation.

Despite a semblance of order having been restored to the main cities and towns, Burma remained beset by insurgencies that raged in the countryside and in the frontier hill regions. Most of these were to continue, at varying degrees of intensity, for the next six decades as Burma paid the highest price possible for Britain's six decades of colonial rule and its well-honed tactic of divide and rule. Yet 'there is a persistent myth' that Burma somehow 'emerged from colonial rule in good shape, with a sound economy and all the attributes necessary for future prosperity', to quote the historian Thant Myint-U (grandson of U Thant), who pointed out that, in 1950, Burma 'was in shambles, and war had been replaced, in many parts, by anarchy'. Myint-U is too polite: British grand strategy destroyed Burma's chances.

If the internal challenges from ethnic and ideological strife weren't enough,

PRASENJIT K. BASU

Burma was additionally ravaged by the backwash from China's civil war. After its defeat by Mao's communists, the KMT found its main refuge on the island of Taiwan. But it is less well known that the KMT's other major redoubt was Burma, and particularly the Shan highlands.

When Japan ruled Burma, Japan's Thai allies had been allowed to occupy the Shan States, particularly because the Shan and Thai languages are closely related. Field Marshal Phin Choonhavan, whose parents were both immigrants to Thailand from the Teochew heartland of Chaoshan, became the military governor of the Shan States. Phin Choonhavan used his strong business ties within the Teochew networks that dominate Thailand's business community to build a very successful opium and heroin export business. As documented by the investigative journalist Sterling Seagrave, Marshal Phin also established strong ties with elements of the KMT, particularly the 93rd Division headed by General Lu Wieng. These ties persisted into the 1950s, when elements of the KMT's 93rd Division invaded the Shan hills as part of the 25,000-strong Chinese Eighth Army led by General Li Mi that hurtled across the Sino–Burmese border from Yunnan into Burma's Wa hills at the end of the Chinese civil war.

In Thailand itself, Prime Minister Plaek Phibunsongkhram, the hero of the Franco–Thai War who had been instrumental in creating the Thai–Japanese alliance, had lost the confidence of Parliament in August 1944 as the tide of war seemed to be turning. His long-standing left-wing rival Pridi Phanomyong became regent to the young king, Ananda Mahidol; this was somewhat ironic, because Pridi had led the civilian wing of the Khana Ratsadon that ended Thailand's absolute monarchy in 1932. The new prime minister was Pridi Phanomyong's protégé Khuang Aphaiwong (who was born of royal Khmer lineage in Battambang, where his father was governor before that region was annexed by France). He was succeeded a year later (soon after the Japanese surrender) by Seni Pramoj, the aristocrat whose mother was from the famed Bunnag family (making him the king's cousin). Seni Pramoj had been ambassador to the US in 1941, refused to declare war on that country, and instead led the Seri Thai movement during the war years. His government initiated war crimes investigations into Phibunsongkhram, Phin Choonhavan and other senior leaders of the wartime regime, and discharged the army units that were occupying parts of neighbouring countries (including the Shan States in Burma). Seni Pramoj helped cement a switch in Thailand's military alliance from Japan to the US after the war, but that regime was ousted in a military coup led by Phin Choonhavan in November 1947—which restored Phibunsongkhram to power after a short stint outside. Although Phin Choonhavan never formally became prime minister himself, he was the power behind the throne of almost every military-dominated government over the next two decades and this central role helped him to consolidate and grow his business empire encompassing the Shan States and the northern part of Thailand (around Chiang Mai).

Initially, General Li Mi's KMT Eighth Army established itself at Tachilek, close to the Thai border where these troops from Yunnan (a Chinese province where the Dai people were formerly dominant) would have felt quite at home amongst Shan and Thai people. The Burmese army recaptured Tachilek in July 1950, but the KMT army regrouped, moving inward where they recruited more Shan and other tribals, and ensconced themselves in the town of Mong Hsat. Although the Chinese army's objective was always to regain territory in China proper, they settled increasingly into Mong Hsat, where the KMT built an airport from which regular flights to Taiwan soon began. American trainers and weaponry began to be flown into the region as well. More ominously for Burma, the KMT army spread increasingly westward into the Shan, Karen and Kachin areas as the prospect of regaining territory in China began to recede. Soon there was an implicit alliance between the KMT remnants and Karen and Kachin rebels in the area, and by March 1953, the KMT forces advanced to within a day's march of the Shan capital city Taunggyi, and were in control of nearly a third of the Union of Burma's official territory.

The Burmese government saw this as an extraordinary joint US–KMT incursion into its national territory, and sought UN intervention. At that time, the KMT still held China's seat at the UN, and so two permanent members of the UN Security Council had effectively invaded Burma's territory. After its UN complaint, a small number of troops (about 2,000) were flown out along with a small amount of arms—with General Chennault's planes providing the transportation. But the Burmese Army concluded from this desultory outcome that the military needed to become much more professional, cohesive and effective. Training methods were greatly improved in collaboration with several major military academies (including Sandhurst, West Point, the IMA at Dehradun, and Sainte-Cyr in France), a psychological warfare directorate established, and the control of Ne Win's loyalists over key positions in the military was tightened. More portentously, the military established the Defence Services Institute which gradually became a kind of holding company for the military's business interests, which soon encompassed major shipping lines, banks and department stores. With members of Ne Win's Fourth Burma Rifles holding all the key jobs within the military, and with its tentacles spreading into a wide business network, Ne Win was building an autonomous power base that was making him immune to democratic or political control.

After a decade in power, the unity of the AFPFL began to fray. That decade had been something of a golden one for Burma's middle class, with new jobs as they replaced the British in government and business, and a widening of educational opportunities as the government facilitated quality education at home and paid for overseas study too. U Nu and his team had delivered a moderate amount of prosperity despite being unable to end all the insurgencies. But in 1958, amid a global economic downturn that was causing disenchantment elsewhere too, Nu's long-standing colleagues Kyaw Nyein and Ba Swe brought a motion of no-confidence against him. U Nu survived this, but only with the help of 'above-ground communists' (i.e., those who participated in parliamentary politics rather than insurrection). This led to grave disgruntlement in the army, and several coup attempts were rumoured in the next few weeks, all supposedly thwarted by Ne Win.

In September 1958, however, U Nu announced that he had requested Ne Win to take the reins of a 'caretaker government'. In this first spell of military rule, Ne Win's regime was noted mainly for its efficiency: the cities were cleaned and homes were newly painted, trains ran on time, prices were stable and the economy recovered strongly. Additionally, corrupt officials were exposed and ousted, and the military took vast strides towards ending the insurgencies. In December 1960, Ne Win (as promised) called a new election: despite the efficient administration provided by Ne Win's technocrat-run regime, his allies lost the election to the ever-popular U Nu, who won a landslide victory. The military retained some of its tentacles across government, but U Nu was now back in power with a more democratic agenda: amongst other issues, a key one he wanted to tackle was the nationalities question, in close consultation with the Shan chiefs who were proposing a federal system with greater powers devolved to the ethnically-dominated regions and highlands.

On 2 March 1962, however, Ne Win put an end to the democratic experiment, as the military violently snatched power, and began setting up the autarkic and isolationist 'Burmese Way to Socialism' with which the country came to be indelibly associated. Until this time, Johns Hopkins' School of Advanced International Studies (SAIS) had a Rangoon campus, the Ford and Asia Foundations had flourishing operations, and Rangoon had a busy, cosmopolitan airport; all this was abruptly ended, the foundations and SAIS expelled, even the Automobile Association and Boy Scouts were banned, as every last shred of Western influence was removed from Burmese society.

And to cement his Burmese chauvinism, Ne Win decided to expel Burma's huge Indian community. Until the 1940s, two-thirds of the population of Rangoon had been of Indian descent; even after the forced departures of thousands during the war, and after the riots of 1937–38, the Indian community in Rangoon was just below half the capital's population in 1962. A weakened

Nehru government uttered not a word of protest, as nearly half a million Indians who had lived and worked in Burma for generations, many of them having built that country and known no other, were summarily expelled in 1963–64 to India (a nation where they no longer had any moorings, and where they now became impoverished refugees, adding to the destitute multitudes already created by Partition in cities like Calcutta). Idi Amin of Uganda expelled a huge Indian population eight years later and, since most of them went to the UK rather than India (the land of Third World solidarity) their plight received substantially greater publicity. Ne Win was emboldened to visit this atrocity upon his Indian minority by what Nehru had already agreed with Ceylon.

Soon after India's southern island neighbour became independent in 1948, the Parliament of Ceylon (later called Sri Lanka) passed a bill disenfranchising about half its Indian (mainly Tamil) population—the 'Indian Tamils' who had been brought to Ceylon as indentured labourers during British rule. They had lived in Ceylon for three or four generations, and had lost all roots in India, but Nehru's India accepted the principle that they would be 'repatriated' to India, and settled in the villages and towns of Tamil Nadu. The expulsions of 'Indian' Tamils reduced the proportion of Tamils in Ceylon's population from close to 30 per cent to 18 per cent over the next eighteen years (with the last expulsion-repatriations occurring during the premiership of Lal Bahadur Shastri in 1965). When combined with S. W. R. D. Bandaranaike's decision in 1956 to make Sinhala the national language and Buddhism the national religion, they lit the spark of the Tamil insurgency that was to engulf Sri Lanka in the 1980s—led, this time, by the Jaffna Tamils whose presence on the island of Ceylon/Lanka had predated that of the Sinhala.

◆

After reasserting control over Malaya, in October 1945 the British fabricated a plan to unite all the disparate pre-War units they had controlled—the Federated Malay States (Perak, Negri Sembilan, Selangor, Pahang), the Unfederated Malay States (Johor, Kelantan, Terengganu, Kedah), the Straits Settlements (Singapore, Penang, Malacca), Brunei, Sabah (owned by the British Borneo Company) and the White Raj of Sarawak—into a centralized Malayan Union. Despite British entreaties to join the European exodus to India after the Japanese invasion, the Malay sultans had stayed on to preside over their kingdoms. This reinforced their legitimacy in the eyes of their Malay subjects, but also meant that they were obliged to 'collaborate' with the Japanese in running their kingdoms. The British decided to pounce on this vulnerability, formulating a scheme that would snatch away the sultans' sovereignty (while letting them retain symbolic authority), dissolve their states' past autonomy, and create a single citizenship for all the people of Malaya.

The only concession to Malay sensibilities was that Singapore (with its overwhelming Chinese majority) was kept out of the Union in order to retain a Malay majority (a census in late 1945 having shown that Malays were 51 per cent of non-Singapore Malaya's population, Chinese 38 per cent and Indians 10 per cent). A colonial official, Harold MacMichael, visited each sultan privately, and coerced all nine sultans to sign on the dotted line before the end of 1945. Sarawak's Rajah Vyner Brooke—who, unlike the Malay sultans during the war, had abandoned his kingdom along with all key members of his family—received a settlement of $4 million to sign on.

The Malayan Union was a naked power grab by the British, who were seeking to tighten their grip on Malaya by replacing their erstwhile 'treaties of protection' with the sultans with a directly colonial relationship. The irony was that the British had abjectly failed to fulfil their obligation to protect the sultans or their subjects in 1941–42. Now they were badly misjudging how the hitherto docile Malays had been transformed by their exposure to the radical nationalist rhetoric of Subhas Bose and the Japanese ideology of 'Asia for Asians'. Writing in 1995, Malaysia's then prime minister, Mahathir Mohamad, was clear: '...there is no denying that the Japanese occupation led ultimately to Malaya gaining its independence from British colonial rule.' Mahathir elaborated, 'In the Pacific War the Japanese proved that the West was not invincible. Previously Asians had thought the West could never be beaten, but the Japanese showed us that the West could be defeated. That convinced us that we, too, could do what Japan did—not fight a war, of course, but develop our country. Despite the wartime atrocities, Japan has been a source of inspiration and confidence.'

The hubristic British colonial authorities were oblivious to these changes in national sensibility, and were completely taken aback by the concerted uproar that greeted their announcement of the scheme to create a unitary Malayan Union. On 30 November 1945, even before Britain's constitutional plans (as embodied in the Malayan Union) were fully known, a left-wing Malay Nationalist Party (Partai Kebangsaan Melayu Malaya, PKMM) was formed to articulate the interests of the Malay nation (bangsa Melayu), which it perceived as transcending British colonial boundaries, and certainly independent of the sovereignty of the 'feudal' sultans, who it disdained. Its leader was Ahmad Boestamam, 24, a former journalistic subordinate of Ibrahim Yaacob who had followed him into the KMM, and similarly advocated an 'Indonesia Raya'. Boestamam had been imprisoned before the war by the British. Released by the Japanese, he received officer training in a Japanese militia and learnt propaganda techniques, emerging after the war as Malaya's most charismatic public speaker. Many compared his rhetorical skills to Sukarno (with whom he was loosely aligned), but Boestamam always insisted that his greatest inspiration was Subhas Chandra Bose.

The Malay Nationalist Party was approached early by an Indonesian agent of the communist MPAJA that was seeking to break out of its straitjacket of being dubbed a mainly Chinese force. Boestamam accepted an investment by the Malayan Communist Party (MCP) of $50,000 into his newspaper, *Suara Rakyat* (*The People's Voice*). But his party—and its militant wing, Angkatan Pemuda Insaf (API), which he directly headed—kept the MCP at arm's length, developing a radical nationalism that sought to serve as a big tent for all strands of Malayan nationalism that were committed to full independence. This goal made it immediately suspect in British eyes, especially given the Malay Nationalist Party (PKMM) leadership's past affiliation with the KMM (seen as Japanese 'collaborators'). However, the PKMM accepted the unitary Malayan citizenship (to all residents of Malaya regardless of race), albeit looking beyond Malaya to a Greater Indonesia as being its ultimate goal.

The instinctive racism of the returning British managed to alienate even their most loyal subjects—the middle class. The Straits Chinese and Eurasian middle class were alienated by the fact that (despite having the right to have British passports) they were not eligible for back pay while all Europeans received back pay and benefits for the years of incarceration by the Japanese; after protests, these civil servants were given three and a half months' pay (still far less than the Europeans). In December 1945, a less radical party was formed by a multi-racial group of intellectuals in Singapore that was named the Malayan Democratic Union (MDU). Although advocating that Malaya remain within the British Commonwealth, it was otherwise closely aligned with, or at least sympathetic to, the PKMM. The MDU's leading lights were either Eurasians (Philip Hoalim, John Eber, Gerald de Cruz) or Chinese (Wu Tian Wang, Lim Hong Bee, Lim Kean Chye) but they were steadfast in their commitment to a non-discriminatory and united Malaya that would include Singapore.

The MPAJA and its successor MCP expected that, after their wartime cooperation with the Allies, they would be rewarded with political pre-eminence in post-War Malaya. Unlike Boestamam's PKMM, the communists did not advocate independence and were quite willing to cooperate with the colonial regime's constitutional plans. The MCP also welcomed the Malayan Union's concept of a unitary citizenship for all Malayans but expressed dismay at the exclusion of Singapore—which was the natural capital of Malaya (and where the British Governor General and Supreme Commander of SEAC were based). The exclusion of Singapore was the first British gambit at divide and rule in Malaya, aimed at reducing the political reach of the MPAJA which, during the war years, had been an overwhelmingly Chinese force (despite its 'tiga bintang', or three-star, badge to represent Malaya's three races). Immediately after the Japanese surrender, there had been reprisal killings and attacks by the MPAJA on the mainly Malay police force (which had helped the Japanese maintain order). The MCP's leader, Lai Teck, was himself a Vietnamese–Chinese, and most of its cadres looked on China as the 'mother country' while asserting their right to Malaya as a home. Lai Teck was exposed in 1947 as a triple agent (he had worked for French, British and Japanese intelligence while staying atop the Communist Party of Malaya (CPM)), but his leadership of the party was already erratic.

While sticking to constitutional means, the CPM believed its primary role was to use those constitutional levers to organize the 'proletariat' (dock workers, plantation labourers, factory hands) to mitigate the unequal pre-War economic arrangements. In January 1946, this led to a series of strikes and industrial actions that, the CPM felt, were very much of a piece with the ethos of the Labour Party in Britain. Mountbatten, too, was anxious not to be seen as too draconian in his response, especially since Chin Peng (a close military ally of the British during the war years) was emerging as a key leader of the CPM, and had just been conferred an OBE. But his cadres had been embittered by the nature of the demobilization in 1945—feeling thoroughly betrayed by the British, who failed to acknowledge the sacrifices they had made in the lonely years of guerrilla war on behalf of the Allies. Employers were reluctant to hire the ex-MPAJA 'troublemakers', which only increased their sense of alienation and disgruntlement. The CPM's call for a general strike on 15 February 1946, which they dubbed National Humiliation Day, to commemorate the fourth anniversary of the fall of Malaya to the Japanese, signified the extent to which relations had broken down. Livid at this intended insult, Mountbatten counter-proposed that the commemoration be on 27 February—to memorialize the Sook Ching massacres by the Japanese troops.

When the CPM and its allies went ahead with the commemoration on 15 February anyway, the British police responded with a brutal crackdown: two people were killed in Singapore and several wounded, while twenty-two were killed in police firing at Labis and Mersing in Johore. This was, after all, when Britain was feeling besieged in India as well, with the naval mutiny underway there. British Malaya's colonial authorities began deporting those perceived as troublesome amongst the Chinese and Indians to their 'native' countries, even if their families had been in Malaya for more than three generations. The 'Malayan Spring' of democratic free expression was over merely four months after it had begun. The repressive 'laws of 1941' that were then re-imposed have never been entirely dismantled in the subsequent seven decades.

By this time, the Malays had also been roused into ferment over the government's White Paper laying out the details of the Malayan Union on 22 January 1946. The Malay elite were furious that the Chinese and Indians would have the full benefits of citizenship, arguing that the 'indigenous' Malays were thus in danger of becoming a minority in their own country. Many Chinese (particularly the Peranakan) and Indians had been in Malaya for several generations, while some 'Malays' were relatively recent arrivals from Sumatra, Java, South Sulawesi (Bugis) and elsewhere, and the non-Malays argued that the only truly indigenous people of Malaya were the aboriginal Orang Asli. Such arguments only made the Malays more intransigent, and 200 leading Malays met at a conference on 1 March, at which a new United Malays National Organization (UMNO) was formed. Dato Onn bin Jaafar, the District Officer whose father and grandfather had been chief ministers to the Johor court and who himself was widely admired for his forthright critiques of Johor's governance, became UMNO's first president. Dato Onn had already questioned the right of Sultan Ibrahim of Johor to sign the MacMichael treaties giving up his sovereignty to a foreign power, and UMNO now extended that argument to the other sultans as well, calling into question the legality of the MacMichael treaties and hence the Malayan Union. But its most important slogan was 'Malaya for the Malays, not Malayans' as it honed in on the citizenship issue as its main tool of mobilization.

By the time Edward Gent, the architect of the Malayan Union scheme, arrived to take charge as high commissioner on 31 March 1946, full-scale rebellion had broken out against it on every side, and UMNO organized a complete boycott of his inaugural ceremony the next day. Within a month of his arrival, Gent was ready to abandon the Malayan Union in favour of a new Federation idea, with abridged citizenship rights for the non-Malays. There were three directions in which the British could have turned for a principal local ally at this stage: (a) they could have supported the MDU with its positive vision of a non-sectarian and all-embracing Malaya, albeit at the risk of having to grant independence early and eventually empowering the MDU's ally, Boestamam's anti-feudal Malay Nationalist Party with its aim of a Greater Indonesia (the novelist James Michener reported in 1951 that this was still the most preferred alternative amongst the Malays, with even Dato Onn bin Jaafar supporting it in a conversation with the novelist); (b) they could have embraced their old wartime allies from the MPAJA, which had been disbanded in December 1945 and substituted by the CPM, but at the risk of seeing Malaya turn increasingly communist; or (c) they could embrace the frankly racist notions of UMNO, privileging the 'special position' and rights of Malays over the other races in Malaya, and creating a race-based Malaya.

At Gent's strong urging, the British chose to side with UMNO and its narrow, racist definition of citizenship that privileged Muslim Malays over other Malayans. This conservative Anglo–Malay alliance, the British recognized, was the easiest route to prolonging their empire in Southeast Asia, and conserving British business interests in the region for the long haul. The ninety-six-year-old Frank Swettenham, the wizened creator of British Malaya, warned that if the Malayan Union wasn't abandoned, 'we would have Indonesia'. Attlee dispatched Malcolm MacDonald (son of Ramsay, the first Labour prime minister) as the Governor General of British Southeast Asia, and he concluded within a week of his arrival that Malay protests were in danger of 'being swept into Indonesian anti-European currents.' The MDU and its ally the PKMM were aiming for Indonesian-style 'Merdeka' (independence), and the best way to hold this off was to re-forge an alliance with the sultans and their conservative allies in UMNO. By mid-1946 this alliance had been cemented with Dato Onn bin Jaafar becoming 'mentri besar', or chief minister, of Johor.

The consequence was a definition of citizenship that disenfranchised most of the Chinese and Indians, albeit giving them the right to 'earn' citizenship over time through residency. The British instinct to divide and rule galvanized the Muslim Malays behind a racist definition of nationhood that gave special rights to a single 'race' (defined as Malay Muslims, who were soon dubbed 'bumiputras' or sons of the soil), even if many of them were later arrivals in Malaya than many of the Chinese and Indians who were now deemed foreigners (despite having no other country that they could legitimately call home). Dato Onn's own mother was a Circassian Turk, both parents of Ahmad Boestamam (real name Abdullah Sani bin Raja Kechil, suggesting mini-royal lineage) had moved to Malaya from Minangkabau in Sumatra, the future prime minister Mahathir was a Jawi Peranakan (Straits-born Indian Muslim) whose father was from Kerala, the future deputy prime minister Musa Hitam's parents were migrants from Bugis, and yet they were all deemed bumiputra, while Eurasians whose Portuguese ancestors had settled in Melaka for more than four centuries, or Peranakans and Straits Chinese who had been in Malaya for several centuries, would forever be defined as outsiders to Malaya.

UMNO, the sultans and the British held secret talks to hammer out the terms of the new Federation over the rest of 1946, and this entailed new treaties being signed, which effectively restored Malay sovereignty. But there was a huge uproar from non-UMNO political forces when the Federation's terms were published in early 1947. The PKMM and MDU strongly protested on behalf of the rakyat jelita (common people) of all races, demanding independence (merdeka). But the British deliberately ignored them as being irrelevant. UMNO had appropriated the rhetoric of Malay nationalism while firmly ruling out Merdeka as a goal in the foreseeable future. The CPM was vociferous in its opposition to the new Federation, but it was in some disarray with the early 1947 unmasking of its leader Lai Teck as a triple agent. Chin Peng, his successor, adopted a more militantly anti-colonial stance, but was hampered in attempts to widen his party's support base by its lack of intellectual heft (he himself having left school at fifteen to join the movement).

Despite being ignored by the British, the MDU and PKMM began wide consultations for a 'People's Constitution', and formed the All-Malayan Council for Joint Action (AMCJA) to bring all the streams of radical opinion under a single umbrella organization. The PKMM immediately faced charges of selling out the Malays (since the MDU was seen as non-Malay, and the CPM was providing tacit support to the AMCJA), so Boestamam's PKMM pulled out and formed a separate coalition called PUTERA, to be headed by the bohemian novelist Ishak Haji Muhammad. Tan Cheng Lock, a sixty-three-year-old whose family had been in Penang since 1771 and who spoke Malay fluently but no Chinese dialect, became chairman of AMCJA–PUTERA. British intelligence dismissed the patrician Tan Cheng Lock (who later founded the conservative Malaysian Chinese Association) as a communist dupe. The People's Constitution devised by AMCJA–PUTERA was premised on PUTERA's notion of a Melayu nation (kebangsaan Melayu) to which people of any race could aspire to belong, as long as they were 'willing to change their bangsa to bangsa Melayu' and sever their ties to other nations. Although 'becoming a Malay' (masuk Melayu) traditionally also meant 'entering' Islam, PUTERA decided that Melayu would have a politico-legal connotation but not a religious one, and the deciding vote on the issue was cast by Boestamam. This creative solution opened up citizenship to the vast majority of Malayans, and the People's Constitution eventually offered citizenship to anyone who had lived in Malaya for eight of the preceding ten years.

Mustapha Hussein, who had been deputy leader of KMM (behind Ibrahim Yaacob), and had been imprisoned by the British for a year after their return to Malaya (only being released after hundreds of people signed a petition mentioning Mustapha's acts of kindness during Japanese rule), played a vital role in the AMCJA–PUTERA alliance, and in drafting the People's Constitution. His assertive interventions ensured that the People's Constitution provided for 55 per cent of the national assembly to comprise Malays for the first nine years, Malay to be the national language, and the Malay rulers to be sovereign albeit constitutional monarchs, with legislatures elected by universal suffrage. Malay religion and customs would be controlled by Malays, and a Council of Races would be responsible for checking discriminatory legislation. But the federation would include both Malaya and Singapore.

The British remained adamantly opposed to this well-crafted People's Constitution—because it provided an alternative, workable and multi-racial framework for governance, in which the British (as 'neutral arbiters') were no longer required. The radical nationalists had managed differences with finesse, and shown how the British proposals of early 1946 for a Malayan Union could actually be made to work.

Naturally, the British rejected this People's Constitution, ignoring it precisely because it was so likely to fashion a genuine Melayu nationalism cutting across race. Instead the colonial authorities published their own Federation proposals unaltered, continuing to excoriate the AMCJA–PUTERA proposals as unrealistic, and as evidence of inexperience in dealing with racial and ethnic disputes (although, ironically, that is precisely what the writers of the People's Constitution had grappled with, and successfully ironed out).

The AMCJA–PUTERA retaliated with a technique perfected by Gandhi in India—a hartal (a complete stoppage, going much further than a general strike), which they called for 20 October 1947, the day the British Parliament was to start deliberating on the proposals for a Malayan Federation. With Chinese businesses fully onside (led in Singapore by Lee Kong Chian, the son-in-law of the pre-War stalwart Tan Kah Kee), and the enthusiastic participation of labour unions, farmers and fishermen across Malaya, the hartal was a monumental success—marking the first time that a political strike in Malaya was observed by people of all races. In the run-up to 20 October, the people of Malaya talked of little else and the hartal became a watershed moment in Malaya's political history.

Except that the British colonial authorities ignored its implications, and went on implacably dividing to rule. Tan Cheng Lock came under relentless pressure for having conceded Malay majority rule in the People's Constitution (although the British proposals enabled even stronger Malay control), and the pro-British press went to town with the alleged communist links of various AMCJA leaders (and the CPM's participation within it). The British succeeded in splitting the Chinese Chambers of Commerce away from the opposition alliance by the end of 1947 and the KMT was presented as an alternative source of loyalty for Chinese businesses. Malayan solidarity was anathema to the British, so loyalty to China's KMT was preferable!

The promising autumn of multi-racial nationalism was soon buried by the restoration of the pre-War Anglo–Malay alliance of elites. On 21 January 1948, it was codified in a new treaty signed between the British and the nine Malay rulers. By the time this formally came into force on 1 February 1948, the British had introduced a draconian new ordinance outlawing most forms of assembly and protest, and allowing 'shooting to kill'. Ahmad Boestamam and most of the leadership of AMCJA–PUTERA were jailed, and the key leaders spent the next seven years imprisoned while the British worked towards arranging political outcomes that suited the interests of British business.

And relentless British pressure, supplemented by pressure from their Chinese towkay peers, successfully peeled Tan Cheng Lock and Lee Kong Chian away from the opposition alliance, ostensibly, for the former, to prevent a major breach between Malays and Chinese. Meanwhile, the illiberal British ordinance brought forth a deluge of industrial action spearheaded by the MCP in the first few months of 1948, with sawmills and rubber factories being burnt, and strike action taken by dock workers, amongst the still relatively thin ranks of Malaya's 'proletariat'. When three British planters were murdered in Perak, the British declared a state of emergency, suspended all civil rights, and formally outlawed their erstwhile wartime allies, the MCP. Inevitably, the old MPAJA morphed into the Malayan Peoples' Anti-British Army before eventually settling on the rather ethnically-optimistic title of Malayan Races' Liberation Army (MRLA).

The twelve-year Malayan Emergency (1948–60) was colonial war by another name, but it made Malaya and Singapore safe for British (and other multinational) businesses. The British deliberately did not call it 'war', as that would cause businesses to lose their insurance cover. One key side effect of that nomenclature was that there was less 'collateral damage' to civilians in the cities—in distinct contrast to Vietnam and Indonesia. The armed forces were careful to aim their fire primarily at the MRLA in their hideouts in Malaya's thick rainforests, where they were largely 'invisible', despite maintaining the full panoply of military facilities including field hospitals, barracks, stores, etc. The MRLA did have considerable support in the countryside, particularly amongst the illegal squatters who had occupied land during and immediately after the war years (and Japanese rule). The British attacked these areas, often destroying entire villages with all their homes and personal possessions; the inhabitants were initially deported to China (and, where appropriate, to India), but soon Mao's regime refused to receive them, and the British then were obliged to resettle them into new communities (which were like concentration camps to begin with, but gradually acquired amenities and became little towns and villages). A total of 750,000 Chinese Malayans were resettled in this way in one of the world's largest attempts at population control.

Throughout the Emergency, the MRLA never had more than 8,000 men under arms at any one time, and over the twelve years, a total of about 7,000 MRLA guerrillas were killed. It was a relatively small, isolated but passionate group committed to a multi-racial and communist Malaya, but hobbled from the start by the fact that it was dominated not by Malays but by Chinese. Ranged against them were 350,000 regular army, navy and air force personnel, police and auxiliaries, as well as special force units. One participant reported that 'one could go a whole year in the jungle without seeing anybody at all'! Like the INA forces on either side of the Burma–India border, more MRLA guerrillas probably died of malaria and starvation than by British firing. And most importantly, the MRLA had no rearguard to fall back on (like the Vietminh had in China and Laos); although they had allies in southern Thailand, the Thai government was harrying communists there as well, so there was no real sanctuary available to them in that country.

Meanwhile, the British shepherded their preferred political allies towards nationhood in a conservative, pro-business policy framework. Dato Onn bin Jaafar, already the chief minister of Johor, began serving as the Malayan member (or understudy to the British minister) for Home Affairs in the federal government. This was despite the fact that Onn had been ousted from his position as leader of UMNO in 1951. Having founded the party to oppose the multi-racial Malayan Union in 1946, Onn bin Jaafar had an epiphany of sorts five years later, and began advocating the idea of opening UMNO membership to all races, by changing its name to the United *Malayan* National Organization. Replacing 'Malays' with 'Malayan' (to denote Malay, Chinese and Indian inhabitants of Malaya) in UMNO was a bridge too far for its membership and, when he threatened to resign at his proposals being challenged, UMNO chose to accept his resignation. Onn bin Jaafar then formed his Negara party to pursue the same multi-ethnic objective, but his party suffered a crushing defeat in the 1952 municipal polls, demonstrating that UMNO's pro-Malay platform (denying full citizenship to Chinese and Indians) was popular amongst Malays.

The affable aristocrat, Tunku Abdul Rahman (half-brother of the sultan of Kedah) had succeeded Onn bin Jaafar as the leader of UMNO. Eccentric but endearing, the Tunku's personality had much in common with Burma's U Nu, but with an additional predilection for the good life (horse racing, for instance). And he proved to be an instinctively effective politician, able to feel and respond to the pulse of Malay opinion. He pulled the first rabbit out of his hat at the 1955 elections, where he worked out an Alliance with the new conservative Chinese party established by Tan Cheng Lock, the Malayan Chinese Association (MCA), to ensure they did not contest against each other. A year before the election, the Alliance was widened to include the Malayan Indian Congress (MIC), which had previously been aligned with Onn's Negara Party; originally formed in 1946 by John Thivy, a former cabinet minister in Subhas Bose's Provisional Government of Free India, the MIC had initially focused on the fight for India's independence, turning to the socio-cultural rights of Malaya's Indians (and especially its Tamil plantation workers) under the leadership of V. T. Sambanthan Thevar, who eventually brought it into the Alliance as a fellow-conservative party (quite different from its initial radical character, the only legacy of which is that the MIC headquarters in Kuala Lumpur is still called Netaji Hall).

Like India in 1935 or Hong Kong in 1995, the British proposed a legislature for Malaya in 1955 where less than half the seats would be chosen through elections. The Tunku negotiated to ensure that a clear majority (52 out of 98) would be directly elected by the people and the Alliance promptly won 51 of the 52 elected seats in the 1955 election, and was thus able to form a stable federal government headed by the Tunku as Malaya's chief minister, who then began trilateral negotiations towards independence with the British and the sultans. The Malay sultans were offered a unique rotating national kingship that would alternate amongst the nine states in turn, with each king (Agong) ruling for five years within a constitutional monarchy, while retaining customary rights over religion and land (some of which were devolved to the elected state legislature). It was a profoundly conservative political framework, with British business interests strongly protected alongside Malay customary and religious rights and privileges.

After a decade of conflict—and eight years of the proxy war of the Emergency—the MRLA also began peace negotiations in 1956, easing British apprehensions about Malaya's independence, which was granted on 31 August 1957. Tunku Abdul Rahman, however, refused to allow the MCP back into the political mainstream, so the peace talks soon collapsed, but by then the MRLA had lost momentum. Even with independence, a considerable British troop presence would remain in Malaya, and a degree of administrative continuity was also provided by the continuing presence of British civil servants at the higher echelons of administration.

Singapore was excluded from the Federation of Malaya, but the election there in 1955 had also resulted in a couple of unexpected outcomes. The two conservative parties—the Progressive Party (favoured by the British commercial establishment) and the Democratic Party (linked to Chinese Chambers of Commerce)—were expected to dominate the election to a legislature that still had a large number of members (7 out of 32) nominated by the British, and would be elected only by 'British subjects' in Singapore (less than a fifth of the total population: the actual number of votes cast was 156,089 out of a total population at the time of 1.305 million). Instead, the Labour Front led by David Saul Marshall (termed a 'Eurasian' in colonial Singapore's system of racial categorization, but whose ancestors were Baghdadi Jews who migrated to Singapore from India) won 13 of the 25 elected seats. And the People's Action Party (PAP) led by Harry Lee Kuan Yew (formerly an election agent of the Progressive Party at the 1951 election, when he worked for his law firm colleague John Laycock) won 3 of the 4 seats it contested (plus another won by Ahmad Ibrahim, a PAP-supported independent in Sembawang), emerging as a clear, strong voice to the left of Marshall's Labour Front. Singapore, with its large British naval base in Sembawang and role as the largest sea- and air-hub in Southeast Asia, had been seen as the final bastion of the British empire in the east, especially with Hong Kong increasingly under the shadow of Mao's Communist China. Suddenly, Singapore's independence was in play, with Marshall leading the charge and Lee snapping at his heels.

Singapore's new chief minister, David Marshall, was strongly anti-communist—his views being largely consonant with those of the British Labour Party—while Lee Kuan Yew was merely a 'non-communist' who was officially ambivalent between colonialism and communism. Both leading Singapore barristers by this time, Lee was willing to represent all radicals (without checking whether or not they were communists) while Marshall refused a brief once he had concluded that a potential client was a communist. In mid-1954, when some University of Malaya students were accused of sedition for articles they had published in an underground newspaper called *Fajar*, Marshall initially agreed to represent them, but afterwards changed his mind, sending them a caustic letter saying they were communists and had misled him about their true beliefs. Lee Kuan Yew not only agreed to represent the students, but also arranged for a radical Queen's Counsel called D. N. Pritt (with whom he had become acquainted during his time as a law student in London and Cambridge) to argue for the students in court, which he did with aplomb, obtaining their acquittal.

But in the longer term, the biggest difference between Marshall and Lee Kuan Yew proved to be their relative ability to reach out to the most vital constituency in Singapore's broader electorate—'the world of the Chinese-educated', as LKY put it pithily. Marshall simply had no entrée into this vital community, while LKY made a determined bid to bring it into his fold, effectively working out his own 'united front' strategy to trump the communists' version of it (that aimed to make him the dupe to be trumped). Colonial Singapore provided English and Malay instruction in primary schools, and English-only instruction in the secondary schools. The majority Chinese and the smaller Indian community were left to fend for themselves. The Chinese-language schools were thus funded privately by wealthy Chinese and by clan associations (promoting their respective dialects and also Mandarin). These were the bastions of KMT support in Singapore, and by the early 1950s had transferred their loyalty wholesale to Mao and the MCP. Soon after the *Fajar* case, a group of middle-school students from the Chinese schools approached LKY to defend them in a case of subversion; although both he and Pritt recognized that the students' case was weak, they took on the case and earned the students' gratitude.

Of the five PAP candidates (including the independent) who ran in the 1955 election, two were communists: Lim Chin Siong and Devan Nair. The latter lost, to the relief of LKY (as expressed decades later in his autobiography). Lim Chin Siong was not comfortable in English, which would limit his ability to debate effectively in the Assembly, and he was thus going to be easier to control than if both communist candidates had entered the legislature. Although the British often suspected LKY of being a crypto-communist, the correct designation for him was non-communist: the colonial Special Branch began keeping an eye on him in London and Cambridge, and he received a frosty reception from the police when he arrived back in Singapore from Cambridge. Although LKY was, like countless other students from the 'third world' and the Commonwealth, attracted to the ideas of Harold Laski, it was to the Fabian end of the latter's ideas (of evolutionary socialism) rather than to his Marxist ones that LKY adhered. The Special Branch soon worked out a modus vivendi with him, recognizing that he opposed the CPM. LKY was willing to 'ride the tiger' of communism but determined to tame that tiger and live to tell the tale. Thus LKY fully engaged with and eventually led a number of industrial actions in 1954–55 by postal, dockyard, bus and other workers' groups, and Lim Chin Siong joined his circle via one of these. But when the PAP held its inaugural party conference in November 1954, Tunku Abdul Rahman (representing UMNO) and Tan Cheng Lock (representing MCA) attended and spoke—in a clear sign that the PAP was recognized as led by a non-communist team.

Marshall led the charge in negotiating Singapore's path to independence and the British wisely chose to play along with him, trying to shield him from the opprobrium of having to take the blame for extending the Emergency regulations to deal with the spate of industrial actions that continued well into 1956. The most serious of these occurred within weeks of the 1955 assembly election—the Hock Lee Bus Company riots of May 1955, after a strike led by the PAP's communist leaders Lim Chin Siong and Fong Swee Suan. LKY recognized afterwards that the Communist United Front (CUF) tactics entailed provoking confrontations with the authorities that would demonstrate a breakdown of order and make a communist takeover seem the only option, with little scope for compromise. Marshall's vacillating responses to the strikes (of which 260 occurred over a twelve-month period) sent weak signals that appeared to encourage the strikers, further aggravating the situation. After just a year in office, Marshall led an all-party delegation for negotiations with the British. The PAP was represented by Lee Kuan Yew and Lim Chin Siong at these London talks, and the two took radically different positions. The communists were determined to have 'full sovereignty' and nothing short of it, and Marshall unwittingly raised the stakes by promising just that before his departure for London, while LKY said at his departure press conference that '75 per cent self-government' was all that could be achieved at these talks, and the PAP's aim remained 'full self-government in five years'.

The talks broke down, with the British insisting on keeping control over internal security (in light of the continuing industrial unrest), apart from foreign affairs and defence. LKY and Lim Chin Siong shared a flat and a car during their London sojourn, and the latter depended on LKY to teach him the niceties of English etiquette. But they took differing positions on the talks, and spent their free time with different groups of people: LKY primarily with his friend and political ally Goh Keng Swee (then working towards a PhD at the London School of Economics), who would become a key PAP minister and had gathered around him several brilliant Singaporean students, including Joe (J. Y.) Pillay, who would become Singapore's finest technocrat, as the founding and long-lasting chairman of Singapore Airlines, and running both the Monetary Authority and Government Investment Corporation after the mid-1980s financial crisis. Lim Chin Siong evidently spent time with John Eber (one of the founders of the MDU, who by this time was a communist) and other communist ideologues. Ironically, only Marshall and Lim Chin Siong were left supporting the demand of 'immediate merdeka' as the conference wound down, with LKY and all other participants broadly agreeing that defence, internal security and foreign affairs must still be in British hands in order to fend off the risk of a communist takeover of the key naval and military base of Singapore, which was still crucial to the defence of Australia and New Zealand. By raising the stakes, Marshall was obliged to resign when his call for immediate independence was rejected, which he did formally by June 1956.

With the full cooperation of Lim Yew Hock, Marshall's former labour and welfare minister, who succeeded him as chief minister, the British initiated a crackdown on the Chinese schools and other supporters and sympathizers of the communists. These turned out to be an eclectic mix, from the Singapore

Women's Federation to the Chinese Brass Gong Musical Society plus a multiplicity of the standard unions, including unions of various types of workers' groups, students and teachers (especially in the Chinese middle schools). Although LKY dismisses him as a 'promoted stenographer', Lim Yew Hock was in fact a product of the Raffles Institution (Singapore's top high school) and had distinguished himself as a trade unionist (much like LKY himself, albeit taking less radical positions) while indeed working primarily as a clerk and stenographer. The PAP publicly decried the use of Emergency regulations, and other curbs on civil rights, to detain communist suspects—but while LKY often made such public statements, he did nothing else to oppose the arrests of several PAP 'communists' such as Lim Chin Siong, Devan Nair and James Puthucheary. The last had traversed an interesting path: an INA war hero, he was part of Gulzara Singh's Azad Brigade which had fought gallantly at Palel and along the Tamu–Moreh–Palel–Imphal road in April–May 1944. After the war, James Puthucheary had taken refuge for several months at the Bose family residence in Calcutta when the Malayan police was seeking him in 1946–47. He then became one of the founders of the MDU, and gradually began urging Indians (and Chinese) to dissociate themselves from their ancestral homelands (unless they chose to migrate back there) and instead give their full loyalty to Malaya during the heyday of the People's Constitution. Enrolling in the University of Malaya, Puthucheary was effectively the leader of the eight *Fajar* students.

The label 'communist' was a convenient one for the colonial Special Branch to use to suppress its most implacable opponents, and LKY uncritically adopted the same label. However, like Sukarno and Ho Chi Minh, many of these anti-colonial activists were open to a wide variety of nationalist ideas and were not necessarily dyed-in-the-wool members of the communist party. Puthucheary's background as an INA war veteran suggests a deep-seated anti-colonialism, which shaded into socialism and further left without necessarily being communist. Graduating with honours in economics from the University of Malaya, James Puthucheary spent this period of detention after 1956 writing a book called *Ownership and Control in the Malayan Economy*, which argued persuasively that the 'idea that Chinese capitalists dominate the economy of Malaya is an optical illusion', because the economy was actually in the thrall of the European 'managing agencies' which operated through a system of colonial exploitation of labour (known then as 'indentured labour', a system that has never been completely dismantled in the former British colonies of Malaya, Singapore, Qatar, UAE, Kuwait, etc.). Puthucheary argued that the correct antidote to Malaya's socio-economic challenges was not to attempt to artificially create a class of Malay capitalists to match the Chinese capitalists, but for widespread state intervention to redress those anomalies. Arguably, today's Petronas (Malaysia's national oil company) and Khazanah Nasional (the reform-oriented holding company for government-owned corporations) are manifestations of the economic vision laid out by James Puthucheary and, ironically, so are Singapore Airlines, and Temasek-owned companies such as DBS, Keppel and ST Group.

Meanwhile, LKY was still in control of the PAP—with seven of the twelve members of the central executive team being his non-communist allies—but Lim Chin Joo (brother of Lim Chin Siong) was now leading a 'second team' of CUF activists who had evidently been instructed by the CPM to try and capture the leadership of the PAP. Lim Yew Hock, widely seen as a British stooge, had proved ineffective in reaching out to the Chinese-educated mainstream of Singapore society, which was still largely pro-communist. Marshall, marginalized since his resignation as chief minister, began to flirt with the communists, regularly taking positions to the left of LKY, and floated the new Workers' Party as a vehicle for his emerging leftist viewpoints.

Lim Chin Joo egged Marshall on, hoping that a raging confrontation between the two stalwarts would diminish both LKY and Marshall and give the communists an opportunity to consolidate their strong base with the Chinese-educated mass of Singaporeans. In 1957, the ordinance that had extended citizenship rights to more than 200,000 individuals who had lived in Singapore for eight of the previous ten years further widened the potential support base of the pro-communists. But Marshall went too far—challenging LKY to contest a by-election against him from LKY's constituency (Tanjong Pagar), which the latter immediately accepted. The challenge was tenable only if Lim Chin Joo threw his support behind Marshall, but the pro-communists lost their nerve, realizing that it was better to have LKY still standing at the head of the PAP, rather than defeated (which would have obliged Lim Chin Joo to formally become PAP leader, quickly removing the 'mask' of non-communism from the PAP and exposing the whole party to a possible colonial ban).

In the end, with Lim Chin Joo's support for him ebbing, Marshall dropped his direct challenge to fight LKY in his constituency and failed to contest Marshall's own seat of Cairnhill in the May 1957 by-elections. Not only did the PAP win LKY's seat, but Lim Yew Hock's Labour Front failed to win Cairnhill either. From then on, there was little doubt that the popular momentum was with LKY and the PAP, albeit with a potent challenge waiting in the prison wings in the form of Lim Chin Siong and his comrades (who LKY was committed to releasing once in power).

The December 1957 election to a revamped City Council clearly demonstrated the PAP's electoral advances. The PAP decided to fight that election via an electoral pact with Lim Yew Hock's Labour Front and UMNO (which still had a strong following amongst Singapore's Malays), with the three parties agreeing not to put up candidates against each other. The PAP won thirteen of the fourteen seats it contested, Lim Yew Hock's Labour Front just four of the sixteen allotted to it, and UMNO won both the seats it contested in Malay-majority areas. The PAP was thus able to have its candidate for mayor elected (in a coalition with UMNO that gave it fifteen of the thirty-two seats in the council). Ong Eng Guan, the Hokkien-speaking PAP man who became mayor, proved to be a populist who was good at rousing a crowd (in the majority dialect of Singapore's Chinese, taking up the mantle of Lim Chin Siong well on this score) but rather ineffective at governance. LKY did not move against him immediately, as he was electorally useful (although the two parted company politically by 1960).

Just prior to this (in August 1957), the pro-communist bloc within the PAP (led by Lim Chin Joo) made an audacious attempt to take over the party's central executive committee. LKY got wind of the plan, which also entailed taking charge of Lim Yew Hock's power base in the Singapore Trade Union Congress (STUC), and merging it with the pro-communist Singapore General Employees' Union (SGEU). Lee Kuan Yew's non-communist group passed party resolutions that committed the PAP to 'an independent, democratic, non-communist, socialist Malaya' but LKY refused to remain PAP secretary general (and Toh Chin Chye the party's chairman) after the party voted to give the pro-communists the same number of executive committee seats (six) as the non-communists. Within a fortnight of the PAP convention, Chief Minister Lim Yew Hock moved against the pro-communist group, arresting Lim Chin Joo and thirty-four other key pro-communists within the PAP. The pro-communists were on the verge of merging the STUC with the SGEU to create a broad front of PAP–Labour Front–Worker's Party (possibly with Marshall as figurehead). The pre-emptive arrests looked like a move by Lim Yew Hock to support the non-communists in the PAP, but LKY was quick to emphasize in an Assembly speech that Lim had acted primarily to defend his own turf—the threat to his political base in the STUC.

In 1958, the MCP's key underground leader in Singapore, 'the Plen' (as LKY and Goh Keng Swee called him until discovering his identity to be Fang Chuan Pi), requested a clandestine rendezvous with Lee Kuan Yew at which they agreed that the MCP would not attempt to dislodge LKY's group from the PAP leadership, on the assurance that Lim Chin Siong and his key comrades would be released if/when the PAP came to power. LKY and the Plen communicated via actions that signalled each side's commitment to its own undertakings to the other side. Having discovered the Plen's identity, LKY was startled to realize that the Plen's twenty-five-year-old sister was one of the PAP's newest assembly members. The PAP was still engaged in a very precarious balancing act. In May 1958, LKY accompanied Chief Minister Lim Yew Hock as part of another all-party delegation to London. By then, British officials were paying increasing attention to LKY, although many were still wary of him. With the pro-communists excluded, it was easier to achieve agreement over '75 per cent self-government', with foreign affairs and defence still in British hands, and an internal security council with a British chair, but comprising three Britishers, three Singaporeans and a representative from the Federation of Malaya (with effectively a pro-British casting vote).

A year later (May 1959), at Singapore's first general election based on universal suffrage as a self-governing territory, the PAP won a decisive mandate—winning more than 53 per cent of the total vote, and 43 of the 51 seats in the legislative assembly, enabling Lee Kuan Yew to become Singapore's first prime minister at the age of just thirty-five. In keeping with his promise to the Plen, LKY was committed to releasing the pro-communist PAP leaders as soon as the party took power. Lee Kuan Yew was determined to release them the day before the PAP took office and, in preparing for that day, he had worked on the five key leaders (Lim Chin Siong, Devan Nair, James Puthucheary, Sidney Woodhull and Fong Swee Suan) at Changi Prison for nearly a year. His aim was for them to conform fully to the PAP's goal of 'an independent, democratic, non-communist Malaya' which implicitly meant a strong commitment to Singapore's merger with Malaya. Devan Nair was the first to come on board, and he helped LKY convince the rest of his comrades, who signed a public pledge on 4 June 1959 of their commitment to create a non-communist Malaya. The next day LKY and his new PAP ministry took office, with Lim Chin Siong as a parliamentary secretary and Puthucheary leading the Industrial Promotion Board.

Lee Kuan Yew and the PAP were particularly keen to merge with Malaya as the surest guarantee against communist insurrection. Subversion was easier within Singapore (with its large Chinese-educated community, including Chinese businessmen who idolized Mao's China) than within Malaya, where the twelve-year-long Emergency had largely suppressed the MCP by then. But Tunku Abdul Rahman was still very wary of LKY and the PAP, who he viewed as crypto-communists. He had made his preferences clear by making Lim Yew Hock a 'Tun' (an exclusive title that can only be held by thirty-five Malayans at any one time). For the next two years, the Tunku's attitude towards LKY remained frosty, as the former remained wary of altering Malaya's demographic balance by bringing Singapore's 1.3 million Chinese into the Federation, thereby reducing the Malay proportion of the population to just below 50 per cent. The conservative aristocrat with a laid-back attitude also found the hard-charging socialist disagreeable: that they had obtained law degrees at Cambridge around the same time, the Tunku barely obtaining a pass degree, while LKY took a double first, hardly helped. But on the merger question, a breakthrough on the demographic impasse occurred in May 1961 when Tunku Abdul Rahman proposed the inclusion of the British territories on Borneo (Sabah, Sarawak and Brunei) along with Singapore to create a united states of Malay*sia*, in which Malays would still retain a comfortable majority.

The Tunku warmed further to LKY after the latter narrowly survived an attempt by the pro-communist faction led by Lim Chin Siong (minus Devan Nair who stayed loyal to LKY) to oust the government in July 1961 via a no-confidence motion. After hectic last-minute parleys and manoeuvres by both sides, the PAP government won 26 of the 51 votes in the legislative assembly, and thirteen pro-communist legislators walked out of the PAP the following month to form an alternative party, the Barisan Sosialis (Socialist Front). Two days before the confidence vote, Lord Selkirk (the British commissioner general for Southeast Asia) hosted Lim Chin Siong and his three closest comrades to an 'Eden Hall tea party' (as LKY sardonically called it in the Assembly). It was a final attempt at divide and rule which, admittedly, the British had done much less of in Singapore and Malaya than their other colonies. If the tea party was supposed to be secret, it was a curious attempt to signal to the pro-communists that they would be acceptable as an alternative; if information was supposed to have leaked out to the public, it was a signal to the legislators that voting against the PAP leadership would not be frowned on by the British.

Having survived the confidence vote, and milked the Selkirk–Lim Chin Siong tea party for all it was worth politically, Lee Kuan Yew was able to greatly burnish his anti-colonial credentials in a way that the Tunku never could (although he did not need to, since Malays saw him and UMNO as the vital bulwark against a communist, and Chinese, takeover). The PAP had spent three years building up an effective grassroots organization to counter the communists, centred around the People's Association (created in June 1960), as well as effective spending on community centres, skills training, education (including opportunities for the Chinese-educated to be prepared for civil service careers), and the start of an effective housing programme through the Housing and Development Board (HDB). So, it was now far better positioned for an all-out fight against Lim Chin Siong and his pro-communist group. LKY gave a series of radio talks (in English, Mandarin and Malay) in September 1961 carefully explaining the case for merger and the creation of a new Malaysia.

Over the next few months, Lee Kuan Yew and Tunku Abdul Rahman worked on building a rapport, helped by the fact that LKY (and his accomplished wife, who had outdone him in two out of three A-level subjects at school) spoke Malay well, sang Indonesian songs in his bath, and otherwise appeared a regular Malayan to the Tunku. In April–May 1962, Lee Kuan Yew set off on a mission to convince the leaders of the developing world—primarily the triumvirate of Nehru (India), Nasser (Egypt) and Tito (Yugoslavia) who had created the Non-Aligned Movement (NAM)—that 'Malaysia' was not an imperialist plot, as Indonesia's Sukarno was insisting. Nehru and Nasser received him and his message warmly. Tito was more suspicious but was grudgingly won over. The mission was a success. In September 1962, Singaporeans voted strongly in favour of merger in a referendum, with 71 per cent in favour of the option that the PAP supported, and only 25 per cent responding to the Barisan Sosialis call to cast blank ballots. It was a decisive win for LKY.

But an unexpected challenge to the notion of Malaysia emerged in little Brunei on 8 December 1962 (the twenty-first anniversary of Japan's invasion). There, a former member of Indonesia's pemuda nationalist forces, A. M. Azahari, launched a 'North Kalimantan Army' aimed at regaining all the territories that Brunei had lost to the British over the previous 120 years—to either create an independent Greater Brunei or merge it with Indonesia. Barisan Sosialis extended him moral support, as did remnants of Ahmad Boestamam's Partai Rakyat, but the British quickly dispatched a team of Gurkhas and other commandos from their naval base in Singapore to crush the attempted rebellion, although it persuaded Brunei's sultan to stay out of Malaysia, and instead retain a closer link to Britain for another twenty-one years.

The Brunei imbroglio also led to a decisive move against the pro-communists in Singapore. The PAP government was ready to move against them in December 1962, but the Tunku demurred, particularly because there were a couple of Malayan MPs who were also to be brought under this security dragnet. Eventually, on 2 February 1963, 'Operation Cold Store' was set in motion, with 370 Singapore police officers (aided by 133 policemen from Johor) fanning out across the island to arrest a total of 169 people deemed to be threats to security for their pro-communist actions and beliefs. They only found 115 (the others having moved from where they were expected to be), but those arrested included key figures like Lim Chin Siong, his brother Chin Joo, James Puthucheary and Sydney Woodhull. After the Brunei scare, and amid increasingly violent rhetoric from Sukarno's Indonesia, the arrests of the pro-communists provoked hardly any protests this time. LKY had taken the additional precaution of not banning Partai Rakyat, so that anti-colonialists would have an alternative political home to turn to other than Barisan Sosialis. For most of those jailed (for long terms), this was the end of their political careers, although a few recanted or were pardoned and became prominent in the PAP later. LKY noted that the CUF did not attempt to replace the jailed leaders with a new set of cadres, and as a goodwill gesture he also offered Lim Chin Siong an opportunity to go into exile in Indonesia (which he turned down).

However, disputes between Malaya (often now represented by Deputy Prime Minister Tun Abdul Razak, the former Raffles College classmate of LKY) and Singapore continued to fester right up to the week preceding merger. While internal security was to be controlled by the federal government, Singapore was to retain full control over labour and education; the disputatious issue of what (if any) share of Singapore's revenues should be the federal share was settled at 28 per cent of Singapore's total revenue (or 40 per cent of its 'national taxes'). On 31 August 1963 (the seventh anniversary of Malaya's independence) LKY unilaterally announced the independence of Singapore, thus taking over its own foreign relations in preparation for handing them over to Malaysia. One piquant upshot of this was that LKY remained prime minister of Singapore throughout the time that the city state was part of Malaysia, while also gaining a foothold (through fifteen seats) in Malaysia's new federal legislature. Despite some disputes still swirling in the background (mainly because Malaya had failed to follow through legislatively on some solemn undertakings given to Singapore's leadership), the creation of Malaysia was joyfully celebrated across the new nation on 16 September 1963, which happened to be LKY's fortieth birthday. (The date was chosen primarily because the Tunku liked the number eight, and sixteen is twice eight; evidently the Tunku was unaware it was LKY's birthday, and might have changed the date had he known.)

Given the unresolved disputes and niggles, LKY called an early election in Singapore to be held during the week following Singapore's merger with Malaysia. When the results were announced on 21 September, the PAP had swept to another resounding victory, winning 37 of the 51 seats (including all three Malay-majority seats that UMNO had hoped to wrest), while the Barisan Sosialis won only thirteen and Ong Eng Guan's UPP only his own seat. The PAP's Fortress Singapore had held!

But since the Tunku had broken his promise not to compete against the PAP in Singapore, LKY decided to put up a 'token contest' at the April 1964 general election in Malaya as well, albeit mainly putting up candidates against the MCA (whose leader, Tan Siew Sin, the son of Tan Cheng Lock and now Malaysia's finance minister, had been especially confrontational in his interactions with the PAP). Singapore finance minister Goh Keng Swee was opposed to putting up a token contest, seeing it as unnecessarily vitiating ties with MCA and the Alliance without any significant benefits to Singapore. But it was the Malaya-born PAP politicians (including Chin Chye and Devan Nair) who were keenest to contest the election. So the PAP put up nine candidates but suffered a severe embarrassment, winning just a single seat (Bangsar, won by Devan Nair). The PAP simply did not have the 'ground game' to compete electorally in Malaya, just as UMNO could not in Singapore.

UMNO retaliated within months, with its secretary general Syed Jaafar Albar acting as the hatchet man. Pre-empting LKY's call for a round-table with all Malay political and social organizations in Singapore, Albar came to Singapore and addressed a gathering of all Malay political parties (including three that were pro-Indonesia, and against the creation of Malaysia) in July 1964, using colourfully provocative language to attack LKY as being anti-Malay. Race riots broke out in Singapore a few days later, with the police (now taking orders from Kuala Lumpur) choosing to stand by, especially when Chinese homes were under attack. Similar riots occurred in September 1964 too, further vitiating the atmosphere.

During the course of 1964, the biggest threat to Malaysia came not from its internal contradictions but from external challenges—first by the Philippines' claim to Sabah and then from Indonesia's increasingly vociferous opposition to its very existence. The Philippines claimed that the Sultan of Sulu (whose descendants were citizens of the Philippines) had merely leased his territories of North Borneo to the British and now that the latter were departing, Sabah should revert to the Philippines rather than become part of Malaysia. Indonesia's claim on Borneo had to do with contiguity, since the larger part of Borneo (Kalimantan) was in its territory and abutted Sabah, Sarawak and Brunei (which were separated by a large stretch of sea from Malaya). And its historical claims to all of Malaya stretched back to the Japanese period (when Malaya, Singapore and Sumatra were administered as a single country called Syonan and the slogan of Indonesia Raya had been propagated by Ibrahim Yaacob and the KMM) as well as to the Srivijaya and Majapahit empires that had encompassed most of Malaya.

◆

Sukarno's Indonesia had gone through a series of existential crises in the 1950s, grappling with diverse definitions of nationhood, how much democracy was appropriate, the extent to which shariah should rule Muslims' lives, the degree of agrarian reform necessary to fulfil its anti-colonial destiny, and several types of secessionism. Capitalism had a bad name in Indonesia because it was strongly associated in the public mind with the worst excesses of colonialism, so virtually all political parties agreed on the need to curtail foreign ownership (both Dutch and Chinese). Yet, with all the technocrats trained at Dutch universities, they were broadly conservative on issues of property rights—thus, for instance, acting in favour of Dutch planters rather than the 'squatters' who had moved into parts of their land during the 1940s, and converted some of the land to farming (from plantation agriculture). In theory, Indonesia had a parliamentary system of government with the prime minister and Cabinet wielding most power, but President Sukarno was the only individual who remained in office throughout the period (1945–65), thereby not only 'reigning' but also ruling to an increasing extent (Mohammad Hatta had the next-longest tenure, as vice president, 1945–56). Ironically, the 'parliament' itself was based on negotiations amongst parties (rather than an election) in the first five years (1950–55), and all the major parties other than the communist PKI participated in coalition governments during the period.

The Dutch colonial system of patronage based on handing out 'licences' and 'concessions' to preferred businessmen continued, including in the attempt to redress the ethnic disadvantages of the 'pribumi' (indigenous) business groups. Typically, the licence or concession became a source of rent-seeking, with the pribumi business group collecting a small fee while outsourcing the concession to another foreign or Chinese-owned business. And while the technocrats advocated fiscal austerity, the exchequer came to be increasingly burdened by the demands of each coalition partner to increase public employment within the ministry that each made its own (the nationalist PNI controlled home affairs, the socialist PSI defence, and orthodox Muslim NU controlled religious affairs, etc.). Sukarno attempted to hold together the disparate ideologies represented in his cabinet through the slogan of NASAKOM (Nationalism, Agama meaning religion, and Communism) that he had first articulated in the mid-1920s. 'Pancasila' (the 'five principles') provided the philosophical underpinning for the Indonesian state, which was to be founded on: (a) belief in the one God ('Maha Esa' being the term used, not the Arabic word Allah); (b) Just and civilized Humanity; (c) Indonesian Unity; (d) Democracy guided by consensus derived from deliberations amongst representatives; and (e) Social Justice for all the people. These, coupled with the magnanimous choice of Melayu Riau (the Malay spoken in the Riau islands) rather than majority Javanese as the official Bahasa Indonesia (Indonesian language) helped bind the nation after the brutalities and colonial divisions that had accompanied its birth.

Yet when the first election was held in 1955, its deeply fractured outcome only sowed additional divisions rather than becoming a binding source of legitimacy. Sukarno's nationalist PNI emerged as the largest party but won only 22.3 per cent of the vote, followed closely by the modernist Muslim Masyumi (associated with Mohammad Hatta) with 20.9 per cent, the orthodox Muslim Nahdlatul Ulama (NU) with 18.4 per cent and communist PKI with 16.4 per cent. Sutan Sjahrir's socialist PSI (which had been very influential since 1945, especially with the Western powers enthused by its role in resisting the Japanese) won merely 2 per cent of the vote. Support for PNI, NU and PKI was concentrated in East and Central Java (with the PNI strong in Bali too). Masyumi was strong in West Java, Sumatra and the outer islands. It was also the only party that advocated the full version of the first of the Pancasila principles: 'Belief in the one God—with the obligation for adherents of Islam to implement the Islamic law (shariah).' The additional words (after the dash in the quote) were to have been included in the 'Jakarta Charter', the first Constitution proclaimed on 18 August 1945 (the day after the independence declaration), but were dropped at the last minute at the behest of the secular and non-Muslim parties. Some Islamists came to view this as a 'magic trick' perpetrated by secular politicians, and were thoroughly embittered by what they perceived as a betrayal of one of the founding principles of the nation. The Darul Islam rebellions of the 1950s (which took up where the 1948 rebellion had left off) were one direct consequence of disillusionment with this theme, particularly amongst the outer islands, which also resented the fact that their commodity export earnings appeared to be largely subsidizing Jakarta and Java. Regional resentments fused with Islamist goals in the rebellions in Central Java in 1955, Aceh in 1957, and West Java in 1962 (by which time Masyumi itself had been banned).

Sukarno had an opportunity to fuse ideology more coherently into policy during the brief period (1952–57) when his prime ministers were from his own PNI rather than from another coalition partner. Wilopo, and especially the Javanese aristocrat Ali Sastroamijoyo, pursued policies more consonant with Bung Karno's vision. Sastroamijoyo had been ambassador to the US, and helped Sukarno organize the Afro-Asian Conference at Bandung in 1955 that marked the high-water mark of non-alignment as a foreign policy principle for the developing world. Zhou Enlai, the prime minister of the then-pariah PRC (which still did not hold China's seat at the United Nations) stole the show, although Sukarno shone too in the reflected glory of Nasser, Nehru, Tito and other stalwarts of the Non-Aligned developing world.

Domestically, they also began to act against the persisting Dutch control over the economy. Bank Indonesia had replaced the Dutch-owned Java Bank as the nation's central bank in 1952, and Sastroamijoyo began putting pressure on Dutch-owned businesses in the plantation and industrial sectors, even as he raised the Irian Jaya (Papua) issue at the United Nations, where the majority of the General Assembly supported Indonesia's position (but not the two-thirds majority required for the UN to commit to taking action). Hatta who, like Sutan Sjahrir, had always maintained that the revolution was completed with the ouster of the Dutch, and Indonesia needed to get on with developing itself socially and economically, resigned as vice president on 1 December 1956. Although he said he was simply tired, the people could see that Sukarno's constant revolution was now a strain on his longest-standing political ally.

In late 1957, to punish the Dutch for their continued intransigence over Irian Jaya, Sukarno began to expropriate Dutch businesses, most of which were initially taken over by their employees, and eventually by the government or military. Most of the remaining Dutchmen in Indonesia were expelled from the country, after being subjected to increasing public harassment. These acts of nationalism (long telegraphed as essential by most anti-colonial activists before independence) now led to Sukarno being labelled 'erratic' in the Western press, much as Mossadegh had been in 1952–53 (after nationalizing the Anglo-Iranian Oil Company in 1951) and Mugabe in more recent times. The Dulles brothers—Secretary of State John Foster and CIA chief Allen—began to pay increasing attention to Indonesia.

John Foster Dulles had already concluded by October 1953 that 'between a territorially united Indonesia which is leaning and progressing towards Communism and a breakup of that country into racial and geographical units, I would prefer the latter...' His brother Allen Dulles' CIA began covert deliveries of arms to Sumatra, where a new military rebellion was underway by late 1957 that, according to its proclamation of 15 February 1958, sought to establish a Revolutionary Government of the Republic of Indonesia (PRRI, to use its Bahasa acronym). Rebels in Sulawesi joined them a couple of days later, calling theirs the Permesta (Piagam Perjuangan Semesta, or Universal Struggle Charter) rebellion. The army commander Abdul Haris Nasution (who had succeeded to the post in January 1950, after Sudirman died of TB) had already advised Sukarno to declare martial law a few months earlier. Now, Sukarno authorized Nasution to mount a full military response to the PRRI-Permesta rebellion. In the east, the Permesta rebels were aided by deployment of twenty-one B–26 bombers and a few P–51 Mustang fighters by the US CIA, whose officers flew covert missions from the Philippines and may also have used the Permesta rebels' main air base in Manado. The CIA suffered a major embarrassment when a B–26 was shot down over Ambon on 18 May 1958; as the huge amount of incriminating evidence inside the bomber demonstrated, the B–26 pilot Allen Pope was clearly a CIA operative.

Nasution's military was able to quickly crush the PRRI–Permesta rebellions—which enhanced both his and Sukarno's prestige. At Nasution's urging, in 1959 Sukarno proclaimed the re-establishment of the 1945 Constitution (which had created a strong presidency) and bid adieu to the Constituent Assembly (which had been meeting for four years since 1955 but remained deadlocked on several issues), and instead inaugurated his era of 'Guided Democracy'. In 1960, an Indonesian court convicted Allen Pope to death by firing squad. The new Kennedy administration sought to intervene to save Pope's life and, in exchange, agreed to use its good offices to oblige the Dutch to vacate Irian Jaya, which they began doing in 1962. JFK apparently believed that, by thus strengthening the pro-Western parts of Sukarno's cabinet, he would reduce the influence of the PKI on him. But the PKI had become too big to restrain by this point. Led by D. N. Aidit, the PKI was the largest communist party outside the main Communist bloc with over 3 million active members, 24 million affiliated supporters and a strong presence across rural Java based on its platform of agrarian reform. Within Indonesia, the military was becoming increasingly wary of the PKI's growing influence, and the conflict between them would come to a head in October 1965.

Apart from overwhelming evidence of CIA involvement in the PRRI–Permesta rebellion, Sukarno had more personal reasons for his leftward tilt. In November 1957, there had been an assassination attempt on Sukarno at his son's primary school, involving a grenade attack that killed several other people but narrowly missed Sukarno himself. Over the next few years, there were at least five more audacious assassination attempts against him—the most astonishing being an aerial bombardment of the presidential palace in 1960. Both the PSI (a socialist party that was strongly anti-communist) and Masyumi (the Islamist party linked to Hatta) were implicated in some of these assassination attempts, explaining why Sukarno banned both parties.

Sukarno had made a valiant attempt to knit together the disparate strains of nationalism in Indonesia during the 1950s, but the international politics of the Cold War rudely intruded into his nationalist idyll. Many of the stalwarts of the young nation's early years succumbed to the various blandishments of foreign powers: in 1958, Sumitro Djojohadikusumo (who, as a socialist acolyte of Sutan Sjahrir, had helped set up Indonesia's representation at the United Nations in the 1940s, and then served as trade and industry minister in PSI-led cabinets and finance minister in another cabinet) exercised his 'personal option of rebellious character' and joined the PRRI–Permesta rebellion. The socialist pemuda leader Adam Malik was to emerge in 1964 as the leader of the anti-communist movement aligned with anti-PKI army officers in the name of Sukarnoism—a claim that was rejected by Sukarno's PNI, most of which preferred to align with the PKI.

Flushed with his success over Irian Jaya, Sukarno (through foreign minister Subandrio) began warning the Malayans in January 1963 that Indonesia strongly opposed the creation of Malaysia, and would counteract it militarily. Sure enough, by late September 1963, Sukarno launched his 'Konfrontasi' (confrontation) in the immediate aftermath of the creation of Malaysia. By this time, however, Indonesia's own military leadership was deeply divided, with the majority of the army lining up in opposition to the growing influence of the communist PKI in Sukarno's NASAKOM alliance that incorporated PNI, NU and PKI, with the last increasingly in the ascendant after the banning in 1961–62 of the Masyumi and socialist PSI (which had, respectively, been the political vehicles of Hatta and Sjahrir—the two other poles of Indonesia's founding triumvirate).

Since about 1957, and especially after the PRRI–Permesta rebellion, the army had taken to 'profit-generating' activities, taking on extensive business interests to supplement the meagre budget and poor pay that the government was able to provide soldiers. Amongst the most prominent of the profit-oriented generals was Brigadier General Suharto, who commanded the Diponegoro Division based in Semarang (and responsible for Yogyakarta and Central Java). In particular, two prominent Chinese businessmen, Liem Sioe Liong (later the founder of the Salim Group conglomerate) and Bob Hasan, had served as close business associates of his in the palm oil and timber trade respectively. In 1959, an army investigation into corruption led to Suharto being implicated in extensive smuggling activities (in association with Salim and Hasan), and suspended from his operational position; he was instead shifted to the Army Staff and Command College in Bandung.

As a capitalist-oriented brigadier, Suharto appears to have caught the attention of Allen Dulles's CIA at this time. Jakarta was by this point a den of intrigue, with the PKI seen as closely aligned to China and the Soviet Union (with the Indonesian air force being its main power centre), and increasingly worried elements in the army deepening ties with the US and UK to counteract the growing menace of the PKI and Islamist forces—both of which the army had battled intermittently since the early uprisings in 1948 which the nationalist army saw as acts of high treason. Nasution and, at a more junior level, Suharto were amongst the early KNIL veterans who remade the Indonesian army into a more professional (as opposed to revolutionary) force after Sudirman's death in January 1950. While the pemuda were very much a part of the army, the KNIL veterans were more dominant, having led it at many of the most crucial battles that kept the republic afloat when most of the political leadership was in Dutch custody. The army had thus developed its own esprit de corps and an officer like Suharto was able to land on his feet despite being implicated for smuggling. Such heterodox business activities were, in fact, the norm amongst many senior officers, so Suharto was quickly rehabilitated, and was promoted to major general at the beginning of 1962, tasked with leading Operation Mandala, a joint army-navy-air force command based in Makassar that was to lead the invasions of Western New Guinea.

Although the Indonesian troops who landed in New Guinea had been quickly captured, the army was able to gain some of the reflected glory from the diplomatic triumph that enabled the 'return' of Irian Jaya (formerly Dutch West New Guinea) to Indonesian hands. Soon after this, General Suharto was placed in overall command of Konfrontasi. This proved, eventually, to be Sukarno's undoing, because Suharto was by this point clearly against the whole idea of confrontation with the Western world (and its post-colonial proxy, Malaysia) as articulated by President Sukarno in his 'Year of Living Dangerously' (from late 1964 onwards). Suharto's key subordinates, Ali Murtopo and Benny Murdani (who were supposed to be at the vanguard of Konfrontasi) contacted the Malaysians clandestinely to express their opposition to Konfrontasi, and gradually began to coordinate their actions with the intelligence agencies of Malaysia, Singapore and Britain (which were officially Indonesia's enemy nations at the time).

In September 1964, about a hundred Indonesian paratroopers landed in the hilly areas of Johor in peninsular Malaysia accompanied by about a dozen Chinese–Malayan defectors, but were soon subdued (almost certainly because the British and Malaysians had received intelligence about them from Suharto's KOSTRAD). Britain began moving its air and naval forces from its Singapore base into Indonesian waters in the Sunda Straits, and war seemed imminent, with the British Foreign Office hinting at following the US precedent of a month earlier (when the Tonkin Gulf Resolution was passed by the US Congress to enable military action in Vietnam). Although the crisis passed, another eighty regular army troops were parachuted into Singapore and southern Malaysia in March 1965, and won some early skirmishes before being overpowered. Although the CPM's rebellion had been defeated by this time, the Indonesians made little attempt to foment dormant CPM cadres in their favour.

Indonesia's anti-colonial rhetoric against Malaysia made little headway at the UN, where Malaysia was elected to (a non-permanent seat on) the Security Council, which voted 9–2 against Indonesia on the issue of Konfrontasi. The Soviet Union vetoed the resolution, thus limiting the embarrassment to

Indonesia, but Indonesia soon became the first country to withdraw from the United Nations. The Non-Aligned Movement had begun fragmenting after the brief India–China War of 1962, and failed to rally to Indonesia's support in 1964–65. Nonetheless, the former pemuda stalwart Adam Malik's anti-PKI activities (in alignment with elements of the military) amid the confrontation with Britain and Malaysia was seen by Sukarno and most of his PNI party as a form of treason. Sukarno responded by welcoming China's foreign minister Chen Yi to Jakarta and encouraged rumours about China helping Indonesia to build a nuclear bomb (after China's own successful nuclear weapons test in 1964).

Although the Soviets had dutifully supported Indonesia at the Security Council, Khrushchev was otherwise largely uninterested in Indonesia. On a visit to the country in 1960, he had addressed public rallies where he appeared to admonish Sukarno, who had responded in kind. Unbeknownst to much of the world, the Sino–Soviet breach was widening sharply at this time, and Sukarno had chosen to align clearly with China rather than the USSR, and he was speaking publicly of an Indonesia–Cambodia–Vietnam–China–North Korea axis.

The events of 30 September–2 October 1965 in Jakarta remain shrouded in mystery to this day. The official line during the Suharto years (and most of the time since) about the events following 30 September 1965 is that there was a communist coup attempt, which was suppressed by the army led by Suharto (the seniormost officer to have survived the coup attempt), and especially the strategic reserve command KOSTRAD that he led. Sukarno, it was hinted, was complicit in the coup aimed at consolidating the communists' hold over his government, and eliminating the remaining pro-Western leaders in the army (who, according to the 30 September coup plotters, had constituted a CIA-backed Council of Generals to oust Sukarno and his leftist allies). While this is the official line that has been accepted in Indonesia since 1965, the 'Cornell Paper' by Benedict Anderson and Ruth McVey (and their subsequent research and writings on the subject) poked some very credible holes in that version of events. First, there was little reason for Sukarno and the PKI's Aidit to mount a 'coup' since they were themselves in power, and the CIA itself quoted Aidit as saying in October 1964 that the PKI was especially well positioned to advance its political programme because of its proximity to the leadership at every level of Indonesia's governance structure.

Second, each of the three leaders of the 30 September Movement (who were supposedly aiming to oust the pro-Western 'Council of Generals') was either serving under Suharto then or had done so very recently. Colonel Abdul Latief had led the army's exercises to test the quality of Jakarta's defences, and he and his key co-plotters—Lieutenant Colonel Untung and Brigadier General Suparjo—would have been well aware of the centrality of KOSTRAD to the capital's defences, especially because of its highly sophisticated communications systems; yet the trio of coup plotters made no attempt whatsoever to attack Suharto or KOSTRAD and disable its communications (although they did disable the civilian communications systems, thereby actually enhancing the strategic importance of KOSTRAD amid the coup). Third, even after the coup, Suharto was *not* the highest-ranking general to have survived; he used KOSTRAD's strategic communications systems to draw power to himself, and specifically repudiated President Sukarno's nomination of Pranoto Reksosamudro (a rival of Suharto's who had been his chief of staff in the Diponegoro Division and the whistle-blower on his smuggling) as the successor to the slain General Ahmad Yani as chief of army staff.

Abdul Haris Nasution, the overall military commander since 1950, had been on the list of seven generals that the coup plotters wanted to arrest or kill. (The elimination of the seven seniormost generals would also have ensured that no general senior to Suharto would survive.) But when the plotters arrived to arrest him, Nasution managed to jump the fence of his house, and landed in the compound of his neighbour (the Iraqi ambassador). Although he fractured his leg as a consequence, Nasution also managed to survive the coup plotters' plans. Curiously, Major General Suharto acknowledged having met one of the three key coup plotters, Colonel Latief, late on 30 September night at a military hospital (where Suharto's baby son, Tommy, or Hutomo Mandala Putra, was being treated for minor burns he had suffered at home from hot soup; in later life, Tommy was to find himself metaphorically in 'hot soup' all too frequently). In some senses, this meeting should not have been too surprising: Latief had served under Suharto during the revolutionary army's assault on Dutch-controlled Yogyakarta in March 1949, and in numerous other postings (having graduated from the army's Staff and Command College one year after Suharto did). Latief had been an honoured guest at the circumcision ceremony of Suharto's son, Sigit, and Suharto had similarly attended the same ceremony for Latief's son. In 1963, Suharto had also travelled all the way to a remote Javanese village to attend Lieutenant Colonel Untung's wedding.

In the original Cornell Paper (circulated within academic circles in January 1966), Anderson and McVey merely asserted that the G30S ('Group 30th September') coup was 'an internal army affair' initiated by a group of officers from the Diponegoro Division based in Semarang, who saw themselves as custodians of Javanese culture, which was threatened by the Westward tilt of leading non-Javanese Dutch-trained generals such as Nasution. The Cornell Paper asserted that the G30S plotters had no prior links to the PKI or to Sukarno, neither of whom initiated or organized the coup, instead each becoming its most prominent victims. Benedict Anderson is amongst the most prominent Marxist-oriented scholars of the past half-century (as is his brother Perry), so his claim that the PKI had nothing at all to do with the coup strains credulity. The PKI mayor of Solo was amongst the first to welcome the G30S coup, and Untung (of the Cakrabirawa presidential guard) was clearly at least influenced by the PKI. But PKI leader D. N. Aidit did nothing to activate his potentially powerful mass organizations in support of the coup—which does suggest that he had scant prior knowledge of the coup plan, although some other members of the PKI leadership may have been more closely involved.

Benedict Anderson published another paper (in the year 2000) containing details of the explosive trial of Colonel Abdul Latief in 1978. Unlike all his co-conspirators, Latief was not killed in 1965–66, but instead tortured and abused relentlessly during his thirteen years in solitary confinement awaiting trial. At his trial, Latief made a powerful presentation, choosing to lay out the 'whole truth' of what G30S was about. Just as Sukarno had made a brilliant indictment of Dutch rule at his early 1930s trial, turning his defence plea into a searing attack on the racist basis of Dutch rule (titled 'Indonesia Accuses!'), so Latief chose to lay out in gory detail what exactly had happened on 30 September and 1 October 1965 (knowing at the trial that his fate was preordained, just as Sukarno's had been in 1930). His accusation was simple: he (Latief) himself had fully briefed his long-standing friend, Major General Suharto, about the Council of Generals' plans to overthrow Sukarno and his cabinet on 5 October 1965, and the 30 September Movement's plans to pre-empt them. Latief (who was then commanding Brigade 1 in Jakarta) also informed his direct boss, Major General Umar Wirahadikusumah, Jakarta's territorial commander. That Suharto and Umar were fully informed in advance of the G30S plans helps explain one of the anomalies the original Cornell Paper had pointed out: that these two (the most important army commanders in Jakarta) were inexplicably left untouched by the G30S plotters, in what appeared to be a fatal strategic error in their plans.

In reality, their error was to have trusted Suharto!

While encouraging his close friends and subordinates to move against all the generals who might be obstacles to his own rise to power (and who these nationalist subordinates believed were plotting against Sukarno at the West's behest), Suharto was secretly in league with Britain, Malaysia and the US through KOSTRAD's intelligence chief, Ali Murtopo, who had used the 1958 coup plotters' networks to reach out to MI6 and the CIA, and Benny Murdani, who deepened those links while masquerading as a Garuda (national airline) representative in Bangkok.

Having had time to reflect on the matter during his years of imprisonment and torture, Latief had concluded by 1978 that Suharto, Ali Murtopo and Benny Murdani themselves comprised the Council of Generals—although Suharto had encouraged the G30S group to believe that Nasution and Yani led that council. The G30S plotters were not entirely naive to have believed this since Nasution was a prominent exponent of the army's profit-generating activities over the previous half-decade, and was seen as an opponent of Sukarno's leftward tilt in the Guided Democracy era. Having been briefed by Latief late on 30 September evening, Suharto allowed Untung to make his self-incriminating broadcast over RRI (Radio Republik Indonesia) at 7.15 a.m. on 1 October 1965 (including the announcement of a 'Revolutionary Council' that was largely fictitious but excluded Sukarno); then Suharto quickly moved to strengthen his own military hold over the capital (while posing as the protector of 'Bung Karno our great leader'). By that afternoon, Suharto had designated himself the new army commander. By this time, the G30S plotters had brought Sukarno ('for his own protection') to their main operational headquarters at Halim Perdanakusuma airbase—where they had also taken Omar Dhani (the air force chief, who was known to be left-leaning) and PKI chief D. N. Aidit. From Halim, President Sukarno sent couriers to Generals Pranoto Reksosamudro and Umar Wirahadikusumah, summoning them to Halim in order to effect the leadership transition in the military. Suharto forbade Umar from going to Halim, and rejected President Sukarno's designation of Pranoto as the next army commander.

While professing to be acting in the name of President Sukarno, Suharto had induced and completed a military coup within twenty-four hours of the start of the G30S rebellion. The plotters had originally planned only to arrest the seven top generals, and present them to Sukarno along with evidence of their plot—to overthrow the government—on which the president would then be able to act. But instead, three of the generals (including the army commander, General Yani) were killed at their homes, apparently because the inexperienced soldiers panicked when faced with resistance or gunfire from within their homes. The Berkeley scholar Peter Dale Scott had a much clearer explanation: he asserted that the entire putsch was organized by troops under Suharto's command, who ensured that all the generals would be killed. (Scott pointed out that, in January 1965, a unity meeting of the army had occurred between 'Yani's inner circle' and a group of officers led by Suharto 'who had grievances against Yani'; the latter all became key leaders of Suharto's new order regime, while all five of those lined up on Yani's side at this meeting were killed by G30S.) Suharto's G30S subordinates had the three other generals shot and all six generals' bodies were then dumped in a well at Halim airbase, which could easily later be linked to PKI, whose cadres had previously been trained at or near that airbase.

As the new military strongman, Suharto banned all newspapers on 2 October, but curiously allowed the PKI newspaper to be published that day, carrying an editorial supporting the G30S coup. Anderson and Scott separately asserted that this editorial was 'planted', with the latter insinuating that it was the handiwork of the CIA. This was, in any case, one of the last issues of that newspaper to ever be published. Additionally, Suharto was briefed on 3 October by the doctors who had carried out autopsies on the six generals' bodies, and those reports all showed that they had died from gunshot wounds at close range. Yet, starting on 4 October, Suharto and his key subordinates began publishing and broadcasting gruesome reports about how members of the PKI women's and students' groups had gouged out the generals' eyes and mutilated their bodies before dumping them in the well. These utterly fanciful reports played a big role in fomenting hatred towards the PKI, and helped provoke the anti-communist (and later anti-Chinese) pogroms that began in Java by mid-October.

Scott also demonstrates that US covert assistance to anti-Sukarno elements of the Indonesian Army was stepped up immediately after President John F. Kennedy's assassination. (JFK had attempted to improve ties with Sukarno, succeeding to a considerable extent.) In December 1963 (a month after JFK's death), the Lyndon B. Johnson administration withdrew all economic aid to Indonesia (reversing flows that JFK had routinely approved), while continuing covert military supplies to favoured elements in the army. Scott alleges that the quadrupling of Indonesian rice prices between July and October 1965 was a direct consequence of economic subversion by the US. At the supposed nadir of US–Indonesia relations in July 1965, the American company Rockwell Standard agreed a contract to supply 200 light aircraft to the Indonesian Army (notably, *not* the Air Force) over the subsequent two months, with Bob Hasan (Suharto's close friend and business partner) acting as the middleman on the transaction.

During his time at the Army Staff and Command College at Bandung (1959–60), Suharto had played a key role in advancing the army's 'civic mission' and the Doctrine of Territorial Warfare that the US was promoting through its PSI (socialist) and Masyumi (modernizing Muslim) allies. The doctrine of civic action for the military was the basis of its US-sponsored counter-revolutionary role before 1965, and eventually became the basis for its 'dwifungsi' (dual function) ideology after 1965 justifying army intervention in all aspects of civil society.

Both Suharto's New Order and its critics (Anderson, McVey and Scott) agree that a shadowy figure called Syam Kamaruzaman was a key coordinator of the G30S plot. While Suharto's New Order regime asserted that Syam headed the PKI's Special Bureau tasked with manipulating the key military leaders of G30S, the critics asserted that Syam was actually a highly effective socialist (PSI) intelligence operative working in close coordination with the CIA. There is little doubt that the PSI became (after 1957–58) the key ally of the US in the PRRI–Permesta rebellion, and later through key personnel such as Sumitro Djojohadikusumo and Adam Malik. During the 1950s, it was impossible for anyone to be a member of both the PKI and PSI since the two had become mortal enemies, especially since the Madiun Revolt of 1948. Although the New Order regime insisted that Syam was primarily a PKI operative, it was much more likely that he was in fact a PSI activist who managed to penetrate the PKI. Syam was used to testify in hundreds of trials of alleged PKI activists over the next three decades, but the official story that he headed the PKI Special Bureau strains credulity. The CIA's own reports pointed out that Aidit did nothing to activate or arouse his formidable mass organizations during the coup attempt, which suggests that he was a captive of the coup plotters (rather than leading them). By the evening of 1 October, Suharto had taken charge of both the military and all key strategic points of Jakarta, and was no longer taking orders from Sukarno. The latter, aware of the numerous assassination attempts against him, appeared to recognize that the situation was well out of his control and refused to accompany Untung to his base in Central Java, retreating instead to his Bogor Palace.

Suharto's loyalist forces turned on the coup plotters (betraying them, in the opinion of Latief) and killed almost all of them over the next fortnight. Latief and Syam were not killed, however, suggesting that they were seen as assets to be used in future trials—and the latter was especially useful in that role. Meanwhile, photographs of the mutilated bodies of the slain generals, and stories of the alleged role of the PKI in fomenting the G30S coup, murdering the generals and violating their bodies were widely broadcast. The reprisal killings of communist sympathizers began in mid-October 1965, fomented almost everywhere by the arrival of an army contingent with provocative stories about specific individuals' roles in the alleged PKI plot.

In the bloodbath that followed over the next three months in particular—continuing over the subsequent half-year with less vigour—at least half a million Indonesians were killed in one of the most gruesome massacres of the gory twentieth century. Anybody with even slight links to the PKI or sympathy for it was a candidate for massacre, and the pogroms quickly spread from communist sympathizers to all ethnic Chinese, who were tarred by ethnic association with Communist China (the ultimate backers of the PKI).

After half a year of relentless bloodletting, Suharto obtained the 'Supersemar' (Surat Perintah Sebelas Maret), or Order of 11 March (1966) from President Sukarno virtually at gunpoint at his Bogor Palace. 'Semar' refers to a central character from Java's wayang puppet theatre (and one of the rare pre-Indic characters not from the Mahabharata), so the name was meant to convey a climactic passing of the torch. While the Order itself merely gave Suharto the authority to take 'whatever measures' he deemed necessary to restore order across the country, it was correctly perceived as an almost complete transfer of authority from Sukarno to Suharto. A week later, Suharto banned the PKI, dismissed fifteen pro-Sukarno members of the Cabinet and effectively became the supreme leader of the country, although Sukarno remained the nominal president, stripped of all effective power. In March 1967, a newly-constituted MPR (parliament) anointed Suharto the acting president, and removed the word 'acting' from his title in 1968.

One of the first actions that Suharto took, even before the end of 1965, was to call an end to Konfrontasi. Although the CIA was never able to officially claim this victory (apart from US Senate hearings in 1975–76 which came close to revealing its role), the British were less reticent in acknowledging their role in one of the West's greatest triumphs of the Cold War. With their experience at 'psyops' (psychological operations) from the Malayan Emergency, the British Foreign Office Information Research Department boasted that it had played the key role in spreading false propaganda about a Communist plan to slaughter the citizens of Jakarta: this story was planted with the BBC, and quickly spread around the world and into Indonesia itself, helping to foment greater venom against the PKI. The British plan to use its high commission in Singapore to spread black propaganda about Sukarno, the PKI and ethnic Chinese in Indonesia was first approved by Tory prime minister Harold Macmillan, and continued under Labour's Harold Wilson.

But the more covert role of the US was far more crucial to the emergence of the pro-Western Suharto as the new dictator of Indonesia, with a readymade doctrine of a 'civic mission' for the military. Scott pointed out, in particular, that several US corporations appeared to have foreknowledge about the impending ouster of Sukarno: in April 1965, Freeport Sulphur reached a preliminary agreement over the exploitation of copper deposits in West Papua (eventually resulting in a US$500 million investment). And even as Western journals reported that Indonesia's oil and gas industry was sinking into a morass, the US partner of Ibnu Sutowo's oil firm, Permina, bought a substantial proportion of shares in the company in September 1965—just days before G30S.

With a pro-Western regime installed in Southeast Asia's largest nation, the five closest US allies (Malaysia, Singapore, Indonesia, the Philippines and Thailand) decided to come together in the Association of South East Asian Nations (ASEAN) in 1967, marking the beginning of an era of economic and strategic cooperation for the region that helped alleviate the political tensions of the early 1960s. In Indonesia itself, Sumitro Djojohadikusumo was quickly brought into Suharto's New Order regime as trade and industry minister, and myriad other rebels of the Sukarno era found themselves rehabilitated after the counter-revolution effected by Suharto. Over the next three decades, Indonesia was to become a near-model student of the World Bank's experiments in development economics and policy.

The month prior to the G30S coup in Indonesia, the twenty-three-month merger of Singapore with Malaysia had ended in tears. Fed up with the rising ethnic tensions resulting from Lee Kuan Yew's call for a 'Malaysian Malaysia', Tunku Abdul Rahman lost patience and decided to expel Singapore, and UMNO led the Malaysian Parliament in a 126–0 vote to endorse expulsion on 9 August 1965 (with the Singapore parliamentarians abstaining). Lee Kuan Yew shed genuine tears while announcing the forced independence of Singapore, as the ultimate goal of his entire political career had been the merger and co-development of the two territories. Singapore's prospects as an independent nation appeared bleak in the absence of its own supplies of water, and the absence of an economic hinterland. With the departure of Singapore, the rest of Malaysia (including Sabah and Sarawak) had a clear Malay majority and a definite preponderance of Malays over Chinese across the country. Devan Nair initially remained in the Malaysian Parliament, and renamed the Malaysian version of the PAP as the Democratic Action Party (DAP), with a slightly different ('rocket') symbol. By 1966, LKY summoned Devan Nair back to Singapore in order not to further vitiate Singapore's fraught relations with Malaysia. The DAP soon became a prominent opposition party; since the 2013 election, it is the second-largest party in Malaysia's Parliament, although this outcome was achieved primarily because of its role in a three-party opposition coalition.

The most tangible consequences of the ethnic tension that had been spawned by the merger of Singapore into Malaysia were the riots of 13 May 1969 in Malaysia. They went on sporadically until 31 July that year and claimed an official toll of 196 dead and 350 wounded (with unofficial estimates being substantially higher). Contagion to Singapore in the form of week-long inter-communal riots there killed 4 people and injured 80, although the police intervened aggressively (and impartially) to restore order quickly in Singapore.

The Malaysia riots had been triggered by the outcome of the 1969 parliamentary election. Held on 10 May, the election resulted in significant gains for the two Chinese-based secular parties, DAP and Gerakan, which together won 21 of the 144 seats, based on their demand for the end to special privileges for bumiputras. DAP also gained half the state assembly seats in Selangor, while Gerakan won a majority in Penang, and PAS (Pan-Malaysian Islamic Party) won a majority in Kelantan. Consequently, the Alliance led by UMNO (52 seats), MCA and MIC (plus some Sabah and Sarawak parties) lost its two-thirds majority in Parliament for the first time and was reduced to 74 of the 144 seats. A DAP–Gerakan celebratory rally in Kuala Lumpur on 12 May resulted in racial slurs being hurled at Malay bystanders. An angry UMNO rally the next day condemned the allegedly aggressive behaviour of Chinese–Malaysians, setting off the orgy of violence.

Tunku Abdul Rahman's authority was severely undermined by his government's inability to contain the violence, and especially the perception that he was dealing with this major crisis in his usual laid-back manner, when much greater urgency was necessary. Instead, a National Operations Council (NOC, or Majlis Gerakan Negara) headed by Tun Abdul Razak took control of restoring law and order, and devising long-term solutions to the ethnic imbalances that were perceived to have led to the riots. Parliament was suspended (until 1971) and a state of emergency was declared. In September 1970, Tun Abdul Razak formally replaced the Tunku as prime minister, and Rahman finally lost the UMNO presidency in June 1971 after a rebellion by a group of UMNO Young Turks led by Mahathir Mohamad and Musa Hitam. Razak then implemented his New Economic Policy (NEP) aimed at redistributing national wealth more equally amongst the races—obtaining Chinese business leaders' acquiescence in the plan, in return for guaranteeing the safety of their persons and businesses. The Malays held 2.4 per cent of the nation's wealth in 1970 (by the NOC's calculations), while 'Other Malaysians' (mainly Chinese) held 33 per cent and foreigners 63 per cent. The NEP aimed to raise the bumiputras' share to 30 per cent by 1991, while allowing 'Other Malaysians' to have 40 per cent and cutting foreigners' share to 30 per cent. Bumiputras would also have guaranteed quotas in the universities, and a slew of other privileges.

Singapore, meanwhile, vigorously began implementing a dynamic economic policy aimed at replicating many of the institutions that had made Japan successful, led by an Economic Development Board (EDB) that was akin to Japan's MITI, except that it sought out foreign direct investments (FDI) into Singapore by leading multinational corporations (MNCs) from around the world. Seeking out MNC investments went completely against the trend in the developing world at the time. The 'dependencia' theory, propounded most prominently by the Brazilian sociologist Fernando Henrique Cardoso, was then in its heyday—arguing that the 'periphery' nations would eternally tie themselves into a subservient relationship to the 'core' ones that dominated the world, especially if the periphery were to depend on FDI from MNCs. Lee Kuan Yew's 'Singapore model', by contrast, aggressively sought to provide incentives for MNCs to invest in Singapore since, LKY argued, Singapore had no other resources apart from its people. Employing his people productively was the only way for Singapore to prosper, he argued, and 'exploitation' of its people by MNCs was a small price to pay in the service of future prosperity.

And, in a nod to his socialist roots but actually much more to the pathways already paved and trodden by Japan, Taiwan and (since 1961) Korea, Lee Kuan Yew also gave a prominent role to government-linked corporations (GLCs) to develop Singapore's physical infrastructure and public services. Prominent amongst these was what became SingTel, as well as the Development Bank of Singapore (now just DBS), a highly effective postal service (that included the Post Office Savings Bank, POSB, yet another nod to a concept pioneered by Japan in the 1870s), a HDB that was tasked with rapidly providing a basic level of universal public housing (to be purchased by citizens at market determined prices), the Port of Singapore Authority and airports authority focused on world-leading technical efficiency, and a number of companies (Keppel, Sembawang) that spearheaded the transformation of the shipyards abandoned by Britain's Royal Navy into the world's leading ship-repair hubs. In 1971, LKY's technocratic whiz kid J. Y. Pillay was tasked with creating Singapore Airlines (SIA) after it split with its Malaysian sister company. Using the examples of Air India and Cathay Pacific, he quickly made SIA a paragon of quality and punctuality, with a distinctive identity built around the qualities of the smiling Singapore Girl and impeccable cabin service.

Singapore's economic dynamism derived from the success of its MNC-driven export model. This began with the usual textiles, garments, shoes and toy manufacturers who employed Singaporeans by the thousands at a time when their skill and education levels were still low. But, emulating Japan's focus on universal literacy and high education standards, Singapore created a meritocratic education system aimed at raising the technical abilities of the labour force, reinforced by a highly effective skills development programme aimed at imparting specific vocational training tailored towards meeting the specific needs of current and future employers. And, in order to attract the best talent into government, Singapore decided that its civil servants and ministers would be paid salaries commensurate with the earnings of the best-paid private sector talent. This was reinforced by a Corrupt Practices Investigation Board that cracked down on any evidence of corruption, which would lead to loss of salary and pension, and severely punitive jail terms for offenders. But a final aspect of the Singapore model entailed a continuation of colonial-era foreign labour recruitment practices that gave Singapore's labour market unusual degrees of flexibility. Work that Singaporeans were not prepared to do—household maids, construction, or cutting hedges in the blazing sun or rain—were performed by foreign workers on one- to three-year contracts that were unchanged from the indentured labour system that had built Malaya's plantations. Eventually, significant parts of Singapore's manufacturing and services (retail, restaurants/ hotels) sectors came to depend crucially on such indentured labour.

STALIN, MAO AND THE CONSEQUENCES OF UNFETTERED DICTATORSHIP

We saw in the last chapter how Stalin's Red Army finally repudiated its non-aggression treaty with Japan, and entered the war on 9 August 1945 (although it was still before midnight on 8 August in Moscow, the deadline for it to enter the war in accordance with the Yalta declarations). At Yalta, Britain and the US had agreed that the Soviet Union would regain Sakhalin and the Kuril Islands from Japan, and would be allowed to reclaim the 'lease' on the naval base at Lushun it had lost to Japan in 1905. Dalian was to be turned into an internationalized city, and the Soviet Union would gain a majority stake in the Japanese (formerly Sino–Russian) railway line through Manchuria. The Allies were still thinking in terms of 'spheres of influence' akin to nineteenth-century European diplomacy, and Chiang Kai-shek was quietly kept out of these deliberations, thereby undermining his authority as a supposed member of the 'Big Four' prosecuting the Asian war.

Having entered the war late, Stalin's Red Army did not stop its rapid advance when Emperor Hirohito announced Japan's surrender on 15 August 1945 and asked his troops to lay down their arms. Instead, the Soviet forces— which had by then taken Inner Mongolia but were less than halfway into Manchukuo—continued to rush forward in the face of minimal resistance from the small minority of Japanese troops who refused to accept their emperor's order to surrender. Their key goal here was to ensure that Japanese ammunition, weapons and equipment would fall into the hands of their allies—the CCP, which Mao Zedong had by then taken complete control of as chairman (with Marshal Zhu De as vice-chairman, reflecting the vital role of the army within the CCP at this time). It was the young Lin Biao who led the CCP's troops into Manchuria on the back of the Soviet invasion. By the time Lin Biao's forces arrived there in September 1945, the Soviets controlled all the main industrial cities, towns, mines and railroads in the rich and industrialized region. The Soviets deposed Puyi as emperor of Manchukuo, and seized large stores of food and machinery (especially power equipment like transformers, electrical motors, etc., the best machine tools, and whole laboratories and hospitals) for themselves, claiming these as reparations for Soviet losses in the European war. But by ensuring that Lin Biao came into possession of almost all of Japan's vast military supplies and weaponry in the region, the USSR gave its ally the CCP a decisive edge in the ensuing Civil War.

As soon as they gained significant territory in Manchuria, the CCP also began implementing a radical programme of land reform—going beyond its past campaigns of rent reductions, to actual transfer of ownership to those who tilled the land. This was relatively easy in Manchuria, as most holders of large tracts of land could be labelled 'collaborators' with the Japanese, apart from some land that was directly Japanese-owned, and could be redistributed with even less disruption. Although they were unable to extend their reach into southern Manchuria's industrial heartland, the CCP established its headquarters at Harbin (a city of 800,000 inhabitants at the time), and busied itself in widening its support base amongst the peasantry by visibly advancing the programme of land redistribution.

The vast landholdings in the frontier territory of Manchuria were complex—as landlords had many intermediate relationships with tenants, assignees, farm workers (who sometimes stayed with the landlord's family and worked in exchange for a share of the crop)—but the CCP gained support by being fairer and less corrupt in their dealings than the KMT. In mid-1946, when KMT forces recaptured all twenty-nine counties in Jiangsu that the CCP had controlled, former landlords returned to their lands and unleashed severe repression on those that had taken possession of their land under CCP auspices. Similar reprisals were meted out on those that had participated in CCP-led land reforms in Hebei, Shandong, Henan and the old CCP stronghold of Yan'an, with at least one member of each such family shot as punishment, and thousands of others imprisoned if they failed to provide ransom money; local populations (especially in Yan'an) were also resentful of the way in which the CCP had abandoned them to their fate when the KMT arrived.

The main battleground of the civil war soon became the resource-rich and industrialized region of Manchuria, which had a population of just 5 million in 1905, but had risen to 45 million by 1945 as Japanese investments rapidly developed the region into the most prosperous part of Asia after Japan itself. While land redistribution in Manchuria helped shore up rural support for the CCP, the communists also used Harbin as a training ground for urban administration—of which they had precious little until that point. Like the Manchu pioneers Nurhaci and Hong Taiji had done in Manchuria in the 1620s, the CCP now used Harbin and Manchuria as the base to learn the techniques and skills to run cities and the whole country. In Harbin, taxes were kept low for grain, fuel and cooking oil, and much higher for luxuries. The CCP faced a severe test when Harbin was confronted with an epidemic of bubonic plague (arising from lab rats left behind by Japanese troops who had been experimenting with germ warfare). Although 30,000 people died, effective quarantine and inoculation—and help from Soviet health experts—capped the disaster.

Chiang Kai-shek's KMT did manage to gain possession of most of Japan's highly-developed industrial base in southern Manchuria, including the vast Anshan steel complex, the Liaoyang cotton mill, numerous hydroelectric plants, and the Fushun coal mines. But both in Manchuria and earlier in Shanghai, the KMT proved inept and corrupt in the process of taking over erstwhile Japanese properties, with officials often renting these out for private gain, while KMT cadres freely looted materials and supplies, earning the ire of the local population. Fatally, the KMT squandered a potential base of support by appointing outsiders from southern China to key positions in each of the three Manchurian provinces of Heilongjiang, Jilin and Liaoning and, most imprudently, bundled off the Young Marshal, Zhang Xueliang (whose selfless patriotism had stalled the Japanese advance into Manchuria and beyond a decade earlier) into exile in Taiwan. In the words of a newspaper correspondent in the key Manchurian city of Mukden (henceforth Shenyang), 'the common people... feel on the one hand that all under heaven belongs to the southerners and on the other that life today is not as good as it was in Manchukuo times'.

Taking advantage of such latent disaffection, the CCP's Lin Biao first built up a conventional army (far larger than the guerrilla force he had led until 1945), and then launched an audacious military manoeuvre in November 1946, crossing the frozen Sungari River in Manchuria to launch a surprise attack on the KMT army's winter lodgings. Although repeatedly beaten back by the KMT's superiority in numbers and air power, Lin Biao continued a series of attacks on the KMT forces over the next half-year—with an attack on the railhead at Siping in May 1947 proving a key turning point. From then on, Lin's CCP forces concentrated on cutting off the KMT armies' links to the key cities they controlled by destroying the railroads that connected them, reducing their access to supplies, and hence undermining morale amongst the KMT's key garrisons.

The communist armies were reinforced by Korean recruits sent from North Korea by Kim Il-sung, who had himself been a guerrilla fighter against the Japanese in Manchuria since the 1930s. The Korean communist troops in Jilin felt they were fighting for their ancient homeland (since the old Koguryo kingdom of Korea had included Jilin and much of Manchuria), and the CCP armies' general level of commitment was much greater because it was locally recruited, while the KMT forces were fighting far from home, in unfamiliar terrain. Morale in the Nationalist (KMT) armies was further undermined by the large disparity in pay between ordinary soldiers and their generals (who had gained most of the riches from the expropriation of Japanese property). Despite their superiority in numbers, the KMT armies adopted a strangely defensive posture, rarely pursuing Lin Biao's army after they had beaten it back from an area. Jung Chang and Jon Halliday assert that this was because Mao had moles in the KMT army. By mid-1947, the communist armies began to make decisive gains, as the Nationalists abandoned besieged towns and cities, with their full panoply of armaments, equipment and supplies falling into communist hands. By the end of 1947, it had become clear that Chiang Kai-shek had disastrously miscalculated in his attempt at invading Manchuria before consolidating his hold over the rest of China.

That hold was being steadily undermined by the KMT's failure to control inflation in China proper. Having taken control of the coastal heartlands that Japan had ruled (Beijing, Shanghai, Nanjing, Tianjin, Jiangsu, Zhejiang, Fujian and Guangdong), Chiang's KMT botched the process of merging the Japanese-era currency with the new 'fabi' currency that the KMT introduced. The exchange rate used (200 units of Japanese-era currency for 1 fabi) effectively impoverished all residents of the former Japanese-ruled areas (including key cities like Shanghai, Nanjing, Beijing and Guangzhou), hugely devaluing their savings while enriching the KMT and their cronies. This utterly unfair exchange rate was engineered by Chiang Kai-shek's prime minister, T. V. Soong (Madame Chiang's brother) immediately after the end of the war with Japan. One of the biggest beneficiaries was H. H. Kung, the seventy-fifth generation descendant of Confucius and a Yale economics graduate who had been a very effective finance minister (and before that, industry minister) to Chiang Kai-shek over the previous two decades and was reputed to already be the richest man in China. (He was also married to Soong Ai-ling, the eldest of the Soong sisters—the other two having married Sun Yat-sen and Chiang Kai-shek.) Dispossessing the middle class of China's main cities— merely because they had lived under Japanese rule and been governed by a Japanese collaborationist regime—was especially impolitic on Chiang's part. Resentment of the way Madame Chiang's family had enriched themselves at the expense of the middle-class residents of China's (formerly Japanese-ruled) cities caused the latter (who should otherwise have been the KMT's natural allies) to turn permanently wary and distrustful of Chiang Kai-shek.

The process of 'returning' businesses and government-run corporations from the hands of the Japanese and their 'collaborators' to their previous owners was a politically-fraught muddle—marred by graft and much political point-scoring amongst long-standing rivals. Wang Jingwei, the president (until November 1944) of the Japanese-backed Republic of China based in Nanjing, had after all been Chiang Kai-shek's rival to succeed Sun Yat-sen as leader of the KMT, and had served as Chiang's prime minister for three years (1932–35). A substantial KMT faction had collaborated with the Japanese, and separating collaborators from 'patriots' was inherently difficult, made all the more complex by the KMT leadership's venality and greed. The demobilization of soldiers and policemen who had worked for the Japanese, and the closure of their armaments factories, contributed to a surge in unemployment, and the KMT responded to shortages of goods by printing more money. In Shanghai, prices tripled between September and November 1945, and had increased tenfold by May 1946. Although the pace of inflation moderated slightly thereafter, it reaccelerated in February 1947 (by which time the general level of prices had risen twenty-nine-fold from the September 1945 level).

Inflation sparked industrial unrest across the KMT's urban strongholds, and the communists were able to infiltrate labour unions in most of the major cities—especially Shanghai, Tianjin, Wuhan and Guangzhou—where they helped foment unrest, to which the KMT invariably responded with repressive violence. By mid-1947, the KMT began taking a more conciliatory approach and began to address the inflation problem with a more realistic set of plans. This included some wage and price controls, alongside effective distribution of essential food and other commodities at fixed prices to government servants, soldiers, students, teachers and some cultural workers, helping to contain the cost of living. For a while in 1948, inflation was brought under control by Chiang Kai-shek's eldest son by his first wife, Chiang Ching-kuo (who had effectively been Stalin's hostage in Moscow for more than a decade, having initially been a classmate of Deng Xiaoping's at the party school there). The younger Chiang helped introduce a new 'gold yuan' to replace the devalued fabi, and mounted a vigorous attempt at curtailing speculation and hoarding, including decisive action against Green Gang warlords and other currency and stock market manipulators. But the promise to limit circulation of the gold yuan to 2 billion units proved impossible to sustain as shortages of key commodities worsened by October 1948 and rumours of new money-printing sparked a new bout of speculative hoarding, followed by actual increases in money supply and a new bout of rapid inflation.

Despite all the disaffection sparked by inflation, the KMT appeared to be winning the Civil War in the first half of 1947. In March, the KMT captured Mao's bastion of Yan'an (with Mao himself escaping in an automobile convoy just ahead of Yan'an's capture, aided by a tip-off from a mole). Over the next three months, the CCP was routed in all its remaining strongholds in China proper and was forced back into its fastness of Manchuria, a region that had not been part of China until the Manchu conquest of China in the seventeenth century. Now, however, Manchuria was the economic powerhouse of the region, and Stalin's help in ensuring that most of the armaments factories, machinery and economic base of Manchuria fell into the CCP's hands, proved to be a decisive factor in turning the tide.

In areas recaptured from the CCP, landlords were allowed to regain their former homes and land, and visit violent reprisals upon those who had participated in the CCP's often-gruesome land reform campaigns. This lent a sharper edge to the fighting, as Mao's CCP came to be seen as being on the side of the peasants and working people, while the KMT were defending the elite. Its reputation for enabling peasants to gain control of land from their landlords proved an effective recruitment device for the CCP, as did coercive ideological campaigns, which denigrated any reluctant participant as a 'class enemy' to be treated with the gruesome brutality reserved for landlords. Ironically Ya'nan was the one area where local people were thoroughly disillusioned with the communists, having been abandoned to their fate upon the CCP's retreat.

With its armies massively augmented by new recruits in the second half of 1947 and early 1948, the CCP turned the tide of the war by capturing the vital industrial cities in Manchuria of Changchun (with its massive automobile complex) and Shenyang (Mukden) after long sieges in the second half of 1948. The six-month siege of Changchun proved particularly brutal, with residents resorting to eating their belts, dead rats and tree bark in the final weeks before its capture. At the end of it, the KMT's elite New First Army (its finest fighting force) had fallen to the CCP with all its superb armaments, heavy equipment and supplies. After that decisive victory in Manchuria, the CCP was able to throw its enlarged army into battle in the heartlands of northern China. Soon thereafter, the CCP captured Jinan and Shandong province and launched its decisive Huaihai Campaign—the most important conventional battle of the Civil War—at the end of which the CCP had secured east-central China. During this campaign (militarily directed by Zhu De), the political mobilization of 2 million peasants to provide logistical support to the military was led by the forty-five-year-old Deng Xiaoping. And in the final, decisive sixty-four-day Pingjin Campaign (referring to Bei*ping* and

Tian*jin*), the CCP conquered Tianjin, Zhangjiakou and Dagu, culminating in the capture of the old imperial capital of Beiping (which was renamed Beijing, although transcribed in English as 'Peking' until the 1970s). During this Pingjin Campaign, a crucial role was assigned to former Japanese soldiers, who had been effectively 're-educated' in communism by the leader of the Japan Communist Party, Nosaka Sanzo, who had spent the war years in Yan'an with Mao and Zhou Enlai, and subsequently unleashed his propaganda blitz amongst demoralized Japanese prisoners of war. With their superior skills and training in gunnery, the Japanese communist soldiers handled almost all the artillery deployed by the People's Liberation Army in the crucial Pingjin Campaign.

The KMT generals did not stand and fight in most of the cities of the North China Plain. Jung Chang and Jon Halliday's investigations provided a clear explanation for this: almost all the KMT's generals were either communist moles or had moles amongst their key staff or family members who ensured that the CCP armies were always one step ahead of them in terms of information flow. As the CCP armies led by Lin Biao approached, the KMT general Fu Tso-yi (Zuoyi) decided to abandon Chengde, Baoding and Qinhuangdao and instead make his stand at Beiping and Tianjin. But Fu's own daughter was a communist informant, and by the time the two armies met at Tianjin, Fu Tso-yi was a psychological wreck, his mind addled by the CCP's seeming omniscience about his tactics and strategy.

Chiang Kai-shek's choice of a supreme commander for the previous Manchuria campaign had also proved catastrophic. Chiang had picked Wei Lihuang, who Chiang himself suspected to be a communist agent. But Wei was regarded highly by the Americans for his wartime victories in Burma, and this factor overwhelmed all others in Chiang's mind. The US had provided the KMT with about US$4.4 billion in military aid, and Chiang hoped that the US would be enthused to provide more by his appointment of a general regarded highly by Stilwell to this crucial command. Wei had sought to join Mao's communists in 1938, but Mao had preferred to allow key generals like Wei to remain in the KMT army while becoming key informants and 'sleepers' for the communists. Wei contacted the Soviet embassy immediately upon receiving his Manchuria appointment and kept his communications with the communists open even after taking up his post. General Wei Lihuang had been known as 'Hundred Victories Wei' for his previous military exploits, but these inexplicably ended as soon as he got to Manchuria. Instead, his military moves there invariably led to large contingents of his troops falling into the hands of Mao's People's Liberation Army (PLA). At least 260,000 of the KMT's elite troops had thus 'fallen into' the PLA's arms, massively augmenting it, before Wei was relieved of his command. By then, it was too late to save even southern Manchuria's key cities for the KMT. Wei was placed under house arrest, but later escaped to Hong Kong and lived until his death (in 1960) in Mao's People's Republic (albeit without receiving much recognition for his perfidy to the KMT as it would have dented Mao's reputation for military genius).

With his bastions in north China quickly falling to the communists, Chiang Kai-shek resigned as President of China on 21 January 1949 (having been re-elected less than a year earlier) but remained chief of the KMT political party to the bitter end, a factor that diluted the credibility of his successor as official head of state. That successor, Vice President Li Zongren (a rival of Chiang's and a KMT general who had won a rare battlefield victory against the Japanese, having been a Guangxi warlord before that) attempted to negotiate a compromise with Mao, who agreed to temporarily halt the fighting but gave a list of 'Eight Demands', which amounted to conditions for the KMT's surrender (starting with 'punish all war criminals', of whom Chiang was designated 'number 1'). Prior to the fall of the old imperial capital of Beiping to the communists, Chiang had sent thousands of crates full of antiques, pottery, art and imperial Qing dynasty archives to the island of Taiwan, where he stationed 300,000 of his crack troops, along with twenty-six gunboats and some aircraft squadrons.

Meanwhile, Mao had ordered his troops to maintain strict discipline, and not disrupt the working of the normal economy. Chinese businessmen were ('temporarily') to be allowed to run their businesses without hindrance (including being allowed 'appropriate capitalist exploitation' of labour), looting was strictly forbidden, and measures were taken to ensure adequate food supplies (and hence contain inflation) in newly-conquered cities. This ensured that Mao's communists faced little opposition from wary publics after they took control of cities, and received grudging admiration relative to the venality that had characterized the retreating KMT. Chiang and Li moved their government headquarters first to Nanjing, then briefly to Shanghai, before moving south to Changsha and then to the old wartime capital of Chongqing. After a ten-week lull in the Civil War, Mao gave Li a five-day ultimatum in mid-April to surrender on the terms contained in his unyielding Eight Demands. When Li failed to respond, the PLA's assault resumed, with Nanjing quickly falling to the communist forces (23 April), Hangzhou and Wuhan soon after, followed in May by Shanghai.

The PLA forces then fanned out across the country, Peng Dehuai leading his armies northwest to the ancient capital of Xian, the rest of Shaanxi and to Lanzhou in the far northwest and then onto Xinjiang in September, where

Soviet forces helped the PLA put down a local rebellion. And Lin Biao headed south, capturing Changsha in August, and then running into severe resistance in the attempt to take the southern redoubt of Canton (Guangzhou), which did not fall until mid-October.

Two weeks earlier, on 1 October 1949, Mao Zedong ascended Beijing's Gate of Heavenly Peace—the main entrance to the imperial palace during the Ming and Qing eras—to proclaim the establishment of the People's Republic of China. Newsreels (and eyewitness accounts) of the occasion show Mao giving a rather pedestrian speech in his heavy Hunan accent, with a long catalogue of ministers, but never uttering the words that hagiographic retellings of the occasion attribute to him: 'The Chinese people have stood up!' The fighting, however, was continuing and Xiamen (the getaway point for those KMT officials and soldiers seeking to escape to Taiwan) finally fell to the communists in late November 1949, as did Chongqing, where Deng Xiaoping was in political control of the forces charged with conquering the southwest (with the army commander being his long-time comrade-in-arms, Liu Bocheng). It was only after the fall of Sichuan's capital, Chengdu, on 10 December 1949 that the core of the KMT government (including Chiang) was evacuated to Taiwan by air.

Six days later, Mao set off on his first trip outside China—going to Moscow as a gesture of thanksgiving and to demonstrate clearly just how much he was 'leaning to one side'. It proved to be a bewildering experience for Mao, as the two communist leaders found each other's imperial visions of their respective national boundaries clashing irretrievably.

Stalin had been especially irritated by the hagiographic myth-making of Mao's propaganda machine (which barely acknowledged the decisively facilitative role in the CCP's revolutionary triumph played by Stalin and the Soviet Union). Far from welcoming his fellow revolutionary hero with a warm bear hug, Stalin barely acknowledged Mao's presence in Moscow for several days. Then a protracted two-month period of negotiation ensued as the two imperialist visions clashed: Stalin, although Georgian by birth, was a committed Russian imperialist with an expansive vision of Soviet territorial ambitions, and Mao matched him with just as imperialist a vision of Chinese imperial boundaries, that must perforce be at least as extensive as the Qing ones. After two months, it was agreed that the Soviet Union (hence Russia) would give up its long-standing control over Port Arthur (Lushun) and Dalian—the two Manchurian prizes that Japan and Russia had tussled over for fifty years— and that China would keep East Turkestan (which the USSR had helped it secure), but that China would have no claim over 'Outer Mongolia', which had been independent (but heavily under Soviet influence) since 1921 (although

'Inner Mongolia' would stay part of China, itself a rather large concession).

Burma was the first nation outside the Soviet bloc to recognize Mao's regime as the legitimate government of China (on 9 December 1949), and India was the second (on 30 December 1949), followed by Pakistan five days later. Soon after India accorded diplomatic recognition to Mao's government, it began to periodically denounce Nehru as a hypocritical imperial lackey. In January 1950, Mao's regime announced that its key unfinished tasks for 1950 included the 'liberation' of Tibet, Hainan island and Taiwan. 'Liberation from whom and what?' the Tibetans plaintively but quite pointedly asked, 'Ours is a happy country with a solvent government.' A representative of the Manchu regime (almost always a Manchu rather than a Han Chinese) had been stationed in Lhasa for about two centuries until 1910 (but there had been no representative, and no relationship, between Tibet and the Ming or any previous Han Chinese dynasty). Even the Manchu representative was essentially an ambassador, although the Qing court—in the imperial manner to which China's courts were accustomed—designated Tibet's rulers as tributaries rather than allies or foreign powers. By 1950, however, Tibet had been completely independent for forty years—with no Chinese diplomat, sentry, postal system, language, newspaper or any other trappings of Chinese-ness visible in Lhasa or elsewhere in Tibet. India and Nepal had always treated Tibet as an independent country, and it was only Curzon who had introduced the notion of 'suzerainty' into discussions about Tibet's relationship with the Manchu regime (uncritically labelled 'Chinese'). Matters were somewhat complicated by the fact that the KMT had used Tibetan (Khampa) warriors in its last stand in Sichuan (the western part of which was, in any case, part of the 'Inner Tibet' that the Qing dynasty had annexed in its final decade, the rest of Inner Tibet being the vast, beautiful plateau of Qinghai sometimes labelled 'Shangri-La').

The fourteenth (and still current) Dalai Lama was not quite fifteen years old, but he urged his government to engage global opinion, to counter Communist China's claim that Tibet was part of China or that somehow it needed to be 'liberated'. In particular, Tibet sent letters to the US, UK and India. Nehru, who had invited a Tibetan delegation to the Asian conference of 1947 now began taking a more conciliatory approach towards China; when repeatedly asked about Tibet, he maintained that India had good diplomatic relations with Tibet and China, but by April 1950 was beginning to use the word 'suzerainty' to describe China's claim over Tibet. (That modern international law does not acknowledge any such concept as 'suzerainty' did not appear to give Nehru pause.) Nehru also kept assuring India's press and Parliament that India's traditional rights in Tibet would be maintained under his formulation of Chinese suzerainty over Tibet. Ironically, China had no real access to Tibet at the time, and India was the only nation that had extensive representation in Tibet (including at Lhasa, Shigatse, Yatung and Gyantse); when a delegation from Beijing travelled to Lhasa in March 1950, they came via Calcutta, then Kalimpong (in India's Darjeeling district) before entering Tibet from the south. The Americans were keen to support Tibet's claim to sovereignty but needed support from India (or possibly Nepal) to solidify the claim. But the proto-communist Nehru (who believed, in his simple heart, that communism was the wave of the future, and the forces of history would inevitably lead to the triumph of communism) contemptuously brushed off the American offer of support. Nehru told his cabinet that it was not possible for India to help Tibet fend off the well-armed PLA (but he did not address the question of whether American support could have augmented the military potential of a combined effort). The Tibetans were on their own, and hence highly vulnerable, having neglected any military preparation during their forty years of full independence.

China, while assuring India that it could retain its traditional rights within Tibet, began pressuring the Tibetan government by late September with a set of 'Three Demands', the first of which was to accept that Tibet was part of China. Accepting these demands would allow the 'peaceful liberation' of Tibet! The Dalai Lama was willing to discuss the other two terms, that China would control Tibet's trade and would oversee its military, but refused to accept the first. And the Tibetans maintained that since there were no foreigners (apart from a single German and a single Briton) in Tibet, there was no need to 'liberate' Tibet from imperialist control and certainly no need for any Chinese troop presence in Tibet. The leader of the Tibetan delegation asserted quite rationally: 'Tibet will remain independent as it is at present, and we will continue to have very close "priest-patron" relations with China. Also, there is no need to liberate Tibet from imperialism, since there are no British, American or KMT imperialists in Tibet, and Tibet is ruled and protected by the Dalai Lama (not any foreign power).' The 'priest-patron' relationship is what Tibet had with the Manchus and the Mongols (but, pointedly, not with the Ming or any other Han Chinese dynasty). It was based on mutual respect, with the Mongols and Manchus respecting the spiritual leadership of Tibet in exchange for some temporal rights. Tibet's tragedy was that the world did not pay attention then, and has not paid much attention since.

Mao knew that, although the PLA was a well-oiled machine, it did not have the ability to fight a war on the high plateau of Tibet should India seriously seek to engage militarily. But it was clear to him (from Zhou Enlai's initial contacts with Nehru) that there was scant chance of India intervening.

So, despite some stout resistance from Khams in the area, Mao sent the PLA into battle across the Jinsha River on 7 October and, after some fierce fighting, the PLA captured the eastern Tibetan town of Chamdo on 19 October 1950. News of this fighting was kept very low-key, and only dim reports appeared in India about a fortnight later, while the rest of the world remained largely oblivious. Nehru, fully engaged in his flights of fancy as an 'honest broker' between the two Koreas, was still insisting that the Chinese would adopt nothing but 'peaceful means' while dealing with Tibet. If he had any intelligence reports about China's invasion, he kept them very much to himself until it was too late. When El Salvador introduced a resolution on behalf of Tibet into the UN, Britain and India shamefully thwarted any discussion of it. (This was especially ironic since the PRC, although recognized by Britain and India, was not a seated member of the UN at the time and regularly launched verbal attacks on Britain and India as arch imperialists.)

On 7 November 1950, Sardar Vallabhbhai Patel, India's home minister, wrote to Nehru, 'The Chinese government have tried to delude us by professions of peaceful intentions.... The final action of the Chinese, in my judgement, is little short of perfidy. The tragedy of it is that the Tibetans put faith in us; they chose to be guided by us; and we have been unable to get them out of the meshes of Chinese diplomacy or Chinese influence.' Patel added tellingly, 'We had a friendly Tibet which gave us no trouble.... We seem to have regarded Tibetan autonomy as extending to (an) independent treaty relationship. The Chinese interpretation of suzerainty appears to be different. We can, therefore, safely assume that very soon they will disown all the stipulations which Tibet has entered into with us in the past.' This was amongst Patel's last communications with his colleague; his health was deteriorating fast, and he died on 15 December. But his warnings proved prescient.

The fourteenth Dalai Lama was enthroned on 17 November 1950, and soon afterwards agreed to send a delegation to negotiate with Beijing. The delegation, far from negotiating, was faced with a seventeen-point set of demands that it was obliged to accept, and given no opportunity to communicate with their government back in Lhasa. After six months of effectively being held hostage, the delegation agreed to the seventeen points on 23 May 1951. It was the first time any representative of Tibet had ever agreed to accept China's sovereignty in any form over Tibet, although the Tibetan government (and its leader the Dalai Lama) had not accepted this. There was little to distinguish this 'acceptance' from Korea's acceptance of Japanese sovereignty over Korea in 1909–10; the acquiescence of Teddy Roosevelt had made Japan's annexation of Korea possible in 1910, and Nehru's acquiescence similarly allowed China to annex Tibet by October 1951 (when its troops entered Tibet). The Dalai Lama first sounded out Nehru on the possibility of obtaining political asylum in India in 1956 and was strongly rebuffed. Eventually, amid the brutal suppression of the Tibetan uprising of March 1959, the Dalai Lama (still only twenty-four years old) escaped on foot to Assam, and was finally granted asylum in India, where he established a 'Little Lhasa' at Dharamsala in Himachal Pradesh, just south of Ladakh, the region that Ranjit Singh and Gulab Singh had annexed from Tibet in the nineteenth century and that is today a redoubt of Buddhism in India. In 1962, an Indian Army that had been starved of funds by the leftist defence minister, Krishna Menon, was given a bloody nose by China's PLA. My newly-married mother was amongst many thousands who donated her jewellery to India's cause but was told to flee north Bengal, as the Chinese swarmed into Assam before suddenly withdrawing after 'teaching India a lesson'.

For Koreans, the Second World War never really ended until 1953 (and even at the end of that period, all Korea got was an armistice rather than a durable peace). Bruce Cumings (a Korea specialist at the University of Chicago) has shown that the end of the World War, and Japan's surrender to the Allies, brought no peace to Korea. Instead, the Soviet Red Army advanced into northern Korea and ensured that a communist faction, led by an undoubted hero of resistance to Japanese rule (primarily in Manchukuo rather than Korea proper), Kim Il-Sung, took power in the northern half of Korea up to the 38th parallel. In the south, left-wing 'people's committees' (mainly comprising those that had resisted Japanese rule) took local control, and sought to purge the government of 'collaborators' with Japanese rule. When the Americans arrived in October 1945, they looked around for more conservative political forces to align themselves with and these typically turned out to be the 'yangban' intellectual and political elite, landlords and businessmen (most of whom had collaborated with the Japanese, and prospered during their rule). This led to civil war in parts of the south, especially in the rice-basket region of southern Cholla and Cheju island.

The end of China's civil war resulted in the repatriation of vast battalions of battle-hardened Korean communist troops to North Korea (Democratic People's Republic of Korea, DPRK) in early 1950. Border clashes became common in the subsequent months. Finally, on 25 June, the DPRK claimed a casus belli in the form of a Republic of Korea Army (ROKA) attack on the isolated Ongjin peninsula into territory north of the 38th parallel. Using that as the excuse, DPRK troops poured into the south and made for the southern capital of Seoul. US Secretary of State Dean Acheson, likening the invasion to Hitler's invasions of Czechoslovakia and Poland, quickly persuaded

President Truman that the defence of South Korea was vital to US national interests and also crucial to the security of America's new ally, Japan. The Soviet Union was then boycotting the UN because it had refused to seat the PRC; so when a resolution condemning North Korea was introduced into the UN Security Council, the Soviet Union abstained; since it had not exercised its customary veto, the resolution passed, and the UN decided to take military action against the DPRK.

It took a few weeks for the UN troops to be galvanized into action under the overall command of Field Marshal Douglas MacArthur. Before that, however, Seoul quickly fell to the DPRK forces on 27 June despite last-minute measures like blowing up the bridge over the Han River, killing hundreds (of the 4,000 refugees) who were crossing the bridge at the time. The ROKA soldiers were ill-disciplined and unmotivated, and developed a reputation for running rather than fighting. The DPRK forces advanced rapidly across South Korea, until just a small area (known as the Pusan Perimeter in South Kyongsang province) still remained in ROKA hands, with President Syngman Rhee also holed up there. This area—including Pohang and Taegu—would become the heart of Korean industrialization in the 1960s, but now it was a precarious redoubt for the US-aligned ROK government.

In early July, a joint US Army–Marine Corps task force set off from Yokohama bound for Inchon, following MacArthur's command to make an amphibious landing in that coastal town just northwest of Seoul, and more than a hundred miles behind the DPRK army's lines. MacArthur's dramatic Inchon landing on 15 September 1950 quickly turned the tide of the war. American forces began to push northwards from the Pusan Perimeter, while the surprise attack from behind their lines disrupted the DPRK army's strategy. Tens of thousands of North Korean troops perished as they were pushed back north. On 29 September 1950, Seoul was recaptured and Syngman Rhee's government was restored to power in its capital.

MacArthur had received explicit orders not to cross the 38th parallel if there was any evidence of Soviet or Chinese involvement in fighting on North Korea's side (to preclude any possibility of a Third World War). Although the Chinese had been threatening to enter the war on North Korea's side since mid-August, they hadn't done so by 1 October 1950 (the first anniversary of China's revolution) and MacArthur ordered his troops to cross into North Korea. Meanwhile, the US Seventh Fleet was already patrolling the Taiwan Straits to prevent any hostilities between the PRC and Taiwan. Pyongyang, the north's capital, fell to the UN–ROKA combined forces on 19 October 1950. Soon thereafter, China's PLA (called the People's Volunteer Army for this purpose) entered the war on the North Korean side. And a stalemate ensued in the war, amid brutal warfare until an armistice was signed in July 1953.

In China itself, the 1950s were characterized by the brutalities of its land reform programme, which unleashed terror on the landlord class. At least 1 million people were killed, and horrific atrocities committed on at least 10 million others designated to be class enemies. Yet much of this was romanticized around the world, as a great peasant revolution. In 1956, Mao launched his 'Hundred Flowers' movement, with the slogan 'let a hundred flowers bloom, let a hundred thoughts contend' with Liu Shaoqi and Deng Xiaoping (then the general secretary of the secretariat) in the vanguard. Then, when criticisms became too loud, Mao abruptly changed course and announced the anti-rightist campaign (aimed at ferreting out those who had been most vocal in the Hundred Flowers phase), followed soon afterwards by the Great Leap Forward—Mao's attempt, from 1958 to 1961, to pull China into rapid industrialization through collectivization. The Great Leap sought to force every spare bit of iron in the country (including ploughs) to be turned into steel in an extreme attempt to emulate both the brutality and the industrial success of Stalin in the 1930s.

In the event, Mao's attempt at industrialization was a spectacular failure, although the brutality surpassed anything that even Stalin had managed. Manchuria, the most industrialized region of the country, suffered most grievously from the famine that followed, killing at least 18 million, and perhaps as many as 45 million people, making it by far the most gruesome massacre of the twentieth century. The most horrific aspect of it was that the rest of the world did not comprehend just how gruesome the famine had been for another two decades. And when China's PLA crossed the Himalayas to attack India in October 1962 (as a classic Maoist diversion from domestic woes), the majority of India's communists chose to support China over India (and became members of the Communist Party of India–Marxist that ruled West Bengal for thirty-four years from 1977).

Liu Shaoqi led the internal dissent against the Great Leap, and he and Deng Xiaoping took the lead in restoring stability to the economy after its three-year contraction. But they were the first ones to be attacked as 'capitalist roaders' and 'running dogs of the imperialists' when Mao decided to counter them with the Cultural Revolution from 1966 onwards, which ran until his death in 1976. Liu and his wife were brutalized in public by the Red Guards, as were Deng and his family (his son Deng Pufang was thrown out of the third-floor window of his college dorm, and was paralysed for the rest of his life), and they along with hundreds of thousands of other intellectuals and gentry were sent off to work in the countryside. The wasted years left China in desperate need of emulating others. Luckily, Japan and its emulators

(Taiwan especially and Korea under Park Chung-hee) were to provide the blueprint for Deng Xiaoping to follow after 1978.

MITI AND THE MAKING OF JAPAN'S ECONOMIC MIRACLE

We saw in Chapter 4 that Japan's industrial policy in the 1930s had been characterized by a constant tussle between the 'self-regulation' of zaibatsu advocated by Ministry of Commerce and Industry (MCI) bureaucrats, and the 'state control' that the military preferred. The latter, in its extreme forms, resulted in widespread nationalization of businesses (especially in Manchukuo) between 1931 and 1936 in the heyday of the anti-zaibatsu movement amongst the militarists. The nationalizations had proven a failure, and the MCI veteran Kishi Nobusuke had been summoned to restore dynamism to Manchukuo industry, which he did by inviting Nissan's Ayukawa to move his firm's car and truck manufacturing to Changchun (in Kirin province; now spelt Jilin).

In October 1941, Prime Minister Tojo appointed Kishi as MCI minister (making him, at forty-six, one of modern Japan's youngest ministers). Amongst the key early initiatives of MCI during the war was a plan for industrial rationalization that involved converting textile firms to munitions manufacturing, as well as the closure of small and medium enterprises (especially those that produced for the domestic market) or their absorption into zaibatsu (as subsidiaries or subcontractors). The conquest of Manchukuo, and more particularly northern and east-coastal China, had ironically resulted in Japan 'losing' one of its main export markets for earning foreign currency (as most of China became part of the yen currency bloc). MCI analysis revealed that most small and medium enterprises were very import-dependent but sold primarily into the domestic market. This made them prime targets for 'rationalization' amid the shortage of foreign exchange.

As the war began to turn less favourable for Japan in mid-1942 (after Midway and Guadalcanal), Kishi discovered that the industrial 'control associations'—each of them run by a zaibatsu chief—were operating like cartels that maximized the profits of the leading zaibatsu (which often cut side deals with the military to keep the arrangement going). Kishi moved to appoint a quasi-government employee (with enforcement powers) as the head of some of the key control associations (replacing the chief executive of the largest zaibatsu within the industry) starting with the vital steel industry (which came to be headed by Admiral Toyoda Teijiro, former MCI minister). And he sought to defuse the tension between the self-regulation and state-control advocates through various forms of mixed public-private corporation. 'Licensed companies' like Toyota and Nissan, and public sector Japan Steel and

South Manchuria Railroad, were amongst the 'national policy companies' that were part of this rubric, but the management foundation ('eidan') eventually became the MCI's favoured device to control a sector without the zaibatsu domination of the control associations. The public part of the Tokyo subway system, for instance, was established in 1941 as the Teito Rapid Transit Eidan, which continued to exist until 2004. During the war years, though, the key eidan was the Industrial Facilities Eidan, created in November 1941 to purchase or lease idle factories and convert them to munitions manufacturing. And it worked closely with the 'Promotion Bureau' of MCI, whose task it was to promote the expansion of companies' scale, especially to encourage small-scale ones to grow larger. Kishi and his vice minister Shiina Etsusaburo also obtained a couple of key imperial ordinances—the Enterprise Licensing Ordinance (prohibiting new businesses without obtaining a government licence) and the Enterprise Readjustment Ordinance, giving the government the right to order any company to convert to the manufacture of munitions.

The Kishi–Shiina team also created an Enterprises Bureau as the nerve centre for industrial reorganization and production-expansion activity. This bureau survived well into the MITI era, and was from the start responsible for capital supply, internal organization, efficiency, and inspecting/controlling financials and accounts of all Japanese enterprises (an extraordinarily wide remit). It supervised the Industrial Facilities Eidan and also dealt with all issues concerning small and medium industries. It began by converting one sector after another to munitions manufacturing, with most of the textile industry in particular being forcibly converted towards aeroplane and plane parts manufacturing. The number of installed spindles declined 82 per cent between 1937 (12.17 million) and February 1946 (2.15 million), and the number of textile mills dwindled from 271 to just 44 over that period. In mid-1943, the cabinet categorized all industries into 'peace industries' (textiles, metals, chemicals), munitions industries (steel, coal, light metals, aircraft and shipbuilding) and 'daily necessities'. The last category was to be largely abolished, and industries in the first category were liable to be converted into the second category. The consequence was that basic consumer goods began to disappear by 1944 and, with Japan's merchant fleet being heavily depleted by Allied bombing during the final year of the war, supply lines to the colonies (especially Malaya and the East Indies) collapsed. Deprivation of food and consumer goods was severe in both Japan and across its empire in the final year of the war, and the memories of deprivation in that period were played up even more by Allied propagandists after the war (neatly ignoring the severe famines in India and Britain's African colonies, and the French colony of Indo-China).

A second consequence was to create an industrial structure that was dominated by heavy and chemical industries. And the industrial economy also became increasingly concentrated in the hands of the zaibatsu, with medium- and small-scale producers increasingly obliged to become subsidiaries or permanent subcontractors of the zaibatsu. In late 1943, Japan's pre-War MCI was relabelled the Ministry of Munitions (MM), and Prime Minister Tojo himself took over additional charge as Minister of Munitions with Kishi as vice minister but also holding the rank of a state minister without portfolio (working directly under Tojo, albeit with similar rank). Secretly, Tojo also gave the same ministerial rank to another ex-zaibatsu official, Fujihara Ginjiro (a former chief executive of the Mitsui-linked Oji Paper Company, who had run the Industrial Facilities Eidan since its creation). Initially after the creation of MM, Kishi was able to separate management from ownership by posting supervisors from the ministry in every factory, and making them (rather than the industrial 'control associations') responsible for meeting targets and following MM rules, while continuing to pay dividends to shareholders. This supervisory authority survived into the MITI era, providing invaluable experience to MITI cadres.

Kishi, however, was furious to discover that Fujihara had been appointed as a kind of zaibatsu monitor over him in MM and immediately offered his resignation to Tojo, who refused to accept it. However, relations between Kishi and Tojo deteriorated as a consequence of this imbroglio, and in July 1944—after the fall of Saipan—Kishi began openly advocating that Japan sue for peace, since a victory in the war was no longer possible. This was a dangerous position for anyone to take, especially because Tojo still controlled the kempeitai (military police). It also brought Kishi closer to Abe Kan, who was the leader of a minor faction in the Diet that had argued during the 1942 election that Japan should call off the war effort. This view was then beginning to gain ground in the navy and with a growing faction in the Imperial Household; reinforced by his network of quiet supporters, Kishi refused to resign when Tojo asked him to in July 1944, and in the ensuing power struggle it was Tojo who was forced out later that month. (Abe Kan died in 1946, but his son Shintaro would marry Kishi's daughter Yoko, and their son Shinzo is the current prime minister of Japan; Abe Kan's closest deputy, Miki Takeo, would become prime minister in 1974.)

Although he survived the struggle with Tojo, Kishi was subsequently eclipsed within MM as his rival Fujihara was appointed munitions minister in the cabinet headed by General Koiso Kuniaki; thereafter Toyoda of the Iron and Steel Control Association succeeded Fujihara as munitions minister in the cabinet of Admiral Suzuki Kantaro, which was officially tasked with bringing the war to an end, and he appointed Kishi's old collaborator Shiina Etsusaburo as vice minister. Shiina remained vice minister even after a new ministry was appointed following Japan's surrender on 15 August 1945, and it was he who moved swiftly before the arrival of the American occupiers to obtain an imperial ordinance abolishing the Ministry of Munitions and replacing it with the old MCI. Since this did not clash with the American occupiers' objectives, the Supreme Commander of the Allied Powers (SCAP, a position held by General Douglas MacArthur) did not attempt to alter these arrangements once the SCAP had taken full control of Japan's government.

The SCAP did move to purge any politician seen as having links to the militarists who had led the war effort—so Kishi, for instance, was initially jailed at Sugamo prison as a 'Class A' war crimes suspect. More important, the SCAP decreed that the zaibatsu and the cartels they had run were primarily responsible for the war economy, and so ordered that the zaibatsu be broken up, their cartels banned, and the influence of their 'control associations' replaced by direct bureaucratic control. In effect, this empowered the MCI bureaucrats and particularly the 'Kishi–Shiina line' within MCI, advocating bureaucratic direction of industrial policy (to replace the euphemism of 'self-regulation' by control associations). However, the MCI bureaucrats' nirvana was continually challenged not so much by the SCAP (which had a 'New Deal' orientation that was largely in accord with the MCI's Kishi–Shiina line) but by Prime Minister Yoshida Shigeru, who was acutely distrustful of Japan's wartime controlled economy, and the bureaucrats who had helped run it.

Yoshida had been a diplomat until 1939, serving as ambassador to Italy and then to the UK, and his key qualification in the eyes of the SCAP was that he spoke English fluently, but was otherwise quite cut off from Japan's mainstream. He succeeded Shidehara Kijuro (prime minister from October 1945 to May 1946), the liberal diplomat and foreign minister of the 1920s and early 1930s whose attempts at engaging the world through 'economic diplomacy' with China had been continually thwarted by the West, thus undermining him domestically. Yoshida was also the son-in-law of Makino Nobuaki, the second son of Okubo Toshimichi (one of the 'three samurai' of 1868 who had led the campaign to oust the Tokugawa shogunate before the Meiji Restoration); unlike most of Japan's political elite (who had links to the old Choshu domain), Yoshida's antecedents were thus in Satsuma (through Okubo). And Yoshida also was thought to be a Catholic, which further distanced him from the majority of his compatriots. Yoshida only became prime minister because the leader of his party in the Diet, Hatoyama Ichiro, was also purged by the SCAP. With the end of the war, Japan suddenly had a surfeit of out-of-work diplomats, and Yoshida was determined to use them to staff key ministries. In particular, he was determined to place reliable foreign ministry officials atop the MCI to oversee the economic bureaucrats he loathed.

But Yoshida lost power after the April 1947 election, in which the Socialists gained a plurality of seats (144 out of 466 seats), albeit with a similar vote share (26.3 per cent) as the Democratic Party (which won 132 seats) and slightly less than the 26.5 per cent won by Yoshida's Liberal Party (which, however, won only 129 seats); the Liberals were effectively the successors to the pre-war Seiyukai party, while the Democratic Party comprised former members of the Minseito. With the SCAP backing them, the Socialists (led by Katayama Tetsu) formed a stable coalition government with the Democrats. During the year that Katayama was prime minister, MCI was able to use the cover of socialism to greatly strengthen its industrial policy toolkit. MCI recreated the 'economic general staff' of the war years, took over the functions previously pooled with the private sector, enacted materials mobilization legislation that was even stronger than in the war years, and vastly expanded its bureaucratic numbers, taking up the third largest share of the budget (after the Prime Minister's Office and Finance Ministry).

In the immediate aftermath of surrender, industrial policy made stealth advances while the government's initial focus fell squarely on the need to combat runaway inflation. Prices leapt 247 per cent in September from the August 1945 level, and by March 1946 the price index was 1085 per cent above the August 1945 level. While production collapsed at the end of the war, and foreign trade came to an abrupt end (sharply reducing the availability of many key commodities), the government kept up its wartime payments to soldiers, contractors and creditors, while also adhering to its guarantees to munitions companies and compensation payments to former owners of factories that had been forcibly converted to arms production. The SCAP believed (as did Bank of Japan—BoJ—governor Ichimada Naoto) that price stabilization was more crucial than the finance ministry's focus on boosting production (and demand), and by July 1946 the SCAP was able to force the finance ministry to halt making those large payments. When the wartime compensation payments ended, however, there was a precipitous decline in production and inflation soared further.

Defying the SCAP, the Japanese government devised a 'priority production system' to restore production of key commodities like coal and steel to at least the pre-war levels. Its key institutions were the Reconstruction Finance Bank (RFB, established in January 1947), the Economic Stabilization Board (ESB, set up in August 1946, as a predecessor to the influential Economic Planning Agency), a Coal Agency to manage supplies of that key resource, and fifteen public corporations ('kodan') to ration commodities and products based on a Temporary Supply and Demand Control Law. In the immediate chaos following the war's end, coal production had plummeted—from 4 million tonnes monthly during the war years to just 0.55 million tonnes in November 1945—primarily because 145,000 Korean and 9,000 Chinese miners were repatriated to their home countries. Japanese miners were shifted from various metal mines to coal, but a virulent labour movement caused a steep rise in production costs and made the mines unviable.

Eventually, the priority production system came into operation in January 1947, aiming to boost output of three 'priority' commodities—coal, steel and fertilizers. The government began buying these commodities from producers at a high price, and selling them on to consumers at a lower price, with the cost of the subsidy being borne by the government's budget. In 1947, these subsidies absorbed about 14 per cent of the general account, rising to 20 per cent in 1948 and 25.6 per cent in 1949. Aided by such subsidies, coal production reached 29.3 million tonnes (97.7 per cent of the target) in the first year, and 34.8 million in 1948. With energy supplies restored, the economy began to hum gradually back to life.

The socialist Katayama administration, however, tried to overreach—by imposing wage and price controls, and attempting to nationalize the coal industry (emulating what the UK's Labour government had done the previous year). Nationalization (introduced as a 'temporary measure' in April 1948) did little to boost coal production beyond the levels that had been achieved in the previous two years of priority production. And price controls inevitably spawned a black market, resulting in an orgy of corruption that eventually culminated in the 'Showa Denko' corruption case that brought down the Socialist government in October 1948. Even earlier, the attempt to impose wage controls resulted in the well-publicized death from starvation in October 1947 of a judge who attempted to live on the new wage while refusing to buy rice on the black market. The period of Socialist rule also enabled the SCAP to have some key legislation passed—including the abolition of the hitherto-powerful Home Ministry, an Anti-Monopoly Law that provided for the dissolution of the zaibatsu, and land reform that gave ownership of land to the tiller (at the expense of absentee landlords). But in the minds of the Japanese electorate, the year of Socialist government became synonymous with food shortages, black markets and spiralling inflation. Katayama had been replaced as prime minister by Ashida Hitoshi of the Democratic Party (Minseito) in March 1948, but the coalition was still seen as a socialist one, and all participants in it were tarred by the Showa Denko scandal (which led to the arrest of Ashida himself) and the stench of inflation. In October

1948, Yoshida regained the prime ministership, and his Liberal Party won a majority in the Diet election of February 1949.

Annual inflation peaked in 1946 at an average of 360 per cent, but remained in triple digits in 1947 and 1948 (i.e., with the level of prices more than doubling each year). Compensation payments to landlords and zaibatsu owners (in cash or shares) rapidly lost value in the inflationary environment, and also spurred the hoarding of products and supplies by many businessmen, exacerbating inflation. The leading economist at Tokyo University, Arisawa Hiromi, had argued that Japan's per capita income levels needed to return to at least 60 per cent of those in the mid-1930s before an aggressive price stabilization could occur, since the requisite monetary contraction could cause the economy to halve in size (to levels that prevailed in 1946, a year in which the Japanese were able to eke out a bare existence). By 1949, per capita income was in fact 69 per cent of the average levels of 1934–36 and real national income was 82 per cent of those levels, with agriculture output at 97 per cent of the mid-1930 levels.

After winning the February 1949 election, Yoshida decided that curbing inflation had to become his top priority and the SCAP agreed, having received instructions from Washington DC in December 1948 to focus on enabling Japan to attain economic self-sufficiency, which would require a credible fixing of its exchange rate. With the communists making advances in China, and Nosaka Sanzo (the Comintern operative who had collaborated with Mao, providing the Japanese cadres who manned CCP artillery during the conquest of Beijing and Tianjin) now attempting to strengthen the Japan Communist Party, Cold War considerations took precedence in US policy—hence the need to stabilize Japan's economy and restore its vitality.

Japan's onerous surrender terms had included a ban on independent international trade and financial transactions. Consequently, the SCAP maintained a complete stranglehold over Japan's exports, imports and all foreign exchange transactions. Until September 1947, the SCAP only allowed government-to-government trade; then, it permitted private foreigners to engage in trade, while private Japanese were only allowed to re-engage in international commerce after December 1949. For the first two years after the surrender, Japan's imports were all channelled through the SCAP, which supplied them to the Board of Trade (BoT) within MCI, and BoT in turn sent Japanese 'exports' to the SCAP. The BoT operated through four fully government-owned corporations (kodans) for textiles, raw materials, food, and minerals and industrial products. As a consequence of these strictures, Japan's annual exports in 1949 were just US$500 million (only 15 per cent of the levels in 1934–36), while its imports were US$900 million (about

30 per cent of the 1934–36 level). The US Treasury financed the resulting deficit, but until April 1949 the SCAP and the BoT also maintained multiple exchange rates—US$1: ¥130 for imports, and US$1: ¥330 for most exports (and ¥500 for some products).

In December 1948, the SCAP, MacArthur, outlined a nine-point agenda of contractionary economic policy, including expanded taxes, lower spending (especially on RFB loans), a balanced budget, monetary restraint and a fixed exchange rate to spur an improved trade balance. Yoshida was keen to pursue this policy line, especially as advocated by Arisawa, and he appointed his close confidant Shirasu Jiro (the UK-educated son-in-law of another Satsuma nobleman) as director general of BoT to help oversee the export promotion drive. Yoshida and Shirasu were committed to the SCAP's goal of spurring international trade, but they preferred to have foreign ministry mandarins run those programmes rather than the industrial policy votaries at MCI. To curtail the latter, Shirasu merged the BoT into MCI to create a new Ministry of International Trade and Industry (MITI) in April 1949, hoping to staff it primarily with foreign service officials. Any credible export promotion strategy, however, required a substantial increase in production, some rationalization of industry, and raising productivity—precisely the skill sets that the MCI mandarins of the 'Kishi–Shiina line' had in abundance. Despite Yoshida's distaste for the MCI, it was they who quickly came to dominate the new MITI and set the course of Japan's industrial strategy.

In February 1949, the SCAP also handed back all control over foreign exchange to the Japanese government and sanctioned the creation of a Foreign Exchange Control Board that would control the allocation of all foreign exchange earned by any Japanese citizen (which had to be handed to the government). The ESB and Foreign Exchange Control Board were both abolished in August 1952 as the occupation wound down, and their powers were transferred to MITI. While they existed, they ran an annual foreign exchange budget that helped allocate capital and technology imports and controlled joint ventures. With the transfer of those powers to MITI, the latter controlled all the elements of industrial policy and management, which it used to direct Japan's successful, tightly-controlled return to international markets and trade.

In April 1949, the former Detroit banker Joseph Dodge became an adviser to the Japanese government, empowered by the SCAP to implement draconian measures to rein in inflation. He shrank the money supply and established a new exchange rate for the yen of US$1: ¥360, which was to last until Nixon's abandonment of the gold standard in 1971. This undervalued exchange rate helped spur a surge in exports (which rose 133 per cent in 1950) while curtailing imports (which expanded 30 per cent in 1950), thus helping to lower the trade deficit within the first year. But the Dodge Line of severe fiscal and monetary austerity caused a sharp reduction in domestic demand that eliminated inflation but reduced output and raised unemployment rates by early 1950. But then the Japanese economy was rescued in June 1950 by the Korean War—resulting in a huge increase in US procurements from Japan of everything from military uniforms to trucks, motorcycles, ships and steel.

Japan's ability to respond to 'Korean War demand' rested primarily on the fact that Japan had enormous idle capacity, and about 12 million unemployed workers who had been repatriated from war theatres. About 7.1 million of them were demobilized soldiers and policemen, 2.6 million workers were from the erstwhile colonies (particularly the Manchurian railways) and 1.6 million released from the armaments industry. Despite the agrarian reform which had given the actual tillers of farmland ownership of it, the size of agricultural holdings was too small for the millions of extra people who had returned to farming in the immediate aftermath of surrender, and the vast majority of agricultural plots remained unviable, with farmers and agricultural workers eager for other jobs. There was thus an 'unlimited supply of labour' available to fuel development in accordance with the model of W. Arthur Lewis (who published his famous paper in 1954) and this labour was well educated, disciplined and skilled. Japan capitalized on this labour supply by focusing initially on labour-intensive exports of textiles, apparel, toys, household goods, chinaware and consumer electronics. Sony was the new exporter of televisions and radios during this period, joining Matsushita (which had suffered a setback when its founder Matsushita Konosuke was purged by the SCAP, although this was overturned after a prolonged appeal process). Others who benefited from the Korean War-induced boom in demand were the carmakers Toyota and Nissan (the latter having moved its manufacturing plants back to Japan from Manchuria) and the electronics maker, Hitachi.

Japan's real GDP—having declined by 44 per cent between 1942 and 1946, and recovered only to 65 per cent of its 1942 size in 1949—expanded by a dramatic 15.9 per cent in 1950, and a further 12.5 per cent and 11.6 per cent in the next two years, thus regaining its 1939 level by 1952, and finally surpassing its previous peak in 1953; real per capita income, however, surpassed its previous (1941) peak only in 1956. Despite the rapid growth, this was a period of great volatility in the Japanese economy, with a four-month 'recession' in late 1951 when a truce was agreed in Korea and demand slumped; the next phase of surging growth (November 1951 to January 1954) was driven by consumption, and this necessarily led to a deterioration in Japan's balance of payments, which was alleviated only by a ten-month recession in 1954. Notably, the Japanese economy was still very dependent on the foreign exchange earned from US 'special procurements' (for military purposes and aid supplies to non-communist Southeast Asian nations) and the spending of US occupation forces and their families: these accounted for 37 per cent of all foreign exchange earned by Japan in financial year (FY) 1952–53, and 11 per cent as late as FY 1959–60 (by which time, most US soldiers were confined mainly to Okinawa).

Tight control over the foreign exchange budget—and especially over the allocation of permits for imports and technological collaborations—gave MITI a decisive influence over capital allocation. At the outset, MITI allowed the imports of raw materials, oil and other minerals that Japan did not produce, and effectively forbade imports of almost all manufactured goods. While there was a good basis for such a prohibition in the early 1950s period of severe foreign exchange shortages, the pattern of imports broadly persisted through the next thirty years, and Japan's imports of manufactured goods are still a lower share of GDP than any other major economy. This effective prohibition on imports of manufactures, of course, provided an extra source of protection to domestic manufacturers.

The 'Lewis model' posits that wages stay low while there is an unlimited supply of labour, boosting returns to capital which can be reinvested in steadily upgrading existing plants (thereby boosting productivity) and expanding into new areas. MITI played the vital role in guiding that capital into specific areas where it perceived a comparative advantage for Japan. The success of the heavy and chemical industrialization drive of the 1930s provided the obvious template, and MITI built on it. Priority sectors were identified by MITI, cheap loans were made available for investment in those sectors, and technology imports permitted based on the achievement of previous targets for exports or output. Apart from the labour-intensive sectors, MITI initially also promoted steel, cement, electric power (these three as basic industries, required as building blocks of infrastructure), electronics, motorcycles and synthetic fibre spinning. After 1956, when MITI began gaining political clout, steel and shipbuilding became complementary sectors of particular focus (as Japan became a pioneer in the building of truly large cargo ships that were able to transport steel across oceans for the first time, making steel a truly internationally-tradable product), as did automobiles, petrochemicals, cameras, radio and television sets, watches, and household appliances.

Bank loans were the crucial element driving Japan's high-speed growth, as Japanese companies relied on bank credit (rather than equity) as their main source of capital from 1950 onwards. While 68 per cent of industrial funds raised in 1935 had come from firms' equity-issuance, this proportion was just 20–30 per cent in the first half of the 1950s (and declined to just 10 per cent by 1963). With equity playing such a small role in their financing, Japanese companies needed to pay much less attention to quarterly profitability, and could instead concentrate on research and product development, gaining foreign market share, and quality control over the long term. The genesis of this system, too, can be traced to the capital shortage of the early 1950s and especially the Bank of Japan's response to the Korean War boom, when it began the practice of what Chalmers Johnson called 'overloaning'. Each of the 'city banks' provided more credit to its group of companies than could be justified by the companies' capacity to repay—sometimes even more than their net worth—and the BoJ, in turn, provided the banks more credit than could be justified by the city banks' capital bases. The BoJ worked closely with MITI's Enterprises Bureau to ensure that city banks' loans were going precisely to the sectors that MITI was seeking to promote (and not others). But the BoJ's first post-war governor, Ichimada (who served from mid-1946 to end-1954) also periodically made known the ceilings on aggregate lending, and adhered strictly to these—particularly because he had served in Germany during the 1930s and was acutely conscious of the factors that had led to hyperinflation in Weimar Germany. This fear of hyperinflation has remained ingrained in career employees at Japan's central bank to this day.

Conflict between the Ministry of Finance and BoJ was also ingrained from the outset in 1950. Ikeda Hayato, a career MoF bureaucrat (1925 to 1948), became Yoshida's finance minister in 1949 and concurrently was MITI minister for various brief spells between 1950 and 1952. Although Ikeda was a fiscal conservative (with views broadly compatible with the SCAP), he was also a votary of rapid economic growth, preferably through more aggressive bank lending. This is where he came into conflict with Ichimada's BoJ, especially when the BoJ's credit limits threatened to stall the economic recovery induced by the demand boom from the Korean War. Ikeda created an Export Bank of Japan that immediately met with the SCAP's approval (and it became Japan's Export-Import Bank once the occupation had ended), but also established the Japan Development Bank in 1951 in the teeth of stiff opposition from the SCAP (which felt it replicated RFB). Two pre-war policy banks were strengthened—Norinchukin Bank (for agriculture cooperatives) and the Bank for Commerce and Industrial Cooperatives—and Ikeda established four other policy banks. These were all funded by a mix of US 'counterpart funds' (in the initial years) and from the postal savings system for small savers that had existed since the 1880s. Since the postal savings deposits were officially held in a trust account of the MoF, they were within Ikeda's bailiwick and he used them to the hilt to create policy banks as the second pillar of Japan's financial system, to complement the 'city banks'.

The SCAP had pushed an Anti-Monopoly Law to enforce the break-up of the zaibatsu, which the US perceived as being at the forefront of Japan's militarist past (quite ironically so, given the militarists' own hostility to the zaibatsu in the 1930s, which had led to numerous assassinations of business leaders and politicians seen as too close to them). Soon enough, however, clusters of corporate borrowers from specific 'city banks' became the basis of 'gurupus' that were based on a 'keiretsu' that horizontally reassembled the old zaibatsu companies by the mid-1950s. Each of the keiretsu gurupus was headed by a large bank, and included a 'sogo shosha' (general trading company) and several industrial firms in each of the main sectors that MITI was promoting; the zaibatsu holding company was outlawed, but instead the major firms within each gurupu had cross-shareholdings in each other.

Thus the DKB (Dai-Ichi Kangyo Bank) gurupu came to encompass the Kawasaki, Furukawa and Hitachi keiretsus, Itochu as its general trading company, three insurance companies (Asahi and Dai-Ichi Mutual, Sompo), Tokyo Electric Power (TEPCO), Asano (now Taiheiyo) Cement, Kao (chemicals), Yokohama Rubber and Seibu Department Store. Itochu had always been the supplier of raw materials to Kawasaki (including Kawasaki Steel and Kawasaki Heavy Industries), but then extended the same role to rival firms within the gurupu such as Kobe Steel and Ishikawajima-Harima Heavy Industries. The 'big six' conglomerate gurupus were clustered around Fuji, Sanwa, Mitsui, Mitsubishi, Sumitomo and Dai-Ichi Kangyo banks. (At the height of the Japanese asset bubble in 1989–90, DKB was the world's largest bank by assets, and nine of the world's ten largest banks were Japanese; in December 1989, Japan's equity market capitalization was 41 per cent of the world's equity market value.) The Mitsubishi, Mitsui and Sumitomo keiretsus simply reconstituted the old zaibatsu of the same name by the second half of the 1950s.

The intense competition amongst the keiretsu groups played a significant role in Japan's industrial successes of the 1960s and 1970s. When MITI set targets for sector export performance, the constituents of each of the keiretsu groups within that sector competed hard to outdo each other in meeting those targets; until 1970, MITI's annual targets for exports and industrial output were invariably exceeded, and usually by very large margins, except in recession years (such as in the post-Olympic year of 1965). In addition, there was a great deal of entrepreneurship outside the keiretsu groups, with Sony (the electronics pioneer) emerging rapidly from its founding in 1946 to compete with Matsushita (with its Panasonic and National brands) in consumer electronics, as well as with Hitachi (part of the DKB group) and

Toshiba (loosely part of the Mitsui keiretsu).

Similarly, Toyota (which had been part of the Mitsui zaibatsu before the war) became independent and built a vertically-integrated keiretsu of its own, which includes small car subsidiary Daihatsu and truck maker Hino. It competed in the automobile (car, truck and van) sector with Nissan (part of the Fuji group), Honda (unaffiliated with any keiretsu), Mitsubishi Motors, Isuzu, Suzuki, Subaru and Mazda. The bank credit-driven model of growth meant that the over-borrowed companies were performing a high-wire act—needing to grow their revenues rapidly in order to service their debt. They focused on quality as a major means to retain market share, with the American professor W. Edwards Deming becoming a cult figure for his statistics-based approach to industrial engineering and quality control. The 'Deming Prize' for quality control was established in 1951, and Japanese companies competed aggressively with each other to win it, and to obtain other independent certifications of quality. That attention to detail and quality became emblematic of Japanese products by 1960, and they built a stellar reputation around the world, especially in the US. Ironically, Deming himself remained largely unknown in the US until the late 1980s, when Japan's economic model was becoming a focus of envy and emulation.

Once the US 'lost' its preferred ally in Asia, with the KMT losing China's civil war to Mao's forces, the Allies signed a peace treaty with Japan in 1952, and the SCAP facilitated the merger of Japan's conservative parties. They eventually formed the Liberal Democratic Party (LDP) in November 1955. In the interim, with the SCAP's blessing, Yoshida's expanded Liberal Party maintained a solid plurality in the Diet, thereby enabling him to remain prime minister until December 1954. In 1945–46, the occupying power had purged more than 255,000 politicians, army and navy officers, bureaucrats and businessmen perceived as being at the forefront of Japan's militarism in the 1940s. In May 1951, General Matthew Ridgway (who had succeeded MacArthur as the SCAP) began to release thousands of individuals from the purge; by the end of that year, over 250,000 had been released, and only 5,500 still remained subject to the purge—including Kishi Nobusuke, who remained purged for a further year at Yoshida's insistence. Despite that antipathy, Kishi (who had been born as Sato Nobusuke in Yamaguchi in the heart of the old Choshu domain, but adopted as a child by the town's wealthier Kishi family) was persuaded to join the Liberals (rather than the socialists) by his biological brother Sato Eisaku, who was already serving as a minister in Yoshida's cabinet.

Soon after he was de-purged in 1952, Kishi formed a right-wing Reform Party that came in second with 18.8 per cent of the vote in the October 1952 election (barely a few months after Kishi had formed that party), although Yoshida's Liberals won a clear majority. The following year, Yoshida allowed Kishi into the Liberal Party, and the latter quickly became the leader of the largest faction within the party arguing for a more robust foreign policy, including rearmament (and constitutional revision to allow it) and economic planning. As their differences mounted, Yoshida expelled Kishi from the Liberal Party. Kishi then combined forces with Hatoyama Ichiro (the former Seiyukai politician who was to have led the Liberals until he was purged) and other conservative notables to form a new Democratic Party, which combined with the two Socialist parties (and defectors from the Liberals) to bring down Yoshida's government in October 1954. Hatoyama became prime minister, although he was widely seen as the 'omikoshi' ('a portable Shinto shrine') being carried/steered by the party's secretary general (and real leader), Kishi. The Democratic Party won 185 seats (with 36.6 per cent of the vote) in the February 1955 election (out of a total of 467 seats), reducing Yoshida's Liberals to 114 seats (26.8 per cent of the vote). Even before the election, Kishi had been in close contact with key members of Yoshida's party, although Hatoyama was opposed to those contacts, as they threatened his own control of the Democratic Party. Kishi's efforts and the active support of US Secretary of State John Foster Dulles culminated in the unification of the two to create the LDP in November 1955. Hatoyama stayed prime minister for just over a year after the unification, and Kishi finally rose to the prime ministership in February 1957, remaining in the job for three and a half years and creating the '1955 system' that ensured uninterrupted LDP governance for the next thirty-eight years. (Half a century later, Hatoyama's grandson was to lead the Democratic Party of Japan, DPJ, to power in 2008 but he lasted barely a year in office, and Kishi's grandson, Abe Shinzo, eventually ousted the DPJ in December 2012, beginning a second, more durable term as prime minister after an unsuccessful one-year term in 2006–07).

While Kishi is associated in the public mind with the 'control bureaucrats' of MITI and its predecessors (MM and MCI), and consequently with their allies in the keiretsu, he actually built his political comeback on his personal alliances with small and medium enterprises (SMEs). And it was as an advocate for SMEs—who, then as now, employ over 70 per cent of all Japanese workers and account for more than 99 per cent of all Japanese companies—that Kishi built his post-War political base. Like their German counterparts, the 'mittelstand', Japan's SMEs are typically family-owned firms that build on traditions of intricate craftsmanship and artisanal skills passed down and built on through the generations. They proliferate in the services sector (any visit to a small, specialist restaurant in Kamakura or a Tokyo basement is a sublime gastronomic experience), but are crucial to the vitality of the manufacturing sector as well. In manufacturing, SMEs are typically tied to large manufacturers as vendors, parts suppliers, and providers of niche skills for specific sub-products. The best and most successful of them grow large enough to become globally competitive providers of services and parts for the world, breaking free of their initial moorings as parts of larger groups. And some SMEs begin as purely innovative manufacturers and grow without specific links to larger firms (Sony, Panasonic and Honda being prime examples).

Japan experienced a modest post-War baby boom (especially in 1948–54), with the population rising from 78 million in 1947 to 88.75 million in 1954, rising more sedately to 94 million in 1960, and reaching 104.33 million by 1970. The domestic market was therefore quite large and it grew rapidly as incomes soared during the first two decades, with real GDP more than doubling between 1951 and 1960, and then tripling between 1960 and 1971. MITI's focus on heavy and chemical industrialization (HCI) therefore benefited from rising domestic demand: initially, MITI encouraged new HCI investment in supplying the domestic market (which was protected from external competition by an effective prohibition on imports of manufactures, plus an undervalued exchange rate that made imports expensive). 'Administrative guidance' by MITI was aimed at creating an oligopolistic structure without excessive market entry, but the presence of six big conglomerates meant that there inevitably were at least six (and sometimes more) players fighting for space within each promoted sector.

MITI's aim was to ensure that the larger, more successful firms within a sector would be able to achieve economies of scale and scope that would substantially reduce the unit cost of production, preferably achieving those scale economies within Japan's domestic economy. As the domestic market got saturated, exports became a growing imperative for the typical keiretsu-based manufacturer. Thus, despite its reputation as an export-led economy, Japan always had the characteristics of a large (usually continent-sized) economy like the US, with exports rarely accounting for more than a tenth of GDP. In 1960, exports were 9.2 per cent of GDP, but they averaged 8 per cent of GDP in the next four years and rose above 9 per cent of GDP in 1965 after a big surge in exports amid a post-Olympics slump in domestic demand. Not until after the oil crisis of 1973 did Japan's export/GDP ratio rise above 11 per cent (having edged above 10 per cent for the first time in 1971, following the 'Nixon shock' of dollar devaluation).

Entrepreneurial companies that were not favoured by MITI and its policy banks were, perforce, more export-oriented from the start. For instance, Sony was started in 1947 by two friends who had briefly served as electronics researchers in the navy: Ibuka Masaru (who had set up a radio repair shop in 1946) and a physics buff, Morita Akio. They began to focus primarily on exports to the US by the second half of the 1950s, after licensing transistor technology from Bell Labs and putting it to civilian use for the first time to produce a pocket transistor radio. Initially known by its initials (TTK), the company made Japan's first tape recorder in 1950, and its name was changed to Sony in 1958 just as it began marketing its new transistor radio in the US. That became a youth sensation in the US by 1960, and Sony was already famed for its quality and reliability; that year, Sony also introduced the world's first transistor-based television. The following year, Sony became the first Japanese firm to list on the New York Stock Exchange through American Depository Receipts. By the 1970s, Sony was the world's leading consumer electronics brand, and was celebrated for introducing a series of innovative products—the Trinitron TV (for which Sony won an Emmy Award in 1973), and the digitized cassette recorder which culminated in the Walkman, the world's first portable audio music player, introduced in 1979 and ubiquitous amongst the world's youth in the 1980s: it can truly be said that the Walkman was to 1980s youth culture what the iPhone and iPad are to today's youth. It was succeeded by the Discman (for CD players) in 1984, and Sony also introduced the world's first video cassette recorders (VCR) in 1975, although its Betamax format was eventually eclipsed by rival Japanese firm JVC's VHS format (introduced the following year).

Japan's successful staging of the 1964 Olympics in Tokyo became the showcase of Japan's post-War economic accomplishments. Perhaps most emblematic of all was the 'shinkansen' or bullet train inaugurated in 1964 that sped from Tokyo to Kyoto and Osaka at speeds that were nearly double those of the express trains elsewhere in the world. Japan's bullet trains have maintained an absolutely spotless reputation for punctuality over the subsequent five decades, and suffered no accidents during that incredibly long period, despite earthquakes and numerous other natural disasters that they were frequently challenged by. (By contrast, the new bullet trains launched by China in the past decade had a couple of spectacular, fatal accidents soon after they were inaugurated.) During the period from 1951–60, Japan's real GDP growth averaged 8.9 per cent annually, but this speeded up even further in the 1960s, with annual average real GDP growth rising to 10.5 per cent during the 1961–70 period, easily the fastest of any major economy on earth, and quite rightly labelled the 'Japanese economic miracle'. By 1970, Japanese cars—Toyotas, Datsuns (the brand name used then by Nissan) and Hondas—were beginning to arrive in the US, and were quickly acquiring a reputation for quality that they built on steadily in the next decade. By the late 1980s, Japanese cars had begun to supplant the venerable brands from the General Motors and Ford stable, and dominated the mass market in the US (and increasingly across the world, although facing severe protectionist barriers in Europe).

Japan's per capita GDP (in constant 1990 US$) was $670 in 1820 (close to India's in 1990, albeit only slightly more than India's in 1820). By 1934, it had risen to US$2,100 and it reached a pre-war peak of US$2,864 in 1942. After falling all the way to US$1,555 in 1946, Japan's per capita GDP rebounded to US$4,000 in 1960 and rose to US$10,000 (equivalent to at least double that in today's dollars) by 1970. Japan had become a fully-developed economy—the first non-European nation to have mastered the process of modern economic growth to achieve the prosperity and abundance that the West had achieved earlier in the century.

TAIWAN AND KOREA'S PATHS DIVERGE, THEN MERGE, AS BOTH EMBRACE THE JAPAN MODEL

Writing in 1956, the International Cooperation Administration (ICA, the predecessor to USAID) was transparent in assessing Taiwan's economic inheritance: 'The legacies of 50 years of development under Japanese rule include an economy more advanced than that of any other geographical region of China, except Manchuria, and a standard of living second only to Japan amongst Far Eastern countries.' Notably, the ICA acknowledged that Manchuria (ruled formally by Japan for fourteen years, and an 'economic colony' heavily under its influence for forty years) was the only region of China that was almost as economically advanced as Taiwan was.

By 1939–40, Taiwan had a primary school enrolment ratio of 60 per cent—double the average for Asia as a whole. In 1935–40, the estimated primary enrolment ratio in India was 12.3 per cent, China 12.4, the Dutch East Indies 13.3, Hong Kong 22, and Malaya (including Singapore) 24.6 per cent. Apart from Japan, only Taiwan, Ceylon (Sri Lanka) and independent Thailand had primary enrolment ratios of over 50 per cent. In addition, there were five Taiwanese managers for every Japanese 'manager' in companies operating in Taiwan, and three Taiwanese technicians for every Japanese 'agricultural technician' and 'medical technician'. The high quality of 'human capital' was a key advantage conferred by Japanese rule.

After undertaking a cadastral survey, the Japanese had undertaken a reform of the agrarian structure, dispossessing an absentee landlord class and instead empowering an intermediate class of local landlords who became key supporters of the regime. It also established cooperatives, landlord-tenant associations and an agricultural extension service that transferred modern farming technology to Taiwanese cultivators—particularly for rice and sugar, of which Taiwan became a key supplier to Japan. By the 1930s, rising wages in Japan prompted the Japanese to invest in numerous industries in Taiwan, including food processing, cement, textiles, wood products including pulp and paper, chemical fertilizers, oil refining, shipbuilding, aluminium and copper smelting. (We have seen in Chapter 4 that the Japanese invested in many of the same industries in Manchuria as well, and additionally in car manufacturing—with Nissan effectively moving its manufacturing headquarters there.) During the long period from 1911 to 1938, Taiwan's real GDP grew 3.8 per cent annually, Korea's 3.6 per cent annually and Japan's 3.4 per cent annually (while British India's grew less than 1 per cent annually, implying a decline in per capita GDP in India over the period). Taiwan's industrial output expanded 6 per cent annually over that entire period, accelerating to 7 per cent annual growth in the 1930s, as Taiwan became a vital cog in the Japanese supply chain, by processing Southeast Asian raw materials for the Japanese market. Although most of its trade was with Japan, Taiwan had become Asia's largest trading nation, with per capita trade amounting to $39 annually for Taiwan in the late 1930s, compared with $26 for Korea, $23 for Japan, $18 for the Philippines and $1 for mainland China.

Japanese-domiciled corporations did own most of Taiwan's industry. Although there were numerous Taiwanese suppliers to the zaibatsu, Taiwan did not develop any of its own large monopolistic corporations. When Chiang Kai-shek and his KMT forces 'retreated' to Taiwan in 1949 after their defeat by Mao's communists in the Chinese Civil War, about 1.5 million mainland Chinese (including much of the intellectual, bureaucratic, financial and commercial elite of China) arrived and effectively became the overlords of Taiwan's 6 million indigenous inhabitants. Most Taiwanese had been favourably disposed towards Japanese rule, during which educated Taiwanese had learnt and spoken both their native Hokkien and Japanese, while many voluntarily adopted Shinto practices.

When the KMT's General Chen Yi arrived on 24 October 1945 to take Taiwan over on behalf of Nationalist China after fifty years of Taiwan's effective incorporation into Japan, he was received with a mix of enthusiasm and trepidation, and the latter sentiment soon became predominant. Chen Yi's KMT took over the Japanese state monopolies of sugar, tobacco, camphor, tea, paper, chemicals, oil refining, mining and cement, and the KMT took control of about 500 Japanese-owned factories and mines. Worse, most Taiwanese senior and middle managers were displaced and replaced by 'carpetbaggers' from the mainland, who then sought to use Taiwan as a cheap supply base for export of products (at extremely low prices) to mainland China (where they made massive profits). In turn, this led to severe food and raw material shortages on Taiwan itself, causing prices to double within the first year, and for inflation to soar past 400 per cent by early 1947.

Taiwanese resentment of this attempted colonization by mainland Chinese led to a Taiwanese revolt that began on 27 February 1947, and was met by a severely repressive KMT military response that began the next day (which is why it is still called the 2–28 Massacre, to refer to 28 February 1947). At least 10,000 (and possibly as many as 30,000) Taiwanese were killed by the KMT's military machine, entrenching Taiwanese nationalism in opposition to the attempt at incorporating the island into China.

This hostility was still palpable when the KMT forces retreated onto Taiwan, and came to dominate it after losing the Civil War on the mainland in 1949. Partly to alleviate that hostility, the KMT undertook a major land reform initiative—transferring ownership of old Japanese-owned land to its tenants, and subsequently also transferring ownership of all holdings above three hectares to their tenant-cultivators. This, coupled with heavy investment in rural infrastructure and irrigation, made Taiwan's agriculture sector highly productive, with rice yields (of 3 tonnes per hectare) by 1960 that were the highest in Asia after Japan. (It is ironic that Japan now must impose high tariffs to protect its rice farmers, but that is because rice cultivation was one area which was not subject to automation in Japan, and the surging productivity of the rest of the economy gradually made rice farming relatively uncompetitive in Japan over the subsequent four decades as the yen appreciated by leaps and bounds.) Rice and sugar remained Taiwan's main exports through the 1950s—a decade during which the Taiwan dollar was kept overvalued, partly to restrain imported input costs for new 'infant industries'. Despite those impediments, Taiwan's agriculture output grew 4.4 per cent annually between 1954 and 1967—the fastest in all of Asia.

By the mid-1950s, import substitution was beginning to advance rapidly, particularly for consumer goods. Gradually, the KMT government began to introduce subsidies to help exporters to overcome currency overvaluation, with companies that exported more being allowed to import larger shares of the machinery they needed, and receiving rebates on their imports in proportion to their exports. Like Japan in the 1920s and 1930s, Taiwan organized the textile industry in order to reduce excessive competition (and resulting 'wastage' of capacity and capital): a government agency would supply raw cotton, provide all their working capital needs, and buy up all production. This was an industry that was quickly established in Taiwan by mainlanders who had moved their textile factories across the Taiwan Straits lock, stock, and barrel at the end of the Civil War. In 1957–58, amid a worldwide recession, Taiwan began to alter its exchange rate to make it more favourable to exporters—and the result was a spectacular increase in textile exports, which rose 38 per cent in 1958 and 200 per cent by the end of 1959, continuing to grow at an average annual pace of 40 per cent for the next five years. By 1961, Taiwan's success in textiles led the US to impose restraints on Taiwan's textile exports, marking the definitive 'arrival' of Taiwan as a globally competitive textile exporter. The US, as the world's largest economy by far, accounted for 34 per cent of Taiwan's textile exports in 1964, with Hong Kong taking 17 per cent and Thailand 12 per cent.

Plastics were another industry that was established with government assistance in the 1950s. The J. G. White Engineering Corporation identified this as suitable for Taiwan in 1953, and K. Y. Yin (the government's chief economic planner) began searching amongst bank depositors for a person with suitable savings and entrepreneurial potential to lead this industry. At the same time, Y. C. Wang—having seen the potential for plastics during his many years spent in Japan—had approached the Industrial Development Bureau in search of investment opportunities, and was already edging towards this sector. The match between government agency and entrepreneur seemed made in heaven: the government constructed the first PVC (polyvinyl chloride) plant in 1957, and handed it over to Y. C. Wang as a going concern. PVC (the material used in ubiquitous plastic bottles worldwide) became the basis of Wang's formidable Formosa Plastics business group.

Professor Robert Wade's pioneering 1990 book, *Governing the Market: Economic Theory and the Role of Government in East Asian Industrialization*, established very clearly just how important the state's role was as a planner and initiator of economic development in Taiwan (and Korea thereafter). Wade showed that the KMT government played the key role in creating the synthetic textiles industry, in order to diversify away from a dependence on cotton alone. Collaborating with an American company called Von Kohorn, the Taiwan government facilitated the creation of a joint venture China Man-Made Fibre Corporation, which brought together Von Kohorn and numerous private and public Taiwanese textile firms to make rayon in 1957. Wade showed that Taiwan used policy instruments such as 'import restrictions, sectoral allocation of foreign exchange, and concessional credit' to facilitate the development of specific industries. These were remarkably similar to what Japan had used, and Taiwan also created a battery of Japan-like government bodies to aid industrial development, including the China Productivity and Investment Centre (for technical assistance), the Industrial Development and Investment Centre (to facilitate FDI, in a slight departure from Japanese practice), and the China Development Corporation (for industrial finance). Taiwan also began to reach out to Overseas Chinese (mainly those in Hong Kong, many of them recent migrants there from the mainland) in 1955; initially, there was scant response from them, but Taiwan improved the incentive structure amid the global recession of 1957, and also depreciated the Taiwan dollar that year to more competitive levels, thereby beginning to attract much more capital inflows from Overseas Chinese.

By early 1950, the US had lost interest in Taiwan and the KMT, seeing the latter as a bothersome failed ally once it had lost the Chinese Civil War. But the Korean War that began in June 1950 quickly altered the US calculus, and Taiwan came to be seen as a vital part of East Asia's strategic perimeter. Thereafter, and especially in the post-Korean War period from 1954 onwards, substantial US military and economic aid flowed to Taiwan. But the Taiwanese were particularly fortunate in having close ties to both the world's largest economy (the US) and its fastest growing one (Japan) in the 1950s. Local Taiwanese had particularly strong ties to Japan, while the mainlanders had deeper connections with the US (but fairly substantial ones with Japan too). For instance, Wade pointed to a late 1980s study that showed that of Taiwan-based businessmen with a foreign education, 75 per cent of the native Taiwanese had been educated in Japan and 23 per cent in the US, while 61 per cent of the mainland-evacuee businessmen were educated in the US and 18 per cent in Japan.

US military and economic aid helped stabilize the Taiwanese economy in the early years, and thereafter the US played an important role in tempering the KMT's étatist state-capitalist instincts, obliging the government to allow technocrats to run the economic bureaucracy, and force through speedy privatizations of state-led companies in order to ensure that they remained competitive. Taiwan, however, lacked a large domestic market so it could not entirely replicate the Japanese model. Cars were one sector where as many as five assemblers were established in Taiwan with government support and Japanese technological assistance after an initial US-assisted company (Yue-Loong) was established in 1953 to assemble cars from completely-knocked-down kits. Despite collaboration with Nissan and Toyota, and several tiers of graduated tariff protection, the small size of the domestic market precluded economies of scale in the automobile sector, and Taiwan never became a truly successful car manufacturer.

By contrast, Taiwanese firms took to electronics manufacturing like ducks to water, especially aided by the generous governmental support they received. Taiwanese firms began to assemble radios with US technology by the late 1940s, and in 1950 import restrictions on radios were introduced to encourage the industry. Domestic infant industry protection was soon extended to transmitters, cables, wire and light bulbs. In 1953, Taiwan's Tatung established an extensive collaboration agreement with a Japanese firm to produce electric watt-metres from domestic components, including the training of Taiwanese engineers in Japan. And over the next decade, at least seven other collaborative ventures were established between Taiwanese and Japanese firms (facilitated by US aid in the early years). By 1962, the Taiwanese government was imposing local content requirements to oblige firms to add more value in Taiwan to their television, air conditioner, refrigerator, car and diesel-engine assembly lines.

As Taiwan began to develop a pool of skilled manpower in basic electronics manufacturing and assembly, Philips (of the Netherlands) established a semiconductor assembly and packaging facility in Taiwan in 1961, effectively inaugurating what came to be called 'outsourcing' of electronics manufacturing, and the globalization of supply chains. Fairchild Semiconductor had established a presence in Hong Kong the same year, and General Instruments arrived in Taiwan with a large manufacturing plant in 1964. The Taiwanese became adept at electronics manufacturing in small factories and assembly plants, developing the artisanal skills essential for effective electronics and semiconductor manufacturing, later put to good use with personal computers too. In 1965, Taiwan created an export processing zone, where foreign firms could operate with almost complete freedom as long as they exported all their output. Between 1964 and 1966, as many as twenty-four US firms rushed in to take advantage of this opportunity and Taiwan's electronics industry was well on the way to becoming world class, with local suppliers working closely with Japanese and American manufacturers who still had the technological edge.

Emulating Japan, Taiwan's planners coordinated production in key industries like electronics (and earlier, in textiles, chemicals, and plastics, amongst others), ensuring that production was in line with the needs of foreign buyers, facilitating marketing, training skilled workers and engineers, reducing bureaucratic red tape, obtaining raw materials and helping to boost quality. Thus the entire gamut of MITI's corporatist functions was replicated in Taiwan, especially in key industries like electronics. Singapore was also doing similar things by the late 1960s, except that Singapore's Economic Development Board primarily provided these services to multinational corporations looking to invest in Singapore, while Taiwan focused primarily on boosting its own entrepreneurs. (The key constraint for Singapore's Lee Kuan Yew was that most of the major Singapore entrepreneurs had been sympathetic to the communists, and so were deemed unsuitable to be the leaders of Singapore's own development.) Taiwan's government organized two major exhibitions in 1967–68 to bring investors and local producers together.

The 1970s were to prove a very challenging decade for Taiwan. In 1971, Taiwan's long-standing ally, the US, began to make the extraordinary decision to switch recognition from the Republic of China (on Taiwan) to Mao's PRC after the arch anti-communist of the 1950s and 1960s, President Richard Nixon, went to meet Mao in February 1972. His Secretary of State, Henry Kissinger, had secretly visited China in March 1971 while on a visit to Pakistan, having feigned illness to explain his non-appearance in Pakistan that day. Following a second fruitful trip by Kissinger, Nixon announced in July 1971 that he would soon be going to China himself. Like Churchill, Kissinger has written his own history and has lionized Nixon's opening up to Communist China as being a strategic master stroke, while glossing over the fact that the US was thus choosing to align itself with one of the great genocidal maniacs of the twentieth century, including (a few years later) his close ally, Pol Pot of Cambodia. Mao was then in the midst of the Cultural Revolution, during which thousands of intellectuals, writers and bureaucrats had been killed, and millions of others sent into the countryside to perform forced labour. It was with this unsavoury regime—then at the height of one of its most gruesome campaigns—that Nixon and Kissinger chose to openly align, using as a go-between the genocidal regime of General Yahya Khan of Pakistan (which was then in the midst of an ethnic cleansing of non-Muslims from East Pakistan, and a murderous rampage against Bengali nationalists there).

Taiwan lost China's seat in the United Nations and with it a permanent seat on the Security Council. Worse, it also lost membership of UN-affiliated institutions like the IMF and World Bank. Japan switched recognition to Mainland China in 1972. After 1971, Taiwan had to maintain macroeconomic stability on its own, with no possibility of any resort to an IMF-led rescue, and so was obliged to be more circumspect in its development strategies. Another of the key consequences was a flood of Taiwanese migrants moving to the US—so Taiwan's loss was most clearly the US technology sector's gain. Taiwanese (both native Taiwanese and displaced mainlanders who were citizens of the Republic of China on Taiwan) provided most of the early wave of technopreneurs and engineers in Silicon Valley and in Massachusetts (clustered around Lowell) in the 1970s. Of the latter, perhaps the most eminent was Wang Laboratories, which became one of the most prominent semiconductor players in the late 1970s and 1980s, and central to the 'Massachusetts Miracle' that propelled Governor Michael Dukakis to the Democratic nomination for president in 1988.

Taiwan did not sit still amid this exodus, instead seeking to harness it by establishing the Industrial Technology Research Institute (ITRI) at Hsinchu in 1973, which was to grow into the flourishing technological hub of Hsinchu Science Park. Both the world-leading semiconductor foundries, Taiwan Semiconductor Manufacturing Corporation (TSMC) and United Microelectronics Corporation (UMC), were spawned by Hsinchu's ITRI. TSMC's Morris Chang, born in Ningbo (mainland China) in 1931, graduated with an engineering degree from Harvard and built a very successful career at Texas Instruments until 1983, when he moved back to Taiwan to run ITRI. Even as he worked at ITRI in Hsinchu, Morris Chang created TSMC in 1987, and it has gone on to become the world's largest chip foundry—an essential partner to the world's leading semiconductor manufacturers. While SMEs are Taiwan's most successful companies (replicating the artisanal aspect of Japan's economy), some larger global champions too emerged with the help of the government planning and coordination mechanisms, prominently Acer computers and Formosa Plastics.

Japan's colonization of Korea was analogous to Britain's approach towards Ireland—while Japanese colonization of Taiwan had been more akin to England's approach towards Wales and Scotland—with similar consequences in terms of the local attitude towards the colonizer. Like the British in Ireland, Japanese settlers played an important role in Korea—taking control of close to half of all agricultural land in Korea and tilling some of it with their own hands (while primarily depending on tenant-peasants to provide the majority of the crop). While this developed Korea's agriculture sector—its output growing at an average annual pace of 2.3 per cent during the thirty-five years of Japanese rule—the ubiquity of Japanese settlers (albeit only 3 per cent of the population) in the upper echelons of society blocked the upward mobility of Koreans.

Whereas opportunities for industrial employment had played an important role in the transformation of Japan's occupational structure in the post-Meiji period, such mobility was much more restricted in Korea. However, during the period of Japanese rule, Koreans sought opportunities outside Korea, and elsewhere within Korea but outside their home regions, creating an unusually mobile labour force, with more than a fifth of the population working outside their home region, including more than a tenth of the Korean population working overseas. A million Koreans each worked in Japan and Manchuria, a further 200,000 in the Russian Far East and over 100,000 in China. Perforce, the overseas workforce developed skills in industry and mining that were to prove useful upon their return to Korea after the end of the World War. In the 1930s, Japan embarked on a crash programme of heavy industrialization in Manchuria and Korea: while this was primarily aimed at producing armaments, it also developed a base level of skills that very few other colonies acquired.

Education was the factor that most distinguished Japan, Korea and Taiwan from other 'late-industrializers'. We have seen that India's illiteracy rate at Independence was a dauntingly lofty 86 per cent; as late as 1954, just 7 per cent of India's population was in school. In that same year (1954, the year after the end of the war that had torn the country asunder), Korea had 17 per cent of its population in school (a higher proportion than Germany's 13 per cent or the 15 per cent in England and Wales), while Japan had 23 per cent of its population in school (just slightly higher than the 22 per cent of the US population that was in school).

The crucial legacy of the period of Japanese rule was this commitment to education and literacy that were vastly superior to the legacy of other colonial regimes. While Korean scholars complain that the Japanese colonial education structure was aimed mainly at producing workers, agronomists and doctors (rather than managers and engineers) for its colonial agriculture and industrial sectors, there is little doubt that the Korean workforce was substantially more educated than those of India (including Pakistan), Vietnam, Malaya and Indonesia. In 1946, slightly more than 60 per cent of Korea's labour force was literate while British India's overall literacy rate was an abysmal 14 per cent and at least four-fifths of its labour force was completely illiterate.

When Japanese rule ended with the abrupt surrender of Japan to the Allies in August 1945, an inchoate Korean People's Republic was established by left nationalists who were committed to rooting out 'collaborationists' with Japanese rule, eliminating Japanese influence over Korean society, and establishing social equality through a more egalitarian (and less 'feudal') allocation of landholdings. Although lacking any real central authority, 'people's committees' took local control across the country. The Soviet Red Army had advanced down to the 38th parallel just north of Korea's capital of Seoul, and Soviet Russia was quite happy to work with the 'People's Republic' in the north, albeit ensuring that a faction amenable to continued Russian influence took centralized control there. Kim Il-Sung had been a guerrilla fighter against Japanese rule in Manchukuo and the communists had provided the main (albeit modest) resistance to Japanese rule there. The Russians worked with Kim to abolish landlordism, redistribute land holdings (especially land that had been Japanese-owned), nationalize industry (i.e., communist control over erstwhile Japanese-owned industry) and eliminate some of the abusive features of the colonial factory system.

When the Americans arrived in Seoul on 6 September 1945, they did not recognize the Korean People's Republic (South) that was led by Yo Un-hyong, and had established a particularly strong base in the perennially rebellious province of South Cholla. That province—known traditionally as the prosperous rice-basket region of Honam—had been the site of the Tonghak rebellion of 1894 against Japanese exporters who were sending the region's rice to Japan and the world beyond. Then, in 1929, South Cholla's capital of Kwangju witnessed a major student uprising against Japanese rule (and, of course, Kwangju rose up against military rule in 1980 as well). When I visited Kwangju in 2002, the difference between it (and southern Cholla in general) and the rest of South Korea was rather stark: it was as if Kwangju and Cholla had been frozen in time, perhaps two decades behind the rest of South Korea (despite a son of Cholla, Kim Dae-jung, being in his fourth year as president of the country at the time). In the autumn of 1945, Cholla's people's committees, some headed by nationalists who had been imprisoned by the Japanese (like Kim Sok, who was in charge of Kwangju after eleven years in Japanese prisons), others headed by miners, some even by landlords, had taken control of the province during the hiatus between Japan's surrender and the arrival of the Americans on 8 October 1945; some small towns remained under the control of police who had served under the Japanese. The young Kim Dae-jung joined a people's committee in the southwestern port of Mokpo (something that future military regimes were to hold against him, as being a sign of communist leanings). The People's Committees in the south had little or no connections with the communist-affiliated ones in North Korea and comprised nationalists of various hues, primarily grouping people who had not collaborated with Japan.

Very few of the American military teams had been specifically trained for Korea, most having been hastily reassigned from Japan. One of the few officers who had been specifically trained for Korea, Lieutenant Colonel Frank Bartlett, urged his men to understand local opinion, and work with the people's committees. But he was the exception. Most American military commanders were suspicious of the people's committees, and Kwangju's leader Kim Sok was arrested by the US Army by end October 1945.

The commander of the US occupation forces in Korea, General Hodge, was a down-to-earth, straightforward soldier with a peerless military record but scant experience with civic affairs (or 'nation-building'). He responded to the disorder he found in southern Korea by reconstituting and strengthening the National Police that had been created by the Japanese colonial authorities, and bolstering the bureaucracy (especially the home affairs department that was responsible for maintaining law and order). By end 1945, Hodge declared war on the Communist Party, and most of the people's committees were labelled

PRASENJIT K. BASU

communist. Instead, the US occupation authorities decided to work with a group of several hundred 'conservatives', most of whom had collaborated with the Japanese colonizers (with some Japanese governors remaining in place for several months after the occupation began). The conservative former collaborators with Japanese rule were assembled into the Korean Democratic Party (KDP). As it was difficult to find anyone amongst them who was not 'tainted' by association with the Japanese, Syngman Rhee (who had lived in exile in the US city of Denver after participating in the March 1919 uprising against Japanese rule) was brought in to lead the KDP.

By May 1946, the US was well on the way to creating a West Point-style military academy for Korean military officers. The second class of graduates from this academy (in the autumn of 1946) included Park Chung-hee (leader of the 1961 coup) and the future head of the Korean Central Intelligence Agency (KCIA) Kim Chae-gyu (who assassinated Park in 1979)—both former officers in the Japanese imperial army in Manchukuo. By the time Syngman Rhee formally became president of the new Republic of Korea in 1948, the regime had ensured almost complete continuity with the Japanese era, reinforced by a new land reform that gave land to the tiller.

In the intervening years, there had been a full-scale rebellion in the south of the country, beginning in South Cholla in October–November 1946, then spreading in early 1948 to the southern island of Cheju (today a major tourist destination), and erupting with great force in the southwestern port of Yosu in October 1948. The revolt was triggered by anger over the suppression of the people's committees in the southeast of the country, and to preclude their suppression in the southwest (Cholla). The historian Bruce Cumings, who examined the record in detail, asserted that communism or the regime in North Korea had nothing to do with the revolt in the south, which was completely homegrown. In Cheju island, indigenous left-wing people's committees governed until early 1948; even Hodge acknowledged that they were left wing but pro-American, and had no links to the communist party in North Korea or the South Korean Workers' Party, although they were separatist. Syngman Rhee's regime, however, labelled the Cheju people's committees 'communist', and sent in right-wing toughs to rein in their left-wing opponents on Cheju—triggering the large-scale rebellion there. Cumings concludes from the historical record that as many as 80,000 of Cheju's 300,000 population were killed in the brutal suppression of the ensuing revolt, and as many as 40,000 of Cheju's people fled to Japan (where they continue to live in the Osaka area).

The US Army Military Government made a vital contribution to Korea's politico-economic future with its agrarian reform programme, which took

Japan's own land reform in Korea of 1910–19 one step further, by taking land from the aristocracy (and former Japanese owners) and handing ownership of land to the ultimate tiller. By 1949, just 7 per cent of Korea's farmers were landless, and the vast majority owned their land, which gave them an incentive to boost its productivity, by using the extensive irrigation and agricultural extension services that had been created during Japanese rule. Enhanced food supplies helped dampen inflation in the immediate aftermath of the Korean War, and the relatively equal distribution of agrarian land ensured a more egalitarian distribution of income in Korea right through the period from 1950–90. With land speculation no longer possible, Korea's wealthy classes could divert their capital to more productive uses. In the 1950s, they primarily participated in the system of patronage created by Syngman Rhee's regime to allocate the scarce products imported using US aid funds, but their capital was soon to be harnessed far more effectively for national purposes by Park Chung-hee's regime. During the early years of Rhee's regime, the greatest opportunity for doling out patronage was the sale of 3,000 Japanese industrial firms and banks at artificially low prices to new Korean owners.

Between 1953 and 1958, South Korea was recognized as a vital front line state in the new Cold War and so received massive amounts of military and economic aid, averaging about 15 per cent of annual GDP over the period. This helped with rapid reconstruction following the Korean War, but also enabled Korea's inchoate cotton textile industry to grow rapidly over the period, and overall industrial growth in Korea was the fastest of any UN member during that period. But South Korea suffered during the global recession of 1958, and severe disputes began to appear between Rhee's regime and the US. The latter demanded less graft, balanced budgets, low inflation, higher interest rates (to induce more savings), and a focus on light industries, while Rhee wanted import substitution to be extended to heavy industries too. The US also emphasized decentralized control and private ownership (including of banks), while the Japanese had been more realistic in pursuing a centralized approach. Three large devaluations of the currency made it difficult to control inflation, obliging Rhee to adopt contractionary policies that led to an unemployment rate of 20 per cent by 1960. (The disputes between Rhee and the US over economic policy read remarkably similar to the disputes that Afghanistan's Hamid Karzai had with successive US administrations in more recent times.) The economic downturn and high unemployment inevitably led to massive labour and student unrest, leading eventually to Syngman Rhee's ouster in 1960. Student unrest persisted even after an election returned a similar slate of candidates.

On 16 May 1961, General Park Chung-hee crossed the Han River into the heart of Seoul with about 5,000 crack troops, and took control of South Korea via a military coup. Having been trained as a young second lieutenant in the Imperial Japanese Army, Park was heavily influenced by Japan, and especially the socio-economic transformation of Japan following the Meiji Restoration. Park explicitly stated, 'The case of the Meiji imperial restoration will be of great help to the performance of our own revolution. My interest in this direction remains strong and constant.' Although Park's policies of promoting exports and investment in heavy industry were almost precisely based on the specific methods adopted by Japan, Park was even more interested in emulating what he perceived to be the key institutional aspects of Japan's model: (a) a nationalistic patriotism that was the ideological underpinning of the Meiji reforms; (b) thus 'Japanizing' foreign ideas that arrived at a challenging time of foreign invasion by steadfastly focusing on the tasks of reform; (c) the centrality of the middle class, achieved by eliminating the role of the feudal lords, and connecting the energetic forces of the middle class directly with the emperor; and (d) to stimulate national capitalism by allowing millionaires to occupy a vital place both economically and politically in an imperial system dominated by the emperor with former noblemen as elder statesmen. At its base, Korea's institutional legacy was Japanese, and Park Chung-hee understood and admired what had made Japan great. Given the common cultural legacy—from elaborate bowing before and after social interactions, to the way in which corporate and other notices are posted and numbers written—it was natural for Korea to emulate and adopt Japanese practices. Grafting US-style free-market principles onto this Japanese-style institutional legacy was unnatural, and hence an uphill struggle in the 1950s.

Park Chung-hee's administration focused its planning effort primarily on achieving rapid export growth, with business conglomerates ('chaebols') that achieved or exceeded export targets receiving enhanced access to subsidized credit, and additional allocations of foreign exchange to enable them to import capital goods in order to expand even faster. Soon after the coup, Park's junta published a Law for Dealing with Illicit Wealth Accumulation—which it used as a stick to discipline the chaebol millionaires, and bring them into line with the junta's objectives; above all to speed up export growth. Businessmen were forgiven their criminal assessments (for malfeasance under the previous regime) if they would commit to create basic industries in export-oriented sectors. With a favourable exchange rate, Korea's exports soared in the first decade after Park Chung-hee took power—rising at an annual average pace of 40 per cent between 1962 and 1970 (both years included), with annual export growth never falling below 34 per cent in eight years (after growing 31.7 per cent in the first year, 1962).

Korea's Economic Planning Board (EPB) was the nodal government agency that played the role that MITI did in Japan, providing fiscal incentives, policy loans and import quotas to those corporates that were able to meet and exceed export targets. The presidential Blue House took a leading role in administering the incentives, far more than in Japan and Taiwan. But the chaebol also developed an esprit de corps through a version of lifetime employment that helped Korean chaebols to build up loyal cadres of engineers and managers who dedicated their lives to building up the corporation. Taiwan's more entrepreneurial culture meant that company-hopping played a bigger role in Taiwan (for instance, Asustek was established as a competitor by defectors from Acer).

Education was another area where Korea strove to emulate Japan. In 1954, Korea already had 17 per cent of the population enrolled in school (reflecting the legacy of literacy from Japanese colonial times) compared with 23 per cent in Japan in the same year, and just 7 per cent in India. By way of comparison, England and Wales had just 9 per cent of the population in school in 1830 (seventy years after the start of the First Industrial Revolution), and only 15 per cent even in 1954. By 1887, the leaders of the Second Industrial Revolution (Germany and the US) had 18 per cent and 22 per cent of the population enrolled in school, helping to explain why they rapidly overtook Britain as industrial powers over the next two decades. But while literacy in Korea was much higher than the colonial norm in 1945, the Japanese colonial education system in Korea emphasized rote learning, and there was less stress on scientific and technical attainment in Japanese-ruled Korea.

Park Chung-hee focused much attention on overcoming this legacy, with an aggressive programme of technical and engineering education, although quality was naturally somewhat mixed in this headlong dash towards the acquisition of skills. By 1965, Korea had 29 per cent of the secondary-age population in secondary schools (the same proportion as India, which had neglected primary education but done well on secondary and tertiary), but behind Singapore on 45 per cent (the year Singapore separated from Malaysia); Turkey and Mexico were well behind at 16 per cent and 17 per cent respectively. By 1978, Park's Korea had raced ahead to a secondary enrolment ratio of 68 per cent, while Singapore was at 57 per cent, India had barely progressed to 30 per cent, falling behind Turkey (34 per cent) and Mexico (37 per cent), while Brazil lagged at 17 per cent. By the late 1970s, Korea had 22 engineers for every thousand in the population, well ahead of Singapore (5.2), India (3), Mexico (6.9) or Turkey (15.9). Teachers had a higher status (and were better compensated) in Korea than in most other developing economies. Starting from a high base (over 60 per cent of the work force had some schooling in 1946), 58.8 per cent of Korea's workforce and 76.2 per cent of its manufacturing workforce had secondary or tertiary education by 1983. It was consequently able to absorb and use technology much better than most other developing nations' work forces. Technology had come to Korea bundled in with military aid from the US until the mid-1960s. Once that dried up, Japan became the main source of technology licensing agreements for Korean firms. From the outset, Korea also emulated Meiji-era Japan's three main sources of technology, skill and knowledge acquisition: (a) a small core of experienced individuals who had acquired leading technologies; (b) overseas training for a select group of young men; and (c) foreign experts and advisers. The last were particularly used to double-check on the quality of the technology being imported from Japan. So, in the 1980s, POSCO and Hyundai Motors used the same Japanese sources for new technology (Nippon Steel and Mitsubishi Motors respectively) as Malaysia's Perwaja and Proton, but the Korean buyers ensured that the technology they were receiving was genuinely at the cutting edge, while the Malaysians received experimental technologies for which they served as guinea pigs.

Korea had first acquired steel capacity in 1941, when the Japanese established two steel mills in southern Korea. Although these were severely damaged during the Korean War, and the steel industry was fragmented and uncompetitive by the early 1960s, there was a considerable pool of experienced personnel with knowledge of steel-making in Korea. Nonetheless, the World Bank strongly opposed Korea's plans to invest in an integrated steel plant in 1968. Park Chung-hee went ahead nonetheless, appointing a proven manager and military protégé of his, General Park Tae-joon, who had already successfully turned around Korea Tungsten Corporation. After several abortive attempts at arranging financing for the large-scale project that the Parks envisaged, the project was financed by reparations from Japan for '36 years of hardship under Japanese rule'. Nippon Steel (then the world's most efficient steel producer) led the 'Japan Group' of engineering consultants to Pohang Iron and Steel Company Limited (POSCO). According to POSCO's own documents, the 'Japan Group, in the name of friendship and economic development, was very enthusiastic about providing assistance at the time.' They agreed to scale-up capacity to 9.1 million tonnes (from the 2.6 million tonnes originally planned) by the time the plant came fully on-stream in 1973, and ensured that the highest quality technology was made available. Park Tae-joon had employed Australia's BHP to obtain a second opinion on the quality of technology, but there was also sufficient in-house expertise to ensure effective technological absorption.

Both features were missing in Malaysia when it sought to embark on a similar collaboration with Nippon Steel in the 1980s. While Korea had had steel mills since 1941 and had experience with the relevant technology, Malaysia (having been a British colony) had been a pure commodity exporter with no prior steel-making experience. From its very first year of full operations in 1973, POSCO was profitable, albeit aided by access to subsidized foreign capital and massive government investment in infrastructure such as roads, harbours and low-cost power. By 1986, POSCO had sufficiently mastered the complex technology of steel-making for it to become the lowest-cost steel manufacturer in the world, and to begin providing technical expertise and consulting services for the refurbishment and modernization of the United States Steel (USX) plant in Pittsburg, California. Spurred on by Japan's help, POSCO had become a world leader, and continued to go from strength to strength. With the rapid growth of the shipbuilding, car and machinery industries, there was excess demand for its products within Korea, but POSCO had a self-imposed target of exporting 30 per cent of its output in order to stay competitive with its global peers.

When Hyundai Heavy Industries (HHI) was building its first very large crude carrier ship, it was able to recruit a large number of engineers from Korea Shipbuilding and Engineering Corporation (KSEC), a government-run shipbuilder originally established in 1937 by Mitsubishi of Japan, that the government had further invested in during the 1950s and 1960s. A knowledge-sharing alliance between KSEC, Seoul National and Yonsei University had also been established, which also aided HHI greatly. When one of its first big shipbuilding orders (for five ships for a Greek buyer) fell through, partly because technical challenges caused delays in production, Hyundai Merchant Marine Corporation (HMMC) was created, and took over the ships.

Subsequently, a heavy engineering company was also established to acquire ship design and engine manufacturing capacity that put HHI on par or ahead of its Japanese competitors. Thereafter, the government ensured that all its oil refinery exports were carried on HMMC ships. But in response, HHI became highly efficient and never again had problems of excess capacity until 1998, becoming the world's largest shipbuilding company by 1984, filling annual orders of 10 million deadweight tonnes (DWT) that year. HHI did not relinquish its status as the world's largest shipbuilder in the subsequent 32 years. During its difficult initial years, HHI also benefited from membership of its chaebol, which cross-subsidized its losses, and also provided managerial personnel (particularly from Hyundai Construction).

Whether steel, shipbuilding or cement, the pioneering investments in Korea were done by Japan during the colonial period. At a minimum, this created a pool of technical personnel that could be tapped by Korea's new industrialists and government in subsequent periods. Nothing comparable existed in India, for instance, which necessitated the vast scale and breadth of investments in the public sector (steel, petrochemicals, oil refineries, heavy machinery manufacturing) that India attempted during the Nehru years. Nehru's mistake was to ignore India's initial comparative advantage in textiles and garments—which withered because protection of other industries drove up the effective exchange rate, pricing out textile exporters. The lack of export earnings, in turn, acted as a constraint on India's ability to import the essential intermediate goods that could not be easily import-substituted. In effect, sequencing was where Nehru went wrong: had he allowed textiles and garment exports to lead (along with existing exports like tea, jute, mica, iron ore), then used those earnings to import the capital goods needed for a more ambitious industrial sector, India may have succeeded sooner. Ironically, the state-owned companies like oil explorer ONGC, steel maker SAIL, and aluminium and zinc companies BALCO and Hindustan Zinc, provided the bulk of the managerial and technical talent for Reliance Industries, ArcelorMittal Steel and the Vedanta group respectively as these private Indian companies became globally competitive.

Korea's real GNP grew a modest 2.2 per cent in the first year after Park took power, as macroeconomic adjustments were made. Thereafter, over the subsequent seventeen years that Park Chung-hee was South Korea's president, real GNP growth averaged 9 per cent annually until 1979, with real GNP consequently more than quadrupling over his term in office. It was one of the most remarkable economic transformations ever achieved, and moved Korea from a poor to a middle income economy in less than two decades. Park's approach differed from Japan and Taiwan's only in one important aspect—it involved much more risk-taking, with inflation remaining high throughout the period, and the current account remaining in deficit in all but two years (with large deficits of 7–10 per cent of GDP for about a third of the years).

Park's government also nationalized the banks—which were close to bankruptcy—in 1961, and this gave the junta even greater control over the allocation of capital. All exporters who met their export targets received access to working capital loans, but longer-term credit for specific industries went to favoured companies that demonstrated particular ability in those industries (or which earned Park's trust early, and lived up to it over time). So the massive integrated steel mill of the state-owned POSCO received ample allocations of credit, while the mini-mills of the colonial era were starved of funds, and Ssangyong Cement (owned by a member of Park's political party) received much more credit than the Japanese-legacy Tongyang Corporation, although the latter had much more expertise in cement at the start of the period. The three leading chaebols—Samsung, Hyundai and Daewoo—received support for machinery building, while Hyundai received the lion's share of loans for the shipbuilding industry. In each of these sectors, multi-year credit support to the leading player(s) gradually caused other competitors to wither away (including seven small but experienced players in the shipbuilding industry). By the time of Park's assassination in 1979, Korea had emerged as a significant steel manufacturer, and its chemicals, shipbuilding and car industries were heading towards global competitiveness.

But the high-wire system, like Bismarck's, clearly required the mastery of Park himself. The year after his assassination, Korea was obliged to take an IMF loan. Thus reinforced, however, Korea followed Japan's path in becoming globally competitive in televisions, cars, ships, steel and petrochemicals over the next decade, as Park's HCI drive of the 1970s began to bear ample fruit (much as Japan's similar drive had done in the 1930s). Gradually, these heavy industries replaced the light industries (textiles, garments, shoes, etc.) in which Korea was becoming uncompetitive as its labour market was being strained. But the full-employment economy meant that absolute poverty had been abolished in South Korea, and the country was comfortably middle income, and approaching prosperity. This culminated in the hosting of the 1988 Olympics in Seoul, a coming-out party much like Japan's in 1964, albeit with less democracy (as the former general Roh Tae-woo won a disputed election the previous year, in the first free election since Park's days).

THE SHORTCOMINGS OF INDIA'S NEHRUVIAN MODEL OF COMPREHENSIVE IMPORT SUBSTITUTION

At independence, India's social indicators were absolutely abysmal—with life expectancy at birth of just 32 years, and a literacy rate of just 14 per cent (also amongst the lowest on earth). But the Congress had been committed to democracy and 'secularism' (or neutrality amongst religions, 'dharma nirapekshata'), and these endured. Neither was a natural legacy of British colonialism: democracy failed to establish itself in Pakistan, or develop genuine roots in the soil of Malaysia, Singapore, Burma, Iraq or in Britain's erstwhile African colonies (Nigeria, Kenya, Uganda, Zambia, Zimbabwe, Egypt), so it could not have been a legacy of British rule.

India's democracy was, in reality, a result of the internal processes established by the Congress party during the independence movement, with issues being debated thoroughly before decisions were made—and that tradition of exhaustive debates transferred automatically into independent India's Parliament. That Congress' democratic procedures ended at the door of the 'high command' also became Indian democracy's Achilles heel, with leadership selection in the Congress and all other political parties remaining thoroughly opaque; the unfortunate experience of 1939, when Gandhi forced Bose to resign the Congress presidency despite winning re-election overwhelmingly over Gandhi's candidate, and of 1946—when Gandhi asked Patel to step aside in favour of Nehru despite the former being strongly preferred by the provincial leaders of Congress—has become the norm across all parties.

Contrary to the resolutions adopted at Congress sessions since 1929 (which had all demanded purna swaraj or complete independence), Nehru accepted dominion status for India in August 1947 (as did Pakistan). Although India became a republic in January 1950, it remained part of the Commonwealth of former British colonies (other than the US and Ireland). One important consequence of this was that most British commercial interests in India were untouched at independence, and continued to function unaltered: so Calcutta remained the headquarters of the global jute textile and tea industries, controlled by British companies ('managing agencies') that employed only Britishers as managerial employees (my father joined one such company on the first day of 1955 as the third Indian recruited as an assistant manager on any of the fifteen tea estates owned by the company; the first two had only joined the previous year).

And as we saw, the Indian army and police were still entirely British-controlled in 1946–47—and these British officers facilitated the pogroms of partition violence. The new Indian Republic was based on a constitution modelled upon the Government of India Act, 1935—with universal suffrage replacing the more limited electorate (14 per cent of the population) under the original Act, and the princely allies of the British losing the two-fifth share of parliamentary seats they had under the 1935 Act (in exchange for 'privy purses' which assured them a large permanent pension). But constitutional continuity meant that laws written for purposes of colonial control remained on the statute books, unless they were specifically withdrawn (and very few were). Colonial attitudes towards administration persisted, with a bureaucracy that had been created for supercilious colonial overlordship suddenly expected to participate in the onerous tasks of development.

During World War II, Britain had drawn resources from India without paying for them—and instead 'purchased' those goods and services by accumulating 'sterling balances' (or future promises to pay). In other words, Britain was acting like a customer who enters a warehouse, empties it of all its food, timber and other resources, but merely makes a promise to pay later. One consequence was that the Reserve Bank of India simply printed more rupees to pay for some of the items purchased from Indian sources, causing inflation to soar to over 70 per cent in 1943 (after 68 per cent growth in money supply in 1942)—which, as we have seen in Chapter 5, was a major contributor to the Indian Famine of 1943. India's sterling balances (i.e., British purchases from India during the war that Britain had failed to pay for) amounted to £1,321 million in 1945 (or US$5.284 billion at the prevailing exchange rate). This was larger than the US$4.4 billion that Britain owed the US under its Lend-Lease agreement—but the latter was a convertible or hard-currency liability, while India was constrained by being part of the sterling area, and having no right even to invest the sterling balances in UK gilts (that might have earned 4 per cent interest, which Britain was unwilling to pay).

Instead India's sterling balances were devalued along with the devaluation of the pound in 1949, which reduced the size of India's balances by the equivalent of US$1.1 billion. And subsequently, 'independent' India agreed to an arrangement under which about a quarter of the sterling balances were used to buy an annuity which would enable India to pay the pensions of British bureaucrats and soldiers who had served in India (although surely, as the colonial power, Britain should have borne these pension bills). Part of the rest was used to buy British military stores and supplies left behind in India, and the rest was used primarily to buy British imports of consumer and capital goods—which effectively meant that India was hurting its own import-competing industries in the early years, by buying goods from the UK that would otherwise not be purchased. This was daylight robbery by a debtor-nation (Britain) sucking a final pound of flesh from its former colony.

Interestingly, Britain paid its debts to Argentina, Portugal and Brazil by selling off its assets (e.g., British ownership of the railways in Argentina). This could surely have been done in India too, but the British claimed that their investments in India were too small to pay off the sterling balances!

India's colonial bureaucrats had a patronizing attitude towards citizens, with a focus on law enforcement and keeping order rather than developing the economy. Those attitudes persisted post-independence because the same people remained in place—with Indians gradually replacing British incumbents over the first 5–10 years, moving into not only their offices but also into their colonial-era homes with all the trappings of power these connoted. In Korea and Taiwan, Japanese-owned companies, banks, farms and other assets were orphaned—and came into the possession of the new governments, who could remake them as they pleased. In India and Pakistan, British ownership of commercial assets persisted, and British attitudes towards the citizenry were adopted and preserved by the bureaucracy. So, as late as 1990, literacy rates in India and Pakistan remained abysmally low (52 per cent and 36 per cent respectively)—and bureaucrats argued that it would be impossible to employ the millions of poor if they were ever to be educated. Japan's developmental state had always been focused on providing the basic public goods—mass education and literacy, basic public health and sanitation, good physical infrastructure—to citizens, first in Japan and then in Taiwan, Manchuria and Korea.

British India's failure to provide education was apparent, and none of the basic public services (primary education and health, policing, sanitation, roads) reached down to the village, where local power-holders were expected merely to ensure that land revenue was collected and delivered (with no reciprocal provision of services by the British–Indian state). The successor state of Congress-ruled India similarly proved utterly unable to extend basic services to the village level: thus, when Narendra Modi took office in May 2014, more than half of Indian households still did not have access to basic sanitation (a toilet at home or in school), and India had yet to achieve universal literacy amongst its primary schoolgoing age cohort, although the literacy rate had risen by about 10 percentage points at each decadal census. As Modi expressed it in his first speech in Parliament, 'when the state fails to provide basic services like education and primary health, the poor suffer most since they cannot afford to buy private services.'

Where Nehru did make a decisively positive impact, however, was in addressing the other major lacuna that most developing economies face—a severe shortage of engineering and managerial talent. The British had only allowed Indians to acquire civil engineering degrees, but the nationalist Madan Mohan Malaviya had established electrical and mechanical engineering degree courses at Banaras Hindu University by the second decade of the twentieth century. Nehru created the Indian Institutes of Technology (IIT, first in Kharagpur near Calcutta, then in Bombay, Kanpur, Madras and Delhi)—which began to produce world-class engineers in the 1950s. Only Korea and Taiwan acquired comparable engineering schools in the developing world, but Nehru and Abul Kalam Azad (India's first education minister) were the pioneers in overcoming this handicap. Nehru also collaborated with MIT's Sloan School of Management in creating the first Indian Institute of Management (IIM) in Calcutta (November 1961), followed the next month by another IIM at Ahmedabad. The IITs and IIMs have ensured that India has far superior supplies of engineers, entrepreneurs and business managers than any other developing economy—and this despite the fact that the vast majority of IIT graduates migrated to the US (or Europe) between 1955 and 1990. The Nehruvian approach to education focused much more on secondary and tertiary education than on primary. So, in 1995, India was still producing six times as many graduates as China was producing—although China has since closed that gap with a tertiary education boom.

The Indian economy grew at an average pace of 3.7 per cent annually between 1950 and 1980—implying per capita income growth of 1.5 per cent annually. This was a lot faster than the 0.7 per cent annual growth of real GDP in the 1900–1950 period (which meant a decline in per capita income over that period). But between 1950 and 1980, India was expanding no faster than the average pace of global GDP growth; since India's population was growing slightly faster than the world's population during that period, India's per capita income was growing marginally less than the world's average growth rate over those three decades. For one of the poorest countries on earth at the start of this period, this was simply not good enough, and India remained amongst the ten poorest nations on earth in 1980. In the first decade (1950–60), real GDP expanded slightly more than 4 per cent annually despite a balance of payments crisis in FY 1957–58, but the wars with China (1962) and Pakistan (1965) sapped the economy's strength in the 1960s.

Real GDP declined 3.7 per cent in FY 1965–66, but the average real GDP growth in the second decade slowed only marginally to 3.9 per cent. The 1970s were the dismal decade for India's economy, with growth slowing to just 2.3 per cent annually in the first half of the decade amid the depredations of Socialism (including a tightening of foreign exchange controls, anti-monopoly rules and bank nationalization, all of which tended to increase corruption)—but improving in the second half of the turbulent 1970s. Overall, though, a 3.5–4 per cent handle for average annual real GDP growth was deplorably anaemic. Nehru attempted to graft a Soviet-style planning approach onto a colonial-era bureaucracy, with mediocre results. Import substituting industrialization (ISI) was the policy recommended by the World Bank in the 1950s—in the hope of stimulating demand for capital goods from the West, while the newly emerging economies would focus on replacing imports of consumer goods with domestic production. India adopted an extreme version of this ISI strategy—by banning virtually all imports of consumer goods, while also attempting (after 1956) to develop heavy and chemical industries via public enterprises that Nehru termed the 'temples of modern India' that would capture 'the commanding heights of the economy'. The extreme protection for consumer goods meant that India produced shoddy consumer products (from toothpaste to soap, watches, cornflakes, bread, whisky, cars, motorcycles, scooters) in the absence of competition—which was restricted via a panoply of licences/controls over the amount and mix of products that each company was allowed to produce. Intermediate goods and parts still needed to be imported for most products, so the 'foreign exchange constraint' was often a binding one on an economy that was characterized by scarcity.

Pervasive tariff and non-tariff barriers to imports implicitly meant an anti-export bias: imported products were expensive, and this raised the costs of exportable products (including consumer goods). Although India also had duty drawback schemes (like Korea and Taiwan) to compensate exporters for the higher cost of imports, the compensation was insufficient for the all-pervading anti-export bias. While Taiwan adopted an explicitly export-promoting policy by 1958, and Korea after 1961, India retained its export pessimism—justifying it by the 'fallacy of composition' (if every developing economy tried to export, they would flood the market, cause export prices to fall and hurt each other even more). India's policymakers made the cardinal mistake of believing that India was a large economy, and should thus focus on domestic demand—although India's economy was only the size of Holland even in 1990.

Had India chosen an export-promoting policy in 1950 or 1960, most of its exports would have had a negligible share of world markets—and would thus have been 'price-takers' rather than causing export prices to fall. The possible exceptions were tea and jute in 1950: these were still dominated by British companies, so India had no particular reason to promote them—although India could have used the sterling balances to take ownership of these companies, and then mounted a serious attempt at controlling the global market for those exports. In textiles and garments, India had a significant global market share in the early 1950s—with that market share having grown rapidly during World War II and in the Korean War. But the overvaluation of the rupee because of the ISI strategy severely weakened India's textile sector, and caused it to lose competitiveness—especially to Japan and Taiwan in the second half of the 1950s, and to Korea, Hong Kong and Singapore in the 1960s. Crucially, the 'infant industry' argument for import protection rested on the notion that a new industry needed to be nurtured when it was an infant—but those protections would eventually be withdrawn as the infant grew to adolescence. India never withdrew or reduced the import protection (even into late middle age), because of persistent export pessimism—which is what caused the economy to wallow in a below 4 per cent growth trap.

Superficially, there were similarities between Nehru's heavy industrialization drive in the 1950s, and what Stalin accomplished in the Soviet Union or Takahashi Korekiyo in Japan in the 1930s. But Nehru (and his adviser Mahalanobis) paid insufficient attention to the financing of the strategy. Stalin squeezed his agriculture sector, attacking the kulaks and appropriating their agricultural surpluses to finance his industrialization drive. The Soviet Union's massive military build-up helped provide a major additional source of demand for the new heavy-industrial products, as did Japan's military machine in the 1930s. But Japan had prepared the way for heavy industrialization through a mass education programme that began half a century earlier. Its land reforms in the 1870s had created a highly productive agricultural sector by the 1920s, which was the basis of Japan's successes as an exporter of silk, cotton textiles and apparel—and rice and sugar from Taiwan. That export-oriented participation in the global market had lifted Japan's per capita incomes (and those of Taiwan, Korea and Manchuria) sufficiently by the 1930s (to about ten times India's per capita income in the 1950s), so that Japan had a substantial domestic market (apart from military demand).

Nehru, on the other hand, was seeking to do everything at once: starting with trying to address dismally low literacy rates and negligible rates of enrolment in tertiary education, Nehru attempted land reforms (which did not entirely succeed across the country) and extension programmes to boost agricultural output, but also sought to import substitute both consumer and capital goods production—while ignoring how he was going to overcome the foreign exchange constraint that would limit the ability to import essential intermediate goods and raw materials that India did not produce. Japan had done all this, but sequentially: land reforms to boost agricultural productivity, alongside mass education, then inducing former daimyo and landlords (who had been compensated with bonds for the loss of their agrarian land) to invest in the new industries (which were labour intensive at first, with state-owned heavy industry only gradually introduced in the third decade after the Meiji Restoration). By attempting to do it all at once (and with a bias towards government rather than private ownership), Nehru achieved mediocre results everywhere, with agriculture suffering both from an overvalued exchange rate (that made imports cheap and exports uncompetitive) and the meagre response to land reform, while consumer goods remained inefficient because of excessive protection, and heavy industry's ability to expand was constrained by the dearth of imported capital goods and technology. In a poor country, national savings were low and could not finance the massive public investment required for Nehru's strategy, while export pessimism meant India did not have the ability to import what it didn't produce.

That the Indian economy had significant potential to expand faster became evident in the second half of the 1970s. When Indira Gandhi imposed the Emergency in June 1975, India had a controlled experiment in East Asian-style authoritarian rule. And, in economic terms, it clearly worked: not only did real GDP grow 9 per cent in FY 1975–76 (the fastest growth for any year until that time), but India also had a current account surplus, the trains and planes ran on time, and the cities were notably cleaner. Growth did run out of momentum in FY 1976–77, and India's electorate chose freedom over bread in the March 1977 election. But one of the best-kept secrets of India's economic trajectory is that the next two years—during Morarji Desai's premiership—saw India's real GDP expand 7.5 per cent and 5.5 per cent in successive years (for an average growth pace of 6.5 per cent, the fastest two-year growth rate achieved by India until that time). Desai was an experienced hand at managing the economy (having presented nine budgets and shepherded India out of its two recessions in 1958 and 1966), and his finance minister H. M. Patel was a skilled former bureaucrat (who had served India as both home and finance secretary). They reduced corporate taxes, eased restrictions on incumbent companies' ability to expand capacity, and removed most price controls. The economy responded with alacrity to the modest deregulation by the Desai–Patel duo. But Morarji Desai was ousted in July 1979 by Charan Singh; the latter, as finance minister since February that year, pursued a quixotic attempt to raise agriculture prices to appease his core farmer constituency. But, the surge in crude oil prices (to US$36/barrel that year, from US$3 in September 1973) led to a severe case of stagflation, as the economy contracted 5 per cent in a year in which inflation was in double digits. It was left to P. V. Narasimha Rao to take Desai's modest reforms and comprehensively transform India's economy after 1991.

JAPAN AND ITS FLYING GEESE; THE ACRIMONIOUS
COLONIAL LEGACY FURTHER WEST

Asia was able to throw off the colonial yoke because one Asian nation, Japan, proved able and willing to stand up to the European powers. Asia owes a deep debt of gratitude to the intrepid perspicacity of the southern samurai of Choshu and Satsuma, who first attempted to battle the Europeans, but soon recognized it would be better to emulate them. The punctilious manner in which they acquired knowledge and institutions from the 'best of the West', while retaining cultural autonomy, enabled Japan to rapidly become a formidable economic and military power. While military conquest was the way all colonizers expanded their dominions (to the universal detriment of those they colonized), Japan prepared itself meticulously for the sociopolitical challenges of imperial rule. Thus, while the Dutch sought to divide Indonesia into numerous fragments (sixteen states were agreed upon in the Renville Agreement of January 1948, with fifteen expected to retain a strong Dutch link), the Japanese immediately freed Sukarno and Hatta once they had conquered the East Indies, and encouraged them to create encompassing national organizations that contributed vitally to moulding an Indonesian national identity.

Burma, the Philippines, Vietnam, Cambodia and Laos all were declared independent of colonial control by Japan during the war (and allowed to be led by their most legitimate leaders). The European imperialists could never completely reverse those declarations in the post-War world. With Japan's assistance, Subhas Bose's Provisional Government of Free India demonstrated that Indians were capable of forming a freedom army of their own, and financing it through their own national bank; in November 1945, when the fog of wartime propaganda was lifted, Indians discovered the gallant story of the INA, which thoroughly undermined the loyalty of the British Indian navy, air force and army—leading to the mutinies of January–February 1946 that forced Britain to abandon its long-term plans for empire, and begin negotiating India's freedom. Once the British Indian military was lost, Britain's paramountcy across West Asia proved untenable, and the edifice of European empire crumbled across Asia.

In Taiwan, Korea and Manchukuo, the Japanese built physical

infrastructure, modernized land tenure, invested in heavy industries (and the skills required to run them), and vastly boosted literacy (using both Japanese and the local language). That legacy proved vital in launching them onto the path of Modern Economic Growth in ways that no European colony was ever equipped to do. The British, Dutch and French colonies had scant infrastructure, and far lower literacy than the Japanese colonies, and consequently were far behind Taiwan, Manchuria and Korea in social indicators such as life expectancy in 1945. In China, the European powers relinquished their treaty port rights in 1943, mainly because all the treaty ports had by then fallen to Japanese control. But at the Yalta Conference (February 1945), the US and UK agreed to restore Russian control of Port Arthur (Lushun) and to make the whole of Dalian an international port (rather than restoring it to Chinese sovereignty). That the Great Powers were still thinking in terms of 'spheres of influence' (precisely as they did in 1919) was evident in the way in which they demarcated who would take the surrender of the Axis powers in various parts of Asia.

So Japan's key wartime legacy was to have liberated East Asia from European dominion by May 1942. (Indeed, had Russia won the Russo–Japanese War of 1904–05, Korea and Manchuria would immediately have come completely under Russian rule, and Asia would most likely have continued to be European-controlled to this day, akin to Francophone Africa or pre–1991 Soviet Central Asia). Newly empowered leaders would not relinquish their freedoms when the European powers tried to use the British Indian Army to restore Dutch control of the East Indies (which Sukarno and Hatta had already renamed Indonesia) or French control of Indo-China (where the Vietminh had seized Vietnam, and royals had declared socialist goals for Cambodia and Laos). The British chiefs of staff produced a White Paper for Churchill in May 1945 laying out the key strategic imperatives to control the Indian Ocean (hence undivided India, Burma and Ceylon) until 1960.

But British hubris went too far. The INA's 'Chalo Delhi' marching song had urged: '"To Delhi" be your Battle Cry / hoisting the national standard high / Fluttering atop the Lal Qila / Let it fly, let it fly', and it was at Delhi's symbolic Lal Qila (Red Fort) that the British decided to hold the INA trials, while simultaneously using Indian troops to launch the reprisal killings against Indonesia's nationalist army in Surabaya. The dormant Congress, crushed by the colonial government since February 1943 (with most of its important leaders imprisoned in the half-year following the launch of the Quit India Movement in August 1942), was revived by the nationalist fervour unleashed by the INA trials. The result was that the three INA stalwarts' life sentences were commuted, but that proved insufficient to preclude the mutinies in the Indian navy, air force and army that finally forced the British Indian empire to its knees. The mutinous sailors and airmen specifically demanded that Indian troops be withdrawn from Indonesia and Vietnam. But South Vietnam was still prised from nationalist control, and it took another three decades before Vietnam was unified and free. In Indonesia, Stalin's failed attempt at a revolution within the revolution in 1948 swung the US behind the nationalists, ending the Dutch bid to restore imperial control.

Stalin did succeed in delivering China to his communist ally, by ensuring that the critical region of Manchuria, with its industrial base and massive caches of Japanese ammunition, fell into Mao and Lin Biao's hands. But once he was in control of China, Mao's imperialist vision for China clashed with the Russian imperialism of Stalin—and the two imperialists came to a grudging agreement, with the Soviets retaining control of Outer Mongolia and a small chunk of Manchuria in exchange for Chinese control of Inner Mongolia and East Turkestan (Xinjiang). Mao inherited Inner Tibet (Qinghai and western Sichuan) when the KMT fled, but invaded Tibet proper in October 1950. Nehru's India did nothing to prevent its annexation. Amid growing repression of Tibet's people, the Dalai Lama escaped to India in 1959, and a Tibetan government in exile was formed at Dharamsala, representing the last unfinished business of the imperialist era in Asia.

Although decolonization became the new norm, the Cold War served as a new fig leaf for brazen power grabs across Asia in the 1950s. Mossadegh's Iran was a particular victim. But Nasser showed in 1956 that Britain without the Indian military was a paper tiger. That soon allowed Iraq to free itself of its British puppet monarchy (1958), and for Malaya and Singapore to become dominions before moving towards true independence. By then, Japan had used the logic of the Cold War to restore the apparatus of a Developmental State (which SCAP had initially wanted to dismantle) and begun its rapid ascent back to economic dynamism, with Taiwan under the KMT gradually following in its wake with similar policies. In 1961, South Korea's Park Chung-hee jumped into the fray as well, energetically emulating every aspect of Japan's policy apparatus, albeit with an extra dash of risk-taking made possible by greater centralized control in his Blue House.

By the end of the 1980s, Japan reached its economic and financial apogee as Brand Japan strode the world like a colossus. Its industrial companies— producing cars (Toyota, Honda, Nissan, Mazda, Suzuki), trucks (Mitsubishi, Hino), tyres (Bridgestone), construction equipment (Komatsu), semiconductors and high-tech electronics (Hitachi, Fujitsu, Toshiba), consumer electronics (Sony, Panasonic, Sharp, Sanyo, Ricoh), watches (Seiko) and cameras (Canon,

Olympus, Yashica)—became ubiquitous as their products became household names across the modern world. Japanese products became peerless for process-efficiency and quality control. High oil prices hurt demand for American gas-guzzlers in the 1970s, spurring mass switching to Toyota, Honda and Nissan cars, which won customers' lasting loyalty through superb after-sales service. To many Americans, it seemed at the time that, although Japan had been defeated in the Second World War, its companies had won the peace. The historian Paul Kennedy argued in a bestselling book that, like the imperial overstretch of other great powers, the US had overextended itself during the Cold War and was bound to pay the price over subsequent decades.

Like other bystanders in great wars (indeed, like the US in World Wars I and II, when its homeland had not been attacked), Japan appeared the real winner of the Cold War, as the two great combatants in that conflict (the US and USSR) exhausted each other like heavyweight boxers in the final rounds of a long fight. Japan's seeming financial dominance was reflected in the fact that the total value of its equity market was approximately double that of the US at the end of 1989. While this was a high-water mark that has never again been attained by Japan's equities, that apogee struck awe into observers around the world—and the consensus then was that Japan was unstoppable, and those stock market valuations simply reflected the likely future dominance of their companies.

The financial predictions proved entirely false, because they were partly predicated upon a massive bubble in the real estate market that had been inflated after 1984 (when Japan fully opened its capital markets), and after Japan agreed—at a meeting of the G7 powers at New York's Plaza Hotel in 1985—to allow the yen to appreciate rapidly (which it did, doubling in value over the next three years, inducing massive capital inflows into Japan that exacerbated the asset bubble). Mieno Yasushi, an unorthodox but determined governor of the BoJ, kept monetary policy on a tight leash from 1990 to 1993—until it was certain that Japan's bubble had most definitely burst. Over the subsequent fifteen years, Japan's property prices declined a precipitous 86 per cent, and Japan suffered persistent consumer price deflation between 1998 and 2012. Extraordinarily, however, Japan's social solidarity held: unlike the US in the 1930s (when unemployment had soared past 25 per cent), Japan's unemployment rate peaked at a modest 5.6 per cent in 2011 as the government bore most of the detrimental burdens of deflation.

Despite that, when Bill Clinton ran for US president in 1992, his campaign was based largely on an economic platform that aimed to emulate Japan's active industrial policy. When he was interviewing candidates to head his Council of Economic Advisers, Clinton rejected the leading liberal economist,

Paul Krugman, and instead picked Laura d'Andrea Tyson, whose academic reputation was primarily that of a 'Japan basher'. The epithet was a trifle unfair, but Tyson had indeed focused on analysing Japan's approach to industrial policy, and her November 1992 book argued for a 'cautious activist' approach to industrial policy in high-technology industries with 'dynamic scale economies' and national security spin-offs.

The Clinton/Tyson approach restored the US to pre-eminence as the world's most powerful economy by the end of the twentieth century. A new high-technology revolution and the restoration of America's fiscal health (partly via a sharp pullback of its military-industrial complex) restored America's economic pre-eminence. The US had finally won the 146-year race with Japan for Asia-Pacific (and global) economic predominance—but it had been a close race, especially between 1975 and 1995, when Japan appeared on track to win.

Korea and Taiwan followed the full array of Japan-style planning mechanisms, and the outcome was world-leading companies, egalitarian societies and relatively equal income distributions. Land reforms under Japanese rule ensured more equal distribution of agrarian holdings in both countries, which consequently became the most successful agricultural economies in Asia during the first half of the twentieth century. They reformed land tenure further after the departure of the Japanese, creating small but economic landholdings—and removing all large landholdings, thereby eliminating the incentive for real estate or Filipino-style plantations to become capitalist pursuits. During their key phase of industrialization (including their pursuit of heavy and chemical industries), both Taiwan and Korea had banking systems that were almost completely government-owned. This ensured that governments could mould key sectors and direct credit to national champions (who emerged through a competitive process, but received support as long as they met export targets), with government ownership of companies being an extra tool in the strategic sectors.

During the 1950s, Japan's MoF and BoJ were opposed to heavy and chemical industries, insisting that static comparative advantage lay in labour-intensive manufacturing, given the huge surplus labour created in the aftermath of war, which had lowered labour costs. But MITI argued that Japan needed to look beyond existing factor endowments, and focus on investments that would introduce new technology and enable Japan to succeed in heavy and chemical industries (as it had done before the war). So MITI successively promoted cars, steel, petrochemicals, semiconductors, and consumer electronics. And MITI became 'the model for its counterparts in both Taiwan and Korea to accept the same responsibility for promoting new industries and advanced technologies'.

The credit for Japan, Korea and Taiwan's egalitarian outcomes is often attributed to the land reforms undertaken under US auspices after 1945. However, the beneficence of US agrarian policies was clearly insufficient to underpin that other US ally of 1955–75, South Vietnam. The region that became South Vietnam (erstwhile Annam and Cochin-China) remained under French control throughout World War II, with Bao Dai reinstated as king in March 1945 without significantly altering the French colonial social structure, which included extended land holdings by the Catholic Church. The departure of the French created an opportunity for Korea/Japan-style agrarian reforms, particularly through redistribution of formerly French- and church-owned land. But Ngo Dinh Diem, South Vietnam's leader from 1954 to 1961, a Catholic steeped in the elite culture of Bao Dai's court, was an unlikely implementer of serious agrarian reform. Although he capped land rents at a quarter of production, only a tenth of all cultivated land in South Vietnam was redistributed from those holding more than 100 acres. This was no match to the Vietminh's generous redistribution of land in North Vietnam.

A crucial difference between South Vietnam, and Japan, Korea and Taiwan was that the latter had already undergone a prior land reform that had redistributed land from the largest landowners (the daimyo in Japan immediately after the Meiji Restoration, the yangban class in Korea following Japan's takeover of the nation in 1910, and large landholders in Taiwan immediately after Japan's conquest in 1895). The newly empowered farmers with clear land titles became key supporters of the new regime, and were energetic users of the agricultural extension services provided by the Japanese state which helped bolster agricultural productivity across all three nations in the Japanese imperium. On the other hand, while the Vichy regime had given the Japanese military right of passage through Vietnam, the Vietnamese nation did not benefit from the type of comprehensive land reform that Japan undertook in Taiwan and Korea since Japan did not take over its governance. South Vietnam's 1970 land reform did boost agricultural productivity for a time, but received a new setback with the communists' attempt at collectivizing agriculture after 1975. A vital reason why South Vietnam failed as a socio-economic entity was the failure of its early land reform, in circumstances that were very similar to Korea or Taiwan in 1945–50 (with key landowners delegitimized because they were foreign). But the prior Japanese land reform had already raised agricultural productivity in Japan, Taiwan and Korea, so the post-war reform under US auspices was only a marginal change, not the drastic leap that needed to be accomplished on the agrarian tabula rasa of South Vietnam in 1955.

Taiwan replicated Japan's economic institutions and planning mechanisms, with the Industrial Development Bureau (IDB) acting as MITI's equivalent. The Council for Economic Planning and Development (CEPD) developed broad policy guidelines, but the IDB then selected the industries that were to be promoted through fiscal incentives, tariffs or import controls, and policy loans. Additionally, it established order in export marketing if excessive competition in an industry prompted complaints from buyers, provided administrative guidance to firms, and oversaw price negotiations in sectors (e.g., petrochemicals) that needed them. Taiwan's IDB thus almost exactly replicated the functions that MITI had in Japan, combining responsibility for trade and foreign investment policy with those of domestic industrial policy.

Taiwan was able to use its government-directed credit mechanisms to build up world-leading shipping lines. In some areas, notably textiles and shoes, Taiwanese firms remained global players long after Taiwan ceased to be a viable manufacturing base for those products: for instance, Yue Yuen remains the world's largest manufacturer of athletic and leisure footwear (producing on an OEM/ODM basis for Nike, Adidas, Puma, Crocs, Reebok, etc.), having moved most of its production lines to Dongguan in China's Pearl River delta and then to Vietnam.

Ultimately, Taiwan's greatest successes came in electronics, We saw how the government-owned ITRI became the base for the creation of TSMC, the world's largest chip foundry, focusing on application-specific integrated chips (ASICs) for the telecommunications and consumer electronic industries. Its domestic rival UMC was also founded from within ITRI, and is now the third largest chip foundry in the world, and the only one apart from TSMC that is consistently profitable. Foxconn (Hon Hai) has become the world's largest electronics contract manufacturer.

Lee Teng-hui, who became Taiwan's president in 1988, was the first 'bensheng ren' (Taiwanese-born) to rise to the top of the KMT. He fundamentally reoriented the framework of economic policy, making it more conducive to the expansion of entrepreneurial companies through a deepening of the venture capital industry. An admirer of the benign and developmental impact of Japan's colonial rule, Lee Teng-hui was instrumental in taking Taiwan onto a more innovative and entrepreneurial path that differentiated the Taiwanese economy quite significantly from the Korean one. Apart from encouraging venture capital funds (which would incubate and bolster SMEs, which were primarily Taiwanese- rather than Mainlander-owned), Lee's administration played a key role in reversing the brain drain, inducing Taiwanese based in California's Silicon Valley to return and build an alternative entrepreneurial hub in Hsinchu.

By Lee Teng-hui's last year in office (2000), the dense ecosystem of

Hsinchu had made Taiwan the home for 224 specialized semiconductor makers. Every part of the personal computer (PC) and components supply chain was dominated by Taiwanese companies, although rarely selling final products that bore their own brands. Acer had emerged as the third largest PC manufacturer in the world. By 2015, Asustek (founded by four former Acer employees) overtook Acer to become the fourth-largest PC vendor by unit sales worldwide, and the world's largest motherboard maker.

Lee Teng-hui was also instrumental in fully democratizing Taiwan, subjecting himself to the first democratic presidential election in 1996 (which he won with 54 per cent of the vote). The CPC felt so threatened by the prospect of a directly elected president in Taiwan that mainland China began a series of military manoeuvres in Fujian province across the Taiwan Straits, including a highly threatening set of missile tests that involved live missiles being fired into the straits. By effectively calling an end to the civil war, and creating an elected Legislative Yuan for Taiwan, Lee Teng-hui had already incurred China's wrath, and this reached a fevered pitch when all major offices in Taiwan were shifted to direct popular election. On reaching his constitutional term limit, Lee stepped down and held a free election that was won by Chen Shui-bian of the opposition Democratic Progressive Party. Chen had previously won the mayoralty of Taipei when that was first opened up to a democratic vote in December 1994, so Lee Teng-hui played the key role in fully democratizing Taiwan, working his way up from the municipality level to nation.

Ethnically and socially more cohesive, Korea replicated Japan's institutional mechanisms almost completely, and achieved similarly stellar results. The only aspect missing in Korea was Japan's version of the mittelstand (artisanal SMEs), but even these began to emerge much more after Kim Dae-jung's reforms of 1998. At the start of its industrialization drive, it was the Japan-inspired Park Chung-hee who provided the vision and cohesive leadership that enabled Korea to achieve spectacular results at great speed. Korea's EPB was the nodal agency that played the role that MITI did in Japan, providing fiscal incentives, policy loans and import quotas to those corporates that were able to meet and exceed export targets. The presidential Blue House took a leading role in administering the incentives, far more than in Japan and Taiwan. Park responded to external shocks not with austerity, but through expansionary policies that increased debts and spurred new investments. Park thus depended on dynamic owner-managers of the chaebols to implement his vision, embrace risk and overcome seemingly insurmountable barriers. He found these men in Chung Ju-yung of Hyundai, Lee Byung-chul of Samsung and most controversially Kim Woo-choong of Daewoo. The chaebol developed an esprit de corps through Japan-style lifetime employment that helped build up loyal cadres of engineer-managers who dedicated their lives to building up the corporation, in contrast to Taiwan, where the culture of entrepreneurship extended to leaving a successful company to set up a competitor (as with Acer and Asustek). By 2015, Samsung Electronics was the world's largest electronics firm, LG a leading consumer electronics brand, and Hyundai Motor the world's fourth-largest car manufacturer.

Japan, Korea and Taiwan also benefited from having a 'hard state' with the capacity to achieve targeted outcomes that was distinctly absent in soft states like India. Hard states not only have the capacity to get things done (and resist interest group pressures), they are also capable of shaping economy and society. Mancur Olson's work on collective action shows the capacity for ossification of interest groups in societies that are stable over long periods; their stranglehold can only be broken by massive social dislocation of the sort that Japan, Taiwan and Korea experienced in 1945–50. As Korea expert Bruce Cumings showed, 2–3 million Koreans returned to their homeland from Manchuria and Japan, and another 4–5 million moved between North and South Korea (in a total population of 25 million), thoroughly disrupting existing social structures, and strengthening the state's capacity relative to society. Mainlander migration to Taiwan was similarly disruptive in 1949–50, and Japan's entire society was destroyed by war. The LDP, once it was allowed to coalesce after 1952, was unusually strong relative to an atrophied civil society after war and occupation, and so was able to institutionalize policy frameworks that moulded the economy over the next four decades with relatively little opposition, as the LDP became the permanent party of government. Taiwan and Korea as dictatorships (from 1949–91 and 1961–88 respectively) were even better positioned than Japan to build corporatist states that were capable of delivering key policy outcomes.

The political economists Acemoglu and Robinson argue in their book *Why Nations Fail* that colonial regimes create 'extractive' rather than 'inclusive' institutions that serve the interests of a narrow colonial elite. The new Malaysia, by keeping almost all aspects of the colonial economy unchanged (apart from the apex of the country's leadership) had superimposed a politically-inclusive system (through the Alliance of the three main race-based parties in a political democracy) upon a base that effectively supported the 'extractive' nature of the colonial economy. One aspect of the solution after the May 1969 riots was the NEP, which created an extensive programme of affirmative action for the Malays (bumiputras) in order to level the playing field of opportunity (in colleges, universities, employment and in share-ownership through the capital markets). The establishment of the national oil company Petronas (formally

Petroliam Nasional) after major crude oil discoveries, and the creation of PNB as a vehicle for pooling and effectively managing bumiputras' savings in the 1970s, created additional inclusive institutions for their benefit.

As prime minister, Mahathir launched his 'Look East' economic policy in 1982, aimed explicitly at emulating Japan—with a slew of industrial projects based on technological collaboration with Japan, and yen-denominated financing by Japanese banks. The most prominent of the projects established at the time was the automobile manufacturing company, Proton (in collaboration with Mitsubishi), Perwaja Steel (in collaboration with Nippon Steel), and various other projects in petrochemicals and fertilizers with Japanese partners. Unlike Korea, which had invested heavily in tertiary education (and inherited substantial engineering expertise from steel, shipbuilding and cement projects incubated by the Japanese), Malaysia had a limited supply of local engineering talent. This proved one impediment to the success of Proton and Perwaja (the latter was also hampered by the transfer of an untried technology by its Japanese partner), but the biggest challenge proved to be the 1985 Plaza Accord which spurred a massive appreciation of the Japanese yen, destroying the financial viability of Malaysia's yen-financed industrial projects.

Lee Kuan Yew adopted a slight variation of the Japan developmental model, giving the lead role to MNCs and GLCs rather than national private sector champions. Leading a purportedly socialist party, LKY began by seeking to build universal public housing—but ensured that these homes had to be purchased individually at market-determined prices. Singapore would have no welfare state, but would be similar to Japan in emphasizing discipline and cleanliness, and the 'Asian values' of filial piety, respect for elders, and familial rather than state-based welfare that Japan advocated in the 1940s. Like Japan, Singapore also decided that the state needed to take an active part in economic planning—and the Economic Development Board was established to spearhead industrialization, with planning processes that were akin to those of Japan's MITI but with a focus on attracting MNCs rather than building national champions. Just as Japan had done in the first two decades after the Meiji Restoration, Singapore established a slew of GLCs—including a Post Office Savings Bank (POSB) that mirrored Japan's postal savings system. Joe Pillay and his team built Singapore Airlines into the world's most admired airline with impeccable service and the ability to charge premium prices for it. And after SingTel was carved out of the Post and Telegraph Department in 1993, it swiftly became one of Asia's most admired and highest quality telecom providers.

There was little doubt that Singapore achieved its spectacular economic success in a political system that was not inclusive, and within an economic system that preserved several key aspects of the colonial extractive economy. The entire construction and household/domestic service sectors were pure legacies of colonialism—with foreign workers continuing to be employed on terms that were little different from the colonial era of 'indentured labour', with virtually no legal recourse for the foreign worker, and the employer having the right to terminate employment on a whim (and deport the foreign worker within 24 hours). Although Singapore achieved a high level of per capita (or average) income, the income distribution stayed extremely skewed: for instance, only about 35 per cent of the population currently earns enough to pay income tax (for which the threshold income level is S$22,000 annually), while the average level of annual income is S$77,000.

In distinct contrast to Korea, Taiwan and Japan—where incomes have been evenly distributed by global standards—Singapore and Malaysia were amongst the Asian countries with the highest degrees of income inequality. Their Gini coefficients (where a coefficient of 0 implies complete equality, and 1 implies extreme inequality) have consistently been in the 0.45–0.50 range, although recent taxes and transfers in Singapore have brought the coefficient slightly below 0.45 in recent years. For both Malaysia and Singapore, the Gini coefficient leaves out migrant foreign workers, whose incomes are even lower, and who would likely take the coefficients towards 0.5 or higher—compared with levels of 0.32–0.36 for Japan, Korea and Taiwan.

Mahathir, after the abortive attempt to emulate Japan and Korea, adopted the Singapore variant of the Japan model by 1986 (allowing full foreign ownership without bumiputra quotas for companies that exported most of their output), as did Thailand under Prem and Indonesia under Suharto. Mahathir also adopted 'Thatcherism with Malaysian characteristics', privatizing utilities and other GLCs to make them more competitive and defray public debt. In giving an outsized and continuing role to the GLCs, Singapore and Malaysia inadvertently adapted the model first proposed by the veteran of the INA (and hence a wartime ally of Japan and Boestamam), James Puthucheary, whose 1956 book advocated the creation of GLCs that would help to offset the outsized importance of the European agency houses that dominated Malaya's economy. Puthucheary's ideas animated the NEP and also the 'dawn raid' that enabled Malaysia to gain control over Sime Darby and Guthrie; he had become a discreet adviser to Malaysia's leaders after being expelled from Singapore in 1963 as part of Operation Coldstore against Barisan Sosialis. But being a backer of a racially-integrated Malaya, Puthucheary would probably have advocated a more complete embrace of Japan's developmental state—with MIDA and EDB focusing much more on developing national champions in manufacturing, not just in financial services.

Mao proved the greatest butcher of a brutish twentieth century, killing more millions in the Great Famine of 1958–61 than even Stalin in 1930s Russia, and Churchill in 1940s India. It fell to his twice-purged revolutionary colleague, Deng Xiaoping, to implement rational market-based pricing in agriculture before using the Chinese diaspora to implement the Singapore variant of the Japanese developmental model. At the outset of his reforms, Deng tipped his hat to their ultimate inspiration: 'As early as the Meiji Restoration the Japanese began to expend a great deal of effort on science, technology and education. The Meiji Restoration was a kind of modernization drive undertaken by the emerging Japanese bourgeoisie. As proletarians, we... can do better.'

Ironically, after 1984 Deng Xiaoping's China adopted most features of the Singapore variant of the Japanese developmental model—rather than the more purely Japanese (domestic company-driven) model that Korea and Taiwan adopted. After the soaring success of his agrarian reforms of 1979–80, centred around the household responsibility system and freedom to sell surplus farm produce on open markets, Deng began to open several special economic zones (SEZs) in cities and regions that were the original homes of the main diasporic Chinese communities. So, in order to attract the Cantonese speakers of Hong Kong and Southeast Asia, Shenzhen and Zhuhai became SEZs, while Shantou in eastern Guangdong was aimed at attracting the Teochew (who were dominant in Thailand's business community, but also had a substantial presence in Hong Kong and Singapore, including leading businessmen Li Ka-shing and Lien Ying Chow). Xiamen (Amoy) in Fujian became an SEZ aimed particularly at attracting Hokkien speakers (who were in a majority in Taiwan and Singapore), and Hainan island became an SEZ to cater to the Hainanese diaspora. The implicit appeal to the Chinese diaspora proved highly effective, and FDI-driven exports from the original SEZs burgeoned rapidly—leading Deng to designate more ports (including the mega-ports of Shanghai and Tianjin) as SEZs.

All the SEZs were located in precisely the old 'treaty ports' of the previous century. Each foreign power had competed hard to develop the physical infrastructure of its treaty port, and the period of Japanese rule had further bolstered the quality of that infrastructure. Consequently, the treaty ports' physical infrastructure was far superior to the rest of the country by 1950—although it was best in the areas that Japan ruled directly for longest, i.e., southern Manchuria. Deng and his acolytes considered SEZs to be experiments in capitalism along the coast—but the laboratories proved such towering successes that the experiments were soon replicated in many more coastal cities.

Deng recognized that the capitalists who had fled Mao's China had built up a world-class financial centre in Hong Kong and a cutting-edge technological manufacturing base on Taiwan—which mainland China could harness to its own advantage. Xiamen and the rest of Fujian province soon became a vital new assembly and processing region for Taiwan's manufacturers, who retained the design, research and capital intensive manufacturing processes in Taiwan but moved assembly and labour-intensive processes to Fujian and then Suzhou (where about a million Taiwanese now reside). Like in Southeast Asia, the foreign-funded enterprises generated the vast bulk of China's exports—importing capital and intermediate goods from the home country of the foreign-funded factory, processing and assembling the final product in China and exporting it to the rest of the world. Thus, while China runs a global trade surplus of US$600 billion annually, it runs a bilateral trade deficit with Taiwan of close to US$100 billion, and the latter grows steadily.

While Deng Xiaoping adopted the Singapore variant of the Japanese developmental model, his successors were more enamoured of the Korean variant (and especially its credit-fuelled chaebol conglomerates). After the huge setback and humanitarian catastrophe of Tiananmen Square in June 1989, Deng turned to the Shanghai duo of Jiang Zemin and Zhu Rongji to reinvigorate economic liberalization. They attempted to remake the state-owned enterprises (SoEs) into chaebols, but had yet to entirely succeed in grafting the Japanese variant onto the Singapore version of the model. China became the factory of the world, but its products did not bear many brand labels that were authentically from the PRC (with most brands coming from Taiwan, Korea, Japan, Hong Kong, Germany or the US).

Zhu Rongji's most important contribution to China's international competitiveness was the 50 per cent devaluation of the renminbi at the beginning of 1994 (to RMB 8.7 to a US dollar, from RMB 5.8 previously)—while simultaneously controlling credit, to end the cycle of devaluation and inflation that China suffered in the previous decade. China's currency had been devalued numerous times over the previous decade (from RMB 2 per US dollar in 1982), but the impact of previous devaluations had been quickly dissipated by the onset of high inflation, as unfettered credit growth caused the classic symptoms of overheating—inflation and current account deficits.

The super-competitive renminbi caused the rest of Asia's export engines to stall, as exports stopped expanding after June 1996 (from 10–30 per cent annual growth in 1986–96). It took another year for Asia's currency quasi-pegs to the US dollar to come undone. It had been possible for Thai companies to borrow in US dollars at interest rates that were 3–5 percentage points lower than baht interest rates—and they borrowed US dollars in droves. By July 1997, Thailand's short-term external debt (due within a year) was about five times the value of its foreign exchange reserves—and the Bank of Thailand allowed the baht to float on 2 July, resulting in a rapid depreciation. The Korean won, Indonesian rupiah, Malaysian ringgit and Philippine peso quickly succumbed to the same affliction, and the Asian financial crisis (AFC) spread mayhem over the next twelve months.

Banking systems in the AFC economies went through a wrenching period of reform, during which they each established asset management companies to buy bad loans from their banks at steep discounts to face value—thus administering huge losses to the banks' shareholders. The purpose of these effective carve-outs of banks' bad assets was to ensure that banks would learn a salutary lesson about the consequences of poor credit appraisal and imprudent lending, as they clearly did with bank credit rarely growing more than 10 per cent annually since 1998.

The contrast with China was stark, where bank credit has typically grown 15–30 per cent virtually every year through the past two decades. Consequently, despite its rapid economic growth, China's banks were on the brink of an even larger crisis than the AFC by 2003. In June that year, Standard & Poor's (S&P) put out a credit report that estimated that China's non-performing loans (NPL) ratio was 50 per cent—far higher than the NPL ratios had ever reached in any of the AFC economies in 1998. Even the official figure for NPLs in China at the time was an astronomical 24 per cent, but S&P's report was seen as far more credible; the latter estimated that China's banking system would need US$500 billion of fresh capital (equal to 40 per cent of China's GDP at the time) if it was to be properly cleaned up. China created four asset management companies that 'bought' the bad assets from the banks at face value, administering no losses whatsoever to China's big state-owned banks.

This only increased 'moral hazard', creating an incentive for banks to be even more imprudent in their lending practices in future, knowing that they were likely to be bailed out by the government. It was extraordinary that the rest of the world allowed China to participate in global trade as a normal member of the WTO despite the fact that its domestic banking system was not operating according to free-market principles. The main consequence of this was that, after 2001, there was very little additional expansion in fixed investment spending anywhere in the world other than China. Between 1996 and 2016, China's fixed asset investment expanded nearly sevenfold, while the entire developed world saw its fixed investment spending expand at a compound annual growth rate of just 2 per cent over that period. In March 2007, Premier Wen Jiabao warned that China's economy was 'unstable, unbalanced, uncoordinated and unsustainable'. But, faced with the global financial crisis of 2008, China reopened the spigot of bank lending, and China's M2 money supply soared from US$6.5 billion in August 2008 to US$23.3 billion by April 2017—the biggest monetary expansion in human history, which created history's greatest bubble of industrial and real estate capacity. China too will eventually succumb to the Achilles heel of East Asia's economic miracles—the feeble foundations of its heavily-distorted financial systems—just as ASEAN and Korea did in 1997, and Japan had done after 1990.

Post-War Japan was supremely civilized, a caring and polite society, but its attitude towards women remained ossified in a nineteenth-century mould. When combined with ruinous asset deflation, the rising dependency ratio and falling birth rates caused Japan's economy to suffer two decades of stagnation and deflation. Early in the process, Japan's political consensus also frayed, with the LDP losing power for the first time since the early 1950s in 1993, when the scion of one of the storied daimyo families of Kumamoto prefecture, Hosokawa Morihiro, led an exodus from the LDP into a newly-formed Japan New Party that won the Diet election in a coalition with seven other parties. Like India's Janata coalition of 1977, this disparate congeries of parties proved quite unable to cohere, and the LDP's Koizumi Junichiro and Abe Shinzo eventually restored Japan's economic health. Despite its two lost decades, life expectancy at birth (85 years) is still higher in Japan than anywhere else in the world, with women's life expectancy at 87 years. And virtually all Japanese are assured a life of prosperity in a beautiful, clean country that is a beacon of environmental leadership. While the challenge of reducing its mountain of public debt will weigh on Japan's economy for decades to come, it will stay near the top of global league tables of per capita income, its companies will remain influential for many decades, and its influence on Asia's remaking will endure.

Japan's magic touch did not extend to India and points west. In the east, even Saipan and the Mariana islands (which Japan ruled in the inter-war years) developed excellent infrastructure and widespread literacy, while the Japanese introduced Tagalog instruction in the Philippines to bind that archipelago and create a sense of nationhood during Japan's brief rule. By contrast, at the end of British rule, India (1947) and Iraq (1958) had the same dismal literacy rate of 14 per cent. After OPEC successfully boosted oil prices in October 1973 (capitalizing on the fact that the US ceased to be the swing producer in world oil markets after it ran out of surplus capacity in 1970), Iraq's de facto leader Saddam Hussein announced the nationalization of the IPC on 1 June 1972. As crude oil prices surged from US$3 per barrel in September 1973 to US$11 in 1974 and US$36 after Iran's Islamic Revolution in 1979, Saddam used the bountiful oil revenues to finance an enormous social development programme focused especially on literacy, and replacing dirt tracks with modern highways. At the end of that decade of soaring oil prices, UNESCO marked its International Literacy Day in September 1979 with a special prize for Iraq, commending its successful campaign against illiteracy. It was another feather in the cap of Saddam Hussein, but he soon let megalomania get the better of him, launching the Iran–Iraq War in September 1980, which bled both countries for eight years, causing a massive run-up in Iraq's debt—which Saddam sought to overcome by invading Kuwait in August 1990.

Socio-economic progress had been throttled during the half-century that the British had a stranglehold over Iran's oil. Mohammad Reza Shah neither extended his father's social reforms nor spread the benefits of the OPEC bounty of the 1970s widely enough to sustain support for his regime. The forces of democratic nationalism first unchained by Iran's 1908 constitution reached a crescendo in 1977–78, as the Shah's notorious SAVAK secret police cracked down hard—especially against the Tudeh (communist) party and the nationalist ideological progeny of Mossadegh who had coalesced around Mehdi Bazargan (the engineer who had headed the National Iranian Oil Company after it was nationalized). The brooding charisma of Ayatollah Khomeini prevailed by February 1979, although he initially helmed a coalition of all anti-Shah forces, at the centre of which was a 'bazaari-mullah' alliance (of merchants and clerics) loosely aligned with (while remaining wary of) the Tudeh party that retained strong links to the Soviet Union. The Khomeini family were immigrants to Iran from Lucknow in India, and the young Ruhollah Khomeini had used the moniker 'al-Hindi' for his radical columns in Tehran's newspapers, but he was ruthless in crushing Tudeh once he had consolidated power.

When the catastrophic Iran–Iraq War ended (20 August 1988), both the countries were heavily indebted. Oil prices collapsed to US$11 per barrel by 1990, further weakening the finances of oil exporters who had ridden the hubris of the 1970s. Iraq's straitened finances tempted Saddam to conquer Kuwait, which he overran between 2 and 4 August 1990. Saddam sought thereby to solve several of his problems at once (like boosting Iraq's oil reserves, raising oil prices, and eliminating the US$40 billion debt that Iraq owed to Kuwait!)—while capitalizing on his self-created image as the 'New Saladin'. Instead, it triggered a ferocious US response, as President George Herbert Walker Bush (a Texas oilman himself, and grandson of two bankers who had been instrumental in creating the OSS, the precursor of the CIA) assembled an inclusive global coalition to overturn the conquest of Kuwait by military means (fully supported by the UN Security Council). Having restored Kuwait's independence after a five-week war in January–February 1991, George H. W. Bush wisely decided not to press on to Baghdad, fearing the consequence of conflict between the majority Shia and the ruling Sunnis that would be an obstacle to national unity for Iraq. Instead, the US (with UN support) established no-fly zones in the Shia-dominated south and the Kurd-dominated northern province of Iraq.

Saddam's dreams of Arab unity under Iraqi leadership lay shattered. And, although he had delivered a decade of superior social outcomes than either the West's puppet Shah in Iran or the predecessor British puppet monarchy in Iraq itself, Saddam's Baathist ideology was only a temporary palliative to Iraq's founding folly: Churchill had suppressed the Shia majority of Iraq, while fusing the Sunni Arabs and Kurds with Christians, Turkmens and Yezidis into an uneasy coalition of minorities. When George W. Bush attacked Iraq anew in March 2003, he quickly toppled a neutered Saddam. But, unlike Japan in 1950–52, where the vast majority of purged politicians were allowed to rejoin the political mainstream, Bush's proconsul Paul Bremer made no such compromise with the Baathists—barring nearly 550,000 of Iraq's soldiers, bureaucrats, teachers and judges from future participation in governance. They were to eventually morph into rebels of varying ideological hues, the Shia joining militias in the south and the Sunnis coalescing around al-Qaeda, and eventually providing the grisly foot soldiers for ISIS/Daesh, especially after the former French colony of Syria collapsed into civil war in 2011.

The British legacy of Divide and Rule was particularly toxic in the Indian subcontinent. Britain was able to partition India in a manner that maximized bitterness between India and Pakistan, fomenting conflict over Kashmir, and ensuring that soldiers and policemen commanded by the British stood aside while the partition riots raged, creating 'facts on the ground' that were bound to embitter relations between the legatee nations. Pakistan's military, funded mainly by the US, ensures that its politicians' desire to normalize relations with India rarely makes progress. General Ayub Khan's military coup of 1958 was expressly aimed at precluding Pakistan's first general election, which appeared set to elect a left-wing government that would be friendly to India.

Neither Pakistan nor India achieved annual real GDP growth much above the world average of 3.5 per cent between 1950 and 1980. Their social structures remained remarkably similar, as both retained the colonial governing apparatus, while attempting to graft developmental objectives upon it. Mass literacy remained dismal in both countries, especially in comparison to East Asia. Although India attempted more land reform, Pakistan was marginally more successful in agriculture until the 1970s, because its policies had less of an anti-export bias than India's. Pakistan's textile sector was also more buoyant in the 1960s, but India had a far more diversified manufacturing sector, albeit primarily focused on meeting domestic rather than export demand. Indira Gandhi nationalized fourteen of India's largest banks in 1969, abolished the 'privy purses' of the ex-princes, and introduced stringent anti-monopoly and exchange control laws that deepened the state's stranglehold over India's economy—but had the practical effect of fostering corruption and crony capitalism.

The wars of 1965 and 1971, albeit brief, were additional setbacks to the economic progress of both countries. When Pakistan finally held its first general election in 1970, Sheikh Mujibur Rahman's Awami League (the spearhead of the movement for Bengali autonomy) won 160 of Pakistan's 300 parliamentary seats—far ahead of the 81 seats won by Zulfiqar Ali Bhutto's Pakistan People's Party (PPP). But Bhutto, despite being ideologically similar to Mujib, raised objections to Mujib becoming prime minister. Jinnah had provoked East Bengali ire on his first visit to Dhaka in March 1948, stating emphatically that Urdu alone would be Pakistan's national language (and denigrating Bengali as a 'Hindu' language), setting off a backlash that culminated in the Language Movement of 1952. The linguistic unity of East Bengalis never flagged (with Colonel M. A. G. Osmani, the senior Bengali officer in the East Pakistan army, introducing popular Bengali songs by Nazrul, Tagore and Dwijendralal Roy into regimental singing), despite the rising military repression between 1958 and 1971. This reached its crescendo with Operation Searchlight on 25–26 March 1971, when at least seven thousand civilians were killed in cold blood by the Pakistani army in Dhaka, and several thousand across other cities of East Pakistan over the next two months.

The genocidal atrocities of the Pakistan Army eventually killed at least 300,000 civilians in 1971 and drove 16 million Bengalis to seek refuge across the border in India. Many of the intellectuals targeted by Pakistan's army (like the economists Anisur Rahman and Rehman Sobhan) were able to use their academic contacts to reach out to liberal US senators (especially Edward Kennedy) to highlight the Bengali plight—but the Nixon administration's support for the genocidal Yahya Khan was unwavering, as it was to be for Mao's protégé Pol Pot in Cambodia later in the decade.

When her brilliant trio of generals—Sam Manekshaw (a Zoroastrian), Jagjit Singh Aurora (a Sikh) and J. F. R. Jacob (an Indian Jew)—forced the Pakistani Army to surrender unconditionally at Dhaka on 16 December 1971, Indira Gandhi's triumph appeared to be complete (aided by her experienced defence minister, Jagjivan Ram, of the formerly 'untouchable' caste). But while Indira Gandhi is portrayed (not least by Kissinger) as a ruthless Machiavellian schemer, her naive idealism undid all the gains of her brilliantly executed victory in 1971. Then, faced with Nixon's implacable opposition (manifested in his dispatch of the US Seventh Fleet into the Bay of Bengal as a shot across the bow to the Indian military), Indira had undermined Nixon through effective use of America's popular culture, culminating in the Concert for Bangladesh in August 1971 at which such musical icons as Joan Baez (with her anthem titled 'Bangladesh' even before that country had come into existence), Bob Dylan, George Harrison, Ringo Starr, and the Bengali duo of Ravi Shankar and Ali Akbar Khan helped mobilize public opinion in opposition to the Pakistani genocide against Bengali nationalists, intellectuals and Hindus that Generals Yahya and Tikka Khan had unleashed with the explicit support of Nixon and Kissinger. The latter fully expected that India would make Bangladesh a colony (or incorporate it fully into India) and even believed that India (after its emphatic naval victory at Karachi harbour) was on the verge of undoing Partition by taking over West Pakistan too.

But, unlike the US (which has kept military bases in Germany, Japan, Korea and elsewhere since 1945, in Iraq since 1991 and Afghanistan since 2001) and the UK (which retained military bases across Asia for more than twenty years after its imperial withdrawal beginning 1947–48), Indira withdrew all Indian military personnel from Bangladesh. And at Shimla in July 1972, she agreed to return 93,000 Pakistani POWs without gaining anything concrete in return, apart from a vague commitment by Pakistan to respect the Line of Control in Kashmir. India's leaders have been especially eager to prove that they accept the finality of Partition—although Pakistan's military leaders propagate the myth that India's primary purpose is to undo Partition. If indeed Indira was the Machiavellian she was made out to be by Kissinger, she could have dismantled Pakistan in 1972–73: in Baluchistan and NWFP, the anti-partition National Awami Party led by Khan Abdul Wali Khan had emerged as the largest party. G. M. Syed's Jiye Sindh secessionist movement was gaining ground in Sindh (despite its leader's long incarceration), as was Ghaus Bux Bizenjo's separatist movement in Baluchistan. But Indira (like Jawaharlal and Lal Bahadur before her) craved global approbation, and wanted to be seen as a 'good global citizen' committed to anti-colonialism and other worthy causes.

Despite the landslide mandate Mujib had received in 1970, and the continuing adulation showered on him by the vast majority of his people, a determined group of anti-India and Islamist military renegades brutally assassinated Mujib and his entire family (apart from two daughters who were overseas) on 15 August 1975, and established martial law by November 1975. Although Pakistan lost its eastern wing, its separation ironically empowered the pro-Pakistan Islamist fringe in Bangladesh. It took Mujib's elder daughter, Sheikh Hasina Wajed, fifteen years of political mobilization before she gained an electoral majority in 1996 in a hostile, military-dominated polity; ousted after five years, Hasina regained power in a landslide in 2009, but remains hemmed in by a steadily more confident jihadist movement that attacks Hindus, Buddhists, atheists and secular intellectuals as it seeks to erode the secularism that Bangladesh was founded on. Despite these persistent existential challenges, Bangladesh became a more successful garment export-based economy in the twenty-first century, and its strong export performance helped Bangladesh's per capita GDP close the wide gap that existed in 1971 between it and West Pakistan. In 2016, Bangladesh's per capita income was only 4 per cent lower than Pakistan's (from being 60 per cent of Pakistan's in 2006, and less than half Pakistan's in 1971).

In Sri Lanka, the legacy of European divide and rule began to manifest itself by 1980, responding to S. W. R. D. Bandaranaike's designation of Sinhala as the only national language and Buddhism as the national religion in 1956. The legacy of a century and a half of Portuguese rule was that Catholic schools dominated Ceylon, although Christians were only about 7 per cent of the population (led by the elite of mixed-race burghers), and the Buddhist majority of the population was deliberately neglected. Ironically, Solomon Bandaranaike himself was born a High Church Anglican, and the leaders of his main rival party (the UNP's Dudley Senanayake and Junius Jayewardene) were also from elite Christian families, but they all ostentatiously converted to Buddhism in order to further their political careers. Bandaranaike outflanked the UNP when he donned the mythical mantle of Dutthagamani (the ancient Sinhala king who had defeated the Tamil king Elara in the second century BCE and united the island), and fought for Sinhala Only in the 1956 election at the head of his newly-created Sri Lanka Freedom Party, which also adopted socialist policies and called for Britain's withdrawal from its naval bases. The UNP quickly agreed to the Sinhala Only policy, alienating the Tamils (Hindus and Moors/Muslims) who had dominated the Ceylon Civil Service through their mastery of English.

By 1983, a full-scale civil war was underway, as the increasingly marginalized Tamils began demanding an 'Eelam' or homeland for themselves in their northern bastion of Jaffna and in the east around Trincomalee. Eventually, the ferocious army of the Liberation Tigers of Tamil Eelam (LTTE) subdued its rivals and led the Eelam struggle. The LTTE's Velupillai Prabhakaran professed to be inspired by Subhas Bose, although his methods were far more brutal—and sectarian (where Bose's approach was inclusive). Although the LTTE was defeated after a 26-year war by the then Sri Lankan president Mahinda Rajapaksa (who also claimed the mantle of Dutthagamani), the Tamils eventually gained autonomy in their devastated homeland. But the peace dividend remained elusive, as tea and tourism proved an insufficient path to economic dynamism.

Despite the oil bounty, the institutional equipment of economic development that Japan had spawned across East Asia never touched West Asia, and its socio-economic development remained stunted by the colonial legacy. The end of Britain's naval sway east of Suez in 1971 also ended the British presence in the Trucial States and its other Gulf protectorates. British companies and personnel retained a strong presence as 'expatriate' executives (with all the trappings of colonial-era privileges, including pay scales substantially higher than those of local employees) not just in the countries of the new GCC but also in the new eastern allies of Malaysia and Singapore, where many features of the colonial economy persisted. In the GCC countries, a system best described as 'neo-Mamluk' emerged, with foreigners (Indians, Pakistanis, Palestinians, Filipinos) doing the work no locals wanted to do, and performing skilled tasks (under British or other European management) while local citizens filled well-paid sinecures in government or as ornamental 'managers' in private companies.

But the end of the British military presence was to have profound consequences over the rest of the decade, altering the security balance irretrievably in the region. The oil-rich emirates were thinly populated and most of their populations were uneducated. The emir of Abu Dhabi, Sheikh Zayed, was himself illiterate. With scant expertise available to run a modern economy, all the former British protectorates, as well as the US ally Saudi Arabia, chose to peg their currencies rigidly to the US dollar, a decision they often regretted as the greenback depreciated once Nixon took it off the gold standard in 1971. Although the British business and expatriate-executive presence endured, the GCC countries switched to the US as their principal security ally. The Saudi oil deal with the US that created Saudi ARAMCO took on a security dimension during World War II and became permanent by the 1970s (when Saudi Arabia and Iran were the 'twin pillars' of US strategy in West Asia), and the rest of the GCC maintained a tight currency and security relationship with the US. Education systems in the GCC (except Kuwait) promoted Salafism, and its most extreme Wahhabi version in Saudi Arabia, from where it was increasingly exported to the rest of the Muslim world, with a particularly pernicious impact on Afghanistan.

In December 1979, the Soviets invaded Afghanistan to curtail the growing turmoil in their backyard, as the southern Muslim cone of the USSR was seen as its soft underbelly. But Afghanistan proved to be the graveyard of the Soviet Red Army—the equivalent of Vietnam to the US, made worse by the collapse of oil prices in the 1980s, which devastated a Soviet economy that was already reeling from its inability to miniaturize the transistor chip. When Pakistan's General Zia ul-Haq began implementing his vision of Pakistan leading the forces of international jihad, Prince Turki al-Faisal (head of the Saudi intelligence agency, Istakhbarat) became Pakistan's vital partner. Between 1982 and 1992, some 35,000 Arab, North African, Uzbek, Uighur and other Asian jihadis travelled to Pakistan for training in jihadist camps before their deployment in Afghanistan. Their most potent leader proved to be the wealthy Yemeni student Osama bin Laden.

After the Soviet withdrawal from Afghanistan in September 1989, Lieutenant General Hamid Gul (head of Pakistan's ISI while Benazir Bhutto was prime minister) became the most ardent ideologue for 'the first Islamic international brigade of the modern era'. When a coalition of mujahideen led by Ahmad Shah Masood and Burhanuddin Rabbani, including the Herat-based Ismael Khan, the Hazara leader Mohammad Mohaqqiq and the KGB-trained Uzbek leader Abdul Rashid Dostum seized control of Kabul in 1992, Pakistan's ISI threw its support behind their rival Gulbuddin Hekmatyar, but by 1995 the ISI shifted fully to Mullah Omar and his fanatical Taliban, which conquered Kabul with Pakistani help (and Saudi coordination) in September 1996. Osama bin Laden formally came under the Taliban's protection in Kandahar in 1997. On 9 September 2001, two Tunisian al-Qaeda operatives (who had received special year-long 'journalist' visas to Pakistan that only the ISI can approve) assassinated Ahmad Shah Masood (who still controlled a quarter of Afghanistan). Two days later, nineteen al-Qaeda operatives (fifteen of them Saudi citizens) hijacked four commercial airliners, crashing two into the iconic World Trade Center towers in New York, and another into the Pentagon, while the fourth (meant to smash into the US Capitol) was crash-landed by passengers who overcame the hijackers. At least 2,996 innocent civilians were killed during the biggest terrorist attack in the US. The horrifically audacious plan had been hatched by the Pakistani Khalid Sheikh Mohammed, and was led in the US by an Egyptian called Mohammed Atta, who received US$100,000 shortly before the attack from General Mahmud Ahmed, head of Pakistan's ISI. Osama bin Laden had inspired the diabolical plot, and the US invaded Afghanistan the following month—but could not nab Osama, who disappeared into Pakistan. It was on 2 May 2011 that the US finally 'got him', as a team of Navy SEALs swooped down on a large compound at Abbottabad, a few hundred metres from Pakistan's elite Kakul military academy, and shot the al-Qaeda leader dead in the third-floor bedroom he shared with his wives.

The toxic legacy of Partition, which had begun in 1905 with Curzon's diabolical plan to set Muslims against Hindus in India, using separate electorates as the instrument to perpetuate discord, continued to endure. But jihadism also ate into the vitals of Pakistan itself, as the Taliban increasingly turned on Pakistan's military for its alleged lack of zeal in jihad's cause in Kashmir or Afghanistan. The wages of jihadism left Pakistan with little to export but terrorism.

Further west, the artificial borders created by Sykes–Picot in 1915–16 collapsed in disarray a century later, as a Great Arab Civil War engulfed Syria, Iraq and Libya from 2011 onwards, spawning an even more vicious terrorist organization called Daesh (or ISIS, for Islamic State in Iraq and al-Shams). European colonialism, and the greed it spawned in the aftermath of the Great War, was still unfurling its venomous legacy in West Asia.

Pamulaparti Venkata Narasimha Rao was an unlikely contender to be India's most consequential leader of the twentieth century, which is what he proved to be. The two-year prime ministership of Morarji Desai had demonstrated India's promise, as real GDP growth averaged 6.5 per cent in 1977–79 after Desai's mild deregulation. After a disastrous year of stagflation under Charan Singh, Indira returned to power promising stability, taking a US$5 billion IMF loan (the largest-ever IMF loan up to that point) that required more piecemeal reforms, which Rajiv Gandhi took forward in 1985–89, but at the expense of an unsustainable rise in external debt. When Narasimha Rao placed India onto the path of export-oriented expansion, he reformed an essentially Anglo–Saxon economy, reducing the degree of financial repression, but not adapting all the features of a Japan-style developmental state.

Rao's astute leadership not only shepherded India past its most treacherous economic shoals, he deftly restored peace in Punjab and Assam, two important border states that had been wracked by insurgency since Indira's final term. India's revealed comparative advantage in software and other services was manifested in a surge of software exports—which expanded at an average annual pace of 60 per cent in the first half-decade, and continued expanding by more than a fifth annually through the next decade. Tata Consultancy Services, Infosys, Wipro and HCL became household names to businesses across the world that depended on them for software, shared services and to run their IT backbones, as India became the 'services back office of the world'. India's exports of all 'invisible' services expanded from US$7.5 billion in FY 1991–92 to US$ 149 billion by FY 2008–09 (or a twentyfold increase in seventeen years). At the same time, exports of goods expanded from US$18.5 billion in FY1991–92 to US$166.2 billion in FY 2008–09 (a ninefold rise in seventeen years) and US$318.6 billion in FY 2014–15 (rising by more than seventeen times in twenty-three years). Goods and services exports together had grown to US$552 billion in FY 2014–15—rising by more than twenty-one times in the twenty-three years since the 1991 reforms, exposing the folly of the export pessimism that had held India back before 1991.

Prime Minister Atal Bihari Vajpayee took additional steps to strengthen the edifice, improving the telecommunications, road and airport infrastructure and making the public sector more efficient. Narendra Modi modernized the state further, and attempted to extend basic services (universal access to banking and microfinance, sanitation, public health and education) to every last household, nearly 150 years after Japan had provided these to its citizens. But his Make in India initiative was still attracting more FDI than domestic investment, because India was wary of deploying the full panoply of developmental state policies for fear that they would spawn corruption and misuse. India thus appeared set to become a middle income country by 2030, but would probably not be able to emulate Japan and Korea's leap to developed economy status in a generation.

With its financial system modelled more along conventional Anglo–Saxon norms, India was also less likely to succumb to the Achilles heel of every East Asian economy—a financial crisis. With India, Vietnam and Indonesia providing new dynamism, the more sedate middle and high income economies of Asia were well positioned to create the complementarities that would ensure that the twenty-first century would be an Asian century, albeit without any single Asian economy being likely to successfully challenge the Pax Americana in the first half of that century.

A continent vanquished and ravaged through the first half of the twentieth century, Asia mounted a stirring comeback in its second half. The pathways were paved by Japan, the solitary Asian nation that had resisted the seemingly inexorable European march of conquest across Asia—but Japan eventually emulated much of the brutality that Europeans had deployed in that conquest. Suitably chastened after 1945, Japan rapidly closed the economic gap with the West; then Taiwan and Korea replicated and occasionally surpassed the trail Japan had blazed, followed by ASEAN, China and India. Financial fragility notwithstanding, Asia had regained its position at the nerve centre of the global economy by the second decade of the twenty-first century. A continent that lay supine and exploited in 1900 had been transformed by 2017 into an industrious, dynamic and increasingly creative force capable of taking humanity to new heights in an Asian twenty-first century.

ACKNOWLEDGEMENTS

This book has been a labour of love that I have been researching for the past two decades, and writing since September 2013. I am grateful to my publisher, David Davidar, who offered me a book contract just six hours after I'd sent him an email containing my Prologue. He and his team (particularly my editor, Pujitha Krishnan, and her associate, Amardeep Banerjee) have been stalwart in their support over the past four years, even as the book grew well past the size they had originally envisaged. They wisely persuaded me to shorten the last chapter into a brief Epilogue, with the promise that the full version will be published early next year as a separate book.

My daughter, Meghna, has been my most important sounding board and supporter throughout the writing of this book. The writing encompassed her four years at Yale-NUS College, where she imbibed the best of East and West intellectually; but both there, and while studying Asian History for her IB diploma, she felt the absence of a comprehensive book about modern Asia. I hope this book will fill that lacuna for students of the immediate future.

I am grateful for the encouragement and advice of Gurcharan Das, and my Asia-hand friends Ajay Kapur and Rahul Jacob, who read early drafts and provided invaluable feedback. I have benefited from conversations and debates with work colleagues over the years, including Tan Sri Azman Mokhtar, Kumagai Mitsumaru, Kasper Bartholdy, Vikas Nath, John Mulcahy, John Doyle, Low Siew Kheng, Steve Hagger, Chia Tse Chern, Lim Jit Soon, Dato' Sri Abdul Wahid Omar, Asit Shah, Rajesh Sundaresan, Lee Chang-hee, Narendra Singh, Lois Quinn and Allen Shiau, and from intellectual interactions with Eric Rice, M. J. Akbar, Rajesh Sachdeva, Vivek Arora, Jomo Kwame Sundaram, Prabhat Shukla, Gautam Banerjee, K. V. Rao, Praveen Kadle, Neel Chowdhury, Sharifatu Laila, Subarno Chattarji, Shobha Tshering Bhalla, Sumita Ambasta, Rakesh Mohan, Frances Dydasco, Vanessa Doneghan, Khiem Do, Richard Tan, M. V. Rajeev Gowda, Sanjeev Sanyal, David Gambrill, Sanjeev Duggal, Murali Srikantaiah and Darren McDermott. I alone, of course, am responsible for the contents of the book.

My interest in East Asia was first sparked when my parents (Prabhash and Swagata Basu) visited Malaysia, Singapore, Bangkok, Manila, Hong Kong, Tokyo and Osaka in 1978, sending wonderful letters and postcard vignettes back to me and my brother Srijit at boarding school in Darjeeling. Upon their return, we became subscribers to the *Far Eastern Economic Review*, that wonderful weekly chronicle of Asia's political and economic ebb and flow. Until its sad demise in 2004, the *Review* was my weekly companion, and a wellspring of Asian insights.

At St Paul's School, Darjeeling, I was privileged to receive a marvellously cosmopolitan education. At the age of ten, I played a wise but battered Tartar prisoner in a play set in the Tsar's court, and at thirteen, I played the Mikado in a staging of the Gilbert & Sullivan opera, *The Mikado*. I'm grateful to Chris Macdonald and Denzil Prince for casting me in these exotic roles that introduced me early to Russia (and its fraught relationship with 'Tartars') and Japan. The late Rector Hari Dang, and teachers like Kailash Dar, Allen Wood, David Howard, Evelyn Morton, Kabir Mustafi, Salil Banerjee, Chandak Chattarji and Horace Stolke widened my intellectual horizons in countless ways.

At St Stephen's College, Delhi, Kalyanjit Roychoudhury and the late Vinod Chowdhury deepened my interest in Economics and History respectively. Conversations on the college lawns with Arup Banerjee, Rajat Modwel, Lalit Vachani and Ranobir Basu spurred me onto a lifetime of learning. At the University of Pennsylvania, teachers like Tom Callaghy, Francine Frankel, Howard Pack, Lawrence Klein, Jim Spady and Jack Nagel stimulated my interest in the comparative analysis of polities and economies, and my debates with Lee Jung-bock (a visiting professor from Seoul National University) got me thinking about the themes that animate this book. I benefited enormously from engaging intellectually with the wide-ranging seminars and conferences held in 1990 during the celebration of the University of Pennsylvania's 250th anniversary.

Living in Singapore and Kuala Lumpur over the past twenty-three years, and working and holidaying across Asia over the past two decades, has helped deepen my understanding of the continent's history. Singapore's two great bookstores on Orchard Road (Kinokuniya, and the late lamented Borders), London's Waterstones and Calcutta's Oxford have been the treasure troves from which I have purchased almost all the wonderful books listed in my Bibliography; even where I strongly disagree with a book's contents, the writing and reading have edified and enriched my thinking, and so I am grateful to every one of the great writers. As a true bibliophile, I resisted Kindle and other technological innovations, preferring to own every book that interested me. When I needed to research anything beyond my own book collection, Singapore's magnificent National Library system unfailingly came to the rescue.

My son Prithviraj and daughter Taarini weren't quite as interested in Baba's project as much as their Didi was, but their cheerful company was always a joy and solace as I plunged deeper into this vast project. My wife Aarti's support and intellectual companionship kept me going amid myriad external challenges that she invariably overcame. She (and my editors) would have preferred a shorter book. But I have stubbornly insisted that Asian nations and peoples need to know each other's histories. Asians know so much about Bismarck, Garibaldi, Cavour and Disraeli, but non-compatriot Asians barely know the names of Ito, Takahashi, Kishi, Park Chung-hee, Aguinaldo, Bose, Phibun, Ahmad Boestamam, Lee Teng-hui and Narasimha Rao. It is to them and the better-known makers and liberators of modern Asia (Sun Yat-sen, Sukarno, Gandhi, Zhou Enlai, Deng Xiaoping, Lee Kuan Yew, Mahathir, Kim Dae-jung and Modi) that I dedicate this book, in the hope that their inspiring stories will become far more widely known and appreciated across Asia and the world.

NOTES AND REFERENCES

INTRODUCTION

ix   **Vietnam (1965-75):** The Vietnam War can be traced back to 1954 to the ouster of France, and South Vietnam basically becoming an American client state, but the conventional US-Vietnam war began only in 1965.

xii   **the nations of East Asia:** East Asia is used in the wider sense and includes both Northeast and Southeast Asia.

xii   **Tibet, Hong Kong:** There is little doubt that Tibet is a nation, albeit one now being occupied by China. Hong Kong was a nation state of sorts (a member of the WTO/GATT for instance, and still is). In theory, it is no longer a separate nation state, but an intermediate category until 2047.

xii   **South Asia (India, Bangladesh, Sri Lanka, Pakistan, Nepal, Bhutan, the Maldives):** 'South Asia' is a Pakistani term aimed at distancing themselves from their Indian heritage, although Pakistani restaurants all over the world quietly call themselves Indian!

xvii   **Tartars (and their Turk Muslim cousins):** Tartar is a broader term than 'Tatar' (which refers to those who speak the Tatar language, and live mainly in the Tatar Autonomous Republic of Russia). 'Tartar' subsumes all speakers of Altaic languages—Turks, Mongols, Manchus. The early conflicts were between Russians and Tartars (Mongols), but those who stayed behind in Russia were Tatars.

CHAPTER 1

2   **Hong Kong and the New Territories:** Hong Kong island was given in perpetuity to Britain after the First Opium War, but the New Territories (which actually comprise 86 per cent of the land in Hong Kong) was leased to Britain for 150 years (ending in 1997).

3   **his elder brother Dara Shukoh:** Most traditional sources use 'Dara Shikoh', but there is a strong and growing view that the name should be rendered 'Dara Shukoh', because 'Shikoh' means 'terror' in Farsi while 'Shukoh' means 'glory', and it is the latter that his name was meant to convey. Gopal Gandhi's play, for instance, is called *Dara Shukoh*.

4   **how 'it crept into our houses':** Niall Ferguson, *Empire: How Britain Made the Modern World*, London: Penguin, 2003, pp. 16-17.

6   **Aurangzeb then declared a jihad:** He declared a jihad in order to provide additional motivation for his Muslim soldiers.

9   **the Nizam ul-Mulk began rallying:** Nizam ul-Mulk literally translates as 'Administrator of the Realm', a title that was given to Asaf Jah I by Emperor Farrukhsiyar in 1713.

10   **became the Nawab of Hyderabad:** Nawab of Hyderabad was the actual title, but the family preferred to use the title Nizam, which gave it greater legitimacy across the Timurid empire, since it was conferred by an emperor in Delhi and made Asaf

Jah I the administrator of all the Timurid realms.

12   **mythology of an 'accidental empire':** The typical phrase is that the 'empire was acquired in "a fit of absence of mind"'. Ferguson, *Empire*, p. 2.

13   **'best provided city in the world':** John Keay, *India: A History,* New York: Atlantic Monthly Press, 2000, p. 304.

14   **'the most faithless and usurping of all mankind':** Ibid., p. 396.

15   **'Citoyen Tipu's' methods:** Ibid., p. 399.

16   **'would not have disgraced Attila':** Ibid., p. 401.

19   **'man of military genius':** Ibid., p. 422.

19   **'army as effective as that of the Company.':** Ibid.

21   **a severe blow to British prestige in India:** General Airey, who ordered the disastrous Charge of the Light Brigade during the Crimean War, is said to have retorted that the disaster was 'nothing to Chillianwala'.

21   **some rulers had chosen to align themselves:** The Rajputs of Rajasthan, for instance, already used to such alliances with the Mughals, were quick to become British allies (although the British proved much more domineering 'allies' than the Mughals ever were after Aurangzeb's time); that Scindia had crushed Jaipur and Jodhpur also made them natural subsidiary allies of the British. With the subjugation of the Sikh empire, the East India Company was master of all India, although it had direct territorial control of about two-thirds of the country, and 'subsidiary alliances' in the rest of the country. (Even in the Punjab, for instance, the Cis-Sutlej states—led by Patiala—had become 'subsidiary allies' of the British long before Ranjit Singh's successors were subdued by the British, and their territory proved strategically vital in that conquest.)

24   **While the tour was described as 'leisurely':** Saul David, *The Indian Mutiny*, London: Penguin, 2003, p. 50.

25   **ignited the rebellion three months too early:** The rebellion was supposed to have begun on 23 June, the hundredth anniversary of Plassey.

30   **'a single shelf of a good European library':** Zareer Masani, *Macaulay: Pioneer of India's Modernization*, Noida: Random House India, 2012, p. 90.

30   **'a class who may be interpreters':** Ibid., p. 101.

38   **'that there is no teacher to be compared with Christ' :** These were the words of John Henry Barrows, chair of the organizing committee of the World Parliament of Religions, quoted in: Uua.org, 'Leader Resource 1: The 1893 Worlds Parliament of Religions' <http://www.uua.org/re/tapestry/adults/river/workshop14/178841.shtml> [accessed 8 May 2017]

37   **'advancing the political, intellectual, and material advancement':** Jogesh Chandra Bagal, *History of the Indian Association 1876-1951*, Calcutta: Indian Association, 1953, p. 13.

43   **'strong reduction of wages':** Colin Brown, *A Short History of Indonesia: The Unlikely Nation?* Crows Nest (New South Wales): Allen & Unwin, 2003, p. 91.

44   **Chinese sources talk of trade:** Ibid., p. 17.

50   **tudungs:** 'tudung' is the Bahasa word for 'head covering'; 'hijab' in Arabic.

52   **37.5 million florins:** A florin was a Florentine coin containing 72 grains of pure ('fine') gold, worth about US$140 today.

54   **55 square miles a** *day*: Karl E. Meyer and Shareen Brysac, *Tournament of Shadows: The Great Game and the Race for Empire in Asia*, London: Little, Brown & Company, 1999, p. 111.

54   **that took the Golden Horde:** The Golden Horde was the northwestern khanate of

the Mongol empire established in 1225 (while Genghis Khan still reigned) by Genghis Khan's grandson Batu Khan.

55   **took just one generation to embrace:** Genghis Khan's grandson Hulegu conquered Iran, Iraq and Syria, but did not become a Muslim; he was a Nestorian Christian who converted to Buddhism, and his successor Abaqa was a Buddhist too—as was Hulegu's brother, Kublai Khan, who became emperor of China. Abaqa's brother and successor Tequder converted to Islam, and became Sultan Ahmed. Hulegu and his successors ensured that Farsi rather than Arabic became the main language of Iran (Persia).

55   **with its capital in Istanbul (old Constantinople):** The city was known as Constantinople at the time, although the Asian parts of the city were known as Stamboul, and the European parts as Pera. Amongst the Turks, the city was already called Istanbul, but the more widely accepted name was Constantinople.

57   **sold a telegraph concession:** The 'concession' gave a monopoly over the new telegraph system to the British.

57   **'obtain, exploit, develop':** Stephen Kinzer, *Reset: Iran, Turkey, and America's Future*, New York: St Martin's Griffin, 2010 (Afterword 2011), p. 25.

60   **political control was limited to Shaanxi:** Shaanxi (formerly romanized as Shensi, with its capital at Xian) and Shanxi (sometimes written 'Shansi', with its capital at Taiyuan) are neighbouring provinces in central China. Shaanxi was the ancient heart of China, and is considered the cradle of Chinese civilization. Xi'an was the capital of many ancient Chinese dynasties, including the Qin, Zhou and Tang.

63   **(including having Six Ministries):** The Ming had six ministries, which was considered the standard practice in China.

65   **'growth without development':** John King Fairbank and Merle Goodman, *China: A New History*, 2nd enlarged edition, Cambridge (Massachusetts): Belknap, 2006, p. 167.

69   **Cohong merchants:** 'Cohong' was the guild of local merchants ('Hongs').

70   **'most important treaty settlement':** Jonathan D. Spence, *The Search for Modern China*, New York: W.W. Norton & Co., 1990, p. 158.

71   **a 'century of unequal treaties':** Fairbank and Goodman, *China*, p. 210.

72   **a 'heavenly kingdom of great peace':** Ibid., p. 207.

76   **(now effectively headed by the Dowager Empress Cixi):** Cixi, as the mother of the infant emperor, was the most powerful personality in the imperial court and she never relinquished the effective power that she acquired when her son was a child.

78   **There were also shamanistic elements:** The highest form of martial arts (such as kung fu) fuse physical with spiritual control, the latter supposedly making the body invulnerable to many types of pain (including knife wounds and perhaps even bullets).

83   **'one of our own':** Nicholas Tarling, *The Cambridge History of Southeast Asia*, Vol. 1, Part 1, 1999, p. 44.

85   **Amitav Ghosh's evocative description:** Amitav Ghosh, *The Glass Palace*, London: HarperCollins, 2000, pp. 39-46.

92   **the only way to achieve 'wealth and strength':** W. G. Beasley, *The Rise of Modern Japan: Political, Economic and Social Change Since 1850*, 3rd edition, London: Phoenix, 2000, p. 47.

92   **'building many more guns and ships':** Ibid., p. 49.

94   **'knowledge will be sought throughout the world':** Ibid., p. 56.

100   **future zaibatsu conglomerates:** Zaibatsu was the term for the large industrial and financial conglomerates that dominated Japan's economy from the 1880s until 1945.

103 **the weakness of the Chosun state:** In the pre-modern era, the royal household demand was often the largest source of demand (everywhere in the world, not just in Korea).

103 **'with the same sovereign rights as Japan':** Beasley, *Rise of Modern Japan*, p. 144.

105 **interests 'to a peculiar degree':** Article 1 of the Anglo-Japanese Treaty of 1902.

CHAPTER 2

111 **Director of the Interior:** Similar to Minister of the Interior, but designated Director since it was a provisional government.

112 **'intelligent' and 'capable of self-government':** John Keay, *Empire's End: A History of the Far East from High Colonialism to Hong Kong*, New York: Scribner, 1997, p. 113.

115 **Bryan's advocacy of 'free silver':** 'Free silver' was the genesis of the idea of a flexible exchange rate, i.e., not tying the dollar's value to gold.

115 **populist emphasis on trust-busting:** 'Trust-busting' refers to anti-monopoly activism, which Teddy Roosevelt was to implement as president.

115 **'the full measure of individual rights and liberties':**William McKinley, 'Benevolent Assimilation Proclamation', Washington: 21 December 1898 <http://www.msc.edu. ph/centennial/benevolent.html> [accessed 19 July 2017]

115 **'fighting, once begun, must go on to the grim end':** Stuart Creighton Miller, *Benevolent Assimilation: The American Conquest of the Philippines*, New Haven: Yale University Press, 1982, p. 62.

117 **'the Philippines were therefore reinvaded':** Keay, *Empire's End*, p. 118.

117 **'greatest turncoat (balimbing) in Philippine history':** Historian Ambeth Ocampo used the term in 'Looking Back: the First Filipino Novel', *Philippine Inquirer*, 4 December 2005.

118 **'invariably followed them with a private apology':** Keay, *Empire's End*, p. 120.

121 **'ensure the survival of the East Asian people':** Chushichi Tsuzuki, *The Pursuit of Power in Modern Japan: 1825-1995*, Oxford, New York: Oxford University Press, 2000, p. 177.

125 **'the reverberations of that victory':** Pankaj Mishra, *From the Ruins of Empire: The Revolt Against the West and the Remaking of Asia*, London: Allen Lane, 2012, p. 1.

125 **'For as long as we rule India':** Keay, *India: A History*, p. 462.

125 **'best of all for the cause of progressive civilization':** Ibid.

126 **'any government which by indiscriminate almsgiving':** Mike Davis, *Late Victorian Holocausts: El Nino Famines and the Making of the Third World*, London: Verso (formerly New Left) Books, 2000, pp. 162 and 164.

130 **'territorial integrity' and 'abstain from interference':** Article 2 of the Convention between Great Britain, China and Tibet, 3 July 1914.

131 **'The best guarantee of the political advantage:** Keay, *India: A History*, p. 464.

131 **'"Divide et impera" was the old Roman motto:** M. J. Akbar, *Nehru: The Making of India*, London: Viking, 1988, p. 33.

131 **'We have maintained our power':** Ibid.

132 **'Bengal united is power':** Anthony Read and David Fisher, *The Proudest Day: India's Long Road to Independence*, New York, W.W. Norton & Co., 1998, p. 88.

133 **'unity they have not enjoyed:** Akbar, *Nehru*, p. 65.

134 **'man of utmost insignificance':** Newworldencyclopedia.org, 'George Nathaniel Curzon'

<http://www.newworldencyclopedia.org/entry/George_Nathaniel_Curzon> [accessed 5 May 2017]

134 'Do you mean...the Tatas propose: Tata.com, 'Quotes: Sir Dorabji Tata', 2008 <http://www.tata.com/aboutus/articlesinside/FX6UE!$$$$!cbFhc=/TLYVr3YPkMU=> [accessed 12 March 2017]

136 'ambassador of Hindu–Muslim unity': Jaswant Singh, *Jinnah: India, Partition, Independence*, New Delhi: Rupa & Co., 2009, p. 6.

136 'a carefully drawn-up petition': Akbar, *Nehru*, p. 66.

137 'I have also asked [my colleagues]: Ibid.

137 'the incalculable benefits conferred by British rule': Ibid., p. 67.

137 'appreciation of the just aims': Ibid., p. 68.

137 '...a very, very big thing has happened today': Ibid.

137 only 'true political voice in the country': Jaswant Singh, *Jinnah* p. 81.

137 'doughtiest opponent': Akbar, *Nehru*, p. 69.

138 'of my two wives': En.banglapedia.org, 'Fuller, Sir Joseph Bampfylde' <http://en.banglapedia.org/index.php?title=Fuller,_Sir_Joseph_Bampfylde> [accessed 5 May 2017]

139 'The Indian National Congress has for its ultimate goal': sriaurobindoashram.org, 'Extracts from the Diary of G. S. Khaparde' http://www.sriaurobindoashram.org/research/show.php?set=doclife&id=11 [accessed 5 May 2017]

140 'Japan's success (in defeating Russia)': T. R. Sareen, 'The Ghadr Party' in *We Fought Together for Freedom: Chapters from the Indian National Movement*, (ed.) Ravi Dayal, New Delhi: Oxford University Press, 1998, p. 62.

141 'Indians, especially educated Hindus': Arthur Herman, *Gandhi & Churchill: The Epic Rivalry that Destroyed an Empire and Forged our Age*, London: Arrow Books, 2009, p. 165.

142 'remind the British people that': Excerpt from a statement in the inaugural issue of the *Indian Sociologist*, reproduced in A. M. Shah, 'The Indian Sociologist 1905–14, 1920–22'. *The Economic and Political Weekly*, 5 August 2006, pp. 34–36.

142 'the finest ever made in the name of patriotism': Herman, *Gandhi & Churchill*, p. 166.

142 'I believe that a nation held down': Deepti Kaul, 'Madanlal Dhingra: Lion-hearted hero from Punjab', in *Connected to India*, 2 March 2017 <http://www.connectedtoindia.com/madan-lal-dhingra-lion-heart-from-punjab-758.html> [accessed 5 May 2017]. Her key source is Vishav Bandhu, *The Life and Times of Madan Lal Dhingra*.

143 'For nearly a quarter of a century': Akbar, 1988, *Nehru*, p. 70.

144 Oriya and Assamese are mutually intelligible, as is Maithili: Maithili (the language of the region in which Sita, the wife of Rama in the Ramayana, was born) has its own Mithilakshar script, which is precisely the same as Bengali and Assamese (with only one letter written slightly differently in the three languages). The Oriya script is different, but the Oriya language is also Pali-influenced like the others and can be learnt by Bengali- and Assamese-speakers within a week or two of intermingling. (Oriya is probably the most ancient of the four east Indian languages, and through trade ties to Southeast Asia, had a profound influence on Thai, Khmer, Laotian, Shan and Burmese—although these tonal languages are no longer mutually intelligible with the east Indian languages.) In the rest of 'Bihar and Chhota Nagpur' sub-province, most urban centres (Patna, Ranchi, Dhanbad, Hazaribagh, Jamshedpur) had Bengali-speaking majorities at the time (and still have Bengali pluralities today).

147 literacy rates had already risen to at least 30 per cent: According to an influential

estimate by Rawski, quoted in Fairbank and Goldman, *China*, p. 261.

151 'turned out to have a startling degree: Spence, *Search for Modern China*, p. 266.
152 'is actually waiting for you: Ibid., p. 267.
153 'a republic is the best political system': Ibid., p. 278.

CHAPTER 3

154 **European Civil War of 1914-18:** The Indian historian K. M. Panikkar was the first to use this phrase in 1955, and other historians including J. M. Roberts have used it more recently.

154 **'The phrase is simply loaded':** Daniel Patrick Moynihan, *Pandaemonium: Ethnicity in International Politics*, New York: Oxford University Press, 1993, p. 81.

155 avoid 'foreign entanglements': George Washington, the first US president, wrote a 'Farewell Address' upon declining a third term, in which he warned his fellow Americans to avoid 'foreign entanglements'.

157 there 'are just eight states on earth': Moynihan, *Pandaemonium*, p. 10.

157 the 'only war aim' for the two major protagonists: Eric J. Hobsbawm, *The Age of Extremes: A History of the World 1914-1991*, New York: Vintage Books (Random House), 1995, p. 30.

158 'American supporters of Irish independence: Moynihan, *Pandaemonium*, p. 12. Moynihan refers to Wilson as 'Scotch-Irish', i.e., of Irish Protestant stock, his ancestors having moved to Ireland from Scotland, and then eventually across the Atlantic.

164 'revolutionary hotbed on the Caspian': Daniel Yergin, *The Prize: The Epic Quest for Oil, Money & Power*, New York: Touchstone (Simon & Schuster), 1992, p. 129.

166 used a 'Jew-baiting' argument: Ibid., p. 162. Watson Rutherford, MP, accused Churchill of 'Jew-baiting', and Churchill later acknowledged that his 'attack on monopolies and trusts...did it'.

166 'attack on monopolies and trusts': Ibid.

167 'want for oil or tankers in case of war': Ibid., p. 163.

167 'floated to victory on a wave of oil': Ibid., p. 183.

170 'fanaticism and intellectual slavery': Kinzer, *Reset*, 2010, p. 32.

171 'fought like a man possessed': Ibid., p. 36.

178 **Marxist theory posited that:** The quotations in this paragraph are taken from: Karl Marx (with Friedrich Engels), *Selected Writings (Communist Manifesto, Wages Price and Profit, Capital, Socialism: Utopian and Scientific)*, London: CRW Publishing Ltd., 2004, and V. I. Lenin, *Imperialism: The Highest Stage of Capitalism*, Sydney: Resistance Books, 1999 (first published in 1917).

180 'should necessity arise': Kinzer, *Reset*, p. 26.

182 'a human cancer': Ibid., p. 40.

182 'The Greek troops then got out of hand': Lord Patrick Kinross, *Atatürk: The Rebirth of a Nation*, London: Phoenix Books, 1995, p. 154.

183 'the establishment in Palestine: Margaret MacMillan, *Paris 1919: Six Months that Changed the World*, New York: Random House, 2001, p. 417.

184 **Armenian entrepreneur Calouste Gulbenkian:** Although he was technically a Turkish-born British citizen, Gulbenkian was Armenian by heritage and proud of his roots. He was born in Istanbul (Constantinople) in 1869 (at a time when Armenia was part of the Ottoman empire), and became a British citizen in 1902.

187 that 'began with the retreat from Vienna': Reşat Kasaba (ed.) *Cambridge History*

of Turkey, Vol. 4, Cambridge: Cambridge University Press, 2008, p. 138.

191 'a dagger pointed at the heart of China': MacMillan, *Paris 1919*, p. 334.

197 (as most elites inevitably do): Scottish nationalists hark back to the heroism of the highland clans which resisted the English intruders in the seventeenth and eighteenth centuries. But a minority of the clan leaders collaborated with the English, and became the new ruling elite—for instance, the Campbells of Loch Lomond who 'betrayed' the Macdonald Scots-nationalists.

198 Prince Ranjitsinhji of Nawanagar: Ranjitsinhji considered himself an honorary Englishman, and played all his cricket with enormous distinction for that country; he expressly forbade his extravagantly talented nephew, Duleepsinhji, to play for India when the opportunity arose in 1932.

198 'successor on the throne of Aurangzeb': MacMillan, *Paris 1919*, p. 403.

199 'the gradual development of self-governing institutions: Read and Fisher, *Proudest Day*, p. 134.

200 'at no time imply any disloyalty': Akbar, *Nehru*, p. 94.

203 with very similar terms of service: Including three-year contracts that conferred almost no rights on the workers, and could be broken at any time by the employer who thus had a disciplinary stranglehold on each worker, who had already been uprooted from his home, and thus lost any customary rights to till those lands.

203 'mission is that of making peace': Akbar, *Nehru*, p. 109.

203 'higher law of our being': Ibid., p. 110.

208 'any Muslim in India to imagine': Ibid., p. 135.

210 'swaraj within a year': Patrick French, *Liberty or Death: India's Journey to Independence and Division*, London: Flamingo (HarperCollins), 1997, p. 37.

212 offer of talks on dominion status: 'The Deshbandhu was beside himself with anger and disgust' over Gandhi's failure to respond to Reading's overture: Subhas Chandra Bose, *The Indian Struggle 1920-1942*, edited by Sisir K. Bose and Sugata Bose, Delhi: Oxford University Press, 1998, p. 75.

212 Maulana Abul Kalam Azad later wrote: Azad had already spent nearly half of the previous decade in British jails because of his steadfast solidarity with nationalist causes—starting in 1907-11 when he was one of the prominent Muslims involved in the occasionally violent uprising against the Partition of Bengal, and then through his nationalist Urdu newspaper *Al-Hilal*.

CHAPTER 4

221 himself an authentic product: Osama bin Laden belonged to a prominent business family of Saudi Arabia, and was educated in Saudi schools: his doctrines were a literalist (perhaps slightly more extreme) version of Wahhabi ideology.

221 backed and funded the Jamaat-e-Islami: The Saudi state extended its support to the Jamaat from the time of ibn Saud, although the funding became more significant after the 1940s as Saudi oil wealth swelled.

222 'greatest Mohammedan power in the world': Christopher Catherwood, *Churchill's Folly: How Winston Churchill Created Modern Iraq*, New York: Carroll & Graf Publishers, 2004, p. 94.

223 'in four or five years...': Ibid., p. 142.

223 'Churchill's scheme was, in effect': Ibid., p. 141.

225-226 at the pre-war parity of US$4.87 to the pound: US productivity had soared during the decade since 1914, while Britain's output and productivity had stagnated (and Britain's inflation had been much higher than in the US). The wide divergence in productivity performance meant that sterling had depreciated against the dollar (and gold). By restoring the pre-war exchange rate, Churchill hobbled British industry, making it totally uncompetitive against US manufacturers in particular. Consequently, British wage rates needed to be cut drastically (or workers laid off in their thousands) if Britain was to regain competitiveness (and the same applied to India, Australia, Canada, etc., who were linked to sterling). This is what spurred the General Strike.

226 'perhaps the most damaging error of modern economic and financial policy': John Kenneth Galbraith, *A Journey Through Economic Time: A Firsthand View*, New York: Houghton Mifflin, 1994, p. 52 and 54 (for the second quote in the sentence).

226 'Roman genius...the greatest law-giver': Richard J. Samuels, *Machiavelli's Children: Leaders and their Legacies in Italy and Japan*, Ithaca: Cornell University Press, 2003, p. 169.

232 'The sun does not rise': Keay, *Empire's End*, p. 33.

232 'the future united Republic': Ibid.

232 'We hear the promise of a life': Ibid.

236 Soviet intelligence as claiming credit for assassinating Zhang Zuolin: Jung Chang and Jon Halliday, *Mao: The Unknown Story*, London: Jonathan Cape, 2005, p. 181 (footnote, where they cite recent Russian intelligence claims that the assassination was organized by Naum Eitington—who was also responsible for Trotsky's death—on Stalin's orders).

239 'One thing is clear': Jawaharlal Nehru, *Glimpses of World History*, Allahabad: Kitabistan (republished by the Jawaharlal Nehru Memorial Fund and Oxford University Press, 2002), 1934, p. 887.

239 'roads, irrigation and agriculture': Ibid., p. 894.

242 'the platitudes associated with the Open Door': Beasley, *Rise of Modern Japan*, p. 163.

243 'to develop and maintain...': Ibid., p. 163 (quoting Article I of the treaty).

244 'enemies of our neighbours': Ibid., p. 164

250 'China is not an organized state': Ibid., p. 174.

252 (the Tibetan form of 'Chakrasamvara Siddhartha'): Siddhartha is the Buddha's given name. Chakrasamvara translates either as the 'Circle of Bliss', or as a tantric deity in Vajrayana Buddhism often depicted with four faces. It's a quintessentially Buddhist name, with Tibetan and Sanskrit origins.

257 as explained in a study: Alice H. Amsden, *Asia's Next Giant: South Korea and Late Industrialization*, New York: Oxford University Press, 1989, pp. 59-61. She quotes G. E. Hubbard's book, *Eastern Industrialization and its Effect on the West*, London: Oxford University Press, 1938.

257 'Keynesian policies as early as 1932': Charles P. Kindleberger, *The World in Depression, 1929-1939*, Berkeley: University of California Press, 1973, p. 192.

257 far more to Takahashi's policy success: Chalmers Johnson, *MITI and the Japanese Miracle: The Growth of Industrial Policy, 1925-1975*, Stanford (California): Stanford University Press, 1982, pp. 6-7.

261 outwitted by Chiang Kai-shek in 1926-27: During this period (1926-27), Wang Jing-wei's closest ally within the KMT (while it was in a united front with the CCP) was Mao Zedong, as explained in Jung Chang and Jon Halliday, pp. 44-46.

263 'the leading organizer of the revolutionary movement': Sugata Bose, *A Hundred Horizons: The Indian Ocean in the Age of Global Empire*, Cambridge, MA: Harvard

University Press, 2006, p. 55.

264 'the most classless country': Subhas Bose, *Indian Struggle*, p. 149.

265 'We have always relied': French, *Liberty or Death*, p. 53.

265 'the phrase "Dominion Status"': Ibid., pp. 53–54.

267 'to make the deaf hear': Bipan Chandra, 'Bhagat Singh and his Comrades' in *We Fought Together for Freedom: Chapters from the Indian National Movement*, edited by Ravi Dayal, New Delhi: Oxford University Press, 1998, p. 144.

267 'The bomb was necessary': Ibid., p. 144.

268 'The man who goes on hunger strike: Sugata Bose, *His Majesty's Opponent: Subhas Chandra Bose and India's Struggle against Empire*, Cambridge, MA: Belknap (Harvard University Press), 2011, p. 76.

270 'The British government in India': Stanley Wolpert, *India*, Oakland: University of California Press, 1999, p. 204.

271 'most remarkable call to war': Herbert A. Miller, 'Gandhi's Campaign Begins', *The Nation*, 23 April 1930.

271 'With this, I am shaking': Mahatma Gandhi, *Selected Political Writings*, (ed.) Dennis Dalton, Indianapolis/Cambridge: Hackett, 1996, p. 72.

272 'Not one of the marchers': Webb Miller, UPI report, 21 May 1930, quoted in Brian Martin, *Justice Ignited*, Lanham: Rowman & Littlefield, 2006, p. 38.

275 'the British nation has we believe': Herman, *Gandhi & Churchill*, p. 350.

275 'Good night, Mr Gandhi': Ibid., p. 353.

276 'It is alarming and also nauseating': Akbar, *Nehru*, p. 233.

285 'for the political uplift of India': Sugata Bose, *His Majesty's Opponent*, 2011, p. 93.

286 'the next phase in world-history': Subhas Bose, *Indian Struggle*, p. 351.

286 'between some form of Communism': Ibid., p. 350.

286 'Samyavada—an Indian word': Ibid., p. 352.

287 'cannot expect to remain at liberty': Mihir Bose, *The Lost Hero: A Biography of Subhas Bose*, New Delhi: Blue Leaf, 2004 (first published by Quartet Books, London, 1982), p. 323.

287 'without humiliating another proud': Sugata Bose, *His Majesty's Opponent*, p. 122.

291 'looked through a telescope': Jaswant Singh, *Jinnah*, p. 248.

291 'is it not enough that the Congress': Sugata Bose, *His Majesty's Opponent*, p. 246–247.

293 'appealing to the good sense of the British': Mihir Bose, *The Lost Hero*, p. 388.

294 'a prospect of a compromise': Ibid., p. 392.

294 '...since I was instrumental': Ibid., pp. 393–394.

294 'it will be a tragic thing': Ibid., p. 395.

295 command Gandhi's 'implicit confidence': Ibid., p. 400.

295 'as politically an elder brother': Ibid., pp. 403–404.

295 any attempt to 'push' Subhas out: Sugata Bose, *His Majesty's Opponent*, p. 162.

297 'This is not the time to bargain': Mihir Bose, *The Lost Hero*, p. 415.

297 'the loyalty of the Muslim community': Narendra Singh Sarila, *The Shadow of the Great Game: The Untold Story of India's Partition*, New Delhi: HarperCollins, 2005, p. 42.

CHAPTER 5

300 'the Japanese regarded China': Christopher Bayly and Tim Harper, *Forgotten Armies: Britain's Asian Empire and the War with Japan*, London: Penguin, 2004, p. 2.

301 'China would one day be the United States of Asia': Ibid.

303 'without dismembering the Chinese republic': Ibid., p. 26.

307 (with 'Greater East Asia' left to Japan): Article II of the pact stated: 'Germany and Italy recognize and respect the leadership of Japan in the establishment of a new order in Greater East Asia.' The territorial extent of 'Greater East Asia' remained undefined.

312 member of the Legislative Yuan: The Legislative Yuan roughly translates as China's parliament, although it was more than a legislature in Sun Yat-sen's political theory, which embraces it as an integral branch of government.

316 rather than elite ones like St John's and St Paul's: Both St Paul's and St John's were amongst the top high schools of Rangoon, although they respectively shared the names of schools in Darjeeling (India) and Kuala Lumpur (Malaya).

323 'In all the war, I never': Herman, *Gandhi & Churchill*, pp. 472–473.

325 'people worship... like a god': Bayly and Harper, *Forgotten Armies*, p. 122.

325 'the majority of the population': Ibid., p. 121.

327 'the most absolute monarchy in the world': Keay, *Empire's End*, p. 138.

328 the Mid-Levels: Hong Kong consists of three main regions—Hong Kong island itself (acquired by the British in 1842), Kowloon (most of which was added in 1860) and the vast but largely uninhabited New Territories (acquired in 1898, on a 99-year lease). Much of the business district is in the Central (and Western) region of Hong Kong island, which is a small but densely populated area, on the edge of which is a steep hillside. The middle section of this hillside comprises the Mid-Levels, and the top of it is called the Peak (both areas are now amongst the highest-priced real estate in the world).

332 Greater East Asian Co-Prosperity Sphere: This is the term the Japanese used for the united Asian bloc that would be free of European control, and instead allied with Japan.

334 'That is the end of the British Empire': Bayly and Harper, *Forgotten Armies*, p. 130.

335 'There must at this stage be': Ibid., p. 142.

336 'worst disaster': Herman, *Gandhi & Churchill*, p. 479.

336 'the Japanese Army will treat you': Sugata Bose, *His Majesty's Opponent*, p. 241.

337 'The fall of Singapore means': Ibid., p. 213.

337 inter-ethnic violence amongst Malays and Chinese: The MPAJA primarily comprised ethnic Chinese Malayans, while many of the Malays collaborated with Japanese rule. So there were some post-war reprisal killings, although the communist MPAJA's alliance with the British didn't much survive the war years either.

337 'Under the Japanese I learnt': Keay, *Empire's End*, p. 230.

345 the Dutch 'threw away their uniforms': Ibid., p. 182.

348 'with the arrival of the Japanese': Pramoedya Ananta Toer, *This Earth of Mankind* (*Bumi Manusia*), translated by Max Lane, New York: Penguin, 1990, p. 74.

348 Nahdlatul Ulama...Muhammadiya: The two largest Muslim organizations in Indonesia (and earlier in the Dutch East Indies). Each represents two divergent tendencies in Indonesian Islam. NU is more traditionalist in that it accommodates syncretic beliefs and venerates Sufi saints—while Muhammadiya seeks to cleanse Indonesian Islam of all these 'traditionalist' accretions (and hence has strong Wahhabi influences, although it prefers to call itself 'modernist'). Masyumi brought them both onto the same platform.

350 chiefs with no 'Injuns': The reference is to an American phrase: Chiefs without any Indians (or Native Americans).

350 'So we had won after all': Sarila, *Shadow of the Great Game*, p. 97, quoting from

Vol. 6 of Churchill's memoir of the Second World War.

350 raise 'the Indian problem': Ibid.
351 'should voluntarily give the Indians': Ibid., p. 103.
351 'Approximately 75 per cent': Ibid., p. 105.
352 'Our ideal remains a united': Ibid., p. 102.
352 'the only long-term policy': Ibid., p. 99.
352 'It goes without saying: Ibid., pp. 56–57.
352 'likes of Cripps and Wedgwood Benn': Ibid., p. 56. Also for the two subsequent quoted phrases.
352 creed of non-violence in the sphere of national defence: Maulana Abul Kalam Azad, *India Wins Freedom (The Complete Version)*, Hyderabad: Orient Longman, 1988, pp. 32–33. Azad points out that the Working Committee endorsed non-violence when it came to issues internal to India, but in a separate resolution agreed to set aside non-violence in matters relating to national defence, while reiterating that 'she could not participate in the war effort of the democracies till she was herself free'. Even this tortured resolution was soon being questioned by some members of the Working Committee.
353 'I think he [Jinnah] was rather': Sarila, *Shadow of the Great Game*, p. 102.
353 'an invitation to the Muslims': Stanley Wolpert, *Shameful Flight: The Last Years of the British Empire in India*, New York: Oxford University Press, 2006, p. 21.
354 'Congress will oppose the scheme': Sarila, *Shadow of the Great Game*, p. 108.
354 domain of 'the British Commander-in-Chief': Ibid., p. 110.
355 a 'post-dated cheque on a crashing bank': Akbar, 1988, p. 339.
355 'analogous to that of the King': Wolpert, *Shameful Flight*, p. 35.
355 'give no approval unless': All quotations in this and the subsequent paragraph from Sarila, *Shadow of the Great Game*.
356 'Subhas Bose's escape to Germany': Azad, *India Wins Freedom*, p. 40.
358 'respect the right of all peoples': Read and Fisher, *Proudest Day*, p. 308.
359 Dr Khan Sahib: Although elected overwhelmingly as chief minister of the NWFP in 1937, Dr Khan Sahib had resigned with the other Congress chief ministers in 1939. The other two were still in office.
364 'extended his best wishes to Bose': Sugata Bose, *His Majesty's Opponent*, p. 220.
364 'While standing for full collaboration': Ibid., p. 222.
365 'passive resistance for the Reich': Ibid., p. 219.
366 'The whole world now sees': Ibid., p. 224.
366 'Quite apart from the demands of war': Bayly and Harper, *Forgotten Armies*, p. 286.
367 having 'no parallel in the annals': Madhusree Mukherjee, *Churchill's Secret War: The British Empire and the Ravaging of India During World War II*, New Delhi: Tranquebar (first published by Basic Books, New York), 2010, pp. 100–101.
367 'good support to the Military authorities': Ibid., p. 103.
367 'I am glad to learn': Ibid., p. 104.
368 'overbreeding and eugenic unfitness': Bayly and Harper, *Forgotten Armies*, p. 286.
371 Tojo pledged 'unconditional support': Sugata Bose, *His Majesty's Opponent*, p. 243.
371 Japan would do 'everything possible': Ibid.
371 'The freedom we shall win': Ibid., p. 244.
371 'when the revolution succeeds': Ibid., p. 245.
372 'Subhas Bose drew crowds': Bayly and Harper, *Forgotten Armies*, p. 322.
372 'Indians outside India': Sugata Bose, *His Majesty's Opponent*, pp. 245–246.
373 'finally kissed the soil of India': Interview by the author, 12–13 August 2006.

373 spoke movingly of the most inspirational person: Rasammah's speech at the INA Retrospective seminar held on 13 August 2006 in Singapore by the India Club.

373 'when Bose really got down': Mukherjee, *Churchill's Secret War*, p. 179.

373 'of course particularly anxious': Ibid.

374 'if you want to know what personality is': Mihir Bose, *The Lost Hero*, p. 625.

376 'held the entire assembly in awe': Sugata Bose, *His Majesty's Opponent*, p. 261, quoting from 'Bose and Japan', a pamphlet released by Japan's foreign ministry.

376 President Laurel's guest: President José Laurel's son Salvador would become vice president of the Philippines in 1986, when the dictator Ferdinand Marcos was democratically ousted by Corazon Aquino (whose husband was the son of Benigno Aquino, Speaker of the Philippines parliament during the war).

377 'The first drop of blood': Sugata Bose, *His Majesty's Opponent*, p. 267.

378 'Arise! We have no time to lose': Hugh Toye, *Subhash Chandra Bose (The Springing Tiger): A Study of a Revolution*, Mumbai: Jaico, 1957, p. 106.

379 Mairembam Koireng Singh: Manipur became a state of India in 1972, its king having acceded to India (rather than to Burma) in September 1949 but it had a chief minister from 1963 onwards, and the post was held by Koireng Singh until 1968.

379 'most of Nagaland as far as Kohima': 'Phizo's Plebiscite Speech', May 1951 <http://www.neuenhofer.de/guenter/nagaland/phizo.html> [accessed 13 April 2017]

380 'a revolt in Bengal and Bihar': Mihir Bose, *The Lost Hero*, p. 671.

380 'the situation is slightly not': Sugata Bose, *His Majesty's Opponent*, p. 281.

381 'surging with revolutionary fervour': Ibid., p. 286.

381 'Imphal has given us the knowledge': Peter Ward Fay, *The Forgotten Army: India's Armed Struggle for Independence, 1942–45*, Ann Arbor: University of Michigan Press, 1993, p. 314.

381 'Tum mujhe khoon do': Ibid., p. 315.

382 'variously reported as between': Ibid., 330.

383 'You are proposing to risk your life': Toye, *Subhash Chandra Bose*, p. 140.

384 'battling with no hope': Fay, *Forgotten Army*, p. 556.

384 'What did you mean, you people': Sugata Bose, *His Majesty's Opponent*, p. 291.

386 'The British Indian Army have now': Toye, *Subhash Chandra Bose* p. 156.

386 'political consciousness which the Indian': Ibid., p. 170.

386 'the majority view is that': Fay, *Forgotten Army*, p. 510.

387 'INA had literally burst upon the country': Ibid., p. 484.

387 'there has seldom been a matter': Ibid.

388 'shrewd but devious and malevolent': Sarila, *Shadow of the Great Game*, p. 173.

388 'not a case of three individuals': Kirsten Stellars, 'Another Meaning of Treason: The Legacy of the Red Fort Trials in International Law', 22 December 2016, *Leiden Journal of International Law*, 2017 (Forthcoming). Available at SSRN: https://ssrn.com/abstract=2568032

389 'their warmest and greatest supporters': Archive.org, 'Full text of I.N.A. Defence' <https://archive.org/stream/inadefence035528mbp/inadefence035528mbp_djvu.txt> [accessed 13 April 2017]

389 'the officer added, in a low': Fay, *Forgotten Army*, p. 493.

389 'a seething mass of humanity': Ibid., p. 495.

390 'as Indian opinion is opposed': Ibid., p. 514.

390 'To regain control of the situation': Ibid., p. 516.

391 'practically all are sure': Ibid., p. 517.

391 'In the autumn of 1945': Ibid., p. 519.

391 'Wherever I went during this period': Azad, *India Wins Freedom*, p. 134.

392 'stand on their own feet economically': Wolpert, *Shameful Flight*, p. 98.

393 'It was the first time since 1857': Akbar, *Nehru*, p. 370.

393 'Mr Basu, your view of why India': Author's discussion with Vayalar Ravi in Singapore on 28 April 2012.

393 25,000 volunteer soldiers: The INA comprised a total of 60,000 members of whom 25,000 to 30,000 comprised civilian recruits from the region.

397 'prompt and utter destruction': 'Potsdam Declaration', 1945 <http://www.atomicarchive.com/Docs/Hiroshima/Potsdam.shtml> [accessed 13 April 2017]

398 Inner Mongolia or Mengjiang: Nei Monggol is the Chinese name for Inner Mongolia, Mengjiang is what it was called when it was semi-independent under Japanese auspices.

399 'communicate to the Governments': 'Hirohito's "Jewel Voice Broadcast"', 15 August 1945 <https://web.archive.org/web/20130910212019/http://www.airforcemag.com/MagazineArchive/Pages/2012/August%202012/0812keeper.aspx> [accessed 13 April 2017]

400 'a new and most cruel bomb': Ibid.

401 'We the people of Indonesia': Keay, *Empire's End*, p. 210. (He uses 'and other matters' rather than 'etc.', but 'etc.' is a more accurate translation.)

CHAPTER 6

410 'not to damage the international relations': Ashis Nandy, 'The Other Within: The Strange Case of Radhabinod Pal's Judgement on Culpability', *New Literary History*, vol. 23, no. 1, p. 49.

410 'each and every one of the accused': Ibid., p. 47.

410 'otherwise than under a due process': Ibid., p. 50.

410 'perhaps not the result': Ibid., p. 51.

410 'did not act as a free and independent': Ibid., p. 52

410 'Japanese Class A war criminal': The phrase is regularly deployed in the Western media when Japanese politicians visit the Yasukuni Shrine in Tokyo, where the souls of nearly 2.5 million Japanese war dead are memorialized, including 14 classified as Class A war criminals.

414 'We extremists, we who revolt': Christopher Bayly and Tim Harper, *Forgotten Wars: The End of Britain's Asian Empire*, London: Allen Lane, 2007, p. 177.

416 'Don't let us be forced to face': Keay, *Empire's End*, p. 256.

416 'Our slogan remains the same': Bayly and Harper, *Forgotten Wars*, p. 179.

423 'I am a federalist, yes': Keay, *Empire's End*, p. 266.

423 the States: There were numerous States separately represented (like the rajas/nawabs of India before Independence), many of which had been previously grouped into the Great East.

425 Shan States: The Shan are ethnically closer to the Thais, but their states were in British Burma, except during the World War, when they had been handed to Thailand.

426 Khuang Aphaiwong: The family's formal noble surname was Abhayavongsa ('fearless clan' in Sanskrit).

426 the Ho Chi Minh Trail: The Ho Chi Minh Trail was an elaborate system of mountain paths, trails and tunnels used to ferry supplies and arms into Cambodia, Laos and South Vietnam by the communist regime in North Vietnam during the Vietnam War. (It is normally thought to have been activated in 1959.)

428 'Fête de l'Indépendance': Translated as 'Independence Celebration' in French.

428 'the Annamite government': Bayly and Harper, *Forgotten Wars*, p. 147.

429 the most 'telling legacy': Keay, *Empire's End*, p. 280.

430 'as between you and the French': Bayly and Harper, *Forgotten Wars*, p. 150.

431 'Gandhi of Indo-China': Keay, *Empire's End*, p. 281.

431 'free state having its own government': Ibid., p. 283.

432 'it is you who will end up': Ibid., p. 286.

436 '...for the last General Election (1934)': Dsal.uchicago.edu, 'VIII.C.5. Major Elections, 1920–45' <http://dsal.uchicago.edu/reference/schwartzberg/pager.html?object=260&view=text> [accessed 19 April 2017]

439 'would have to continue responsibility': Sarila, *Shadow of the Great Game*, p. 170.

439 'Congress made a deliberate effort': Ibid., p. 171.

440 'The USSR is the only major power': Ibid., p. 181, quoting from the top-secret report of the Post-Hostilities Planning Staff, available in the Oriental and Indian Collection at the British Library, London.

440 'the Indian Ocean area': Ibid., p. 182.

440 Britain 'must ensure that': Ibid.

440 '[His Majesty's Government] must be most cautious': Ibid., p. 190.

440 'It was most unlikely': Ibid.

440-1 'own judgement...that Jinnah': Ibid.

441 'proceeded on the assumption': Ibid., pp. 190–191.

442 'most brilliant' student he ever had: R. K. Bhatnagar, 'Was Krishna Menon a Sick Man?', *Asian Tribune*, 17 October 2009.

443 'We are now faced in India': Sarila, *Shadow of the Great Game*, p. 193.

444 'Many things that have been done': Ibid., p. 200.

444 'I am so glad you are as convinced': Ibid., p. 201.

444 'My dear Stafford': Ibid., pp. 201–202.

445 'If the Mission can avoid a discussion': Ibid., p. 207.

446 two 'possible bases of agreement': Ibid., p. 208.

446 'you may work for an agreement': Ibid.

446 'was in fact militarily unsound': Ibid., p. 210.

446 'the way things have shaped': Azad, *India Wins Freedom*, p. 162.

446 (quoting Alan Campbell-Johnson's memoirs): Campbell-Johnson was a public relations executive and Liberal politician, who served as a key staff member to Lord Louis Mountbatten from 1942 to 1948, serving with him at SEAC headquarters in Delhi and Kandy until 1946, and then as press attaché to the Viceroy of India in 1947–48.

446 '...for many years that Jawaharlal': Akbar, *Nehru*, p. 371.

446 'international outlook': French, *Liberty or Death*, pp. 262–263.

447 had an open marriage: Alex von Tunzelmann, *Indian Summer: The Secret History of the End of an Empire*, London: Simon & Schuster (Pocket Books), 2008, chapter 5.

448 'northwest and northeast' of India: Wolpert, *Shameful Flight*, p. 106.

449 'independence without a violent': Azad, *India Wins Freedom*, p. 164.

449 'completely unfettered by agreements': Ibid.

450 He acts with childlike innocence: Sarila, *Shadow of the Great Game*, p. 237.

450 'It was in Ramzan': Ibid., p. 224.

451 'had seen to police arrangements': Ibid., p. 223, quoting from Bengal governor Burrows's report to Wavell and Pethick-Lawrence sent on 22 August 1947.

451 'it is the unanimous decision': Ibid., pp. 223–224.

451 'communal disorder' was 'a natural': Ibid., p. 225.

452 'saddle Indians with responsibility': Ibid., p. 229.

453 'was, to take a charitable view': Azad, *India Wins Freedom*, p. 199.

453 'We all like our admirers': Ibid., p. 198.

454 'in the interests of communal peace': Sarila, *Shadow of the Great Game*, p. 235.

456 'would like to suggest...the necessity': Ibid., p. 239.

457 'any halt in the constitutional process': Ibid., p. 257.

457 The professional diplomat Girija Shankar Bajpai: Bajpai was British India's representative in Washington DC (called 'Agent General') from 1943 until the appointment of Asaf Ali as the Interim Government's first ambassador.

457 India's 'indebtedness to the British': Sarila, *Shadow of the Great Game*, p. 257.

458 'whether or not Brit are disposed': Ibid., p. 261.

458 if 'a constitution will not': Ibid.

458 '[His Majesty's Government's] powers and obligations': Ibid.

459 a division of Punjab: Ibid., p. 264.

461 'India will continue to be dependent': Ibid., p. 243.

461 'Indian problem could be solved': Ibid., p. 277.

462 unable to 'obtain the agreement': Ibid.

462 'far out of it': Wolpert, *Shameful Flight*, p. 140.

462 'the new Pakistan is almost certain': Sarila, *Shadow of the Great Game*, p. 278.

462 'I do not care how little': Ibid.

462 'for psychological and emotional': Ibid., p. 279.

462 'it would not be right to impose': Ibid., 280.

464 independence-minded Nawab of Bhopal: The Bhopal nawab's son-in-law, Iftekhar, the Nawab of Pataudi, had captained India's cricket team to England merely a year earlier (in 1946).

465 'It is a matter of life and death': Sarila, *Shadow of the Great Game*, p. 296.

465 'an effective acceptance of dominion status': Ibid.

466 'preached "non-violence"': Bl.uk, 'Minutes of the Meeting of the Viceroy with the Indian Leaders, 3 June 1947' <http://www.bl.uk/reshelp/findhelpregion/asia/india/indianindependence/indiapakistan/partition6/index.html> [accessed 19 April 2017]

466 'had no hand' in partition: Read and Fisher, *Proudest Day*, p. 461.

467 Mountbatten acknowledged afterwards: Sarila, *Shadow of the Great Game*, p. 308.

468 'the Khudai Khidmatgars to the wolves': Azad, *India Wins Freedom*, p. 210.

469 'In exchange for Indian acceptance': Sarila, *Shadow of the Great Game*, p. 314.

471 'would help to consolidate Britain': Ibid., p. 15.

471 'British air power could threaten': Ibid., p. 22.

472 '[t]he area of Pakistan is strategically': Ibid., p. 28.

472 'The Indus Valley, western Punjab': Ibid., p. 29.

473 Of the 21 million Bengali Hindus: Census of India 1941 showed that the Hindu population of what became East Pakistan was 28 per cent of the total (which was 75 million in 1947).

473 as late as 1970, nearly 20 per cent: Home.iitk.ac.in, 'Hindu Genocide in East Pakistan' <http://home.iitk.ac.in/~hcverma/Article/Genocide%20of%20Hindus%20in%20banglasdesh.pdf> [accessed 19 April 2017].

473 Muslims comprise over 25 per cent: Censusindia.gov.in, 'Religion' <http://censusindia.gov.in/Census_And_You/religion.aspx> [accessed 16 June 2017]

476 Jinnah specifically requested them: Alice Albinia, *Empires of the Indus: The Story of a River*, New York: W. W. Norton, 2010, pp. 2–25.

479 'assurances from the Indian leaders': Sarila, *Shadow of the Great Game*, pp. 343–344.

480 'As soon as law and order': Ibid., p. 354.

480 'the decision to hold a plebiscite': Ibid., footnote on the page.

482 protesting the 'change' in: Ibid., p. 358.

482 'three battalions of the Pakistan Army': Ibid., pp. 360–361.

484 'deny all help to the raiders': Ibid., p. 371.

485 Philip John Noel-Baker was Britain's: Noel-Baker happened to have obtained a First in his Economics Tripos from Cambridge the same year as my grandfather did; there were just four Firsts that year, the other two named Robertson and Henderson.

485 written an 'appreciation' for the British: Sarila, *Shadow of the Great Game*, p. 374.

485 'should be very careful to guard': Ibid., p. 374.

486 '77 per cent Muslim': Ibid., p. 376.

487 Angus Maddison's authoritative data: Angus Maddison, *The World Economy: A Millennial Perspective*, Paris: Development Centre of the OECD, 2001, p. 30.

488 Maddison estimates that India: Ibid., p. 261.

489 China's 25 per cent in 1700: Ibid., p. 263.

490 'Wages were fifty cents': Stephen Kinzer, *All the Shah's Men: An American Coup and the Roots of Middle East Terror*, Hoboken, NJ: Wiley, 2003, p. 67.

491 'try being prime minister himself': Ibid., p. 82.

492 'that in 1948, according to accounts: Ibid., p. 123.

500 'Your heroes of those days': Sugata Bose, *His Majesty's Opponent*, p. 12.

501 'notorious Quisling', Aung San: Thant Myint-U, *The River of Lost Footsteps: Histories of Burma*, London: Faber and Faber, 2006, p. 239.

502 'representative council': Bayly and Harper, *Forgotten Wars*, p. 65.

508 'unknown' persons: Ibid., p. 313. The quotations in this paragraph comprise terms used by Rance in his report to London. Thant Myint-U (2006) says that it became clear after the assassination that the arms had been released to U Saw's men.

510 'White Paper of May 1945': The quotations in this paragraph are taken from Hansard. millbanksystems.com, 'Burma Independence Bill', 5 November 1947 <http://hansard. millbanksystems.com/commons/1947/nov/05/burma-independence-bill> [accessed 19 April 2017]

512 'You'll be the Lenin of Burma': Thant Myint-U, *River of Lost Footsteps*, p. 268.

512 'there is a persistent myth': Ibid., pp. 269–270.

513-4   grow his business empire: Phin's son, Chatichai Choonhavan, inherited his father's business and political empire, and became prime minister of Thailand in the late 1980s, until ironically being ousted in a military coup in 1991.

517 '...there is no denying that': Mahathir Mohamad and Shintaro Ishihara, *The Voice of Asia: Two Leaders Discuss the Coming Century*, Tokyo: Kodansha, 1995, p. 17.

517 'In the Pacific War the Japanese': Ibid., pp. 122–123.

518 but Boestamam always insisted: Bayly and Harper, *Forgotten Wars*, p. 195.

518 British Governor General and Supreme Commander of SEAC were based: SEAC was headquartered in Kandy until September 1945, when Mountbatten moved to Singapore after the formal Japanese surrender there.

519 while staying atop the Communist Party of Malaya: Confusingly, the party's acronym was either MCP (Malayan Communist Party) or CPM (Communist Party of Malaya), with the two names/acronyms used interchangeably, as I have done in this paragraph to reflect the gradual transition to the use of CPM.

521 'being swept into Indonesian': Bayly and Harper, *Forgotten Wars*, p. 216.

522 'willing to change their bangsa to bangsa Melayu': The phrase meant 'changing your nation to the Melayu (or Malayan) nation' by severing ties to other nations

(like China, India or Indonesia). 'Bangsa' means 'nation' in Malay, although it can also be translated as 'race'. It was clear that 'bangsa' here meant 'nation', because 'bangsa Melayu' was translated explicitly into English as 'Melayu nation' (the word order in Malay is the opposite of English).

524 **Chinese towkay peers:** Towkay is a Hokkien word meaning 'boss' that colloquially refers to prominent businessmen in Malaya (Singapore and today's Malaysia).

525 **'one could go a whole year':** Keay, *Empire's End*, p. 307.

527 **The majority Chinese and the smaller Indian community were left to fend for themselves:** Much is made of the fact that Japanese was made compulsory in Korea, but that was no different to English-only instruction in Singapore and the Philippines, and Korean was soon introduced as a parallel stream of education in Japanese-ruled Korea, unlike in Singapore and the Philippines, where the majority-language was ignored by the colonizing power.

529 **'75 per cent self-government':** Lee Kuan Yew, *The Singapore Story: Memoirs of Lee Kuan Yew*, Singapore: Singapore Press Holdings (Times Editions), 1998, p. 230.

530 **'promoted stenographer':** Ibid., p. 240.

530 **the 'idea that Chinese capitalists':** Nilanjana Sengupta, *A Gentleman's Word: The Legacy of Subhas Chandra Bose in Southeast Asia*, Singapore: ISEAS Publishing, 2012, p. 186.

532 **'an independent, democratic, non-communist':** Lee Kuan Yew, *Singapore Story*, p. 269.

535 **Partai Rakyat:** This was the new socialist party that Ahmad Boestamam established after his release from prison in 1955. It never gained much electoral traction, as Boestamam's eight-year incarceration had provided ample room for UMNO and its Alliance to deepen their electoral stranglehold with tacit British support.

538 **'Maha Esa' being the term used:** 'Maha Esa' translates as 'Almighty', and has the advantage of being neutral amongst religions—close enough to the Hindu Iswar and the Christian Isa for Christ.

540 **'between a territorially united Indonesia':** Theodore Friend, *Indonesian Destinies*, Cambridge, MA: Belknap (Harvard University Press), 2003, p. 61.

541 **'personal option of rebellious character':** Ibid., pp. 62–63.

543 **Suharto's KOSTRAD:** KOSTRAD is the Indonesian army's Strategic Reserve Command, which was established in March 1961 to spearhead the takeover of West New Guinea, with Suharto as KOSTRAD's first commander. It was to play a vital strategic role in many key events in Indonesia's history over the subsequent half-century.

546 **Cakrabirawa presidential guard:** Sukarno named his presidential guard Cakrabirawa/ Tjakrabirawa after 'Prabu Kresna's' (Lord Krishna's) secret weapon from Javanese wayang mythology based on the Mahabharata: he was either referring to 'chakravyuh' (the elaborately layered defensive formation), or Lord Krishna's Sudarshan Chakra (discus).

547 **'Yani's inner circle':** Peter Dale Scott, 'The United States and the Overthrow of Sukarno', *Pacific Affairs*, vol. 58, 1985.

550 **Ibnu Sutowo's oil firm, Permina:** Permina was founded by the military in 1957 after the nationalization of remaining Dutch oil assets, and Ibnu Sutowo was appointed its first chief. He remained in that role until 1966, when he became Suharto's first minister of mines, oil and natural gas—and remained in charge of Permina and its successor as national oil company, Pertamina, until 1976, when Pertamina collapsed under the weight of its mounting debts, which amounted to US$10.5 billion at the

time.

556 'the common people... feel': Spence, *Search for Modern China,* p. 495.

558 Stalin's hostage in Moscow for more than a decade: Ching-kuo was sent to study in Moscow, but Stalin never let him return, holding him as a kind of hostage he could use to pressurize Chiang Kai-shek. Ching-kuo married a Russian woman during this time.

562 'leaning to one side': Spence, *Search for Modern China,* p. 524.

563 'Liberation from whom and what?': Ibid., p. 525.

564 'Tibet will remain independent': This statement by Tibet's finance minister and head of delegation Tsepon W. D. Shakabpa is quoted in Melvin C. Goldstein, *A History of Modern Tibet: The Calm Before the Storm, 1951–55*, vol. 2, Berkeley: University of California Press, 2009, p. 46.

565 The Chinese government have tried: Ajay B. Agrawal, *India, Tibet & China: The Role Nehru Played*, Mumbai: NA Books International, 2003, p. 20.

566 'teaching India a lesson': Zhou Enlai is widely reported to have used these words, which are attributed to him by, for instance: Brahma Chellaney, 'How China Fights: Lessons from the 1962 Sino-Indian War', *Newsweek*, 29 October 2012.

585 'The legacies of 50 years: Robert Wade, *Governing the Market: Economic Theory and the Role of Government in East Asian Industrialization*, Princeton: Princeton University Press, 1990, p. 75.

588 'import restrictions, sectoral allocation': Ibid., pp. 191–192.

597 'The case of the Meiji imperial': Alice H. Amsden, p. 52, quoting from Park Chung-hee, *The Country, the Revolution and I*, translated by I. Sinder, Seoul: Hollym Corporation, 1963, pp. 120–121.

598 18 per cent and 22 per cent of the population: Ibid., p. 217.

598 Korea had 22 engineers: Ibid., p. 218.

598 Starting from a high base: Ibid., p. 222.

599 Korea also emulated Meiji-era Japan's: Ibid, p. 227.

599 '36 years of hardship': Ibid., p. 295, quoting a POSCO company document from 1984.

599 the 'Japan Group, in the name': Ibid.

605 'when the state fails to provide': Narendra Modi's speech in the Lok Sabha, 11 June 2014.

EPILOGUE

611 Port Arthur (Lushun): It was known as Port Arthur (especially internationally) until 1953, when China's sovereignty was restored—and its Chinese name Lushun became prevalent. During Japanese rule, it was known as Ryojun, but the rest of the world still called it Port Arthur (including in the Yalta documents).

611 The INA's 'Chalo Delhi' marching song: Chalo Dilli pukar ke / qaumi-nisham sambhal ke / Lal Qile pe gaarh ke / lehrae ja lehrae ja (composed by the Gurkha bandmaster, Captain Ram Singh Thakuri of the Azad Hind Fauj).

613 New York's Plaza Hotel: The fabled Plaza Hotel is owned (as of early 2017) by India's Sahara group, but amongst its previous owners was Donald Trump (whose second wedding, and the only one to a non-immigrant American, was solemnized there) and Singapore's CDL Hotels.

614 her November 1992 book argued: The book was titled *Who's Bashing Whom? Trade Conflict in High-Technology Industries.*

614   high-technology industries: Such as semiconductors, high-definition TV, and aircraft.

614   an extra tool in the strategic sectors: Thus Korea and Taiwan had POSCO and China Steel respectively, like Japan Steel in the early twentieth century.

614   'the model for its counterparts': Wade, *Governing the Market*, p. 326.

615   received a new setback: Rice output fell to a low of less than 10 million tonnes by 1979, before a liberalization of Vietnam's agriculture began in 1981. Output then rebounded to 15.1 million tonnes in 1987 and more than doubled to 32.5 million tonnes by 2000 as Vietnam once again became a major rice exporter.

616   IDB then selected the industries: Wade, *Governing the Market*, p. 202.

616   Taiwan's IDB thus almost exactly: Ibid., p. 203. In 1979, when the second OPEC oil crisis caused a surge in oil prices, and there was a dispute between downstream and upstream petrochemical producers over imports, the IDB played a vital role in adjudicating the dispute, and obtaining the result that it felt best suited Taiwan's long-term interests.

616   producing on an OEM/ODM basis: OEM stands for original equipment manufacturer, which manufactures products based on the client's design and specifications. An ODM (original design manufacturer) designs and fabricates the product based on the client's ideas and specifications.

617   the third largest PC manufacturer: Acer couldn't hold on to third place, but it remained amongst the world's top six for the next fifteen years, while many other rivals fell by the wayside, including two big American ones that Acer acquired, Packard-Bell and Gateway.

617 224 specialized semiconductor makers: Including 115 in IC design, 5 IC mask makers, 3 wafer manufacturers, 6 IC chemicals makers, 20 IC fabrication plants, 30 IC testing plants, 36 IC packagers, and 9 lead frame manufacturers.

617   Kim Woo-choong of Daewoo: Daewoo repeatedly had to be rescued by the state after becoming overleveraged. But in the end, it was the only one of the 'big 5' chaebols that actually went bankrupt in 1997-98 (and this time wasn't rescued by Park's old political opponent, Kim Dae-jung).

617-8   The chaebol developed an esprit de corps: The role of highly educated engineer-managers in developing corporate loyalty is described in Amsden, *Asia's Next Giant*, Chapters 7 and 9.

618   LG a leading consumer electronics brand: LG is the world's second-largest TV manufacturer, just behind Samsung. In 1996, Daewoo was the world's largest TV maker.

618   Mancur Olson's work on collective action: Mancur Olson, *The Rise and Decline of Nations: Economic Growth, Stagflation and Social Rigidities*, New Haven: Yale University Press, 1982, Chapters 2 and 3.

618   As Korea expert Bruce Cumings showed: Bruce Cumings, *The Korean War: A History*, New York: Modern Library (Random House), 2010, pp. 104-106.

618   Taiwan and Korea as dictatorships: Wade, *Governing the Market*, pp. 337–342.

618   establishment of the national oil company: Both Petronas and PNB were spearheaded by Tengku Razaleigh when he was finance minister in the 1970s.

619   'Asian values' of filial piety: These were the values that animated Japan's Greater East Asia Co-Prosperity Sphere.

620   Guthrie: The successful dawn raid on Guthrie was launched on 7 September 1981, just a few months after Mahathir became prime minister. It marked him out for particularly harsh treatment in the British press ever afterwards.

621   'As early as the Meiji restoration': Hobsbawm, *Age of Extremes*, p. 461.

623 **asset management companies:** E.g. KAMCO in Korea, Danaharta in Malaysia and IBRA in Indonesia.

623 **the latter estimated that China's:** Phelim Kyne, 'S&P Says Chinese Banks Need Bailout Estimated at $500 Billion', *Wall Street Journal*, 23 June 2003 <https://www.wsj.com/articles/SB105639308053775200> [accessed 28 April 2017]

623 **after 2001:** i.e., following the dot-com related technology boom, which was followed by China's accession to the WTO in 2001.

624 **China's M2 money supply:** M2 is a broad measure of money supply that is commonly used around the world: it comprises notes and coins in circulation, demand and time deposits of banks and other financial institutions.

624 **attitude towards women remained ossified:** The plight of Crown Princess Michiko epitomized what Japanese women faced. A high-flying international trade negotiator, Michiko was obliged to do little else but focus on producing a male heir once she married the Crown Prince.

624 **dismal literacy rate of 14 per cent:** Will Durant interrupted the writing of his magisterial *The Story of Civilization* to write a brief but searing book called *The Case for India*, which he published in October 1930. He was moved to do so, he said, because 'I have seen a great people starving to death before my eyes... due... to the most sordid and criminal exploitation of one people by another in all recorded history.' Shashi Tharoor's *An Era of Darkness* (Aleph, 2016) provides a brilliant update of Durant's critique of Britain's role in India.

625 **launching the Iran-Iraq War:** Saddam was, of course, egged on by the US, especially once the Reagan administration was in place.

625 **the 'New Saladin':** That great warrior hero was also born in Tikrit, like Saddam, albeit of Kurdish rather than Arab heritage.

626 **politicians' desire to normalize relations:** Nawaz Sharif has publicly advocated normalization of relations with India since the 1996 election, which he fought primarily on that plank. Sharif won in a landslide that year, but the promising Lahore Declaration of February 1999 (when Vajpayee and Sharif established a bond) was upended by the Kargil invasion led by General Pervez Musharraf two months later. Similarly, the bonhomie established by Modi visiting Sharif on his birthday in 2015 was followed a few days later by the ISI-sponsored terrorist attack on Pathankot in India.

627 **160 of Pakistan's 300 parliamentary seats:** Mujib's Awami League won 39.2 per cent of the national vote, while Bhutto's PPP won 18.6 per cent.

627 **Language Movement of 1952:** This eventually led to the commemoration of 21 February as International Mother Language Day by the UN.

627 **crescendo with Operation Searchlight:** 'Operation Searchlight' <http://en.banglapedia.org/index.php?title=Operation_Searchlight> [accessed 27 April 2017]

628 **explicit support of Nixon and Kissinger:** Princeton.edu, 'The Blood Telegram: Nixon, Kissinger, and a Forgotten Genocide', 2013 <http://wws.princeton.edu/faculty-research/research/item/blood-telegram-nixon-kissinger-and-forgotten-genocide> [accessed 20 June 2017]

628 **apart from two daughters:** The two daughters, Hasina and Rehana, were in Germany at the time. Hasina is now prime minister of Bangladesh, and Rehana's daughter Tulip Siddiq was elected the (Labour) MP for Hampstead and Kilburn in the 2015 UK general election.

629 **alienating the Tamils:** Nehru agreed to 'repatriate' the Tamil plantation workers (who were 12 per cent of the population and had been in Ceylon for three to four generations) to Tamil Nadu (where they no longer had any real links). This reduced

the Tamil population to 27 per cent (about a third of them 'Moors'). The family of movie icon and Tamil Nadu chief minister M. G. Ramachandran was from Kandy, where he was born.

629 **inspired by Subhas Bose:** 'Prabhakaran', 21 May 2009, *Economist* <http://www.economist.com/node/13687889> [accessed 27 April 2017]

630 **Gulf protectorates:** The British protectorates included Kuwait, Aden, Qatar, Bahrain, Abu Dhabi, Dubai and the smaller Emirates of Eastern Arabia, plus ally Oman.

630 **deal with the US that created Saudi ARAMCO:** Led primarily by Standard Oil of California.

630 **southern Muslim cone of the USSR:** The Soviets referred to their southern flank as a Muslim Cone, although 'Southern Cone' usually refers to a region in Latin America.

631 **inability to miniaturize the transistor chip:** The key technological failing that undid the Soviet Union is now recognized to have been their inability to miniaturize—while the Soviets remained quite effective at large construction works. Miniaturizing the transistor enabled the US to produce semiconductors of increasing sophistication (and decreasing size), ultimately undermining the Soviets technologically.

631 **wealthy Yemeni student Osama bin Laden:** Osama's father Mohammad, a close friend of Saudi king Faisal, had made a fortune through contracts to expand the mosques and other complexes of the holy cities of Mecca and Medina.

631 **'the first Islamic international brigade':** Ahmed Rashid, *Taliban: Militant Islam, Oil and Fundamentalism in Central Asia*, New Haven: Yale University Press, 2000, p. 129.

631 **the US finally 'got him':** President Barack Obama said, 'We got him', as he watched the events unfold live from the White House Situation Room.

632 **as real GDP growth averaged 6.5 per cent in 1977-79:** April 1977 to March 1979 (two fiscal years; Charan Singh became finance minister in February 1979, just as Khomeini was taking power in Iran). This was India's best two-year economic performance until that point, surpassing the 6 per cent growth during Indira's Emergency period. In the Charan Singh-led financial year 1979–80, India had its worst year of economic performance, with real GDP contracting 5 per cent while inflation soared. Indira thus won a landslide in that year's general election.

632 **all 'invisible' services:** Including BPO, or business process outsourcing, and remittances from overseas Indians.

632 **exports of goods expanded:** Goods exports were led by engineering goods, gems and jewellery, textiles, pharmaceuticals, refined oil and vehicles.

633 **still attracting more FDI:** But the FDI commitments to Modi's India were truly spectacular. *The Financial Times*' FDI magazine, which compiles authoritative figures on global FDI flows, reported that India received the largest FDI commitments of any single country worldwide in 2015 and 2016. In fact, India had never ranked amongst the top 5 before 2014. India had thus displaced long-time leaders: the US and China.

BIBLIOGRAPHY

Abreu, Marcelo de Paiva, *Britain as a Debtor: Indian Sterling Balances, 1940–53, The Economic History Review*, 31 July 2016.

Acemoglu, Daron and Robinson, James, *Why Nations Fail: The Origins of Power, Prosperity and Poverty*, Crown Business (Random House), New York, 2012.

Agrawal, Ajay B., *India Tibet & China: The Role Nehru Played*, NA Books International, Mumbai, 2003.

Ahmad, Riaz, *Muslim Punjab's Fight for Pakistan: League's Agitation against the Coalition Ministry of Sir Khizr Hayat Khan Tiwana, January-March 1947*, Pakistan Journal of History and Culture (Vol. XXVIII, No. 1), Islamabad, 2007.

Ahmed, Akbar S., *Jinnah, Pakistan and Islamic Identity: The Search for Saladin*, Routledge, London, 1997.

Akbar, M. J., *Nehru: The Making of India*, Viking, London, 1988.

_____, *India: The Siege Within, Challenges to a Nation's Unity*, Penguin, Harmondsworth (Middlesex), 1985.

_____, *The Shade of Swords: Jihad and the Conflict between Islam and Christianity*, Routledge, London, 2002.

_____ *Tinderbox: The Past and Future of Pakistan,* Harper Collins, New Delhi, 2011.

Albinia, Alice, *Empires of the Indus: The Story of a River*, John Murray, London, 2008.

Amsden, Alice H., *Asia's Next Giant: South Korea and Late Industrialization*, OUP, New York, 1989.

_____, *The Rise of "The Rest": Challenges to the West from Late-Industrializing Economies*, OUP, New York/Oxford, 2001.

_____, *Escape from Empire: The Developing World's Journey through Heaven and Hell*, The MIT Press, Cambridge (MA), 2007.

Anderson, Benedict, *Petrus Dadi Ratu*, New Left Review 3, May-June 2000.

_____ and Ruth McVey, *What happened in Indonesia?*, New York Review of Books, 1 June 1978.

Armstrong, Karen, *Islam: A Short History*, Phoenix Press (Orion Publishing), London, 2000.

Arjomand, Said Amir, *The Turban for the Crown: The Islamic Revolution in Iran*, Oxford University Press, New York, 1988.

Azad, Maulana Abul Kalam, *India Wins Freedom: the Complete Version*, Orient Longman, Hyderabad/New Delhi, 1988.

Baechler, Jean, Hall, John A. & Mann, Michael (eds.), *Europe and the Rise of Capitalism*, Basil Blackwell, Oxford, 1989.

Badrinath, Chaturvedi, *Swami Vivekananda: the Living Vedanta*, Penguin, New Delhi, 2006.

Baker, Nicholson, *Human Smoke: The Beginnings of World War II, the End of Civilization*, Simon & Schuster, London, 2008.

Banglapedia, *National Encyclopedia of Bangladesh*, en.banglapedia.org.

Baru, Sanjaya, *The Accidental Prime Minister of India: The Making and Unmaking of Manmohan Singh*, Penguin India, New Delhi, 2014.

Basu, Prasenjit K., Chellaney, Brahma, Khilnani, Sunil and Khanna, Parag, *India as a New Global Leader*, Foreign Policy Centre, London, 2005.

Bayly, Christopher and Harper, Tim, *Forgotten Wars: The End of Britain's Asian Empire*,

Allen Lane, London, 2007.

_____, *Forgotten Armies: Britain's Asian Empire and the War with Japan*, Penguin, London, 2004.

Beasley, W. G., *The Rise of Modern Japan: Political, Economic and Social Change since 1850* (3rd edition), Phoenix, London, 2000.

Bose, Mihir, *The Lost Hero: A Biography of Subhas Bose*, Blue Leaf, New Delhi, 2004 (first published by Quartet Books, London, 1982).

Bose, Subhas Chandra, *The Indian Struggle 1920-1942* (eds. Sisir K. Bose and Sugata Bose), Oxford University Press, Oxford, 1997.

Bose, Sugata, *His Majesty's Opponent: Subhas Chandra Bose and India's Struggle against Empire*, Belknap (HUP), Cambridge (MA), 2011.

_____, *A Hundred Horizons: The Indian Ocean in the Age of Global Empire*, Harvard University Press, Cambridge, 2006.

Brown, Colin, *A Short History of Indonesia: The Unlikely Nation?* Allen & Unwin, Crows Nest (NSW), 2003.

Catherwood, Christopher, *Churchill's Folly: How Winston Churchill Created Modern Iraq*, Carroll & Graf Publishers, New York, 2004.

Chang, Jung and Halliday, Jon, *Mao: The Unknown Story*, Jonathan Cape, London, 2005.

Chua, Amy, *World on Fire: How Exporting Free Market Democracy Breeds Ethnic Hatred and Global Instability*, Anchor Books (Random House), New York, 2004.

Clapham, Christopher, *Third World Politics: An Introduction*, The University of Wisconsin Press, Madison, 1985.

Coedes, George, *The Making of South East Asia*, University of California Press, Berkeley and Los Angeles, 1966.

Cumings, Bruce, *The Korean War: A History*, Modern Library (Random House), New York, 2010.

Dalrymple, William, *The Last Mughal: The Fall of a Dynasty, Delhi 1857*, Viking (Penguin), New Delhi, 2006.

Das, Gurcharan, *India Grows at Night: A Liberal Case for a Strong State*, Allen Lane, New Delhi, 2012.

_____, *India Unbound*, Viking (Penguin India), New Delhi, 2000.

Dasgupta, Subrata, *Awakening: The Story of the Bengal Renaissance*, Random House India, Noida, 2011.

Datta-Ray, Sunanda K., *Looking East to Look West: Lee Kuan Yew's Mission India*, Viking (Penguin) ISEAS, New Delhi / Singapore, 2009.

David, Saul, *The Indian Mutiny: 1857*, Penguin, London, 2003.

Davis, Mike, *Late Victorian Holocausts: El Nino Famines and the Making of the Third World*, Verso (formerly New Left) Books, London, 2000.

Dayal, Ravi (ed.), *We Fought Together for Freedom: Chapters from the Indian National Movement*, OUP, New Delhi, 1998.

Dhar, Anuj, *What Happened to Netaji?*, Vitasta Publishing, New Delhi, 2015.

Dower, John, *Embracing Defeat: Japan in the Aftermath of World War II*, Penguin, London, 1999.

Duara, Prasenjit, *The Global and Regional in China's Nation-Formation*, Routledge, London, 2009.

Eaton, Richard M., *The Rise of Islam and the Bengal Frontier: 1204-1760*, University of California Press, Berkeley, 1993.

Editors and writers, *The Economist* (all weekly editions, including Special Reports), London, 1988–2016.

Elegant, Robert, *Pacific Destiny: Inside Asia Today*, Avon Books, New York, 1990.

Embree, Ainslie T. (ed.), *Alberuni's India* (abridged edition, trans. Sachau, Edward C.), W. W. Norton & Co, New York, 1971.

Enright, Michael J., Scott, Edith E. and Chang, Ka-mun, *Regional Powerhouse: The Greater Pearl River Delta and the Rise of China*, John Wiley & Sons, Singapore, 2005.

Evans, Peter B., *Embedded Autonomy: States and Industrial Transformation*, Princeton University Press, Princeton (NJ), 1995.

Evans, Richard, *Deng Xiaoping and the Making of Modern China*, Penguin, London, 1995.

Fairbank, John King and Goodman, Merle, *China: A New History* (Second Enlarged edition), Belknap, Cambridge (MA), 2006.

Fay, Peter Ward, *The Forgotten Army: India's Armed Struggle for Independence, 1942–45*, University of Michigan Press, Ann Arbor, 1993.

Fenby, Jonathan, *The Penguin History of Modern China: The Fall and Rise of a Great Power 1850–2008*, Allen Lane, London, 2008.

Ferguson, Niall, *Colossus: The Rise and Fall of the American Empire*, Penguin, London, 2004.

_____, *Empire: How Britain Made the Modern World*, Penguin, London, 2003.

Fernandez-Armesto, Felipe, *Millennium: A History of the Last Thousand Years*, Scribner, New York, 1995.

Frank, Katherine, *Indira: The Life of Indira Nehru Gandhi*, HarperCollins, London, 2001.

Frankel, Francine, *India's Political Economy 1947–2004: The Gradual Revolution* (Second edition), OUP, New Delhi, 2005.

French, Patrick, *Liberty or Death: India's Journey to Independence and Division*, Flamingo (HarperCollins), London, 1997.

_____, *India: A Portrait*, Penguin, New Delhi, 2014.

Friend, Theodore, *Indonesian Destinies*, Belknap (HUP), Cambridge (MA), 2003.

Fukuyama, Francis, *Trust: The Social Virtues and the Creation of Prosperity*, Free Press Paperbacks, New York, 1996.

_____, *The Origins of Political Order: From Prehuman Times to the French Revolution*, Profile Books, London, 2011.

Galbraith, John Kenneth, *A Journey through Economic Time: A Firsthand View*, Houghton Miflin, New York, 1994.

_____, *The World Economy Since The Wars: A Personal View*, Mandarin Books, London, 1995.

Gall, Carlotta, *The Wrong Enemy: America in Afghanistan 2001–2014*, Penguin India, Gurgaon, 2014.

Gandhi, Rajmohan, *Understanding the Muslim Mind*, Penguin, New Delhi, 1987.

_____, *A Tale of Two Revolts: India 1857 and the American Civil War*, Penguin (Viking), New Delhi, 2009.

Ghosh, Amitav, *River of Smoke,* John Murray, London, 2011.

_____, *Sea of Poppies,* John Murray, London, 2008.

_____, *The Glass Palace,* Harper Collins, London, 2000.

Gilpin, Robert, *Global Political Economy: Understanding the International Economic Order*, Princeton University Press, Princeton, 2001.

Godement, François (trans. Parcell, Elisabeth J.), *The New Asian Renaissance: from Colonialism to Post-Cold War,* Routledge, London, 1997.

Gomez, Edmund Terence, and K. S., Jomo., *Malaysia's Political Economy: Politics, Patronage and Profits*, CUP, Cambridge, 1997.

Gowda, M. V. Rajeev and Sridharan, Eswaran, *Reforming India's Party Financing and*

Election Expenditure Laws, Election Law Journal, Vol. 11, No. 2, 2012.

Haggard, Stephan, *Pathways from the Periphery: The Politics of Growth in the Newly Industrializing Countries*, Cornell University Press, Ithaca, 1990.

Hajari, Nisid, *Midnight's Furies: The Deadly Legacy of India's Partition*, Houghton Mifflin Harcourt, New York, 2015.

Halberstam, David, *The Best and the Brightest* (20th anniversary edition), Ballantine Books (Random House), New York, 1992.

Herman, Arthur, *Gandhi & Churchill: The Epic Rivalry that Destroyed an Empire and Forged our Age*, Arrow Books, London, 2009.

Hobsbawm, Eric J., *Industry and Empire (The Pelican Economic History of Britain, Vol. 3)*, Penguin, London, 1969.

_____, *The Age of Empire: 1875-1914*, Weidenfeld & Nicholson, London, 1987.

_____, *The Age of Extremes: A History of the World 1914-1991*, Vintage Books (Random House), New York, 1995.

Hourani, Albert, *A History of the Arab Peoples*, Belknap (Harvard University Press), Cambridge (MA), 1991.

Howard, Michael and Wm. Roger Louis, *The Oxford History of the Twentieth Century*, OUP, Oxford, 1998.

Huang, Yasheng, *Capitalism with Chinese Characteristics: Entrepreneurship and the State*, Cambridge University Press, New York, 2008.

Huntington, Samuel P., *The Clash of Civilizations and the Remaking of World Order*, Simon and Schuster, New York, 1996.

Hutton, Will, *The Writing on the Wall: China and the West in the 21st Century*, Abacus, London, 2008.

Jenner, W. J. F., *The Tyranny of History: The Roots of China's Crisis*, Allen Lane, London, 1992.

Johnson, Chalmers, *MITI and the Japanese Miracle: The Growth of Industrial Policy, 1925-1975*, Stanford University Press, Stanford (CA), 1982.

_____, *Japan: Who Governs? The Rise of the Developmental State*, W. W. Norton, New York/London, 1995.

Jomo, Kwame Sundaram and Hui, Wee Chong, *Malaysia @ 50: Economic Development, Distribution, Disparities*, Strategic Information and Research Development Centre, Petaling Jaya, 2014.

Keay, John, *Empire's End: A History of the Far East from High Colonialism to Hong Kong*, Scribner, New York, 1997.

_____, *The Honourable Company: A History of the English East India Company*, Harper Collins, London, 1991.

_____, *India: A History*, Atlantic Monthly Press, New York, 2000.

_____, *Sowing the Wind: The Seeds of Conflict in the Middle East*, John Murray, London, 2003.

Kennedy, Paul, *The Rise and Fall of the Great Powers: Economic Change and Military Conflict from 1500 to 2000*, Random House, New York, 1987.

Kindleberger, Charles P., *Manias, Panics and Crashes: A History of Financial Crises* (3rd edition), Wiley, New York, 1999.

_____, *World Economic Primacy: 1500-1990*, Oxford University Press, New York, 1996.

_____, *The World in Depression, 1929-1939*, University of California Press, Berkeley, 1973.

Kinross, Lord Patrick, *Atatürk: The Rebirth of a Nation*, Phoenix Books, London, 1995.

Kinzer, Stephen, *All the Shah's Men: An American Coup and the Roots of Middle East Terror*, Wiley, Hoboken (NJ), 2003.

_____, *Reset: Iran, Turkey, and America's Future*, St. Martin's Griffin, New York, 2010 (Afterword 2011).

Kissinger, Henry A., *Diplomacy*, Simon and Schuster, New York, 1994.

_____, *On China*, Penguin, New York, 2012.

Koo, Richard, *Balance Sheet Recession: Japan's Struggle with Uncharted Economics and its Global Implications*, Wiley, Singapore, 2003.

Kotter, John P., *Matsushita Leadership: Lessons from the 20th Century's Most Remarkable Entrepreneur*, The Free Press, New York, 1997.

Krugman, Paul, *The Return of Depression Economics*, Penguin, London, 1999.

_____, *The Age of Diminished Expectations: US Economic Policy in the 1990s*, The MIT Press, Cambridge (MA), 1992.

Kwarteng, Kwasi, *Ghosts of Empire: Britain's Legacies in the Modern World*, Bloomsbury, London, 2011.

_____, *War and Gold: A Five-Hundred-Year History of Empires, Adventures and Debt*, Bloomsbury, London, 2014.

Landes, David S., *The Wealth and Poverty of Nations: Why Some Are So Rich And Some So Poor*, Little Brown & Co., London, 1998.

Lawrence, Robert Z., *Can America Compete?* The Brookings Institution, Washington DC, 1984.

Lee Kuan Yew, *The Singapore Story: Memoirs of Lee Kuan Yew*, Singapore Press Holdings (Times Editions), Singapore, 1998.

_____, *From Third World to First: The Singapore Story: 1965–2000*, Singapore Press Holdings (Times Editions), Singapore, 2000.

Lenin, V. I., *Imperialism: The Highest Stage of Capitalism*, Resistance Books, Sydney, 1999.

Lewis, W. Arthur, *Development with Unlimited Supplies of Labour*, The Manchester School, Vol. 22, Issue 2. 1954.

Louis, William Roger, *Ends of British Imperialism: The Scramble for Empire, Suez and Decolonization*, I. B. Tauris, London, 2006.

Macintyre, Andrew (ed.), *Business and Government in Industrializing Asia*, Cornell, Ithaca, 1994.

MacMillan, Margaret, *Paris 1919: Six Months that Changed the World*, Random House, New York, 2001.

Maddison, Angus, *The World Economy: A Millennial Perspective*, Development Centre of the OECD, Paris, 2001.

Magaziner, Ira and Patinkin, Mark, *The Silent War: Inside the Global Business Battles Shaping America's Future*, Random House, New York, 1989.

Mahbubani, Kishore, *Can Asians Think?*, Times Books International, Singapore, 1998.

Martin, Brian, *Justice Ignited*, Rowman & Littlefield, Lanham, 2006.

Martinez-Diaz, Leonardo, *Globalizing in Hard Times: The Politics of Banking-Sector Opening in the Emerging World*, Cornell University Press, Ithaca, 2009.

Marx, Karl (with Engels, Friedrich), *Selected Writings (Communist Manifesto, Wages Price and Profit, Capital, Socialism: Utopian and Scientific)*, CRW Publishing Ltd., London, 2004.

Masani, Zareer, *Macaulay: Pioneer of India's Modernization*, Random House India, Noida, 2012.

McGregor, Richard, *The Party: The Secret World of China's Communist Party*, Harper, New York, 2012.

Meyer, Karl E. and Brysac, Shareen, *Tournament of Shadows: The Great Game and the Race for Empire in Asia*, Little, Brown & Company, London, 1999.

Meyer, Karl E., *The Dust of Empires: The Race for Mastery in the Asian Heartland*, Century Foundation (Public Affairs), New York, 2003.

Mishra, Pankaj, *From the Ruins of Empire: The Revolt against the West and the Remaking of Asia*, Allen Lane, London, 2012.

Mikuni, Akio and Murphy, R. Taggart, *Japan's Policy Trap: Dollars, Deflation, and the Crisis of Japanese Finance*, Brookings Institution Press, Washington (DC), 2002.

Miller, Stuart Creighton, *Benevolent Assimilation: The American Conquest of the Philippines*, Yale University Press, New Haven, 1982.

Mitter, Rana, *A Bitter Revolution: China's Struggle with the Modern World*, OUP, Oxford, 2004.

Mohamad, Mahathir bin, *The Malay Dilemma*, Times Books International, Singapore, 1970.

_____, *A New Deal for Asia*, Pelanduk Publishing, Subang Jaya (Selangor, Malaysia), 1999.

_____ and Ishihara, Shintaro, *The Voice Of Asia: Two Leaders Discuss the Coming Century*, Kodansha, Tokyo, 1995.

Morgan, David, *The Mongols*, Basil Blackwell, Cambridge (MA), 1987.

Morris, Ian, *Why the West Rules—For Now: The Patterns of History and What They Reveal about the Future*, Profile Books, London, 2010.

Moynihan, Daniel Patrick, *Pandaemonium: Ethnicity in International Politics*, OUP, New York, 1993.

Mukherjee, Madhusree, *Churchill's Secret War: The British Empire and the Ravaging of India During World War II*, Tranquebar, New Delhi (first published by Basic Books, NY), 2010.

Myint-U, Thant, *The River of Lost Footsteps: Histories of Burma*, Faber and Faber, London, 2006

_____, *Where China Meets India: Burma and the New Crossroads of Asia*, Faber & Faber, London, 2011.

Nandy, Ashis, *Return from Exile: Alternative Sciences, Illegitimacy of Nationalism, The Savage Freud*, OUP, Delhi, 1998.

Nehru, Jawaharlal, *Glimpses of World History*, Kitabistan, Allahabad, 1934 (republished by the Jawaharlal Nehru Memorial Fund and Oxford University Press, 2002).

Noland, Marcus, *Pacific Basin Developing Countries: Prospects for the Future*, Institute for International Economics, Washington (DC), 1990.

_____ and Pack, Howard, *Industrial Policy in an Era of Globalization: Lessons from Asia*, Institute for International Economics, Washington (DC), 2003.

North, Douglass C., *Structure and Change in Economic History*, W. W. Norton & Co, New York, 1981.

Olson, Mancur, *The Rise and Decline of Nations: Economic Growth, Stagflation, and Social Rigidities*, Yale University Press, New Haven, 1982.

_____, *Power and Prosperity: Outgrowing Communist and Capitalist Dictatorships*, Basic Books, New York, 2000.

Phillips, Kevin, *American Dynasty: Aristocracy, Fortune and the Politics of Deceit in the House of Bush*, Penguin, London, 2004.

Pilling, David, *Bending Adversity: Japan and the Art of Survival*, Penguin, New York, 2014.

Prasad, Rajendra, *India Divided*, Penguin, New Delhi, 2010 (first published, 1946).

Priestley, H. E., *The Awakening World (Book 1: The Vision of Freedom, 1750-1815)*,

Frederick Muller, London, 1966.

Pringle, Robert, *Understanding Islam in Indonesia: Politics and Diversity*, Editions Didier Millet, Singapore, 2010.

Rai, Vinod, *Not Just an Accountant: The Diary of the Nation's Conscience Keeper*, Rupa, New Delhi, 2014.

Rajan, Raghuram, *Fault Lines: How Hidden Fractures Still Threaten the World Economy*, Princeton University Press, Princeton, 2010.

_____ and Zingales, Luigi, *Saving Capitalism from the Capitalists: Unleashing the Power of Financial Markets to Create Wealth and Spread Opportunity*, Crown Business, New York, 2003.

Rashid, Ahmed, *Taliban: Militant Islam, Oil & Fundamentalism in Central Asia*, Yale University Press, New Haven, 2000.

Read, Anthony and Fisher, David, *The Proudest Day: India's Long Road to Independence*, W. W. Norton & Co., New York, 1998.

Riddle, Peter, *Islam and the Malay-Indonesian World: Transmission and Responses*, Horizon Books, Singapore 2001.

Roberts, J. M., *The Penguin History of the Twentieth Century: The History of the World, 1901 to the Present*, Penguin, London 1999.

Rodrik, Dani (ed.), *In Search of Prosperity: Analytic Narratives on Economic Growth*, Princeton University Press, Princeton (NJ), 2003.

Rodrik, Dani, *The Globalization Paradox: Democracy and the Future of the World Economy*, W. W. Norton & Co., New York, 2011.

Rohwer, Jim, *Asia Rising: How History's Biggest Middle Class will Change the World*, Butterworth-Heinemann Asia, Singapore, 1995.

Samuels, Richard J., *Kishi and Corruption: An Anatomy of the 1955 System*, Japan Policy Research Institute (Working Paper no. 83), December 2001.

_____, *Machiavelli's Children: Leaders and Their Legacies in Italy and Japan*, Cornell University Press, Ithaca, 2003.

Sarila, Narendra Singh, *The Shadow of the Great Game: The Untold Story of India's Partition*, Harper Collins India, New Delhi, 2005.

Sarkar, Jadunath, *Shivaji and His Times*, Orient Blackswan (5th revised edition), 2010.

Schwarz, Adam, *A Nation in Waiting: Indonesia in the 1990s*, Allen & Unwin, Sydney, 1994.

Scott, Peter Dale, *The United States and the Overthrow of Sukarno*, Pacific Affairs 58, Summer 1985.

Seagrave, Sterling, *Lords of the Rim: The Invisible Empire of the Overseas Chinese*, Corgi Books, London, 1995.

Sen, Mohit, *A Traveller and the Road: The Journey of an Indian Communist*, Rupa & Co., New Delhi, 2003.

Sen, Amartya, *The Argumentative Indian: Writings on Indian History, Culture and Identity*, Allen Lane, London, 2005.

Sengupta, Nilanjana, *A Gentleman's Word: The Legacy of Subhas Chandra Bose in Southeast Asia*, ISEAS Publishing, Singapore, 2012.

SenGupta, Nitish, *Bengal Divided: The Unmaking of a Nation (1905-1971)*, Viking (Penguin), New Delhi, 2007.

Shennan, Margaret, *Out in the Midday Sun: The British in Malaya, 1880-1960*, John Murray, London, 2000.

Sharma, Ruchir, *Breakout Nations: In Pursuit of the Next Economic Miracles*, Penguin Books, London, 2012.

Singh, Jaswant, *Jinnah: India – Partition – Independence*, Rupa & Co., New Delhi, 2009.

Singh, Khushwant, *Train to Pakistan*, Ravi Dayal Publisher (Permanent Black), New Delhi, 1988 (first published by Orient Longman, 1956).

Snow, Edgar, *Red Star over China* (Revised and Enlarged edition, with Introduction by John K. Fairbank), Pelican Books, London, 1972 (first published by Victor Gollancz 1937).

Snow, Philip, *The Fall of Hong Kong: Britain, China and the Japanese Occupation*, Yale University Press, New Haven/London, 2004.

Spence, Jonathan D., *The Search for Modern China*, W. W. Norton & Co., New York, 1990.

Studwell, Joe, *How Asia Works: Success and Failure in the World's Most Dynamic Region*, Profile Books (paperback edition), London, 2014.

Terrill, Ross, *The New Chinese Empire: And What It Means for the United States*, Basic Books, New York, 2003.

Tharoor, Shashi, *The Great Indian Novel*, Penguin, London, 1989.

_____, *An Era of Darkness: The British Empire in India*, Aleph, New Delhi, 2016.

Toer, Pramoedya Ananta, *This Earth of Mankind* (*Bumi Manusia*, translated by Lane, Max), Penguin (USA), New York, 1996.

Toye, Hugh, *Subhash Chandra Bose (The Springing Tiger): A Study of a Revolution*, Jaico, Mumbai, 1957.

Tudor, Daniel, *Korea: The Impossible Country*, Tuttle Publishing, New Clarendon (VT), 2014.

Vien, Nguyen Khoc, *Vietnam: A Long History*, The Gioi Publishers, Hanoi, 2003.

Von Tunzelman, Alex, *Indian Summer: The Secret History of the End of an Empire*, Simon & Schuster (Pocket Books), London, 2008.

Wade, Robert, *Governing the Market: Economic Theory and the Role of Government in East Asian Industrialization*, Princeton University Press, Princeton, 1990.

Walter, Carl E. and Howie, Fraser J. T., *Red Capitalism: The Fragile Financial Foundation of China's Extraordinary Rise*, Wiley, Singapore, 2012.

Wheatcroft, Andrew, *Infidel: A History of the Conflict between Christendom and Islam*, Penguin, London, 2004.

_____, *The Ottomans*, Viking (Penguin), London, 1993.

Wilson, Jon, *India Conquered: Britain's Raj and the Chaos of Empire*, Simon & Schuster, London, 2016

Wolpert, Stanley, *Shameful Flight: The Last Years of the British Empire in India*, Oxford (OUP Inc.), New York, 2006.

Yergin, Daniel, *The Prize: The Epic Quest for Oil, Money & Power*, Touchstone (Simon & Schuster), New York, 1992.

_____, *The Quest: Energy, Security, and the Remaking of the Modern World*, Allen Lane, London, 2011.

INDEX

Abdali, Ahmad Shah, 11, 17
Abdulhamid II, Sultan, 169
Afghanistan, 1, 319, 630–631
Aguinaldo, General Emilio, 39–40,
   111–119, 136, 343, 339
Akbar, Emperor, 2, 20
   alliance with the Rajput warriors, 2–3
   Din-i Ilahi religion, 5
Alam II, emperor Shah, 11–12
al-Din, Muzaffar, 57
al-Din, Naser, 57
Alexander VI, Pope, 41
Ali, Asaf, 365, 389, 452, 457
Ali, Haidar, 13–15
Ali, Maulana Muhammad, 200, 211
Ali al-Gaylani, Rashid, 357
Ambedkar, B. R., 487
American Civil War (1861–65), 72
Amherst, Lord William, 66
Amritsar Treaty, 18
Anglo–Afghan War, 19
Anglo–Burmese War of 1852, 83
Anglo–French–Israeli alliance, 494
Anglo–Iranian Oil Company (AIOC),
   489–494
Anglo–Iraqi Treaty of 1930, 224–225,
   357
Anglo–Iraqi War of 1941, 357–359
Anglo–Japanese Treaty, 1902, 120, 167,
   242, 329
Anglo–Maratha Wars, 12
   First (1775–82), 14
   Second (1803–05), 17
Anglo–Mysore Wars, 12
   First (1767–69), 13
   Fourth (1799), 16
   Second (1780–84), 15
Anglo–Persian Oil Company (APOC),
   166
Anglo–Siamese Treaty of 1909, 86
Anglo–Sikh Wars, 12, 20
Anglo–Soviet invasion of Persia, 1941,
   357

Anglo–Thai Peace Treaty, 1946, 425
Angre, Admiral Kanhoji, 7
Annam, 84, 402, 424, 426–429, 431–
   433, 615
Ansari, M.A., 214
anti-Brahmin movement, 215
Anti-Imperialist League, 114
Antoinette, Marie, 15
Anushilan Samiti, 140
Aquino, Servillano, 116
Arab revolt, 167–174
ARAMCO, 222, 490, 630
Arjunawiwaha (Mpu Kanwa), 44
Arya Samaj, 38
Attariwala, Sher Singh, 21
Aurangzeb, Emperor, 3, 8, 47
   defeat of Sambhaji, 5–6
   jihad against the Marathas, 6
   jizya tax on non-Muslims, 3
   temple-destruction, 3
Ayutthaya, 80
Azad, Maulana Abul Kalam, 141, 214,
   284, 353–354, 356, 439, 443, 446,
   453, 456, 468

Baghdad Pact, 472, 495, 499
Bakht, Mirza Jawan, 26
Bakr, Mirza Abu, 27
Balfour, Prime Minister, 125
Balfour Declaration of 1917, 183, 223
Balkan Wars of 1912–13, 159
Bandaranaike, Sirimavo, 315
Bandaranaike, Sir Solomon Dias, 314
Banerjea, Surendranath, 37, 133, 215
Bangladesh, 627–629
banking systems in the AFC economies,
   623
Bataan Death March, 343
battles
   of Buxar, 1764, 11–12
   of Chillianwala, 1849, 21
   of Java Sea, 346–347
   of Legyi, 384

of Manila Bay, 1898, 112–113
of Mukden, 1905, 121
of Panipat, 11
of Plassey, 1757, 4
of Sakarya River, 187
of Shakar Kheda, 9
of Singapore, 345
of Surabaya, 1945, 417
of Talikota, 1565, 13
of Tsushima Strait, 1905, 121
Bengal Chemical Works, 134
Bengal famines, 126
Bengali Hindus and Muslims, 132,
    143–144, 318
Bengal Revolutionary Society, 140
Bengal textile industry, 16
Bentinck, William, 31
Besant, Annie, 210
Bharathi, Subramania, 134
Bhonsles, 18
Bismarck, Otto von, 10, 157
Black Dragon Society, 247
Bólivar, Simón, 109
Bolshevik Revolution, 177–181
Bonaparte, Napoleon, 16, 49, 106
Bonifacio, Andrés, 110–111
Bonjol, Tuanku Imam, 51
Bonnerjee, Womesh Chandra, 37, 131
Boone, Charles, 7
Bordoloi, Gopinath, 290
Bose, Jagadish Chandra, 38
Bose, Khudiram, 140
Bose, Rash Behari, 175–177, 343, 370
Bose, Subhas Chandra, 262–299, 356,
    363–394, 436, 500–501
  in Andaman and Nicobar Islands,
    376–377
  Bose–Huq alliance, 292–293
  Bose–Jinnah talks, 291
  in Burmese prisons, 264
  'Chalo Delhi' (On to Delhi), 372, 378,
    386, 611
  close ties to Edvard Beneš, 285–286
  food aid during famine of 1942–45,
    369
  'Forward Bloc,' 296, 318, 320, 373
  Free India Centre, 319
  INA, 370–394
  Indian POWs and, 319

political outlook and views, 364–365
practical vision for India, 286, 289
Provisional Government of Free India,
    375–376
reforms land tenure, 288
rift with Gandhi, 262–299
support to Gandhi's Quit India, 365
Boston Tea Party, 1773, 35
Bowring Treaty, 1855, 83
Boxer Protocol, 1901, 79, 120
Boxer Uprising, 1899–1901, 78–79
Brahmo Samaj, 38
Bridgeman, Henry, 6
Britain's decolonization, 436–487
British Crescent, 309–314
British East India Company, 2–3, 12, 14,
    21, 33, 67–68
British Malaya, 309–314
Brooke, Sir James, 83, 326
Bryan, William Jennings, 115, 119
Buddhism, 59
Buddhists, 2
Bukhara, 19
Bunnag, Tish, 82
Bunnags, 82–83
Burlingame Treaty, 190
Burma
  between 1886 and 1936, 315–316
  Britain's declaration of war, 316
  conquest of, 83–84
  evacuation from Rangoon, 349–350
  Japanese assault on, 349–352
  Japanese military leadership and
    independence of, 360–363
  Muslim–Buddhist riots, 316
Burma National Army (BNA), 383–384
Burnes, Alexander, 20

Cabinet Mission Plan, 445–450, 454
Cambodia, 44, 82, 84–85, 307–308, 362,
    402, 424–426, 429, 433–436, 488,
    591, 610–611, 627
Cambodian Hindu kingdom, 44
Campbell, Sir Colin, 28
caste system, 31
CENTO (Central Treaty Organization),
    472
Central Asia, 54–55, 60, 81
Chaki, Prafulla, 140

468–469, 499

Khan, Abtai Sain, 59

Khan, Aga, 137

Khan, Altan, 59

Khan, Amanullah, 205

Khan, Azimullah, 24

Khan, Bakht, 26, 28

Khan, Genghis, 54, 61

Khan, Husain Ali, 9

Khan, Ismail, 87

Khan, Kartalab, 8

Khan, Kublai, 41, 45, 60

Khan, Lhabzang, 128

Khan, Murshid Quli, 8–9

Khan, Reza, 181

Khan, Shaista, 8

Khan, Siddi Yakut, 6

Khan, Sir Sikandar Hayat, 359

Khan, Sir Syed Ahmed, 136

Khan, Zafrullah, 487

Khilafat republics, 211

Khudai Khidmatgars, 271–272, 468, 499

Khyber-Pakhtunkhwa region, 19

Kido Koin of Choshu, 90, 92–94, 96–97

Kim Dae-jung, 107, 594, 617

Kingsford, Douglas, 140

Kipling, Rudyard, 32, 114

Kitchener, Lord Herbert, 127

KMM (Kesatuan Melayu Muda, Union of Malay Youth) movement, 311

KMT, 180, 192, 196, 229, 232–233, 235–236, 244, 249, 253–256, 261, 302, 312–313, 328, 330–331, 333, 362, 405–406, 424, 430, 434, 461, 487, 513–514, 526, 555–564, 581, 586–589, 612, 616

Komagata Maru incident, 176

Korea, 1, 120, 197, 611, 614–615, 620
  adoption of Japan's economic model, 585–602
  China's influence over, 103–104
  Japanese reforms in, 123
  Japan's influence, 1870s and 1880s, 102
  Koryo dynasty (918–1392), 102
  Mongol invasion in 1231, 103
  primitive distribution networks, 103
  Samil (1 March 1919) Movement in, 246

Silla kingdom, 102
  socio-cultural homogeneity, 102
  treaty between Japan and, 1876, 103
  Yi (or Chosun/Joseon) dynasty, 103–104

Kotewall, Robert, 329

Krishak Praja Party, 320

Krishnadevaraya, King, 13

Ladakh, 19

Lahore Conspiracy Case, 267–268

Lahore Resolution, 1940, 292

Lake, General, 17

Lakshmibai (Rani of Jhansi), 24, 28, 30, 372

La Liga Filipina, 110

Laos, 84–85, 307–308, 362, 402, 424–426, 433–436, 488, 511, 525, 610–611

Lapu-Lapu, Datu, 41

Laski, Harold, 442–443

Lawrence, T. E., 172

Lee Kuan Yew, 74, 99, 334, 527, 529, 532–535, 551, 553, 590, 619

Lee Teng-hui, 106, 616–617

Lenin, Vladimir, 177

Liberation Tigers of Tamil Eelam (LTTE), 629

life expectancy at birth, 488–489

Li Hongzhang, President, 75 76, 79, 103–104, 146, 193

Linggadjati Agreement, 419

Linlithgow, Viceroy, 288, 293, 296–298, 352–354, 360, 368

Lin Zexu, 68–69

Liu Shaoqi, 256, 568

London Naval Treaty of 1930, 247–248, 251–252

Louis XVI, 15

Lucknow, siege of, 28

Lucknow Pact, 200, 266, 459

MacArthur, Douglas, 117

MacArthur, Lieutenant General Arthur, 112, 116

Macartney, Lord George, 66

Macaulay, Thomas, 30
  Minute on Education', 30, 130

Macdonald, Brigadier General James, 126

Macdonald, David, 129
Mahal, Zinat, 26
Mahayana Buddhist empire of Srivijaya, 44
Majapahit, 46
Majapahit kingdom, 45
Make in India initiative, 633
Malaviya, Madan Mohan, 134, 212
Malaysia, 2, 40, 46, 51, 106–107, 304, 311–312, 334, 349, 373, 488, 517, 531, 534–537, 542–544, 550–553, 598–600, 602, 618–620, 623
  Mahathir's 'Look East' policy of 1980s, 107
Malhotra, Uttam Chand, 319
Malvar, General Miguel, 116
Mamluk (slave) dynasty in Egypt, 55, 501
Manaf, Hashim ibn Abd, 172
Manchu–Mongol alliance, 1935, 253
Manchu rulers of China, 1
Mao Zedong, 119, 301, 311–313, 317, 434, 554, 612
Maratha resistance, 3
Marathas, 25
'martial races and castes,' concept, 36
Massie, Joseph, 32
Mataram, 44, 47–48
McKinley, President William, 40
Meckel, Major Klemens, 96
Meligeni, Fernando, 40
Menon, V. K. Krishna, 442–443, 453, 464
Menon, V. P., 457, 464–465, 470
Mill, James, 30
  The History of British India, 30
Minangkabau, 43
Ministry of Commerce and Industry (MCI), 569–570
Minto, Lord, 135
Mirza, Iskander, 469
Mitsubishi, 99, 101
Model T car, 159–160
Modi, Prime Minister Narendra, 605, 633
Mohamad, Prime Minister Mahathir, 107, 517, 521, 552, 619–620
Mohammed, Dost, 20
Mongkut (Rama IV), King, 82

Montagu–Chelmsford Reforms, 199–201, 393
Mookerjee, Shyama Prasad, 292, 367, 466
Morales, Evo, 41
'most favoured nation' (MFN) principle, 71, 90
Motilal Nehru Committee, 265
Mountbatten, Lord Louis, 55, 158, 354, 404–406, 408, 412, 424–425, 439, 441, 447, 454–455, 458–470, 472–476, 479–487, 503, 505, 510, 519
Mughal, Prince Mirza, 26
Mughal–Maratha conflict, 5–7
Mughals, 2
Mukden incident, 249
Mukherjee, Jatindra, 140, 175, 177
Mulraj, Diwan, 21
Munro, Major General Thomas, 12
Murshidabad, 8
Musharraf, Pervez, 471, 474
Muslim League, 133, 137, 200, 203, 210–211, 264–266, 281–284, 287–288, 290–293, 297–298, 318, 320, 352, 359, 367, 369, 385–386, 388, 437–439, 444–445, 449–458, 460, 463, 467, 469, 473, 475, 477, 504
mutiny of 1857, 23–26, 39
Mysore kingdom, 12–13

Nalwa, Hari Singh, 19
Nanjing Massacre, 409
Nansen, Fridtjof, 54
Naoroji, Dadabhai, 131
Napier, Major General Sir Charles, 20
Napoleonic Wars, 50–51
National Iranian Oil Company (NIOC), 491, 493–494
nationalism (1901–13), 108
  Curzon's partition of Bengal, 125–144
  Japan's victory over Russia in 1904–05, 119–125
  Philippine War of Independence, 108–119
  Sino–British treaty, 1893, 128
nation-building without nationality, 114
Nawab of Arcot, 22

Malaya, 516–537
Singapore, 551–554
Pottinger, Sir Henry, 70
Prasad, Rajendra, 203
'provincial option,' principle of, 351

Qajars, 56–57
Qasim, Nawab Mir, 12
Qianlong, emperor, 80
Qishan, Governor General, 69–70
Queue Order', 64
Quezon, Manuel, 118–119

Raffles, Thomas Stamford, 50, 53
Rahman, Habibur, 402–403
Rai, Lala Lajpat, 134, 266
Rajagopalachari (Rajaji), C., 272
Raja of Tanjore, 22
Rajaram, King, 5–6
Rajputs of Mewar, 4
Rama IV (Mongkut), King, 83
Rama V (Chulalongkorn), King, 83
Rana, Jang Bahadur, 29
Rao, P. V. Narasimha, 632
Rao, Raghunath, 17
Rao I, Peshwa Baji, 8, 10
Rao II, Peshwa Baji, 17–18, 24
Rathore of Jodhpur, Ajit Singh
    (Governor), 8
Ray, Dwijendralal, 134
Ray, Prafulla Chandra, 38, 134
Red Fort, 11
Renville Agreement, 421–422
Republic of the United States of
    Indonesia (RUSI), 422–423
Restoration Society, 146
Reuter, Baron Paul Julius von, 57
Ricarte, Artemio, 116, 343
Risley, Sir Herbert, 132
Rizal, José, 39, 109–110, 135
Rockefeller, John D., 160–161
Rohillas, 11
Roosevelt, President Franklin D., 321,
    339
Roosevelt, President Theodore, 116,
    161
Rowlatt Act, 201, 204–206, 269, 298
Roy, Raja Rammohun, 38
Royal Dutch/Shell, 163–167

Royal Netherlands East Indies Army
    (KNIL), 53
Russia, 1
    annexation of Manchuria, 120
    Tsarist Russia's expansionary motives,
        120–122
Russian–Ottoman struggle, 55
Russian–Tartar struggle, 54–55
Russo–Japanese rivalry, 105
Russo–Japanese War of 1904–05, 108

Sadiq, Mirwaiz, 87
Safavids, 56–57
Saigo Takamori of Satsuma, 90, 92–94,
    96–97
Sailendra dynasty, 44
Saionji Kinmochi, Prince, 189
Sakdalista uprising, 341–342
Salimullah, Nawab, 133
Samarkand, 19
Sambhaji, King, 5
Samuel, Marcus, 52
San, Aung, 317
San, Saya, 315
Saraswati, Sri Dayananda, 37–38
Sarawak, 325–327
Satichaura massacre, 24
Saud, Abdul Aziz ibn, 216–218, 220–221
Sayyids, 9
Schlieffen Plan, 159
Scindia, Daulat Rao, 17
Scindia, Mahadji, 11, 14, 17
Scindias (Shindes) of Gwalior, 10–11
self-determination, 119, 154, 183, 189–
    218, 222–223, 225, 227, 269–270,
    275, 298, 351, 389
Sen, Keshub Chandra, 38
Sen, Rajanikanta, 134
Sengupta, Jatindra Mohan, 274
Sèvres Treaty, 184–185
Shah, Akbar, 318
Shah, Emperor Muhammad, 10
Shah, King Hussain, 132
Shah, Naser al-Din, 57
Shah I, Bahadur, 7
Shah Jahan, Emperor, 2
Shahuji, Prince, 6–7
Shammar, Jabal, 156
Shastri, Prime Minister Lal Bahadur, 516

PRASENJIT K. BASU

Shell Transport and Trading Company, 52

Shidehara Kijuro, 243–244

Shiite dynasty, 56

Shivaji, Chhatrapati, 3–4
  alliance with Qutb Shahi dynasty, 5
  land power, 5
  unitary state under, 5

Shuja-ud-Daulah, Nawab, 12

Siam, conquest of, 80–86

Siamese State Bank, 86

Sikh kingdom, 8

Sikkim–Tibet border, delineation of, 125–144

Simla Convention of 1914, 130

Simon Commission, 269, 274, 439

Singapore, 2, 164, 310, 324–325, 327, 335, 337, 425, 516, 619–620

Singh, Bhagat, 214, 267–268

Singh, Zorawar, 19

Sino–French War, 1883, 84

Sino–Japanese War of 1894–95, 104–105, 123–124

Siraj-ud-Daulah, Nawab, 4, 11

Soetardjo Petition, 1936, 340

Sook Ching massacre, 409

Soomro, Allah Bux, 353, 359–360

Spanish–American War, 40

Spirit Boxers, 78

Sri Lanka (Ceylon), 2, 314, 629–630
  Tamil community of, 314–315

Srivijaya, 44

Stalin, Joseph, 554, 612

Standard Oil trust, 160–166, 221

Stirling, Sir James, 89

Straits of Shimonoseki, 92

Straits Settlements, 164, 309–311, 362, 516

subsidiary allies, 21–22

Suez crisis of 1956, 494–497

Suhrawardy, Hussain Shaheed, 263, 291, 369, 450–451, 454, 465–466, 472–473

Sukarchakia, Ranjit Singh, 18

Sukarno, 107, 231–232, 337, 340, 347

Sultan, Mirza Khizr, 27

Sultan, Tipu, 13, 15
  diplomatic mission to Constantinople, 15

Sun Yat-sen, 74, 144–153, 192, 312, 332

Supreme Commander of Southeast Asia Command (SEAC), 404–406, 408, 412–419, 424, 428

Suzuki Keiji, Colonel, 303, 317

Swadeshi and Boycott movements, 133–142

Swadeshi Steam Navigation Company, 134

Sykes–Picot Agreement, 219, 632

Taft, William Howard, 116

Tagore, Dwarkanath, 37

Tagore, Maharshi Debendranath, 38

Tagore, Rabindranath, 134, 210

Tagore, Satyendranath, 36

Taiping Rebellion (1850–64), 72–75

Taishi, Esen, 59

Taiwan, 105–106, 611, 614–615, 620
  adoption of Japan's economic model, 585–602, 615–616
  Japan's influence, 124
  Lee Teng-hui's era, 616–619

Taksin the Great, King, 81–82

Talaat, Mehmed, 170

Tan Kah Kee, 312–313

Tata Steel, 134

Tea Act of 1773, 35

Thailand, 1
  Chakri dynasty, 82
  cultural assimilation with Chinese, 306
  Pridi Phanomyong's period, 425
  1930s, 304–309

Thai–Burman relations, 80–82
  war on the Allies, 1942, 309

Thakins, 316

Than Tun, Thakin, 363

Thibaw, King, 85

Thura, General Maha Thira, 81

Tibet, 612

Tilak, 'Lokmanya' Bal Gangadhar, 134, 138–139, 141, 200, 264

Timurids, 2, 7–8, 10, 25

Tjokroaminoto, H.O.S., 124

Togo Heihachiro, Admiral, 121

Tojo Hideki, Prime Minister, 322–323

Toledo, Alejandro, 41

Tonkin, 84–85, 401–402, 424, 426–428, 431–434

CPSIA information can be obtained
at www.ICGtesting.com
Printed in the USA
BVHW031102280122
627070BV00014B/51/J